Environmental Regulation

Environmental Regulation

Law, Science, and Policy

Robert V. Percival
*Associate Professor of Law and
Director, Environmental Law Program
University of Maryland School of Law*

Alan S. Miller
*Executive Director, Center for Global Change
University of Maryland*

Christopher H. Schroeder
*Professor of Law
Duke University School of Law*

James P. Leape
*Senior Vice President
World Wildlife Fund*

Little, Brown and Company
Boston   Toronto   London

Library of Congress Catalog Card No. 92-70815

ISBN 0-316-69901-2

Fourth Printing

MV-NY

Published simultaneously in Canada
by Little, Brown & Company (Canada) Limited

Printed in the United States of America

To my international family,
Barbara, Marita, and Richard.

R.V.P.

To Sue, to my parents, and to the
many students who suffered
through the early drafts of this
book.

A.S.M.

For Herb and Jane Schroeder—
their dispositions of love and care
for others embody the best we could
bring to the problems of public
affairs.

C.H.S.

To Suki, Benjamin, and Jonathan.

J.P.L.

Summary of Contents

Contents

ix

— 2 —
‖ *Environmental Law: A Structural Overview* ‖   *71*

— 3 —

|| *Waste Management and Pollution Prevention* || *199*

— **4** —

‖ *Regulation of Toxic Substances* ‖   *425*

— 5 —
‖ *The Regulatory Process* ‖   *657*

— 7 —
‖ *Water Pollution Control* ‖   *865*

— 8 —
‖ *Protection of Public Resources* ‖   *1021*

— 9 —
‖ Protection of the Global Environment ‖   *1141*

|10|
‖ *Conclusion* ‖ *1239*

— **APPENDIX A** —

‖ *Glossary* ‖

— **APPENDIX B** —

‖ *List of Acronyms* ‖

Preface

American law has changed in profound ways in response to environmental concerns. Public concern for the environment fueled much of the development of administrative law. It now animates the creation of a modern regulatory state in which law plays a prominent role in articulating public values. The explosive growth of environmental law has created a vast and fiercely complex web of regulation that is changing the way we live, work, and do business.

The rapid growth of environmental law has been a mixed blessing for educators. While the demand for environmental education has increased, the expanding breadth and complexity of environmental regulation has made a difficult subject even more challenging to teach. Thus, it is hardly surprising to find widespread dissatisfaction with current approaches to teaching environmental law. This dissatisfaction stems in part from a perception that the work of environmental lawyers increasingly is divorced from the concerns that inspired the environmental movement. Sax, Environmental Law in the Law Schools: What We Teach and How We Feel About It, 19 Envtl. L. Rep. 1-251 (June 1989). While this perception undoubtedly reflects, at least in part, larger concerns about the role of lawyers in society, it may also be symptomatic of the narrow vision of law often employed in environmental law courses.

A "Second Generation" Approach to Environmental Law

This textbook is founded on the conviction that a "second generation" approach to environmental law is necessary because of the dramatic changes that have occurred in our understanding of environmental problems and society's responses to them. This text seeks to broaden students' vision by inviting them to explore how law relates to the larger problems society seeks to solve through collective action. That transformation is reflected in the book's title, which emphasizes the value of approaching environmental law through a regulatory policy focus that explores the full range of forces that shape the way law affects human behavior.

By focusing on regulation, viewed expansively as embracing all forms of collective action to protect the environment, this text seeks to enhance understanding of the way law affects the behavior of institutions and individuals. This requires far more than "black letter" mastery of environmental law; it also demands an appreciation of the complex processes by which political, economic, and ethical concerns shape regulatory policy in this field. Thus, the text consistently focuses not only on the substance of environmental statutes, but also on how they are translated into regulations and the factors that shape their real world consequences.

Science plays an important role in environmental policymaking, as new practitioners of environmental law soon discover. While environmental lawyers need not be scientists, it is vital that they be able to appreciate the importance of scientific information and to understand how to work with scientists, economists, and other professionals on environmental matters. Thus, the text highlights the role of science and the impact of scientific information on environmental policy. Each chapter begins with a review of what we know about the nature and sources of the environmental problems it addresses and how what we don't know complicates policymaking. The text introduces the increasingly important risk assessment paradigm and explores the impact of scientific uncertainty on regulatory policy decisions. It examines how society decides, in the face of uncertainty, that particular problems warrant a collective response, and it explores the forces that shape what that response will be.

Two decades of federal environmental regulation have provided considerable experience with alternative approaches to regulation. Economists long have criticized "command and control" regulation as inefficient, while others have defended it on ethical or practical grounds. The text seeks to help students understand both the value and limitations of economic analysis for regulatory policy and the relevance of ethical and practical concerns. Experience with the first generation of environmental regulation has stimulated considerable innovation in regulatory policy. Environmental regulation now increasingly embraces a rich mix of alternative approaches including informational regulations, taxes, liability schemes, and insurance requirements. The text explores why these developments make this an exciting time to study environmental regulations and their larger implications for regulatory policy.

Accessibility as a Response to Complexity

An environmental law text must be accessible precisely because environmental regulation generally is not. The fearsome complexity of environmental regulation can deter even well-motivated students. Students need a guide through the regulatory jungle that can help them discover why environmental policy is far too exciting to be lost in regulatory minutiae. The text seeks to introduce the "big picture" of environmental law by placing regulation in the larger context of societal efforts to control environmental risk. It then explores how scientific, political, and economic concerns affect the impact of law and regulatory policy on the behavior of individuals and institutions.

Students cannot be expected to master the details of all the major environmental statutes in a single survey course. But it is important for students to learn where to turn when a particular problem makes it necessary to learn such details. To assist students in understanding the statutes, the text includes charts outlining the principal provisions of the major federal laws. Problems and questions also are included throughout the text. Often based on actual environmental controversies, the problems and questions give students an opportunity to experience for themselves the role that law can play in addressing social problems and the many "extralegal" factors that influence policy.

Research in environmental law can be a particular challenge now that environmental regulation has become as complex and specialized as tax law. Important information often is generated by unfamiliar sources; crucial regulatory interpretations frequently are buried in obscure documents. To assist students in learning where to turn for further information, a "Pathfinder" is included in each chapter that directs students where to find the statutes, regulations, and other crucial source materials and provides suggestions concerning how to keep abreast of important developments in the field. A Glossary (Appendix A) is provided to assist students in understanding scientific and legal terms, as well as a List of Acronyms (Appendix B) to help students with the ever-growing number of acronyms infecting the field.

Organization of the Text

Teaching environmental law poses some fundamental organizational dilemmas, including the perennial tradeoff between breadth and depth of coverage. While this text cannot promise any magical solutions to the organizational dilemma, it has been designed to make it easier for the teacher to cope with the inevitable tradeoffs. The chapters have been organized to maximize the individual teacher's flexibility in deciding what to cover and in what order. As described in the teacher's manual for this text, the material may be covered in a variety of sequences, depending on the length of the course and the teacher's desired subject matter emphases.

Chapter 1 begins by focusing on the nature and sources of environmental concerns. Students are invited to explore the roots of environmental values and alternative perspectives on how society should respond to environmental problems. Before delving into the details of any particular regulatory scheme, Chapter 2 provides a broad overview of how the legal system has responded to environmental concerns by exploring the sources of environmental law, the development of modern environmental legislation, and alternative approaches to regulation. By providing students with a broad framework for understanding the role of public law in environmental protection and for evaluating alternative approaches to regulation, the materials emphasize that environmental problems are not a series of hermetically sealed issues, but rather an interrelated set of problems that defy any one, narrow regulatory solution.

Exploration of the substantive law of environmental protection commences in Chapter 3, which focuses on the increasingly central role of waste management and pollution prevention strategies in environmental regulation. The materials analyze efforts to prevent and to remediate environmental contamination by comparing and contrasting two types of approaches to pollution prevention: regulatory approaches, as represented by "cradle-to-grave" federal regulation of hazardous waste, and liability approaches, as embodied in the "Superfund" legislation's imposition of strict, joint, and several liability on a broad class of parties involved in the release of hazardous substances. We seek to demystify these complex statutory schemes by providing case studies and problem exercises that give students opportunities to examine how these statutes are applied in practice. Students also are challenged to critique current policy and to explore alternative strategies for pollution prevention through source reduction, recycling, and efforts to change consumer behavior.

Chapter 4 focuses on the other major set of problems that have become a focus of environmental protection policy in recent years: efforts to protect public health from exposure to toxic substances. The materials explore the tension between law and science that is a product of society's desire to prevent harm before it occurs, despite considerable scientific uncertainty about what is harmful and how harmful it is. Students are introduced to the development and use of risk assessment techniques that have assumed an increasingly significant role in regulatory decisions under the major federal statutes. Alternative approaches to answering the "how safe is safe" question are compared and contrasted, including the risk-benefit balancing approaches of FIFRA and TSCA, feasibility-based standards required by OSHA and the Safe

Drinking Water Act, and the purely health-based standards required by the Delaney Clauses of the Food, Drug, and Cosmetic Act and section 112 of the Clean Air Act. The chapter concludes by emphasizing the emergence of new approaches to toxic substance control, including burden-shifting and informational approaches and the revival of common law actions.

Chapter 5 focuses on the complicated processes by which environmental laws are translated into regulations. Rather than simply introducing the administrative law of environmental protection, the materials also explore how agencies set regulatory priorities and the increasingly important role of the Executive Office of the President in supervising federal regulation. Expanding beyond the focus of traditional casebooks, the chapter also considers how congressional oversight committees, interest groups, and other participants in the regulatory process seek to influence agency policy decisions. The materials provide case studies illustrating the glacial pace of the process and the increasing use of action-forcing mechanisms to influence agency behavior. Students are challenged to explore why the products of the regulatory process often diverge from statutory promises and to evaluate proposals for improving the rulemaking process through regulatory negotiation and generic rulemaking. The role of the judiciary in the regulatory process also is explored by considering changing standards governing citizen access to courts and the scope of judicial review of agency action.

The remaining chapters provide detailed coverage of the principal medium-specific environmental schemes. Chapter 6 focuses on the variety of regulatory strategies employed to combat air pollution as modified by the Clean Air Act's far-reaching 1990 Amendments. After a brief survey of the historical development of the Act, the chapter introduces the structure of the Act and explores how it seeks to protect ambient air quality. The tension between federal standards and state implementation is then explored, including the 1990 Amendments' response to the perennial problem of nonattainment. The chapter then focuses on interstate air pollution and the innovative emissions trading program established by the 1990 Amendments. It then explores efforts to force the development of cleaner fuels and cars and how the Act attempts to prevent deterioration of air quality in areas that already meet national standards. The chapter concludes by discussing how the air toxics provisions of the 1990 Amendments seek to stimulate source reduction by encouraging early reductions in toxic emissions.

Chapter 7 focuses on regulations to control water pollution. After reviewing federal statutory authorities for controlling water pollution, the chapter explores the Clean Water Act's comprehensive permit program for controlling point sources of water pollution. In addition to including traditional coverage of the development of effluent limitations, the chapter provides expanded coverage of four major issues that have become critically important to water pollution control now that technology-based controls on point sources have been implemented: water quality-based controls and the regulation of toxics, the pretreatment program, control of pollution from nonpoint sources, and regulation of dredge and fill operations to protect wetlands. The chapter concludes by using the Clean Water Act to illustrate how environmental enforcement is conducted by federal and state authorities and through citizen suits.

The universe of environmental law is not limited to the complex web of statutes and regulations designed to control pollution and to protect public health against exposure to toxics. Issues of public resource management, which were the focus of environmental concern a century ago, remain an important aspect of environmental law that often is ignored in contemporary materials. Chapter 8 introduces students to public resource management issues by focusing on the National Environmental Policy Act and the Endangered Species Act. While these programs are but a small part of the legislation that governs management of public resources, they are enormously important for illustrating alternative approaches for affecting agency policy decisions and for reconciling other public values with environmental concerns. It concludes by examining conflicts between public resource management and the environment such as the spotted owl controversy.

Chapter 9 focuses on protection of the global environment through international environmental law. Perhaps the most stunning change in the past two decades of environmental concern has been the realization that environmental problems have now become global in scope. As daunting as the challenges facing domestic environmental policy are, international policy faces an even more daunting task: that of reconciling diverse national interests. Yet the perceived urgency of the threat to the global environment has produced remarkable international initiatives to protect the global environment. The chapter begins with an introduction to international environmental law. It then considers efforts to protect the global atmosphere from ozone depletion and global warming and climate change; the impact of international trade liberalization on the environment; the regulation of international trade in hazardous substances; and the influence of international financial institutions on global development policies.

The materials conclude in Chapter 10 by focusing on what environmental regulation has accomplished and its prospects for the future. After exploring contrasting assessments of the results of environmental regulation, the chapter considers how corporate policies are changing as a result of environmental regulation.

This book has been under development for nearly four years. It is the product of materials used to teach environmental law at a dozen schools in a score of courses during that period. Because it is designed to be accessible to students with a variety of backgrounds, the text also has been used in graduate public policy courses. The authors welcome comments and reactions.

We are grateful to the many people who assisted us with this project. We particularly would like to thank: Oscar Gray, who put us in touch with Little, Brown and reminded us of the roots of environmental law; our colleagues who used drafts of the manuscript at a dozen schools during the last four years (and their students who suffered through the early versions); and Rich Ossias and his colleagues at EPA's Office of General Counsel, who provided helpful comments on the Clean Air chapter. Bob Percival would like to thank the many students and recent graduates who assisted him with research, including Carol Iancu, Safia Kadir, John Kalas, Kristin Klein, Mary Raivel, and particularly Maureen O'Doherty, who also provided remarkable assistance with final production tasks. He appreciates the enthusiastic support provided to the project by the school's administration, including former dean Mike Kelly and acting dean Alan Hornstein, and the assistance provided by research librarian Maxine Grosshans and Marilyn Heath. Alan Miller thanks Pamela Wexler, Donna Kopsidas, and the librarians at Widener School of Law. Chris Schroeder also thanks a number of Duke law students and recent graduates who have assisted ably in compiling and researching these materials, including Don Frost, Evy Jarrett, Jennifer Alvey, Kimberle Dunn, Michele Kirk, Lee Roach, Jeremy Weiss, and Brian Kelly. June Hubbard, editorial assistant at Duke Law School, skillfully prepared a number of the graphics. Special appreciation is due to the administration at Duke Law School, especially Dean Pamela Gann, for administrative and financial support.

We owe a considerable debt to the remarkable people at Little, Brown & Company who guided the book to completion, including Carol McGeehan, who understood what we were about from the start and provided invaluable advice and support; Jane Zanichkowsky, our manuscript editor, who always found a way to accommodate our efforts to improve the final product; and Kurt Hughes, design administrator, who enthusiastically tackled the unusual demands of the project. Finally, all of us are especially grateful to Laura Mrozek, secretary for Maryland's Environmental Law Program, who shepherded assembly of the book from start to finish with extraordinary skill and grace. Laura performed prodigous feats of typing, proofing, and xeroxing, coordinated the permissions process, and continually kept us out of trouble whenever the demands of the project seemed impossible. We are immensely grateful to her.

Robert V. Percival
Alan S. Miller
Christopher H. Schroeder
James P. Leape

May 1992

Acknowledgments

The authors gratefully acknowledge the permissions granted to reproduce the following materials.

Acton, Understanding Superfund: A Progress Report (chart), Rand Corporation R-3838-1CJ (1989). Reprinted with permission.

Auer and Gould, Carcinogenicity Assessment and the Role of Structure Activity Relationship (SAR) Analysis Under TSCA Section 5. Reprinted from 5 Journal of Environmental Science and Health (1987), Table IV by courtesy of Marcel Dekker, Inc.

Aufderheide and Rich, Environmental Reform and the Multilateral Banks, World Poly. J. 303-305, 307 (Spring 1988). Reprinted with permission.

Bauman, How Government Regulations Are Made (cartoon), The Guardian (1985). Reprinted with permission from the artist.

Baumol and Oates, Economics, Environmental Policy, and the Quality of Life 71-79 (1979). Reprinted by permission of Prentice Hall, Englewood Cliffs, New Jersey.

Bean, We Don't Know the Benefits Side of the Equation, 1990 Envtl. Forum 28 (July-Aug. 1990). Copyright © 1990 The Environmental Forum. Reprinted by permission.

Benedick, Ozone Diplomacy 5-7 (1991). Reprinted by permission of the publishers from Ozone Diplomacy by Richard Elliott Benedick, Cambridge, Mass.: Harvard University Press, copyright © 1991 by the World Wildlife Fund and The Conservation Foundation and the Institute for the Study of Diplomacy, Georgetown University.

Bevis, Northern Spotted Owl (photo), 1989 Wilderness 48 (Spring 1989). Reprinted with permission of the photographer.

Broder, Beyond Folk Songs and Flowers, Wash. Post, April 22, 1990, p.B7. Copyright © 1990 by the Washington Post Writers Group. Reprinted with permission.

Bryk, The Montreal Protocol and Recent Developments to Protect the Ozone Layer, 15 Harv. Envtl. L. Rev. (1991). Reprinted with permission from the author.

Commoner, Failure of the Environmental Effort, 18 Envtl. L. Rep. 10195 (1988). Barry Commoner is Director of the Center for the Biology of Natural Systems, Queens College, City University of New York. Reprinted with permission.

Conserve Oil—and Wilderness (editorial), N.Y. Times, Feb. 19, 1991, p.A16. Copyright © 1991 by The New York Times Company. Reprinted with permission.

EPA's Assessment of Top Environmental Concerns and the Public's Ranking (chart), in Counting on Science at EPA, 249 Science 616 (1990). Copyright © 1990 by the AAAS. Reprinted with permission of Science.

Flavin, Slowing Global Warming: A Worldwide Strategy, Worldwatch Paper 91, p.66 and chart. Reprinted with permission.

Fortuna and Lennett, Hazardous Waste Regulation: The New Era (chart), p.67. Copyright © 1986. Material is reproduced with permission of McGraw-Hill, Inc.

Hall, The Evolution and Implementation of EPA's Regulatory Program to Control the Discharge of Toxic Pollutants to the Nation's Waters, 10 Nat. Resources Law. 507 (1978). Copyright © 1977 the American Bar Association. Reprinted by permission of the American Bar Association and the author.

Hardin, The Tragedy of the Commons, 168 Science 1243 (1968). Copyright © 1968 by the AAAS. Reprinted with permission of Science.

Harter, The Dilemma of Causation in Toxic Torts. Material originally prepared for the Program on Financial Compensation, Institute for Health Policy Analysis, Washington, D.C. Reprinted with permission.

Houck, Ending the War: A Strategy to Save America's Coastal Zone, 47 Md. L. Rev. 358 (1988). Reprinted with permission.

Ignoring Pleas of Environmentalists, Kansas Man Digs Up Virgin Prairie, N.Y. Times, Nov. 23, 1990, p.B18. Copyright © 1990 by The New York Times Company. Reprinted with permission.

Intergovernmental Panel on Climate Change, Working Group I, Scientific Assessment (1990). Reprinted with permission from Cambridge University Press.

Johnson, The Basel Convention: The Shape of Things to Come for United States Waste Exports?, 21 Envtl. L. 299 (1991). Reprinted with permission.

Liberty, The Oregon Planning Experience: Repeating the Success and Avoiding the Mistakes, 1 Md. Poly. Stud. 45 (Aug. 1988). Reprinted with permission.

"Where the Water Is Tainted" and "Where the Air Is Bad" (maps), N.Y. Times, Oct. 13, 1991, p.F10. Copyright © 1991 by The New York Times Company. Reprinted by permission.

Wilson, Biophilia. Reprinted by permission of the publishers from Biophilia by Edward Wilson, Cambridge, Mass.: Harvard University Press. Copyright © 1984 by the President and Fellows of Harvard College.

Wilson, Toward a Lasting Conservation Ethic (statement before congressional committee reviewing the Endangered Species Act) (1980). Reprinted by permission.

World Wildlife Fund and The Conservation Foundation, excerpt from comments made by Donald Kennedy on December 5, 1978, when Kennedy was Commissioner of the Food and Drug Administration. Reprinted from Risk Assessment and Risk Control, Washington, D.C.: The Conservation Foundation (1987).

World Wildlife Fund and The Conservation Foundation, State of the Environment: A View Toward the Nineties 54-73, 87-95, 101-105, 136 and charts (1987). Reprinted with permission.

Environmental Regulation

=1=

Environmental Values and Policies: An Introduction

[A]t one level, the environmentalists have swept away all opposition. The "conservation ethic" has become one of the fixed guiding stars of American politics—a "value question" that permits only one answer from anyone who hopes to be part of the public dialogue. What all this suggests is that the argument is no longer about values. That's over, and the environmentalists have won. The argument now is about policies. And those with the best evidence and the best arguments, not just the purest hearts, will prevail.

—*David S. Broder**

Behind all the studies, the figures, and the debates, the environment is a moral issue. We can and should be nature's advocate.

—*George Bush***

The spectacular growth of public concern for the environment has transformed American law during the past quarter-century. In the space of a single generation, environmental law has grown from a sparse set of common law precedents and local ordinances to encompass a vast body of national legislation. Numerous federal and state agencies now implement these laws through breathtakingly complex regulations that affect virtually every aspect of our lives. In addition, as environmental concerns increasingly transcend national boundaries, environmental law now is serving as a catalyst for the development of new regimes of international law.

This book provides a comprehensive introduction to environmental law. Chapter 1 considers the concerns that have animated its meteoric rise and the values these concerns reflect. After a brief historical sketch,

---

*Beyond Folk Songs and Flowers, Wash. Post, Apr. 22, 1990, at B7.
**Speech of June 8, 1989, quoted in Council on Environmental Quality, Environmental Quality—Twenty-First Annual Report xv (1991).

1

the diverse values embodied in American environmentalism are reviewed, followed by an examination of how environmental problems are viewed from the perspectives of economics and ecology. The chapter explores why there is broad agreement that some form of collective action is necessary to address environmental problems but considerable conflict over the precise form such action should take. The substance of environmental law is explored in subsequent chapters.

A. ENVIRONMENTAL PROBLEMS AND PROGRESS

As law mirrors society, environmental law's rapid growth surely reflects changes in social values. Once considered by many to be the province of a fringe movement, environmental concerns are now becoming firmly embedded in the mainstream of American culture. Throughout the past decade the annual New York Times-CBS poll has found sizeable and increasing majorities of the public agreeing that "protecting the environment is so important that requirements and standards cannot be made too high, and continuing environmental improvement must be made regardless of cost." By 1989 this remarkable conclusion was endorsed by a margin of more than four to one. Environmental values are now capturing formerly hostile ground in some corporate boardrooms. During the twentieth anniversary celebration of Earth Day on April 22, 1990, even companies that had vigorously opposed environmental regulation felt compelled to proclaim their concern for the environment; many now court consumers with claims that their products are environmentally friendly.

While a time traveler from the early 1960s might be surprised to find that environmental concerns have moved so firmly into the mainstream, it is not hard for us to understand why. Human activity is altering the environment at an unprecedented rate. In the past 40 years more people and more pollution have been added to the planet than in the preceding 10,000 years! Despite considerable uncertainty over the timing and consequences of environmental change, scientists are warning that the accumulating residues of an industrial society pose an unprecedented threat to the health of the planet. As scientists struggle to assess the dimensions of this threat, the public repeatedly is confronted with more visible evidence of mankind's capacity to damage the environment. Twenty years after the 1969 Santa Barbara oil spill galvanized the American environmental movement, the *Exxon Valdez* joined Chernobyl and Bhopal as symbols of environmental disasters spawned by the intersection of human carelessness and modern technology. Reinforced by these symbols of catastrophe, mounting evidence of damage to the global atmosphere has moved environmental concerns to the forefront of international attention. An increasingly sophisticated public now understands that environmental protection no longer means simply keeping pollution out of their backyards; for problems such as global warming, ozone depletion, and the loss of tropical rain forests, the entire planet is their backyard, and many are convinced that its health is in jeopardy.

The breadth of public concern for the environment is hardly surprising, since the quality of life on earth ultimately depends on the health of the planet. But what *does* seem surprising is that two decades of unprecedented growth in environmental regulation have not softened the public's demand for environmental protection. This reflects both the scope of the problems and the difficulty of translating public support into effective policies. To be sure, two decades' worth of regulation has had a significant impact on the quality of life in the United States, as can easily be seen by comparing conditions here with the environmental devastation in eastern Europe. Yet environmental law has not delivered on many of its ambitious promises. Beneath the veneer of broad public support for environmental protection run strong currents of dissatisfaction. Many believe that much more needs to be done; others argue that it can be done far more efficiently if we select our tools more carefully.

These and other developments have led some to predict that we are on the threshold of a new era in environmental policy. Early indications suggest that the 1990s may rival the 1970s in American and international public action to address environmental problems. By overwhelming bipartisan majorities, Congress adopted the Clean Air Act Amendments of 1990, continuing the explosive growth of environmental legislation that has been the hallmark of the last two decades. These Amendments mandate the most detailed and comprehensive environmental regulations in history. To achieve the 90 percent reductions in auto emissions and releases of industrial toxins required by the Amendments, fundamental changes will be required in technology and product design. By casting the regulatory net far wider than ever before, this legislation singlehandedly ensures that environmental regulation will be a growth industry for decades to come. While the Clean Air Act Amendments may brighten employment prospects for environmental law students, their price tag—estimated by the Environmental Protection Agency (EPA) to be $25 billion annually—promises to intensify the quest for new approaches to reduce the cost of environmental progress.

Considerable policy change already is under way in the field of environmental regulation. Some innovative approaches are mandated by provisions in the new Clean Air Act Amendments; other important changes are being initiated at the state level. Debate over the future direction of environmental policy will be informed and influenced by our experience with existing law and policy in important ways. This text explores and critiques that law and policy and raises questions about our unfinished environmental business. To appreciate current law and policy it is essential to understand its origins. Thus, it is useful at the outset to provide a highly telescoped view of how contemporary environmental law developed.

April 22, 1970, the first Earth Day, has become the standard date used to mark the beginning of the modern Environmental Era. Samuel Hays reminds us, however, that Earth Day was "as much a result as a cause" of modern environmental consciousness. It had been preceded by at least a decade of growing awareness of environmental damage and of changing attitudes toward environmental well-being. Hays, From Conservation to Environment: Environmental Politics in the U.S. Since World War II, 6 Env. Rev. 24 (1982). It also was preceded by a number of vivid events highlighting obvious, and almost self-defining, environmental problems. Rachel Carson had written Silent Spring in 1962, exposing the bioaccumulative character of DDT; in 1963 the federal government had floated a plan to dam the Colorado River so as to flood part of the Grand Canyon, enraging David Brower of the Sierra Club and serving as a great mobilizing cause; in the mid-sixties methyl mercury had been discovered in the flesh of swordfish, and studies in California had firmly linked automobile exhaust to urban smog; in the later sixties the SST was under development as well as under attack for contributing to noise pollution and ozone depletion, and oil had spilled into the beautiful Santa Barbara channel in early 1969, with television sending pictures of oil-drenched shore and sea birds across the country.

Still, the tremendous outpouring of concern and interest in these and other environmental questions that Earth Day prompted took the environmental movement in new directions. Something new was afoot in the country. The sense of newness was reinforced by the fact that leadership for the event came largely from outside the ranks of the traditional conservation and preservationist organizations such as the Sierra Club, the Audubon Society, the Izaak Walton League, the National Wildlife Federation, or the Wilderness Society. The call to action focused not so much on the natural resources concerns of such longstanding groups as on issues of pollution, security, and survival. Enthusiasm that crystallized on Earth Day was even by then spawning a number of new environmental organizations dedicated to addressing these problems directly. The Environmental Defense Fund (EDF), for instance, had been organized by a group of concerned scientists in 1967 to take up Rachel Carson's cause of banning DDT and related pesticides, as well as other toxic water pollution issues. Wanting to take more aggressive stands on environmental issues, Friends of the Earth (FOE) had spun off from the Sierra Club in 1969, and the Environmental Policy Institute later spun off from FOE. The Natural Resources Defense Council (NRDC) came next in 1970, concentrating on air pollution and nuclear power. Environmental Action was initially created as the organizing entity for Earth Day, and it has continued as a broad-based membership organization since that time.

Environmental issues had hardly been mentioned by either candidate during the 1968 presidential campaign; in the years that followed politicians could not ignore the surging popularity of environmental concerns. At the end of 1969 Congress approved the National Environmental Policy Act (NEPA), the basic charter of national environmental policy and the first truly significant federal environmental protection legislation. Declaring that "each person should enjoy a healthful environment," NEPA announced that it would be the "continuing policy of the Federal Government . . . to use all practicable means and measures . . . to create and maintain conditions under which man and nature can exist in productive harmony." Embracing a broad range of environmental values as national goals, the legislation pledged to "assure for all Americans safe, healthful, productive, and esthetically pleasing surroundings." President Nixon signed NEPA into law in front of a national television audience on New Year's Day, 1970, ushering in what has been called "the environmental decade."

Environmental issues enjoyed enormous popularity as the 1970s began. In his description of the 1972 presidential campaign, Theodore White writes that by 1970 "the environment[al] cause had swollen into the favorite sacred issue of all politicians, all TV networks, all good-willed people of any party." T. White, The Making of the President 45 (1973). Public opinion polls showed that "environmental protection had become a *consensual* issue . . . as majorities of the public expressed pro-environment opinions and typically only small minorities expressed opinions in the anti-environment direction." Dunlap, Public Opinion and Environmental Policy, in Environmental Politics and Policy 87, 98 (J. Lester, ed. 1990). A Harris poll conducted in 1970 found that Americans rated pollution as "the most serious problem" facing their communities. The environment was named the "issue of the year" for 1970 by Time magazine.

As the first celebration of Earth Day approached in early 1970, the media reported that politicians were "vying for a spot in the vanguard of the environmental crusade." Some were recent converts. "Typical of the political maneuvering is the situation in California, where Governor Ronald Reagan, accused by critics of being a 'Johnny-come-lately' to environmental problems, has proposed a program for 'an all-out war against the debauching of the environment.'" King, Pollution Fight Pressed Across Nation, N.Y. Times, Feb. 24, 1970, at 1. The Sierra Club's president complained that environmental concerns had become so politically irresistible that they even were receiving support from unwelcome quarters such as "politicians paying lip service, industrialists laying down public relations smokescreens," and anarchists seeking to subvert democratic institutions.

Partially spurred by and partially leading public opinion, the country's politicians pursued the problems highlighted by Earth Day. Some changes were purely symbolic, as when the Small Business Administration announced in July 1970 that it was removing the smoke from the smokestack depicted on its official seal. Other changes were more substantive. In a major environmental message to Congress, President Nixon proposed a host of environmental protection measures including a tax designed to spur the elimination of lead additives in gasoline and federal research to develop a pollution-free automobile engine. Congress countered by proposing ambitious environmental initiatives of its own. Within a six-year period, 1970-1976, the United States Congress enacted nearly all of the basic environmental legislation studied in this course, most of it by overwhelming bipartisan majorities. We will discuss the broad outlines of these laws in more detail in Chapter 2; their specific provisions are discussed in subsequent chapters. For now, let us consider how we might assess their impact.

When Ed Koch was mayor of New York City, he regularly asked his constituents, "How am I doing?" This is certainly a pertinent question to ask about environmental law as well, for the dominant rationale for environmental regulation is to achieve results that improve environmental quality. In this casebook we will try to supply information that, when added to what you have and are learning elsewhere, will improve your ability to answer that question. We want to do this, furthermore, in a way that improves your ability to decide whether the laws we have enacted and the regulations we have written are the best we can do in achieving that goal or whether improvements can be made.

Because detailed information about progress must await our treatment of specific environmental regimes, we reserve most of it for Chapter 10's conclusion. Preliminarily, we want to warn you to be cautious consumers of environmental progress reports, especially in using them to draw conclusions about the efficacy of environmental legislation. What Myrick Freeman says in the context of evaluating water quality progress is generalizable: "The relevant question is not how much some measure of water quality has changed at some location . . .; this is a before-and-after question. The right question is: How much better was actual water quality than [it] would have been . . . without clean-up requirements, . . . given the same economic conditions, weather and rainfall? This is the with-and-without question." M. Freeman in Public Policies for Environmental Protection 111 (P. Portney, ed. 1990). The with-and-without question is very hard to answer; sometimes it will make a better case for environmental legislation than the before-and-after question does, while at other times it will suggest that other legislative or regulatory strategies might have been much more successful. Sometimes it is virtually impossible to tell (although it is rarely hard to find people willing to argue each side).

Pollution controls on automobiles appear to have been an enormous success when one considers the rapid growth in automobile use. CEQ reported in 1990 that total national emissions of hydrocarbons and carbon monoxide, which had been growing rapidly prior to 1970, declined by 28 percent and 38 percent respectively between 1970 and 1989 despite a 56 percent increase in the number of automobiles on U.S. roads during that period. Controls on the use of lead additives in gasoline have been even more successful: total annual emissions of lead declined 96 percent from 1970 to 1987. CEQ, Environmental Quality—Twentieth Annual Report 8-9 (1990).

Even when environmental policy has achieved significant reductions in pollution, the reductions may not be sufficient to reach health-based goals. Despite substantial progress in reducing air pollution, millions of Americans still live in areas that exceed national health-based standards for ozone and carbon dioxide. Policies that control particular sources of a pollutant may not prevent other sources of it from causing substantial harm. The phasedown of lead in gasoline has reduced average levels of lead in children's bodies dramatically, but an estimated three million children still have dangerously high levels of exposure to lead. A substantial portion of this exposure comes from products that have now been banned or severely restricted—lead-based paint, gasoline lead additives, lead plumbing—but that continue to be sources of lead exposure through soil, dust, air, or drinking water.

As scientific knowledge has improved, the environmental agenda has expanded. Contamination of the environment is far more pervasive, and vastly more difficult to remediate, than first thought. For example, it is now estimated that contamination around the handful of the nation's nuclear weapons production facilities is so serious that it will cost substantially more than $100 billion to clean up; cleanup of the thousands of toxic dump sites throughout the country will be vastly more costly. Scientific advances also are revealing that some health-based environmental standards are insufficiently protective. For example, scientists have discovered that children suffer permanent neurological damage from exposure to low levels of lead that previously were thought to be safe; tests on other pollutants such as ozone and sulfur dioxide suggest that adverse health effects may occur at lower levels than known when the standards were set.

Even when existing law and policy get a passing mark, another cautionary note is raised by those who argue that the progress made so far cannot be read as a harbinger of future successes. They suggest that early successes came because we had created an economy that did so much environmental harm that easy targets of opportunity for cleanup abounded. Remaining problems may be much more intractable. What is more, the problems that have not been addressed adequately may be the most environmentally significant.

Some of the divergence in assessments of our progress results from differences of opinion about what environmental problems are the most urgent. Pessimistic assessments come from some groups that stress population growth and climate stabilization, two issues that are scarcely addressed by any American environmental laws. Observers also disagree about what constitutes success for environmental laws. Should the country's environmental policies be aimed at efficient resource uses, as was suggested by President Reagan's Council on Environmental Quality; should it be aimed at achieving "zero discharge" of pollution into the country's waters, as the Clean Water Act states; or should it be nothing less than saving the planet, as Worldwatch insists (and if so, what steps does that entail)?

Different perspectives on environmentalism would produce different lists of unfinished business, but almost all would agree with the assessment of the Conservation Foundation, which is that "the need for environmental action is at least as great as it has ever been." In 1987, the Environmental Protection Agency undertook a self-study that resulted in its own report, entitled Unfinished Business, and its own list of topics demanding further attention. The list is presented in Figure 1.1.

Why is this list so long? We already have alluded to one part of the explanation, which may lie in what we can call the "second generation thesis." The list of unfinished business is the consequence of starting with the easiest targets of opportunity: the most serious environmental problems that could be most easily cured get addressed first. We are now working our way down the list to problems that are either less serious or more intractable. The criteria of seriousness and tractability point in the same direction in their recommendations for public action, but for very different reasons. One suggests that projects remain unfinished because they are not so serious—we have more important things to do. The other intimates that problems remain unsolved because we lack the combination of capacity and will necessary to address them, even though they are of tremendous significance. Ought we to be prepared to triage environmental problems, taking the most manageable ones first, acknowledging that we are unable to address others and that still others are only worth addressing once we have finished with other business? We will return to some of these questions in Chapter 5, in the analysis of various proposals to prioritize the nation's environmental agenda.

Some versions of the "second generation thesis" identify a specific qualitative difference between first- and second-generation problems:

Environmental concerns have evolved since the heady days of the modern environmental movement, 1968 to 1972. Early legislation concentrated on

FIGURE 1.1
Agenda of "Unfinished Business" Identified by EPA

Inactive hazardous waste sites
Active hazardous waste sites
Accidental releases of toxics from chemical plants
Pesticide applications in farming
Other pesticide risks
Discharges of point sources directly into water systems
Indirect discharges of point sources into water systems
Nonpoint source (irrigation runoff, stormwater runoff, etc.) discharge
    into water systems
Criteria air pollutants (including acid rain)
Hazardous air pollutants
Other air pollutants
Occupational exposure to chemicals
Pesticide residues in food
Drinking water contamination
Genetic engineering
Mining wastes
Radon—indoor air pollution
Indoor air pollution other than radon
Indoor air pollution from consumer products
The greenhouse effect
Stratospheric ozone depletion
Contaminated sludge disposal
Wetlands preservation
Nonhazardous waste sites—municipal
Nonhazardous waste sites—industrial
New toxic chemicals
Releases from storage tanks
Other groundwater contamination
Accidental releases from oil tankers
Non-nuclear radiation
Estuaries, coastal waters, and oceans

Source: EPA, Unfinished Business (1987).

the impact of man's activities on the environment and the more obvious sources of pollution: air contaminants such as sulfur oxides and photo-chemical smog and water pollutants such as dissolved organic chemicals and pesticides. These were plainly hazards that affected many of us and our surroundings and were visible or had acute effects (seen in a relatively brief time). As we moved into the late 1970s and 1980s, the center of concern shifted to a more difficult and tenuous problem. Information gathered earlier suggested the possibility that exposure to substances in the air, land, and water, in consumer products, and in the workplace might affect us years later. To make matters worse, we were exposed to those substances in small amounts, in parts per million or even parts per billion. The focus, in short, shifted from hazard (which affects all of us) to risk (which affects some of us). [M. Rushefsky, Elites and Environmental Policy, in Environmental Politics and Policy 261, 262 (J. Lester, ed. 1990).]

Is Rushefsky arguing that older pollution problems were situations in which pollution was harming everyone? If so, is that correct? In distinguishing between hazard and risk, he argues that risk affects only some of us. In what sense is this correct? Consider, as examples, the risks of global warming and the risk of cancer from exposure to toxics. Assuming that one characteristic of (some) risks is that they affect only some of us, why does that make public policy concerning them "difficult and tenuous"? Do you find the distinction between hazard and risk helpful in distinguishing among different problems on the EPA's list of unfinished business?

In a moment we will turn to other analyses that suggest additional reasons, perhaps more persistent, for our rather long list of unfinished business. Many of the traditions frequently subsumed by the label Deep Ecology indicate that environmental problems reflect structural problems in society's basic orientation toward nature. First, however, consider the views of syndicated columnist David Broder, who suggested at the time of the twentieth anniversary celebration of Earth Day that, whatever the reasons for having more to do, American society has at last coalesced on some clear environmental goals or principles.

Broder, Beyond Folk Songs and Flowers
Wash. Post, Apr. 22, 1990, at B7

[A]t one level, the environmentalists have swept away all opposition. The "conservation ethic" has become one of the fixed guiding stars of American politics—a "value question" that permits only one answer from anyone who hopes to be part of the public dialogue. . . . [During Earth Week] I went to a press conference with the National Association of Manufacturers, the Business Roundtable and the representatives of many of the industries environmentalists love to hate—coal, chlorine, chemicals, compressed gas, electric power, plastics and rubber. They were gathered to proclaim their pride in the environmental advances of the past 20 years. Alexander Trowbridge, former secretary of commerce and former NAM president, said: "A clean environment is not just a desired . . . but a realistic goal, to which American industry is committed."

Banished, at least for the moment, were 20 years of business warnings that environmental standards could be achieved only at a huge cost in jobs, in productivity and in competitiveness. Environmental protection is "good business," Trowbridge declared. . . . All is not that benign, of course. As the business spokesmen readily conceded, they will be hard at work in the House of Representatives trying to weaken some provisions of the Senate-passed Clean Air bill. Their recognition that the values embodied in Earth Day have prevailed actually puts them in a better position to challenge the environmentalists in specific cases.

Because this Earth Day got so overblown, because the environmental message was so hyped with song and slogan, even the press and television, which normally give short shrift to the other side of the argument, were shamed into admitting that not all these issues offer neat solutions.

There was far more in the press in the last few days about the major NASA study, questioning the global-warming alarms, than there had been when it was published. I saw popular journals expressing skepticism for the first time about the need for the costly asbestos-removal program. A few iconoclasts, like Berkeley's Aaron Wildavsky, even were quoted as suggesting that some in the political Left are simply using environmentalism as a handy tool for achieving more government control of the economy. . . .

What all this suggests is that the argument is no longer about values. That's over, and the environmentalists have won. The argument now is about policies. And those with the best evidence and the best arguments, not just the purest hearts, will prevail.

NOTES AND QUESTIONS

1. Do you agree with Broder that the "conservation ethic" has prevailed in this country? If so, is it because, as Broder argues, the country has internalized a consensual position on the need to improve environmental quality and all that is now in dispute are the best programs or policies to accomplish this? Or, rather, might it be because a term like "conservation ethic" can be many things to many people, so that consensus is more apparent or verbal than real?

2. Consider the following observation made by environmental historian Joseph Petulla a decade before Broder's commentary:

> If we listen to environmental debate, it will appear that there is even some kind of consensus regarding values. Yet when you scratch the surface, when individuals—executives, labor officials, factory workers, teachers, professional workers, farmers, travelling salesmen—begin to tell you their own life stories, their hopes, needs, feelings, and opinions, you get a glimpse of the complexity of the problem of values. Very often the same person holds contradictory attitudes. Values seem to arise from economic interests,

yet many of the oldest and most deeply imbedded ones, like those prevalent
for centuries in religious thought, enjoy an existence virtually independent
of economic conditions. Attitudes toward [the environment] can be understood as only a small cluster in the vast constellation of values coming
from hundreds of cultural sources—family, religion, economic beliefs,
even personality and character. [J. Petulla, American Environmentalism
3 (1980).]

Is Petulla's observation still accurate, or has there been a fundamental
change in the past decade in the way people view the environment? How,
if at all, can Petulla's observation be reconciled with Broder's statements?

3. In April 1990, when Broder wrote his column, a nationwide
public opinion poll conducted by the Wall Street Journal and NBC News
found that when people were asked which was more important—protecting the environment or keeping prices down—80 percent chose "protect the environment," while only 13 percent chose "keep prices down."
When the same question had been asked in October 1981, only 51 percent had chosen protecting the environment, while 38 percent had chosen keeping prices down. Does this indicate a fundamental shift in the
public's values? Although there is wide agreement that protecting the
environment in the abstract is a desirable goal, consensus often breaks
down when the public is polled about specific policies. The April 1990
poll found limits to the public's environmental good intentions. By a 50
to 48 margin, the public rejected a "20 cent per gallon increase in the
price of gasoline for cleaner fuels," while "closing pollution-producing
factories, resulting in loss of jobs" was spurned by a 59 to 33 margin.
Rosewicz, Americans Are Willing to Sacrifice to Reduce Pollution, They
Say, Wall St. J., April 20, 1990, at A1.

4. Public opinion analyst Riley Dunlap describes support for environmental protection as a "passive consensus" where there is "widespread but not terribly intense public support" and the "government has
considerable flexibility in pursuing the goal and is not carefully monitored by the public." R. E. Dunlap, Political Opinion and Environmental
Policy, in Environmental Politics and Policy: Theories and Evidence 131
(J. Lester, ed. 1987). Do you agree? What evidence would support this
view? What implications would it have for designing an effective environmental policy?

5. Broder suggests that the country is in basic agreement that the
environment is worth saving, protecting, or enhancing. Before you can
move from this argument to matters of policy—where, in Broder's opinion, the action is—you have to be more specific than this. In particular,
you need some idea of where and what the environmental problems are.
What needs saving, protecting, and enhancing, and why? Reflect for a
moment more on the idea of an "environmental problem."

The problems identified in 1970—problems such as air pollution, water pollution, solid waste disposal, energy extraction and consumption patterns, natural resources preservation and management, agricultural land management, urban congestion, ocean fisheries depletion, and ocean waste dumping—are united by a single characteristic. They are all aspects of The Earth as Modified by Human Action, to borrow the title of an influential book by George Perkins Marsh published in 1874. Yet the earth is being modified in a great variety of ways at every moment. What further characteristics enable us to isolate some of these interactions, to label them problems and then to seek solutions to them? A preliminary thought: Perhaps we could classify human modifications of the earth according to whether they have harmful effects on the environment. Yet this thought prompts another: What constitutes a harmful environmental effect? While the answer may seem obvious in cases of egregious damage, a great deal of environmental harm occurs slowly and through complex and often poorly understood mechanisms. As we will see throughout this casebook, because it is difficult to determine with precision environmental causes and effects, even the most sophisticated scientific assessments of environmental impact are very uncertain. This has important implications for environmental policy-making that we will explore in greater detail later.

6. Assuming we have agreed that a given phenomenon constitutes an adverse environmental effect, assessing the significance of that effect proves to be an equally troublesome task. Since World War II, the magnitude of human effects on the environment has grown dramatically, as has the public's attitude toward the significance of those effects. Samuel Hays has argued that changes in environmental values are part of a still larger complex of changes in social attitudes and values:

> [Changes in environmental attitudes] are but one aspect of massive social changes that include television and the computer, new realms of production beyond manufacturing, new attitudes about the relationships between men and women, new levels of income and education, and new intensities of information acquisition and exchange. . . .
>
> While one could easily focus on the crisis aspect of pollution problems (and this usually was the tone of media coverage), on a more fundamental level the notion of pollution as a problem arose far more from new attitudes that valued both smoothly functioning ecosystems and higher levels of human health. . . .
>
> While preventive medicine had made impressive accomplishments in vaccination against infectious diseases, it now seemed to be less interested in the limitations on optimum health that might come from environmental causes. . . . Hence, a major aspect of the public's concern for chemical pollution was either to take matters into their own hands and avoid contaminants by means of new personal lifestyles, or to demand public action to prevent exposure. [S. Hays, Three Decades of Environmental Politics, in Government and Environmental Politics 19, 20, 25, 35 (M. J. Lacey, ed. 1989).]

Expanding on Hays, is it fair to conclude that the entire concept of "adverse environmental impact" is a perceptual concept, not some feature of the physical world? For instance, is it right to think that when some people affirm wilderness preservation and see great environmental harm from cutting down trees, while others affirm forest land as a productive human resource and see little environmental harm from cutting (perhaps followed by reforestation), their disagreement rests in part on a disagreement about values?

This is not to deny that physical alterations of the world are not "real"; it is only to suggest that humans interact with the world in two ways relevant to environmental policy. Their physical actions alter the world in measurable ways, and they also organize, categorize, and evaluate that world through the conceptual schemes and value perspectives they inhabit. This understanding of the role of values in interpreting the world suggests that terms like "adverse environmental impacts" and "environmental problems" are concepts constructed by and of human beings. Different value perspectives may construct a term differently, and hence different worldly phenomena may be included within it. Once one begins to see how many different value perspectives intertwine to form the environmental movement, and hence how many different understandings of adverse impacts and environmental problems may be coexisting in American thought, perhaps one should be a little suspicious of David Broder's suggestion that we are all environmentalists now.

B.　AMERICAN ENVIRONMENTALISM: SOURCES AND VALUES

The roots of American environmentalism are complex and rich. Interwoven much like actual plant roots, they constitute a variety of value systems and perspectives on humans and the environment that are at some times tightly joined and congruent and at other times far apart and divergent. It is impossible to do them justice through any short treatment. Still, some introduction to the major themes—actually a reminder of them, for you will all have encountered indications of these themes in the culture—is an essential prelude to the study of environmental law and policy. In a responsive democratic system, law and policy will embody attitudes, values, and objectives of the citizens. When those attitudes, values, and objectives merge in what John Rawls has termed an "overlapping consensus," law and policy may proceed without much overt attention to the tensions that exist elsewhere; when they diverge, law and policy will exhibit those tensions and, perhaps, paralysis or stalemate will result. Such moments may or may not reveal the full dimensions of the disagreements. Yet it may be impossible to understand completely the nature of the localized policy dispute unless you are aware that the disputants are speaking from within different traditions or are coming to the arena along different pathways.

Even the basic question of what constitutes an environmental problem (and consequently what issues ought to be on the country's unfinished environmental agenda) cannot be approached except from within some set of values that provides perspective and definition. One such perspective (a highly influential one) is provided by the discipline of economics and its associated value structure. The economic perspective posits that the paramount social value for public policy is the maximization of human satisfaction, or utility. It treats all features of the world, including the natural environment, as potential sources of satisfaction or dissatisfaction. Consequently, an environmental problem becomes defined as a state of affairs in which some feature of the environment is being used in a way that fails to take maximum advantage of its ability to satisfy human wants. If we take "pollution" to refer to undesired discharges into the environment, then the economic perspective will conceive of pollution problems as cases in which the benefits of polluting activities are not as great as the harm being done by that pollution to people's use of the environment. Pollution problems are viewed as cases of *inefficiency,* cases in which the use of resources could be altered so as to provide a better mix of harms and benefits. "To assert that there is a pollution problem or an environmental problem is to assert, at least implicitly, that one or more resources is not being used so as to maximize human satisfaction. Environmental problems are economic problems, and better insight can be gained by the application of economic analysis." W. Baxter, People or Penguins: The Case for Optimal Pollution 17 (1974). The economic perspective regards the goal of environmental policy to be improving the mix and, ideally, achieving the maximum or optimal amount of human satisfaction possible, given all the conflicting demands on the natural resources at stake.

Contrast with this Aldo Leopold's land ethic. Building on an understanding of humanity as but one part of a dynamic ecosystem, Leopold wrote that "a thing is right when it tends to preserve the integrity, stability, and beauty of the biotic community. It is wrong when it tends otherwise." A. Leopold, A Sand County Almanac 201, 224-225 (1968). Much of Leopold's work was devoted to expressing the value of aspects of the environment that had no obvious economic value. "To sum up," he wrote, "a system of conservation based solely on economic self-interest is hopelessly lopsided. It tends to ignore, and thus eventually to eliminate, many elements in the land community that lack commercial value, but that are (as far as we know) essential to its healthy functioning. It assumes, falsely, I think, that the economic parts of the biotic clock will function without the uneconomic parts." Id. at 213. Leopold plainly thought that polluting discharges may "tend otherwise" at levels well below those that are optimum from the economic perspective. For Leopoldians, the environmental problem of pollution can arise in situations in which the economic perspective would see no problem.

In particular, Leopold and other ecologists tend to believe that the *scale* of man's actions constitutes its most destructive quality. "The combined evidence of history and ecology seems to support one general deduction: the less violent the man-made changes, the greater the probability of successful readjustment in the [ecosystem]. Violence, in turn, varies with human population density; a dense population requires a more violent conversion. In this respect, North America has a better chance for permanence than Europe, if she can contrive to limit her density." Id. at 220. From the economic perspective, in contrast, large-scale disruptions of natural order are not necessarily to be avoided; it all depends on what costs and benefits to human beings are associated with those disruptions.

Economics provides an example of a homocentric perspective; Leopold's land ethic exemplifies a biocentric or ecocentric ethic. The difference is significant for an understanding of the country's environmental tradition and concerns.

The economic perspective is the quintessential example of a homocentric ethic, because the environment has value solely because it is used by humans in a way that satisfies their wants and desires. However, homocentric ethics do not have to be utilitarian in structure, as the economic perspective is, and some of them can be quite protective of the environment. Economic analysis itself has been employed frequently to argue *against* environmentally disruptive acts. Preservationist ideals, discussed below, are widely thought to be even more environmentally benign, yet a major theme within preservationist thought is also homocentric in orientation, insofar as the environment is being valued as a source of individual spiritual renewal. As a final example, some ethics of stewardship, many of them theological in origin, teach that humankind's responsibility is to husband and conserve resources that God has made available to us. Yet this, too, can have a homocentric orientation. "God as the wise conservator and superintendent of the natural world made humans caretakers and stewards in his image. Stewardship ethics, however, is fundamentally a homocentric ethic. Humans must manage nature for the benefit of the human species, not for the intrinsic benefit of other species." Merchant, Environmental Ethics and Political Conflict: A View from California, 12 Envtl. Ethics 45, 54-55 (1990).

In contrast, "environmental ethics" as a category of thought about the human-environment relationship has become identified as any "ethic which holds that natural entities and/or states of affairs are intrinsically valuable, and thus deserve to be the object of our moral concern," irrespective of whether they are useful or valuable to us in meeting *our* needs. Thompson, A Refutation of Environmental Ethics, 12 Envtl. Ethics 147, 148 (1990). Defined this way, environmental ethics are often referred to as biocentric or ecocentric ways of thinking, to contrast them with the homocentric ethics so familiar to our Western traditions (strictly speaking, these are not identical terms; biocentric ethics center on living things, ecocentric ethics on the entire ecosystem, living and nonliving).

In recent years, the science of ecology has had an influence on both homocentric and nonhomocentric systems of environmental values. NEPA's call for "systematic, interdisciplinary" analysis of "the profound impact of man's activity on the interrelationships of all components of the natural environment" is very much a call with ecological origins. Ecology's central orientation is to view "living organisms and this non-living (abiotic) environment [as] inseparably interrelated and inter-act[ing] upon each other." E. Odum, Fundamentals of Ecology 10 (2d ed. 1959). Ecological study provides a warning that if humans want to retain the relatively hospitable surroundings the earth has so far provided, we must become much more cognizant of the ecological ramifications of our actions. Leopold's land ethic evolved from his reflections as an applied ecologist studying the diversity and resilience of local ecosystems.

Perhaps most significant, seen as a way of understanding the human-environment relationship, ecology serves as a unifying thread for a number of different biocentric and ecocentric points of view. Its stress on relationships among mutually dependent components lends itself to an emphasis on harmony and cooperation that a variety of perspectives have found congenial. Leopold's land ethic is the starting point for many contemporary efforts to develop a picture of ethical behavior that is not centered on humans. For an investigation of the land ethic's meaning and its influence, see Companion to A Sand County Almanac (J. B. Callicott, ed. 1987).

While the science of ecology by itself cannot generate a moral imperative, the language of ecology has undoubtedly provided the non-homocentric vocabulary many see as essential to describe such an imperative. Even religious organizations, whose traditional views have frequently been analyzed as ignoring or diminishing the status of non-human species, have increasingly been expressing the importance of environmental issues in ecological terms. In January 1990, for example, Pope John Paul II issued a message entitled "Peace with All Creation." In it he explained that alongside the arms race, regional conflicts, and domestic injustice, world peace is threatened "by a lack of due respect for nature, by the plundering of natural resources and by a progressive decline in the quality of life." Throughout the message, the Pope employed the vocabulary of ecology.

[A] new ecological awareness is beginning to emerge which, rather than being downplayed, ought to be encouraged to develop into concrete programs and initiatives. . . . The profound sense that the earth is "suffering" is shared by those who do not profess our faith in God. Indeed, the increasing devastation of the world of nature is apparent to all. It results from the behavior of people who show a callous disregard for the hidden, yet perceivable requirements of the order and harmony which govern nature itself.

People are asking anxiously if it is still possible to remedy the damage which has been done. Clearly, an adequate solution cannot be found merely in a better management or more rational use of the earth's resources, as important as these may be. Rather, we must go to the source of the problem and face in its entirety that profound moral crisis of which the destruction of the environment is only one troubling aspect. . . . Theology, philosophy and science all speak of a harmonious universe, of a "cosmos" endowed with its own integrity, its own internal, dynamic balance. This order must be respected. The human race is called to explore this order, to examine it with due care and to make use of it while safeguarding its integrity.

Other religious organizations have also spoken out on the importance of ecological awareness. For example, the World Council of Churches organized a World Convocation on Justice, Peace, and the Integrity of Creation emphasizing the ecological themes of integrity and interconnection. Dr. Norman Jackson, executive director of the United Church of Christ Council of American Indian Ministry, stressing an Indian interpretation of the scriptures, writes that "humanity is understood to be an integral part of creation like everything else, with no authority or powers for domination and subduing creation. The integrity of creation means living in integral harmony with creation. . . ."

Such statements ought to be seen in the context of the controversy, alluded to a moment ago, concerning whether Western religions have been part of the environmental problem or part of the solution. In 1967, Lynn White wrote an influential essay entitled The Historical Roots of Our Ecological Crisis, in which he argued that much of the blame for our current situation rests with the biblical account of the Creation, in which God set humankind apart from the rest of creation, gave men and women dominion over creation, and instructed them to subdue it. White, The Historical Roots of Our Ecological Crisis, 155 Science 1203 (Mar. 10, 1967). White's analysis was supported soon thereafter in John Passmore's Man's Responsibility for Nature (1974). Ever since, environmentally concerned theologians have been retrieving the biblical tradition of stewardship as a counterweight to these accusations.

Another distinctive value system whose influence you will see in American policy and law is that of the preservationist. Preservationists may emphasize historical continuity, within our culture, our traditions, and our relationships with the natural environment. They may, however, also demand the preservation of certain places because they provide the context and catalyst for contemporary revelation and self-understanding. "Why should we not also enjoy an original relation with the universe?" asks Emerson.

> Why should not we have a poetry and philosophy of insight and not of tradition, and a religion by revelation to us, and not the history of theirs? Embosomed for a season in nature, whose floods of life stream around and through us, and invite us, by the powers they supply, to action proportioned to nature, why should we grope among the dry bones of the past . . . ? The sun shines today also. There is more wool and flax in the fields. There are new lands, new men, new thoughts. Let us demand our own works and law and worship.

Where are these insights found? By communing with nature itself, for "[u]ndoubtedly, we have no questions to ask which are unanswerable."

> We must trust the perfection of creation so far as to believe that whatever curiosity the order of things has awakened in our minds, the order to things can satisfy. . . . [N]ature is already, in its forms and tendencies, describing its own design. Let us interrogate the great apparition that shines so peacefully around us. Let us inquire, to what end is nature? . . . In the woods, we return to reason and faith. There I feel that nothing can befall me in life—no disgrace, no calamity (leaving me my eyes), which nature cannot repair. Standing on the bare ground—my head bathed by the blithe air and uplifted into infinite space—all mean egotism vanishes. I become a transparent eyeball; I am nothing; I see all; the current of the Universal Being circulates through me; I am part or parcel of God. [R. W. Emerson, "Nature" (1836), reprinted in New World Metaphysics 171, 171-174 (G. Gunn, ed. 1981).]

The writings of Emerson, Thoreau, and other Transcendentalists firmly graft into American literary history the connection between spiritual renewal and nature, so that one recurring argument for wilderness preservation urges doing so "because our lives and our conception of ourselves will be enhanced—in a spiritual sense—if we learn to appreciate [nature] for what it is and we learn how to live in harmony with it." J. Thompson, Preservation of Wilderness and the Good Life, in Environmental Philosophy (R. Elliot and A. Gare, eds. 1983).

These thoughts may misleadingly suggest that preservationists are necessarily homocentric thinkers, valuing nature for what it provides for the human spirit. For many in this tradition, nature is to be valued first for itself; it then turns out that human contemplation of nature proves a source of inspiration as well. This biocentric idea is well expressed by the naturalist John Muir, founder of the Sierra Club:

The world, as we are told, was made especially for man—a presumption not supported by the facts. . . . Now it never seems to occur to [many people] . . . that Nature's object in making animals and plants might possibly be first of all the happiness of each of them, not the creation of all for the happiness of one. Why should man value himself as more than a small part of the one great unit of creation?

Some argue that the kind of intrinsic value Muir attributes to non-humankind supports the conclusion that those nonhumans possess rights that environmental policy ought to respect. David Brower, when he was chairman of the Sierra Club, expressed his agreement with Muir by announcing, "I believe in the rights of creatures other than man." However, animal rights advocates disagree over the precise source of those rights. Peter Singer and others argue for an animal welfare ethic, basing their views on the capacity of animals to experience pleasure and pain, and on that basis extending a homocentric ethic, Benthamite utilitarianism, to cover nonhuman species. See P. Singer, Animal Liberation (2d ed. 1990). Tom Regan, on the other hand, rejects the utilitarian approach and instead finds support for animal rights in the idea that living beings who have the capacity to experience life in certain qualitative ways (including having beliefs and desires, perceptions, memory, and a sense of the future) possess inherent value that gives them a right to respect, independent of the pleasures or pains they may experience. See T. Regan, The Case for Animal Rights (1983).

Whether a case for animal rights can ultimately be made out is still being debated. Others seek to pretermit the question. Paul Taylor, for instance, argues that, once one accepts an ecological perspective, seeing species in addition to humankind as integral elements of the biota, each pursuing their own good in their own way, one must become committed to an attitude of respect for nature. Such an attitude requires, among other things, that we act "out of consideration and concern for the good of wild living things." P. Taylor, Respect for Nature 84 (1986). For additional views, see J. B. Callicott, Hume's Is/Ought Dichotomy and the Relation of Ecology to Leopold's Land Ethic, in In Defense of the Land Ethic: Essays in Environmental Philosophy (Callicott, ed. 1989). However wide the disagreements among these environmental ethicists, they remain on the biocentric and ecocentric side, seeking to articulate "not an ethic for the *use* of the environment, a 'management ethic,' but an ethic *of* the environment." J. B. Callicott, The Case Against Moral Pluralism, 12 Envtl. Ethics 99, 99 (1990).

ENVIRONMENTAL PHILOSOPHY: A PATHFINDER

Environmental ethics has become an important field in its own right in recent years. It has spawned a vast literature concerning alternative justifications for respecting the environment on philosophical grounds. These debates are extraordinarily valuable for, as Christopher Stone notes, once one begins a serious inquiry into the philosophical basis for environmental protection, it rapidly "bores to the very bedrock of law and morals." C. Stone, Earth and Other Ethics (1987).

In addition to influential classics such as G. P. Marsh, The Earth as Modified by Human Action (1874); A. Leopold, A Sand County Almanac (1949); R. Carson, Silent Spring (1963); C. Stone, Should Trees Have Standing? Toward Legal Rights for Natural Objects, 45 S. Cal. L. Rev. 450 (1972); E. F. Schumacher, Small Is Beautiful (1973); and L. H. Tribe, Ways Not to Think About Plastic Trees: New Foundations for Environmental Law, 83 Yale L.J. 1315 (1974), the historical development of American environmental thought is summarized in S. P. Hays, Conservation and the Gospel of Efficiency: The Progressive Conservation Movement, 1890-1920 (1959); R. Nash, Wilderness and the American Mind ⟵ (1967); J. Petulla, American Environmentalism (1980); and ⟶ R. Nash, The Rights of Nature (1989), which contains an excellent annotated bibliography.

The classic statement of the economic perspective on environmental issues is J. H. Dales, Pollution, Property, and Prices (1968). This perspective is also outlined in simplified form in W. Baxter, People or Penguins: The Case for Optimal Pollution (1974); R. Posner, The Economics of Law (1987); and A. M. Polinsky, An Introduction to Law and Economics (1983). Mark Sagoff has done some of the most interesting work critiquing the economic perspective on environmental issues. Much of his work is summarized in M. Sagoff, The Economy of the Earth (1988).

Useful introductory anthologies to environmental philosophy include W. T. Blackstone, ed., Philosophy and the Environmental Crisis (1974); T. Regan, ed., Earthbound: New Introductory Essays in Environmental Ethics (1984); D. Scherer and T. Attig, eds., Ethics and the Environment (1983); D. VanDeVeer and C. Pierce, People, Penguins and Plastic Trees: Basic Issues in Environmental Ethics (1986); and B. G. Norton and H. Shue, eds., The Preservation of Species (1986).

In addition to the works already cited above or in the text, proposals to develop an ethic of the environment are developed in R. Attfield, The Ethics of Environmental Concern (1983); H. Rolston III, Philosophy Gone Wild: Essays in Environmental Ethics (1986) and Environmental Ethics: Duties to and Values in the Natural World (1988); E. C. Hargrove, Foundations of Environmental Ethics (1989); A. Brennan, Thinking About Nature: An Investigation of Nature, Value and Ecology (1988); and P. Wenz, Environmental Justice (1988).

Much of the important literature in this rapidly developing field (which now includes animal rights, Deep Ecology, and ecofeminist movements) is contained in a periodical that often is difficult to find in law libraries: Environmental Ethics, a journal published quarterly by the Department of Philosophy at the University of Georgia.

Other perspectives that are not exclusively oriented toward the environment also play significant roles in the debate over environmental policy. A prominent characteristic of many environmental issues is that they impose costs or risks on individuals that are not of those individuals' choosing. The residents of Love Canal did not choose to be exposed to toxic substances; citizens all over the world did not choose to run the risks of global warming. Undisclosed trace elements of carcinogens in food create risks to consumers that they did not choose. In a society such as ours, it is possible to argue that "the principal value informing public law for the workplace and the environment—as well as private behavior—may be *autonomy,* not *efficiency,*" as Mark Sagoff has written:

> An efficient society promotes the ability of the individuals in it to satisfy their wants and desires; it promotes freedom in the sense that refers to an individual's welfare. This sense of freedom—"negative" freedom or freedom from interference in one's pursuit of happiness—has no necessary connection with autonomy. Freedom, in this sense, has to do with getting what you want or doing what you like; autonomy, on the other hand, consists in your ability to get or to do these things on your own, without being beholden to any other person, without accepting favors, and without having the important background decisions made by somebody else. . . . [T]he public's primary goal . . . may not be efficiency; it may be autonomy. People want to determine the background level of risk; they do not want the working conditions of their lives to be determined by others. It does not matter how cost-beneficial risks are; it is a question, rather, of who controls them. [Sagoff, On Markets for Risks, 41 Md. L. Rev. 755, 761-762, 764 (1982).]

Another current within the broader environmental movement connects environmental issues to a larger agenda of social justice. Social activist environmentalists focus on the connections between environmental policy and issues of poverty, discrimination, and other historical concerns of a progressive social agenda. They are frequently critical of some of the best-known national environmental organizations because, in their opinion, "national environmental groups are out of touch with certain pivotal realities in the industrialized world—issues of racism, social justice, economic fairness and democracy. . . . As long as it has poor communities to dump on, corporate America will have no incentive to reduce waste production or substitute safe materials. Grassroots activism brings the people face to face with the corporate polluter, bypassing the compromise-ridden regulatory apparatus." Toward a New Environmentalism, 15 Greenpeace 2 (July-Aug. 1990). Social activists have coined terms such as "environmental racism" to express the link they see between their race discrimination concerns and environmental issues. See, e.g., The Integrity of Justice, 19 Sojourners 22 (Feb.-Mar. 1990).

These concerns focus on the notion that environmental risks are not evenly distributed across racial and ethnic groups and income classes. Studies have shown that minorities and the poor suffer disproportionately high levels of exposure to toxic substances. For example, the Agency for Toxic Substances and Disease Registry found that levels of lead in children's blood vary inversely with income and that a substantially greater proportion of minority children than white children had dangerously high blood lead levels. While 17 percent of all American children had dangerously high blood lead levels, the proportion of poor African-American children in the inner city with such lead levels was 67.8 percent. Agency for Toxic Substances and Disease Registry, The Nature and Extent of Lead Poisoning in the United States (1988).

Studies also have shown that the location of hazardous waste disposal facilities is disproportionately concentrated in minority communities. In 1983 the General Accounting Office found that most hazardous waste landfills in the Middle Atlantic states were located in predominately African-American communities. General Accounting Office, Siting of Hazardous Waste Landfills and Their Correlation with Racial and Economic Status of Surrounding Communities (June 1983). A more comprehensive study by the United Church of Christ Commission for Racial Justice concluded that the single variable best able to explain the location of commercial hazardous waste facilities in the United States was the racial composition of the community. Toxic Wastes and Race in the United States: A National Report on the Racial and Socio-Economic Characteristics of Communities Surrounding Hazardous Waste Sites (1987). Even after controlling for community income and other socio-economic factors, the study found that the proportion of the population that was African-American was the best predictor of communities' likelihood to be located near a dump.

The social justice agenda shares some points with the ideal of autonomy mentioned earlier; it also emphasizes participatory democracy as a decisionmaking ideal that should be applied to environmental problems as well as all others that affect the lives of the poor and other marginalized groups. "Creating a sustainable society cannot be accomplished without the consent and participation, indeed the leadership, of those who are marginalized and victimized." Toward a New Environmentalism, at 2. Indeed, it is for expository purposes only that we can isolate the different strands of environmentalism from one another, because the vast majority of environmentally conscious Americans hold to some blend or another of the views we have summarized, with the single possible exception of the economic perspective, because many environmentalists define themselves in opposition to the cost-benefit perspective of economics.

The more transformative strands of American environmentalism come together under the umbrella of the Deep Ecology movement. In the words of one practitioner, "the inherent contradiction—passionate identification with nature, and the simultaneous exploitation of natural resources—is at the heart of the deep ecology issue." Tobias, Introduction, in Deep Ecology v (M. Tobias, ed. 1988). In arguing for greater attention to mankind's identification with nature, Deep Ecologists elaborate a critique of society's apparent decision to give in to the exploitative urge, a critique that picks up many of the themes just reviewed, seeing in them a "minority tradition" within the American heritage. Figure 1.2, compiled from two of the seminal articles of the Deep Ecology Movement, shows some of the major thematic differences that deep ecologists stress.

Some or all of these aspects will frequently converge, agreeing that some human action raises an environmental concern. Opposition to the proposal in the 1960s to dam the Colorado River near the Grand Canyon was a dramatic example of such a consensus. The proposal raised obvious preservationist concerns because of the expanse of inspiring natural formations and wilderness area that would be lost to view and to human appreciation. The land ethicist saw the action as one whose scale and impact would drastically destabilize the many ecosystems included within the Canyon or dependent on the free running of the Colorado through it. People standing within the economic perspective could see that human costs would be incurred from damming the river that made the enterprise questionable, especially in terms of recreational opportunities foregone.

Even when different aspects of environmentalism agree on immediate aims or programs, however, an underlying tension remains. Some of these aspects—mainly the biocentric or ecocentric ones, but also some parts of preservationism and the ethics of stewardship—bring a moral or ethical intensity to environmental problems. They tend to produce feelings of outrage and to demand prompt solutions. Other aspects—the economic perspective chief among them—tend to view environmental problems as instances of mismanagement or institutional

FIGURE 1.2
Comparison of Dominant and Minority Traditions in American Life

Dominant tradition	Minority tradition
centralized authority	authority decentralized; nonhierarchical; democratic
bureaucratization	small-scale community
police power	local autonomy
individualism (subjectivism)	self-responsibility
leadership by holding instruments of violence	leadership by example
competitiveness	helping others; mutual aid; communalism
frequent encouragement to "produce more; consume more"	simplicity of "wants"
government regulation	self-regulation; nonviolence practiced in a "professional" way
secular authority	respect for spiritual-religious mentors
church monopolization of religious ritual	full community participation in rituals
tendency toward monopoly of ideology whether religious or secular	tolerance of variety of approaches to being (religious experiences)
perception of nature as "data" or as "natural resources"	open communication with nature
narrow definition of citizenship; all other inhabitants of place are slaves or disenfranchised	broad definition of community (including animals, plants); intuition of organic wholeness
natural diversity valued as a resource to be used	natural diversity accorded its own (intrinsic) value
belief that it is nonsense to talk about value except as value for humankind	belief that equating value with value for humans reveals a racial prejudice
belief that pollution should be decreased if it threatens economic growth	belief that decrease of pollution has priority over economic growth

Sources: B. Devall and G. Sessions, Deep Ecology: Living as If Nature Mattered 18-19 (1985); A. Naess, Identification as a Source of Deep Ecological Attitudes, in Deep Ecology 256, 257 (M. Tobias, ed. 1988).

failure. They are less outraged because they tend not to criticize the underlying motivations and preferences that produce environmental degradation, wanting instead to concentrate on removing the opportunities for those preferences to operate unchecked. A founder of Deep Ecology has framed the contrast this way:

Deep ecology, unlike reform environmentalism, is not just a pragmatic short-term social movement with a goal like stopping nuclear power or cleaning up waterways. Deep ecology first attempts to question and present alternatives to conventional ways of thinking in the modern West. Deep ecology understands that some of the "solutions" of reform environmentalism are counter-productive. Deep ecology seeks transformation of values and social organization. [Devall, The Deep Ecology Movement, 1980 Natural Resources J. 299, 303.]

Nor do the different aspects even always agree on short-term aims. From the economic perspective, for example, it is very difficult to see the loss of old-growth forest and the endangerment of the northern spotted owl in the Pacific Northwest as an environmental problem when weighed against the economic benefits of continuing the lumbering of old-growth forests. For the preservationist or land ethicist it is hard to find a more dramatic issue.

The varying traditions within the environmental movement of the United States also struggle within and among themselves to achieve consensus on tactics. Lately, some elements of the Deep Ecology movement and grassroots environmental groups have become disenchanted with the program of the national environmental groups that will be the main representatives of American environmentalism confronted in these pages. For Deep Ecologists, these organizations—the Natural Resources Defense Council, the Environmental Defense Fund, the Sierra Club— have become too cozy with the institutions of power and too used to the tactics of negotiation and compromise. Lois Gibbs of the Citizens' Clearinghouse for Hazardous Waste charges that the national groups have "the same mentality as government and industry" because they fight environmental battles "in intellectual terms," while "[p]eople at the grassroots level live these fights." Weisskopf, From Fringe to Political Mainstream, Wash. Post, April 19, 1990, at A1, A16.

Indeed, the national organizations do have a continuing presence in Washington; they are regular participants in the processes of legislation drafting, agency rulemaking, and litigation in the federal courts. They are relied on by politicians to represent the environmental point of view. Thus, they have tremendous power, but they also shoulder an appreciable responsibility, because the approval of these environmental organizations for a government action such as new clean air legislation or a controversial regulation greatly enhances the credibility of the action among the environmentally concerned voting public and also practically assures that no more stringent measure will be forthcoming. One group of scholars has even suggested that the extremely tough-talking legislation of the early 1970s can be traced to the *absence* of such environmental groups of national stature. Because there were no such organizations with whom the politicians could negotiate, the politicians competed with each other to perfect tougher and tougher legislation, rather than seeking a more modest consensus for which they could claim credit after it had received the stamp of approval of the recognized environmental organizations. See Ackerman, Elliot, and Millian, Toward a Theory of Statutory Evolution: The Federalization of Environmental Law, 1 J. L. Econ. & Org. 313 (1985).

An identifiable component of the Deep Ecology movement equates such participation in mainstream political and legal structures with eventual co-optation by them. No individual's career exemplifies the tension between the tactics of participation and those of confrontation better than David Brower's. Brower was the first full-time executive director of the Sierra Club. By pressing an aggressive agenda of protecting the national parks and forests, he transformed the Sierra Club from an established preservationist organization with membership concentrated primarily in California to a national organization with a significant voice in national policy. Opposition to the government's proposal to dam the Grand Canyon proved the most visible and dramatic rallying point for the Club. Eventually, however, the board of the Sierra Club and Brower disagreed over tactics, and Brower left to form the more confrontational Friends of the Earth. After years with FOE, Brower has once again moved on.

Whereas Brower is an excellent example of a life dedicated to environmental protection through aggressive, noncompromising demands, Edward Abbey is the author who has most significantly inspired the direct action wing of environmentalism through his writings, nonfiction and fiction. One direct action strategy has been labeled "ecotague" and even "ecoterrorism." It manifests itself in such actions as spiking trees in old-growth forests to prevent their destruction by lumber companies. Direct action environmentalism is associated with groups such as Earth First!, whose slogan is "No compromise in defense of Mother Earth," although most Earth First! members disavow such tactics as tree spiking. Prior to this ecotague was known as "monkeywrenching," taking its name from Abbey's The Monkeywrench Gang (1976), the fictional bible of militant environmentalism. Whereas Brower's tactics consist of unwavering insistence that environmental principles not be compromised or negotiated away, Abbey's monkeywrench gang sought to disrupt development projects and other kinds of environmental degradation by engaging in a kind of guerrilla warfare against them. The gang cut down billboards with chainsaws or blew them up with explosives, pulled up surveyor's stakes around highway construction projects, ruined heavy equipment by pouring sand in gas tanks, and planned the blowing up of a dam.

To explore how different value perspectives influence attitudes toward environmental policy we turn now to a contemporary controversy that almost everyone would classify as "environmental."

PROBLEM EXERCISE: SHOULD THE ARCTIC NATIONAL WILDLIFE REFUGE BE OPENED TO OIL EXPLORATION AND DEVELOPMENT?

Along the northeast coast of Alaska 200 miles north of the Arctic Circle lies a pristine wilderness area. Sometimes called North America's Serengeti, the area is home to a vast herd of porcupine caribou whose migratory range extends over 96,000 square miles. It is the kind of place most Americans encounter only in the pages of National Geographic, which describes it as "a land of mountains and broad, lake-filled plains, where caribou have worn trails in rock and geese have traced paths in the sky over millennia of rhythmic wandering; where ice holds the sea and frost the land until a brief, glorious burst of flowering summer; . . . a roadless land, a part of the North little touched by the 20th century, or the 19th, or the first." Lee, Oil in the Wilderness: An Arctic Dilemma, National Geographic, Dec. 1988, at 858.

To an oil company geologist the area is inspirational for a very different reason. Located 40 miles east of North America's largest oil field at Prudhoe Bay, the area represents "the chance of a lifetime to search for 'elephants'—oil fields with more than a hundred million barrels of producible reserves—in perhaps the last major hunting ground on North America's mainland." Id. at 863.

In 1960 Congress recognized the special character of Alaska's northeastern coastal plain by establishing a nine-million-acre Arctic National Wildlife Range there. When it subsequently enacted legislation governing the disposition of Alaskan public lands (the Alaska National Interest Lands Conservation Act), Congress expanded the protected area along the coastal plain into the 19-million-acre Arctic National Wildlife Refuge (ANWR). The legislation set aside nearly half of ANWR as wilderness area, while directing the Secretary of the Interior (in section 1002) to report on whether 1.5 million acres of the coastal plain ("section 1002 lands") should be opened to oil development or preserved as wilderness and wildlife habitat.

In response to this directive, field staff from the Interior Department prepared a draft report assessing the impact of oil exploration and development on the section 1002 lands. They concluded that "[l]ong-term losses in fish and wildlife resources, subsistence uses, and wilderness values would be the inevitable consequences" of development, which "will result in widespread, long-term changes in wildlife habitats, wilderness environment, and Native community activities" and possibly "a major population decline" in the caribou herd. However, the final report issued by Secretary of the Interior Donald P. Hodel in 1987 reached sharply different conclusions. It stated that "[i]mpacts predicted for exploration and development drilling were minor or negligible on all wildlife resources on the 1002 area." While conceding that "there is a risk that a decline could occur" in the caribou population, it found that "no appreciable population decline is expected as a result of oil development." Secretary Hodel's report recommended that the area be opened immediately to oil exploration and development.

Following the release of the Interior Department report, the U.S. Fish and Widlife Service was asked by a member of Congress to evaluate whether the environmental impact of oil development in nearby Prudhoe Bay had been as benign as predicted in the government's environmental impact statement. A draft of their report was leaked to Congress in May 1988. The draft report found that the environmental impact of oil drilling in Prudhoe Bay had been far greater than estimated in the environmental impact statements prepared 15 years earlier. It noted that 11,000 acres of wildlife habitat had been destroyed, nearly twice what had been predicted, and that the populations of bears, wolves and other predators, and most bird species had declined. Although caribou had increased in number, the report attributed this increase to a decline in the numbers of bears and other caribou predators. It noted that more than 200 million gallons of fresh water unexpectedly were being withdrawn from lakes and streams by oil operations each year and that erosion, sedimentation, and oil spills had done far more damage to water quality than anticipated.

After the Fish and Wildlife report was leaked to Congress, a House committee chair charged that for political reasons the Interior Department had been deliberately suppressing it since its completion in December 1987. Officials of the Interior Department denied this charge and claimed that the report had not been released because of internal disagreement over the validity of its conclusions. Shabecoff, Alaska Oilfield Report Cites Unexpected Harm to Wildlife, N.Y. Times, May 11, 1988, at 1. During the ensuing controversy, the following editorial appeared in the New York Times.

‖ *Risks Worth Taking for Oil* ‖
N.Y. Times, June 2, 1988, at A26

Can Big Oil and its Government regulators be trusted with the fragile environment of Alaska's Arctic Wildlife Refuge? Congress, pressed by the Reagan Administration to allow exploratory drilling in what may be North America's last great oil reserve, has been wrestling with the question for years. Then, last month, opponents' skepticism was heightened by a leaked report from the Fish and Wildlife Service saying that environmental disruption in the nearby North Slope oil fields is far worse than originally believed.

The North Slope development has been America's biggest test by far of the proposition that it is possible to balance energy needs with

sensitivity for the environment. The public therefore deserves an independent assessment of the ecological risks and an honest assessment of the energy rewards.

No one wants to ruin a wilderness for small gain. But in this case, the potential is enormous and the environmental risks are modest. Even if the report's findings are confirmed, the likely value of the oil far exceeds plausible estimates of the environmental cost.

The amount of oil that could be recovered from the Wildlife Refuge is not known. But it seems likely that the coastal plain, representing a small part of the acreage in the refuge, contains several billion barrels, worth tens of billions of dollars. But drilling is certain to disrupt the delicate ecology of the Arctic tundra.

Some members of Congress believe that no damage at all is acceptable. But most are ready to accept a little environmental degradation in return for a lot of oil. Hence the relevance of the experience at Prudhoe Bay, which now yields 20 percent of total U.S. oil production.

Last year, Representative George Miller, a California Democrat and opponent of drilling within the refuge, asked the Fish and Wildlife Service to compare the environmental impact predicted in 1972 for Prudhoe Bay with the actual impact. The report from the local field office, never released by the Administration, offers a long list of effects, ranging from birds displaced to tons of nitrous oxide released into the air.

According to the authors, development used more land, damaged more habitat acreage and generated more effluent than originally predicted. The authors also argue that Government monitoring efforts and assessment of long-term effects have been inadequate.

It's important to find out whether these interpretations are sensible and how environmental oversight could be improved. The General Accounting Office, a creature of Congress, is probably the most credible agency to do the job. But even taken at face value, the report's findings hardly justify putting oil exploration on hold.

No species is reported to be endangered. No dramatic permanent changes in ecology are forecast. Much of the unpredicted damage has arisen because more oil has been produced than originally predicted. Even so, the total acreage affected by development represents only a fraction of 1 percent of the North Slope wilderness.

The trade-off between energy and ecology seems unchanged. If another oil field on the scale of Prudhoe Bay is discovered, developing it will damage the environment. That damage is worth minimizing. But it is hard to see why absolutely pristine preservation of this remote wilderness should take precedence over the nation's energy needs.

Question One.   The editorial argues in favor of opening ANWR to drilling. Do you find its arguments to be persuasive? The editorial does not favor drilling for oil in *all* circumstances. When would the editorial writers be opposed to drilling in a wilderness area? Do you agree? Are there additional circumstances in which you would oppose drilling? The editorial suggests that anyone supporting "absolutely pristine preservation" of the Wildlife Refuge mistakenly gives wilderness "precedence over the nation's energy needs." Is that correct? For someone concerned about endangered species or ecological damage, is it sufficient that "no species is reported to be endangered" and that "[n]o dramatic permanent changes in ecology are forecast"?

After the *Exxon Valdez* oil spill occurred on March 24, 1989, Congress refused to endorse oil drilling in the Arctic National Wildlife Refuge. The editorial staff of the New York Times apparently had second thoughts as well. In an editorial on July 22, 1989 the Times declared that the "whole sorry episode sends a powerful warning to those who would seek oil in fragile areas without first rebuilding public confidence in the industry's capacity to drill and deliver the oil safely and cleanly." The Times endorsed a congressional proposal to impose a temporary moratorium on offshore oil drilling, noting that the public "wants time to weigh the risks of drilling in fragile areas against the benefits." The Wider Stain of Spilled Oil, N.Y. Times, July 22, 1989. Responding to environmental concerns, President Bush in June 1990 imposed a broad moratorium on drilling and leasing off much of the nation's coastline. However, he has continued to push for opening ANWR to oil drilling.

Question Two.   Did the *Exxon Valdez* disaster change the nature or magnitude of the risks of Alaskan oil development, or did it simply make people more aware of those risks so that they took them into account in new ways? Students of cognitive psychology have concluded that we increase our sense of the probability that some catastrophe will occur when one has occurred in the recent past, because an example of the catastrophe is more available to us.

Question Three.   Once a wilderness area has been developed, it will never again be wilderness, or at least not for a very, very long time. So the decision to develop cannot be reversed. On the other hand, a decision to place an area off limits can later be reversed. Following Iraq's invasion of Kuwait in August 1990, Alaska's congressional delegation seized the opportunity to urge that ANWR be opened for drilling to reduce American dependence on foreign oil. How should the apparent irreversibility of a decision to open a wilderness area to development be factored into the decisionmaking process?

Question Four. Environmental decisions inevitably occur in the context of uncertainty over the consequences of those decisions; to a considerable degree we are ignorant even of the applicable probabilities to associate with adverse consequences. What role should either type of uncertainty play in environmental decision-making? Is this issue related to the issue of irreversibility? We address these questions in greater detail in Chapter 4.

In February 1991, and while hostilities were continuing in the Persian Gulf, President Bush announced his administration's National Energy Strategy. Placing much less emphasis on the use of energy efficiency and energy conservation measures than environmentalists had been urging, the Strategy included a proposal to open ANWR to exploratory drilling. The Strategy forecast that in 2005 ANWR will produce 4 percent of the oil consumed in the United States, declining to less than 1 percent after the year 2010. Even if ANWR is opened to oil development, the Strategy predicts that the United States will be importing 60 percent of its oil by 2030.

At the time of the release of the National Energy Strategy, the Times addressed the ANWR debate again.

Conserve Oil—and Wilderness
N.Y. Times, Feb. 19, 1991, at A16

The Arctic National Wildlife Refuge forms only a small part of Alaska. Smaller still is the coastal plain of the refuge, a narrow wilderness that flanks the Beaufort Sea. The frozen plain is home to maybe 200 Eskimos, 180,000 caribou and dozens of rare Arctic species. It may also contain the biggest undiscovered oilfield in the United States.

President Bush wants to open the plain for exploration. The proposal symbolizes everything that's wrong with what is known of Mr. Bush's energy strategy, which will be unveiled this week. It's not so much that he would exploit an ecological treasure, although to many environmentalists that is the heart of the matter. What's wrong is that he would do so even though conservation could achieve the same results without risk to the environment.

The oil industry, which is running out of places to drill, makes a strong case for exploring the refuge. It says that only 12,700 acres of the plain—less than 1 percent—would be marred by the usual detritus: rigs, pipelines, drilling mud, airfields. Meanwhile, the Interior Department figures the odds are one in five of finding as much as 3.4 billion barrels of oil. By industry standards, those are good odds promising a huge return. By 2005, assuming quick discovery, the field could reach peak production of 800,000 barrels a day. That's 10 percent of all present U.S. production.

These numbers are almost big enough to obscure two counterarguments. One: The oil under the plain is not a renewable resource. Soon it will be gone. Two: If the objective is to reduce reliance on foreign oil and create a rational long-range energy policy—and Mr. Bush says it is—there may be far better ways of achieving it.

For example, assuming that the number of cars increases only slightly, a gradual increase in fuel economy standards from 27.5 miles per gallon to 40 could reduce demand by two million barrels of oil per day by 2005. That's far more than the coastal plain could produce. Besides, the conservation saving would be permanent.

Mandating tough fuel standards may not be the most fair or effective way to save oil. A good case can be made for a stiff gasoline tax that goes to the root of America's addiction to petroleum. In the bargain, it would raise money to develop other energy sources. Yet neither alternative is mentioned in the energy proposals now circulating in Washington. Nor is there more than a hint that consumption may be part of the energy equation. Give me the refuge, the President seems to say, and we will drill our way out of dependency.

Perhaps, someday, a stronger case can be made for exploring this fragile terrain. But Mr. Bush hasn't begun to make it. Until he does, the man who asks to be known as the Environment President sounds like the Expedient President instead.

Question Five. Now the Times's editors seem opposed to ANWR exploration until the Bush Administration has exhausted more environmentally benign means of achieving the same energy gains. Why didn't that consideration appear to influence their first editorial position? Does the more recent editorial indicate that decision-makers should consider whether alternative means are available to satisfy societal ends at less cost to the environment? If so, many environmental decisions would appear to depend on the current state of technology, which determines the costs and availability of alternatives. In the minds of many, one important objective of environmental laws is to encourage the development of even better technologies, so that we can find ways around current impasses such as the energy-environment conflict presented in the first Times editorial. For further discussion of the objective of encouraging the development of better technologies, see pages 165 to 173, in Chapter 2.

Question Six. Given the shifting positions reflected in the editorials, what role do you now think irreversibility considerations should play in such decisions?

Question Seven. Scientists have continually emphasized the uncertainty of projections concerning the environmental impact of development at ANWR. Faced with this uncertainty, both sides in the debate over ANWR offer sharply different projections based largely on the same data. For example, proponents of opening ANWR to drilling argue that the growth of the Central Arctic caribou herd in the vicinity of the Prudhoe Bay oil field from 5,000 to 18,000 head during the past 15 years demonstrates that drilling will not cause unacceptable harm to the environment. Opponents argue that caribou herds have grown worldwide in the past decade as part of a cyclical increase that scientists do not fully understand. They note that calving has fallen sharply within a half mile of the roads and facilities at Prudhoe Bay, and they argue that drilling at ANWR would threaten its much larger 180,000-head porcupine caribou herd, which is dependent on a much smaller area of land. Scientists emphasize that the long-term, cumulative impacts of development at Prudhoe Bay will take decades to assess. How much confidence in projections of environmental impact should be required before a decision concerning a major development project is based on them? Should it depend on the likely magnitude of the consequences? On their reversibility?

Question Eight. Is the ANWR controversy primarily a dispute over values (between adherents of the economic and ecological perspectives) or a factual dispute that turns on differing predictions of the likely consequences of drilling? Consider the following contrasting descriptions of ANWR offered by opponents and proponents of drilling during March 1991 congressional hearings. Brooks Yeager, vice president of the National Audubon Society, described ANWR as "one of the earth's last great dynamic ecosystems." Accusing environmentalists of distorting the facts about ANWR, Walter Hickel, governor of Alaska, described it as "a barren, marshy wilderness in the summer, infested with uncountable mosquitoes, and locked in temperatures of 60 and 70 degrees below zero for up to nine months of the year." What explains these sharply contrasting descriptions of ANWR? Are they the product of differences in values or of different views concerning what "the facts" are? Do our values inevitably influence our willingness to accept certain propositions as "facts" and to draw certain conclusions from them?

Question Nine. Native Americans living in remote villages near ANWR have a very different perception of what the ANWR battle is about. To Sarah James, a Gwich'in from Artic Village, Alaska, it "is not just an environmental issue." Rather,

[i]t is about the survival of the ancient culture that depends on the caribou. It is about the basic tribal and human rights to continue [our] way of life.

For thousands of years we have lived with the caribou right where we are today. We are talking about an Indian nation that still lives on the land and depends on the herd. In my village 75 percent of protein comes from caribou. It's not just what we eat. It is who we are. Caribou are our life. It's in our stories and songs and the whole way of the world. [Sarah James, Testimony before a Subcomm. of the Senate Environment and Public Works Comm. (Mar. 1991).]

How should Ms. James's concerns be factored into the ANWR decision? Should preservation of a way of life be an important goal of environmental policy? Ms. James notes her tribe always protected the habitat of the caribou "[e]ven during hard times." They feel a moral "responsibility to keep this land pure and pass it on to our children, grandchildren and so on for generations yet to come."

In contrast to the Gwich'in, Inupiat Eskimos argue that ANWR should be opened to oil exploration because of the economic benefits development will provide. The Arctic Slope Regional Corporation, which represents the Inupiat of the North Slope, owns 92,000 acres of land that they wish the oil companies to develop. An Inupiat representative argues that as a result of development at Prudhoe Bay,

[r]evenues from the only economy we have—the oil industry—have provided high schools in each of our eight villages for the first time in our history. We now have health clinics, utilities, a local senior citizens' home and other basic public services that most Americans take for granted. [Letter from Brenda Itta-Lee, Vice President for Human Resources, Arctic Slope Regional Corporation, to the editors, Wash. Post, Aug. 28, 1991.]

How would you respond to her concerns?

Question Ten.   Both sides in the ANWR controversy have sought to bolster their positions by arguing that more is at stake than the future of ANWR alone. Invoking the specter of a previous battle that rallied the environmental movement, a Sierra Club representative asks, "If they can drill here, where can't they drill? If we're going to develop this, we might as well go ahead and dam the Grand Canyon." On the other side, Energy Secretary James D. Watkins warns that by the next decade declining production at Prudhoe Bay will threaten the viability of the Trans-Alaska Pipeline unless new sources of oil are found in northern Alaska. While efforts to open ANWR to drilling failed to win approval in Congress in 1991, the Bush Administration's budget proposals for fiscal year 1993 include the opening of ANWR, ensuring further controversy. Given what you know about the ANWR controversy, how would you vote and why?

C. ECONOMICS AND THE ENVIRONMENT

Each of the value systems we have canvassed has associated with it a distinctive discourse and set of concepts within which its problems are formulated and debated. The semi-official discourse of much environmental decision-making is economics, in which problems are expressed in terms of consumer satisfaction, efficiency, externalities, and public goods. As noted above, William Baxter, writing from this perspective, has argued that "to assert that there is a pollution problem or an environmental problem is to assert, at least implicitly, that one or more resources is not being used so as to maximize human satisfactions. Environmental problems are economic problems, and better insight can be gained by the application of economic analysis." W. Baxter, People or Penguins: The Case for Optimal Pollution 17 (1974).

Users of other value systems relevant to environmental policy disagree with this statement to varying degrees. They object to the value premises implicit in the economic approach, they reformulate environmental problems in their own discourses, and they engage in technical criticisms of economic methods to show that those methods are seriously incomplete, misleading, or inaccurate. Because economic concepts and terminology are so prevalent in this field, however, it is vital that everyone approaching environmental law be conversant with those concepts and terminology—if only so that criticism of them can be informed and astute. Throughout this course try to keep in mind two distinct tasks: (1) to understand how the discipline of economics approaches environmental problems and (2) to understand the critiques of the economic approach that can be advanced from other perspectives. Understanding of environmental policy disputes can be greatly enhanced by attending to these two related, but distinct, endeavors.

The next two readings serve to introduce the economic approach to environmental problems. The first is an introduction into the economic view of environmental problems. The second is a classic in the environmental literature, depicting one prevalent form in which environmental problems arise.

	Baumol and Oates, Economics,	
	Environmental Policy and the	
	Quality of Life	
	71-79 (1979)	

THE MECHANISM OF ENVIRONMENTAL DAMAGE IN A FREE ENTERPRISE ECONOMY

[T]here are features in our economic system that act as systematic inducements to environmental abuse. Without an understanding of the nature of these inducements, the design of environmental programs is likely to go awry. That is why it is necessary to examine the relation between environmental damage and the incentive structure of the economy.

In its production of consumer goods—shirts, dishwashers, and pinball machines—the performance of our economy has been remarkable. Never before and nowhere else has an economy spewed forth so many consumer products so efficiently. As Marx and Engels put it, "[t]he Bourgeoisie, during its rule of scarce one hundred years, has created more massive and more colossal productive forces than have all previous generations together." This contrasts sharply with our economy's very mixed performance in providing some of the other amenities usually considered part of the good society. The free enterprise system has obviously not done so well as a supplier of pure air and water or quiet surroundings.

Both sides of the matter—the economy's outstanding efficiency in producing consumer goods and its mediocre performance in providing social benefits—have long been studied by economists. In 1776 Adam Smith's Wealth of Nations explained why a free enterprise system is so responsive to consumers' demands in the marketplace. In 1920 another British economist, A. C. Pigou, showed why the performance of a profit system in supplying social amenities is apt to be less satisfactory. It is important to understand the logic of both of these analyses, because it indicates how we can repair the operation of a free market economy to provide the proper incentives for the protection of the environment.

We must note first that economists generally do not set themselves up as arbiters of any "correct" quantity of resources to devote to environmental programs. They do not argue that people *should* want to devote fewer resources to, say, turning out motorcycles and television sets and that people *ought* to use these resources instead to clean up the air and water. Economists emphasize that they have not been granted any privileged knowledge about the ideal allocation of resources. The analyses we describe in this chapter rest on no such presumption. Pigou's logic shows clearly that, because of features inherent in its structure, a free enterprise economy will respond inadequately *to the wishes of the general public* in its supply of social amenities. In an affluent society, the public's wish for dayglow Frisbees or goosedown parkas will be the business world's command. But if the public wants purer air just as strongly, the response of business will be virtually nil.

1. The Competitive Price System as an Invisible Hand

In a free enterprise system the more efficiently a business firm satisfies the demands of consumers, the more it profits. If its products do not meet the specifications of the public or if it does not produce its commodity as inexpensively as possible, competitors will take its business away. These competitive pressures are a remarkably powerful inducement for the efficient provision of consumer goods and services. Every firm must constantly be on the lookout, not only for a better mousetrap, but also for ways to produce it less expensively. Note that producers serve the consumer not out of a sense of morality or commitment to public service, but out of their own self-interest, and sometimes even as a matter of economic survival.

Prices play a fundamental role in this process. They guide three critical functions of the economy: they match the output of goods and services to consumer desires; they apportion the limited supply of commodities; and they prevent waste. We need not linger over the first of these functions since it will not play a critical role in our discussion; moreover, the mechanism involved is fairly obvious. The basic point is that if consumer tastes change, switching, for example, from high-cholesterol lamb to lower-cholesterol veal, the price of lamb will fall and that of veal will rise. Farmers will consequently be forced to shift their investment from one product to the other to obey the wishes of consumers.

More important for our purposes is the role of prices in doling out and conserving scarce items. When a commodity becomes scarce, its market price will inevitably rise. This immediately implies something which may strike the noneconomist as paradoxical, if not downright perverse: the public can sometimes benefit from a rise in prices!

How can it ever be possible for consumers to benefit from price rises? . . .

The critical role of the price mechanism in relation to goods in limited supply is that it sends those supplies *where* they are needed most and makes them available *when* they are needed most. If grain is abundant in one area and scarce in another, the price differential that will arise will induce a flow of grain from the place of comparative abundance to the area of shortage. If there is a fair amount of grain in the warehouses from last year's crop but the crop about to be harvested is poor, the "futures price" (the price for delivery in later months) will rise relative to the current price. Grain will consequently be held back from current consumption and saved until later when the need for it will be greater. In this way the market mechanism husbands the available supplies of goods and gets them to the persons to whom they matter most, when and where they are needed most.

There have been times when society was unwilling to accept the social consequences of the unimpeded operation of the price mechanism. Price controls during war (and other) times, ceilings on interest rates, and rent controls in some cities are all recent examples of restraints on the price system. Historically, each limitation on price has been accompanied by a shortage of the good in question. In these cases, distribution of the limited supply has sometimes degenerated into chaos, with goods going predominantly to individuals with "the right connections." In other cases, chaos has been prevented by the imposition of direct rationing as a substitute for the price system. Often black markets come into being and commodities are sold at high illegal prices. In this latter case, prices are effectively restored as the apportioning mechanism (but in a way that is more costly and less efficient than if the pricing system had been left to its own in the first place).

The apportionment produced by the price system has much to be said for it. Consider the extreme opposite case: fixed rationing that takes no account of varying consumer preferences. Everyone is assigned a half pound of cheese and a half dozen eggs whether or not he or she happens to love the former and detest the latter. The apportionment that is achieved by the price system, in contrast, gets more of the available eggs to those who prefer eggs and more of the cheese to cheese lovers. Customers spend their money on the commodities they like. The pricing system thus tends to allocate goods and services according to individual tastes and incomes. On the other hand, apportionment by price always weighs most heavily upon the poor. When goods are scarce, rising prices hit hardest at the poor who are most vulnerable to the pressures for reduced consumption. This is the most effective rallying point of those who advocate alternative means to deal with shortages.

An important function of the price mechanism for our study is its ability to discourage wasteful use of resources in the production process. Business firms devote a great deal of effort and research to reduce the quantity of expensive resources used in making their products. In fact, input prices can have a profound effect on their usage. In economies where wages are low there is little investment in labor-saving equipment, while in high-wage societies there is a constant search for new machines to replace human labor. There are remarkable examples of great care and expense laid out to prevent waste in precious metal industries. In platinum-using industries, the clothing of workers is cleaned every day in order to reclaim the bits of this precious metal which have lodged in the cloth. We emphasize that a competitive, free enterprise system virtually necessitates such cost-minimizing efforts. For without them the firm will be unable to match the prices of competitors.

In summary, inherent in the price system are extremely important incentives that guide resources to the production of those goods and services that consumers want to buy, incentives that encourage efficient methods of production. As we shall see next, there are good reasons to expect that this mechanism will not work nearly so well when it comes to the provision of the social amenities.

2.   The Shortcomings of the Price System in Supplying Social Amenities

There are many services that the general public desires, but for which it is very difficult to charge an appropriate price. An extreme case includes goods and services, called *pure public goods,* which if supplied to any one consumer are automatically provided to many others. A classic example is pesticide spraying to destroy malaria-bearing mosquitoes in a particular area. There is no way a mosquito-free neighborhood can be provided to some residents of the area without making it available, simultaneously, to everyone else who lives there. But if a profit-making business is to sell its product, it must be able to exclude nonpurchasers from the consumption of that product. In the case of malaria elimination, a pesticide spray company cannot charge individual residents since all the nonpayers in the region will also benefit from the spraying. For the same reason, no private business firm will undertake the supply of national defense, public health measures, the elimination of crime in a city, or any of the other services which can be considered public goods. There is simply (under existing institutions) no way to market such a good or service.

A less extreme version of this problem crops up in a much broader category of economic activities. These are activities that affect not only the welfare of the supplier and the purchaser of a product, but also (unintentionally) yield incidental benefits or cause incidental injuries to some third party or parties not directly involved in the exchange. These unintended side effects are called *externalities* or *spillovers,* that is, these activities spill over upon persons outside the immediate transaction. An example of an external *benefit* is the case where a business decides to bury high tension electric lines in order to avoid the high maintenance costs of overhead wires. Other people in the area benefit not only because an eyesore has been removed, but also because there is some reduction in personal danger during storms.

In our discussion we are interested primarily in the *detrimental* externalities or spillovers that constitute the source of many of our most serious environmental problems. Air pollution is a prime example. A factory that pours smoke into the atmosphere does not do so as an end in itself, but as an incidental side effect of the process of production. The smoke that increases laundry costs in the neighborhood, that reduces the pleasure of living there, and that may constitute a health hazard is a spillover effect; it is omitted entirely from the firm's calculations of its receipts and costs. The fact that the business that causes a detrimental externality pays no part of its cost helps to explain why the market mechanism does such an imperfect job of protecting the environment. One can think of the cleanliness of the air, the purity of the water, and the attractiveness of a neighborhood as public resources that can be used up by production processes. Just as the manufacture of some product may require x ounces of steel or y kilowatt hours of electricity, it may use up z units of pure air through its discharges of smoke. There is, however, an important difference in the way in which the firm treats these inputs. The company has to pay for the steel and electricity it uses. But under most current arrangements, the use of the atmosphere is usually free of charge to the firm, and is not considered in its cost calculations.

We may, then, describe the externalities with which we are concerned to be products of an institutional arrangement under which a number of society's resources are given away free. Landlords who let their properties deteriorate "use up" the quality of the neighborhood, difficult though measurement of that quality may be, just as surely as a steel maker uses up society's coal resources. Fresh air, clean water, and attractiveness of the neighborhood are all available for the taking, and that is precisely where the difficulty lies, for a zero price is an invitation to the user to waste the resources for which he pays nothing.

The problem of externalities can be viewed as one involving the absence of well-defined *property rights*. No one owns our clean air or water and, as a result, there is no price placed upon it. Though it is abundantly clear that we do not have unlimited quantities of clean air and water, we have failed to use the price system to apportion these scarce resources properly. This suggests one obvious instrument that policy makers can use to deal with externalities. By *requiring* the generators of externalities to bear the cost—by making the polluters pay—society can discourage the flow of undesirable spillovers. This is an approach to the matter favored by many economists. We will see that there is reason to expect this approach to be effective in many cases. But it may be able to do more than that. It may bring to the provision of social amenities all of the responsiveness to consumer demands, and all of the pressures for efficiency in the use of resources that the price mechanism enforces in the production of ordinary consumer goods. If a system of charges upon the generators of externalities can come anywhere near to matching this claim, it will indeed have much to be said in its favor.

The following classic article broadens the focus of the economic argument in favor of environmental protection measures by considering its application to the management of public lands known as "the commons."

Hardin, The Tragedy of the Commons
168 Science 1243 (1968)

The tragedy of the commons develops in this way. Picture a pasture open to all. It is to be expected that each herdsman will try to keep as many cattle as possible on the commons. Such an arrangement may work reasonably satisfactorily for centuries because tribal wars, poaching, and disease keep the numbers of both man and beast well below the carrying capacity of the land. Finally, however, comes the day of reckoning, that is, the day when the long-desired goal of social stability becomes a reality. At this point, the inherent logic of the commons remorselessly generates tragedy.

As a rational being, each herdsman seeks to maximize his gain. Explicitly or implicitly, more or less consciously, he asks, "What is the utility to me of adding one more animal to my herd?" This utility has one negative and one positive component.

(1) The positive component is a function of the increment of one animal. Since the herdsman receives all the proceeds from the sale of the additional animal, the positive utility is nearly $+1$.

(2) The negative component is a function of the additional overgrazing created by one more animal. Since, however, the effects of overgrazing are shared by all the herdsmen, the negative utility for any particular decisionmaking herdsman is only a fraction of -1.

Adding together the component partial utilities, the rational herdsman concludes that the only sensible course for him to pursue is to add another animal to his herd. And another, and another. . . . But this is the conclusion reached by each and every rational herdsman sharing a commons. Therein is the tragedy. Each man is locked into a system that compels him to increase his herd without limit in a world that is limited. Ruin is the destination toward which all men rush, each pursuing his own best interest in a society that believes in the freedom of the commons. Freedom in a commons brings ruin to all. . . .

In an approximate way, the logic of the commons has been understood for a long time, perhaps since the discovery of agriculture or the invention of private property in real estate. But it is understood mostly only in special cases which are not sufficiently generalized. Even at this late date, cattlemen leasing national land on the western ranges demonstrate no more than an ambivalent understanding, in constantly pressuring federal authorities to increase the head count to the point where overgrazing produces erosion and weed-dominance. Likewise, the oceans of the world continue to suffer from the survival of the philosophy of the commons. Maritime nations still respond automatically to the shibboleth of the "freedom of the seas." Professing to believe in the "inexhaustible resources of the oceans," they bring species after species of fish and whales closer to extinction.

The National Parks present another instance of the working out of the tragedy of the commons. At present, they are open to all, without limit. The parks themselves are limited in extent—there is only one Yosemite Valley—whereas population seems to grow without limit. The values that visitors seek in the parks are steadily eroded. Plainly, we must soon cease to treat the parks as commons or they will be of no value to anyone.

What shall we do? We have several options. We might sell them off as private property. We might keep them as public property, but allocate the right to enter them. The allocation might be on the basis of wealth, by the use of an auction system. It might be on the basis of merit, as defined by some agreed upon standards. It might be by lottery. Or it might be on a first-come, first-served basis, administered to long queues. These, I think, are all the reasonable possibilities. They are all objectionable. But we must choose—or acquiesce in the destruction of the commons that we call our National Parks. . . .

In a reverse way, the tragedy of the commons reappears in problems of pollution. Here it is not a question of taking something out of the commons, but of putting something in—sewage, or chemical, radioactive, and heat wastes into water; noxious and dangerous fumes into the air; and distracting and unpleasant advertising signs into the line of sight. The calculations of utility are much the same as before. The rational man finds that his share of the cost of the wastes he discharges into the commons is less than the cost of purifying his wastes before releasing them. Since this is true for everyone, we are locked into a system of "fouling our own nest," so long as we behave only as independent, rational, free-enterprisers.

The tragedy of the commons as a food basket is averted by private property, or something formally like it. But the air and waters surrounding us cannot readily be fenced, and so the tragedy of the commons as a cesspool must be prevented by different means, by coercive laws or taxing devices that make it cheaper for the polluter to treat his pollutants than to discharge them untreated. We have not progressed as far with the solution of this problem as we have with the first. Indeed, our particular concept of private property, which deters us from exhausting the positive resources of the earth, favors pollution. The owner of a factory on the bank of a stream—whose property extends to the middle of the stream—often has difficulty seeing why it is not his natural right to muddy the waters flowing past his door. The law, always behind the times, requires elaborate stitching and fitting to adapt it to this newly perceived aspect of the commons.

NOTES AND QUESTIONS

1. Hardin's story of the commons is a "tragedy" because a dynamic is at work within the story that is leading to eventual disaster, disaster for all. What is that dynamic?

Insofar as the dynamic relates to the desire of "each herdsman to maximize his gain," is the tragedy unavoidable? Many who disagree with the economic approach to environmental problems do so because they believe humans ought not, and need not, pursue their own "gain" singlemindedly. Aldo Leopold, for one, claimed that anyone approaching the environment as exclusively an object for personal gain in effect treated it as a piece of property, "entailing privileges but not obligations." In arguing for a "land ethic," he argued for a change in humanity's disposition toward the environment, one that "changes the role of Homo sapiens from conqueror of the land-community to plain member and citizen of it. [This] implies respect for his fellow-members, and also respect for the community as such." A. Leopold, A Sand County Almanac 204 (1968). This idea has been widely influential among environmentalists. For summaries and appraisals, see Meyers, An Introduction to Environmental Thought: Somes Sources and Some Criticisms, 50 Ind. L.J. 426 (1975); Heffernan, The Land Ethic: A Criticial Appraisal, 4 Envtl. Ethics 235 (1982); C. Stone, Earth and Other Ethics (1987).

2. As Baumol and Oates suggest, one technique for dealing with externalities is to make the generator of the externality pay for them—the "polluter pays" principle. This has the effect of internalizing the externality, because the environmental disamenities are now something the polluter has to take into account—they have been internalized into his decisionmaking process—by virtue of having to pay for them. By ensuring that the costs of production reflect the costs of environmental damage, efforts to internalize externalities can lead to more efficient resource allocation by making the price of goods reflect the true social costs of production. The difficulties of internalizing externalities by implementing the "polluter pays" principle are well explored in F. Anderson, et al., Environmental Improvement Through Economic Incentives (1982).

3. The "polluter pays" principle is powerful and attractive, but it has not gone unchallenged in theory. In an important article, Ronald Coase argued that problems such as pollution are two-sided, because they involve a conflict between competing uses of a resource. Because they are two-sided, environmental problems can be solved in either of two ways, by making the polluter pay or by giving the polluter a right to pollute that the victims of pollution can then purchase, if they wish. Under Coase's Theorem, if bargaining is costless (what economists call assuming no transaction costs), either approach should result in an efficient outcome because the pollution will be abated only if it is cheaper to control than the damage it causes its victims. For example, if the peace of mind of the residents who live near Three Mile Island Unit 1 is worth more than the value of operating the plant, then the plant would not be restarted either because the residents could gain by paying the plant not to operate (if the plant had a right to do so) or because it would not be economical for the plant to compensate residents for their fears (if the residents had a right to be free from the danger of accident). In principle, either solution will result in solving the environmental problem, economically viewed, because it will eliminate the undesirable externality aspects of the situation. See Coase, The Problem of Social Cost, 3 J.L. & Econ. 1 (1960). Properly viewed, Coase's argument is not one against the "polluter pays" principle, but rather one for remembering that the economic perspective does not require application of the "polluter pays" principle to all externalities.

4. Coase's views have been particularly influential in the privatization movement, because one application of Coase's argument is to urge that sometimes pollution problems can be left to private market solutions, where polluter and pollutee can bargain for the appropriate level of polluting activity relatively free from governmental interference. See, e.g., T. L. Anderson and D. R. Leal, Free Market Environmentalism (1991); The Heritage Foundation, Protecting the Environment: A Free Market Strategy (D. Bandow, ed. 1986); J. Baden and R. Stroup, eds., Bureaucracy v. Environment (1981); Runge, The Fallacy of "Privatization," 7 J. Contemp. Stud. 3 (1984). One of the earliest, and still among the most valuable, essays on the advantages of markets for pollution rights is J. H. Dales, Pollution, Property and Prices (1968).

5. In addition to noting the obvious unreality of the zero-transaction-cost assumption, critics of Coase's Theorem are quick to point out that the initial allocation of rights (whether to pollute or to be free from pollution) can have a significant impact on the distribution of income. The distribution of income in turn affects tastes and alters the ultimate outcomes produced by market economies. While extolling the importance of efficiency, economists have tried to dismiss such distributional concerns by arguing that they should be dealt with by general tax and welfare policies or by assuming that winners and losers are approxi-

mately the same when more efficient policies are pursued. Noting that Coase himself emphasized that all market transactions have costs (Coase argued that the very existence of firms illustrated that nonmarket mechanisms can be cheaper in some circumstances than market ones), Dean Guido Calabresi maintains that "distributional issues cannot, even in theory, be avoided." Calabresi, The Pointlessness of Pareto: Carrying Coase Further, 100 Yale L.J. 1211, 1215 (1991). Calabresi argues that transaction costs, "no less than existing technology, define the limits of what is currently achievable in society," id. at 1212, and that "there is no difference, in theory or in practice, between the reduction or elimination of these impediments and any other innovation in knowledge or organization which might make us all better off." Id. at 1218. Thus, he maintains that the real challenge for social policy is to decide which impediments to a better life to invest in removing, which inevitably requires explicit consideration of distributional concerns.

A Note on Environmental Problems and the Prisoner's Dilemma

1. The Commons and Welfare Economics. Recall Baumol and Oates's discussion of detrimental, or *negative, externalities,* which they define as "unintended side effects . . . [that] spill over upon persons outside the immediate transaction." The commons as described by Hardin is an instance of negative externalities. In the case of the commons, the relevant transaction is the placing of an additional head of cattle on the commons by any of the herders. It may seem like an odd transaction, because the herder does not have to "transact" with anyone in order to take that action, but that is precisely the problem here. When a herder transacts with the commons by bringing an additional animal onto it, the act produces both a positive component and a negative component, but much of that negative component is not experienced by the actor— it is largely external to his relationship to the commons resource, and spills over onto all the other herders through its adverse effects on the size of their herds or of the cattle within those herds. If the herder were required to transact with the other herders before increasing the herd size, they presumably would ask to be compensated for these adverse effects. Do you see why this would defuse the "tragedy" in the commons story?

Hardin's commons also exhibits features of a public good: If any individual refrains from placing a head of cattle on the commons, that action produces a good by enhancing the condition of the entire herd, but that good is experienced by everyone, so supplying this good to any single member of the commons makes it available to all. The concepts of being public and of being negative externalities can be combined so that we can also speak of the act of placing an additional head on the commons as producing a *public bad*. Placing an additional head on the commons produces an externality that is experienced by everyone on the commons.

A number of important pollution and natural resources problems share practically all the characteristics of Hardin's commons. Consider air pollution from automobile exhausts, litter along a roadside or a hiking trail, camping in Toulumne Meadows in Yosemite National Park, a traffic jam in Yellowstone, air pollution in small Vermont valleys from the nearly universal use of wood stoves by homeowners, and the use of national forest land for grazing cattle by ranchers. How about air pollution from a power plant or factory, chemical emissions from a dry cleaning establishment, or the discharge of dioxin into a river by a paper mill? Do these share characteristics with the commons, or are they distinguishable in some important way?

2. The Commons, the Prisoner's Dilemma, and Collective Action. The phenomena at work in the commons are frequently analyzed with the use of a model of behavior known as the Prisoner's Dilemma, named for the story that was first used to illustrate the behavior. In that story, illustrated in Figure 1.3, two suspects of a serious crime are separately offered the same deal by a district attorney. Each is told that if she testifies against her colleague she will go free, as long as the other suspect doesn't also turn state's evidence, in which case each will receive a moderate sentence. If neither suspect testifies, then each will be convicted of a lesser crime, for which the district attorney already has sufficient evidence. Each will then receive a light sentence for the lesser crime. However, if one suspect keeps quiet while the other testifies, the silent suspect will receive a harsh sentence.

FIGURE 1.3
The Prisoner's Dilemma
(severity of sentence in boxes)

	Suspect #1 Act in individual interest ("fink")	Suspect #1 Act in joint interest (do not "fink")
Suspect #2 Act in individual interest ("fink")	#1: Moderate #2: Moderate	#1: Harsh #2: Light
Suspect #2 Act in joint interest (do not "fink")	#1: Light #2: Harsh	#1: Light #2: Light

The behavior being modeled here is a species of what we now know as strategic behavior, which simply means that the interaction of the behavior of an actor and the behavior of others determines the outcome for the actor. If the actor is going to achieve the best possible results for herself, she must take into account how those others are likely to behave. The Prisoner's Dilemma represents an important kind of strategic interaction. Notice that from the perspective of any single actor there is no individual dilemma at all. Each suspect gets a shorter sentence by testifying against the other, regardless of what the other one does. Thus the strategy of testifying "dominates" any other strategy that an actor could choose, and any suspect interested in minimizing his or her sentence should adopt it. (You should satisfy yourself that this is so: Put yourself in the shoes of a suspect, then ask yourself (1) What course of action gets me the lightest possible sentence, assuming that my co-suspect testifies? and (2) What course of action gets me the lightest possible sentence, assuming that my co-suspect keeps quiet?)

The Dilemma materializes when you realize that the final result of both actors' following this dominant strategy is that they each get moderate sentences, which is worse for each of them than if they had both kept silent. The result is an outcome that is "individually rational and collectively deficient." B. Barry and R. Hardin, Rational Man and Irrational Society? 25 (1982). It is individually rational because each player chooses her dominant strategy, which is the rational thing to do. It is collectively deficient because there exists another outcome that would leave *each suspect* better off than the outcome if both testify.

This conclusion, "individually rational and collectively deficient," has become identified as the problem of collective action: "[I]t may be in everyone's individual interest not to cooperate in a collective effort even though everyone would be better off if everyone cooperated." Id. The problem of collective action, in fact, can be treated as an expanded Prisoner's Dilemma in which there are not just two players, but larger numbers, up to indefinitely many, or n players, so that collective action situations can sometimes be modelled as n-person Prisoner's Dilemmas. See generally, R. Hardin, Collective Action (1982), especially chapter 2, "Collective Action and the Prisoner's Dilemma."

Hardin's commons is thus understandable as an n-person Prisoner's Dilemma. Each herder is faced with a choice between adding a head of cattle to the commons or not adding a head. Now as long as the size of the total herd remains small relative to the commons' carrying capacity, the payoff to each herder is independent of whatever the others do, so there is no strategic interaction of the sort that marks the Dilemma. Eventually, however, the behavior of the herds will begin to interact, because the commons constitutes a scarce resource for grazing. Once carrying capacity is reached, the payoff to any herder will be dependent on whether the others choose to add a head of cattle or not. At this point, is it fair to say that the dominant strategy for any herder is to add a head of cattle, so this is what he should do regardless of what the others do? If so, then you might say that the "tragedy" in the Tragedy of the Commons is identical to the "dilemma" in the Prisoner's Dilemma: Actions that are individually rational produce a result that is collectively deficient.

Speaking generally, the collective action necessary to defuse the commons tragedy can be viewed either as the provision of a public good, diminishing the herd size, or the elimination of a public bad, augmenting the herd size. In either case, the analysis of public goods or bads is linked to the analysis of the Prisoner's Dilemma in that some collective action is typically required to produce such goods or diminish such bads, and the individuals involved typically have individually rational reasons for refusing to participate in that action that can be illuminated using the Prisoner's Dilemma model. Does it matter whether the problem is viewed as one of public goods or public bads? See part 3(f) of this Note, below.

Modern game theory has greatly enriched our appreciation for the workings of n-person Prisoner's Dilemmas, and it also has developed a number of important distinctions and variations within the basic model. Two of the classics in the field are Mancur Olson's The Logic of Collective Action (1965) and Russell Hardin's Collective Action (1982). Olson's focus was on political organization and interest groups, as he sought to explain why some groups that could benefit from jointly pursuing some concerted action nevertheless fail to do so, while others succeed. Hardin showed that Olson's formulation of the logic of collective action was equivalent to an n-person's Prisoner's Dilemma, thus linking two bodies of work that had been proceeding somewhat independently. In the ensuing years, the model has been applied to a vast array of situations, including analyses of the antiwar and civil rights movements, the environmental movement, problems of natural resource depletion (such as the commons), pollution, citizens' turning out to vote, and lobbying by industrial associations, trade organizations, and labor unions.

3. *Solutions.* Many can agree that "collectively deficient" results ought to be avoided if possible. Such agreement barely gets the issue of solutions off the ground, however, because analysts have suggested a wide array of possible solutions, about which people are not at all indifferent.

a. *Cooperation I.* If we can see that individually rational behavior leads to collectively deficient results, the participants may be able to see the same thing. If they do, shouldn't they be able to see the wisdom of cooperation, because cooperation will be better for everyone?

Sometimes yes, sometimes no. Even if the district attorney allows the suspects to talk to one another, the classic Prisoner's Dilemma looks quite resistant to cooperation, because the incentives to welch on an agreement not to testify are the same as the incentives for testifying in the first case. How about the commons situation described by Hardin? Welching might be less of a problem here, assuming an initial agreement could be achieved. For one thing, if the commons were small enough, and the cattle identified by owner (as they presumably would be), it would be possible for the herders to monitor one another. If herders adopted a policy of "I won't add to the commons flock if you don't," that policy might have a chance of maintaining the herd at or below carrying capacity, because each herder would know that a violation by her would be followed by a violation by the others, which would harm her herd as well as those of the others.

The argument for cooperation in such cases requires that the participants face a succession of opportunities to choose whether to continue cooperating or to welch, because it is the recognition of future retaliation by others when they get the chance that encourages a herder to cooperate. There is no such chance in a so-called one-shot, or single-play, Prisoner's Dilemma. Where there are such chances, in cases that are called iterated Prisoner's Dilemmas, cooperation sometimes becomes plausible as an individually rational strategy. Not always, however. It depends on whether a herder's short-term gains from welching outweigh her long-term losses from the others' retaliating. That, in turn, depends on a herder's estimation of the influence her choices will have on others. If other herders will welch anyway, whether or not the actor does, or if they will *not* welch anyway, or if the short-term gains are substantial enough, welching becomes the individually rational strategy even in an iterated situation. As indicated, the commons case described by Hardin represents an iterated *n*-person Prisoner's Dilemma, because the commons does not go to ruin all at once, but only after a series of decisions leading to severe overgrazing. Hardin seems to think that the herders will conclude that cooperation is not the individually rational strategy in such a case. Do you agree? Why or why not?

   b. Cooperation II.   Another line of attack on Prisoner's Dilemmas produces talk of cooperation, but from another angle. In reflecting on commons cases especially, some have suggested that the cause of commons depletion stems from a disintegration of community solidarity, community spirit, or a shared appreciation of the sacred character of the natural resources that permits commons users to relate to the common resource primarily as a source of individual gain. Aldo Leopold, for instance, identified the idea that land and the environment were viewed by modern civilization as private property, to be consumed like any other economic resource, as a prime contributor to wilderness depletion and deterioration.

Other students of the commons observe that commons have existed for centuries and continue to exist, and that the record as to their deterioration is mixed—some have deteriorated, while others either haven't or didn't for long periods of time. As one study suggests, "[p]erhaps what existed in fact was not a 'tragedy of the commons' but rather a triumph: that for hundreds of years—and perhaps thousands, although written records do not exist to prove the longer era—land was managed successfully by communities." Cox, No Tragedy on the Commons, 7 Envtl. Ethics 49, 60 (1985). Cultural anthropologists, including especially but not limited to students of Native American cultures, have identified cultural and ideological explanations for husbanding commons resources.

These views tend to question the behavioral premise, or the engine, that drives the tragedy of the commons: They deny that people necessarily behave in the individually rational way posited by the Prisoner's Dilemma model, at least some of the time and in some circumstances. You might connect this line of argument with the Deep Ecology movement, which urges the retrieval of norms that respect and revere nature or that emphasize community solidarity, and hence offer to defeat the tragedy of the commons, or unravel the dilemma of the prisoners, by instilling and cultivating cooperative community spirit.

   c. Cooperation III.   Although this casebook deals with situations in which government intervention has been employed to address collective action problems (hence the word "Regulation" in the title), the importance of cooperative solutions should not be underestimated. Cooperation has distinct advantages over government intervention, especially in avoiding coercion or threatened coercion by the state. Consider also that some of the most intractable environmental problems of the future and near future are going to be international in scope. The greenhouse effect and ozone depletion are two obvious examples. Each will require actions by many nations. Lacking an international governing body with coercive powers, the international community must seek cooperative solutions.

   d. Government intervention—generally.   Some have urged that interceding in Prisoner's Dilemmas constitutes the primary function of government. Mancur Olson, for instance, writes that "[a] state is first of all an organization that provides public goods for its members, the citizens." M. Olson, The Logic of Collective Action 15 (1965). (Bear in mind, in considering Olson's views, that national defense, public highways, law enforcement and the criminal and civil court systems, and public education are but some of the governmental services that exhibit public goods characteristics.) Long before the problem of collective action became identified as such, theorists had observed that such cases were ones in which government might legitimately intervene, and even writers not otherwise associated with interventionist views about government have concluded that Prisoner's Dilemma cases provide a legitimate occasion for intervention. For example, John Stuart Mill wrote:

> There are matters in which interference of law is required, not to overrule
> the judgment of individuals respecting their own interest, but to give effect
> to that judgment; they being unable to give effect to it except by concert,
> which concert again cannot be effectual unless it receives validity and
> sanction from the law. [J. S. Mill, Principles of Political Economy, bk. V.,
> chap. XI, sec. 12.]

Mill is suggesting that "I would rather cooperate than welch, but only
if you cooperate" is an individually rational judgment in some circumstances, and that it may require legal sanction to ensure universal cooperation, which all seem to desire.

    Assuming some government assistance is conceded, the form that
assistance takes still must be decided. There are a number of possibilities,
and debate about them can be heated. The minimal amount of intervention is legal enforcement of consensual contracts. If the participants
all came together to agree on a policy of mutual self-restraint in grazing
on the commons, government sanctions in the form of judicial relief via
a private lawsuit for breach of contract would enable such cooperative
solutions to work. However, the consensual contract itself presents another sort of collective action problem, because it takes time and effort
to produce universal agreement. It may not be worth any individual's
time to negotiate and obtain the consent of all others. What is more,
those negotiations are subject to another kind of strategic behavior: Some
necessary party to the agreement might play particularly hard to get
(this is called "holding out" in the collective action literature), thinking
that she might be able to extract some special advantage—a signing
bonus, perhaps—from the others if she bargained hard enough. Thus,
other forms of intervention are sometimes urged above and beyond
contract enforcement. For a recent argument that consensual contracts
are a promising solution to some significant collective action problems,
see D. Schmidtz, The Limits of Government: An Essay on the Public
Goods Argument (1991).

    e. Defining property rights.   Recall Baumol and Oates's conclusion
that many cases of detrimental, or negative, externalities were the result
of an inadequate definition of property rights. We have too much air
pollution, for instance, because we have not defined property rights in
air sufficiently. In the case of Hardin's commons, overgrazing might be
avoided if the commons were divided into individual parcels and owners
of cattle were restricted to grazing cattle on their own land. Do you see
why?

    Parsing out a commons into individual shares and requiring indi-
viduals to compensate others for detrimental externalities, also suggested
by the Baumol and Oates reading (see Note 1, above) are both solutions

of the "define property rights" variety. The parceling-out solution grants a property right in land, while the compensate-for-negative-externalities solution grants a property right in cattle, protecting them from certain kinds of interference. Practically speaking, it would be feasible to enforce the parceling-out solution by insisting that would-be violators obtain the prior consent of each landowner before they use each person's land, because land boundaries are relatively easy to define and maintain, and negotiations can be carried on one at a time for each parcel whose use is desired.

In contrast, it is unlikely that the second kind of solution could be administered by insisting that each would-be violator obtain prior agreement on the amount of compensation to be paid. Such a negotiation would amount to obtaining a consensual contract with every herder, and would be subject to the same practical difficulties. The second kind of solution could more practically be enforced by insisting on after-the-fact compensation. If that were the method of enforcement, the solution of paying for negative externalities would closely resemble the common law tort system and its action for nuisance. Thus common law remedies in tort can be viewed as one device for solving Prisoner's Dilemmas of the commons variety. The classic source for viewing property rights as a means of controlling externalities is Demsetz, Toward a Theory of Property Rights, 57 Am. Econ. Rev. 347 (Pap. & Proc. 1967). For analysis of tort and property rules in this vein, start with Calabresi and Melamed, Property Rules, Liability Rules, and Inalienability: One View of the Cathedral, 85 Harv. L. Rev. 1089 (1972). Demsetz uses several commons examples to illustrate his thesis, while Calabresi and Melamed employ pollution situations to illustrate theirs.

f. Command-and-control regulation.   Tort remedies themselves may be inadequate, however, because of further collective problems internal to the decision by victims to bring tort litigation in the first place. If litigation is conducted by individual plaintiffs, it may not require actors to pay for the total negative externalities they cause. On the other hand, conducting litigation on behalf of everyone, say, through a class action, amounts to the creation of a collective good, the ultimate court award of damages in which everyone shares. Because litigation is costly and risky, individual victims may want to sit back and rely on the efforts of others to prosecute the case and secure the victory. If enough victims react this way (behavior the collective action literature terms "free-riding"), total effort and resources may be inadequate to succeed.

In such circumstances, petitioning government to impose regulations may stand a better chance of success. While still presenting collective action problems, petitioning government may be less costly than litigating because a few leaders of victims can get politicians' attention largely by pointing to the number of people affected, instead of requiring significant financial contributions from them, and because government possesses investigatory resources that can be marshaled in ways that do not occur in private litigation.

Russell Hardin has suggested several characteristics of commons situations that increase the likelihood people will pursue regulatory solutions to their problems. Most important is whether a problem is seen as one of eliminating a public bad rather than of providing a public good. R. Hardin, Collective Action chs. 4, 5. Hardin concedes that the distinction between a bad and a good "will wither under a persistent philosophical glare," but replies that it is nevertheless a prominent piece of ordinary discourse. Perhaps the distinction we make in ordinary conversation is reflecting the further characteristics that Hardin notes. (1) If the problem is a bad, the goal the group wants to achieve "is likely to be more clearly focused, for example opposing a specific refinery or highway project rather than supporting 'some constructive effort.' " (2) The costs for controlling bads are typically imposed on the producer of the bad; the costs for producing goods are typically imposed on the beneficiaries. Thus the gains to victims may be large in the case of bads. (3) Bads frequently come from sources external to the victim group, so that a moral sense of unfairness that someone is harming innocent group members may motivate action. (Contrast the commons to the air-polluting factory.) (4) Even if the bads are internal to the group, individuals within the group may be more willing to cooperate if the issue is framed as one of trying to avoid harming someone else, not as one of cooperating to provide a benefit to someone. (5) Some psychologists suggest that people are more motivated to prevent losses from current welfare positions than they are to achieve comparable gains. This phenomenon, termed "hysteresis," is famously noted by David Hume: "[People] generally fix their affections more on what they are possess'd of, than on what they never enjoy'd: For this reason, it would be greater cruelty to dispossess a [person] of any thing than not to give it [to her or him.]" D. Hume, A Treatise of Human Nature, bk. 3, pt. 2, sec. 1, at 482 (L. A. Selby-Bigge and P. H. Nidditch, eds., 1978).

g. Taxes.   When the public good at issue is to be purchased, taxes are one method for the coordinated extraction of necessary sums for payment. Think of national defense, for example. Taxes may also be used as a signal of negative externalities: By imposing a properly calibrated pollution tax on emission sources, government can make those sources aware of the negative externalities of their activities in the same way that a tort award would.

h. Marketable permits.   The 1990 Clean Air Act Amendments seek to control emissions that contribute to acid rain by establishing a total annual ceiling for such emissions and then requiring that sources of these emissions have a permit to emit in order to stay in operation. The total annual ceiling will be maintained by limiting the total amount of permitted emissions to that amount or less. Sources with permits will be allowed to sell them to other emitters. A comparable strategy for Hardin's commons would have a government overseer of the commons setting a total annual grazing ceiling, then allowing individual herders to add heads of cattle to the commons only if they had a permit to do so. Limiting the total number of permits to the annual grazing ceiling ensures that the ceiling is met (assuming no cheating).

i. Incentives.   Alfred Kahn, an economist who served in several positions in the Carter Administration, often urged his colleagues "to keep the hand of government as invisible as possible." Sometimes government can reallocate resources in such a manner that actors can be motivated to choose actions that are not collectively deficient, without experiencing the situation as involving government coercion. Dedicating one highway lane to car pools and buses during rush hours is an example. Individual drivers may now be motivated to choose car pooling or riding the bus because that is a better decision for them, from their individual point of view, than driving their own cars. Favorable electrical rates for using power during off-peak hours, or for permitting the utility company to interrupt power to air conditioners if necessary to serve peak demand, are other examples. These examples share the characteristic that the incentives effectively rearrange the pay-off structure of the Prisoner's Dilemma by making cooperating sufficiently attractive to individuals that they prefer it to not cooperating.

4. Refinements and Complications.   The Prisoner's Dilemma model is a powerful tool for appreciating how some environmental problems arise even when it seems that everyone would be better off if the problem were eliminated. It suggests a reason for government assistance in resolving environmental disputes based on the preferences of the individuals involved, which is a powerful sort of justification in a polity that values individual liberty and tolerance for different preferences.

There may be few *pure* Prisoner's Dilemmas in the environmental field, however, so additional considerations must always be taken into account. Recall the example of an air-polluting factory. From the perspective of the factory, the situation is not a Prisoner's Dilemma at all, because the solution of "everyone cooperate" by not polluting harms the factory while benefitting the victims. Unlike the Prisoner's Dilemma, then, solutions here are likely to have winners and losers. If the factory is overpolluting in the sense of causing more harm than the costs the factory is saving by not controlling its emissions, there is theoretically a sum of money that the victims could pay the factory that would leave everyone better off—a sum, in other words, that would reduce harm to victims more than it cost them and that would produce gain for the factory more than the costs of abating the pollution. So winners and losers are not inevitable, but this assumes that it is appropriate to have victims in such circumstance pay for harm avoidance, and the basis of that judgment cannot be found within the Prisoner's Dilemma model.

The factory example exhibits two ways in which the Prisoner's Dilemma model is frequently incomplete: It is an incomplete description of some important cases of overuse of resources, and it is an incomplete basis for determining what solution type should be employed to reduce overuse. For further reading on complications and refinements to the Prisoner's Dilemma model as applied to problems of public policy and the environment, see, in addition to the works already cited in this note, W. Poundstone, Prisoner's Dilemma (1992); M. Santos, Managing Planet Earth (1990); G. Hardin and J. Baden, Managing the Commons (1977).

One further merit of the Prisoner's Dilemma model deserves mention, a merit that should be ascribed to game theory as a whole. The dilemma teaches the importance of thinking strategically by taking into account reactions of others to actions taken. Environmental policy-making is strewn with instances of well-meaning legislation to which regulated entities and others then react in ways that undermine the legislation's effectiveness, sometimes even resulting in counterproductive effects. Intelligent policy-making in this field cannot proceed without learning the lessons of strategic behavior.

D. ECOLOGICAL PERSPECTIVES

The root of the prefix "eco" in the word "ecology" derives from the Greek *oikos,* meaning "household." The modern interpreters of the term "ecology" are intent on expanding our appreciation of what constitutes our "household" and on helping us to see the interconnections between ourselves, our actions, and all constituents of our household, or ecosystem. This ecological vision is apparent in Aldo Leopold's definition of ethics itself. "All ethics," he wrote, "rest upon a single premise: that the individual is a member of a community of interdependent parts. . . . The land ethic simply enlarges the boundaries of the community to include soils, waters, plants, and animals, or collectively: the land." A Sand County Almanac 203 (1968).

The science of ecology constitutes one method for bringing this interdependence to bear on environmental policy. As a science, ecology seeks to understand the functioning of ecosystems, both on a small scale (such as the ecosystem of a small freshwater wetland) and on a grand scale (such as the global oxygen-carbon dioxide-water cycle, which plays a vital role in world climate and climate changes). Through studying ecosystems, ecologists seek knowledge about the entire process of life by synthesizing chemical, geological, and meteorological information about the environment and biological and chemical information about living organisms and combining them into a single system. The leading textbook on the science of ecology is E. Odum, Fundamentals of Ecology (3d ed. 1971).

This drive to comprehensiveness derives from the overarching idea of interdependence, which is further reflected in such ecological slogans as "you can never do just one thing" and "everything is connected to everything else." A major portion of the ecological research agenda concerns tracing the consequences of actions through successively widening sequences of effects. Often these actions will be described as the introduction of an outside force or constituent into a currently functioning ecosystem. Ecosystems themselves are seen as dynamic, changing processes that tend toward *homeostasis,* that is, that have the characteristics of being self-regulating and self-maintaining in that they contain the ingredients and mechanisms to return to equilibrium after they have been disturbed. Thus a "functioning" ecosystem is one exhibiting this homeostatic capacity.

Ecologists have traditionally believed that this homeostatic condition is potentially ubiquitous—that all ecosystems will exhibit an inherent balance unless they are upset by outside disturbances. It is a dynamic equilibrium, with prey and predator, competition and coexistence within the system; nevertheless, over the system as a whole and over time, the diversity and complexity of functioning ecosystems produce a stability, or balance. In any ecosystem, the "presence and success of an organism depend upon the completeness of a complex of conditions," while in turn individual organisms contribute to the stability of the system itself by occupying an ecological "niche"—performing a function that contributes to the stability of the system. See E. Odum, Fundamentals of Ecology (3d ed. 1971).

The capacity to self-regulate and equilibrate is by no means without limit, however. The idea of an ecosystem's "carrying capacity," or the extent of disruption it could absorb without losing its homeostatic capacity, played an important role in debates surrounding the environmental laws passed in the early 1970s.

By studying the mechanisms that enable restorative reactions to outside influences, ecologists seek to understand when and how those mechanisms can be overstressed to the point of exceeding carrying capacity so that ecosystem stability is threatened. Here important concepts are *unintended consequences* and *scale of action.* Because ecosystem interconnections can be complex and multifarious, an ecological rule of thumb is that seemingly simple actions typically will have non-obvious and unintended consequences that may culminate in a threat to ecosystem stability. Introduce a new organism into an ecosystem and it may function as a virulent pathogen, like the measles that decimated the Eskimos and South Sea Islanders following their first contacts with Western civilization. Bioaccumulation provides another mechanism through which seemingly discrete actions can have unintended consequences. Chemicals, such as the pesticide DDT, accumulate in the tissue of animals that consume other animals, plants, or water containing the chemical. When these animals are consumed in their turn by still others, the chemicals can continue to accumulate or concentrate until they reach dangerous, even fatal proportions. Both the American condor and the bald eagle populations have suffered because plants and insects sprayed with pesticides were consumed by rodents and snakes that were then consumed by the predator birds, eventually producing pesticide contamination in them sufficient to weaken their egg membranes so that their young died before birth.

A second rule of thumb for ecologists is that smaller actions have less drastic consequences on functioning ecosystems than larger actions do. Recall the statement from Leopold that we referred to earlier: "The combined evidence of history and ecology seems to support one general deduction: the less violent the man-made changes, the greater the probability of successful readjustment in the [ecosystem]. Violence, in turn, varies with human population density; a dense population requires a more violent conversion. In this respect, North America has a better chance for permanence than Europe, if she can contrive to limit her density." A Sand County Almanac at 220.

The lessons of unintended consequences, scale, and others from ecology's study of interconnectedness and interdependence can to some extent be incorporated into the economic perspective on environmental problems. In theory, these lessons can improve our ability to assess the costs and benefits of human action. "Look before you leap" is perfectly sound economic advice; someone committed to the economic perspective can hear many of ecology's lessons as warnings to look *harder* before we leap, because there are going to be additional costs (ecology's lessons tend to be on the cost side, although theoretically unintended consequences could be beneficial ones) beyond those we have appreciated thus far. One of the first pieces of modern-era environmental legislation, the National Environmental Policy Act, was partly premised on the idea that interdisciplinary ecological study ought to precede major federal actions in order that the unintended environmental effects of actions could be better represented in an overall cost-benefit assessment of the action. See, for example, section 102(2)(A)-(B), requiring federal agencies to "utilize a systematic, interdisciplinary approach which will insure the integrated use of the natural and social sciences and the environmental design arts in planning [and to] insure that presently unquantified environmental amenities and values may be given appropriate consideration in decisionmaking. . . ."

Many students of ecology, however, derive lessons that are in greater tension with the economic outlook. A basic tenet involved in applying economics to public policy is that one should be guided by the best assessments of costs and benefits that one can produce. Even if those assessments are highly imperfect, decisions based on them amount to the best that we can do if, over time, we expect to maximize the net of benefits over costs. Some students of ecology advocate a quite different operating principle: Smaller action is (almost) always the better action. These students emphasize how little we grasp the full complexity of ecosystem interaction and interdependence. Accordingly, they think it overwhelmingly likely that large-scale actions will swamp some or another important, stability-contributing aspect of the relevant ecosystem.

At this level, preferring small actions to large ones combines a counsel of caution with an underlying judgment that the ways of nature ought to be respected. The methodological principle of ecology, seeing humans as one constituent member of ecosystems composed of many interdependent parts rather than as a dominant, qualitatively distinct member, combines with an admiration for the homeostatic qualities of "natural" systems to produce a prescription for humans: Live in harmony with nature, not at odds with it. Do not maximize, but rather harmonize. The natural equilibrations of functioning ecosystems come to constitute a norm, and to provide a sense of normality, that humans are urged to respect. A good collection of essays touching on some of ecology's broader implications is The Subversive Science: Essays Toward an Ecology of Man (P. Shepard and D. McKinley, eds. 1969).

At yet another level, the preference for smallness blossomed into an entire worldview in the late 1960s and 1970s, stimulated by the publication of E. F. Schumacher's Small Is Beautiful (1973) and I. Illich's Tools for Conviviality (1973). As described by Schumacher,

> To strive for smallness means to try to bring organizations and units of production back to a human scale. . . . There are many reasons for favoring smallness. Small units of production can use small resources—a very important point when concentrated, large resources are becoming scarce or inaccessible. Small units are ecologically sounder than big ones: the pollution or damage they may cause has a better chance of fitting into nature's tolerance margins. Small units can be used for decentralized production, leading to a more even distribution of the population, a better use of space, the avoidance of congestion and of monster transport. Most important of all: small units, of which there can be a great number, enable more people "to do their own thing" than large units of which there can only be a few. Smallness is also conductive to simplicity. Simplicity . . . is a value in itself. [E. F. Schumacher, The Age of Plenty: A Christian View, in Economics, Ecology and Ethics 126, 133 (H. Daly, ed. 1980).]

Notice how Schumacher's defense of smallness invokes, in addition to ecology, many of the other strands of environmentalism noted in Part B of this Chapter.

This brief review has traced some of the more significant influences of ecology, starting with its methodology for scientific study of complex natural systems, then going on to examine some implications for assessing the costs and benefits of environmentally disruptive actions, and finally to some ethical or normative claims about appropriate human behavior. In recent years, some of the assumptions held by the science of ecology have been changing. As you read the following excerpt, ask yourself what implications the changes it describes in the science of ecology may have on ecology's policy significance and the normative claims associated with it.

> ### Stevens, New Eye on Nature: The Real Constant Is Eternal Turmoil
> **N.Y. Times, July 31, 1990, at C1**

In a revision that has far-reaching implications for the way humans see the natural world and their role in it, many scientists are forsaking one of the most deeply embedded concepts of ecology: the balance of nature. . . .

This concept of natural equilibrium long ruled ecological research and governed the management of such natural resources as forests and fisheries. It led to the doctrine, popular among conservationists, that nature knows best and that human intervention in it is bad by definition.

Now an accumulation of evidence has gradually led many ecologists to abandon the concept or declare it irrelevant, and others to alter it drastically. They say that nature is actually in a continuing state of disturbance and fluctuation. Change and turmoil, more than constancy and balance, is the rule. As a consequence, say many leaders in the field, textbooks will have to be rewritten and strategies of conservation and resource management rethought.

The balance-of-nature concept "makes nice poetry, but it's not such great science," said Dr. Steward T. A. Pickett, a plant ecologist at the Institute of Ecosystem Studies of the New York Botanical Garden at Millbrook, N.Y. . . . While the shift in thinking has not yet produced a coherent new theory to replace the old one, Dr. Pickett characterizes what is going on as "a major revision of one of our basic assumptions of how the natural world works." The developing conviction that nature is ruled more by flux and disturbance is "becoming the dominant idea," he said. . . .

Some scientists now say that ecological communities of plants and animals are inherently unstable, largely because of idiosyncratic differences in behavior among communities and individuals in them. A super-aggressive wolfpack leader, for example, can greatly increase the pack's hunting efficiency and destabilize the ecosystem—just as the death of a pack leader can promote instability.

But even if ecological communities do display some sort of internal equilibrium, many scientists believe, external disturbances like climatic change, year-to-year variations in weather patterns, fires, windstorms, hurricanes and disease seldom, if ever, give the communities a chance to settle into a stable state. In this view, the climax forest, the neatly symmetrical predator-prey relationship and the bumper fish population become transient conditions at best, even in the absence of human intervention.

Scientists are finding this to be true on many scales of time and space, from the glacial and global to the seasonal and local, and in parts of the world long considered the most pristine and stable like the tropical rain forests of South and Central America, for instance, or the north woods of Canada and the northern United States.

In the natural landscape, "there is almost no circumstance one can find where something isn't changing the system," said Dr. George L. Jacobson Jr., who, as a paleoecologist at the University of Maine, studies ecological change as it is revealed in ancient sediments and rocks. And while there may be a tendency toward a stable equilibrium, he said, "it's never allowed to get there, so we might as well not expect it to exist."

A Difficulty—Posing a Question: What Is Natural?

In this developing new perspective, humans are emerging as just one of many sources of ecological disturbance that keep nature in a perpetual state of uproar. The question of whether humans should intervene in natural processes is moot, ecologists say, since humans and their near-human ancestors have been doing so for eons, and ecological systems around the world bear their indelible imprint.

The supposedly pristine rain forests of Latin America, for instance, owe some of their character to the intervention of humans who planted and transplanted trees and other plants throughout the jungle. And the supposedly unspoiled Serengeti plain of Africa, some ecologists are convinced, owes its tremendous abundance of grazing animals at least partly to human-set fires that created savanna habitats.

The real question, ecologists say, is which sort of human interventions should be promoted and which opposed.

One of the biggest human interventions, some say, is taking place now as people pour heat-trapping chemicals, mainly carbon dioxide, into the atmosphere. Many climatologists expect that this will cause the

Earth's climate to warm significantly, causing especially widespread ecological dislocation.

The temperature of the earth has shifted up and down many times in past eons, ecologists point out, and ecosystems have always adjusted. But this human intervention, scientists say, threatens to force, in a century or less, vast climatic and ecological changes that have usually taken millennia. Ecologists fear that this time, ecosystems will not adjust rapidly enough to stave off catastrophe for many species.

Moreover, some ecologists say, natural disruptions promote diversity of species in a forest, for example, by opening up gaps and patches where different plants can grow than grew before. But they say also that people are eliminating some of this diversity. "We threaten that variability because we want to manage everything like cornfields," said Dr. Julie Denslow, a tropical ecologist at Tulane University. There is, she said, "a whole camp of us" opposed to this "horrible homogenizing."

The new view of nature poses difficulties for conservationists and environmentalists who want to preserve things in their natural condition, scientists say, since the question now becomes: If change is constant, what is the natural state?

What, for instance, is the natural condition of the Adirondacks, where a spirited argument is going on about whether "rough" fish like suckers, shiners and chubs should be killed and removed from some ponds to make way for trout. People on one side of the argument, citing a state policy that aims to "perpetuate natural aquatic ecosystems" in the area, say that the rough fish represent the natural condition and that the ponds should be preserved in that condition. Others say that at least some rough fish are descendants of baitfish brought in by humans and that they have crowded out trout that flourished there earlier.

Is either of these alternative conditions "the" natural state? Or is the natural state the way the Adirondacks were when Europeans first arrived? Or, for that matter, the way they were in the millennia when the region was buried under an ice-age glacier? Or in the succession of different forests, animals and ecosystems that followed?

"Nature can be in many conditions," said Dr. Daniel B. Botkin, an ecologist at the University of California at Santa Barbara who is a leader of the reassessment effort. Because of that, he said, conservationists and resource managers will be required to analyze a given situation more carefully than in the past and then choose which natural condition to promote rather than simply insist that humans should not upset a supposed balance of nature.

"I think he's right," said Rupert Cutler, the president of the Defenders of Wildlife, a major conservation organization. He said that the shift in thinking "suggests that the responsibility for protecting nature will require a much higher level of intense application of science than it was ever assumed to require in the past."

EMPTY THEORY: OBSERVATIONS FIND NO NEAT BALANCE

In its classic formulation, the balance-of-nature concept holds that an ecosystem maintains a constant equilibrium and when disturbed, it returns to its former status when the cause of the disturbance is removed.

Many scientists now say it is clear that this is not the way things work. "We can say that's dead for most people in the scientific community," said Dr. Peter L. Chesson, a theoretical ecologist at Ohio State University. . . .

Many observations of the behavior of animal populations in the wild, says Dr. Botkin, do not support the assumption of neat balance predicted by traditional ecological theory. One aspect of the theory says that when a population of animals moves into an area, it grows gradually to a level of abundance at which its environment will allow it to be sustained indefinitely, and then remains at that level. Another says that predator and prey populations in a given ecosystem oscillate in numbers, with one population at a peak while the other is at a low point and vice versa, thereby creating an equilibrium over time.

But in real life, says Dr. Botkin, "when you introduce a population to a new area it goes up and then crashes, and then it doesn't remain constant. The long-term numbers vary and are much lower" than predicted by the theory. Similarly, he said, a number of studies and observations, in the laboratory as well as the wild, show that predator-prey populations do not oscillate stably and predictably. Instead, they either fluctuate wildly and unpredictably or the prey species is eliminated and the predator species dies of starvation. In one famous experiment, paramecium microbes increased rapidly. When predator microbes were introduced, they increased, too. But in the end, the paramecia were exterminated and the predators died of starvation.

Attempts to apply the classical equilibrium principle to the management of marine fisheries led to disaster, according to Dr. Botkin. For years, he said, international regulators of commercial fishing determined allowable annual catches by calculating maximum sustainable yields according to equilibrium theory. The theory was such a poor guide, Dr. Botkin said, that population after population of commercial fish suffered catastrophic declines in the 1950's and 1960's and some have not yet recovered.

Managers of fisheries are trying to move away from that strategy now, he said, by analyzing the more complicated factors that actually determine fish populations. Among these, for example, are the environmental disturbances that largely determine the size of a given year's hatching of young fish. By estimating and keeping track of these varying "year classes," managers hope to adjust catch quotas year-by-year and avoid wiping out an entire class.

Some scientists are not quite ready to abandon entirely the concept of an inherent tendency toward equilibrium in ecosystems. A kind of equilibrium, they say, may exist on some scales of time and space.

Scale, in fact, may be very important. While there may be enormous, unbalancing disturbances and fluctuations among small populations in small ecosystems, says Dr. Pickett, the fluctuations may be dampened when the larger picture is considered, where a sort of medium-scale equilibrium might apply. An animal population that fails in one environment might not do so if allowed to range over a wider area. Dr. Botkin also said it is quite possible that while a given locality's ecology would change markedly over thousands of years, there could be recurring similarities—and thus a kind of floating equilibrium—at medium-range time scales.

That, in fact, is what Dr. Chesson, the theoretician, postulates. There may, for instance, be a limited range in which an animal population fluctuates over several hundred years. An equilibrium could be calculated by taking the average of the fluctuations. But it would be a "real mistake," said Dr. Chesson, to equate this with anything "remotely like" the classical idea of the balance of nature.

CONSTANT CHANGE—OUTSIDE FACTORS SHAPE ECOSYSTEMS

Perhaps the most outstanding evidence favoring an ecology of constant change and disruption over one of static balance comes from studies of naturally occurring external factors that dislocate ecosystems.

For a long time, says Dr. Meyer of the University of Georgia, these outside influences were insufficiently considered. The emphasis, she said, was "on processes going on within the system," even though "what's happening is driven by what's happened outside." Ecologists, she said, "had blinders on in thinking about external controlling factors."

Climate and weather appear foremost among these factors. By studying the record laid down in ocean and lake sediments, scientists know that climate, in the words of Dr. Davis of the University of Minnesota, has been "wildly fluctuating" over the last two million years, and the shape of ecosystems with it. The fluctuations take place not only from eon to eon, but also from year to year and at every scale in between. "So you can't visualize a time in equilibrium," said Dr. Davis.

Dr. Jacobson said there is virtually no time when the overall environment stays constant for very long. "That means that the configuration of the ecosystems is always changing."

NOTES AND QUESTIONS

1. Those views of environmental ethics that draw on ecology stress that humans are but one element in a complex, interrelated system of elements, each of which is entitled to respect. Adherents of such eco-centric perspectives contrast their views with the homocentric principle that actions are good or bad insofar as they benefit or harm humans alone. How, if at all, do you think the "new ecology" as described in the preceding article might affect ecocentric perspectives on environmental ethics?

2. In his book Ecology and the Politics of Scarcity, William Ophuls provides the following statement of "the essential message of ecology."

> [A]lthough it is possible in principle to exploit nature rationally and rea-sonably for human ends, man has not done so. Because he has not been content with the portion naturally allotted him, man has invaded the bi-ological capital built up by evolution. Moreover, due to man's ignorance of nature's workings, he has done so in a peculiarly destructive fashion. . . . We must learn to work with nature and to accept the basic ecological trade-offs between protection and production, optimum and maximum, quality and quantity. This will necessarily require major changes in our life, for the essential message of ecology is limitation: there is only so much the biosphere can take and only so much it can give, and this may be less than we desire. [Ecology and the Politics of Scarcity 43 (1977).]

How must Ophuls's "essential message" be modified, if at all, if the new ecology is sound?

3. How will ecology's contribution to the assessment of the conse-quences of human actions be affected by the new ecology? Has the science of ecology been made less relevant or more relevant to a careful evaluation of costs and benefits of large-scale human action? If there are no "natural" states to use as benchmarks, does calculating harm and benefit become more difficult, less difficult, or remain the same? How about deciding what is a harm or a benefit in the first place?

4. The inhabitants of Nantucket Island have been arguing over the fate of Frog Pond. The fairly large pond comes at one point within 150 feet of the ocean, but has been entirely cut off from the ocean for about 80 years by a small dune system. It supports an entirely freshwater marshlands ecoculture, including large quantities of mosquitoes—which support the frogs that give the pond its name. Previously, the pond was regularly inundated by the ocean, and its ecosystem was that of a saline marsh (no mosquitoes). Neighbors of Frog Pond are saying they want to return the Pond to its natural condition by cutting a channel through to the ocean. Others on the island say they want to guarantee that the Pond stay in its natural state, which seems to mean that it remain fresh-water until a natural circumstance, such as a major storm, breaches the

dune system. How do you analyze this conflict in light of the old ecology? In light of the new ecology?

5. The new ecology emphasizes biologists' inability to make meaningful and reliable forecasts about the conditions of ecosystems. David Ehrenfeld, a professor of biology at Rutgers University, argues that scientists have responded to this problem in two unsatisfying fashions, which he calls the "Horoscope Method" and the "Dignified Retreat." Ehrenfeld, Environmental Protection: The Expert's Dilemma, Phil. & Pub. Poly. 8 (Spring 1991). When pressed by policymakers for predictions concerning the ecological impact of alternative actions, some scientists maintain the pretense that scientific models can predict environmental impacts by making unreliably specific or hopelessly general predictions (the "Horoscope Method"). Others refuse to consider the policy implications of scientific research or limit their recommendations to general calls for additional research (the "Dignified Retreat"). Professor Ehrenfeld argues that neither approach is a satisfactory response to the need to make policy choices in the face of uncertainty. He argues that experts should be more willing to acknowledge the limitations of scientific knowledge and to share what they do know with the public in a more interactive and mutually respectful manner.

6. Even if we could determine what is truly "natural," does it necessarily follow that our goal should be to preserve the environment in its "natural" state? Some natural conditions threaten human health. For example, consider radon, a naturally occurring radioactive gas that seeps into homes and other buildings from underground. EPA estimates that radon causes thousands of cases of lung cancer each year. Or consider the condition of Lake Nyos, a deep lake in the crater of a dormant volcano in northwest Cameroon. Dissolved carbon dioxide entering the lake from the volcano killed an estimated 1,700 people in 1986 when it was released in a giant bubble that had accumulated underwater. Scientists warn that an unstable natural dam holding the Lake's water back may collapse and drown nearby residents, but they are afraid that lowering the lake's water level will trigger another lethal burst of carbon dioxide. Sean Kelly, Lethal Lake Nyos Again Threatens Doom for Neighbors in Cameroon, Wash. Post, July 20, 1991, at A15. What principles should govern our responses to such problems?

7. Isn't the ultimate objective of environmental policy to answer the question Christopher Stone poses: What sort of planet will this be? Stone argues that while technology and resource constraints define the range of future options that we realistically can seek, environmental ethics seeks to tell us which of these alternative futures we *ought* to select. Environmental law, then, seeks to determine how we can arrange our social institutions in order to achieve the future that we want. C. Stone, Earth and Other Ethics 15-16 (1987). What obligation do we have toward future generations when making choices concerning what sort of planet

this will be? Do we have an obligation to leave future generations at least the same range of choices that we have? Or do we owe them some lesser obligation because they depend on us for their existence and their values will be influenced by the state of the world we choose to leave them? How would proponents of the economic perspective approach these questions? The ecological perspective?

E. ENVIRONMENTAL POLICY: SOME INTRODUCTORY THEMES

As you read through these materials, you are likely to discover that several themes run through our discussion of environmental law and policy. It is appropriate to conclude this chapter by identifying two of the most important of these themes. Each has considerable relevance for understanding the difficulties that confront environmental policy-makers. The first theme emphasizes the consequences of the tension inherent in the competing value perspectives that may be brought to bear on environmental questions. We have grouped these perspectives into two simplified categories that we call "moral outrage" and "cool analysis." The second theme emphasizes the importance of considering how law and policy respond to uncertainty, which makes policy judgments particularly difficult in the environmental area.

1. *Moral Outrage versus Cool Analysis*

We began this chapter with David Broder's optimistic claim that environmental disputes no longer involve value questions. Yet we then reviewed sharply contrasting value perspectives that play an important role in environmental controversies. The competing perspectives inevitably affect, if only in subtle ways, which phenomena we identify as environmental problems, how seriously they concern us, and what we view as appropriate responses to them. A considerable amount of the policy debate that animates environmental law exhibits a tension between what could be called "moral outrage" and "cool analysis." The moral outrage perspective has deep roots in American environmentalism, which often grounds a concern about environmental policy on moral or ethical commitments; a good many environmentalists also seek, as an ultimate objective, a transformed social structure and culture in which human ambitions with respect to the use of natural resources would conflict with their preservation a great deal less than do our current structure and culture. As we will see, the ethical aspects are reflected in numerous places in the environmental laws, for example (1) in NEPA's promise that each person should enjoy a healthy environment; (2) in the statutes that set aside portions of wilderness for the enjoyment of all citizens; and (3) in the general reluctance to treat environmental concerns as fungible with purely individual preferences. The transformative aspects come through dimly in statutes that seek to force the development of improved pollution control technology, although the sort of social transformation at the heart of portions of the Green movement and the "small is beautiful" movement that preceded it implicates more basic social and cultural orientations.

These ethical and transformative aspects of environmentalism are frequently caricatured (perhaps accurately) as totalitarian in their implications. Yet it is clear that public attitudes toward environmental issues commonly do exhibit moral concern and the desire to reshape human stances on nature (witness the overwhelming support for the proposition that "continuing environmental improvement must be made regardless of cost"), and that most environmental advocates believe they can *persuade* others of the wisdom of their proposals rather than impose them.

The opposing tradition of cool analysis is represented by welfare economics and cost-benefit analysis and by the tendency to treat environmental problems as conflicts among uses of equal status (jobs v. health, income v. environmental quality, and so on). While agreeing that environmental problems exist, cool analysts characterize those problems as strictly similar to all other issues of managing scarce resources. This characterization raises two points of tension between the cool analysis approach and the moral outrage approach: (1) the cool analyst takes a decidedly amoral approach to environmental problems, treating them as no different than a question of how much white bread versus whole-wheat bread to produce—all such questions are essentially questions of aggregating individual preferences, and the analyst has nothing of interest to say about how those preferences are produced, whether a product of individual morality, whim, quirks, or self-interest; (2) the cool analyst wants to apply a methodology to the solution of environmental problems that corresponds to her amoral treatment of them, a methodology that equates a preference for environmental quality to a preference for cosmetic cream or dog biscuits.

The tension between the moral outrage and cool analysis perspectives is reflected in legislators' fondness for writing statutes that declare idealistic ends as an expression of moral outrage while delegating the task of achieving those ends to specialized agencies more inclined to cool analysis. This may result in considerable disparity between the declared intentions of the environmental laws and their results. However, the laws' expression of moral outrage undoubtedly has some influence on public values by articulating the kind of society to which we aspire and the kind of planet we seek.

2. *Decision-making Under Uncertainty*

At virtually every turn, environmental policy must confront problems of *decision-making under uncertainty.* Environmental problems are caused by a wide variety of human activities whose effects are dispersed over space and time through complex interactions that often are poorly understood. Environmental damage may take years to become apparent, and it may occur at locations and through mechanisms far removed from the action that initiates it. Thus, even when efforts are made to anticipate and to prevent harm, policymakers often are not aware of the full range of environmental consequences until after considerable damage has occurred. Predictions of future ecological impacts and human health effects are fraught with uncertainty because of the complexity of the effects, data limitations, and incomplete scientific understanding of processes. Improved understanding of the probabilistic nature of certain environmental effects has made the concept of risk increasingly influential in environmental policymaking, but officials still must confront enormous uncertainties when making environmental decisions.

These uncertainties complicate efforts to resolve environmental disputes. While differences in values animate many environmental conflicts, factual uncertainty provides ample ammunition for disputants. The moral outrage and cool analysis perspectives reflect a recognition that environmental disputes often turn on conflicts between competing values. However, policymakers are reluctant to make explicit choices between competing values, perhaps because social norms discourage them from acknowledging that some values must be compromised. Instead, most environmental controversies are waged as factual disputes that focus on competing interpretations of the nature and magnitude of environmental effects and the social consequences of alternative policies. Such seemingly "factual" disputes are virtually inevitable in light of the tremendous uncertainties that surround not only the assessment and characterization of environmental effects, but also predictions about the availability and cost of control technologies over time.

Differences in value perspectives may influence not only perceptions and interpretations of "the facts," but also views concerning the appropriate responses to uncertainty. For example, the ecological substratum of environmentalism predicts that the unknown and unintended consequences of our actions will systematically be more detrimental than not, and thus counsels caution in the face of uncertainty. The economic substratum, which stresses adaptability and the favorable side of innovative change, characteristically draws just the opposite conclusion. Which counsel is heeded when burdens of proof are assigned will be determinative of the policy outcome when uncertainty is too great to be overcome.

Whichever conclusion one adopts, an appropriate appreciation of uncertainty counsels that we should constantly be striving to know more. Thus, it is vital that environmental lawyers become conversant in other disciplines that are more likely to increase our knowledge about the real world of environmental consequences than is the law. Yet we must also bear in mind that the quest for information is itself costly and at some point its costs will exceed whatever benefits improved information may have for decision-making. The trick for policymakers is to determine what is a tolerable level of uncertainty, that is, one that permits informed decision-making while avoiding what has been called "paralysis by analysis."

The chapters that follow illustrate these and other themes that are important to an understanding of the complex and politically charged arena in which environmental law and policy is made. Chapter 2 will introduce you to the complex body of laws and regulations that has been developed to respond to the environmental problems society has identified.

= 2 =

Environmental Law: A Structural Overview

The last two decades of environmental policy in this country have been similar in some ways to [the Space Invaders] video game: Every time we saw a blip on the radar screen, we unleashed an arsenal of control measures to eliminate it.

—*EPA Administrator William Reilly**

If you have traveled in the remote parts of the Deep South, I am sure you have seen the architecture of Tobacco Road—shacks built of whatever materials were available at the time, often by a series of owners. Maybe the roof is corrugated tin, but one wall is made from a billboard and the door step is a cinder block. No part matches any other part, and there are holes here and there. Still, it provides a measure of basic shelter, and there comes a point where it is easier to tack a new board over a gap that appears than to redesign the entire structure.

—*Ronald Outen***

Environmental law is structurally complex. Its complexity stems in part from its diverse roots: centuries of evolving common law doctrine, a welter of federal and state statutes with a vast array of implementing regulations, and even agreements between sovereign states. Like the video game mentioned in the quotation above from William Reilly, most environmental statutes respond to particularly visible manifestations of broader problems. When considered together, it is apparent that they provide regulatory authority that is at once piecemeal and overlapping. Thus, even though the environmental laws articulate some of society's

---

*Quoted in Clarke, Looking at Risk, Envtl. Forum 12, 14 (Mar.-Apr. 1991).
**Environmental Pollution Laws and the Architecture of Tobacco Road, in National Research Council, Multimedia Approaches to Pollution Control: Symposium Proceedings 139 (1987).

noblest aspirations, their architecture much more closely resembles a shack on Tobacco Road than a Gothic cathedral.

The complex architecture of environmental law reflects not only the circumstances of its birth, but also the complexity of the problems it addresses and the difficulty of reconciling the competing values environmental policy implicates. Although there is a remarkable cross-disciplinary consensus in favor of collective action to address problems caused by "individually rational but collectively deficient" behavior, often there is sharp disagreement concerning the precise form that action should take. No one wants to bear the brunt of environmental regulation, though everyone wants to enjoy its benefits. The diverse philosophies that animate environmental concerns and the immense uncertainties that confront policymakers provide ample opportunity for controversy. When regulatory policy is developed and implemented, tensions submerged in ambiguous statutory language often are resolved in ways that contribute further to the extraordinary complexity of environmental regulation.

This chapter is designed to introduce the "big picture" of environmental law by providing a roadmap of sorts to help you navigate this legal labyrinth. After reviewing the roots of environmental law, it explores the principal federal environmental statutes and the wide range of alternative regulatory strategies they employ. The chapter concludes with a brief introduction to the process by which statutes are translated into regulations.

A. SOURCES OF ENVIRONMENTAL LAW

What we call environmental law is a complex combination of common law, legislation, and international agreements. After centuries of wrestling with environmental conflicts, the common law has now been eclipsed by an explosion of environmental statutes. The public law that has come to dominate the field generally declares broad environmental goals while delegating to administrative agencies substantial responsibility for developing and implementing policy. Despite the ascendancy of public law, environmental law's common law roots remain important for several reasons. They articulate principles that have been highly influential in the development of public law, and they retain considerable vitality in their own right as common law actions make a resurgence in some areas today. Moreover, an appreciation of the inadequacies of the common law is crucial to understanding the rapid growth of public law and to evaluating its effectiveness in protecting the environment.

1. Common Law Roots

Prior to the explosion of environmental legislation in the 1970s, the common law was the legal system's primary vehicle for responding to environmental disputes. For centuries common law courts had wrestled with what is perhaps the quintessential question of environmental law: how to harmonize conflicts that inevitably occur when human activity interferes with the interests of others in the quality of their physical surroundings. The common law relied largely on nuisance law doctrines to resolve environmental controversies, although conduct that resulted in a physical invasion of property could be addressed as a trespass. Nuisance law is designed to protect against invasions of interests in the use and enjoyment of land, while trespass protects against invasions of interests in the exclusive possession of land.

A leading treatise's declaration that nuisance law is an "impenetrable jungle," W. Prosser, Handbook of the Law of Torts §86, at 571 (4th ed. 1971), no doubt reflects, in some respects, the difficulties courts face in attempting to harmonize the competing interests at stake in environmental controversies. The history of nuisance law illustrates the tension between the competing perspectives on environmental problems that we call "moral outrage" and "cool analysis." The early common law of nuisance held actors strictly liable when their actions interfered with property rights held by others. This common law version of moral outrage focused largely on whether certain interests had been invaded, not on the conduct that produced the invasion. As the Industrial Revolution intensified environmental conflicts, the common law more frequently employed balancing approaches, similar to the cool analysis perspective, that considered not only the nature of the interference with property rights but also the nature and utility of the conduct that generated the interference.

While applicable to related problems, private and public nuisance actions have distinct legal roots. Private nuisance actions focus on invasions of interests in the private use and enjoyment of land. Public nuisances were common law crimes that involved offenses against the state arising from actions that interfered with public property (e.g., obstruction of the king's highway, encroachment on the royal domain) or that endangered the health or property of large numbers of people. Actions to abate private nuisances could be brought by private parties damaged by them. Public nuisances were subject to abatement actions by governmental authorities or by private parties who suffered special injury.

A. PRIVATE NUISANCE

Nontrespassory invasions of another's interest in the private use
and enjoyment of land are actionable as *private nuisances.* Unlike intentional trespass, where liability attaches even in the absence of a showing
of harm, private nuisance liability requires a showing of significant harm.
Moreover, the interference with property rights must be intentional and
unreasonable or actionable under rules imposing strict liability on those
engaging in abnormally dangerous activities as in Fletcher v. Rylands,
L.R. 3 H.L. 330 (1868). As the Restatement of Torts explains, these
requirements reflect a recognition that some conflicts are inevitable in
a modern society:

> Life in organized society, and especially in populous communities, involves
> an unavoidable clash of individual interests. Practically all human activities
> unless carried on in a wilderness, interfere to some extent with others or
> involve some risk of interference, and these interferences range from the
> mere trifling annoyances to serious harms. It is an obvious truth that each
> individual in a community must put up with a certain amount of risk in
> order that all may get together. The very existence of an organized society
> depends upon the principle of "give and take, live and let live," and there-
> fore the law of torts does not attempt to impose liability or shift the loss
> in every case where one person's conduct has some detrimental effect on
> another. Liability is imposed only in those cases where the harm or risk
> to one is greater than he ought to be required to bear under the circum-
> stances at least without compensation. [Restatement of Torts (Second) §822
> comment g (1978).]

Nuisance law has long wrestled with the difficult question of how to
determine the level of harm or risk that requires compensation.

Actions for private nuisance evolved from the ancient assize of
nuisance, which was designed to secure the free enjoyment of property.
In the early fifteenth century the assize of nuisance was displaced by an
action on the case for nuisance. While procedurally simpler than the
assize, actions on the case provided only a damages remedy. Suits in
equity were necessary in order to obtain injunctions ordering the abatement of private nuisances; such actions were rarely brought prior to the
mid-nineteenth century.

An influential early case in the development of nuisance law was
a seventeenth-century decision involving a pig sty built adjacent to William Alred's property. In Alred's Case, 77 Eng. Rep. 816 (1611), the pig
sty was held to be a private nuisance because the wretched stench that
it generated interfered with Alred's enjoyment of his property. While
the decision did not imply that all unpleasant odors emanating from the
property of others were actionable, it established that if a nontrespassory
invasion of property rights was sufficiently great, air pollution was ac-

tionable as a private nuisance. As Lord Holt explained in declaring a nuisance the failure to repair a wall separating a privy from a neighbor's property, "every man must so use his own as not to damnify another." Tenant v. Goldwin, 92 Eng. Rep. 222 (1702).

As the Industrial Revolution progressed, environmental insults became more difficult to avoid. This created a tension between common law notions of strict liability and approaches that would balance the value of activities that generated pollution against the rights of victims. The clearest example of this tension is the 1858 decision of the Court of Common Pleas in Hole v. Barlow, 4 C.B.N.S. 334 (1858). Citing fears that nuisance actions could bring industry to a halt in England's great manufacturing towns, the court refused to hold a brickmaking operation liable as a private nuisance despite the pollution it produced. The court upheld a jury instruction that "no action lies for the use, the reasonable use, of a lawful trade in a convenient and proper place even though some one may suffer annoyance from its being carried on." While this sharp departure from precedent threatened to eviscerate private nuisance doctrine, it was soon overruled. The decision in Bamford v. Turnley, 122 Eng. Rep. 27 (1862), returned to the strict liability premise that private property may not be used to cause harm to another. The court held that pollution from a brick kiln erected by a defendant while constructing a house was actionable as a nuisance. The court rejected the defendant's argument that operation of the brick kiln was justified because of its convenience for the defendant. But it left open the prospect that pollution caused by factories might not be held to a similarly strict standard.

While not deviating from the black-letter principle of Alred's Case, the common law gradually tempered private nuisance doctrines by increasing the severity of harm required and by adjusting notions of reasonableness. As industrialization changed the conditions of urban environments, courts expected individuals to become more tolerant of discomfort produced by industrial activity. To qualify as a private nuisance, the degree of interference with a plaintiff's "comfortable and convenient enjoyment" of land had to be substantial. Because the standards of substantiality and reasonableness could vary with the location and circumstances of the pollution, nuisance law became a kind of zoning device. As Lord Thesiger explained in Sturgess v. Bridgman, L.R. 11 Ch. D. 852 (1879): "What would be a nuisance in Belgrave Square would not necessarily be one in Bermondsey." Judges observed that plaintiffs were not entitled to pollution-free air, but rather to "air not rendered to an important degree less compatible, or at least not rendered incompatible, with the physical comfort of human existence." Walter v. Selfe, 4 De G. & Sm. 315, 322 (1851).

In St. Helens Smelting Co. v. Tipping, 11 H.L.C. 642 (1865), the owner of a large estate one and one-half miles from a copper smelter alleged that the smelter's emissions had damaged his trees, crops, and animals and caused him substantial personal discomfort. The area around the smelter had been singled out in a report by the Lords Select Committee on Noxious Vapors in 1863 as a "scene of desolation" caused by pollution from heavy industry. The report had stated that "[f]arms recently well-wooded, and with hedges in good condition, have now neither tree nor hedge left alive; whole fields of corn are destroyed in a single night, especially when the vapours fall upon them while in bloom; orchards and gardens, . . . have not a fruit tree left alive. . . ." Brenner, Nuisance Law and the Industrial Revolution, 3 J. Legal Stud. 403, 416 (1974). The court rejected the company's argument that smelting may be carried on with impunity if the smelter is in a suitable location. As the lord chancellor explained: "The word 'suitable' unquestionably cannot carry with it this consequence, that a trade may be carried on in a particular locality, the consequence of which trade may be injury and destruction to the neighboring property." The court held the company liable only for damage to the property that could be shown "visibly to diminish [its] value," and not for mere personal discomfort that the pollution may have caused Tipping.

American courts initially followed the English common law's refusal to balance the value of polluting activity against the harm to the victim. Like the British courts, many American courts rejected the "coming to the nuisance" doctrine, which would have barred recovery to victims who complained about conditions that existed prior to their moving into an area. Relying on the principle that any unreasonable use of property to the injury of others is a nuisance, the Maryland Court of Appeals in 1890 explained its rejection of balancing approaches in the following terms:

> The law, in cases of this kind, will not undertake to balance the conveniences, or estimate the difference between the injury sustained by the plaintiff and the loss that may result to the defendant from having its trade and business, as now carried on, found to be a nuisance. No one has a right to erect works which are a nuisance to a neighboring owner, and then say he has expended large sums of money in the erection of his works, while the neighboring property is comparatively of little value. The neighboring owner is entitled to the reasonable and comfortable enjoyment of his property, and, if his rights in this respect are invaded, he is entitled to the protection of the law, let the consequences be what they may. [Susquehanna Fertilizer Co. v. Malone, 73 Md. 268, 20 A. 900, 902 (1890).]

Thus, Maryland's highest court upheld a judgment that noxious vapors from a large fertilizer factory that damaged the health and property of a neighboring family were a nuisance, even though several other fertilizer plants were located in the area.

While decisions like *Susquehanna Fertilizer Co.* represented an application of the ancient maxim "Let justice be done, though the heavens may fall," courts were less inclined to follow this approach in fashioning remedies than they were in defining rights. In determining what relief to award, American courts generally were more inclined to balance environmental damage against the value of polluting activities than English courts. This has been interpreted by some legal historians as reflecting the American legal system's efforts to promote industrial growth in the nineteenth century, L. Friedman, A History of American Law (1973); M. Horwitz, The Transformation of American Law, 1780-1860 (1977), though others have found a more mixed picture. Schwartz, Tort Law and the Economy in Nineteenth-Century America: A Reinterpretation, 90 Yale L.J. 1717 (1981). In any event, it is clear that courts increasingly were confronted by conflicts caused by the environmental impact of industrial activity. In a society that encouraged industrial growth, many courts were reluctant to award injunctions against private nuisances if they involved activities that had considerable economic value, as indicated in the decision below. The case arose from a series of lawsuits brought by landowners who lived in the vicinity of two copper smelters located in Ducktown, Tennessee, near the Georgia-Tennessee border. Charging that the smelters were private nuisances, the residents sued the two companies that owned the smelters, the Ducktown Sulphur, Copper & Iron Co. and the Tennessee Copper Company, and asked the court to issue an injunction prohibiting their operation. In each case, the court of chancery appeals had directed that operation of the smelters be enjoined, reversing the trial court's refusal to issue an injunction. Appeals were then heard by the Tennessee Supreme Court.

Madison v. Ducktown Sulphur, Copper & Iron Co.
113 Tenn. 331, 83 S.W. 658 (1904)

MR. JUSTICE NEIL delivered the opinion of the Court.

The bills are all based on the ground of nuisance, in that the two companies, in the operation of their plants at and near Ducktown, in Polk county, in the course of reducing copper ore, cause large volumes of smoke to issue from their roast piles, which smoke descends upon the surrounding lands, and injures trees and crops, and renders the homes of complainants less comfortable and their lands less profitable than before. The purpose of all the bills is to enjoin the further operation of these plants. . . .

Ducktown is in a basin of the mountains of Polk county, in this State, not far from the State line of the States of Georgia and North Carolina. This basin is six or eight miles wide. The complainants are the owners of small farms situated in the mountains around Ducktown.

The method used by the defendants in reducing their copper ores is to place the green ore, broken up, on layers of wood, making large open-air piles, called "roast piles," and these roast piles are ignited for the purpose of expelling from the ore certain foreign matters called "sulphurets." In burning, these roast piles emit large volumes of smoke. This smoke, rising in the air, is carried off by air currents around and over adjoining land. . . .

The general effect produced by the smoke upon the possessions and families of the complainants is as follows, *viz.:*

Their timber and crop interests have been badly injured, and they have been annoyed and discommoded by the smoke so that the complainants are prevented from using and enjoying their farms and homes as they did prior to the inauguration of these enterprises. The smoke makes it impossible for the owners of farms within the area of the smoke zone to subsist their families thereon with the degree of comfort they enjoyed before. They cannot raise and harvest their customary crops, and their timber is largely destroyed. . . .

The court of chancery appeals finds that the defendants are conducting and have been conducting their business in a lawful way, without any purpose or desire to injure any of the complainants; that they have been and are pursuing the only known method by which these plants can be operated and their business successfully carried on; that the open-air roast-heap is the only method known to the business or to science by means of which copper ore of the character mined by the defendants can be reduced; that the defendants have made every effort to get rid of the smoke and noxious vapors, one of the defendants having spent $200,000 in experiments to this end, but without result.

It is to be inferred from the description of the locality that there is no place more remote to which the operations referred to could be transferred.

It is found, in substance, that, if the injunctive relief sought be granted, the defendants will be compelled to stop operations and their property will become practically worthless, the immense business conducted by them will cease, and they will be compelled to withdraw from the State. It is a necessary deduction from the foregoing that a great and increasing industry in the State will be destroyed, and all of the valuable copper properties of the State become worthless. . . .

While there can be no doubt that the facts stated make out a case of nuisance, for which the complainants in actions at law would be entitled to recover damages, yet the remedy in equity is not a matter of course. Not only must the bill state a proper case, but the right must be clear, and the injury must be clearly established, as in doubtful cases the party will be turned over to his legal remedy; and, if there is a reasonable doubt as to the cause of the injury, the benefit of the doubt will be given to the defendant, if his trade is a lawful one, and the injury is not the necessary and natural consequence of the act; and, if the injury can be adequately compensated at law by a judgment for damages, equity will not interfere. . . .

In addition to the principles already announced, the following general propositions seem to be established by the authorities: If the case made out by the pleadings and evidence shows with sufficient clearness and certainty grounds for equitable relief it will not be denied because the persons proceeded against are engaged in a lawful business. (Tipping v. St. Helens Smelting Co., 11 H.L. Cas., 642; Susquehanna Fertilizer Co. v. Malone, 73 Md., 268, 282, 20 Atl. 900), or because the works complained of are located in a convenient place, if that place be one wherein an actionable injury is done to another (Susquehanna Fertilizer Co. v. Malone, 73 Md., 268, 277, 278, 20 Atl., 900, and cases cited; Tipping v. St. Helens Smelting Co., supra); nor will the existence of another nuisance of a similar character at the same place furnish a ground for denying relief if it appear that the defendant has sensibly contributed to the injury complained of (Tipping v. St. Helens Smelting Co., supra). Nor is it a question of care and skill, but purely one of results. Fletcher v. Rylands, 1 L.R., Exch., 289. . . .

But there is one other principle which is of controlling influence in this department of the law, and in the light of which the foregoing principle must be weighed and applied. This is that the granting of an injunction is not a matter of absolute right, but rests in the sound discretion of the court to be determined on a consideration of all of the special circumstances of each case, and the situation and surroundings of the parties, with a view to effect the ends of justice.

A judgment for damages in this class of cases is a matter of absolute right, where injury is shown. A decree for an injunction is a matter of sound legal discretion, to be granted or withheld as that discretion shall dictate, after a full and careful consideration of every element appertaining to the injury. . . .

The question now to be considered is, what is the proper exercise of discretion, under the facts appearing in the present case? Shall the complainants be granted, in the way of damages, the full measure of relief to which their injuries entitle them, or shall we go further, and grant their request to blot out two great mining and manufacturing enterprises, destroy half of the taxable values of a county, and drive more than 10,000 people from their homes? We think there can be no doubt as to what the true answer to this question should be.

In order to protect by injunction several small tracts of land, aggregating in value less than $1,000, we are asked to destroy other property worth nearly $2,000,000, and wreck two great mining and manufacturing enterprises, that are engaged in work of very great importance, not only to their owners, but to the State, and to the whole country as well, to depopulate a large town, and deprive thousands of working people of their homes and livelihood, and scatter them broadcast. The result would be practically a confiscation of the property of the defendants for the benefit of the complainants—an appropriation without compensation. The defendants cannot reduce their ores in a manner different from that they are now employing, and there is no more remote place to which they can remove. The decree asked for would deprive them of all of their rights. We appreciate the argument based on the fact that the homes of the complainants who live on the small tracts of land referred to are not so comfortable and useful to their owners as they were before they were affected by the smoke complained of, and we are deeply sensible of the truth of the proposition that no man is entitled to any more rights than another on the ground that he has or owns more property than that other. But in a case of conflicting rights, where neither party can enjoy his own without in some measure restricting the liberty of the other in the use of property, the law must make the best arrangement it can between the contending parties, with a view to preserving to each one the largest measure of liberty possible under the circumstances. We see no escape from the conclusion in the present case that the only proper decree is to allow the complainants a reference for the ascertainment of damages, and that the injunction must be denied to them. . . .

NOTES AND QUESTIONS

1. How can you reconcile the Tennessee Supreme Court's refusal to enjoin the copper smelters in Ducktown with the conclusion by Maryland's highest court in Susquehanna Fertilizer Co. v. Malone that a property owner is "entitled to the reasonable and comfortable enjoyment of his property, and, if his rights in this respect are invaded, he is entitled to the protection of the law, let the consequences be what they may?"

2. Copper had been discovered near Ducktown in 1849. The mines were developed in the early 1850s, and the area thrived until 1879 when the mines were closed due to economic conditions. After the bankruptcy of the Union Consolidated Mining Company, which had operated a copper smelter, thousands abandoned Ducktown, leaving it a virtual ghost town. In 1891, the Ducktown Sulphur, Copper & Iron Company, a British corporation, purchased the assets of Union, reopened the mines, and made major investments in rebuilding the operation. When it was first named as the defendant in ten nuisance actions, the Ducktown Company responded with indignation, arguing that it was responsible for resuscitating a depressed area to the delight of most of the population. The company filed its own countersuit against the plaintiffs who had sued it. It charged that the plaintiffs were disgruntled because they had been rejected for jobs and that they had "fraudulently confederated

together to vex, harass and annoy" the company. Ducktown sought an injunction to bar prosecution of the suits against it. The company maintained that the plaintiffs had entered "into a champertous and illegal contract with certain attorneys" to prosecute the cases on a contingent fee. Ducktown maintained that the litigation would cost more than the plaintiffs' lands were worth and that it was unfair for it to have to pay substantial court costs that the plaintiffs could escape by pleading the pauper's oath. The company also cited the fact that the residents had not sued the American company that owned the other smelter. After more than 30 depositions were taken, 4 of the plaintiffs dropped their lawsuits, and the trial court barred another from further prosecution after finding that his contract with his attorneys was "champertous and illegal." Ducktown Sulphur, Copper & Iron Co. v. Barnes, 60 S.W. 593 (1900). When the residents later brought a single action against both Ducktown and the American company that owned the other smelter, the Tennessee Copper Company, the companies succeeded in having the case dismissed for misjoinder of defendants who had not acted in concert. Swain v. Tennessee Copper Co., 111 Tenn. 430, 78 S.W. 93 (1903). A subsequent lawsuit culminated in the *Madison* decision in 1904.

3. During the previous litigation, Ducktown had argued in the trial court that it had acquired prescriptive rights to pollute the air because copper smelters had operated for decades in the area. The residents argued that the previous smelter "used charcoal in reducing the ore, which gave out no poisonous vapors or smoke in injurious quantities," while Ducktown "uses large quantities of stone coal in reducing a low grade of ore," with far more damaging pollutants. Ducktown Sulphur, Copper & Iron Co. v. Barnes, 60 S.W. 593, 596 (1900). The trial court rejected the company's argument, and its decision was upheld on appeal by the Tennessee Supreme Court. Citing the common law's rejection of the "coming to the nuisance" defense, the court declared that it was no defense to charges of nuisance to argue that similar establishments existed previously. 60 S.W. at 606.

4. The Tennessee Supreme Court's decision in *Madison* demonstrates that landowners could recover damages in private nuisance actions when pollution caused sufficient harm to their property. In *Madison* there was virtually no discussion of the issue that has proved to be the most substantial obstacle to common law recovery in environmental cases today: proof of causal injury. Plaintiffs must prove that defendant's actions are the legal cause of the invasion of their property rights and that that invasion is substantial, i.e., more than a slight inconvenience or annoyance. Why was the causation issue not litigated more vigorously by defendants in *Madison*?

5. While the court in *Madison* awarded the plaintiffs damages, it refused to enjoin operation of a smelter that had considerable economic value to the community even though the smelter generated pollution

that caused significant damage. In what respects does the court's decision reflect the moral outrage perspective on environmental issues? In what respects does it reflect the perspective of cool analysis?

6. While private nuisance actions offered some prospect of redress for pollution damage, their promise was largely illusory, particularly when substantial industrial establishments were involved. A study of private nuisance actions in late nineteenth-century England concluded that the law simply "was not being applied in industrial towns." Brenner, Nuisance Law and the Industrial Revolution, 3 J. Legal Stud. 403, 419 (1974). Several factors diminished the practical value of nuisance law. Recovery generally was only permitted for actual, physical damage to property that caused a decline in its market value. Property values generally increased with industrialization even in contaminated areas, making recovery difficult. Lawsuits were prohibitively expensive for the average British worker. Environmental conditions in most factory towns were so bad that the requirement that nuisances be evaluated in light of the "state of the neighborhood" actually "militated against the recognition by the common law of minimum standards of comfort and health." Id. at 420. Fearful of discouraging industrialization, courts held factories liable only in rare cases where the pollution was so devastating that it produced a "scene of desolation" for miles around, as in Tipping's case. Id. at 416. Moreover, many of the largest polluters were public or quasi-public enterprises that were protected from liability because their actions were authorized by statute.

7. While courts in the United States have been more disposed to award damages than to enjoin private nuisances, private parties occasionally have been successful in shutting down polluters in cases where environmental damage was quite severe. See, e.g., McClung v. North Bend Coal & Coke Co., 1 Ohio Dec. 187 (C. P. Hamilton 1892), affd., 9 Ohio C.C. 259 (1895) (injunction obtained against coking operations that destroyed more than 200 evergreen trees and impaired the health of persons on the ancestral estate of President William Henry Harrison).

8. The use of private nuisance actions to redress more generalized environmental damage is limited by the common law's focus on protection of private property interests. While the property rights and privileges protected by the common law include more than possessory interests, they do not include interests in public property. Thus, private nuisance actions could not be used to redress damage to the commons—air and water held in common by the public at large. Private parties could recover for public nuisances only if they could show that they had suffered special damage not shared in common with the rest of the public. Thus, a fisherman seeking to recover because a paper mill's pollution of the Roanoke River interfered with his ability to catch fish was told that his "complaint is fatally defective for the reason that the plaintiff did not

own either the River or the fish therein." Hampton v. North Carolina Pulp Co., 49 F. Supp. 625 (E.D.N.C. 1943).

9. Although principles of common law nuisance are applicable to all types of pollution, some courts have treated water pollution as an interference with riparian rights rather than under nuisance principles. Thus pollution of surface waters could be actionable if it interfered with the rights of riparian owners to receive a flow of water in its natural state of purity. Wisdom, The Law on the Pollution of Waters (1966). See, e.g., Indianapolis Water Co. v. Strawboard, 53 F. 970 (D. Ind. 1893) (enjoining a strawboard factory from discharging into a river straw, lime, and muriatic acid, which killed fish and made the water unfit for cattle to drink, because it damaged plaintiff's riparian water rights).

10. The early common law did not provide much protection against pollution of groundwater. Only in the rare cases where landowners could prove that a specific source of pollution caused groundwater to reach their land in a polluted condition were nuisance principles applied. Ballard v. Tomlinson, 29 Ch. D. 115 (1885) (common law liability for sewage discharged into well that resulted in pollution of the well of another). For similar reasons, the common law has not proved adequate for redressing nonpoint source pollution. See Columbia Avenue Saving Fund Co. v. Prison Commission of Georgia, 92 F. 801 (W.D. Ga. 1899) and cases cited therein (refusing to enjoin prison construction because the damage it would cause to nearby streams would be the product of nonpoint source pollution); United States v. Brazoria County Drainage District No. 3, 2 F.2d 861 (S.D. Tex. 1925) (drainage ditch that contributed to erosion not a common law nuisance).

11. The Restatement of Torts (Second) defines private nuisance as "a non-trespassory invasion of another's interest in the private use and enjoyment of land." Restatement of Torts (Second) §821D (1978). Only those who have property rights and privileges with respect to the use and enjoyment of the land may recover, and only if the harm they suffer is significant. Why does nuisance law require a showing of significant harm, while trespass law does not? The Restatement provides that to constitute a private nuisance the invasion of property rights must be either "intentional and unreasonable; or unintentional and otherwise actionable under the rules governing liability for negligent, reckless or ultrahazardous conduct." §822. Why do intentional invasions of property rights that cause significant harm have to be unreasonable in order to be actionable as a private nuisance?

12. In defining what constitutes an intentional invasion of property rights, the Restatement focuses on the foreseeability of harm. For certain kinds of activities that result in environmental harm, this may have important consequences. For example, the Restatement deems pollution of groundwater to be far less foreseeable than surface water pollution.

It notes that invasions of property rights that result from discharges to lakes, streams, and surface waters ordinarily should be considered intentional, because such discharges are substantially certain to cause such an invasion, particularly if the pollution is continued for any length of time. However, invasions resulting from the pollution of groundwater "are ordinarily not intentional since the course of such waters is usually unknown and the actor can thus foresee no more than a risk of harm in most cases." Restatement of Torts (Second), §832 comment f. Do you agree with this distinction? If actions that cause groundwater pollution are not deemed intentional it would be necessary under the Restatement's approach to prove that they are the result of negligence or abnormally dangerous activity in order to recover in a private nuisance action.

Harmonizing Conflicting Interests: To Balance or Not to Balance?

The early common law assessed nuisance claims by focusing almost exclusively on the nature of the interference pollution caused to the property rights of its victims. Yet defendants continued to press courts to balance the hardship of pollution abatement against the damage to victims when considering requests for equitable relief. By 1927, this debate had reached the point where Judge Learned Hand described the state of nuisance law as one of "great confusion" with U.S. courts split over whether or not to balance comparative hardships between polluters and victims. Smith v. Staso Milling Co., 18 F.2d 736 (2d Cir. 1927). In *Staso Milling* Judge Hand explained why he believed that the balancing approach was reasonable, particularly when courts were considering whether to grant injunctions against private nuisances:

> The very right on which the injured party stands in such cases is a quantitative compromise between two conflicting interests. What may be an entirely tolerable adjustment, when the result is only to award damages for the injury done, may become no better than a means of extortion if the result is absolutely to curtail the defendant's enjoyment of his land. Even though the defendant has no power to condemn, at times it may be proper to require of him no more than to make good the whole injury once and for all. [Id. at 738.]

Yet a balancing approach does not necessarily preclude injunctions against nuisances. In *Staso Milling* Judge Hand affirmed an injunction barring a slate processing mill from polluting a stream. Even though construction of the plant had altered "the balance of convenience" in a manner that might normally preclude an injunction, Hand noted that prior to building the plant the plant's owners specifically had promised nearby property owners that it would not pollute the stream. Noting that no similar promise had been made with respect to air pollution, Hand indicated that an injunction barring the plant from releasing dust could be modified if the plant could demonstrate that no better technology was available for controlling emissions of dust.

While many American courts have enthusiastically embraced the balancing approach, some tension between strict liability and balancing has persisted in private nuisance cases. The evolution of the Restatement of Torts' position illustrates this tension. The First Restatement adopted an explicit balancing approach for determining whether an interference with property rights was unreasonable. Section 826 of the First Restatement provided that intentional invasions of another's interest in the use or enjoyment of land are unreasonable unless the utility of the actor's conduct outweighs the gravity of the harm. This encouraged courts to balance the social value of a polluting activity against the damage it caused. After criticism of the First Restatement's formulation, the Second Restatement added an alternative criterion of unreasonableness in section 826(b). It states that an intentional invasion is unreasonable if *either* the gravity of the harm outweighs the utility of the actor's conduct *or* "the harm caused by the conduct is serious and the financial burden of compensating for this and similar harm to others would not make the continuation of the conduct not feasible." This has supplemented what appeared to be a kind of risk-benefit calculus of reasonableness with an alternative test focusing on the financial feasibility of controls. A further embellishment was added by section 829 of the Second Restatement. It states that even in cases where compensation is beyond the financial capacity of an enterprise, an invasion should be deemed unreasonable if the harm it causes "is severe and greater than the other should be required to bear without compensation." As a result, the Second Restatement's definition of unreasonableness now embraces notions of fairness or moral outrage as well as feasibility and risk-benefit balancing. Each of these three notions is represented in current regulatory approaches for controlling pollution, as we will see in subsequent chapters.

Economists emphasize that because environmental problems involve interactions between polluters and victims, efficient solutions to nuisance problems involve remedies that minimize the joint costs or maximize the joint value of the interacting activities. If only the polluters determine the extent of harm, then a rule holding polluters strictly liable for the damages they cause is efficient because it will induce them to take the efficient amount of care while ensuring that the prices of their goods reflect their full social costs. However, if the victim's behavior can affect the extent of damage (e.g., by moving away or by investing in measures that shield her from the effects of pollution), economists argue that strict liability is only efficient if a defense of contributory negligence is recognized, because victims otherwise will have no incentive to take actions that can avoid damage more cheaply. These arguments are explained in clear and nontechnical terms for the noneconomist in A. M. Polinsky, An Introduction to Law and Economics 92-93 (1983).

William Landes and Judge Richard Posner argue that the common law is best understood as an attempt by judges to promote efficient resource allocation. They argue that efficiency dictates that liability for private nuisances be imposed only "where the nuisance causes substantial damage that exceeds the cost of eliminating it and where, moreover, the defendant (injurer) can eliminate the nuisance at a lower cost than the plaintiff (victim)." W. Landes and R. Posner, The Economic Structure of Tort Law 49 (1987). Landes and Posner conclude that nuisance law generally, but not always, conforms to this principle, particularly now that courts frequently balance the value of competing land uses, the suitability of the conduct to the character of the locality, and the relative costs of avoiding harm. They note that the requirement that harm be substantial serves to screen out cases in which damage is too small to warrant resort to the legal system for abating the nuisance. Id. at 49. Landes and Posner criticize as inefficient the alternative test of unreasonableness articulated in section 826(b) of the Second Restatement, but they note that few American courts have adopted it.

As noted in Chapter 1, the Coase Theorem states that if bargaining is costless and cooperative then any choice of an entitlement or remedy will lead to an efficient outcome. This observation is premised on the notion that parties can engage in exchanges that will lead to efficient outcomes. Ours, however, is not a world of zero transaction costs; imperfect information and strategic behavior make it difficult to reach efficient outcomes. Estimates of the damages caused by pollution, the benefits of polluting activity, and the costs of control alternatives are fraught with uncertainty. Polluters and their victims can gain strategic advantages by misrepresenting these parameters or by providing estimates that fall at different ends of the range of uncertainty. Moreover, as Judge Hand noted in *Staso Milling*, if victims always are entitled to injunctions against pollution they could use this entitlement as "a means of extortion" to hold out for more than the efficient level of compensation. In theory the common law offers a flexible, case-by-case assessment of liability that could permit courts to overcome some of the problems of strategic behavior. Economists argue that the common law can promote efficient outcomes by placing liability on the party that is the cheapest cost avoider. See Michelman, Pollution as a Tort: A Non-Accidental Perspective on Calabresi's *Costs*, 80 Yale L.J. 647 (1971). This approach, however, may require courts to obtain accurate estimates of the damages and benefits of polluting activities, information that is not always readily available. For suggestions concerning how courts can minimize the impact of such uncertainty, see A. M. Polinsky, An Introduction to Law and Economics 24 (1983).

One approach for coping with imperfect information is for courts to structure flexible remedies that take advantage of market forces to determine which party can control pollution most efficiently. See Calabresi and Melamed, Property Rules, Liability Rules and Inalienability: One View of the Cathedral, 85 Harv. L. Rev. 1089 (1972); Rabin, Nuisance Law: Rethinking Fundamental Assumptions, 63 Va. L. Rev. 1209 (1977). The conditional injunction approach has been recommended on these grounds. It was used by the New York Court of Appeals in the famous decision of Boomer v. Atlantic Cement Co., 26 N.Y.2d 219, 257 N.E.2d 870 (1970). The court in *Boomer* issued a conditional injunction barring the operation of a cement plant whose air emissions had caused substantial damage to nearby property until the plant paid surrounding residents the full value of their permanent damages if the plant continued operation. The theory behind this approach was that the plant would opt to continue operations only if the operations had more economic value than the cost of the damage they produced.

The notion that rights and liabilities should be allocated in a manner that promotes efficiency can be controversial because of its distributional consequences. Viewed from the moral outrage perspective, the Tennessee Supreme Court's refusal to enjoin the Ducktown smelter's emissions and the New York court's decision to permit the cement plant in *Boomer* to purchase the right to continue operation may seem outrageous to the victims of the pollution, even though they ultimately may receive damages. After all, as Judge Hand noted in *Staso Milling*, the polluter "has no power to condemn" the victim's property, but a damage award that allows the pollution to continue produces virtually the same result. Despite courts' concern for achieving efficient outcomes, distributional concerns also play a significant role in shaping environmental policy, as we will see throughout this casebook.

While the common law offers some prospect for resolving conflicts between a single source of pollution and a few neighbors, there is wide agreement that private nuisance actions are grossly inadequate for resolving the more typical pollution problems faced by modern industrialized societies. But see T. L. Anderson and D. R. Leal, Free Market Environmentalism (1991); The Heritage Foundation, Protecting the Environment: A Free Market Strategy (D. Bandow, ed. 1986) (arguing for resuscitation of the common law by creating tradeable private rights in certain common resources). When numerous and diverse pollutants emanating from widely dispersed sources affect large populations the common law is simply inadequate for providing redress, as even staunch advocates of the economic perspective concede. See, e.g., R. Posner, Economic Analysis of Law 46-47 (2d ed. 1977). The difficulty plaintiffs

face is well described in the Report of the Lords Select Committee on
Noxious Vapors in 1862, which noted that "partly in consequence of the
expense such actions occasion, partly from the fact that where several
works are in immediate juxtaposition, the difficulty of tracing the damage to any one, or of apportioning it among several, is [so] great as to
be all but insuperable." H.L. Select Committee on Noxious Vapours at
v, quoted in Brenner, Nuisance Law and the Industrial Revolution, 3 J.
Legal Stud. 403, 425 (1974). Even when the *aggregate* damage caused by
pollution is quite large, the damage to any individual victim may be
insufficient to make a lawsuit worthwhile. While the class action device
offers some mechanism for dealing with such problems, it has not played
a significant role in redressing environmental damage. In cases where
pollution interferes with rights held in common by the public, the common law's response has been to rely on public nuisance actions, to which
we now turn.

B. PUBLIC NUISANCE

The common law offers somewhat greater promise for protecting
the environment when used by governmental entities to protect their
citizens against *public* nuisances. The Second Restatement defines a public nuisance as "an unreasonable interference with a right common to
the general public." Restatement of Torts (Second) §821B (1978). As
with the doctrine of private nuisance, with public nuisance not all invasions of rights are actionable, only unreasonable ones. In determining
whether interference with a public right is unreasonable, the Restatement directs courts to consider whether the conduct: (1) involves a
significant interference with the public health, safety, comfort, or convenience; (2) is illegal; or (3) is of a continuing nature or has produced
a long-lasting effect on the public right that the actor has reason to know
will be significant.

The doctrine of public nuisance was used most frequently in the
early common law to prosecute those who obstructed public highways
or encroached on the royal domain. The doctrine later expanded to
embrace actions against those who fouled public waters or emitted noxious fumes. Following the Industrial Revolution, public nuisance actions
were rarely prosecuted to abate pollution. When such actions were
brought, courts were not "eager to find large enterprises guilty of public
nuisances, because they feared the economic consequences of a policy
of strict enforcement." Brenner, Nuisance Law and the Industrial Revolution, 3 J. Legal Stud. 403, 421 (1974). It is not surprising that many
of the public nuisance actions that were brought by governmental authorities targeted nonresident polluters, as illustrated in the decisions
below.

Two early Supreme Court decisions involve public nuisance actions brought by state authorities against out-of-state polluters. The first grew out of the burgeoning sewage disposal problem faced by many rapidly expanding American cities. In the late nineteenth century, most cities disposed of their sewage by simply dumping it untreated into the nearest lake or stream. As one American court had noted, "the history of sewers shows that from time immemorial the right to connect them with navigable streams has been regarded as part of the jus publicum." Newark v. Sayre Co., 60 N.J. Eq. 361, 45 A. 985 (1900). Not surprisingly, with rapid urbanization, sewage disposal became a major source of environmental conflict among cities and states that shared public waterways.

In one of the two early cases, Missouri v. Illinois, 200 U.S. 496 (1906), the facts were as follows: Chicago dumped its raw sewage into the Chicago River, which flowed into Lake Michigan. By the mid-1860s the Chicago River, "being a sluggish stream in its lower reaches, had become so offensive because of receiving the sewage of a rapidly growing city, that for its immediate relief the municipal authorities" agreed to pump additional fresh water into it from a pumping station serving a nearby canal. Wisconsin v. Illinois, 278 U.S. 367, 402 (1929). This plan ultimately failed, and the river "again became grossly polluted." Id. The Illinois Drainage and Water Supply Commission then proposed a more ambitious solution that involved the construction of a large canal to the Des Plaines River that would "produce a magnificent waterway between Chicago and the Mississippi River" through which Chicago's sewage would flow. The plan was approved and a new Sanitary District of Chicago was organized in 1890. Construction of the canal commenced in 1892, and it was opened in January 1900. The flow of the Chicago River ultimately was reversed; it now flows away from Lake Michigan and toward the Mississippi River.

Though hundreds of miles away, residents of St. Louis, Missouri became upset when they learned that the Mississippi River, their source of drinking water, would now become the recipient of the raw sewage from two million Chicago residents. Missouri filed a common law nuisance action against Illinois in the United States Supreme Court. Arguing that the sewage would endanger the health of its citizens, Missouri asked the Supreme Court to enjoin Illinois and the Sanitary District of Chicago from discharging sewage through the canal.

Illinois tried to have the case dismissed on jurisdictional grounds, arguing that it was not really a dispute between states subject to the Supreme Court's original jurisdiction. The Supreme Court rejected Illinois's arguments and held that it had jurisdiction. Missouri v. Illinois, 180 U.S. 208 (1901). As Justice Holmes later explained:

> The nuisance set forth in the bill was one which would be of international importance—a visible change of a great river from a pure stream into a

polluted and poisoned ditch. The only question presented was whether as
between the States of the Union this court was competent to deal with a
situation which, if it arose between independent sovereignties, might lead
to war. Whatever differences of opinion there might be upon matters of
detail, the jurisdiction and authority of this court to deal with such a case
is not now open to doubt. Missouri v. Illinois, 200 U.S. 496, 518 (1906).

The Supreme Court appointed a special commissioner to hear evidence in the case, which dragged on for years as Chicago's sewage poured
through the canal and on to the Mississippi. Missouri's lawyers argued
that disease-producing bacteria contained in Chicago's sewage had caused
a 77-percent increase in typhoid fever deaths in St. Louis after the canal
was opened in January 1900. Illinois argued that any increase in deaths
from typhoid fever was an artifact of a change in reporting practices
that for the first time had consolidated a host of fever-related deaths
under the classification of typhoid fever. Illinois's lawyers argued that
the drainage canal actually had improved water quality in the Mississippi's tributaries by increasing their volume and rate of flow. They maintained that any injury caused by bacteria in the Mississippi was the product
of sewage dumped by other Missouri cities upriver from St. Louis. Missouri responded that any increase in the volume or rate of flow of the
river's tributaries served only to hasten the delivery of Chicago's sewage
and its accompanying bacteria.

|| *Missouri v. Illinois* ||
|| **200 U.S. 496 (1906)** ||

MR. JUSTICE HOLMES delivered the opinion of the court.

This is a suit brought by the State of Missouri to restrain the discharge of the sewage of Chicago through an artificial channel into the
Desplaines River, in the State of Illinois. That river empties into the
Illinois River, and the latter empties into the Mississippi at a point about
forty-three miles above the city of St. Louis. It was alleged in the bill
that the result of the threatened discharge would be to send fifteen
hundred tons of poisonous filth daily into the Mississippi, to deposit
great quantities of the same upon the part of the bed of the last-named
river belonging to the plaintiff, and so to poison the water of that river,
upon which various of the plaintiff's cities, towns and inhabitants depended, as to make it unfit for drinking, agricultural, or manufacturing,
purposes. . . .

Before this court ought to intervene the case should be of serious
magnitude, clearly and fully proved, and the principle to be applied
should be one which the court is prepared deliberately to maintain against
all considerations on the other side. See Kansas v. Colorado, 185 U.S.
125.

As to the principle to be laid down the caution necessary is manifest. It is a question of the first magnitude whether the destiny of the great rivers is to be the sewers of the cities along their banks or to be protected against everything which threatens their purity. To decide the whole matter at one blow by an irrevocable fiat would be at least premature. If we are to judge by what the plaintiff itself permits, the discharge of sewage into the Mississippi by cities and towns is to be expected. We believe that the practice of discharging into the river is general along its banks, except where the levees of Louisiana have led to a different course. The argument for the plaintiff asserts it to be proper within certain limits. These are facts to be considered. Even in cases between individuals some consideration is given to the practical course of events. In the black country of England parties would not be expected to stand upon extreme rights. St. Helen's Smelting Co. v. Tipping, 11 H.L.C. 642. See Boston Ferrule Co. v. Hills, 159 Massachusetts, 147, 150. Where, as here, the plaintiff has sovereign powers and deliberately permits discharges similar to those of which it complains, it not only offers a standard to which the defendant has the right to appeal, but, as some of those discharges are above the intake of St. Louis, it warrants the defendant in demanding the strictest proof that the plaintiff's own conduct does not produce the result, or at least so conduce to it that courts should not be curious to apportion the blame.

We have studied the plaintiff's statement of the facts in detail and have perused the evidence, but it is unnecessary for the purposes of decision to do more than give the general result in a very simple way. At the outset we cannot but be struck by the consideration that if this suit had been brought fifty years ago it almost necessarily would have failed. There is no pretence that there is a nuisance of the simple kind that was known to the older common law. There is nothing which can be detected by the unassisted senses—no visible increase of filth, no new smell. On the contrary, it is proved that the great volume of pure water from Lake Michigan which is mixed with the sewage at the start has improved the Illinois River in these respects to a noticeable extent. Formerly it was sluggish and ill smelling. Now it is a comparatively clear stream to which edible fish have returned. Its water is drunk by the fishermen, it is said, without evil results. The plaintiff's case depends upon an inference of the unseen. It draws the inference from two propositions. First, that typhoid fever has increased considerably since the change and that other explanations have been disproved, and second, that the bacillus of typhoid can and does survive the journey and reach the intake of St. Louis in the Mississippi.

We assume the now prevailing scientific explanation of typhoid fever to be correct. But when we go beyond that assumption everything is involved in doubt. The data upon which an increase in the deaths from typhoid fever in St. Louis is alleged are disputed. The elimination of other causes is denied. The experts differ as to the time and distance within which a stream would purify itself. No case of an epidemic caused by infection at so remote a source is brought forward, and the cases which are produced are controverted. The plaintiff obviously must be cautious upon this point, for if this suit should succeed many others would follow, and it not improbably would find itself a defendant to a bill by one or more of the States lower down upon the Mississippi. The distance which the sewage has to travel (357 miles) is not open to debate, but the time of transit to be inferred from experiments with floats is estimated at varying from eight to eighteen and a half days, with forty-eight hours more from intake to distribution, and when corrected by observations of bacteria is greatly prolonged by the defendants. The experiments of the defendants' experts lead them to the opinion that a typhoid bacillus could not survive the journey, while those on the other side maintain that it might live and keep its power for twenty-five days or more, and arrive at St. Louis. Upon the question at issue, whether the new discharge from Chicago hurts St. Louis, there is a categorical contradiction between the experts on the two sides.

The Chicago drainage canal was opened on January 17, 1900. The deaths from typhoid fever in St. Louis, before and after that date, are stated somewhat differently in different places. We give them mainly from the plaintiff's brief: 1890, 140; 1891, 165; 1892, 441; 1893, 215; 1894, 171; 1895, 106; 1896, 106; 1897, 125; 1898, 95; 1899, 131; 1900, 154; 1901, 181; 1902, 216; 1903, 281. It is argued for the defendant that the numbers for the later years have been enlarged by carrying over cases which in earlier years would have been put into a miscellaneous column (intermittent, remittent, typho-malaria, etc., etc.), but we assume that the increase is real. Nevertheless, comparing the last four years with the earlier ones, it is obvious that the ground for a specific inference is very narrow, if we stopped at this point. The plaintiff argues that the increase must be due to Chicago, since there is nothing corresponding to it in the watersheds of the Missouri or Mississippi. On the other hand, the defendant points out that there has been no such enhanced rate of typhoid on the banks of the Illinois as would have been found if the opening of the drainage canal were the true cause.

Both sides agree that the detection of the typhoid bacillus in the water is not to be expected. But the plaintiff relies upon proof that such bacilli are discharged into the Chicago sewage in considerable quantities; that the number of bacilli in the water of the Illinois is much increased, including the *bacillus coli communis*, which is admitted to be an index of contamination, and that the chemical analyses lead to the same inference. To prove that the typhoid bacillus could make the journey an experiment was tried with the *bacillus prodigiosus*, which seems to have been unknown, or nearly unknown, in these waters. After preliminary trials, in which these bacilli emptied into the Mississippi near the mouth of the Illinois were found near the St. Louis intake and in St. Louis in times varying from three days to a month, one hundred and seven barrels of the same, said to contain one thousand million bacilli to the cubic centimeter, were put into the drainage canal near the starting point on November 6, and on December 4 an example was found at the St. Louis intake tower. Four others were found on the three following days, two at the tower and two at the mouth of the Illinois. As this bacillus is asserted to have about the same length of life in sunlight in living waters as the *bacillus typhosus*, although it is a little more hardy, the experiment is thought to prove one element of the plaintiff's case, although the very small number found in many samples of water is thought by the other side to indicate that practically no typhoid germs would get through. It seems to be conceded that the purification of the Illinois by the large dilution from Lake Michigan (nine parts or more in ten) would increase the danger, as it now generally is believed that the bacteria of decay, the saprophytes, which flourish in stagnant pools, destroy the pathogenic germs. Of course the addition of so much water to the Illinois also increases its speed.

On the other hand, the defendant's evidence shows a reduction in the chemical and bacterial accompaniments of pollution in a given quantity of water, which would be natural in view of the mixture of nine parts to one from Lake Michigan. It affirms that the Illinois is better or no worse at its mouth than it was before, and makes it at least uncertain how much of the present pollution is due to Chicago and how much to sources further down, not complained of in the bill. It contends that if any bacilli should get through they would be scattered and enfeebled and would do no harm. The defendant also sets against the experiment with the *bacillus prodigiosus* a no less striking experiment with typhoid germs suspended in the Illinois River in permeable sacs. According to this the duration of the life of these germs has been much exaggerated, and in that water would not be more than three or four days. It is suggested, by way of criticism, that the germs may not have been of normal strength, that the conditions were less favorable than if they had floated down in a comparatively unchanging body of water, and that the germs may have escaped, but the experiment raises at least a serious doubt. Further, it hardly is denied that there is no parallelism in detail between the increase and decrease of typhoid fever in Chicago and St. Louis. The defendants' experts maintain that the water of the Missouri is worse than that of the Illinois, while it contributes a much larger proportion to the intake. The evidence is very strong that it is necessary for St. Louis to take preventive measures, by filtration or otherwise, against the dangers of the plaintiff's own creation or from other sources than Illinois. What will protect against one will protect against another. The presence of causes of infection from the plaintiff's action makes the case weaker in principle as well as harder to prove than one in which all came from a single source. . . .

We might go more into detail, but we believe that we have said enough to explain our point of view and our opinion of the evidence as it stands. What the future may develop of course we cannot tell. But our conclusion upon the present evidence is that the case proved falls so far below the allegations of the bill that it is not brought within the principles heretofore established in the cause.

NOTES AND QUESTIONS

1. Why did Missouri fail to convince the Supreme Court that Chicago's sewage discharges constituted a public nuisance? Did the discharge of raw sewage into a canal that eventually flows into the Mississippi affect the quality of drinking water in St. Louis? If so, was it an unreasonable interference with the rights of Missouri's citizens? Should it make any difference that Chicago's sewage would not have reached the Mississippi but for construction of the canal?

2. What is the relevance of Justice Holmes's statement that "[e]ven in cases between individuals some consideration is given to the practical course of events. In the black country of England parties would not be expected to stand upon extreme rights"? Does this suggest that some balancing of interests is appropriate in public nuisance cases?

3. How persuasive was the statistical evidence Missouri presented to demonstrate that the sewage discharges had caused a substantial increase in typhoid fever deaths in St. Louis? What other evidence could Missouri have presented to demonstrate that the sewage discharges had harmed its residents?

4. Justice Holmes notes that Missouri's own cities, including cities upstream of St. Louis, routinely discharge raw sewage into the Mississippi. What impact do you think this observation should have had on the result in this case? Would the outcome have been any different if Missouri had required its cities to employ more sophisticated treatment technology to protect the Mississippi from pollution?

5. Like Chicago, several New Jersey cities discovered shortly after the turn of the century that their sewage discharges had overwhelmed the carrying capacity of the Passaic River. They decided to build a large sewer line that would transport their raw sewage directly into New York Bay. By 1911, New Jersey was discharging 120 million gallons of sewage per day, over the protests of New York authorities. Like Missouri, New York filed a common law nuisance action in the Supreme Court. Extensive testimony concerning the impact of the sewage disposal was presented before a special master. The testimony was concluded in June 1913. After the case was argued in 1918, the Court asked the parties to update the record concerning the impact of the sewage discharges. In the meantime the federal government had intervened and negotiated

an agreement requiring New Jersey to adopt improved treatment technology—coarse screens to remove floating matter and sedimentation
basins with scum boards. In 1921, the Supreme Court denied New York's
request for an injunction. The Court observed that

> the burden upon the state of New York . . . is much greater than that
> imposed upon a complainant in an ordinary suit between private parties.
> Before this court can be moved to exercise its extraordinary power under
> the Constitution to control the conduct of one state at the suit of another,
> the threatened invasion must be of serious magnitude and it must be
> established by clear and convincing evidence. [New York v. New Jersey,
> 256 U.S. 296, 309 (1921).]

While noting that New York was free to renew its action if conditions
changed, the Court emphasized that New York had failed to prove that
there were visible suspended particles, odors, or a reduction in the dissolved oxygen content of the Bay sufficient to interfere with aquatic life.
It also observed that New York discharged its own sewage from 450
sewers directly into the adjacent waters.

6. In May 1929, New Jersey filed its own public nuisance action in
the Supreme Court against New York City. New Jersey asked the Court
to prohibit the city from dumping garbage, that then washed onto New
Jersey beaches, into the ocean. New York argued that other cities dumped
garbage in the ocean and that it was impossible to tell the origin of the
garbage found on New Jersey's shores. A special master appointed by
the Court ultimately found that enough garbage had washed up on New
Jersey's beaches to fill 50 trucks and that the garbage had made swimming impracticable and had damaged fish nets. The master concluded
that ocean dumping by New York City was the primary source of the
garbage because the amount dumped by other cities was negligible in
comparision to New York's massive quantities. Until 1918 New York City
had incinerated its garbage, but it commenced ocean dumping after the
incinerator was destroyed by fire. By 1929 the city had 20 incinerators,
but they were unable to handle all the city's garbage disposal needs. The
master recommended that New York be enjoined from ocean dumping,
with the injunction to take effect after the city was given a reasonable
time to construct more incinerators. The Court approved this recommendation in New Jersey v. City of New York, 283 U.S. 473 (1931) and
remanded the case to the master to decide how much time the city needed
to construct additional incinerators.

On December 7, 1931, the Supreme Court issued an injunction
prohibiting New York City from dumping garbage off the coast of New
Jersey effective June 1, 1933. New Jersey v. City of New York, 284 U.S.
585 (1931). The decree required the city in the meantime "to operate
and utilize the existing incinerators and other facilities for the final

disposition of garbage and refuse in such a manner as to reduce to the lowest practicable limit the amount of garbage dumped at sea." Id. at 586. The city was directed to file progress reports with the Court every six months. On May 8, 1933, less than a month before the deadline for New York to stop ocean dumping, New Jersey moved that the city be held in contempt for failing to commence construction of additional incinerators. New York argued that construction of the incinerators had been unavoidably delayed because of a lack of funds, and it asked the Court to extend the deadline to April 1, 1934. In October 1933, the special master reported that the city had begun construction of two incinerators, but that they would not be operable until April 21 and June 30, 1934 respectively. The Court then extended the deadline to July 1, 1934 and specified that violations would result in a penalty of $5,000 per day to be paid by New York to New Jersey. New Jersey v. City of New York, 290 U.S. 237 (1933).

7. Is the judiciary an appropriate institution for formulating pollution control policy, or is such a task better left to administrative agencies with more specialized expertise? As we will see, a major obstacle to effective pollution control has been the reluctance of politically accountable officials to implement policies that may adversely affect local industries. Could judges, who are more insulated from political forces, do a more effective job of formulating environmental policy?

8. Governmental entities have themselves been among the most persistent violators of environmental regulations. As we will see in Chapter 7, efforts to force governmental entities (e.g., municipal sewage treatment plants) to comply with the environmental laws perennially come up against the argument that there isn't enough money to do so. Confronted with this argument in a public nuisance action in 1858, a British court said of local authorities: "If they have not funds enough to make further experiments, they must apply to Parliament for power to raise more money. If, after all possible experiments, they cannot [dispose of their sewage] without invading the Plaintiff's rights, they must apply to Parliament for power to invade his rights." A.G. v. Birmingham Borough Council, 70 Eng. Rep. 220, 4 K. & J. 528, 541 (Vice Ch. Ct. 1858).

9. A year after it decided Missouri v. Illinois, the Supreme Court was again confronted with a common law nuisance action involving interstate pollution. This time the controversy involved a source of pollution already familiar to us—sulfur dioxide emissions from the very Ducktown, Tennesee copper smelters involved in Madison v. Ducktown Sulphur, Copper & Iron Co. Invoking the Court's original jurisdiction, the state of Georgia brought a common law nuisance action against the smelters, which, as you may recall, were located directly across the Georgia-Tennessee border. In 1904, the year that the Tennessee Supreme Court had decided not to enjoin operation of the smelters, Georgia filed suit in the Supreme Court, complaining that the smelters'

emissions crossed the border and caused considerable property damage in Georgia. Georgia asked the Supreme Court to enjoin operation of the smelters. In response to Georgia's lawsuit, the companies pledged to change their method of operation to reduce their emissions. Georgia then agreed to dismiss its lawsuit without prejudice. But after the smelters installed tall smokestacks that simply transported the pollution across a wider swath of territory, Georgia again filed suit.

Georgia v. Tennessee Copper Co.
206 U.S. 230 (1907)

MR. JUSTICE HOLMES delivered the opinion of the court.

This is a bill in equity filed in this court by the State of Georgia, in pursuance of a resolution of the legislature and by direction of the Governor of the State, to enjoin the defendant Copper Companies from discharging noxious gas from their works in Tennessee over the plaintiff's territory. It alleges that in consequence of such a discharge a wholesale destruction of forests, orchards and crops is going on, and other injuries are done and threatened in five counties of the State. It alleges also a vain application to the State of Tennessee for relief. A preliminary injunction was denied, but, as there was ground to fear that great and irreparable damage might be done, an early day was fixed for the final hearing and the parties were given leave, if so minded, to try the case on affidavits. This has been done without objection, and, although the method would be unsatisfactory if our decision turned on any nice question of fact, in the view that we take we think it unlikely that either party has suffered harm.

The case has been argued largely as if it were one between two private parties; but it is not. The very elements that would be relied upon in a suit between fellow-citizens as a ground for equitable relief are wanting here. The State owns very little of the territory alleged to be affected, and the damage to it capable of estimate in money, possibly, at least, is small. This is a suit by a State for an injury to it in its capacity of quasi-sovereign. In that capacity the State has an interest independent of and behind the titles of its citizens, in all the earth and air within its domain. It has the last word as to whether its mountains shall be stripped of their forests and its inhabitants shall breathe pure air. It might have to pay individuals before it could utter that word, but with it remains the final power. The alleged damage to the State as a private owner is merely a makeweight, and we may lay on one side the dispute as to whether the destruction of forests has led to the gullying of its roads.

The caution with which demands of this sort, on the part of a State, for relief from injuries analogous to torts, must be examined, is dwelt upon in Missouri v. Illinois, 200 U.S. 496, 520, 521. But it is plain that some such demands must be recognized, if the grounds alleged are proved. When the States by their union made the forcible abatement of outside nuisances impossible to each, they did not thereby agree to submit to whatever might be done. They did not renounce the possibility of making reasonable demands on the ground of their still remaining quasi-sovereign interests; and the alternative to force is a suit in this court. Missouri v. Illinois, 180 U.S. 208, 241.

Some peculiarities necessarily mark a suit of this kind. If the State has a case at all, it is somewhat more certainly entitled to specific relief than a private party might be. It is not lightly to be required to give up quasi-sovereign rights for pay; and, apart from the difficulty of valuing such rights in money, if that be its choice it may insist that an infraction of them shall be stopped. The States by entering the Union did not sink to the position of private owners subject to one system of private law. This court has not quite the same freedom to balance the harm that will be done by an injunction against that of which the plaintiff complains, that it would have in deciding between two subjects of a single political power. Without excluding the considerations that equity always takes into account, we cannot give the weight that was given them in argument to a comparison between the damage threatened to the plaintiff and the calamity of a possible stop to the defendants' business, the question of health, the character of the forests as a first or second growth, the commercial possibility of reducing the fumes to sulphuric acid, the special adaption of the business to the place.

It is a fair and reasonable demand on the part of a sovereign that the air over its territory should not be polluted on a great scale by sulphurous acid gas, that the forests on its mountains, be they better or worse, and whatever domestic destruction they have suffered, should not be further destroyed or threatened by the act of persons beyond its control, that the crops and orchards on its hills should not be endangered from the same source. If any such demand is to be enforced this must be, notwithstanding the hesitation that we might feel if the suit were between private parties, and the doubt whether for the injuries which they might be suffering to their property they should not be left to an action at law.

The proof requires but a few words. It is not denied that the defendants generate in their works near the Georgia line large quantities of sulphur dioxid[e] which becomes sulphurous acid by its mixture with the air. It hardly is denied and cannot be denied with success that this gas often is carried by the wind great distances and over great tracts of Georgia land. On the evidence the pollution of the air and the magnitude of that pollution are not open to dispute. Without any attempt to go into details immaterial to the suit, it is proper to add that we are satisfied by a preponderance of evidence that the sulphurous fumes cause and threaten damage on so considerable a scale to the forests and vegetable life, if not to health, within the plaintiff State as to make out a case within the requirements of Missouri v. Illinois, 200 U.S. 496. Whether Georgia by insisting upon this claim is doing more harm than good to her own citizens is for her to determine. The possible disaster to those outside the State must be accepted as a consequence of her standing upon her extreme rights.

It is argued that the State has been guilty of laches. We deem it unnecessary to consider how far such a defense would be available in a suit of this sort, since, in our opinion, due diligence has been shown. The conditions have been different until recent years. After the evil had grown greater in 1904 the State brought a bill in this court. The defendants, however, already were abandoning the old method of roasting ore in open heaps and it was hoped that the change would stop the trouble. They were ready to agree not to return to that method, and upon such an agreement being made the bill was dismissed without prejudice. But the plaintiff now finds, or thinks that it finds, that the tall chimneys in present use cause the poisonous gases to be carried to greater distances than ever before and that the evil has not been helped.

If the State of Georgia adheres to its determination, there is no alternative to issuing an injunction, after allowing a reasonable time to the defendants to complete the structures that they now are building, and the efforts that they are making, to stop the fumes. The plaintiff may submit a form of decree on the coming in of this court in October next.

Injunction to issue.

NOTES AND QUESTIONS

1. Why did Georgia succeed in getting an injunction from the United States Supreme Court when plaintiffs in Madison v. Ducktown Sulphur, Copper & Iron Co. had been refused such relief by the Tennessee Supreme Court? Justice Holmes suggests that in fashioning a remedy for a public nuisance, the Court has less latitude to balance the equities because the plaintiff is a sovereign state. What is his rationale for this conclusion? Is this why the Court ultimately held that Georgia was entitled to an injunction?

2. Why did Georgia succeed in the *Tennessee Copper* case when Missouri failed to get the Supreme Court to enjoin Chicago's discharge of sewage in Missouri v. Illinois? Did Georgia simply have better evidence than Missouri that the pollution had caused damage to its citizens? Did it make any difference that the defendants in *Tennessee Copper* were two private companies rather than another sovereign state?

3. In *Tennessee Copper* Justice Holmes warned: "Whether Georgia by insisting upon this claim is doing more harm than good to her own

citizens is for her to determine. The possible disaster to those outside the State must be accepted as a consequence of her standing upon her extreme rights." What did he mean by this? Recall Justice Holmes's comment in Missouri v. Illinois that if Missouri had won the case many other suits would follow and Missouri might find itself a defendant in cases brought by downstream states.

4. In a separate opinion, Justice John Marshall Harlan argued that the Court should apply the same standard in nuisance cases brought by public authorities as it would in private nuisance actions. He wrote: "If this were a suit between private parties, and if, under the evidence, a court of equity would not give the plaintiff an injunction, then it ought not to grant relief, under like circumstances, to the plaintiff, because it happens to be a state, possessing some powers of sovereignty." However, he concurred in the majority's decision, explaining that "Georgia is entitled to the relief sought, not because it is a state, but because it is a party, which has established its right to such relief by proof." Do you agree that courts should apply the same standard in deciding nuisance cases regardless of whether or not the plaintiff is a public entity? Why do you think the common law developed different standards to govern public and private nuisances?

5. In addition to actions by governmental authorities, public nuisance actions can be brought by private parties if they can demonstrate that the nuisance has harmed them in a manner not shared with the general public. William Prosser notes that the traditional "special injury" requirement for private actions derived from the ancient notion that private parties should not be able to vindicate the rights of the sovereign and from a desire to prevent a multitude of actions to redress the same nuisance. Prosser, Private Action for Public Nuisance, 52 Va. L. Rev. 997 (1966). As courts and legislatures broadened citizen rights of action to redress environmental damage, the special injury requirement has come under fire and has been relaxed in some instances. Bryson and Macbeth, Public Nuisance, the Restatement (Second) of Torts, and Environmental Law, 2 Ecology L.Q. 241 (1972). For example, the Restatement (Second) of Torts suggested that the special injury requirement should not bar actions seeking equitable relief or class actions brought against public nuisances by private individuals. Restatement (Second) of Torts §821C and comment j (1978). See Hodas, Private Actions for Public Nuisance: Common Law Citizen Suits for Relief from Environmental Harm, 16 Ecology L.Q. 883 (1989). American and Canadian courts are said to favor the traditional requirement that private parties be required to show that they have suffered damage of a different kind than that suffered by the general public, while English courts are said to require only that the damage be of a greater degree than that suffered by the general public. Kodilnye, Public Nuisance and Particular Damage in the Modern Law, 6 Legal Stud. 182, 193 (1986).

6. Faced with the threat of an injunction, the Tennessee Copper Company eventually settled with the state of Georgia by setting up a fund to compensate those injured by its emissions and by agreeing to restrict its operations during warmer months. The other smelting company, the Ducktown Sulphur, Copper & Iron Company, refused to restrict its operations, claiming that it already had spent $600,000 constructing "purifying works" to reduce the percentage of sulfur emitted from the ores from 85.5 percent to 41.5 percent. Despite this investment, Ducktown released more than 13,000 tons of sulfur emissions in 1913. Georgia applied to the Supreme Court for a final injunction against Ducktown. While noting that it could not determine precisely how much of a reduction in Ducktown's emissions would be necessary to prevent harm to property in Georgia, the Court issued a final injunction on June 1, 1915. Georgia v. Tennessee Copper Co., 237 U.S. 474 (1915). The Court specified that no more than 20 tons of sulfur per day could be emitted during the period from April to October and no more than 40 tons per day during the rest of the year. 237 U.S. at 678. The Court appointed Dr. John T. McGill of Vanderbilt University as an inspector to monitor Ducktown's emissions. In light of its conclusion that it could not determine what level of emissions reduction would prevent harm to property in Georgia, what basis do you think the Supreme Court had for specifying emissions limits in its injunction?

The Supreme Court's injunction ultimately stimulated the smelter owners to develop new pollution control technology. "Out of the Ducktown litigation came a great industrial achievement—the design, erection and successful operation of an adaptation of the lead chamber process to convert sulfur dioxide from copper smelting operations to sulfuric acid." Rodgers, Tacoma's Tall Stack, Nation, May 11, 1970, at 553, 555. A half century later, "the Ducktown smelter is cited as a model for pollution abatement." Id. In his article, Rodgers contrasts the result in Ducktown with the situation in Tacoma, Washington in 1970 where an ASARCO copper smelter built in 1905 was then discharging more than 22 tons of sulfur dioxide *per hour,* in contrast with the 20 tons *per day* permitted of the Ducktown smelter under the Supreme Court's injunction.

7. Interstate pollution remains a serious problem, but the Supreme Court no longer is in the business of establishing emissions limits in federal common law nuisance actions. Why would the Supreme Court be reluctant to hear such actions? Consider the following comment by the Court in refusing the injunction sought by New York against New Jersey's sewage disposal practices:

We cannot withhold the suggestion, inspired by the consideration of this case, that the grave problem of sewage disposal presented by the large and growing populations living on the shores of New York Bay is one more likely to be wisely solved by cooperative study and by conference and mutual concession on the part of the representatives of the States so vitally interested in it than by proceedings in any court however constituted. [New York v. New Jersey, 256 U.S. 296, 313 (1921).]

Do you agree with the Court's conclusion?

8. In Illinois v. City of Milwaukee, 406 U.S. 91 (1972) (*Milwaukee I*), the Supreme Court confirmed that federal common law nuisance actions could be brought against polluting governmental entities, but it reversed its previous willingness to hear such actions under its original jurisdiction. The Court held that the federal district courts were the proper forum for hearing a nuisance action by Illinois charging four Wisconsin cities with polluting Lake Michigan. While rejecting the argument that new federal environmental legislation had preempted federal common law, the Court noted:

It may happen that new federal laws and new federal regulations may in time pre-empt the field of federal common law of nuisance. But until that comes to pass, federal courts will be empowered to appraise the equities of the suits alleging creation of a public nuisance by water pollution. While federal law governs, consideration of state standards may be relevant. Thus, a State with high water-quality standards may well ask that its strict standards be honored and that it not be compelled to lower itself to the more degrading standards of a neighbor. There are no fixed rules that govern; these will be equity suits in which the informed judgment of the chancellor will largely govern. [406 U.S. at 107-108.]

Not long after this decision, the explosion of federal environmental protection legislation led the Court to slam the door on most federal common law actions, as we will see below.

9. Even in cases of public nuisance, the common law has proved to be a crude mechanism at best for controlling the onslaught of modern-day pollution. Thus, most of what we study today as environmental law consists of public law—federal and state environmental statutes, which often create elaborate regulatory schemes implemented by administrative agencies. Common law principles, however, have had an important impact on many current regulatory programs. And as scientific advances make it easier to measure pollutants and to trace their impacts on the environment, common law actions may become more popular (as already seems to be occurring in certain areas). Thus, although most of our attention will be focused on the large and complex body of environmental statutes, it is important not to lose sight of the big picture that includes the common law, which can still serve as an important tool for addressing regulatory gaps left by public law.

2. *The Public Law of Environmental Protection*

A. ENVIRONMENTAL STATUTES: A HISTORICAL PERSPECTIVE

Virtually all the major federal statutes on which these materials focus are a product of a remarkable burst of legislative activity that began with the first Earth Day in 1970. Yet environmental legislation has a much longer history. Ordinances designed to improve sanitation in urban areas had existed in England for centuries. See, e.g., 12 Rich. 2 c. 13 of 1338 (fourteenth-century ordinance prohibiting the throwing of dung, filth, or garbage into ditches, rivers, or other waters near any city borough or town). Wisdom, The Law on the Pollution of Waters 7 (1966). The impact of industrialization on conditions in English urban areas in the nineteenth century spurred considerable legislation directed at improving sanitation by restricting emissions of smoke and noxious fumes and discharges of sewage. However, "the significance of these acts . . . was restricted largely to their number" because they did not establish specific standards, and they provided for neither inspection nor significant penalties for violations. Brenner, Nuisance Law and the Industrial Revolution, 3 J. Legal Stud. 403, 425 (1974). The Smoke Abatement Act of 1853 required companies to use "the best practicable means" to control smoke emissions but did not specify what these were. Several national Nuisances Removal Acts proscribed the maintenance of conditions "injurious to health," but required proof that injury had occurred before violations could be prosecuted. "Only when Parliament confined its regulatory efforts to specific industries did its antipollution legislation begin to acquire force." Id. at 426-427. For example, the Alkali Acts enacted between 1863 and 1874 specified precise pollution control standards (condensation of not less than 95 percent of the muriatic acid) and emissions limits (0.2 grain muriatic acid per cubic foot of escaping gas) for alkali manufacturing plants.

In nineteenth-century America, regulatory legislation was left largely to state and local governments. Aside from an unusual federal statute enacted in 1838 in response to explosions of steamship boilers, the federal role in protecting public health and safety remained largely a nonregulatory one. State laws and local ordinances to protect public health and to require the abatement or segregation of public nuisances were common, although they were poorly coordinated and rarely enforced in the absence of a professional civil service. Like the early English antipollution laws, American smoke abatement ordinances did not clearly specify what level of emissions was proscribed. See, e.g., Sigler v. Cleveland, 4 Ohio Dec. 166 (C.P. Cuyahoga 1896) (holding that an ordinance outlawing "dense smoke" was unconstitutionally overbroad because it was so vague that it could ban all smoke).

Most federal legislation that affected the environment did so by promoting development of natural resources. The Homestead Act of 1862 and the Mining Act of 1872 unabashedly encouraged rapid development of public resources by authorizing private parties to lay claim to public land and the mineral resources on it. Land grants to encourage railroad construction turned over up to 180 million acres of public lands to private developers. R. Robbins, Our Landed Heritage: The Public Domain, 1776-1970 (1976). While the concerns of preservationists and conservationists helped spur establishment of the first national park in 1872, support also came from the railroads, which were seeking to promote tourism and to further the development of western lands. The establishment of the national forest system in 1891 marked a turning point of sorts, for it withdrew forest lands from development under the Homestead Act.

In 1899, Congress enacted the Refuse Act, which prohibited the discharge of refuse into navigable waters without a permit from the Secretary of the Army. But this legislation, part of the Rivers and Harbors Act, was inspired by commercial rather than environmental concerns. Congress wanted to ensure that the waterways of commerce were kept free from barriers to navigation. The Act had little impact on environmental quality until environmentalists discovered in the late 1960s that it could be used to bring citizen suits to stop pollution of surface waters.

At the federal level, efforts to reconcile environmental concerns with policies favoring development of public resources consistently met with difficulties. Environmental interests prevailed only infrequently until the 1960s, when the growing popularity of outdoor recreation and concern over the environmental impact of public works produced landmark legislation. In 1960, Congress adopted the Multiple Use, Sustained Yield Act, which directs federal agencies to manage the National Forests to serve the multiple uses of "recreation, range, timber, watershed, and wildlife and fish purposes." Growing concern for the preservation of natural areas was reflected in the subsequent enactment of the Wilderness Act of 1964, the Wild and Scenic Rivers Act in 1968, and the Federal Land Policy and Management Act of 1976. Other federal laws reflected public interest in protecting social and cultural values from the impact of public works programs. Particularly significant was section 4(f) of the Department of Transportation Act of 1966, which required that special effort be made to prevent federally funded construction projects from damaging parks, recreation areas, wildlife refuges, and historic sites. Like the Fish and Wildlife Coordination Act of 1958, which required that federal agencies consult the U.S. Fish and Wildlife Service in connection with water projects, this legislation focused on incorporating environmental concerns into resource management decisions.

To the extent that federal law was regulatory in character prior to 1970, most the targets of environmental regulation were government agencies rather than private industry. In legislation like the National Historic Preservation Act of 1966, Congress sought to ensure that government agencies respected social and cultural values when pursuing development projects. These laws laid the groundwork for the subsequent enactment of the landmark National Environmental Policy Act of 1969, which required federal agencies to take environmental concerns into account when taking any action with a significant impact on the environment.

Although federal law imposed few regulations on private industry that were animated by environmental concerns, after World War II the federal government became involved in encouraging states to adopt pollution control measures. The Federal Water Pollution Control Act of 1948 authorized research and federal funding for state water pollution control programs. It declared interstate water pollution that endangered public health or welfare to be a public nuisance actionable by the Attorney General following a cumbersome procedure involving a hearing conducted by the Surgeon General. Subsequent legislation offered progressively larger carrots and an occasional stick to encourage states to act. Congress authorized federal grants for the construction of sewage treatment plants over the opposition of President Eisenhower. In 1956 it required states to submit pollution control plans as a condition for obtaining such grants.

The federal programs in the 1950s and 1960s were premised on the notion that environmental problems were the responsibility of state and local governments. The primary federal role was to assist with research and funding while letting the states decide how to control pollution. With expanding economic activity in the post-World War II era, the interstate character of pollution became increasingly apparent. The notion that pollutants do not respect state or even national boundaries was brought home by scientists' warnings that the entire planet was being dangerously poisoned by radiation from nuclear tests in the atmosphere. The premise that the federal role in pollution control should be a nonregulatory one became increasingly tenuous.

When Congress adopted legislation in 1955 directing the Department of Health, Education and Welfare (HEW) to conduct a five-year program of research on the effects of air pollution, it continued to emphasize that pollution control was primarily a state responsibility. By 1960 Congress had begun to appreciate the national dimensions of the air pollution problem. Recognizing that a large percentage of the pollution came from products marketed nationwide, Congress mandated a federal study to determine what levels of automobile emissions were safe. In 1963, when it enacted an early version of the Clean Air Act, Congress acknowledged the need for federal involvement in efforts to protect interstate air quality. The Act directed HEW to publish national air quality criteria, and it also authorized another cumbersome conference procedure for dealing with interstate air pollution problems.

The federal environmental laws of the 1960s were the precursors of the laws today that mandate comprehensive national regulation—the Clean Air Act, the Clean Water Act, and the Resource Conservation and Recovery Act (RCRA). But prior to the 1970s, this legislation was largely nonregulatory, with the federal role confined to the provision of modest grants to assist states with environmental planning. That changed dramatically beginning in 1970.

To be sure, the use of public law by the federal government to regulate private industry was not an entirely new development. Throughout the twentieth century, the federal government had pursued extensive economic regulation to protect consumers and to preserve competition. Federal antitrust law developed in the late nineteenth century; a federal food and drug law was enacted as early as 1906. The first federal pesticide legislation, the Insecticide Act of 1910, 36 Stat. 331, was designed to protect consumers from adulterated or misbranded pesticides. However, the regulatory schemes established by the pollution control legislation of the last two decades mandate a far more ambitious and pervasive form of federal regulation than ever before.

The federal role in environmental policy changed dramatically during the 1970s due to two distinct, but interrelated, developments. First, the National Environmental Policy Act, the Endangered Species Act, and major federal pollution control legislation were enacted in rapid succession. These statutes established the ground rules for environmental protection efforts by mandating that environmental impacts be considered explicitly by federal agencies, by prohibiting actions that jeopardize endangered species, and by requiring the establishment of the first comprehensive controls on air and water pollution, toxic substances, and hazardous waste. Second, the explosion of environmental legislation in the 1970s was accompanied by a parallel opening up of the courts to judicial review of agency decisions that affected the environment. This gave concerned citizens sorely needed tools for challenging agency action and for ensuring that previously unresponsive agencies implemented the ambitious new legislative directives.

A chronology of the major federal environmental statutes is presented below. While the statutes listed are among the principal statutes covered in this casebook, they are by no means a comprehensive catalog of all federal environmental legislation. In addition to the laws identified below, other statutes represent more specific responses to particular environmental problems, for example, the Lead-Based Paint Poisoning

Prevention Act, the Nuclear Waste Policy Act, the Low-Level Radio,
Waste Policy Act, the Uranium Mill Tailings Radiation Control Ac\
Plastic Pollution Control Act, and the Art and Craft Materials Labe
Act.

CHRONOLOGY OF SIGNIFICANT FEDERAL ENVIRONMENTAL LEGISLATION

1. National Environmental Policy Act (NEPA): Signed into
law on January 1, 1970; establishes broad national environmental policy goals; requires federal agencies to assess environmental impacts of significant actions; established Council
on Environmental Quality.

2. Clean Air Act: Clean Air Amendments of 1970 establish basic framework for federal regulation of air pollution;
replace Clean Air Act of 1963 and Air Quality Act of 1967,
which had authorized HEW to publish air quality criteria to
be used by states in setting standards; set deadlines for EPA
to promulgate national ambient air quality standards to be
implemented by the states, national emission standards for
hazardous air pollutants, and auto emission standards; authorizes citizen suits. The Act was substantially amended in
1977 and 1990 to require implementation of more stringent
controls in areas that had failed to attain national standards,
to address the acid rain problem (in 1990), and to make other
substantial changes in the framework for federal regulation
of air pollution.

3. Federal Water Pollution Control Act (Clean Water Act):
Enacted in 1972, it bans the unpermitted discharge of pollutants into surface waters, requires application of technology-
based controls on dischargers, and establishes a national permit
program, the National Pollutant Discharge Elimination System (NPDES), which is implemented by states subject to EPA
supervision; authorizes grants to states for construction of
sewage treatment plants; authorizes citizen suits. Reauthorized and substantially amended by the Clean Water Act
Amendments of 1977 and the Water Quality Act of 1987.

4. Federal Insecticide, Fungicide, and Rodenticide Act
(FIFRA): 1972 Federal Environmental Pesticide Control Act,
which amended 1947 legislation, establishes basic framework
for pesticide regulation; requires registration of pesticides and
authorizes EPA to ban unreasonably dangerous pesticides.
Amended in 1988 to require more expeditious review of pesticides previously registered.

5. *Marine Protection, Research, and Sanctuaries Act of 1972* (Ocean Dumping Act): Prohibits ocean dumping of wastes except with a permit at sites designated by EPA.

6. *Endangered Species Act:* Enacted in December 1973, this legislation prohibits federal action that jeopardizes the habitat of species in danger of extinction and prohibits the taking of any such species by any person.

7. *Safe Drinking Water Act:* Enacted in 1974; requires EPA to set limits for maximum allowable levels of contaminants in public drinking water systems; amended in 1986 to require more expeditious promulgation of standards.

8. *Toxic Substances Control Act of 1976* (TSCA): Provides EPA with comprehensive authority to regulate or prohibit the manufacture, distribution, or use of chemical substances that pose unreasonable risks; requires premanufacture notification of EPA for new chemicals or significant new uses of existing chemicals.

9. *Resource Conservation and Recovery Act of 1976* (RCRA): Directs EPA to establish regulations ensuring the safe management of hazardous waste from cradle to grave. Reauthorized and substantially amended by the Hazardous and Solid Waste Amendments of 1984 (HSWA), which impose new technology-based standards on landfills handling hazardous wastes, require phaseout of land disposal for certain untreated hazardous wastes, and increase federal authority over disposal of nonhazardous solid wastes.

10. *Comprehensive Environmental Response, Compensation, and Liability Act of 1980* (CERCLA): Establishes strict liability system for releases of hazardous substances and creates a "Superfund" to finance actions to clean up such releases. Amended by the Superfund Amendments and Reauthorization Act of 1986 (SARA), which increases the size of Superfund, imposes numerical goals and deadlines for cleanup of Superfund sites, and specifies standards and procedures to be followed in determining the level and scope of cleanup actions.

11. *Emergency Planning and Community Right-to-Know Act* (EPCRTKA): Enacted in 1986, this statute requires corporations to provide local authorities with detailed information concerning their use of any of more than 300 toxic substances and to report annually the quantities of such chemicals released into the environment.

As difficulties arose in the implementation of the first federal regulatory statutes, Congress reacted by adopting new laws as well as lengthy amendments to existing statutes that broadened the scope of agency responsibilities and imposed new and more specific obligations for agency action. Today environmental legislation is taken up by every Congress. Indeed, between the signing of NEPA into law on New Year's Day 1970 and the passage of CERCLA (the Superfund legislation) on December 11, 1980, Congress passed over 20 major laws concerning environmental quality. During the 1980s, many of these statutes have been updated, broadened, and substantially strengthened by amendments. Comprehensive amendments to RCRA were adopted in 1984, to CERCLA and the Safe Drinking Water Act in 1986, and to the Clean Water Act in 1987. Curtis Moore has calculated that the cumulative length of just seven major federal environmental statutes increased from less than 200 pages in 1975 to nearly 1,000 pages in 1988. Moore, Second Step on a Thousand Mile Journey: The Case for Creating a Department of Environmental Protection 56 (draft, 1989). And this figure does not include the 800 pages of Clean Air Act Amendments adopted in 1990 after 13 years of legislative gridlock.

The federalizing of environmental law began with President Nixon signing the National Environmental Policy Act (NEPA), 42 U.S.C. §§4321-4370a, on national television on January 1, 1970. Declaring that "each person should enjoy a healthful environment," the statute established as "the continuing policy of the Federal Government . . . to use all practicable means and measures . . . to create conditions under which man and nature can exist in harmony. . . ." NEPA revolutionized environmental policymaking not by imposing any substantive environmental controls, but rather by mandating changes in the decisionmaking process of federal agencies. The statute requires agencies to incorporate environmental concerns into their decisionmaking by requiring them to perform detailed assessments of the environmental impacts of, and to consider alternatives to, any "major Federal actions significantly affecting the quality of the human environment." While NEPA only mandated *consideration* of environmental impacts, Congress soon declared certain impacts to be presumptively unacceptable when it forbade the taking of endangered species of fish, wildlife, or plants by enacting the Endangered Species Act in 1973. Once it became clear that citizens could enforce these requirements in court, they became a powerful new tool for challenging development projects.

Following the enactment of NEPA, Congress launched a succession of far-reaching regulatory programs to control pollution. In December 1970, Congress adopted the Clean Air Act, 42 U.S.C. §§7401-7642, and in October 1972 the Federal Water Pollution Control Act, 33 U.S.C. §§1251-1376, popularly known as the Clean Water Act. These statutes replaced what had been relatively modest federal research and financial assistance programs with comprehensive regulatory schemes to control air and water pollution throughout the nation. The Environmental Protection Agency (EPA), established by executive order in 1970, was directed to identify air pollutants that threatened public health or welfare and to establish national ambient air quality standards to be implemented by the states. In the Clean Water Act, Congress prohibited all unpermitted discharges of pollutants into surface waters, it required EPA to implement technology-based effluent limits on dischargers, and it established a national permit system to be implemented by EPA or states subject to EPA supervision. Both acts spawned breathtakingly complex national regulatory programs. These programs have grown even more complicated over time as Congress, EPA, and state regulators have made adjustments in them in response to problems with their implementation.

While the first federal environmental statutes focused on control of conventional pollutants, growing public concern over toxic substances spurred enactment of a series of additional statutes that focused on protection of public health. Congress enacted the Safe Drinking Water Act (SDWA) in 1974, and in 1976 it enacted both the Toxic Substances Control Act (TSCA), 15 U.S.C. §§2601-2629, and the Resource Conservation and Recovery Act (RCRA), 42 U.S.C. §§6901-6987. The Safe Drinking Water Act requires EPA to establish regulations to protect public health from contaminants in public water supplies. TSCA authorizes the most explicitly far-reaching regulatory controls, which can be imposed on any chemical substance found by EPA to present an unreasonable risk to health or the environment. RCRA (which is a part of legislation also known as the Solid Waste Disposal Act) requires EPA to establish controls ensuring the safe management of hazardous waste from "cradle to grave."

Although EPA was formed in 1970 to consolidate environmental protection responsibilities in a single federal agency, EPA is not the only regulatory agency with substantial responsibilities for protecting public health and the environment, as indicated by Figure 2.1. The Food and Drug Administration, which is now under the direction of the Department of Health and Human Services, has long been responsible for ensuring the safety of food, drugs, and cosmetics under the federal Food, Drug, and Cosmetic Act. In 1970 Congress created the Occupational Safety and Health Administration as part of the Department of Labor and charged it with ensuring the safety of the workplace. The Nuclear Regulatory Commission and the Department of Energy are responsible for protecting the public from risks posed by atomic material under the Atomic Energy Act. While the laws administered by these agencies usually are referred to as health and safety laws rather than environmental legislation, they are extremely important for the control of substances, products, and activities that pose environmental risks. Other agencies with substantial environmental responsibilities include the Department of the Interior, which is responsible for managing most public lands; the Department of Transportation, which regulates the transport of hazardous materials under the Hazardous Materials Transportation Act;

FIGURE 2.1
Executive Agencies with Environmental Responsibilities

President

The Executive Office of the President

White House Office	Council on Environmental Quality	Office of Management and Budget
Overall policy Agency coordination	Environmental policy coordination NEPA oversight Environmental quality reporting	Budget Agency coordination and management

Environmental Protection Agency	Department of the Interior	Department of Agriculture	Department of Commerce	Department of State
Air and water pollution Pesticides Radiation Solid waste Superfund Toxic substances	Public lands Energy Minerals National parks	Forestry Soil Conservation	Oceanic and atmospheric monitoring and research	International environment

Department of Justice	Department of Defense	Department of Energy	Department of Transportation	Department of Housing and Urban Development
Environmental litigation	Civil works construction Dredge and fill permits Pollution control from defense facilities	Energy policy coordination Petroleum allocation Research and development	Mass transit Roads Airplane noise Oil pollution	Housing Urban parks Urban planning

Department of Health and Human Services	Department of Labor OSHA	Nuclear Regulatory Commission	Tennessee Valley Authority
Health	Occupational health	License and regulate nuclear power	Electric power generation

Source: CEQ, Environmental Quality 1985 (1986).

the Council on Environmental Quality, charged with coordinating federal environmental policy and assisting federal agencies with NEPA compliance; the U.S. Army Corps of Engineers, which operates a permit program for dredge and fill activities under section 404 of the Clean Water Act; and the Department of Energy, which administers the National Energy Policy and Conservation Act.

A chronic problem with environmental regulation has been that the responsibilities of administrative agencies have grown far more rapidly than agency resources. This became apparent soon after the enactment of the Clean Air Act in 1970 and the Clean Water Act in 1972. EPA officials told a Senate committee in 1974 that the Agency could not possibly carry out all its regulatory responsibilities because its budget had been determined independently of any assessment of what would be required to implement the new environmental laws. See Environmental Protection Agency's Budget Request for Fiscal Year 1975, Hearings before the Senate Comm. on Public Works, at 210-211 (Feb. 1974) (statement of EPA Administrator Russell Train). The gap between agency resources and responsibilities was exacerbated by the Reagan Administration's use of the budgeting process to promote "regulatory relief." Although the administration could not convince Congress to relax the environmental statutes, it did succeed in substantially reducing EPA's budget. Between 1980 and 1983, EPA's budget was slashed by one-third and its personnel by more than 20 percent. Even though the budget cuts were restored during Reagan's second term, by the time the administration left office in 1989, EPA had roughly the same number of employees as it did in 1977. Moore, Second Step on a Thousand Mile Journey: The Case for Creating a Department of Environmental Protection 51 (draft, 1989). Yet the agency's statutory responsibilities had multiplied severalfold.

Most of the environmental laws on which this casebook focuses are administered by EPA, although the laws generally impose environmental responsibilities on all federal agencies who operate facilities that generate pollution. Facilities operated by federal agencies, such the nuclear weapons plants operated by the Defense Department and the Department of Energy, are now major targets of environmental regulation. Indeed, the General Accounting Office has estimated that federal agencies now spend more money to ensure that their own facilities comply with environmental laws than they spend on applying such laws to private industry.

B. THE IMPACT OF PUBLIC LAW ON COMMON LAW ACTIONS TO PROTECT THE ENVIRONMENT

With the advent of comprehensive federal regulatory statutes, courts soon faced questions concerning the impact of public law on common law actions. While statutes may supplant common law if legislative bodies so intend, legislative intent is often deliberately left murky because legislators are loath to disturb the products of decades of judicially developed doctrine. Thus, the relationship between the public law and the common law of environmental protection can be a complicated one. A simplified way of looking at this question is represented in Figure 2.2. Common law actions can be preempted by environmental statutes, as shown by the portion of the common law circle that is obscured by the public law circle. But in other areas the two can coexist. Common law actions can serve as a supplement for addressing the very problems targeted by environmental statutes and regulations (as indicated by the shaded area where the two circles overlap) or they can fill in gaps not addressed by public law (as indicated by the portion of the common law circle that does not overlap with the public law circle). Courts have wrestled with the question of defining the proper boundaries of these circles, as we will see.

As noted above, the Supreme Court in Illinois v. City of Milwaukee, 406 U.S. 91 (1972) (*Milwaukee I*) delegated jurisdiction over federal common law nuisance actions between states to the federal district courts. Thus, following the Supreme Court's decision in *Milwaukee I*, Illinois pursued its common law nuisance action in federal district court. In the meantime, the federal Clean Water Act had been enacted. This legislation established a comprehensive regulatory scheme to control water

FIGURE 2.2
The Relationship Between the Public Law and the Common Law of Environmental Protection

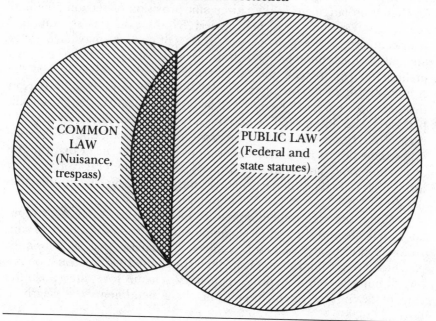

COMMON LAW
(Nuisance, trespass)

PUBLIC LAW
(Federal and state statutes)

pollution by requiring all dischargers of pollutants into surface waters to obtain a permit, usually from a state environmental agency operating under federal oversight. Milwaukee ultimately obtained a permit limiting the discharges from its sewage treatment plants. While Milwaukee argued that the permit precluded Illinois's nuisance action, Illinois maintained that the permit limits were too lax and that the discharges remained a nuisance at common law.

In 1977, the district court rejected Milwaukee's defense, ruling that Milwaukee's discharge of inadequately treated sewage was a nuisance under federal common law and ordering the city to control its discharges more stringently than required by its Clean Water Act permit. The Seventh Circuit affirmed the district court's holding that the Clean Water Act had not preempted the federal common law of nuisance, but it held that the district court should not have required more stringent limits on discharges of treated sewage than required by the city's permit. The case then returned to the Supreme Court, which addressed the impact of the Clean Water Act's regulatory scheme on federal common law nuisance actions in City of Milwaukee v. Illinois, 451 U.S. 304 (1981) (*Milwaukee II*).

In *Milwaukee II* the Supreme Court held that Illinois's federal common law nuisance action had been preempted by the federal Clean Water Act. Writing for the Court, Justice Rehnquist noted that legislative preemption of *federal* common law did not implicate the same federalism concerns that require clear expressions of congressional intent before state law may be preempted. Illinois had argued that there was clear evidence that Congress had not intended to preempt federal common law based on language in the citizen suit provision of section 505(e) of the Clean Water Act, which provides: "Nothing in this section shall restrict any right which any person (or class of persons) may have under any statute or common law to seek enforcement of any effluent standard or limitation or to seek any other relief (including relief against the Administrator or a State agency)." However, the Supreme Court read this language narrowly to mean "that nothing *in §505*, the citizen-suit provision, should be read as limiting any other remedies which might exist. . . . [I]t means only that the provision of such suit does not revoke other remedies. It most assuredly cannot be read to mean that the Act as a whole does not supplant formerly available federal common-law actions but only that the particular section authorizing citizen suits does not do so." 451 U.S. at 328-329 (emphasis in original).

Citing the comprehensive nature of the Clean Water Act's regulatory scheme and the technical complexities courts would have to confront to formulate pollution control standards, Justice Rehnquist concluded that Congress implicitly had supplanted federal common law by adopting a comprehensive regulatory scheme for water pollution control. "Congress' intent in enacting the Amendments was clearly to establish an all-encompassing program of water pollution regulation. *Every* point source discharge is prohibited unless covered by a permit, which directly subjects the discharger to the administrative apparatus established by Congress to achieve its goals." Justice Rehnquist concluded that "[t]he establishment of such a self-consciously comprehensive program by Congress, which certainly did not exist when Illinois v. Milwaukee was decided, strongly suggests that there is no room for courts to attempt to improve on that program with federal common law." *Milwaukee II,* 451 U.S. at 318-319 (emphasis in original). He went on to note that application of federal common law would be "peculiarly inappropriate in areas as complex as water pollution control. . . . Not only are the technical problems difficult—doubtless the reason Congress vested authority to administer the Act in administrative agencies possessing the necessary expertise—but the general area is particularly unsuited to the approach inevitable under a regime of federal common law. Congress criticized past approaches to water pollution control as being 'sporadic' and 'ad hoc,' S. Rep. No. 92-414, p. 95 (1971), 2 Leg. Hist. 1511, apt characterizations of any judicial approach applying federal common law, see Wilburn Boat Co. v. Fireman's Fund Ins. Co., 348 U.S. 310, 319 (1955)." *Milwaukee II,* 451 U.S. at 325.

Justice Rehnquist noted that Illinois was free to pursue its case for more stringent controls on Milwaukee's discharges before the Wisconsin state agency responsible for issuing Milwaukee a permit under the Clean Water Act. But he maintained that "[i]t would be quite inconsistent with this scheme if federal courts were in effect to 'write their own ticket' under the guise of federal common law after permits have already been issued and permittees have been planning and operating in reliance on them."

NOTES AND QUESTIONS

1. The Supreme Court's decision in *Milwaukee II* effectively ended the use of federal common law nuisance actions for controlling interstate water pollution. Justice Blackmun, joined by two other dissenting Justices, argued that this was a particularly unfortunate result because it would encourage states to resort to state law to handle interstate pollution problems ("Instead of promoting a more uniform federal approach to the problem of alleviating interstate pollution, I fear that today's decision will lead States to turn to their own courts for statutory or common-law assistance in filling the interstices of the federal statute." 451 U.S. at 353-354 (Blackmun, J., dissenting)).

2. An important part of the rationale for preemption in *Milwaukee II* was the pervasive regulatory scheme provided by the Clean Water Act's NPDES permit program. The Act requires permits for all dis-

charges of pollutants to surface waters from point sources. The Ninth Circuit in National Audubon Society v. Department of Water, 869 F.2d 1196 (9th Cir. 1989), held that the Clean Water Act preempts a federal common law nuisance action against the Los Angeles Department of Water and Power for damage it caused by diverting water from Mono Lake. The court, however, reserved judgment on the question whether the federal Clean Air Act would preempt a federal common law nuisance action against the Department for air pollution. The Ninth Circuit held that a federal common law action was not available under the facts of the case because, unlike the situation in Georgia v. Tennessee Copper Co., there was no interstate dispute involved. A dissenting judge argued that there is a uniquely federal interest in preserving air quality even in intrastate disputes. Plaintiffs had argued that a federal common law nuisance action for interstate water pollution should be available to them because the Clean Water Act does not apply to the action they challenged since no NPDES permit was required for the water diversions they challenged. Although the Supreme Court has not determined whether the federal Clean Air Act preempts federal common law nuisance actions for interstate air pollution, the Second Circuit has held that it does not. In New England Legal Foundation v. Costle, 666 F.2d 30 (2d Cir. 1981), the court explained that the Clean Air Act does not preempt such action because it, unlike the Clean Water Act, does not regulate pollution from all sources. Prior to enactment of the 1990 Amendments, the Clean Air Act did not employ a federal permit program. Now that it does, would a different result be likely in New England Legal Foundation v. Costle?

3. In other areas, federal common law remains alive. For example, Congress occasionally has indicated that common law principles should be used to supplement federal environmental statutes. When the Comprehensive Environmental Response, Compensation, and Liability Act (CERCLA) was enacted in 1980, Congress created a strict liability scheme for persons involved in the release of hazardous substances. Although CERCLA does not expressly specify that it imposes joint and several liability, it has been interpreted to do so as a result of statements by its sponsors that "issues of liability not resolved by the Act, if any, shall be governed by traditional and evolving principles of common law." 126 Cong. Rec. S14964 (Nov. 24, 1980); 126 Cong. Rec. H11787 (Dec. 3, 1980).

C. FEDERALISM, STATE PROGRAMS, AND FEDERAL PREEMPTION OF STATE ENVIRONMENTAL LAW

While the growth of environmental regulation largely has been driven by federal legislation, state law retains considerable importance in environmental protection. While Congress clearly has the power to preempt state law, Garcia v. San Antonio Metropolitan Transit Authority, 469 U.S. 528 (1985), it generally has been careful not to exercise it when enacting federal environmental legislation except in certain narrow circumstances discussed below. State common law can be a significant tool for addressing pollution, and some of the most innovative regulatory legislation to protect the environment, such as California's Proposition 65 and New Jersey's Environmental Cleanup and Responsibility Act, has been the product of state legislation.

Michigan was a pioneer in using legislation to encourage the development of a state common law of environmental protection. The Michigan Environmental Protection Act (MEPA), enacted in 1970, authorizes "any person" to sue for declaratory and equitable relief "for the protection of the air, water, and other natural resources and the public trust therein from pollution, impairment or destruction." Mich. Comp. Laws Ann. §691.1201 et seq. Suits may be brought against the state, its agencies, corporations, individuals, or other private entities. MEPA, which was the first "citizen suit" legislation in the country, was designed to challenge courts to develop a "common law of environmental quality." It provides that if a plaintiff makes a prima facie showing that a defendant has or is likely to "pollute, impair or destroy the air, water or other natural resources," the defendant must either rebut this showing or demonstrate as an affirmative defense that there is "no feasible and prudent alternative to the defendant's conduct and that such conduct is consistent with the promotion of the public health, safety and welfare in light of the state's paramount concern for the protection of its natural resources." Courts are directed not to authorize or approve conduct likely to pollute, impair, or destroy such resources "so long as there is a feasible and prudent alternative." If a court finds that the challenged conduct is subject to an existing environmental standard that the court finds "to be deficient," the court can "direct the adoption of a standard approved and specified by the court." For a discussion of the impact of MEPA, see Slone, The Michigan Environmental Protection Act: Bringing Citizen-Initiated Environmental Suits into the 1980's, 12 Ecology L.Q. 271 (1985).

Efforts to use state common law to address interstate pollution have been more problematical. In International Paper Co. v. Ouellette, 479 U.S. 481 (1987), the Supreme Court addressed the question whether the federal Clean Water Act preempted a *state* common law nuisance action brought by Vermont plaintiffs against a New York discharger. The Court held that federal courts can apply state common law to address interstate pollution in light of the savings clause in section 510 of the Clean Water Act, which specifies that states may adopt and enforce more stringent limits on discharges than required by federal standards. However, the Court required that the state law to be applied be that of the discharging state rather than the receiving state. Fearing that downstream states otherwise could apply unreasonably stringent standards to dischargers in upstream states, the Court explained that a state's common law is preempted to the extent that it "stands as an obstacle to the accomplishment and execution of the full purposes and objectives of Congress."

The Supreme Court's holding in *Ouellette* preserves the possibility of using state common law to address interstate pollution as long as the state law that is applied is the law of the discharging state. In Her Majesty the Queen v. City of Detroit, 874 F.2d 332 (6th Cir. 1989), the Sixth Circuit affirmed that MEPA was not preempted by the federal Clean Air Act. Thus, it permitted the Province of Ontario and national environmental organizations to bring a MEPA challenge in state court to a decision to approve a municipal incinerator that would contribute to interstate pollution.

While state law can be an important source of environmental regulation, the driving force behind expansion of the regulatory net has been an explosion of federal legislation. The federalization of environmental law was a product of concern that state and local authorities lacked the resources and political capability to control problems that were becoming national in scope. Federal environmental legislation has employed three different approaches in defining federal-state relationships. The first model, which proved largely inadequate for controlling interstate pollution, restricted the federal role to provision of financial or regulatory incentives to encourage states to adopt their own environmental standards. This approach is still used for encouraging state and local land use and solid waste management planning under the Coastal Zone Management Act, the Clean Water Act, and subtitle D of the Resource Conservation and Recovery Act. But in other areas it has been largely supplanted by two other models incorporating more aggressive federal regulatory roles.

The model most frequently employed by the environmental statutes makes federal agencies responsible for establishing environmental standards that then may be administered and enforced by state authorities. The principal federal pollution control schemes, such as RCRA, the Clean Air Act, and the Clean Water Act, required EPA to establish uniform national standards that can be implemented and administered by states subject to federal supervision. Most federal environmental statutes specify that the standards they require are minimum standards that must be met by every state, while expressly authorizing states to establish more stringent pollution controls if they so desire. For example, section 510 of the Clean Water Act specifies that states may adopt and enforce more stringent limits on discharges than required by the federal government.

Statutes that require the establishment of minimum federal standards are designed to prevent competition for industry among states from undermining environmental protection while allowing states that place a higher value on a clean environment to impose stricter controls. Economists often have criticized the use of uniform national standards as inefficient, although in some circumstances businesses favor national standards that preempt state law to avoid the high cost of complying with 50 different standards. Indeed, it has been argued that one of the major forces behind the auto emission controls included in the original Clean Air Act was the desire of automobile manufacturers to avoid having to cope with a multiplicity of state standards. See Ackerman, Elliot, and Millian, Toward a Theory of Statutory Evolution: The Federalization of Environmental Law, 1 J. L. Econ. & Org. 313 (1985).

A major difficulty with state administration of federal standards has been the problem of program responsibilities outpacing agency resources. The federal government increasingly has delegated responsibility for environmental programs to the states, even as federal grants for administering those programs have been reduced sharply. Most states failed to replace the lost federal funds for environmental programs with funds of their own. J. P. Lester, A New Federalism? Environmental Policy in the States, in N. Vig and M. Kraft, eds., Environmental Policy in the 1990s 67 (1990). The quality of state environmental programs and the resources devoted to them varies dramatically from state to state. While EPA has the authority to withdraw a delegation of program authority to any state that is not meeting federal standards, the agency has little incentive to do so since it would add to EPA's responsibilities without providing additional resources to implement them. As the burden of environmental expenditures increasingly falls on state and local governments that are strapped for funds, see EPA, A Preliminary Analysis of the Public Costs of Environmental Protection: 1981-2000 (1990), the quality of state administration of federal programs is likely to become even more variable.

A third model eschews state administration of federal standards in favor of federal control. This approach is employed for national regulation of chemicals under the Toxic Substances Control Act (TSCA), for national pesticide registration under the Federal Insecticide, Fungicide, and Rodenticide Act (FIFRA), and in certain provisions of the Clean Air Act governing vehicle emissions. Under these programs, which are used to regulate products distributed nationally, federal standards can preempt inconsistent state standards.

Issues of federal preemption of state common law actions to control environmental hazards have arisen in toxic tort litigation, see, e.g., Silkwood v. Kerr-McGee Corp., 464 U.S. 238 (1984) (holding that award of punitive damages under state law for exposure to nuclear material not preempted by the Atomic Energy Act); Cippollone v. Liggett Group, Inc., 789 F.2d 181 (3d Cir. 1986) (Federal Cigarette Labeling and Advertising Act preempts state common law action for failure to warn of

dangers of cigarette smoking), and in response to state regulatory initiatives that allegedly interfere with federal programs. See, e.g., Huron
Portland Cement Co. v. Detroit, 352 U.S. 440 (1960) (upholding municipality's smoke abatement ordinance as applied to ships on the Great
Lakes against claims that it interfered with interstate commerce and that
it was preempted by federal safety regulation of seagoing vessels); Bur-
bank v. Lockheed Air Terminal, Inc., 411 U.S. 624 (1973) (holding that
the Noise Control Act and the Federal Aviation Act preempt a local noise
abatement ordinance that effectively barred jet aircraft from taking off
at night); Pacific Gas & Electric v. California Energy Commission, 461
U.S. 190 (1983) (upholding a California state initiative that blocked the
licensing of new nuclear power plants in the state pending the development of a facility for disposal of high-level nuclear waste on the ground
that it is an economic measure rather than a safety regulation in conflict
with the Atomic Energy Act).

The Supreme Court has held that respect for federalism requires
that federal preemption not be inferred lightly. For federal regulatory
programs to preempt state law, Congress must either expressly indicate
its intent to preempt state law or the state law must be implicitly
preempted. Implicit preemption can occur in three ways. First, state
regulation can be preempted if federal regulation is so pervasive as to
make it reasonable to infer that there is no room for state action (as in
Milwaukee II). Second, if federal law regulates a field in which the federal
interest is sufficiently dominant to preclude state enforcement (as in
regulation of nuclear safety), state laws on the same subject are preempted.
Third, if the goals of the federal regulatory scheme and the requirements
it imposes indicate an intent to preclude state authority, state regulation
can be preempted.

Implicit preemption is not lightly inferred. The judicial reluctance
to preempt state regulation is based on federalism concerns as articulated
by Justice Rehnquist in *Milwaukee II*:

> In considering [whether federal law preempts state law] "we start with the
> assumption that the historic police powers of the States were not to be
> superseded by the Federal Act unless that was the clear and manifest
> purpose of Congress." Jones v. Rath Packing Co., 430 U.S. 519, 525 (1977)
> (quoting Rice v. Santa Fe Elevator Corp., 331 U.S. 218, 230 (1947)). While
> we have not hesitated to find pre-emption of state law, whether express
> or implied, when Congress has so indicated, see Ray v. Atlantic Richfield
> Co., 435 U.S. 151, 157 (1978), or when enforcement of state regulations
> would impair "federal superintendence of the field," Florida Lime & Av-
> ocado Growers, Inc. v. Paul, 373 U.S. 132, 142 (1963), our analysis has
> included "due regard for the presuppositions of our embracing federal
> system, including the principle of diffusion of power not as a matter of
> doctrinaire localism but as a promoter of democracy." San Diego Building

Trades Council v. Garmon, 359 U.S. 236, 243 (1959). [City of Milwaukee v. Illinois, 451 U.S. 304, 316 (1981).]

Preemption can be inferred if it is impossible to comply with both federal and state regulations or if application of the state regulatory scheme would serve as an obstacle to achievement of the federal purpose. As the Supreme Court stated in English v. General Electric Co., 110 S. Ct. 2270, 2278 (1990) in discussing whether a law that targeted health and safety hazards unrelated to radiation was preempted by federal regulation of nuclear safety: "[F]or a state law to fall within the preempted zone, it must have some direct and substantial effect on the decisions made by those who build or operate nuclear facilities concerning radiological safety levels."

In cases where courts have found state regulations to be preempted, Congress can always act to remove the preemptive impact of federal regulation. For example, in Exxon Corp. v. Hunt, 475 U.S. 355 (1986), the Supreme Court held that states' "superfunds" were preempted to the extent that they were used to fund the cleanup of hazardous substance releases covered by the federal Superfund legislation. Even this holding was a narrow one, however, because the Court indicated that states could use such funds to pay their required contributions to federal cleanups. Congress promptly amended the Superfund legislation in 1986 to clarify that states could require companies to contribute to state funds even if they were used for activities covered by the federal legislation.

Even statutes (such as FIFRA) that expressly prohibit states from imposing labeling or packaging requirements different from those imposed by federal regulation have not been interpreted to preempt other types of state or local regulation. In Wisconsin Public Intervenor v. Mortier, 111 S. Ct. 2476 (1991), the Supreme Court unanimously held that FIFRA did not preempt municipal ordinances requiring that a permit be obtained before a pesticide is applied to certain private lands. FIFRA prohibits the use of pesticides unless they are registered by EPA. The Court noted that FIFRA provides that a state may not regulate the labeling or packaging of pesticides and authorizes states to regulate the sale or use of registered pesticides only to the extent that they do not permit a sale or use prohibited by federal law. The Court found that FIFRA was not a sufficiently comprehensive statute to infer that Congress intended to exclude state regulation.

Despite legislative history indicating that Congress had rejected an amendment expressly designed to authorize further local regulation of pesticides, the Court in *Mortier* noted that there was no actual conflict between the local permitting ordinance and federal regulation under FIFRA. The Court concluded that FIFRA "does not equate registration and labeling requirements with a general approval to apply pesticides throughout the Nation without regard to regional and local factors like climate, population, geography, and water supply." 59 U.S.L.W. at 4759. The National Pest Control Association, an industry trade association, had argued that uniformity was necessary to avoid a "jumble of overlapping, conflicting, confusing and unnecessary local ordinances" that "would severely impair, if not make impossible, delivery of timely, cost-effective pest control." But the Court found that Congress has not intended to preclude states from permitting local regulation, noting that "FIFRA implies a regulatory partnership between federal, state, *and* local governments." Thus, even in circumstances where potentially inconsistent state and local regulation may make national marketing more difficult, courts are reluctant to preempt state regulation unless Congress has expressly so directed.

As national regulation expands in scope, the range of potential conflicts between federal and state environmental regulation may increase. One response to this problem has been to adopt a kind of hybrid approach to preemption that establishes conditions that must be satisfied before state or local governments can adopt regulations that go beyond minimum federal standards. For example, the Clean Air Act amendments now authorize states to adopt stricter auto emissions standards than the federal minimum, but only if those standards conform to the stricter standard that California has been allowed to adopt. The rationale behind this provision is that it will increase state flexibility to meet federal Clean Air standards while requiring vehicle manufacturers only to meet a standard that they already must comply with in the California market. This approach is designed to give states greater flexibility in tailoring standards to their environmental needs while avoiding the creation of several different standards that would be expensive for national manufacturers to meet.

Aside from the problems inconsistent state standards cause national manufacturers, states generally have been given the freedom to adopt stricter environmental standards than the federal minimum on the assumption that the state would have to bear the costs of the more stringent regulation. This theory is reflected in CERCLA, the Superfund legislation, which allows states to apply their own stricter standards for cleanup of toxic waste sites, but only if the states agree to pay the additional costs of meeting the state rather than the federal standards. When the cost of meeting stricter standards would be borne largely by dischargers in other states this theory does not apply, which may explain the Supreme Court's unwillingness in International Paper Co. v. Ouellette, 479 U.S. 481 (1987), to permit a downstream state to apply its own common law standards to water pollution originating in an upstream state with less stringent standards.

As you will see when we examine specific regulatory statutes, questions of federal-state relations arise frequently in the development and implementation of environmental standards. For now, you should simply be aware of this issue and the continuing tension between federal and state authorities it generates, a tension that may increase as states adopt increasingly aggressive environmental standards.

3. *International Law and the Environment*

As the global dimensions of environmental problems receive increasing attention, so does international environmental law. Beginning with bilateral agreements to protect migratory fish and game and to resolve transboundary pollution disputes, international environmental law now has expanded to involve virtually the entire community of nations in multilateral agreements to address global problems. The need to develop a coordinated policy for protecting the planet's atmosphere against ozone depletion and the greenhouse effect has spurred remarkable advances in international law. While these and other international initiatives are discussed in more detail in Chapter 9, it is useful to preview their place in the structure of environmental law and to consider their relationship to domestic environmental policy.

International environmental law has been described by Professor Lynton Caldwell as "the collective body of agreements among states regarding mutual rights and obligations affecting the environment." He notes that it has multiple roots and sometimes ill-defined contours:

> It is embodied in conventions among states (treaties) and, to lesser effect, in international declarations, collective principles, opinions of jurists, and generally accepted practices among states. Enforcement of its provisions, customary or specified by treaty, are usually sought through negotiations (e.g., diplomacy) rather than through adjudication. Its boundaries are definable only in broad terms because new scientific findings and enlarging perceptions of man-biosphere relationships have continually if unevenly expanded its frontiers. [L. Caldwell, International Environmental Policy: Emergence and Dimensions 102 (1984).]

While principles of customary international law provide some basis for actions to protect the global environment, they rarely have been used successfully. Actions based on principles of customary law must confront the same obstacles that make recovery difficult in common law actions. Proof of causation and damages must be shown, and injury to the global commons is unlikely to be found to constitute a sufficient basis for recovery. Even in cases where injury to a country's citizens or property can be demonstrated to constitute a sufficient invasion of a sovereign's legally protected interest, problems of jurisdiction and enforcement are formidable obstacles to recovery. Countries may simply refuse to appear in the World Court or to recognize the jurisdiction of national tribunals, as the government of France did when a court in the Netherlands held French defendants liable for salt pollution of the Rhine. 11 Intl. Env. Rep. 652 (Dec. 14, 1988).

Only a handful of environmental disputes between nations have been resolved by international tribunals, and these were the product of bilateral agreements between neighboring states. The most prominent example is the Trail Smelter decision, 3 R. Intl. Arb. Awards 1905 (1941), which has served as an important precedent for the development of international environmental law. The Trail Smelter case involved a dispute between the United States and Canada over emissions from a lead and zinc smelter in Trail, British Columbia. The smelter discharged 300 tons of sulfur per day into the air ten miles from the U.S. border. The United States claimed that the pollution was causing severe damage in the state of Washington. After the United States complained to Canada, the two countries agreed to submit the dispute to an International Joint Commission (composed of representatives from the United States, Canada, and Belgium) convened under procedures that had been established by the two countries in the Boundary Waters Treaty of 1909.

One of the difficulties such tribunals face is to determine what standards of liability to apply. In the Trail Smelter case the International Joint Commission looked for guidance from the laws of each country concerning transboundary pollution. An influential U.S. precedent that helped convince the Commission to rule in favor of the United States was the Supreme Court's decision in Georgia v. Tennessee Copper Co., 206 U.S. 230 (1907), discussed above. In its decision the Commission declared that "no State has the right to use or permit the use of its territory in such a manner as to cause injury by fumes in or to the territory of another or the properties of persons therein, when the case is of serious consequence and the injury is established by clear and convincing evidence." Trail Smelter. The Canadian government was found liable for $350,000 in damages. However, in calculating these damages the tribunal found that the reduced value of businesses or property caused by the pollution was too remote an element of damages to be included in the award.

Plaintiffs victimized by transboundary pollution occasionally have resorted to courts in the source country. For example, in Michie v. Great Lakes Steel Division, 495 F.2d 213 (6th Cir.), cert. denied, 419 U.S. 997 (1974), a group of 37 residents of Canada were allowed to bring a nuisance action against three steel companies located in the United States based on the diversity jurisdiction of the federal courts. The Canadian government also has used the federal courts to try to force action to control acid rain and international air pollution.

The most promising avenue for international environmental protection efforts appears to be international agreements between sovereign states. While these treaties bind only the signatories, under U.S. law they can override inconsistent state regulations. A bilateral treaty to protect migratory birds that travel between the United States and Canada was the focus of an important decision by the Supreme Court in 1920. In Missouri v. Holland, 252 U.S. 416 (1920), a state challenged the federal government's authority to enforce regulations adopted by the Secretary of Agriculture to enforce the Migratory Bird Treaty of 1916. The treaty had pledged the United States and Canada to restrict the killing, capturing, or selling of certain migratory birds. Missouri argued that federal regulations enforcing the treaty were an infringement of its rights under the Tenth Amendment to regulate property within its borders.

Justice Holmes, writing for the Court, noted that the power to make treaties is expressly delegated to the president by Article II, section 2 of the Constitution and that laws enacted by Congress to implement treaties are the supreme law of the land under the Supremacy Clause of Article VI. While noting that but for the treaty the state would be free to regulate the killing of birds within its territory, Justice Holmes rejected the state's claim that it owned the birds. "Wild birds are not in the possession of anyone; and possession is the beginning of ownership. The whole foundation of the State's rights is the presence within their jurisdiction of birds that yesterday had not arrived, tomorrow may be in another State and in a week a thousand miles away." 252 U.S. at 434. He concluded:

> Here a national interest of very nearly the first magnitude is involved. It can be protected only by national action in concert with that of another power. The subject-matter is only transitorily within the State and has no permanent habitat therein. But for the treaty and the statute there soon might be no birds for any powers to deal with. We see nothing in the Constitution that compels the Government to sit by while a food supply is cut off and the protectors of our forests and our crops are destroyed. It is not sufficient to rely upon the States. The reliance is vain, and were it otherwise, the question is whether the United States is forbidden to act. We are of opinion that the treaty and statute must be upheld. [252 U.S. at 435.]

The decision in Missouri v. Holland is an important constitutional law decision because it confirmed that a treaty made by the president and ratified by the Senate is part of "the supreme law of the land" and overrides any conflicting state laws. A previous attempt by Congress to regulate the killing of migratory birds had been struck down in two federal district court cases, which the Supreme Court cited in another portion of the Missouri v. Holland decision without expressing any view on their validity. Questions concerning the limits of the federal government's ability to override local laws through exercise of the treaty power were of greater concern prior to decisions confirming the breadth of

Congress's power to preempt state laws pursuant to the Commerce Clause of Article I, section 8.

.In recent years there has been a surge in multilateral agreements to protect the global environment. As of May 1989, the United Nations Environment Program had identified 140 international environmental agreements (addressing subjects from white lead to tropical timber), nearly two-thirds of which were signed after 1970. A catalyst for international environmental initiatives was the Stockholm Conference on the Human Environment sponsored by the United Nations in 1972. The conference, which was attended by representatives of 133 nations, culminated in the issuance of a Declaration on the Human Environment that recognized the urgency of global action to protect the environment and the duty of all countries to prevent transboundary environmental damage. The Stockholm Conference led to establishment of the U.N. Environment Programme (UNEP) and the initiation of an environmental planning process involving developing and industrialized countries in a series of future conferences. A follow-up conference held in Nairobi in 1982 on the tenth anniversary of the Stockholm Conference helped spur the U.N.'s creation of the World Commission on Environment and Development. Scores of world leaders will attend an "Earth Summit" held by the U.N. in Rio de Janeiro in June 1992 to celebrate the twentieth anniversary of the Stockholm Conference.

ENVIRONMENTAL LAW: A PATHFINDER

Environmental law is like a jungle, though it need not be an impenetrable one. But the rapid pace of developments in the field and the importance of nontraditional sources of information can make research in environmental law a considerable challenge.

Most environmental regulation is now the product of elaborate regulatory schemes established pursuant to *federal statutes*. To become familiar with the principal federal statutes, students can consult the U.S. Code. West's Selected Environmental Statutes—Educational Edition contains the most accessible compilation of federal environmental statutes and is updated annually.

Most federal environmental *regulations* are found in Title 40 of the Code of Federal Regulations. As of July 1991 it occupied 15 volumes, only three less than the number allotted the IRS for tax regulations. Persons interested in contemporary regulatory developments can read the daily Federal Register, which includes all proposed and final regulations by EPA and other agencies, as well as announcements concerning public meetings and the availability of studies and other documents. Even those who read the Federal Register religiously may not learn of crucial regulatory developments until it is too late. The best way to keep up with current developments is to read the Current Developments section of BNA's weekly Environment Reporter, which provides comprehensive coverage of a broad range of issues at both the federal and state levels. A useful way to monitor EPA activities is to read Inside EPA, a weekly publication by Inside Washington Publishers, which reports the latest rumors and developments from within the Agency.

Significant developments in *environmental litigation* often occur long before a reported decision appears in the Federal Reporter or Federal Supplement. The Environmental Law Reporter, published monthly by the Environmental Law Institute, contains summaries of pending litigation, and its companion, Environmental Reporter Cases, includes settlement agreements and unpublished judicial decisions in environmental cases.

Comprehensive environmental law *treatises* include Sheldon Novick's The Law of Environmental Protection published by Clark, Boardman and William Rodgers's Environmental Law, published by West. A highly readable introductory treatise on environmental law is David Sive and Frank Friedman, A Practical Guide to Environmental Law, published by ALI-ABA. There has been an astonishing proliferation of environmental *periodicals*. Among the most useful are ELI's Environmental Forum, an entertaining bimonthly publication that reports on environmental policy developments, and Environment magazine. In light of the importance of scientific developments for environmental policy, regular reading of Science magazine is also very useful. Leading environmental *law journals* include Ecology Law Quarterly, the Columbia Journal of Environmental Law, the Harvard Environmental Law Review, and the Yale Journal on Regulation. During the Bush Administration, the annual report of the Council of Environmental Quality has again become a very useful update on developments in environmental law and policy.

Each February ELI and ALI-ABA host an annual environmental law *conference* in Washington that provides one of the best mechanisms for staying abreast of current developments in the field. The ABA, state bar associations, and law schools also sponsor numerous conferences.

Research advice on more specialized environmental topics is included in subsequent chapters.

UNEP-sponsored international negotiations have produced significant multilateral agreements initiating measures to protect the global environment. These include the 1985 Vienna Convention for Protection of the Ozone Layer, the 1987 Montreal Protocol on Substances that Deplete the Ozone Layer, and the 1989 Basel Convention on Transboundary Movements of Hazardous Waste and Their Disposal. Negotiation of an international climate convention began in 1991. Other international organizations also have played an influential role in the development of international environmental protection measures. The European Community (EC) and the Organization for Economic Cooperation and Development (OECD), whose members include the 19 European countries, the United States, Canada, Japan, and Australia and New Zealand, are involved in a variety of initiatives to coordinate environmental policy. These include OECD's declarations concerning mutual acceptance of chemical test data and the establishment of minimum premarketing data sets for chemical assessment.

Although international law is having increasing influence on the environmental policies of the United States and other countries, national legislation continues to be the dominant source of environmental law. We now consider the wide range of approaches to regulation employed by these laws and the lively current debate over regulatory alternatives.

B. APPROACHES TO REGULATION: ASSESSING THE OPTIONS

1. *Regulation and Its Alternatives*

Regardless of the philosophic perspective one brings to environmental policy, there is broad agreement that some form of collective action should be undertaken to address environmental problems for reasons explored in Chapter 1. While this can provide a powerful rationale for government regulation, it is important to bear in mind that collective action can assume a wide variety of forms, not all of which involve centralized action by government. Some communities are able to avoid the depletion of common resources without government involvement by using informal and private means to discourage overuse. These may include efforts to discourage outsiders from using the commons, see, e.g., To Protect Resources, Many Communities Use Informal Regulations, Wash. Post, July 17, 1989, at A2 (noting that lobster trappers avoid depletion of the lobster stock by using surreptitious violence to keep outsiders away), or community norms that regulate its use by neighbors. See Ellickson, Of Coase and Cattle: Dispute Resolution Among Neighbors in Shasta County, 38 Stan. L. Rev. 623 (1986) (study of cattle grazing patterns). Natural resources also can be protected from environmental damage by privatizing them—by creating enforceable property rights owned by someone with an incentive to protect the resource. The Nature Conservancy, for example, has been enormously successful in buying environmentally significant properties in order to preserve them.

Informal, community-based controls are most likely to protect common resources where such resources are concentrated in a small area and there is strong community support for limiting exploitation. If entry into the commons is difficult to control or community support is lacking, informal controls are unlikely to work. See, e.g., Ingrassia, Overfishing Threatens to Wipe Out Species and Crush Industry, Wall St. J., July 16, 1991, at A1 (failure of informal controls to halt the depletion of fish stocks in the North Atlantic); Kerr, Geothermal Tragedy of the Commons, 253 Science 134 (July 12, 1991) (depletion of northern California geothermal resources). Privatization is more likely to succeed in protecting resources such as land (in which property rights can be easily defined) than in protecting the quality of air or water.

Thus, one should be cautious about drawing the simplistic conclusion that government regulation is always the appropriate response to the circumstances described by Hardin's "Tragedy of the Commons." One need not quarrel with the problem Hardin identifies—that truly unrestricted use of the commons will tend to deplete common resources—to appreciate the diversity of approaches, both governmental and nongovernmental, that can be used to combat it.

Kip Viscusi has identified four institutional mechanisms that may be used to control environmental risk: market forces, government regulation, liability, and social insurance. Viscusi, Toward a Diminished Role for Tort Liability: Social Insurance, Government Regulation, and Contemporary Risks to Health and Safety, 6 Yale J. on Reg. 65 (1989). These categories provide a useful framework for organizing our discussion of society's options for responding to environmental problems. Each of the institutions Viscusi identifies plays a role in environmental policy with varying emphasis depending on the nature of the problem to be addressed.

While most of the focus of environmental policy has been on government regulation, nonregulatory alternatives are becoming increasingly important complements to regulatory policy. Indeed, government now frequently uses regulation to enhance the effectiveness of the other institutional mechanisms for protecting the environment. For example, some regulatory legislation now requires information disclosure to harness the market power of informed consumers as a means to prevent environmental damage. Other regulations require that insurance be purchased by those engaging in activities that create environmental risk to ensure that the liability system can provide compensation for environmental damage. Thus, these four institutional mechanisms are best viewed not as discrete alternatives, but rather as part of a web of societal responses to environmental problems.

As illustrated in Figure 2.3, each of the four institutions has its own strengths and weaknesses as a vehicle for controlling environmental risks. Market forces can respond more quickly and flexibly than government regulation to discourage consumption of products that cause environmental damage, but markets are likely to be effective only when consumers are sufficiently well-informed about the link between a product and environmental damage to induce the marketing of less damaging substitutes. Unlike regulation, the liability system can provide compensation to victims of environmental damage. This provides an incentive for potentially liable parties to prevent harm, the goal regulation seeks to pursue more directly by requiring or prohibiting certain conduct. The effectiveness of the liability system, both in providing compensation and deterring harm, is limited by the financial capability of parties, which can be expanded through the purchase of insurance. The availability of insurance may tend to reduce the insured's incentives to prevent harm, though premiums priced to reflect differences in the riskiness of insured activity provide some incentive for investments in preventive measures.

When consumers are well-informed and free to choose, market forces can generate remarkably effective pressure to stop practices that cause environmental damage. For example, although the Marine Mammal Protection Act limits the number of dolphins that tuna fishers can kill each year, environmentalists had long complained that the law was poorly enforced, particularly on foreign boats. They launched a boycott of tuna that succeeded when a major seafood processor announced that it would no longer purchase tuna that had been captured using fishing practices that result in harm to dolphins. The company attributed the decision to lobbying by environmentalists, the two-year boycott, and an "almost theological" debate among its board of directors. Ramirez, "Epic Debate" Led to Heinz Tuna Plan, N.Y. Times, April 16, 1990, at D1.

In the absence of informed consumers, seafood processors who used "dolphin-safe" methods would be placed at a competitive disadvantage because it is more expensive to catch tuna using methods that avoid harm to dolphins who swim nearby. Indeed, the company that first announced the new policy stated that tuna prices may rise by 2 to 10 cents a can because of the higher costs of purchasing tuna caught using dolphin-safe methods. Because of their higher cost, companies could not be expected to employ dolphin-safe fishing methods in the absence of consumer pressure. The company that decided to adopt the dolphin-safe policy did so less than two months after consumer tracking surveys had shown a jump in awareness of the issue to 60 percent of

FIGURE 2.3
Comparison of Institutional Mechanisms for Controlling
Environmental Risks

Institutional mechanism	Advantages	Drawbacks
Market Forces	Can control risks rapidly and efficiently when consumers are well-informed and have a choice of alternatives	Inadequate incentives to generate and disclose accurate information to consumers; many risks not tradeable in markets due to absence of transferable property rights
Common Law Liability	Can provide compensation to victims of environmental damage; more efficient than regulation when private parties have better information than government about nature of risks and how to control them	Inadequate incentives to control risks due to difficulties of proving causal injury and recovering for harm that is widely dispersed or in excess of source's capacity to provide compensation
Government Regulation	Can efficiently prevent environmental harm by internalizing external costs of risky activity; can be used to respond to equity concerns by altering the distribution of risks and benefits; can be used to generate better information about risks	Does not provide compensation to victims of environmental damage; difficult to tailor regulation to take into account relevant differences within classes of regulatory targets; can be counterproductive in the absence of accurate information about the nature of risks and control options
Insurance	Helps ensure that compensation will be available for victims of environmental damage	Can reduce incentives to prevent environmental damage

consumers surveyed. The enormous influence of consumer preferences was demonstrated when, within hours of the announcement, the company's two leading competitors announced similar policies of purchasing only tuna caught using dolphin-safe methods. As a result, firms marketing more than 70 percent of the canned tuna sold in the United States have pledged to purchase only dolphin-safe tuna and are now labeling their products as dolphin-safe (see Figure 2.4).

Not everyone was enthusiastic about the tuna processors' decision. An editorial in the Wall Street Journal harshly criticized the companies and suggested that an antitrust investigation might be in order in light of "the instant consensus among competitors to offer more costly tuna." Protectionist the Dolphins, Wall St. J., April 17, 1990, at A22. The editorial implied that the companies' true motive was not to protect dolphins but to protect themselves against foreign competition. In 1991 an international tribunal ruled that a U.S. embargo on imports of non-dolphin-safe tuna imposed under the Marine Mammal Protection Act violated the General Agreement on Tariffs and Trade. Despite this ruling, pressure from U.S. consumers helped convince the government of Mexico to require its tuna fleet to implement some dolphin protection measures.

While consumer boycotts generally have a mixed record of success, consumer pressure occasionally can be very effective in changing corporate policies, particularly when it stems from a perception that a product threatens the health of consumers. For example, in 1989, apple sales plummeted after a national television report that apples treated with daminozide, or Alar, a fumigant used as a growth regulator, contained residues of a powerful carcinogen. For 17 years EPA had been concerned that Alar might break down into a carcinogenic substance, but it had not acted to suspend the product's registration under FIFRA pending the results of additional testing. Consumer reaction to the televised report caused such a devastating plunge in apple sales that growers pledged to discontinue use of Alar. The product quickly was withdrawn, and its registration was canceled by EPA without contest from the manufacturer. More recently, an environmental group helped convince the McDonald's Corporation to adopt fundamental changes in the packaging of its fast food products, replacing polystyrene packaging with paper.

FIGURE 2.4
Tuna Label Logo

Monitoring compliance with corporate pledges of voluntary action can be difficult when highly visible practices (like the packaging of hamburgers) are not involved. For example, during the Alar controversy, many apple vendors announced that they only purchased apples from growers who did not use Alar. Testing by Consumers Union, however, found Alar residues on a significant percentage of apples sold by such vendors. Some supermarket chains have announced that they will adopt strict standards for products making environmental claims in order to respond to consumer concerns about misleading advertising. They plan to hire an independent consulting firm to review the claims and award a "Green Seal" of approval to certain products. Smith, Four Store Chains to Set Strict Standards for Environmental Claims for Products, Wall St. J., April 13, 1990, at A2. Environmentalists recently have formed their own organization, called Green Seal Inc., to award seals of approval to "environmentally friendly" products. Smith, Group to Award Environmental Seals of Approval, Wall St. J., June 14, 1990, at B4.

Common law liability has been the principal alternative to government regulation for protecting the environment. Even the staunchest supporters of market mechanisms for controlling risk, who describe themselves as "free market environmentalists," emphasize the importance of liability standards for defending property rights against environmental insults. As discussed at the beginning of this chapter, the difficulties involved in proving a causal link between a particular action and damage to a particular plaintiff have limited the effectiveness of common law liability as a mechanism for controlling environmental risk. One strength of liability approaches is that they offer some prospect of compensating victims after damage is done, which the regulatory system does not. And the prospect of having to pay compensation can serve as a powerful deterrent to spur investment in efforts to prevent environmental harm.

Economists argue that the decision concerning the relative emphasis to place on liability and regulation is analogous to a choice between letting the market regulate the price of outputs and organizing a firm to control inputs into the production process. Liability rules establish the price of environmental damage (the output), while regulations seek to control the activities (inputs) that create such damage. While the former approach might seem more appealing to market enthusiasts, regulation of inputs is not as unusual as it might seem. Indeed, the very reason why firms are organized is that resort to markets has its own costs, and companies find it is cheaper to control inputs into the production process by resorting to a nonmarket substitute, the formation of firms. As Guido Calabresi explains:

> . . . neither market nor nonmarket forms of organization are primary; rather, they are two approaches which interrelate in oddly symmetrical ways as (a) people seek to find the most efficient (least costly) way of

structuring their relationships, and, given that both approaches exist, (b) people try to use the power (wealth or authority) which each approach gives them to accrue maximum benefits to themselves. [Calabresi, The Pointlessness of Pareto: Carrying Coase Further, 100 Yale L.J. 1211 (1991).]

In some circumstances it is simply more efficient to resort to nonmarket mechanisms to achieve our goals. Of course, in the environmental area the choice is not really between free markets and government regulation. Instead, as Judge Richard Posner notes, "the choice is between two methods of public control, the common law system of privately enforced rights and the administrative system of direct public control." R. A. Posner, Economic Analysis of Law 271 (2d ed. 1977). The question of how to find the proper mix of liability and regulation is one of the fundamental challenges facing environmental policymakers.

Economist Steven Shavell argues that four factors should be considered in assessing the relative efficiency of liability and regulation as mechanisms for controlling risk. Shavell, Liability for Harm Versus Regulation of Safety, 13 J. Legal Stud. 357 (1984). The first is the relative knowledge of private parties and the public concerning the benefits of risky activities and the costs of reducing risks. Shavell argues that liability tends to be more efficient than regulation in controlling risk when a private actor is in a better position than the government to assess the risks of an activity and to determine the level of care to exercise. Regulation is favored when the government is in a better position than a private actor to assess risks and to determine what precautions to employ.

The second factor Shavell identifies is the capacity of private parties to provide compensation for the full amount of harm their actions produce. If an activity can cause more damage than the actor is capable of repaying, fear of liability will not provide sufficient incentive for private investment in an efficient level of precautions. Shavell's third consideration is the chance that some private parties will escape suit for the harm that they do. Parties unlikely to be held liable for harm they produce, such as those who cause harm that is widely dispersed or difficult to trace, will not have adequate incentive to reduce risks to an efficient level in the absence of regulation.

The fourth consideration Shavell identifies is the relative administrative costs of the tort system and of direct regulation. Despite complaints about the administrative costs of the tort system, Shavell notes that the liability system's administrative costs usually are incurred only if harm occurs, while the administrative costs of regulation are incurred regardless of the occurrence of harm. Applying these factors, Shavell suggests that it makes sense to emphasize regulation to prevent a variety of environmental harms where the government has a superior capability to assess risks and private parties are likely to escape liability for the harm caused by their actions.

We now turn to a contemporary case study that illustrates the range of choices available to policymakers in determining the relative emphases to place on liability and regulation in preventing environmental damage.

Case Study: Liability, Regulation, and the Prevention and Remediation of Oil Spills

Large oil spills, like the Santa Barbara Channel blowout in 1969 and the *Exxon Valdez* spill two decades later, generate considerable public outrage. Yet few realize that more than 6,000 oil spills occur every year in amounts large enough to be reported to the U.S. Coast Guard. The total amount of oil spilled in U.S. waters in some years equals or exceeds the more than 10 million gallons spilled by the *Exxon Valdez*.

For decades liability for oil spills in U.S. waters was governed by a confusing patchwork of laws including five federal laws, three international conventions, three private international agreements, and dozens of state laws. The federal laws and international agreements were designed largely to limit the liability of shipowners in the event of a major spill, with the precise liability limits depending on where the oil came from (e.g., the Trans-Alaska Pipeline Act) or where it was spilled (e.g., the Deepwater Port Act, the Outer Continental Shelf Lands Act). The most extreme of these acts, the aptly named Limitation of Liability Act of 1851, limited liability to the value of the vessel after the casualty occurred. Courts strained to interpret this pre-Civil War relic expansively because of its potentially extreme consequences. For example, in the case of the wreck of the *Torrey Canyon*, which spilled 100,000 tons of crude oil into the English Channel in 1976, liability would be just $50—the value of the sole lifeboat that survived the wreck.

Proposals to rationalize this patchwork of oil spill laws were bottled up in Congress for nearly two decades. This legislative gridlock finally was overcome only after the *Exxon Valdez* disaster. Consider the issues that confronted Congress in determining what mix of liability and regulation to impose when it enacted the Oil Pollution Prevention, Response, Liability, and Compensation Act of 1990 (OPA 90), 104 Stat. 484 (1990).

Question One: Who Should Be Held Liable for Oil Spills? Environmentalists argue that both shipowners and the oil companies that own the cargo should be held strictly liable for oil spills. If cargo owners are liable, oil companies will have a powerful incentive to avoid shipping their oil in "rust buckets" manned by untrained crews. (Because Exxon happened to be the owner of the *Exxon Valdez*, this would not have made any difference with respect to liability for that spill). Oil companies argue vigorously that only the owners and operators of vessels should be held strictly liable for spills. The oil companies maintain that holding cargo owners liable for oil spills would be akin to making persons who ship something by Federal Express responsible for damages in the event a Federal Express cargo plane crashed. With whom do you agree? Is the Federal Express analogy an apt one? Should the nature of the cargo make any difference?

During the debate leading to enactment of OPA 90, the Royal Dutch/Shell Group announced that it would stop using its own tankers to carry oil to the United States except for an offshore terminal near Louisiana. The company explained that it took this move because a "shipowner who is involved in a pollution incident in the U.S.A., even when he has behaved properly, responsibly and without negligence, may face claims which far outweigh the potential commercial reward from such trade." Wald, Oil Companies Rethink Risk of Having Tankers, N.Y. Times, June 13, 1990, at A26. Does this reinforce the case for extending liability to cargo owners? By contrast, Arco Marine, a subsidiary of Atlantic Richfield, announced that it will ship oil only in its own ships. "We think we have better control that way, and therefore, have some control over the liability," explained Jerry Aspland, president of Arco Marine. Id. Which decision is more likely to expose the company to liability—Royal Dutch/Shell's or Arco Marine's? Which decision is likely to reduce the chances that the company's oil would be involved in a spill?

Question Two: Should Liability Be Limited?   Liability limits, such as that embodied in the Limitation of Liability Act of 1851, were designed originally to facilitate the rapid development of shipping trade by reducing the risks facing shipping companies. Critics argue that liability limits unfairly subsidize giant oil companies by relieving them of responsibility for paying the full costs of the environmental damage they have wrought. They maintain that the liability limits that existed prior to enactment of OPA 90 were absurdly low in light of the enormous damage that can be done by a large oil spill. For example, section 311 of the Clean Water Act, 33 U.S.C. §1321, limited liability to $150 per gross ton per vessel, which would have limited the liability of the *Exxon Valdez* to between $15 and $31 million for a spill that cost billions to clean up. (The Act makes liability unlimited if the spill results from "willful negligence.")

Oil companies argue that unlimited liability creates an uninsurable risk that makes doing business extremely risky. Noting that the cost of the *Valdez* cleanup could come to between 3 and 4 billion dollars, which is more than the net worth of many oil companies, the president of the American Petroleum Institute asks, "Could you afford to risk your whole company every time you move a ship?" Wald, Oil Companies Rethink Risk of Having Tankers, N.Y. Times, June 13, 1990, at A26. Is there any justification for a liability cap? If so, at what level should the cap be set?

Question Three: Should State Oil Spill Liability Laws Be Preempted? At the time OPA 90 was enacted, two dozen states had their own oil spill liability laws, including 19 coastal states with laws that provide for unlimited liability. Disagreement over whether Congress should preempt these laws was largely responsible for the legislative gridlock that blocked enactment of new oil spill liability legislation for nearly two decades. The oil industry and the Bush Administration argued that the United States should join the most recent international protocol, which would limit a shipowner's liability to $61 million and preempt state laws providing for greater liability. The administration argued that foreign shippers would simply stop shipping to U.S. ports if state laws providing for unlimited liability were not preempted. (Five international and two domestic shipping companies announced during the debate over OPA 90 that they would no longer ship oil to ports in states with unlimited liability laws.) Opponents of preemption, led by Senate Majority Leader George Mitchell of Maine, argued that states should be free to impose higher standards of care and that adoption of the international liability limits would unfairly transfer the costs of spills from the polluters to the taxpayers. Lippman, Oil Spill Bill: Mitchell Prevails Over Shippers, Wash. Post, July 24, 1990, at A4. Opponents of preemption argue that the shippers are bluffing, noting that oil had been shipped for years to states with unlimited liability laws. Proponents of preemption respond that the *Exxon Valdez* spill has changed everything because now shippers realize that cleanup costs from a single spill could be several billion dollars. Should state laws providing for unlimited liability be preempted?

Question Four: What Role Should Regulation Play in Prevention of Oil Spills? Liability is a crude instrument for affecting behavior; by itself it cannot ensure that the appropriate amount of care is exercised in all circumstances. Regulation can avoid damage that liability alone will not deter. As Steven Shavell notes, regulation is more efficient than liability for preventing accidents caused by those likely to escape responsibility for their actions. This factor usually weighs in favor of regulation as a means for deterring environmental damage because of the difficulty of proving causation under the common law. Large oil spills are another matter, however, because their causes are difficult to conceal, although assessments of the damage that they wreak are difficult. Professor Shavell notes that regulation is more efficient than liability for deterring accidents that cause more damage than responsible parties are capable of repaying. Except in circumstances where major multinational oil companies are the responsible parties, large oil spills certainly are capable of causing damage that exceeds the capacity of private parties to provide compensation. Indeed, arguments in favor of limited liability are premised on the notion that spills may be so expensive to clean up that it will be impossible to get adequate insurance to pay the full costs of a spill. In these circumstances, what regulations, if any, should be imposed to prevent oil spills or to minimize the damage they cause? From an economist's perspective, regulation should be used to stimulate investment in safety to the point where further investment would cost more than the reduction in damage it would produce. See, e.g., Stigler, What an Oil Spill Is Worth, Wall St. J., April 17, 1990, at A22. How would you apply this principle to regulations designed to prevent oil spills?

Congress previously had directed the Secretary of Transportation to consider whether or not to require oil tankers operating in U.S. waters to have double hulls. The oil and shipping industries had fiercely resisted a double hull requirement, and no action was taken to impose one. Proponents of a double hull requirement argue that had the *Exxon Valdez* been equipped with a double hull, far less oil would have been spilled. Shipowners argue that the cost of outfitting ships with double hulls would be prohibitive, particularly if existing ships have to be retrofitted with them. Understandably more enthusiastic, the Shipbuilders Council of America claims that double bottoms could be added to the entire existing American fleet for less than $2 billion, less than the amount Exxon already has spent cleaning up the Alaskan spill, although they admit that retrofitting all ships with double hulls would be far more expensive. Lowey, In '88, 6 Oil Spills Every 7 Days, N.Y. Times, June 22, 1990, at A27. In the wake of the *Valdez* spill, one major oil company stunned the industry by announcing that it was ordering double hulls for all its new tankers. Should double hulls be required? If so, should they be required only on new ships, or should existing ships be retrofitted?

Congress ultimately addressed these issues when it enacted OPA 90, whose provisions are outlined below, after a long and bitter legislative struggle. Compare your ideas on these issues with the resolution reached by Congress.

PROVISIONS OF THE OIL POLLUTION PREVENTION, RESPONSE, LIABILITY, AND COMPENSATION ACT OF 1990

Parties Liable. OPA 90 makes owners and operators of vessels or facilities that discharge oil strictly liable for cleanup costs and damages caused by such discharges. Owners of oil carried in bulk are made partially liable for amounts not otherwise recovered.

Limitation of Liability. OPA 90 increases the federal liability limit to $1,200 per gross ton, an eight-fold increase over the cap formerly provided in section 311 of the Clean Water Act. OPA 90 also creates a new $1 billion compensation fund, funded by a five-cent-per-barrel tax on oil, to pay for cleanup costs that exceed the liability limit. The entire $1 billion fund can be paid out for a single spill, with up to $500 million available for payments for damage to natural resources. Section 311 of the Clean Water Act formerly had authorized a $35 million compensation fund, but the fund contained only $4 million at the time of the *Exxon Valdez* spill.

State Liability Laws. OPA 90 does *not* preempt state laws that provide for unlimited liability for oil spills.

Regulations to Prevent Oil Spills. Congress ultimately opted to impose a double hull requirement on virtually all oil tankers operating in U.S. waters. For existing ships, the double hull requirement is to be phased in over the next 20 years on a schedule that varies based on tankers' size and age. The older and larger the ship, the sooner the requirement phases in. For example, beginning on January 1, 1995, single-hull tankers of at least 30,000 gross tons that are at least 28 years old would have to be retrofitted or retired, as would smaller tankers that are at least 40 years old. Barges of less than 5,000 tons operating on inland waterways and ships that transfer their oil to smaller ships more than 60 miles offshore are exempt from the requirements.

NOTES AND QUESTIONS

1. Judgments concerning the value of any regulatory scheme require thorough assessment of the real-world consequences of regulation. While careful studies of the impact of regulation are relatively new, the regulated community can be surprisingly innovative in developing strategies for avoiding regulatory requirements. "Avoidance behavior" by the targets of regulation can render regulatory strategies self-defeating or even counterproductive. Prominent examples of this phenomenon are discussed in Sunstein, Paradoxes of the Regulatory State, 57 U. Chi. L. Rev. 407 (1990). Is OPA 90 likely to engender such problems? For example, because OPA 90 increases the liability of shipowners, some oil companies may simply sell tankers they now own in order to avoid full

liability. One way to prevent such avoidance behavior is to broaden the coverage of regulations. For example, if OPA 90 had extended full liability to cargo owners, as the bill passed by the House would have done, oil companies could not have escaped full liability simply by selling their ships. Yet consider the following report about how some companies responded to the prospect that cargo owners would become liable:

> Shipping and oil executives are devising strategies to circumvent the biggest threat they face from new oil spill legislation—unlimited liability in case of an accident. Already at least one international oil company has been parking the title to some of its oil in transit with a willing outside party, a company controlled by fugitive oil trader Marc Rich in Switzerland. Refiners also are shunning legal ownership until the oil arrives at their plants, instead of accepting it in the seller's port as before. At the same time, some shippers are getting ready to subdivide their fleets into single-ship companies, each with minimal assets, to protect the rest of their operations from any one claim. . . . Shipping and oil-industry specialists predict that this continued possibility of open-ended claims under state laws will scare away legitimate companies unwilling to risk their assets each time they ship a load of oil to the U.S. Instead, tanker owners without the resources to cover cleanup costs or satisfy damage claims will be attracted to the trade, the experts contend. The likely results, they say, will be higher oil prices and more oil spills. [Sullivan, Oil Firms, Shippers Seek to Circumvent Laws Setting No Liability Limit for Spills, Wall St. J., July 26, 1990, at B1.]

How should regulators respond to this problem?

2. Because avoidance behavior by the regulated community may defeat the purposes of regulation, it is important that attempts to create exemptions or loopholes in regulatory schemes be scrutinized carefully. For example, one critical exemption from the double hull requirement under OPA 90 is that tankers will be exempt from the requirement if they transfer their oil to smaller ships at least 60 miles offshore. Yet many observers believe that this practice actually will result in more frequent oil spills during transfer operations.

The problem of avoidance behavior by the targets of environmental regulation is one that we will encounter frequently throughout this casebook. Indeed, a great many of the cases that have interpreted the environmental statutes arise in response to efforts by the regulated community to escape regulation under the statutes. When statutes and regulations are developed it is important to think about ways to deal with the problem of avoidance behavior. Perhaps this helps explain why interest is increasing in nonregulatory strategies to supplement environmental regulation.

3. Despite the increasing interest in nonregulatory strategies to increase the effectiveness of environmental controls, there is wide agree-

ment that some form of regulation is essential to prevent environmental degradation. We now turn to the question of what form that regulation should take. This has become a topic of considerable controversy in recent years as proponents of regulatory approaches that employ economic incentives harshly criticize approaches employing command-and-control regulation, which frequently are incorporated in the environmental laws.

2.   The Regulatory Options

Environmental law has become so complicated in recent years that the field is beginning to resemble tax law, where practitioners must be specialists in order to comprehend fully the meaning of regulations. Before examining any particular scheme of environmental regulation, it is useful to step back for a moment and try to identify some essential components of regulation, even if in highly idealized form, to provide a framework for comparing alternative options.

Figure 2.5 illustrates some of the essential elements of environmental regulation. Regulation usually is undertaken in response to a perception that a problem exists that requires a collective response. How societies become aware of problems and develop sufficient concern about them to initiate regulatory action is perhaps the most important, but most poorly understood, part of the process. Regulatory action often is initiated in response to highly visible incidents of harm or widely publicized problems. For example, in 1954, public concern over unidentified flying objects inspired the French village of Chateauneuf-du-Pape, well-known for its famous wine of the same name, to pass an ordinance prohibiting flying saucers from landing within the village limits.* While this ordinance apparently has achieved its goal—no flying saucers have landed in the village—there is considerable concern that regulation often is not directed to the problems most deserving of attention. This issue is considered in Chapter 5's discussion of the way environmental agencies set regulatory priorities.

Once it has been determined that a problem deserves some form of collective response, three important issues must be confronted: (1) What conduct or activity should be targeted for collective action? (2) On what basis should judgments be made about how that conduct should be altered? (3) What form of collective action should be employed in an

---

*This incident has been made famous by a California winery, Bonny Doon Vineyards, which has named one of its wines "Le Cigare Volant" (The Flying Cigar) because it is based on the traditional grape blend that comprises Chateauneuf-du-Pape.

FIGURE 2.5
The Components of Regulation

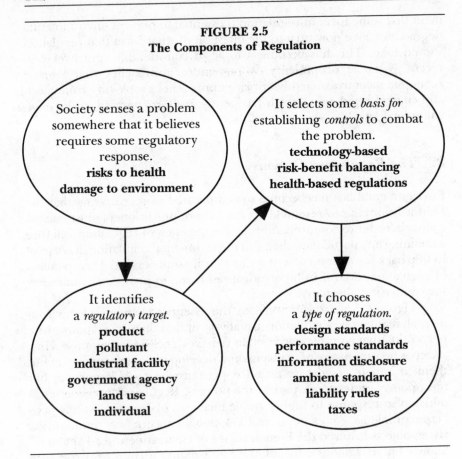

Society senses a problem somewhere that it believes requires some regulatory response.
risks to health
damage to environment

It selects some *basis for* establishing *controls* to combat the problem.
technology-based
risk-benefit balancing
health-based regulations

It identifies a *regulatory target.*
product
pollutant
industrial facility
government agency
land use
individual

It chooses a *type of regulation.*
design standards
performance standards
information disclosure
ambient standard
liability rules
taxes

effort to alter that conduct? These issues are not an exhaustive catalog of all the components of regulation, and decisions concerning them need not be made in any particular sequence. But the classifications can serve as a useful starting point for study of environmental regulation by isolating some of the major points of dispute over the strengths and weaknesses of various regulatory alternatives. Thus, for present purposes we can think of an environmental regulation as a government directive given to a particular *regulatory target* based on some finding (*basis for controls*) that prohibits or requires some type of action (depending on the *type of regulation* employed).

Regulation can assume many forms, and it can be implemented through a wide array of instrumentalities. To understand how environmental regulation works it is useful to outline the range of possible options for each of the three components of regulation identified above.

A. REGULATORY TARGETS

The environmental statutes generally define what activities (products, pollution, land uses) or entities (industrial facilities, individuals, government agencies) can be regulated. The categories listed below are all well-represented within the current universe of environmental regulation, as shown in Figure 2.6.

Products. Legislation aimed at products ranges from the very broad, such as the Toxic Substances Control Act (TSCA), under which EPA can regulate virtually any aspect of the life cycle of "any chemical substance or mixture" (manufacture, processing, distribution, use, or disposal); to the rather specific, such as the Federal Insecticide, Fungicide, and Rodenticide Act (FIFRA), governing just the substances mentioned in the Act's title; to the very specific, such as the Lead-Based Paint Poisoning Prevention Act or the provisions of TSCA directed at particular substances (e.g., asbestos or PCBs).

Pollutants. Virtually all damaging residuals from industrial, commercial, and some domestic activities fall within the jurisdiction of some federal environmental statute, although it also seems that regulation never quite covers the entire universe of residuals, as illustrated by periodic outcries when a heretofore unregulated substance or activity causes widely publicized environmental damage (e.g., accidental chemical releases, medical waste washing onto public beaches).

Industrial Facilities. Federal regulation targeted at industrial facilities is perhaps the best known, and seemingly the easiest, form of regulation to enforce, for facilities are fewer in number than individuals. Consider the difference, for example, between the EPA's requiring the automobile industry to install emission control devices at the factory and a regulation imposing no obligation on automobile manufacturers but requiring each car owner to install a comparable device. Industrial facilities may be a more attractive target for federal regulators because enforcement against them raises none of the federalism concerns that arise when the federal government tries to coerce state and local government into action. As environmental regulation becomes more comprehensive, small businesses more frequently are becoming regulatory targets (e.g., gas station owners whose underground storage tanks are now regulated by RCRA subtitle I, dry cleaners affected by both RCRA and the 1990 Clean Air Act Amendments).

Government Agencies. In many cases government entities are regulated because they own certain kinds of facilities that have become part of the pollution problem (e.g., public water supply systems, sewage treat-

FIGURE 2.6
The Principal Federal Environmental Laws Classified by Type of Statute and Regulatory Targets

1. Waste management and pollution control laws	*Regulatory targets*
Clean Air Act	Emissions of air pollutants
Clean Water Act	Discharges of pollutants into the navigable waters of the United States
Resource Conservation and Recovery Act	Generation, transportation, treatment, storage, and disposal of hazardous wastes
Comprehensive Environmental Response, Compensation and Liability Act	Liability for responses to releases of hazardous substances and damage to natural resources
Safe Drinking Water Act	Contaminants in public drinking water supplies, underground injection of hazardous wastes
Ocean Dumping Act	Ocean dumping of material
Surface Mining Control and Reclamation Act	Surface coal mining operations on nonfederal lands

2. Health and safety laws	*Regulatory targets*
Occupational Safety and Health Act	Workplace hazards
Toxic Substances Control Act	Manufacture, processing, use, or disposal of any chemical substance or mixture except for pesticides, tobacco, food, and drugs
Federal Insecticide, Fungicide, and Rodenticide Act	Distribution, sale, and use of pesticides
Emergency Planning and Community Right-to-Know Act	Storage and releases of hazardous substances by manufacturing industries
Hazardous Materials Transportation Act	Transportation of hazardous materials
Consumer Product Safety Act	Dangerous consumer products
→Food, Drug, and Cosmetic Act	Food additives, drugs, and cosmetics
Atomic Energy Act	Atomic materials

3. Resource management laws	*Regulatory targets*
National Environmental Policy Act	Major federal actions significantly affecting the environment
Endangered Species Act	Actions that threaten endangered species
Federal Land Management and Policy Act	Management of federal lands
Coastal Zone Management Act	Development in coastal zones
Outer Continental Shelf Lands Act	Leasing of outer continental shelf
Wild and Scenic Rivers Act	Wild and scenic rivers
Wilderness Act of 1964	Wilderness areas

ment plants, nuclear weapons production plants, schools with asbestos-containing materials). Regulations aimed at government *qua* government also have been an important component of the environmental laws from the enactment of NEPA, which required federal agencies to change their decisionmaking processes to incorporate environmental concerns, to the implementation of federal regulatory programs under the label of "cooperative federalism." A primary example of the latter is the process by which EPA establishes national ambient air quality standards under section 109 of the Clean Air Act, then passes to the states the job of implementing those standards under section 110 via specific regulations aimed at polluting facilities. One advantage Washington seeks to gain through such partnerships is the enlistment of state regulatory officials to augment the somewhat less ample supply of federal enforcement personnel.

Individuals. There are few extant examples of federal regulation of private individuals who are not doing business as firms. Among the important exceptions are federal prohibitions generally applicable to all persons, such as the ban on unpermitted dredging and filling of wetlands and the federal prohibition on the taking of endangered species. Regulation of individual conduct is less popular for both political and practical reasons. Early attempts by EPA to solve some of the air pollution problem by imposing transportation control plans on cities in ways that would directly affect individual driving habits were barred by Congress after vehement protests, and the nonpoint source control program of the Clean Water Act has been largely a silent (if not an entirely dead) letter in substantial part because land use controls require the regulation of many individual activities rather than a few centralized ones. Even when not directly regulated, individuals increasingly will be affected by regulations that change the availability or design of the products they buy (e.g., clean fuel requirements, prohibitions on the sale or use of lighter fluid in heavily polluted areas, programs to develop automobiles powered by unconventional means, and other steps taken to implement the 1990 Clean Air Act Amendments).

Land Uses. The major pieces of federal lands legislation establish rules governing the management of public lands. While most private land use decisions are regulated only at the local level, some of the federal environmental laws contain provisions that affect land use decisions, such as the Clean Water Act's requirements that permits be obtained before dredge-and-fill operations are conducted in wetlands and its provisions for areawide land use planning to address pollution from nonpoint sources.

The choice of regulatory target can be a crucial determinant of the success of a regulatory scheme. When it identifies regulatory targets, environmental law inevitably creates winners and losers in distributing the costs and benefits of regulation. This has important political and practical consequences. Politically powerful regulatory targets are more likely to be successful in lobbying against environmental regulation that will affect them. When such lobbying fails, the potential high costs of compliance give the regulated community powerful incentives to seek avenues of escape from the regulatory net. As a result, the implementation and enforcement of environmental regulation can affect in dramatic ways how regulatory targets are identified and defined. A program that seeks to regulate a few easily identified targets will be much easier to implement and to enforce than one that attempts to regulate numerous, poorly identified, or widely dispersed entities.

B.   BASES FOR CONTROLS

Although environmental regulations ultimately are aimed at improving environmental quality, the terms of each specific regulation are founded on methodologies that have different starting points, or bases. The environmental statutes employ three major approaches for determining how far to go in controlling a regulatory target.

Health (or Environment).   Some statutes direct that controls be established on the basis of what is required to achieve a goal stated exclusively in health- or environment-related terms. For example, the Clean Air Act instructs EPA to set ambient air quality standards at a level requisite to protect human health with an "adequate margin of safety." At least the first part of that instruction—requisite to protect human health—takes EPA on a search for a level of ambient air quality based on a medical assessment of the effects of air pollution on human health. In setting that level, EPA is not supposed to examine other issues that might be germane to setting a standard, such as how much it will cost to achieve that level of control or whether technology exists to do so. The Delaney Clauses of the federal Food, Drug, and Cosmetic Act also impose controls on a purely health-related basis by directing that no food or color additives be approved if they have been found to induce cancer in man or in animals.

Technology (or Feasibility).   Other statutes tie the ultimate regulatory standard to the capabilities of technology. These might be viewed as the opposite of health-based standards, because instead of asking what is needed to protect health they ask what it is possible to do. For example, under the Clean Air Act (CAA), EPA issues performance standards for new sources that are based on the best control technology that has been adequately demonstrated (CAA §111(a)(1)(C)). Other statutes employ a hybrid approach that directs that health be protected to the extent feasible. For example, the Occupational Safety and Health Act directs OSHA to ensure "to the extent feasible" that no worker "will suffer material impairment of health or functional capacity." Since it limits health-based regulation to what is feasible, this approach is best described as a feasibility-limited, health-based approach.

   Balancing.   While this category can capture a variety of values that may serve as bases for controls, they all share the common attribute of requiring some comparison of the gains of a proposed standard with its costs. For example, the Toxic Substances Control Act requires EPA to protect against "unreasonable risks" to be determined by balancing the environmental and health effects of chemicals against the economic consequences of regulation.

   Consider how the three bases for controls relate to one another. Figure 2.7 supplies a rough schematic representation that facilitates comparison of how each of the three options operate when used to control a pollutant that harms human health.

   The figure shows two graphs, the right-hand one of which has been flipped on its *y*-axis so that the two curves drawn can be shown intersecting. The line descending from left to right is the health curve. It indicates that the adverse health effects of pollution generally decline as emissions are reduced. The shape of the curve as drawn is suggestive

---

FIGURE 2.7
Bases for Controls: Health-Based, Technology-Based,
and Balancing Approaches

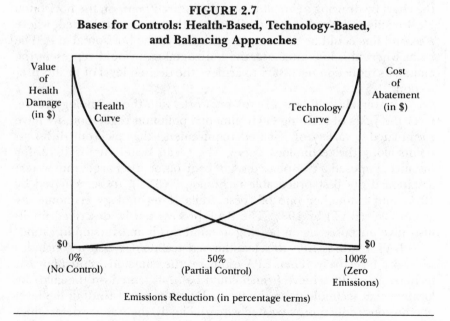

Emissions Reduction (in percentage terms)

only; many other configurations are possible. In the toxics field, one particular aspect of the curve as drawn is, however, salient: Current federal policy assumes that there is no safe level of exposure to most toxic air pollutants. Accordingly, you cannot get to zero health effects until you get to zero emissions.

In depictions of this kind, the line emanating from the left-hand origin, labeled "Technology," is frequently designated "Costs of Abatement." Costs, however, are determined by the underlying technologies available for abating, so it is fair to designate this the technology curve. Each point on this curve implies an underlying technology, which produces the stipulated pollution reduction at that (incremental) cost, but the same technology need not underlie each point. A rudimentary and inexpensive technology may suffice to eliminate 80 percent of emissions, for example, but after that point this becomes ineffective and another must be selected.

The health and technology curves are employed in health-based (H-based) and technology-based (T-based) regulation, respectively. H-based regulation is concerned with controlling emissions until a certain level of health-related safety is achieved—in other words, until a certain point along the left-hand y-axis has been reached. The process can be understood graphically as long as one understands this is an idealized simplification of the actual standard-setting procedures. An H-based regulator would first determine how much health protection is required (as represented by the desired point on the vertical axis), and then determine how to achieve it. This determination could be represented on the chart by drawing a line out from the desired point on the horizontal Health axis and parallel to it until the health curve is intersected, where a second line could be drawn perpendicular to the horizontal axis. The point where this line intersects the horizontal axis would represent the emissions reduction necessary to achieve the desired level of health protection.

Conversely, a T-based regulator works with the technology curve. Over the years of refining environmental pollution regulation, we have formulated a variety of T-based requirements that pick out different points along the technology curve. The Clean Water Act of 1972, for instance, imposed a two-phased set of controls on discharges into water: a standard of "best practicable technology" (BPT), to be achieved by 1977, and a tougher one of "best available technology economically achievable" (BAT) by 1983. The BAT process can be described for illustrative purposes, again bearing in mind this is an oversimplification.

BAT requires EPA to select the best technology that it concludes will work effectively. Then EPA estimates the emissions reduction that technology could achieve (which could be represented on the chart by locating that technology on the technology curve and finding the level of emissions reduction associated with it). Finally, the Agency determines whether bearing those costs is "economically achievable" by industry. If they are, the level of control corresponding to the chosen technology (represented, again, by extending a line through the correct point on the technology curve, perpendicular to the horizontal axis) becomes the regulatory standard; if not, EPA must proceed leftward along the technology curve until an economically achievable point is reached.

Other T-based regulations use the technology curve in different ways, but they all share the essential feature of ignoring the health curve, just as H-based regulations ignore the technology curve. In contrast, regulations based on balancing approaches are concerned with both curves, particularly where they intersect. The central idea behind balancing approaches is to determine, at least approximately, where to set emission controls so that any stricter control is not justified, because the costs of control are greater than the value of the health gains, and any more lenient controls are likewise unjustified, because the health losses would be greater than the savings in control costs. This point can be represented as the point where the two curves intersect.

In addition to depicting the three bases for controls graphically, Figure 2.7 suggests why there are only these three general categories. Pollution is a problem because it causes harm or creates a risk of harm. It is a hard problem because stopping it is expensive—were it easy and cheap to stop pollution, we would have done so long ago. So when some pollutant becomes a policy issue, the natural questions to ask are: (1) How much harm is it causing? and (2) What can be done about it? Logically, these two questions can have only one of three relationships: answers to the first can trump the second, in which case we have H-based regulation; answers to the second can trump the first, leading to T-based regulation; or the answers can be compared in some fashion and balanced against each other, leading to balancing approaches to regulation.

C.   TYPES OF REGULATION

Regulations must be expressed in directives that are specifically understandable by the regulatory target and enforceable by subsequent government intervention, if necessary. Among the major types of regulation (not all of them germane to all the categories of regulated activity) are:

Design Standards.   These specify how a certain plant, piece of machinery, or facility (such as a pollution control apparatus) should be designed and engineered. OSHA has written numerous design standards, such as the standard of 36 inches' clearance between library shelves in law libraries. EPA writes fewer design standards, although some of its performance standards become de facto design standards. This can occur when EPA's regulation is predicated on technology (see above). If EPA has written a regulation on the assumption that a particular technology exists whose performance can meet the regulation, a regulatory target may prudently decide its safest course to compliance is to install that technology. Then, should the target fail to comply, it can defend by attempting to place responsibility on EPA.

Performance Standards. These set an objective, or performance level, for the regulatory target to meet, without specifying how this should be done. EPA's new-source performance standards under the Clean Air Act and its various effluent limitations under the Clean Water Act are simply a few of the many environmental regulations that are nominally performance standards—but bear in mind that some of these routinely devolve into de facto design standards.

Ambient Standards. A very different type of performance standard than emissions limits, these play a significant enough role in regulatory decision-making to merit separate mention. These establish a level of environmental quality to be achieved or maintained in some environment, be it a lake or stream, an airshed or an underground aquifer. As such, ambient standards are incomplete, because they are not directed at a particular regulatory target. Typically, federal ambient standards are contained in legislation that instructs the states to achieve those levels within a certain time period, but without specifying how the states are to do this—this is why ambient standards can be viewed as performance standards (whose target is the states).

Emissions Limits. These are a kind of performance standard that specify the rate, amount, and kind of pollutants that may be emitted from a given source over a specific period of time.

Use Instructions (Including Prohibitions). These prohibit an activity or limit it to certain specified occasions or localities. They arise typically in connection with the regulation of products, such as pesticides or food additives, but they are also a land use strategy, as when the National Park Service bans autos in Yosemite National Park during certain times of the day or bans off-road vehicles from specified back roads or wilderness areas. In occupational settings, use instructions can be directed at workers.

Marketable Allowances. Economists have been longtime advocates of marketable allowances, which would permit companies to buy and sell emission rights in order to use market forces to ensure that pollution is reduced in the least costly manner. The 1990 Amendments to the Clean Air Act embrace this approach by providing that electric utilities will be issued tradeable allowances to emit sulfur dioxide. These allowances are based on the theory that companies that can reduce emissions most cheaply will do so and sell their allowances to companies for whom such reductions would be more expensive.

Taxes or Emissions Charges. Economists also have supported the use of environmental taxes or emissions charges as a means for internalizing the social costs of activities that damage public health or the environment. One of the earliest examples of the imposition of such a tax was the Esch Act of 1909, which imposed a tax on white phosphorus to induce manufacturers of matches to use a safer, but previously more expensive, substitute. Congress recently has become more enthusiastic about environmental taxes. After EPA mandated the phaseout of chlorofluorocarbons (CFCs), Congress in 1989 imposed an escalating tax on CFC production to accelerate both the phaseout of these ozone-depleting chemicals and the development of substitutes for them. Taxes used to fund environmental programs are occasionally based on the polluter-pays principle, to provide added incentive for emissions reductions. For example, the 1990 Clean Air Act Amendments seek to assist in defraying the cost of administering a new permit program by imposing an emissions charge of at least $25 per ton on sources needing permits.

Subsidies. Subsidies are the converse of taxes. Corporate investments that are beneficial to the environment can be encouraged by providing companies with public funds, tax breaks, or other benefits to subsidize such activity. In the past, government subsidies frequently promoted environmentally destructive activities. The elimination of government subsidies for activities such as the development of wetlands or logging on public lands can also be an effective means to promote environmental protection objectives.

Deposit-Refund Schemes. Combining elements of both taxes and subsidies, deposit-refund schemes impose a fee that later can be refunded when a product is returned for recycling or disposal in an environmentally responsible manner. Several states have enacted "bottle bills" that impose a deposit on beverage containers that is refunded when they are returned. Deposit-refund schemes help reduce litter. They also could serve as a disincentive for "midnight dumping" that taxes on waste disposal otherwise might encourage.

Liability Rules and Insurance Requirements. Some statutes strengthen common law rules imposing liability on those responsible for environmental damage. CERCLA imposes strict, joint, and several liability for environmental cleanup costs and natural resource damages. Regulations issued under other statutes seek to increase the effectiveness of liability rules by requiring that facilities seeking permits to handle hazardous materials have sufficient insurance or other resources to pay for potential damage caused by their activities. In return for limiting liability for nuclear accidents, the Price Anderson Act requires utilities to purchase $150 million of private insurance per reactor and to contribute to a second-tier federal compensation fund totaling $7 billion.

Planning or Analysis Requirements. Beginning with NEPA's directive that federal agencies prepare environmental impact statements, environmental regulation occasionally requires that certain information be gathered and analyzed or that certain plans be prepared prior to undertaking environmentally significant decisions. Efforts to encourage states to control nonpoint source pollution and to improve the management of nonhazardous solid waste have relied largely on requirements for more comprehensive planning.

Information Disclosure (Labeling) Requirements. These require the regulatory target to disseminate information. Their usual objective has been to inform persons of hazards they can avoid through proper conduct, such as wearing ear protection in noisy areas or avoiding foods containing sodium when on a low-sodium diet. Disclosure requirements may be subdivided into design and performance categories. Congress has specified the precise wording of cigarette warning labels (a design standard). California's Proposition 65 requires businesses employing toxic chemicals to give "clear and reasonable warning" to exposed individuals (a performance standard). Informational regulation now also is being used to generate public pressure for emissions reductions, as illustrated by the Emergency Planning and Community Right-to-Know Act's requirement that manufacturing facilities publicly report their annual releases of toxic substances.

The choice of what mix of controls to employ is likely to be influenced by the nature of the regulatory targets and the chosen basis for control. Some types of controls are better suited for certain regulatory targets and bases for control than are others. For example, information disclosure and labeling requirements are more likely to be effective when the regulatory target is a product that informed consumers can decline to purchase than when it is widely dispersed sources of air pollution. Statutes that require that controls be based on the capabilities of a certain level of technology may not leave much room for choice concerning the type of control to employ. While regulators can set performance standards that reflect the capabilities of a given level of technology, regulatory targets may choose to play it safe by simply installing the particular technology used to derive the standard. Unless regulators are extraordinarily prescient in determining appropriate levels of emissions charges

able to foresee

or environmental taxes, they cannot ensure that pollution will be limited to any specific level, such as that required by health-based standards.

Like the choice of regulatory targets, the choice of which type of control to impose will create winners and losers because it will not affect every member of the regulated community in the same way. By requiring companies to pay for emissions they previously could discharge for free, emissions charges may transfer wealth from polluters to regulators. Yet these same polluters may be winners under a marketable permit scheme because the scheme would allow them to sell rights to pollute that previously were not transferable. Advocates of marketable permits claim this is a virtue because it creates an incentive for emission reductions beyond the minimum that otherwise would be required by regulation. Opponents note that because the source of this incentive is the ability to transfer rights to pollute, aggregate levels of pollution will not be any lower and pollution actually may increase around facilities purchasing pollution rights.

Regulatory policy debates are often heated because of differences in values and the uneven manner in which alternative approaches to regulation distribute risks and benefits. Opponents of marketable permits express moral outrage at the notion that anyone could possess, much less be able to sell, such a thing as a "right to pollute." Proponents are equally outraged at the inefficiency of requiring the same level of pollution control regardless of cost differentials.

3. Criteria for Comparison

The choice of which regulatory strategy to employ is a matter for Congress. The environmental statutes generally identify regulatory targets by defining the jurisdictional reach of the authorities they delegate to agencies. Congress also usually specifies the bases for control and types of regulation agencies may employ to implement the environmental laws. For example, when air pollution became politically salient, Congress chose to regulate by establishing *health-based performance standards,* the national, uniform ambient air standards (see sections 108 and 109 of the Clean Air Act), through an instruction *targeted at the states,* instructing each state to develop a plan outlining how it would achieve those standards. When it enacted the Clean Water Act, Congress required EPA to impose *technology-based effluent standards* targeted directly at the *industrial facilities* that discharge pollutants into surface waters.

Dissatisfaction with the performance of executive agencies in implementing the environmental laws has encouraged Congress to write regulatory legislation with increasing specificity. Congress now often specifies deadlines for implementing action by agencies, and occasionally it spells out precise regulatory consequences should an agency fail to meet a deadline. For example, the 1984 amendments to the Resource Conservation and Recovery Act (RCRA) provided that the land disposal of broad classes of hazardous wastes would be banned automatically after certain deadlines unless EPA specified levels of treatment that would render such disposal safe.

Despite the increasing specificity with which Congress writes the environmental statutes, executive agencies inevitably have considerable discretion in defining the precise contours of the regulatory strategy used to implement statutory commands. Thus, both legislators and executive officials face important choices in choosing among the available regulatory options. Given the high stakes of these choices (for both the regulated community and the environment) and the rich mix of available options, it is not suprising that assessments of regulatory alternatives can be highly controversial. Indeed, dissatisfaction with existing regulatory strategies has ignited a lively debate between proponents of approaches that rely on economic incentives and defenders of the traditional command-and-control approach. Before exploring this debate, it is important to identify the various criteria available for assessing regulatory options.

Many different criteria can be used to evaluate the merits of alternative regulatory strategies. Professor Thomas McGarity has identified six such criteria: (1) administrative feasibility, (2) survivability (under existing conditions of judicial and political review), (3) enforceability, (4) efficiency, (5) fairness and equity, and (6) ability to encourage technological advance. McGarity, Media-Quality, Technology, and Cost-Benefit Balancing Strategies for Health and Environmental Regulation, 46 Law & Contemp. Probs. 159 (Summer 1983). McGarity found that each regulatory strategy scores high under some of these six criteria but not under others. As a result, one's view of the relative merits of health-based, technology-based, and balancing approaches to setting regulatory standards may depend heavily on the relative importance one attaches to each criterion. For example, because efficiency is enormously important to most economists, they are harshly critical of command-and-control regulations that generally do not vary regulatory standards to take into account differences in compliance costs. Proponents of command-and-control regulation may recognize its inefficiency, but believe that it scores high on administrative simplicity, enforceability, and equity, which they may view as more important values than efficiency.

One way to appreciate the diverse values implicated by efforts to evaluate regulatory alternatives is to work through a problem. The following is an admittedly oversimplified problem designed to illustrate how these issues arise in a specific factual context.

PROBLEM EXERCISE: SELECTING AN AIR POLLUTION CONTROL STRATEGY

Assume that you work for a U.S. consulting firm that has been asked by the leaders of one of the new regimes in Eastern Europe to advise them concerning what environmental laws to establish. No air pollution control legislation has yet been enacted. The new government wants to know what kind of national strategy to employ to control the air pollution that became very serious under the country's former communist leadership.

To keep matters simple, the Problem asks you to focus on only one airborne pollutant, which we will call "scary stuff," and one source of that pollutant. Let us suppose that the source of the pollutant is two factories, one in an urban setting, the other in a rural setting. Both are owned by the same company, one of the new private enterprises that purchased assets formerly owned by the government. The factories are the same size, each emitting 60 tons of scary stuff per hour and each operating approximately 2,000 hours per year. In the urban setting, 750,000 people live within a 25-km radius of the factory, while in the rural setting 1,000 people live within such a radius. The pollutant is sufficiently heavy that we assume virtually all of it falls to earth within that radius under most meteorological conditions (although sufficiently high winds can carry it farther afield).

Four groups are involved in lobbying and advising the new government on the air pollution issue. As the facts unfold, consider the various questions posed. From time to time, the questions ask you to react from the perspective of one or more of four interest groups. They are:

> NAP (Neighbors Against Pollution)—a group of environmentally aware citizens who all live within the 25-km radius of the urban factory, and many of whom live within 4 blocks of the factory's property line.
>
> GORP (Group of Organized Rural People)—a smaller group of citizens who live within 25 km of the rural factory.
>
> POLLUTCO—the newly formed private corporation that owns and operates both facilities, which formerly had been owned by the communist government.
>
> STAFF—the staff of your consulting firm, which consists largely of former EPA employees who hope that your advice to the new government eventually will produce lucrative consulting contracts with whatever administrative bureaucracy is charged with implementing a new air pollution control law.

Act One: STAFF has been doing some preliminary investigations into the health effects associated with the scary stuff. So far, it has been determined that the pollutant has adverse effects on the respiratory system, especially for asthmatics. It also impairs the growth of wheat, corn, and alfalfa. At fairly high levels its causes severe neurological damage. It is also a suspected human carcinogen; because of this, medical ethical protocols preclude human experimentation that might produce more definitive information on its other health effects, including neurological effects.

Question One. The new government wants to enact legislation to regulate air pollution, but it also wants to encourage the development of private industry. On the basis of what you know about the scary stuff, which basis for control should the new law employ—a health-based, technology-based, or a balancing approach? Which approach do you think would be favored by NAP? By GORP? By POLLUTCO? Is there any additional information you would want to obtain before making a recommendation concerning which approach to employ?

Act Two: STAFF also has been considering the various strategies that might be employed to control the scary stuff. They have studied two pollutant control technologies. Technology One is currently in use at several facilities in the United States and Canada and has shown itself generally reliable until it is required to achieve greater than a 94 percent pollutant reduction, when the equipment becomes increasingly unreliable. When Technology One is out of operation, the entire factory must shut down. STAFF has used industry-supplied figures to produce a table of pollutant reduction costs (see the chart below).

TECHNOLOGY ONE		TECHNOLOGY TWO	
At this level of pollution removal	*The cost for each ton of pollutant removed is (in thousands of dollars)***	*At this level of pollution removal*	*The cost for each ton of pollutant removed is (in thousands of dollars)***
70%	4	70%	50
75	5	75	50
80	8	80	45
85	12	85	40
90	17	90	40
95	32	95	45
96	*	96	45
97	*	97	45
98	*	98	45
99	*	99	45
99.5	*	99.5	60
99.9	*	99.9	120

*Costs are not displayed for levels above 95 percent for Technology One because it becomes too unreliable above that level.

**These are average cost figures, not marginal cost figures. They are expressed as the net present value of all future costs including amortized capital costs and repair and maintenance costs over the life of the technology. To obtain total costs at each level, calculate how many total tons of pollutant are being removed and multiply by the number in this column. You may assume that the plants are in operation 2,000 hours per year.

Technology Two is a newer, more experimental design, and it is much more capital-intensive than Technology One. It has not been installed in any full-scale facility in the country, but a couple of 1/10 scale model experiments have been conducted. Although the technology eventually failed in each of these tests, each failure appeared attributable to a specific malfunction that engineers think they can correct. STAFF has used engineering studies and its own projections to produce an estimated table of pollutant reduction costs for Technology Two. (Notice that Technology Two is so capital-intensive that it actually costs more to operate per pound of pollutant removed when operating at low removal figures. See the chart.) The only way to eliminate pollution entirely is to close both plants.

Question Two.   On these facts, should STAFF recommend that the government favor a technology-based standard or a health-based standard? Or would you favor not regulating at all until still more information is available? If you favor waiting for more information, what information do you want to have, and how would you use it? How would NAP, GORP, and POLLUTCO answer the same questions?

Question Three.   Assume you conclude that a technology-based standard is called for here. Recall that under that approach, you are not to prescribe a technology that industry must use, but instead must identify a level of pollution reduction that industry must achieve based on the technology that you determine to be the "best," or the "best practicable," or the "best available." (These qualifiers are not synonymous.) Why, do you think, are technology-based standards typically written in that way? From the perspective of POLLUTCO, might you prefer the government simply to name a specific technology that you must employ? Why? What impact, if any, would this have on incentives for the development of new pollution control technologies?

Question Four.   Assume the government instructs you that it wants to use a "best practicable technology" standard. Which technology, One or Two, would you recommend that it use as the basis of the technology-based standard, and what specific level of pollution reduction would you recommend? You might think about the following observation by Professor McGarity:

> EPA's technology-based standards have taken a terrible beating in the courts of appeals. The agency's initial effort in the mid-1970's to promulgate national technology-based effluent limitations for new and existing sources under the Clean Water Act precipitated more than 250 court challenges. After many of these cases were consolidated, the courts of appeals across the country decided sixteen appeals, all but three of which resulted in remands to the agency on one or more substantive issues. . . .
> The agency has been most successful when it can point to an existing source which currently meets its proposed effluent limitation. Similarly, when the EPA can point to an existing pilot plant that can meet its proposed limitation, the agency can usually survive judicial review. However, when

the EPA cannot point to an exemplary or pilot plant in the same industrial category or subcategory and therefore relies upon its prediction that an existing treatment technology will transfer from one industry to another, the courts are more skeptical, and the agency usually loses. In the rare cases in which the EPA has gone beyond existing technology to project that the industry will be able to develop a technology capable of meeting the prescribed effluent limitations at some future date, the EPA has lost two out of three appeals. [McGarity, Media-Quality, Technology and Cost-Benefit Balancing Strategies for Health and Environmental Regulation, 46 Law & Contemp. Probs. 159, 212-213 (1983).]

While our hypothetical country has no tradition of judicial review comparable to that in the United States, the government has indicated that it wants to do everything it can to encourage foreign investment. How, if at all, would this influence your recommendation?

Act Three: After thinking it over, the government decides that it does not want to turn to technology-based standards except as a last resort. It tells you to have STAFF develop some risk assessment information before making further recommendations concerning the regulatory options.

Dutifully, STAFF engages in a risk assessment.* Concurrently, they commission additional laboratory research on the carcinogenicity of the scary stuff and some meteorological modeling of the dispersion of this pollutant from factories the same size as POLLUTCO's. They have decided to ignore the respiratory effects and the neurological effects of the pollutant because at low levels they seem much less significant than the cancer-related risks.

STAFF returns with some preliminary estimates. They have been able to make some calculations of exposures based on some very simplified assumptions. First, for various emission levels they have estimated the exposure of a person living at either of the factory boundary lines, 24 hours a day, for a 70-year life span. (In regulatory parlance, this is the so-called Maximum Exposed Individual, or MEI.) Second, they have

---

*Risk assessment concepts are introduced in Chapter 4. Students who are interested in learning more about how risk assessments are performed may wish to preview some of that material there. For now, however, all that you need to know about risk assessment is that it is the process of assessing and characterizing the nature and magnitude of risk posed by a particular substance. Quantitative risk assessments can express risk in terms of either individual risk (chances of any one individual's experiencing the harmful effect, e.g., chances of 1 in 100,000 that an individual exposed to the substance for a lifetime of 70 years would get cancer) or population risk (total number of individuals predicted to experience the harmful effect, calculated by multiplying the individual risk number by the number of people exposed, e.g., if one million people are exposed to a risk of cancer of 1 in 100,000, then the population risk would be ten cases of cancer).

estimated the average exposure over the entire area within a 25-km radius of the plant. Then they have taken those exposure figures, combined them with the low-dose response projections derived from one of the available dose response models, and produced estimates of the increased risk to the MEI as well as the average increased risk for people living within 25 km of the plant. The following table summarizes their estimates.

Emissions from plant (in tons/year)	Cancer risk for MEI	Average cancer risk
120,000 (No control)	.0002 (1 in 5,000)	.00002 (1 in 50,000)
6,000 (95% Removal)	.0001 (1 in 10,000)	.00001 (1 in 100,000)
600 (99.5% Removal)	.00005 (1 in 20,000)	.000005 (1 in 200,000)
120 (99.9% Removal)	.000025 (1 in 40,000)	.0000025 (1 in 400,000)

Question Five. A health-based regulatory approach seeks to control pollutant emissions until some desired low level of risk is reached. A risk-balancing approach would balance risk reduction benefits against costs. As STAFF, which approach would you recommend to the government? If you choose a risk-balancing approach, what level of pollution reduction would you recommend? If you choose a health-based approach, do you establish the desired low level of risk on the basis of cancer risk to the MEI or average cancer risk?

Question Six. From the position of NAP and GORP, which regulatory approach do you favor? Will a risk-balancing approach seem as attractive to GORP as it does to NAP?

Question Seven. Recall Professor McGarity's six criteria for assessing the value of different approaches to regulation: efficiency, administrative feasibility, survivability (under existing conditions of judicial and political review), enforceability, fairness and equity, and ability to encourage technological advance. With the scary stuff example as your point of reference, how would you assess each of the three principal approaches to regulation under each of these criteria?

A. UNCERTAINTY, FLEXIBILITY, AND COMPLEXITY

The difficulties involved in formulating regulatory policy take a quantum leap when one's focus is expanded beyond a single pollutant or a single source to encompass the design of national regulatory programs. In addition to enormous uncertainties concerning the sources and impacts of various pollutants, regulators confront a fundamental dilemma between flexibility and complexity in regulatory design. How can a national regulatory scheme be sufficiently flexible to take into account the differential impacts of different pollutants and the diversity of circumstances among firms in the regulated industry without being so complex as to be administratively unworkable?

The tension between regulators' desire for flexibility and their aversion to complexity is reflected in much of the debate over regulatory policy. It has particular significance in the context of environmental regulation, which must confront a vast universe of sources discharging a myriad of pollutants whose impacts are difficult to assess with precision. As Eugene Bardach and Robert Kagan explain: "The difficulty of the regulatory task—and hence the degree to which the agency risks being accused of ineffectiveness or unreasonableness—increases to the extent that the harms to be prevented are of uncertain degree or origin, and secondly, to the extent that the regulated enterprises to be controlled are diverse (in technology, cooperativeness, and ability to afford compliance)." E. Bardach and R. Kagan, Social Regulation: Strategies for Reform 11 (1982).

Given the pervasive uncertainty that surrounds environmental problems and the enormous diversity of regulatory targets encompassed by the environmental laws, the task confronting regulators is indeed a difficult one. The legal system seeks to formulate general rules to be applied to certain classes of activities and enterprises. Yet the diversity of regulatory targets implies that it will be virtually impossible to design regulations that take into account relevant differences between individual targets. This has important consequences for enforcement policy as well. As Bardach and Kagan note, the ultimate goal of many regulatory programs "is to induce a general attitude of 'social responsibility' whereby plant managers . . . are continually alert and sensitive to all of the diverse harmful acts that may result from their technologies and their employees' activities." Id. at 13. Yet because regulations have to focus on objective measures that often are not very good proxies for the underlying attitude of carefulness they seek to promote, they may have difficulty achieving their intended goals.

There are several strategies available for adjusting regulations to account for the diversity of regulated entities. Consider the following possibilities. Uniform regulations can be issued with a procedure for granting variances. Regulations can be designed to apply to a smaller class of activities or entities that have similar characteristics. Or regulations can rely on case-by-case decision-making to permit consideration of individual circumstances. See T. J. Sullivan, Tailoring Government Response to Diversity, in id. at 120. While case-by-case review can be valuable if the number of regulatory targets is small, it is likely to prove extremely cumbersome if there are large numbers of regulated firms. Coping with uncertainties surrounding the sources and impacts of pollutants is even more difficult, as we will see in subsequent chapters. Each regulatory strategy places different informational demands on regulators, and each has its own practical and political consequences. It is important to keep these in mind when assessing alternative regulatory strategies.

Uniform, technology-based controls initially were thought to be easier to develop and monitor. Thus, it is not surprising that some form of nationally uniform, technology-based controls are an essential component of the Clean Air Act, the Clean Water Act, and RCRA. Risk-balancing and health- or media-based standards were thought to be more difficult to implement and administer because they require considerable information about health effects and economic impacts that are difficult to assess with precision.

A Case Study: Oil Spill Liability and Section 311 of the Clean Water Act

The regulatory tradeoff between flexibility and complexity is well illustrated by the history of federal regulation of discharges of oil spills and hazardous substances under section 311 of the Clean Water Act. This experience, on which the strict liability provisions of the Superfund legislation (CERCLA) are modeled, began in 1970 with the precursor of today's Clean Water Act. In 1970 Congress established a national policy that "there should be no discharges of oil or hazardous substances into or upon the navigable waters of the United States." As originally written, section 311 of this Act prohibited and required the reporting of all discharge of "harmful quantities" of oil. While this sounds like a relatively straightforward prohibition, it required the Secretary of the Interior, who at that time administered the statute, to determine what constituted "harmful quantities" of oil. Given the enormous uncertainties that surround assessments of the impact of pollutants on aquatic life, any regulation that required actual proof of harm would be extremely difficult to enforce. For small discharges of oil or hazardous substances, the costs of demonstrating harm surely would exceed any likely recovery. As a result, the Secretary of the Interior opted for a simpler, but less flexible, interpretation of section 311. He promulgated what came to be known as the "sheen test" for oil discharges. Under that test, any oil spill that caused "a film or sheen upon or discoloration of the surface of the water or adjoining shorelines" was deemed a harmful quantity prohibited by the statute.

The sheen test was challenged by dischargers, who argued that section 311 required evidence that small spills actually had caused harm. In United States v. Boyd, 491 F.2d 1163 (9th Cir. 1973), the Ninth Circuit held that the "harmful quantities" language in the statute meant that de minimis discharges were not illegal if they were not actually harmful. As a result, defendants charged with spilling oil could contest whether the discharges actually had caused harm. In a subsequent case, United

States v. Chevron Oil Co., 583 F.2d 1357 (5th Cir. 1978), the Fifth Circuit held that the sheen test was only a rebuttable presumption of harm to the environment. The court emphasized that Congress had not chosen to prohibit *all* discharges of oil, but rather only discharges in "harmful quantities." Under the Fifth Circuit's approach, defendants were free to contest whether their discharges had caused harm, but they bore the burden of showing that the discharge had not actually been harmful.

In 1978 Congress amended section 311 to provide that environmental officials could prohibit any discharge of oil or hazardous substances that they found "may be harmful to the public health or welfare of the United States." After extensively considering alternative approaches for determining what discharges may be harmful, EPA in 1987 again promulgated the sheen test. The sheen test again came under judicial scrutiny when challenged by defendants charged with releasing oil. After the Coast Guard assessed civil penalties ranging from $250 to $1,000 against Chevron for 12 discharges of oil that created oil sheens, the company successfully argued in court that the discharges were not illegal under section 311 because the impact of the spills on the ecosystem was de minimis at most. On appeal, the Fifth Circuit reversed. The court held that the 1978 amendments had authorized EPA to prohibit spills that "may be harmful" regardless of whether or not they caused actual harm. In holding that spills that violated the sheen test violated the statute regardless of whether or not they caused harm, the court explained that EPA could adopt a less flexible approach to regulation in order to avoid the administrative expense of a more complicated inquiry: "In sum, the agency may both proscribe incipient injury and measure its presence by a test that avoids elaborated inquiry. While it is apparent that such an approach sometimes overregulates, it is equally apparent that this imprecision is a trade-off for the administrative burden of case-by-case proceedings." Chevron U.S.A., Inc. v. Yost, 919 F.2d 27 (5th Cir. 1990).

NOTES AND QUESTIONS

1. Why do you suppose that Congress did not simply prohibit *all* discharges of oil in section 311? What was to be gained by prohibiting only discharges in harmful quantities? Does the use of the sheen test effectively sacrifice these ends by prohibiting even discharges that may not be harmful?

2. If you determined that only discharges of oil or hazardous substances that are harmful should be prohibited, who should bear the burden of proof concerning the impact of the discharge: the discharger

or enforcement officials? What effect is the allocation of the burden of proof likely to have on the enforceability of the prohibition?

3. Should it matter whether the discharger believed that the discharge would be harmful? Criminal prohibitions generally require some element of intentional conduct, though it need not necessarily be an intent to cause harm to the environment. By contrast, strict liability provisions impose liability without regard to fault. What impact would an intent requirement have on incentives to prevent discharges? What impact would a strict liability standard have on such incentives?

Uniformity versus Flexibility: The Case of Technology-Based Regulation

Observers of environmental regulation have reached divergent conclusions about the relative merits of technology-based and media-quality-based regulatory designs. Critics of technology-based approaches have emphasized their inefficiencies. For example, Bruce Ackerman and Richard Stewart argue that experience with best available technology (BAT) controls has demonstrated the following:

1. Uniform BAT requirements waste many billions of dollars annually by ignoring variations among plants and industries in the costs of reducing pollution and by ignoring geographic variations in pollution effects. A more cost-effective strategy of risk reduction could free up enormous resources for additional pollution reduction or for other purposes.

2. BAT controls, and the litigation that they provoke, impose disproportionate penalties on new products and processes. A BAT strategy typically imposes far more stringent controls on new sources because there is no risk of shutdown. Also, new plants and products must run the gauntlet of lengthy regulatory and legal proceedings to win approval; the resulting uncertainty and delay discourage new investment. By contrast, owners of existing products and processes can use the legal process to postpone or water down compliance requirements. Also, BAT strategies impose disproportionate burdens on more productive and profitable industries because they can "afford" more stringent controls. This "soak the rich" approach inhibits growth and international competitiveness.

3. BAT controls can ensure the diffusion of established control technologies. But they do not provide strong incentives for the development of new, environmentally superior strategies and may actually discourage their development. Such innovations are essential if we are to maintain economic growth in the long run without simultaneously increasing pollution and other forms of environmental degradation.

4. BAT involves centralized, uniform determination of complex scientific, engineering, and economic issues involving the feasibility of con-

trols on hundreds of thousands of pollution sources. Such determinations impose massive information-gathering burdens on administrators and provide fertile ground for litigation, producing reams of technical data, complex adversary rulemaking proceedings, and protracted judicial review. Given the high cost of regulatory compliance and the potential gains from litigation brought to defeat or delay regulatory requirements, it is often more cost effective for industry to invest in litigation than in compliance.

5. A BAT strategy is inconsistent with intelligent priority-setting. Simply regulating to the hilt whatever pollutants or problems happen to get on the regulatory agenda may preclude an agency from dealing adequately with other more serious problems that come to scientific attention later. The BAT strategy also tends to reinforce regulatory inertia. Foreseeing that "all or nothing" regulation of a given substance under BAT will involve very large administrative and compliance costs, and recognizing that resources are limited, agencies will seek to limit the number of substances on the agenda for regulatory action. Ackerman and Stewart, Reforming Environmental Law: The Democratic Case for Market Incentives, 13 Colum. J. Envtl. L. 171, 173-175 (1988).

Howard Latin argues that proposals for more flexible regulatory approaches are based on "an excessive preoccupation with theoretical efficiency" while "inadequate emphasis" is placed "on actual decision-making costs and implementation constraints." Latin, Ideal Versus Real Regulatory Efficiency: Implementation of Uniform Standards and "Fine-Tuning" Regulatory Reforms, 37 Stan. L. Rev. 1267, 1270 (1985). Latin contends that because "[a]ny system for environmental regulation must function despite the presence of pervasive uncertainty, high decision-making costs, and manipulative strategic behavior resulting from conflicting private and public interests," the "indisputable fact that uniform standards are inefficient does not prove that any other approach would necessarily perform better."

Latin stresses "numerous advantages of uniform standards in comparison with more particularized and flexible regulatory strategies." He argues that these advantages include

decreased information collection and evaluation costs, greater consistency and predictability of results, greater accessibility of decisions to public scrutiny and participation, increased likelihood that regulations will withstand judicial review, reduced opportunities for manipulative behavior by agencies in response to political or bureaucratic pressures, reduced opportunities for obstructive behavior by regulated parties, and decreased likelihood of social dislocation and "forum shopping" resulting from competitive disadvantages between geographical regions or between firms in regulated industries.

Latin also argues that proposed "fine-tuning" reforms actually would prove infeasible in many contexts and that the effectiveness of existing regulations often could be improved "by reducing even the degree of 'fine-tuning' that is currently attempted." Id. at 1271.

B. REGULATION, TECHNOLOGICAL INNOVATION, AND "TECHNOLOGY FORCING"

Our discussion so far has assumed that the balance of costs and benefits represents an inflexible trade-off: Greater environmental protection can only be achieved at the expense of greater costs. However, costs are not in fact fixed but reflect the technology available for pollution control. Improving technology can increase the level of reductions achievable *and* lower costs. Technological innovation that expands the menu, increases the capability, or reduces the cost of available pollution control technology is commonly viewed as a desirable goal. The impact of regulation on technological innovation and the potential for regulation to stimulate such innovation are crucial issues that must be considered in designing any regulatory scheme.

While using regulation to force the development of improved pollution control technology may sound like a new and radical concept, the old common law nuisance cases frequently had a technology-forcing flavor. The Supreme Court's injunction in Georgia v. Tennessee Copper Co. stimulated the development of improved pollution control technology by limiting the emissions of the Ducktown copper smelters to levels that could not be achieved using existing technology. Prior to issuance of the injunction, the companies that owned the smelters had little reason to search for methods to control their emissions of sulfur dioxide and other air pollutants, particularly after the Tennessee Supreme Court refused to enjoin their virtually uncontrolled emissions. Although the smelters' emissions were damaging surrounding property severely, the prospect of providing compensation to the owners of small tracts of nearby mountain lands estimated to be worth between $66 and $180 provided little reason to search for improved pollution control technology. However, after the Supreme Court ordered emissions reductions, the companies were forced to develop new technology to reduce their emissions.

Many of the other early common law cases reflect a concern for requiring companies at least to employ the best available technology for preventing environmental damage. For example, the injunction issued by the Supreme Court in New Jersey v. City of New York was designed to force New York City to build incinerators as an alternative to dumping garbage in the ocean off the New Jersey shore. Even though the slate mill in *Staso Milling* already had installed technology to control 99 percent of the dust it emitted, Judge Learned Hand affirmed an injunction prohibiting all emissions of dust from the mill. He told the company to try to do better, noting that they could later apply for a modification of the decree if they could demonstrate that "there are no better arresters extant, that it operates those it has at maximum efficiency," and that the mill's only alternative would be to shut down. 18 F.2d 737, 739. In DeBlois v. Blowers, 44 F.2d 621 (D. Mass. 1930), a major factor in the court's decision holding that emissions from a steel galvanizing plant were a nuisance was the conclusion that the company had not done everything reasonably practicable to prevent damage to its neighbors because it had not erected tall smokestacks. Courts often modified injunctions to give companies time to develop or install new technology to control their emissions. Arizona Copper Co. v. Gillespie, 230 U.S. 46 (1913) (trial court has the discretion to permit a temporary modification of an injunction to permit the company to experiment to determine if settling basins will adequately control discharges of tailings and slimes); Storley v. Armour & Co., 107 F.2d 499 (8th Cir. 1939) (order barring a meat packing plant from polluting a river stayed for one year to give the company time to find additional means to treat waste).

The common law cases and most technology-based regulation generally have involved efforts to require companies to employ a technology already in existence. Opponents of technology-based regulation argue that one of its most pernicious features is that it actually retards technological innovation by reducing incentives to develop better control measures. Judge Richard Posner notes that regulations that prescribe specific technologies to be employed by regulatory targets discourage the target from searching for the most efficient method of pollution control. He argues that technology-based regulation also encourages inefficient strategic behavior by the regulated industry:

> In the deliberations before the legislature or agency leading to the formulation of the standard, the affected industry has an incentive to propose the cheapest pollution-control method, regardless of its efficacy, and to deny the existence of any more costly devices (even if they are more efficient because of the amount of pollution eliminated). Once the specified measure is adopted, the industry has no incentive to develop better devices unless they happen also to be cheaper. Worse, the members of the industry have an incentive to collude to withhold from the legislature or agency information concerning the technical and economic feasibility of pollution control and even, as alleged in recent antitrust actions against the automobile manufacturers, to conspire to delay the development of pollution-control technology. [R. A. Posner, Economic Analysis of Law 279 (2d ed. 1977).]

Regulations that establish performance standards without specifying the technology to be used to meet them avoid some of these problems by preserving incentives for the development of improved pollution control technology. They do not, however, avoid the problem of strategic behavior by the regulated community during the time performance standards are under consideration. Regulatory targets have an incentive to exaggerate the costs of complying with proposed performance standards in an effort to convince regulators not to adopt them. As a result it is difficult to get accurate estimates from industry of prospective compliance costs. Once performance standards are adopted, the regulated community has an incentive to develop more efficient technology for achieving them, absent a belief that regulators can be convinced to relax the standards.

Experience with environmental regulation has demonstrated that industry estimates of prospective compliance costs prove to be far too pessimistic. EPA Assistant Administrator William G. Rosenberg notes: "Historically, actual costs are generally much lower than projections because of improved technology. For example, in 1971 the oil industry estimated that lead phase-out would cost 7 cents a gallon, or $7 billion a year. In 1990, with 99 percent of lead phaseout accomplished, actual costs are only $150 million to $500 million a year, 95 percent less than earlier estimates." Rosenberg, Clean Air Amendments, 251 Science 1546, 1547 (1991).

Environmental writings display some ambivalence toward technology. While industrialization is the cause of much environmental disruption, the innovation that has accompanied it has improved the technology available for combatting many environmental problems. See generally J. Ausubel and H. Sladovich, eds., Technology and the Environment (1989). A desire to influence the development of "appropriate technologies" is reflected in the National Environmental Policy Act, 42 U.S.C. §4331(b)(3), and the creation of the Office of Technology Assessment as an arm of Congress. See S. Novick, The Law of Environmental Protection §3.02(1).

Both the Clean Air Act and the Clean Water Act incorporated the concept of "technology forcing," the idea that laws could force industry to come up with innovative solutions by adopting standards more stringent than those attainable by then-available technology. Id. §3.02. "Technology forcing" is sometimes distinguished from "action forcing," the implication in the latter being that technology is available but not being widely used for economic or other reasons. The effluent limitations in the Clean Water Act, which are based on "best available technology economically achievable," are a good example of action-forcing standards. In interpreting this term, EPA focuses on the state of the art in an industry and occasionally looks to transfer technology used by other industries, but does not demand more than is in use by some facility. See LaPierre, Technology-Forcing and Federal Environmental Protection Statutes, 62 Iowa L. Rev. 771 (1977). The attraction of technology forcing is the opportunity it offers to eliminate, or at least ameliorate, the regulatory dilemma by achieving desired environmental goals while minimizing their economic cost.

The desirability of using regulation to induce the development of improved technology is widely accepted, as illustrated by the many technology-forcing provisions incorporated in the 1990 Clean Air Act Amendments. The debate now centers on how best to design regulations to stimulate improved technology.

Congress's initial approach to technology-forcing regulation was to engage automakers in a high-stakes game of chicken. Title II of the 1970 Clean Air Act mandated emission standards for automobiles that were "a function of the degree of control required, not the degree of technology available today." S. Rep. No. 91-1198, 91st Cong., 2d Sess. 24 (1970). The Act required automobile manufacturers to slash vehicle emissions by 90 percent in order to be able to continue selling cars in the United States after a specified deadline, subject to a one-year extension. Not surprisingly, the automobile manufacturers fought hard to convince EPA to extend the deadline on the ground that the necessary technology for reducing vehicle emissions was not yet available. After EPA Administrator William Ruckelshaus shocked the industry by refusing to extend the deadline, the auto industry convinced a court to order him to reconsider. International Harvester v. Ruckelshaus, 478 F.2d 615 (D.C. Cir. 1973). The following article describes some of the lessons of this experience as viewed from the perspective of the renewed debate over auto emission controls that occurred when the 1990 Clean Air Act Amendments were enacted.

Weisskopf, Auto Pollution Debate Has Ring of the Past
Wash. Post, Mar. 26, 1990, at A1

In 1967, when Dick Klimisch of General Motors Corp. began delving into the black art of "catalysis" as a possible cure for auto pollution, he attracted few believers.

Working in a tiny GM laboratory, Klimisch spent the next six years and $1 billion of GM's money to prove the skeptics wrong. Nicknamed "Captain Catalyst," he searched the periodic table until he found the right chemical combination to catalyze, or trigger, a reaction in the exhaust system of an automobile that rendered noxious emissions into harmless gases.

The "catalytic converter," encased in a stainless steel vessel and connected to the engine of virtually every new car since 1975, not only assured that the auto industry could comply with the ambitious tailpipe standards of the 1970 Clean Air Act. It also became the nation's most powerful weapon against urban smog—a signal contribution still trumpeted by Detroit as proof of its ingenuity and commitment to clean air.

But the history of catalytic converters reveals another side of Detroit. The industry refined the technology only after Congress imposed strict limits and deadlines and foreign car makers threatened to develop cleaner engines. It lobbied forcefully against passage of the standards in 1970, calling them unobtainable, disastrously expensive and environmentally unnecessary. It pressed its case right up to the date of installing the first catalytic converters, and even after the devices put millions of cars into compliance, it fought to have the standards relaxed for cars and not extended to trucks.

Now as Congress attempts to strengthen the Clean Air Act, Detroit's ability to take another big slice out of tailpipe pollution is a major issue. Once again, automakers and their powerful political sponsors in Washington insist that it is not feasible or necessary and that congressional dictates to do so would be financially ruinous. They say the catalytic converter has done just about everything it can do.

To critics, it is a familiar refrain from the industry capable of changing only when forced by statutory deadline.

"We have to look at industry's arguments in light of our past experiences," said Michael Walsh, former director of the Environmental Protection Agency's mobile source program. "Their public posture is always much more pessimistic than technical reality. No place is that more evident than with the catalytic converter." . . .

. . . [T]wenty years ago . . . Senator Edmund S. Muskie (D-Maine) was Congress's most influential voice on clean air. Impatient with earlier anti-smog efforts, Muskie decided to force the production of clean cars by setting standards based on the health needs of cities, not on Detroit's view of what was feasible.

His legislation, passed by Congress in 1970, called for 90 percent cuts in hydrocarbons and carbon monoxide by 1975 and the same for nitrogen oxides by 1976.

It was a few years earlier that the possibility of using catalytic converters as an anti-pollution device first attracted attention. The idea came from independent suppliers of the devices to oil refineries for use in transforming petroleum into high-octane gasoline. Why not use the same catalysts to neutralize the byproducts of gasoline burned in car engines?

Detroit was not receptive. The main problem was lead, then injected into gasoline to reduce engine knock and boost octane. Industry officials argued that lead would ruin the devices. Anyway, they argued, catalytic converters would never survive the jostling they would receive in cars.

Whether Detroit gave catalysts a fair hearing is open to dispute. In 1969, the automakers were charged with conspiring to delay the development of antipollution devices. The antitrust suit was settled later that year when the companies, without conceding wrongdoing, agreed to stop any illegalities.

At GM, meanwhile, interest in catalysts grew with the hiring in 1967 of Klimisch, then 28 and fresh from a job at E. I. DuPont de Nemours and Co. experimenting with cheaper ways of catalyzing petroleum molecules into synthetic fabric for women's underwear.

In two years, Klimisch found by trial and error that a catalyst containing precious metals—platinum and palladium—retains enough oxygen when exposed to the high temperatures of engine exhaust to convert hydrocarbons into water vapor and harmless carbon dioxide.

When the converter, then a vessel of ceramic beads coated in precious metals, survived an in-house road test of 50,000 miles, "We couldn't believe it," Klimisch recalled. "The conventional wisdom was that we'd never get it to last so long."

The breakthrough persuaded GM President Edward Cole to issue a historic and startling statement on January 15, 1970. Speaking to the Society of Automotive Engineers, he called on oil companies to take lead out of gasoline to facilitate the use of catalytic converters in cars. Throwing down the gauntlet, he announced that starting with 1971 models, all GM cars would be able to run on unleaded gasoline.

In Washington, however, GM joined Chrysler Corp. and Ford Motor Co. in opposing standards proposed by Muskie that seemed obtainable in Klimisch's lab. Lee A. Iacocca, then Ford's executive vice president, said in September 1970 that the limits "could prevent continued production of automobiles" and "do irreparable damage to the American economy."

Opposition persisted in the early 1970s as Detroit pleaded with the EPA to suspend the standards under a waiver clause in the 1970 law. By 1973, Chrysler President John J. Riccardo called the limits still "beyond the capability of known technology." His company attempted to muzzle an independent catalyst manufacturer from lobbying for the technology by threatening loss of Chrysler business, informed sources said.

And a GM official testified at a spring 1973 EPA hearing that forcing Detroit to install the devices in 1975 models would be technically and economically disastrous.

In May 1973, the EPA agreed to relax the standards for two years. But with catalytic converters proving to be a boon to fuel efficiency and performance, GM announced six weeks later that all of its 1975 models would be equipped with the devices. . . .

"I came out of the whole exercise with catalytic converters as a technological optimist in what the industry can do," said Walsh, the EPA's top auto pollution expert in the 1970s and now a private consultant. "When you give them a challenge, they meet it."

NOTES AND QUESTIONS

1. The courts played an important role in the auto emissions story. EPA initially refused to grant a waiver, expressing the conclusion that the requisite technology was available but might require "major changes in the kinds of automobiles produced for sale in the United States. . . ." EPA's decision was reversed in International Harvester Co. v. Ruckelshaus, 478 F.2d 615 (D.C. Cir. 1973). Noting that the effect of the standards could be to discourage consumer purchases of new cars and consequently prolong use of older, more polluting cars, the court concluded that the environmental costs of a one-year suspension were modest and had to be balanced against the potential economic and ecological risks of an erroneous judgment that the technology was sufficiently developed.

2. The auto emissions experience is one of several instances in which Congress refused to back down in the face of industry assertions that economic catastrophe was imminent; it is surprisingly difficult to find any evidence of serious adverse consequences in any of them. Easterbrook, Everything You Know About the Environment Is Wrong, New Republic, April 30, 1990, at 14. Technology has proved to be remarkably adaptable once regulation has created the proper incentives. The chemical industry publicly denied the availability of reasonable substitutes for chlorofluorocarbons (CFCs), chemicals that damage the ozone layer, until regulation became imminent after the discovery of the Antarctic ozone hole and the development of an international consensus that CFCs should be phased out. Since regulations were announced, substitutes have become available at a remarkable rate. Miller, Policy Responses to Global Warming, 14 So. Ill. L. Rev. 187 (1990). See also Ashford and Ayres, Using Regulation to Change the Market for Innovation, 9 Harv. Envtl. L. Rev. 419 (1985); Note, Technology Forcing: The Clean Air Act Experience, 88 Yale L.J. 1713 (1979) (copper smelter experience).

3. The economic and political risks are nevertheless such that Congress has only rarely chosen to threaten the shutdown of an entire industry should emissions standards prove unachievable. The issue is more often what form of regulation is most conducive to innovation. In particular, fixed emissions standards based on current assessments of technology are widely faulted for the absence of incentives for further innovation. An industry regulated by a "best available technology" standard may rightly question the benefits of research on new pollution control methods, knowing that the costs could increase. Moreover, once the required level of emissions reduction has been achieved, there is no remaining incentive for efforts to go still further. See Dudek and Palmisano, Emissions Trading: Why Is This Thoroughbred Hobbled?, 13 Colum. J. Envtl. L. 217, 234-236 (1988); F. Anderson et al., Environmental Improvement Through Economic Incentives 3 (1977); J. Bonine,

The Evolution of Technology-Forcing in the Clean Air Act, 6 Env. Rep. (BNA) Monograph No. 21 (July 25, 1975); Stewart, Regulation, Innovation, and Administrative Law: A Conceptual Framework, 69 Calif. L. Rev. 1259 (1981).

4. By what criteria should we decide whether technology forcing has been successful as applied to a particular industry? For example, if it were possible to make cars that achieved zero emissions but the cost was $10,000 per car, would such a policy be considered successful? See, for example, R. Crandall et al., Regulating the Automobile (1986), arguing that "even if [the Clean Air Act] has improved air quality substantially compared with what it would have been, the marginal costs greatly exceed the marginal benefits." Id. at 115.

5. Determining the circumstances in which courts will uphold regulations that require some evolution in technology is a complex task. While in theory an agency need only show that technology will *become* available, "[i]n practice, this showing is difficult to make, given a rule-making procedure in which the EPA must disclose its data and analysis, meet the criticisms of industry, and survive a 'hard look' standard of review." Stewart, Regulation, Innovation, and Administrative Law: A Conceptual Framework, 69 Cal. L. Rev. 1259, 1300 (1981). Would more precise statutory language help? Suppose that instead of "best available technology," a statute required achievement of the "maximum technologically feasible level" of pollution control unless the agency could justify a less stringent level on economic grounds. See NRDC v. Herrington, 768 F.2d 1355, 1391-1400 (1985).

6. How should other trade-offs associated with redesigning products to meet environmental requirements be taken into account? For example, what if cars made lighter to meet fuel efficiency requirements are less safe in collisions with heavier vehicles? Some controls on emissions and changes made to promote efficiency have also reduced engine performance. On the other hand, as Weisskopf notes, the transition to catalytic converters resulted in improved performance because it eliminated the need for carburetor adjustments previously made for emission control purposes.

7. Is there any way to judge the innovation potential in particular industries in advance of technology-forcing requirements? Some technologies appear to be mature, in the sense that they have been in use for decades and improvements over time might readily be expected to approach theoretical limits. Consider, for example, the relative potential for improving computers and the gasoline combustion engine. On the other hand, technology forcing may lead to a necessary examination of alternative fuels that offer significant opportunities for improvement. See, e.g., The Greening of Detroit, Business Week, April 8, 1991, at 54-60. Another example is steelmaking, an industry that goes back more than 200 years. Dramatic reductions have been achieved in the energy

requirements and emissions associated with conventional steelmaking. Nevertheless, much more advanced methods of steelmaking are now being developed that would produce better-quality steel using lower-quality (and less expensive) coal, while also reducing energy needs and emissions. J. Goldemberg, Energy for a Sustainable World 67-69 (1987).

8. Advocates of increased reliance on economic incentive approaches to regulation argue that they are better suited for stimulating technological innovation than the "game of chicken" approach Congress employed in dealing with the auto industry in the early 1970s. Pollution taxes and emissions trading schemes create a continuous incentive for innovations that reduce emissions while giving companies flexibility to meet emissions limits however they can, including process changes and other alternatives to conventional end-of-pipe technology. Others are more skeptical of the impact of economic incentive approaches on technological innovation. They argue that such approaches are best suited for stimulating cost savings rather than improvements in pollution control. Should this matter? A study of emissions trading under the Clean Air Act suggests that flexibility has led to innovation in the form of cost-saving modifications as opposed to new hardware or exotic technologies. Dudek and Palmisano, supra question three, at 235-236. While we examine the emissions trading experience in more detail in Chapter 6, we now conclude our discussion of approaches to regulation by examining economic incentive approaches.

C. ECONOMIC INCENTIVE APPROACHES TO REGULATION

While contemporary interest in economic incentive approaches to environmental regulation makes them appear to be a recent invention, they actually have been the subject of high-level debate from the start of the federalization of environmental law. In 1965 the Economic Pollution Panel of the president's Science Advisory Committee discussed pollution taxes in their report Restoring the Quality of the Environment. In 1966, the president's Council of Economic Advisers (CEA) proposed the use of effluent charges to create incentives for dischargers to reduce pollution, with the revenue raised to be used to pay for municipal treatment plants. CEA, Economic Report of the President, 1966, at 124 (1966). In his Environmental Message of 1971 President Nixon proposed that Congress impose a charge on sulfur dioxide emissions, and he pushed for a stiff tax on gasoline lead additives to encourage their rapid phase-out. These proposals were not given serious consideration by Congress.

In his final appearance before Congress in 1977, outgoing EPA administrator Russell Train strongly endorsed the use of economic incentive approaches to regulation. He concluded that the command-and-control approach to regulation initially employed by Congress had been sensible, despite its inefficiency. As he explained:

The thrust of these statutes . . . has been to set deadlines that were tough, mandate standards that were tough, force technology and the state of the art. I have fully supported that approach. I think it has made complete good sense. It has succeeded in getting the country off the mark, so to speak, in dealing with the problems. It probably carries with it certain penalties in terms of efficiency, both technological efficiency and economic efficiency. But I think that up to now these have been costs that have been well worth paying in order to get the country moving on these programs. If we had started to fine tune from the beginning, I think we would still be fine tuning and we would have very little progress in terms of cleanup. [Train, Status of the Programs and Policies of the Environmental Protection Agency, Hearing before the Subcomm. on Environmental Pollution of the Senate Comm. on Public Works, 95th Cong., 1st Sess. 9 (1977).]

Train concluded that the time had now come to explore the use of economic incentive approaches to regulation in a few selected areas such as sulfur dioxide emissions and automobiles that failed to comply with emissions standards. Train noted that the "nuclear device of not being able to sell cars" was "not a very practical kind of sanction" to encourage the development of better emissions control technology. He argued that effluent charges would create a continuous financial incentive to reduce pollution while avoiding arguments over the feasibility of complying with emissions limits.

One of the most important reasons why Congress did not quickly embrace incentive-based approaches to regulation was its awareness that a shift to such policies would create losers as well as winners. As Figure 2.8 indicates, each of the principal incentive-based approaches has advantages and drawbacks that reflect, at least in part, how they alter the distribution of the costs and benefits of regulation. In addition, a study of congressional staff discovered that neither proponents nor opponents of effluent charges really understood the theory behind them. S. Kelman, What Price Incentives? Economists and the Environment 100-101 (1981).

Necessity eventually proved to be the mother of invention for the first major use of incentive-based regulation by EPA when it established an emissions trading program under the Clean Air Act. Faced with the dilemma of how to permit new sources of air pollution in areas that had not complied with national air quality standards, EPA developed an offset program that encouraged an early form of emissions trading subsequently endorsed by Congress in the nonattainment provisions of the 1977 amendments to the Clean Air Act. EPA subsequently broadened emissions trading possibilities by adopting a "bubble policy" upheld by the Supreme Court in Chevron U.S.A. v. NRDC, 467 U.S. 837 (1984). While few emissions trades actually occurred, see Dudek and Palmisano, Emissions Trading: Why Is This Thoroughbred Hobbled?, 13 Colum. J. Envtl. L. 217 (1988), economists have estimated that the program may

FIGURE 2.8
Comparison of Uniform, National Regulatory Approaches with
Incentive-based Approaches to Regulation

	Pros	*Cons*
1. *Uniform, National Regulation*	Arguably easier to establish Assures protection of health Precludes relocation to avoid controls	Inefficient since ignores differences in marginal control costs Provides no incentive to reduce emissions beyond maximum permitted
2. *Effluent Charges*	Creates incentives for dischargers to reduce emissions in the most cost-effective manner Provides funds to cover social costs of pollution	No guarantee sufficiently protective levels of control will be achieved Difficult to determine socially efficient level of such charges Increases cost of production Creates incentive for midnight dumping
3. *Marketable Permits*	Creates incentives for dischargers to reduce emissions in the most cost-effective manner Overall allowable level of pollution can be determined in advance by allocation of permit rights	Can result in less equitable distributions of pollutants Some believe it is unfair to permit polluters to profit from sale of rights to pollute
4. *Deposit-Refund Schemes*	Reduces incentive for midnight dumping	Administrative costs of collecting and refunding deposits reduce attractiveness
5. *Provision of Subsidies for Investments in Pollution Controls*	Assists small and less profitable firms in bearing costs of compliance	Penalizes firms that already have invested in compliance technology Redistributes income from taxpayers to polluting activities

Source: Adapted from Congressional Research Service, Pollution Taxes, Effluent Charges and Other Alternatives for Pollution Control 2-8 (May 1977).

have saved industry between $5 and $12 billion. Hahn and Hester, Where Did All the Markets Go? An Analysis of EPA's Emissions Trading Program, 6 Yale J. Reg. 109 (1989). A program adopted by EPA in 1982 that authorized gasoline refiners to trade rights to use lead additives was far more popular in the industry, with more than half of all refineries making trades. See Hahn and Stavins, Incentive-Based Environmental Regulation: A New Era from an Old Idea?, 18 Ecology L.Q. 1 (1991). The 1990 Clean Air Act Amendments have now substantially expanded the use of economic incentive approaches by creating a system of tradeable allowances to emit sulfur dioxide and by imposing a tax on each ton of such emissions. These programs are discussed in Chapter 6.

Why has environmental policy eschewed the use of incentive approaches to regulation until recently? Opposition to these approaches has come from both environmentalists and, surprisingly, from industry. Many environmentalists have perceived effluent charges or pollutant taxes as licenses to pollute. They note that effluent charges cannot guarantee that pollution will be limited to any particular level and that they could create inequities by exposing citizens in areas where the pollution control costs are high to greater levels of pollution. Industry has opposed effluent charges and pollution taxes in part because they make dischargers pay for what formerly had been free. Proponents of economic incentive approaches now recognize that part of the opposition to such policies is due to concern over their distributional implications, that is, the fact that they, like other forms of regulation, create losers as well as winners. Hahn and Stavins, supra, at 39-41. Thus, more attention is now being paid to the development of mechanisms for compensating losers. See, e.g., Butraw, Compensating Losers When Cost-Effective Environmental Policies Are Adopted, Resources 3 (Summer 1991). For example, because the emissions trading provisions of the 1990 Clean Air Act Amendments will reduce demand for high-sulfur coal, a program to provide benefits to coal miners who lose their jobs was included in the amendments.

Considerable debate has focused on whether economic incentive approaches to regulation are more difficult or easier for regulatory authorities to administer. Bruce Ackerman and Richard Stewart argue that such approaches are "feasible and effective" and that critics have underestimated the enormity of the benefits that would accrue from replacing current regulatory schemes that do not work and whose "malfunctions" will only get worse. While rejecting the claim that economic incentive approaches necessarily will impose greater burdens on administrators, they argue that the real question "is whether increased administrative costs are outweighed by greater benefits for society as a whole." Citing EPA's development of the "bubble" policy, they contend that the "additional information-gathering, analysis, and other effort" required to develop the policy was a worthwhile investment because it "saved over

$700 million and stimulated new ways of cleaning up pollution." Ackerman and Stewart conclude that "[i]t is time for environmental lawyers to stop celebrating the statutory revolution of the 1970s and to start building a statutory structure worthy of the year 2000." Ackerman and Stewart, Reforming Environmental Law, 37 Stan. L. Rev. 1333, 1364-1365 (1985).

A report by a group calling itself Project 88 proposing economic incentive approaches to environmental regulation was instrumental in generating support for the inclusion of such provisions in the 1990 Clean Air Act Amendments. Project 88: Harnessing Market Forces to Protect Our Environment (Dec. 1988). The bipartisan group that sponsored the report, chaired by Senator Timothy Wirth and the late Senator John Heinz, has issued a followup study that proposes the use of market-based regulatory strategies for dealing with global climate change, solid and hazardous waste management, and management of natural resources. A major advance in this report is its explicit consideration of how to deal with the equity issues raised by the use of economic incentive approaches to regulation. Project 88—Round II: Incentives for Action: Designing Market-Based Environmental Strategies (May 1991). The pros and cons of these proposals and other regulatory alternatives are explored in greater detail in subsequent chapters.

4. Regulatory Authorities

To develop an understanding of how the various federal regulatory schemes relate to one another, it is useful to construct a rough sketch of their jurisdictional reach. Jurisdictional terms in the statutes are very important because they determine the statutes' coverage—which products or activities can be subject to regulation under which statutes. They are a source of frequent battles between regulators and the regulated community because regulation almost inevitably creates incentives for avoidance behavior by regulatory targets. Thus, as we will see when we examine individual statutes, jurisdictional terms often have to be defined through litigation.

Figure 2.9 provides a crude illustration of the jurisdictional reach of some of the major federal environmental laws. It illustrates that the regulatory authorities available for responding to an environmental problem generally depend on location or the medium affected by the problem or the characteristics of the pollutant or product thought to be the source of the problem. For example, the Occupational Safety and Health Administration has jurisdiction over workplace hazards; the Consumer Product Safety Commission has authority to regulate hazards in consumer products; foods, drugs, and cosmetics are regulated by the federal Food and Drug Administration (FDA).

FIGURE 2.9
Legislative Authorities Affecting the Life Cycle of a Chemical

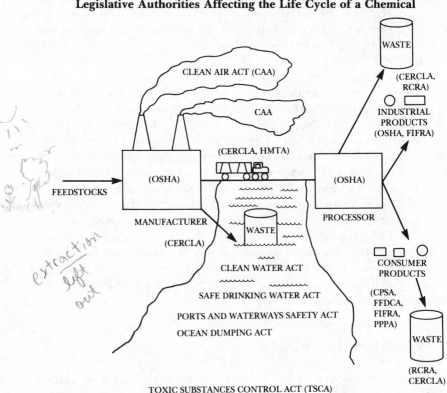

CERCLA: Comprehensive Environmental Response, Compensation, and Liability Act
FFDCA: Federal Food, Drug, and Cosmetic Act
RCRA: Resource Conservation and Recovery Act
FIFRA: Federal Insecticide, Fungicide, and Rodenticide Act
CPSA: Consumer Product Safety Act
OSHA: Occupational Safety and Health Act
HMTA: Hazardous Materials Transportation Act
PPPA: Poison Prevention Packaging Act

The regulatory authorities available to EPA to control pollution are largely dependent on where pollutants are discharged and the nature and source of each pollutant. The Clean Air Act authorizes the use of ambient air quality standards to control pollutants that come from numerous or diverse sources and that threaten public health or welfare. The types of controls that can be imposed depend on whether the source is a mobile or a stationary source of pollution; more stringent controls are imposed on new sources than on existing sources. EPA's jurisdiction under the Clean Water Act covers virtually all discharges of pollutants into the "waters of the United States," although the Army Corps of Engineers is given jurisdiction under the Act over the discharge of dredged or fill material into navigable waters. The Ocean Dumping Act gives EPA jurisdiction over the transport and dumping in ocean waters of materials other than dredged material. The Safe Drinking Water Act gives EPA jurisdiction over contaminants in public water supply systems, while FIFRA allows EPA to regulate the licensing and use of pesticides.

In theory the Toxic Substances Control Act (TSCA) is the broadest source of EPA's regulatory authority because it authorizes EPA to ban or to restrict the manufacture, marketing, use, or disposal of any "chemical substance or mixture" (with the exception of pesticides and products regulated by the FDA). TSCA thus authorizes EPA to regulate chemicals through all phases of their "life cycle" from manufacture through use and disposal in any environmental medium. Thus it appears to cover all of the activities shown in the diagram. While RCRA's coverage is somewhat more narrowly confined to solid wastes that are deemed hazardous by EPA, it too authorizes extensive controls since it mandates regulation of hazardous wastes from "cradle to grave," including controls on disposal of it in any environmental medium (e.g., land disposal, incineration). Although EPA has exempted from RCRA's reach certain disposal or treatment practices (e.g., recycling activities and the disposal of waste in sewers), its coverage is still quite broad. Although broadly interpreted, the term "solid wastes" has been difficult to define precisely. Congress has specified that it is not limited to materials that actually are in solid form, but can also include "liquid, semisolid or contained gaseous material." The cradle-to-grave controls imposed under subtitle C of RCRA apply only to solid wastes that are "hazardous," another hard-to-define term. CERCLA makes broad classes of responsible parties jointly and severally liable for the costs of cleaning up releases of an enormous universe of "hazardous substances." While CERCLA's liability approach stands in sharp contrast to the regulatory schemes employed by other statutes, it is likely to have a significant impact on the generation and management of hazardous substances.

Complaints are often heard that the fragmented structure of environmental law makes it difficult to pursue coordinated regulatory responses to cross-media contamination. Often there is considerable overlap among the various laws that may be used to address a particular environmental problem. Congress has not laid out a single grand scheme or unifying principle that establishes priorities for regulation under the various statutes. Rather, it has directed that environmental agencies implement a variety of programs under several statutes, while urging agencies to try to coordinate their actions with other agencies and within themselves.

Efforts to rationalize the environmental laws into a unified whole, for example, by enacting an organic act combining all the statutory authorities of the Environmental Protection Agency have not generated much enthusiasm, although EPA Administrator William Reilly has expressed support for the concept. Reilly, The Future of Environmental Law, 6 Yale J. on Reg. 351 (1989). EPA has proposed that cross-media reduction of environmental risk be considered a central organizing principle for environmental regulation. A thoughtful explanation of the political obstacles to such an approach is provided by R. Outen, Environmental Pollution Laws and the Architecture of Tobacco Road, in National Research Council, Multimedia Approaches to Pollution Control: A Symposium Proceedings 139 (1987). Outen concludes that "it is easier to tack a new board over a gap that appears than to redesign the entire structure."

Outen notes that the existing highly fragmented structure of law and regulation is mirrored in the fragmented structure of EPA, the environmental community, and the congressional committees with jurisdiction over the environment. Cross-media analysis is expensive, complex, and time-consuming, and the "political reward structure favors piecemeal solutions to newly identified problems." Moreover, the law that authorizes the most comprehensive, cross-media approach to regulation of risks—TSCA—has been implemented far less successfully than have narrower, technology-based approaches that do not require complex, cross-media analyses. Id. at 141-142. Despite political obstacles to structural changes in environmental law, there is a growing recognition that environmental regulation should place far more emphasis on pollution prevention as a cross-cutting strategy for reducing environmental risks. EPA has embraced this concept, noting that environmental contamination is far more difficult and expensive to remediate than it is to prevent.

A Case Study: Public Law and the Control of Lead Poisoning

One reason why environmental law has become so complicated is the complexity of what it seeks to regulate. Pollutants do not adhere to tidy jurisdictional boundaries as they work their way through the environment. This is well illustrated by efforts to control human exposure to lead, a toxic substance that can cause substantial damage to human health even at low levels of exposure. Although humans have known of lead's acute dangers since ancient times, sources of human exposure to lead remain. Figure 2.10 represents an attempt by the National Academy of Sciences (NAS) in its 1980 report Lead in the Human Environment to diagram the multiple environmental pathways that result in human exposure to lead. As the chart indicates, occupational exposure to lead

FIGURE 2.10
Sources and Environmental Pathways That Can Result in Exposures of Human Populations to Lead

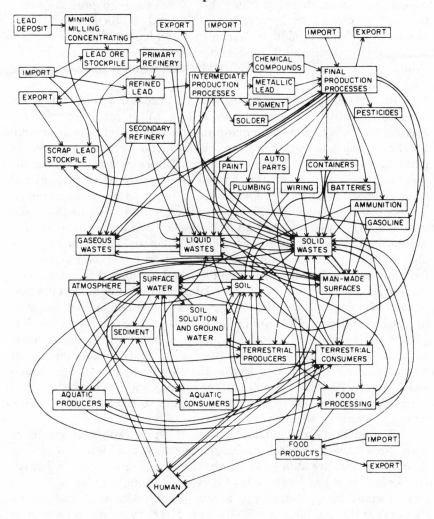

Source: NAS, Lead in the Human Environment 35 (1980).

may occur when lead is mined, milled, concentrated, and refined and during the process of manufacturing products that use lead, such as lead acid batteries, gasoline lead additives, pesticides, and inks. Each of these processes also generates lead wastes that may be in solid, liquid, or gaseous form and that may contaminate the air, surface water, soil, and groundwater. Consumers may be exposed to lead not only as a result of their use of products that contain lead, but also as a result of breathing air contaminated with lead emissions from gasoline combustion and industrial processes, drinking water that passes through plumbing containing lead pipe or lead solder, or eating food products derived from plants, animals, or aquatic organisms that had ingested lead or that are packaged in containers soldered with lead. Children may ingest lead by eating soil, by breathing lead dust, and by chewing on surfaces containing lead-based paint.

In 1980 the NAS report stressed the need for a coordinated approach to control all sources of human exposure to lead. Yet given the fragmented structure of the environmental statutes, efforts to prevent human exposure to lead have been the product of regulatory actions by many agencies using different statutory authorities. For example, the Food and Drug Administration limited the leachable content of glazed ceramic products in 1971. EPA mandated phased reductions in the allowable lead content of gasoline under the Clean Air Act in 1973, and in 1985 it virtually eliminated lead from gasoline by adopting even tougher standards. The Department of Housing and Urban Development promulgated regulations governing abatement of lead-based paint hazards in federally assisted housing in 1976 under the Lead-Based Poisoning Prevention Act. The Consumer Product Safety Commission limited the lead content of paints and banned the use of lead in certain articles intended for use by children in 1978 under the authority of the Consumer Product Safety Act. In 1978 EPA promulgated a national ambient air quality standard for lead under the Clean Air Act and OSHA established limits on occupational exposure to lead under the Occupational Health and Safety Act. In 1991 EPA established regulations under the Safe Drinking Water Act designed to require municipalities to reduce lead contamination in drinking water over the next two decades.

Despite all these regulatory efforts, it is now estimated that more than three million children under the age of 6 have levels of lead in their bodies that are above the threshold for medical concern. Scientists now believe that low levels of lead previously thought to be safe are in fact associated with potentially serious neurological damage. In 1991 the Centers for Disease Control (CDC) lowered its definition of lead toxicity from 25 micrograms of lead per deciliter of blood to 10 μg/dl. Because of the many sources of exposure to lead, CDC recommends that all children be screened for lead poisoning.

The choice of which statutes to employ in combatting an environmental problem can make a great deal of difference for the stringency of controls because different statutes employ different criteria for establishing regulatory standards. While regulation has focused on preventing releases of lead into the environment, lead already present in the environment (in paints, pipes, and soil) continues to poison millions of children. Current regulatory authorities are poorly designed for clean-ing up existing lead contamination, in part because of the high cost of lead abatement. Some statutes (such as the Delaney Clause of the Food, Drug, and Cosmetic Act and section 112 of the Clean Air Act, which governs regulation of hazardous air pollutants) require agencies to set standards solely on the basis of health considerations, without consid-ering the costs of controls. Other laws (such as TSCA and FIFRA) require regulators to balance the costs of controls against their benefits to human health and the environment. Still others (such as the Occupational Safety and Health Act and the Safe Drinking Water Act) direct agencies to set controls to protect health as stringently as is feasible given current tech-nology. Thus, the choice of which statute to use may have a significant impact on the regulatory outcome.

For example, the primary statute regulating the workplace envi-ronment is the Occupational Safety and Health Act. It requires that OSHA regulate to protect workers against material impairment of health or functional capacity to the extent feasible. Yet even the controls that OSHA deems to be the most stringent feasible are admittedly insufficient to protect the health of workers from lead exposure in certain manu-facturing processes, such as the production of lead acid batteries. As a result, workers in certain occupations are exposed to levels of lead that threaten the health of their offspring. This is reflected in the Supreme Court's decision in International Union, United Automobile, Aerospace and Agricultural Implement Workers of America v. Johnson Controls, 111 S. Ct. 1196 (1991), which struck down a "fetal protection" policy barring women of childbearing age from battery manufacturing jobs. The Court found that this policy constituted sex discrimination in violation of Title VII of the Civil Rights Act, in part because of evidence that exposure to lead damages both male and female reproductive systems.

The difficulty of establishing coordinated regulatory responses us-ing individual environmental statutes is painfully apparent in dealing with pervasive problems like lead poisoning. Several alternative ap-proaches for reducing human exposure to lead are currently under consideration. A national environmental organization has proposed that Congress impose a substantial excise tax on the production and impor-tation of lead and that the revenues be placed in a National Lead Paint Abatement Trust Fund. Environmental Defense Fund, Legacy of Lead: America's Continuing Epidemic of Childhood Lead Poisoning (Mar. 1990). It argues that a lead tax will create an economic incentive for industry to substitute less harmful alternatives for lead while helping to defray the enormous costs of abating existing contamination.

In 1991 EPA proposed a strategy for using its existing regulatory authority in a coordinated fashion to reduce significantly the number of children with blood lead levels above 10 μg/dl. EPA proposed to: (1) develop methods to identify geographic "hot spots" of lead exposure;

(2) develop and disseminate cost-effective methods to abate in-place lead exposure sources; (3) implement lead pollution prevention programs by exploring market-based incentives to limit or eliminate lead use and by using regulatory mechanisms such as the TSCA to reduce the use of lead in current and future products; (4) minimize human and environmental exposures through traditional control mechanisms by clustering together current and prospective regulatory activities that deal with lead; (5) encourage environmentally sound recycling; (6) develop and implement a public information and education program; (7) initiate a cross-media lead enforcement initiative; and (8) coordinate research programs concerning lead. While EPA's cross-media enforcement initiative resulted in administrative fines of $10 million being imposed on twelve companies, Lead Polluters Get Punished, 253 Science 621 (1991), the agency subsequently backed off on new regulatory initiatives.

Question One.   Why did regulation fail to prevent widespread human exposure to lead? What are the strengths and weaknesses of current approaches for preventing lead poisoning? How could they be improved? Do regulatory agencies need new statutory authority to control lead poisoning, or do they just need to be more aggressive in implementing existing authorities?

Question Two.   EPA exercised its authority under TSCA to deal with a similarly pervasive health threat when it prohibited virtually all mining, importation, manufacturing, and use of asbestos, based on an assessment of the life cycle of environmental risks posed by that substance. Although the asbestos ban has been largely reversed by a federal appeals court, could such an approach be an effective strategy for preventing lead poisoning?

Question Three.   The CDC recommends that all children be screened for lead poisoning. The proponents of this approach argue that it will generate political pressure for more effective regulatory action when parents throughout the country discover that their children are being disadvantaged by exposure to lead. Under what circumstances would you agree that lead screening of children should be required?

Question Four.   Is an excise tax likely to be effective in reducing the amount of lead use? If the revenues from such a tax were used to fund lead poisoning abatement efforts, could this actually generate opposition to proposals that EPA ban lead use under TSCA because it could eliminate a crucial source of abatement funds? Should it be done on a national basis?

Question Five.   In light of the *Johnson Controls* decision, which effectively prohibits "fetal protection" policies, what additional measures could be required to protect workers in lead acid battery plants from exposure to reproductive risks?

In the chapters that follow we will review many of the regulatory actions that have been taken under the environmental statutes to reduce lead emissions. When you encounter these examples, consider why despite these actions more than three million American children have dangerously high levels of lead in their blood.

C. THE REGULATORY PROCESS: A PREVIEW

The regulatory process is the arena in which law is translated into policy. This occurs in large part through the actions of administrative agencies operating under the watchful eye of the judiciary. We defer detailed consideration of this process until Chapter 5 in order to give you an opportunity first to gain some familiarity with the regulatory statutes that make this process so important. However, to gain a complete picture of the structure of environmental law, it is useful to review here how the regulatory process fits into that overall structure.

1. Law, Policy, and Agency Decision-making

Whenever Congress decides to confront an environmental issue, its options can be visualized as a "policy space," in the parlance of our policy sciences colleagues. Each point within that space represents a discrete, defined program for action, including the action of doing nothing. The statutes Congress enacts seldom point to a single unique location within the policy space, however. Instead, Congress identifies a target area, a subset of all the available options, and instructs an administrative agency to implement the statute by resolving all the remaining issues necessary to produce a definitive governmental decision.

To translate the environmental laws into regulations, administrative agencies must choose a regulatory alternative within the policy space established by law and develop, propose, and promulgate regulations. The Administrative Procedure Act and the environmental laws under whose authority the agency acts outline the ground rules for agency action, but agencies generally have considerable discretion over both the substance of regulatory policy and the procedures used to formulate it. How agency discretion is exercised within the policy space identified by the environmental statutes determines the precise contours of environmental policy and, presumably, the level of environmental protection the laws actually provide. Thus, study of the rulemaking process and agency decision-making is critical to understanding environmental policy.

Courts also play an important role in the regulatory process, but it is a limited one. In the 1970s we relearned that the *best* one can expect from the courts in their review of agency decisions is that they will ensure the agency stays within the section of policy space designated by Congress. If, for example, Congress told EPA to set air pollution levels for lead "requisite to protect the public health with an adequate margin of safety" (see §109(b)(1) of the Clean Air Act), litigation may ensure that the EPA does not consider how expensive compliance with that standard would be when it decides what the correct standard is, because Congress excluded such considerations when it directed the EPA to consider only the health effects of the pollutant. See Lead Industries Assn. v. EPA, 647 F.2d 1330 (D.C. Cir.), cert. denied, 449 U.S. 1042 (1980).

That determination scarcely terminates the interest that environmentally aware persons have in what EPA does, however. Such persons want to influence the specific policy point that the agency selects from among the considerable number remaining after Congress has spoken and the courts have ensured that the agency is listening. In the case of airborne lead, for example, industry urged EPA to use the exposure levels at which "clearly harmful" effects are apparent in order to fix the specific pollution level and insisted that a "medical consensus" exist about the harmful nature of such effects before the agency acted. Others supported EPA's acting before it conclusively determined that an observed effect was harmful. EPA eventually decided to base its airborne lead pollution level on a study showing a correlation between lead exposure and increases in blood cells of an enzyme named erythrocyte protoporphyrin, which indicated that the chemical process for forming hemoglobin was being impaired by the presence of lead. In retrospect, this has proved fortunate, because more recent work demonstrates a strong correlation between lead and adverse health effects at even lower levels of exposure.

A great deal of the practical significance of the Clean Air Act's regulation of lead turned on whether EPA chose industry's proposal, the proposal it eventually did choose, or yet some other one to specify what constituted protecting public health for purposes of its final action. Notwithstanding the extensive statute Congress had written, the Clean Air Act did not speak conclusively to that area of "detail." There were multiple points within the target area, any one of which EPA could have chosen.

Lawsuits are frequently necessary to set the agenda and get the attention of the agency. A fair amount of actual policy formation occurs as the interested parties "bargain within the shadow of the law." The lesson of the last two decades is simply that influencing agency action within its target area plays as substantial a part in the practice and the substance of environmental law as what courts do in defining and defending the target area boundaries Congress has established. This casebook characterizes both parts of environmental law as worthy of study; indeed, it would be misleading to focus too heavily on the activities of courts, the doctrines of judicial review, standing, and statutory interpretation. This is doubly true in light of a general retrenching of federal judicial scrutiny of agency decison-making, as appears to be occurring under the auspices of a more deferential Supreme Court. The effect of such deference is to enlarge the policy space available for agency discretionary behavior.

Theories of agency decision-making abound. The model implicit in conventional descriptions of the environmental statutes could be called the New Deal model of *agency expertise:* Environmental agencies are responsible for applying their independent expertise to achieve the objectives outlined in the laws. Yet dissatisfaction with the product of agency expertise played a major role in the early development of environmental statutes. Much of federal environmental law represents a reaction against the failure of executive agencies to respond to the environmental concerns of the public. When it enacted the environmental laws, Congress was aware of the extensive literature suggesting that regulatory agencies tend to become the captives of the regulated industry. To resist this *agency capture* model of the process, action-forcing provisions such as citizen suits and provisions for judicial review were incorporated in the environmental statutes.

In his influential book Defending the Environment, Joe Sax argued in 1970 that mission-oriented administrative agencies had become prime obstacles to environmental protection. The New Deal model of entrusting policy-making to the expertise of "an incredible tangle of agencies with noble-sounding mandates and small budgets" had failed, Sax argued, because the "expert" agency had supplanted the public to such an extent that "[t]he public itself is thought to possess *no* expertise about the public interest." Despite the Administrative Procedure Act, the "public remains an outsider, to be tolerated as a recipient of notices and participant at formal hearings, but not as central player." J. Sax, Defending the Environment 60-61 (1970). Sax argued for opening up the courts to stricter scrutiny of agency decisions.

NEPA already had mandated a fundamental change in agency decisionmaking processes, presaging other, very different, action-forcing provisions in the regulatory statutes that soon followed. Rather than responding to demands for reform with more elaborate hearing procedures, NEPA had the potential to alter the internal decisionmaking structure of agencies to foment change from within. The Clean Air Act, which soon followed, dealt a body blow to the notion of unquestioning deference to administrative expertise by establishing "a tightly interlocking schedule of deadlines, timetables, and specific targeted air quality goals." Rabin, Federal Regulation in Historical Perspective, 38 Stan. L. Rev. 1189, 1291 (1986). As Rabin notes, the congressional reluctance to engage in "blank-check delegation" was not without precedent, and the standards required by the Clean Air Act left considerable room for agency discretion. As Sax had conceded, agency discretion was inevitable for many environmental issues where "legislatures will never be able to do more than state large policy choices. . ." . Id. at 234. But he maintained that judicial scrutiny of agency action could provide the key check to ensure that agencies acted in the public interest.

As the courts opened to the public and the "hard look" doctrine of judicial review arrived, perhaps the most influential model of the contemporary administrative process has been developed by Richard Stewart. Stewart argues that the administrative process has shifted to an *interest representation model* where agency decisions are in large part a product of input from competing private interest groups. Stewart, The Reformation of American Administrative Law, 88 Harv. L. Rev. 1669 (1975); Stewart and Sunstein, Public Programs and Private Rights, 95 Harv. L. Rev. 1195 (1982). The environmental statutes and judicial review encourage public access to and participation in the rulemaking process, while not providing any guarantees that any particular group's interest will prevail.

To explain how agencies respond to input from private interests, Roger Noll has proposed an *external signals theory* of agency behavior. Noll argues that agencies seek to reinforce favorable signals from interest groups external to the agency while minimizing unfavorable signals. Congress and the president reward agencies that receive favorable signals and punish those that receive unfavorable ones. Noll's theory is consistent with the observation that agencies rarely seek to be the initiators of bold regulatory initiatives and are eager to embrace alternatives that postpone the need to reconcile conflicts among interest groups.

Economists have argued that regulation usually is employed as a means for special interest groups to disguise transfers of wealth from one group to another under the cloak of the "public interest." See Stigler, The Theory of Economic Regulation, 2 Bell J. Econ. & Mgmt. Sci. 3 (1971); Peltzman, Toward a More General Theory of Regulation, 19 J. Law & Econ. 211 (1976). While some environmental regulations have been described as conforming to this model, Ackerman and Hassler, Clean Coal, Dirty Air (1981) (arguing that the Clean Air Act's new source performance standards for coal-burning power plants are a massive subsidy to high-sulfur coal producers), this criticism is far more relevant to economic regulation than it is to environmental protection measures. But see Hazardous Waste Treatment Council v. EPA, 861 F.2d 277 (D.C. Cir. 1988), cert. denied, 109 S. Ct. 3157 (1989) (*HWTC I*) (denying standing to trade association representing hazardous waste treatment companies who sought to challenge EPA RCRA regulations as too lax on the ground that RCRA does not protect competitor interests).

Regardless of which theory of regulation one subscribes to, it is clear that private interest groups now have an enormous impact on how agencies implement the environmental statutes. The broad model of public participation in rulemaking embodied in our administrative process facilitates fierce contests between interest groups when important regulatory decisions are at issue. Although they ensure that everyone can be heard, notice-and-comment procedures provide no guarantees concerning the value of the public's input. Describing a particularly high-stakes battle over an air pollution regulation in Sierra Club v. Costle, 657 F.2d 298 (1981), Judge Wald noted that "[c]onflicting interests play fiercely for enormous stakes, advocates are prolific and agile, obfuscation runs high, common sense correspondingly low" and "the public interest is often obscured." As one gains an appreciation for the complexity of the environmental statutes, it becomes easier to understand why even enormously popular legislation leaves so much room for private interests to maneuver during the implementation stage.

Drawing on the lessons of biology, William Rodgers describes the process by which "consensus" environmental legislation is transformed into a regulatory battleground by relating the story of the red squirrel. To discourage predators like the horned owl, the red squirrel developed an effective strategy of chattering because owls will not waste their time attacking prey that is alert to their presence. But chattering suddenly becomes a spectacularly poor strategy when the squirrel is confronted with a different predator—humans armed with rifles. Rodgers argues that legislators respond to private interests like prey responding to predators by pursuing strategies that hide in "consensus" environmental legislation provisions that will later undercut its effective implementation. These include process entitlements, vague and ambiguous terms, and delegations that permit legislators to embrace environmentally pure ends while quietly undercutting the means for their attainment in the name of federalism or procedural fairness. Rodgers, The Lesson of the Red Squirrel: Consensus and Betrayal in the Environmental Statutes, 5 J. Cont. Health L. & Poly. 161 (1989).

As Rodgers describes the process, following the enactment of popular environmental legislation the apparent "consensus" behind the law swiftly disappears. The statute "suddenly means what lawyers and others say it means as it undergoes translation in the world at large." In other words, "statutory instructions immediately will be put to use as interpretations in legal gameplaying in a host of different arenas." Rodgers, The Lesson of the Owl and the Crows: The Role of Deception in the Evolution of the Environmental Statutes, 4 J. Land Use & Envtl. L. 377, 382 (1989). Among the "long list of surprising readings and tactics" that then appear are "betrayals of sidebar agreements not recorded in the legislation, the invention of legislative history after-the-fact, and the attribution of meanings scorned by the negotiating principals." Id. at 383.

Some argue that problems with the regulatory process often are the result of Congress's enactment of statutes with unrealistic aspirational goals to be implemented by agencies whose reach far exceeds their political grasp. This forces the agencies to delay and to dissemble rather than implement commands that conflict with economic realities. See, e.g., Dwyer, The Pathology of Symbolic Legislation, 17 Ecology L.Q. 233 (1990).

Additional support for Rodgers's thesis comes from instances in which legislative delegations of difficult policy choices have permitted legislators to play both sides of the fence. Drawing on his experience as an NRDC lawyer working on implementation of the Clean Air Act, David Schoenbrod relates that "the same legislators that had reaped political credit, sometimes with our help, for protecting the environment by enacting the legislation, were urging EPA to go easy and thus getting more political credit and campaign contributions from constituents threatened with emission controls." Schoenbrod, Environmental Law and Growing Up, 6 Yale J. on Reg. 357, 363 (1989). Schoenbrod explains that

> [w]hat enabled legislators to be all things to all interests was the enactment of legislation that delegated the essential legislative task of making rules of conduct—the emission limitations—and to save for itself the task of establishing goals and rules of procedure. Setting goals is attractive to legislators because they need only set the popular ones. Making rules of procedure is also desirable because the procedure obscures the failure to make tough choices. [Id. at 364.]

Schoenbrod argues that Congress "could have solved most of the air pollution problem" it perceived at the time the Clean Air Act was enacted if it had simply specified the emissions limits in the statute, rather than delegating the decision to EPA to be made through a lengthy and complicated process. Id. at 365. Rather than insulating environmental decisions from politics, "delegation shifted decisionmaking from a highly visible political arena, Congress, to less visible ones" within the agencies. Because the public has a greater capacity to influence the legislative arena, the regulated community benefits from delegation of policy choices to less visible administrative forums.

2. *The Judicial Role in the Regulatory Process*

The 1970s brought major developments within the federal courts. When the Supreme Court in Citizens to Preserve Overton Park v. Volpe, 401

U.S. 402 (1971), reversed a decision to authorize the expenditure of federal funds to build an interstate highway through a park, the decision was a surprise for two reasons: it indicated that courts were willing (1) to review a wide range of agency actions and (2) to scrutinize more carefully the rationale behind agency decisions. Federal judges had become sensitized to frequent charges that federal agencies, especially those whose business was public works (such as the Army Corps of Engineers, the Bureau of Land Reclamation, and the Atomic Energy Commission), largely ignored legitimate environmental concerns in making their administrative decisions. As these claims were pressed in court by loosely knit public interest organizations, federal judges began to transform administrative law to provide greater superintendence of agency decision-making. First the doctrines of standing, which govern who is entitled to challenge agency action in court, were transformed in a series of landmark cases involving environmental challenges to decisions to construct major works, making it easier for persons concerned about the environment to litigate. See Stewart, The Reformation of American Administrative Law, 88 Harv. L. Rev. 1669 (1975).

With environmental cases easier to bring under more expansive standing rules, courts began scrutinizing agency responsibilities much more closely. They found "law to apply," that is, substantive standards against which to judge agency actions, where previously they would have held that choices about whether to proceed were committed to the agency's discretion and hence unreviewable by a federal court. Judicial review of agency decision-making reached its zenith with the D.C. Circuit's "hard look" doctrine, which counseled agencies to examine carefully the factors made relevant by statute prior to taking action. (A succinct summary of the hard look doctrine is contained in Sunstein, Deregulation and the Hard Look Doctrine, 1983 Sup. Ct. Rev. 181-184 (1983)).

Although these developments in administrative law were significant for the entire gamut of federal agency activity and owed their new existence to currents broader than environmentalism, it is also clear that a major portion of the important administrative law judicial decisions of the late 1960s and the 1970s were formed and litigated by environmental strategists, and that administrative law innovation and environmentalism were substantially intertwined.

Today judicial review is well accepted, but judicial scrutiny of agency action has become substantially more deferential to agency decision-making. Following the Supreme Court's decision in Vermont Yankee Nuclear Power Corp. v. NRDC, 435 U.S. 519 (1978), courts have been deferential to the procedures used by agencies in making regulatory policy decisions as long as they comport with the minimal requirements of the Administrative Procedure Act. Judicial deference was expanded dramatically in Chevron U.S.A. v. NRDC, 467 U.S. 837 (1984), to include deference to agency interpretations of statutory provisions except when they are contrary to unambiguous statutory commands.

Despite courts' more deferential approach to judicial review, such review continues to play an important role in regulatory policy, particularly in the environmental area. The major federal environmental statutes specifically authorize judicial review of agency action taken pursuant to them, and they also specify the procedures for obtaining judicial review. See, e.g., RCRA §7006(a), 42 U.S.C. §6976; TSCA §19, 15 U.S.C. §2618; CWA §509(b), 33 U.S.C. §1369(b); CAA §307(b), 42 U.S.C. §7607(b). These statutes, coupled with the judicial review provisions of the APA, 5 U.S.C. §§701-706, lay out the ground rules for challenging agency decisions in the federal courts. They generally permit private parties to obtain judicial review of final agency action (as distinguished from "preliminary, procedural, or intermediate agency action," which may be reviewed only when the final action is taken, APA §704) as long as it is not "committed to agency discretion by law" (such as a decision whether or not to initiate enforcement action, Heckler v. Chaney, 470 U.S. 821 (1985)), §701(a)(2). Plaintiffs seeking judicial review also must have exhausted their administrative remedies by raising their objections in the rulemaking proceeding before the agency whose actions they seek to challenge in court. The agency's action also must be deemed sufficiently "ripe for review" by courts, who seek to avoid premature adjudication of issues that have not crystallized to the point at which they are having more than a hypothetical impact on prospective litigants.

Virtually all of the federal environmental statutes also authorize *citizen suits* (FIFRA is the principal exception) against governmental agencies who fail to perform their statutory duties and against those who violate the statutes. It is important not to confuse the citizen suit provisions of the environmental statutes with the statutes' judicial review provisions. The citizen suit provisions generally authorize two types of lawsuits: action-forcing lawsuits against the agency for failure to perform a nondiscretionary duty and citizen suits against anyone who violates the environmental laws. The *judicial review* provisions of the environmental statutes authorize courts to review agency actions, such as the issuance or repeal of environmental regulations. The use of litigation to force administrative agencies to act is discussed in Chapter 5, which examines the regulatory process in greater detail. Citizen suits are examined in the context of environmental enforcement efforts in Chapter 7.

Having started from little federal activity and no "law to apply" and grown to a complex of federal laws, regulations, and judicial review, environmental law is changing again. In the third phase of environmental law, which characterizes our present situation, prominent environmental litigation is not over, but that litigation is changing shape. Agencies will still be sued, but companies are also being sued directly for "toxic torts." Even when agencies are the focal point of environmental attention, we will see a need to lobby and negotiate that is at least as strong as the need to litigate.

Accordingly, as we examine the substance of environmental law in the chapters that follow you will confront as many "policy problems" as you do appellate decisions. The course seeks to develop your skills at arguing for positions on those policy issues and for criticizing policy judgments.

This casebook is not targeted exclusively at federal regulation under the aegis of federal statutes. After a period of relative quiet, common law initiatives are once again emerging as important matters in the growth of environmental law, especially in the field of toxics exposure. In important ways, common law litigation represents a decentralization of environmental decision-making. Other reflections of decentralization include the revitalized role of state and local governments, as well as grass roots organizations, in challenging land-use decisions relating to hazardous waste disposal and clean-up. We will explore these common law initiatives, their interaction with federal statutory law, and the broader questions of institutional design raised by the prospect of using private litigation and the private marketplace as a replacement for centralized regulation.

Finally, just as an important decentralizing impetus is currently holding sway, an equally important internationalizing impetus is also on the rise. Ozone depletion and the greenhouse effect are the two most news-commanding current examples of environmental issues that must be approached on a multilateral basis if humankind is to be at all successful in addressing them. We will examine aspects of this internationalizing impetus as well.

D. ENVIRONMENTAL REGULATION: SOME ADDITIONAL THEMES

At the close of Chapter 1, we introduced two of the most important themes in environmental law and policy: the contrasting perceptions of environmental problems through the lenses of what we called "moral outrage" and "cool analysis," and the impact of uncertainty. Now that we have surveyed the history and structure of environmental regulation, these themes can be supplemented with some additional insights. First, the observation that regulation produces losers as well as winners has important consequences for understanding environmental policy that often are overlooked. Second, the rich mixture of regulatory strategies environmental policy employs reflects both different assessments of the goals and objectives of policy and different assessments of the appropriate means for pursuing those goals. Third, regardless of whether one views environmental policy issues from the perspective of moral outrage or cool analysis, environmental law is a field in which implementation and institutional concerns play an important role in shaping regulatory policies and constraining regulatory alternatives.

1.   Winners and Losers

In the 1990s, it is undeniably obvious in a way that it was not in 1970 that environmental policy produces winners and losers and, generally, that it has significant costs. EPA has estimated that the United States currently is investing $115 billion per year to protect the environment. EPA, Environmental Investments: The Cost of a Clean Environment (Dec. 1990). These costs are expected to rise sharply (to between $171 and $185 billion by the year 2000) as new regulatory requirements take effect and as policymakers continue to respond to strong, unsatisfied demands for further environmental protection measures.

The high stakes involved in environmental regulation—for both the regulated community and a concerned public—make it important to pay close attention to the distributional impact of regulation. To understand the development and implementation of environmental policy, it is necessary to consider not only how efficient policies are, but also how equitable. While economists argue that some environmental regulations are needlessly inefficient, their prescriptions for improving regulation have, until recently, failed to consider distributional concerns. This has limited the influence of economists on policy because in some circumstances the distribution of the risks and benefits of regulation may be even more important to policy outcomes than the aggregate levels of either.

The importance of distributional issues is a reflection of some of the values that generally animate environmental concern. Just as regulation creates winners and losers, so too do environmental problems. Efforts to control pollution are inspired in large part by concern over its distributional impact. Victims of environmental insults resent what they consider to be the unfairness of invasions of their personal autonomy. The notion that victims must tolerate such assaults if they are produced by activities that are too costly to control in the aggregate is highly unpopular. Because it often is easier to discern who bears the costs of environmental regulation than it is to see who bears the costs of environmental problems, efforts to use regulation to address distributional concerns have not always been successful.

The fact that environmental policy causes winners and losers has to be taken into account in understanding the influence of interest groups in the shaping and implementation of policy. Significant portions of environmental law owe their current shape at least in part to the influence of special pleading and the ability of particular groups and subgroups to shift costs onto someone else. Thus, the fact that regulation creates winners and losers implies that environmental law as it presently exists cannot be understood as simply the hermetically sealed interaction of considerations of aggregate environmental ends and means. The relative visibility and power of the winners and losers of certain policies has a major effect on ultimate policy outcomes.

2. Regulatory Strategies Reflect Different Assessments of Goals and Means

Under the combined influence of value perspectives and institutional concerns, environmental policy displays a rich mix of regulatory strategies, which must be understood as reflecting *both* different assessments of the goals and objectives of environmental policy (e.g., the goals suggested by moral outrage or cool analysis) *and* different assessments of the appropriate institutional mechanisms for pursuing those goals (e.g., technology-based approaches, significant risk approaches, balancing approaches, tort law, information disclosure strategies, and so on). In understanding and appraising the form of environmental law and policy, it is necessary to consider the influence of *both* differing interpretations of the goals of policy and differing interpretations of the appropriate means for implementing policy.

A considerable part of the debate between proponents and critics of different approaches to regulation reflects both differences in value perspectives and differences concerning the appropriate means for achieving policy goals. The moral outrage perspective finds pollution deeply offensive, particularly when it threatens human health. Cool analysts are offended by the notion that societal resources are being wasted on inefficient programs. As one economist complained, "When you're carrying out a crusade, you don't ask what's the cost of the religion." Morgenstern and Eisenstodt, Profits Are for Rape and Pillage, Forbes, Mar. 5, 1990, at 96. While believing their cool analysis to be value-neutral, economists are perceived by many environmentally concerned persons to be equally determined crusaders.

Even when clear goals can be agreed on, differences in value perspectives can affect assessments of the appropriate means for achieving such goals. Critics of emissions trading schemes are outraged by the notion that polluters should be allowed to sell "rights to pollute." Advocates of economic incentive approaches to regulation maintain that if such policies more effectively achieve environmental ends, policymakers should not be concerned with how they do so. Each perspective has a different assessment of how to respond to the flexibility-versus-complexity tradeoff, based on how their own interests are likely to be affected.

3. Implementation and Institutional Concerns

Environmental law is a field in which implementation and institutional concerns loom very large. Both shape regulatory policies and constrain practicable alternatives to existing practices. There are at least three dimensions to these concerns:

1. *Institutional.*   Environmental law has to "fit in" to a preexisting institutional structure of separation of powers among Congress, the president, and the judiciary that has shaped environmental law in important ways. For example, congressional suspicion of the executive branch provides one explanation for the use of the command-and-control regulatory format. Judicial deference to agency judgments, as well as judicial refusal to compel agencies to act when they refuse to do so (save when the obligation to act has been made nondiscretionary) pushes Congress toward even more specific command and control. The traditional institutional relationship between government as a whole and American industry, whereby government only rarely tells industry how to structure its internal production processes, helps explain why environmental policy has continued to place heavy reliance on end-of-the-pipe controls, despite an awareness that these will in many instances be inadequate.

2. *Federalism-related.*   Respect for federalism concerns and for preserving state and local autonomy has played a major role in shaping the evolution and structure of national environmental policy. Compare the Supreme Court's emphasis on protecting the rights of a sovereign state from interference by an out-of-state company in Georgia v. Tennessee Copper with its reluctance to umpire environmental disputes between coequal states in New York v. New Jersey. The evolution of environmental law into a national regulatory system occurred against a backdrop of growing interstate pollution problems. Yet the major federal statutes are structured in important ways to preserve state autonomy even at the price of weakening their implementation.

3. *Context-related.*   Regulatory responses to environmental problems need to be, and to a certain extent have been, sensitive to the unique dimensions of environmental problems. Different contexts have called for different regulatory and institutional responses, as we will see when we examine the major statutes individually. Environmental regulation employs a rich mix of regulatory strategies in large part because of the complexity of environmental problems and the uncertainty that inevita-

bly surrounds them. The result is a regulatory edifice that does not look coordinated and comprehensive, but that, like a shack on Tobacco Road, is often better served by inserting a new board than by rebuilding the structure.

Because of the importance of these implementation and institutional concerns, this book encourages students to become sophisticated consumers and critics of regulatory policy. It emphasizes the importance of policy analysis more than litigation skills because our operating assumption is that many of the skills normally associated with legal education can be applied to influencing agency choices in better ways than winning lawsuits. Environmentalists have always expressed the faith that ideas and principles are as real and important as actions and results, and this belief expresses a piece of our shared faith that there are lawyers' skills worth learning here. Importantly, we believe that skills of argumentation and criticism can make a difference in the regulatory arena, and hence that working the halls of the bureaucracy does not always degenerate into interest group politics and horsetrading. By argumentation we mean the capacity to marshal facts and reasons in the most persuasive manner possible. By criticism we include the capability not simply to accept the limitations on policy choices left by the Congress, but to challenge those limitations on reasoned grounds. Criticism is obviously useful to one in a position to critique legislative proposals *before* they become law. What may be less apparent is the relevance of such criticism once an agency has been assigned the task of implementing legislative judgments. Nevertheless, the history of environmental implementation reveals a surprising number of instances in which agencies have slowed implementation of legislative designs, or even sought to circumvent them, because the agency had become convinced the options left open by the legislation were unwise or ill-considered.

=3=
Waste Management and Pollution Prevention

We recognized from the very beginning that, in terms of technology, lasting environmental progress must come, not from "add-on" controls, but from basic changes in industrial and automotive processes themselves. Pollution is essentially a form of waste. . . . [W]e need to develop economic as well as regulatory approaches to environmental protection that—together with rising energy and raw materials costs—will make it increasingly more costly and less profitable to waste energy and other raw materials and thus produce pollution.

—EPA administrator Russell Train in 1977*

The Congress hereby declares it to be the national policy of the United States that pollution should be prevented or reduced at the source whenever feasible; pollution that cannot be prevented should be recycled in an environmentally safe manner, whenever feasible; pollution that cannot be prevented or recycled should be treated in an environmentally safe manner whenever feasible; and disposal or other release into the environment should be employed only as a last resort and should be conducted in an environmentally safe manner.

—Pollution Prevention Act of 1990, 42 U.S.C. §13101(b)

Pollution, by its very nature, is waste. Thus, the first pollution control laws had a direct impact on waste disposal practices. By restricting discharges of pollutants into air and water, the Clean Air Act and Clean Water Act encouraged the development of "end-of-the-pipe" technologies to reduce emissions. The limitations of an end-of-the-pipe approach became apparent as the residues captured by pollution control devices and the sludges generated by wastewater treatment plants created their own waste disposal problems. Environmental officials rec-

---

*Train, Statement before the Subcomm. on Environmental Pollution of the Senate Public Works Comm. (Jan. 18, 1977).

ognized that a truly effective pollution control strategy would require comprehensive measures that did not simply shift pollutants from one medium to another. Congress eventually responded by enacting laws requiring "cradle-to-grave" regulation of hazardous waste and imposing strict liability on parties responsible for releases of hazardous substances.

As regulations restricting waste disposal have increased in stringency, the unpleasant tradeoffs posed by existing disposal alternatives have become more visible. As a result, a consensus is emerging that environmental policy should shift its focus from controlling end-of-the pipe discharges to preventing the generation of pollution at its source. This shift has become one of the most significant trends in contemporary environmental policy. The Council on Environmental Quality predicted in 1990 that "[t]he term 'pollution prevention' may well become the hallmark of environmental policy in the 1990s and beyond." CEQ, Environmental Quality—Twentieth Annual Report 215 (1990). Later that year Congress declared pollution prevention to be national policy when it inserted the Pollution Prevention Act into omnibus budget reconciliation legislation. Pollution prevention has rapidly achieved "buzzword" status. Transforming it into an operational reality will require far more than declarations of national policy or changes in waste disposal practices. Rather, it will require changes in the very processes of production. The question of how best to stimulate pollution prevention presents a substantial challenge to policymakers.

This chapter explores the rich mix of regulatory strategies that the environmental laws employ to ensure proper management of waste and to stimulate investments in pollution prevention. We begin by examining the nature and scope of the waste management problem and why it poses such a difficult challenge for regulatory policy. We then consider how the federal environmental statutes use both regulatory and liability approaches to control waste management practices.

Two federal statutes—the Resource Conservation and Recovery Act (RCRA) and the Comprehensive Environmental Response, Compensation, and Liability Act (CERCLA)—provide comprehensive authority over waste management practices. After considering how RCRA and CERCLA fit into the larger scheme of federal environmental law, these statutes are then used to illustrate how regulatory and liability approaches can be used to prevent mismanagement of waste and to remediate environmental damage. The chapter concludes by exploring how these and other approaches are being used to encourage pollution prevention and to ensure that an appropriate mix of waste disposal options is employed.

A. WASTE MANAGEMENT AND THE POLLUTION PROBLEM

After World War II, the volume and toxicity of industrial and municipal waste streams increased dramatically with industrial growth and the rise of the synthetic chemical industry. Yet it was not until 1976 that concern over disposal of toxic waste led to the enactment of comprehensive federal regulatory authority over waste management. Hazardous waste problems now rank near the top of the public's environmental concerns.

Waste management became a national concern only after the mounting legacy of past mismanagement became visible. The practice of dumping toxic waste in whatever location was "out of sight/out of mind" was irrevocably altered in 1978 when a chemical soup seeped into a New York residential community called Love Canal. While environmental regulations now restrict toxic waste disposal to certain sites, the amount of waste generated by human activity continues to grow. Many believe that hazardous waste continues to threaten public health and the environment and that a shortage of waste disposal capacity soon will create a national crisis. Others argue that the problem is principally a political one and that the public consistently has overreacted to localized problems rarely shown to pose significant health risks.

Despite this divergence of views, there is wide agreement that past waste management practices have left an expensive legacy of environmental contamination. The enactment of broad statutory authorities to prevent mismanagement of waste has yet to ameliorate this problem. Estimates of the number of sites where cleanup will be required are staggering and continue to grow. In 1985, the Office of Technology Assessment (OTA) reported that up to 10,000 sites could need to be placed on the National Priorities List (NPL), the list of the most dangerous dump sites eligible for cleanup under the Superfund program. At that time, 538 sites had been placed on the NPL, and EPA estimated that about 2,000 sites eventually would be placed on the list. OTA estimated that total Superfund cleanup costs "could easily be $100 billion— out of total costs to the Nation of several hundred billion dollars, and it could take 50 years to clean 10,000 sites." OTA, Superfund Strategy 3 (April 1985). Five years later, the Office of Management and Budget estimated that the cost of cleaning up already-identified waste disposal problems just at *federal* facilities will be on the order of $140 to $200 billion over the next 30 years. OMB, Budget of the United States Government FY 1991, at 16 (1990). Other estimates of the total cost of environmental cleanup have ranged from $500 billion to more than $1 trillion, far more than the $8.5 billion allocated to Superfund over the last five years.

The report that follows presents EPA's perspective on the waste management problem. It describes the many types of wastes humans generate and the potential hazards they pose.

EPA, Environmental Progress and Challenges: EPA's Update
79 (1988)

More than six billion tons of agricultural, commercial, industrial, and domestic waste are produced in the United States each year. Most waste presents few health or environmental problems. Half the total, for example, is agricultural waste, primarily crop residues, most of which is plowed back into the land. Other waste, particularly that from industrial sources, can imperil both public health and the environment. . . . Leaks from underground storage tanks and chemical emergencies also contribute to contamination of the land and ground water.

If not properly disposed, even common household wastes can cause environmental problems ranging from foul-smelling smoke from burning trash to breeding grounds for rats, flies, and mosquitoes. Even at properly run disposal sites, land contamination can contribute to air and water pollution because small quantities of toxic substances such as pesticides, paints, or solvents may be dumped with other household wastes. Rain water seeping through the buried wastes may form "leachate" that percolates down through soil and may contaminate ground water. Other organic wastes such as garbage and paper products decompose and can form explosive methane gas.

Industrial wastes may present particularly troublesome problems. Many components of these wastes, such as dioxins, may present serious health or environmental threats by themselves; others are hazardous only in combination with other substances. Potential health effects range from headaches, nausea, and rashes, to acid burns, serious impairment of kidney and liver functions, cancer, and genetic damage. . . .

CLEANING UP EXISTING WASTE PROBLEMS

The problem of past hazardous waste disposal was brought to national attention in a series of incidents and the resulting news stories in the late 1970s. The first major incident was Love Canal in Niagara Falls, New York, where people were evacuated from their homes after hazardous waste buried for over 25 years seeped to the surface and into basements. Times Beach, Missouri represents another prominent story of hazardous waste mismanagement. There, oil contaminated with dioxin was used on roads and subsequently contaminated the soil and ground water in the community. . . .

SOURCES OF THE PROBLEM AND EPA's APPROACH

. . . [E]very major sector of the economy contributes to producing waste in the United States. The kinds of wastes produced by these sources and their effects vary greatly. As a result, wastes need different levels and types of control. The principal sources of waste are discussed below.

INDUSTRIAL HAZARDOUS WASTES

The chemical, petroleum, metals, and transportation industries are major producers of hazardous industrial waste. . . . Ninety-nine percent of the hazardous waste produced and managed under the RCRA program is produced by facilities that generate large quantities (more than 2,200 pounds) of hazardous waste each month.

A much smaller amount of hazardous waste, about one million tons per year, comes from small quantity generators that each produce between 220 and 2,200 pounds of waste per month. These include automotive repair shops, construction firms, laundromats, dry cleaners, and equipment repair shops. Over 60 percent of these wastes are derived from lead batteries. The remainder include acids, solvents, photographic wastes, and dry cleaning residues.

The large majority of hazardous waste is managed in the more highly industrialized areas of the United States, particularly those areas with active chemical and petroleum industries. The quantity of RCRA-regulated hazardous waste handled in the Rocky Mountains and the far west is much smaller than the amount in the eastern, southern, and midwestern states. . . .

MUNICIPAL WASTES

Municipal wastes include household and commercial wastes, demolition materials, and sewage sludge. Solvents and other harmful household and commercial wastes are generally so intermingled with other materials that specific control of each is virtually impossible. Leachate resulting from rain water seeping through municipal landfills may contaminate underlying ground water. While the degree of hazard presented by this leachate is often relatively low, the volume produced is so great that it may contaminate ground water. EPA issues requirements for municipal facilities under its program to regulate nonhazardous waste. State and local governments then are responsible for ensuring compliance.

Industrial societies with smaller farming populations and higher incomes produce considerably more waste per person than do developing countries. . . . The United States produces the most waste per person among industrial nations [4.0 pounds per person per day versus 3.0 in Tokyo, 2.4 in Paris, and 1.5 in Rome]. Taking certain materials out of those headed for the dump and recycling them is one way to manage the large volumes of waste generated. EPA encourages state and local governments to set up recycling programs, and has set a four year goal to achieve a nationwide 25 percent rate of recycling of nonhazardous wastes at their source.

Sewage sludge is the solid, semisolid, or liquid residue produced from treating municipal wastewater. Some sewage sludges contain high levels of disease-carrying microorganisms, toxic metals, or toxic organic chemicals. Because of the large quantities generated, sewage sludge is a major waste management problem in a number of municipalities. . . .

MINING WASTES

A large volume of all waste generated in the United States is from mining coal, phosphates, copper, iron, uranium, and other minerals and from ore processing and milling. These wastes consist primarily of overburden, the soil and rock cleared away before mining, and tailings, the material discarded during ore processing.

Mining wastes are a source of environmental problems particularly in a few western and southwestern states. Although mining wastes are generally considered to present low hazards, they present a disposal problem because of the estimated 2.34 billion tons generated per year. Runoff from these wastes increases the acidity of streams and pollutes them with toxic metals. Furthermore, the tremendous amounts of overburden generated in surface mining can pose local management problems. . . .

OTHER WASTES

Of the six billion tons of waste generated each year, more than half are from agriculture and forestry. Most of this waste poses relatively small health and environmental hazards. Much of forestry waste is now burned for energy, and agricultural waste is mostly plowed back into the fields or burned. Some agricultural wastes, such as unused pesticides and empty pesticide containers, do require safe treatment and disposal and are regulated by EPA. . . .

Utilities also contribute to the nation's waste production. The principal wastes produced by electric power plants are sludges from processes designed to prevent air and water pollution. Ninety percent (over 70 million tons annually) of all combustion waste generated in the U.S. is from coal-fired power plants. These wastes are generated in large amounts but generally are of low risk. . . .

UNDERGROUND STORAGE OF SUBSTANCES

Leaking underground storage tanks are another source of land contamination that can contribute to ground-water contamination. The majority of these tanks do not store waste, but instead store petroleum products and some hazardous substances. Most of the tanks now in place are bare steel and subject to corrosion. Many are old and near the end of their useful lives. Hundreds of thousands of these tanks are thought to be leaking, with more expected to develop leaks in the next five to ten years. Leaking tanks can contaminate local ground-water supplies, may endanger local drinking water systems, or may lead to explosions and fires.

NOTES AND QUESTIONS

1. When the Conservation Foundation attempted to estimate the amount of waste generated each year by residents of the United States, they discovered that this was an extraordinarily difficult task. Although the concept of waste is easy to understand, it is not so easy to define with precision. One person's trash may be another's raw material. As the Foundation's report noted:

> When a material becomes a waste is often not clear. If an industrial plant reprocesses some of the waste materials produced in one operation (for instance, a metal fabrication plant returning metal cuttings to its smelter) the materials are often not counted as wastes. If, however, the plant producing the materials ships them to another facility for resmelting, they may well be counted as wastes that are recycled. The question of what should be counted as an agricultural waste is even more uncertain. Is animal manure that is spread on fields as a soil conditioner and fertilizer a waste? . . .
>
> Classification and measurement are further complicated because many waste management systems transform waste or transfer it to a point where it may be counted again. Thus, contaminants can be removed from a wastewater stream and either dumped on the ground—creating solid

wastes—or incinerated—creating both air wastes and, with the remaining ash, solid wastes. Similarly, air pollution control devices can create solid wastes or water wastes. In some cases, waste may be chemically or physically converted to a form no longer counted as waste, even though it may still cause problems. For example, both air and water pollution control devices frequently convert organic (that is, carbon-containing) wastes to carbon dioxide (CO_2) and water, which they release into the atmosphere. In most cases, this CO_2 disappears from the accounting system. Yet it is still a waste product, for it contributes to the atmospheric CO_2 overload. [Conservation Foundation, State of the Environment: A View Toward the Nineties 106-107, 411 (1987).]

After wrestling with these problems and surveying the available data, the Conservation Foundation concluded that about 50,000 pounds of waste is produced each year for each person in this country. The report noted that even this rough figure is misleadingly small because it assumes that the water has been removed from liquid wastes. Households were estimated to generate only 3 percent of all waste, but even this tiny percentage represented 3,600 pounds of garbage per household, 120,000 gallons of wastewater that creates 180 pounds of sludge, 64 pounds of air pollutants from wood stoves, and 210 pounds of air pollutants from automobiles.

2. As indicated by Figure 3.1, the Conservation Foundation estimated that wastes from water runoff form the largest category of waste by volume, followed by non-coal-mining wastes and agricultural wastes. The volumes in which wastes are generated, however, do not provide a complete picture of the degree of hazard the wastes pose. Some wastes are more toxic, more mobile, and more difficult to neutralize than others; others may be relatively benign in composition or may decompose naturally into harmless or even beneficial substances. Efforts to control waste disposal also may alter the form and volume of waste as well as the medium in which the waste ultimately will be disposed. Note the volumes of wastes produced as air pollution control sludges, water pollution control sludges, and incinerator residues. These wastes illustrate that emission controls in a given medium create wastes that ultimately must be disposed of elsewhere.

3. While RCRA and CERCLA are the most comprehensive statutory responses to the waste management problem, they are not the only laws that affect waste disposal practices. Before we examine the RCRA and CERCLA programs, it is useful to consider briefly the wide variety of other statutes that are used to regulate waste management practices.

FIGURE 3.1

Estimated Annual Waste Production in the United States

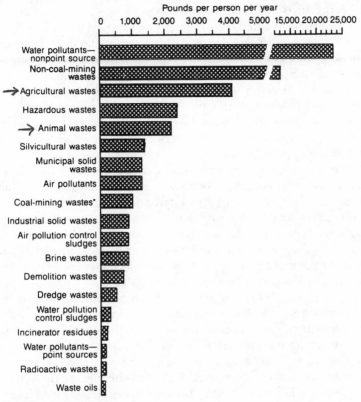

Pounds per person per year

* Underground coal mining only.
All values are estimated dry weights except for "Hazardous wastes." Some wastes may
be double-counted.

Source: Conservation Foundation, State of the Environment: A View Toward the
Nineties 408 (1987).

B. STATUTORY AUTHORITIES AFFECTING WASTE MANAGEMENT

Congress has long recognized that the best strategy for preventing
pollution is to reduce the generation of waste while encouraging recycling. Yet environmental regulations have focused almost exclusively on
waste *disposal* practices, influencing waste *reduction* only indirectly by
raising disposal costs. Wastes are generated at many stages in the production process. Wastes are generated by the extraction of raw materials
as well as during refining and fabrication. Some wastes generated during

manufacturing are recycled as scrap that is fed back into the crude materials refining process to be transformed into a form usable in further product manufacturing. The rest become industrial waste. Manufactured products are themselves sources of waste when capital goods are demolished and when consumer goods and packaging are discarded as litter or household and commercial wastes. Although the design of production processes and finished products determines the volume and composition of waste streams, waste disposal considerations often have not been incorporated into product design decisions.

The variety and complexity of activities that generate and dispose of wastes are reflected in the patchwork way in which the environmental laws control various waste management activities. Nearly a dozen major federal statutes control some aspect of waste disposal. These include not only the principal pollution control laws, listed previously, but also other statutes designed to control radioactive wastes and uranium mill tailings. These statutes are summarized in Figure 3.2. The chart lists the pollutants or wastes covered by each law (what we have called "regulatory targets"), the type of regulations they impose, and the basis for imposing controls. The chart also identifies how each law may produce cross-media transfers of wastes (e.g., air pollution controls may generate sludge and incinerator residues that are disposed of on land).

As the chart confirms, the environmental statutes focus on diverse regulatory targets. The extent of regulatory authority over waste management practices varies depending on the activity or product that generates the waste, the characteristics of the waste, and the location or method of waste disposal. For example, wastes burned or vented into the air may be subject to regulation under the Clean Air Act. Wastes discharged into inland or coastal waters are regulated under the Clean Water Act, while wastes dumped into the open ocean are controlled by the Marine Protection, Research, and Sanctuaries Act (MPRSA, also known as the Ocean Dumping Act). Radioactive wastes and uranium mill tailings are covered by their own separate statutes: the Nuclear Waste Policy Act regulates the most highly radioactive wastes generated by nuclear power plants; the Low Level Radioactive Waste Policy Act controls other radioactive wastes, such as those generated by hospitals and laboratories; the Uranium Mill Tailings Radiation Control Act sets standards for the cleanup of wastes from uranium mines. The Safe Drinking Water Act regulates contaminants that are found in public drinking water supplies as well as hazardous wastes disposed of through underground injection in deep wells.

The nature of the activity that generates a waste also may have a significant influence on the way the waste is regulated. For example, wastes generated by households have been exempted from RCRA's hazardous waste regulations because of concern over the difficulty of extending the federal regulatory system into everyone's backyard. Because mineral extraction operations generate wastes in such large volumes, Congress temporarily exempted them from federal hazardous waste regulations pending further study. Recycling activities also have been exempted from hazardous waste regulation in order to encourage efforts to reduce the volume and toxicity of waste streams.

Although Figure 3.2 might give one the impression that federal regulation has long dominated the waste management field, solid waste disposal was not regulated at the federal level until relatively recently. Garbage disposal and other forms of waste management have traditionally been the exclusive concern of local and state governments, especially municipalities. Indeed, virtually all of the other major federal environmental legislation antedates the enactment of the principal federal laws regulating waste disposal. But concern over the environmental damage caused by improper waste disposal has rapidly produced in RCRA and CERCLA two of the most far-reaching federal environmental laws. RCRA provides for cradle-to-grave regulation of hazardous waste, while CERCLA imposes strict liability for the cleanup of releases of hazardous substances. While the two statutes have complementary objectives—RCRA to prevent releases of hazardous wastes and CERCLA to clean up releases of a broader class of hazardous substances—they each employ very different means to pursue their goal. RCRA employs a regulatory approach, while CERCLA is founded on a strict liability scheme.

REGULATION OF WASTE MANAGEMENT: A PATHFINDER

The principal statutory authorities that regulate waste management practices are contained in the Resource Conservation and Recovery Act (RCRA), codified at 42 U.S.C. §§6901-6992k, and the Comprehensive Environmental Response, Compensation, and Liability Act (CERCLA), codified at 42 U.S.C. §§9601-9675. Because RCRA was originally enacted as an amendment to the largely nonregulatory Solid Waste Disposal Act, it is sometimes referred to by that name, though practitioners and courts generally use the RCRA acronym. Because CERCLA creates the federal Superfund, it is often referred to as the Superfund legislation. RCRA was substantially revised in 1984 by the Hazardous and Solid Waste Amendments (HSWA). As of 1992, Congress is considering reauthorization, and significant amendments may be adopted. CERCLA was substantially amended in 1986 by the Superfund Amendments and Reauthorization Act (SARA). It was reauthorized without substantial amendment in 1990. Because disposal of nonhazardous solid waste is largely governed

FIGURE 3.2
Major Federal Laws Regarding Waste

Statute	Waste management objective	Pollutants/wastes covered	Regulatory approach†	Basis for controls	Primary transfers to another medium
Clean Water Act: 33 U.S.C. §1251 et seq.	Protect and improve surface water quality	All discharges to surface waters, including 126 priority toxic pollutants	Performance standards (emissions limits); ambient standards	Technology with health-based backup*	Sludge to land; air emissions from treatment plant and sludge incineration
Marine Protection Research and Sanctuaries Act: 16 U.S.C. §1401 et seq.	Limit dumping into ocean	All wastes except oil and sewage in the ocean	Use restrictions (prohibited unless done with permit)	Balancing, with health-based backup	
Safe Drinking Water Act: 40 U.S.C. §§300f-300j-10 (Supp. 1977); P. L. 99-339	Protect public drinking water supply	Contaminants found in drinking water and wastes injected into deep wells	Ambient standards, design and performance standards	Technology*	
Clean Air Act: 42 U.S.C. §7401 et seq.	Protect and improve air quality	All emissions to air	Ambient standards; performance standards (emissions limits)	Health; technology*	Sludge and incinerator residues to land
Resource Conservation and Recovery Act: 42 U.S.C. §6901 et seq.	Control hazardous and solid wastes; encourage waste reduction and recycling	Hazardous and solid wastes	Use restrictions, design and performance standards; information disclosure	Health	Air through incineration; water through sewage treatment plants

		All hazardous wastes found at sites	Performance and design standards	Health, with cost-effectiveness constraint	Air through volatilization, incineration, and dust
Comprehensive Environmental Response, Compensation, and Liability Act: 42 U.S.C. §9601 et seq.; P. L. 99-499	Cleanup of abandoned hazardous waste sites; emergency response	All hazardous wastes found at sites	Performance and design standards	Health, with cost-effectiveness constraint	Air through volatilization, incineration, and dust
Surface Mining Control and Reclamation Act: 30 U.S.C. §1201 et seq.	Control pollution from surface coal mines	Surface coal mining wastes	Performance standards	Health (or environment)	Releases to water
Nuclear Waste Policy Act: 42 U.S.C. §10101 et seq.	Control disposal of high-level radioactive wastes	Commercial high-level radioactive waste	Use restrictions	Health (or environment)	
Low Level Radioactive Waste Policy Act: 42 U.S.C. §2021b et seq.	Control disposal of low-level radioactive waste	Commercial low-level radioactive waste	Use restrictions, performance and design standards	Health (or environment)	
Uranium Mill Tailings Radiation Control Act: 42 U.S.C. §7901 et seq.	Manage uranium mill tailings	Uranium mill tailings	Performance standards	Health (or environment)	Air from dust
Toxic Substances Control Act: 15 U.S.C. §2601 et seq.	Prevent unreasonable risk from chemical substances	Wastes from production or use of industrial chemical substances	Use restrictions	Balancing	

†Lists the major approaches for each statute. Some statutes use nearly all the approaches identified in Chapter 2B2.

*Some or all of these are feasibility-limited technology standards (see Chapter 4D2).

Source: Adapted from Conservation Foundation, State of the Environment: A View Toward the Nineties 426-427 (1987).

211

by state law and municipal ordinances, it is important to consult sources of such law and to pay attention to the policies of state (and local) environmental officials.

EPA waste management regulations are codified at 40 C.F.R. pts. 240-281. Regulations governing management of hazardous waste begin at 40 C.F.R. pt. 260. While CERCLA has largely been a nonregulatory program, it is beginning to generate a substantial body of regulations contained in 40 C.F.R. pts. 300-311. The list of CERCLA hazardous substances appears at 40 C.F.R. pt. 302. Significant regulatory interpretations often are found in EPA guidance documents rather than in the Federal Register, which makes it difficult to keep track of significant changes in EPA policy. The American Bar Association sponsors a satellite seminar each year to update practitioners on RCRA and CERCLA developments.

EPA maintains dockets containing important information about sites eligible for cleanup under CERCLA. These include a Federal Facilities Docket, a National Priority List (NPL) Docket, and Superfund Administrative Records, which include Records of Decision (RODs) concerning site cleanups. EPA also maintains a toll-free hotline at EPA headquarters in Washington that can provide answers to questions about the RCRA and CERCLA programs. Outside of the District of Columbia the number for the RCRA/Superfund Hotline is 800-424-9346. In the District of Columbia the hotline number is (703) 920-9810. EPA also has established a Pollution Prevention Information Clearinghouse accessible through this hotline.

Background information concerning the RCRA program can be found in EPA, The Nation's Hazardous Waste Management Program at a Crossroads (July 1990), EPA/530-SW-90-069; D. Lennett and R. Fortuna, Hazardous Waste Regulation: The New Era (1987). Useful background information on CERCLA can be found in the Environmental Law Institute's Superfund Deskbook (1990 ed.); Jan Paul Acton, Understanding Superfund (1989), published by the Rand Corporation's Institute for Civil Justice; the symposium Superfund: Waste or Waste Cleanup?, in the Winter 1992 issue of Natural Resources and Environment, published by the ABA's Section of Natural Resources, Energy, and Environmental Law.

Despite differences in their initial purposes and approaches, the RCRA and CERCLA programs are closely linked. Section 7003 of RCRA, 42 U.S.C. §6973, authorizes government actions to enjoin anyone who has contributed to waste-handling practices that may present an "imminent and substantial endangerment to health or the environment." This authority foreshadowed the enactment in 1980 of CERCLA's cleanup authorities. As congressional dissatisfaction with EPA's implementation of these programs produced major legislative revisions of each program (RCRA in 1984 and CERCLA in 1986), their interrelationship has become more important. Congress has recognized that the success or failure of RCRA's preventative regulations will have a major impact on the number of dump sites that the CERCLA program will have to clean up in the future. Thus, as we will see below, Congress has directed that RCRA's regulatory program be used to phase out the most dangerous land disposal practices while requiring operating RCRA facilities to clean up prior releases of hazardous substances as a condition for obtaining a RCRA permit.

In addition to the regulatory authorities mentioned above, Congress has acted to encourage voluntary efforts to reduce the generation of waste. The Pollution Prevention Act of 1990 represents a step in this direction. Inserted into the Omnibus Budget Reconciliation Act of 1990 during conference committee, the legislation was not contained in either the House or Senate budget bill. The conference committee report describes it as "a first step to maximize voluntary reduction of hazardous wastes and other pollutants created during the manufacturing process by improving the quality of information available to industry, states, and local and Federal officials."

The Act declares it "to be the national policy of the United States that pollution should be prevented at the source whenever feasible." In cases where pollution cannot feasibly be prevented, it declares recycling to be the preferred alternative, followed by treatment, and only then disposal. The Act requires EPA to establish a Pollution Prevention Office and a Source Reduction Clearinghouse to facilitate source reduction. The Act also requires EPA to develop a Pollution Prevention Strategy. The strategy, which EPA announced in January 1991, is designed to establish standard methods for measuring source reduction and measurable goals by which progress can be judged. As part of this strategy, EPA has targeted 15 to 20 high-risk chemicals whose generation can be reduced, and it has established a voluntary goal of reducing total environmental releases of these chemicals by 33 percent by the end of 1992 and by 50 percent by the end of 1995. EPA, Pollution Prevention Strategy (Jan. 1991).

EPA has emphasized that voluntary pollution prevention programs are not intended to substitute for strong regulatory and enforcement programs. Indeed, the Agency has indicated that it is investigating more creative use of its existing regulatory authorities to encourage source reduction, and it is committed to seeking the adoption of source reduction plans as a means for settling enforcement cases.

The Pollution Prevention Act is designed mainly to create an improved information base that can facilitate future decisions about regulatory action to prevent pollution. The Act requires companies that already must file annual reports on environmental releases pursuant to the Emergency Planning and Community Right-to-Know Act to include in these reports descriptions of their source reduction and recycling activities. This information, which will be made available to the public, is to include estimates of the amount of source reduction each company expects to achieve during the next two years.

C. THE RCRA REGULATORY PROGRAM

1. RCRA: An Introduction

A. HISTORY OF THE RCRA PROGRAM

The Solid Waste Disposal Act of 1965 had established a modest program of research on solid waste management centered in the old Department of Health, Education, and Welfare. In 1970 this legislation was expanded to authorize federal grants to support the development of new technology for solid waste management. Congress concluded that solid waste management was primarily a local responsibility, and it continued to define the federal role as a nonregulatory one.

By 1976, this had changed. RCRA was enacted after congressional committees had received estimates that the volume of solid waste generated in the United States was much greater than previously imagined. An estimated 3 to 4 billion tons of solid waste were reportedly being generated annually, and the amount was growing at an estimated 8 percent per year. The House committee report accompanying the legislation noted that each year Americans discarded 71 billion cans, 38 billion jars and bottles, 35 million tons of paper, 7.6 million televisions, 7 million cars and trucks, and 4 million tons of plastics. H.R. Rep. 94-1491, 94th Cong., 2d Sess. at 10-11 (1976).

After 1980, the history of RCRA became tightly intertwined with that of CERCLA. Mounting evidence of lax disposal practices prompted Congress to become actively involved in cleaning up the mistakes of the past and preventing their reoccurrence. By and large, RCRA has become the locus of Congress's prevention concerns, while CERCLA tackles the problems of cleaning up past mistakes, although there are important areas of overlapping responsibility. Under section 7003 of RCRA, for instance, the government can sue to enjoin activities causing "imminent and substantial endangerment," and thus can compel some cleanups. In addition, RCRA's "corrective action" requirements impose cleanup responsibilities as a condition for maintaining a current operating permit. In this section we concentrate on the predominant prevention aspects of the statute. We discuss RCRA's corrective action authorities in section E2 of this chapter.

The 1976 Act established a basic statutory structure, which continues to the present: a system for identifying and listing hazardous wastes, a cradle-to-grave tracking system, standards for generators and transporters of hazardous wastes and for operators of treatment, storage, and disposal (TSD) facilities, a permit system to enforce these standards, and a procedure for delegating to states the administration of the permitting program. This complicated structure reflects RCRA's distinct, though interrelated, objectives.

First, RCRA aimed at making land disposal of wastes far safer than it had been previously. The "overriding concern" of Congress in enacting RCRA, as expressed in the House committee report accompanying the legislation, was "the effect on the population and the environment of the disposal of discarded hazardous wastes—those which by virtue of their composition or longevity are harmful, toxic, or lethal." The report noted that "[w]ithout a regulatory framework, such hazardous waste will continue to be disposed of in ponds or on the ground in a manner that results in substantial and sometimes irreversible pollution of the environment."

The RCRA structure provided such a regulatory framework. The identification and listing system would notify generators, transporters, and operators as to which wastes came under the Act's safeguards for hazardous wastes; the tracking system would ensure that compliance could be monitored and responsibility for future problems fixed; the standards, especially for TSD operators, would minimize the environmental costs of disposal, while the permitting system would put operators on clear notice of those standards.

RCRA represented a significant departure from the approach of end-of-the-pipe pollution control statutes such as the Clean Air Act and Clean Water Act by regulating the entire life cycle of hazardous waste management activities. Congress recognized that environmental regulations should do more than simply transfer pollution from one medium to another. As the House committee that reported out the RCRA legislation explained:

> At present the federal government is spending billions of dollars to remove pollutants from the air and water, only to dispose of such pollutants on the land in an environmentally unsound manner. The existing methods of land disposal often result in air pollution, subsurface leachate and surface run-off, which affect air and water quality. This legislation will eliminate this problem and permit the environmental laws to function in a coordinated and effective way.

Indeed, the committee optimistically declared that RCRA "eliminates the last remaining loophole in environmental law, that of unregulated land disposal of discarded materials and hazardous wastes." H.R. Rep. 94-1491, 94th Cong., 2d Sess., at 4 (1976). While the RCRA regulatory program has focused on protecting groundwater from contamination by hazardous wastes leaching from land disposal facilities, RCRA requires regulation of all avenues for treatment, storage, and disposal of hazardous waste, including incinerators and air emissions from hazardous waste landfills.

Second, RCRA aimed at technology forcing. The statute, through the regulations that EPA was instructed to promulgate, requires TSD operators to employ technologies for landfill disposal "as may be necessary to protect human health." §3004(a). Beyond this, however, RCRA evinces a concern that landfills were being used excessively because they were far cheaper than alternative disposal techniques. As one analyst notes: "It is not difficult to see why firms and others faced with the costs of incineration to render wastes less harmful (estimated to range from $300 to $1,000 per ton) or of burying the wastes in landfills (perhaps as little as $50 per ton) would choose the latter." R. Dower, Hazardous Wastes, in Public Policies for Environment Protection 154 (P. Portney, ed. 1990). Imposing stricter safety requirements on landfills would raise the costs of such disposal; Congress believed that this would force the development of superior alternative technologies.

The desire to promote alternative disposal techniques has become even more apparent as Congress has revisited the 1976 legislation, first in 1980 and again in 1984. For instance, as Senator Chafee (R-R.I.) explained during debate on the 1984 Amendments:

> [L]and disposal is extremely cheap when compared with the available alternatives such as incineration or chemical-physical treatment. Therefore, we should not be surprised to find that land disposal and treatment in land disposal facilities such as surface impoundments are being utilized much more frequently than the newer, high-tech options. . . . What we do not have, and will not have as long as cheap land disposal options are available, is a viable market to support the development and expansion of new, safer treatment and disposal technologies. [130 Cong. Rec. S30697 (daily ed. Oct. 5, 1984).]

The 1984 Amendments reflected a new level of congressional effort to force technological change because Congress was no longer relying on market forces to express the increased costs of land disposal and hence to stimulate that change. As Representative Lent (R-N.Y.) said, "I believe it is appropriate for the Congress to intervene at this time and to establish a new policy which calls for a review of known hazardous wastes and a determination whether these wastes are appropriate for land disposal." 130 Cong. Rec. H29490 (daily ed. Oct. 3, 1984). The most dramatic such interventions are the 1984 Amendments' land disposal ban provisions, analyzed later in this section.

Third, RCRA aimed at waste reduction. "Waste reduction" encompasses any techniques that adjust basic manufacturing processes so that waste is not generated in the first place. One incentive for waste reduction is provided by increasing the costs of waste disposal. Beyond this, initial elements of a waste reduction program were rudimentary at best and, in the press of implementing the regulatory aspects of RCRA, essentially ignored. There are some signs this situation is changing. We return to waste reduction strategies in section F below.

One reason waste reduction was not more directly addressed by the 1976 statute involves the fourth objective of RCRA: Congress wanted to minimize direct regulation of American production processes. As the committee report accompanying the House version of the 1976 Act explained the provisions applicable to generators of hazardous wastes, "rather than place restrictions on the generation of hazardous waste, which in many instances would amount to interference with the production process itself, the committee has limited the responsibility of the generator for hazardous waste to one of providing information." H.R. Rep. No. 94-1491, 94th Cong., 2d Sess., at 26 (1976). The jurisdictional trigger of the statute reflects this intention, in that the statute defines "solid wastes" as "discarded material." §1004(27).

American Mining Congress v. EPA, excerpted below, involves some of the interpretational and implementational issues created by the desire of Congress to steer EPA away from direct regulation of normal production processes. As that decision suggests, some of the most significant problems arise with respect to the fifth objective of the statute: encouraging recycling. As a method for addressing the solid waste problem, recycling, or resource recovery, can be seen as standing between waste reduction and treatment, storage, and disposal. While waste reduction adjusts primary production processes so that waste is eliminated before it is generated, and TSD facilities dispose of or otherwise care for the generated wastes that remain, recycling takes generated wastes and returns all or part of them to primary production processes. Congress understood that increased recycling was yet another way to minimize environmental and public health damage from waste disposal and meant to encourage it. As the House report said, "an increase in reclamation and reuse practices is a major objective of the Resource Conservation and Recovery Act." H.R. Rep. No. 94-1491 at 2.

Although the desire to encourage recycling has been clear from the beginning, the status of recycling activities under RCRA's regulatory authorities has been problematic. Many of the problems relate to the distinction between "the production process itself" and "discarded material." If they are awaiting processing through a recycling facility, are piles of industrial residue from manufacturing "discarded materials" or are they part of "the production process itself"? Does it matter whether or not the recycling processes actually employed were being employed as part of production processes before RCRA was enacted (even if not employed as extensively as we would like)? From time to time, EPA has said that it "did not believe [its] authority extends to certain types of recycling activities that are shown to be similar to normal production processes. . . ." 50 Fed. Reg. at 614. In other places, however, it has been more aggressive, interpreting RCRA as "providing authority over hazardous wastes being used, reused, recycled, or reclaimed." 48 Fed. Reg. at 14,502. The line-drawing exercise here is important, because regulated firms have a substantial interest in being exempt from governmental regulation. This is precisely what was at stake in *American Mining Congress*. That litigation is also typical of a fair amount of litigation under RCRA. Because being caught by the RCRA regulatory net is financially onerous, and because the statute contains so many definitions and exemptions, we have witnessed considerable litigation about its jurisdictional boundaries.

Finally, RCRA sought to maintain substantial state responsibility for the solid waste problem. The legislation explicitly acknowledged that "the collection of solid wastes should continue to be primarily the function of State, regional and local agencies," §1002(a)(4). While it mandated comprehensive federal regulation of "hazardous wastes," it provided for the delegation of permitting responsibilities to qualifying state agencies. Thus, RCRA reflected the tendency of 1970s environmental legislation to leave politically divisive implementation of federal substantive legislation to the states. Some of this divisiveness emerges during controversies surrounding the siting of hazardous waste related facilities. See section F1, below.

While keeping the basic structure of the 1976 Act intact, Congress revisited RCRA with major amendments in 1984 called the Hazardous and Solid Waste Amendments (HSWA). HSWA sought to strengthen EPA's regulatory hand in accomplishing RCRA's primary objectives. Congress made more apparent its conviction that land disposal should be the disposal option of last resort and expressed its dissatisfaction with the slow pace of RCRA implementation.

Defining which of the myriad chemical waste streams are hazardous and what management practices will ensure that no damage is done to the environment proved to be far more difficult than anyone had imagined. These inherent difficulties were exacerbated in 1981 when the Reagan Administration's regulatory relief program brought RCRA implementation to a temporary standstill. EPA's promulgation of final permitting standards for TSDs was delayed for years while existing TSDs were allowed to continue in operation as RCRA "interim status" facilities with minimal environmental controls. To qualify for "interim status" facilities were only required to notify EPA of their existence and to conduct minimal groundwater monitoring.

The 1984 Amendments mandated a major shift in the philosophy behind RCRA regulation. EPA previously had recognized that all landfills eventually leak, but it had focused most of its regulatory attention on measures to contain such leakage. The 1984 Amendments sought not only to speed EPA's development of regulatory standards and to close certain loopholes in EPA's existing regulations, but also to fundamentally change waste disposal practices by phasing out land disposal and by forcing the development and use of improved technology to detoxify hazardous wastes.

To speed EPA's implementation of RCRA, Congress imposed scores of new statutory deadlines for the promulgation of regulations by EPA. EPA had failed to meet most such deadlines in the original RCRA legislation. Indeed, most of the significant RCRA regulations, such as permitting standards for TSDs, were issued under court orders as a result of citizen suits brought by environmental groups. To ensure that the most significant new deadlines established by the 1984 Amendments were met, Congress coupled them with "hammer" provisions specifying what regulations would automatically take effect if EPA failed to act.

The principal thrust of the 1984 Amendments was to shift hazardous waste disposal away from the land and to encourage the development of more sophisticated treatment technologies. To minimize the land disposal of untreated wastes, Congress directed that such disposal be banned in stages unless EPA determined that there would be "no migration" of hazardous constituents as long as the waste remains hazardous. Recognizing that severe contamination already had occurred at many TSDs, Congress required facilities obtaining RCRA permits to take corrective action to clean up all prior releases of hazardous wastes and their constituents. To hasten the closing of interim status facilities that would not qualify for final permits, Congress required all TSDs to apply for final RCRA permits by October 1986 and to certify compliance with groundwater monitoring and financial responsibility requirements. As a result of these provisions, a majority of the existing treatment and storage facilities and incinerators opted to close, as did the vast majority of land disposal facilities. In 1990 EPA reported that 1,273 RCRA land disposal facilities were closing, while only 194 were either applying for, or had received, permits; 1,559 RCRA treatment and storage facilities were closing, while 1,251 were either applying for, or had received, permits; and 130 RCRA incinerators were closing, while 120 were seeking permits. EPA, The Nation's Hazardous Waste Management Program at a Crossroads 43 (July 1990).

The 1984 Amendments substantially strengthened the RCRA program, focusing EPA's regulatory arsenal on discouraging the land disposal of hazardous waste. Although EPA has made substantial progress in implementing the 1984 Amendments, many problems remain. EPA met only 27 of the 66 HSWA deadlines that expired in April 1988. In 1990, EPA stated that it would not complete all of the regulatory actions required by the 1984 Amendments until early in the next century, although court-ordered deadlines may accelerate this schedule.

B. Structure of the RCRA Program

To understand how the RCRA program operates, it is useful to begin by sketching in greater detail the basic structure of the regulatory scheme the statute creates, rather than plunging headlong into what one court has called a "mind-numbing journey" (American Mining Congress v. EPA, 824 F.2d 1177, 1189 (D.C. Cir. 1987)) through EPA's complicated RCRA regulations. The structure of RCRA is outlined below. When studying RCRA, bear in mind what targets EPA generally may regulate under the statute (those who generate, transport, treat, store, or dispose of hazardous solid waste) and the basis for controls specified in the statute ("as may be necessary to protect human health or the environment").

STRUCTURE OF THE RESOURCE CONSERVATION AND RECOVERY ACT

§1002. Goals: outlines statutory goals, including the principle that land disposal should be the least favored method for managing hazardous wastes.

Subtitle C: Hazardous Waste Management (§§3001-3020)
§3001. Identification and Listing of Hazardous Waste: requires EPA to develop criteria for determining what is a hazardous waste and to list wastes determined to be hazardous.

§3002. Regulation of Generators of Hazardous Waste: requires EPA to establish recordkeeping requirements and a manifest system to be used to track shipments of hazardous waste from point of generation.

§3003. Regulation of Transporters of Hazardous Waste: requires transporters of hazardous waste to use the manifest system.

§3004. Regulation of Facilities that Treat, Store, or Dispose of Hazardous Waste (TSDs): requires EPA to set standards for TSDs to ensure safe handling of hazardous waste, sets minimum requirements for such standards, prohibits the land disposal of untreated wastes unless EPA spe-

cifically determines that such disposal is protective of human health and the environment, establishes minimum technology requirements for certain facilities, and requires corrective action for all releases of hazardous wastes or constituents.

§3005. Permit Requirements for TSDs: requires TSDs to obtain a permit from EPA or states that incorporates the requirements of section 3004.

Subtitle D: State or Regional Solid Waste Plans

§§4001-4010: require EPA to establish guidelines for state solid waste management plans and to set minimum requirements for state plans including a ban on new open dumps, require EPA to establish criteria for classifying facilities as sanitary landfills, prohibit open dumping of solid waste except in sanitary landfills, and require EPA to establish minimum regulatory standards for municipal landfills to be implemented by the states.

Enforcement, Citizen Suit, and Judicial Review Provisions

§3008: provides federal enforcement authorities including criminal, civil, and administrative penalties.

§7002: authorizes citizen suits against those who violate RCRA regulations or permits, against anyone who has contributed or is contributing to the past or present handling of any solid or hazardous waste that may present an imminent and substantial endangerment to health or the environment, and against the EPA administrator for failure to perform any nondiscretionary duty.

§7003: authorizes suits by EPA to restrain anyone who has contributed or is contributing to the past or present handling of any solid or hazardous waste that may present an imminent and substantial endangerment to health or the environment.

§7006: authorizes judicial review of RCRA regulations in the D.C. Circuit.

Subtitle I: Regulation of Underground Storage Tanks

§9002: requires owners of underground storage tanks to notify state authorities.

§9003: requires EPA to issue regulations governing detection, prevention, and correction of leaks from underground storage tanks, including financial responsibility requirements and new tank performance standards.

Subtitle J: Demonstration Medical Waste Tracking Program

§11003: requires EPA to establish a demonstration program for tracking medical wastes in certain states.

As you can see, RCRA is divided into two major parts: (1) subtitle C, a regulatory program covering *hazardous* solid wastes, and (2) subtitle D, a largely nonregulatory program to encourage states to improve their management of *nonhazardous* solid waste. Subtitle C of RCRA requires EPA to regulate generators of hazardous waste (§3002), transporters (§3003), and facilities that treat, store, or dispose of hazardous waste (§3004). Operating standards for TSD facilities are to be implemented through a permit system (§3005).

RCRA's subtitle C regulations are contained in 40 C.F.R. pts. 260-272. While they are too complicated to be reviewed in detail here, some idea of the general types of requirements they impose on generators, transporters, and TSD facilities is provided in Figure 3.3. Generators are responsible for determining if their wastes are hazardous. Those who accumulate more than 100 kilograms of hazardous waste per month—an estimated 200,000 firms—are subject to regulation under subtitle C. These generators must obtain an identification number for their hazardous waste. To ensure that shipments of hazardous waste can be traced, generators must complete a multiple-copy manifest form to accompany the waste to its ultimate destination at a licensed TSD. The generator must notify authorities if a copy of the manifest form is not returned certifying that the waste reached its intended destination. 40 C.F.R. pt. 262.

Transporters also must use the manifest system, and they must mark and label their shipments of hazardous waste. 40 C.F.R. pt. 263. Transporters of hazardous waste must comply not only with EPA's manifest requirements, but also with regulations on hazardous materials transportation established by the Department of Transportation pursuant to the Hazardous Materials Transportation Act.

Facilities that treat, store, or dispose of hazardous waste must obtain a permit that incorporates minimum national standards established in EPA's regulations. 40 C.F.R. pt. 270. See Figure 3.4. These include not only general administrative requirements for recordkeeping, personnel training, and emergency preparedness, but also specific design, performance, and operating requirements for each category of facility. New units, replacement units, and lateral expansions of existing landfills and surface impoundments must meet certain minimum technology requirements. (For example, landfills must have double liners and a leachate collection system.) Facilities also must prepare closure plans describing how the facilities ultimately will be closed, and they must demonstrate

FIGURE 3.3

Summary of RCRA Subtitle C Regulations Applicable to Hazardous Waste Generators, Transporters, and Treatment, Storage, and Disposal Facilities

RCRA requirements	Generators	Transporters	Treatment, storage, disposal facilities[a]
Determine if wastes are hazardous	X		X
Notify EPA if RCRA hazardous waste handler and obtain identification number	X	X	X
Train personnel in waste management procedures and emergency response	X	X	X
Preparedness and prevention measures and notification of releases	X	X	X
Contingency planning and emergency procedures	X		X
Inspect facility operations periodically	X		X
Track waste with manifest system	X	X	X
Recordkeeping and reporting	X		X
Package marking, labeling, and transport vehicle placarding		X	X
Physical security			X
Use and manage containers, landfills, and other operating areas properly[b]			X
Design and operate waste handling areas adequately[b]			X
Groundwater monitoring			X
Closure and postclosure care			X
Ensure financial responsibility for closure and postclosure care			X

[a]Treatment, storage, or disposal facilities in operation on or before November 19, 1980, could continue operating under "interim status" until a hazardous waste permit was issued, at which time the facility must be in compliance with the final permit regulations.

[b]This includes the design and operation of tanks, surface impoundments, waste piles, land treatment facilities, landfills, incinerators, and injection wells.

Source: GAO, New Approach Needed to Manage the Resource Conservation and Recovery Act, July 1988, at 24.

FIGURE 3.4
A Capsule Description of RCRA's Subtitle C Program

EPA and the states share the responsibility for regulating newly generated hazardous waste under RCRA. RCRA was created to minimize the risks from hazardous wastes at all points in their life cycle, from their generation to their disposal. It was also designed to require safeguards; to encourage the proper disposal of municipal, commercial, and industrial waste; to eliminate or reduce waste; and to conserve energy and natural resources.

Hazardous Waste and "Cradle to Grave" Management

RCRA involves a "cradle to grave" effort covering the generation, transportation, storage, treatment, and disposal of newly generated hazardous waste. EPA's system includes five basic elements:

- **Identification**—Generators and the types of waste that they produce must be initially identified.
- **Tracking**—A uniform "manifest" describing the waste, its quantity, the generator, and receiver, must accompany transported hazardous waste from the point at which it is generated to its final off-site destination and disposal.
- **Permitting**—All hazardous waste treatment, storage, and disposal facilities will be issued permits to allow EPA and the states to ensure their safe operation. There are about 7,000 facilities that must receive permits in order to continue operating.
- **Restrictions and controls**—Hazardous waste facilities must follow EPA's

rules and guidance specifying acceptable conditions for disposal, treatment, and storage of hazardous wastes.
- **Enforcement and compliance**—Generators, transporters, and facilities are penalized if they do not comply with the regulations.

The cradle to grave system works through requirements for hazardous waste treatment, storage, and disposal facilities. Key to this system are RCRA operating permits. Basic operating permits identify administrative and technical standards with which facilities must comply. For example, the permits require operators of hazardous waste landfills to keep thorough records of the types and quantities of wastes they manage.

Hazardous Waste Manifest Trail

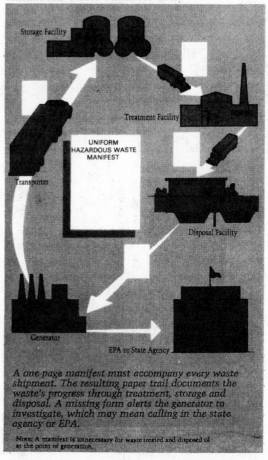

A one-page manifest must accompany every waste shipment. The resulting paper trail documents the waste's progress through treatment, storage and disposal. A missing form alerts the generator to investigate, which may mean calling in the state agency or EPA.

Note: A manifest is unnecessary for waste treated and disposed of at the point of generation.

Source: EPA, Environmental Progress and Challenges: EPA's Update 88 (Aug. 1988).

that they have sufficient financial resources to compensate third parties for damages as well as to undertake safe closure and to conduct postclosure monitoring and maintenance.

Another significant requirement of the 1984 Amendments is that RCRA permits now must require facilities to take "corrective action for all releases of hazardous waste or constituents from any solid waste management unit" at the facility. Thus, TSD facilities that wish to continue operation must clean up any prior contamination at their facility regardless of when or where it occurred. TSDs also must conduct regular groundwater monitoring and take corrective action if contamination is detected. When closing, TSDs must take precautions designed to ensure that their facilities will not leak in the decades to come, and they must ensure their financial responsibility to clean up releases that occur during postclosure care. Generators, transporters, and TSDs must all train their personnel in waste management and emergency response procedures, and they must notify the authorities of releases of hazardous substances.

The process for obtaining a RCRA permit is complex and extraordinarily lengthy. In 1990 EPA reported that the average length of time for issuance of a RCRA permit was four and one-half years for an incinerator, four years and two months for a land disposal facility, two years and nine months for a treatment facility, and two and one-half years for a storage facility. EPA, The Nation's Hazardous Waste Management Program at a Crossroads 50 (July 1990).

The regulatory program established by RCRA can be viewed as essentially a two-tiered scheme: "hazardous wastes" are to be regulated stringently under subtitle C (from generation through transport to disposal), while all other solid wastes are subject to subtitle D and left largely untouched by federal regulation (although municipal solid waste landfills are now subject to minimum federal standards under subtitle D). Rather than attempting to vary the degree of regulation to match the degree of hazard posed by a particular waste, the RCRA program with few exceptions leaves only two regulatory options: comprehensive regulation with little regard for cost considerations, or no federal regulation at all. If a facility is found to be treating, storing, or disposing of a hazardous waste, it generally must comply with all permit requirements regardless of the degree of hazard its waste poses. Thus, RCRA properly can be viewed as mandating a form of health-based regulation, but one that does not vary once the regulatory threshold of "hazardousness" has been crossed.

To be sure, there is another provision in RCRA that gives EPA more discretion to tailor the extent of regulation to the degree of hazard involved. Section 7003 of RCRA authorizes EPA to sue to enjoin any person who has contributed to, or is contributing to, any solid or hazardous waste management practices that "may present an imminent and substantial endangerment to health or the environment." This was used extensively by the government to address the need to clean up abandoned dump sites prior to the enactment of CERCLA in 1980.

As we will see below, EPA's implementation of the land disposal ban provisions of the 1984 Amendments to RCRA has now moved the RCRA program much closer to technology-based regulation. While the land ban appears to be a health-based standard on paper (it prohibits the disposal of untreated hazardous wastes unless it can be shown with a reasonable degree of certainty that there will be no migration of the waste as long as it remains hazardous), EPA has chosen to implement it by requiring that facilities use the best demonstrated available treatment technology (BDAT) before disposing of wastes on land.

Most of the dump site cleanup problem is a legacy of the inadequacy of controls on waste disposal practices in the past. But few people are confident that even new, tougher controls on hazardous waste disposal can ensure that existing facilities regulated under subtitle C of RCRA will not eventually become Superfund sites. This lack of confidence stems not only from the fact that a certain amount of illegal dumping undoubtedly occurs, but also from gaps in subtitle C's coverage. As a result, HSWA amended subtitle D of RCRA, which covers nonhazardous solid wastes, to require EPA to establish minimum regulatory standards to be used by the states in regulating municipal landfills. While these regulations, which we examine in section C6, will subject management practices for nonhazardous solid wastes to their first significant dose of regulation, subtitle C's regulations remain far stricter, particularly in light of the land disposal ban.

As a result of the 1984 Amendments, the universe of facilities regulated under RCRA has expanded dramatically. In 1990 EPA estimated that 4,700 treatment, storage, and disposal facilities were regulated under subtitle C. EPA, The Nation's Hazardous Waste Management Program at a Crossroads 7 (July 1990). EPA estimates that these facilities consist of 81,000 separate waste management units. By bringing generators of small quantities of hazardous waste into the RCRA system, the 1984 Amendments more than doubled the number of generators subject to subtitle C from less than 100,000 to more than 211,000. Id.

In the sections that follow we consider how far RCRA's jurisdiction extends by exploring the meaning of the terms that are the crucial jurisdictional triggers for RCRA regulation: "solid waste" and "hazardous waste." To be regulated under RCRA a substance must be a *solid waste;* only solid wastes that are *hazardous* are subject to regulation under the onerous subtitle C.

2. What Substances Are "Solid Wastes"?

RCRA's jurisdiction extends to all "solid waste." A waste does not have to be in solid form in order to be considered a "solid waste" for purposes of RCRA jurisdiction. Section 1003(27) of RCRA defines "solid waste" as including "any garbage, refuse, sludge from a waste treatment plant, water supply treatment plant, or air pollution control facility and other discarded material, including solid, liquid, semisolid or contained gaseous material, resulting from industrial, commercial, mining, and agricultural operations, and from community activities." 42 U.S.C. §6903(27).

Certain categories of waste have been exempted from RCRA by EPA or Congress by excluding them from the definition of solid waste. As illustrated in Figure 3.5, Congress has exempted domestic sewage, industrial wastewater discharges that are subject to regulation as point sources under section 402 of the Clean Water Act, irrigation return flows, mining wastes not removed from the ground, and certain nuclear materials covered by the Atomic Energy Act. EPA by regulation also has exempted other categories of waste including household wastes (i.e., the garbage we generate at home), fertilizer used in agricultural operations, and certain categories of high-volume wastes that Congress had directed EPA to study (e.g., certain mining wastes). These exclusions can have significant environmental consequences because the wastes removed from the RCRA regulatory program include millions of gallons of hazardous materials whose disposal is largely unregulated.

A particularly troublesome issue for EPA has been the extent to which RCRA covers recycled materials. If material that otherwise would be discarded is recycled, can it be considered a solid waste? If a generator maintains that materials that otherwise would be considered wastes are being stored for future recycling should the materials be covered by RCRA's regulations?

On January 4, 1985 EPA issued a definition of "solid waste" that required 54 pages of explanation in the Federal Register, 50 Fed. Reg. 614. Under EPA's definition, materials are considered solid wastes if they are abandoned by being disposed of, burned, or incinerated; or stored, treated, or accumulated before or in lieu of those activities. EPA determined that certain materials used in recycling also might fall within RCRA's jurisdiction depending on the nature of the material and the recycling activity involved. This resulted in a legal challenge by representatives of the mining and petroleum industries. They argued that EPA's jurisdiction under RCRA could not extend to materials that eventually would be reused because such materials were not wastes. The D.C. Circuit decided this challenge to EPA's definition of solid waste in the case that follows.

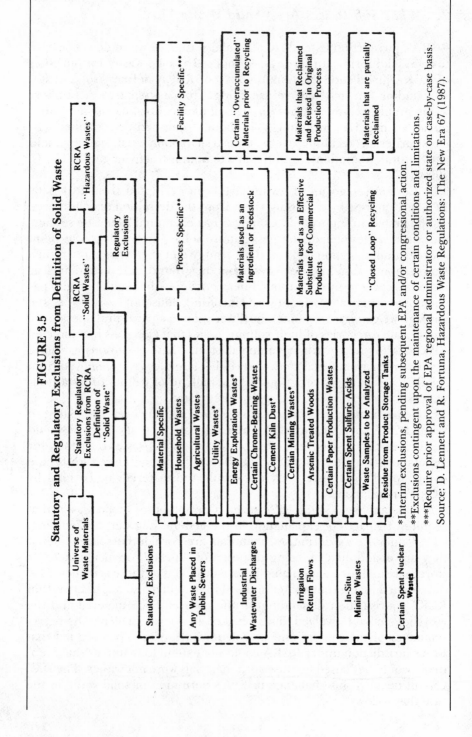

FIGURE 3.5
Statutory and Regulatory Exclusions from Definition of Solid Waste

*Interim exclusions, pending subsequent EPA and/or congressional action.
**Exclusions contingent upon the maintenance of certain conditions and limitations.
***Require prior approval of EPA regional administrator or authorized state on case-by-case basis.
Source: D. Lennett and R. Fortuna, Hazardous Waste Regulations: The New Era 67 (1987).

|| *American Mining Congress v. EPA* ||
|| 824 F.2d 1177 (D.C. Cir. 1987) ||

Before STARR and MIKVA, Circuit Judges, and McGOWAN, Senior Circuit Judge.

STARR, Circuit Judge:

These consolidated cases arise out of EPA's regulation of hazardous wastes under the Resource Conservation and Recovery Act of 1976 ("RCRA"), as amended, 42 U.S.C. §§6901-6933 (1982 & Supp. III 1985). Petitioners, trade associations representing mining and oil refining interests, challenge regulations promulgated by EPA that amend the definition of "solid waste" to establish and define the agency's authority to regulate secondary materials reused within an industry's ongoing production process. In plain English, petitioners maintain that EPA has exceeded its regulatory authority in seeking to bring materials that are not discarded or otherwise disposed of within the compass of "waste."

I

RCRA is a comprehensive environmental statute under which EPA is granted authority to regulate solid and hazardous wastes. . . .

Congress' "overriding concern" in enacting RCRA was to establish the framework for a national system to insure the safe management of hazardous waste. H.R. Rep. No. 1491, 94th Cong., 2d Sess. 3 (1976), U.S. Code Cong. & Admin. News 1976, pp. 6238, 6240, 6241. . . .

RCRA includes two major parts: one deals with nonhazardous solid waste management and the other with hazardous waste management. Under the latter, EPA is directed to promulgate regulations establishing a comprehensive management system. Id. §6921. EPA's authority, however, extends only to the regulation of "hazardous waste." Because "hazardous waste" is defined as a subset of "solid waste," id. §6903(5), the scope of EPA's jurisdiction is limited to those materials that constitute "solid waste." That pivotal term is defined by RCRA as

> any garbage, refuse, sludge from a waste treatment plant, water supply treatment plant, or air pollution control facility *and other discarded material,* including solid, liquid, semisolid or contained gaseous material, resulting from industrial, commercial, mining, and agricultural operations, and from community activities. . . .

42 U.S.C. §6903(27) (emphasis added). As will become evident, this case turns on the meaning of the phrase, "and other discarded material," contained in the statute's definitional provisions.

EPA's interpretation of "solid waste" has evolved over time. On May 19, 1980, EPA issued interim regulations defining "solid waste" to include a material that is "a manufacturing or mining by-product and sometimes is discarded." 45 Fed. Reg. 33,119 (1980). This definition contained two terms needing elucidation: "by-product" and "sometimes discarded." In its definition of "a manufacturing or mining by-product," EPA expressly *excluded* "an intermediate manufacturing or mining product which results from one of the steps in a manufacturing or mining process and is typically processed through the next step of the process within a short time." Id.

In 1983, the agency proposed narrowing amendments to the 1980 interim rule. 48 Fed. Reg. 14,472 (1983). The agency showed especial concern over *recycling* activities. In the preamble to the amendments, the agency observed that, in light of RCRA's legislative history, it was clear that "Congress indeed intended that materials being recycled or held for recycling can be wastes, and if hazardous, hazardous wastes." Id. at 14,473. The agency also asserted that "not only can materials destined for recycling or being recycled be solid and hazardous wastes, but the Agency clearly has the authority to regulate recycling activities as hazardous waste management." Id.

While asserting its interest in recycling activities (and materials being held for recycling), EPA's discussion left unclear whether the agency in fact believed its jurisdiction extended to materials recycled in an industry's on-going production processes, or only to materials disposed of and recycled as part of a waste management program. In its preamble, EPA stated that "the revised definition of solid waste sets out the Agency's view of its jurisdiction over the recycling of hazardous waste. . . . Proposed section 261.6 then contains exemptions from regulations for those hazardous waste recycling activities that we do not think require regulation." Id. at 14,476. The amended regulatory description of "solid waste" itself, then, did not include materials "used or reused as effective substitutes for raw materials in processes using raw materials as principal feedstocks." Id. at 14,508. EPA explained the exclusion as follows:

> [These] materials are being used essentially as raw materials and so ordinarily are not appropriate candidates for regulatory control. Moreover, when these materials are used to manufacture new products, the processes generally are normal manufacturing operations. . . . The Agency is reluctant to read the statute as regulating actual manufacturing processes.

Id. at 14,488. This, then, seemed clear: EPA was drawing a line between discarding and ultimate recycling, on the one hand, and a continuous or ongoing manufacturing process with on-site "recycling," on the other. If the activity fell within the latter category, then the materials were not deemed to be "discarded."

After receiving extensive comments, EPA issued its final rule on January 4, 1985. 50 Fed. Reg. 614 (1985). Under the final rule, materials are considered "solid waste" if they are abandoned by being disposed of, burned, or incinerated; or stored, treated, or accumulated before or in lieu of those activities. In addition, certain recycling activities fall within EPA's definition. EPA determines whether a material is a RCRA solid waste when it is recycled by examining both the material or substance itself and the recycling activity involved. The final rule identifies five categories of "secondary materials" (spent materials, sludges, by-products, commercial chemical products, and scrap metal). These "secondary materials" constitute "solid waste" when they are disposed of; burned for energy recovery or used to produce a fuel; reclaimed; or accumulated speculatively. Id. at 618-19, 664.[1] Under the final rule, if a material constitutes "solid waste," it is subject to RCRA regulation *unless* it is directly reused as an ingredient or as an effective substitute for a commercial product, or is returned as a raw material substitute to its original manufacturing process.[2] Id. In the jargon of the trade, the latter category is known as the "closed-loop" exception. In either case, the material must not first be "reclaimed" (processed to recover a usable product or regenerated). Id. EPA exempts these activities "because they are like ordinary usage of commercial products." Id. at 619.

II

Petitioners, American Mining Congress ("AMC") and American Petroleum Institute ("API"), challenge the scope of EPA's final rule. Relying upon the statutory definition of "solid waste," petitioners con-

---

1. Under the final rule, a "use constituting disposal" is defined as direct placement on land of wastes or products containing or derived from wastes. A material is "accumulated speculatively" if it is accumulated prior to being recycled. If the accumulator can show that the materials feasibly can be recycled, and that during a one-year calendar period the amount of material recycled or transferred for recycling is 75% or more of the amount present at the beginning of the year, the materials are not considered solid wastes. A material is "reclaimed" if it is processed to recover a usable product, or if it is regenerated. Id.

2. Specifically, the final rule excludes materials recycled by being: "(1) [u]sed or reused as ingredients in an industrial process to make a product, *provided the materials are not being reclaimed;* or (2) [u]sed or reused as effective substitutes for commercial products; or (3) [r]eturned to the original process from which they are generated, without first being reclaimed." Id. (emphasis added). In the third category, the material must be returned to the original manufacturing process as a substitute for raw material feedstock, and the process must use raw materials as principal feedstocks.

tend that EPA's authority under RCRA is limited to controlling materials that are *discarded or intended for discard.* They argue that EPA's reuse and recycle rules, as applied to in-process secondary materials, regulate materials that have not been discarded, and therefore exceed EPA's jurisdiction.

[The court then describes how petroleum refineries use a complex retrieval system to recapture escaping hydrocarbons and return them to appropriate parts of the refining process. The court also states that mining facilities reprocess ore and recapture for reuse in the production process metal- and mineral-bearing dusts released during processing. The court notes that the materials recaptured by petroleum refineries and mining facilities are considered "solid waste" under EPA's rule.]

III . . .

. . . Congress, it will be recalled, granted EPA power to regulate "solid waste." Congress specifically defined "solid waste" as "discarded material." EPA then defined "discarded material" to include materials destined for reuse in an industry's *ongoing* production processes. The challenge to EPA's jurisdictional reach is founded, again, on the proposition that in-process secondary materials are outside the bounds of EPA's lawful authority. Nothing has been *discarded,* the argument goes, and thus RCRA jurisdiction remains untriggered.

The first step in statutory interpretation is, of course, an analysis of the language itself. As the Supreme Court has often observed, "the starting point in every case involving statutory construction is 'the language employed by Congress.'" CBS v. FCC, 453 U.S. 367, 377 (1981) (quoting Reiter v. Sonotone Corp., 442 U.S. 330, 337 (1979)). In pursuit of Congress' intent, we "start with the assumption that the legislative purpose is expressed by the ordinary meaning of the words used." Securities Industry Ass'n v. Board of Governors, 468 U.S. 137, 149 (1984) (quoting Richards v. United States, 369 U.S. 1, 9 (1962)). These sound principles governing the reading of statutes seem especially forceful in the context of the present case. Here, Congress defined "solid waste" as "discarded material." The ordinary plain-English meaning of the word "discarded" is "disposed of," "thrown away" or "abandoned." Encompassing materials retained for immediate reuse within the scope of "discarded material" strains, to say the least, the everyday usage of that term. . . .

. . . [A] complete analysis of the statutory term "discarded" calls for more than resort to the ordinary, everyday meaning of the specific language at hand. For, "the sense in which [a term] is used in a statute must be determined by reference to the purpose of the particular legislation." Burnet v. Chicago Portrait Co., 285 U.S. 1, 6 (1932). . . .

. . . RCRA was enacted in response to Congressional findings that the "rising tide of scrap, discarded, and waste materials" generated by consumers and increased industrial production had presented heavily populated urban communities with "serious financial, management, intergovernmental, and technical problems in the disposal of solid wastes." Id. §6901(a). . . .

The question we face, then, is whether, in light of the National Legislature's expressly stated objectives and the underlying problems that motivated it to enact RCRA in the first instance, Congress was using the term "discarded" in its ordinary sense—"disposed of" or "abandoned"—or whether Congress was using it in a much more open-ended way, so as to encompass materials no longer useful in their original capacity though destined for immediate reuse in another phase of the industry's ongoing production process.

Leg.

For the following reasons, we believe the former to be the case. RCRA was enacted, as the Congressional objectives and findings make clear, in an effort to help States deal with the ever-increasing problem of solid waste *disposal* by encouraging the search for and use of alternatives to existing methods of disposal (including recycling) and protecting health and the environment by regulating hazardous wastes. To fulfill these purposes, it seems clear that EPA need not regulate "spent" materials that are recycled and reused in an *ongoing* manufacturing or industrial process. These materials have not yet become part of the waste disposal problem; rather, *they are destined for beneficial reuse or recycling in a continuous process by the generating industry itself.*

Hist.

The situation in this case thus stands in sharp contrast to that in *Riverside Bayview,* another post-*Chevron* case. There, the Corps of Engineers had defined "the waters of the United States" within the meaning of the Clean Water Act, 33 U.S.C. §§1311, 1362 (1972), to include "wetlands." Recognizing that it strained common sense to conclude that "Congress intended to abandon traditional notions of 'waters' and include in that term 'wetlands' as well," the Court performed a close and searching analysis of Congress' intent to determine if this counterintuitive result was nonetheless what Congress had in mind. Id. at 461-65. The Court based its holding (that the agency's expansive definition of "waters of the United States" was reasonable) on several factors: Congress' acquiescence in the agency's interpretation; provisions of the statute expressly including "wetlands" in the definition of "waters"; and, importantly, the danger that forbidding the Corps to regulate "wetlands" would defeat Congress' purpose since pollutants in "wetlands" water might well flow into "waters" that were indisputably jurisdictional. Id. at 465. Thus, due to the nature of the water system, the very evil that Congress sought to interdict—the befouling of the "waters of the United States"—would likely occur were the Corps of Engineers' jurisdiction to stop short of wetlands. *Riverside Bayview,* 106 S. Ct. at 463. . . .

. . . EPA's regulation of in-process materials . . . seems to us an effort to get at the same evil (albeit, very broadly defined) that Congress had identified by extending the agency's regulatory compass, rather than, as with the regulation of wetlands, an attempt to reach activities that if left unregulated would sabotage the agency's regulatory mission. We are thus not presented with a situation in which Congress likely intended that the pivotal jurisdictional term be read in its broadest sense, detached from everyday parlance; instead, we have a situation in which Congress, perhaps through the process of legislative compromise which courts must be loathe to tear asunder, employed a term with a widely accepted meaning to define the materials that EPA could regulate under RCRA. See *Dimension Financial,* 106 S. Ct. at 689. And it was that term which the Congress of the United States passed and the President ultimately signed into law. . . .

IV

We are constrained to conclude that, in light of the language and structure of RCRA, the problems animating Congress to enact it, and the relevant portions of the legislative history, Congress clearly and unambiguously expressed its intent that "solid waste" (and therefore EPA's regulatory authority) be limited to materials that are "discarded" by virtue of being disposed of, abandoned, or thrown away. While we do not lightly overturn an agency's reading of its own statute, we are persuaded that by regulating in-process secondary materials, EPA has acted in contravention of Congress' intent. Accordingly, the petition for review is Granted.

MIKVA, Circuit Judge, dissenting:
. . . In my opinion, the EPA's interpretation of solid waste is completely reasonable in light of the language, policies, and legislative history of RCRA. See United States v. Riverside Bayview Homes, 474 U.S. 121 (1986). Congress had broad remedial objectives in mind when it enacted RCRA, most notably to "regulat[e] the treatment, storage, transportation, and disposal of hazardous wastes which have adverse effects on the environment." 42 U.S.C. §6902(4). The disposal problem Congress was combatting encompassed more than just abandoned materials. RCRA makes this clear with its definition of the central statutory term "disposal":

> the discharge, deposit, injection, dumping, spilling, leaking, or placing of any solid waste or hazardous waste into or on any land or water so that such solid waste or hazardous waste or any constituent thereof may enter

the environment or be emitted into the air or discharged into any waters, including ground waters.

42 U.S.C. §6903(3). This definition clearly encompasses more than the everyday meaning of disposal, which is a "discarding or throwing away." Webster's Third International Dictionary 654 (2d ed. 1981). The definition is *functional:* waste is disposed under this provision if it is put into contact with land or water in such a way as to pose the risks to health and the environment that animated Congress to pass RCRA. Whether the manufacturer subjectively intends to put the material to additional use is irrelevant to this definition, as indeed it should be, because the manufacturer's state of mind bears no necessary relation to the hazards of the industrial processes he employs.

Faithful to RCRA's functional approach, EPA reasonably concluded that regulation of certain in-process secondary materials was necessary to carry out its mandate. The materials at issue in this case can pose the same risks as abandoned wastes, whether or not the manufacturer intends eventually to put them to further beneficial use. As the agency explained, "[s]imply because a waste is likely to be recycled will not ensure that it will not be spilled or leaked before recycling occurs." The storage, transportation, and even recycling of in-process secondary materials can cause severe environmental harm. Indeed, the EPA documented environmental disasters caused by the handling or storage of such materials. It also pointed out the risk of damage from spills or leaks when certain in-process secondary materials are placed on land or in underground product storage. . . .

. . . [I]n this case the EPA has interpreted solid waste in a manner that seems to expand the everyday usage of the word "discarded." Its conclusion, however, is fully supportable in light of the statutory scheme and legislative history of RCRA. The agency concluded that certain on-site recycled materials constitute an integral part of the waste disposal problem. This judgment is grounded in the EPA's technical expertise and is adequately supported by evidence in the record. The majority nevertheless reverses the agency because it believes that the materials at issue "have not yet become part of the waste disposal problem." Maj. op. at 1186. This declaration is nothing more than a substitution of the majority's own conclusions for the sound technical judgment of the EPA. The EPA's interpretation is a reasonable construction of an ambiguous statutory provision and should be upheld.

NOTES AND QUESTIONS

1. Do you agree with EPA that the definition of "solid waste" should employ a functional approach that focuses on whether materials have

become part of the waste disposal problem? Does the court agree with this principle? Given the enormous variety of ways in which materials are processed and the diversity of substances that emerge at various stages of manufacturing processes, is it realistic to expect that an agency could define a concept like "solid waste" with precision and clarity? How would you propose to do so?

2. To what extent, if any, should the definition of "solid waste" turn on an assessment of whether or not a substance poses a risk warranting regulation? If such judgments are relevant for definitional purposes, who should make them—EPA or the courts? Note that in his dissent Judge Mikva challenged the majority's statement that materials stored on-site for possible future reclamation "have not yet become part of the waste disposal problem." What basis did he have for questioning their statement? Did the majority give sufficient deference to EPA's conclusion that such materials are an integral part of the waste disposal problem? Should EPA's judgment on this factual issue make any difference to a court reviewing the scope of EPA's regulatory authority?

3. Should EPA be able to define "solid waste" broadly to encompass materials that it believes need to be regulated to prevent deliberate evasion of RCRA regulations? Consider, for example, whether gaseous materials can be regulated under RCRA. Congress defined "solid waste" in section 1003(27) of RCRA to include "solid, semisolid or *contained gaseous material*," 42 U.S.C. §6903(27) (emphasis supplied). While this language suggests that RCRA extends only to gases in containers, EPA has expressed concern that "a plant could evade regulation by designing a [production] process to keep the process emissions in a gaseous state," 54 Fed. Reg. 50,973 (1989). EPA notes that the Bhopal tragedy occurred when a volatile liquid (methyl isocyanate) was released as a gas. Thus, EPA initially declared that only "true gases," defined as "those which are not capable of being condensed and which remain gaseous at standard temperature and pressure," were exempt from RCRA when released in uncontained form. Under this interpretation, gases capable of being condensed and materials that are not gases at standard temperature or pressure would be subject to subtitle C of RCRA when released in uncontained form. Is this position consistent with the statutory definition of "solid waste"? EPA subsequently reconsidered its position and now states that its RCRA authority "is limited to containerized or condensed gases." 54 Fed. Reg. 50,973 (1989). Which interpretation is more consistent with the statutory language? Which is more consistent with the goals of RCRA? If a facility deliberately heats a solid waste until it becomes a gas and is released into the air, can EPA regulate this activity under subtitle C? See 54 Fed. Reg. 50,973 (col. 2). Why or why not? If a facility designs its production process so that this occurs, can a RCRA permit be required? See id.

4. Five months after the D.C. Circuit's *AMC* decision, EPA pro-

posed a new definition of "solid waste" in response to the court's decision. 53 Fed. Reg. 519 (Jan. 8, 1988). While EPA proposed to exclude from the definition materials reclaimed in a "closed loop," it concluded that the court's decision did not affect its authority to regulate materials "recycled in ways where the recycling activity itself is characterized by discarding," 53 Fed. Reg. at 520. Thus, EPA indicated that it would consider several factors in deciding whether materials recycled without passing through "a continuous, ongoing manufacturing process" were solid wastes. These factors include: (1) whether the material is typically discarded on an industry-wide basis, (2) whether the material replaces a raw material when it is recycled and the degree to which its composition is similar to that of the raw material, (3) the relation of the recovery practice to the principal activity of the facility, (4) whether the material is handled prior to reclamation in a secure manner that minimizes loss and prevents releases to the environment, and (5) other factors, such as the length of time the material is accumulated. 53 Fed. Reg. 35,415. How are each of these factors relevant to the question whether a material should be considered a solid waste?

5. EPA received more than 130 comments on its proposal to modify its prior regulations. Representatives of the American Mining Congress charged that EPA had interpreted the *AMC* decision far too narrowly. In an unusual move, they asked the D.C. Circuit to hold EPA in contempt of court for failing to abide by the decision even though EPA had not taken any final action on its proposal. The D.C. Circuit denied their motion.

6. As a result of the *AMC* decision, industry representatives argued that a number of substances that EPA has regulated under subtitle C of RCRA are not "solid wastes." For example, can EPA regulate sludge from wastewater stored in a surface impoundment if the sludge may at some time in the future be reprocessed for metals recovery? EPA said yes because it is the product of wastewater and it is stored in an impoundment that can threaten harm to the environment. The D.C. Circuit agreed in American Mining Congress v. EPA (*AMC II*), 907 F.2d 1179 (D.C. Cir. 1990). The court distinguished *AMC* in the following terms:

> *AMC*'s holding concerned only materials that are "destined for *immediate reuse* in another phase of the industry's ongoing production process," id. at 1185 (emphasis added), and that "have not yet become part of the waste disposal problem," id. at 1186. Nothing in *AMC* prevents the agency from treating as "discarded" the wastes at issue in this case, which are managed in land disposal units that *are* part of wastewater treatment systems, which *have* therefore become "part of the waste disposal problem," and which are *not* part of ongoing industrial processes. Indeed, [we have] explicitly rejected the very claim that petitioners assert in this case, . . . namely, that under RCRA, potential reuse of a material prevents the agency from classifying it as "discarded." [907 F.2d at 1186.]

7. If the owner of the surface impoundment could guarantee EPA that *all* the sludge in the surface impoundment eventually would be removed for metals reclamation, could the sludge be considered a solid waste while it was still in the impoundment? What if it had leached hazardous constituents into the soil beneath the impoundment?

8. Can materials that are in fact recycled be considered wastes at the time of recycling? Citing *AMC*, EPA determined that materials inserted into a metals reclamation process cease to be solid wastes for purposes of RCRA regulation at the time they arrive at a reclamation facility because they are no longer "discarded materials." 53 Fed. Reg. 11,753 (1988). The materials involved were wastes that EPA had required to be treated through metals reclamation. Environmentalists successfully challenged this interpretation in American Petroleum Institute v. EPA, 906 F.2d 792 (D.C. Cir. 1990). The court explained that

> *AMC* is by no means dispositive of EPA's authority to regulate [such waste]. Unlike the materials in question in *AMC,* [the waste] is indisputably "discarded" *before* being subject to metals reclamation. Consequently, it *has* "become part of the waste disposal problem"; that is why EPA has the power to require that [it] be subject to mandatory metals reclamation. See 53 Fed. Reg. 11,752-53 (recognizing this point). Nor does anything in *AMC* require EPA to cease treating [the material] as "solid waste" once it reaches the metals reclamation facility. [The material] is delivered to the facility not as part of an *"ongoing* manufacturing or industrial process" within "the generating industry," but as part of a mandatory waste treatment plan prescribed by EPA. [906 F.2d at 741 (emphasis in original).]

Noting that Congress consciously had decided not to regulate the *generation* of waste when it adopted RCRA due to concerns about interfering with production processes, EPA had maintained that it could not regulate material undergoing metals reclamation because that would interfere with an ongoing production process. Regulating furnaces used to recover metals from zinc-laden waste "would be like directly regulating the industrial production of zinc from ore," EPA argued. Rejecting this argument, the court explained: "The two forms of regulation might be 'like' each other, but they are by no means one and the same." 906 F.2d at 741 n.15. The court emphasized that even if the treatment process produced something of value—reclaimed metals—the important distinction for purposes of RCRA jurisdiction was whether the material being processed had been discarded, not whether the process extracted valuable products from the discarded material. 906 F.2d at 741 n.16.

9. In Chapter 2 we discussed the problem of defining regulatory targets given the regulated community's incentive to escape regulation. This is nowhere better illustrated than by the problem of defining "solid waste." Because *AMC* created uncertainty concerning a key jurisdictional

term—the definition of "solid waste"—the regulated community sought to embrace it as a major loophole for avoiding RCRA regulation. Under the most extreme interpretation of *AMC*, a company might escape RCRA regulation simply by asserting that it eventually would recycle waste material that otherwise would be regulated. However, in light of the decisions in *American Petroleum Institute* and *AMC II*, EPA staff now believe that *AMC*'s holding has been sharply limited. Do you agree? As a result, they no longer feel compelled to promulgate a new definition of "solid waste." While EPA will solicit further public comment on this issue, agency officials now indicate that it is unlikely that EPA will take final action on its proposed redefinition of "solid waste." They now believe that EPA's previous definition is legal and enforceable and that the D.C. Circuit's decisions in *American Petroleum Institute* and *AMC II* have vindicated the agency's position, which focuses on whether materials are part of the waste disposal problem. Do you agree with this conclusion?

10. Two ex-EPA officials formerly in charge of solid waste programs have commented:

> [T]he regulatory distinction between wastes and products has led to discrepancies that are not defensible from an environmental standpoint. For example, certain pesticides that can be applied directly to the land at high concentrations cannot be legally disposed in state-of-the-art hazardous waste landfills until they have been pretreated. . . . Similarly, chemical treatment processes that are part of chemical production are relatively unregulated compared with chemical waste processes that are part of waste disposal. . . .
>
> [These discrepancies] grow even more problematic as recycling becomes a desirable component of waste management.
>
> Historically, a facility performing "legitimate" recycling has been exempt from many of the environmental management standards that apply to facilities deemed to be managing hazardous waste. . . . Yet a long list of recycling facilities, including oil refiners, battery recyclers, and scrap metal recyclers, have ended up as Superfund sites. Moreover, some facilities that claimed the recycling exemption (e.g., certain thermal facilities) look amazingly similar to hazardous waste treatment facilities, yet the same recycling facilities are allowed to reuse their ash as product while the hazardous waste incinerator must continue to treat it as hazardous waste, regardless of how clean that ash is. [Williams and Cannon, Rethinking RCRA for the 1990s, 21 Envtl. L. Rev. 10063, 10067 (1991).]

Are there any legitimate justifications for these discrepancies?

11. In order to be subject to the cradle-to-grave regulations of RCRA's subtitle C, a material must be not only a "solid waste" but also a "hazardous" one. We now turn to the question of what solid wastes are hazardous for purposes of RCRA.

3. Identifying "Hazardous Waste"

Although Congress required EPA to regulate hazardous waste under subtitle C of RCRA, it did not specify how the agency was to determine what wastes were hazardous. "Hazardous waste" is defined by section 1004(5) of RCRA as

> a solid waste, or combination of solid wastes, which because of its quantity, concentration, or physical, chemical, or infectious characteristics may—
>> (A) cause or significantly contribute to an increase in mortality or an increase in serious irreversible, or incapacitating reversible, illness; or
>> (B) pose a substantial present or potential hazard to human health or the environment when improperly treated, stored, transported, or disposed of, or otherwise managed.

Section 3001 of RCRA requires EPA to promulgate regulations identifying the characteristics of hazardous waste and listing particular wastes as hazardous "taking into account toxicity, persistence, and degradability in nature, potential for accumulation in tissue, and other related factors such as flammability, corrosiveness, and other hazardous characteristics."

EPA has implemented these provisions (40 C.F.R. pt. 261) by establishing two principal avenues for solid waste to be deemed "hazardous": by exhibiting one of four hazardous characteristics ("characteristic wastes") or by being specifically listed as a hazardous waste in EPA's regulations ("listed wastes"). Waste streams can be specifically listed as hazardous if EPA determines that they routinely contain hazardous constituents or exhibit hazardous characteristics. As indicated in Figure 3.6, EPA has established four general categories of listed wastes (the "F," "K," "P," and "U" lists). By the end of 1990, EPA had listed more than 760 types of wastes as hazardous by placing them in one of these four categories.

To prevent generators from evading hazardous waste regulations by diluting or otherwise changing the composition of listed waste streams, EPA in 1980 adopted two important rules: the "mixture rule" and the "derived-from" rule. The mixture rule provides that any mixture of a listed waste with another solid waste is itself considered to be a hazardous waste. The derived-from rule provides that wastes derived from the treatment, storage, or disposal of a listed waste (such as the ash residue from incineration of a listed waste) are deemed to be hazardous wastes. 40 C.F.R. §261.3(c)(2)(i). Thus, listed wastes would be deemed to remain hazardous unless they are specifically "delisted" by EPA.

Although some industry groups maintained that the mixture and derived-from rules unlawfully expanded EPA's jurisdiction under RCRA,

FIGURE 3.6
RCRA Hazardous Waste Classifications

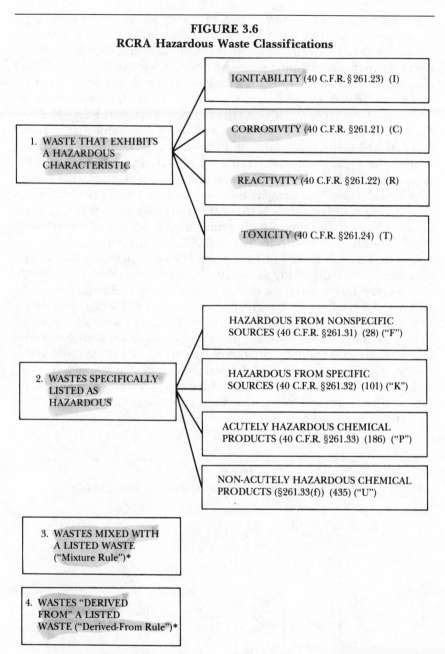

1. WASTE THAT EXHIBITS A HAZARDOUS CHARACTERISTIC
   - IGNITABILITY (40 C.F.R. § 261.23) (I)
   - CORROSIVITY (40 C.F.R. §261.21) (C)
   - REACTIVITY (40 C.F.R. §261.22) (R)
   - TOXICITY (40 C.F.R. §261.24) (T)

2. WASTES SPECIFICALLY LISTED AS HAZARDOUS
   - HAZARDOUS FROM NONSPECIFIC SOURCES (40 C.F.R. §261.31) (28) ("F")
   - HAZARDOUS FROM SPECIFIC SOURCES (40 C.F.R. §261.32) (101) ("K")
   - ACUTELY HAZARDOUS CHEMICAL PRODUCTS (40 C.F.R. §261.33) (186) ("P")
   - NON-ACUTELY HAZARDOUS CHEMICAL PRODUCTS (§261.33(f)) (435) ("U")

3. WASTES MIXED WITH A LISTED WASTE ("Mixture Rule")*

4. WASTES "DERIVED FROM" A LISTED WASTE ("Derived-From Rule")*

*Regulations temporarily reinstated, 57 Fed. Reg. 7628 (1992), aft on procedural grounds in Shell Oil v. EPA, 950 F.2d 741 (D.C. Cir. 1

the rules became an important part of the RCRA program while legal challenges to the rules were held in abeyance for more than a decade. When the D.C. Circuit finally addressed the issue in December 1991, it struck down the mixture and derived-from rules without deciding whether they exceeded EPA's authority. Surprisingly, the court held that EPA had not provided adequate notice and opportunity for comment when it proposed the rules in 1978. Shell Oil Co. v. EPA, 950 F.2d 741 (D.C. Cir.) (Dec. 6, 1991). The court rejected EPA's argument that industry had suffered no prejudice from this 13-year-old procedural defect, even though the Agency maintained that it had considered and rejected the very criticisms industry would have made had adequate notice been provided. Noting "the dangers that may be posed by a discontinuity in the regulation of hazardous wastes," the court suggested that EPA reenact the rules on an interim basis under the "good cause" exception to the Administrative Procedure Act, 5 U.S.C. §553(b)(3)(B).

EPA has now done so by temporarily reinstating the rules while it conducts a new rulemaking to consider them. 57 Fed. Reg. 7628 (1992).

Figure 3.6 identifies the different classifications of hazardous waste and the places where EPA regulations pertaining to them appear in the Federal Register. Wastes not specifically listed as hazardous must be managed as hazardous wastes if they exhibit one of the four hazardous characteristics (ignitability, corrosivity, reactivity, or toxicity) that are illustrated in Figure 3.7. These "characteristic wastes" are considered hazardous only until they no longer exhibit the hazardous characteristic. Unlike listed wastes, characteristic wastes are not subject to the mixture or derived-from rules. If they are mixed with a substance other than a

---

FIGURE 3.7
Characteristics That Identify a Waste as Hazardous

Ignitability   Corrosivity   Reactivity   Toxicity

Source: GAO, New Approach Needed to Manage the Resource Conservation and Recovery Act 18 (July 1988).

listed waste they need to be managed as a hazardous waste only as long as they continue to exhibit a hazardous characteristic. Substances derived from a characteristic waste are considered hazardous only if they continue to exhibit a hazardous characteristic.

Thus, the extensive regulatory standards prescribed by subtitle C of RCRA are applicable to solid wastes that are hazardous, which include: (1) wastes specifically listed as hazardous, (2) wastes that exhibit any of the four hazardous characteristics, and (3) wastes mixed with or derived from a listed waste (pending the outcome of the rulemaking initiated by EPA in response to the *Shell Oil* decision).

During the first decade of RCRA implementation, EPA's slow progress in identifying and listing hazardous wastes was criticized frequently. Although EPA studied more than a dozen other potential characteristics that could be used to classify a waste as hazardous (including carcinogenicity, infectiousness, and organic toxicity), it did not adopt any of these other characteristics because it was unable to identify suitable tests for them. In 1981 EPA instead focused on studying 1,100 industrial production processes to expand its category of "listed wastes." But the Agency promulgated new waste listings for only five wastes, finding that it had insufficient information to determine whether other waste streams should be listed. In 1986 EPA abandoned its plan to do more studies and shifted its focus to revising its hazardous characteristics. EPA based this decision on its conclusion that the industry study process was too expensive and had resulted in few waste listings.

The 1984 Amendments to RCRA directed EPA to identify additional hazard characteristics by November 1986 and to improve the existing toxicity characteristic test by March 1987. EPA missed these deadlines by three years. On March 5, 1990, the Agency promulgated far-reaching revisions to its procedures for identifying toxic characteristic wastes. EPA added 25 organic chemicals (including benzene, vinyl chloride, and chloroform) to the 8 metals and 6 pesticides on its existing list of substances which if found as constituents in waste in certain concentrations render the waste hazardous under the toxicity characteristic. EPA also promulgated a new, more sensitive test, known as the toxicity characteristic leaching procedure, or TCLP, to be used to determine whether a solid waste contains these hazardous constituents. It is estimated that these changes will subject more than 17,000 additional waste generators to regulation under subtitle C of RCRA, including many companies in the pulp and paper, petroleum refining and marketing, organic chemicals, pharmaceuticals, plastics, rubber, lumber, and textile industries. EPA estimates that the cost of complying with the new rules will range from $250 to 400 million per year, largely because the rules will increase the volume of material considered to be hazardous waste by some 1.8 million metric tons. 55 Fed. Reg. 11,798 (1990).

Former EPA staffer William Pedersen has argued that the RCRA system is both overinclusive and underinclusive. Pedersen argues that RCRA is overinclusive because the mixture and derived-from rules result in the regulation of many wastes that are far less toxic than wastes excluded from the system. Pedersen, The Future of Federal Solid Waste Regulation, 16 Colum. J. Envtl. L. 109, 120 (1991). While EPA has acknowledged problems with the mixture and derived-from rules, prior to the *Shell Oil* decision it had been reluctant to propose any de minimis exception for fear that this would simply encourage dilution of wastes. See Gaba, The Mixture and Derived-from Rules Under RCRA: Once a Hazardous Waste Always a Hazardous Waste?, 21 Envtl. L. Rep. 10033 (1991). Pederson maintains that RCRA is underinclusive because more truly hazardous waste is excluded from the RCRA system than is included. He notes that while data on hazardous waste generation are notoriously unreliable, only a small fraction of the waste that is generated is listed as hazardous and that special exemptions (such as those for mining waste, household waste, and waste placed in public sewers) exclude more waste that possesses a hazardous characteristic than is included in the RCRA system. Id. at 118-119.

Pedersen maintains that the RCRA program's failure to provide more comprehensive coverage of hazardous waste is a result of the "stigma and drastic regulatory burden that attend listing a waste." Although the D.C. Circuit has held that concern over the stigma attached to a waste's being listed as hazardous is an insufficient basis for refusing to list an otherwise hazardous waste, Hazardous Waste Treatment Council v. EPA, 861 F.2d 270 (D.C. Cir. 1988) (rejecting argument that used oil should not be listed as a hazardous waste because it would discourage recycling), EPA has resisted efforts to expand the coverage of RCRA listings except when expressly required by Congress.

NOTES AND QUESTIONS

1. EPA has taken the position that "[h]azardous waste listings are retroactive, so that once a particular waste is listed, all wastes meeting that description are hazardous wastes no matter when disposed." 53 Fed. Reg. 31,147 (1988). Why would EPA take this position? Is it fair to owners of land disposal facilities that contain wastes not considered to be hazardous at the time of disposal? Does this constitute improper "retroactive" rulemaking? See Chemical Waste Management, Inc. v. EPA, 869 F.2d 1526 (D.C. Cir. 1989).

2. EPA's derived-from rule provides that "any solid waste generated from the treatment, storage, or disposal of a hazardous waste, including any sludge, spill residue, ash, emission control dust, or leachate (but not including precipitation run-off) is a hazardous waste." 40 C.F.R. §261.3(c)(2)(i). Why do you think EPA promulgated this regulation? As

a result of the derived-from rule, would the residue left over after hazardous waste is treated to reduce its toxicity itself be a hazardous waste? Would soil, groundwater, or any other environmental medium become a hazardous waste when it comes into contact with a listed waste? See Chemical Waste Management, Inc. v. EPA, 869 F.2d 1526 (D.C. Cir. 1989).

3. Do you agree with Pedersen that the mixture and derived-from rules are likely to require that many nonhazardous materials be managed as a hazardous waste? How could EPA narrow the scope of these rules without encouraging dilution? Should EPA exempt waste that does not have a certain threshold concentration of hazardous constituents?

4. Note that the derived-from rule includes leachate (except for precipitation runoff). Leachate is produced when liquids (including rainwater) seep through wastes buried in landfills, producing a fluid that contains constituents of the original waste. State-of-the-art landfills have liners and leachate collection systems to keep hazardous constituents from escaping in the form of leachate. Would leachate collected from a hazardous waste landfill have to be managed as a hazardous waste under the derived-from rule? See id. What about rainwater runoff?

5. The derived-from and mixture rules applied only to listed waste. Yet determinations of whether materials that are not listed as hazardous waste have a hazardous characteristic also can be difficult. The following problem is designed to help you appreciate the difficulty of determining whether or not a waste is hazardous (and therefore subject to regulation under RCRA subtitle C) as a result of the toxicity characteristic. It is based on an actual controversy. Read the facts carefully; consult the statute and the EPA regulations reproduced in the problem before preparing your answers.

PROBLEM EXERCISE: INCINERATOR ASH AND RCRA

As landfill space disappears, many cities are building incinerators to dispose of municipal garbage. More than 160 municipal waste incinerators burn about 13 percent of the 160 million tons of garbage generated in the United States each year. Dozens more are under construction. Municipal incinerators now generate more than 4 million tons of ash (approximately 25 percent by volume of the original waste stream). Ash residues include fly ash captured by emission control equipment, bottom ash, and the products of incomplete combustion. Heavy metals are present in the ash residues, and occur in particularly large quantities in the fly ash.

As noted above, one of the four characteristics that can make a waste "hazardous" for purposes of subtitle C regulation is toxicity. Toxicity is determined by a procedure designed to measure the potential for a waste to leach hazardous constituents. The test procedure, formerly called the "extraction procedure" and now called the "toxicity characteristic leaching procedure" (TCLP), analyzes the extract from a sample of the waste for any of 40 chemical contaminants. If the extract has any of these substances in concentrations above specified levels (generally 100 times greater than levels allowed under the Safe Drinking Water Act), the waste is considered to be toxic and must be managed as a hazardous waste. Figure 3.8 lists the maximum concentration of contaminants for the toxicity characteristic.

EPA's regulations require a person who generates a solid waste to "determine if that waste is a hazardous waste," 40 C.F.R. §262.11 (see Figure 3.9). If a waste is not a hazardous waste specifically listed in subpt. D of 40 C.F.R. pt. 261, the person must determine whether the waste is hazardous because of its characteristics by either testing the waste or "[a]pplying knowledge of the hazard characteristic of the waste in light of the materials or the processes used." 40 C.F.R. §262.11(c)(2).

When tested using EPA's toxicity test, fly ash and bottom ash from municipal waste incinerators frequently have been found to contain lead and cadmium at concentrations greater than the 5 and 1 milligram per liter cutoff levels for the toxicity characteristic. Fly ash fails the test 80 to 90 percent of the time, bottom ash fails 20 to 25 percent of the time, and combined ash fails about 50 percent of the time. Only a handful of municipal incineration facilities test their ash regularly.

In March 1987 an environmental group reviewed the results of tests performed on ash residues from more than 20 incinerators around the country. The group concluded that the data showed that "ash residues commonly contain lead and cadmium at levels well above the toxicity limits." It sent a letter summarizing the test results to the owners and operators of 100 incinerators. The letter stated:

> We are enclosing a summary of these test results for your examination because they have important consequences for your obligations under federal law. Federal regulations require that the owner or operator of a facility generating solid waste must test the waste by using the extraction procedure toxicity test unless it can be determined that the waste is not toxic based on "knowledge of the hazard characteristic of the waste in light of the materials or the processes used." 40 C.F.R. 262.11. The enclosed test results demonstrate that ash residues from incineration fail the toxicity test with sufficient frequency to require, at a minimum, that the owners and operators of such facilities test all ash residues. The results show that even if some samples of an incinerator's ash "pass" the test, others will not. Thus, a "passing" sample does not provide any assurance that other ash residues are non-hazardous. Accordingly, even if you previously have tested ash samples that did not fail the toxicity test, you are not relieved of your continued testing obligation. If a facility that you own or operate is cur-

FIGURE 3.8
Maximum Concentration of Contaminants for the Toxicity Characteristic

EPA HW No.[1]	Contaminant	CAS No.[2]	Regulatory level (mg/L)
D004	Arsenic	7440-38-2	5.0
D005	Barium	7440-39-3	100.0
D018	Benzene	71-43-2	0.5
D006	Cadmium	7440-43-9	1.0
D019	Carbon tetrachloride	56-23-5	0.5
D020	Chlordane	57-74-9	0.03
D021	Chlorobenzene	108-90-7	100.0
D022	Chloroform	67-66-3	6.0
D007	Chromium	7440-47-3	5.0
D023	o-Cresol	95-48-7	[4]200.0
D024	m-Cresol	108-39-4	[4]200.0
D025	p-Cresol	106-44-5	[4]200.0
D026	Cresol		[4]200.0
D016	2,4-D	94-75-7	10.0
D027	1,4-Dichlorobenzene	106-46-7	7.5
D028	1,2-Dichloroethane	107-08-2	0.5
D029	1,1-Dichloroethylene	75-35-4	0.7
D030	2,4-Dinitrotoluene	121-14-2	[3]0.13
D012	Endrin	72-20-8	0.02
D031	Heptachlor (and its epoxide)	76-44-8	0.008
D032	Hexachlorobenzene	118-74-1	[3]0.13
D033	Hexachlorobutadiene	87-68-3	0.5
D034	Hexachloroethane	67-72-1	3.0
D008	Lead	7439-92-1	5.0
D013	Lindane	58-89-9	0.4
D009	Mercury	7439-97-6	0.2
D014	Methoxychlor	72-43-5	10.0
D035	Methyl ethyl ketone	78-93-3	200.0
D036	Nitrobenzene	98-95-3	2.0
D037	Pentrachlorophenol	87-86-5	100.0
D038	Pyridine	110-86-1	[3]5.0
D010	Selenium	7782-49-2	1.0
D011	Silver	7440-22-4	5.0
D039	Tetrachloroethylene	127-18-4	0.7
D015	Toxaphene	8001-35-2	0.5
D040	Trichloroethylene	79-01-6	0.5
D041	2,4,5-Trichlorophenol	95-95-4	400.0
D042	2,4,6-Trichlorophenol	88-06-2	2.0
D017	2,4,5-TP (Silvex)	93-72-1	1.0
D043	Vinyl chloride	75-01-4	0.2

[1]Hazardous waste number.

[2]Chemical abstracts service number.

[3]Quantitation limit is greater than the calculated regulatory level. The quantitation limit therefore becomes the regulatory level.

[4]If o-, m-, and p-Cresol concentrations cannot be differentiated, the total cresol (D026) concentration is used. The regulatory level of total cresol is 200 mg/l.

rently generating ash residue, it is vital that you comply with federally-mandated standards for testing ash and for managing ash in accordance with subtitle C requirements if it is found to be toxic. Failure to perform such tests and failure to comply with subtitle C requirements could subject you to severe civil and criminal penalties.

Question One.   Few municipal waste combustion facilities regularly test their ash using the toxicity test. Do you think the owners and operators of such incinerators are required to do so pursuant to 40 C.F.R. section 262.11? Why or why not? If they are required to test, must they test all the ash, just the fly ash, or both the fly ash and the combined ash? How frequently, if at all, must they conduct such tests?

Question Two.   Why do you think the environmental group sent the letters? What is the relevance of the test data enclosed with the letter? If a sample of ash is tested and "fails" the toxicity test, how must the

---

FIGURE 3.9
RCRA Regulations

§ 262.11   Hazardous waste determination.

A person who generates a solid waste, as defined in 40 CFR 261.2, must determine if that waste is a hazardous waste using the following method:

(a) He should first determine if the waste is excluded from regulation under 40 CFR 261.4.

(b) He must then determine if the waste is listed as a hazardous waste in subpart D of 40 CFR part 261.

NOTE: Even if the waste is listed, the generator still has an opportunity under 40 CFR 260.22 to demonstrate to the Administrator that the waste from his particular facility or operation is not a hazardous waste.

(c) For purposes of compliance with 40 CFR part 268, or if the waste is not listed in subpart D of 40 CFR part 261, the generator must then determine whether the waste is identified in subpart C of 40 CFR part 261 by either:

(1) Testing the waste according to the methods set forth in subpart C of 40 CFR part 261, or according to an equivalent method approved by the Administrator under 40 CFR 260.21; or

(2) Applying knowledge of the hazard characteristic of the waste in light of the materials or the processes used.

ash be managed? How do you think the owners and operators of municipal incinerators responded to this letter? How would you advise them to respond?

Question Three. Less than two weeks after the letters were sent, a congressional committee held hearings to consider the regulatory status of incinerator ash. At the hearing, representatives of incinerator owners and operators argued that incinerator ash should be exempt from subtitle C of RCRA pursuant to section 3001(i), which had been added by the 1984 Amendments. Section 3001(i) provides that a "facility recovering energy from the mass burning of municipal solid waste shall not be deemed to be treating, storing, disposing of, or otherwise managing hazardous wastes for the purposes of regulation under [subtitle C]" if the facility (1) receives and burns only household waste and nonhazardous waste from commercial and industrial sources, (2) does not accept hazardous waste identified or listed under subtitle C, and (3) "has established contractual requirements or other appropriate notification or inspection procedures to assure that hazardous wastes are not received at or burned in such facility." Do you agree that this provision exempts incinerator ash from regulation under subtitle C? What advice would you give owners and operators of incinerators to enhance their chances of taking advantage of this exemption? How would you advise the owners of the 40 incinerators that are not used to generate energy?

Question Four. Representatives of owners and operators of municipal incinerators also argued that because fly ash routinely is mixed with bottom ash, which has much lower concentrations of toxic metals, the combined ash will not fail the toxicity test as frequently. Because fly ash is acidic and bottom ash is alkaline, mixing the ash may produce a buffering effect that decreases the ash's tendency to leach metals. Recall EPA's mixture rule. Were fly ash a specifically listed waste, the product of mixing fly ash with bottom ash would itself be considered a hazardous waste under the mixture rule. However, because fly ash is only a characteristic waste, the mixture rule is not applicable. Combined ash samples fail the toxicity test with less frequency than fly ash samples do. Is mixing the two ash streams the answer to the problems of incinerator owners and operators?

Question Five. The metals in ash are a result of their presence in products that make up a large portion of the municipal solid waste stream. Lead is present in colored printing inks, paints, insecticides, and batteries; cadmium in colored printing inks and small batteries; mercury in newspaper and batteries; arsenic in wood preservatives and pesticides. What regulatory authorities other than RCRA could EPA use to reduce the presence of these metals in ash?

Question Six. While this controversy was under way, EPA proposed to lower the maximum contaminant level for lead, one of the constituents of concern for the toxicity test, as part of regulations implementing the Safe Drinking Water Act. 53 Fed. Reg. 31,516 (1988). How, if at all, could this have an effect on the status of incinerator ash under RCRA?

Question Seven.   Municipal officials argue that if incinerator ash must routinely be managed as a hazardous waste, the large volume of ash would rapidly consume all available subtitle C disposal capacity within three or four years. Moreover, EPA estimates that the amount of ash produced by municipal incinerators will more than quadruple to 17 million tons per year by the year 2000. How would you respond to concern that incinerator ash would overwhelm the RCRA system if subject to subtitle C regulation? Is new legislation necessary to deal with the ash "problem"? Should EPA issue new regulations to clarify the status of incinerator ash under RCRA?

NOTES AND QUESTIONS

1. Because of the vast size and variability of regulatory targets, environmental regulation relies heavily on the regulated community to determine what activities are subject to regulation and even for monitoring compliance. This makes the development of clear tests for determining whether a substance or activity is subject to regulation enormously important. EPA now recognizes that regulations that permit generators to avoid testing if they simply do not think their waste is hazardous are problematic, particularly when it comes to enforcement. After conducting a comprehensive review of the RCRA program, EPA found that

> [t]he RCRA regulations (40 C.F.R. §262.11) allow potential generators of hazardous waste to *apply knowledge* of their process when determining whether they are generating a hazardous waste. This provision has hindered enforcement efforts aimed at regulating generators and potential generators of individual waste streams under RCRA. There is no self-reporting mechanism to identify generators who claim to eliminate characteristic hazardous waste from the RCRA system. To take an enforcement action, EPA or the state must sample and analyze the waste to determine if the waste exhibits any of the hazardous waste characteristics. [EPA, The Nation's Hazardous Waste Management Program at a Crossroads 39 (1990) (emphasis in original).]

How should EPA respond to this problem?

2. When it promulgated the RCRA land disposal ban, which we will examine shortly, EPA decided not to require generators to test their wastes to determine whether or not they were subject to the land ban. The Agency instead allowed generators to rely on their own knowledge of waste characteristics, while requiring treatment and disposal facilities

who received wastes to conduct testing. The D.C. Circuit upheld this decision when environmentalists challenged it in court. The court stated: "[W]e find it neither nonsensical nor absurd to expect that generators may to some extent 'know their waste' without testing each batch produced." The court emphasized that the testing requirements for treatment and disposal facilities would serve as a useful check on generators' certifications that wastes meet applicable standards. Hazardous Waste Treatment Council v. EPA, 886 F.2d 355, 369, 371 (D.C. Cir. 1989). Is this situation different in any important respects from the situation involving the testing of ash from municipal incinerators?

3. Environmental regulation generates an enormous demand for tests that can quickly, reliably, and inexpensively detect and measure hazardous constituents in environmental media. Because of the multitude of chemicals present in waste streams, the RCRA program has faced a particularly daunting challenge. "The large number of chemicals listed as toxic and hazardous and the broad universe of waste types and environmental media far exceeded the analytical state of the art in the early 1980s." EPA, The Nation's Hazardous Waste Management Program at a Crossroads 104 (1990). Methods have been developed for analyzing EPA's initial list of RCRA hazardous constituents; the quality of EPA's measurement methods, however, often is criticized. As the universe of substances regulated under RCRA expands to embrace organic chemicals, EPA faces a continuing struggle to fill serious gaps in its analytical capabilities.

Incinerator Ash: A Postscript

EPA did not agree with municipalities that ash from municipal incinerators is automatically exempt from subtitle C of RCRA due to section 3001(i). In July 1985 EPA had stated that it interpreted section 3001(i) to mean that incinerators were not managing hazardous waste when they incinerated municipal solid waste, but that ash or other byproducts generated by the incineration process were not exempt from subtitle C. Although EPA noted that it did not have evidence "to indicate that these ash residues are hazardous under existing rules," it concluded that such residues "would be hazardous under present EPA regulations if they exhibited a [hazardous waste] characteristic." 50 Fed. Reg. 28,725. Citing the enormous cost of managing ash as a hazardous waste, owners and operators of incinerators vigorously lobbied EPA to reinterpret section 3001(i) to exempt ash from subtitle C. EPA did not do so.

A national environmental group eventually filed suit against two incineration facilities, arguing that their failure to manage their ash in accordance with subtitle C violated RCRA. Confronted with the argument that management of incinerator ash as a hazardous waste would be enormously costly, each district court held that the ash is exempt if facilities comply with the requirements of section 3001(i). On appeal the Second Circuit affirmed, Environmental Defense Fund v. Wheelabrator Technologies, Inc., 931 F.2d 211 (2d Cir. 1991), while the Seventh Circuit reversed, Environmental Defense Fund v. City of Chicago, 948 F.2d 345 (7th Cir. 1991). While the split in the circuits may encourage the Supreme Court to decide the issue, a legislative resolution also is possible. In the 1990 Clean Air Act Amendments Congress barred EPA from regulating incinerator ash until November 1992, while indicating that this amendment was not intended to affect the outcome of the appeals.

EPA officials have supported the development of a special program for ash management that would not require compliance with full RCRA subtitle C requirements, but that would impose more than the minimal requirements for subtitle D landfills. This "D plus" approach would entail mixing fly ash and bottom ash and disposing of it in monofills— landfills that contain only one kind of waste and that do not contain hazardous waste or municipal solid waste. Several bills have been introduced in Congress to require EPA to regulate incinerator ash as a "special" waste subject to hybrid requirements. EPA is conducting research and formulating an ash management strategy. Technical and scientific aspects of the ash controversy are discussed in R. Denison and J. Ruston, eds., Recycling and Incineration: Evaluating the Choices 177-200 (1990).

4.   Avoiding TSD Status

The regulated community perceives RCRA's subtitle C regulations to be extremely burdensome, particularly for TSDs. Thus, companies go to great lengths to avoid being caught in the subtitle C net. Despite the breadth of its coverage, subtitle C leaves many avenues for escape. Consider the following advice from an industry lawyer well versed in the subtleties of RCRA. As you read this excerpt, recall the difficulties EPA faced in defining "solid waste" as reflected in American Mining Congress v. EPA, 824 F.2d 1177 (D.C. Cir. 1987) and subsequent litigation.

> ### Stoll, Coping with the RCRA Hazardous Waste System: A Few Practical Points for Fun and Profit
> #### 1 Envtl. Hazards 6 (July 1989)

Subtitle C of the federal Resource Conservation and Recovery Act (RCRA) establishes the famous "cradle to grave" framework for managing today's hazardous waste activities. Along with EPA's ever-changing and ever-expanding regulations, Subtitle C has probably expedited the trip from cradle to grave for more than one environmental manager.

It is fashionable to write and talk about how horrible the Subtitle C system has become. Words and phrases like "corrective action," "criminal convictions," "land bans," "financial assurance," "hammers," "post-closure care," and—perhaps the most spine-chilling of all—"permitting" are thrown about to scare poor readers and audiences.

In truth, the system can be horrible and most of the fear-mongering is fair. There are paths in the regulations, however, through which manufacturing companies may greatly reduce the pain and save lots of money. I would like to pass on a few hypothetical examples and pointers.

One key theme is that a reasonably logical reading of EPA's regulation might cause one to reject an otherwise attractive option. In some situations, however, happy results and great cost savings can be achieved through a more careful reading of EPA's regulations, an awareness of EPA's rulings (often unpublished) and creative thinking. Before turning to the examples, a few Subtitle C fundamentals should be reviewed.

Exclusions.   Statutory and/or regulatory provisions exclude certain materials or practices from Subtitle C jurisdiction. A few of the more notable are materials disposed into a public sewer system; industrial discharges subject to Clean Water Act permits; residues from fossil fuel combustion; and certain "mining" wastes.

Definitions of "Solid Waste" and "Hazardous Waste."   A material may be hazardous but not a "waste" or a material may be a waste but not "hazardous." In either case, there would be no Subtitle C jurisdiction. A material must be *both* a waste and hazardous to trigger Subtitle C jurisdiction.

EPA's regulations for determining what is a "waste" contain some of the most puzzling English word patterns ever devised. The regulations endeavor to prescribe tests—based on the type of material and on the type of management activity—for determining whether a material is a product (and therefore exempt from RCRA) or a waste (and therefore covered). 40 C.F.R. §§260.22 et seq.; 261.1; 261.2; 261.4.

EPA's regulations for determining whether a waste is "hazardous" are somewhat simpler. A waste may be hazardous either because it is on a "list" or because—when tested—it fails one of several hazard "characteristic" protocols. 40 C.F.R. §261.3(a).

Vast Differences in Coverage Among Types of Waste Management.
The "cradle-to-grave" system regulates the following types of parties involved with hazardous waste: (a) generators; (b) transporters; and (c) owners/operators of treatment, storage or disposal facilities ("TSD" facilities). One point cannot be overemphasized: *by several orders of magnitude, the system is much harsher on TSD facilities.* Permits, corrective action,

post-closure, financial assurance, and many other burdens are part of the TSD game and do not apply to those who only generate and or transport.

HYPOTHETICAL EXAMPLES

Below are examples where a plant manager seeks ways to cut costs and/or increase revenues and avoid onerous RCRA burdens. One central theme is a follow-up to the third point above: it is often acceptable to stay in the Subtitle C system so long as TSD status can be avoided, and there are several ways (generally unpublicized) to accomplish this. Another key theme is that important RCRA interpretations appear in strange places.

1. Obtaining Useful Feedstock from Others' Wastes.   Alpha Company buys Chemical A at $5.00 per pound for use as a degreasing and cleaning solvent. Once used, their "spent" solvent is a listed RCRA hazardous waste.

The Alpha plant manager develops a plan to save millions of dollars. He would buy others' spent solvents, "regenerate" or "reclaim" the solvents to make virgin-quality Chemical A, and use the reclaimed material as a feedstock. He figures he can obtain spent Chemical A at $1.00 per pound.

He runs this by his environmental people, who find the RCRA regulations quite discouraging for two reasons. (a) The spent Chemical A is a "waste." While EPA's regulations provide that certain types of materials are not wastes if they are "reclaimed," they specify that *spent* materials are wastes even if reclaimed. 40 C.F.R. §261.2(c). (b) The reclamation at Alpha's facility would trigger TSD status because (i) the reclamation is "treatment" of hazardous waste, and (ii) storage of the spent chemical A prior to reclamation would independently trigger T/S/D status.

The plant manager, upon checking with corporate management, is glum. Management has concluded that even the millions in savings are not worth TSD status.

Unfortunately these people do not realize that Alpha can have its cake and eat it too. While part (a) of the foregoing analysis is correct (the spent Chemical A must be regarded as a hazardous waste), part (b) is based upon a misunderstanding of the regulations and an unnecessary factual assumption. *Even though the spent Chemical A will be a hazardous waste when generated and transported, Alpha may be able to reclaim it without triggering TSD status.*

First, even though the reclamation may be "treatment," it is also "recycling." EPA's regulations specify: "The recycling process itself is exempt from RCRA." 40 C.F.R. §261.6(c)(1). (EPA buried this fundamental in a parenthetical near the end of a paragraph dealing with storage.)

Second, Alpha might recycle the spent Chemical A *without first storing it.* EPA's regulations contemplate this, and make clear that engaging in this practice will avoid TSD status. 40 C.F.R. §261.6(c)(2). For example, Alpha may arrange a system by which trucks enter its facility, park at the reclamation device, and off-load the spent Chemical A through hoses connected directly from the truck to the reclamation device. EPA has on several occasions affirmed that in such a situation, no "storage" is involved.

If Alpha could accomplish this recycling without storage, it would avoid all of the permitting and other horrors of TSD status. It would only need to file a "notification" of its hazardous waste activity and comply with the manifesting (paper trail) requirements. 40 C.F.R. §261.6(c)(2).

2. Reclaiming Feedstock from One's Own Wastes Without a "Closed Loop" System.

Beta Company uses Chemical A as a feedstock, and a secondary material from Beta's process is "spent" Chemical A. Spent Chemical A is a listed hazardous waste. Beta must pay $5.00 per pound to purchase virgin Chemical A. Beta has been paying $2.00 per pound to have a commercial incinerator destroy spent Chemical A.

The plant manager would like to save millions of dollars by devising a system to reclaim and reuse her spent Chemical A. With a recycling system, she could both drastically reduce the volume of virgin Chemical A she has to buy and eliminate her off-site disposal costs entirely.

Her environmental people tell her that in EPA's definition of solid waste, there is a "closed loop" exemption which such a recycling practice might fit. If spent material is reclaimed and returned to the original process and the entire process is "closed" through interconnected tubes and pipes, the material will not be a RCRA "waste" at all. 40 C.F.R. §261.4(a)(8).

The plant manager is glum. There is only one suitable location on her property for the reclamation process, and it is thousands of yards from the place where the spent Chemical A is generated. Because of the layout of the facility, the costs of such a "closed loop" system would be prohibitive.

Here again, the analysis has been correct, as far as it goes, but the plant people have been overlooking some basic points. Even though Beta cannot avoid being a generator, it can still avoid TSD status.

Beta may be able to collect the spent Chemical A in drums, and, *always within 90 days* of the date of generation, recycle the spent Chemical A. In this manner, no TSD status is triggered. First, as described in [the first example], the recycling process is exempt. Second, EPA's regulations have long provided that a generator may accumulate its own hazardous wastes in tanks or containers for up to 90 days without triggering TSD status. 40 C.F.R. §262.34. Thus, so long as Beta keeps "rotating" drummed waste so that no drum is stored more than 90 days before it is recycled, TSD status can be avoided.

Caution: This result can only be achieved if the storage takes place at the same facility where the waste was generated. For instance, if Beta installed its reclamation device on a nearby but separate parcel of land, it could not store drums at all on the separate parcel without triggering TSD. The 90-day exemption applies only to the generating facility; once off-site, storage of hazardous waste for *any* period of time will trigger TSD. If the reclamation device were on a separate parcel, Beta could avoid TSD only by some form of direct off-loading from transport vehicles as described in [the first example].

3. Other Treatment Avoiding TSD.

Gamma Company generates a hazardous waste and sends it off-site for treatment at a cost of $2.00 per gallon. The plant manager learns that there is a simple and inexpensive treatment process he could use in tanks at his facility which would render the waste nonhazardous. If he could do this, he could save millions of dollars per year in off-site transport and treatment costs.

His environmental people look for regulatory exemptions under which "treatment" would not trigger TSD status. They find three: (1) where wastes which are hazardous only because they are "corrosive" are being neutralized; (2) where waste waters are being treated as part of a Clean Water Act discharge; and (3) where the treatment is part of a "totally enclosed" recycling system. 40 C.F.R. §270.1(c)(2).

The plant manager is glum. His proposal would not fit any of these three narrow exemptions. He drops his idea, because the millions in cost savings will not justify TSD status.

Unfortunately for Gamma, its people missed a paragraph in the middle of a long EPA Federal Register preamble on an unrelated topic and were unaware of an EPA letter to a Wisconsin consulting firm. With such inimitable administrative procedure, EPA has ruled that generators may "treat" hazardous waste in containers or tanks for no more than 90 days at the generating facility and not trigger TSD status. Thus, so long as treatment occurs on-site in tanks that are emptied at least every 90 days, millions in off-site disposal costs can be saved and TSD status can be avoided.

4. Recycling One's Own Hazardous Wastewater.

Delta Company plans to conduct a chemical tank steam-cleaning operation, and will need a million gallons of water a month. The plant manager would like to save money by reusing the same water after treating it, but does not want to trigger TSD status. She is told by her environmental people that the wastewater would clearly be a RCRA hazardous waste (as it will be mixed with commercial chemicals on EPA's RCRA "lists").

But they read the first three hypotheticals in this article and are now thinking creatively. They develop the following logic: (i) always store the hazardous waste in tanks or containers for less than 90 days so "storage" will not trigger TSD, then (ii) reclaim the wastewater through treatment into reusable water and this "recycling" of hazardous waste will be exempt from RCRA.

They are further comforted by language in EPA's regulations which says that materials reclaimed beneficially are not thereafter RCRA wastes (unless burned for energy recovery or placed in or on the land). 40 C.F.R. §261.3(c)(2)(i). Certainly the reclaimed wastewater fits this description.

At this point, however, a lawyer throws cold water on the idea. She discovers language in EPA's 1985 Federal Register preamble to the foregoing regulation which strongly suggests that EPA did not intend for wastewater to be protected by it. ["We caution, though, as we did in the proposal, that this principle does not apply to reclaimed materials that are not ordinarily considered to be commercial products, such as wastewaters or stabilized wastes." 50 Fed. Reg. 634 (Jan. 4, 1985).] At this point, the plant manager is glum.

But then the lawyer uses her head. She figures anything that EPA published as far back as 1985 could be suspect, and phones some EPA people. Lo and behold, she finds that EPA headquarters recently sent a memo to one of EPA's regional offices ruling that wastewater can be protected by the regulatory language. [Memorandum from Sylvia K. Lowrance, EPA Office of Solid Waste Director, to David A. Wagoner (Region VII) (Oct. 27, 1988).]

Again, TSD could be avoided and millions of dollars saved only if one were aware of an unpublished EPA interpretation. EPA's last Federal Register words on the subject would in fact have tended to squelch the idea.

QUICK POINTERS

Here are a few other quick pointers for avoiding or curtailing Subtitle C exposure:

Redirect Stream to POTW or NPDES.   You may be able to redirect certain RCRA waste streams to a public sewer system and/or a point source discharge to the navigable waters. While this may trigger additional Clean Water Act pretreatment and/or NPDES requirements, such requirements may not be nearly as costly and onerous as RCRA requirements.

Change Manufacturing Process.   If you generate a waste that is hazardous because it fails a characteristic (i.e., non-"listed"), you may be able to alter your manufacturing process (through chemical and/or engineering changes) to produce a material that does not fail the characteristic and is therefore no longer hazardous. (This approach would not work for a "listed" waste.)

Delisting.   If you generate a "listed" waste, you may be able to secure a "delisting" if you can show EPA that at your particular facility, the waste is not truly hazardous. The delisting process is expensive, time consuming, and involves notice-and-comment rulemaking in the Federal Register. Nevertheless, many facilities have successfully utilized this process. While serious delays were prevalent a few years ago, EPA is now usually able to process a delisting petition in about a year.

Export.   Many companies have found that they can reduce costs by shipping their wastes to Canada or other countries for ultimate treatment and disposal. EPA regulations expressly allow for such "exports" of hazardous waste. In fact, Canada and the U.S. have a bilateral agreement under which many U.S. companies are now shipping their wastes to Canada.

Reclaim Non-Listed Sludges and By-Products.   EPA's "waste" definition draws major distinctions among "spent materials," "sludges," and "by-products." If you generate a spent material, it will always be a "waste" (even if reclaimed). But if you generate a "sludge" or "by-product," *and* it is not a "listed" waste, then it will *not* be a waste if it is reclaimed. 40 C.F.R. §261.2(c).

Thus, assume a facility in Maine generates a hazardous by-product which is not "listed." If the by-product were disposed a mile away it would be a RCRA hazardous waste. If, however, it were shipped to Arizona for reclamation it would be totally outside RCRA jurisdiction and no generator, transporter, manifesting and/or T/S/D requirements would apply.

NOTES AND QUESTIONS

1. The more stringent the regulation, the greater the incentive for avoidance behavior by the regulated community. Because the regulations imposed by subtitle C of RCRA are perceived as particularly onerous, the regulated community has exerted extraordinary effort to escape subtitle C. While some of the strategies cited by Stoll would subject TSDs to other, presumably less onerous, forms of federal regulation (e.g., the

Clean Water Act's permit program if waste is discharged into surface waters or the Act's pretreatment program if it is discharged into sewers), in other cases the consequences of escaping subtitle C are avoidance of federal regulation altogether. Stoll believes that the strategies he identifies for escaping subtitle C "are not really suggestive of 'loopholes' in the RCRA system." He argues instead that "they show that recycling is something that is generally encouraged by RCRA" and that his strategies should result in "a national reduction in potential health and environmental risks." Do you agree that the strategies Stoll recommends will result in greater protection of the environment than management of hazardous waste in facilities with RCRA permits?

2. Why, do you suppose, has EPA exempted from TSD status those who accumulate hazardous waste in tanks or containers for no more than 90 days? Even if each batch of hazardous waste in the containers is emptied at least once every 90 days, the containers can contain hazardous waste almost continuously. Does it make any difference from the standpoint of environmental risk whether each batch of waste has been there for no more than 90 days?

3. Some of the strategies recommended by Stoll are possible because of EPA's fear that recycling of hazardous waste would be discouraged if the recycling process were subject to RCRA requirements. Yet there is a fine line between activities that truly recycle waste by transforming it into a usable product and those that simply alter the waste in some way and then attempt to market the residue. For example, if an incinerator that burns hazardous waste sells its ash residue as a material for use in highway construction, can it be considered a recycling operation exempt from subtitle C's TSD regulations? Arguing that this is "sham recycling," the federal government has filed suit against a Louisiana company that made such a claim. The government is charging the company, which incinerated more than 200 million pounds of hazardous waste a year, with violating RCRA and is seeking to close the facility and impose a $50 million fine. United States v. Marine Shale Processors Inc., No. 90-1240 (W.D. La.).

4. Stoll emphasizes that surprising avenues for avoiding subtitle C regulations are buried in obscure places: cryptic statements in unrelated Federal Register notices, unpublished correspondence with EPA, or memoranda from EPA officials. For example, the solution to Gamma Company's problem appeared in a Federal Register notice concerning rules for small-quantity generators. 51 Fed. Reg. 10,146 (1986). As Stoll explains:

Half-way through a lengthy preamble discussion labelled "Part 264/265 Facility Standard Issues," EPA explained that generators could treat (if accumulating less than 90 days) without triggering T/S/D. Id. at 10168, col. 3. EPA based this surprising ruling on 40 C.F.R. §262.34, which says that accumulation for more than 90 days would trigger storage (not "treatment" requirements). RCRA practitioners had always assumed that the 90-day rule protected storage only. A Wisconsin consultant wrote to EPA to seek confirmation and a clarification as to whether the ruling applied to all generators (not just "small quantity," which the rule specifically addressed). EPA's Solid Waste Director responded by confirming that preamble position and clarifying that it applied to all generators. [Letter from Marcia E. Williams to Kevin A. Lehner (July 25, 1986).]

Is this an appropriate procedure for informing the public about an interpretation of such potential importance to the regulated community? What should practitioners do to keep abreast of future EPA interpretations of subtitle C regulations? In August 1990 EPA's general counsel announced that he would attempt to issue written legal opinions to make the agency's interpretations of regulations more accessible to the public. EPA's Office of General Counsel had not issued any opinions since 1985.

5. In 1990 EPA conducted a comprehensive review of the RCRA program that tried to identify why RCRA regulations seem so complicated and confusing. One problem EPA identified was that RCRA program staff tend to substitute lengthy Federal Register preambles for clear regulatory language. For example, the proposed regulation revising the definition of solid waste contained 8 pages of regulatory language, but a 47-page preamble. Regulations governing used oil, hazardous waste in tanks, and hazardous waste exports had preambles three to four times longer than the regulatory language. While preambles are necessary to respond to comments and to illustrate what regulatory language means, EPA's study concluded that the RCRA program should "[w]rite regulations simply and clearly, with the aim of their being understood without a preamble." EPA, The Nation's Hazardous Waste Management Program at a Crossroads 37 (July 1990). For now, RCRA practitioners ignore preambles at their peril.

6. As Stoll mentions, wastes listed as hazardous can be delisted if a generator can demonstrate to EPA's satisfaction that the waste stream is not in fact hazardous at a particular facility. To obtain a delisting, a generator must petition EPA. Prior to enactment of the 1984 Amendments to RCRA, environmentalists complained that the procedure for delisting wastes had been abused by the regulated community. Many wastes were granted "temporary" delistings, which continued in effect indefinitely, without giving the public any notice and without providing an opportunity for public comment. Other waste streams were delisted because of evidence that they did not contain the specific constituents for which they had been listed, but without any consideration of what other hazardous constituents they might contain. To correct these perceived abuses, section 3001(f) was added to RCRA by the 1984 Amend-

ments. This section requires EPA, when evaluating delisting petitions, to consider any other factors that could cause the waste to be hazardous in addition to those for which the waste originally was listed. EPA must publish in the Federal Register a proposal to grant or deny a delisting petition within a year of receiving the petition; final action must be taken within two years. The 1984 Amendments also terminated all "temporary" delistings effective November 8, 1986 unless EPA, after soliciting public comment, promulgated them in final form. In 1988 EPA granted six delisting petitions and denied eight others.

7. Exports of hazardous waste to another country are regulated under section 3017 of RCRA, which was added by the 1984 Amendments. This section prohibits the export of hazardous waste unless the consent of the receiving country's government has been obtained. Persons who intend to export hazardous waste must give EPA advance notice. The Secretary of State then must inform the government of the recipient country and request its consent to accept the waste. Canada has entered into an agreement with the United States that governs the export of hazardous waste. What impact does this agreement have on exporters' obligations under section 3017 of RCRA? See §3017(f).

8. Incentives for escaping RCRA's coverage have become even greater as a result of the land disposal ban mandated by the 1984 Amendments. Congress attempted to phase out hazardous waste disposal practices that could not be demonstrated to be safe in order to provide greater incentives for the development of new waste treatment and disposal technologies, as discussed in the next section.

5. The RCRA Land Disposal Ban

When it amended RCRA in 1984, Congress attempted to work fundamental changes in the nation's waste disposal practices. Mounting evidence that even some of the best-designed land disposal units eventually leaked contaminants convinced Congress that extraordinary measures were needed to shift waste disposal away from the land. Thus, Congress established a new national policy that "to avoid substantial risk to human health and the environment, reliance on land disposal should be minimized or eliminated, and land disposal, particularly landfill and surface impoundment, should be the least favored method for managing hazardous wastes," RCRA §1002(b)(7). To accomplish this goal, Congress enacted a staged prohibition on the land disposal of all untreated hazardous wastes unless the EPA administrator "determines the prohibition of one or more methods of land disposal of such waste is not required in order to protect human health and the environment for so long as the waste remains hazardous," RCRA §3004(d)(1). In making these determinations, the EPA administrator was directed to take into account the characteristics of the waste, "the long-term uncertainties associated with land disposal," and the importance of encouraging proper management of hazardous waste in the first instance. But Congress limited EPA's discretion by specifying that

> a method of land disposal may not be determined to be protective of human health and the environment . . . unless, upon application by an interested person, it has been demonstrated to the Administrator, to a reasonable degree of certainty, that there will be no migration of hazardous constituents from the disposal unit or injection zone for as long as the wastes remain hazardous. [RCRA §§3004(d)(1), (e)(1), (g)(5).]

Congress did not entirely ban the land disposal of wastes unable to meet this exacting standard. It provided an exception for wastes that had been treated to "substantially diminish the toxicity of the waste or substantially reduce the likelihood of migration of hazardous constituents from the waste so that short-term and long-term threats to human health and the environment are minimized." §3004(m). EPA was directed to promulgate treatment standards specifying how waste otherwise subject to the land disposal ban could satisfy this standard. Thus, the land disposal ban in reality applies to *untreated* hazardous wastes and is a vehicle for EPA to require pretreatment of wastes that cannot be shown to be capable of safe disposal on land in untreated form.

When the 1984 Amendments were adopted, it was widely believed that it would be extremely difficult, if not impossible, for anyone to satisfy the burden of demonstrating "no migration" of hazardous constituents. Thus, virtually all untreated hazardous wastes would eventually be barred from land disposal. The only escape from the RCRA land ban would be compliance with the treatment standards for hazardous waste mandated by RCRA section 3004(m). Wastes treated in compliance with these standards could only be managed in land disposal facilities that meet the minimum technology requirements of new section 3004(o), which require landfills and surface impoundments to have double liners, a leachate collection system, and groundwater monitoring.

Congress directed that the land disposal ban would become effective in stages over a period of three and one-half years beginning on November 8, 1986 and ending on May 8, 1990. RCRA §3004(g). EPA was required first to determine whether wastes containing solvents or dioxins and other wastes thought to be most hazardous ("California list wastes") could safely be land disposed in untreated form and, if not, to promulgate treatment standards. Congress then instructed EPA to divide all other hazardous waste into three "thirds," and to make similar determinations concerning wastes in each of the three categories by specified deadlines. If EPA failed to meet the deadlines for the first two thirds of the waste, a "soft hammer" would fall requiring that the waste be disposed of only in facilities that meet the minimum technology requirements of section 3004(o) (requiring the use of double liners and a leachate collection system). For any waste for which EPA had not made a determination or promulgated a treatment standard by May 8, 1990, a "hard hammer" would fall prohibiting all land disposal of the waste. If EPA determined that "adequate alternative treatment, recovery, or disposal capacity which protects human health or the environment" was not available, the agency was authorized to extend the effective date of the land disposal ban for up to two years. RCRA §3004(h).

As a result, the thrust of the land ban is to require pretreatment of most wastes prior to land disposal. To ensure that the land ban does not backfire by simply encouraging indefinite storage of waste, section 3004(j) of RCRA prohibits the storage of wastes subject to the land ban "unless such storage is solely for the purpose of the accumulation of such quantities of hazardous waste as are necessary to facilitate proper recovery, treatment or disposal."

A. EPA's Initial Effort to Implement the RCRA Land Ban

On January 14, 1986, EPA proposed treatment standards for the first group of wastes subject to RCRA's land ban, primarily solvents and dioxin-containing wastes. 51 Fed. Reg. 1602. EPA proposed a hybrid approach employing a technology-based treatment standard (based on what EPA determined to be the Best Demonstrated Available Technology (BDAT) for treating wastes) capped by a risk-based ("screening") approach favored by the Office of Management and Budget. The risk-based screening approach would cap the level of treatment required by BDAT by specifying that wastes need not be treated beyond levels at which "the maximum concentration (of a hazardous constituent) [is] below [the level at] which the Agency believes there is no regulatory concern for the land disposal program." Id. at 1611. EPA's risk-based screening levels were determined by modeling the concentrations of hazardous constituents that could be detected 500 feet from disposal units. EPA proposed to require that treatment satisfy whichever of the two approaches was less stringent in a given application. Thus, BDAT would not be required if it resulted in treatment beyond risk-based screening levels, but if BDAT could not achieve screening levels, facilities generally would not be required to go beyond BDAT.

EPA's proposal generated considerable controversy because it was viewed as an important precedent for how EPA would implement the entire land ban program. Eleven members of Congress who had been on the conference committee that shaped the 1984 Amendments to RCRA denounced the proposal in a letter to EPA Administrator Lee M.

Thomas. What was particularly galling to them was the impression that EPA's risk-based approach had converted the explicit "no migration" standard into one that would tolerate migration unless risk models showed it to be unacceptable.

To justify inclusion of the risk-based approach OMB had favored, EPA focused on "Congress' inclusion of the clause 'for as long as the wastes remain hazardous' as a modifier to what otherwise would have been a strict no migration standard, i.e., 'no migration of hazardous constituents from the disposal unit.'" They proposed "to interpret inclusion of this modifying clause as implying that the statutory standard allows for some migration of hazardous constituents beyond the immediate confines of the disposal unit, as long as such migration does not present any threat to human health and the environment." The former congressional conferees rejected this interpretation. Arguing that it was "hard to imagine how we could have more clearly expressed our intent," they stated: "To construe these words in a way that sanctions the escape of hazardous constituents from the disposal unit suggests that the agency has either misunderstood Congress' directive or is attempting to rewrite the statute to suit its own purposes." They explained:

> The requirement for proof of "no migration" is to be interpreted literally. . . . We specifically rejected the concept of an acceptable level of migration because of the scientific uncertainties associated with determining what is an "acceptable" level. For example, predicting the character and rate of migration, the fate and transport of the contaminants, and points of present and future human and environmental exposure are subject to significant error. The scientific uncertainty makes reliance on such predictions inconsistent with the statutory presumption against land disposal and in favor of treatment. [Letter from Rep. Dingell, Sen. Chafee, et al. to Lee M. Thomas 4-5 (Mar. 4, 1986).]

Two congressional hearings were held to examine EPA's proposal. In the face of substantial pressure from Congress and environmental groups, EPA abandoned the risk-based screening approach when it adopted a final rule in November 1986. EPA adopted the BDAT approach while delaying for two years the effective date of the land ban for seven wastes for which it did not believe adequate treatment capacity was available. EPA also waived application of the land ban to certain wastes including dilute solvents, wastes from small-quantity generators, and wastes from CERCLA or RCRA cleanup actions.

Disappointed that EPA had abandoned the proposed risk-based approach for treatment standard, the Chemical Manufacturers Association (CMA) and others challenged EPA's final rule, as indicated in the following case.

	Hazardous Waste Treatment	
	Council v. EPA	
	886 F.2d 355 (D.C. Cir. 1989)	

Before WALD, Chief Judge, SILBERMAN and D. H. GINSBURG, Circuit Judges.

Opinion PER CURIAM.

Opinion concurring in part and concurring in the result filed by Circuit Judge SILBERMAN.

In 1984, Congress amended the Resource Conservation and Recovery Act ("RCRA"), 42 U.S.C. §§6921-6991 (1982 & Supp. IV 1986), to prohibit land disposal of certain hazardous solvents and wastes containing dioxins except in narrow circumstances to be defined by Environmental Protection Agency ("EPA") regulations. See Hazardous and Solid Waste Amendments, §201(a), 42 U.S.C. §6924(e) (Supp. IV 1986). In these consolidated cases, petitioners seek review of EPA's final "solvents and dioxins" rule published pursuant to Congress' 1984 mandate. . . .

In January 1986, EPA issued a notice of proposed rule-making announcing its draft implementation of the land disposal prohibition for solvents and dioxins. See 51 Fed. Reg. 1602 (1986) (hereinafter "Proposed Rule"). Approximately ten months later, after receiving extensive public commentary on the draft blueprint, EPA published a final solvents and dioxins rule differing in some respects from its draft approach. See 51 Fed. Reg. 40,572 (1986) (hereinafter "Final Rule"). These differences were especially striking in EPA's implementation of section 3004(j) and section 3004(m) of RCRA, governing the storage prohibition and treatment standards, respectively, for solvents and dioxins. . . .

In the Proposed Rule, EPA announced its tentative support for a treatment regime embodying both risk-based and technology-based standards. The technology-based standards would be founded upon what EPA determined to be the Best Demonstrated Available Technology ("BDAT"); parallel risk-based or "screening" levels were to reflect "the maximum concentration [of a hazardous constituent] below which the Agency believes there is no regulatory concern for the land disposal program and which is protective of human health and the environment." Proposed Rule at 1611. . . .

EPA invited public comment on alternative approaches as well. The first alternative identified in the Proposed Rule (and the one ultimately selected by EPA) was based purely on the capabilities of the "best demonstrated available technology." Id. at 1613. . . .

The Agency received comments supporting both approaches, but ultimately settled on the pure-technology alternative. Of particular importance to EPA's decision were the comments filed by eleven members of Congress, all of whom served as conferees on the 1984 RCRA amendments. As EPA recorded in the preamble to the Final Rule:

> [These] members of Congress argued strongly that [the health screening] approach did not fulfill the intent of the law. They asserted that because of the scientific uncertainty inherent in risk-based decisions, Congress expressly directed the Agency to set treatment standards based on the capabilities of existing technology.
>
> The Agency believes that the technology-based approach adopted in (the) final rule, although not the only approach allowable under the law, best responds to the above stated comments.

Final Rule at 40, 578.

EPA also relied on passages in the legislative history supporting an approach under which owners and operators of hazardous waste facilities would be required to use "the best (technology) that has been demonstrated to be achievable" (quoting 103 Cong. Rec. S9178 (daily ed. July 25, 1984) (statement of Senator Chafee)). And the agency reiterated that the chief advantage offered by the health-screening approach—avoiding "treatment for treatment's sake"—could "be better addressed through changes in other aspects of its regulatory program." Id. As an example of what parts of the program might be altered, EPA announced that it was "considering the use of its risk-based methodologies to characterize wastes as hazardous pursuant to section 3001 [of RCRA]." Id.; see 42 U.S.C. §6921 (1982 & Supp. IV 1986).

Petitioner CMA challenges this aspect of the rule as an unreasonable construction of section 3004(m)'s mandate to ensure that "short-term and long-term threats to human health and the environment are minimized." 42 U.S.C. §6924(m) (1982 & Supp. IV 1986). In the alternative, CMA argues that EPA has failed to explain the basis—in terms of relevant human health and environmental considerations—for its BDAT regime, which allegedly requires treatment in some circumstances to levels far below the standards for human exposure under other statutes administered by EPA. Thus, CMA claims that EPA's action in promulgating a technology-based rule is arbitrary and capricious. . . .

We repeat the mandate of §3004(m)(1): the Administrator is required to promulgate "regulations specifying those levels or methods of treatment, if any, which substantially diminish the toxicity of the waste or substantially reduce the likelihood of migration of hazardous constituents from the waste so that short-term and long-term threats to human health and the environment are minimized." 42 U.S.C. §6924(m)(1).

CMA reads the statute as requiring EPA to determine the levels of concentration in waste at which the various solvents here at issue are "safe" and to use those "screening levels" as floors below which treatment would not be required. CMA supports its interpretation with the observation that the statute directs EPA to set standards only to the extent that "threats to human health and the environment are minimized." We are unpersuaded, however, that Congress intended to compel EPA to rely upon screening levels in preference to the levels achievable by BDAT.

The statute directs EPA to set treatment standards based upon either "levels or methods" of treatment. Such a mandate makes clear that the choice whether to use "levels" (screening levels) or "methods" (BDAT) lies within the informed discretion of the agency, as long as the result is "that short-term and long-term threats to human health and the environment are minimized." To "minimize" something is, to quote the Oxford English Dictionary, to "reduce [it] to the smallest possible amount, extent, or degree." But Congress recognized, in the very amendments here at issue, that there are "long-term uncertainties associated with land disposal," 42 U.S.C. §6924(d)(1)(A). In the face of such uncertainties, it cannot be said that a statute that requires that threats be minimized unambiguously requires EPA to set levels at which it is conclusively presumed that no threat to health or the environment exists. . . .

This is not to say that EPA is free, under §3004(m), to require generators to treat their waste beyond the point at which there is no "threat" to human health or to the environment. That Congress's concern in adopting §3004(m) was with health and the environment would necessarily make it unreasonable for EPA to promulgate treatment standards wholly without regard to whether there might be a threat to man or nature. That concern is better dealt with, however, at *Chevron*'s second step; for, having concluded that the statute does not unambiguously and in all circumstances foreclose EPA from adopting treatment levels based upon the levels achievable by BDAT, we must now explore whether the particular levels established by the regulations supply a reasonable resolution of the statutory ambiguity.

. . . Is EPA's Interpretation Reasonable?

The screening levels that EPA initially proposed were not those at which the wastes were thought to be entirely safe. Rather, EPA set the levels to reduce risks from the solvents to an "acceptable" level, and it explored, at great length, the manifest (and manifold) uncertainties inherent in any attempt to specify "safe" concentration levels. The agency discussed, for example, the lack of any safe level of exposure to carcinogenic solvents, 51 Fed. Reg. at 1,628; the extent to which reference dose levels (from which it derived its screening levels) understate the dangers that hazardous solvents pose to particularly sensitive members of the population, id. at 1,627; the necessarily artificial assumptions that accompany any attempt to model the migration of hazardous waste from a disposal site, id. at 1,642-53; and the lack of dependable data on the effects that solvents have on the liners that bound disposal facilities for the purpose of ensuring that the wastes disposed in a facility stay there, id. at 1,714-15. Indeed, several parties made voluminous comments on the Proposed Rule to the effect that EPA's estimates of the various probabilities were far more problematic than even EPA recognized. . . .

CMA suggests, despite these uncertainties, that the adoption of a BDAT treatment regime would result in treatment to "below established level of hazard." It relies for this proposition almost entirely upon a chart in which it contrasts the BDAT levels with (1) levels EPA has defined as "Maximum Contaminant Levels" (MCLs) under the Safe Drinking Water Act; (2) EPA's proposed "Organic Toxicity Characteristics," threshold levels below which EPA will not list a waste as hazardous by reason of its having in it a particular toxin; and (3) levels at which EPA has recently granted petitions by waste generators to "delist" a particular waste, that is, to remove it from the list of wastes that are deemed hazardous. CMA points out that the BDAT standards would require treatment to levels that are, in many cases, significantly below these "established levels of hazard."

If indeed EPA had determined that wastes at any of the three levels pointed to by CMA posed no threat to human health or the environment, we would have little hesitation in concluding that it was unreasonable for EPA to mandate treatment to substantially lower levels. In fact, however, none of the levels to which CMA compares the BDAT standards purports to establish a level at which safety is assured or "threats to human health and the environment are minimized." Each is a level established for a different purpose and under a different set of statutory criteria than concern us here; each is therefore irrelevant to the inquiry we undertake today. . . .

In sum, EPA's catalog of the uncertainties inherent in the alternative approach using screening levels supports the reasonableness of its reliance upon BDAT instead. Accordingly, finding no merit in CMA's contention that EPA has required treatment to "below established levels of hazard," we find that EPA's interpretation of §3004(m) is reasonable. . . .

WAS EPA'S EXPLANATION ADEQUATE?

The Supreme Court has made it abundantly clear that a reviewing court is not to supplement an agency's reasons for proceeding as it did, nor to paper over its plainly defective rationale: "The reviewing court should not attempt itself to make up for such deficiencies [in the agency's explanation]; we may not supply a reasoned basis for the agency's action that the agency itself has not given." Motor Vehicles Manufacturers Ass'n v. State Farm Mut. Auto Ins. Co., 463 U.S. 29, 43 (1983) (citing SEC v. Chenery Corp., 332 U.S. 194, 196 (1947)). "We will, however, 'uphold a decision of less than ideal clarity if the agency's path may reasonably be discerned.' " Id. (quoting Bowman Transportation, Inc. v. Arkansas-Best Freight System, Inc., 419 U.S. 281, 286 (1974). Accordingly, in order to determine whether we can affirm EPA's action here, we must parse the language of the Final Rule to see whether it can be interpreted to make a sensible argument for the approach EPA adopted. We find that it cannot. . . .

[A]fter EPA issued the Proposed Rule, some commenters, including eleven members of Congress, chastised the agency on the ground that the use of screening levels was inconsistent with the intent of the statute. They stated that because of the uncertainties involved, Congress had mandated that BDAT alone be used to set treatment standards. EPA determined that the "best respon[se]" to those comments was to adopt a BDAT standard. It emphasized, however, that either course was consistent with the statute (and that it was therefore not *required* to use BDAT alone). Finally, it asserted, without explanation, that its major purpose in initially proposing screening levels "may be better addressed through changes in other aspects of its regulatory program," and gave an example of one such aspect that might be changed.

This explanation is inadequate. It should go without saying that members of Congress have no power, once a statute has been passed, to alter its interpretation by post-hoc "explanations" of what it means; there may be societies where "history" belongs to those in power, but ours is not among them. In our scheme of things, we consider legislative history because it is just that: *history.* It forms the background against which Congress adopted the relevant statute. Post-enactment statements are a different matter, and they are not to be considered by an agency or by a court as legislative history. An agency has an obligation to consider the comments of legislators, of course, but on the same footing as it would those of other commenters; such comments may have, as Justice Frankfurter said in a different context, "power to persuade, if lacking power to control." Skidmore v. Swift & Co., 323 U.S. 134 (1944).

It is unclear whether EPA understood this fundamental point. On the one hand, it suggested that the adoption of a BDAT-only regime "best respond[ed]" to the comments suggesting that the statute required such a rule. On the other hand, EPA went on at some length to establish that the comments were in error, in that screening levels are permissible under the statute. EPA's "rationale," in other words, is that several members of Congress (among others) urged upon it the claim that Proposition

X ("Congress mandated BDAT") requires Result A ("EPA adopts BDAT"), and that although Proposition X is inaccurate, the best response to the commenters is to adopt Result A.

Nor is anything added by EPA's bald assertion that its reason for initially preferring Result B (screening levels) "may be" better served by other changes in the statutory scheme. In its Proposed Rule, EPA had, after extensive analysis of the various alternatives, come to the opposite conclusion. It is insufficient, in that context, for EPA to proceed in a different direction simply on the basis of an unexplained and unelaborated statement that it might have been wrong when it earlier concluded otherwise.

In the entire relevant text of the Final Rule, EPA neither invokes nor discusses the uncertainties inherent in the land disposal process in support of its determination to use BDAT. EPA's only mention of the concept is in its description of the commenters' argument that, because of such uncertainties, Congress mandated BDAT—an argument that EPA rejected. While it may be that EPA intended that reference to act as an incorporation of all the uncertainties it outlined in its Proposed Rule, or all the many challenges to its assumptions that commenters submitted in response to the Proposed Rule, that intent, if indeed it exists, is so shrouded in mist that for this court to say that we could discern its outlines would be as illogical as the agency's explanation in the Final Rule itself. Accordingly, we grant the petitions for review in this respect.

SILBERMAN, Circuit Judge, concurring in part and concurring in the result: . . .

It would appear that EPA, faced with formidable political forces opposing its Proposed Rule, simply acquiesced in the approach desired by those forces, but was unwilling to offer *as its own* a statutory/policy rationale to justify its acquiesence. In the Final Rule, EPA in effect stated that it recognized, and subordinated itself to, the senators and congressmen who protested against EPA's Proposed Rule without in any way affirming the legal (or policy) superiority of the legislators' position. My colleagues acknowledge EPA's behavior is intolerable as a matter of administrative law, . . . but nevertheless "rescue" EPA from its predicament by supplying the statutory/policy analysis which, if it had been adopted by EPA, would have obviated the need for a remand. Under the circumstances, I do not know why the court's remand is other than an empty gesture, one which conforms to principles of judicial review of agency policymaking only in form.

NOTES AND QUESTIONS

1. Why did the court think that it was wrong for EPA to respond to the congressional criticism as it did? Members of Congress often try to influence agency policies. The congressional reaction to the land ban proposal was particularly vociferous: committees in both the House and the Senate immediately scheduled hearings to criticize EPA's proposal. While congressional committees frequently hold oversight hearings to review EPA's performance, it is unusual for committees in both houses of Congress to review a single notice of proposed rulemaking. What impact should the post-enactment views of members of Congress have on EPA's interpretation of environmental statutes? Should it make any difference that the members who criticized EPA's land ban proposal included the conferees and principal authors of the 1984 Amendments?

2. What difference does it make whether EPA uses a BDAT approach or risk-based screening levels to implement the land disposal ban? How would each approach deal with the large uncertainties that exist concerning the long-term fate and transport of hazardous constituents in waste? What statutory basis did EPA have for adopting a BDAT approach?

3. The court suggests that it would be inappropriate to require treatment below levels at which there no longer are threats to human health and the environment. 886 F.2d at 336. Can you think of any justification for requiring that wastes be treated to levels that are below those required by drinking water regulations? EPA has taken the position that it need not construe the levels at which a waste no longer meets the toxicity characteristic ("characteristic levels") as levels below which no further minimization of threats be required. 886 F.2d at 362. Thus, in promulgating the fifth set of land ban regulations, 55 Fed. Reg. 22,520, EPA asserted that it had the authority under RCRA to require application of section 3004(m) treatment standards to waste containing hazardous constituents in concentrations below characteristic levels. 886 F.2d at 362 n.7. However, EPA refused to exercise this authority, precipitating a lawsuit by environmental groups and a waste treatment trade association.

4. The court notes EPA's statement that the major advantage of a risk-based screening approach—avoiding "treatment for treatment sake"—could best be pursued through "considering the use of its risk-based methodologies to characterize wastes as hazardous pursuant to section 3001 [of RCRA]." For several years EPA has indicated that it would consider adopting a rule that allowed listed wastes to escape regulation when their concentrations of hazardous constituents fell below certain levels deemed de minimis. Such a rule would, in effect, provide a self-implementing alternative to the cumbersome delisting process. Would you favor such an approach? What information would EPA need in order to be able to determine what levels of hazardous constituents

should be considered to be de minimis? While the Agency has yet to propose such an approach, it has indicated that any de minimis levels it adopts "will cap treatment standards if they are higher than the treatment standards." 55 Fed. Reg. 22,520.

5. Residues from treating listed wastes are usually considered listed wastes due to the derived-from rule of 40 C.F.R. section 261.3(c)(2). Thus all residues from treatment of listed waste are banned from land disposal unless they in turn meet section 3004(m) treatment standards or are exempted by a no migration or capacity variance. The same is not true for treatment of characteristic wastes. EPA has taken the position that "[r]esidues from the treatment of characteristic waste, however, are not automatically considered the characteristic waste; these residues are considered characteristic if they still display the original characteristic, or if they display another characteristic." 55 Fed. Reg. 22,520.

6. EPA's land disposal regulations also were challenged by environmentalists. The Natural Resources Defense Council challenged EPA's implementation of section 3004(j) of RCRA, which prohibits storage of wastes subject to the land ban except for the purpose of accumulating such quantities "as are necessary to facilitate proper recovery, treatment, or disposal." Noting that most wastes are removed from the site of generation within 90 days, EPA initially proposed to allow generators to accumulate waste for up to 90 days. After commenters criticized this period as too short, EPA ultimately adopted a presumption that storage for up to one year was proper unless EPA can prove that wastes are not being stored to facilitate proper recovery, treatment, or disposal. 51 Fed. Reg. 40,643. The final rule shifts the burden of proof to the facility to justify storage for longer than a one-year period. Recall Stoll's advice concerning the use of the 90-day storage rule for avoiding subtitle C. Will EPA's new one-year rule offer similar opportunities for postponing compliance with the land ban?

In another portion of the per curiam opinion, the court rejected NRDC's challenges to EPA's one-year storage regulation. NRDC had argued that section 3004(j)'s flat prohibition of the storage of waste subject to the land ban "unless such storage is solely for [proper purposes]" requires generators to bear the burden of proving that any storage was proper. By shifting the statutory burden of proof to itself for wastes stored up to one year, EPA "effectively allows a one year override of the statutory prohibition," NRDC argued. How do you think the court responded to NRDC's argument? See 886 F.2d at 366 (Section III of decision).

7. Prior to enactment of the RCRA land ban, what incentives, if any, existed for generators to have their hazardous waste treated to substantially reduce its toxicity and the likelihood of migration of hazardous constituents? In the absence of a market for hazardous waste treatment services, what incentives existed for TSDs to invest in new

treatment technologies? What impact do you think the enactment of the RCRA land ban would have on the development of new treatment capacity? Why did Congress provide for a possible two-year extension of the effective date of the land ban based on the unavailability of adequate alternative treatment capacity?

8. Do you agree with Judge Silberman's criticism of the majority? Why do you think the majority indicated that the uncertainty rationale could justify choice of a BDAT approach? How do you suppose EPA responded to the court's decision on remand? An excerpt from EPA's response is presented below.

EPA, *Hazardous Waste Management System: Land Disposal Restrictions*
55 Fed. Reg. 6640 (1990)

Before addressing the issue of justification of EPA's choice of technology-based BDAT in the final solvents and dioxin rules, EPA wishes to address the ultimate resolution it envisions for the section 3004(m) treatment standards. EPA accepts, and agrees with the Court's admonition that EPA may not establish treatment standards "wholly without regard to whether there might be a threat to man or nature." See 886 F.2d at 362; also concurring opinion, id. at 372. EPA believes that the best way ultimately to achieve this objective is not to require further treatment of prohibited wastes containing threshold levels of hazardous constituents at which listed wastes themselves would no longer be deemed hazardous, within the broad meaning of RCRA section 3001.

EPA is presently unable to promulgate such levels, however. This is an issue that has bedeviled the Agency for years and one that remains an Agency priority. Many of the very uncertainties discussed below that determine the Agency's policy preferences for technology based standards instead of the screening level approach proposed initially likewise have not been resolved fully enough to promulgate threshold concentration levels.

EPA's eventual intention to use threshold hazardous waste levels concurrently under development to cap the section 3004(m) treatment standards still leaves the question of which standards to apply in the interim. If no treatment standards are in effect, then the various statutory prohibitions in sections 3004(d), (e) and (on May 8, 1990) (g) ("hammers") would take effect, and most hazardous waste disposal would thus be prohibited unless it occurs in a land disposal unit determined by EPA to satisfy the statutory "no migration" test. Since this would leave most hazardous waste without a legal management option, EPA believes it imperative to have treatment standards in place. . . . EPA has determined that the soundest choice for the interim is to retain its original choice of technology-based treatment standards based on performance of BDAT. The Agency's reasons are based on both legal analysis and the Agency's determination that its choice of options is consistent with and furthers the Congresisonal intent and policy objectives in promulgating the land disposal restrictions provisions. . . .

A. LEGAL ANALYSIS

It is now established that section 3004(m) does not dictate that treatment standards be either technology-based or risk-based. See 886 F.2d at 361-64. Clearly, the requirement in section 3004(m) that treatment standards minimize threats to human health and the environment is ambiguous as to the precise extent of treatment.

Even more important in the Agency's view, is the indication that Congress expected the Agency to adopt a different approach in establishing treatment standards than the approach used heretofore by the Agency in establishing subtitle C regulatory standards. Those standards implement the statutory directive to establish hazardous waste management standards at a level "as may be necessary to protect human health and the environment," see, e.g., section 3004(a). EPA has implemented this strategy by developing regulations that are based on ascertaining a level of risk that EPA deems acceptable and crafting controls that seek to ensure that this level of risk is not exceeded.

Section 3004(m), in contrast, does not require that treatment standards be protective of human health and the environment, but rather commands that those standards ultimately substantially diminish waste toxicity or mobility in order that "short-term and long-term threats to to human health and the environment be minimized." EPA believes that this language can reasonably be interpreted to require more than the normal subtitle C regulatory command that standards be those necessary to protect human health and the environment. This conclusion is reinforced by the many statutory provisions that were part of the 1984 amendments stressing the inherent uncertainties associated with assessing the safety of land disposal of hazardous wastes, RCRA §§1002(b)(7), 3004(d)(1)(A), 3004(e)(1)(A), 3004(g)(5), and the Congressional determination that the only protective land disposal units are those for which EPA has determined, with a "reasonable degree of certainty," that "there will be no migration of hazardous constituents from the disposal unit for as long as the wastes remain hazardous."

The legislative history of §3004(m) also provides support for the interpretation that Congress intended something other than treatment standards reflecting EPA-determined acceptable levels of risk normally used in establishing subtitle C regulations. . . .

[EPA then discusses the legislative history and concludes that "Congress did not provide clear guidance on the meaning of "minimize threats."] Hence, EPA believes that it has discretion to adopt an interpretation that emphasizes the need for certainty in reducing the risks of and disposal of hazardous wastes and that allows EPA to prefer technology-based standards over capping levels that incorporate unacceptable levels of uncertainty.

B. EPA's POLICY PREFERENCE

EPA's intepretation of section 3004(m) also serves Congress' goals. EPA views Congress' objectives in adopting the Land Disposal Restrictions Program as seeking to assure safety by removing as many of the uncertainties associated with land disposal of hazardous waste as possible, and to a lesser degree as forcing use of existing treatment capacity. See RCRA §§1002(b)(7), 3004(d)(1), (e)(1), (g)(1), and S. Rep. No. 284, 98th Cong. 1st Sess. at 19. Congress also intended that "reliance on land disposal should be minimized or eliminated, and land disposal, particularly landfill and surface impoundment, should be the least favored method for managing hazardous wastes." See §1002(b)(7).

These objectives are well served by retaining the technology-based treatment standards that the Agency has implemented until EPA can establish acceptably certain threshold levels that identify constituent concentration levels at which wastes are not hazardous. The "long-term uncertainties association with land disposal" (section 3004(d)(1)(A)) are reduced by using treatment technologies whose performance is objective rather than predictive. Technology-based standards also better further the Congressional goal of using existing treatment capacity. This is because the risk-based screening level approach proposed initially would have served to cap treatment, and thus at least to some extent, decreased use of treatment capacity. See 51 FR 1612-13. For the same reason, use of the screening level approach would not have minimized hazardous waste land disposal to the same extent as technology-based standards because more wastes could permissibly be land disposed without treatment (or with less treatment).

The legislative history also shows that another of Congress' objectives was the promulgation of treatment standards that were at least roughly equivalent (in terms of stringency of control) to standards required under the Clean Water Act and Clean Air Act. The Senate Report provides:

> A requirement for treatment of hazardous constituents under other statutes is another factor that may be considered. For example, the Administrator should impose, as a condition of land disposal, a treatment requirement that is consistent with categorical pretreatment standards re-

quired pursuant to the Clean Water Act. It makes little sense to improve or accelerate regulations under those statutes only to have environmental goals frustrated by loopholes allowed less stringent treatment under [RCRA].

S. Rep. No. 284 at 16.

The categorical pretreatment standards under the Clean Water Act cited above are technology-based regulations. The Clean Air Act also establishes regulatory programs—the New Source Performance Standards and Prevention of Significant Deterioration—that are technology based. EPA is concerned that the screening levels proposed in 1986, with their reliance on predictive modelling to stimulate dispersion and attenuation in the environment, might result in levels of control that are significantly less stringent than the levels imposed under either of these other programs. Such a result would clearly fail to service this particular objective.

There are also other problems with the proposed approach which cause EPA to prefer the technology-based rule adopted. The proposed rule attempted to take into account the waste's behavior in the land disposal environment after it is land disposed. Since promulgation of the final rule in November 1986, EPA has in fact abandoned the predictive model that was used as the basis for screening levels due to inadequacies relating to wastes' migratory potential in landfill environments and aquifer dispersion characteristics. Because the screening levels proposed in 1986 incorporated a modelling approach to dilution and attenuation in the environment based on a model which EPA now believes is superseded, EPA views promulgation of those levels as insufficiently certain at this time to satisfy Congress' immediate goals for land disposal treatment standards.

Even without predictive modelling, uncertainties currently remain relating to assessing wastes' toxicity. See generally 51 FR at 1714-20 (January 14, 1986). These problems, while not insurmountable over a long term, have posed difficulties in developing threshold levels in the short-term that could be used to assess when threats of hazardous waste land disposal are minimized with enough assurance to cap treatment standards. The difficulties that remain involve dealing with the large number of hazardous constituents controlled under the RCRA subtitle C program (which exceed by several times even the extensive list of priority pollutants under the Clean Water Act), assessing and possibly devising exposure scenarios for the air and environmental (rather than human) exposure pathways, developing analytical detection methods for over 100 hazardous constituents, and determining an approach when threshold levels are less than the pollutant's limit of detection.

EPA must grapple with each of these issues, determining which are substantial enough to play a significant role in the selection of any capping levels, and how to work with the factors that it finds to be significant.

Although EPA has begun work on a rule that will consider these issues, that rule is not yet ready for proposal, much less promulgation.

EPA prefers to further the statutory objective of assuring safety by eliminating as much of the inherent uncertainty of hazardous waste land disposal by retaining the current approach of technology-based treatment standards until it develops concentration thresholds for determining when wastes are hazardous. It therefore is the Agency's decision to retain treatment standards that are based on performance of BDAT until it develops acceptably certain threshold concentration levels. This approach not only better mirrors Congressional intent, but better fulfills the Congressional objectives in promulgating the land disposal restrictions provisions.

NOTES AND QUESTIONS

1. How does EPA's new explanation of its reasons for deciding to require BDAT differ from the Agency's previous explanation? What justification does EPA offer for refusing to adopt risk-based screening levels? Does EPA reject the concept of risk-based regulation for hazardous waste? Do you think the new explanation is adequate to satisfy the objections of the court in Hazardous Waste Treatment Council v. EPA?

2. In Hazardous Waste Treatment Council v. EPA, the court suggested that there is a limit to EPA's authority to require treatment as hazardous constituents approach de minimis levels. Would EPA have the authority to require BDAT if a lesser technology could reduce hazardous constituents in a waste to such levels? How does EPA deal with this issue in justifying BDAT standards?

3. Note that EPA reveals that it has abandoned the model on which it based its proposed risk-based screening levels. What is the significance of this revelation? In light of the uncertainties that surround the fate and transport of hazardous constituents in soil and groundwater, do you think EPA will ever be able to have sufficient confidence in modeling to support a risk-based screening approach?

4. Why does EPA refer to treatment standards established under other environmental statutes, such as the Clean Water Act and Clean Air Act? What is the significance of the fact that certain portions of these acts require technology-based treatment standards?

B. FURTHER IMPLEMENTATION OF THE RCRA LAND BAN

EPA has now issued land disposal ban determinations and treatment standards for all listed or characteristic hazardous waste identified at the time of the 1984 Amendments. As required by the 1984 Amendments, EPA accomplished this in five stages between November 8, 1986 and May 8, 1990—addressing solvents and dioxins first, California list wastes second, and then each of the three thirds of the remaining universe of hazardous waste.

The D.C. Circuit, the exclusive venue for judicial review of RCRA regulations (§7006(a)(1)), has upheld various aspects of EPA's implementation of the land ban. In NRDC v. EPA, 907 F.2d 1146 (D.C. Cir. 1990), the court rejected the chemical industry's argument that a ban on deep injection of hazardous waste could not take effect until EPA specifically determined that such wastes could not safely be disposed in that manner. The court explained that Congress had presumed that land disposal of untreated wastes was unsafe unless EPA made a determination to the contrary:

> Nothing in [RCRA] requires the [EPA] Administrator to determine that a method of land disposal is not safe before prohibiting it. Rather, the statute commands the Administrator to promulgate prohibitory regulations unless he has made an affirmative demonstration of safety. . . . It seems indisputable to us that Congress did not require the EPA, before banning methods of land disposal, to determine affirmatively that they were not safe. Congress had already legislatively assumed that fact, subject only to the Administrator's decision otherwise. [907 F.2d at 1153-1154.]

i. Treatment Standards

The treatment standards promulgated by EPA are based on determinations concerning the capabilities of BDAT for destroying, extracting, or immobilizing hazardous constituents in waste. Incineration seems to be EPA's favored treatment technology, though the treatment standards also are expected to encourage source reduction and recycling of hazardous waste. For some of the wastes, EPA established "no land disposal" as the treatment standard based on evidence that the waste can be totally recycled or that it no longer is being land disposed.

In determining what technology constitutes BDAT, EPA initially indicated that it would perform comparative risk analysis to consider if the risks generated by treatment of a waste with a particular technology were greater than the risks of land disposal of the same waste. EPA soon concluded that this approach was not particularly useful because land disposal is presumptively disfavored by RCRA. 53 Fed. Reg. 31,190 (1988). Noting that the alternative to promulgating treatment standards for a waste was an automatic prohibition on land disposal, EPA abandoned the comparative risk approach. Id. This decision was upheld in American Petroleum Institute v. EPA, 906 F.2d 729 (D.C. Cir. 1990).

Although the treatment standards EPA has promulgated to implement section 3004(m) are technology-based, the Agency has written most of them in performance terms. For example, many standards specify the levels to which hazardous constituents must be reduced as a result of treatment. In other cases the standards specify a certain technology to be used for treatment based on a conclusion that one technology is clearly superior. EPA has attempted to encourage the development of alternative treatment technology by permitting generators or treaters to make waste-specific or site-specific demonstrations that an alternative treatment method can achieve a level of performance equivalent to that of the specified treatment method. 40 C.F.R. §268.42(b); 55 Fed. Reg. 22,520.

One form of "treatment" that EPA has rejected is the petroleum industry's claim that "land treatment" could constitute BDAT for some wastes. EPA concluded that

Congress has specifically voided the consideration of land treatment as BDAT by defining it to be land disposal in §3004(k) of RCRA as amended. . . . Land treatment is a type of land disposal, and prohibited wastes must meet a treatment standard before they are land disposed, unless they are disposed in no-migration units. [Response to Comments Related to the First-Third Wastes Treatment Technologies and Associated Performance, vol. V, Doc. No. LDR7-SOO1E, at 01621; vol. VI, Doc. No. LDR9-SOO1F, at 01755, 01758.]

This decision was upheld by the D.C. Circuit in American Petroleum Institute v. EPA, 906 F.2d 729 (D.C. Cir. 1990). As the court explained:

In simple terms, land treatment is a form of land disposal involving the placement of hazardous waste directly on the ground (rather than, for example, in a landfill or surface impoundment) with the expectation that the hazardous constituents will eventually become less hazardous. Thus, in a "land treatment facility," the treatment of hazardous wastes occurs only *after* the waste has been land disposed. [906 F.2d at 735 (emphasis in original).]

EPA promulgated land ban determinations and treatment standards for the final set of pre-1984 hazardous wastes on May 8, 1990. EPA's "third third" rule was controversial because the agency asserted the authority to require that characteristic wastes be treated with BDAT that would reduce hazardous constituents even below levels at which such wastes no longer would be considered hazardous. While environmental groups praised this determination, they harshly criticized EPA for refusing to exercise such authority for numerous wastes. EPA's final rule requires treatment below characteristic levels for 15 wastes, but for 23 others it caps levels of required treatment at characteristic levels. Calling the latter a "total capitulation" to the oil and chemical industries that "guts the land ban program," 21 Env. Rep. 149 (May 11, 1990), the Hazardous Waste Treatment Council and three environmental groups have sought judicial review. NRDC v. EPA, No. 90-1245 (D.C. Cir.).

EPA is now concentrating on promulgating treatment standards for wastes that have become subject to subtitle C after the 1984 Amendments. For a waste newly identified or listed after the enactment of the 1984 Amendments, EPA is required to determine whether it safely can be disposed of on land within six months of the date of listing.

ii.   "No-Migration" Variances

As noted above, the EPA administrator cannot permit the continued disposal of untreated hazardous wastes on land unless the owner or operator of the facility receiving the waste demonstrates "that there will be no migration of hazardous constituents from the disposal unit or injection zone as long as the wastes remain hazardous." §§3004(d)(1), (e)(1), (g)(5). EPA has promulgated regulations codifying this requirement and specifying procedures for handling petitions for no-migration variances. 51 Fed. Reg. 40,572 (1986), as amended by 53 Fed. Reg. 31,138 (1988). Standards for handling no-migration petitions for underground injection wells were promulgated in July 1988. 53 Fed. Reg. 28,122 (1988). They are codified at 40 C.F.R. pt. 148. Standards for no-migration petitions for other land disposal units are codified at 40 C.F.R. §268.6.

EPA's interpretation of the no-migration provisions as applied to deep injection of hazardous waste was upheld in large part in NRDC v. EPA, 907 F.2d 1146 (D.C. Cir. 1990). The court upheld EPA's determination that a petitioner seeking a no-migration variance for deep injection would have to show that the waste would not migrate out of a geological formation for the shorter of either 10,000 years or the period of time the waste remained hazardous. The court found that the 10,000 year alternative time limit was reasonable and consistent with the statute "because it would be long enough to insure that the 'no migration' standard would be met, and yet short enough to come within the limitations of predictability." 907 F.2d at 1158.

A closer question involved what had to be shown not to migrate— hazardous constituents or hazardous waste. The statutory language refers to "no migration of hazardous *constituents* . . . for so long as the *wastes* remain hazardous." EPA interpreted this to mean no migration of constituents in concentrations at which they would be considered a hazardous waste. Thus, EPA's interpretation would permit some migration of hazardous constituents as long as the constituents were not themselves at levels sufficient to be a hazardous waste. While conceding that it was a close call, a panel of the D.C. Circuit upheld EPA's interpretation in a 2-1 decision. The court noted that "read literally, the 'no migration' standards would seem to prohibit the migration of even a single molecule (or perhaps an appropriate de minimis amount) for the statutory time

period, even though the migrating waste is itself not hazardous at all."
After finding the statute ambiguous (and noting that in another portion
of RCRA Congress had prohibited migration of "*any* hazardous constituent," §3005(j)), the court deferred to EPA's interpretation.

In dissent, Judge Wald argued that the majority had failed to respect the clear statutory language, which reflected "not some wild, counterintuitive result that we should strain to avoid, but rather . . . the
natural result of a belief that migration is an inherently uncertain process." 907 F.2d at 1173. Joined by two other judges in a dissent from a
denial of rehearing en banc, Judge Wald asserted that the decision would
have a "far-reaching impact upon the *entire* land disposal schemata for
hazardous waste contained in §3004 of the Resource Conservation and
Recovery Act." Id.

EPA has approved no-migration variances for some deep injection
of untreated hazardous waste. By April 1990, EPA had received 65 no-
migration petitions for underground injection wells and 24 for other
land disposal units. 55 Fed. Reg. 13,068 (1990). By June 1990 EPA had
granted 12 variances for deep injection and had proposed to grant 15
others. Because of the enormous depths at which it inserts wastes into
the ground, EPA has indicated that as long as the Safe Drinking Water
Act regulations governing underground injection are followed, some
wastes can be safely disposed. 55 Fed. Reg. 22,520 (1990).

The D.C. Circuit has ruled that EPA's approval of a petition for a
no-migration variance is not subject to direct judicial review by that court
because it does not involve the promulgation of a regulation. Hazardous
Waste Treatment Council v. EPA, 910 F.2d 974 (D.C. Cir. 1990).

NOTES AND QUESTIONS

1. Can you think of any justification for requiring that hazardous
waste be treated beyond levels at which it would no longer be deemed
hazardous? Is "treatment for treatment's sake" the inevitable result of
applying BDAT in circumstances where technology is capable of reducing risks beyond levels deemed safe? Recall the following statement in
Hazardous Waste Treatment Council v. EPA, 886 F.2d 355 (D.C. Cir.
1989): "That Congress' concern in adopting §3004(m) was with health
and the environment would necessarily make it unreasonable for EPA
to promulgate treatment standards wholly without regard to whether
there might be a threat to man or nature." Is it legal for EPA to require
treatment beyond levels at which a waste is no longer deemed hazardous?

2. The term "hazardous constituent" refers to a chemical substance
(listed in Appendix VIII to 40 C.F.R. pt. 261) that may cause a waste to
be considered hazardous when present in a sufficient concentration. By

upholding EPA's interpretation that some migration of chemicals was permissible as long as the chemicals were not sufficiently concentrated to be considered a hazardous waste, the court sanctioned a less protective standard for land disposal. Judge Wald maintained that even if a standard allowing no migration of any *constituents* seemed harsh, Congress had intended to adopt an overly stringent standard to respond to uncertainties concerning the fate and transport of hazardous waste:

> The "no migration" standard is an *over*protective standard, inserted by Congress to ensure that not even hazardous constituents migrate from a body of waste known to be hazardous. . . . It reflects Congress' evident concern that once hazardous constituents are known to be migrating from a body of waste known to be hazardous, the uncertainties involved are too great to allow the EPA to determine that the migration is at an "acceptable" level. [907 F.2d at 1172 (emphasis in original).]

Is uncertainty the only justification that can be offered for adopting an "overprotective" standard?

3. Does EPA's decision that some migration of hazardous constituents is permissible achieve part of what the Agency originally had sought when it proposed the use of risk-based screening levels for determining BDAT? Recall that EPA was severely criticized by members of Congress for proposing an approach that would have allowed some migration from disposal units based on models demonstrating that hazardous constituents would not be at levels that would threaten health. How does EPA's interpretation of the "no-migration" variance compare with its ill-fated risk-based screening approach to determining BDAT?

4. Underground injection is used to dispose of a substantial portion of the nation's hazardous waste. Given the enormous uncertainties that surround forecasts of the fate and transport of pollutants, how can anyone demonstrate that wastes will not migrate from the injection zone for 10,000 years? EPA is planning to issue a regulation providing further guidance concerning how to obtain no-migration variances. Petitioners are required to characterize the environmental media in question and to model the environmental pathways along which constituent migration may occur. EPA has granted some conditional no-migration variances. For example, DOE obtained one for placement of radioactive waste at DOE's Waste Isolation Pilot Plant (WIPP) for a maximum of ten years. 55 Fed. Reg. 47,700 (1990). EPA found that DOE had demonstrated, to a reasonable degree of certainty, that hazardous constituents will not migrate from the WIPP disposal unit during the testing period proposed by DOE. If it cannot demonstrate the long-term acceptability of the site, DOE will be required to remove the hazardous wastes by the end of the test period. Is the approach of granting temporary, conditional no-migration variances consistent with the statute?

5. The Office of Management and Budget has been a vigorous critic of the land disposal ban, largely because the ban is not a product of cost-benefit balancing. OMB estimated that compliance with the land ban's "first third" regulations would cost more than $4 billion for every death averted by preventing groundwater contamination, making the regulation one of the most expensive (in dollars per life saved) ever promulgated. CEQ, Environmental Quality—Twenty-First Annual Report 283 (1991). How would you respond to OMB's concern? Do you think OMB has accurately assessed the true value of the land ban to society? If you accept OMB's estimate, does it necessarily follow that the land ban is an extremely poor environmental policy?

6. Subtitle D and the Regulation of "Nonhazardous" Municipal Waste Disposal

Subtitle D of RCRA, which addresses solid wastes that are not considered hazardous, encompasses a far broader volume of waste than subtitle C. While 200 to 300 million tons of wastes are regulated as hazardous under subtitle C each year, the other 12 billion tons of solid waste falls under the jurisdiction of subtitle D. As discussed above, responsibility for controlling the management of these wastes has remained largely the province of state and local governments. Mining waste, garbage generated by households, nonhazardous industrial waste, and waste from small generators of hazardous waste has not been regulated under subtitle C of RCRA. These wastes instead are subject only to subtitle D's prohibition of "open dumping" of waste at sites that are not classified as sanitary landfills under EPA's subtitle D criteria. With the exception of its "open dumping" ban and EPA's new minimum standards for municipal landfills, subtitle D of RCRA has not been a federal regulatory program, but rather a modest program of financial assistance to encourage states to engage in areawide waste management planning.

Soon after the enactment of RCRA, it became apparent that even landfills that had not received wastes classified as hazardous under subtitle C could pose a substantial threat to ground water. In 1984, EPA estimated that there were approximately 93,000 such landfills in the United States. Approximately 75,000 of these were located at industrial sites and another 18,500 served as municipal dumps. EPA, A Ground-Water Protection Strategy for the Environmental Protection Agency 14 (1984). Very little was known about these sites, and only a handful of states required any regular groundwater monitoring even though most dumps were located near aquifers.

When EPA conducted a Surface Impoundment Assessment in 1984, it identified more than 180,000 surface impoundments, most of which were unlined. About 40 percent of municipal and industrial impoundments were found to be "located in areas of thin or permeable soils, over aquifers currently used for drinking or that could be used for drinking." Id. at 38.

There are several reasons why nonhazardous waste landfills can pose substantial threats to human health and the environment. Prior to enactment of RCRA, hazardous wastes from industrial operations were often sent to municipal landfills. With the growth of the synthetic chemical industry after World War II, many highly toxic and persistent chemicals were added to this waste disposal stream. Most landfills were located in whatever seemed at the time to be the most convenient site, with little or no concern given to long-term environmental consequences. There was scant investment in technology for treating or containing wastes. Society simply assumed that nature would take care of any problems and that wastes that were placed out of sight were best left out of mind.

Even after RCRA was enacted, a considerable amount of hazardous waste continued to be sent to municipal landfills. In 1985 the Congressional Budget Office estimated that more 26 million tons of hazardous wastes was placed in nonhazardous waste landfills in the United States in 1983. Office of Technology Assessment, Superfund Strategy 126 (1985). A considerable portion of this waste consisted of hazardous waste from households and small-quantity generators, which were exempt from regulation under subtitle C. While these exemptions may have made good sense from the standpoint of administrative convenience, they make less sense from an ecological standpoint. Households and small-quantity generators generate hazardous wastes in small quantities, but these quantities add up. While it may take longer for such wastes to cause environmental problems, eventually they will.

Another reason why nonhazardous waste disposal sites pose environmental threats is the problem of midnight dumping. In addition to receiving wastes dumped surreptitiously, many landfills have not done a thorough job of inspecting incoming waste, and it is often difficult to determine the precise chemical composition of wastes sent to landfills. As subtitle C regulations have increased the cost of hazardous waste disposal, the incentive for midnight dumping has increased.

When Congress adopted the 1984 Amendments to RCRA, it recognized that even municipal dumps that managed solid waste not regulated under subtitle C could pose serious environmental hazards. Thus the 1984 Amendments made an important change in the federal role regarding solid waste management under subtitle D. The Amendments took the first steps toward a federal regulatory role. The Amendments added section 4010(c), which requires EPA to revise its subtitle D criteria for facilities that may receive hazardous household wastes or hazardous wastes from small-quantity generators. The revised criteria must require that such facilities at least perform groundwater monitoring and undertake corrective action as appropriate. Congress also required states to adopt "a permit program or other system of prior approval and conditions" to assure compliance with EPA's revised subtitle D criteria. RCRA §4005(c). In states that do not adopt adequate programs, EPA is authorized to enforce its own criteria.

To implement these new requirements, EPA proposed revisions to its criteria for solid waste disposal facilities in August 1988. 53 Fed. Reg. 33,314 (1988). While proposing to require groundwater monitoring at such facilities, EPA did not propose to establish any specific design or operation standards for landfills. EPA found that only 15 percent of landfills have liners; fewer than one-third perform groundwater monitoring; and at least 35 percent violate state groundwater protection standards. The Agency estimated that compliance with the revised criteria would cost an average of $43,600 per year per landfill, or about $11 per year per household. With the compliance costs to be borne by new landfills included, EPA estimated that the total cost of compliance eventually would reach $880 million a year. See Molotsky, First Federal Rules Proposed Governing Garbage Landfills, N.Y. Times, Aug. 25, 1988, at A1.

While the measures EPA proposed for solid waste landfills were modest compared to the Agency's subtitle C standards for hazardous waste facilities, they represented an important first step in what may prove to be an expanding regulatory role for the federal government. EPA's proposal touched off a bitter battle with the Office of Management and Budget, which reviews all EPA regulations prior to publication. OMB maintained that the proposed regulations would cost more than $19 billion for every life they saved. CEQ, Environmental Quality—Twenty-First Annual Report 283 (1991). OMB estimated that groundwater contamination from solid waste facilities posed a risk of cancer to exposed individuals of less than one in one million.

Because of OMB's objections, it took EPA more than three years to promulgate the new standards for municipal landfills. The regulation was promulgated under court order in October 1991. Even after the regulation had been signed by EPA Administrator William Reilly, OMB's involvement resulted in at least ten additional modifications' being made to the regulation prior to its publication in the Federal Register. 22 Env. Rep. 1542 (Oct. 11, 1991).

The final rule adopted by EPA establishes standards for siting, design, operation, and closure of municipal landfills. Landfills also will be required within five years to conduct regular groundwater monitoring and to take corrective action to clean up contamination. The rules provide a flexible menu of design standards that states may elect based on their hydrogeological and other characteristics. For example, while the criteria base compliance monitoring on contamination detected at landfill boundaries, they authorize states to adopt alternative compliance points up to 150 meters from facility boundaries. The rules exempt from design standards, groundwater monitoring, and corrective action requirements small landfills (those receiving less than 20 tons of garbage per day) in regions where rainfall is light (less than 25 inches per year). 56 Fed. Reg. 50,978 (1991).

States are required to establish permit programs to incorporate the subtitle D standards. States must comply with the regulations by October 1993. If a state approves a landfill that has less stringent design standards than required by the federal criteria, the regulation gives EPA only 30 days in which to object. EPA is authorized to impose federal standards directly in states that fail to submit acceptable state programs.

When it issued the subtitle D standards in October 1991, EPA estimated that there were approximately 6,000 nonhazardous waste landfills then operating. These landfills handle the vast majority of the 160 million tons of municipal solid waste generated each year. Because most of these landfills do not have adequate environmental protection measures, EPA estimates that the new subtitle D regulations will cost municipalities approximately $330 million per year to implement and that approximately 3,000 landfills will close within five years.

The dispute between EPA and OMB over the revised subtitle D reflects a broad philosphical difference between the two agencies. OMB generally believes that specific preventive measures should not be required unless it can be demonstrated through risk assessment and cost-benefit analysis that the measures will cost less than the environmental benefits they will produce. OMB assumes that unless it can be shown that people will die from drinking contaminated groundwater, landfill design standards are a poor investment. OMB does not view environmental releases as inherently undesirable, unless they can be predicted to produce damage greater than the costs of preventing them.

In contrast, EPA believes that it should prevent environmental contamination before it occurs. Given the enormous uncertainties that make it virtually impossible to predict the fate and transport of pollutants in groundwater, EPA is less willing to assume that groundwater contamination will not be a serious problem regardless of what a risk assessment model that focuses only on cancer risks may predict. EPA is more favorably disposed to preventive measures than OMB. In part, this reflects the notion that an ounce of prevention is worth a pound of cure. Because it is so difficult and expensive to clean up environmental release, EPA believes that even expensive preventive measures are sound investments.

NOTES AND QUESTIONS

1. While existing landfill capacity is disappearing rapidly, several states are in the process of adopting standards for municipal landfills that are more stringent than those adopted by EPA. For example, Penn-

sylvania, New York, Connecticut, and Maine require landfills to have double liners, a requirement not included in EPA's criteria. When OMB argued against including double liners in the federal criteria on cost-benefit grounds, their analysis failed to reflect the fact that many states already require them. 22 Env. Rep. 1140 (Aug. 23, 1991).

2. Subtitle D's evolution from a modest financial assistance program to a program establishing minimum federal standards for municipal landfills follows what has become a relatively consistent pattern for federal environmental programs. As national awareness of environmental problems grows, federal programs to encourage state planning gradually evolve into national regulatory programs. Because waste management has been viewed as almost a quintessential state and local responsibility, subtitle D took longer to follow this path. The recognition that solid waste management is a significant problem that requires national regulation reflects the increasingly tenuous nature of RCRA's attempt to distinguish between hazardous and nonhazardous waste. RCRA's two-tier system of imposing subtitle C's onerous regulatory requirements on waste deemed hazardous while allowing all other forms of solid waste to escape significant federal regulation is now eroding and seems destined to erode further. What do you think accounts for this development? Can one infer from it that EPA's efforts to identify the universe of truly hazardous wastes have not been successful?

3. It already is extremely difficult, if not virtually impossible, to site new landfills. What impact will increasingly stringent regulation have on the availability of landfill capacity in the future? These and other issues will be explored in more detail when we discuss the future of waste management in section F of this chapter.

4. The philosophic differences between EPA and OMB are also reflected in their attitudes toward corrective action for environmental contamination. EPA tends to believe in the principle that environmental releases of hazardous substances should be cleaned up. OMB believes that it may not be worthwhile to do so in all cases because cleanup costs may exceed the benefits of remediation. Whose position would create greater incentives for preventing environmental releases—EPA's or OMB's? Congress has mandated stringent corrective action requirements for facilities seeking permits under RCRA subtitle C. We will examine these in section E2 of this chapter, after we examine the other major strategy for preventing and remediating releases of hazardous substances—the liability approach embodied in CERCLA.

D. CERCLA LIABILITY

1. *Introductory History*

When it enacted RCRA in 1976 Congress thought it had closed the last remaining loophole in environmental law. Yet Congress soon discovered that the consequences of decades of poor waste management practices were just beginning to appear. The billions of tons of hazardous waste that had been dumped on the land and into ponds, pits, lagoons, and drums had spread into the soil and was now contaminating ground and surface waters at thousands of sites. Communities felt threatened by discoveries of toxic chemicals in close proximity to their homes, schools, and sources of drinking water.

Shortly after RCRA was enacted, the Love Canal disaster was discovered. In 1953, the Hooker Chemical and Plastics Corporation had transferred title to a 16-acre site to the Niagara Falls Board of Education for the sum of one dollar. The company acknowledged that it had buried chemicals on the site, which it had covered with a layer of clay, and the deed of sale stated that the company would not be responsible for any injuries that might occur. A school and 100 homes were built on the site, which became known as Love Canal. Following heavy rains in 1978, a chemical soup began seeping into residential basements. More than 80 chemical compounds were found, including many known carcinogens. Ultimately, 1,000 families were relocated and homes along the canal were demolished.

Love Canal became a national media event that crystallized a festering problem in terms that provoked an emotional response from the public. The public response contributed to a political climate that produced the Comprehensive Environmental Response, Compensation, and Liability Act (CERCLA), the most comprehensive new federal approach to environmental protection since the enactment of NEPA. Even though the story of Love Canal will forever be associated with CERCLA, it is important to understand that in many respects CERCLA represents a natural adaptation of centuries of common law developments as extended by modern environmental statutes.

CERCLA is a direct extension of common law principles of strict liability for abnormally dangerous activities. CERCLA is modeled directly on the Clean Water Act's oil spill liability program established in 1972. As discussed in Chapter 2, section 311 of the Clean Water Act applies the principle of strict liability to persons responsible for releases of "harmful quantities" of oil. This provision, coupled with emergency response authorities contained in section 504(b) of the Act, established a national oil spill response program that made persons responsible for the spills strictly liable for response costs. In 1978, Congress broadened section 311 to encompass not only oil spills, but also releases of other hazardous substances in navigable waters. Congress also made dischargers liable not only for cleanup costs but also for damages to natural resources.

After Love Canal focused national attention on hazardous waste dumps in 1978, it became apparent that existing authorities were not well-suited for responding to releases of hazardous substances on land. EPA and the Justice Department filed several lawsuits under RCRA section 7003 seeking to require the abatement of hazards at abandoned hazardous waste dump sites. At the time, section 7003 authorized suits to abate situations in which "any solid or hazardous waste is presently an imminent and substantial endangerment to health or the environment." Although EPA previously had taken the position that section 7003 applied only to active hazardous waste facilities regulated under subtitle C, the government attempted to adapt the statute to respond to abandoned dumps.

In June 1979 the Carter Administration introduced legislation to authorize the government to respond to releases of hazardous substances at dump sites and to provide for recovery of response costs. Broader legislation (which was opposed vigorously by the chemical industry but eventually approved by two Senate committees) also provided for compensation to victims of exposure to hazardous substances. These proposals became known as "Superfund" bills because they provided for a trust fund to finance government response costs, like the oil spill trust fund. While the House of Representatives in September 1980 approved legislation creating a fund to clean up hazardous waste dump sites and to broaden the fund for responding to oil and hazardous substance spills in navigable waters, the Senate did not vote on its own legislation until after the November 1980 election.

Following President Carter's defeat, the Senate reconvened in a lame duck session. While the Republicans had won control of the Senate, their new majority leader-elect, Senator Howard Baker, was committed to enactment of Superfund legislation and Senator Robert Stafford, who would become the new chairman of the Senate Environment Committee, was a committed environmentalist. The bill approved by the Senate committees had provided for a $4.1 billion superfund, which was scaled back to $1.6 billion after negotiations on the floor and a threatened filibuster by Senator Jesse Helms. Cummings, Completing the Circle, Envtl. Forum 11, 14-15 (Nov.-Dec. 1990). Provisions for compensating victims of exposure to hazardous substances also were eliminated.

On November 24, 1980, the Senate adopted its own bill as a substitute for the House-passed legislation by a vote of 78-9. After tough negotiations, the House agreed to accept the Senate version of the legislation without holding a conference committee. On December 3, 1980 the House passed the Senate bill 274-94. After two years of debate and escalating public concern over toxic waste, Congress had enacted the Comprehensive Environmental Response, Compensation, and Liability Act (CERCLA), which President Carter signed into law on December 11, 1980.

The principal provisions of CERCLA are outlined below. While most of the public attention devoted to CERCLA focuses on its remedial aspects, its most fundamental contribution to environmental policy is its comprehensive liability scheme, which provides the most powerful incentives for preventing releases of hazardous substances that are contained in any federal statute. As Philip Cummings, the chief counsel of the Senate Environment Committee when CERCLA was drafted, writes: "CERCLA is not primarily an abandoned dump cleanup program, although that is included in its purposes." Instead,

> The main purpose of CERCLA is to make spills or dumping of hazardous substances less likely through liability, enlisting business and commercial instincts for the bottom line in place of traditional regulation. It was a conscious intention of the law's authors to draw lenders and insurers into this new army of quasi-regulators, along with corporate risk managers and boards of directors. [Id. at 11.]

CERCLA's liability provisions are contained in section 107. The question of how broadly CERCLA's liability net is cast is examined below.

PRINCIPAL PROVISIONS OF CERCLA

§101. Definitions: the term "hazardous substance" is defined in section 101(14); "release" is defined in section 101(22).

§103. Notification Requirements: requires reporting of releases of hazardous substances to the National Response Center.

§104. Response Authorities: authorizes the president to undertake removals or remedial action consistent with the National Contingency Plan to respond to actual or potential releases of hazardous substances.

§105. National Contingency Plan: requires establishment of National Priorities List (NPL) of facilities presenting the greatest danger to health, welfare, or the environment based on a hazard ranking system (HRS) and requires revision of National Contingency Plan (NCP).

§106. Abatement Actions: authorizes issuance of administrative orders requiring the abatement of actual or potential releases that may create imminent and substantial endangerment to health, welfare, or the environment.

§107. Liability: imposes liability on (1) current owners and operators of facilities where hazardous substances are released or threatened to be released, (2) owners and operators of facilities at the time substances were disposed, (3) persons who arranged for transportation or disposal or treatment of such substances, and (4) persons who accepted such substances for transport for disposal or treatment. These parties are liable for: (a) all costs of removal or remedial action incurred by the federal government not inconsistent with the NCP, (b) any other necessary costs of response incurred by any person consistent with the NCP, (c) damages for injury to natural resources, and (d) costs of health assessments.

§111. Superfund: authorizes $8.5 billion Superfund for period from 1986-1991, extended through 1994 with a $5.1 billion appropriation approved in 1990.

§116. Cleanup Schedules: establishes schedules for evaluating and listing sites on NPL, commencement of remedial investigation and feasibility studies (RI/FSs), and commencement of remedial action.

§121. Cleanup Standards: establishes preference for remedial actions that permanently and significantly reduce the volume, toxicity, or mobility of hazardous substances and requires selection of remedial actions that are protective of health and the environment and cost effective, using permanent solutions to maximum extent practicable; requires cleanups to attain level of "legally applicable or relevant and appropriate standard, requirement, criteria or limitation" contained under any federal environmental law or more stringent state law.

§122. Settlements: sets standards for settlements with potentially responsible parties.

In addition to creating incentives for preventing releases of hazardous substances, CERCLA is designed to ensure that such releases are cleaned up. To accomplish this goal, section 105 of CERCLA initially directed the president to establish a list of at least 400 sites needing cleanup (the National Priorities List, or NPL). To guide remediation efforts, section 105 directed that the National Contingency Plan (NCP), originally prepared by the Council on Environmental Quality to implement section 311 of the Clean Water Act, be revised to establish more comprehensive procedures for dealing with hazardous substance releases.

To accomplish its remediation goals, CERCLA authorizes the government to respond to environmental releases by spending money in the Superfund which then can be reimbursed by parties made strictly liable for such releases. Section 111 of CERCLA creates a revolving trust fund (the Superfund), funded initially through a tax on chemical feed-stocks, to finance governmental cleanup activities. Section 104 of CERCLA authorizes the president to respond to releases of hazardous substances by undertaking short-term removal actions or longer-term remedial actions and to obtain reimbursement for the costs of these actions from parties held responsible under section 107. Section 106 also authorizes the government to issue orders requiring private parties to undertake actions to abate actual or potential releases of hazardous substances that may create imminent and substantial endangerment. While CERCLA is one of the few environmental statutes that delegate implementation authority to the president, this authority has largely been transferred to EPA by executive order.

EPA's initial implementation of CERCLA was highly controversial, to say the least. The Reagan Administration, which assumed office shortly after CERCLA was signed into law, was hostile toward the program, and its appointees were slow to implement its provisions. EPA sought to avoid spending money in the Superfund and to encourage responsible parties to undertake cleanups through negotiations. After a scandal involving the alleged political manipulation of Superfund expenditures led to the resignation of EPA Administrator Anne Gorsuch Burford in 1983, returning EPA administrator William Ruckelshaus pledged more vigorous implementation of the program. Five years after CERCLA had been enacted, critics of EPA noted that the Agency had succeeded in "cleaning up" only six of the hundreds of sites on the NPL.

The controversy over implementation of CERCLA played a major role in the reauthorization of RCRA in 1984. The enactment of tough new regulatory measures to prevent mismanagement of hazardous waste in the 1984 Amendments to RCRA reflected in part the realization that it was far more difficult to clean up environmental contamination than previously thought.

Two years after substantially altering RCRA, Congress in 1986 made major changes in CERCLA when it enacted the Superfund Amendments and Reauthorization Act (SARA). SARA was the culmination of a prolonged struggle over how to correct widely recognized problems in the CERCLA program. Bipartisan dissatisfaction with EPA's slow progress in cleaning up dump sites, and a growing recognition that the dump site cleanup problem was of far greater scope than Congress previously had envisioned, produced stringent new requirements for Superfund cleanups.

In the wake of SARA, CERCLA has achieved a degree of complexity sufficient to deter all but the hardiest students of statutory analysis from casual browsing in the U.S. Code. Because CERCLA's most important contribution to environmental law is its liability provisions, we focus on them first.

2. Liability Provisions of CERCLA

CERCLA makes a broad class of parties liable for the costs of responding to the release, or the substantial threat of a release, of "any hazardous substance." It does so by authorizing responses to such releases (or to releases of "any pollutant or contaminant which may present an imminent and substantial danger to the public health or welfare") in section 104, and then by specifying in section 107 the parties liable for response costs.

The term "hazardous substance" is broadly defined by section 101(14) to include hazardous wastes subject to regulation under subtitle C of RCRA, toxic water pollutants regulated under section 307 of the Clean Water Act, hazardous air pollutants listed under section 112 of the Clean Air Act, imminently hazardous chemicals regulated under section 7 of TSCA, substances subject to section 311 of the Clean Water Act (governing oil and hazardous substance spills in navigable waters), and additional substances designated by EPA. Thus, it is considerably broader than the universe of hazardous wastes regulated under subtitle C of RCRA. While the definition of "hazardous substance" encompasses just about any toxic substance, section 104 also provides CERCLA jurisdiction over substances not listed in any of the categories of "hazardous substances" if it is a "pollutant or contaminant which may present an imminent and substantial danger to the public health or welfare." Thus, the release of a substance that does not happen to fall within CERCLA's broad definition of "hazardous substances" can still generate CERCLA liability if it presents "an imminent and substantial danger."

"Release" is broadly defined in section 101(22) to cover just about any means for a substance to escape into the environment. Not all releases of hazardous substances fall within CERCLA's broad jurisdiction. Section 107(i) of CERCLA exempts the application of pesticides registered under FIFRA, and section 107(j) exempts "federally permitted releases." The latter are defined in section 101(10) to include discharges authorized by permits issued under the Clean Water Act, RCRA, the Ocean Dumping Act, the Safe Drinking Water Act, the Clean Air Act, and the Atomic Energy Act, and certain fluid injection practices for producing oil or natural gas.

The enormous publicity directed at CERCLA's remediation provisions (examined below) has obscured the fact that CERCLA's liability provisions also are designed to serve preventive ends. While some have argued that the CERCLA cleanup process has become so bureaucratic as to make the program resemble a traditional command-and-control regulatory program, Coalition on Superfund, Coalition on Superfund Research Report ix (1989), CERCLA's liability provisions remain the heart of the statute. By imposing strict liability on a broad class of potentially responsible parties, Congress intended to create a powerful new incentive for waste reduction and more careful handling and disposal of waste. As the Senate committee report on the original CERCLA legislation stated, "By holding the factually responsible person liable, [the bill] encourages that person—whether a generator, transporter, or disposer of hazardous substances—to eliminate as many risks as possible." S. Rep. No. 848, 96th Cong., 2d Sess. 33 (1980).

Thus, CERCLA pursues dual goals: to prevent environmental contamination and to ensure that it is cleaned up when it occurs. While some argue that CERCLA's liability scheme has delayed the cleanup of dump sites and wasted resources on litigation, any evaluation of CERCLA's liability provisions should be done in the context of the Act's dual objectives. Regardless of how rapidly EPA proceeds with dump site cleanups, the CERCLA program could still be a success if its liability provisions are effective in deterring environmental releases. Fear of CERCLA liability undoubtedly is stimulating some voluntary reductions in the volume and toxicity of waste generated, an increase in recycling of waste, and an increase in the care with which waste is managed and ultimately disposed. As a report for the Rand Corporation noted:

> By exposing firms to unlimited liability for prior waste handling, Superfund sets up strong signals that equally stringent regulations will operate in the future as well. This should lead to more conservative waste-handling practices both today and in the future and may lead business to reduce its use of toxic materials—and to increase recycling of these substances. [Acton, Understanding Superfund: A Progress Report 19 (1989).]

What is not known is precisely how significant CERCLA's liability provisions have been in stimulating such behavior. It seems clear that the Act *should* provide powerful incentives for investing in prevention. In the sections that follow we consider how CERCLA's liability provisions operate.

3.   *"Release of Hazardous Substance"*

As noted above, the trigger for a CERCLA response action under section 104 is the release or substantial threat of a release of a hazardous substance (or of something not considered a hazardous substance that nonetheless presents imminent and substantial danger). The sections that follow consider how broadly "hazardous substance" has been defined and what constitutes an environmental "release."

A.   HAZARDOUS SUBSTANCES

EPA has listed more than 700 substances as "hazardous substances" for purposes of CERCLA. 40 C.F.R. §302. The question of how broadly

CERCLA's definition of "hazardous substances" should be interpreted was addressed by the D.C. Circuit in the following case. Congress had temporarily exempted certain mining wastes from regulation under subtitle C of RCRA. In the case that follows the mining industry argued that this exemption also should exempt it from liability under CERCLA.

Eagle-Picher Industries v. EPA
759 F.2d 922 (D.C. Cir. 1985)

STARR, Circuit Judge:

This case calls on us to examine the complex web of "Superfund" legislation passed by Congress in the waning days of 1980. Specifically, we are presented with contentions pressed by certain mining companies and an electric utility that their facilities were improperly included by the Environmental Protection Agency on a nationwide list of priority sites under the Comprehensive Environmental Response, Compensation and Liability Act of 1980, 42 U.S.C. §§9601 et. seq. (1982) ("CERCLA" or "the Act").

CERCLA was designed to address the growing problem of inactive hazardous waste sites throughout the United States. The Act authorizes the Environmental Protection Agency ("EPA") to respond to the release of both "hazardous substances" and those "pollutants or contaminants" the release of which may present "an imminent and substantial danger to the public health or welfare," as those terms are defined in the Act. A response by EPA can be of two kinds: removal, or remedial action. Removal actions involve the actual cleanup of a release, 42 U.S.C. §9601(23). Remedial actions are those actions consistent with a permanent remedy to prevent or minimize the release of hazardous substances. Id. §9601(24).

To enable EPA to respond to those sites most urgently in need of cleanup, EPA is required under section 105(8)(B), 42 U.S.C. §9605(8)(B), to compile the National Priorities List ("NPL") of releases or threatened releases throughout the United States. The petitioners in these consolidated cases object to the placement of their respective facilities on the NPL and advance various arguments as to why the EPA's actions were purportedly in error. . . .

Petitioners first claim that mining wastes and fly ash are not "hazardous substances" within the meaning of CERCLA. The pivotal term, "hazardous substance," is defined rather elaborately in section 101(14) of the Act, 42 U.S.C. §9601(14):

"[H]azardous substance" means (A) any substance designated pursuant to section 1321(b)(2)(A) of title 33, (B) any element, compound, mixture, solution, or substance designated pursuant to section 9602 of this title, (C) any hazardous waste having the characteristics identified under or listed pursuant to section 3001 of the Solid Waste Disposal Act [42 U.S.C. §6921] (but not including any waste the regulation of which under the Solid Waste Disposal Act [42 U.S.C. §6901 et seq.] has been suspended by Act of Congress), (D) any toxic pollutant listed under section 1317(a) of title 33, (E) any hazardous air pollutant listed under section 112 of the Clean Air Act [42 U.S.C. §7412], and (F) any imminently hazardous chemical substance or mixture with respect to which the Administrator has taken action pursuant to section 2606 of title 15. The term does not include petroleum, including crude oil or any fraction thereof which is not otherwise specifically listed or designated as a hazardous substance under subparagraphs (A) through (F) of this paragraph, and the term does not include natural gas, natural gas liquids, liquefied natural gas, or synthetic gas usable for fuel (or mixtures of natural gas and such synthetic gas). . . .

Petitioners ground their claim on the parenthetical clause found in subclause (C) of this complex provision, which expressly refers for its definitional purposes to several other federal statutes. That parenthetical clause applies by its terms to petitioners, inasmuch as both mining wastes and fly ash have been suspended from regulation under the Solid Waste Disposal Act (which includes the subsequently passed statute known as "RCRA"). See 42 U.S.C. §§6921(3)(A)(i), 6921(3)(A)(ii) (1982). From this exclusion, petitioners draw the conclusion that mining wastes and fly ash are thus excluded as well from CERCLA's definition of "hazardous substances."

Notwithstanding its superficial appeal, petitioners' argument suffers from a mortal flaw, namely that their interpretation does not comport with the plain meaning of the entire statutory provision. As EPA notes, a substance is a "hazardous substance" within the meaning of CERCLA if it qualifies under *any* of the several subparagraphs of section 101(14). The exception for mining wastes and fly ash is found only in a parenthetical clause in subparagraph (C). The ordinary, straightforward reading of that exception is that it applies only to subparagraph (C), not to any of the other five subparagraphs. Had Congress intended to exempt mining wastes and fly ash from the entirety of section 101(14), it obviously could have placed the exemption at the beginning or end of the section, not in one of the several subparagraphs. Indeed, this is precisely what Congress did do with respect to other specific substances. At the conclusion of section 101(14), a *general exception* from the definition of "hazardous substance" is carved out for petroleum and natural gas products. Had Congress intended to create a similarly broad exception for mining wastes and fly ash, the Legislature readily could have placed that exception alongside the petroleum and natural gas exceptions.

Petitioners argue that such an interpretation must be rejected for two reasons: first, that the interpretation would render meaningless the exception in subparagraph (C), and second, that the legislative history of CERCLA clearly shows that the subparagraph (C) exception was meant to exempt totally such wastes from the term "hazardous substance."

As to the first argument, petitioners observe that EPA labels as "hazardous substances" the mining wastes and fly ash produced by petitioners because those wastes contain substances, such as arsenic, cadmium, and selenium, which are regulated under one or more of the several environmental statutes referred to in section 101(14). Petitioners claim that virtually all mining wastes and fly ash contain at least trace amounts of substances that qualify as "hazardous substances" under one of section 101(14)'s subparagraphs. Thus, they argue, EPA's interpretation would render all or virtually all mining wastes and fly ash CERCLA-covered "hazardous substances," with the effect of denuding the exception in subparagraph (C) of any efficacy whatsoever. Since, petitioners argue, courts should under settled principles reject a proffered statutory interpretation which renders any part of the statute meaningless where a reasonable alternative interpretation exists, we should be constrained to embrace their proposed construction which breathes life into all of CERCLA's definitional provisions.

Unfortunately for petitioners, they have cited nothing in CERCLA, its legislative history, or the record in this case demonstrating that all or virtually all mining wastes and fly ash have constituents which are "hazardous substances." We have nothing more than petitioners' bare assertions on this point. Likewise, petitioners have presented nothing demonstrating that Congress was of the view that all or almost all mining wastes and fly ash contain hazardous substances. It is quite possible that Congress was unconvinced that enough was known about mining wastes and fly ash for EPA to decide that those substances, as a general rule, posed a threat to the environment, but at the same time Congress may have been willing to bring any mining wastes and fly ash found to contain "hazardous substances" within the ambit of section 101(14). Without a showing that Congress believed that the regulation of mining wastes and fly ash under other subparagraphs of section 101(14) would render the exception in subparagraph (C) meaningless, we are disinclined to reject the plain meaning of section 101(14).

[The court then denied the petitions for review.]

NOTES AND QUESTIONS

1. A vast number of activities can been interpreted to be "releases of hazardous substances" because of the large number of substances that contain constituents considered to be "hazardous substances" under CERCLA. Courts have held that a substance is a "hazardous substance" for purposes of CERCLA if it contains chemical constituents that are

hazardous substances, regardless of their quantity or concentration. As the court in United States v. Carolawn Co., 21 Envtl. Rep. Cases 2124, 2126 (D.S.C. 1984) explained, "If a waste material contains hazardous substances, then the waste material itself is a hazardous substance for purposes of CERCLA." CERCLA's definition of hazardous substances "does not distinguish hazardous substances on the basis of quantity or concentration." Id. More than 700 toxic substances are considered to be "hazardous substances" under CERCLA's definition of the term.

2. Note that the petitioners argued that the subparagraph (C) exception would be meaningless if mining wastes and fly ash were not deemed to be expressly exempted from CERCLA's definition of "hazardous substances." In response to this argument, the court notes that it has nothing more to go on than petitioners' "bare assertions" that virtually all mining wastes and fly ash have constituents that are "hazardous substances." How difficult do you think it would be to demonstrate that virtually all mining waste and fly ash have hazardous constituents? Would this case have been decided differently if the petitioners had been able to make such a demonstration?

3. While the first word in CERCLA's title is "Comprehensive," not all substances that create environmental hazards are covered under the Act. Petroleum products were expressly exempted from the general definition of "hazardous substance" in section 101(14) of CERCLA. One reason for this exemption is that oil spills in navigable waters already were covered by section 311 of the Clean Water Act and it was anticipated that this program eventually would be broadened to cover oil spills on land. Congress has responded to the latter problem in piecemeal fashion.

The 1984 Amendments to RCRA added a new subtitle I to create a special program for responding to leaking underground storage tanks, funded through a separate trust fund. Legislation enacted in 1990 also requires regulations to prevent spills from land-based oil pipelines. Courts have tended to interpret the petroleum exclusion to CERCLA narrowly so that it does not exempt hazardous substances added to oil during or after its use. City of New York v. Exxon Corp., 766 F. Supp. 177 (S.D.N.Y. 1991) (petroleum exclusion does not cover oil that has acquired hazardous constituents through manufacturing processes rather than through refining). See also Bellack, Distilling a Useful Petroleum Exclusion, 6 Nat. Resources & Env. 35 (1992).

B. "RELEASE OR SUBSTANTIAL THREAT OF RELEASE"

Section 104(a)(1) of CERCLA authorizes the government to respond whenever "any hazardous substance is released or there is a substantial threat of such a release into the environment." The term "release" is broadly defined in section 101(22) to mean any spilling, leaking, pumping, pouring, emitting, emptying, discharging, injecting, escaping, leaching, dumping, or disposing into the environment (including the abandonment or discarding of barrels, containers, and other closed receptacles containing any hazardous substance or pollutant or contaminant). [§101(22).]

Specifically exempted from the definition of "release" are releases that result only in workplace exposures, emissions from vehicle exhaust, releases of material from a nuclear incident, and the normal application of fertilizer.

To alert emergency response authorities to potentially dangerous situations, section 103 of CERCLA requires reporting of releases of hazardous substances in quantities that exceed thresholds (called "reportable quantities") established by EPA. Releases are to be reported to the National Emergency Response Center. Although section 104 gives EPA the authority to respond not only to releases of hazardous substances, but also to conditions that pose a "substantial threat" of a release, section 103's notification requirement applies only to "releases."

Despite section 101(22)'s broad definition of "release," courts have indicated that there are limits to the kinds of conditions that EPA may consider to be "releases" for which notification can be required under section 103. In The Fertilizer Institute v. EPA, 935 F.2d 1303 (D.C. Cir. 1991), the D.C. Circuit held that EPA had adopted an overly expansive definition of "release" when it promulgated regulations establishing reportable quantities (RQs) for radionuclides. Because actual radionuclide releases are difficult to measure and there are more than 1,500 different radionuclides, EPA had concluded that notification was required if material containing certain quantities of radionuclides were placed into "any unenclosed containment structure wherein the hazardous substance is exposed to the environment." 54 Fed. Reg. 22,526 (1989). The Agency explained that because "[a]n unenclosed containment structure may allow the hazardous substance to emit, escape, or leach into the air, water, or soil," its placement there "would constitute a 'release' regardless of whether an RQ of the substance actually volatilizes into the air or migrates into surrounding water or soil." Id.

The D.C. Circuit noted that the placement of a substance in a location where it was *exposed to the environment* was conceptually distinct from the movement of a substance *into the environment* because the mere exposure of a substance to the environment does not always result in a release (e.g., a nonvolatile substance could be placed in an open-air container without escaping into the air). The court rejected EPA's argument that certain substances posed such a great threat of a release that the Agency was justified in treating their placement into an unenclosed containment structure as an actual release. The court found it significant that section 103's notification requirement, unlike section

104's response authorities, extends only to "releases" and not to conditions that create a "substantial threat" of a release. The court held that under CERCLA's provisions, nothing less than the actual release of a hazardous material into the environment triggers its reporting requirements.

Other courts have indicated that releases that do not exceed naturally occurring levels of hazardous substances (background levels) at a site, United States v. Ottati & Goss, Inc., 900 F.2d 429, 438 (1st Cir. 1990), or levels that correspond to CERCLA cleanup standards, Amoco Oil Co. v. Borden, Inc., 889 F.2d 664, 670 (5th Cir. 1989), may not give rise to CERCLA liability. Note that CERCLA section 104(a)(3) bars response actions for releases of "naturally occurring" substances where found naturally, except in emergencies.

NOTES AND QUESTIONS

1. Why did EPA want to define "release" to encompass the unenclosed storage of a hazardous substance?

2. Can EPA still require the reporting of actual releases of radionuclides? What if EPA determines that it is simply too difficult or impracticable to measure such releases?

3. Are there good reasons for EPA to want to be alerted to potential releases of hazardous substances? Why do you suppose that CERCLA does not require reporting of potential releases?

4. Does *Fertilizer Institute* imply that the mere presence of wastes containing hazardous substances at an abandoned dump site is not sufficient to establish liability under section 107 of CERCLA unless the government can prove that the hazardous substances actually are being released into the environment? In response to the decision, an industry attorney predicted that because "people are desperate to escape liability . . . you'll see this language popping up" in future CERCLA cases. Court Overturns EPA Definition of Hazardous "Release" Under Superfund, Inside EPA, June 21, 1991, at 6.

5. Suppose that copper ore slag from a smelter is dumped on the ground in an industrial yard where logs are stored by a lumber company. The slag is considered a hazardous substance because it contains copper, lead, zinc, and arsenic, which themselves are hazardous substances. The smelter owner argues that the slag is actually a useful commercial product because it can be sold as a ballast substitute. Can the smelter slag trigger CERCLA liability? See Louisiana-Pacific Corp. v. Asarco, Inc., 735 F. Supp. 358 (W.D. Wash. 1990).

6. Because occupational exposures to toxic substances and harmful physical agents are already regulated by OSHA, CERCLA's definition of "release" expressly exempts "any release which results in exposure to

persons solely within a workplace, with respect to a claim which such persons may assert against the employer of such persons." §101(22)(A), 42 U.S.C. §9601(22)(A). Suppose that employees of a thermometer manufacturing plant are exposed to mercury at work, which is transported on their clothing and in their bodies to their homes and eventually is discharged into their septic systems and to public sewers. Can the owner of the plant be made liable under CERCLA for the mercury discharges? See Vermont v. Staco, Inc., 684 F. Supp. 822 (D. Vt. 1988).

4. Strict, Joint, and Several Liability

References to "strict, joint, and several liability" are nowhere to be found in CERCLA. Yet courts almost uniformly have found that CERCLA imposes strict, joint, and several liability on responsible parties. This result seems odd to some, particularly since express references to strict, joint, and several liability were deleted from the Senate bill that became CERCLA shortly before the Senate floor vote.

The only reference to a standard of liability is in the definitional section of CERCLA. Section 101(32) states that the "term 'liable' or 'liability' under this subchapter shall be construed to be the standard of liability which obtains under section 1321 of Title 33 [§311 of the federal Clean Water Act]." Philip Cummings, who was then chief counsel of the Senate Environment and Public Works Committee, explains that this was the final compromise prior to Senate passage of CERCLA. He tells the following story:

> The committee staff had argued that strict, joint, and several liability, explicitly referred to in S. 1480 and the November 18 substitute, was not radical but was the standard of liability under §311 of the CWA. Alan Simpson (R-Wyoming) was skeptical; if that were so, he countered, why not just say that. The committee staff agreed to put in the reference to the standard of liability under §311 that is now §101(32) of CERCLA. [Cummings, Completing the Circle, Envtl. Forum 11, 15 (Nov.-Dec. 1990).]

Most courts have interpreted section 101(32) as authorizing the imposition of strict, joint, and several liability on defendants who cannot demonstrate that the harm caused by their wastes is divisible. United States v. Chem-Dyne Corp., 572 F. Supp. 802, 810 (S.D. Ohio 1983); United States v. Bliss, 667 F. Supp. 1298 (E.D. Mo. 1987); United States v. Monsanto, 858 F.2d 160 (4th Cir. 1988). This was the approach that had been followed by courts interpreting section 311 of the Clean Water Act and it is grounded in common law principles reflected in the Restatement (Second) of Torts.

Strict liability relieves the government of the obligation to prove that hazardous substances were released as the result of negligence or that the defendant's conduct was intentional and unreasonable. As experience with oil spill liability had demonstrated, strict liability was necessary if the government was to have a realistic chance of recovering response costs. Section 311's oil spill liability program provided for strict liability premised on the notion that the burden of environmental injuries of this sort should be placed on the industry that created the risk.

While oil spills typically come from a single source, hazardous substances released at dump sites can be a complex mixture of wastes from many sources. The application of joint and several liability is designed to avoid disputes over apportionment of CERCLA liability from delaying the cleanup of environmental contamination. Recognizing that many dump sites had been abandoned or were owned by companies that were bankrupt or insolvent, Congress broadened the class of potentially liable parties in section 107 of CERCLA.

To ensure that those whose actions generated the hazardous substances would contribute to the costs of cleaning them up, and to prevent the government from having to bear the lion's share of cleanup expenses, section 107 extended strict, joint, and several liability to generators of hazardous substances. This has been one of the most controversial aspects of CERCLA. While the courts had been uncertain whether the government's abatement authority for cases of "imminent and substantial endangerment" under section 7003 of RCRA extended to generators of hazardous waste, section 107 of CERCLA imposed joint and several liability on generators who arranged for disposal of their waste.

In many cases responsible parties have argued that it is unfair to hold them jointly and severally liable because they made only a small contribution to the total harm. Consider how such arguments were addressed in the case that follows.

O'Neil v. Picillo
883 F.2d 176 (1st Cir. 1989)

COFFIN, Senior Circuit Judge:

In July of 1977, the Picillos agreed to allow part of their pig farm in Coventry, Rhode Island to be used as a disposal site for drummed and bulk waste. That decision proved to be disastrous. Thousands of barrels of hazardous waste were dumped on the farm, culminating later that year in a monstrous fire ripping through the site. In 1979, the state and the Environmental Protection Agency (EPA) jointly undertook to clean up the area. What they found, in the words of the district court, were massive trenches and pits "filled with free-flowing, multi-colored, pungent liquid wastes" and thousands of "dented and corroded drums containing a veritable potpourri of toxic fluids." O'Neil v. Picillo, 682 F. Supp. 706, 709, 725 (D.R.I. 1988).

This case involves the State of Rhode Island's attempt to recover the clean-up costs it incurred between 1979 and 1982 and to hold responsible parties liable for all future costs associated with the site. The state's complaint originally named thirty-five defendants, all but five of whom eventually entered into settlements totalling $5.8 million, the money to be shared by the state and EPA. After a month-long bench trial, the district court, in a thorough and well reasoned opinion, found three of the remaining five companies jointly and severally liable under section 107 of the Comprehensive Environmental Response, Compensation, and Liability Act of 1980, 42 U.S.C. §9601 et seq. ("CERCLA") for all of the State's past clean-up costs not covered by settlement agreements, as well as for all costs that may become necessary in the future. The other two defendants obtained judgments in their favor, the court concluding that the state had failed to prove that the waste attributed to those companies was "hazardous," as that term is defined under the Act.

Two of the three companies held liable at trial, American Cyanamid and Rohm and Haas, have taken this appeal. Both are so-called "generators" of waste, as opposed to transporters or site owners. See §107(a)(3), 42 U.S.C. §9607. Neither takes issue with the district court's finding that some of their waste made its way to the Picillo site. Rather, they contend that their contribution to the disaster was insubstantial and that it was, therefore, unfair to hold them jointly and severally liable for all of the state's past expenses not covered by settlements. They further contend that it was error to hold them liable for all future remedial work because the state has not demonstrated that such work ever will be necessary. . . .

. . . We . . . confine our discussion to appellants' arguments concerning the unfairness of holding them jointly and severally liable for the government's past and future clean-up costs.

JOINT AND SEVERAL LIABILITY

Statutory Background

It is by now well settled that Congress intended that the federal courts develop a uniform approach governing the use of joint and several liability in CERCLA actions. The rule adopted by the majority of courts, and the one we adopt, is based on the Restatement (Second) of Torts: damages should be apportioned only if the *defendant* can demonstrate that the harm is divisible. See, e.g., United States v. Chem-Dyne Corp., 572 F. Supp. 802, 809-11 (S.D. Ohio 1983); United States v. Monsanto

Co., 858 F.2d 160, 171-73 (4th Cir. 1988); United States v. Bliss, 667 F. Supp. 1298, 1312-13 (E.D. Mo. 1987).

The practical effect of placing the burden on defendants has been that responsible parties rarely escape joint and several liability, courts regularly finding that where wastes of varying (and unknown) degrees of toxicity and migratory potential commingle, it simply is impossible to determine the amount of environmental harm caused by each party. See, e.g., United States v. Chem-Dyne, 572 F. Supp. at 811; *Monsanto*, 858 F.2d at 172-73. It has not gone unnoticed that holding defendants jointly and severally liable in such situations may often result in defendants paying for more than their share of the harm. Cf. United States v. Monsanto, 858 F.2d at 173. Nevertheless, courts have continued to impose joint and several liability on a regular basis, reasoning that where all of the contributing causes cannot fairly be traced, Congress intended for those proven at least partially culpable to bear the cost of the uncertainty. See, e.g., United States v. Chem-Dyne, 572 F. Supp. at 809-810.

In enacting the Superfund Amendments and Reauthorization Act of 1986 ("SARA"), Congress had occasion to examine this case law. Rather than add a provision dealing explicitly with joint and several liability, it chose to leave the issue with the courts, to be resolved as it had been— on a case by case basis according to the predominant "divisibility" rule first enunciated by the *Chem-Dyne* court. See, e.g., United States v. Monsanto, 858 F.2d at 171 n.23 (*Chem-Dyne* decision endorsed by Congress); cf. Garber, Federal Common Law of Contribution Under the 1986 CER-CLA Amendments, 14 Ecol. L.Q. 365, 374-75 (1987). Congress did, however, add two important provisions designed to mitigate the harshness of joint and several liability. First, the 1986 Amendments direct the EPA to offer early settlements to defendants who the Agency believes are responsible for only a small portion of the harm, so-called de minimis settlements. See §122(g). Second, the Amendments provide for a statutory cause of action in contribution, codifying what most courts had concluded was implicit in the 1980 Act. See §113(f)(1). Under this section, courts "may allocate response costs among liable parties using such equitable factors as the court determines are appropriate." We note that appellants already have initiated a contribution action against seven parties before the same district court judge who heard this case.

While a right of contribution undoubtedly softens the blow where parties cannot prove that the harm is divisible, it is not a complete panacea since it frequently will be difficult for defendants to locate a sufficient number of additional, solvent parties. Moreover, there are significant transaction costs involved in bringing other responsible parties to court. If it were possible to locate all responsible parties and to do so with little cost, the issue of joint and several liability obviously would be of only marginal significance. We, therefore, must examine carefully appellants' claim that they have met their burden of showing that the harm in this case is divisible.

Divisibility

The district court issued two rulings on joint and several liability. First, the court held appellants jointly and severally liable for all of the state's past costs not covered by settlements, roughly $1.4 million including prejudgment interest. According to appellants, this money was spent exclusively on "removal" costs or "surface cleanup" (e.g., sampling the waste, contacting responsible parties, and ultimately, *removing* the barrels and contaminated soil), and not on remedying the alleged damage to groundwater and other natural resources ("remedial" costs). Second, the district court held appellants jointly and severally liable for all future removal costs to be incurred by the state, as well as for all cost-efficient remedial action the state (and EPA) may deem necessary after conducting further tests. The parties discuss the two holdings separately and we shall do likewise.

I.   Past Costs

industry

Appellants begin by stressing that the state's past costs involved only surface cleanup. They then argue that because it was possible to determine how many barrels of waste they contributed to the site, it is also possible to determine what proportion of the state's removal expenses are attributable to each of them simply by estimating the cost of excavating a single barrel. The EPA advances two reasons why this approach is incorrect. First, it claims that it was not possible to determine how many barrels were traceable to appellants, nor was it possible to determine how much of the contaminated soil removed by the state was attributable to each appellant, and therefore, that it is impossible to apportion the state's removal costs. Second, it argues that even if it were possible to determine what proportion of the state's removal costs are attributable to appellants, joint and several liability still would have been proper because the "harm to be apportioned is not the cost but the environmental contamination that prompts the response action." We shall discuss the EPA's two arguments in reverse order.

We state at the outset that we have some trouble with the EPA's second argument. Assuming the government ultimately undertakes remedial action to clean the groundwater in the area and then seeks to recover the costs of doing so, it will have in effect submitted two separate bills, one for the cost of removing the barrels and soil, and one for cleaning the water. We think it likely that the harm to the water will be indivisible, and therefore, that appellants could properly be held jointly and severally liable for the cost of this remedial action. But simply because the costs associated with cleaning the groundwater cannot be apportioned does not mean that we should decline to apportion the costs of removing the barrels and soil if those costs are in fact divisible. This would seem to follow from the basic common law principle that defendants not be held responsible for those costs traceable to others. We think that the EPA would have to accept as much. Nonetheless, the Agency adheres to the position that it is irrelevant whether or not the costs of *removal* can be apportioned.

The reason the Agency takes this position is not because the environmental harm that *actually* occurred was indivisible, but because the additional environmental harm that the government *averted* would have been indivisible had it occurred. This argument gives us pause because it appears to contravene the basic tort law principle that one pays only for the harm that was, and not for the harm that might have been.

Assume that it costs the government $1 million to remove all of the barrels from a site, but of this million, only $300,000 were spent removing the defendant's barrels. Also assume that had the barrels not been removed, the additional damage to the environment would have been $5 million and that this five million would not have been divisible. The government certainly would not take the position that it could recover $5 million in such a situation. Instead, it would ask only for the $1 million that it actually spent. Yet when it comes to apportioning that million, the Agency argues that we should look to whether the $5 million of averted harm would be divisible.

If we were to accept the EPA's "averted harm" argument, it appears that apportionment would be appropriate only in the highly unlikely event that (1) all of the barrels were empty and no further environmental harm was possible; (2) the individual barrels were sufficiently far apart that even if further spillage occurred, there would be no commingling of wastes and thus no difficulty determining whose waste caused what damage; or (3) every barrel contained precisely the same type of waste so that even if there was further spillage and commingling, the environmental harm could be apportioned according to the volumetric contribution of each defendant. As the EPA undoubtedly recognizes, it rarely, if ever, will be the case that one of these three conditions is present. As a practical matter, then, joint and several liability will be imposed in *every* case.

Because we believe Congress did not intend for joint and several liability to be imposed without exception, we are troubled by the practical implications of the Agency's argument, the more so because it seems to find no support in common law tort principles, which were to be one of our benchmarks in developing a uniform approach to govern the imposition of joint and several liability. At oral argument, the Agency did not claim, however, that its theory fit within the common law framework of joint and several liability, but instead, took the position that these CERCLA cases are not standard tort suits. Although we recognize that Congress deviated from certain tort principles, see New York v. Shore Realty Corp., 759 F.2d 1032, 1044 (2d Cir. 1985), we had thought that on the issue of joint and several liability we were to take our lead from evolving principles of common law. It would seem incumbent upon the Agency, then, to demonstrate that on this *particular* question of joint and several liability, Congress intended for us to abandon the common law.

Having said all that, we choose not to resolve the issue in this case. Had appellants met their burden of showing that the costs *actually incurred* by the state were capable of apportionment, we would have had no choice but to address the EPA's theory. But because we do not believe appellants have done so, we can, and do, choose to leave the question for another day. We turn now to the EPA's first contention that the state's removal costs are not capable of apportionment.

Removal Costs. The state's removal efforts proceeded in four phases (0-3), each phase corresponding roughly to the cleanup of a different trench. The trenches were located in different areas of the site, but neither party has told us the distance between trenches. Appellants contend that it is possible to apportion the state's removal costs because there was evidence detailing (1) the total number of barrels excavated in each phase, (2) the number of barrels in each phase attributable to them, and (3) the total cost associated with each phase. In support of their argument, they point us to a few portions of the record, but for the most part are content to rest on statements in the district court's opinion. Specifically, appellants point to the following two sentences in the opinion: (1) "I find that [American Cyanamid] is responsible for ten drums of toxic hazardous material found at the site"; and (2) as to Rohm and Haas, "I accept the state's estimate [of 49 drums and 303 five-gallon pails]." Appellants then add, without opposition from the government, that the ten barrels of American Cyanamid waste discussed by the district court were found exclusively in Phase II, and that the 303 pails and 49 drums of Rohm and Haas waste mentioned by the court were found exclusively in Phase III. They conclude, therefore, that American Cyanamid should bear only a minute percentage of the $995,697.30 expended by the state during Phase II in excavating approximately 4,500 barrels and no share of the other phases, and that Rohm and Haas should be accountable for only a small portion of the $58,237 spent during Phase III in removing roughly 3,300 barrels and no share of the other phases. We disagree.

The district court's statements concerning the waste attributable to each appellant were based on the testimony of John Leo, an engineer hired by the state to oversee the cleanup. We have reviewed Mr. Leo's testimony carefully. Having done so, we think it inescapably clear that the district court did not mean to suggest that appellants had contributed only 49 and 10 barrels respectively, but rather, that those amounts were all that could be *positively attributed* to appellants.

Mr. Leo testified that out of the approximately 10,000 barrels that were excavated during the four phases, only "three to four hundred of the drums contained markings which could potentially be traced." This is not surprising considering that there had been an enormous fire at the site, that the barrels had been exposed to the elements for a number of years, and that a substantial amount of liquid waste had leaked and eaten away at the outsides of the barrels. Mr. Leo also testified that it was not simply the absence of legible markings that prevented the state from identifying the overwhelming majority of barrels, but also the danger involved in handling the barrels. Ironically, it was appellants themselves who, in an effort to induce Mr. Leo to lower his estimate of the number of barrels attributable to each defendant, elicited much of the testimony concerning the impossibility of accurately identifying all of the waste.

In light of the fact that most of the waste could not be identified, and that the appellants, and not the government, had the burden to account for all of this uncertainty, we think it plain that the district court did not err in holding them jointly and severally liable for the state's past removal costs. Perhaps in this situation the only way appellants could have demonstrated that they were limited contributors would have been to present specific evidence documenting the whereabouts of their waste at all times after it left their facilities. But far from doing so, appellants deny all knowledge of how their waste made its way to the site. Moreover, the government presented evidence that much of Rohm and Haas' waste found at the site came from its laboratory in Spring House, Pennsylvania and that during the relevant years, this lab generated over two thousand drums of waste, all of which were consigned to a single transporter. Under these circumstances, where Rohm and Haas was entrusting substantial amounts of waste to a single transporter who ultimately proved unreliable, we simply cannot conclude, absent evidence to the contrary, that only a handful of the 2,000 or more barrels reached the site.

II. Future Liability

The district court held appellants jointly and severally liable for all further removal costs taken by the state, as well as for all necessary remedial actions. Appellants have two principal objections. First, they claim that it was error to hold them responsible for the removal of certain piles of soil because the settling parties had agreed to undertake this cost. The state represents to us that these parties have now taken care of the piles and we therefore find the issue moot.

Second, appellants contend that it was improper to hold them liable for future remedial action because the state has not shown that such work will ever be needed. They do not claim, however, that if remedial action is shown to be necessary, it would be a mistake to assume that their waste contributed to the damage. We see no problem with the court giving the state (and EPA) time to conduct further tests. If after conducting the necessary tests, the government concludes that there was in fact no harm to the area's groundwater, then appellants will have nothing to worry about. Moreover, the district court ruled that under section 107 of the Act, the state may take only such measures as are cost-efficient. Appellants, therefore, will have an opportunity to challenge the state's chosen remedial measures at the appropriate time.

Appellants have argued ably that they should not have been held jointly and severally liable. In the end, however, we think they have not satisfied the stringent burden placed on them by Congress. As to all other issues, we affirm substantially for the reasons set out by the district court. Appellants should now move on to their contribution action where their burden will be reduced and the district court will be free to allocate responsibility according to any combination of equitable factors it deems appropriate. Indeed, there might be no reason for the district court to place any burden on appellants. If the defendants in that action also cannot demonstrate that they were limited contributors, it is not apparent why all of the parties could not be held jointly and severally liable. However, we leave this judgment to the district court. See, e.g., Developments, Toxic Waste Litigation, 99 Harv. L. Rev. 1458, 1535-43 (1986).

Affirmed.

NOTES AND QUESTIONS

1. Although the court criticized EPA's "averted harm" theory of apportionment for the removal costs, it did not reach this issue because it held that the defendants had not met their burden of "showing that the costs actually incurred were capable of apportionment." Why was the court so reluctant to rule on this issue? What would American Cyanamid and Rohm and Haas have had to show in order to demonstrate that the removal costs actually incurred were capable of apportionment? Would the outcome in this case have been any different if the companies could prove that they had made arrangements to ship only 10 and 49 drums, respectively, to the site? What if they could prove they had only generated a total of 10 and 49 such drums respectively?

2. As the court notes in *Picillo*, Congress did seek to ease the burden of joint and several liability when it amended CERCLA in 1986 by enacting a de minimis settlement provision in section 122(g) and by providing a statutory cause of action for contribution in section 113(f)(1).

Suppose the 30 other responsible parties in this case had settled pursuant to the de minimis contributor provisions of section 122(g). What impact would this have had on the ability of American Cyanamid and Rohm and Haas, the appellants in *Picillo,* to recover in a contribution suit against the other responsible parties? See section 122(g).

3. The 30 other responsible parties in *Picillo* entered into settlements totaling $5.8 million, for an average of less than $200,000 per party. Do you think that the defendants American Cyanamid and Rohm and Haas were being penalized for their unwillingness to enter into settlements? What impact is joint and several liability likely to have on the willingness of defendants to settle? Will it make them more disposed to settlement for fear of being held liable for all the costs and damages, or will it make them fight harder to avoid any liability?

4. Is it fair to hold a defendant responsible for all response costs in circumstances where it is not possible to demonstrate that the harm is divisible? Would it be reasonable to require the government to bear the burden of showing that the harm is not divisible? What impact would this have on the government's ability to recover CERCLA response costs and damages? If joint and several liability were abolished in CERCLA cases what would the government have to demonstrate in order to recover response costs?

5. During the debates over CERCLA reauthorization that culminated in 1986 with the enactment of SARA, the insurance industry and others lobbied for repeal of strict, joint, and several liability. Citing studies indicating that a great deal of money was being spent on CERCLA litigation, these companies argued that administrative costs would be lower and more funds would be available for actual cleanup if strict, joint, and several liability were abolished. How would you respond to these arguments? What additional information, if any, would you like to have to evaluate them? Although the Reagan Administration was not sympathetic to environmental regulation, its Justice Department successfully opposed efforts to repeal CERCLA's liability standard.

6. When provisions for victim compensation were dropped from the legislation that eventually became CERCLA, Congress added section 301(e)'s directive that a study be made of the adequacy of existing common law and statutory remedies. This study, known not surprisingly as the "section 301(e) study," identified three major barriers to recovery of personal injuries for exposure to hazardous substances: (1) the difficulty of proving causation, (2) statutes of limitations that may operate to bar suits before damage is discovered, and (3) the difficulty of apportioning damages among multiple tortfeasors. How does CERCLA's liability standard address these factors in the context of recovering response costs? Congress has been concerned that application of CERCLA's liability standard to recovery of damages for personal injury would open up the floodgates to enormous numbers of claims, many of which would be

meritless. Thus, when it enacted SARA in 1986, Congress narrowly rejected a proposal for a pilot program to provide administrative compensation to victims of exposure to hazardous substances. It did, however, deal with the statute of limitations problem by adding section 309, which tolls state statutes of limitations in cases involving exposures to hazardous substances until injury is or should have been discovered.

7. The section 301(e) study concluded that strict liability standards were a useful mechanism for transferring the costs of environmental damage to those in the best position to reduce or eliminate environmental risks. The study found that strict liability would help ensure that those who engage in activities that inevitably create some environmental damage would bear the costs of such damage through insurance premiums and higher disposal costs. Considerable debate has continued concerning the question of how broadly the liability net should be cast.

8. Although there is broad support for Congress's judgment that parties involved in the creation and handling of toxic wastes should be held strictly liable for the costs of remediating the damage they cause, joint and several liability is far more controversial. In addition to expressing concerns about its fairness, Richard Epstein argues that joint and several liability actually dilutes the incentives for those handling toxic waste to take precautions to prevent releases because they know that ultimately liability may be broadly shared. Epstein, The Principles of Environmental Protection: The Case of Superfund, 2 Cato J. 9 (1982). Epstein notes that efforts by any one party to take greater precautions reduce the ultimate liability of all parties, while careless actions that result in additional releases only increase the damage that ultimately may be shared by all. Epstein, Two Fallacies in the Law of Joint Torts, 73 Geo. L.J. 1377 (1985). How would you respond to these concerns?

9. In theory joint and several liability should tend to reduce the transaction costs of CERCLA cleanups by reducing the importance of arguments over the relative degree of fault among PRPs. Some have argued, however, that by making any PRP potentially liable for the total costs of cleanup, joint and several liability actually increases transaction costs by making PRPs more resistant to settlement. During the reauthorization process that culminated in the enactment of SARA, a number of industry lobbyists cited the transaction costs of early CERCLA litigation and the potential unfairness of joint and several liability in support of proposals to abolish it. What impact would abolition of joint and several liability have on EPA's ability to recover response costs from PRPs? Insurance companies have been vocal opponents of CERCLA's liability scheme, and they have been successful in some cases in having their comprehensive general liability policies interpreted to exclude coverage of CERCLA response costs, Continental Insurance Co. v. Northeastern Chemical & Pharmaceutical Co., 842 F.2d 977 (8th Cir.) (en banc), cert. denied, 488 U.S. 821 (1988); Maryland Casualty Co. v. Armco,

Inc., 822 F.2d 1348 (4th Cir. 1987), cert. denied, 484 U.S. 1008 (1988), while losing in many others. See O'Leary, Coming Full CERCLA: The Release of Superfund Insurance Coverage Decisions from State Supreme Courts, 6 Nat. Resources & Envt. 31 (Winter 1992) (federal and state courts sharply divided on issues of insurance coverage for CERCLA response costs).

10. Joint and several liability also reflects concern that the public not be required to bear cleanup costs when any party responsible for a hazardous substance release remains solvent. The potential for unfair burdens being imposed on parties only minimally responsible for releases remains a major concern. We now turn to the questions of which parties are responsible under CERCLA.

5. Responsible Parties

CERCLA embodies a liability approach to regulation. Rather than directing EPA to specify through regulations what actions persons must take to prevent environmental damage, CERCLA specifies the potential consequences if hazardous substances are released or if conditions posing a substantial threat of such a release are created. CERCLA's approach is intended not only to provide a means for financing the cleanup of environmental damage, but also to deter mismanagement of hazardous substances. Crucial to CERCLA's value as a deterrent is how the Act defines potentially liable parties. Section 107 of CERCLA broadly defines the parties potentially liable for response costs.

A. OWNERS AND OPERATORS

The case that follows is one of the most influential early interpretations of CERCLA's liability provisions. As you read it, consider what impact it is likely to have on incentives to prevent releases of hazardous substances in the future. Consider also whether its strict interpretation of CERCLA could lead to unfair results in other circumstances.

|| *New York v. Shore Realty Corp.* ||
|| **759 F.2d 1032 (2d Cir. 1985)** ||

Before FEINBERG, Chief Judge, OAKES and NEWMAN, Circuit Judges. OAKES, Circuit Judge:

This case involves several novel questions about the scope of the Comprehensive Environmental Response, Compensation, and Liability Act of 1980, 42 U.S.C. §§9601-9657 (1982) ("CERCLA"), and the interplay between that statute and New York public nuisance law. CERCLA

. . . was intended to provide means for cleaning up hazardous waste sites and spills, and may generally be known to the public as authorizing the so-called Superfund, the $1.6 billion Hazardous Substances Response Trust Fund, 42 U.S.C. §§9631-9633.

On February 29, 1984, the State of New York brought suit against Shore Realty Corp. ("Shore") and Donald LeoGrande, its officer and stockholder, to clean up a hazardous waste disposal site at One Shore Road, Glenwood Landing, New York, which Shore had acquired for land development purposes. At the time of the acquisition, LeoGrande knew that hazardous waste was stored on the site and that cleanup would be expensive, though neither Shore nor LeoGrande had participated in the generation or transportation of the nearly 700,000 gallons of hazardous waste now on the premises. . . .

LeoGrande incorporated Shore solely for the purpose of purchasing the Shore Road property. All corporate decisions and actions were made, directed, and controlled by him. By contract dated July 14, 1983, Shore agreed to purchase the 3.2 acre site, a small peninsula surrounded on three sides by the waters of Hempstead Harbor and Mott Cove, for condominium development. Five large tanks in a field in the center of the site hold most of some 700,000 gallons of hazardous chemicals located there, though there are six smaller tanks both above and below ground containing hazardous waste, as well as some empty tanks, on the property. The tanks are connected by pipe to a tank truck loading rack and dockage facilities for loading by barge. Four roll-on/roll-off containers and one tank truck trailer hold additional waste. And before June 15, 1984, one of the two dilapidated masonry warehouses on the site contained over 400 drums of chemicals and contaminated solids, many of which were corroded and leaking.

It is beyond dispute that the tanks and drums contain "hazardous substances" within the meaning of CERCLA. 42 U.S.C. §9601(14). The substances involved—including benzene, dichlorobenzenes, ethyl benzene, tetrachloroethylene, trichloroethylene, 1,1,1-trichloroethylene, chlordane, polychlorinated biphenyls (commonly known as PCBs), and bis (2-ethylhexyl) phthalate—are toxic, in some cases carcinogenic, and dangerous by way of contact, inhalation, or ingestion. . . .

CERCLA was designed "to bring order to the array of partly redundant, partly inadequate federal hazardous substances cleanup and compensation laws." It applies "primarily to the cleanup of leaking inactive or abandoned sites and to emergency responses to spills." And it distinguishes between two kinds of response: remedial actions—generally long-term or permanent containment or disposal programs—and removal efforts—typically short-term cleanup arrangements.

CERCLA authorizes the federal government to respond in several ways. EPA can use Superfund resources to clean up hazardous waste sites and spills. 42 U.S.C. §9611. The National Contingency Plan ("NCP"), prepared by EPA pursuant to CERCLA, id. §9605, governs cleanup efforts by "establish[ing] procedures and standards for responding to releases of hazardous substances." At the same time, EPA can sue for reimbursement of cleanup costs from any responsible parties it can locate, id. §9607, allowing the federal government to respond immediately while later trying to shift financial responsibility to others. Thus, Superfund covers cleanup costs if the site has been abandoned, if the responsible parties elude detection, or if private resources are inadequate. . . . In addition, CERCLA authorizes EPA to seek an injunction in federal district court to force a responsible party to clean up any site or spill that presents an imminent and substantial danger to public health or welfare or the environment. 42 U.S.C. §9606(a). In sum, CERCLA is not a regulatory standard-setting statute such as the Clean Air Act. Id. §§7401-7642. Rather, the government generally undertakes pollution abatement, and polluters pay for such abatement through tax and reimbursement liability. . . .

Congress intended that responsible parties be held strictly liable, even though an explicit provision for strict liability was not included in the compromise. Section 9601(32) provides that "liability" under CERCLA "shall be construed to be the standard of liability" under section 311 of the Clean Water Act, 33 U.S.C. §1321, which courts have held to be strict liability, see, e.g., Steuart Transportation Co. v. Allied Towing Corp., 596 F.2d 609, 613 (4th Cir. 1979), and which Congress understood to impose such liability, see S. Rep. No. 848, 96th Cong., 2d Sess. 34 (1980) [hereinafter cited as Senate Report], reprinted in 1 CERCLA Legislative History, supra, at 308, 341. Moreover, the sponsors of the compromise expressly stated that section 9607 provides for strict liability. . . . Strict liability under CERCLA, however, is not absolute; there are defenses for causation solely by an act of God, an act of war, or acts or omissions of a third party other than an employee or agent of the defendant or one whose act or omission occurs in connection with a contractual relationship with the defendant. 42 U.S.C. §9607(b). . . .

Covered Persons. CERCLA holds liable four classes of persons:

(1) the owner and operator of a vessel (otherwise subject to the jurisdiction of the United States) or a facility,

(2) any person who at the time of disposal of any hazardous substance owned or operated any facility at which such hazardous substances were disposed of,

(3) any person who by contract, agreement, or otherwise arranged for disposal or treatment, or arranged with a transporter for transport for disposal or treatment, of hazardous substances owned or possessed by such person, by any other party or

entity, at any facility owned or operated by another party or
entity and containing such hazardous substances, and

(4)   any person who accepts or accepted any hazardous substances
for transport to disposal or treatment facilities or sites selected
by such person.

42 U.S.C. §9607(a). As noted above, section 9607 makes these persons
liable, if "there is a release, or a threatened release which causes the
incurrence of response costs, of a hazardous substance" from the facility,
for, among other things, "all costs of removal or remedial action incurred
by the United States Government or a State not inconsistent with the
national contingency plan."

Shore argues that it is not covered by section 9607(a)(1) because it
neither owned the site at the time of disposal nor caused the presence
or the release of the hazardous waste at the facility. While section
9607(a)(1) appears to cover Shore, Shore attempts to infuse ambiguity
into the statutory scheme, claiming that section 9607(a)(1) could not have
been intended to include all owners, because the word "owned" in section
9607(a)(2) would be unnecessary since an owner "at the time of disposal"
would necessarily be included in section 9607(a)(1). Shore claims that
Congress intended that the scope of section 9607(a)(1) be no greater
than that of section 9607(a)(2) and that both should be limited by the
"at the time of disposal" language. By extension, Shore argues that both
provisions should be interpreted as requiring a showing of causation.
We agree with the State, however, that section 9607(a)(1) unequivocally
imposes strict liability on the current owner of a facility from which there
is a release or threat of release, without regard to causation.

Shore's claims of ambiguity are illusory; section 9607(a)'s structure
is clear. Congress intended to cover different classes of persons differently. Section 9607(a)(1) applies to all current owners and operators,
while section 9607(a)(2) primarily covers prior owners and operators.
Moreover, section 9607(a)(2)'s scope is more limited than that of section
9607(a)(1). Prior owners and operators are liable only if they owned or
operated the facility "at the time of disposal of any hazardous substance";
this limitation does not apply to current owners, like Shore. . . .

Shore's causation argument is also at odds with the structure of the
statute. Interpreting section 9607(a)(1) as including a causation requirement makes superfluous the affirmative defenses provided in section
9607(b), each of which carves out from liability an exception based on
causation. Without a clear congressional command otherwise, we will
not construe a statute in any way that makes some of its provisions
surplusage. . . .

Furthermore, as the state points out, accepting Shore's arguments
would open a huge loophole in CERCLA's coverage. It is quite clear that
if the current owner of a site could avoid liability merely by having

purchased the site after chemical dumping had ceased, waste sites certainly would be sold, following the cessation of dumping, to new owners who could avoid the liability otherwise required by CERCLA. Congress had well in mind that persons who dump or store hazardous waste sometimes cannot be located or may be deceased or judgment-proof. See, e.g., Senate Report, supra, at 16, reprinted in 1 CERCLA Legislative History, supra, at 323. We will not interpret section 9607(a) in any way that apparently frustrates the statute's goals, in the absence of a specific congressional intention otherwise. . . .

Affirmative Defense.   Shore also claims that it can assert an affirmative defense under CERCLA, which provides a limited exception to liability for a release or threat of release caused solely by

> an act or omission of a third party other than an employee or agent of the defendant, or than one whose act or omission occurs in connection with a contractual relationship, existing directly or indirectly, with the defendant (except where the sole contractual arrangement arises from a published tariff and acceptance for carriage by a common carrier by rail), if the defendant establishes by a preponderance of the evidence that (a) he exercised due care with respect to the hazardous substance concerned, taking into consideration the characteristics of such hazardous substance, in light of all relevant facts and circumstances, and (b) he took precautions against foreseeable acts or omissions of any such third party and the consequences that could foreseeably result from such acts or omissions.

42 U.S.C. §9607(b)(3).

We disagree. Shore argues that it had nothing to do with the transportation of the hazardous substances and that it has exercised due care since taking control of the site. Who the "third part(ies)" Shore claims were responsible is difficult to fathom. It is doubtful that a prior owner could be such, especially the prior owner here, since the acts or omissions referred to in the statute are doubtless those occurring during the ownership or operation of the defendant. Similarly, many of the acts and omissions of the prior tenants/operators fall outside the scope of section 9607(b)(3), because they occurred before Shore owned the property. In addition, we find that Shore cannot rely on the affirmative defense even with respect to the tenants' conduct during the period after Shore closed on the property and when Shore evicted the tenants. Shore was aware of the nature of the tenants' activities before the closing and could readily have foreseen that they would continue to dump hazardous waste at the site. In light of this knowledge, we cannot say that the releases and threats of release resulting of these activities were "caused solely" by the tenants or that Shore "took precautions against" these "foreseeable acts or omissions."

NOTES AND QUESTIONS

1. Why do you think Congress chose to extend CERCLA liability to current owners and operators of facilities where hazardous substances had been deposited? Is it fair to hold persons who were not involved in the creation of environmental hazards liable for the costs of cleaning them up? If the court had accepted Shore's argument that section 107(a)(1) covered only owners and operaters at the time of disposal, what impact would it have had on the government's ability to obtain reimbursement for Superfund response costs? What impact is the court's decision likely to have on future purchasers of property containing hazardous substances?

2. At the time Shore Realty purchased the property at issue in this case, Shore was aware that the tanks and drums on the site contained hazardous substances. Suppose Shore had known only that there were tanks and drums on the site, but not that they contained hazardous substances. Would this have made any difference for Shore's liability under CERCLA? Would it have made any difference if the tanks and drums had been buried on the property and Shore had not even been aware of their existence? Should innocent purchasers be absolved from CERCLA liability? If they are, what impact would this have on incentives for investigating potential contamination of property?

3. When CERCLA was amended in 1986, Congress sought to deal with the problem of innocent purchasers by clarifying the defense provided in section 107(b)(3). It did so not by amending section 107(b)(3), but by adding in section 101(35) of CERCLA a new definition of the term "contractual relationship" used in section 107(b)(3). Consider the language of section 101(35), 42 U.S.C. §9601(35). How, if at all, would this new amendment have affected the result in *Shore Realty*?

4. The district court in *Shore Realty* had also exercised pendent jurisdiction to entertain the state's common law nuisance claims. The district court had issued an injunction against Shore supported in the alternative by finding that Shore was liable for having a common law nuisance on its property. The Second Circuit upheld this decision in another portion of Judge Oakes's opinion. Judge Oakes noted that a property owner who is aware of a nuisance on the property can be held liable under New York law if the nuisance has not been abated despite the owner's having had a reasonable opportunity to do so. Citing the Restatement (Second) of Torts, the court noted that this common law nuisance liability is founded not on responsibility for the creation of the harmful condition but on the property owner's exclusive control over the land and the things done on it, which creates a responsibility for taking reasonable measures to remedy nuisances that threaten harm to others. Judge Oakes concluded that Shore could be found strictly liable under two common law nuisance theories. Because hazardous wastes

were present on the property without the necessary permits having been obtained, Shore was guilty-of a per se nuisance for violating state regulations. Second, the presence of corroding drums of toxic waste was an abnormally dangerous activity that made Shore strictly liable in nuisance under New York law.

5. CERCLA's liability provisions were designed to ensure that responsible parties reimburse the government for the lion's share of cleanup expenses. The amounts recovered by the government in CERCLA cost recovery actions initially were disappointing. During the first five years of CERCLA enforcement, government cost recovery actions succeeded in recovering only $32 million of the $1.3 billion spent on the Superfund program. The government now pursues a more aggressive approach to cost recovery. As EPA's Director of the Office of Waste Programs Enforcement has observed, EPA now operates under "the assumption that people who never expected to be will find themselves involved in toxic-waste cases." Generally, EPA "will seek out everyone associated with the contaminated property and send them a notice letter of potential liability." Lucero, EPA's Role in and Perspective on Property Transfer and Financing Liabilities, in ABA, Burdens of Environmental Regulation on Private Property Ownership and Business Transactions: Reasonable or Unreasonable? 18 (May 1987).

SARA and the Innocent Purchaser Problem

Concern about the potential liability of innocent purchasers of contaminated land under section 107(a)(1) led Congress to make some adjustments when CERCLA was amended by SARA in 1986. Landowner defendants often had attempted to invoke the third-party defense of section 107(b)(3), which relieves a party of liability for hazardous substance releases that are solely the result of an act or omission of a third party other than an employee or agent of the defendant or one with whom the defendant had a direct or indirect contractual relationship. To escape liability under this provision, the defendant has to prove by a preponderance of evidence that she exercised due care with respect to the hazardous substance and took precautions against the third party's foreseeable acts or omissions. SARA added section 101(35) to clarify that innocent purchasers of contaminated property can assert the third-party defense of section 107(b)(3) if they can establish that: (1) they did not have actual or constructive knowledge of the presence of hazardous substances at the time the land was acquired, (2) they are a government entity acquiring the property through involuntary transfer, or (3) they acquired the land by inheritance or bequest.

These provisions create even more explicit incentives for purchasers of property to conduct environmental assessments at the time of purchase. To establish a lack of constructive knowledge of the presence of hazardous substances on the land when it was acquired, CERCLA provides that a purchaser "must have undertaken, at the time of acquisition, all appropriate inquiry into the previous ownership and uses of the property consistent with good commercial or customary practice in an effort to minimize liability," §101(35)(B). Courts are directed to consider the purchaser's specialized knowledge or experience, the relationship of the purchase price to the value of uncontaminated property, reasonably ascertainable information about the property, the obviousness of the likely presence of contamination, and the ability to detect such contamination by appropriate inspection. By creating a defense to liability for purchasers who undertake the appropriate inquiry, these provisions will encourage more thorough inspections of property at the time of purchase.

SARA's innocent purchaser clarification has been criticized as too vague to provide genuine assistance to the real estate community because it does not specify precisely how much investigation of a property is necessary to avoid liability. Wagner, Liability for Hazardous Waste Cleanup: An Examination of New Jersey's Approach, 13 Harv. Envtl. L. Rev. 245, 254 (1989). While some real estate lawyers have given it at least grudging praise as a step in the right direction, it is unclear whether it will relieve many purchasers of liability. See also Glass, The Modern Snake in the Grass: An Examination of Real Estate and Commercial Liability Under Superfund and SARA and Suggested Guidelines for the Practitioner, 14 B.C. Envtl. Aff. L. Rev. 381 (1987).

A Note on Property Transfer Statutes

As a result of CERCLA's liability provisions, environmental assessments are now performed frequently in connection with real estate transactions. Thus, it is becoming increasingly difficult for landowners responsible for past contamination to unload their properties on unwitting purchasers. Another strategy for preventing innocent purchasers from being duped into buying contaminated properties is to require that information concerning environmental contamination be disclosed to the purchaser when property is transferred.

In order to ensure that the federal government did not itself dupe innocent purchasers, SARA added section 120(h) to CERCLA. Section 120(h) requires federal agencies to notify purchasers of federal property of the type and quantity of any hazardous substance known to have been stored (for one year or more), released, or disposed on the property. Federal agencies are required to disclose such information to the extent that it is "available on the basis of a complete search of agency files." Notice must be included not only in the contract for the sale, but also in the deed to the property. Section 120(h), however, provides even more protection to purchasers than simply disclosing environmental hazards. It also requires federal agencies to enter into covenants warranting that remedial action has been taken to clean up the property and promising that the government will undertake further remedial action if necessary after the property is transferred.

In 1990 EPA promulgated regulations applying section 120(h)'s notice requirements only to properties on which hazardous substances were stored, released, or disposed when the property was owned by the federal government. EPA believed that Congress had enacted section 120(h) largely out of concern for property, such as former military facilities, on which the government itself had placed hazardous substances, and it sought to "avoid imposing unfair and unmanageable obligations on federal agencies that had no role" in bringing the hazardous substances to the property. 55 Fed. Reg. 14,210. In Hercules, Inc. v. EPA, 938 F.2d 276 (D.C. Cir. 1991), the D.C. Circuit held that EPA's interpretation was contrary to the express terms of the statute, which requires that the federal government disclose what it knows about hazardous substances on the property regardless of when the substances were placed there. The court dismissed EPA's concern about imposing unfair and unmanageable obligations on federal agencies by noting:

> CERCLA explicitly supports the imposition of remediation obligations on parties who were not responsible for contamination and who have no experience in the handling or remediation of hazardous substances, as when it imposes liability on the sole basis that a party is the current owner or operator of a site contaminated by some previous owner or operator. [938 F.2d at 281.]

Moreover, the court observed that section 120(h) limits agencies' obligations to the disclosure of information contained in agency files.

Several states, including Illinois, California, and Indiana, have statutes requiring sellers to disclose information about known or suspected contamination on property being sold. Connecticut requires that sellers certify that any hazardous wastes discharged on the property have been cleaned up. New Jersey's statute is the most far-reaching because it requires both an environmental assessment and, if necessary, a cleanup as conditions for property transfer. New Jersey's Environmental Cleanup Responsibility Act (ECRA) took effect on December 31, 1984. ECRA requires that an environmental assessment be made when industrial property is being sold and that a cleanup plan be implemented if the property is found to be contaminated. The Act requires that the seller transfer to the buyer either (1) a "negative declaration" approved by state environmental authorities that declares either that no hazardous substances have been released on the site or that any discharge has been cleaned up or (2) an approved cleanup plan accompanied by financial assurances that the plan will be implemented. If a seller fails to comply with ECRA, the buyer may void the transaction, and the seller is strictly liable for response costs and damages for failure to implement the cleanup.

When ECRA was first implemented, New Jersey authorities discovered far more contaminated properties than they had anticipated. This resulted in lengthy delays in property transfers and considerable criticism of ECRA from industry. In response to this criticism, New Jersey environmental officials wrote new regulations authorizing the completion of transactions prior to cleanup and permitting the sale of uncontaminated portions of a larger property without full ECRA review.

New Jersey officials maintain that ECRA has produced significant environmental benefits, including far more dump site cleanups in that state than the Superfund program has produced. Paul, Environmental Exams Become Common, Wall St. J., Oct. 13, 1987, at 6. In the first six years of its operation, ECRA is credited with more than $207 million in privately funded cleanups. Motiuk and Sheridan, New Jersey's ECRA: Problems, Policies, Future Trends, 21 Envtl. Rep. 549 (1990). For fiscal year 1990 alone, the New Jersey Department of Environmental Protection approved 234 cleanup plans costing more than $178 million. N.J. Dept. of Environmental Protection, ECRA Update, July 1990, at 2.

ECRA has been highly unpopular with real estate agents because it has produced considerable delays in the settlement of real estate transactions. See Wagner, Liability for Hazardous Waste Cleanup: An Examination of New Jersey's Approach, 13 Harv. Envtl. L. Rev. 245, 254 (1989). It is unpopular with business not only because it delays and complicates property transfers but also because it imposes new cleanup obligations. A lawyer who has handled ECRA transactions argues that "[b]ecause of the statute, some industrial facilities will sit forever, neither closed nor sold, since no one wants to be stuck with cleanup costs." English, ECRA, Envtl. Forum 15, 17 (Mar.-April 1989). Nevertheless, he deems ECRA "the wave of the future," given the pervasiveness of environmental contamination problems. Id. at 18.

NOTES AND QUESTIONS

1. If you were a prospective purchaser of property, which approach to property transfer laws would you prefer—a pure disclosure approach or ECRA's mandatory cleanup approach? Which would you prefer if you owned contaminated property that you wished to sell? Which if you owned property that you were certain was free of contamination?

2. Which approach is more likely to protect truly innocent purchasers—CERCLA's or ECRA's? If you are purchasing property in a state without any of the kinds of property transfer laws described above,

how much investigation do you need to undertake to ensure that you will escape future CERCLA liability? Who bears the cost of this investigation? If you are purchasing property in New Jersey, how much investigation do you need to undertake? Who bears the cost?

3. The U.S. Defense Department has announced that the requirement that it clean up toxic contamination before selling federal property is making it difficult to close 86 military bases it was directed to close in 1988. Schneider, Toxic Cleanup Stalls Transfer of Military Sites, N.Y. Times, June 30, 1991, at A1. Officials estimate that it will cost more than $1 billion and take nearly a decade just to remediate these 86 sites. This will offset some of the $5.6 billion the base closings were projected to save the government over the next 20 years. Id. The Bush Administration's budget request for fiscal year 1993 included a total of $3.7 billion to clean up pollution at closed and active military bases and $5.5 billion for cleaning up contamination from DOE's nuclear weapons program. This budget request for military cleanups substantially exceeds EPA's total fiscal year 1993 budget request of $7 billion. Cushman, Bush to Ask More for Base Cleanups, N.Y. Times, Jan. 24, 1992, at A15.

4. As we have seen in O'Neil v. Picillo, owners of contaminated properties are not the only parties subject to liability under section 107 of CERCLA. The companies who generated the waste disposed at the Picillos' pig farm were held liable under section 107(a)(3) of CERCLA. We now consider the liability of generators of hazardous substances.

B.   GENERATORS

Perhaps CERCLA's most substantial modification of common law liability is the imposition of liability on the nonnegligent generators of hazardous substances that are released. By casting the liability net so expansively, CERCLA created powerful new incentives for generators of hazardous substances to manage them carefully. Generators who formerly were delighted to let the cheapest waste hauler relieve them of their hazardous residues now must select treatment and disposal options, and monitor their implementation, with care. For if the generator's hazardous substances are sent to a site where a release occurs or is threatened, the generator could be held strictly, jointly, and severally liable for response costs and natural resource damages.

Generator liability is covered in section 107(a)(3) of CERCLA, which imposes liability on

> any person who by contract, agreement, or otherwise arranged for disposal
> or treatment, or arranged with a transporter for transport for disposal or
> treatment, of hazardous substances owned or possessed by such person,
> by any other party or entity, at any facility or incineration vessel owned

or operated by another party or entity and containing such hazardous substances. [CERCLA §107(a)(3), 42 U.S.C. §9607(a)(3).]

The statutory language provides little guidance to courts seeking to determine the proper scope of generator liability. As O'Neil v. Picillo illustrates, although it may be possible to tie generators directly to waste contained in marked drums, it is virtually impossible to prove which generator's waste comprises which part of the chemical soup typically formed under the surface of a hazardous waste dump site. Because the language of section 107(a)(3) refers to "any facility . . . *containing such hazardous substances*" (emphasis supplied), the statute suggests that the government has some obligation to prove that the generator's waste is at a facility where releases occur. But it is unclear if this obligation requires the government to prove that the generator's wastes were part of the release in question.

Recognizing the difficulty the government would face if required to prove whose wastes are physically present in a given release, courts have interpreted section 107(a)(3) broadly to promote the remedial purposes of Congress. In one influential early case, United States v. South Carolina Recycling and Disposal, Inc., 21 Envtl. Rep. Cases 1577 (D.S.C. 1984), the court held that the prerequisites for proving generator liability were that the generator arranged for its wastes to be disposed of at, or transported to, a facility where a release occurred or is threatened and that wastes of the same type as those sent by the generator are present at the site. See United States v. Mottolo, 695 F. Supp. 615, 625 (D.N.H. 1988).

The potentially expansive nature of generator liability and its larger ramifications for waste management policy are illustrated by the following unusual case.

United States v. Aceto Agricultural Chemicals Corp.
872 F.2d 1373 (8th Cir. 1989)

LARSON, Senior District Judge:

This case arises from efforts by the Environmental Protection Agency (EPA) and the State of Iowa to recover over $10 million dollars in response costs incurred in the clean up of a pesticide formulation facility operated by the Aidex Corporation in Mills County, Iowa. Aidex operated the facility from 1974 through 1981, when it was declared bankrupt. Investigations by the EPA in the early 1980s revealed a highly contaminated site. Hazardous substances were found in deteriorating containers, in the surface soil, in fauna samples, and in the shallow zone of the groundwater, threatening the source of irrigation and drinking water for area residents. Using funds from the "Hazardous Substance Superfund," see 26 U.S.C. §9507, the EPA, in cooperation with the State of Iowa, undertook various remedial actions to clean up the site.

The EPA now seeks to recover its response costs from eight pesticide manufacturers who did business with Aidex, in particular, who hired Aidex to formulate their technical grade pesticides into commercial grade pesticides. The complaint alleges it is a common practice in the pesticide industry for manufacturers of active pesticide ingredients to contract with formulators such as Aidex to produce a commercial grade product which may then be sold to farmers and other consumers. Formulators mix the manufacturer's active ingredients with inert materials using the specifications provided by the manufacturer. The resulting commercial grade product is then packaged by the formulator and either shipped back to the manufacturer or shipped directly to customers of the manufacturer.

The complaint alleges that although Aidex performed the actual mixing or formulation process, the defendants owned the technical grade pesticide, the work in process, and the commercial grade pesticide while the pesticide was in Aidex's possession. The complaint also alleges the generation of pesticide-containing wastes through spills, cleaning of equipment, mixing and grinding operations, and production of batches which do not meet specifications is an "inherent" part of the formulation process. . . . Plaintiffs . . . allege that six of the eight companies are liable under section 9607(a)(3) of the Comprehensive Environmental Response, Compensation, and Liability Act (CERCLA), because by virtue of their relationships with Aidex they "arranged for" the disposal of hazardous substances. See 42 U.S.C. §9607(a)(3).

The defendants have moved to dismiss the action under Fed. R. Civ. P. 12(b)(6), arguing that they contracted with Aidex for the processing of a valuable product, not the disposal of a waste, and that Aidex alone controlled the processes used in formulating their technical grade pesticides into commercial grade pesticides, as well as any waste disposal that resulted therefrom. . . . The court denied the motion under CERCLA, . . . holding that principles of common law in conjunction with the liberal construction required under CERCLA could support liability under section 9607(a)(3). 699 F. Supp. 1384.

We granted all parties leave to file interlocutory appeals, and the case is now before us for decision. . . .

CERCLA places the ultimate responsibility for clean up on "those responsible for problems caused by the disposal of chemical poisons," Dedham Water Co. v. Cumberland Farms Dairy, Inc., 805 F.2d 1074, 1081 (1st Cir. 1986), by authorizing suit against four classes of parties: (1) the owners and operators of a facility at which there is a release or threatened release of hazardous substances; (2) the owners or operators of such a facility any time in the past when hazardous substances were disposed of; (3) any person who "arranged for" the treatment or disposal of a hazardous substance at the facility; and (4) the persons who transported hazardous substances to the facility. 42 U.S.C. §9607(a). Most courts have held CERCLA imposes strict liability and joint and several liability. See e.g., *NEPACCO*, 810 F.2d at 732 n.3; *Shore Realty Corp.*, 759 F.2d at 1042; United States v. Chem-Dyne Corp., 572 F. Supp. 802, 808-10 (S.D. Ohio 1983). Only a limited number of statutorily-prescribed defenses are available. See 42 U.S.C. §9607(b); United States v. Hooker Chemicals & Plastics Corp., 680 F. Supp. 546, 549 (W.D.N.Y. 1988); *Bliss*, 667 F. Supp. at 1304; United States v. Ward, 618 F. Supp. 884, 893 (E.D.N.C. 1985).

. . . Tailored particularly to hazardous waste sites, CERCLA liability may attach only to those responsible for "hazardous substances" as defined in the statute. See 42 U.S.C. §9601(14). Three of the pesticide wastes found at the Aidex site are *not* alleged to be "hazardous substances" under CERCLA. For this reason, plaintiffs have sued only six of the eight defendants under CERCLA. . . .

LIABILITY UNDER CERCLA

To establish a prima facie case of liability under CERCLA, plaintiffs must establish

(1) the Aidex site is a "facility";
(2) a "release" or "threatened release" of a "hazardous substance" from the Aidex site has occurred;
(3) the release or threatened release has caused the United States to incur response costs; and
(4) the defendants fall within at least one of the four classes of responsible persons described in section 9607(a).

Bliss, 667 F. Supp. at 1304; *Conservation Chemical Co.*, 619 F. Supp. at 184.

The complaint adequately alleges facts which would establish the first three elements, and defendants do not challenge these allegations for purposes of this appeal. At issue in this appeal is whether the defendants "arranged for" the disposal of hazardous substances under the Act, and thus fall within the class of responsible persons described in section 9607(a)(3). In finding plaintiffs' allegations sufficient to hold defendants liable as responsible persons, the district court relied on the principle that CERCLA should be broadly interpreted and took guidance from common law rules regarding vicarious liability. In particular, the district court found that defendants could be liable under common law for the abnormally dangerous activities of Aidex acting as an independent contractor, see Restatement (Second) of Torts §427A (1965), holding that the common law was an appropriate source of guidance when the statutory language and legislative history of CERCLA prove inconclusive. . . .

"Arrange for" is not defined by the statute, but "disposal" is. "Disposal" includes "the discharge, deposit, injection, dumping, spilling, leaking, or placing" of any hazardous substance such that the substance "may enter the environment." 42 U.S.C. §6903(3). See 42 U.S.C. §9601(29).

Citing dictionary definitions of the word "arrange," defendants argue they can be liable under section 9607(a)(3) only if they intended to dispose of a waste. Defendants argue further the complaint alleges only an intent to arrange for formulation of a valuable product, and no intent to arrange for the disposal of a waste can be inferred from these allegations. We reject defendants' narrow reading of both the complaint and the statute.

Congress used broad language in providing for liability for persons who "by contract, agreement, or otherwise arranged for" the disposal of hazardous substances. See A & F Materials, 582 F. Supp. at 845. While the legislative history of CERCLA sheds little light on the intended meaning of this phrase, courts have concluded that a liberal judicial interpretation is consistent with CERCLA's "overwhelmingly remedial" statutory scheme. NEPACCO, 810 F.2d at 733. See Dedham Water Co., 805 F.2d at 1081; Conservation Chemical Co., 619 F. Supp. at 192; United States v. Mottolo, 605 F. Supp. 898, 902 (D.N.H. 1985).

Both the First and Second Circuits have declared they "will not interpret section 9607(a) in any way that apparently frustrates the statute's goals, in the absence of a specific congressional intent otherwise." Dedham Water Co., 805 F.2d at 1081; New York v. Shore Realty Corp., 759 F.2d 1032, 1045 (2d Cir. 1985). We thus interpret the phrase "otherwise arranged for" in view of the two essential purposes of CERCLA:

> First, Congress intended that the federal government be immediately given the tools necessary for a prompt and effective response to the problems of national magnitude resulting from hazardous waste disposal. Second, Congress intended that those responsible for problems caused by the disposal of chemical poisons bear the costs and responsibility for remedying the harmful conditions they created.

Dedham Water Co., 805 F.2d at 1081 (citing United States v. Reilly Tar & Chemical Corp., 546 F. Supp. 1100, 1112 (D. Minn. 1982)).

The second goal—that those responsible should pay for clean up—would be thwarted by acceptance of defendants' argument that the allegations in plaintiffs' complaint do not sufficiently allege they "arranged for" disposal of their hazardous substances. While defendants characterize their relationship with Aidex as pertaining solely to formulation of a useful product, courts have not hesitated to look beyond defendants' characterizations to determine whether a transaction in fact involves an arrangement for the disposal of a hazardous substance. In *Conservation Chemical,* for example, the court found defendants' sale of lime slurry and fly ash byproducts to neutralize and treat other hazardous substances at a hazardous waste site could constitute "arranging for disposal" of the lime slurry and fly ash. 619 F. Supp. at 237-41. Denying defendants' motions for summary judgment, the court reasoned that defendants contracted with the owner of the site "for deposit or placement" of their hazardous substances on the site, and thus could be found liable under the statute. Id. at 241.

Other courts have imposed CERCLA liability where defendants sought to characterize their arrangement with another party who disposed of their hazardous substances as a "sale" rather than a "disposal." See New York v. General Electric Co., 592 F. Supp. 291, 297 (N.D.N.Y. 1984); *A & F Materials,* 582 F. Supp. at 845. In the *G.E.* case, General Electric had sold used transformer oil to a dragstrip, which used the oil for dust control. The oil contained PCBs and other hazardous substances, and the State of New York sought to recover costs for clean up of the site from G.E. *G.E.,* 592 F. Supp. at 293-94. In denying G.E.'s motion to dismiss, the court emphasized G.E. allegedly arranged for the dragstrip to take away its used transformer oil with "knowledge or imputed knowledge" that the oil would be deposited on the land surrounding the dragstrip. Id. at 297. Stating that CERCLA liability could not be "facilely circumvented" by characterizing arrangements as "sales," the *G.E.* court cited CERCLA's legislative history: "[P]ersons cannot escape liability by 'contracting away' their responsibility or alleging that the incident was caused by the act or omission of a third party." Id. at 297 (and authorities cited therein). See *A & F Materials,* 582 F. Supp. at 845.

Courts have also held defendants "arranged for" disposal of wastes at a particular site even when defendants did not know the substances would be deposited at that site or in fact believed they would be deposited elsewhere. See *Ward,* 618 F. Supp. at 895; State of Missouri v. Independent Petrochemical Corp., 610 F. Supp. 4, 5 (E.D. Mo. 1985); United States v. Wade, 577 F. Supp. 1326, 1333 n.3 (E.D. Pa. 1983).

Courts have, however, refused to impose liability where a "useful" substance is sold to another party, who then incorporates it into a product, which is later disposed of. E.g., Florida Power & Light Co. v. Allis Chalmers Corp., 27 Env't Rep. Cas. (BNA) 1558 (S.D. Fla. 1988); United States v. Westinghouse Electric Corp., 22 Env't Rep. Cas. 1230 (BNA) (S.D. Ind. 1983). See also Edward Hines Lumber Co. v. Vulcan Materials Co., 685 F. Supp. 651, 654-57 (N.D. Ill.), aff'd on other grounds, 861 F.2d 155 (7th Cir. 1988). Defendants attempt to analogize the present case to those cited above, but the analogy fails. Not only is there no transfer of ownership of the hazardous substances in this case (defendants retain ownership throughout), but the activity undertaken by Aidex is significantly different from the activity undertaken by, for example, Florida Power & Light. Aidex is performing a process on products owned by defendants for defendants' benefit and at their direction; waste is generated and disposed of contemporaneously with the process. Florida Power & Light, on the other hand, purchased electrical transformers containing mineral oil with PCBs from defendant Allis Chalmers, used the transformers for approximately 40 years, and then made the decision to dispose of them at the site in question. *Florida Power & Light,* 27 Env't Rep. Cas. (BNA) at 1558-60. Allis Chalmers was thus far more removed from the disposal than the defendants are in this case. . . .

Finally, defendants' contention that the district court erred in looking to the common law must also be rejected. As the Seventh Circuit has recently held, the sponsors of CERCLA anticipated that the common law would provide guidance in interpreting CERCLA. Edward Hines Lumber Co. v. Vulcan Materials Co., 861 F.2d 155, 157 (7th Cir. 1988). See Colorado v. ASARCO, Inc., 608 F. Supp. 1484, 1488-89 (D. Colo. 1985) (citing legislative history); United States v. Chem-Dyne, 572 F. Supp. 802, 808 (S.D. Ohio 1983). While the *Edward Hines* court refused to find a company was an "operator" of a facility when the common law did not provide for liability, 861 F.2d at 157-58, in this case, the common law supports the imposition of liability on defendants. See Restatement (Second) of Torts §§413, 416, 427 and 427A (1965).

For all of the reasons discussed above, accepting plaintiffs' allegations in this case as true and giving them the benefit of all reasonable inferences therefrom, we agree with the district court that the complaint states a claim upon which relief can be granted under CERCLA. Any other decision, under the circumstances of this case, would allow defendants to simply "close their eyes" to the method of disposal of their hazardous substances, a result contrary to the policies underlying CERCLA.

NOTES AND QUESTIONS

1. What impact will this decision have on efforts by pesticide manufacturers to ensure that their products do not create environmental contamination? The attorney who represented defendants in the *Aceto* case has written an article criticizing the decision. Garrett, The Aceto Case: CERCLA Liability for Products?, 20 Env. Rep. 704 (1989). He argues that CERCLA liability should be limited to parties intentionally disposing of wastes because these are the only parties in a position to control the risks of environmental contamination. Do you agree? What could the pesticide manufacturers do to control the risks of contamination of the sort that occured in *Aceto*?

2. Mr. Garrett argues that a decision in favor of his client would "have no adverse environmental effects; it would simply leave liability with the company that generated the wastes and controlled their disposal." Id. at 704, 706. Do you agree? How would a decision in favor of the defendant pesticide manufacturers in the *Aceto* case have affected cleanup efforts at the site? What impact would it have had on the manufacturers' incentives for ensuring that in the future their products do not contaminate the environment during the formulation process?

3. What is the crucial factor permitting the court to impose "arranged for" liability on the pesticide manufacturers? Is it that they had the capacity to control Aidex's disposal practices? That they knew Aidex would have to dispose of hazardous byproducts or waste? That the products Aidex produced were sold or shipped to customers of the pesticide manufacturers rather than to independent customers of Aidex? To help you think about these issues, consider the following situations.

4. General Battery Corporation (GBC) sold used batteries to Brown, the owner and operator of a battery breaking facility. Brown broke the batteries, washed the cases, and returned the scrap from the inside to GBC to reuse. Brown's property becomes a Superfund site because spent casings as well as battery acid contaminated with lead were present in substantial quantities on the site. The EPA joins GBC as a defendant. Is GBC a PRP under section 107 of CERCLA? Does it matter that GBC was fully aware of the process of battery breaking, which necessarily involves a risk that battery acid might be spilled onto the ground? Would the result be diferrent if the scrap material was not returned to GBC but was sold on the open market?

5. Next, consider Edward Hines Lumber Co. v. Vulcan Materials Co., 685 F. Supp. 651 (N.D. Ill.), affd. on other grounds, 861 F.2d 155 (7th Cir. 1988), cited in *Aceto*. Hines owned a wood products facility in which he treated wood with various toxic chemicals supplied by Vulcan. Hines was notified by the government that his property was contaminated and ordered to clean up the site. Hines sued Vulcan, claiming Vulcan was a PRP too. Vulcan had assisted in designing and building Hines's facility, had trained the employees, and had licensed Hines to use Vulcan's trademark, and Vulcan's employees had full access to the Hines facility. The court dismissed the complaint against Vulcan, holding that liability for arranging for disposal "attaches only to parties who transact in a hazardous substance in order to dispose of or treat the substance." 685 F. Supp. at 654. "[Vulcan] did not decide how the hazardous substance would be disposed of after its use in the wood treatment process. That [it] knew . . . that Hines stored the process runoff in a holding pond . . . [is not enough to establish] liability." Id. at 656.

Is *Hines* consistent with *Aceto*? Does the *Hines* requirement for PRP status that someone transact in a hazardous substance "in order to dispose of" the substance mean that courts must examine the party's subjective state of mind? If so, is that consistent with CERCLA's being a strict liability statute?

6. Arco manufactures various rubber products from neoprene feedstock supplied by du Pont. The manufacturing process, which was recommended to Arco by du Pont, leaches the products in water, producing a wastewater that contains hazardous substances, including toluene. The wastewater is discharged into a seepage pond owned by Arco. The seepage from the pond contaminates a groundwater aquifer, and Arco is ordered to clean up. Du Pont is joined as a potentially responsible party, and then brings a motion to dismiss on the ground that it does not come within any of the four categories of PRPs of section 107. What result under *Hines*? Under *Aceto*? See Kelley v. Arco Indust. Corp., 739 F. Supp. 354 (W.D. Mich. 1990).

7. A company known as 3550 Stevens Creek Associates, the owner of a commercial property at that address, has spent over $100,000 in the past four years removing asbestos insulation from the building in the course of remodelling. It brings a private recovery action under section 107(a) of CERCLA against Monsanto, the manufacturer of the asbestos, and against the Barclays Bank, the original owner of the building, claiming that Monsanto had arranged for the disposal of asbestos (an admittedly hazardous substance) and that Barclays was the owner and operator within the meanings of section 107(a). What result? (Note that the government is precluded by statute from spending Superfund monies to respond to a release or threat of release "from products which are part of the structure of, and result in exposure within . . . business . . . structures. . . ." §104(a)(3)(B). This limitation against government action, however, has been held inapplicable to private recovery actions.) See 3550 Stevens Creek Associates v. Barclays Bank of California, 915 F.2d 1355 (9th Cir. 1990). Suppose that Stevens Creek Associates had not remodeled the building but instead had sold it to Ace Demolition, knowing that Ace was going to raze the building so that new construction could proceed on the site. After state inspectors halt the demolition until Ace has removed and properly disposed of the asbestos, Ace sues Stevens Creek to recover its response costs. Same result? Compare CP Holdings v. Goldberg-Zoino & Associates, 769 F. Supp. 432 (D.N.H. 1991).

8. Consider the following hypothetical: A private individual took his car to a service station to have the brakes checked. The mechanic examined the brakes and decided that, in connection with brake repairs, the brake fluid needed to be replaced. The old fluid was removed and placed into a leaky tank at the service station, along with hazardous substances from other sources, eventually resulting in federal cleanup expenditures. Would the automobile owner be liable under section 107(a)(3)? See Garrett, The Aceto Case: CERCLA Liability for Products?, 21 Env. Rptr. 704 (1989). Would it matter whether the auto owner had taken this environmental law course?

9. Should suppliers of raw materials who have no reason to know that their materials will produce hazardous substance releases be treated like innocent purchasers of contaminated land? Note that section 107(b)(3) provides a defense to a party exercising due care who took precautions against foreseeable acts or omissions of third parties if the defendant can show that a release was caused solely by "an act or omission of a third party other than an employee or agent of the defendant." However, the defense expressly does not apply if the "act or omission occurs in connection with a contractual relationship," foreclosing this defense to most generators. Recall that the potential liability of innocent purchasers of contaminated land under section 107(a)(1) led Congress to clarify the circumstances under which the section 107(b)(3) defense can be invoked by innocent purchasers when it enacted SARA in 1986. Consider section 101(35). Should a similar provision be enacted to protect truly innocent generators?

exception to 3rd party rule

10. In *Aceto,* the United States also charged the defendants under section 7003 of RCRA, which imposes liability on anyone who has "contributed to" the handling, storage, treatment, or disposal of hazardous wastes that pose an imminent and substantial endangerment to health or the environment. The court found the facts were sufficient to sustain liability under this remedial statute as well. Although it did not decide the issue, the court found it at least arguable that "contributed to" liability under RCRA required less involvement in the acts of disposal than "arranged for" liability under CERCLA.

11. One way to gain a better appreciation for the way CERCLA's liability provisions operate is to work through a problem. The problem below introduces you to a few new aspects of CERCLA as well.

PROBLEM EXERCISE: CERCLA LIABILITY

Scientific Disposal Services, Inc. (Scientific) has owned a hazardous waste disposal site since 1970. Scientific contracts with toxic waste generators to dispose of their wastes, safely and securely, on its premises. All its contracts certify that Scientific will use the highest degree of skill and diligence in securing and maintaining the security of these wastes.

Scientific disposes of its liquid wastes in 55-gallon drums and its solid wastes in thick bags lined with plastic liners. Underneath the entire facility is a double layer of plastic liners. On receipt of waste shipments, it codes each drum and bag and records the source of the shipment, its contents as indicated by the generator (Scientific does not perform its own tests on the contents of these shipments for financial reasons), and its storage location within the facility.

Scientific does most of its business with several large companies. Amalgamated Pesticides, Inc. (Amalgamated) ships primarily liquid wastes containing 2,3,4-T (trichlorophenoxy acetic acid), 2,4-D (dichlorophenoxy acetic acid), and 2,3,7,8-TCDD (tetrachloro-p-dibenzo dioxin) (also called "dioxin"). True Value Pesticides (True Value) ships the same wastes as Amalgamated. Large Chemical Company's (Chemical) shipments include mercury, asbestos, TCE (trichloroethylene), and benzene. Another company, Insolvent, has shipped major amounts of a variety of chemicals to the site, but it has gone out of business in the past year. Scientific has also received very small shipments from other companies. Experimental Labs, Inc. (Experimental) has shipped 2,3,4-T, 2,4-D, and dioxin, and Toxicology Lab (Toxicology) has shipped a small quantity of arsenic in an insulated metal box—arsenic that had become contaminated and hence unusable in some health studies it had under way at its laboratory. Together Amalgamated, True Value, and Chemical account for about 80 percent of the total volume of wastes Scientific has processed at the site, while Insolvent shipped about 18 percent.

Experimental in particular was concerned that its wastes be treated safely. Before employing Scientific, it sent employees to study Scientific's operations for several days. It carefully reviewed Scientific's procedures and studied its daily operations. Satisfied that Scientific was operating a state-of-the-art facility, Experimental sent its waste there.

Prior to Scientific's owning the site, it and three acres of contiguous land were owned by an industrial concern. Two acres of land were sold off by the concern in 1953 to its president, who built a residence on them. The third acre was sold in 1959 to the plant manager, who did the same thing. The president's property is now owned by his sole heir, his son, Junior, who inherited the property in 1965 and has long since ceased to use it as a residence. It is currently unoccupied. The plant manager's parcel was sold in 1970 to Innocent, but has since been totally abandoned; it was recently acquired by the city at a foreclosure sale for nonpayment of taxes. The industrial operation sold out to a foreign competitor in 1969, and that competitor made a business decision to close the plant and sell the property to Scientific.

Unknown to Scientific or to any of its client companies until recently, the industrial concern had disposed of the wastes from its operations by dumping them on its property, without taking any precautions and apparently in many cases without even realizing the wastes may have been hazardous. Very sketchy records of the concern just discovered by Scientific reveal that wastes were dumped on all parts of the concern's property, including what became the president's and the plant manager's properties. The records indicate that the wastes include a great number of the substances now handled by Scientific.

Dioxin has been found in soil in residential areas adjacent to the site and in a nearby stream. Soil studies indicate that a number of toxic wastes have migrated from the Scientific site to the neighboring properties. These wastes have been detected in wells used for drinking water as much as a mile away.

Question One. A neighborhood group has become terribly concerned about the potential health hazards posed by the Scientific site. It wants to urge EPA to act under the Superfund statute, but not wanting just to blindly petition EPA, it comes to you for an analysis of EPA's options. What can EPA do to get the site cleaned up? See sections 104 and 107 of CERCLA. If EPA decides to place the site on the NPL and then use Superfund monies to clean up the site, from whom can it recoup those costs? See sections 107 and 101. Consider specifically:

1. Scientific (see section 107(a)(1));
2. Junior (consider also sections 107(b)(3) and 101(35)(A)(iii));
3. Innocent (consider sections 101(20)(A), 101(35)(A)(i), and 101(35)(B));
4. the city (consider section 101(35)(A)(ii));
5. the foreign competitor (see sections 107(a)(2) and 101(29)); and
6. each of Scientific's current clients (for Toxicology Lab see United States v. Monsanto, 858 F.2d 160 (4th Cir. 1988)).

Question Two. Assume no off-site contamination has been found. Instead, one day, while operating one of Scientific's forklifts, an employee negligently spears three neighboring drums. The ensuing chemical interaction causes an explosion. The city fire department rushes to the scene and proceeds to fight the fire. The struggle continues for six days. Two firefighters are injured and eventually must be placed on full disability by the city. You are the city attorney. The mayor wants an opinion as to whether the Superfund legislation will allow the city to recoup the costs of fighting the fire and of paying for the disability leave. What is your advice? See especially sections 107(a)(4)(B), 101(23), and 101(25) of CERCLA.

Question Three. Now assume you are the attorney for Experimental Labs, Inc., which had shipped to the site exactly one drum of chemicals that it said contained a "soup" of 2,3,4-T, 2,4-D, and dioxin. Experimental has gotten wind of the EPA's proposed cleanup. Advise Experimental on its potential exposure and what it must try to do to minimize it. See particularly section 122(g).

C. How Expansively Should CERCLA's Liability Net Be Cast?

As the decisions in *Shore Realty* and *Aceto* illustrate, courts have interpreted the liability provisions of CERCLA expansively, rejecting efforts to create exceptions to owner-operator and generator liability. Although section 107(a)(4) of CERCLA also imposes liability on certain transporters, this provision has been less controversial because it has now been limited to transporters who play a role in selecting where the hazardous substances are disposed ("any person who accepts . . . any hazardous substances for transport to disposal or treatment facilities . . . or sites *selected by such person*," §107(a)(4) (emphasis supplied)).

The most controversial applications of CERCLA liability have occurred in the context of lending institutions and state and local governments. Each category of institution has lobbied vigorously for the creation of a special exemption from CERCLA liability, as discussed below.

i. Lender Liability

One major source of controversy is the CERCLA liability of a financial institution that has an interest in property secured by it. Section 101(20)(A) of CERCLA addresses this issue by providing that CERCLA's "owner or operator" liability does not extend to "a person who, without participating in the management of a vessel or facility, holds indicia of ownership primarily to protect his security interest in the vessel or facility." This provision would appear to exempt from CERCLA liability financial institutions who merely hold mortgages on property.

A more difficult problem may arise, however, if the lender forecloses on the property and acquires title to it or otherwise participates in the management of the property. Consider the following decision.

	United States of America v. Fleet	
	Factors Corp.	
	901 F.2d 1550 (11th Cir. 1990)	

KRAVITCH, Circuit Judge:

FACTS

In 1976, Swainsboro Print Works ("SPW"), a cloth printing facility, entered into a "factoring" agreement with Fleet in which Fleet agreed to advance funds against the assignment of SPW's accounts receivable. As collateral for these advances, Fleet also obtained a security interest in SPW's textile facility and all of its equipment, inventory, and fixtures. In August, 1979, SPW filed for bankruptcy under Chapter 11. The factoring agreement between SPW and Fleet continued with court approval. In early 1981 Fleet ceased advancing funds to SPW because SPW's debt to Fleet exceeded Fleet's estimate of the value of SPW's accounts receivable. On February 27, 1981, SPW ceased operations and began to liquidate its inventory. Fleet continued to collect on the accounts receivable assigned to it under the Chapter 11 factoring agreement. In December, 1981, SPW was adjudicated a bankrupt under Chapter 7 and a trustee assumed title and control of the facility.

In May, 1982, Fleet foreclosed on its security interest in some of SPW's inventory and equipment, and contracted with Baldwin Industrial Liquidators ("Baldwin") to conduct an auction of the collateral. Baldwin sold the material "as is" and "in place" on June 22, 1982; the removal of the items was the responsibility of the purchasers. On August 31, 1982, Fleet allegedly contracted with Nix Riggers ("Nix") to remove the unsold equipment in consideration for leaving the premises "broom clean." Nix testified in deposition that he understood that he had been given a "free hand" by Fleet or Baldwin to do whatever was necessary at the facility to remove the machinery and equipment. Nix left the facility by the end of December, 1983.

On January 20, 1984, the Environmental Protection Agency ("EPA") inspected the facility and found 700 fifty-five gallon drums containing toxic chemicals and forty-four truckloads of material containing asbestos. The EPA incurred costs of nearly $400,000 in responding to the environmental threat at SPW. On July 7, 1987, the facility was conveyed to Emanuel County, Georgia, at a foreclosure sale resulting from SPW's failure to pay state and county taxes.

The government sued Horowitz and Newton, the two principal officers and stockholders of SPW, and Fleet to recover the cost of cleaning up the hazardous waste. The district court granted the government's summary judgment motion with respect to the liability of Horowitz and Newton for the cost of removing the hazardous waste in the drums. The government's motion with respect to Fleet's liability, and the liability of Horowitz and Newton for the asbestos removal costs, was denied. Fleet's motion for summary judgment was also denied. The district court, sua sponte, certified the summary judgment issues for interlocutory appeal and stayed the remaining proceedings in the case. Fleet subsequently brought this appeal challenging the court's denial of its motion for summary judgment. . . .

The government contends that Fleet is liable for the response costs associated with the waste at the SPW facility as either a present owner and operator of the facility, see 42 U.S.C. §9607(a)(1), or the owner or operator of the facility at the time the wastes were disposed, see 42 U.S.C. §9607(a)(2).

The district court, as a matter of law, rejected the government's claim that Fleet was a present owner of the facility. The court, however, found a sufficient issue of fact as to whether Fleet was an owner or operator of the SPW facility at the time the wastes were disposed to warrant the denial of Fleet's motion for summary judgment. On appeal each party contests that portion of the district court's order adverse to their respective interests.

A.   *Fleet's Liability Under Section 9607(a)(1)*

CERCLA holds the owner or operator of a facility containing hazardous waste strictly liable to the United States for expenses incurred in responding to the environmental and health hazards posed by the waste in that facility. See 42 U.S.C. §9607(a)(1); S. Rep. No. 848, 96th Cong., 2d Sess. 34 (1980). This provision of the statute targets those individuals presently "owning or operating such facilit[ies]." See 42 U.S.C. §9601(20)(A)(ii). In order to effectuate the goals of the statute, we will construe the present owner and operator of a facility [to be] that individual or entity owning or operating the facility at the time the plaintiff initiated the lawsuit by filing a complaint.

On July 9, 1987, the date this litigation commenced, the owner of the SPW facility was Emanuel County, Georgia. Under CERCLA, however, a state or local government that has involuntarily acquired title to a facility is generally not held liable as the owner or operator of the facility. Rather, the statute provides that

> in the case of any facility, title or control of which was conveyed due to bankruptcy, foreclosure, tax delinquency, abandonment, or similar means to a unit of State or local government, [its owner or operator is] any person who owned, operated or otherwise controlled activities at such facility immediately beforehand.

42 U.S.C. §9601(20)(A)(iii).

Essentially, the parties disagree as to the interpretation of the phrase "immediately beforehand." The district court reasoned that Fleet could not be liable under section 9607(a)(1) because it had never foreclosed on its security interest in the facility and its agents had not been on the premises since December 1983. The government contends that the statute should be interpreted to refer liability "back to the last time that someone controlled the facility, however long ago." Appellee's Brief at 23. Thus, according to the government, the period of effective abandonment of the site by the trustee in bankruptcy (from December 1983 to the July 1987 foreclosure sale) should be ignored and liability would remain with Fleet since it was the last entity to "control" the facility.

We agree with Fleet that the plain meaning of the phrase "immediately beforehand" means without intervening ownership, operation, and control. Fleet, therefore, cannot be held liable under section 9607(a)(1) because it neither owned, operated, or controlled SPW immediately prior to Emanuel County's acquisition of the facility. It is undisputed that from December 1981, when SPW was adjudicated a bankrupt, until the July 1987 foreclosure sale, the bankrupt estate and trustee were the owners of the facility. Similarly, the evidence is clear that neither Fleet nor any of its putative agents had anything to do with the facility after December 1983. Although Fleet may have operated or controlled SPW prior to December 1983, its involvement with SPW terminated more than three years before the county assumed ownership of the facility. The fact that the bankrupt estate or trustee may not have effectively exercised their control of the facility between December 1983 and July 1987 is of no moment. It is undisputed that Fleet was not in control of the facility during this period. Although a trustee can obviously abdicate its control over a bankrupt estate, it cannot in such a manner unilaterally delegate its responsibility to a previous controlling entity. To reach back to Fleet's involvement with the facility prior to December 1983 in order to impose liability would torture the plain statutory meaning of "immediately beforehand."

Not responsible [handwritten]

B. *Fleet's Liability Under Section 9607(a)(2)*

CERCLA also imposes liability on "any person who at the time of disposal of any hazardous substance owned or operated any . . . facility at which such hazardous substances were disposed of . . ." 42 U.S.C. §9607(a)(2). CERCLA excludes from the definition of "owner or operator" any "person, who, without participating in the management of a . . . facility, holds indicia of ownership primarily to protect his security interest in the . . . facility." 42 U.S.C. §9601(20)(A). Fleet has the burden of establishing its entitlement to this exemption. *Maryland Bank & Trust,* 632 F. Supp. at 578; see United States v. First City National Bank of Houston, 386 U.S. 361, 366 (1967). There is no dispute that Fleet held an "indicia of ownership" in the facility through its deed of trust to SPW, and that this interest was held primarily to protect its security interest in the facility. The critical issue is whether Fleet participated in management sufficiently to incur liability under the statute.

are responsible [handwritten]

The construction of the secured creditor exemption is an issue of first impression in the federal appellate courts. The government urges us to adopt a narrow and strictly literal interpretation of the exemption that excludes from its protection any secured creditor that participates in any manner in the management of a facility. We decline the government's suggestion because it would largely eviscerate the exemption Congress intended to afford to secured creditors. Secured lenders frequently have some involvement in the financial affairs of their debtors in order to insure that their interests are being adequately protected. To adopt the government's interpretation of the secured creditor exemption could expose all such lenders to CERCLA liability for engaging in their normal course of business.

Fleet, in turn, suggests that we adopt the distinction delineated by some district courts between permissible participation in the financial management of the facility and impermissible participation in the day-to-day or operational management of a facility. In United States v. Mirabile, the first case to suggest this interpretation, the district court granted summary judgment to the defendant creditors because their participation in the affairs of the facility was "limited to participation in financial decisions." No. 84-2280, slip op. at 3 (E.D. Pa. Sept. 6, 1985) (available on WESTLAW as 1985 WL 97). The court explained "that the participation which is critical is participation in operational, production, or waste disposal activities. Mere financial ability to control waste disposal practices . . . is not . . . sufficient for the imposition of liability." *Mirabile*, No. 84-2280, slip op. at 4; accord United States v. New Castle County, 727 F. Supp. 854, 866 (D. Del. 1989); Rockwell International v. IU International Corp., 702 F. Supp. 1384, 1390 (N.D. Ill. 1988); see also Coastal Casting Service v. Aron, No. H-86-4463, slip op. at 4 (S.D. Tex. April 8, 1988) (complaint alleging that secured creditor's entanglement with facility's management surpassed mere financial control held sufficient). The court concluded that "before a secured creditor . . . may be held liable, it must, at a minimum, participate in the day-to-day operational aspects of the site. [Here, the creditor] . . . merely foreclosed on the property after all operations had ceased and thereafter took prudent and routine steps to secure the property against further depreciation." Id. at 12; accord United States v. Nicolet, Inc., 712 F. Supp. 1193, 1204-05 (E.D. Pa. 1989).

The court below, relying on *Mirabile*, similarly interpreted the statutory language to permit secured creditors to

> provide financial assistance and general, and even isolated instances of specific management advice to its debtors without risking CERCLA liability if the secured creditor does not participate in the day-to-day management of the business or facility either before or after the business ceases operation.

United States v. Fleet Factors Corp., 724 F. Supp. 955, 960 (S.D. Ga. 1988); accord *Guidice*, at 561-62; *Nicolet*, 712 F. Supp. at 1205. Applying this standard, the trial judge concluded that from the inception of Fleet's relationship with SPW in 1976 to June 22, 1982, when Baldwin entered the facility, Fleet's activity did not rise to the level of participation in management sufficient to impose CERCLA liability. The court, however, determined that the facts alleged by the government with respect to Fleet's involvement after Baldwin entered the facility were sufficient to preclude the granting of summary judgment in favor of Fleet on this issue.

Although we agree with the district court's resolution of the summary judgment motion, we find its construction of the statutory exemption too permissive towards secured creditors who are involved with toxic waste facilities. In order to achieve the "overwhelmingly remedial" goal of the CERCLA statutory scheme, ambiguous statutory terms should be construed to favor liability for the costs incurred by the government in responding to the hazards at such facilities. *Allis Chalmers*, 893 F.2d at 1317; see *Maryland Bank & Trust Co.*, 632 F. Supp. at 579 (secured creditor exemption should be construed narrowly); Note, When a Security Becomes a Liability: Claims Against Lenders in Hazardous Waste Cleanup, 38 Hastings L.J. 1261, 1285-86, 1291 (1987) (same) [hereinafter Claims Against Lenders]. The district court's broad interpretation of the exemption would essentially require a secured creditor to be involved in the operations of a facility in order to incur liability. This construction ignores the plain language of the exemption and essentially renders it meaningless. Individuals and entities involved in the operations of a facility are already liable as operators under the express language of section 9607(a)(2). Had Congress intended to absolve secured creditors from ownership liability, it would have done so. Instead, the statutory language chosen by Congress explicitly holds secured creditors liable if they participate in the management of a facility.

Although similar, the phrase "participating in the management" and the term "operator" are not congruent. Under the standard we adopt today, a secured creditor may incur section 9607(a)(2) liability, without being an operator, by participating in the financial management of a facility to a degree indicating a capacity to influence the corporation's treatment of hazardous wastes. It is not necessary for the secured creditor actually to involve itself in the day-to-day operations of the facility in order to be liable—although such conduct will certainly lead to the loss of the protection of the statutory exemption. Nor is it necessary for the secured creditor to participate in management decisions relating to hazardous waste. Rather, a secured creditor will be liable if its involvement with the management of the facility is sufficiently broad to support the inference that it could affect hazardous waste disposal decisions if it so chose. We, therefore, specifically reject the formulation of the secured creditor exemption suggested by the district court in *Mirabile*. See, No. 84-2280, slip op. at 4.

This construction of the secured creditor exemption, while less permissive than that of the trial court, is broader than that urged by the government and, therefore, should give lenders some latitude in their dealings with debtors without exposing themselves to potential liability. Nothing in our discussion should preclude a secured creditor from monitoring any aspect of a debtor's business. Likewise, a secured creditor can become involved in occasional and discrete financial decisions relating to the protection of its security interest without incurring liability.

Our interpretation of the exemption may be challenged as creating disincentives for lenders to extend financial assistance to businesses with potential hazardous waste problems and encouraging secured creditors to distance themselves from the management actions, particularly those related to hazardous wastes, of their debtors. See *Guidice*, at 562; Note, Interpreting the Meaning of Lender Management Under Section 101(20)(A) of CERCLA, 98 Yale L.J. 925, 928, 944 (1989). As a result the improper treatment of hazardous wastes could be perpetuated rather than resolved. These concerns are unfounded.

Our ruling today should encourage potential creditors to investigate thoroughly the waste treatment systems and policies of potential debtors. If the treatment systems seem inadequate, the risk of CERCLA liability will be weighed into the terms of the loan agreement. Creditors, therefore, will incur no greater risk than they bargained for and debtors, aware that inadequate hazardous waste treatment will have a significant adverse impact on their loan terms, will have powerful incentives to improve their handling of hazardous wastes.

Similarly, creditors' awareness that they are potentially liable under CERCLA will encourage them to monitor the hazardous waste treatment systems and policies of their debtors and insist upon compliance with acceptable treatment standards as a prerequisite to continued and future financial support. Claims Against Lenders, supra, at 1294; Note, The Liability of Financial Institutions for Hazardous Waste Cleanup Costs Under CERCLA, 1988 Wis. L. Rev. 139, 185 (1988) [hereinafter Liability of Financial Institutions]. Once a secured creditor's involvement with a facility becomes sufficiently broad that it can anticipate losing its exemption from CERCLA liability, it will have a strong incentive to address hazardous waste problems at the facility rather than studiously avoiding the investigation and amelioration of the hazard.

In *Maryland Bank & Trust Co.*, the court aptly described and weighed the competing policy interests of creditors and the government in interpreting the secured creditor exemption:

> In essence, the defendant's position would convert CERCLA into an insurance scheme for financial institutions, protecting them against possible losses due to the security of loans with polluted properties. Mortgagees, however, already have the means to protect themselves, by making prudent loans. Financial institutions are in a position to investigate and discover potential problems in their secured properties. For many lending institutions, such research is routine. CERCLA will not absolve them from responsibility for their mistakes of judgment.

632 F. Supp. at 580.

We agree with the court below that the government has alleged sufficient facts to hold Fleet liable under section 9607(a)(2). From 1976 until SPW ceased printing operations on February 27, 1981, Fleet's involvement with the facility was within the parameters of the secured creditor exemption to liability. During this period, Fleet regularly advanced funds to SPW against the assignment of SPW's accounts receivable, paid and arranged for security deposits for SPW's Georgia utility services, and informed SPW that it would not advance any more money when it determined that its advanced sums exceeded the value of SPW's accounts receivable.

Fleet's involvement with SPW, according to the government, increased substantially after SPW ceased printing operations at the Georgia plant on February 27, 1981 and began to wind down its affairs. Fleet required SPW to seek its approval before shipping its goods to customers, established the price for excess inventory, dictated when and to whom the finished goods should be shipped, determined when employees should be laid off, supervised the activity of the office administrator at the site, received and processed SPW's employment and tax forms, controlled access to the facility, and contracted with Baldwin to dispose of the fixtures and equipment at SPW. These facts, if proved, are sufficient to remove Fleet from the protection of the secured creditor exemption. Fleet's involvement in the financial management of the facility was pervasive, if not complete. Furthermore, the government's allegations indicate that Fleet was also involved in the operational management of the facility. Either of these allegations is sufficient as a matter of law to impose CERCLA liability on a secured creditor. The district court's finding to the contrary is erroneous.

With respect to Fleet's involvement at the facility from the time it contracted with Baldwin in May 1982 until Nix left the facility in December 1983, we share the district court's conclusion that Fleet's alleged conduct brought it outside the statutory exemption for secured creditors. Indeed, Fleet's involvement would pass the threshold for operator liability under section 9607(a)(2). Fleet weakly contends that its activity at the facility from the time of the auction was within the secured creditor exemption because it was merely protecting its security interest in the facility and foreclosing its security interest in its equipment, inventory, and fixtures. This assertion, even if true, is immaterial to our analysis. The scope of the secured creditor exemption is not determined by whether the creditor's activity was taken to protect its security interest. What is relevant is the nature and extent of the creditor's involvement with the facility, not its motive. To hold otherwise would enable secured creditors to take indifferent and irresponsible actions toward their debtors' hazardous wastes with impunity by incanting that they were protecting their security interests. Congress did not intend CERCLA to sanction such abdication of responsibility.

CONCLUSION

We agree with the district court that Fleet is not within the class of liable persons described in Section 9607(a)(1). We also conclude that the court properly denied Fleet's motion for summary judgment. Although the court erred in construing the secured creditor exemption to insulate Fleet from CERCLA liability for its conduct prior to June 22, 1982, it correctly ruled that Fleet was liable under Section 9607(a)(2) for its subsequent activities if the government could establish its allegations. Because there remain disputed issues of material fact, the case is remanded for further proceedings consistent with this opinion.

Affirmed and remanded.

NOTES AND QUESTIONS

1. Why was Fleet held liable? What could Fleet have done differently to avoid liability? Could Fleet have preserved its security interest in SPW and at the same time avoid CERCLA liability? How?

2. Would Fleet's liability have been affected if it had not foreclosed on its security interest in the facility's inventory and equipment? If it had not contracted to auction off the inventory and equipment?

3. How will *Fleet Factors* affect the relationships between financial institutions and borrowers who manage hazardous substances? Will facilities that have a poor environmental record have a harder time obtaining loans as a result of this decision, or will it simply make it more difficult for *all* facilities that manage hazardous substances to obtain loans, regardless of their environmental records? If you were an attorney for a financial institution, what steps would you advise the institution to take to avoid CERCLA liability in circumstances similar to those in *Fleet Factors*?

4. The Ninth Circuit took a different view of the circumstances in which lenders could be held liable under CERCLA in In re Bergsoe Metal Corp., 910 F.2d 668 (9th Cir. 1990). The Port of St. Helens, a municipal corporation, agreed to issue industrial development bonds to finance the construction of a lead recycling operation owned by Bergsoe Metals Corporation. Through a sale-and-leaseback arrangement, the Port was given the deed to Bergsoe's property, which the company then leased back, paying rent to the bank that held the Port's bonds in amounts equal to the principal and interest due on the bonds. Bergsoe later went bankrupt, and the site became the subject of a CERCLA cleanup. Although the Port of St. Helens held the deed to the property, it argued that it was not an owner for purposes of CERCLA because it held the deed solely to protect its security interest under section 101(20)(A). Declining to follow *Fleet Factors*'s suggestion that the *capacity* to influence

waste disposal decisions was sufficient for CERCLA liability, the Ninth Circuit held that "whatever the precise parameters of 'participation,' there must be *some* actual management of the facility before a secured creditor will fall outside the exception." 910 F.2d at 672. Thus, the court concluded that the Port fell within the secured creditor exemption and was not liable for cleanup costs under CERCLA.

The Aftermath of *Fleet Factors*

In *Fleet Factors* the Justice Department indicated that any provision of management advice by a financial institution to a borrower who is an owner or operator of property for which response costs are incurred may be sufficient to create liability under CERCLA. Yet in successfully opposing Fleet's petition for certiorari before the Supreme Court, the solicitor general argued that "the government has rarely sought to hold lenders liable under CERCLA and—as demonstrated in this case—has generally sought such relief only where the lender's participation in the management of the facility is extensive." Solicitor General's Brief in Opposition, Fleet Factors Corp. v. United States, No. 90-504, Dec. 14, 1990. The solicitor general argued that even if "capacity to control" is not the proper test of participation in management, the result would have been the same because Fleet actively participated in management and a trial would have been necessary to resolve factual disputes concerning the nature of Fleet's involvement.

Financial institutions have aggressively used *Fleet Factors* to argue that Congress should exempt them from CERCLA liability. In an amicus brief in support of Fleet's petition for certiorari, lenders argued that *Fleet Factors*'s "capacity to control" test had eviscerated the secured creditor exemption of section 101(20)(A). Noting that lenders were parties to 36 CERCLA suits and that 60 more had been named as potentially responsible parties by EPA, the lenders told the Supreme Court that their liability could exceed $100 billion.

The lenders found natural allies in two government agencies, the Federal Deposit Insurance Corporation (FDIC) and the Resolution Trust Corporation (RTC). Both agencies are responsible for properties seized by the government from failed savings and loan institutions. Stung by the discovery that section 120(h) of CERCLA would require the cleanup of contamination at all properties sold by the federal government, the FDIC and RTC have sought a legislative exemption from CERCLA liability. The FDIC identified 238 properties in its inventory that have hazardous waste problems and has estimated that for 117 of these properties, cleanup costs may range from 100 to 150 percent of the market value of the properties. 21 Env. Rep. 2254 (April 19, 1991). The RTC has discovered that 300 of its properties have contamination problems and estimates that this number might double. Labaton, Pollution Raises Cost of Bailout, N.Y. Times, July 20, 1990, at D1, D4.

EPA has opposed the efforts of lending institutions to obtain a legislative exemption from CERCLA. In testimony before a Senate committee in April 1991, EPA officials noted that private lending institutions have received only 8 out of 18,392 formal notices of potential CERCLA liability issued by EPA and that only 1 of the 8 institutions has asserted an innocent landowner defense. 21 Env. Rep. 2254 (April 19, 1991). Claiming that the FDIC and RTC have overreacted to unreasonable fears of potential future liability, EPA officials have opposed any legislative exemption.

In an effort to forestall a legislative exemption, EPA pledged to issue new regulations clarifying the ways in which lenders can protect themselves. In June 1991 EPA proposed a new interpretation of CERCLA's secured creditor exemption, which is contained in section 101(20)(A). 56 Fed. Reg. 28,798 (1991). The Agency acknowledged a tension between a security holder's need to protect its security interest by ensuring that a borrower's properties are properly managed and EPA's duty to recover funds spent on CERCLA cleanups. EPA specified a broad range of activities that a lender may undertake without forfeiting its exemption. These included providing "periodic financial or other advice to a financially distressed debtor," undertaking "loan workout" activities, foreclosing on the security (including taking a deed in lieu of foreclosure), winding-up operations, and liquidating or selling off assets. EPA cautioned, however, that while these activities would not void section 101(20)(A)'s exemption from the definition of "owner" or "operator," lenders could still be liable under section 107(a)(3)-(4) if they arranged for the disposal or transport of hazardous substances. Under EPA's proposed rule, lenders who foreclose on properties may retain their exemption even if they continue the operation of a facility, as long as they do not "fail to take reasonable actions to sell the property" or reject or fail to act on "a written, bona fide offer for a value equal to or exceeding the outstanding loan obligation." 56 Fed. Reg. at 28,801. EPA specified that, within 12 months of foreclosure, security holders must list the property for sale, advertise it at least monthly, and act on any "written, bona fide, firm offer of fair consideration for the property." Id.

Noting that the exemption for properties involuntarily acquired by governmental units in section 101(20)(D) of CERCLA applies only to state and local governments, EPA also stated that federal agencies who acquired properties in this manner could qualify for the security interest exemption by "standing in the shoes" of the prior security holder.

NOTES AND QUESTIONS

1. Should EPA's proposed rule be sufficient to ease the lenders' fears of CERCLA liability? What actions would you now advise a lender to take in order to avoid CERCLA liability?

2. If lenders were successful in obtaining a legislative exemption from CERCLA liability, what impact would such an exemption have on their lending practices? Would they be more likely to lend money to firms with a poor environmental record? If lending institutions were exempt from CERCLA liability, could they purchase contaminated property at bargain basement prices, insist that the government pay to clean it up, and then sell the more valuable decontaminated property at a profit?

3. Issues remarkably similar to those in the lender liability debate arise with respect to the liability of parent corporations for the actions of their subsidiaries. In United States v. Kayser-Roth, Inc., 910 F.2d 24 (1st Cir. 1990), cert. denied, 111 S. Ct. 957 (1991), a parent corporation was held liable as an "operator" under CERCLA because it exercised "pervasive" control over a wholly owned subsidiary responsible for a release. Yet in other cases courts have refused to hold parent corporations liable under CERCLA when they have not exercised active control over their subsidiaries' actions. Joslyn Manufacturing Co. v. T. L. James & Co., Inc., 893 F.2d 80 (5th Cir. 1990), cert. denied, 111 S. Ct. 1017 (1991).

4. The prospect of creating special exemptions from CERCLA liability, whether by regulation or legislation, is disturbing to many. Lobbyists for other industries caught in the CERCLA liability net have opposed creating an exemption for lenders because they fear that it will simply increase the burden CERCLA places on other companies. As one industry representative said, "The only thing fair about Superfund is that it is unfair to everyone." EPA Issue Rules on Superfund Liability, Legal Times, June 17, 1991, at S28. Similar arguments are being made in opposition to proposals to exempt state and local governments from CERCLA liability, as discussed below.

ii. Liability of State and Local Governments

One of the more successful strategies used by potentially responsible parties (PRPs) has been to expand the class of parties required to contribute to CERCLA cost recovery actions by suing state and local governments for contribution. Section 113(f) of CERCLA authorizes a private right of action for contribution from parties liable or potentially liable under section 107(a). A number of PRPs have used this provision to seek contribution from government agencies by arguing that such agencies are liable as owners, operators, or generators.

In Pennsylvania v. Union Gas Co., 491 U.S. 1 (1989), the Supreme Court held that the Eleventh Amendment did not prohibit states from being held liable to private parties under CERCLA. The Court noted that section 101(21) of CERCLA expressly includes state and local governments within the definition of persons subject to CERCLA and that section 101(20)(D) provided a very narrow exclusion from "owner or operator" liability for state and local governments who acquire facilities involuntarily.

In United States v. Dart Industries, 847 F.2d 144 (4th Cir. 1988), the Fourth Circuit rejected industry claims that the South Carolina Department of Health and Environmental Control should be held liable under CERCLA as the "owner" or "operator" of an abandoned dump site regulated by the state. The court concluded that performance of regulatory responsibilities is insufficient to make a state agency an owner or operator. Similar arguments were rejected in United States v. New Castle County, 727 F. Supp. 854 (D.C. Del. 1989). The court noted that the site was not controlled by the county "with any proprietary or financial interest at stake." The county also was held not to be liable under the "arranged for" provisions of section 107(a)(3). Relying on the reasoning of New York v. City of Johnstown, 701 F. Supp. 33 (N.D.N.Y. 1988), the court noted that the county had not owned or possessed the waste sent to a landfill. The court distinguished cases where non-owners were held liable as arrangers by noting that they involved officers or plant supervisors of companies that had generated the waste. By contrast, in United States v. Stringfellow, 31 E.R.C. 1315 (C.D. Cal. 1990), the state of California was found to be liable as a result of its actions in selecting a site for hazardous waste dumping and controlling all actions at the site.

Other courts have held that municipalities can be liable under CERCLA for having arranged to dispose of municipal solid waste at sites where CERCLA response actions are undertaken. In B. F. Goodrich v. Murtha, 754 F. Supp. 960 (D. Conn. 1991), affd., —F.2d— (2d Cir. 1992), a district court refused to dismiss a suit brought by the B. F. Goodrich Company, General Electric, Atlantic Richfield, and the Upjohn Company against 24 small Connecticut towns that sent municipal waste to a dump that became a CERCLA site. The court held that even though municipal solid waste is not regulated as hazardous under RCRA due to the household waste exemption, it can contain hazardous substances that would subject the municipality to CERCLA liability. On appeal the Second Circuit affirmed. The court explained that it was "aware that holding the municipal defendants as responsible parties and including municipal solid waste within the definition of hazardous substances will have far-reaching implications." The court noted, however, that "burdensome consequences are not sufficient grounds to judicially graft an exception onto a statute, a graft that would thwart the language, purpose, and agency interpretation of the statute." B. F. Goodrich v. Murtha, —F.2d—, — (2d Cir. 1992).

Lawsuits against municipalities have now become a popular strategy for PRPs. Because municipal waste is present at more than 25 percent of the approximately 1,200 sites on the NPL, and often in large volumes, the liability of municipalities is potentially quite great. Moses and Woo, Municipal Liability Under Superfund Seen, Wall St. J., Mar. 13, 1992, at B3.

Some municipalities and small businesses have agreed to settlements. More than 400 small businesses and 41 towns and school districts near Utica, New York have agreed to contribute $1.8 million to a pharmaceutical manufacturer and a metal fabricator who sued 603 defendants for contribution to clean up a landfill where municipal waste had been disposed. Id.

Recognizing the potential liability of municipalities under CERCLA, EPA in 1989 had announced a Municipal Settlement Policy. While confirming that municipalities were subject to CERCLA liability, the policy stated that EPA generally would not identify generators and transporters of municipal solid waste as PRPs unless the Agency had reason to believe that their waste was more hazardous than normal. In July 1991 EPA announced that it would develop national guidelines for allocating response costs when municipal solid waste is found at CERCLA sites. 22 Env. Rep. 647 (July 19, 1991). While EPA officials maintain that they have no authority to exempt municipalities from CERCLA, they state that the new policy will make it easier for municipalities to reach early settlements of CERCLA liability suits by clarifying how much weight their contributions to waste at a site should be given. EPA also announced that it will not bring CERCLA enforcement actions against owners of residential properties. Id.

NOTES AND QUESTIONS

1. Does the growing controversy over municipal liability under CERCLA confirm Richard Epstein's argument that joint and several liability dilutes individual incentives for preventing environmental damage? What impact will the prospect of CERCLA liability have on the way municipalities manage their waste? Are governmental entities more or less likely to be concerned about potential liability than private corporations? Is the fear of CERCLA liability likely to increase or decrease the popularity of incineration as an option for municipal waste management? What impact will it have on the popularity of recycling?

2. Municipalities are lobbying Congress for an exemption from CERCLA liability. How would you vote on their request? Why? What impact would an exemption have on how municipalities manage their

waste? One proposal would give EPA the exclusive authority to bring contribution actions against municipalities. 22 Env. Rep. 828 (Aug. 2, 1991). Is this an appropriate compromise? Industry representatives argue that it is unfair to give any group a special exemption from CERCLA liability. They argue that because EPA has concentrated on deep pocket defendants, large companies are forced to file contribution actions against municipalities and small generators. Municipalities maintain that these suits instead are a ploy to make CERCLA's liability provisions look so unreasonable that Congress eventually will scrap them.

3. Are each of us as individuals potentially liable under CERCLA as generators who arrange for disposal of waste containing hazardous substances by taking out our garbage? What about wastes we personally transport to a landfill? Note that while EPA has announced that it will not bring CERCLA actions against individual owners of residential property, PRPs remain free to do so.

4. Suppose that a group like the League of Women Voters conducts a program to collect hazardous household waste such as old paint cans and weed killers, and they contract with a licensed RCRA subtitle C facility to dispose of the wastes they collect. If the company hired to transport the waste to the facility instead dumps it by the side of the road, is the League potentially liable under CERCLA? Are individuals whose paint cans and weed killers were dumped liable?

5. The contribution provision of section 113(f)(1) of CERCLA directs courts to "allocate response costs among liable parties using such equitable factors as the court determines are appropriate." Should a court apportion CERCLA liability on the basis of the relative volumes of waste generators contributed to a site or on the basis of the wastes' relative toxicity? Large companies tend to favor volumetric apportionment when municipal solid waste is involved at a site, while municipalities reject it by arguing that their waste is far less toxic than industrial waste. How would you respond to these arguments?

6. How should liability be apportioned as between owner-operators and generators? What factors should a court consider in addressing this issue? These and other questions are addressed below.

A Note on Settlements and the Right to Contribution

Although courts have been relatively uniform in interpreting CERCLA to provide for joint and several liability, they diverge with respect to how it should be applied and the circumstances under which equitable apportionment may be appropriate. Compare United States v. Chem-Dyne Corp., 572 F. Supp. 802 (S.D. Ohio 1983) (placing burden on defendants to demonstrate that response costs can be apportioned) with United States v. A & F Materials, 578 F. Supp. 1249 (S.D. Ill. 1984) (listing six factors to be considered in apportioning damages even when joint and several liability could appropriately be applied).

As noted above, Congress did seek to ease the burden of joint and several liability when it amended CERCLA in 1986 by enacting a de minimis settlement provision in section 122(g) and by providing a statutory cause of action for contribution in section 113(f)(1). In United States of America v. Cannons Engineering Corp., 899 F.2d 79 (1st Cir. 1990), nonsettling defendants challenged consent decrees between the government and certain responsible parties. EPA had first offered to reach administrative settlements with all de minimis contributors under section 122(g) who would agree to pay 160 percent of their projected share of all past and future response costs based on calculations of the amount of waste by volume that each had contributed to the site. The Agency explained that the 60 percent premium was intended to cover unexpected costs or unforeseen conditions. Three hundred generators agreed to such settlements, which released them from all liability and exempted them from suits for contribution under section 122(g)(5). EPA then filed suits against 84 other potentially responsible parties, settling with 47 of them who were major PRPs in one consent decree and with 12 de minimis PRPs (who previously had rejected the administrative settlement) in another. The 12 de minimis PRPs agreed to pay 260 percent of their volumetric share of projected response costs, with the additional 100 percent premium representing a penalty for delay.

The First Circuit upheld the settlement in the face of challenge from nonsettling PRPs. Noting that "a party should bear the cost of the harm for which it is legally responsible," the court opined that "settlement terms must be based upon, and roughly correlated with, some acceptable measure of comparative fault. . . ." While noting that "[t]here is no universally correct approach," the court approved EPA's use of volumetric shares, applying a deferential arbitrary and capricious standard of review. The court indicated that EPA could seek to encourage prompt settlements by offering to settle for a smaller amount, while seeking larger settlements in return for releasing parties from uncertain future liability.

The court rejected the plaintiffs' arguments that EPA should have based its apportionment of liability on the relative toxicity of the wastes rather than on their volumetric shares. "Having selected a reasonable method of weighing comparative fault, the agency need not show that it is the best, or even the fairest, of all conceivable methods. The choice of the yardstick to be used for allocating liability must be left primarily to the expert discretion of the EPA, particularly when the PRPs involved are numerous and the situation is complex." 899 F.2d at 88. As the decision in *Cannons Engineering* indicates, EPA has considerable flexibility in how it structures its settlement strategy for apportioning CERCLA liability as long as it can justify its actions. We now examine what costs parties are liable for in CERCLA actions.

6. Response Costs and Damages to Natural Resources

Section 107(a) of CERCLA makes responsible parties liable for four types of costs: (1) all costs of government response actions not inconsistent with the national contingency plan (NCP), (2) any other necessary response costs incurred by any other person consistent with the NCP, (3) damages to natural resources including the reasonable costs of assessing such damages, and (4) the costs of any health assessment studies carried out pursuant to section 104(i).

Considerable litigation has focused on recovery of response costs under CERCLA. The statute expressly authorizes the government to recover the costs of removals or remedial actions, which have been held to include the costs of both planning and implementation. United States v. Northeastern Pharmaceutical & Chemical Co., 579 F. Supp. 823, 850 (W.D. Mo. 1984). Costs of investigation, testing, monitoring, hiring experts, and site security also have been held to be recoverable. Ascon Properties, Inc. v. Mobil Oil Co., 866 F.2d 1149, 1154 (9th Cir. 1989); Cadillac Fairview/California v. Dow Chemical Co., 840 F.2d 691, 695 (9th Cir. 1988).

Although a number of early decisions provided that medical expenses, relocation costs, and damage to private property were recoverable, see, e.g., Williams v. Allied Automotive Autolite Division, 704 F. Supp. 782, 784 (N.D. Ohio 1988), more recent cases suggest that medical monitoring costs and private property damage may not be recoverable. Artesian Water Co. v. New Castle County, 851 F.2d 643, 648-649 (3d Cir. 1988). The latter view is premised on the notion that the congressional intent was remediation of hazardous substances; Congress rejected the use of CERCLA for victim compensation.

A difference in the language of section 107(a)(4)(A) (authorizing government recovery of response costs "not inconsistent with" the NCP) and section 107(a)(4)(B) (authorizing private recovery of "other necessary costs of response . . . consistent with" the NCP) suggests a difference in who bears the burden of proving that response costs were consistent with the NCP. When the government seeks to recover its response costs, defendants have the burden of demonstrating that they are not consistent with the NCP. United States v. Conservation Chemical Co., 619 F. Supp. 162, 186 (W.D. Mo. 1985). When private parties seek reimbursement for response costs, they have been held to bear the burden of proving consistency. City of Philadelphia v. Stepan Chemical Co., 544 F. Supp. 1135, 1144 (E.D. Pa. 1982).

While some courts require that private parties demonstrate "strict compliance" with the NCP, Almand Properties Corp. v. Aluminum Co. of America, 711 F. Supp. 784 (D.N.J. 1989), others have applied a "substantial compliance" standard. The latter would permit some deviation from strict compliance with the NCP when consistent with the NCP's basic purposes. Wickland Oil Terminals v. ASARCO, Inc., 792 F.2d 887, 891 (9th Cir. 1986). In its 1990 revision of the NCP, EPA rejected the "strict compliance" standard while emphasizing the need for substantial compliance with requirements for a "CERCLA Quality Clean-up" in section 121(b)(1) of CERCLA.

Some of the most conceptually difficult issues arise with respect to determination of damages to natural resources. To simplify the recovery of such damages, Congress directed that regulations be promulgated to govern the assessment of damages to natural resources, CERCLA section 301(c), and that assessments made pursuant to these regulations will be entitled to a rebuttable presumption of validity in cost recovery proceedings. CERCLA section 107(f)(2)(C). The case that follows involves challenges to the natural resource damages regulations that were issued belatedly by the Department of the Interior.

State of Ohio v. Department of the Interior
880 F.2d 432 (D.C. Cir. 1989)

WALD, Chief Judge, and SPOTTSWOOD W. ROBINSON III and MIKVA, Circuit Judges:

CERCLA provides that responsible parties may be held liable for "damages for injury to, destruction of, or loss of natural resources, including the reasonable costs of assessing such injury, destruction, or loss resulting from such a release." §107(a)(C), 42 U.S.C. §9607(a)(C). Liability is to "the United States Government and to any State for natural resources within the State or belonging to, managed by, controlled by, or appertaining to such State." §107(f)(1), 42 U.S.C. §9607(f)(1). The Act provides for the designation of federal and state "trustees" who are authorized to assess natural resources damages and press claims for the recovery of such damages, both under CERCLA and under §311 of the Federal Water Pollution Control Act (commonly referred to as the "Clean Water Act"), 33 U.S.C. §1321. CERCLA §107(f)(2), 42 U.S.C. §9607(f)(2).

Congress conferred on the President (who in turn delegated to Interior) the responsibility for promulgating regulations governing the assessment of damages for natural resource injuries resulting from releases of hazardous substances or oil, for the purposes of CERCLA and the Clean Water Act's §311(f)(4)-(5) oil and hazardous substance natural resource damages provisions, 33 U.S.C. §§1321(f)(4)-(5). These regulations originally were required to be in place by December 1982. §301(c), 42 U.S.C. §9651(c). CERCLA prescribed the creation of two types of procedures for conducting natural resources damages assessments. The regulations were to specify (a) "standard procedures for simplified assessments requiring minimal field observation" (the "Type A" rules), and (b) "alternative protocols for conducting assessments in individual cases" (the "Type B" rules). §301(c)(2), 42 U.S.C. §9651(c)(2). Both the Type A and the Type B rules were to "identify the best available procedures to determine such damages." Id. The regulations must be reviewed and revised as appropriate every two years. §301(c)(3), 42 U.S.C. §9651(c)(3). Under the Act, a trustee seeking damages is not required to resort to the Type A or Type B procedures, but CERCLA as amended provides that any assessment performed in accordance with the prescribed procedure is entitled to a rebuttable presumption of accuracy in a proceeding to recover damages from a responsible party. §107(f)(2)(C), 42 U.S.C. §9607(f)(2)(C).

In August 1986, Interior published a final rule containing the Type B regulations for natural resource damage assessments, the subject of this lawsuit. Shortly thereafter, in October 1986, Congress adopted SARA, amending the natural resources damages provisions of CERCLA in several respects. For example, SARA provided that assessments performed by state as well as federal trustees were entitled to a rebuttable presumption, it provided for the recovery of prejudgment interest on damage awards, and it proscribed "double recovery" for natural resources damages. §§107(f)(2)(C), 107(a), 107(f)(1), 42 U.S.C. §§9607(f)(2)(C), 9607(a), 9607(f)(1). SARA also amended §301(c) to require Interior to adopt any necessary conforming amendments to its natural resource damage assessment regulations within six months of the effective date of the amendments, "[n]otwithstanding the failure of the President to promulgate the regulations required under this subsection on the required [December 1982] date." §301(c)(1), 42 U.S.C. §9651(c)(1). . . .

The most significant issue in this case concerns the validity of the regulation providing that damages for despoilment of natural resources shall be "the *lesser of:* restoration or replacement costs; or diminution of use values." 43 C.F.R. §11.35(b)(2) (1987) (emphasis added).

State and Environmental Petitioners challenge Interior's "lesser of" rule, insisting that CERCLA requires damages to be at least sufficient to pay the cost in every case of restoring, replacing or acquiring the equivalent of the damaged resource (hereinafter referred to shorthandedly as "restoration"). Because in some—probably a majority of—cases lost-use-value will be lower than the cost of restoration, Interior's rule will result in damages awards too small to pay for the costs of restoration. Petitioners point to a section of CERCLA providing that recovered damages must be spent only on restoration as evidence that Congress intended restoration cost-based damages to be the norm. As further proof of such a norm, the same section goes on to state that the measure of damages "shall not be limited by" the sums which can be used for restoration. Petitioners maintain that the "shall not be limited by" language clearly establishes restoration costs as a "floor" measure of damages. Petitioners also rely on the legislative history of CERCLA and of SARA, claiming that it reinforces the sense of the text and documents Congress' primary emphasis on restoration of natural resources. In particular, they point to a House report on SARA, insisting that it, together with the other statutory indicators, proves conclusively that Congress intended restoration costs to be a minimum measure of damages in natural resource cases.

Interior defends its rule by arguing that CERCLA does not prescribe any floor for damages but instead leaves to Interior the decision of what the measure of damages will be. DOI acknowledges that all recovered damages must be spent on restoration but argues that the amount recovered from the responsible parties need not be sufficient to complete the job. DOI suggests two alternative meanings of the "shall not be limited by" phrase that do not construe it as a damages floor. Finally, DOI argues that the legislative history, like the statutory text, is ambiguous and that Interior's rule for measuring damages is a reasonable one.

Although our resolution of the dispute submerges us in the minutiae of CERCLA text and legislative materials, we initially stress the enormous practical significance of the "lesser of" rule. A hypothetical example will illustrate the point: imagine a hazardous substance spill that kills a rookery of fur seals and destroys a habitat for seabirds at a sealife reserve. The lost use value of the seals and seabird habitat would be measured by the market value of the fur seals' pelts (which would be approximately $15 each) plus the selling price per acre of land comparable in value to that on which the spoiled bird habitat was located. Even if, as likely, that use value turns out to be far less than the cost of restoring the rookery and seabird habitat, it would nonetheless be the only measure of damages eligible for the presumption of recoverability under the Interior rule.

After examining the language and purpose of CERCLA, as well as its legislative history, we conclude that Interior's "lesser of" rule is directly contrary to the expressed intent of Congress. . . .

Section 107(f)(1) and the Measure of Damages

The strongest linguistic evidence of Congress' intent to establish a distinct preference for restoration costs as the measure of damages is contained in §107(f)(1) of CERCLA. That section states that natural resource damages recovered by a government trustee are "for use only

to restore, replace, or acquire the equivalent of such natural resources."
42 U.S.C. §9607(f)(1). It goes on to state: "The measure of damages in
any action under [§107(a)(C)] shall not be limited by the sums which can
be used to restore or replace such resources." Id.

Limitation on Uses of Recovered Damages

By mandating the use of all damages to restore the injured resources, Congress underscored in §107(f)(1) its paramount restorative
purpose for imposing damages at all. It would be odd indeed for a
Congress so insistent that all damages be spent on restoration to allow
a "lesser" measure of damages than the cost of restoration in the majority
of cases. Only two possible inferences about congressional intent could
explain the anomaly: Either Congress intended trustees to commence
restoration projects only to abandon them for lack of funds, or Congress
expected taxpayers to pick up the rest of the tab. The first theory is
contrary to Congress' intent to effect a "make-whole" remedy of complete restoration, and the second is contrary to a basic purpose of the
CERCLA natural resource damage provisions—that polluters bear the
costs of their polluting activities. It is far more logical to presume that
Congress intended responsible parties to be liable for damages in an
amount sufficient to accomplish its restorative aims. Interior's rule, on
the other hand, assumes that Congress purposely formulated a statutory
scheme that would doom to failure its goals of restoration in a majority
of cases.

In this connection, it should be noted that Interior makes no claim
that a "use value" measure will provide enough money to pay for *any*
of the three uses to which all damages must be assigned: restoration,
replacement *or acquisition of an equivalent resource.* Nor could Interior
make such a claim, because its "lesser of" rule not only calculates use
value quite differently from restoration or replacement cost but it also
fails to link measurement of use value in any way to the cost of acquiring
an equivalent resource. For example, Interior could not possibly maintain that recovering $15 per pelt for the fur seals killed by a hazardous
substance release would enable the purchase of an "equivalent" number
of fur seals.

The "Shall Not Be Limited By" Language

The same section of CERCLA that mandates the expenditures of
all damages on restoration (again a shorthand reference to all three listed
uses of damages) provides that the measure of damages "shall not be
limited by" restoration costs. §107(f)(1), 42 U.S.C. §9607(f)(1). This pro-

vision obviously reflects Congress' apparent concern that its restorative purpose for imposing damages not be construed as making restoration cost a damages ceiling. But the explicit command that damages "shall not be limited by" restoration costs also carries in it an implicit assumption that restoration cost will serve as the basic measure of damages in many if not most CERCLA cases. It would be markedly inconsistent with the restorative thrust of the whole section to limit restoration-based damages, as Interior's rule does, to a minuscule number of cases where restoration is cheaper than paying for lost use. . . .

Settlement Provision

CERCLA's settlement provision provides that a federal trustee may settle a natural resource damages case only "if the potentially responsible party agrees to undertake appropriate actions necessary to protect and restore the natural resources damaged by [the] release or threatened release of hazardous substances." §122(j)(2), 42 U.S.C. §9622(j)(2). Interior's "lesser of" rule is out of step with this settlement provision as well: taken together, they establish a ragged-edged scheme whereby a responsible party can settle only if it pays restoration costs, but those restoration costs will usually be more than it stands to lose by trying the case, if damages are awarded in court under the "lesser of" rule. Normally, a rational polluter would not settle for an amount larger than its potential liability. Thus, we should be reluctant to attribute to Congress a Machiavellian intent to allow Interior to undermine its own settlement provision. The fact that Congress insisted on restoration costs as a floor for settlements shows it must have intended a similar measure of damages to operate in the litigation itself. . . .

CERCLA AND THE COMMON-LAW MEASURE OF DAMAGES

DOI and Industry Intervenors argue that Congress intended that damages under CERCLA would be calculated according to traditional common-law rules. Accepting for the sake of argument the contention that the "lesser of" rule reflects the common law, support for the proposition that Congress adopted common-law damage standards wholesale into CERCLA is slim to nonexistent. DOI contends that Congress meant to adopt traditional methods of damage measurement, "[i]n the absence of clearly expressed Congressional intent to deviate from [the] common law rule." 51 Fed. Reg. at 27,705. The legislative history illustrates, however, that a motivating force behind the CERCLA natural resource damage provisions was Congress' dissatisfaction with the common law. Indeed, one wonders why Congress would have passed a new damage provision at all if it were content with the common law. . . .

CERCLA AND ECONOMIC EFFICIENCY

Alternatively, Interior justifies the "lesser of" rule as being economically efficient. Under DOI's economic efficiency view, making restoration cost the measure of damages would be a waste of money whenever restoration would cost more than the use value of the resource. Its explanation of the proposed rules included the following statement:

> [I]f use value is higher than the cost of restoration or replacement, then it would be more rational for society to be compensated for the cost to restore or replace the lost resource than to be compensated for the lost use. Conversely, if restoration or replacement costs are higher than the value of uses foregone, it is rational for society to compensate individuals for their lost uses rather than the cost to restore or replace the injured natural resource.

50 Fed. Reg. at 52,141. See also 51 Fed. Reg. at 27,704 ("lesser of" rule "promotes a rational allocation of society's assets").

This is nothing more or less than cost-benefit analysis: Interior's rule attempts to optimize social welfare by restoring an injured resource only when the diminution in the resource's value to society is greater in magnitude than the cost of restoring it. And, acknowledgedly, Congress did intend CERCLA's natural resource provisions to operate efficiently. For one thing, the Act requires that the assessment of damages and the restoration of injured resources take place as cost-effectively as possible. Moreover, as we have indicated, there is some suggestion in the legislative history that Congress intended recovery not to encompass restoration cost where restoration is infeasible or where its cost is grossly disproportionate to use value. . . .

The fatal flaw in Interior's approach, however, is that it assumes that natural resources are fungible goods, just like any other, and that the value to society generated by a particular resource can be accurately measured in every case—assumptions that Congress apparently rejected. As the foregoing examination of CERCLA's text, structure and legislative history illustrates, Congress saw restoration as the presumptively correct remedy for injury to natural resources. To say that Congress placed a thumb on the scales in favor of restoration is not to say that it foreswore the goal of efficiency. "Efficiency," standing alone, simply means that the chosen policy will dictate the result that achieves the greatest value to society. Whether a particular choice is efficient depends on *how the various alternatives are valued*. Our reading of CERCLA does not attribute to Congress an irrational dislike of "efficiency"; rather, it suggests that Congress was skeptical of the ability of human beings to measure the true "value" of a natural resource. Indeed, even the common law recognizes that restoration is the proper remedy for injury to property where measurement of damages by some other method will fail to compensate fully for the injury. Congress' refusal to view use value and restoration cost as having equal presumptive legitimacy merely recognizes that natural resources have value that is not readily measured by traditional means. Congress delegated to Interior the job of deciding at what point the presumption of restoration falls away, but its repeated emphasis on the primacy of restoration rejected the underlying premise of Interior's rule, which is that restoration is wasteful if its cost exceeds— by even the slightest amount—the diminution in use value of the injured resource. . . .

The regulations establish a rigid hierarchy of permissible methods for determining "use values," limiting recovery to the price commanded by the resource on the open market, unless the trustee finds that "the market for the resource is not reasonably competitive." 43 C.F.R. §11.83(c)(1). If the trustee makes such a finding, it may "appraise" the market value in accordance with the relevant sections of the "Uniform Appraisal Standards for Federal Land Acquisition," see 43 C.F.R. §11.83(c)(2). Only when neither the market value nor the appraisal method is "appropriate" can other methods of determining use value be employed, see 43 C.F.R. §11.83(d).

Environmental petitioners maintain that Interior's emphasis on market value is an unreasonable interpretation of the statute, under the so-called "second prong" of Chevron U.S.A., Inc. v. Natural Resources Defense Council, Inc., 467 U.S. 837, 845 (1984), and we agree. While it is not irrational to look to market price as *one* factor in determining the use value of a resource, it is unreasonable to view market price as the *exclusive* factor, or even the predominant one. From the bald eagle to the blue whale and snail darter, natural resources have values that are not fully captured by the market system. See Commonwealth of Puerto Rico v. SS Zoe Colocotroni, 628 F.2d 652, 673-74 (lst Cir. 1980), cert. denied, 450 U.S. 912 (1981). DOI's own CERCLA 301 Project Team recognized that "most government resources, particularly resources for which natural resource damages would be sought[,] may often have no market." DOI has failed to explain its departure from this view. Indeed, many of the materials in the record on which DOI relied in developing its rules regarding contingent valuation expressed the same idea; it is the incompleteness of market processes that gives rise to the need for contingent valuation techniques. Courts have long stressed that market prices are not to be used as surrogates for value "when the market value has been too difficult to find, or when its application would result in manifest injustice to owner or public," United States v. Commodities

Trading Corp., 339 U.S. 121, 123 (1950); see United States v. Cors, 337 U.S. 325, 332 (1949) (warning against making "a fetish" of market value "since that may not be the best measure of value in some cases"). As we have previously noted in the context of the "lesser of" rule, market prices are not acceptable as primary measures of the use values of natural resources. See generally Anderson, National Resources Damages, Superfund, and the Courts, 16 Envtl. Aff. 405, 442-46 (1989). We find that DOI erred by establishing "a strong presumption in favor of market price and appraisal methodologies." 51 Fed. Reg. 27,720 (1986). . . .

THE TEN PERCENT DISCOUNT RATE

State and Environmental Petitioners next challenge Interior's decision to use a discount rate to calculate the present value of an expected future injury. Petitioners challenge both the decision to discount a future injury for present value and Interior's choice of a ten percent rate. See 43 C.F.R. §11.84(e). As petitioners point to no CERCLA provision addressing the precise question in issue, their burden is to show that the imposition of the discount rate was unreasonable or contrary to the statutory purpose.

Petitioners' central argument appears to be that discounting for present value will by its nature "severely undervalue[]" long-term injury to natural resources. But this argument is misplaced: the point of the CERCLA natural resource damage provisions is to make polluters pay the costs of restoring or replacing damaged resources or acquiring their equivalent. If a release of hazardous substances will necessitate a restoration project costing x dollars five years from now, CERCLA requires that the responsible party pay a sum sufficient to cover those costs *at that time*. Due to the inherent time-value of money (coupled with the effects of inflation), an amount significantly less than x dollars invested today will yield CERCLA's required x dollars at the time the restoration costs are incurred five years from now. Using the proper interest rate as a discount rate, it is possible to calculate how much money must be collected today to equal x dollars in the future. The danger of undervaluation arises from an underestimate of the *future* cost of restoration or from an incorrect discount rate, not from the basic process of discounting itself.

State and Environmental Petitioners' two additional concerns are therefore closer to the target. First, they argue that there is uncertainty as to the correct discount rate. Second, they argue that natural resources will tend to become scarcer over time and hence more valuable; consequently, there is too much uncertainty as to the future cost of restoring or replacing damaged resources to permit an accurate discount rate.

As to the first point, a discount rate by its nature involves a predictive judgment about future rates of interest. Apart from the truism that the proper discount rate is always a matter of uncertainty, petitioners have given us no reason to substitute our judgment for that of Interior and of the Office of Management and Budget, whose circular provided the ten percent figure chosen. 43 C.F.R. §11.84(e)(2). While DOI's explanation of its decision to adopt the Office of Management and Budget figure certainly was terse, we decline to step in and undermine what is first and foremost a policy choice.

As to the second point, we agree that Interior should take into account the possibility that the value of a particular resource or the cost of particular restoration project will increase over time, as a function of scarcity, faster than the rise in the general price level. If such an increase can be reasonably foreseen, it should be reflected in the estimate of the *future* cost of a restoration project; if the estimated future cost is reasonably accurate, then the application of a discount rate to arrive at a *present* value cannot itself be objectionable. Interior's regulations provide that uncertainties as to the cost of future restoration are to be considered in the assessment process and factored into the analysis. So long as the trustee performing the assessment takes into account—as the regulations provide it should—the possibility that restoration costs might rise faster than the general price level, State and Environmental Petitioners' arguments against the use of a discount rate are without merit.

NOTES AND QUESTIONS

1. In a companion case, Colorado v. Department of the Interior, 880 F.2d 481 (D.C. Cir. 1989), the Department of the Interior's Type A regulations for assessing natural resource damages from small-scale hazardous substance releases (through simplified assessments requiring minimal field observation) were remanded for essentially the same reasons the Type B regulations were struck down.

2. Why did the Department of the Interior promulgate the lesser-of rule in the first place? If the regulations had been upheld, what impact would they have had on the size of the liability faced by PRPs? How would this have affected incentives for PRPs to take precautions to prevent future releases of hazardous substances?

3. The Department of the Interior argued that Congress had acquiesced in Interior's lesser-of rule because in 1986, shortly after the regulation had been promulgated, Congress had amended the natural resources damages provision of CERCLA and had not expressly repudiated it. In response to the acquiescence-by-reenactment argument, the D.C. Circuit noted that a committee report on SARA "stated unequivocally that damages recoverable under CERCLA 'include both' restoration cost and lost use value for the period between the spill and the completion

of restoration." 880 F.2d at 458. The court concluded that "Congress apparently declined to amend the pertinent language of §107(f)(1) precisely because it deemed the language to have been clear all along," noting that no member of Congress "even *proposed* a change in the relevant statutory language." Id. The court also expressed its antipathy for acquiescence-by-reenactment arguments, noting that Congress should not have to "reiterate an already clear statutory command in order to fend off an impermissible interpretation" and citing the general principle that repeals by implication are disfavored. Id.

4. In State of Ohio v. Department of the Interior the court held that Congress had expressed "a distinct preference for restoration costs" as the measure of recovery for natural resource damages. Suppose restoration of damaged natural resources is simply infeasible or prohibitively costly in relation to the use value of the resources. In such cases should the measure of damages be altered in any way?

5. The state and environmental petitioners in State of Ohio v. Department of the Interior also challenged a provision in the DOI regulations that permits PRPs to perform damage assessments. They compared it to "appointing the defendant in a tort suit as a special master to decide on the proper amount of damages." Do you agree with this criticism? Why do you think the regulations included this provision? The court upheld this portion of the DOI regulations.

6. In order to determine whether a hazardous substance release caused injury to a particular natural resource, the Department of the Interior's regulations established a set of "acceptance criteria." These provide that to prove causation the natural resource trustee must show that

> (1) the injury alleged to have occurred is a "commonly documented" response to releases of such hazardous substances; (2) the hazardous substance is "known to cause" such an injury in field studies; (3) the hazardous substance is "known to cause" such an injury in controlled experiments; and (4) the injury can be measured by practical techniques and has been "adequately documented in scientific literature." [43 C.F.R. §11.62(f)(2).]

The state and environmental petitioners argued that these acceptance criteria were "extraordinarily burdensome" because they require "virtually absolute scientific proof" of causation. They argued that these criteria were inconsistent with CERCLA because they require greater evidence of causation than the common law requires. Do you agree? The court noted that the legislative history of CERCLA reveals "Congress' general concern for liberalizing the standards of the common law," but it concluded that "CERCLA is ambiguous on this point," and it upheld the acceptance criteria.

7. There are several difficulties inherent in attempts to quantify

intangible values. See Cross, Natural Resource Damage Valuation, 42 Vand. L. Rev. 269 (1989). One technique for quantifying the seemingly unquantifiable is the use of "contingent valuation," a process that attempts to determine the value people place on intangible resources by asking how much they would be willing to pay for them. DOI's natural resource damage assessment regulations permit the use of contingent valuation techniques in situations where damaged resources or their equivalents are not traded in a market. The regulations authorized contingent valuation to determine use value, option values (value of reserving the option to use a resource in the future), and existence values (value of the knowledge that the resource exists and will continue to exist in a certain state). Industry petitioners challenged DOI's authorization of contingent valuation techniques on the grounds that they are inconsistent with common law principles for assessing damage and are not the "best available procedure." They argued that contingent valuation methodology would permit recovery for speculative injuries, which is at odds with common law principles, and that individuals would exaggerate their valuation of resources when asked hypothetical questions about their willingness to pay. The court rejected these arguments, noting that DOI had recognized the need to perform contingent valuations carefully and professionally and that it had rejected the use of "willingness-to-accept" as a contingent valuation measure for fear that it would yield disproportionately high dollar assessments. 880 F.2d at 476-477 n.82.

8. Discount rates are used in cost-benefit analyses in order to enable costs and benefits that accrue over time to be compared by expressing them in terms of net present value. The higher the discount rate, the smaller will be the present value of damages (or costs) that will be incurred in the future. Use of a high discount rate will tend to discourage investments that require expenditures today but whose benefits accrue over time. The Office of Management and Budget was criticized severely when it heavily discounted the value of preventing deaths from exposure to asbestos because asbestos-related diseases have a long latency period. By applying a 10 percent discount rate over a period of 40 years, OMB argued that each asbestos death prevented was worth only $22,094.93 (based on a $1 million valuation for each life). Subcomm. on Oversight and Investigations, House Comm. on Energy and Commerce, 99th Cong., 1st Sess., Comm. Print 99-V, EPA's Asbestos Regulations 78-79 (Oct. 1985). Economists have a very difficult time dealing with issues of intergenerational equity that arise when the risks and benefits of public investments are distributed unevenly over time. For example, if one looks sufficiently far into the future and uses a sufficiently high discount rate, discounting may reveal that it is "worth very little" for society to take action now to prevent the entire destruction of the human race hundreds of years from now. What impact will the use of a 10 percent discount

rate for natural resource damages assessments have on the amount of damages assessed? What difference would a lower discount rate, say, 4 percent, make?

In Corrosion Proof Fittings v. EPA, 947 F.2d 1201 (5th Cir. 1991), the Fifth Circuit approved EPA's use of a 3 percent discount rate in performing a cost-benefit analysis of an asbestos ban under TSCA, noting in a footnote that "[b]ecause historically the real rate of interest has tended to vary between 2% and 4%, this figure was not inaccurate." 947 F.2d at 1218 n.19. The court indicated, however, that EPA must discount future benefits even when they are measured in human lives in order to avoid "skew[ing] the results to discount only costs," 947 F.2d at 1218.

9. The belated appearance and subsequent remand of Interior's natural resource damages regulations deterred some trustees from filing actions for recovery of such damages. Courts have held that the failure of EPA and Interior to promulgate the regulations on time tolled the running of the three-year statute of limitations on such claims. Idaho v. Howmet Turbine Component Co., 814 F.2d 1376 (9th Cir. 1987). In October 1991 a settlement agreement providing $1 billion to restore natural resources damaged by the *Exxon Valdez* oil spill was approved. Prior to that settlement, $50 million had been recovered in two years of settlements of natural resource damages claims for other releases. See Campbell, Economic Valuation of Injury to Natural Resources, 6 Nat. Resources & Envt. 28 (Winter 1992).

10. Interior has now proposed new regulations in response to the decision in State of Ohio v. Department of the Interior, 56 Fed. Reg. 19,756 (1991). The proposal uses the term "compensable value" to embrace "all of the public economic values associated with an injured resource, including use values and nonuse values such as option, existence and bequest values." 56 Fed. Reg. at 19,760. Thus, the concept of "compensable value" recognizes that resources are valued for many different reasons, not all of which are reflected accurately in market prices.

11. Even with damage assessment regulations in place, assessments of natural resource damages are likely to be expensive. Federal and state trustees spent $108 million performing assessments of damage caused by the *Exxon Valdez* spill. Campbell, above, at 56.

Because only governmental entities can recover natural resource damages, the impact of section 107(f) of CERCLA will depend on the vigor with which federal and state trustees pursue claims for such damages. In 1990 the National Oceanic and Atmospheric Administration (NOAA), which serves as the trustee for coastal resources, filed several lawsuits against companies that discharged PCBs and DDT into Los Angeles Harbor. NOAA Files Suit Against Eight Companies for Natural Resource Damage in California, 21 Env. Rep. 362 (1990). Although NOAA reached a $12 million settlement with Los Angeles County sanitation districts in a similar suit, its actions against several chemical companies initially were dismissed. A district judge held that NOAA must prove that the defendants' discharges were a "substantially contributing factor" in damaging the resources. United States and California v. Montrose Chemical Corp., No. 90-3122 (C.D. Cal. 1991). The decision, which implies that NOAA must demonstrate which pollutant from which source caused damage to each resource, applied a higher standard of proof of causation than in previous cases involving natural resource damages where courts required only a showing that defendants' discharges were a "contributing factor." The government has filed a new complaint in an attempt to meet the "substantially contributing factor" test. Justice Department Files Revised Complaint in California Natural Resource Damage Case, 22 Env. Rep. 1189 (1991).

E. REMEDIATION OF ENVIRONMENTAL CONTAMINATION UNDER CERCLA AND RCRA

1. The CERCLA Cleanup Process

Having explored CERCLA's liability provisions, we now examine the complicated process it establishes for cleaning up contaminated sites. To finance government-directed cleanup efforts, CERCLA creates a revolving trust fund (dubbed "Superfund"). As authorized by CERCLA section 115, the president has delegated primary responsibility for carrying out the Superfund program to EPA. Executive Order 12,580 (Jan. 23, 1987).

CERCLA requires the establishment of a National Priorities List (NPL) of sites presenting the greatest dangers to public health, welfare, or the environment, based on evaluation through a hazard ranking system (HRS). §105. A National Contingency Plan (NCP) governs response actions. CERCLA authorizes two kinds of responses: (1) short-term removal actions designed to alleviate immediate dangers to public health or the environment and (2) longer-term remedial actions designed to provide a permanent remedy to the maximum extent practicable. §104. CERCLA gives the government two major avenues for ensuring that hazardous substance releases are cleaned up. The government can order potentially responsible parties to perform the cleanup under section 106, or the government may perform the cleanup itself pursuant to section 104 and then sue responsible parties for reimbursement under section 107. EPA more frequently relies on actions brought under sections 104 and 107 than on section 106.

Superfund has been mired in controversy almost since its inception. The Reagan Administration's initial hostility to the program, which played a leading role in the EPA scandal that forced the resignation of EPA Administrator Anne Gorsuch Burford in 1983, was among the many factors that contributed to the program's painfully slow start. As one of the principal congressional authors of CERCLA described the situation,

> Congress set ambitious goals for the Superfund program; essentially Congress wanted a specific list of abandoned toxic waste sites across the country cleaned up. Notwithstanding the optimistic language in the statute, no one expected a perfect agency response free of the false starts and delays normal for any bureaucratic undertaking. But, Congress did expect an all out effort to attack the problem aggressively with all the resources provided by the legislation. Instead, Congress got long explanations of technical and legal problems, and after five years and over $1.6 billion, EPA could not identify a single site it had completely cleaned up. [Florio, Foreword— Superfund and Hazardous Wastes, 6 Stan. Envtl. L.J. 1, 5 (1987).]

The dump site cleanup problem also was far broader and more difficult than envisioned by Congress when CERCLA was enacted. In the first five years of the program, the average response cost per site increased from $2.5 million to $8.3 million. S. Rep. No. 11, 99th Cong., 1st Sess. 2 (1985). As noted previously, the Office of Technology Assessment (OTA) in 1985 estimated that 10,000 sites eventually might need to be placed on the National Priorities List and that it could take 50 years and more than $100 billion to clean them up. OTA, Superfund Strategy 3 (April 1985). Thus, when the Superfund reauthorization process began, there was widespread agreement that the program would have to be expanded substantially.

After a three-year legislative struggle, Congress in 1986 amended CERCLA with the Superfund Amendments and Reauthorization Act (SARA or 1986 Amendments), which expanded the size of the fund to $8.5 billion while imposing stringent new requirements to address problems in EPA's implementation of the program. Among SARA's significant new provisions were the establishment of detailed cleanup standards (§121(d)), provisions to expand the involvement of states and citizen groups in the decisionmaking process (§§121(f) and 117), new settlement procedures (§122), and the establishment of mandatory schedules for federal facility compliance (§120).

Since SARA's enactment, the number of NPL sites has continued to grow rapidly. By July 1987, 802 sites had been listed and another 149 sites had been proposed for listing. EPA, Progress Toward Implementing Superfund Fiscal Year 1987, at 31 (April 1989). NPL sites are located in every state. The states with the most NPL sites in 1987 were New Jersey with 100, Pennsylvania with 80, Michigan with 69, and New York with 67. By April 1989 the number of NPL sites had increased to 890 final sites and 273 proposed sites, for a total of 1,163. EPA Adds 101 Sites in 33 States to Superfund, 20 Env. Rep. 2569 (1989). As of January 1990, 1,010 sites were listed on the NPL and another 209 sites had been proposed for inclusion, for a total of 1,219 listed and proposed sites. More than 100 additional sites (including 23 federal facilities) were added to the NPL in August 1990, raising the total to 1,187 listed sites. As of July 1991 a total of 1,211 final or proposed sites were listed on the NPL, including 116 sites at federal facilities. 56 Fed. Reg. 35,840 (1991).

SARA has not quieted the controversy that surrounds the Superfund program. In the years since the 1986 Amendments were enacted, EPA has continued to receive harsh criticism from many sources. Environmentalists charge that EPA has not aggressively implemented its authorities and that Superfund cleanups have eschewed more permanent solutions in favor of short-term remedies. The Office of Technology Assessment reports that Superfund cleanups remain "largely ineffective and inefficient," OTA, Are We Cleaning Up? (June 1988), a charge echoed by a coalition of waste treatment firms and environmental groups in their report Right Train, Wrong Track: Failed Leadership in the Superfund Program (June 1988). Members of Congress have been equally harsh in their assessment of EPA's implementation of CERCLA. Congressional reports have criticized EPA for failing to aggressively pursue private party cleanups and cost recovery actions and for failing to comply with some of the provisions of the 1986 Amendments. Comm. on Appropriations, U.S. House of Representatives, Environmental Protection Agency's Management of the Superfund Program (Dec. 1988); F. Lautenberg and D. Durenberger, Cleaning Up the Nation's Cleanup Program (1989). While these critics believe the basic structure of CERCLA to be sound, parties made liable by CERCLA disagree. Some insurance and chemical industry officials have been campaigning to replace CERCLA's liability scheme with a no-fault public works program funded by a flat fee on commercial and industrial insurance. Greenberg, Needed: A Fee on Commercial and Industrial Insurance to Finance Hazardous Waste Cleanup, 19 Envtl. L. Rep. 10254 (1989). CED, Who Should Be Liable? (1989).

In response to criticisms of EPA's implementation of the program, EPA Administrator William Reilly conducted a 90-day management review of the CERCLA program in 1989. Reilly, Management Review of the Superfund Program (June 1989). As a result of this review, Administrator Reilly pledged to pursue a more aggressive "enforcement first" policy to implement CERCLA. Yet when he appeared before a House oversight committee in October 1991, members of Congress charged that little progress had been made in the intervening two years. As of October 1991 only 34 sites had been removed from the NPL despite the expenditure of $9 billion. While remedial action had begun at more than

600 sites, renewed pledges from EPA to speed up the 10-year-long cleanup process were dismissed as "the same ideas that EPA committed to back in 1989." Lautenberg, Dingell Blast Superfund Studies, 22 Env. Rep. 1531 (1991).

Before considering in more detail the problems with Superfund program, it is important to understand the basic structure of the CERCLA cleanup process. As Figure 3.10 indicates, the process has many steps that can take considerable time to complete. After citizens or state authorities notify EPA of possible environmental problems at a site, EPA performs a preliminary assessment to determine if the site warrants further investigation. Sites that do are then inspected, and some are more formally evaluated through a Hazard Ranking System (HRS) that assigns a numerical score. Sites that receive a sufficiently high score are then placed on the National Priorities List (NPL) for Superfund cleanup following notice and an opportunity for public comment. The Superfund cleanup process then requires the performance of a remedial investigation and feasibility study to provide a detailed determination of the extent of contamination and alternative approaches to remediate it. EPA then issues a Record of Decision (ROD) outlining what action will be taken to clean up the site. The cleanup then proceeds through remedial design and remedial action until the cleanup is completed.

The administrative costs of the CERCLA cleanup process have been high. A study by the Rand Corporation found that of the $2.6 billion actually paid out by EPA through September 1988, only $1.6 billion actually went for remedial investigations and response actions at sites. J. Acton, Understanding Superfund: A Progress Report (1989). The other 38 percent of Superfund spending went for overhead expenses:

FIGURE 3.10

Average Time Between Principal Steps in the Superfund Process

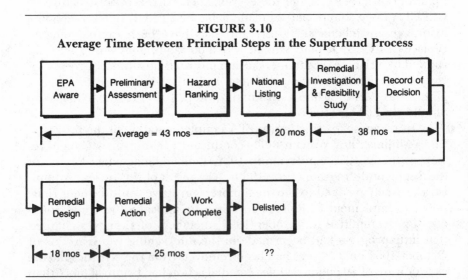

administration, management, laboratory, and litigation costs. The study found that EPA had recovered $230 million in past expenditures through settlements at 328 sites, and that it expected to seek to recover another $824 million at 366 sites. EPA had written off $483 million in spending at another 920 sites for which it had determined not to seek cost recovery. The report offers the following possible explanations for why cost recoveries and actual spending on cleanups have been so low: "reluctant leadership at the outset of the program; the need for time to elapse before certain sites 'mature' to the state at which major expenditures are warranted; the program's emphasis on liability and cost recovery; and program rigidities and its efficiency of operation." Id. at viii.

The Rand report finds that, on average, eight years have elapsed between the time a site came to EPA's attention and the time remedial work began. The report notes that substantial delays can occur if legal challenges are brought by some of the parties while the process is still under way. As a result, courts have resisted efforts by PRPs to create avenues for pre-enforcement review of EPA actions. Congress has provided that judicial review of response actions under section 104 and abatement orders under section 106 may occur only in certain circumstances. See §113(h).

In an effort to speed up the Superfund cleanup process, SARA imposed goals, timetables, and deadlines for various EPA activities. EPA was directed to complete preliminary assessments for the 4,700 sites in the EPA data system by January 1, 1988 and to complete all site inspections for these facilities by January 1, 1989. SARA directed EPA to commence 275 Remedial Investigation/Feasibility Studies (RI/FSs) and 175 new remedial actions within three years of enactment and an additional 200 of each in the following two years. EPA's record in meeting these other SARA deadlines has been mixed.

A report released by EPA's inspector general in May 1991 stated that EPA had misled Congress by overstating its progress in meeting SARA's deadlines. When the deadline of October 17, 1989 expired, EPA had announced that it had commenced 178 remedial actions, three more than required by the SARA deadline. But an audit by the inspector general found that 28 of those sites should not have been counted. EPA Overstated 1989 Site Cleanup Count, Misled Congress, Inspector General Finds, 22 Env. Rep. 220 (1991). Moreover, the audit found that 40 percent of the sites on which remedial action was counted as having commenced were among the least contaminated sites on the NPL. EPA denied the inspector general's charges.

Former EPA general counsel E. Donald Elliot agrees that the CERCLA cleanup process is too slow and that too much money is spent on administrative expenses rather than on actual cleanup. Elliot, Superfund: EPA Success, National Debacle?, 6 Nat. Resources & Envt. 11 (Winter 1992). Elliot notes that while it takes an average of ten years to clean up a site, only three years of that time is spent on actual cleanup. He maintains that a simplified, standardized approach to remedy selection should replace the extraordinarily complicated process currently used. Id. at 48-49.

Has Superfund Worked?

In recent years, the Superfund program has come to follow an almost predictable pattern: receipt of vigorous criticism from all sides, followed by pledges of reform from EPA and subsequent disappointment. For example, in January 1989 the House Appropriations Committee harshly criticized EPA's administration of the Superfund program, concluding that EPA's failure to use its enforcement authorities more aggressively to pursue private cleanups and cost recoveries has "destroyed" the Superfund program's enforcement credibility. House Appropriations Committee Knocks EPA, Says Superfund Program "Simply Not Working," 20 Env. Rep. 2056 (1989). A report by Clean Sites, Inc., a coalition of industry, environmental, and government officials, recommended in January 1989 that the new administration increase Superfund enforcement actions against recalcitrant PRPs. The report recommended that EPA file more cost recovery actions earlier in the process when government funds have been used for response actions and that EPA should pursue nonsettling parties aggressively after settlements are reached and penalize nonsettlors by making them pay more in subsequent litigation. Clean Sites, Inc., Making Superfund Work (1989). The Rand Corporation report found that EPA had issued a total of 653 administrative orders from the inception of the Superfund program through September 30, 1988. Of these, 347 involved NPL sites and 306 involved non-NPL sites. EPA had made a total of 139 judicial enforcement referrals for enforcement of administrative orders under section 106 (including 26 in fiscal year 1988) and 236 for cost recovery under section 107 (including 59 in fiscal year 1988). Acton, Understanding Superfund: A Progress Report 41 (1989).

Following a report coauthored by two senators that was harshly critical of EPA's administration of Superfund (Lautenberg and Durenberger, Cleaning Up the Nation's Cleanup Program (1989)), EPA Administrator William Reilly announced "a new long-term strategy for Superfund" on June 13, 1989. Reilly, A Management Review of the Superfund Program i (1989). Reilly characterized this strategy as an "enforcement-first policy" with the objective "to get the parties responsible for the contamination to do the majority of cleanups up front." EPA Chief Pledges to Force Polluters to Pay Rather Than Rely on Trust Fund for Cleanups, 21 Envtl. Rep. 428 (1989). Specifically, the strategy involved (1) increasing the use of section 106 administrative orders to require private parties to conduct cleanups, (2) establishing strict time limits for negotiating settlements to be followed by enforcement actions if negotiations are not successfully completed, and (3) adding an additional 500 persons and $75 million to the Superfund enforcement arsenal.

Nearly two years later, the Superfund program again came under fire for excessive administrative costs when it was disclosed that nearly one-third of the $200 million spent by the federal government to clean up waste sites was actually being spent on administrative expenses for private contractors. Weisskopf, Administrative Costs Drain "Superfund," Wash. Post, June 19, 1991, at A1. While this result should hardly seem surprising in light of the earlier Rand report's finding that 38 percent of Superfund expenditures went for overhead expenses, EPA nevertheless responded to this report by appointing a task force to conduct a review of the program. As a result of that review, EPA announced yet another batch of new reforms designed to triple the number of cleanups by 1993 and to reduce administrative costs to 20 percent of expenditures. Weisskopf, EPA Plans to Cut Payments to Superfund Contractors, Wash. Post, Oct. 3, 1991, at A23. Congressional oversight committees responded with harsh criticism of the new proposals.

The persistent criticism of EPA's perceived poor performance in completing dump site cleanups has been eagerly embraced by those members of the regulated community who want to abolish CERCLA's strict, joint, and several liability scheme. A major insurance company has launched a national ad campaign advocating that CERCLA be replaced by a public works program that is not based on fault. Others with far less obvious financial interests at stake have joined in the chorus of criticism. The editor of Science magazine deems CERCLA a "toxic law" and decries "a wasteful and inept program." Koshland, Toxic Chemicals and Toxic Laws, 253 Science 949 (1991). A former EPA general counsel argues that Superfund "threatens to become a major debacle, one that could discredit environmental protection programs in the United States for years to come," Elliot, Superfund: EPA Success, National Debacle?, 6 Nat. Resources & Envt. 11 (Winter 1992). Even a respected environmentalist who is vice president for the World Resources Institute observes that the Superfund cleanup program "is threatening to become an exorbitant boondoggle." Mathews, Superfund Boondoggle, Wash. Post, Sept. 6, 1991, at A21.

These criticisms suggest that the Superfund program suffers from both overly high expectations and chronic underperformance. This tension in large part reflects society's difficulty in coming to grips with making hard choices between competing goals, particularly when the tradeoffs involve explosive issues of human health or seemingly irreplaceable natural resources and when the degree of uncertainty is high. As many observers have noted, there is a fundamental tension between

CERCLA's multiple goals of achieving rapid cleanup of dump sites, making responsible parties pay for such cleanups, assuring long-term protection of public health and the environment, and deterring mismanagement of hazardous substances in the future. The hard choices society must make are reflected in the difficulty both CERCLA and RCRA have in answering the "how clean is clean" question, to which we will turn after briefly examining another expensive cleanup program, EPA's RCRA corrective action authorities.

2. RCRA Corrective Action Requirements

When Congress amended RCRA in 1984, among the most significant new amendments were requirements that corrective action be undertaken by facilities in the RCRA program. EPA's initial RCRA regulations imposed relatively minimal requirements on facilities engaged in the treatment, storage, or disposal of hazardous waste (TSDs). Recognizing that it would take some time to establish permanent standards governing TSDs, Congress authorized EPA to allow existing facilities to continue in operation as "interim status" facilities. Pending the development of final regulations governing the operation of TSDs, existing facilities could be granted interim status by doing very little beyond simply notifying EPA of their existence. As EPA repeatedly missed deadlines for promulgating regulations governing TSDs under RCRA, many facilities operating under interim status continued to cause severe environmental contamination. The prospect of permitted RCRA facilities' becoming future Superfund sites spurred Congress to add corrective action requirements to RCRA when it was reauthorized in 1984. See H.R. Rep. No. 198, 98th Cong., 1st Sess. 20, reprinted in 1984 U.S. Code Cong. & Admin. News 5576, 5579, 5620.

Congress mandated that EPA require all facilities seeking RCRA permits to undertake corrective action to clean up any prior contamination at their sites. Section 3004(u) of RCRA provides that permits issued after enactment of the 1984 Amendments "shall require corrective action for all releases of hazardous waste or constituents from any solid waste management unit at a treatment, storage, or disposal facility seeking a permit under this subchapter, regardless of the time at which waste was placed in such unit." 42 U.S.C. §6924(u). If corrective action cannot be completed prior to issuance of a permit, the permit must contain "schedules of compliance for such corrective action" and "assurances of financial responsibility for completing such corrective action."

Although section 3004(u) requires corrective action only for facilities applying for RCRA permits, Congress also gave EPA authority to require corrective action by interim status facilities that chose to close rather than apply for a final RCRA permit. Congress added section

3008(h) to RCRA, which gives EPA the authority to issue corrective action orders against interim status facilities if EPA "determines that there is or has been a release of hazardous waste into the environment" from such a facility. Section 3008(h) also authorizes EPA to file civil suits against interim status facilities to require corrective action. Facilities may be required to take corrective action even beyond the boundaries of their facility unless they can demonstrate to EPA's satisfaction that they have been "unable to obtain the necessary permission to undertake such action," despite their best efforts. §3004(v).

In a wide-ranging Federal Register notice describing its interpretation of the 1984 Amendments (known as the "First Codification Rule" because it amended EPA's regulations to codify changes required by the 1984 Amendments), EPA interpreted its new RCRA corrective action authorities broadly. Noting that section 3044(u) did not restrict corrective action to releases from *hazardous waste* management units, EPA stated that contamination from *any* waste management unit on the property where a facility seeking a RCRA permit was located would require corrective action. 50 Fed. Reg. 28,702 (1985). EPA adopted a regulation that required a facility seeking a TSD permit to "institute corrective action . . . for all releases of hazardous waste or constituents from any solid waste management unit at the facility, regardless of the time at which waste was placed in such unit." 40 C.F.R. §264.101 (1986). EPA interpreted section 3004(u) to require corrective action on "all contiguous property under the owner or operator's control." 50 Fed. Reg. at 28,712. Industry representatives challenged this interpretation in court, arguing that it was an unreasonably broad construction of the term "facility" that would require massive cleanups, particularly when facilities seeking a RCRA permit were located on large properties.

In United Technologies Corp. v. EPA, 821 F.2d 714 (D.C. Cir. 1987), the D.C. Circuit upheld EPA's interpretation. Noting that Congress sought to ensure that facilities receiving RCRA permits would not be contributing to groundwater contamination from inactive units not covered by permit requirements, the court concluded: "Section 3004(u), in essence, creates the broad duty to take corrective action as a quid pro quo to obtaining a permit. Given this purpose, it appears that the EPA's construction of 'facility' is fully consistent with congressional intent."*

---

*Compare this interpretation of the term "facility" with EPA's adoption of a far narrower interpretation of the term in section 3004(o) of RCRA. In Mobil Oil Corp. v. EPA, 871 F.2d 149 (D.C. Cir. 1989), the court upheld EPA's decision that the term "facility" in section 3004(o) applied only to an individual waste management unit and not to an entire waste management complex. This interpretation expanded the disposal options available for waste governed by section 3004(o)'s minimum technology requirements. The court offered a functional justification

RCRA's broad corrective action requirements create powerful incentives for avoidance behavior by the regulated community. Richard Stoll advises companies to "go for the smallest and cleanest 'facility' " if you must own a RCRA TSD. He recommends locating the TSD on the smallest piece of property that is not contiguous to other property owned by the owner-operator. Stoll, Coping with the RCRA Hazardous Waste System: A Few Practical Points for Fun and Profit, 1 Envtl. Hazards 6 (May 1989). As Stoll explains:

> [A]ssume a manufacturing plant has property on a 1000 acre parcel on which there is not now a TSD facility. If the company placed a TSD facility on 100 square feet anywhere within the parcel, the *entire 1000 acres* would be subject to corrective action.
>
> Depending upon what you know (or suspect) about the 1000 acres, the wisest business move might be to buy a (very) small nearby piece of property—but not contiguous to the existing 1000 acres—on which to locate the TSD. This new property could be thoroughly assessed before purchase, and the potential for corrective action disasters could be greatly reduced. [Id. at 9 (emphasis in original).]

In *United Technologies* industry petitioners argued that if EPA's interpretation were upheld, EPA could intrude into their production processes and areas of their property not used for waste management. They argued that EPA could require a company even to clean up contamination that could not be linked to a solid waste management unit. EPA rejected this argument, noting that the Agency would not interpret section 3004(u) to require corrective action for a spill from a truck traveling through a facility because it would not constitute a release from a solid waste management unit. 50 Fed. Reg. 28,702, 28,713-28,714.

In December 1987 EPA adopted a Second Codification Rule, 52 Fed. Reg. 45,788 (1987), that added further important details to the Agency's interpretation of the 1984 Amendments. In the Rule EPA stated that solid wastes temporarily exempt from subtitle C regulation under the Bevill-Bentsen amendments, section 3001(b)(3)(A) (including wastes from "the extraction, beneficiation and processing of ores and minerals"), were nonetheless subject to RCRA's corrective action requirements. This interpretation was upheld by the D.C. Circuit in American Iron & Steel Institute v. EPA, 886 F.2d 390 (D.C. Cir. 1989).

While EPA's broad interpretation of its new corrective action authorities has the potential to produce significant environmental cleanup, a major obstacle to their implementation is the lack of comprehensive

---

for this apparent inconsistency with its *United Technologies* decision, stating that "[i]f the agency believes that the legislative purposes will best be satisfied by construing the term to mean different things in different contexts, then it may act upon the premise." 871 F.2d at 153.

information about the extent of contamination of soil and groundwater at existing RCRA facilities. EPA is requiring facilities applying for RCRA permits to provide it with information about the extent of such contamination. However, extensive noncompliance with EPA's previous groundwater monitoring requirements coupled with hydrogeological uncertainties will make assessment extremely difficult. In 1987 a report by the General Accounting Office found that EPA had been slow to implement a corrective action program. GAO, Hazardous Waste: Corrective Action Cleanups Will Take Years to Complete (1987). Another GAO report in 1988 predicted that

> [t]he RCRA corrective action program could take until at least the year 2025 to complete and may be as large as the Superfund cleanup program, which EPA estimates may require cleanup of about 2,500 sites at an estimated cost of up to $22.7 billion. In the meantime, the longer EPA waits to actually implement corrective action at RCRA facilities, the greater the risk will become that the contamination at the leaking facilities will worsen and that a number of these facilities will have to be cleaned up under Superfund. In fact, EPA estimates that about 800 RCRA facilities may have to be transferred to the Superfund program for cleanup. [GAO, New Approach Needed to Manage the Resource Conservation and Recovery Act 28 (July 1988).]

OMB prevented EPA from issuing proposed regulations implementing the RCRA corrective action requirements for nearly two years. OMB maintained that sweeping corrective action standards would be too costly and that EPA should focus primarily on groundwater contamination at a facility's boundary, not at the contamination's source. When finally allowed to issue proposed regulations in July 1990, EPA proposed a corrective action program strikingly similar to the CERCLA cleanup process, but with its own set of acronyms. Facilities will have to perform a RCRA Facility Assessment (RFA) to get an initial assessment of conditions at the facility. If there is evidence of prior releases, facilities will have to perform a RCRA Facility Investigation (RFI) to characterize the sources of contamination found. This is to be followed by a Corrective Measures Study (CMS) to identify remedies that then will be incorporated into new or modified orders or permits. OMB has required EPA to perform a detailed cost-benefit analysis before adopting final regulations. As a result, it may be several years before final regulations are adopted. Nevertheless, EPA plans to operate in the interim as though the proposed rule has been adopted.

3.   How Clean Is "Clean"?: CERCLA Cleanup Standards

An issue that has bedeviled efforts to clean up environmental contamination can be expressed in the form of the seemingly simple question, how clean is clean? CERCLA initially did not address how extensive cleanup of contaminated dump sites had to be. EPA's regulations ducked this thorny issue as the Agency made cleanup decisions on a case-by-case basis. This virtually guaranteed that the extent of cleanup would vary from site to site. In 1985 an influential report by the Office of Technology Assessment summarized seven alternative approaches for answering this pesky question. The seven approaches included: (1) continued use of current ad hoc practices, (2) site-specific risk assessments, (3) national goals for residual contamination, (4) cleanup to background or "pristine" levels, (5) technology-based standards such as best available technology or best engineering judgment, (6) cost-benefit approaches, and (7) site classification approaches that would determine cleanup levels based on present and projected future uses of a site. OTA, Superfund Strategy 113 (April 1985).

Of these seven alternatives, OTA concluded that the "site classification" approach "would be the most nationally cost-effective approach" for Superfund cleanups. Under this approach, sites where cleanups were deemed to be more valuable because of their present or projected future uses could be restored, while others could be written off by restricting public access to them. Although OTA's report was influential in the debate that culminated in the enactment of SARA, Congress chose to leave EPA with substantial discretion in making cleanup decisions while requiring the application of federal and state environmental standards and criteria to cleanup decisions. This section considers CERCLA's cleanup standards and EPA's experience implementing them.

As noted above, section 104 of CERCLA authorizes EPA to undertake two types of cleanup actions: removal actions and remedial actions. Removals are short-term responses to deal with the immediate dangers at a site, while remedial actions are designed to ensure that the site will not pose any risks to public health or the environment in the future. Removal actions can be undertaken based on a preliminary assessment, while remedial actions are undertaken only after an extensive remedial investigation and feasibility study (RI/FS) is performed to evaluate the long-term threat posed by the hazardous substances and the feasibility of alternative cleanup measures.

EPA has enjoyed broad discretion in determining how extensive remedial actions need to be at Superfund sites. CERCLA initially required only that EPA select an "appropriate" remedial action that, to the extent practicable, complied with the National Contingency Plan and that provided "a cost-effective response which provides a balance between the need for protection of public health and welfare and the environment . . . and the availability of amounts from the Fund," §104(c)(4). EPA ultimately adopted regulations requiring RI/FSs to evaluate the applicability and relevance of other environmental standards to cleanup decisions and generally to follow such standards in taking remedial action—with several exceptions, such as where compliance with the standards would be technically impracticable.

The enactment of SARA in 1986 added section 121 to CERCLA, which addresses the "how clean is clean" question for the selection of remedial actions under sections 104 and 106. This provision has been credited with (or accused of) increasing the costs of the average CERCLA cleanup at least threefold. D. W. Stever, Law of Chemical Regulation and Hazardous Waste §6.06[2][d][iii][B] (1991 ed.). Yet Congress chose to leave EPA with substantial discretion in determining cleanup levels, even though it required consideration of other environmental standards. EPA is still required to select "appropriate remedial actions" that are in accordance with the NCP "to the extent practicable" and that "provide for cost-effective response." §121(a). Congress wanted Superfund cleanups to involve measures that would reduce hazards permanently rather than simply shift the contaminants from one landfill to another. Thus, section 121(b) establishes the following general rule:

> Remedial actions in which treatment [that] permanently and significantly reduces the volume, toxicity or mobility of the hazardous substances, pollutants and contaminants is a principal element, are to be preferred over remedial actions not involving such treatment. The offsite transport and disposal of hazardous substances or contaminated materials without such treatment should be the least favored alternative remedial action where practicable treatment technologies are available.

In determining the appropriate remedial action, EPA is directed to assess alternative treatment technologies "that, in whole or in part, will result in a permanent and significant decrease in the toxicity, mobility, or volume of the hazardous substance, pollutant or contaminant." Section 121(b) requires that EPA "select a remedial action that is protective of human health and the environment, that is cost-effective, and that utilizes permanent solutions and alternative treatment technologies to the maximum extent practicable."

Section 121(d) of CERCLA specifies the degree of cleanup to be required based on consideration of other environmental standards. It provides that remedial actions under CERCLA must assure "protection of human health and the environment" and "be relevant and appropriate under the circumstances," §121(d)(1). They also must provide a level of cleanup that attains that required by any "legally applicable or relevant and appropriate . . . standard, requirement, criteri[on], or limitation under any Federal environmental law" and "any promulgated standard, requirement, criteri[on], or limitation under a State environmental or facility siting law that is more stringent than any Federal" provision when identified by the state in a timely manner. §121(d)(2). These are commonly referred to as ARARs.

There are several exceptions to the requirement that remedial actions achieve cleanup levels consistent with those required by other environmental standards. These include cases in which (1) the remedial action is only one part of a larger remedial action that ultimately will comply with the relevant standards, (2) compliance would increase risks to human health and the environment, (3) compliance is technically impracticable, (4) alternative action will attain an equivalent standard of performance, (5) state standards have not been consistently applied in similar circumstances, or (6) the costs of compliance would be disproportionate in terms of environmental benefit when weighed against the availability of funds to respond to other sites. §121(d)(4). EPA is required to give states opportunities for involvement in selecting remedial actions, and states are authorized to challenge in federal district court decisions not to require compliance with applicable or relevant and appropriate standards. If EPA's decision not to require remedial actions to conform with such standards is upheld, a state nonetheless may require that more extensive cleanup be undertaken if the state agrees to pay for its additional cost. §121(f).

EPA's actual performance in conforming remedial actions to §121(d) has been severely criticized by a number of reports that reviewed records of decision (RODs) at NPL sites. RODs document EPA's reasons for selecting particular cleanup remedies at these sites. The Office of Technology Assessment examined 10 case studies chosen from more than 100 RODs. OTA concluded that these case studies "illustrate in concrete ways some disturbing trends . . . that compromise the ultimate protection of human health and the environment." OTA, Are We Cleaning Up? Ten Superfund Case Studies (June 1988). OTA found that the quality of information to support the selection of remedies in RODs often is poor. "It is not uncommon to have a multimillion-dollar cleanup decision made without any technical data to support it, either from the technical literature or from tests done on site material." Id. at 10.

OTA found that many RODs that claim to select permanent remedies actually involve the use of impermanent or untested technologies. "Impermanent remedies, which provide less protection than permanent ones and do not assuredly meet cleanup goals, are often selected purely because they are cheaper in the short run," OTA concluded. Yet "in the long run [such remedies] are very likely to be more expensive." The OTA study noted that EPA has tolerated levels of residual excess lifetime cancer risk ranging from 1 in 10,000 to 1 in 10 million. Compromises in levels of health protection often are made to reduce cleanup costs. Permanent technologies to eliminate the source of the risks may be eschewed in favor of measures to reduce exposure to the risk "such as capping a site, or institutional controls, such as deed restrictions that have uncertain future implementation." Id. at 14. EPA often cites as reasons for not choosing a permanent technology the fact that sites either have too little contamination to justify such a remedy or too much contamination to make such a remedy practicable. OTA also found that the amendments added by SARA had not eliminated the practice of shifting wastes from one NPL site to another potential NPL site.

When it issued a revised NCP in March 1990, EPA established a new policy of considering nine factors to screen alternatives for remedial action. These include: overall protection of health and the environment; compliance with ARARs; long-term permanence and effectiveness; reduction of toxicity, mobility, or volume; short-term effectiveness; cost, ease of implementation; state acceptance; and community acceptance. 40 C.F.R. §300.430(e), (f). After initial screening, EPA then assesses two criteria: whether a remedial alternative provides overall protection of health and the environment and whether it is consistent with an ARAR. The Agency then balances the five other factors (excepting state and community acceptance), giving greater weight to permanence and reduction of toxicity, mobility, or volume. Finally, EPA considers whether to modify the selection on the basis of state or community acceptance. The use of ARARs in selecting a remedy is criticized in Temkin, Cleaning Up ARARs: Reflections from the Field, 6 Nat. Resources & Envt. 18 (Winter 1992).

PROBLEM EXERCISE: HOW CLEAN IS CLEAN?

Suppose that the Scientific Disposal Services site discussed in the previous problem exercise has been listed on the National Priorities List for cleanup under Superfund. You represent a party potentially responsible for response costs.

Question One.   Consider the seven alternative approaches to the "how clean is clean?" question that OTA identified: (1) continued use of current ad hoc practices, (2) site-specific risk assessments, (3) national goals for residual contamination, (4) cleanup to background or "pristine" levels, (5) technology-based standards such as best available technology or best engineering judgment, (6) cost-benefit approaches, and (7) site classification approaches that would determine cleanup levels based on present and projected future uses of a site. Which approach would you favor for the Scientific Disposal site? What advantages and disadvantages can you identify for the various approaches? OTA concluded that the site classification approach "would be the most nationally cost-effective approach" for Superfund cleanups. Do you agree?

Question Two.   Suppose a new technology is proposed for use in remedial action at the Scientific Disposal Services site. Although it has not been used previously at any other NPL site with similar characteristics, the proponents of the technology argue that it will result in permanent detoxification of the waste. EPA doubts that the untried technology will be as effective as its proponents claim. However, the vendors of the technology have convinced both the PRPs and the community groups active at the site that their claims of permanent detoxification are correct. Despite the advice of EPA's technical experts, EPA selects the new technology because of the intense pressure from parties involved in the site. Did EPA act properly? Is it legal for EPA to give in to community pressure and adopt a remedy that is contrary to its experts' best professional judgment? See §121(b)(2).

Question Three. Suppose that hazardous wastes at the Scientific Disposal Services site have seeped into an aquifer that is a source of drinking water for a small community. EPA determines that although it is not technologically impossible to clean up the aquifer, it would be prohibitively expensive to do so. Because there is doubt concerning whether or not the source of the contamination can ever be effectively contained on a permanent basis, EPA is unwilling to invest the enormous resources that would be required to clean up existing contamination in the aquifer. Thus the ROD selects as a remedial action the permanent closing of the town's wells and provision of an alternative drinking water supply that will be trucked into the town daily. Has EPA acted legally under CERCLA? See §§121(b), (d). What must EPA do to justify its actions? See §121(d)(4). What continuing obligation, if any, does EPA have with respect to the site? See §121(c).

NOTES AND QUESTIONS

1. Do you agree with the criticisms by OTA and others of EPA's approach to the "how clean is clean" issue? How important do you think it is for remedial actions to achieve levels of cleanup that are consistent from site to site? How should EPA deal with the tension between CERCLA's preferences for permanent remedies and treatment and its cost-effectiveness requirement?

2. Some observers have attributed the controversy over EPA's implementation of Superfund to a lack of consensus over the proper goals of CERCLA and inherent tension between CERCLA's goal of promptly and effectively cleaning up hazardous substance releases and its goal of shifting cleanup costs to responsible parties. According to consultants for an industry coalition on Superfund:

> [B]ecause the general goal of cleanup may be simply unachievable either from a technological or a cost standpoint, it is difficult to articulate national and workable cleanup objectives. Even after Section 121 of SARA addressed the "how clean is clean" issue, the exact level of required cleanup has not been specified by Congress, the EPA or the courts. Also, this country has now had wide experience with the articulation of unachievable

goals in environmental legislation, a form of environmental brinksmanship. There is an emerging consensus among policy analysts that the concept has outlived its early utility as a means of building public support for environmental programs and for effectively achieving the basic objectives of any program of pollution reduction, but the idea retains considerable currency in some quarters. Section 121 of SARA adopts technology-forcing cleanup standards, but does not define a level of expected technology development and discharge reduction goals comparable to definitions in the Clean Air and Water Acts. To complicate matters further, Section 121 embodies the same uncertainty about the relevance of economic analysis in setting and achieving standards of other environmental programs. [Coalition on Superfund, Coalition on Superfund Research Report 3-23-24 (1989).]

Do you agree that Superfund's goals are too ambitious? How, if at all, should they be modified? Does EPA's difficulty in finding a satisfactory answer to the "how clean is clean" problem stem from an inherent tension between CERCLA's preference for remedies that are both permanent and cost-effective?

3. In October 1989 OTA reported that about three-quarters of all Superfund cleanups are unlikely to be successful over the long term and that EPA is spending far too much money on administrative and transaction costs and too little on reducing immediate risks at NPL sites. OTA, Coming Clean: Superfund Problems Can Be Solved (Oct. 1989). OTA also concluded that Congress's failure to define more precisely what it means by "permanence" in CERCLA's preference for permanent remedies has allowed EPA too much flexibility to pursue impermanent remedies, which are often selected in order to reach settlements when PRPs or the government are unwilling to spend more money on remedial action. PRPs are estimated to have saved about 50 percent ($1 billion) in ultimate cleanup costs in fiscal year 1988 due to EPA's willingness to agree to impermanent remedies. OTA now estimates that it will cost $500 billion over the next 50 years to clean up all Superfund sites. EPA has criticized some of the data in the OTA report.

4. The OTA study recommended that EPA eliminate its policy of allowing potentially responsible parties (PRPs) to perform remedial investigation/feasibility studies (RI/FSs) because PRPs downplay the extent of contamination and are less likely to recommend the use of permanent cleanup technologies. OTA found that in fiscal year 1988 only 14 percent of RI/FSs performed by PRPs recommended the use of permanent cleanup technologies, compared to 44 percent for studies performed by EPA. EPA ultimately decided to bar PRPs from performing risk assessments, a decision challenged in a lawsuit brought by the Chemical Manufacturer's Association. In December 1991 EPA agreed to settle the lawsuit by seeking public comment on its decision, which it agreed to review. A former EPA general counsel argues that PRPs should not

perform *either* RAs or FSs. Elliot, Superfund: EPA Success, National Debacle?, 6 Nat. Resources & Envt. 11, 49 (Winter 1992).

5. When EPA revised the National Contingency Plan (NCP) that governs Superfund cleanups, one issue the Agency confronted was the extent to which Superfund cleanups must be consistent with standards established under the Safe Drinking Water Act (SDWA). The SDWA requires the establishment of two sets of standards: maximum contaminant level goals (MCLGs), which must be "set at the level at which no known or anticipated adverse effects on the health of persons occur and which allows an adequate margin of safety," and maximum contaminant levels (MCLs), which are to be set as close to the MCLGs as is feasible. Some argue that because MCLGs are set at zero for a number of pollutants, in many cases it would be technically impossible for Superfund cleanups to attain MCLGs. Others maintain that because MCLGs are the health-based standard, while MCLs are limited by considerations of feasibility, MCLGs should at least be considered as the goals to be achieved by Superfund cleanups where possible. With which view do you agree? A study by EPA of 19 NPL sites concluded that existing technology for cleaning contaminated groundwater by pumping it out, treating it, and returning it to the aquifer cannot ensure attainment of health-based goals such as the MCLGs. Memorandum from Jonathan Cannon, Acting Assistant Administrator for Solid Waste and Emergency Response (Oct. 18, 1989). EPA ultimately decided to require that MCLGs be used when they are set at levels other than zero but that MCLs be used if the MCLG is set at zero.

6. Concerned that CERCLA cleanup actions were simply requiring that waste be dug up from one leaking site and trucked to another, Congress restricted the offsite transfer of contaminated soil. Section 122(d)(3) of CERCLA provides that offsite transfers that are the result of removals or remedial actions shall only be made to facilities operating in accordance with RCRA's TSD and permit regulations and certified not to be releasing any hazardous substances to ground or surface waters.

A Note on the Limitations of Groundwater Remediation Technologies

One source of disenchantment with the Superfund cleanup program is the realization that the long-term effectiveness of existing groundwater remediation technology remains highly uncertain. The typical technology for cleaning up contaminated groundwater is to pump it out of the ground, treat it, and reinject it. Pumping and treating is the remedy used in more than two-thirds of all Superfund RODs. Officials remain quite reluctant to mandate that cleanups achieve stringent levels of environmental performance because the results achieved by pump-and-treat technology have given rise to concerns about their long-term effectiveness. An EPA study of 19 sites where groundwater has been subject to continuous pumping and treating for up to a decade found that although considerable quantities of contaminants had been removed, there had been "little success in reducing concentration to target levels." Abelson, Inefficient Remediation of Ground-Water Pollution, 250 Science 733 (1990).

A study by the National Research Council, Ground Water and Soil Contamination: Toward Compatible Science, Policy, and Public Perception (1990), found that it might take 100 to 200 years of pumping and treating to restore water quality to acceptable levels in certain aquifers. Given the enormous quantities of chemicals that have seeped into the earth, comprehensive remediation of groundwater may be a virtually hopeless task. Philip Abelson points out that a large portion of the more than 14 billion pounds of perchloroethylene and 12 billion pounds of trichloroethylene that were used by dry cleaners and machine shops between 1945 and 1984 may be contaminating groundwater. Noting that just one barrel of TCE could contaminate 10 billion gallons of water at the level of 5 ppb (the MCL under the Safe Drinking Water Act), Abelson suggests that the "present practical solution for water supplies may be to treat water at the time it enters the supply system," rather than cleaning it up in advance. Abelson, Inefficient Remediation of Ground-Water Pollution, 250 Science 733 (1990).

F. THE FUTURE OF WASTE MANAGEMENT

Since 1976, when RCRA was enacted, EPA has acknowledged that federal policy should encourage waste reduction as the most desirable approach to the waste management problem. Waste reduction involves measures to reduce the volume and toxicity of waste through changes in the production processes of waste generators. 41 Fed. Reg. 35,050 (1976). EPA identified recycling and waste treatment as the next most desirable options, respectively. Land disposal, the predominant form of waste disposal, was deemed the least desirable approach because of its continuing potential for environmental damage.

As federal policy has regulated land disposal with increasing stringency, this option is rapidly increasing in cost. RCRA's minimum technology standards for subtitle C facilities and the new subtitle D standards for municipal dumps will reduce the supply, and increase the cost, of land disposal facilities. The RCRA land ban now provides explicit, technology-based incentives for treatment of hazardous wastes. By restricting the use of land disposal facilities, the land ban and regulations that raise the costs of land disposal, along with the fear of CERCLA liability, have substantially increased incentives for waste reduction and recycling. But some waste will remain to be disposed, and there is growing concern that the nation's rapidly shrinking disposal capacity will not be sufficient to meet the nation's future disposal needs. The next sections examine the search for disposal alternatives and efforts to stimulate greater reductions in the volume and toxicity of the waste stream.

1. The Search for Disposal Alternatives

Waste reduction initiatives are becoming more important as awareness of the environmental hazards of current disposal practices increases. The choices faced by policymakers searching for new waste disposal alternatives are increasingly stark. Existing landfills are nearly full, while the establishment of new landfills is extraordinarily difficult, if not impossible, due not only to more stringent environmental regulations, but also to "not-in-my-backyard" opposition to the siting of new facilities. While some argue that incineration is a partial "answer," municipalities are discovering that construction and siting of incinerators is difficult and expensive and that incinerators have their own environmental risks including huge quantities of ash, which is itself waste.

Many believe the nation is rapidly approaching a "solid waste crisis" as landfill capacity shrinks in the face of expanding waste streams. EPA has estimated that 80 percent of existing landfills will close within the next 20 years as older landfills reach capacity or are phased out due to the cost of meeting new environmental requirements. OTA, Facing America's Trash: What Next for Municipal Solid Waste? 1 (June 1989).

Pressures to export waste are meeting with unprecedented resistance as the environmental hazards of waste disposal become more widely recognized. In 1988 a garbage-filled barge became a national symbol of the waste disposal problem as it traveled 6,000 miles over 5 months searching for a place to dispose of 3,186 tons of waste from Islip, New York. Six states and three countries refused to accept the cargo, which eventually was returned to New York and incinerated. Later that same year, the *Karin B.*, a ship carrying toxic waste from Italy, had to retrieve its cargo after the Nigerian government threatened to arrest the owners for dumping its cargo in Koko, Nigeria. The ship wandered the sea for months and was refused by France, Britain, Spain, West Germany, and the Netherlands because of its toxic cargo. See Greenhouse, Toxic Waste Boomerang: Ciao Italy!, N.Y. Times, Sept. 3, 1988, at A4. The waste subsequently disappeared without explanation, the ship was sold, and the new owners quickly changed the vessel's name. Philadelphia thought it had solved its ash disposal problem when it signed a contract to dispose of the city's ash in Panama. Panama subsequently canceled the contract, and two more ships began plying the seas seeking a dump site. Baltimore's "poo poo choo choo," a trainload of 12,000 tons of human sewage sludge, traveled through several southern states in a fruitless search for a landfill to call home before the waste ultimately was returned to Baltimore for disposal.

Many in the waste management industry viewed ocean incineration as a promising means for expanding hazardous waste disposal capacity while avoiding difficult siting issues. However, opposition from environmental and community groups located near ports where waste would be transported has led EPA to defer indefinitely the issuance of regulations that would have established permitting procedures for ocean incineration off the coast of the United States. The prospects for ocean incineration subsequently received a near-fatal blow when the London Dumping Convention, an international treaty that governs ocean dumping, was amended to phase out incineration of hazardous waste at sea by 1994. We will explore the international dimensions of the waste disposal problem in more detail in Chapter 9.

By requiring that waste disposal be conducted closer to the point of waste generation, prohibitions on waste exports and ocean incineration make it easier to monitor disposal practices and to place responsibility for mismanagement of wastes, but they also may increase public exposure to hazards generated by waste disposal. While states have broad police powers to regulate waste disposal, courts have recognized legal limits on local efforts to pass the disposal buck through regulations inspired by local opposition to siting.

A. COMMERCE CLAUSE LIMITATIONS

Banning exports is an exercise in self-discipline. Banning imports seems much more attractive, especially when a state is receiving much more waste than it is shipping. For instance, Emelle, Alabama is the home of one of the nation's largest commercial hazardous waste facilities. In 1989, 17 percent of the landfilled hazardous waste in the country was shipped to Emelle. Owned and operated by Chemical Waste Management, the Emelle facility received 341,000 tons of out-of-state hazardous waste in 1985, and the amount increased to 788,000 tons in 1989. In 1989, over 90 percent of all the tonnage landfilled at Emelle was from outside Alabama. See Hunt v. Chemical Waste Management, Inc., 584 So. 2d 1367 (1991), cert. granted, 60 U.S.L.W. 3208 (1992).

The situation for nonhazardous waste is similar. For example, residents of Center Point, Indiana have been monitoring and documenting a pronounced shift in the usage of their municipal sanitary landfill. As recently as 1988, their landfill received approximately two truckloads of local trash daily. By 1991, it was receiving 20 to 30 semitrailers carrying out-of-state garbage. In the first 3 months of 1991, 75 percent of the trash coming into the Center Point landfill was from New York, New Jersey, and the Philadelphia area. Overall, the National Solid Wastes Management Association estimates that in 1989, 15 million tons of non-hazardous waste was shipped between states, more than 50 percent of it from New Jersey and New York. Gutfeld, Smelly Imports, Wall St. J., April 26, 1991, at A1.

These disparities are likely to increase as the supply of available disposal space dwindles. New Jersey, for instance, has only 11 open sanitary landfills, down from over 300 at the beginning of the decade. See id. Accordingly, states that still have storage or disposal capacity are understandably concerned with preserving it for their own needs.

In the face of these circumstances, some states have attempted to close their borders to out-of-state wastes of various kinds. Their strategies face significant constitutional obstacles. The Constitution vests in the Congress the power "to regulate commerce . . . among the several states." Early on, the Supreme Court interpreted the Commerce Clause to imply a limitation on the states' power to regulate interstate commerce even when the Congress had not itself acted. The Clause, as it is sometimes said, speaks with a negative voice ("states may not regulate interstate commerce—at least in certain ways") as well as in a positive voice.

The Court's treatment of the Clause's negative voice is quite intricate. In the following decision, it had the opportunity to determine how the Commerce Clause bore on an early attempt by one state to restrict the importation of out-of-state waste.

Philadelphia v. New Jersey
437 U.S. 617 (1978)

MR. JUSTICE STEWART delivered the opinion of the Court.

A New Jersey law prohibits the importation of most "solid or liquid waste which originated or was collected outside the territorial limits of the State. . . ." In this case we are required to decide whether this statutory prohibition violates the Commerce Clause of the United States Constitution.

I

The statutory provision in question is ch. 363 of 1973 N.J. Laws, which took effect in early 1974. In pertinent part it provides:

No person shall bring into this State any solid or liquid waste which originated or was collected outside the territorial limits of the State, except garbage to be fed to swine in the State of New Jersey, until the commissioner [of the State Department of Environmental Protection] shall determine that such action can be permitted without endangering the public health, safety and welfare and has promulgated regulations permitting and regulating the treatment and disposal of such waste in this State. N.J. Stat. Ann. 13:1I-10 (West Supp. 1978).

[Private landfill owners in New Jersey, as well as several out-of-state cities, including Philadelphia, all of whom had disposal contracts with New Jersey landfills, sued in state court. The New Jersey Supreme Court upheld the statute as a legitimate health and safety statute that did not economically discriminate against interstate commerce and only slightly burdened it. The United States Supreme Court first remanded the case to the New Jersey court, instructing it to consider whether the New Jersey statute had been preempted by the newly enacted Resources Conservation and Recovery Act of 1976. The New Jersey court found no preemption. The plaintiffs appealed once again. After agreeing that no preemption had occurred, the Supreme Court proceeded to the Commerce Clause issues.]

II

[First, the Court held that out-of-state wastes are "commerce" within the meaning of the Commerce Clause. Cases upholding quarantine laws that prohibited the importation of, for example, disease-carrying animal carcasses, sometimes stated that these items were "not legitimate subjects of trade and commerce." The Court explained that in so stating, such cases were "stating [a] conclusion, not the starting point of [their] reasoning."]

III

A

Although the Constitution gives Congress the power to regulate commerce among the States, many subjects of potential federal regulation under that power inevitably escape congressional attention "because of their local character and their number and diversity." South Carolina State Highway Dept. v. Barnwell Bros., Inc., 303 U.S. 177, 185. In the absence of federal legislation, these subjects are open to control by the States so long as they act within the restraints imposed by the Commerce Clause itself. See Raymond Motor Transportation, Inc. v. Rice, 434 U.S. 429, 440. The bounds of these restraints appear nowhere in the words of the Commerce Clause, but have emerged gradually in the decisions of this Court giving effect to its basic purpose. That broad purpose was well expressed by Mr. Justice Jackson in his opinion for the Court in H. P. Hood & Sons, Inc. v. DuMond, 336 U.S. 525, 537-538:

> This principle that our economic unit is the Nation, which alone has the gamut of powers necessary to control of the economy, including the vital power of erecting customs barriers against foreign competition, has as its corollary that the states are not separable economic units. As the Court said in Baldwin v. Seelig, 294 U.S. [511], 527, "what is ultimate is the principle that one state in its dealings with another may not place itself in a position of economic isolation."

The opinions of the Court through the years have reflected an alertness to the evils of "economic isolation" and protectionism, while at the same time recognizing that incidental burdens on interstate commerce may be unavoidable when a State legislates to safeguard the health and safety of its people. Thus, where simple economic protectionism is effected by state legislation, a virtually per se rule of invalidity has been erected. See, e.g., H. P. Hood & Sons, Inc. v. DuMond, supra; Toomer v. Witsell, 334 U.S. 385, 403-406; Baldwin v. G.A.F. Seelig, Inc., supra; Buck v. Kuykendall, 267 U.S. 307, 315-316. The clearest example of such legislation is a law that overtly blocks the flow of interstate commerce at a State's borders. Cf. Welton v. Missouri, 91 U.S. 275. But where other legislative objectives are credibly advanced and there is no patent discrimination against interstate trade, the Court has adopted a much more flexible approach, the general contours of which were outlined in Pike v. Bruce Church, Inc., 397 U.S. 137, 142:

> Where the statute regulates evenhandedly to effectuate a legitimate local public interest, and its effects on interstate commerce are only incidental, it will be upheld unless the burden imposed on such commerce is clearly excessive in relation to the putative local benefits . . . If a legitimate local purpose is found, then the question becomes one of degree. And the extent of the burden that will be tolerated will of course depend on the nature of the local interest involved, and on whether it could be promoted as well with a lesser impact on interstate activities.

See also Raymond Motor Transportation, Inc. v. Rice, supra, at 441-442; Hunt v. Washington Apple Advertising Comm'n, 432 U.S. 333, 352-354; Great A&P Tea Co. v. Cottrell, 424 U.S. 366, 371-372.

The crucial inquiry, therefore, must be directed to determining whether ch. 363 is basically a protectionist measure, or whether it can fairly be viewed as a law directed to legitimate local concerns, with effects upon interstate commerce that are only incidental.

B

The purpose of ch. 363 is set out in the statute itself as follows:

The Legislature finds and determines that . . . the volume of solid and liquid waste continues to rapidly increase, that the treatment and disposal of these wastes continues to pose an even greater threat to the quality of the environment of New Jersey, that the available and appropriate land fill sites within the State are being diminished, that the environment continues to be threatened by the treatment and disposal of waste which originated or was collected outside the State, and that the public health, safety and welfare require that the treatment and disposal within this State of all wastes generated outside of the State be prohibited.

The New Jersey Supreme Court accepted this statement of the state legislature's purpose. The state court additionally found that New Jersey's existing landfill sites will be exhausted within a few years; that to go on using these sites or to develop new ones will take a heavy environmental toll, both from pollution and from loss of scarce open lands; that new techniques to divert waste from landfills to other methods of disposal and resource recovery processes are under development, but that these changes will require time; and finally, that "the extension of the lifespan of existing landfills, resulting from the exclusion of out-of-state waste, may be of crucial importance in preventing further virgin wetlands or other undeveloped lands from being devoted to landfill purposes." 68 N.J., at 460-465, 348 A.2d, at 509-512. Based on these findings, the court concluded that ch. 363 was designed to protect, not the State's economy, but its environment, and that its substantial benefits outweigh its "slight" burden on interstate commerce. Id., at 471-478, 348 A.2d, at 515-519.

The appellants strenuously contend that ch. 363, "while outwardly cloaked 'in the currently fashionable garb of environmental protection,' . . . is actually no more than a legislative effort to suppress competition and stabilize the cost of solid waste disposal for New Jersey residents. . . ." They cite passages of legislative history suggesting that the problem addressed by ch. 363 is primarily financial: Stemming the flow of out-of-state waste into certain landfill sites will extend their lives, thus delaying the day when New Jersey cities must transport their waste to more distant and expensive sites.

The appellees, on the other hand, deny that ch. 363 was motivated by financial concerns or economic protectionism. In the words of their brief, "[n]o New Jersey commercial interests stand to gain advantage over competitors from outside the state as a result of the ban on dumping out-of-state waste." Noting that New Jersey landfill operators are among the plaintiffs, the appellee's brief argues that "[t]he complaint is not that

New Jersey has forged an economic preference for its own commercial interests, but rather that it has denied a small group of its entrepreneurs an economic opportunity to traffic in waste in order to protect the health, safety and welfare of the citizenry at large."

This dispute about ultimate legislative purpose need not be resolved, because its resolution would not be relevant to the constitutional issue to be decided in this case. Contrary to the evident assumption of the state court and the parties, the evil of protectionism can reside in legislative means as well as legislative ends. Thus, it does not matter whether the ultimate aim of ch. 363 is to reduce the waste disposal costs of New Jersey residents or to save remaining open lands from pollution, for we assume New Jersey has every right to protect its residents' pocketbooks as well as their environment. And it may be assumed as well that New Jersey may pursue those ends by slowing the flow of *all* waste into the State's remaining landfills, even though interstate commerce may incidentally be affected. But whatever New Jersey's ultimate purpose, it may not be accomplished by discriminating against articles of commerce coming from outside the State unless there is some reason, apart from their origin, to treat them differently. Both on its face and in its plain effect, ch. 363 violates this principle of nondiscrimination.

The Court has consistently found parochial legislation of this kind to be constitutionally invalid, whether the ultimate aim of the legislation was to assure a steady supply of milk by erecting barriers to allegedly ruinous outside competition, Baldwin v. G.A.F. Seelig, Inc., 294 U.S., at 522-524; or to create jobs by keeping industry within the State, Foster-Fountain Packing Co. v. Haydel, 278 U.S. 1, 10; Johnson v. Haydel, 278 U.S. 16; Toomer v. Witsell, 334 U.S., at 403-404; or to preserve the State's financial resources from depletion by fencing out indigent immigrants, Edwards v. California, 314 U.S. 160, 173-174. In each of these cases, a presumably legitimate goal was sought to be achieved by the illegitimate means of isolating the State from the national economy.

Also relevant here are the Court's decisions holding that a State may not accord its own inhabitants a preferred right of access over consumers in other States to natural resources located within its borders. West v. Kansas Natural Gas Co., 221 U.S. 229; Pennsylvania v. West Virginia, 262 U.S. 553. These cases stand for the basic principle that a "State is without power to prevent privately owned articles of trade from being shipped and sold in interstate commerce on the ground that they are required to satisfy local demands or because they are needed by the people of the State." Foster-Fountain Packing Co. v. Haydel, supra, at 10.

The New Jersey law at issue in this case falls squarely within the area that the Commerce Clause puts off limits to state regulation. On its face it imposes on out-of-state commercial interests the full burden of conserving the State's remaining landfill space. It is true that in our previous cases the scarce natural resource was itself the article of commerce, whereas here the scarce resource and the article of commerce are distinct. But that difference is without consequence. In both instances, the State has overtly moved to slow or freeze the flow of commerce for protectionist reasons. It does not matter that the State has shut the article of commerce inside the State in one case and outside the State in the other. What is crucial is the attempt by one State to isolate itself from a problem common to many by erecting a barrier against the movement of interstate trade.

The appellees argue that not all laws which facially discriminate against out-of-state commerce are forbidden protectionist regulations. In particular, they point to quarantine laws, which this Court has repeatedly upheld even though they appear to single out interstate commerce for special treatment. See Baldwin v. G.A.F. Seelig, Inc., supra, at 525; Bowman v. Chicago & Northwestern R. Co., 125 U.S., at 489. In the appellees' view, ch. 363 is analogous to such health-protective measures, since it reduces the exposure of New Jersey residents to the allegedly harmful effects of landfill sites.

It is true that certain quarantine laws have not been considered forbidden protectionist measures, even though they were directed against out-of-state commerce. See Asbell v. Kansas, 209 U.S. 251; Reid v. Colorado, 187 U.S. 137; Bowman v. Chicago & Northwestern R. Co., supra, at 489. But those quarantine laws banned the importation of articles such as diseased livestock that required destruction as soon as possible because their very movement risked contagion and other evils. Those laws thus did not discriminate against interstate commerce as such, but simply prevented traffic in noxious articles, whatever their origin.

The New Jersey statute is not such a quarantine law. There has been no claim here that the very movement of waste into or through New Jersey endangers health, or that waste must be disposed of as soon and as close to its point of generation as possible. The harms caused by waste are said to arise after its disposal in landfill sites, and at that point, as New Jersey concedes, there is no basis to distinguish out-of-state waste from domestic waste. If one is inherently harmful, so is the other. Yet New Jersey has banned the former while leaving its landfill sites open to the latter. The New Jersey law blocks the importation of waste in an obvious effort to saddle those outside the State with the entire burden of slowing the flow of refuse into New Jersey's remaining landfill sites. That legislative effort is clearly impermissible under the Commerce Clause of the Constitution.

Today, cities in Pennsylvania and New York find it expedient or necessary to send their waste into New Jersey for disposal, and New Jersey claims the right to close its borders to such traffic. Tomorrow, cities in New Jersey may find it expedient or necessary to send their waste into Pennsylvania or New York for disposal, and those States might then claim the right to close their borders. The Commerce Clause will protect New Jersey in the future, just as it protects her neighbors now, from efforts by one State to isolate itself in the stream of interstate commerce from a problem shared by all. The judgment is Reversed.

MR. JUSTICE REHNQUIST, with whom THE CHIEF JUSTICE joins, dissenting.

A growing problem in our Nation is the sanitary treatment and disposal of solid waste. For many years, solid waste was incinerated. Because of the significant environmental problems attendant on incineration, however, this method of solid waste disposal has declined in use in many localities, including New Jersey. "Sanitary" landfills have replaced incineration as the principal method of disposing of solid waste. In ch. 363 of the 1973 N.J. Laws, the State of New Jersey legislatively recognized the unfortunate fact that landfills also present extremely serious health and safety problems. First, in New Jersey, "virtually all sanitary landfills can be expected to produce leachate, a noxious and highly polluted liquid which is seldom visible and frequently pollutes . . . ground and surface waters." The natural decomposition process which occurs in landfills also produces large quantities of methane and thereby presents a significant explosion hazard. Landfills can also generate "health hazards caused by rodents, fires and scavenger birds" and, "needless to say, do not help New Jersey's aesthetic appearance nor New Jersey's noise or water or air pollution problems."

The health and safety hazards associated with landfills present appellees with a currently unsolvable dilemma. Other, hopefully safer, methods of disposing of solid wastes are still in the development stage and cannot presently be used. But appellees obviously cannot completely stop the tide of solid waste that its citizens will produce in the interim. For the moment, therefore, appellees must continue to use sanitary landfills to dispose of New Jersey's own solid waste despite the critical environmental problems thereby created.

The question presented in this case is whether New Jersey must also continue to receive and dispose of solid waste from neighboring States, even though these will inexorably increase the health problems discussed above. The Court answers this question in the affirmative. New Jersey must either prohibit *all* landfill operations, leaving itself to cast about for a presently nonexistent solution to the serious problem of disposing of the waste generated within its own borders, or it must accept waste from every portion of the United States, thereby multiplying the health and safety problems which would result if it dealt only with such wastes generated within the State. Because past precedents establish that the Commerce Clause does not present appellees with such a Hobson's choice, I dissent.

The Court recognizes that States can prohibit the importation of items "which, on account of their existing condition, would bring in and spread disease, pestilence, and death, such as rags or other substances infected with the germs of yellow fever or the virus of smallpox, or cattle or meat or other provisions that are diseased or decayed, or otherwise, from their condition and quality, unfit for human use or consumption." Bowman v. Chicago & Northwestern R. Co., 125 U.S. 465, 489 (1888). See Baldwin v. G.A.F. Seelig, Inc., 294 U.S. 511, 525 (1935); Sligh v. Kirkwood, 237 U.S. 52, 59-60 (1915); Asbell v. Kansas, 209 U.S. 251 (1908); Railroad Co. v. Husen, 95 U.S. 465, 472 (1878). As the Court points out, such "quarantine laws have not been considered forbidden protectionist measures, *even though they were directed against out-of-state commerce.*"

In my opinion, these cases are dispositive of the present one. Under them, New Jersey may require germ-infected rags or diseased meat to be disposed of as best as possible within the State, but at the same time prohibit the *importation* of such items for disposal at the facilities that are set up within New Jersey for disposal of such material generated *within* the State. The physical fact of life that New Jersey must somehow dispose of its own noxious items does not mean that it must serve as a depository for those of every other State. Similarly, New Jersey should be free under our past precedents to prohibit the importation of solid waste because of the health and safety problems that such waste poses to its citizens. The fact that New Jersey continues to, and indeed must continue to, dispose of its own solid waste does not mean that New Jersey may not prohibit the importation of even more solid waste into the State. I simply see no way to distinguish solid waste, on the record of this case, from germ-infected rags, diseased meat, and other noxious items.

The Court's effort to distinguish these prior cases is unconvincing. It first asserts that the quarantine laws which have previously been upheld "banned the importation of articles such as diseased livestock that required destruction as soon as possible because their very movement risked contagion and other evils." According to the Court, the New Jersey law is distinguishable from these other laws, and invalid, because the concern of New Jersey is not with the *movement* of solid waste but with the present inability to safely *dispose* of it once it reaches its destination. But I think it far from clear that the State's law has as limited a focus as the Court imputes to it: Solid waste which is a health hazard when it reaches its destination may in all likelihood be an equally great health hazard in transit.

Even if the Court is correct in its characterization of New Jersey's concerns, I do not see why a State may ban the importation of items whose movement risks contagion, but cannot ban the importation of items which, although they may be transported into the State without undue hazard, will then simply pile up in an ever increasing danger to the public's health and safety. The Commerce Clause was not drawn with a view to having the validity of state laws turn on such pointless distinctions.

Second, the Court implies that the challenged laws must be invalidated because New Jersey has left its landfills open to domestic waste. But, as the Court notes, this Court has repeatedly upheld quarantine laws "even though they appear to single out interstate commerce for special treatment." The fact that New Jersey has left its landfill sites open for domestic waste does not, of course, mean that solid waste is not innately harmful. Nor does it mean that New Jersey prohibits importation of solid waste for reasons other than the health and safety of its population. New Jersey must out of sheer necessity treat and dispose of its solid waste in some fashion, just as it must treat New Jersey cattle suffering from hoof-and-mouth disease. It does not follow that New Jersey must, under the Commerce Clause, accept solid waste or diseased cattle from outside its borders and thereby exacerbate its problems.

The Supreme Court of New Jersey expressly found that ch. 363 was passed "to preserve the health of New Jersey residents by keeping their exposure to solid waste and landfill areas to a minimum." 68 N.J. 451, 473, 348 A.2d 505, 516. The Court points to absolutely no evidence that would contradict this finding by the New Jersey Supreme Court. Because I find no basis for distinguishing the laws under challenge here from our past cases upholding state laws that prohibit the importation of items that could endanger the population of the State, I dissent.

NOTES AND QUESTIONS

1. When Is Discrimination Justifiable?   What was the fatal flaw in the New Jersey statute? Could New Jersey prohibit the importation of out-of-state waste if the state could establish that such waste was more hazardous than wastes generated in-state? In rejecting the quarantine theory on which Justice Rehnquist premises his dissent, Justice Stewart notes that the New Jersey statutes did not require "that waste must be disposed of as soon and as close to its point of generation as possible." Had New Jersey imposed such a requirement, could a ban on waste imports survive constitutional scrutiny?

2. Could All In-State Disposal Be Banned?   New Jersey's law banned only imports of waste; it did not restrict exports of New Jersey's waste to other states. Suppose New Jersey had enacted a statute that banned all waste disposal within the boundaries of the state regardless of where the waste was generated. Such a law effectively would have required that all waste generated in New Jersey be exported. Could such a law survive constitutional scrutiny under the Commerce Clause?

3. *Access to Natural Resources.*   Justice Stewart cites several Supreme Court opinions dealing with attempts by states to protect natural resources within the state from consumption by out-of-state consumers. In Pennsylvania v. West Virginia, 262 U.S. 553 (1923), for instance, the Supreme Court struck down a West Virginia statute requiring producers of natural gas to give West Virginia residents preference over nonresident consumers in the purchase of natural gas. The West Virginia legislature had wanted to insulate state residents in the case of gas shortages and believed this was permissible because the gas originated in West Virginia. However, the Court stated that "[n]atural gas is a lawful article of commerce, and its transmission from one state to another for sale and consumption in the latter is interstate commerce." Id. at 596. West Virginia's stated interest in conserving natural resources could not justify the measure because "the purpose of its conservation is in a sense commercial—the business welfare of the State, as coal might be, or timber. . . . If the States have such power a singular situation might result. Pennsylvania might keep its coal, the Northwest its timber, the mining states their minerals. . . . [C]ommerce will be halted at state lines." Id. at 599. See also Hughes v. Oklahoma, 441 U.S. 322 (1979), striking down an Oklahoma law prohibiting the interstate sale of minnows because nonresidents of the state cannot be forced "to bear the full costs of conserving" when other equally effective measures are available.

4. *State-created Resources.*   In another line of decisions, the Supreme Court has taken a more permissive view of efforts by states to ensure that state-created resources be reserved for use by their citizens. For example, in Reeves v. Stake, 447 U.S. 429 (1980), the Supreme Court upheld a South Dakota statute reserving all cement produced by a state-owned cement plant for use by state residents, in the event orders exceeded supply. According to the Court, "[c]ement is not a natural resource, like coal, timber, wild game, or minerals . . . It is the end product of a complex process whereby a costly physical plant and human labor act on raw materials. South Dakota has not sought to limit access to the State's limestone or other materials used to make cement." Id. at 443-444. The Court acknowledged that South Dakota's policies "reflect the essential and patently unobjectionable purpose of state government—to serve the citizens of the State." Id. at 442.

5. *Conservation.*   In a case that some have thought hard to square with the rest of the Supreme Court's recent Commerce Clause decisions, the Supreme Court has held that Montana could charge an out-of-state license fee for hunting Montana elk that was 25 times larger than the fee charged in-staters. Baldwin v. Fish and Game Commission of Montana, 436 U.S. 371 (1978) (Burger, C.J., concurring). *Baldwin* was decided under the Privileges and Immunities Clause, not the Commerce Clause. The Court recognized that states are not "obliged to share those things held in trust for their own people." Id. at 384. Moreover, such policies "manifest the State's special interest in regulating and preserving wildlife for the benefit of its citizens." Id. at 392. However, in a concurring opinion, Chief Justice Burger limited the majority holding by stating that if the wildlife became involved in interstate commerce, then access cannot be restricted in a manner that violates the Commerce Clause.

Professor Tribe has the following to say about *Baldwin:*

> There . . . appear to be some goods and services that a state's citizens, having created or preserved for themselves, are entitled to keep for themselves. Thus Montana's carefully-tended elk herds are akin to public libraries, public schools, state universities, state-supported hospitals, and public welfare programs—things that the Court has suggested that a state may reserve for the use or enjoyment of its citizens. The Court implied in *Baldwin* that it would approve even a total exclusion of non-resident hunters upon a showing by the state that any additional hunting opportunities beyond those Montana chose to reserve to its citizens would endanger the elk population to the point of extinction. [L. Tribe, American Constitutional Law 539 (2d ed. 1988).]

A year after *Baldwin,* the Court decided Hughes v. Oklahoma, 441 U.S. 322 (1979). At issue was an Oklahoma statute banning the export of minnows caught in state waters. The state defended the ban as a conservation measure. The Court struck down the statute in a 7-2 decision, with the justices aligned exactly as they were in Philadelphia v. New Jersey. Once wild animals or other natural resources became objects in interstate commerce, said the Court, state laws concerning them had to be judged by the same Commerce Clause standards that are applicable to other items of commerce. While recognizing that conservation was a legitimate state interest, the majority held that the state had not shown its ban to be the least discriminatory means of furthering that interest. "Far from choosing the least discriminatory alternative, Oklahoma has chosen to 'conserve' its minnows in the way that most overtly discriminates against interstate commerce." 441 U.S. at 337-338.

6. The Quarantine Cases.   Chief Justice Rehnquist's dissent in the principal case cites a number of decisions called the Quarantine Cases, in which certain blatantly discriminatory legislation has been upheld as a valid exercise of a state's police power to prohibit harmful materials from entering the state. In Maine v. Taylor, 477 U.S. 131 (1986), the Court upheld a Maine statute prohibiting the importation of a type of baitfish. On its face, the "statute restricts interstate trade in the most direct manner possible, blocking all inward shipments of live baitfish at the State's border." Id. at 137. Maine argued that the particular type of fish banned by the statute carried parasites not currently found in Maine waters that would seriously damage the indigenous fish population. The Supreme Court recognized a legitimate state interest, saying "even overt discrimination against interstate trade may be justified where, as in this case, out-of-state goods or services are particularly likely for some reason to threaten the health and safety of a State's citizens or the integrity of its natural resources." Id. at 149. The Court indicated that "[n]ot all intentional barriers to interstate trade are protectionist, and the Commerce Clause is not a guaranty of the right to import into a state whatever one may please . . . regardless of the effect . . . upon the whole community." Id.

7. Philadelphia Revisited. Suppose New Jersey had presented evidence that it had been engaging in stringent waste reduction programs, both voluntary and mandatory, in order to reduce the production of in-state waste as much as possible. Should it then be permitted to ban out-of-state wastes in order to minimize the adverse environmental effects of landfills? Would it matter whether Philadelphia was or was not employing similarly stringent waste reduction programs?

One commentator has concluded that "there is always an implicit assumption in [the Quarantine Cases] either that the problem the quarantine is aimed at . . . does not exist locally, or else that local measures for control and suppression of the problem are in force that are generally comparable in their impact to the embargo on imports." Regan, The Supreme Court and State Protectionism: Making Sense of the Dormant Commerce Clause, 84 Mich. L. Rev. 1091, 1270 (1986).

Suppose the New Jersey legislature decided to develop a system of state-owned landfills. Relying on Reeves v. Stake, could it limit access to those facilities for the benefit of its own citizens? See Note, Recycling Philadelphia v. New Jersey: The Dormant Commerce Clause, Postindustrial Natural Resources and the Solid Waste Crisis, 137 U. Pa. L. Rev. 1309 (1989).

8. New Controversy. Local opposition to waste disposal sites has only intensified in the years since Philadelphia v. New Jersey. Location opposition (dubbed the "not in my backyard" or NIMBY syndrome by its opponents) has successfully defeated or delayed numerous attempts to establish new facilities to handle waste. In this environment, it is no surprise that states have persisted in efforts to restrict waste imports in an attempt to diminish the need for these divisive, difficult facilities. Recently Alabama attempted to exploit some perceived cracks in Philadelphia v. New Jersey, enacting a ban on the importation of hazardous waste from certain states. The legislation, known as the Holley bill, was challenged in the following case.

National Solid Wastes Management
Assn. v. Alabama
910 F.2d 713 (11th Cir. 1990)

EDMONDSON, Circuit Judge.

The United States' largest and Alabama's only commercial hazardous waste management facility is located at Emelle, Alabama. The owner and operator of this facility, Chemical Waste Management, Inc. ("ChemWaste"), along with the National Solid Wastes Management Association, a trade association representing the waste management industry, brought this action seeking declaratory and injunctive relief, against [Alabama].

The suit challenges Ala. Code §22-30-11 (Supp. 1989), known as the "Holley Bill," which prevents commercial waste management facilities like Emelle from accepting hazardous wastes generated in states other than Alabama unless the other states have met certain statutory requirements. . . . Plaintiffs challenge [the Holley Bill] on [the ground] that [it] violate[s] the commerce clause of the United States Constitution.

A.   BACKGROUND

In 1980, the United States Congress enacted [CERCLA], designed to accomplish the clean up of hazardous waste sites. . . .

"A critical step in the implementation of a rational, safe hazardous waste program is the creation of new [hazardous waste disposal] facilities." 132 Cong. Rec. S14,924 (daily ed. Oct. 3, 1986) (statement of Sen. Chafee). Because Congress perceived that few states had developed programs to assure continued disposal capacity in the long run, Congress amended CERCLA in 1986 by enacting [SARA]. . . . "Congress was concerned that certain states, because of political pressures and public opposition, were not able to create and to permit sufficient facilities within their borders to treat and securely dispose of (or manage) the amounts of wastes produced in those states." Office of Solid Waste and Emergency Response, U.S. EPA, Assurance of Hazardous Waste Capacity: Guidance to State Officials [hereinafter EPA Guidance Doc.], at 2 (Dec. 1988). See S. Rep. No. 11, 99th Cong., 1st Sess. 22 (1985) ("Pressures from local citizens place the political system in an extremely vulnerable position. . . . The broader social need for safe hazardous waste management facilities often has not been strongly represented in the . . . process [of creating new facilities]. A common result has been . . . no significant increase in hazardous waste capacity over the past several years.").

The provision of SARA at issue in this case, section 104(c)(9), requires that each state present a proposal to EPA showing that the state will have adequate capacity available to dispose of the hazardous wastes generated within the state for the next twenty years. If the state does not provide such capacity assurances deemed adequate by EPA, the state is prohibited from receiving Superfund money for remedial cleanup actions taken within the state.

Congress recognized that—because of geological factors or for other reasons—every state may not be able to create new disposal facilities within its borders and will not be able to dispose of its own wastes within its own borders for the next twenty years. SARA contemplates that a state may meet its section 104(c)(9) capacity assurance requirements by planning to use other states' disposal facilities and privately owned disposal facilities. 132 Cong. Rec. S14,924 (daily ed. Oct. 3, 1986) (statement of Sen. Chafee). Section 104(c)(9) provides that a state may base its capacity assurance plan on such facilities if the state has entered into an agreement for the use of those facilities. For example, a state that cannot safely dispose of its wastes within its borders (an exporting state) may reach agreements with another state or group of states (importing states) under which the importing states agree to allocate a portion of their disposal capacity to the exporting state. An exporting state may also contract with a privately owned waste management facility. . . . SARA places the burden of making capacity assurances on the exporting (waste generating) state, and not on the importing state. SARA nowhere requires that an importing state enter into interstate or regional agreements, but most states will need to enter into such agreements because most states lack the capacity to dispose of all types of hazardous wastes within their own borders.

In the light of SARA's capacity assurance requirement and the concern of Alabama's leaders over the large amounts of other states' hazardous wastes being disposed of in Alabama, the Alabama legislature in 1989 enacted . . . the "Holley Bill." This provision prohibits the owner or operator of a commercial hazardous waste management facility located in Alabama from treating or disposing of hazardous wastes generated in a state other than Alabama, if the other state either (1) prohibits the treatment or disposal of hazardous waste within its borders and has no facility for such; or (2) has no facility existing within that state for the treatment or disposal of hazardous waste and has not entered into an interstate or regional agreement for the disposal of its wastes to which Alabama is a signatory. The Holley Bill also prohibits commercial waste management facilities in Alabama from contracting with a state other than Alabama to satisfy the other state's capacity assurance obligation.

Under authority of this bill, Alabama has issued a "blacklist" which, on September 13, 1989 (the effective date of the Holley Bill), precluded Emelle from accepting hazardous wastes from twenty-two states and the District of Columbia. Between January 1, 1989 and October 1, 1989,

Emelle received wastes from seventeen of the twenty-two states on the Holley Bill's blacklist. In addition, Emelle has ongoing contracts with waste generators in most of the banned states.

B. THE COMMERCE CLAUSE

Plaintiffs contend that the Holley Bill violates the commerce clause of the United States Constitution. We agree. As discussed below, we hold that hazardous waste is an object of commerce, that the Holley Bill erects a barrier to the interstate movement of hazardous wastes, and that Congress did not—by enacting the SARA amendments to CERCLA—authorize this restriction on interstate commerce.

1. Object of Commerce

"All objects of interstate trade merit Commerce Clause protection; none is excluded by definition at the outset." City of Philadelphia v. New Jersey, 437 U.S. 617, 622 (1978). But when the dangers inhering in an object's movement "far outweigh[]" its worth in interstate commerce, a state can prohibit transportation of the object across state lines. Id. For example, the Supreme Court has said that a state may restrict interstate movement of an object when, on account of the object's "existing condition, [it] would bring in and spread disease, pestilence, and death." Bowman v. Chicago & Northwestern R. Co., 125 U.S. 465, 489 (1888) (striking down state prohibition on interstate state movement of liquor); see also Clason v. State of Indiana, 306 U.S. 439, 442 (1939) (upholding Indiana's prohibition against interstate transportation of large dead animals because "obvious purpose of the enactment [was] to prevent the spread of disease and the development of nuisances").

The Supreme Court in City of Philadelphia v. New Jersey expressly concluded that the interstate movement of solid and liquid waste is commerce. 437 U.S. at 621-23. In that case, the Court rejected the lower court's conclusion that the waste was not an object of commerce because it was valueless and could not be put to effective use. The Court held that the innate danger of the solid and liquid waste did not outweigh its worth in interstate commerce.

Although the hazardous waste involved in this case may be innately more dangerous than the solid and liquid waste involved in City of Philadelphia, we cannot say that the dangers of hazardous waste outweigh its worth in interstate commerce. Congress has defined hazardous waste as "a solid waste . . . which . . . may . . . cause, or significantly contribute to a significant increase in mortality or an increase in serious . . . illness, or . . . pose a substantial present or potential hazard to human health or the environment when *improperly* treated, stored, transported, or disposed of, or otherwise managed." 42 U.S.C. §6903(5) (emphasis added). The legislative and executive branches of the federal government together with the separate states have developed a comprehensive scheme for regulating the management of hazardous waste. Waste generators, transporters, and managers must comply with highly technical and rigid rules designed to ensure that the movement of hazardous waste is accomplished with a minimum of danger to the public and to the environment. To the extent these rules can and do provide for the safe transportation of hazardous waste, the dangers associated with hazardous waste movement do not outweigh the value of moving hazardous waste across state lines. . . .

2.   Barrier to Interstate Commerce

Because hazardous waste is an object of commerce and because the Constitution gives Congress the power to regulate the interstate movement of hazardous waste, a state's restriction of that movement is subject to constitutional scrutiny. See *City of Philadelphia*, 437 U.S. at 622-23, 985 S. Ct. at 2535. To determine whether the Holley Bill erects a barrier to interstate commerce, we follow the test set out by the Supreme Court in *City of Philadelphia:*

> [W]here simple economic protectionism is effected by state legislation, a virtually per se rule of invalidity has been erected. The clearest example of such legislation is a law that overtly blocks the flow of interstate commerce at a State's borders. But where other legislative objectives are credibly advanced and there is no patent discrimination against interstate trade, the Court has adopted a much more flexible approach, the general contours of which were outlined in Pike v. Bruce Church, Inc., 397 U.S. 137, 142 Id. at 624, (citations omitted). The crucial inquiry, therefore, is whether the Holley Bill is basically a protectionist measure, or whether it is based on legitimate local concerns with effects on interstate commerce that are only incidental. [Id. at 624.]

The district court below concluded that the Holley Bill was directed toward a legitimate state concern: complying with SARA's capacity assurance requirements. The district court said that the Holley Bill was "not an effort to isolate Alabama from the national economy." National Solid Wastes Management Ass'n v. Alabama Dep't of Envtl. Management, 729 F. Supp. 792, 804 (N.D. Ala. 1990). We disagree. First, the Holley Bill is not required for Alabama to comply with section 104(c)(9)'s capacity assurance requirement. According to the Senate Report on SARA and the EPA Guidance Document, Alabama may satisfy its capacity assurance requirements by any combination of three measures: (1) creating new disposal capacity within the state, (2) entering into interstate or regional agreements allowing Alabama to use capacity located in other states, and (3) contracting with private waste management facilities. S. Rep. No. 11, 99th Cong., 1st Sess. 22 (1985); EPA Guidance Doc. at 3. If Alabama's capacity assurance plan depends on capacity provided by a commercial, privately owned management facility such as Emelle, the state should contract with the private facility for that capacity, instead of blocking the private facility from accepting wastes from other states.

Second, while the Alabama legislature made a finding that large volumes of hazardous waste entering the state increased the likelihood of accidents and the risk to Alabama's citizens and environment, see Ala. Act. No. 89-788, Alabama did not ban the shipment of all hazardous wastes into the state, but only shipments from certain states. "[T]he evil of protectionism can reside in legislative means as well as legislative ends." *City of Philadelphia*, 437 U.S. at 626. Even if Alabama's purpose in enacting the Holley Bill was to protect human health and the environment in Alabama, that purpose "may not be accomplished by discriminating against articles of commerce coming from outside the State unless there is some reason, apart from their origin, to treat them differently." Id. at 626-27. Plaintiffs presented testimony undisputed by defendants that the types of wastes accepted at the Emelle facility did not vary based upon the states in which the wastes were generated. The Holley Bill plainly distinguishes among wastes based on their origin, with no other basis for the distinction.

Because Alabama's law is a protectionist measure not based adequately on a legitimate local concern, the district court was wrong to apply the Pike v. Bruce Church, Inc. balancing test. The Holley Bill does not regulate "evenhandedly" and its effects on interstate commerce are not merely incidental. See *Pike*, 397 U.S. 137, 142 (1970). On its face, the Holley Bill discriminates among out-of-state waste generators and imposes on these generators the burden of conserving Alabama's remaining hazardous waste disposal capacity. We reject the district court's conclusion that, because Alabama closed its borders to only some states and not all states, Alabama is not hoarding its disposal capacity. Alabama has attempted to "isolate itself from a problem common to many by erecting a barrier against the movement of interstate trade." *City of Philadelphia*, 437 U.S. at 628.

Contrary to defendants' arguments, the Holley Bill does not fall within an exception to the commerce clause carved out by the so-called "quarantine cases." In these cases, the Supreme Court upheld state legislation that facially discriminated against out-of-state commerce involving articles that were highly dangerous. For example, the Court upheld a Maine statute that prohibited the importation of a certain type of baitfish not native to Maine because the baitfish contained a parasite that could have a serious detrimental effect on Maine's fisheries. Maine

v. Taylor, 477 U.S. 131 (1986). Such state laws do not discriminate against interstate commerce, however, but "simply prevent[] traffic in noxious articles, whatever their origin." *City of Philadelphia*, 437 U.S. at 629.

Alabama's selective ban on out-of-state hazardous waste is no quarantine law. Alabama did not ban hazardous wastes from all other states on the ground that the wastes were dangerous to some human health or environmental aspect which Alabama has a right to regulate. Alabama's ban does not distinguish on the basis of type of waste or degree of dangerousness, but on the basis of the state of generation. The Holley Bill discriminates against interstate commerce.

3. Congressional Authorization

A state statute that erects a barrier to interstate commerce may nonetheless be upheld where Congress authorizes the state to regulate in such a manner. "Where state or local government action is specifically authorized by Congress, it is not subject to the Commerce Clause even if it interferes with interstate commerce." White v. Massachusetts Council of Constr. Employers, Inc., 460 U.S. 204 (1983). "Congress may redefine the distribution of power over interstate commerce by permitting the states to regulate the commerce in a manner which would otherwise not be permissible." South-Central Timber Devel., Inc. v. Wunnicke, 467 U.S. 82, 87-88 (1984). Such congressional intent or authorization for states to affect interstate commerce, however, must be "expressly stated" and "unmistakably clear." Id. at 91.

. . . Defendants contend that SARA's section 104(c)(9) effected a redistribution of power over interstate commerce. According to defendants, the SARA amendments to CERCLA gave the states more responsibility for hazardous waste management, including an obligation to develop increased treatment and disposal capacity. But nothing in SARA evidences congressional authorization for each state to close its borders to wastes generated in other states to force those other states to meet federally mandated hazardous waste management requirements. SARA places the burden of making capacity assurances for future hazardous waste management on the *generating state* and imposes a sanction on that state for failure to satisfy its obligation. Congress has not, in our opinion, authorized Alabama to restrict the free movement of hazardous wastes across Alabama's borders. See State of Alabama v. United States EPA, 871 F.2d at 1555 n.3 ("Although Congress may override the commerce clause by express statutory language, it has not done so in enacting CERCLA." (citing *Wunnicke*, 467 U.S. at 82)). If Congress intended to allow the states to restrict the interstate movement of hazardous wastes as Alabama has tried to do, Congress could (and still can) plainly say so. . . .

C. Conclusion

Minimizing the dangers to public health and the environment created by uncontrolled and untreated hazardous wastes is an important task facing society. But Alabama's statute banning wastes selectively, based on state of origin, . . . cannot stand in the face of the Constitution's commerce clause. However honorable and well intentioned Alabama's leaders might be in coming to grips with environmental problems, "it is the duty of the courts to guard vigilantly against any needless intrusion" on "the protection afforded [interstate commerce] by the federal Constitution." *Bowman,* 125 U.S. at 492. The Constitution, here specifically the commerce . . . clause[], may not be encroached upon, even in an attempt to do something good for the environment.

We VACATE summary judgment for defendants, REMAND to the district court, and—because no material issues of fact remain—instruct the district court to enter summary judgment for plaintiffs.

NSWMA v. Alabama: The Alabama Legislature Strikes Back

Alabama has persisted in its efforts to control the flow of out-of-state waste into the Emelle facility. In April 1990 the Alabama legislature enacted new legislation that (a) imposes a "base fee" of $25.60 per ton on all hazardous wastes disposed of in the state, regardless of state of origin; (b) imposes an "additional fee" of $72.00 per ton on all out-of-state waste disposed of in the state; (c) places a cap on the amount that could be disposed of in any Alabama facility in any one-year period. The cap provision applies to all facilities that dispose of over 100,000 tons per year. Alabama has only one such facility: Emelle.

Accompanying these provisions were a number of detailed legislative findings, including the following:

(8) Since hazardous wastes and substances generated in the state compose a small proportion of those materials disposed of at commercial disposal sites located in the state, present circumstances result in the state's citizens paying a disproportionate share of the costs of regulation of hazardous waste transportation, spill cleanup and commercial disposal facilities. Persons, firms or corporations which generate and dispose of such waste and substances in Alabama presently are among the taxpaying citizens of this state who must bear the burden of regulation, inspection, control and clean-up of hazardous waste sites; addressing the public health problems created by the presence of such facilities in the state; and, preserving this state's environment while those generating this waste in other states and shipping it to Alabama for disposal presently are not. This act attempts to resolve that inequity by requiring all generators of waste being disposed

of in Alabama to share in that financial burden. [Ala. Act No. 90-326, §1, Code §22-30B-1.1 Legislative Findings.]

Shortly after the Act became law, Chemical Waste Management, Inc. challenged it on a number of grounds, including Commerce Clause grounds. The trial court upheld the base fee and cap provisions but found that the additional fee provision violated the Commerce Clause. The decision of the Alabama Supreme Court follows.

Hunt v. Chemical Waste Management, Inc.
584 So. 2d 1367 (1991), cert. granted, 60 U.S.L.W. 3208 (1992)

Judge SHORES delivered the opinion of the court.

[The court first addressed the constitutionality of the base fee and cap provisions. Chemical Waste Management (CWM) argued that the base fee violated the Commerce Clause despite being nondiscriminatory on its face, because substantially all of its impact was on interstate commerce. The court rejected CWM's argument, stating that] if no facial discrimination is involved, a "balancing test" is applied to determine the constitutional validity of statutes:

> Where the statute regulates evenhandedly to effectuate a legitimate local public interest, and its effects on interstate commerce are only incidental, it will be upheld unless the burden imposed on such commerce is clearly excessive in relation to the putative local benefits. [Pike v. Bruce Church, 397 U.S. 137 (1970).]

If a legitimate local purpose exists, "the extent of the burden that will be tolerated will of course depend on the nature of the local interest involved, and on whether it could be promoted as well with a lesser impact on interstate activities." Id.

CWM has failed to establish that the Base Fee has discriminatory effects on interstate commerce. The mere fact, as CWM argues, that most of its customers are out-of-state generators does not establish discrimination against interstate commerce. The United States Supreme Court has stated that even if the burden of a state regulation falls most often on out-of-state companies, this burden "does not, by itself, establish a claim of discrimination against interstate commerce." . . .

In balancing the interests at stake, the Court finds that the burden the Base Fee imposes on interstate commerce is not clearly excessive in relation to the benefits it produces. The fee benefits the state, on the other hand, by compensating it for the financial responsibilities and risks it bears on account of commercial hazardous waste disposal activities. Thus, a comparison of the Base Fee's local benefits to its alleged burden on interstate commerce establishes that any such burden is not clearly excessive. Furthermore, to the extent that the Base Fee does deter hazardous waste landfilling, the fee is a proper instrument of deterrence. Finally, in view of the financial, safety, environmental and other objectives of Act No. 90-326 and the fact that the Base Fee falls evenhandedly on interstate and intrastate waste, it is difficult to imagine how these objectives could be accomplished in ways that have a lesser impact on interstate activities. . . .

[The cap provision was similarly upheld against a Commerce Clause challenge.]

We next consider whether the trial court erred in holding that the Additional Fee of Act No. 90-326 discriminates against interstate commerce in violation of the Commerce Clause.

The Commerce Clause does not invalidate all state restrictions on commerce. . . .

In New Energy Co. v. Limbach, 486 U.S. 269, at 278 (1988), the United States Supreme Court stated the test in which a facially discriminatory statute may be found to be valid under the Commerce Clause:

> Our cases leave open the possibility that a State may validate a statute that discriminates against interstate commerce by showing that it advances a legitimate local purpose that cannot be adequately served by reasonable nondiscriminatory alternatives. This is perhaps just another way of saying that what may appear to be a "discriminatory" provision in the constitutionally prohibited sense—that is, a protectionist enactment—may on closer analysis not be so. However it be put, the standards for such justification are high. Cf. Philadelphia v. New Jersey, 437 U.S. 617, 624 (1978) ("where simple economic protectionism is effected by state legislation, a virtually per se rule of invalidity has been erected"); Hughes v. Oklahoma, 441 U.S., at 337 (1979) ("[F]acial discrimination by itself may be a fatal defect" and "[a]t a minimum . . . invokes the strictest scrutiny").

The trial court concluded that City of Philadelphia v. New Jersey, supra, compelled the conclusion that the legislation involved here was foreclosed by the Commerce Clause. We believe that that case is distinguishable under the facts here. That case involved a New Jersey statute that banned the movement of liquid or solid waste (but not hazardous waste) into the state. The purpose of that legislation was found to be economic protectionism, which was in violation of the Commerce Clause. CWM argues that the holding in City of Philadelphia v. New Jersey precludes state and local governments from responding to real and substantial public health and environmental dangers by controlling the importation of wastes. However, the United States Supreme Court cases make a distinction between state measures that discriminate arbitrarily against out-of-state commerce in order to give in-state interests a commercial advantage, i.e., simple economic protectionism, and state measures that seek to protect public health or safety or the environment. Maine v. Taylor, 477 U.S. 131, 148 n.19 (1986). . . .

In Maine v. Taylor, 477 U.S. 131 (1986), the United States Supreme Court made it clear that environmental measures are entitled to greater deference than ordinary legislative acts. The Court upheld a facially discriminatory state statute that banned all importation of live baitfish. The Court stated:

> The Commerce Clause significantly limits the ability of States and localities to regulate or otherwise burden the flow of interstate commerce, but it does not elevate free trade above all other values. As long as a State does not needlessly obstruct interstate trade or attempt to "place itself in a position of economic isolation," . . . it retains broad regulatory authority to protect the health and safety of its citizens and the integrity of its natural resources. The evidence in this case amply supports the District Court's findings that Maine's ban on the importation of live baitfish serves legitimate local purposes that could not adequately be served by available nondiscriminatory alternatives. This is not a case of arbitrary discrimination against interstate commerce; the record suggests that Maine has legitimate reasons "apart from their origin, to treat [out-of-state baitfish] differently. . . ." 477 U.S. at 151-52.

The Supreme Court in Maine v. Taylor cited City of Philadelphia v. New Jersey for the proposition that "[s]hielding in-state industries from out-of-state competition is almost never a legitimate local purpose, and state laws that amount to 'simple economic protectionism' consequently have been subject to a 'virtually per se rule of invalidity,' " while stating that, in contrast to City of Philadelphia v. New Jersey, "there is little reason in this case to believe that the legitimate justifications the State has put forward for its statute are merely a sham or a 'post hoc rationalization.' " Maine v. Taylor, 477 U.S. at 148-49.

The Additional Fee provision in the Act advances a legitimate local purpose that cannot be adequately served by reasonable nondiscriminatory alternatives. It has not been enacted for the purpose of economic protectionism. In enacting the Additional Fee, the Alabama legislature was not banning the collection and acceptance of hazardous waste; it was merely asking the states that are using Alabama as a dumping ground for their hazardous wastes to bear some of the costs for the increased risk they bring to the environment and the health and safety of the people of Alabama. As in Maine v. Taylor, the problem is already with us. Millions of tons of hazardous wastes have been buried at Emelle. The State of Alabama has a legitimate justification, apart from their origin, for treating the out-of-state wastes differently.

Because this waste is *permanently* stored in Alabama, the risk to the health and safety of the people of Alabama will continue in perpetuity. The costs to the state of regulation and monitoring of the facility will continue in perpetuity. A disproportionate share of these costs will be borne by the taxpayers of the State of Alabama for the wastes dumped by other states.

The Additional Fee serves these legitimate local purposes that cannot be adequately served by reasonable nondiscriminatory alternatives: (1) protection of the health and safety of the citizens of Alabama from toxic substances; (2) conservation of the environment and the state's natural resources; (3) provision for compensatory revenue for the costs and burdens that out-of-state waste generators impose by dumping their hazardous waste in Alabama; (4) reduction of the overall flow of wastes traveling on the state's highways, which flow creates a great risk to the health and safety of the state's citizens.

The testimony before the trial court showed that in 1985 some 341,000 tons of hazardous waste were buried in the Emelle facility. By 1989 the tonnage had grown to 788,000 tons per year. While CWM estimates that there is capacity for storage at Emelle for 100 years, the increase in tonnage has more than doubled in four years. . . .

Unlike the situation in City of Philadelphia v. New Jersey, where there was questionable environmental concern, there is legitimate concern here in Alabama. There is no dispute that the wastes dumped at Emelle include known carcinogens and materials that are extremely *hazardous* and can cause birth defects, genetic damage, blindness, crippling, and death. These wastes are far more dangerous to the people of Alabama than rags infected with small-pox or yellow fever.

This Court takes judicial notice of the fact that there is a finite capacity for storage of hazardous waste at the Emelle facility and that the capacity is rapidly being reached. The record reflects that 85% to 90% of the tonnage that is *permanently* buried at Emelle is from out-of-state. There is nothing in the Commerce Clause that compels the State of Alabama to yield its total capacity for hazardous waste disposal to other states. To tax Alabama-generated hazardous waste at the same rate as out-of-state waste is not an available non-discriminatory alternative, because Alabama is bearing a grossly disproportionate share of the burdens of hazardous waste disposal for the entire country. Here, the statute that creates the Additional Fee does not needlessly obstruct interstate trade, nor does it constitute economic protectionism. It is a responsible exercise by the State of Alabama of its broad regulatory authority to protect the health and safety of its citizens and the integrity of its natural resources.

. . . For the reasons stated above, the judgment of the trial court is due to be affirmed as to all issues save the Additional Fee and reversed and the cause remanded as to the issue of the Additional Fee.

Affirmed in part; reversed in part; and remanded.

NOTES AND QUESTIONS

1. Is Hunt v. Chemical Waste Management consistent with Philadelphia v. New Jersey? Has the Alabama Supreme Court adequately considered the Supreme Court's position that "the evil of protectionism can reside in legislative means as well as legislative ends"?

2. Has the legislature of Alabama brought its statute within the rationale of Maine v. Taylor by showing that Alabama has "legitimate reasons apart from their origin, to treat [out-of-state hazardous waste] differently . . ."? Does legislative finding (8) help in this regard?

3. In 1989 Indiana had enacted a series of measures applicable to nonhazardous waste. First, all vehicle operators presenting themselves at an Indiana landfill were required to present a certificate of the state of origin of the waste. Second, if the waste originated in Indiana, the certificate must include the county of origin; if the waste originated out of state, it must also contain a statement from a state or local public health or environmental officer certifying the waste as nonhazardous and noninfectious. Third, it established a flat fee, or tipping fee, of $.50 per ton, but out-of-state waste was to be charged a tipping fee equal to that charged by the site closest to the point of origin of the waste or $.50, whichever is larger.

In Government Suppliers Consolidating Services v. Bayh, 753 F. Supp. 769 (D. Ind. 1990), the court struck down all three provisions. As to the two-tier tipping fee, Indiana argued that the extra funds would be used to fund hazardous waste cleanup. The court found this argument to be a pretext, because "there is no evidence to support any connection between the amount of harm threatened by out of state waste and the size of the tipping fee." 753 F. Supp. at 775. The court acknowledged that Indiana could impose a fee to advance a legitimate interest in deterring solid waste disposal, but held that this interest could be accomplished by a means less restrictive of interstate commerce, namely a single-tier system. Can you suggest how Indiana might re-establish a two-tier fee system in light of Hunt v. Chemical Waste Management? How do you suppose the court ruled on the state of origin certificate and the public health or environmental officer certificate requirements? What facts would be relevant to the court's decision?

4. Consider the constitutional implications of other tactics that are being employed to discourage disposal of out-of-state waste. Can a state that has required that certain items be removed from municipal solid waste ban the disposal of out-of-state wastes that contain such items? Minnesota has adopted legislation that bans the inclusion of tires, lead acid batteries, used motor oil, and major appliances in the municipal solid waste stream. It has now adopted legislation that provides that solid waste generated in another state cannot be disposed in Minnesota unless it meets all solid waste management regulations in the state of generation

and contains no items banned from Minnesota's solid waste stream. Governor Signs Measure to Boost Enforcement of State Pollution Laws, 22 Env. Rep. 315, 316 (1991). Is this legislation constitutional?

5. If a state authorizes its counties to adopt ordinances prohibiting the disposal of waste generated outside the county, can such ordinances be upheld against Commerce Clause attack even though they effectively bar disposal of out-of-state waste in counties adopting such ordinances? Michigan has enacted such a law, which has been upheld by the Sixth Circuit on the ground that it treats out-of-state waste no differently from waste originating in other areas of the state. Kettlewell Excavating, Inc. v. Michigan Department of Natural Resources, 931 F.2d 413 (6th Cir. 1991), cert. granted sub nom. Fort Gratiot Sanitary Landfill v. Michigan Department of Natural Resources, 60 U.S.L.W. 3465 (1992). The court noted, however, that the result might be different if all counties in the state banned out-of-county wastes because that would result in a de facto ban on all out-of-state waste. The court rejected a takings claim made by a landfill owner by reasoning that the landfill still could be used to dispose of waste generated in the county. The Supreme Court has agreed to review the Sixth Circuit's decision.

6. As the Eleventh Circuit noted in National Solid Waste Management Assn. v. Alabama, under its plenary power to regulate commerce Congress is free to grant states the power to discriminate against out-of-staters. In this regard, the Eleventh Circuit contrasted SARA with the Low-Level Radioactive Waste Policy Act, 42 U.S.C. §§2021b-2021j (1982 & Supp. V 1987) (LLRWPA). In the LLRWPA, "states are encouraged to enter into regional compacts to provide for the establishment and operation of regional disposal facilities for low-level radioactive waste. 42 U.S.C. §2021d. In this Act, which predates SARA, Congress expressly authorized states that enter into such compacts to ban waste shipments from states that neither enter into a compact nor meet federal deadlines for establishing their own facilities. 42 U.S.C. §2021e(e)(2), (f)(1)." 910 F.2d at 722 n.19.

Should Congress now amend SARA and follow the approach of the LLRWPA, allowing states like Alabama to restrict out-of-state waste? Ironically, Justice Stewart's observation in *City of Philadelphia* that New Jersey may find it necessary to export its waste in the future has proved prescient. Due to stricter environmental standards imposed on landfills by New Jersey, the state now exports a large percentage of its garbage. States that receive New Jersey's wastes are complaining loudly. In 1990, legislation that would authorize states to ban imports of out-of-state garbage or to charge higher fees for the disposal of garbage that originated out of state passed the Senate but did not survive a House-Senate conference committee. New Jersey's congressional delegation is now a vocal opponent of these proposals because the state ships so much of its solid waste to Pennsylvania, Ohio, Kentucky, and Indiana for disposal.

Gold, New Jersey Officials Defend Policy of Exporting Trash, N.Y. Times, July 19, 1990, at B1.

7. Some environmentalists oppose federal legislation that would authorize states to ban waste imports on the ground that such laws discourage the development of better technologies for waste disposal. See, e.g., Congress Should Not Allow States to Ban Interstate Transport of Waste, Industry Says, 22 Env. Rep. 107 (1991). Do you agree? Grass-roots environmental organizations look more favorably on proposals to authorize waste import bans. Environmentalists Release RCRA Wish List; Interstate Transport, Medical Waste Left Out, 22 Env. Rep. 334 (1991). Why do you think the views of the national groups diverge from those of the local groups on this subject?

8. Spurred in part by the NIMBY syndrome, local governments may be inclined to use their land use authorities to ban *all* land disposal of certain kinds of wastes, especially hazardous wastes, regardless of point of origin. These efforts face no Commerce Clause obstacles. Interestingly, however, federal legislation—which some states are hoping will *authorize* certain waste disposal bans (bans on out-of-state wastes)— may now operate to *prohibit* other kinds of waste disposal bans. The issue is whether a federal statute addressing a particular disposal problem preempts state and local authorities, as discussed in the section that follows.

B. LIMITS ON LOCAL OPPOSITION TO SITING

State and local regulations that discriminate against waste disposal on environmental grounds have been more successful in preventing the fouling of backyards, though waste management firms have tried hard to find legal avenues for combatting the NIMBY syndrome, as illustrated by Rollins Environmental Services, Inc. v. Parish of St. James, 775 F.2d 627 (5th Cir. 1985). In that case a Louisiana parish sought to block operation of a PCB transfer facility in Union, Louisiana first by adopting an ordinance that flatly prohibited such facilities. PCBs are one of the few wastes regulated under TSCA. TSCA is unusual because it is administered exclusively by EPA and it contains provision that preempt more stringent state regulations (TSCA §19, 15 U.S.C. §2617). After the owner of the facility filed suit claiming that TSCA preempted the local ordinance, the parish quickly repealed it and adopted a new law styled "An Ordinance Regulating Commercial Solvent Cleaning Businesses in St. James Parish." The ordinance prohibited the operation of any "commercial solvent cleaning business" within one mile of any school (the PCB transfer facility was located a quarter-mile from an elementary school) or in any "area of special environmental concern."

Although the parish argued that the new ordinance was not

preempted by TSCA because it did not address PCBs specifically, the Fifth Circuit held that it was "a sham." Noting that the law had been immediately preceded by an express ban on PCB disposal activities, the court concluded that "it has the illegitimate objective of regulating a field preempted by Congress." It held the ordinance to be preempted by section 18(a)(2) of TSCA and existing federal regulations that did not prohibit the operation of PCB transfer facilities. The court noted that section 18(b) of TSCA establishes a procedure by which exemptions may be obtained from TSCA's preemption provisions.

A clear problem with the ordinance was that the parish had done a poor job of concealing its true motivation. The parish probably would have had a stronger legal position had it not adopted the first ordinance, which expressly banned PCB transfer facilities. If the second ordinance (purporting to regulate such facilities) had been on the books for several years prior to Rollins's decision to build a PCB disposal facility, the case might have come out differently.

Local opposition remains a formidable obstacle to the siting of hazardous waste disposal facilities. Communities often seem adamantly opposed to such facilities, regardless of what experts may say about safety. Politicians inevitably are influenced by how strongly their constituents feel about these matters. The following case raised the issue of whether adverse public sentiment is in itself a legally cognizable ground for rejecting a facility.

	Geo-Tech Reclamation Industries, Inc.	
	v. Hamrick	
	886 F.2d 662 (4th Cir. 1989)	

ERVIN, Chief Judge:
    . . . West Virginia, like many other states, has enacted a statutory scheme governing solid waste disposal. In accordance with the provisions of the state's Solid Waste Management Act ("the Act"), W. Va. Code §§20-5F-1 to 20-5F-8 (Supp. 1989), landfills are regulated by the Department of Natural Resources ("the Department"). The Act flatly prohibits the operation of open dumps and requires landfill operators to obtain a permit from the Department before constructing, operating, or abandoning any solid waste disposal facility. W. Va. Code §20-5F-5. Permits may be issued by the Department's Director, after notice and opportunity for a public hearing, and may contain reasonable terms and conditions for the operation of a proposed waste facility. W. Va. Code §20-5F-4(b). . . .

[T]he director may deny the issuance of a permit on the basis of information in the application or from other sources including public comment, if the solid waste facility may cause adverse impacts on the natural resources and environmental concerns under the director's purview in chapter twenty of the Code, destruction of aesthetic values, destruction or endangerment of the property of others or is significantly adverse to the public sentiment of the area where the solid waste facility is or will be located. W. Va. Code §20-5F-4(b).

It is the final clause of this section—giving the Director authority to deny a permit solely because it is "significantly adverse to the public sentiment"—which is at issue in this case.

The facts relevant to this consolidated appeal are undisputed and straightforward. Geo-Tech Reclamation Industries, Inc. ("GRI") and LCS Services, Inc. ("LCS") desire to operate a landfill on a site in West Virginia's panhandle country near the North Mountain community. GRI obtained an option to purchase the 331 acre site in 1986 and subsequently filed an application for a landfill operating permit. Its application was denied by the Director of the Department of Natural Resources on the ground that the proposed landfill had engendered "adverse public sentiment." The Director's letter terminating the permit application process stated:

the Department has received approximately 250 letters representing individual citizens, businesses, and groups in the Hedgesville area. All are vehemently opposed to the project. We have also received a petition in which similar feelings were expressed by many more hundreds of local citizens. . . . Due to the significant concern voiced by the residents of the area, I believe it is inappropriate to continue further technical review and am denying the permit application on the basis of adverse public sentiment, as prescribed in §20-5F-4(b). The staff review of the Part I application has not revealed any insurmountable technical problems with the site.

Subsequently, LCS acquired an option to purchase the site in 1987. Its application to operate a solid waste disposal facility was also rejected because of adverse public sentiment. In his letter denying LCS' permit application, however, the Director added "destruction of aesthetic values, and the destruction and endangerment of the property of others" as further reasons for denial. LCS appealed the decision to the West Virginia Water Resources Board pursuant to W. Va. Code §20-5F-7. During hearings before the Board, Robert D. Seip, a former Department employee who supervised the technical review of LCS' application, testified that LCS' site was particularly well suited to serve as a landfill and that LCS' plan had no significant technical failings. Based in part on this testimony, the Board ruled that neither aesthetic or property value related concerns would justify the denial of LCS' application. It affirmed, though, the Director's decision on the basis of adverse public sentiment.

After the State Water Resources Board upheld the Director's decision, LCS and GRI brought declaratory judgment actions challenging §20-5F-4(b)'s constitutionality. LCS and GRI argued that §20-5F-4(b) violated due process by impermissibly delegating legislative authority to local citizens. They also argued that the statute exceeded the state's police power. On cross motions for summary judgment, the district court found §20-5F-4(b) to be unconstitutional. Relying on decisions by the Supreme Court in Eubank v. City of Richmond, 226 U.S. 137 (1912) and Washington Ex Rel. Seattle Title Trust Co. v. Roberge, 278 U.S. 116 (1928), the court accepted the plaintiffs' argument that "this provision is on its face violative of due process rights guaranteed under the United States Constitution insofar as it allows a few citizens to deny an individual the use of his property." Geo-Tech Reclamation Industries, Inc. v. Potesta, No. 2:87-0671, slip op. at 3 (S.D.W. Va. Dec. 22, 1988). . . .

We see no reason, however, to decide whether §20-5F-4(b) works an impermissible delegation of power to local residents because the statute suffers from a more profound constitutional infirmity. It is well settled that land-use regulations "must find their justification in some aspect of the police power, asserted for the public welfare." Euclid v. Ambler Realty Co., 272 U.S. 365 (1926). West Virginia strenuously argues that it acts well within the broad confines of its police power in regulating the development of solid waste disposal facilities. With this we certainly agree. No one would question the state's power to impose a broad array of restrictions on an activity, such as the operation of a landfill, which was recognized as a nuisance even by the early common law.

West Virginia also argues that within this broad array of restrictions, the state may legislate to protect its communities against not only such tangible effects as increased traffic, noise, odors, and health concerns, but also against the possibility of decreased community pride and fracturing of community spirit that may accompany large waste disposal operations. Here again, we do not quarrel with the state's position. "The concept of the public welfare is broad and inclusive. The values it represents are spiritual as well as physical, aesthetic as well as monetary." Berman v. Parker, 348 U.S. 26 (1954). Accord Village of Belle Terre v. Boraas, 416 U.S. 1 (1974). West Virginia may undoubtedly regulate the siting and operation of solid waste disposal facilities so as to eliminate or at least alleviate the deleterious effects of such facilities on more inchoate community values.

The question raised in this case, however, is whether §20-5F-4(b) does in fact further this laudable purpose or whether it is instead "arbitrary and capricious, having no substantial relation" to its purported goal. See Euclid, 272 U.S., at 395. The state argues that the statute's adverse public sentiment clause promotes its stated purpose by allowing citizens to comment upon a proposed landfill's impact on community pride, spirit, and quality of life. But, with commendable candor, the state also recognizes that many who may speak out against a landfill will do so because of self-interest, bias, or ignorance. These are but a few of the less than noble motivations commonly referred to as the "Not-in-My-Backyard" syndrome.

West Virginia argues that §20-5F-4(b) nonetheless protects the administrative permit process from such base criteria for decision-making by vesting final authority in the Director who must exercise his or her discretion in determining whether adverse public sentiment is "significant." We are unable, however, to discern within the language of §20-5F-4(b) any meaningful standard by which the Director is to measure adverse sentiment. Indeed, the facts of these consolidated cases plainly show that the Director made no effort to cull out the wheat from the chaff of public opposition to these permits. And in the absence of any such effort, whether it be mandated by the statute or attempted as a matter of administrative policy, we can find no substantial or rational relationship between the statute's goals and its means. "Where property interests are adversely affected by zoning, the courts generally have emphasized the breadth of municipal power to control land use and have sustained the regulation if it is rationally related to legitimate state concerns. . . . But an ordinance may fail even under that limited standard of review." Schad v. Mt. Ephraim, 452 U.S. 61, 68 (1981). Nothing in the record suggests, nor can we conceive, how unreflective and unreasoned public sentiment that "a dump is still a dump" is in any way rationally related to the otherwise legitimate goal of protecting community spirit and pride. . . .

Accordingly, we find that §20-5F-4(b)'s clause authorizing the Director to reject permits that are "significantly adverse to the public sentiment" bears no substantial or rational relationship to the state's interest in promoting the general public welfare. The district court's decision is therefore affirmed.

NOTES AND QUESTIONS

1. Note that the West Virginia statute did not *require* that a permit be denied if public sentiment was opposed to it; rather, it authorized a permit to be denied for this reason. Should this have made any difference? Is public opinion an illegitimate ground for making permit decisions? Should state officials disregard public opinion? Is this desirable in a democratic society? Would the decision to deny a permit have been upheld if it had also rested on environmental grounds? Would it have made any difference if the permit denial had been based on aesthetic concerns?

2. Is it inevitable that poor communities will be less successful in opposing the siting of dumps in their backyard? Some economists have

proposed that communities be allowed to bid to avoid dumps, with the losing community being compensated by payments from the winners. What do you think. For a description of the enormous pressures to site dumps in rural areas of Appalachia, see Cornett, Will Appalachian Spring Go Down a Sewer?, N.Y. Times, Sept. 26, 1988, at A23.

3. Recall that concern over the availability of hazardous waste treatment and disposal capacity led Congress in the 1986 Amendments to CERCLA to require states to provide EPA with assurances that adequate capacity would continue to exist. As amended by SARA, section 104(c) of CERCLA required states to provide EPA by October 17, 1989 with assurances that their hazardous waste treatment and disposal capacity will be adequate for the next 20 years. The assurances must be in the form of a contract or cooperative agreement between the state and the federal government. Hazardous waste treatment or disposal facilities covered by the assurances must be located "within the State or outside the State in accordance with an interstate agreement or regional agreement or authority," and they must be in compliance with RCRA subtitle C requirements. States that fail to provide such assurances cannot receive the benefit of any remedial actions by EPA pursuant to section 104 of CERCLA. This provision is designed to put pressure on state authorities to ensure the siting of new hazardous waste treatment and disposal facilities in their states.

The capacity assurance plans filed under section 104(c) of CERCLA indicate that 37 states and the District of Columbia are net exporters of hazardous waste, while 13 other states are net importers of hazardous waste. What implications might this have for the chances of federal legislation authorizing states to adopt hazardous waste import bans? EPA's review of the capacity assurance plans found that many were not realistic in their assumptions concerning future disposal capacity.

4. The difficulties of siting waste disposal facilities increase exponentially when the waste involved is radioactive. The disposal of spent fuel from nuclear power plants and high-level radioactive waste generated by nuclear weapons plants is governed by the Nuclear Waste Policy Act (NWPA). This law, enacted by Congress in 1982, is designed to establish permanent disposal facilities for the thousands of tons of high-level radioactive waste that have accumulated throughout the nation. Recognizing the intense regional opposition that would make siting a single facility difficult, Congress provided that two facilities would be opened—one by 1998 and a second by 2003. Congress anticipated that the wastes would be deposited permanently into rock formations 1,000 to 4,000 feet underground and that one facility would be sited in a western state and the second in the East. The Act provides for extensive public participation in the site selection process, and it permits local authorities to veto site selections.

In 1986, 3 sites in the West were nominated by DOE for the first repository—Yucca Mountain, Nevada; Hanford, Washington; and Deaf Smith, Texas—and 12 sites were proposed for the eastern repository. After fierce public opposition from residents in the vicinity of each site, DOE postponed indefinitely plans for siting a second repository east of the Mississippi. The Yucca Mountain site in Nevada eventually was chosen as DOE's preferred site, and the state was offered $10 million per year in compensation. Opposition to the site from Nevada authorities is intense, and it is unclear whether the site will ever open there. In an effort to force state authorities to accept the facility, DOE has filed a lawsuit against the state of Nevada, which had blocked DOE's application to dig an exploratory shaft into Yucca Mountain. DOE now estimates that no facility will be opened until the year 2010 at the earliest. In the meantime, a pilot waste isolation site in New Mexico that is designed to serve as an interim solution prior to opening of the high-level repository, has encountered technical and legal problems, and the nation appears little closer to solving the nuclear waste disposal problem than it was a decade ago.

5. Disposal of low-level radioactive waste, which includes substances that have become contaminated with small amounts of radioactive materials, is governed by the Low-Level Radioactive Waste Policy Act. This Act (LLRWPA), which was enacted by Congress in 1980, is designed to solve the siting dilemma by encouraging states to enter into regional compacts to handle disposal of such waste. Disposal sites for radioactive waste remain in operation in only three states, South Carolina, Nevada, and Washington, which have become increasingly resistant to serving as dumping grounds for the rest of the nation. Thus, Congress specified that each state must be responsible for the disposal of low-level radioactive waste generated by nonfederal facilities within its borders, either by constructing its own disposal site or by entering into a regional disposal compact. As amended in 1985, the LLRWPA provides that each state must either join a regional waste disposal compact or develop its own site for disposal of low-level radioactive waste. States can prohibit the disposal of low-level radioactive wastes generated in any state that has not joined it in a regional waste disposal compact. Compact regions must identify a host state for a disposal site, and the host state is authorized to impose surcharges on wastes generated in the other states. Existing disposal sites also are permitted to collect escalating surcharges for waste from states that have not met certain milestones specified by Congress. DOE is to distribute funds generated by these surcharges to states that have met the milestones as a financial incentive for expeditious compliance with the Act. By sharply increasing the cost of disposal of low-level waste, the surcharges also encourage waste reduction.

States that have failed to comply with the Act by January 1, 1993 are required to take title to all low-level waste generated within their borders and to assume liability for all damages incurred by the generator as a result of the state's failure to take possession of the waste. In New York v. United States, 942 F.2d 114 (2d Cir. 1991), cert. granted, 60 U.S.L.W. 3475 (1992), the Second Circuit rejected New York's claim that the "take title" provision in the Act infringes on state sovereignty so greatly as to violate the Tenth Amendment. The court observed that the LLRWPA and its amendments "are paragons of legislative success, promoting state and federal comity in a fashion rarely seen in national politics." 942 F.2d at 119. Noting that New York's senators had supported the legislation, the court relied on Garcia v. San Antonio Metropolitan Transit Authority, 469 U.S. 528 (1985), which directed states to rely on the political process to protect their sovereign interests rather than "judicially created limitations on federal power." 469 U.S. at 552. The Supreme Court has agreed to review the Second Circuit's decision. Although many states have missed some of the deadlines contained in the LLRWPA, it has resulted in the creation of several regional compacts and the selection of a number of host states for new disposal facilities. No new low-level radioactive waste facilities are expected to become commercially available until the mid-1990s, but the Act has clearly sped up the siting of new facilities.

6. States that operate federal environmental programs under a delegation of authority from EPA are required to meet minimum federal standards. EPA has the authority to revoke a state's delegated authority if the state fails to operate its program in accordance with federal law. The traditional understanding has been that while states must meet minimum federal standards they are free to adopt regulations more stringent than the federal minimum. In November 1987, EPA for the first time initiated proceedings to withdraw a state's authorization to operate a RCRA program. Ironically, EPA's proposal to withdraw North Carolina's RCRA authorization was not inspired by the state's failure to impose sufficiently stringent controls on waste disposal; it was because a state law would have regulated discharges from hazardous waste disposal facilities so stringently as to prevent the construction of a major facility planned by the GSX Corporation. EPA alleged that because the state law required a thousand-fold dilution of discharges of toxics upstream of public drinking water supplies, it acted as a barrier to the construction of new hazardous waste disposal capacity and was inconsistent with federal policy. Environmentalists criticized the EPA move, claiming that the North Carolina ordinance was a legitimate effort to protect public health and that CERCLA section 104(c), rather than RCRA, is the appropriate vehicle for ensuring adequate state disposal capacity. An administrative law judge and EPA's regional administrator ultimately rejected the proposed withdrawal of North Carolina's authorization. The D.C. Circuit upheld this decision in Hazardous Waste Treatment Council v. Reilly, 938 F.2d 1390 (D.C. Cir. 1991). The court concluded that the state law would be inconsistent with RCRA if it resulted in a total ban

on a particular waste treatment technology in the state. The court found, however, that the law would have permitted the facility to be located in other parts of the state.

7. A major waste disposal company has launched a new initiative to help resolve the siting problem. Browning-Ferris Industries, whose chairman is former EPA administrator William Ruckelshaus, has asked New York communities to compete against one another for the right to host a new solid waste disposal facility. The company has offered to negotiate with interested communities a benefits package that could include jobs, an increased tax base, host fees, property value protection guarantees, and the cleanup of old landfills in the vicinity of the community. As Browning-Ferris's chief financial officer states, this is a sharp contrast with the industry's old approach to siting, which was: "Sneak around, option land, get a permit and shazam! Guess what folks—we're putting a landfill next to the school." Trash Troubles, Wall St. J., May 14, 1991, at A1, A14. New York state officials have warmly embraced the company's efforts to try a new approach to the landfill siting problem. But others have expressed concern that it would simply reinforce the trend of having poor communities shoulder a disproportionate share of the burden of environmental hazards. Gold, Wanted, Land for Dump Sites; Benefits Offered, N.Y. Times, July 20, 1990, at B4. What do you think of the idea of explicitly offering "compensation" as a means for addressing the siting problem? Despite distributing a videotaped promotional package featuring Mr. Ruckelshaus to 1,200 local communities, Browning-Ferris has had no takers. Local officials are quoted as saying that agreeing to a site "would be political suicide" and that "you'd have a hard time finding anybody who would [take one]." Trash Troubles, Wall St. J., May 14, 1991, at A1, A14.

8. Recall the discussion in Chapter 1 of the studies showing that hazardous waste disposal facilities are located disproportionately in minority communities. Could a siting decision be successfully opposed on the ground that it is a product of racial discrimination in violation of the equal protection clause of the Fourteenth Amendment? See R.I.S.E., Inc. v. Kay, 768 F. Supp. 1144 (E.D. Va. 1991) (rejecting such a claim because plaintiffs had failed to establish that placement of a landfill in a predominantly black area of a county was the product of *intentional* discrimination).

2. Waste Reduction: Federal and State Initiatives

Efforts to stimulate greater source reduction and recycling are receiving renewed attention as the limitations of "end-of-the pipe" approaches to pollution control shift the focus of environmental policy toward pollution prevention. As noted above, EPA concluded as early as 1976 that waste reduction and recycling should be the preferred strategies for coping with hazardous and solid waste. 41 Fed. Reg. 35,050 (1976). Both are pollution prevention strategies because they reduce the volume and toxicity of waste that must be treated or disposed. In 1990 Congress declared it to be national policy that "pollution should be prevented at the source wherever feasible." In 1991 EPA established a national goal of reducing the solid waste stream by 25 percent by 1992 and by 50 percent by 1997. While many state and local governments are undertaking exciting initiatives to stimulate source reduction and recycling, there is considerable debate concerning the precise role government should play in pursuing waste reduction initiatives.

Market forces have not produced a socially optimal mix of waste management practices because consumers and producers do not bear the full social costs of their contributions to waste disposal problems. Environmental considerations have rarely been incorporated into product design decisions because producers traditionally have not been responsible for waste disposal. Consumers generally are unaware of the true costs of municipal waste disposal since most local governments do not charge consumers based on the volume of waste they generate.

As government regulation increases the cost (and reduces the availability) of traditional waste disposal options, many officials perceive a waste disposal "crisis" that will force a desperate search for new alternatives. But there is no guarantee that society will invest in the optimal mix of waste management strategies, particularly when a perceived crisis looms. Faith in large-scale, high-tech solutions to problems tends to obscure the more complex reality that a combination of smaller-scale alternatives may be the socially optimal response. Fears of electricity shortages in the early 1970s spawned a massive nuclear power plant construction program that environmentalists argued was an inferior economic choice to investments in greater end-use efficiency and small-scale capacity additions. Although many municipalities are considering whether to build incinerators, is is unlikely that any single alternative will provide the optimal solution to waste management problems. Instead it is likely that some mix of alternatives—source reduction, recycling, incineration, and land disposal—will provide the most economical, and most flexible, response to the "waste disposal crisis."

Broad agreement that source reduction is the environmentally preferred approach leaves open important questions concerning how much of it can be achieved, through what means, and at what cost. The principal policy debate today concerns what role government should play in stimulating greater source reduction. Should reductions in the size of the waste stream be mandated by regulations? Should government provide financial incentives to encourage waste minimization? Or should it simply provide information and technical assistance?

A. THE FEDERAL ROLE

EPA initially believed that a strong regulatory program for waste disposal would stimulate waste reduction efforts. While Congress substantially strengthened the federal regulatory program for hazardous wastes in 1984, it also took the first steps toward an expanded federal role in waste reduction efforts. In the 1984 Amendments to RCRA Congress added a waste minimization certification provision. Section 3005(h) of RCRA requires that RCRA permits for TSDs who generate hazardous waste on-site must include an annual certification by the generators that they have "a program in place to reduce the volume and toxicity of such waste to the degree determined by the generator to be economically practicable." Reluctant to get involved in second-guessing production processes, EPA has stated that it does not interpret this provision as imposing any new obligations on generators to undertake waste minimization programs and that it does not expect to question any certifications it receives.

In the 1984 Amendments to RCRA Congress also directed EPA to consider how a national policy of minimizing the volume and toxicity of hazardous waste could be implemented. In October 1986 EPA responded by issuing a report to Congress entitled Minimization of Hazardous Waste. The report concluded that mandatory waste minimization measures were not yet feasible because more information on waste minimization had to be gathered and evaluated. EPA instead recommended an aggressive nonregulatory program to encourage voluntary waste reduction through the provisions of technical assistance and information.

Other studies confirmed wide agreement concerning the desirability of waste reduction efforts, but found that the absence of a comprehensive framework for encouraging it was hindering its development. Environmental Defense Fund, Approaches to Source Reduction (1986); Office of Technology Assessment, Serious Reduction of Hazardous Waste (1986). In 1987, the Office of Technology Assessment issued a study that found that waste reduction could reduce the generation of hazardous waste by up to 50 percent in five years if a comprehensive program were adopted. OTA, From Pollution to Prevention: A Progress Report on Waste Reduction (1987). OTA recommended that EPA establish an Office of Waste Reduction to serve as the focal point for programs that could be encouraged through technical assistance grants to states and the adoption of voluntary waste reduction goals.

Many of the recommendations made by OTA have now been implemented with the enactment of the Pollution Prevention Act of 1990. EPA has established a pollution prevention office, is operating a data exchange program, and has established national goals for waste reduction.

As required by the Pollution Prevention Act, EPA announced a Pollution Prevention Strategy in January 1991. A cornerstone of EPA's strategy is the establishment of voluntary targets for emissions reductions by industries releasing hazardous chemicals. EPA announced that it planned to target 15 to 20 "high risk" chemicals and to establish "a voluntary goal of reducing total environmental releases of these chemicals by 33 percent by the end of 1992, and at least 50 percent by the end of 1995." EPA, Pollution Prevention Strategy 2 (1991).

By setting broad targets for voluntary source reduction, EPA avoids any direct intervention into production processes, leaving it up to dischargers to decide how best to reduce the amount of pollutants they generate. At the same time, the Pollution Prevention Act now requires companies who must report annual emissions of toxic substances to provide information concerning their projected plans for annual emissions reductions. While nothing in this legislation *requires* companies to reduce emissions, EPA will have a means for monitoring the progress companies are making with source reduction because reporting on waste reduction plans is mandatory. EPA also is seeking to effect voluntary reductions in air emissions by encouraging companies to upgrade their facilities with more energy-efficient lighting. EPA estimates that this "green lights" program will produce voluntary emissions reductions of 235 million tons of air pollution per year. 21 Env. Rep. 1705 (1991).

As Congress considers amendments to RCRA, further initiatives to encourage waste reduction are under consideration. For example, one proposal would amend RCRA to prohibit releases of hazardous substances that constitute more than 5 percent of production throughput. This standard could be waived on a plant-by-plant basis if further waste reduction efforts were shown to be infeasible.

The imposition of taxes to encourage recycling also is receiving increasing attention. A bill that would impose a tax of $7.50 per ton on the manufacture of paper, plastics, glass, aluminum, metal, and other products made with virgin materials has received some support in Congress. The revenue collected from this tax would go into a trust fund to assist states with recycling and waste reduction efforts. While preparing the fiscal year 1991 budget, Bush Administration officials briefly floated the idea of a similar tax on virgin materials, but it was quickly abandoned after protests that it was inconsistent with the administration's supposed "no new taxes" policy.

B. STATE AND LOCAL WASTE REDUCTION INITIATIVES

Ambitious programs to encourage waste reduction have been adopted by several states, and proposals for further initiatives abound.

Oregon and Massachusetts were the first states to require companies to undertake pollution reduction planning and reporting. Several other states (including New York, Connecticut, Maine, New Hampshire, Wisconsin, Vermont, Rhode Island, and Iowa) have adopted a law specifying certain toxic materials that must be phased out of product packaging. The legislation requires manufacturers to phase out the use of lead, mercury, cadmium, and hexavalent chromium in product packaging over four years to reduce the toxicity of the solid waste stream. It is widely expected that the legislation will have a national impact on product packaging because it would be expensive for national manufacturers to make separate products to be marketed in different states.

By 1990, 38 states had enacted laws to promote recycling using a variety of strategies. Many state programs establish overall recycling goals while leaving to counties and municipalities the task of determining how to achieve them. In 1987, New Jersey adopted a mandatory statewide source separation and recycling law designed to reduce the solid waste stream by 25 percent. New Jersey Session Laws, 202d Legis., ch. 102 (1987). The legislation requires counties to implement programs to achieve the 25 percent goal. California has adopted a beverage container deposit law that requires the establishment of recycling centers in shopping centers to make recycling more accessible. A unique provision of this legislation is that the size of the required deposit will increase automatically if recycling goals are not achieved. New York's program couples stringent landfill controls with recycling quotas for municipalities.

Recycling programs have faced difficulties finding markets for recycled materials. Programs are sometimes victims of their own success, as prices for recycled materials plunge when recyclables are collected in large quantities. Allen, As Recycling Surges, Market for Materials Is Slow to Develop, Wall St. J., Jan. 17, 1992, at A3. The waste management industry is promoting the notion that investments in a recycling infrastructure will be encouraged if standards requiring a minimum recyclable content in consumer products are established. Oregon has established standards for the recycled content of glass, newsprint, telephone books, and rigid plastic containers. A coalition of Massachusetts businesses has proposed legislation that would require that packages used in Massachusetts contain at least 25 percent recycled materials, be reusable at least five times, be made of materials that are recycled at a 25 percent rate in the state, or contain at least 10 percent less material by weight than five years previously. Stipp, Massachusetts Business Groups Propose a Broad Recycling and Packaging Law, Wall St. J., Sept. 18, 1991, at B6. The Project 88 coalition has recommended that tradeable permits be considered to provide flexibility for individual firms in meeting overall industry-wide minimum content standards. Project 88—Round II, Incentives for Action: Designing Market-Based Environmental Strategies 55 (1991). Firms could elect either to use the required percentage of recycled materials or to buy credits from other firms who exceeded the minimum-content standard.

Recycling programs can be victims not only of their own success, but also of the construction of new waste disposal capacity that relieves immediate pressures on disposal capacity. Some municipalities have signed contracts with the operators of new incinerators guaranteeing that the incinerators will receive a certain volume of garbage. Such contracts reduce the incentive for municipalities to promote waste reduction and recycling efforts. To counter this problem, EPA had proposed a requirement that 25 percent of a broad class of wastes received by incinerators be recycled, but the proposal was abandoned after objections from the President's Council on Competitiveness.

The environmental impact of consumer products containing plastics has long been a contentious issue between manufacturers and environmentalists. In response to campaigns by environmentalists, a handful of cities have adopted ordinances that ban the use of certain plastic materials in consumer products. This has helped fuel industry efforts to recycle plastics. These efforts have gained momentum recently as several manufacturers have announced plans to build plants to recycle polyethylene, polystyrene, and other plastic materials. Ironically, manufacturers who have sought to promote the introduction of "biodegradeable plastics" as an environmentally preferable alternative have been attacked by environmentalists, who note that such materials are not recyclable. Despite vigorous opposition from the plastics industry, Minneapolis and St. Paul, Minnesota have enacted legislation requiring that plastic containers for consumer products be recycled. This legislation will prohibit the use of plastic containers that cannot be recycled.

The Project 88 coalition has proposed a series of measures to create economic incentives for source reduction and recycling. Project 88—Round II, Incentives for Action: Designing Market-Based Environmental Strategies (1991). They note that if more municipalities levied curbside waste collection charges that varied with the amount of waste consumers discard, consumers would have a powerful incentive to reduce the quantity of waste they generate. Id. at 49-50. By placing differential charges on separated recyclables, source separation and recycling can be encouraged as well. Project 88 notes that concerns about encouraging illegal dumping and the impact of waste collection charges on lower income groups would need to be addressed, but that these are not insurmountable problems.

Project 88 also recommends that consideration be given to retail surcharges, levied when products are sold to reflect their disposal costs, and surcharges for the use of virgin materials levied at the point of production. These surcharges would provide an incentive for consumers and producers to take waste disposal into account when making purchasing and production decisions. Id. at 53-54.

G. PREVENTION VERSUS REMEDIATION: SOME CONCLUDING THEMES

The evolution of environmental policy from a focus on pollution *control* to a focus on pollution *prevention* reflects lessons learned from two decades of environmental regulation. Environmental regulation has produced a dramatic shift in notions of public responsibility for waste management. By establishing the legal principle that generators are responsible for what happens to their waste after it leaves them, CERCLA's broad liability provisions demolished the notion that waste that was out of sight ever could be out of mind. Regulation has encouraged pollution prevention indirectly by raising the costs of pollution control and by requiring expensive efforts to remediate environmental contamination. As regulation has increased the cost of responsible disposal alternatives, notions of environmental responsibility have begun to affect product design decisions more directly.

While pollution prevention has become popular in large part because of the realization that it usually is far cheaper to prevent environmental contamination than to try to clean it up, it is important to appreciate that interrelationship between remediation and prevention. Pollution prevention clearly affects the ultimate scope of remediation because the less contamination there is, the smaller will be the scope of the necessary cleanup.

What is not as clearly understood, however, is that remediation standards have a major impact on incentives to invest in pollution prevention. How liability for environmental contamination is allocated, and how stringently contamination must be remediated, will have a substantial impact on the level of care taken to avoid the creation of future environmental risks. If it is understood that environmental policy requires strict remediation of hazardous substance releases at the expense of those who generate and discharge such substances, the costs of environmentally risky activities will be internalized in the parties most capable of avoiding the creation of the risks. The primary lesson of Superfund's dismal record as a cleanup program is not that strict liability schemes are doomed to failure, but rather that environmental contamination is so difficult and expensive to remediate that society should redouble its efforts to prevent environmental releases.

However, if society decides that contaminated aquifers can simply be written off because it costs more to clean them up than they are worth, incentives for dischargers to invest in prevention will be reduced in the absence of some countervailing liability scheme. Indeed, in some circumstances perverse incentives to pollute an aquifer beyond its economic point of no return actually may be created. Workers can be given some protection from workplace toxins by wearing respirators, and wells served by contaminated aquifers can be fenced off. But we have come to appreciate that humans lose a precious portion of their freedom and autonomy if forced to protect themselves from environmental contamination rather than preventing contamination before it occurs. The shift of policy emphasis toward pollution prevention reflects this appreciation.

=4=

Regulation of Toxic Substances

Some risks are plainly acceptable and others are plainly unacceptable. If, for example, the odds are one in a billion that a person will die from cancer by taking a drink of chlorinated water, the risk clearly could not be considered significant. On the other hand, if the odds are one in a thousand that regular inhalation of gasoline vapors that are 2% benzene will be fatal, a reasonable person might well consider the risk significant and take appropriate steps to decrease or eliminate it.

—*Industrial Union Dept., AFL-CIO v. American Petroleum Institute, 448 U.S. 607, 655 (1980) (Stevens, J., plurality opinion)*

[T]he statutes administered by many federal regulatory agencies typically force some action when scientific inquiry establishes the presence of a risk, as for example, when a substance present in the environment, or the workplace, or the food chain, is found to cause cancer in animals. . . .

When the action so forced has dire economic or social consequences, the person who must make the decision may be sorely tempted to ask for a "reinterpretation" of the data. We should remember that risk assessment data can be like a captured spy: if you torture it long enough, it will tell you anything you want to know.

—*William Ruckelshaus**

Although the first wave of federal environmental legislation focused primarily on control of conventional pollution, regulation of toxic substances has been a major theme of federal environmental law since 1976. This chapter focuses on these regulatory authorities and how they have been applied to control toxic substances.

Few people would quarrel with the notion that society should seek to reduce involuntary exposure to environmental risk. Most of the con-

---

*Risk in a Free Society, 14 Envtl. L. Rep. 10190 (1984).

troversy over toxic substance regulation centers on how to protect public health in the face of the enormous uncertainties surrounding the identification and assessment of environmental risks. These uncertainties are particularly significant because of the extremely serious adverse effects associated with toxic exposure combined with the long latency periods that often occur between exposure and manifestation of the effects.

We begin by reviewing the nature and scope of the toxics problem, highlighting the large quantities of potentially toxic substances in the environment and the enormous uncertainties concerning their effects on human health. The regulatory authorities designed to respond to these problems are introduced next. Although the laws authorize regulation to prevent harm, toxic substance regulation generally has been reactive rather than preventive, largely because of the difficulty of predicting harm before it becomes manifest. Efforts by regulatory authorities and the courts to grapple with this dilemma and to determine how much protection to provide to public health are then explored. The chapter concludes with a discussion of alternative approaches to regulation, including informational regulation and common law liability.

A.   THE TOXIC SUBSTANCE PROBLEM

1.   Introduction

Humans are exposed to a bewildering array of potentially toxic chemicals. Due to rapid growth in the production of synthetic chemicals after World War II, more than 70,000 chemicals now are used in pesticides, food additives, cosmetics, drugs, and other commercial products. More than 1,000 new chemicals are introduced every year. It is estimated that nearly 225 billion pounds of synthetic organic chemicals were produced in 1985, nearly 45 percent more than a decade before. Conservation Foundation, State of the Environment: A View Toward the Nineties 141 (1987). Inorganic chemicals, many of which occur naturally (e.g., radon), are present in the environment in large quantities. These include toxic metals that are mined, processed, and used in commercial products. Yet comprehensive information about toxicity, exposure, and potential human health effects is sorely lacking for the vast majority of such chemicals.

It is known that some chemicals build up in the body tissues of humans and animals over time. In 1980, 3 federal agencies reported that more than 200 industrial chemicals and pesticides had been found in measurable amounts in human body tissue. Interagency Collaborative Group on Environmental Carcinogens, Chemicals Identified in Human

Biological Media: A Data Base (Mar. 1980). For a few substances it is known that high levels of exposure in the past are now causing substantial damage to human health. Thousands of deaths occur each year as a result of past exposure to asbestos, which causes lung cancer, mesothelioma, and asbestosis. Millions of children have elevated levels of lead (which is causing permanent neurological damage) in their bodies due to past use of lead in paint and plumbing, the presence of lead in soil, and continued use of lead in gasoline additives and a variety of other products. While what we know about exposure to toxic substances causes considerable concern, what we don't know also is cause for concern. The following report outlines the problem.

Conservation Foundation, State of the Environment: A View Toward the Nineties 136 (1987)

TOXIC SUBSTANCES . . .

Most of the [eight million different] chemicals [listed by the Chemical Abstracts Service] are not thought of as toxic under normal usage. Some are necessary to life or have been developed to cure illnesses. The National Institute of Occupational Safety and Health Registry of Toxic Substances lists almost 60,000 substances that are known to have toxic effects at some level of exposure. Toxic effects include irritation, mutation, reproductive effects, carcinogenesis, and death. Thus it lists water because people drown in it.

TESTING AND REGULATION

Distressingly little is known about the toxic effects of many chemicals. Manufacturers typically test for acute problems such as skin rashes, eye sensitivity, and immediate mortality of fish, algae, or the insect *Daphnia*. But chronic problems such as cancer, birth defects, and neurological damage are much more difficult to assess. A National Academy of Sciences (NAS) committee evaluated a sample of commercial chemicals to determine the adequacy of the testing done to measure possible human toxicity. It found that fewer than 2 percent of the chemicals had been sufficiently tested to allow a complete health hazard assessment to be made. Sufficient information to support even a partial hazard assessment existed for another 12 percent. Adequate testing was most likely to have been conducted for drugs and pesticides. Even for those substances, however, complete or partial health assessments had been carried out on only about one-third of the chemicals. For most categories, the number of substances lacking any data is much greater than the number for which the data are considered to be minimally adequate. In short, the committee found that, for 70 percent of the substances they reviewed, no information on possible effects on human health existed. For another 16 percent, there was some information, but it was less than the amount needed for a partial hazard assessment. Chemical industry officials say that the lack of data is exaggerated because the NAS study did not include confidential test data in company files. They also point out that the committee analyzed a randomly selected subset of chemicals, and these may not be the substances in greatest use or providing the most exposure.

The NAS committee also found, however, that the frequency and quality of testing are unrelated either to the production volume or to a given substance's potential toxic effects based on its physiochemical properties (as assessed by the committee). For 20 percent of the substances reviewed, the committee had serious concerns about potential adverse human health effects; for another 32 percent, the committee had moderate concerns.

Moreover, the NAS committee only looked at human health risk. In general, much less information is available on environmental hazards and effects of exposure on wildlife than is available on human health risks.

In part because of this lack of data, the number of substances regulated is quite small in comparison with the total number in use. The U.S. Environmental Protection Agency's (EPA's) regulations implementing the Resource Conservation and Recovery Act (RCRA) identify as hazardous approximately 500 process wastes and specific chemicals, along with any wastes that have the characteristics of ignitability, corrosivity, reactivity, and "EP Toxicity." As amended in 1977, the Clean Water Act lists 126 chemical compounds as priority pollutants. The 1986 amendments to the Safe Drinking Water Act (SDWA) require EPA to promulgate regulations for some 80 contaminants, in addition to the 20 already regulated. EPA has regulated only 7 substances under the toxic contaminants section of the Clean Air Act.

The use of 4 existing substances (asbestos, PCBs [polychlorinated biphenyls], chlorofluorocarbons, and dioxins) as well as 60 to 70 "new" chemicals has been restricted under TSCA. (Manufacturers withdrew notice to produce another 80-some chemicals that were likely to be restricted.) EPA also has restricted or banned the use of 50-some pesticides under the Federal Insecticide, Fungicide and Rodenticide Act, although all pesticides are also effectively restricted by the terms of their registration. The Occupational Safety and Health Administration (OSHA) adopted 400 existing standards for air contaminants in 1971. Only 23 substances (at least 13 of which were among the original 400) have since been further restricted due to their highly toxic or carcinogenic nature. . . .

MONITORING PROGRAMS

If little is known about the toxicity of chemical substances, even less is known about the extent of human and environmental exposure. Some information is available on production. The U.S. International Trade Commission, the U.S. Bureau of the Census, the Federal Reserve Board, and some trade associations collect data on imports, exports, and domestic production of many synthetic organic chemicals. The U.S. Bureau of Mines collects information on mineral production and consumption. EPA has 1977 production information for the 63,000 chemicals in the TSCA inventory and is collecting updated information for 15,000 chemicals of greatest concern.

But much less information is available about the extent to which these chemicals exist in the environment. SDWA only requires that public water authorities serving communities over 25 people monitor drinking water for the contaminants regulated under that law. The U.S. Food and Drug Administration (FDA) performs a "Total Diet Study" annually to estimate the U.S. population's dietary intake of some 70 pesticides, industrial chemicals, inorganic compounds, and radionuclides. The U.S. Department of Agriculture is responsible for monitoring antibiotics, pesticide residues, and other substances in meat and poultry. EPA and the states monitor for a few toxic air pollutants, and the U.S. Geological Survey (and some states) monitor for a few toxic surface water pollutants on a widespread basis. But most information on toxic air and water pollution comes from one-time surveys.

Two other periodic surveys provide information on human exposure to toxic substances. Since 1970 EPA has conducted the National Human Adipose Tissue Survey (NHATS) to monitor selected pesticides and certain other toxic substances such as PCBs in human adipose tissue. The National Center for Health Statistics sponsors the National Health and Nutrition Examination Survey (NHANES), which measures levels of lead and some pesticides in human blood and urine, among other health factors. The NHANES results indicate the extent to which the test subjects have recently been exposed to toxic compounds, particularly those that are water soluble. The NHATS results are more indicative of long-term exposure to fat-soluble compounds. . . .

Progress in controlling toxic chemicals is impeded by a lack of basic environmental data, a deficit that monitoring programs are designed to correct. Yet the programs have several limitations. First, current monitoring efforts continue to focus on substances, such as PCBs, DDT, and lead, that have attracted interest in the past and are currently regulated.

Little is being done to identify other toxic substances that may pose enough risk to the environment to warrant monitoring. Part of this lack of action stems from the costs and time required to test new and existing chemicals for their toxicity. Second, most programs are better suited to measure persistent organochlorines than to measure other potentially toxic, yet rapidly degrading, substances. Third, except for the whole animal and human adipose monitoring programs, most programs focus on only one medium of exposure. Fourth, important gaps exist in information derived through monitoring; data exist concerning emissions or ambient concentrations of toxic substances and concerning the presence of those substances in people, animals, and plants, but little is known about the exact channels through which organisms take in those substances. Finally, no system has been established to coordinate and use all the data that are being generated from all these programs within the United States, let alone the data produced by other countries. Thus, much current information is not used by all agencies involved in toxic pollutant control.

NOTES AND QUESTIONS

1. By the end of 1990, three years after the Conservation Foundation report, the number of known chemical compounds worldwide had increased to more than 10 million and the number of chemicals in EPA's TSCA Inventory had risen to 68,000. EPA, Meeting the Environmental Challenge 18 (Dec. 1990). The report's conclusions concerning the lack of toxicity data remained as relevant as ever.

2. Legislation to control human exposure to toxic substances was enacted largely due to concern about the unknown. The perception that workers were being exposed to many new and potentially toxic substances helped inspire enactment of the Occupational Safety and Health Act of 1970. The Senate report on the legislation noted that workers not only suffered from "ancient industrial poisons such as lead and mercury," but also that

> technological advances and new processes in American industry have brought new hazards to the workplace. . . . Indeed, new materials and processes are being introduced into industry at a much faster rate than the present meager resources of occupational health can keep up with. It is estimated that every 20 minutes a new and potentially toxic chemical is introduced into industry. [S. Rep. 91-1282, at 2 (1970).]

To combat these "occupational health problems of unprecedented complexity," Congress created the Occupational Safety and Health Administration (OSHA) and directed it to regulate toxic substances in the workplace.

3. Concern over the unknown health effects of toxic substances also animated enactment of the Toxic Substances Control Act (TSCA) in 1976. TSCA was designed to permit EPA to identify chemical hazards before substantial human exposure occurred. Thus section 5 of TSCA requires any person who intends to manufacture or process a new chemical substance to give EPA at least 90 days' advance notice. If EPA determines that the chemical presents an unreasonable risk or that there are insufficient data to assess its impact on public health or the environment, EPA may seek to prohibit the manufacture or use of the chemical pending the development of sufficient data or the promulgation of rules to control the risk.

4. Incentives for conducting toxicity testing are affected by how the regulatory system allocates the burden of proof. If products must be shown to be safe before they can be used, those seeking to manufacture a new product will gather data to establish the product's safety. But if substances can be marketed and used without restriction until they have been demonstrated to pose a threat to human health, manufacturers actually may be discouraged from gathering data on the toxicity of their products. Because EPA has not required that any specific toxicity tests be performed prior to submission of premanufacture notices (PMNs), section 5 of TSCA has not ensured that adequate toxicity data are gathered for new chemicals. While EPA requires that manufacturers submit whatever toxicity data have been gathered, the majority of PMNs lack any toxicity data, and those that have data frequently have only minimal information. EPA received more than 10,000 PMNs between 1976 and 1987, but it required the manufacturers of only 149 new chemicals to conduct additional testing. TSCA stands in sharp contrast to the federal Food, Drug, and Cosmetic Act, which requires extensive testing and express approval before food additives and therapeutic drugs can be marketed or used.

5. In one respect, data concerning toxic substances have improved significantly since the Conservation Foundation report. While formerly very little was known about the nature and scope of releases of toxics into the environment, the Emergency Planning and Community Right to Know Act (EPCRTKA), 42 U.S.C. §§11001-11050, now requires most companies to disclose annually releases of any of more than 300 hazardous substances. These companies must estimate how much of each chemical they released and the environmental media (e.g., air, surface waters, land, TSD facility, sewers) into which the releases occurred. These data are used to prepare a Toxics Release Inventory (TRI), which is available to the public, as described below.

2. Toxic Substances: How Great a Problem?

A. What Is a "Toxic Substance"?

Toxic substance regulation has been controversial because it involves fundamental issues concerning protection of human life in the face of daunting uncertainties. Even the most basic question—how to define the term "toxic"—can start a contentious debate. The regulated community is quick to cite the observation made by the Swiss alchemist Paracelsus in the sixteenth century that "the dose makes the poison." While it is true that even seemingly innocuous substances (such as water) can be toxic to humans when ingested in sufficiently high doses, this tends to obscure toxicologists' growing understanding that some substances pose far greater risks to humans or the environment than others.

Toxic substances "might be loosely defined as substances capable of causing adverse human health or environmental effects under anticipated conditions of exposure"—a definition loose enough, we can add, to reach almost all the pollutants covered by the environmental statutes. M. Shapiro, Toxic Substances Policy, in Public Policies for Environmental Protection 195, 196 (P. Portney, ed. 1990). Without stumbling unduly over definitions, provisionally you can take "toxic" as a term applied on the basis of a substance's ability to cause serious adverse health and environmental effects at *low* levels of exposure, because the utility of considering toxic substances separately from other pollution problems comes from the fact that toxic substances create a common policy problem stemming in large part from this characteristic.

Of course, even the question of what constitutes an "adverse health or environmental effect" can be controversial. Efforts to assess the risks posed by toxic substances are complicated by the wide range of responses that toxic substances may induce in humans. While a great deal of regulatory effort has been devoted to preventing cancer, toxic substances can cause an enormous variety of significant noncancer health risks that are poorly understood, including damage to the cardiovascular or respiratory systems, neurological disorders, and reproductive damage.

The environmental laws generally give administrative agencies considerable discretion in defining what substances are considered toxic for regulatory purposes. For example, section 112 of the Clean Air Act defines "hazardous air pollutants" as pollutants that "cause, or contribute to, air pollution which may reasonably be anticipated to result in an increase in mortality or an increase in serious irreversible, or incapacitating reversible, illness." The Resource Conservation and Recovery Act employs a very similar definition, then expands it to include any solid waste that may "pose a substantial present or potential hazard to human health or the environment when improperly handled." §1004. The Toxic

Substances Control Act, which never mentions the term "toxic" outside of its title (neither do the preceding two statutes, for that matter), covers chemicals that "may present an unreasonable risk of injury to health or the environment."

Because agencies frequently drag their feet in making discretionary decisions, Congress increasingly is specifying precisely what substances should be considered "toxic" for regulatory purposes. For example, the Emergency Planning and Community Right to Know Act specified an initial list of more than 300 substances that were to be considered "toxic chemicals" for reporting purposes, while giving EPA authority to revise the list. EPCRTKA §302(a), 42 U.S.C. §11002(a). As a result, beginning on July 1, 1987, a large segment of U.S. industry was required to disclose for the first time their annual releases of any of 329 toxic chemicals.

B. ENVIRONMENTAL RELEASES OF TOXIC SUBSTANCES

When EPA released the results of EPCRTKA's first Toxics Release Inventory in April 1989, Agency officials were stunned by the results. The 18,500 companies who reported disclosed that they had released 10.4 billion pounds of toxic chemicals in 1987. A total of 3.9 billion pounds were released into landfills, 3.3 billion pounds were sent to treatment and disposal facilities, 2.7 billion pounds were released into the air, and 550 million pounds were discharged into surface waters. EPA Assistant Administrator Linda Fisher described the totals as "startling," "unacceptably high," and "far beyond" EPA's expectations. Weisskopf, EPA Finds Pollution "Unacceptably High," Wash. Post, April 13, 1989, at A33. Even some companies who filed the reports expressed surprise at the large volumes of toxics they were releasing. After refinements were made in the data (some mining companies discovered that they were not required to report), EPA estimated that approximately 7 billion pounds of toxics had been released in 1987 by reporting companies. The TRI data and the impact of EPCRTKA reporting are discussed in more detail in section E1b of this chapter.

After falling to 4.5 billion pounds for 1988, reported releases for 1989 rose to 5.7 billion pounds—2.4 billion into the air, 1.2 billion into underground injection wells, 445 million pounds into landfills, and 189 million pounds into surface waters. Release of Toxic Chemicals in 1989 Reached 5.7 Billion Pounds, EPA Reports, 22 Env. Rep. 223 (1991). While some viewed this data as encouraging because more facilities (22,650) filed reports for 1989 and industrial production had risen by 7 percent, an environmental organization disagreed, arguing that the TRI data do not include 95 percent of all toxic releases due to noncompliance and limitations on the types of chemicals and facilities that must report. NRDC, The Right to Know More (1991).

C. SIGNIFICANCE OF TOXIC RELEASES

The volume of toxic releases does not provide a very clear indication of their environmental significance. The extent to which toxic substances pose a risk to human health depends on the magnitude and nature of human exposure, about which relatively little is known. Many eminent scientists believe that the toxics problem itself has been vastly overstated. These scientists concede that toxic exposures may on occasion be locally significant, but they argue that by and large overall risks from them are low and certainly lower than other sources of risk such as smoking or diet.

Proponents of this view frequently cite evidence that age-adjusted cancer incidence is generally declining. They also note that prominent epidemiologists attribute only 2 percent of cancer mortality to environmental pollution and 4 percent to occupational exposures. Doll and Peto, The Causes of Cancer: Quantitative Estimates of Avoidable Risks of Cancer in the United States Today, 66 J. Natl. Cancer Inst. 1191 (1981); Gough, Environmental Exposures and Cancer Risks, Resources 9 (Winter 1990).

Other scientists are skeptical of these estimates, see, e.g., 54 Fed. Reg. 2,781 (because Doll and Peto excluded cancers that occurred in people over age 65, OSHA notes that it may be reasonable to assume that 10 percent of all cancers are occupationally induced), and they note new studies detecting alarmingly rapid increases in certain kinds of cancer—brain cancer, breast cancer, melanoma, multiple myeloma, and non-Hodgkins lymphoma—throughout the industrialized world. Davis, Hoel, Fox, and Lopez, International Trends in Cancer Mortality in France, West Germany, Italy, Japan, England and Wales and the USA, 336 Lancet 474 (1990). Critics of this view attribute reported increases in cancer incidence to better detection and reporting. Marshall, Experts Clash Over Cancer Data, 250 Science 900 (1990).

While there is ample reason for skepticism on either side, debates over cancer incidence illustrate how regulatory policy has tended to place far more emphasis on controlling cancer risks than other environmental health risks. Risk assessment techniques are better developed for cancer than for neurological, reproductive, or developmental risks, and regulators often assume that regulations to protect against cancer will also protect against other health risks. Scientists are now beginning to question the accuracy of such assumptions. Gibbons, Reproductive Toxicity: Regs Slow to Change, 254 Science 25 (1991).

3. The Evolution of Regulatory Policy

Toxics policy in this country is still evolving. Indeed, it is one of the most volatile components of American environmental policy. By any measure, the volume of toxic chemicals released into the U.S. environment each year is enormous. This suggests that significant gaps remain in the regulatory system despite two decades of federal regulation. The relatively simple formulations of toxic regulations found in early statutes such as the 1970 Clean Air Act and the 1972 Clean Water Act are being replaced by more complex and comprehensive provisions, and both Congress and the executive branch have been and are working to plug the holes in the regulatory program. One issue the materials in this chapter should help you explore is why these holes still exist in a policy area where Congress long ago supposedly signalled its desire to be "precautionary." (See Ethyl Corp. v. EPA, below.) A variety of explanations have been proposed, among them that:

1—Early on, Congress misunderstood the nature and scope of the toxics problem; hence it wrote statutes inappropriate to deal with the problems as we now understand them.

2—Congress perhaps did not so much misunderstand the problem as it manipulated it, writing largely symbolic but unrealistic legislation in order to send favorable political messages to a mobilized environmental constituency, producing unrealistic legislation that has proved almost impossible to implement. *Symbolic*

3—As a society, we as yet have no consensus of how strictly we want to control toxics; in such circumstances it is understandable in a responsive system of representative government that neither EPA nor Congress has been able to articulate coherent and effective policy.

4—The issues raised by toxics are genuinely hard and to a certain extent novel in the American experience; they implicate both the frontiers of scientific knowledge and Americans' basic attitudes toward relatively uncontrolled entrepreneurial expansion as well as their confidence, or lack thereof, that government can ameliorate social problems without creating worse ones in the process. *We don't trust gov't today.*

For some of the extensive commentary on these possibilities, see F. Cross, Environmentally Induced Cancer and the Law (1989); J. Mendelhoff, The Dilemma of Toxic Substance Regulation (1988); Ingram, The Political Rationality of Innovation: The Clean Air Act Amendments of 1970, in Approaches to Controlling Air Pollution (A. Friedlander, ed. 1978); Elliott, Ackerman, and Millian, Toward a Theory of Statutory Evolution: The Federalization of Environmental Law, 1 J.L. Econ. & Org. 313 (1986); Merrill, FDA's Implementation of the Delaney Clause: Repudiation of Congressional Choice or Reasoned Adaptation to Scientific Progress?, 5 Yale J. on Reg. 1 (1985); Dwyer, The Pathology of Symbolic Legislation, 17 Ecology L.Q. 233 (1990).

NOTES AND QUESTIONS

1. Is it surprising to you that such a large volume of toxic materials continues to be released into the environment despite nearly two decades of rapid growth in federal environmental legislation? Based on the discussion of RCRA in Chapter 3, how would you explain why most hazardous substances that are released are not sent to treatment and disposal facilities with RCRA permits?

2. How would you characterize the seriousness of the toxics "problem"? Is it a result of society's fear of the unknown, or is it the product of unpleasant surprises that have been discovered only after substantial damage has been done? What additional information would you wish to obtain before deciding how to allocate additional resources to toxic chemical regulation?

We now turn to examination of the provisions of the environmental laws that were written specifically to address the toxics problem.

B. STATUTORY AUTHORITIES FOR REGULATING TOXIC SUBSTANCES

A complex array of statutory authorities can be used to address the risks presented by toxic chemicals. The most comprehensive regulatory authority is contained in the Toxic Substances Control Act (TSCA), which gives EPA authority over any chemical substance or mixture (other than pesticides regulated by FIFRA and food products, drugs, and cosmetics, regulated by the Food and Drug Administration). The Federal Insecticide, Fungicide, and Rodenticide Act (FIFRA) governs EPA's regulation of pesticides; the Safe Drinking Water Act (SDWA) governs EPA regulation of contaminants in public drinking water systems; section 112 of the Clean Air Act requires EPA to regulate emissions of hazardous air pollutants; and sections 304(*l*) and 307 of the Clean Water Act require EPA to regulate toxic water pollutants.

Agencies other than EPA also have significant authority to regulate toxic substances. The Food and Drug Administration (FDA), which is part of the Department of Health and Human Services, has jurisdiction over foods, drugs, cosmetics, and medical devices under the federal Food, Drug, and Cosmetic Act (FDCA). The Labor Department's Occupational Safety and Health Administration (OSHA) is responsible for protecting workers against toxic chemical hazards in the workplace pursuant to the Occupational Safety and Health Act (OSH Act). Workers in mines are protected separately under the federal Mine Safety and Health Act (MSHA), which is administered by the Department of Labor and its National Institute of Occupational Safety and Health. The Consumer Product Safety Commission (CPSC) regulates hazardous consumer products pursuant to the Consumer Product Safety Act (CPSA), and it also administers the Federal Hazardous Substances Act and the Poison Prevention Packaging Act, which require labeling of hazardous and poisonous substances. The Nuclear Regulatory Commission is responsible for regulating radioactive substances under the Atomic Energy Act.

This is by no means an exhaustive list. Several other statutes address specific aspects of the toxic substances problem. In 1985, the Office of Science and Technology Policy identified 21 different statutes that may be used by 12 different agencies just to regulate carcinogens.

Statutory authorities for regulating toxics differ greatly in the extent to which they require review or approval prior to the manufacture or use of such substances. The federal Food, Drug, and Cosmetic Act requires FDA approval prior to the marketing of new food additives, drugs, and cosmetics. EPA must approve the registration of new pesticides under FIFRA and, as noted above, the Agency must be notified under section 5 of TSCA 90 days prior to the manufacture of a new chemical or the application of an old chemical to a significant new use. While TSCA is rarely used to prevent products from reaching the market, FIFRA and the FDCA are "licensing laws" that require some form of express licensing or approval prior to introducing a chemical into commerce. A broader class of statutes, "standard-setting laws," require agencies to establish standards limiting toxic emissions, controlling worker exposure to toxics, or mandating warning labels on products. These include the OSH Act, the Safe Drinking Water Act, the Consumer Product Safety Act, TSCA, and the provisions of the Clean Air and Clean Water Acts that deal with toxic substances.

The statutes that authorize regulation of toxic substances employ different approaches for determining how to set standards. As indicated in Figure 4.1, these approaches are of three general types, mirroring the three bases for regulatory controls discussed in Chapter 2, pages 146 to 149. Some statutes (e.g., TSCA and FIFRA) require that regulators balance the threat to public health against the cost of regulation when setting regulatory standards—thus, they are balancing statutes. Others (e.g., the OSH Act and the Safe Drinking Water Act) direct that threats to health be regulated as stringently as is feasible. Such statutes are a special case of the standards called technology-based in Chapter 2. Because the concern with toxics exposure at any level is so great that Congress frequently expresses the desire to eliminate exposure if only it were feasible, such standards as those of the OSH Act and the SDWA can also be termed technology- or feasibility-*limited*, rather than feasibility-based. We sometimes use that terminology here. A third approach (which is embodied in section 112 of the Clean Air Act and the Delaney

FIGURE 4.1
Summary of Federal Laws Regulating Toxic Substances

BALANCING STATUTES

Law	Type of controls	Threshold finding	Basis for controls
Food, Drug, and Cosmetic Act (FDCA)	controls levels of natural components of foods	"poisonous or deleterious . . . does not ordinarily render it injurious to health"	balances risk against need for plentiful and affordable food
FDCA	controls levels of environmental contaminants in foods	"poisonous or deleterious . . . does not ordinarily render it injurious to health"	balances risk against whether required, unavoidable, or measurable
FDCA	regulates introduction of new drugs and biologics	"substantial evidence that [it is] safe and effective"; "no imminent hazard to public health"	balances risk against efficacy and impact on health
Federal Insecticide, Fungicide, and Rodenticide Act ✶ FIFRA	prohibits use of pesticides unless registered by EPA; EPA may restrict or condition usage	"will not generally cause any unreasonable risk to man or the environment"	balances adverse impacts of pesticide on human health and the environment against benefits of pesticide
Toxic Substances Control Act	restricts or prevents production, use, or disposal of existing chemicals (§6); requires testing of existing chemicals where data are inadequate to assess risk (§4); prohibits introduction into commerce of chemicals that will present unreasonable risk (§5)	"reasonable basis to believe presents or will present an unreasonable risk of injury to human health or the environment"	balances risk posed by chemicals against economic consequences of regulation
Consumer Product Safety Act	authorizes bans of unreasonably dangerous consumer products	"an unreasonable risk of injury"	balances risk against product utility, cost, and availability

TECHNOLOGY- or FEASIBILITY-LIMITED STATUTES

Occupational Safety and Health Act	sets limits on worker exposure to toxic substances in the workplace	existence of a significant risk that can be reduced appreciably by regulation	ensures that no worker suffers material impairment of health or functional capacity to the extent feasible

FIGURE 4.1
Continued

Law	Type of controls	Threshold finding	Basis for controls
Safe Drinking Water Act	limits contaminants in public drinking water supplies	"may have an adverse effect on the health of persons"	reduces contaminants as closely as feasible to levels where no adverse health effects will occur and which allow an adequate margin of safety
Clean Water Act	sets effluent standards for discharges of toxic pollutants into surface waters	"identifiable effects on health and welfare"	uses best available technology to control discharges with health-based water quality standards as backstop

HEALTH-BASED STATUTES

Law	Type of controls	Threshold finding	Basis for controls
§112 of the Clean Air Act	establishes emission standards for hazardous air pollutants	substance is one of 189 chemicals on initial list specified in statute or added to list on finding that it may present "a threat of adverse human health effects"	sets limits that "provide an ample margin of safety to protect the public health" if technology-based controls fail to do so after 8 years
FDCA	controls levels of added substances in food	"any poisonous or deleterious substance which may render it injurious to health"	prohibition
FDCA	controls levels of added substances in food	"induce[s] cancer in laboratory animals"	prohibition

Clauses of the FDCA) is to require that standards be based exclusively on concerns for protecting public health (health-based statutes). As amended in 1990, section 112 now requires that technology-based controls (reflecting the maximum achievable control technology, or MACT) be applied initially to control hazardous air pollutants, supplemented with purely health-based controls after eight years.

The statutes that employ these three approaches differ substantially in the amount and kind of evidence that must be shown before a substance can be regulated and in the type of controls that they authorize regulators to impose. Some laws authorize outright prohibitions on the manufacture or use of certain chemicals (e.g., TSCA, FIFRA, FDCA), while others authorize the establishment of emission standards or ambient concentration limits (CAA, CWA, OSH Act), restrictions on use, and labeling, warning, or reporting requirements (TSCA).

Figure 4.1 offers a rough comparison of the statutory authorities for regulating toxics. The choice of which statutory authorities to use and how to employ them can make a significant difference in the stringency and effectiveness of regulation. The sections that follow explore how several of these statutes have been applied to control particular toxic substances. A key issue in these regulatory decisions has been how much and what kind of information is necessary before regulatory action can be taken. Most of the statutes do not specifically address this issue. Except for section 112 of the Clean Air Act, which specifies precisely what pollutants must be regulated, the statutes outline general criteria to guide regulatory decisions while giving agencies considerable leeway in determining whether and what to regulate. Courts reviewing agency decisions have grappled with the difficult issue of how to ensure that agency discretion is properly exercised in the face of considerable scientific uncertainty. Given the great uncertainties that surround assessment of environmental risks, the allocation of burdens of proof can have an enormous impact on regulatory outcomes.

C. UNCERTAINTY AND THE DILEMMA OF PREVENTATIVE REGULATION

The demand for environmental regulation is overwhelmingly a demand to *prevent* harm. However, it is difficult to predict precisely what activities will cause what harm. Often the first clue that something is harmful is provided by the discovery that harm has occurred. Scientific uncertainty makes this "dilemma of preventative regulation" particularly acute with respect to regulation of toxic substances.

Faced with this pervasive uncertainty, decisionmakers have increasingly relied on a two-step process for making environmental policy decisions. "Risk assessment" is the process used to characterize the environmental effects of exposure to hazardous materials or situations. "Risk management" is the process of weighing policy alternatives to select the most appropriate regulatory action, if any, for responding to these risks. It is not surprising that there are different approaches to characterizing risks. There is just as wide a divergence of opinion concerning the proper approach to risk management. The "cool analysts" would employ an augmented form of cost-benefit analysis to determine what activities are worth regulating and how stringently to regulate them. The "morally outraged" would regulate without regard to cost considerations, based either on the technologies available for controlling risks or on purely environmental or health-based goals.

As you examine our experience in regulating toxics, consider what portion of the controversy stems from disagreements about items we generally consider to be facts, such as the nature of the adverse health effects associated with toxic exposure, the amount of exposure occurring, or the relationships between different levels of exposure and adverse health effects, and what portion stems from disputes about how to respond to the "facts" as we currently understand them.

1.   Defining and Identifying Risks

Before an agency or court is authorized to regulate any substance or product, some threshold finding must be made, almost always with respect to the harmful potential of the substance or product. For instance, the agency might be instructed to act when it had definitive proof that a substance or product will in fact cause harm if exposure continues. Section 108 of the Clean Air Act, for example, originally ordered EPA to establish ambient air quality criteria for certain pollutants "which, in the judgment [of the administrator], [have] an adverse effect on public health or welfare." This was viewed as requiring proof of actual harm before agency action could be taken. Ethyl Corp. v. EPA, 541 F.2d 1, 14 (D.C. Cir. 1976). One implication of such a threshold requirement in the toxics area is that one is thereby committed to "counting the dead bodies," as environmentalists like to say, before regulating, because definitive evidence of harm to humans typically comes only when actual deaths or illnesses can be linked to past exposure to toxics.

One striking characteristic of modern statutes regulating toxic substances is their manifest unwillingness to wait for definitive proof. They instruct agencies and courts to act in advance of such proof; in other words, when either the harmful nature of a substance or the magnitude of the harm that it will cause, or both, are still doubtful. The crucial question then is: What must we know before it is appropriate to regulate?

Historical experience—as opposed to regulatory theory—indicates that until recently we have still waited for "dead bodies" before implementing strict regulation. Relatively few substances have been subject to regulation because of their chronic health effects. Most of the chemicals that have been regulated on this basis became the focus of regulatory attention only after highly publicized incidents in which high-level, acute exposures caused visible and substantial harm. See E. Silbergeld and R. Percival, The Organometals: Impact of Accidental Exposures and Experimental Data on Regulatory Policies, in Neurotoxicants and Neurobiological Function: Effects of Organoheavy Metals 328 (H. Tilson and S. Sparber, eds. 1987). For example, regulatory action to restrict mercury discharges was undertaken soon after the discovery that children in Minimata, Japan had suffered severe birth defects from mercury that had accumulated in fish from waste discharges between 1953 and 1960.

In other cases opportunities to prevent significant, chronic health damage were missed despite highly publicized incidents involving acute exposures. In October 1924 the use of lead additives in gasoline became a source of considerable public controversy after five workers in a tetra-ethyl lead processing plant in Elizabeth, New Jersey died from acute lead poisoning. Several cities banned the use of tetraethyl lead, which was taken off the market while a panel convened by the Surgeon General studied the health effects of lead additives. After a study was quickly prepared showing that gas station attendants where leaded gasoline was sold did not have higher levels of lead in their blood, tetraethyl lead returned to the market. Rosner and Markowitz, A Gift of God?: The Public Health Controversy over Leaded Gasoline During the 1920s, 75 Am. J. Pub. Health 344 (1985). While the Surgeon General recognized that the study was inadequate for assessing the long-term effect of lead additives on human health, recommended followup studies were not undertaken. It was not until several decades later that regulatory attention focused on the effects of lead emissions on children's health.

One of the early important cases addressing the issue of how much must be known before we can regulate was Reserve Mining Co. v. EPA, 514 F.2d 492 (8th Cir. 1975) (en banc). In that case, the federal government, joined by Minnesota, Wisconsin, Michigan, and several environmental groups, had brought suit under the Clean Water Act, the Rivers and Harbors Act, and the federal common law of nuisance against the Reserve Mining Company for discharging taconite tailings. An Eighth Circuit panel stayed a district court order requiring the company immediately to cease discharging taconite tailings into Lake Superior and into the ambient air around its iron ore processing plant. Reserve Mining Co. v. United States, 498 F.2d 1073 (8th Cir. 1974). The district court had found that both air and water discharges "substantially endanger" the surrounding population, despite the inconclusiveness of evidence concerning their effects on human health. Although it was known that the taconite tailings contained asbestiform fibers extremely similar to those known to cause diseases in occupational settings, there was no evidence that exposures experienced by the population surrounding the plant had increased the incidence of such diseases. A study commissioned by the court had found that the body tissues of recently deceased residents of the area were virtually free of such fibers.

In announcing the stay, the Eighth Circuit stated:

> The discharges may or may not result in detrimental health effects, but, for the present, that is simply unknown. The relevant legal question is thus what manner of judicial cognizance may be taken of the unknown.
> We do not think that a bare risk of the unknown can amount to

proof in this case. Plaintiffs have failed to prove that a demonstrable health hazard exists. This failure, we hasten to add, is not reflective of any weakness which it is within their power to cure, but rather, given the current state of medical and scientific knowledge, plaintiffs' case is based only on medical hypothesis and is simply beyond proof. [498 F.2d at 1083-1084.]

Federal and state environmental officials responded to this decision with alarm. A bill was introduced in Congress to shift the burden of proof to polluters to prove the safety of their discharges once it was shown that they presented "a reasonable risk of being a threat to public health." Supporting this proposed legislation, then-CEQ chairman Russell W. Peterson explained the problem in the following terms:

> Because of the latent health effects of carcinogens it will be more than 10 years before the magnitude of the health risk to the people of Duluth and Silver Bay will be fully realized, and unfortunately it will be based upon the fate of over 200,000 people. Even a few more days of additional exposure pose an unnecessary and unacceptable risk to the residents of the area. [Peterson, letter to Hon. Wallace H. Johnson, reprinted in Burdens of Proof in Environmental Litigation, Hearing before the Subcomm. on Environment of the Senate Commerce Comm., 93d Cong., 2d Sess. 8 (1974).]

Despite the absence of evidence of actual harm to health, in its subsequent en banc decision the Eighth Circuit ultimately endorsed precautionary regulation. The court concluded that the "public's exposure to asbestos fibers in air and water creates some health risk" that justified "abatement of the health hazard on reasonable terms as a precautionary and preventive measure to protect the public health." 514 F.2d at 520. In fashioning its relief, the court sought to "strike a proper balance between the benefits conferred and the hazards created by Reserve's facility" by giving the company time to establish an alternative disposal site for the tailings on land. 514 F.2d at 535.

A second influential early decision was *Ethyl* Corp. v. EPA, 541 F.2d 1 (D.C. Cir. 1976) (en banc). *Ethyl Corp.* involved part of the Clean Air Act that at the time of the decision authorized EPA to regulate gasoline additives if their emissions products "will endanger the public health or welfare" (§211(c)(1)(A)). The EPA reviewed a number of suggestive, but inconclusive, studies on the effects of lead emissions from gasoline exhausts on urban populations, especially children. The administrator concluded that lead in gasoline presented "a substantial risk of harm," and on that basis ordered reductions in the lead content of gasoline.

Ethyl Corp. highlighted the uncertainty that dogs risk analyses. It was impossible for the EPA to demonstrate conclusively that lead was harmful at the levels being considered; nor could EPA determine precisely the probability that lead at such levels was harmful. So, just as important as the question of how to select a course of action in the face of a known risk, the administrator had to decide how to proceed in the face of uncertain risk.

The lead additive manufacturers sought judicial review of EPA's decision. They claimed the statute required EPA to have "proof of actual harm" from auto emissions of lead before it could order limits on the amount of lead in gasoline. In December 1974, a three-judge panel of the D.C. Circuit, with one dissent, struck down the regulations. The panel held that there was insufficient evidence to prove that lead emissions "will endanger the public health or welfare," as required by the Clean Air Act. The majority stated that "the case against auto lead emissions is a speculative and inconclusive one at best."

EPA sought a rehearing en banc, and the full court agreed to hear the case. In March 1976, the court reversed the panel decision in a 5-4 decision. The majority's decision was written by the late Judge J. Skelly Wright.

Ethyl Corp. v. EPA
541 F.2d 1 (D.C. Cir. 1976) (en banc)

WRIGHT, Circuit Judge:

. . . Case law and dictionary definition agree that endanger means something less than actual harm. When one is endangered, harm is *threatened;* no actual injury need ever occur. Thus, for example, a town may be "endangered" by a threatening plague or hurricane and yet emerge from the danger completely unscathed. A statute allowing for regulation in the face of danger is, necessarily, a precautionary statute. Regulatory action may be taken before the threatened harm occurs; indeed, the very existence of such precautionary legislation would seem to *demand* that regulatory action precede, and, optimally, prevent, the perceived threat. . . .

The Administrator read [§211(c)(1)(A)] [as a precautionary statute], interpreting "will endanger" to mean "presents a significant risk of harm." We agree with the Administrator's interpretation. . . .

While the dictionary admittedly settles on "probable" as its measure of danger, we believe a more sophisticated case-by-case analysis is appropriate. Danger, the Administrator recognized, is not set by a fixed probability of harm, but rather is composed of reciprocal elements of risk and harm, or probability and severity. . . . That is to say, the public health may properly be found endangered both by a lesser risk of a greater harm and by a greater risk of a lesser harm. Danger depends upon the relation between the risk and harm presented by each case, and cannot legitimately be pegged to "probable" harm, regardless of whether that harm be great or small. . . .

Where a statute is precautionary in nature, the evidence difficult to come by, uncertain, or conflicting because it is on the frontiers of scientific knowledge, the regulations designed to protect the public health, and the decision that of an expert administrator, we will not demand rigorous step-by-step proof of cause and effect. Such proof may be impossible to obtain if the precautionary purpose of the statute is to be served. Of course, we are not suggesting that the Administrator has the power to act on hunches or wild guesses. . . . [H]is conclusions must be rationally justified. . . . However, we do hold that in such cases the Administrator may assess risks. He must take account of available facts, of course, but his inquiry does not end there. The Administrator may apply his expertise to draw conclusions from suspected, but not completely substantiated, relationships between facts, from trends among facts, from theoretical projections from imperfect data, from probative preliminary data not yet certifiable as "fact," and the like. We believe that a conclusion so drawn—a risk assessment—may, if rational, form the basis for health-related regulations under the "will endanger" language of Section 211.[58]

---

58. It bears emphasis that what is herein described as "assessment of risk" is neither unprecedented nor unique to this area of law. To the contrary, assessment of risk is a normal part of judicial and administrative fact-finding. Thus EPA is not attempting to expand its powers; rather, petitioners seek to constrict the usual flexibility of the fact-finding process. Petitioners argue that the Administrator must decide that lead emissions "will endanger" the public health solely on "facts," or, in the words of the division majority, by a "chain of scientific facts or reasoning leading [the administrator] ineluctably to this conclusion. . . ." Petitioners demand sole reliance on *scientific* facts, on evidence that reputable scientific techniques certify as certain. Typically, a scientist will not so certify evidence unless the probability of error, by standard statistical measurement, is less than 5%. That is, scientific fact is at least 95% certain.

Such certainty has never characterized the judicial or the administrative process. It may be that the "beyond a reasonable doubt" standard of criminal law demands 95% certainty. But the standard of ordinary civil litigation, a preponderance of the evidence, demands only 51% certainty. A jury may weigh conflicting evidence and certify as adjudicative (although not scientific) fact that which it believes is more likely than not. . . . Inherently, such a standard is flexible; inherently, it allows the fact-finder to assess risks, to measure probabilities, to make subjective judgments. Nonetheless, the ultimate finding will be treated, at law, as fact and will be affirmed if based on substantial evidence, or, if made to a judge, not clearly erroneous.

The standard before administrative agencies is no less flexible. . . . Thus, as a matter of administrative law, the Administrator found as *fact* that lead emissions "will endanger" the public health. That in so doing he did not have to rely solely on proved scientific fact is inherent in the requirements of legal

NOTES AND QUESTIONS

1. *Reserve Mining* and *Ethyl Corp.* differ in several respects. For one thing, in *Reserve* a federal court was asked in the first instance to regulate potentially harmful behavior, while in *Ethyl Corp.* an administrative agency had taken the initial step, which then came before the court for judicial review. In section E2 of this chapter we discuss the role of courts as regulators of toxic exposure through toxic tort litigation that seeks damages or injunctions.

Second, *Reserve* involved a substance, taconite mill tailings, that had not yet been shown to cause adverse health effects, although it was judged physically indistinguishable at the fiber level from asbestos fibers, which had been. The medical concern in *Reserve* was based on a medical opinion, found by the district court to be "reasonable," that such similarity was enough to raise a public health concern. *Ethyl Corp.*, in contrast, involved lead, an element known to be "toxic, causing anemia, severe intestinal cramps, paralysis of nerves, fatigue, and even death." 541 F.2d at 8. The question for the EPA administrator, however, was not whether lead was toxic; rather, as carefully framed by the court, it was whether "the automotive emissions caused by leaded gasoline present 'a significant risk of harm' to the public health." 541 F.2d at 7. The answer to this question was much less clear than the question of whether lead was toxic, because inhalation of airborne lead (auto emissions contributed 90 percent of the total lead in urban air) was only one of several significant sources of lead exposure for urban children (ingestion of lead-based paint, diet, and ingestion of lead in dirt and dust were others), because it was unclear how much inhaled lead contributed to the total body burden of lead, and because it was uncertain at what level of total body burden it became appropriate to conclude lead was having an adverse health effect.

2. EPA had based its decision to require reductions in lead additives on three conclusions: (1) based on a preliminary determination that levels of 40 μg/dl of lead in blood is indicative of a danger to health, a significant part of the population was currently experiencing a dangerous condition because blood lead levels in excess of 40 μg/dl existed to a small but significant extent in the general adult population and to a very great extent among children; (2) airborne lead is directly absorbed in the body through respiration to a degree that constitutes a significant risk to public health; and (3) airborne lead falls to the ground, where it mixes with

---

fact-finding. Petitioners' assertions of the need to rely on "fact" confuse the two terminologies. We must deal with the terminology of law, not science. At law, unless the administrative or judicial task is peculiarly factual in nature, or Congress expressly commands a more rigorous finding, assessment of risks as herein described typifies both the administrative and the judicial fact-finding function, and is not the novel or uprecedented theory that petitioners contend.

dust and poses a significant risk to the health of urban children. The court observed that while no specific blood lead level could be identified as the threshold for danger, the 40-μg level was a conservative standard, and that studies of the blood lead levels of workers who work outside and whose only exposure to lead is through the ambient air justified EPA's second conclusion. The court found that theoretical, epidemiological, and clinical studies also supported the second conclusion, and it upheld the third conclusion as a hypothesis that is consistent with known information about the behavior of children and the presence of high lead concentrations in urban soil and dust.

3. Shortly after the *Ethyl Corp.* decision, Congress amended the Clean Air Act to change the standard for regulating fuel additives from "will endanger public health or welfare" to "may reasonably be anticipated to endanger the public health or welfare." Is the new statutory standard more consistent with what the EPA administrator actually found in support of the lead phasedown decision than the "will endanger" standard is?

4. The idea that danger or risk is a composite of the probability of harm occurring and the magnitude of the harm that might occur, which was embraced by Judge Wright in *Ethyl Corp.* when he wrote that "danger" is composed of "reciprocal elements of risk and harm or probability and severity," has proved widely influential.

As explained earlier, a federal agency must make some threshold finding about a toxic substance before regulation is appropriate. Very often that finding will be related to the danger posed by the substance— sometimes that the substance poses a "significant risk" or an "unreasonable risk," sometimes that the substance "will endanger public health," as in *Ethyl Corp.*, sometimes that the substance "may reasonably be anticipated to endanger public health," as section 211 was subsequently amended to read. (We will return to explore the differences between these and other formulations in Section D of this chapter.)

Whatever the threshold happens to be, the idea that danger is composed of reciprocal elements of probability and severity has the implication that two exposures might both satisfy the threshold finding, even though the probability of one causing harm is much less than the probability of the other one causing harm, as long as the severity of the harm associated with the first is correspondingly greater than that associated with the second. In an article published shortly after *Ethyl Corp.*, Talbot Page employed the image of a seesaw to depict the underlying concept. See Page, A Generic View of Toxic Chemicals and Similar Risks, 7 Ecology L.Q. 207 (1978). We will adopt the same imagery here.

In both Figure 4.2 and Figure 4.3 the Threshold Finding can represent any of the various formulations mentioned above. The regulator's initial task is to determine whether the substance under review exceeds that threshold level of concern or, in seesaw terms, whether the left side

FIGURE 4.2

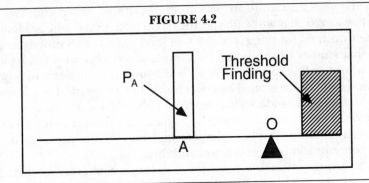

FIGURE 4.3

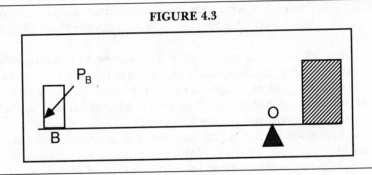

outweighs the right side. The seesaw gives us two variables, distance from the pivot and the weight placed on the seesaw. We can let the distance from the seesaw (OA in Figure 4.2, OB in Figure 4.3) represent the severity of harm associated with the substances under review, and we can let the weight placed on the seesaw (P_A in Figure 4.2, P_B in Figure 4.3) represent the probability (P) that harm will actually occur. Then, according to the physics we all learned as children playing on seesaws, the left side will outweigh the right as long as the combination of the weight on the left side and the distance that weight is from the pivot are great enough. Therefore, it is possible that both substance A and substance B, which has a lower probability of causing harm than Substance A but will cause more harm if it turns out to be harmful, will exceed the threshold finding.

Straightforward as this idea may initially seem, it has powerful implications. One of the most dramatic arises with substances that exceed the relevant threshold even though they have fairly low probabilities of causing harm, because that harm would be catastrophic should it occur. Suppose, for example, that the harm that might occur because of some exposure was 10 times greater than a harm that we would want to prevent if we were certain the smaller harm would occur. Then the seesaw concept of risk or danger would urge us to regulate that exposure even though we thought it only 10 percent likely that the harm would actually occur. Figures 4.2 and 4.3 show why. If in Figure 4.2 OA represents the smaller, certain harm and is 1/10 of the larger, feared harm, and P_A represents 100 percent probability, then, on the assumption that substance A exceeds the threshold finding, so will substance B, as long as P_B is at least 1/10 of P_A, or 10 percent. Each should be regulated.

Now suppose that we have a number of substances like substance B—substances that may cause substantial harm, but as to which we are relatively uncertain whether they will. Will following the indications of the seesaw make sensible policy? In terms statisticians (and environmental lawyers) use, following this policy means that we will expect to see more "false positives," chemicals regulated that turn out not to cause the anticipated harm, than "false negatives," chemicals not regulated that turn out to cause harm. This is so because our policy is to regulate such substances when there is only a small chance that the exposure will prove harmful in the feared way. Using the numbers from our example, regulating when there is a 10 percent chance the harm will occur means that over a number of different regulatory decisions we are actually expecting to be wrong 90 percent of the time. Over time, in other words, the ratio of "guilty" chemicals to "innocent" chemicals should approach 1 to 9.

This is just the opposite of the criminal law, in which we typically argue that we prefer that 10 guilty persons go free (false negatives) than to have a single innocent person wrongfully convicted (a false positive). Talbot Page argues that these contrasting policies are justified by the different values at stake in each case:

Limiting false positives is the guiding principle of criminal law. The objective is to limit the chance of a false conviction. . . . A principal reason for this is that liberty is a primary good, i.e., a good for the deprivation of which there is no adequate compensation. The asymmetrical results achieved by the criminal justice system are intentional and follow from the exceptional value placed on liberty. . . .

The costs of false negatives and false positives are asymmetrical for environmental risk [that is, risk in which the feared harm greatly exceeds the benefits of the risky activity, but the probability of the risk materializing is small] as well, but the asymmetry is in reverse order. For environmental risk, the asymmetrically high cost arises from a false negative; in criminal law from a false positive. Similarly, just as a primary good, liberty, is an important concern in criminal law, so another primary good, health, is an important concern in environmental risk management, but again the roles are reversed.

The analogy between criminal risk and environmental law requires that the roles of negatives and positives be reversed. [Page, A Generic View of Toxic Chemicals and Similar Risks, 7 Ecology L.Q. 207, 233-234 (1978).]

5. EPA's lead phasedown regulations ultimately generated the best evidence concerning the impact of lead emissions from gasoline on lead levels in children's blood. After long delays, the phasedown produced a significant reduction in levels of lead emissions from gasoline. Epidemiologists investigating changes in levels of lead in children's blood discovered an astonishingly high degree of correlation between these changes and changes in gasoline lead emissions, as indicated in Figure 4.4. They found that when gasoline lead use peaked sharply each summer, blood lead levels peaked sharply as well. They concluded that this could only be explained by changes in the levels of lead emissions from gasoline because other major sources of lead (lead paint and food) are roughly constant year-round. This and other evidence that had developed subsequent to the *Ethyl Corp.* decision proved so striking that

FIGURE 4.4
Lead Used in Gasoline Production and Average NHANES II
Blood Lead Levels
(Feb. 1976-Feb. 1980)

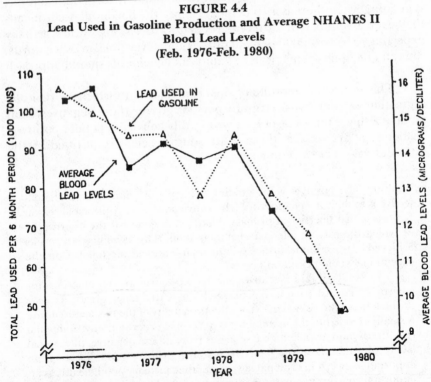

Source: Small Refiner Lead Phasedown Task Force v. EPA, 705 F.2d 506, 528 (D.C. Cir. 1983).

the D.C. Circuit subsequently stated, in a case reviewing even stricter lead limits imposed by EPA in 1982, that "the demonstrated connection between gasoline lead and blood lead, the demonstrated health effects of blood lead levels of 30 μg/dl or above, and the significant risk of adverse health effects from blood lead levels as low as 10-15 μg/dl, would justify EPA in banning lead from gasoline entirely." Small Refiner Lead Phasedown Task Force v. EPA, 705 F.2d 506, 531 (D.C. Cir. 1983). In 1985, EPA went almost that far by requiring reductions in levels of lead in gasoline to one-fifteenth the level upheld in the *Ethyl Corp.* decision. Ironically, EPA's decision virtually to eliminate lead additives from gasoline was based largely on the results of a cost-benefit analysis that showed that the benefits to health from reduction of lead emissions would greatly outweigh increased costs to petroleum refiners.

2. *Coping with Uncertainty: The Road to Risk Assessment*

A. INTRODUCTION: REMEDIES IN *RESERVE* AND *ETHYL CORP.*

Deciding that some toxic exposure creates an appropriate occasion for regulation only begins a regulator's task. The regulator must also decide what to do about it. This issue of remedy—or how stringently to regulate—has become known as the question of "how safe is safe?" It has received a great deal of attention lately, and we return to it in detail in section D, beginning on page 520. Relatively speaking, however, it was not the subject of major concern for either the district court in *Reserve* or the court of appeals in *Ethyl Corp.*, both of which were preoccupied with the prior question of whether sufficient evidence of an actionable risk had been presented by the facts of the case. The question of how stringently to regulate in the face of considerable uncertainty concerning the magnitude and likelihood of harm received more attention in the appellate review in *Reserve*. Before remarking on the more contemporary debates, it is instructive to review how these earlier controversies treated this question prior to the widespread use of risk assessment techniques.

First, *Reserve.* After finding that the air and water pollution from Reserve's plant posed a reasonable medical concern, the district court ordered the facility closed immediately. Reserve appealed to the Eighth Circuit, which first stayed the injunction and then modified it. The court of appeals concluded "the evidence is insufficient to support the kind of demonstrable danger to the public health that would justify the immediate closing of Reserve's operations." Reserve Mining Co. v. EPA, 514 F.2d 492, 507 (8th Cir. 1975). While referring approvingly to Judge Wright's analysis of risk in *Ethyl Corp.* (as expressed in Judge Wright's dissent to the initial 2-1 panel decision), the court concluded that "it cannot be said that the probability of harm is more likely than not," and that "it cannot be forecast that the rates of cancer will increase" as a result of the air and water pollution. 514 F.2d at 520. The court continued:

> In fashioning relief in a case such as this involving a possibility of future harm, a court should strike a proper balance between the benefits conferred and the hazards created by Reserve's facility. In its pleadings Reserve directs our attention to the benefits arising from its operations. [Reserve represented a $350 million capital investment with an annual payroll of $32 million, which supported 3,367 employees. Its production of taconite was 12 percent of the U.S. total.]
>
> [On the other side], the hazard in both the air and water can be measured in only the most general terms as a concern for the public health resting on a reasonable medical theory. Serious consequences could result if the hypothesis on which it is based should ultimately prove true. [514 F.2d at 535-536.]

In speaking of the need to balance "the benefits conferred and the hazards created" by Reserve, did the court explain how to strike such a balance? How can one strike a balance if one "cannot . . . forecast" the amount of harm that might occur? In fact, what did the court mean when it said that an increase in cancer rates cannot be forecast? Does it imply that a court must be *certain* that harm will occur before it can enjoin? Would that be consistent with Judge Wright's approach to risk analysis? What is the implication of the court's conclusion that harm was less than likely? Is it that the probability of harm must be greater than 50 percent before a court should enjoin? Would that be consistent with Judge Wright's approach to risk analysis?

Suppose villagers living in a valley below an earthen dam convince a court that there is a one-in-ten chance that the dam would fail. Would the court be justified in enjoining the dam owner *either* to drain the dam completely *or* to reinforce the dam, and to do so immediately? Is your answer consistent with *Reserve*? With *Ethyl Corp.*? Suppose the dam operator complained that fixing or draining the dam immediately would cause it grievous financial loss, whereas a phased, three-year improvement and reinforcement plan could be accomplished at much lower costs. Would that influence your answer?

Next, *Ethyl Corp.* EPA's rule had ordered a graduated phasedown of the lead content in gasoline, beginning with a refinery average of 1.7 grams per gallon as of January 1, 1975 down through five steps to a final average of 0.5 grams after January 1, 1979. 38 Fed. Reg. 33,734 (1973). The court upheld EPA's phasedown order without closely examining its details or the agency rationale for choosing this particular phasedown instead of any of the counterproposals of industry. (Industry protested the rule's use of a refinery average instead of a company average; they also protested EPA's requirement that averages be computed quarterly, preferring semiannual or annual averaging.) Not only did the court not scrutinize the details of the phasedown, it did not deliberate over the final target figure, 0.5 grams per gallon, that EPA issued. In its proposal for the phasedown rule, EPA had stated:

> Based on the available evidence, the Administrator has concluded that airborne lead levels exceeding 2 micrograms per cubic meter, averaged over a period of 3 months or longer, are associated with a sufficient risk of adverse physiologic effects to constitute endangerment of public health. . . . [A]ttainment of a 2-microgram level will require a 60 to 65 percent reduction in lead from motor vehicles. [37 Fed. Reg. 3,882 (1972).]

Does EPA seem to be saying here that 2 micrograms or less is not an "endangering" level of exposure? If so, it was initially justifying the phasedown from 1.7 to 0.5 (a 70 percent reduction) as necessary to achieve nonendangering exposure.

In issuing its final rule, EPA appeared to shift ground:

> [I]t is difficult, if not impossible, to establish a precise level of airborne lead as an acceptable basis for a control strategy. . . . [However,] [s]trong evidence existed which supported the view that through these routes [air and dust] airborne lead contributes to excessive lead exposure in urban adults and children. In light of this evidence of health risks, the Administrator concluded that it would be prudent to reduce preventable lead exposure. [38 Fed. Reg. 33,734 (1973).]

To buttress its determination that a 70 percent reduction in the amount of lead used in gasoline was possible, EPA lengthened its initial reduction schedule from 4 to 5 years, so as to "moderate the economic and technological impacts of the regulations during the period over which the reduction would be accomplished." That done, EPA wrote that "though the benefits associated with the . . . lead reductions have not been quantified, the Administrator has concluded that this approach is not unreasonably costly and will prudently prevent unnecessary exposure to airborne lead." Costs, in fact, were projected to be less than 0.1 cent per gallon refined, adding only between $82 million and $133 million to the total of $1.5 billion the industry was to invest in refining capacity through the year 1980. 38 Fed. Reg. 33,734, 33,739 (1973).

Thus, EPA appeared to switch from the health-based rationale outlined in its proposed rule to a feasibility-limited approach in its final rule. What considerations could have contributed to the shift? If 70 percent were "preventable," would 80 or 90 percent have been? EPA did not examine this question. Instead, it expressed the aim of determining the most cost-effective approach to the reduction of lead exposure from any source, whether airborne or not. Unfortunately, EPA had previously conceded that because the relative contribution of lead exposure from any one source could not be precisely quantified, "the most cost-effective approach to the aggregate prevention of excessive lead exposure has not been defined." 38 Fed. Reg. 1,258, 1,259 (1973). EPA continued, "the lead in gasoline issue presents particular difficulties regarding the cost-effectiveness of reducing lead contents below the level of 0.5 grams per gallon." So apparently EPA used its misgivings about whether removing lead from gasoline below 0.5 grams was cost-effective, when compared to other techniques for reducing the total body burden of lead, as a reason to stop at that point. Cost-effectiveness is occasionally a requirement for EPA action, but more often it is not. When it is not, EPA is instructed to regulate a route of exposure notwithstanding that the control of other exposure routes might be cheaper.

If EPA thought it "difficult, if not impossible" to determine an acceptable level of airborne lead, should it have ordered an immediate removal of all lead from gasoline? This would have been akin to the district court injunction in *Reserve,* whereas what EPA actually did more nearly resembled the court of appeals's decision there. If EPA had ordered immediate removal, should the court of appeals have reversed?

A Risk by Any Other Name: A Warning About Terminology

In writing in *Ethyl Corp.* that "danger was composed of reciprocal elements of risk and harm or probability and severity," Judge Wright was inadvertently alerting you to a potential source of confusion in the field of toxics regulation: terminology. A variety of terms are employed to describe the concepts involved in the regulation of risk; unfortunately, they aren't always used in the same way. "Risk" itself sometimes refers to the probability that something will happen; at other times it refers to the probability and the harm considered together. As the phrase "risk assessment" has come to be understood, "risk assessment" refers to a process of estimating expected harm, so that "risk" can mean a number of different things, depending on what methodology is being used to "assess" the risk. When a medical statistician employs a dose-response model to calculate the incidence of cancers at low doses, she really doesn't know what the probability is that she has chosen the correct one. Rather, the particular model employed is the result of some policy judgment. A standard reason advanced for choosing one model over another is that it provides a conservative estimate, that is, an estimate the real consequences are unlikely to exceed. These and other difficulties will be explored as the chapter proceeds. Initially, it is wise to be aware of the terminological problems you may confront.

B. DECIDING WHAT RISKS ARE WORTH REGULATING

In neither *Reserve* nor *Ethyl Corp.* did the decisionmaker of first instance quantify the harm that was being avoided because of its decision. When Judge Wright refers to an "assessment of risk," then, you should understand that he did not mean what the term has come to mean: a statement of the projected magnitude and likelihood of harm. See the Note "A Risk by Any Other Name," above. Indeed, the climate in Washington in the 1970s was relatively inhospitable to efforts to apply quantitative methods to regulatory issues involving health and safety, especially when those efforts were ultimately directed toward use in a cost-benefit or risk-benefit analysis. In such analyses the quantitative results of risk assessments are put together with estimates of the costs of regulation so that policymakers can judge whether the gains in risk reduction are worth their costs.

In 1976, the same year as *Ethyl Corp.,* a House subcommittee issued a report critical of risk-benefit and cost-benefit analyses. After examining risk assessment practices in a variety of agencies, including the EPA, the report concluded that there were so many uncertainties involved that

[a]t this juncture risk/benefit analysis as a technique to aid decisionmaking breaks down. The number of unknowns contributing to the measurement of risk make the measurement in the Environmental Protection Agency's terms 'only rough indications of effect.' Efforts to precisely measure risk posed by individual cancer-causing agents currently involve so many obstacles that they are an essentially useless exercise. . . . The limitations on the usefulness of benefit/cost analysis in the context of health, safety, and environmental regulatory decisionmaking are so severe that they militate against its use altogether. [Report of the Subcomm. on Oversight and Investigations of the Comm. on Interstate and Foreign Commerce, H. Rep., 94th Cong., 2d Sess. 510-511, 515 (1976).]

Two years later, a major study of federal regulation by the Senate Committee on Government Affairs concluded that

[w]here economic regulation is concerned, impact analysis [i.e., cost-benefit analysis] can be more easily applied, since there the consequences are usually capable of being reduced to dollar and cent terms. Such is not always the case with health, safety and environmental regulation. Here it is extremely difficult to quantify benefits since they are subject to great uncertainty and often become apparent only with the passage of time. In addition, some important benefits—such as recreational or aesthetic values—are difficult if not impossible to quantify in any meaningful way. Finally, there is the question of how the value of risks of human life, injury and suffering are computed. At present, there is no generally accepted method for evaluating such losses. Therefore, there are serious limitations

to the use of economic impact analysis in the health and safety area. . . .
[D]ecisionmaking to protect the public from serious hazards should not
be reduced to those terms. [Study on Federal Regulation, vol. VI, Committee on Governmental Affairs, U.S. Senate, 96th Cong., 1st Sess. xxiv
(1978).]

Some of these reservations are directed toward the demand of cost-
benefit analysis that risks eventually be measured in dollars, so that they
can be compared to costs measured the same way. Others are addressed
to the processes of quantifying risks in the first place, and they parallel
the sentiments evident in both *Reserve* and *Ethyl Corp.* that such quantification is not at all a prerequisite to preventative regulation.

The 1980s saw increasing momentum in Washington and among
policy analysts to seek more sophisticated means to perform quantitative
risk assessment. An important milestone along that path came in one of
the few cases in which the Supreme Court has participated in the debate
over how much information regulators must have before they regulate
and, just as important, how they can regulate after they have that information. The case involved the regulation of toxic exposures in the
workplace by the Occupational Health and Safety Administration (OSHA)
of the Department of Labor.

The Occupational Safety and Health Act requires OSHA to establish standards to control workplace exposures to toxic substances. Section
6(b) of the OSH Act directs OSHA to "set the standard which most
adequately assures, to the extent feasible, on the basis of the best available
evidence, that no employee will suffer material impairment of health or
functional capacity even if such employee has regular exposure to the
hazard dealt with by such standard for the period of his working life."
29 U.S.C. §655(b)(5). The OSH Act initially authorized OSHA to set
exposure limits based on previously established national consensus standards. Thus, in 1971 OSHA adopted the threshhold limit values (TLVs)
recognized by the American Council of Government Industrial Hygienists (ACGIH) and approximately 20 consensus standards established by
the American National Standards Institute (ANSI). To assist OSHA in
promulgating permanent exposure limits, the OSH Act established the
National Institute for Occupational Safety and Health (NIOSH), a research agency charged with recommending occupational safety and health
standards to OSHA.

In October 1976 NIOSH strongly recommended that OSHA promulgate an emergency temporary standard (ETS) to protect employees
from "grave danger" from exposure to benzene. NIOSH based this
recommendation on epidemiological studies showing that workers exposed to benzene were suffering an unusually high incidence of cases
of leukemia. After OSHA issued an ETS of 1 ppm effective May 1977,
the standard was invalidated by the U.S. Court of Appeals for the Fifth

Circuit. OSHA then conducted a rulemaking to promulgate a permanent permissible exposure limit (PEL) for benzene of 1 ppm, which again was struck down by the Fifth Circuit.

The Fifth Circuit held that OSHA had not demonstrated that the costs of the standard bore a reasonable relationship to its benefits. OSHA then obtained Supreme Court review to consider whether such cost-benefit balancing was required under the OSH Act. A badly divided Supreme Court then surprised the parties by deciding the case on other grounds, as indicated in the opinions below.

Industrial Union Dept., AFL-CIO v. American Petroleum Institute
448 U.S. 607 (1980) (the Benzene decision)

Mr. Justice STEVENS announced the judgment of the Court and delivered an opinion, in which THE CHIEF JUSTICE and Mr. Justice STEWART joined and in Parts I, II, III-A, III-B, III-C AND III-E of which Mr. Justice POWELL joined.

The Occupational Safety and Health Act of 1970 (Act), 84 Stat. 1590, 29 U.S.C. §651 et seq., was enacted for the purpose of ensuring safe and healthful working conditions for every working man and woman in the Nation. This litigation concerns a standard promulgated by the Secretary of Labor to regulate occupational exposure to benzene, a substance which has been shown to cause cancer at high exposure levels. The principal question is whether such a showing is a sufficient basis for a standard that places the most stringent limitation on exposure to benzene that is technologically and economically possible.

The Act delegates broad authority to the Secretary to promulgate different kinds of standards. The basic definition of an "occupational safety and health standard" is found in §3(8), which provides:

> The term "occupational safety and health standard" means a standard which requires conditions, or the adoption or use of one or more practices, means, methods, operations, or processes, reasonably necessary or appropriate to provide safe or healthful employment and places of employment. 84 Stat. 1591, 29 U.S.C. §652(8).

Where toxic materials or harmful physical agents are concerned, a standard must also comply with §6(b)(5), which provides:

> The Secretary, in promulgating standards dealing with toxic materials or harmful physical agents under this subsection, shall set the standard which most adequately assures, to the extent feasible, on the basis of the best available evidence, that no employee will suffer material impairment

of health or functional capacity even if such employee has regular exposure to the hazard dealt with by such standard for the period of his working life. Development of standards under this subsection shall be based upon research, demonstrations, experiments, and such other information as may be appropriate. In addition to the attainment of the highest degree of health and safety protection for the employee, other considerations shall be the latest available scientific data in the field, the feasibility of the standards, and experience gained under this and other health and safety laws. 84 Stat. 1594, 29 U.S.C. §655(b)(5).

Wherever the toxic material to be regulated is a carcinogen, the Secretary has taken the position that no safe exposure level can be determined and that §6(b)(5) requires him to set an exposure limit at the lowest technologically feasible level that will not impair the viability of the industries regulated. In this case, after having determined that there is a causal connection between benzene and leukemia (a cancer of the white blood cells), the Secretary set an exposure limit on airborne concentrations of benzene of one part benzene per million parts of air (1 ppm), regulated dermal and eye contact with solutions containing benzene, and imposed complex monitoring and medical testing requirements on employers whose workplaces contain 0.5 ppm or more of benzene. 29 CFR §§1910.1028(c), (e) (1979).

On pre-enforcement review pursuant to 29 U.S.C. §655(f), the United States Court of Appeals for the Fifth Circuit held the regulation invalid. American Petroleum Institute v. OSHA, 581 F.2d 493 (1978). The court concluded that the Occupational Safety and Health Administration (OSHA) had exceeded its standard-setting authority because it had not shown that the new benzene exposure limit was "reasonably necessary or appropriate to provide safe or healthful employment" as required by §3(8), and because §6(b)(5) does "not give OSHA the unbridled discretion to adopt standards designed to create absolutely risk-free workplaces regardless of costs." Reaching the two provisions together, the Fifth Circuit held that the Secretary was under a duty to determine whether the benefits expected from the new standard bore a reasonable relationship to the costs that it imposed. Id., at 503. The court noted that OSHA had made an estimate of the costs of compliance, but that the record lacked substantial evidence of any discernible benefits. . . .

I

Benzene is a familiar and important commodity. It is a colorless, aromatic liquid that evaporates rapidly under ordinary atmospher[ic] conditions. Approximately 11 billion pounds of benzene were produced in the United States in 1976. Ninety-four percent of that total was produced by the petroleum and petrochemical industries, with the remainder produced by the steel industry as a byproduct of coking operations. Benzene is used in manufacturing a variety of products including motor fuels (which may contain as much as 2% benzene), solvents, detergents, pesticides, and other organic chemicals. 43 Fed. Reg. 5918 (1978).

The entire population of the United States is exposed to small quantities of benzene, ranging from a few parts per billion to 0.5 ppm, in the ambient air. Over one million workers are subject to additional low-level exposures as a consequence of their employment. The majority of these employees work in gasoline service stations, benzene production (petroleum refineries and coking operations), chemical processing, benzene transportation, rubber manufacturing, and laboratory operations.

Benzene is a toxic substance. Although it could conceivably cause harm to a person who swallowed or touched it, the principal risk of harm comes from inhalation of benzene vapors. When these vapors are inhaled, the benzene diffuses through the lungs and is quickly absorbed into the blood. Exposure to high concentrations produces an almost immediate effect on the central nervous system. Inhalation of concentrations of 20,000 ppm can be fatal within minutes; exposures in the range of 250 to 500 ppm can cause vertigo, nausea, and other symptoms of mild poisoning. 43 Fed. Reg. 5921 (1978). Persistent exposures at levels above 25-40 ppm may lead to blood deficiencies and diseases of the blood-forming organs, including aplastic anemia, which is generally fatal.

Industrial health experts have long been aware that exposure to benzene may lead to various types of nonmalignant diseases. By 1948 the evidence connecting high levels of benzene to serious blood disorders had become so strong that the Commonwealth of Massachusetts imposed a 35 ppm limitation on workplaces within its jurisdiction. In 1969 the American National Standards Institute (ANSI) adopted a national consensus standard of 10 ppm averaged over an 8-hour period with a ceiling concentration of 25 ppm for 10-minute periods or a maximum peak concentration of 50 ppm. Id., at 5919. In 1971, after the Occupational Safety and Health Act was passed, the Secretary adopted this consensus standard as the federal standard, pursuant to 29 U.S.C. §655(a).

As early as 1928, some health experts theorized that there might also be a connection between benzene in the workplace and leukemia. In the late 1960's and early 1970's a number of epidemiological studies were published indicating that workers exposed to high concentrations of benzene were subject to significantly increased risk of leukemia. In a 1974 report recommending a permanent standard for benzene, the National Institute for Occupational Safety and Health (NIOSH), OSHA's research arm, noted that these studies raised the "distinct possibility" that benzene caused leukemia. But, in light of the fact that all known cases had occurred at very high exposure levels, NIOSH declined to recommend a change in the 10 ppm standard, which it considered sufficient to protect against nonmalignant diseases. NIOSH suggested that further studies were necessary to determine conclusively whether there was a link between benzene and leukemia and, if so, what exposure levels were dangerous.

Between 1974 and 1976 additional studies were published which tended to confirm the view that benzene can cause leukemia, at least when exposure levels are high. In an August 1976 revision of its earlier recommendation, NIOSH stated that these studies provided "conclusive" proof of a causal connection between benzene and leukemia. Although it acknowledged that none of the intervening studies had provided the dose-response data it had found lacking two years earlier, id., at 9, NIOSH nevertheless recommended that the exposure limit be set low as possible. As a result of this recommendation, OSHA contracted with a consulting firm to do a study on the costs to industry of complying with the 10 ppm standard then in effect or, alternatively, with whatever standard would be the lowest feasible.

In October 1976, NIOSH sent another memorandum to OSHA, seeking acceleration of the rulemaking process and "strongly" recommending the issuance of an emergency temporary standard pursuant to §6(c) of the Act, 29 U.S.C. §655(c), for benzene and two other chemicals believed to be carcinogens. NIOSH recommended that a 1 ppm exposure limit be imposed for benzene. Apparently because of the NIOSH recommendation, OSHA asked its consultant to determine the cost of complying with a 1 ppm standard instead of with the "minimum feasible" standard. It also issued voluntary guidelines for benzene, recommending that exposure levels be limited to 1 ppm on an 8-hour time-weighted average basis wherever possible.

In the spring of 1976, NIOSH had selected two Pliofilm plants in St. Marys and Akron, Ohio, for an epidemiological study of the link between leukemia and benzene exposure. In April 1977, NIOSH forwarded an interim report to OSHA indicating at least a fivefold increase in the expected incidence of leukemia for workers who had been exposed to benzene at the two plants from 1940 to 1949. The report submitted to OSHA erroneously suggested that exposures in the two plants had generally been between zero and 15 ppm during the period in question. As a result of this new evidence and the continued prodding of NIOSH, OSHA did issue an emergency standard effective May 21, 1977, reducing the benzene exposure limit from 10 ppm to 1 ppm, the ceiling for exposures of up to 10 minutes from 25 ppm to 5 ppm, and eliminating the authority for peak concentrations of 50 ppm. 42 Fed. Reg. 22516 (1977). In its explanation accompanying the emergency standard, OSHA stated that benzene had been shown to cause leukemia at exposures below 25 ppm and that, in light of its consultant's report, it was feasible to reduce the exposure limit to 1 ppm. Id., at 22517, 22521.

On May 19, 1977, the Court of Appeals for the Fifth Circuit entered a temporary restraining order preventing the emergency standard from taking effect. Thereafter, OSHA abandoned its efforts to make the emergency standard effective and instead issued a proposal for a permanent standard patterned almost entirely after the aborted emergency standard. Id., at 27452.

In its published statement giving notice of the proposed permanent standard, OSHA did not ask for comments as to whether or not benzene presented a significant health risk at exposures of 10 ppm or less. Rather, it asked for comments as to whether 1 ppm was the minimum feasible exposure limit. Ibid. As OSHA's Deputy Director of Health Standards, Grover Wrenn, testified at the hearing, this formulation of the issue to be considered by the Agency was consistent with OSHA's general policy with respect to carcinogens. Whenever a carcinogen is involved, OSHA will presume that no safe level of exposure exists in the absence of clear proof establishing such a level and will accordingly set the exposure limit at the lowest level feasible. The proposed 1 ppm exposure limit in this case thus was established not on the basis of a proven hazard at 10 ppm, but rather on the basis of "OSHA's best judgment at the time of the proposal of the feasibility of compliance with the proposed standard by the [a]ffected industries." Given OSHA's cancer policy, it was in fact irrelevant whether there was any evidence at all of a leukemia risk at 10 ppm. The important point was that there was no evidence that there was *not* some risk, however small, at that level. The fact that OSHA did not ask for comments on whether there was a safe level of exposure for benzene was indicative of its further view that a demonstration of such absolute safety simply could not be made.

Public hearings were held on the proposed standard, commencing on July 19, 1977. The final standard was issued on February 10, 1978. 29 CFR §1910.1028 (1979). In its final form, the benzene standard is designed to protect workers from whatever hazards are associated with low-level benzene exposures by requiring employers to monitor workplaces to determine the level of exposure, to provide medical examinations when the level rises above 0.5 ppm, and to institute whatever engineering or other controls are necessary to keep exposures at or below 1 ppm. . . .

The permanent standard is expressly inapplicable to the storage, transportation, distribution, sale, or use of gasoline or other fuels subsequent to discharge from bulk terminals. This exception is particularly significant in light of the fact that over 795,000 gas station employees, who are exposed to an average of 102,700 gallons of gasoline (containing up to 2% benzene) annually, are thus excluded from the protection of the standard.

As presently formulated, the benzene standard is an expensive way of providing some additional protection for a relatively small number of employees. According to OSHA's figures, the standard will require capital investments in engineering controls of approximately $266 million, first-year operating costs (for monitoring, medical testing, employee training, and respirators) of $187 million to $205 million and recurring annual costs of approximately $34 million. 43 Fed. Reg. 5934 (1978). The figures outlined in OSHA's explanation of the costs of compliance to various industries indicate that only 35,000 employees would gain any benefit from the regulation in terms of a reduction in their exposure to benzene. Over two-thirds of these workers (24,450) are employed in the rubber-manufacturing industry. Compliance costs in that industry are estimated to be rather low, with no capital costs and initial operating expenses estimated at only $34 million ($1,390 per employee); recurring annual costs would also be rather low, totalling less than $1 million. By contrast, the segment of the petroleum refining industry that produces benzene would be required to incur $24 million in capital costs and $600,000 in first-year operating expenses to provide additional protection for 300 workers ($82,000 per employee), while the petrochemical industry would be required to incur $20.9 million in capital costs and $1 million in initial operating expenses for the benefit of 552 employees ($39,675 per employee). Id., at 5936-5938.

Although OSHA did not quantify the benefits to each category of worker in terms of decreased exposure to benzene, it appears from the economic impact study done at OSHA's direction that those benefits may be relatively small. Thus, although the current exposure limit is 10 ppm, the actual exposures outlined in that study are often considerably lower. For example, for the period 1970-1975 the petrochemical industry reported that, out of a total of 496 employees exposed to benzene, only 53 were exposed to levels between 1 and 5 ppm and only 7 (all at the same plant) were exposed to between 5 and 10 ppm.

II

The critical issue at this point in the litigation is whether the Court of Appeals was correct in refusing to enforce the 1 ppm exposure limit on the ground that it was not supported by appropriate findings.

Any discussion of the 1 ppm exposure limit must of course begin with the Agency's rationale for imposing that limit. The written explanation of the standard fills 184 pages of the printed appendix. Much of it is devoted to a discussion of the voluminous evidence of the adverse effects of exposure to benzene at levels of concentration well above 10 ppm. This discussion demonstrates that there is ample justification for regulating occupational exposure to benzene and that the prior limit of 10 ppm, with a ceiling of 25 ppm (or a peak of 50 ppm) was reasonable. It does not, however, provide direct support for the Agency's conclusion that the limit should be reduced from 10 ppm to 1 ppm.

The evidence in the administrative record of adverse effects of benzene exposure at 10 ppm is sketchy at best. OSHA noted that there was "no dispute" that certain nonmalignant blood disorders, evidenced by a reduction in the level of red or white cells or platelets in the blood, could result from exposures of 25-40 ppm. It then stated that several studies had indicated that relatively slight changes in normal blood values could result from exposures below 25 ppm and perhaps below 10 ppm. OSHA did not attempt to make any estimate based on these studies of how significant the risk of nonmalignant disease would be at exposure of 10 ppm or less. Rather, it stated that because of the lack of data concerning the linkage between low-level exposures and blood abnormalities, it was impossible to construct a dose-response curve at this time.[33] OSHA did conclude, however, that the studies demonstrated that the current 10 ppm exposure limit was inadequate to ensure that no single worker would suffer a nonmalignant blood disorder as a result of benzene exposure. Noting that it is "customary" to set a permissible exposure limit by applying a safety factor of 10-100 to the lowest level at which adverse effects had been observed, the Agency stated that the evidence supported the conclusion that the limit should be set at a point "substantially less than 10 ppm" even if benzene's leukemia effects were not considered. 43 Fed. Reg. 5924-5925 (1978). OSHA did not state, however, that the nonmalignant effects of benzene exposure justified a reduction in the permissible exposure limit to 1 ppm.[34]

OSHA also noted some studies indicating an increase in chromosomal aberrations in workers chronically exposed to concentrations of benzene "probably less than 25 ppm." However, the Agency took no definitive position as to what these aberrations meant in terms of demonstrable health effects and stated that no quantitative dose-response

---

33. . . . OSHA's comments with respect to the insufficiency of the data were addressed primarily to the lack of data at low exposure levels. OSHA did not discuss whether it was possible to make a rough estimate, based on the more complete epidemiological and animal studies done at higher exposure levels, of the significance of the risks attributable to those levels, nor did it discuss whether it was possible to extrapolate from such estimates to derive a risk estimate for low-level exposures.

34. OSHA did not invoke the automatic rule of reducing exposures to the lowest limit feasible that it applies to cancer risks. Instead, the Secretary reasoned that prudent health policy merely required that the permissible exposure limit be set "sufficiently below the levels at which adverse effects have been observed to assure adequate protection for all exposed employees." 43 Fed. Reg. 5925 (1978). While OSHA concluded that application of this rule would lead to an exposure limit "substantially less than 10 ppm," it did not state either what exposure level it considered to present a significant risk of harm or what safety factor should be applied to that level to establish a permissible exposure limit.

relationship had yet been established. Under these circumstances, chromosomal effects were categorized by OSHA as an "adverse biological event of serious concern which may pose or reflect a potential health risk and as such, must be considered in the larger purview of adverse health effects associated with benzene." Id., at 5932-5934.

With respect to leukemia, evidence of an increased risk (i.e., a risk greater than that borne by the general population) due to benzene exposures at or below 10 ppm was even sketchier. Once OSHA acknowledged that the NIOSH study it had relied upon in promulgating the emergency standard did not support its earlier view that benzene had been shown to cause leukemia at concentrations below 25 ppm, there was only one study that provided any evidence of such an increased risk. That study, conducted by the Dow Chemical Co., uncovered three leukemia deaths, versus 0.2 expected deaths, out of a population of 594 workers; it appeared that the three workers had never been exposed to more than 2 to 9 ppm of benzene. The authors of the study, however, concluded that it could not be viewed as proof of a relationship between low-level benzene exposure and leukemia because all three workers had probably been occupationally exposed to a number of other potentially carcinogenic chemicals at other points in their careers and because no leukemia deaths had been uncovered among workers who had been exposed to much higher levels of benzene. In its explanation of the permanent standard, OSHA stated that the possibility that these three leukemias had been caused by benzene exposure could not be ruled out and that the study, although not evidence of an increased risk of leukemia at 10 ppm, was therefore "consistent with the findings of many studies that there is an excess leukemia risk among benzene exposed employees." 43 Fed. Reg. 5928 (1978). The Agency made no finding that the Dow study, any other empirical evidence, or any opinion testimony demonstrated that exposure to benzene at or below the 10 ppm level had ever in fact caused leukemia. See 581 F.2d, at 503, where the Court of Appeals noted that OSHA was "unable to point to any empirical evidence documenting a leukemia risk at 10 ppm. . . ."

In the end OSHA's rationale for lowering the permissible exposure limit to 1 ppm was based, not on any finding that leukemia has ever been caused by exposure to 10 ppm of benzene and that it will *not* be caused by exposure to 1 ppm, but rather on a series of assumptions indicating that some leukemias might result from exposure to 10 ppm and that the number of cases might be reduced by reducing the exposure level to 1 ppm. In reaching that result, the Agency first unequivocally concluded that benzene is a human carcinogen. Second, it concluded that industry had failed to prove that there is a safe threshold level of exposure to benzene below which no excess leukemia cases would occur. In reaching this conclusion OSHA rejected industry contentions that certain epidemiological studies indicating no excess risk of leukemia among workers exposed at levels below 10 ppm were sufficient to establish that the threshold level of safe exposure was at or above 10 ppm. It also rejected an industry witness' testimony that a dose-response curve could be constructed on the basis of the reported epidemiological studies and that this curve indicated that reducing the permissible exposure limit from 10 to 1 ppm would prevent at most one leukemia and one other cancer death every six years.

Third, the Agency applied its standard policy with respect to carcinogens, concluding that, in the absence of definitive proof of a safe level, it must be assumed that *any* level above zero presents *some* increased risk of cancer. As the federal parties point out in their brief, there are a number of scientists and public health specialists who subscribe to this view, theorizing that a susceptible person may contract cancer from the absorption of even one molecule of a carcinogen like benzene.

Fourth, the Agency reiterated its view of the Act, stating that it was required by §6(b)(5) to set the standard either at the level that has been demonstrated to be safe or at the lowest level feasible, whichever is higher. If no safe level is established, as in this case, the Secretary's interpretation of the statute automatically leads to the selection of an exposure limit that is the lowest feasible. Because of benzene's importance to the economy, no one has ever suggested that it would be feasible to eliminate its use entirely, or to try to limit exposures to the small amounts that are omnipresent. Rather, the Agency selected 1 ppm as a workable exposure level, see n.14, supra, and then determined that compliance with that level was technologically feasible and that "the economic impact of . . . [compliance] will not be such as to threaten the financial welfare of the affected firms or the general economy." 43 Fed. Reg. 5939 (1978). It therefore held that 1 ppm was the minimum feasible exposure level within the meaning of §6(b)(5) of the Act.

Finally, although the Agency did not refer in its discussion of the pertinent legal authority to any duty to identify the anticipated benefits of the new standard, it did conclude that some benefits were likely to result from reducing the exposure limit from 10 ppm to 1 ppm. This conclusion was based, again, not on evidence, but rather on the assumption that the risk of leukemia will decrease as exposure levels decrease. Although the Agency had found it impossible to construct a dose-response curve that would predict with any accuracy the number of leukemias that could be expected to result from exposures at 10 ppm, at 1 ppm, or at any intermediate level, it nevertheless "determined that the benefits of the proposed standard are likely to be appreciable." 43 Fed. Reg. 5941 (1978). In light of the Agency's disavowal of any ability to determine the numbers of employees likely to be adversely affected by exposures of 10 ppm, the Court of Appeals held this finding to be unsupported by the record. 581 F.2d, at 503.

It is noteworthy that at no point in its lengthy explanation did the

Agency quote or even cite §3(8) of the Act. It made no finding that any of the provisions of the new standard were "reasonably necessary or appropriate to provide safe or healthful employment and places of employment." Nor did it allude to the possibility that any such finding might have been appropriate.

III

Our resolution of the issues in these cases turns, to a large extent, on the meaning of and the relationship between §3(8), which defines a health and safety standard as a standard that is "reasonably necessary and appropriate to provide safe or healthful employment," and §6(b)(5), which directs the Secretary in promulgating a health and safety standard for toxic materials to "set the standard which most adequately assures, to the extent feasible, on the basis of the best available evidence, that no employee will suffer material impairment of health or functional capacity. . . ."

In the Government's view, §3(8)'s definition of the term "standard" has no legal significance or at best merely requires that a standard not be totally irrational. It takes the position that §6(b)(5) is controlling and that it requires OSHA to promulgate a standard that either gives an absolute assurance of safety for each and every worker or reduces exposures to the lowest level feasible. The Government interprets "feasible" as meaning technologically achievable at a cost that would not impair the viability of the industries subject to the regulation. The respondent industry representatives, on the other hand, argue that the Court of Appeals was correct in holding that the "reasonably necessary and appropriate" language of §3(8), along with the feasibility requirement of §6(b)(5), requires the Agency to quantify both the costs and the benefits of a proposed rule and to conclude that they are roughly commensurate.

In our view, it is not necessary to decide whether either the Government or industry is entirely correct. For we think it is clear that §3(8) does apply to all permanent standards promulgated under the Act and that it requires the Secretary, before issuing any standard, to determine that it is reasonably necessary and appropriate to remedy a significant risk of material health impairment. Only after the Secretary has made the threshold determination that such a risk exists with respect to a toxic substance would it be necessary to decide whether §6(b)(5) requires him to select the most protective standard he can consistent with economic and technological feasibility, or whether, as respondents argue, the benefits of the regulation must be commensurate with the costs of its implementation. Because the Secretary did not make the required threshold finding in these cases, we have no occasion to determine whether costs must be weighed against benefits in an appropriate case.

A

Under the Government's view, §3(8), if it has any substantive content at all, merely requires OSHA to issue standards that are reasonably calculated to produce a safer or more healthy work environment. Apart from this minimal requirement of rationality, the Government argues that §3(8) imposes no limits on the Agency's power, and thus would not prevent it from requiring employers to do whatever would be "reasonably necessary" to eliminate all risks of any harm from their workplaces. With respect to toxic substances and harmful physical agents, the Government takes an even more extreme position. Relying on §6(b)(5)'s direction to set a standard "which most adequately assures . . . that no employee will suffer material impairment of health or functional capacity," the Government contends that the Secretary is required to impose standards that either guarantee workplaces that are free from any risk of material health impairment, however small, or that come as close as possible to doing so without ruining entire industries.

If the purpose of the statute were to eliminate completely and with absolute certainty any risk of serious harm, we would agree that it would be proper for the Secretary to interpret §§3(8) and 6(b)(5) in this fashion. But we think it is clear that the statute was not designed to require employers to provide absolutely risk-free workplaces whenever it is technologically feasible to do so, so long as the cost is not great enough to destroy an entire industry. Rather, both the language and structure of the Act, as well as its legislative history, indicate that it was intended to require the elimination, as far as feasible, of significant risks of harm.

B

By empowering the Secretary to promulgate standards that are "reasonably necessary or appropriate to provide safe or healthful employment and places of employment," the Act implies that, before promulgating any standard, the Secretary must make a finding that the workplaces in question are not safe. But "safe" is not the equivalent of "risk-free." There are many activities that we engage in every day—such as driving a car or even breathing city air—that entail some risk of accident or material health impairment; nevertheless, few people would consider these activities "unsafe." Similarly, a workplace can hardly be considered "unsafe" unless it threatens the workers with a significant risk of harm.

Therefore, before he can promulgate *any* permanent health or safety standard, the Secretary is required to make a threshold finding that a place of employment is unsafe—in the sense that significant risks are present and can be eliminated or lessened by a change in practices.

This requirement applies to permanent standards promulgated pursuant to §6(b)(5), as well as to other types of permanent standards. For there is no reason why §3(8)'s definition of a standard should not be incorporated by reference into §6(b)(5).

. . . This interpretation of §§3(8) and 6(b)(5) is supported by the other provisions of the Act. Thus, for example, §6(g) provides in part that

> [i]n determining the priority for establishing standards under this section, the Secretary shall give due regard to the urgency of the need for mandatory safety and health standards for particular industries, trades, crafts, occupations, businesses, workplaces or work environments.

The Government has expressly acknowledged that this section requires the Secretary to undertake some cost-benefit analysis before he promulgates any standard, requiring the elimination of the most serious hazards first. If such an analysis must precede the promulgation of any standard, it seems manifest that Congress intended, at a bare minimum, that the Secretary find a significant risk of harm and therefore a probability of significant benefits before establishing a new standard.

Section 6(b)(8) lends additional support to this analysis. That subsection requires that, when the Secretary substantially alters an existing consensus standard, he must explain how the new rule will "better effectuate" the purpose of the Act. If this requirement was intended to be more than a meaningless formality, it must be read to impose upon the Secretary the duty to find that an existing national consensus standard is not adequate to protect workers from a continuing and significant risk of harm. Thus, in this case, the Secretary was required to find that exposures at the current permissible exposure level of 10 ppm present a significant risk of harm in the workplace.

In the absence of a clear mandate in the Act, it is unreasonable to assume that Congress intended to give the Secretary the unprecedented power over American industry that would result from the Government's view of §§3(8) and 6(b)(5), coupled with OSHA's cancer policy. Expert testimony that a substance is probably a human carcinogen—either because it has caused cancer in animals or because individuals have contracted cancer following extremely high exposures—would justify the conclusion that the substance poses some risk of serious harm no matter how minute the exposure and no matter how many experts testified that they regarded the risk as insignificant. That conclusion would in turn justify pervasive regulation limited only by the constraint of feasibility. In light of the fact that there are literally thousands of substances used in the workplace that have been identified as carcinogens or suspect carcinogens, the Government's theory would give OSHA power to impose enormous costs that might produce little, if any, discernible benefit.

If the Government were correct in arguing that neither §3(8) nor §6(b)(5) requires that the risk from a toxic substance [to] be quantified sufficiently to enable the Secretary to characterize it as significant in an understandable way, the statute would make such a "sweeping delegation of legislative power" that it might be unconstitutional under the Court's reasoning in A. L. A. Schechter Poultry Corp. v. United States, 295 U.S. 495, 539, and Panama Refining Co. v. Ryan, 293 U.S. 388. A construction of the statute that avoids this kind of open-ended grant should certainly be favored.

C

The legislative history also supports the conclusion that Congress was concerned, not with absolute safety, but with the elimination of significant harm. The examples of industrial hazards referred to in the Committee hearings and debates all involved situations in which the risk was unquestionably significant. For example, the Senate Committee on Labor and Public Welfare noted that byssinosis, a disabling lung disease caused by breathing cotton dust, affected as many as 30% of the workers in carding or spinning rooms in some American cotton mills and that as many as 100,000 active or retired workers were then suffering from the disease. It also noted that statistics indicated that 20,000 out of 50,000 workers who had performed insulation work were likely to die of asbestosis, lung cancer, or mesothelioma as a result of breathing asbestos fibers. . . .

D

Given the conclusion that the Act empowers the Secretary to promulgate health and safety standards only where a significant risk of harm exists, the critical issue becomes how to define and allocate the burden of proving the significance of the risk in a case such as this, where scientific knowledge is imperfect and the precise quantification of risks is therefore impossible. The Agency's position is that there is substantial evidence in the record to support its conclusion that there is no absolutely safe level for a carcinogen and that, therefore, the burden is properly on industry to prove, apparently beyond a shadow of a doubt, that there *is* a safe level for benzene exposure. The Agency argues that, because of the uncertainties in this area, any other approach would render it helpless, forcing it to wait for the leukemia deaths that it believes are likely to occur before taking any regulatory action.

We disagree. As we read the statute, the burden was on the Agency to show, on the basis of substantial evidence, that it is at least more likely than not that long-term exposure to 10 ppm of benzene presents a significant risk of material health impairment. Ordinarily, it is the proponent of a rule or order who has the burden of proof in administrative proceedings. See 5 U.S.C. §556(d). In some cases involving toxic substances, Congress has shifted the burden of proving that a particular substance is safe onto the party opposing the proposed rule.[61] The fact that Congress did not follow this course in enacting the Occupational Safety and Health Act indicates that it intended the Agency to bear the normal burden of establishing the need for a proposed standard.

In this case OSHA did not even attempt to carry its burden of proof. The closest it came to making a finding that benzene presented a significant risk of harm in the workplace was its statement that the benefits to be derived from lowering the permissible exposure level from 10 to 1 ppm were "likely" to be "appreciable." The Court of Appeals held that this finding was not supported by substantial evidence. Of greater importance, even if it were supported by substantial evidence, such a finding would not be sufficient to satisfy the Agency's obligations under the Act.

The inadequacy of the Agency's findings can perhaps be illustrated best by its rejection of industry testimony that a dose-response curve can be formulated on the basis of current epidemiological evidence and that, even under the most conservative extrapolation theory, current exposure levels would cause at most two deaths out of a population of about 30,000 workers every six years. In rejecting this testimony, OSHA made the following statement:

> In the face of the record evidence of numerous actual deaths attributable to benzene-induced leukemia and other fatal blood diseases, OSHA is unwilling to rely on the hypothesis that at most two cancers every six years would be prevented by the proposed standard. By way of example, the Infante study disclosed seven excess leukemia deaths in a population of about 600 people over a 25-year period. While the Infante study involved higher exposures than those currently encountered, the incidence rates found by Infante, together with the numerous other cases reported in the literature of benzene leukemia and other fatal blood diseases, make it difficult for OSHA to rely on the [witness's] hypothesis to assure the statutorily mandated protection of employees. In any event, due to the

---

61. See Environmental Defense Fund, Inc. v. EPA, 548 F.2d 998, 1004, 1012-1018 (1977), cert. denied, 431 U.S. 925, where the court rejected the argument that the EPA has the burden of proving that a pesticide is unsafe in order to suspend its registration under the Federal Insecticide, Fungicide, and Rodenticide Act. The court noted that Congress has deliberately shifted the ordinary burden of proof under the APA, requiring manufacturers to establish the continued safety of their products.

fact that there is no safe level of exposure to benzene and that it is impossible to precisely quantify the anticipated benefits, OSHA must select the level of exposure which is most protective of exposed employees. 43 Fed. Reg. 5941 (1978).

There are three possible interpretations of OSHA's stated reason for rejecting the witness' testimony: (1) OSHA considered it probable that a greater number of lives would be saved by lowering the standard from 10 ppm; (2) OSHA thought that saving two lives every six years in a work force of 30,000 persons is a significant savings that makes it reasonable and appropriate to adopt a new standard; or (3) even if the small number is not significant and even if the savings may be even smaller, the Agency nevertheless believed it had a statutory duty to select the level of exposure that is most protective of the exposed employees if it is economically and technologically feasible to do so. Even if the Secretary did not intend to rely entirely on this third theory, his construction of the statute would make it proper for him to do so. Moreover, he made no express findings of fact that would support his 1 ppm standard on any less drastic theory. Under these circumstances, we can hardly agree with the Government that OSHA discharged its duty under the Act.

Contrary to the Government's contentions, imposing a burden on the Agency of demonstrating a significant risk of harm will not strip it of its ability to regulate carcinogens, nor will it require the Agency to wait for deaths to occur before taking any action. First, the requirement that a "significant" risk be identified is not a mathematical straitjacket. It is the Agency's responsibility to determine, in the first instance, what it considers to be a "significant" risk. Some risks are plainly acceptable and others are plainly unacceptable. If, for example, the odds are one in a billion that a person will die from cancer by taking a drink of chlorinated water, the risk clearly could not be considered significant. On the other hand, if the odds are one in a thousand that regular inhalation of gasoline vapors that are 2% benzene will be fatal, a reasonable person might well consider the risk significant and take appropriate steps to decrease or eliminate it. Although the Agency has no duty to calculate the exact probability of harm, it does have an obligation to find that a significant risk is present before it can characterize a place of employment as "unsafe."

Second, OSHA is not required to support its finding that a significant risk exists with anything approaching scientific certainty. Although the Agency's findings must be supported by substantial evidence, 29 U.S.C. §655(f), §6(b)(5) specifically allows the Secretary to regulate on the basis of the "best available evidence." As several Courts of Appeals have held, this provision requires a reviewing court to give OSHA some leeway where its findings must be made on the frontiers of scientific knowledge. See Industrial Union Dept., AFL-CIO v. Hodgson, 162 U.S. App. D.C. 331, 340, 499 F.2d 467, 476 (1974); Society of the Plastics Industry, Inc. v. OSHA, 509 F.2d 1301, 1308 (CA2 1975), cert. denied, 421 U.S. 992. Thus, so long as they are supported by a body of reputable scientific thought, the Agency is free to use conservative assumptions in interpreting the data with respect to carcinogens, risking error on the side of overprotection rather than underprotection.

Finally, the record in this case and OSHA's own rulings on other carcinogens indicate that there are a number of ways in which the Agency can make a rational judgment about the relative significance of the risks associated with exposure to a particular carcinogen.[64]

[In a concurring opinion, Justice POWELL indicated that although he would not rule out the possibility that OSHA's regulation of benzene could have been upheld on the basis of a properly promulgated generic cancer policy, OSHA had not adopted such a policy at the time it established its revised PEL for benzene. Justice Powell indicated that he agreed with the Fifth Circuit's decision below that the "reasonably necessary" language of §3(8) required OSHA to establish that the costs of its regulations were not disproportionate to their benefits.]

Mr. Justice REHNQUIST, concurring in the judgment.

. . . I believe that this litigation presents the Court with what has to be one of the most difficult issues that could confront a decisionmaker: whether the statistical possibility of future deaths should ever be disregarded in light of the economic costs of preventing those deaths. I would also suggest that the widely varying positions advanced in the briefs of the parties and in the opinions of Mr. Justice STEVENS, THE CHIEF JUSTICE, Mr. Justice POWELL, and Mr. Justice MARSHALL demonstrate, perhaps better than any other fact, that Congress, the governmental body best suited and most obligated to make the choice confronting us in this litigation, has improperly delegated that choice to the Secretary of Labor and, derivatively, to this Court. . . .

. . . Read literally, the relevant portion of §6(b)(5) is completely

---

64. . . . In other proceedings, the Agency has had a good deal of data from animal experiments on which it could base a conclusion on the significance of the risk. . . .

In this case the Agency did not have the benefit of animal studies, because scientists have been unable as yet to induce leukemia in experimental animals as a result of benzene exposure. It did, however, have a fair amount of epidemiological evidence, including both positive and negative studies. Although the Agency stated that this evidence was insufficient to construct a precise correlation between exposure levels and cancer risks, it would at least be helpful in determining whether it is more likely than not that there is a significant risk at 10 ppm.

precatory, admonishing the Secretary to adopt the most protective standard if he can, but excusing him from that duty if he cannot. In the case of a hazardous substance for which a "safe" level is either unknown or impractical, the language of §6(b)(5) gives the Secretary absolutely no indication where on the continuum of relative safety he should draw his line. Especially in light of the importance of the interests at stake, I have no doubt that the provision at issue, standing alone, would violate the doctrine against uncanalized delegations of legislative power. . . .

[Justice Rehnquist then discussed why he believed that additional constraints on OSHA's authority cannot be ascertained from the legislative history or context of §6(b)(5). He termed that section's feasibility requirement "a legislative mirage" that could assume "any form desired by the beholder." He then concluded that this was not a question of whether such an unconstrained delegation was necessary.]

. . . It is difficult to imagine a more obvious example of Congress simply avoiding a choice which was both fundamental for purposes of the statute and yet politically so divisive that the necessary decision or compromise was difficult, if not impossible, to hammer out in the legislative forge. Far from detracting from the substantive authority of Congress, a declaration that the first sentence of §6(b)(5) of the Occupational Safety and Health Act constitutes an invalid delegation to the Secretary of Labor would preserve the authority of Congress. If Congress wishes to legislate in an area in which it has not previously sought to enter, it will in today's political world undoubtedly run into opposition no matter how the legislation is formulated. But that is the very essence of legislative authority under our system. It is the hard choices, and not the filling in of the blanks, which must be made by the elected representatives of the people. When fundamental policy decisions underlying important legislation about to be enacted are to be made, the buck stops with Congress and the President insofar as he exercises his constitutional role in the legislative process.

. . . Accordingly, for the reasons stated above, I concur in the judgment of the Court affirming the judgment of the Court of Appeals.

Mr. Justice MARSHALL, with whom Mr. Justice BRENNAN, Mr. Justice WHITE, and Mr. Justice BLACKMUN join, dissenting. . . .

[T]oday's decision represents a usurpation of decisionmaking authority that has been exercised by and properly belongs with Congress and its authorized representatives. The plurality's construction has no support in the statute's language, structure, or legislative history. The threshold finding that the plurality requires is the plurality's own invention. It bears no relationship to the acts or intentions of Congress, and it can be understood only as reflecting the personal views of the plurality as to the proper allocation of resources for safety in the American workplace.

The plurality is obviously more interested in the consequences of its decision than in discerning the intention of Congress. But since the language and legislative history of the Act are plain, there is no need for conjecture about the effects of today's decision. "It is not for us to speculate, much less act, on whether Congress would have altered its stance had the specific events of this case been anticipated." TVA v. Hill, 437 U.S., at 185. I do not pretend to know whether the test the plurality erects today is, as a matter of policy, preferable to that created by Congress and its delegates: the area is too fraught with scientific uncertainty, and too dependent on considerations of policy, for a court to be able to determine whether it is desirable to require identification of a "significant" risk before allowing an administrative agency to take regulatory action. But in light of the tenor of the plurality opinion, it is necessary to point out that the question is not one-sided, and that Congress' decision to authorize the Secretary to promulgate the regulation at issue here was a reasonable one.

In this case the Secretary found that exposure to benzene at levels [of] about 1 ppm posed a definite, albeit unquantifiable, risk of chromosomal damage, nonmalignant blood disorders, and leukemia. The existing evidence was sufficient to justify the conclusion that such a risk was presented, but it did not permit even rough quantification of that risk. Discounting for the various scientific uncertainties, the Secretary gave "careful consideration to the question of whether th[e] substantial costs" of the standard "are justified in light of the hazards of exposure to benzene," and concluded that "these costs are necessary in order to effectuate the statutory purpose . . . and to adequately protect employees from the hazards of exposure to benzene." 43 Fed. Reg. 5941 (1978).

In these circumstances it seems clear that the Secretary found a risk that is "significant" in the sense that the word is normally used. There was some direct evidence of chromosomal damage, nonmalignant blood disorders, and leukemia at exposures at or near 10 ppm and below. In addition, expert after expert testified that the recorded effects of benzene exposure at higher levels justified an inference that an exposure level about 1 ppm was dangerous. The plurality's extraordinarily searching scrutiny of this factual record reveals no basis for a conclusion that quantification is, on the basis of "the best available evidence," possible at the present time. If the Secretary decided to wait until definitive information was available, American workers would be subjected for the indefinite future to a possibly substantial risk of benzene-induced leukemia and other illnesses. It is unsurprising, at least to me, that he concluded that the statute authorized him to take regulatory action now.

Under these circumstances, the plurality's requirement of identification of a "significant" risk will have one of two consequences. If the plurality means to require the Secretary realistically to "quantify" the risk in order to satisfy a court that it is "significant," the record shows that the plurality means to require him to do the impossible. But regulatory inaction has very significant costs of its own. The adoption of such a test would subject American workers to a continuing risk of cancer and other serious diseases; it would disable the Secretary from regulating a wide variety of carcinogens for which quantification simply cannot be undertaken at the present time.

There are encouraging signs that today's decision does not extend that far. My Brother POWELL concludes that the Secretary is not prevented from taking regulatory action "when reasonable quantification cannot be accomplished by any known methods." The plurality also indicates that it would not prohibit the Secretary from promulgating safety standards when quantification of the benefits is impossible. The Court might thus allow the Secretary to attempt to make a very rough quantification of the risk imposed by a carcinogenic substance, and give considerable deference to his finding that the risk was significant. If so, the Court would permit the Secretary to promulgate precisely the same regulation involved in these cases if he had not relied on a carcinogen "policy," but undertaken a review of the evidence and the expert testimony and concluded, on the basis of conservation assumptions, that the risk addressed is a significant one. Any other interpretation of the plurality's approach would allow a court to displace the agency's judgment with its own subjective conception of "significance," a duty to be performed without statutory guidance.

The consequences of this second approach would hardly be disastrous; indeed, it differs from my own principally in its assessment of the basis for the Secretary's decision in these cases. It is objectionable, however, for three reasons. First, the requirement of identification of a "significant" risk simply has no relationship to the statute that the Court today purports to construe. Second, if the "threshold finding" requirement means only that the Secretary must find "that there is a need for such a standard," the requirement was plainly satisfied by the Secretary's express statement that the standard's costs "are necessary in order to effectuate the statutory purpose . . . and to adequately protect employees from the hazards of exposure to benzene." 43 Fed. Reg. 5941 (1978). Third, the record amply demonstrates that in light of existing scientific knowledge, no purpose would be served by requiring the Secretary to take steps to quantify the risk of exposure to benzene at low levels. Any such quantification would be based not on scientific "knowledge" as that term is normally understood, but on considerations of policy. For carcinogens like benzene, the assumptions on which a dose-response curve must be based are necessarily arbitrary. To require a quantitative showing of a "significant" risk, therefore, would either paralyze the Secretary into inaction or force him to deceive the public by acting on the basis of assumptions that must be considered too speculative to support any realistic assessment of the relevant risk. See McGarity, Substantive and Procedural Discretion in Administrative Resolution of Science Policy Questions: Regulating Carcinogens in EPA and OSHA, 67 Geo. L.J. 729, 806 (1979). It is encouraging that the Court appears willing not to require quantification when it is not fairly possible.

Though it is difficult to see how a future Congress could be any more explicit on the matter than was the Congress that passed the Act in 1970, it is important to remember that today's decision is subject to legislative reversal. Congress may continue to believe that the Secretary should not be prevented from protecting American workers from cancer and other fatal diseases until scientific evidence has progressed to a point where he can convince a federal court that the risk is "significant." Today's decision is objectionable not because it is final, but because it places the burden of legislative inertia on the beneficiaries of the safety and health legislation in question in these cases. By allocating the burden in this fashion, the Court requires the American worker to return to the political arena and to win a victory that he won once before in 1970. I am unable to discern any justification for that result. . . .

In passing the Occupational Safety and Health Act of 1970, Congress was aware that it was authorizing the Secretary to regulate in areas of scientific uncertainty. But it intended to require stringent regulation even when definitive information was unavailable. In reducing the permissible level of exposure to benzene, the Secretary applied proper legal standards. His determinations are supported by substantial evidence. The Secretary's decision was one, then, which the governing legislation authorized him to make.

In recent years there has been increasing recognition that the products of technological development may have harmful effects whose incidence and severity cannot be predicted with certainty. The responsibility to regulate such products has fallen to administrative agencies. Their task is not an enviable one. Frequently no clear causal link can be established between the regulated substance and the harm to be averted. Risks of harm are often uncertain, but inaction has considerable costs of its own. The agency must decide whether to take regulatory action against possibly substantial risks or to wait until more definitive information becomes available—a judgment which by its very nature cannot be based solely on determinations of fact.

Those delegations, in turn, have been made on the understanding that judicial review would be available to ensure that the agency's determinations are supported by substantial evidence and that its actions do not exceed the limits set by Congress. In the Occupational Safety and Health Act, Congress expressed confidence that the courts would carry out this important responsibility. But in these cases the plurality has far exceeded its authority. The plurality's "threshold finding" requirement is nowhere to be found in the Act and is antithetical to its basic purposes.

"The fundamental policy questions appropriately resolved in Congress . . . are *not* subject to re-examination in the federal courts under the guise of judicial review of agency action." Vermont Yankee Nuclear Power Corp. v. NRDC, 435 U.S. at 558 (emphasis in original). Surely this is no less true of the decision to ensure safety for the American worker than the decision to proceed with nuclear power. See ibid.

Because the approach taken by the plurality is so plainly irreconcilable with the Court's proper institutional role, I am certain that it will not stand the test of time. In all likelihood, today's decision will come to be regarded as an extreme reaction to a regulatory scheme that, as the Members of the plurality perceived it, imposed an unduly harsh burden on regulated industries. But as the Constitution "does not enact Mr. Herbert Spencer's Social Statics," Lochner v. New York, 198 U.S. 45, 75 (1905) (Holmes, J., dissenting), so the responsibility to scrutinize federal administrative action does not authorize this Court to strike its own balance between the costs and benefits of occupational safety standards. I am confident that the approach taken by the plurality today, like that in *Lochner* itself, will eventually be abandoned, and that the representative branches of government will once again be allowed to determine the level of safety and health protection to be accorded to the American worker.

NOTES AND QUESTIONS

1. What did OSHA fail to do in the benzene case that in the Court's view was necessary for promulgating a revised PEL for benzene that would withstand judicial review? As a result of the Court's decision, what must OSHA do differently in the future?

2. In light of the *Benzene* decision, who bears the burden of proving that the risk to be regulated is "significant"? How does Justice Stevens justify this allocation of the burden of proof? How can this burden be discharged?

3. Why did OSHA fail to prepare a dose-response curve for benzene prior to promulgating the revised PEL? Did OSHA believe that its revised PEL for benzene would have significant benefits? Must OSHA prepare a dose-response curve in the future?

4. Must OSHA perform a quantitative risk assessment? What if it is not possible for OSHA to assess risks in quantitative terms?

5. In most cases involving the regulation of potentially toxic substances there is considerable uncertainty over the magnitude and nature of the substance's impact on health. One means of coping with uncertainty is to use default assumptions or a "safety factor" approach that errs on the side of caution to protect health. Is OSHA free to use such conservative assumptions after *Benzene*? How much confidence must

OSHA have in its finding that a risk is significant before it will withstand judicial review?

6. What is the principal point of disagreement between Justice Stevens's plurality opinion and Justice Marshall's dissent? In cases in which a substance is known to pose a risk but it is impossible to quantify the *magnitude* of the risk, what would happen under Justice Stevens's approach? Under Justice Marshall's?

7. How "significant" must a risk be in order to satisfy Justice Stevens? His plurality opinion notes that "safe" does not mean "risk free." He later states that a risk of one in a billion of dying from drinking chlorinated water is "clearly not significant," while a risk of one in a thousand that benzene inhalation might be fatal might well lead a reasonable person to consider the risk "significant." Where is the line between "significant" and "insignificant" risks to be drawn and by whom? Does Justice Marshall advocate a zero risk approach? Would he permit OSHA to regulate truly trivial risks? We will return to the question of "how safe is safe" in section D of this chapter.

8. Only three other Justices (Chief Justice Burger, Justice Stewart, and Justice Powell) joined in Justice Stevens's plurality opinion. Justice Powell did not join Part III-D of Justice Stevens' opinion, which discussed how to define and allocate the burden of proving the significance of a risk. In a concurring opinion, Justice Powell noted that he "would not rule out the possibility that the necessary findings [of significant risk] could rest in part on generic policies properly adopted by OSHA," but he noted that OSHA's cancer policy was not promulgated until after the benzene regulations were issued. Justice Powell, however, also expressed the view that OSHA was required "to determine that the economic effects of its standard bear a reasonable relationship to the expected benefits."

9. Justice Stevens's plurality opinion bases the requirement that OSHA determine that risks to be regulated are "significant" on an interpretation of section 3(8) of the OSH Act, 29 U.S.C. §652, which defines the term "occupational safety and health standard." What impact, if any, is the Court's decision likely to have on the regulation of toxic substances by EPA and other agencies operating under different statutory authorities?

10. Justice Rehnquist argues that section 6(b)(5) of the OSH Act is an unconstitutional delegation of legislative power to OSHA, a position that is not accepted by any other member of the Court. What do you think Congress would have to do to satisfy Justice Rehnquist's concern?

11. As a result of the unusual 4-4-1 split, what is the actual "holding" in this case? In future cases that present similar issues, how would you expect the Court to rule?

12. The Fifth Circuit had struck down OSHA's benzene PEL largely because OSHA had failed to demonstrate that the benefits of the standard bore a reasonable relationship to its costs. When the case was briefed

and argued in the Supreme Court, it was widely expected that the Court would determine whether or not some form of cost-benefit balancing was required by the OSH Act. Why did the Supreme Court refuse to decide this issue? One year after the *Benzene* decision the Court again was faced with the question whether the OSH Act required some balancing of costs and benefits. In American Textile Manufacturers Institute, Inc. v. Donovan, 452 U.S. 488 (1981) (the Cotton Dust case), see page 541 below, the Court held that the OSH Act did not require cost-benefit balancing. The case was argued the day after the Reagan Administration assumed office. The Justice Department asked the Court for a voluntary remand because the Reagan Administration disagreed with OSHA's former position that cost-benefit balancing was not required. The Court refused to remand the case and decided it in favor of OSHA. The vote was 5-3, with the majority opinion being written by Justice Brennan and Justice Powell not participating in the case. Which Justice from the *Benzene* decision plurality do you think voted in favor of OSHA in the Cotton Dust case?

A Note on Regulation of Benzene by OSHA Following the *Benzene* Decision

Justice Marshall's prediction that the plurality decision would "eventually be abandoned" proved inaccurate. In fact, Justice Stevens's opinion has had a tremendous impact on the practices of federal regulatory agencies even outside the context of OSHA. It has provided considerable impetus for the use of risk assessments by regulatory agencies, many of which already had begun to perform such assessments prior to the *Benzene* decision. Indeed, OSHA already had completed a risk assessment for the cotton dust standard, which meant that it did not have to be withdrawn following the *Benzene* decision.

Justice Marshall's dissent was prescient in one respect. He argued that the outcome in the *Benzene* decision could subject American workers to continuing exposure to substances that increased risks of cancer and other serious diseases. In the years that followed, OSHA performed several assessments of the risks of benzene exposure to humans. These assessments, which were based on a wealth of new epidemiological data, confirmed that benzene posed extremely serious risks to workers. In 1982, the International Agency for Research on Cancer concluded that workers exposed to 10 to 100 ppm of benzene faced excess leukemia risks of 170 per 1,000. Based on the results of five risk assessments, OSHA eventually concluded that workers exposed to 10 ppm of benzene faced excess leukemia risks ranging from 44 to 152 per 1,000, and that even workers exposed to 1 ppm of benzene faced excess leukemia risks ranging from 5 to 16 per 1,000.

OSHA noted that these estimates were among the most conservative of the estimates that could be derived from studies of benzene exposure. Studies performed by the Chemical Manufacturers Association, Dow Chemical, and NIOSH all found substantial excess leukemia risks from benzene exposure (88 per 1,000 at 10 ppm and 9.5 per 1,000 at 1 ppm). Experimental bioassays also revealed that benzene induces multiple site cancers in both sexes of two species of rodents, evidence that had not been available when the *Benzene* decision was decided. New studies showed that benzene was associated with chromosomal aberrations in exposed workers.

Despite all this data, OSHA took several years to promulgate a new PEL for benzene. In April 1983, a group of unions petitioned OSHA to issue an emergency temporary standard of 1 ppm for benzene. OSHA denied this petition, claiming that the risk assessments needed additional review and that no emergency existed because 90 percent of workers were believed to be exposed to less than 1 ppm of benzene. After an abortive effort by OSHA at regulatory negotiation between the unions and the affected industry, the United Steelworkers of America sought a writ of mandamus in December 1984 to compel OSHA to regulate benzene on an expedited basis.

Fully a year later, when oral argument was heard on the union lawsuit, OSHA lawyers told the court that a proposed rule had just been sent to the Federal Register. Holding that OSHA's issuance of a notice of proposed rulemaking had made the case moot, the court subsequently dismissed the union's lawsuit.

OSHA held hearings on its proposed PEL in March and April 1986 and compiled a 36,000-page record prior to promulgating a new PEL in September 1987. The new standard, effective December 1987, lowered the benzene PEL from 10 ppm to 1 ppm as an 8-hour average, while lowering the short-term exposure limit (STEL) from 25 ppm to 5 ppm as a 10-minute average.

OSHA based its new PEL on risk assessments showing that exposure to 10 ppm of benzene posed a risk of 95 additional leukemia deaths per 1,000 workers, a level greatly in excess of both other toxic substance risks OSHA had deemed significant (including arsenic, ethylene oxide, and ethylene dibromide) and the risk of accidental death in high- and average-risk industries (where death risks ranged from 30 to 3 in 1,000). OSHA estimated that the new PEL would prevent at least 326 deaths from leukemia and other blood diseases and that the actual number of deaths prevented would be considerably greater.

What OSHA left unsaid was that, due to judicial intervention, it had taken ten years to lower the benzene PEL to the very levels the Agency had sought to adopt on an emergency basis in May 1977. (That ETS had been abandoned by OSHA after it had been struck down by the U.S. Court of Appeals for the Fifth Circuit.) The PEL ultimately promulgated by OSHA was at the same level as the PEL vacated by the Supreme Court in 1980 in the *Benzene* decision. Thus, if OSHA's risk assessments are accurate, by delaying promulgation of the stricter PEL judicial intervention has resulted in the exposure of thousands of workers to risks that will result in scores of additional deaths.

C. INTRODUCTION TO RISK ASSESSMENT TECHNIQUES

In the *Benzene* decision, one point of disagreement between the plurality opinion of Justice Stevens and the dissenting opinion of Justice Marshall lay in the apparent assumption of Justice Stevens that risks could be quantified, at least roughly. Justice Marshall, on the other hand, thought that an insistence on quantification would prevent OSHA from performing its regulatory mission. For Justice Stevens to be correct, it must be the case that techniques of quantitative risk assessment work at least tolerably well. Here is a short course on the risk assessment process as currently understood and practiced.

The National Research Council's influential study, Risk Assessment in the Federal Government: Managing the Process (1983), identified four principal steps in the risk assessment process:

- *Hazard identification:* Is the item under study (e.g., a chemical) causally linked to particular health (or public welfare) effects?
- *Dose-response assessment:* What is the relationship between the magnitude of exposure and the probability that the health (or public welfare) effects will occur?
- *Exposure assessment:* What is the level of exposure of humans (or the environment) to the hazard?
- *Risk characterization:* What is the overall magnitude of the risk?

Figure 4.5 illustrates the conventional way of viewing the risk assessment and risk management processes. As the chart illustrates, each of the first three steps in the risk assessment process requires the use of research data to estimate the types of hazard posed (hazard identification), the probability a hazard will occur (dose-response assessment), and the number of people exposed and their levels of exposure (exposure assessment). These three elements are then combined in the process of risk characterization.

Risks can be characterized either in quantitative or qualitative terms. *Quantitative* risk assessments generally specify either the total numbers of people likely to experience the adverse effect or the likelihood that any one individual exposed to the hazard would suffer the adverse effect. The former is referred to as "population risk" (e.g., 100 additional cases of cancer in the exposed population), the latter "individual risk" (e.g.,

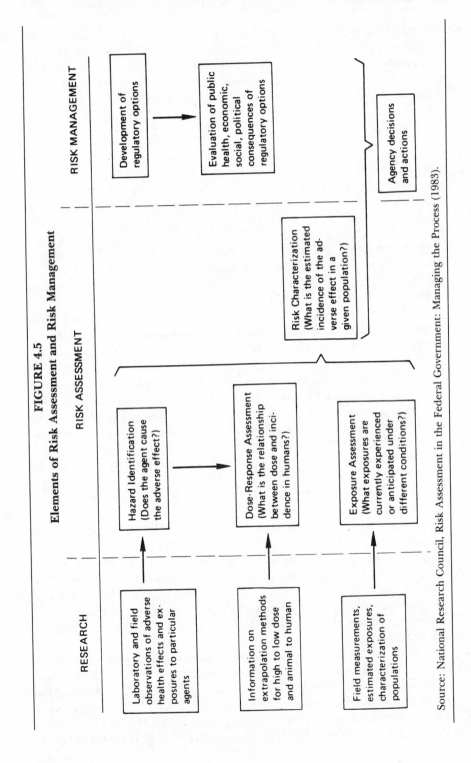

FIGURE 4.5
Elements of Risk Assessment and Risk Management

Source: National Research Council, Risk Assessment in the Federal Government: Managing the Process (1983).

an exposed individual faces a 1-in-10,000 chance of developing cancer). _Qualitative_ risk assessments characterize risks in nonquantitative terms (e.g., the risk is small or large). They are used occasionally to provide rough rank orderings of the seriousness of different risks, a practice referred to as _comparative_ risk assessment (which also is used at times to compare quantitative estimates to assess their significance).

An excellent nontechnical introduction to risk assessment is Conservation Foundation, Risk Assessment and Control (1985). As this report notes, "almost all risk assessments are plagued by inadequate data." Id. at 4. They explain the uncertainties that make risk assessment a risky business in the following terms:

> Virtually all elements of risk assessment are clouded with uncertainty, basically of two kinds. First, the various scientific disciplines involved in assessing risk are not sufficiently developed either to explain the mechanisms by which particular causes produce particular effects or to provide good quantitative estimates of cause-and-effect relationships. Second, the data needed to analyse particular risk are usually not available. [Id. at 5.]

The difficulties of using existing data and techniques for performing risk assessments were highlighted in 1987 when EPA asked its staff to assess the Agency's priorities by performing rough risk assessments of the 31 environmental problems listed in Chapter 1, Figure 1.1. EPA sought to compare the seriousness of these problems by assessing the risks they posed in four areas: cancer risks, noncancer health effects, damage to public welfare (economic damage), and ecological risks. This exercise produced a study, entitled Unfinished Business, that described some of the obstacles to performing risk assessments:

> The best information available is for cancer risk. Even there, however, it was not nearly as good as one might expect.
> The data and methods available for assessing noncancer health effects are poor. Exposure data are surprisingly poor, even on chemicals that are objects of major regulatory efforts.
> There is no general methodology for assessing noncancer health risks. There is no generally applicable methodology for ecological risk assessment. The number of different types of ecological systems, the relative scarcity of ecosystem exposure data and methods, and scientific uncertainties compound the problem. Moreover, the extraordinary complexity of ecological systems prohibits objective assessment of ecological risks.
> While there are generally accepted methods for assessing welfare effects, there is a general scarcity of data and analysis in this area. [EPA, Unfinished Business 98-99 (1987).]

Consider how uncertainty affects the various steps in the risk assessment process.

Hazard Identification.   Regulatory agencies today have a far more difficult task than the first federal safety agency, the Steamboat Inspection Service (see page 486), which was charged with preventing boilers on steamships from exploding. Exploding boilers are a clearly identifiable problem, and the causes of such are reasonably amenable to investigation and discovery. Not so with respect to many modern environmental hazards. Cancer, far and away the most studied and feared health hazard, is still not well understood by scientists. Furthermore, it is difficult even to tell whether a given chemical is actually a human carcinogen. All the potential sources of information have their deficiencies and uncertainties, as described below.

Epidemiologic data.   After incidences of disease are noted in a given segment of the population, well-conducted epidemiologic studies of that segment can sometimes find an association between a causative agent and that disease. Because epidemiology would provide direct evidence in human beings of the hazard, in theory this would be a most valuable source of reliable information. Such evidence, however, is extremely limited. Except in occupational exposure settings, it is extremely difficult to identify population subgroups whose characteristics are virtually identical save for in their exposure to a substance being investigated. Even when such groups can be identified, historic levels of exposure actually experienced by each group are difficult to determine with precision. High background levels of common diseases like cancer mask all but the most catastrophic associations between diseases and particular causative agents. There may simply be too many variables—potential causes of the disease—in the population's history to sort out relative influences. Epidemiologic analysis, furthermore, requires that a disease manifest itself, yet the ideal function of environmental protection is to prevent disease.

Experimental data.   Experimental data have significant advantages over epidemiological data in that they permit scientists to assess environmental hazards in carefully controlled circumstances before widespread human exposure has occurred. Because ethical considerations preclude human exposure to substances that threaten health, most experimental data are derived from in vitro tests or animal bioassays.

Short-term studies and molecular comparisons.   Certain short-term tests of chemicals (e.g., for mutagenicity) have been shown to be highly correlative to carcinogenicity; thus performing such tests can provide some evidence of whether the suspected hazard is a carcinogen. However, scientists now know that not all mutagens are carcinogens and that many nonmutagenic substances may play an important role in the complex process by which cancer develops. Short-term screening tests thus have proved more useful for identifying cancer initiators than for screening cancer promoters or receptors. Scientists also have sought to infer that certain chemicals may be carcinogens by analyzing their molecular structure to determine if it is similar to that of known carcinogens. This is called inference from structure-activity relationships and has been used for limited purposes such as determining whether to require additional testing of certain chemicals for carcinogenicity. Neither of these sources of information assists in estimating the potency of the hazard.

Animal bioassays. This is the most commonly available evidence. Exposure of animals under controlled conditions to a suspected hazard allows researchers to control for other variables and thus isolate the hazard potential of the suspect. Bioassay data are necessarily skimpy, however, because of the enormous sample sizes that are required to detect the risks posed by low-level exposures to toxic substances. Hazard identification frequently relies on just one or two experiments in a single species of rodent. Furthermore, while the validity of translating animal findings into conjectures of human reactions is widely accepted (indeed, fundamental to the entire toxicological research effort), the precise formulae for translating such findings remain disputed and depend on inferences that cannot be scientifically validated. Moreover, there are occasions when observations in animals are of very limited relevance to humans. Still, such studies remain the backbone of governmental and industry research in hazard identification. They are expensive and time-consuming—two years and $2.5 million is typical for a single rodent bioassay—so we should expect such data to be limited.

Dose-Response Assessment. Experimental or epidemiological data never exist for exactly the levels of exposure in question. Scientists therefore must extrapolate from the available data the relationship between the doses relevant to regulation and the human health or environmental effects (the response) to assess the potency of a hazard.

Uncertainties in dose-response assessment come from a variety of sources. With epidemiological data, the population as a whole typically contains subpopulations that are likely to be more susceptible to disease than the population studied, for instance, children, pregnant women, fetuses, and the elderly. It is often unclear how to translate epidemiological data to predict the effects of exposure on such groups.

Animal bioassays present further problems, as noted above. There is no scientific consensus on how to transfer information about animal reactions to suspected hazards and human reactions, even holding the dose constant. Because body weight, body metabolism, differences in immune systems, and other variables are thought to be relevant to the study of how an organism responds to exposures, responses of humans and laboratory animals are likely to differ, but scientists are unsure as to how.

Bioassays also present the problem of extrapolating from higher doses to regulation-relevant, lower doses. Indeed, in order to induce laboratory responses animals are exposed to extremely high doses. This makes it difficult to gauge the adverse response, even among the animal population itself, to much lower doses. This difficulty arises because scientists do not yet have a reliable model of how cancer is caused. There are in fact a variety of competing models, each with its theoretical supporters. Figure 4.6 depicts the typical results of five different extrapolation models, all starting with the same experimental data (the point in the upper right corner of the graph).

Exposure Assessment.   Often the weakest data link in the chain of steps in the risk assessment process is meaningful exposure data. Exposure assessments usually require the use of fate and transport models. Because exposures may occur through several different pathways, particularly for nonoccupational exposures, these models must employ crude assumptions concerning the complex processes of transport and conversion of pollutants and patterns of usage of consumer products. The characteristics of population groups potentially exposed to certain substances also may have a significant impact on risk assessment because some types of people are more susceptible than others to certain hazards. Data on the synergistic effects of exposure to mixtures of substances is generally unavailable.

Hazard Identification Then and Now: Exploding Boilers versus Cancer-Causing Substances

The following is an excerpt from comments made by Donald Kennedy on December 5, 1978, when Kennedy was commissioner of the Food and Drug Administration.

The way we regulate the complex and refractory must, unfortunately, differ from the way in which we regulate the comparatively straightforward. To show you what I mean, let me refer you to the very first federal regulatory agency. That agency—the Steamboat Inspection Service—was founded in 1836. It was called into being to address a specific problem: exploding boilers on steamboats. This was what one might call an unequivocal problem. Boilers exploded, or they did not. Given the explicit nature of explosion, the results were inescapable: there was noise, fire, usually followed quite rapidly by the lapping of water around one's ankles. I hope you don't take it as an extreme statement if I say that people detested having the boilers on their steamboat explode. There was no constituency that favored, let's say from motives of overwhelming ennui, the excitement that followed your run-of-the-mill boiler explosion. No one had organized the survivors into a committee for freedom of choice. And the causes of these unfortunate occurrences were well understood. . . .
Even private enterprise saw [the profit advantages in being able to offer

FIGURE 4.6
Dose-Response Models: What a Difference They Make

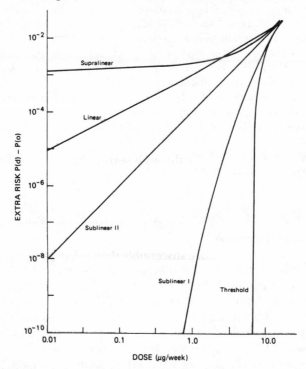

Results of alternative extrapolation models for the same experimental data. NOTE: Dose-response functions were developed (Crump, in press) for data from a benzopyrene carcinogenesis experiment with mice conducted by Lee and O'Neill (1971).

To give you some appreciation for how significant the choice among dose-response models is, consider a hypothetical chemical tested in the laboratory on both mice and rats of both sexes, at doses of 0 mg/kg/day (the control group), 125, 250, 500, and 1,000 mg/kg/day, and found to produce liver cancer in male rats. With 50 rats in each group, the incidence of liver cancer was, respectively, 0, 0, 10, 25, and 40 cases. What do these data imply for fairly low doses—say, 1 mg/kg/day? This depends on which mathematical dose-response model you ask. Here are the results from five models used frequently:

Model	Lifetime risk for male rats at 1 mg/kg/day
One-hit	1 chance in 17,000
Multistage	1 in 167,000
Multihit	1 in 230,000
Weibull	1 in 59 million
Probit	1 in 5.2 billion

Source: EPA, Principles of Risk Assessment: A Nontechnical Review IV-5 to IV-7 (1985).

safer travel to passengers]. So, there we have the father of federal regulation, just oozing common sense. Today, people fear cancer more than, I imagine, our floating ancestors feared boiler explosions. But we do not have a single agency dealing in a comparatively straightforward way with the problem. Nor are we aware of the initiation of the carcinogenic process; we are not really certain how it happens; we do not by any means have a complete inventory of the environmental causes; we do not understand the matrix of reactions between outer and inner environment; we understand practically nothing about interaction among carcinogens and co-carcinogens, potentiation of carcinogens by other substances, and a host of other complex problems of this nature; nor do we have any real proof about threshold or linearity, and if we did we could not be sure that your threshold was the same as mine due to differences in genetic background and our inventory of habits, bad and good. [The Conservation Foundation, Risk Assessment and Control 3 (1985).]

D. A RISK ASSESSMENT CASE STUDY: THE ALAR CONTROVERSY

The Federal Insecticide, Fungicide, and Rodenticide Act (FIFRA), which governs regulation of pesticides, is a risk-benefit balancing statute. FIFRA prohibits the marketing of pesticides that are not registered with EPA. Thus, it is a licensing type of statute that requires premanufacture review of the risks posed by pesticides. Before a new pesticide can be registered with EPA, the Agency must review information about the risks and benefits of the product. More than 50,000 pesticides have been registered since FIFRA was enacted in 1947. These pesticides contain some 1,500 active ingredients and 900 inert ingredients. Many existing pesticide products were registered at a time when very little information was available about their long-term effects on the environment. With the publication of Rachel Carson's book Silent Spring in 1962, public attention was focused on the environmental damage that pesticides like DDT could wreak. Thus, when FIFRA was amended in 1972, EPA was directed to reevaluate or reregister existing pesticides. However, EPA was slow to do this. In 1986 the General Accounting Office reported that none of the active ingredients in older pesticides had been fully tested and assessed for health and environmental effects and that the potential toxicity of inert ingredients had been almost completely ignored. GAO, Pesticides: EPA's Formidable Task 3 (1986).

When EPA determines that an existing pesticide may pose a particularly significant hazard, it may undertake what is called a "special review" of the product. If the Agency determines that the pesticide poses an unreasonable risk, EPA may issue a notice of intent to cancel the product's registration. However, if a pesticide manufacturer requests a hearing within 30 days of a notice of cancellation, FIFRA requires that a formal adjudicatory hearing be held. These hearings may take several years to complete while the pesticide remains on the market unless EPA determines that the risks posed by the product are so severe that an immediate suspension is warranted. EPA has suspended, canceled, or restricted the use of approximately 50 pesticides, including DDT, aldrin, dieldrin, and ethylene dibromide (EDB).

In addition to the slow pace of reregistration and cancellation proceedings, a major problem with FIFRA as originally written was that it required EPA to reimburse pesticide manufacturers and users for the costs of canceled or suspended products. Environmentalists argued that this provision deterred EPA action to remove dangerous products from the market. In addition, EPA had to assume responsibility for the disposal of canceled pesticides. As EPA discovered when it halted the use of EDB in 1984, disposal of existing stocks of pesticides can be difficult and expensive. EPA spent more than $1 million trying to dispose of stocks of EDB, only to discover that the disposal method it had chosen would not work. EPA estimated that the cost of disposing of dinoseb, another pesticide it sought to cancel, would exceed $100 million.

FIFRA was amended in 1988 to address these and other problems. The new amendments establish a schedule for EPA to complete the reregistration of 600 older active ingredients, and they require manufacturers to pay fees to help finance the reregistration process. The amendments provide that only end users of canceled products will be reimbursed, and they require manufacturers to assume the responsibility for storage and disposal of pesticides whose registration is canceled.

PRINCIPAL PROVISIONS OF FIFRA

§3. Registration of Pesticides—requires all pesticides to be registered with EPA based on applications demonstrating that they will perform their intended functions without causing "unreasonable adverse effects on the environment."

§4. Reregistration of Registered Pesticides—requires EPA to reregister pesticides containing active ingredients first registered before November 1, 1984.

§6. Suspension and Cancellation of Registration

§6(a)—provides for automatic cancellation of a pesticide's registration after five years unless the registrant requests that it be continued.

§6(b)—authorizes EPA to cancel the registration of pesticides after adjudicatory hearings if the pesticide is found generally to cause "unreasonable adverse effects on the environment."

§6(c)—EPA may suspend the registration of any pesticide pending completion of formal cancellation hearings if the agency determines that suspension "is necessary to prevent an imminent hazard to human health." If EPA determines that immediate suspension is necessary "to prevent an imminent hazard during the time required for cancellation" the suspension can take effect immediately unless the registrant requests an expedited hearing or if EPA "determines that an emergency exists" that does not permit time for a hearing.

Despite amendments to FIFRA, the process of canceling a pesticide remains fraught with considerable procedural difficulties, as illustrated by the Alar controversy, in which competing risk assessments were the centerpiece of a fierce public controversy. Early in 1989, a strong public outcry followed a report from the Natural Resources Defense Council (NRDC), featured on the popular television program "60 Minutes," that a byproduct of a chemical widely used as a growth regulator on apples was a powerful carcinogen. Using a public relations firm and celebrities to publicize its study, NRDC spread the alarm concerning the chemical daminozide, known by the trade name Alar. As a result of this publicity, several school districts removed apples from school lunch menus. Representatives of EPA, the Food and Drug Administration, and the Department of Agriculture sought unsuccessfully to reassure the public that the food supply was safe and that Alar need not be removed from the market immediately.

The principal dispute between NRDC and government health officials centered on differences between the risk assessments on which they each relied. The following problem exercise focuses on why these two risk assessments differed, based on information drawn from: NRDC, Intolerable Risk: Pesticides in Our Children's Food (Feb. 27, 1989); Pesticides and Kids, 243 Science 1280 (1989); Alar: The Numbers Game, 243 Science 1430 (1989); OUR FOOD SUPPLY IS SAFE, N.Y. Times, April 5, 1989, at A11 (advertisement); Bad Apples, 54 Consumer Reports 288 (May 1989); Rosen, Much Ado About Alar, Issues in Science & Technology 87 (Fall 1990); L. Zeise, P. Painter, P. Berteau, A. Fan, and R. Jackson, Alar in Fruit: Limited Regulatory Action in the Face of Uncertain Risks, in The Analysis, Communication, and Perception of Risk 275 (B. Garrick and W. Gekler, eds. 1991); and Marshall, A Is for Apple, Alar, and . . . Alarmist?, 254 Science 20 (1991).

PROBLEM EXERCISE: THE CASE OF ALAR

The following discussion is meant to be as factually accurate as possible, although we have simplified occasionally where doing so does not materially distort the questions posed. Place yourself in the position of the EPA administrator and answer the questions raised by the text.

Alar is the trade name for daminozide, a plant growth regulator used to keep ripening apples on the tree and to keep apples firm and red during storage. Alar is considered a pesticide and was registered by EPA under FIFRA in 1963. When used on apples, some Alar penetrates the apple skin and remains after harvest and cannot be washed off. Alar decomposes over time into other chemicals including 1,1-(unsymmetrical) dimethylhydrazine (UDMH), which is used as a component in rocket fuel. Alar contains about 1 percent UDMH and it hydrolyzes into additional UDMH, particularly when heated, as in the preparation of applesauce or apple juice, and when ingested in the bodies of mammals.

UDMH was first identified as a potential carcinogen in 1967 when lung tumors were found in mice exposed to UDMH. In 1973 further studies found tumors of the lung, liver, kidney, and blood vessels in mice exposed to UDMH. A study published in 1977 found that when mice were exposed to high levels of Alar, they developed a high incidence of the same type of tumors as the mice exposed to UDMH.

In 1980 EPA announced that it would conduct a special review of Alar, but later it abandoned the effort after meeting with representatives of Alar's manufacturer, the Uniroyal Company. After environmentalists sued EPA, the Agency reinstated the special review. In 1985 EPA staff proposed canceling the registration of Alar for use on food. This action would have had the effect of banning such use (following lengthy administrative hearings that could take a year or two). EPA's proposal was then reviewed by a science advisory panel that severely criticized the methodology used in the animal studies of Alar and UDMH, which had been performed prior to EPA's establishment of "good laboratory practice procedures" in 1979. Because these studies were flawed, EPA withdrew its cancellation proposal in January 1986 and instructed Uniroyal to conduct new studies using a better methodology. Because of publicity concerning the potential hazards of Alar, many apple growers announced that they would voluntarily stop using it.

In January 1989 results from the first year of Uniroyal's new two-year bioassay were reported to EPA. Although the study did not show any increased tumors in mice or rats exposed to Alar, it found tumors in those exposed to high levels of UDMH. Based on these data, the Natural Resources Defense Council prepared its own risk assessment that concluded that between 4,700 and 6,000 preschool children of a population of 22 million (or roughly 1 in every 4,200), will get cancer from exposure to Alar in their first 6 years of life. After this information was publicized on "60 Minutes" on February 26, 1989, a tremendous public outcry ensued.

Suppose that you are the EPA administrator. Your staff analyzes the NRDC report and the Uniroyal data and perform their own risk assessment. They find that of the 22 million children in the cohort examined by NRDC, 5.5 million are currently predicted to get cancer eventually from causes other than Alar. Children, of course, are not the only exposed population. Practically everyone eats apples. NRDC, however, has studied food consumption patterns as part of its analysis, relying largely on Department of Agriculture surveys. It found that fruits of all kinds comprise 34 percent of a preschooler's diet but only 20 percent of a mother's. Furthermore, the average preschooler consumes 6 times more fruit, overall, than an adult woman between 22 and 30, 7 times more apples and applesauce, 7 times more grape products, and 18 times more apple juice. Your staff calculates that the risk of cancer attributable to Alar is 9 in 1 million, 25 times lower than NRDC's estimate. They say the different calculations stem from several sources:

1. *Exposure Period.* EPA has calculated exposure only for a period of 18 months, which it estimates is the likely length of the administrative hearings that would have to be held before Alar uses could be halted unless you determine that an "imminent hazard" exists; NRDC's figures are for exposure during the 6-year period when children are between ages 0 to 6 years.

2. *Dose-Response.* Quantitative risk assessment requires an estimate of how much harm will come from given doses. NRDC thinks Alar a more potent carcinogen than does your staff. Part of the difference comes from different models of cancer causation employed. NRDC used a "time-dependent multistage model" that takes into account the longer latency periods available when one is exposed to a carcinogen when one is young. EPA's model is time-independent and assumes that the risk from a given dose is the same whether one is 5 years old or 70 years old. NRDC also argues that children are more vulnerable to cancer risk for physiological reasons (and hence any exposure amount is more potent for them). For one thing, children weigh less than adults. Therefore, the weight of fruit and its accompanying chemicals relative to body weight is greater than for an adult, and such differences increase the risk of cancer under most current models of cancer causation. NRDC also claims that children are even more susceptible to cancer than adults because their cells are dividing rapidly as a natural part of the growth process and because their enzymatic detoxification systems are not as fully developed as an adult's. There is some evidence these latter claims are true, although there is no scientific consensus. Finally, estimates of potency are extrapolations from the discrete findings of animal experiments. EPA used the interim data from the Uniroyal study, which NRDC adjusted upward because Uniroyal is just one year into a two-year study. NRDC claims that doubling the duration of exposure can be expected to increase the cumulative incidence of tumors by a factor of 32 rather than the factor of 8 used by EPA. Thus, because a far greater proportion of the adverse effects are likely to appear in the second year than EPA had adjusted for, NRDC's estimate of the slope of the dose-response curve is higher, consistent with the findings of the pre-1985 studies that the science advisory board found methodologically flawed.

3. *Exposure.* NRDC assumes that children consume more apples than EPA assumes. EPA's apple consumption estimates rely on a survey of 30,000 people conducted by the U.S. Department of Agriculture (USDA) in 1977-1978; NRDC is using the results of a USDA survey of 2,000 people conducted from 1985-1986 that shows a 30 percent jump in fruit consumption since the 1977-1978 data were compiled. EPA discounts the significance of the more recent survey because the sample size is small. Data from USDA's larger 1986-1987 study were not yet available.

FIFRA gives EPA the authority to ban the use of Alar on apples if such use poses "unreasonable adverse effects" to human health or the environment. However, the statute permits the manufacturer of Alar to challenge such a decision during lengthy administrative hearings that sometimes last for years (see 7 U.S.C. §136d(b)). During these hearings the manufacturer can keep the product on the market unless you determine that an "imminent hazard" exists (see 7 U.S.C. §§136d(c)(1), 136*l*). Even then, the product may remain on the market during expedited hearings unless you declare that an "emergency" requires its immediate removal (see 7 U.S.C. §136d(c)(3)). EPA has been studying Alar for more than 17 years.

Question One. Suppose that you are the EPA administrator. Several members of Congress have called your office demanding to know what you are going to do about Alar. Can you declare an emergency and order that Alar be removed from the market immediately? What would you tell the farmers who may lose an entire apple crop if you take such an action?

Question Two. As EPA administrator, how do you evaluate the differences between NRDC's estimates of risk and the estimates by your own staff? Recall the previous discussion about the impact of data uncertainties on risk assessments. What uncertainties does EPA face for each of the four elements of the Alar risk assessments? Which type of uncertainty affects each of them? Which differences between EPA's estimates and NRDC's estimates stem from the use of different models? Which stem from different assumptions? Whose models, assumptions, and estimates are more reasonable, NRDC's or EPA's?

Question Three. School districts are calling you, wondering whether they should pull apples off school cafeteria lines. Nationwide, purchases by schools account for nearly 25 percent of apple sales. What do you tell them? (As it happened, several school districts, including New York City's and Los Angeles's, did pull apples for a time, then reinstated them.)

Question Four. In other contexts, EPA has suggested that it will aim to reduce excess cancer risk to the level of one in one million or lower. NRDC is pushing for an immediate ban on Alar; your staff has recommended proceeding with administrative hearings to cancel the use of Alar on apples while awaiting the completion of Uniroyal's study and the release of the larger USDA survey data on food consumption before making a final decision. What should you do? Does the law provide a clear answer concerning the proper course of action?

Question Five. On April 5, 1989, a full-page advertisement sponsored by the American Council on Science and Health, a nonprofit organization funded largely by industry contributions, appeared in several major newspapers. Declaring that "OUR FOOD SUPPLY IS SAFE!," the ad condemned "efforts of certain environmental groups to exaggerate risk and cause needless anxiety." In order to "set the record straight," the ads made the following four assertions: (1) "There is no scientific evidence that residues in food from regulated and approved use of pesticides have ever been the cause of illness or death in either adults or children." (2) Charges that pesticide residues cause cancer have "no scientific merit" because they "are based exclusively on studies that expose rats and mice to enormous doses of chemicals. Humans would have to eat tons of produce every day for many years to ingest similar amounts." (3) Pesticides have helped make our food supply "the safest and most plentiful in the world," and if Americans "go 'back to nature,' they will have to coexist with vermin and insects and the diseases they bring." (4) Citing AIDS, smoking, and drug abuse, the ad argued that "[i]t is dangerous to focus on unsubstantiated claims when real risks to our health abound." N.Y. Times, April 5, 1989, at A11. Based on what you know about risk assessment procedures, how would you evaluate the accuracy of each of these claims? Are they misleading in any respects? How would you respond to them?

A Postscript on the Alar Controversy

The denouement of the Alar controversy came quickly. Alar was removed from the apple market by its manufacturer, not primarily because of any regulatory requirements imposed by EPA, but because of consumer pressure. The rapid decline in apple consumption that followed the "60 Minutes" report on February 26, 1989 led apple growers to pressure the manufacturer of Alar to remove it from the market.

Uniroyal, the sole manufacturer of Alar, agreed in June 1989 to halt voluntarily all domestic sales of Alar for food uses. EPA had issued a preliminary determination to cancel all food uses of Alar under FIFRA on May 24, 1989. 54 Fed. Reg. 22,558 (1989). But rather than force EPA to go through cancellation proceedings, Uniroyal formally requested a voluntary cancellation of all food use registrations of Alar on October 11, 1989. EPA issued a cancellation order that became effective on November 17, 1989. 54 Fed. Reg. 47,493 (1989).

The Alar controversy left many apple growers bitter. See Egan, Apple Growers Bruised and Bitter After Alar Scare, N.Y. Times, July 9, 1991, at A1. In November 1990 a group of apple growers in Yakima County, Washington filed a product defamation suit against NRDC, "60 Minutes," and NRDC's public relations firm. The lawsuit seeks $200 million in damages for dissemination of "false, misleading, and scientifically unreliable statements about red apples." Ironically, because the apple industry is currently enjoying record harvests and high prices, "[o]ne tricky point the growers will have to explain is why the apple business has done so well since Alar was taken off the market." Marshall, A Is for Apple, Alar, and . . . Alarmist?, 25 Science 20, 21 (1991).

Now that the Alar bioassay has been completed, EPA reportedly has estimated that Alar is only half as potent a carcinogen as the Agency had estimated in its 1989 risk assessment. Id. at 20. If this report is accurate, EPA's risk assessment would indicate that Alar would pose an individual risk on the order of 4 in 1 million for an exposed person. Should this have changed the outcome of the Alar controversy? EPA's deputy administrator for pesticides and toxics says no. The new data do "not change EPA's earlier conclusion that, although Alar has some benefits, its dietary risks from historical exposures are unacceptably high." While "Alar appears less risky than [EPA] thought in 1989, that lower cancer potency estimate would not lead EPA to reverse [its] regulatory position." Kimm, Alar's Risks, 254 Science 1276 (1991).

Had EPA decided instead that Alar posed an "imminent hazard" warranting immediate suspension of its registration, would its decision have been upheld in court? See National Coalition Against the Misuse of Pesticides v. EPA, 867 F.2d 636 (D.C. Cir. 1989).

Balancing Uncertainty and the Gravity of Potential Harm

Like FIFRA's "imminent hazard" provisions, most of the other statutes that authorize regulation of toxic substances have provisions authorizing immediate regulatory action for substances found to pose very serious risks. Statutes authorizing emergency action generally require a higher threshold showing of immediate risk. For example, section 4(f) of TSCA requires EPA to initiate regulatory action within 180 days of receiving any information that indicates that a chemical "presents or will present a significant risk of serious or widespread harm to human beings from cancer, gene mutations, or birth defects . . .". The Administrative Procedure Act permits agencies to take rulemaking actions without notice and an opportunity for public comment "when the agency for good cause finds" that such procedures "are impracticable, unnecessary, or contrary to the public interest." 5 U.S.C. §553(b). The OSH Act authorizes OSHA to establish emergency temporary standards that take effect immediately if "employees are exposed to grave danger from exposure to substances or agents determined to be toxic or physically harmful or from new hazards" and if an ETS "is necessary to protect employees from such danger." 29 U.S.C. §655(c)(1).

Agencies have been reluctant to use their authority to take immediate action, in part because of fear of judicial intervention. As noted above, OSHA promulgated an ETS lowering the PEL for benzene in 1977, but it abandoned the ETS after the Fifth Circuit struck it down. OSHA also used an ETS to reduce the permissible exposure limit for asbestos from 12 fibers/cubic centimeter to 5 f/cc. This action was not challenged, and the Agency subsequently lowered the PEL to 2 f/cc. However, when OSHA adopted an ETS to lower the PEL from 2.0 f/cc to 0.5 f/cc in 1983, the Fifth Circuit struck it down. Asbestos Information Assn./North America v. OSHA, 727 F.2d 415 (5th Cir. 1984). Although the court did not explicitly reject OSHA's finding that the ETS would save 80 lives over a period of six months, the court based its decision on the conclusion that the ETS was not "necessary" because employees could instead be required to use respirators. OSHA then conducted rulemaking proceedings to promulgate a new PEL. In June 1986 OSHA promulgated a final rule lowering the PEL for asbestos to 0.2 f/cc. This decision was challenged by the asbestos industry, which filed a petition for review in the Fifth Circuit. However, the case was transferred to the D.C. Circuit, where a union had also filed a petition for review challenging the standard as too weak. The court ultimately rejected the asbestos industry's challenge to the PEL, but it agreed with the union that OSHA should consider tightening the standard in some respects, including lowering the PEL to 0.1 f/cc for some industries and adopting a short-term exposure limit (STEL). Building & Construction Trades Dept. v. Brock, 838 F.2d 1258 (D.C. Cir. 1988). OSHA adopted a 0.1 f/cc STEL averaged over 30 minutes in September 1988. 53 Fed. Reg. 35,610 (1988).

Suppose that evidence before EPA indicates that a pesticide that produces only modest benefits poses very substantial environmental risks, but the precise size of these risks is uncertain. Must EPA await further study prior to suspending the pesticide's registration? Howard Latin has argued that regulation will not achieve timely and effective protection of public health if inevitable scientific uncertainties must be explored in detail prior to regulatory decisions' being reached. He notes that "by mandating individualized analyses of any potentially relevant scientific theories or data in each proceeding," EPA's guidelines for carcinogenic risk assessment offer numerous opportunities for opponents of regulation to delay regulatory decisions. Latin, Good Science, Bad Regulation and Toxic Risk Assessment, 5 Yale J. on Reg. 89 (1988).

In 1982 a major scandal rocked EPA's FIFRA program when it was revealed that a laboratory that had prepared a considerable amount of the data submissions for FIFRA registrants had routinely falsified health and safety studies submitted in support of applications for registration. EPA had assigned only one full-time staff member to audit all pesticide testing laboratories for evidence of fraud or misreporting. Thus, many existing pesticide products are registered on the basis of false or invalid data. EPA and FDA have now established "Good Laboratory Practice" guidelines for data audits to prevent a recurrence of this problem. McGarity, Public Participation in Data Audits, 1 Accountability in Res. 47 (1989).

E. ANIMAL BIOASSAYS AND THE ASSESSMENT OF RISKS TO HUMAN HEALTH

The use of quantitative risk assessments as a basis for regulatory decisions has grown substantially in recent years. In light of the enormous uncertainties inherent in risk assessment and the high cost of regulation, it is not surprising that the regulated community would seek to challenge the results of risk assessments. One area of increasing controversy is the relevance of animal bioassays for assessments of risks to humans.

While "mice are not little men," the use of animal bioassays to assess carcinogenic risks is well-accepted in the scientific community. Scientists generally require positive results from tests of both sexes of at least two species of experimental animals before considering a substance carcinogenic. Experimental data demonstrate that virtually all of the substances that have been identified through epidemiological studies as human carcinogens also produce positive results in animal bioassays. Tomatis, Aitio, Wilbourn, and Shuker, Human Carcinogens Identified So Far, 80 Jap. J. Cancer Res. 795 (1989). Yet epidemiological studies have only been performed for a tiny fraction of the chemicals in use that have been identified as carcinogenic through animal bioassays. Karstadt, Bobal, and Selikoff, A Survey of Availability of Epidemiologic Data on Humans Exposed to Animal Carcinogens, in Quantification of Occupational Cancer 223 (R. Peto and M. Schneiderman, eds. 1981) (complete epidemiological data available for only 8 of 75 animal carcinogens).

The case that follows involves a challenge to OSHA's use of animal bioassays to perform a risk assessment for regulatory purposes. The risk assessment supported OSHA's decision to establish a 1 ppm permissible exposure limit (PEL) for ethylene oxide (EtO), a gas used in manufacturing and for the sterilization of hospital instruments. OSHA applied a mathematical model to data provided by animal bioassays ("the Bushy Run rat study") to develop quantitative estimates of the risks posed by EtO.

The Bushy Run rat study involved researchers' exposing rats to EtO at concentrations of 100, 33, and 10 ppm for 6 hours per day, 5 days per week at the Bushy Run Research Center in Pittsburgh. Although the study indicated that EtO exposure was associated with the development of various types of cancer, industry commentators criticized the results on several grounds. Some commentators argued that because the rats had suffered a viral infection during the study, it could have adversely affected their immune system and invalidated the results. OSHA, however, accepted the testimony of a pathologist from the National Cancer Institute that the infection had no substantial effect on the study's results. The Ethylene Oxide Industry Council also argued that because the types of tumors that appeared in the test rats were types that occur in rats spontaneously, EtO might be a tumor promoter rather than a tumor initiator. But OSHA concluded that this did not invalidate the study's relevance because tumor promoters can simultaneously be tumor initiators and because promoters ultimately might be as dangerous as initiators.

The Association of Ethylene Oxide Users (AEOU) challenged OSHA's risk assessment before the U.S. Court of Appeals for the D.C. Circuit. The court's decision is of considerable importance for its discussion of how regulatory agencies can cope with the inevitable problems of scientific uncertainty in developing quantitative risk assessments from experimental data.

Public Citizen Health Research Group
v. Tyson
796 F.2d 1479 (D.C. Cir. 1986)
(the Ethylene Oxide case)

Before ROBINSON, Chief Judge, WRIGHT, Circuit Judge, and McGOWAN, Senior Circuit Judge.

McGOWAN, Senior Circuit Judge:

In these consolidated cases, we review the Occupational Safety and Health Administration's rule limiting exposure to ethylene oxide, a chemical widely used in manufacturing and in hospital instrument sterilization.

[OSHA determined, on the basis of several epidemiological and experimental studies, that EtO is carcinogenic, cytogenic, and mutagenic and that it is a hazard to human reproduction. After reviewing the studies relied on by OSHA, the court upheld OSHA's findings that EtO posed human health hazards. In response to claims by the Association of Ethylene Oxide Users (AEOU) that there were deficiencies in the studies OSHA relied on, the court noted that "[w]hile some of OSHA's evidence suffers from shortcomings, such incomplete proof is inevitable when the agency regulates on the frontiers of scientific knowledge."] . . .

Once OSHA determined that EtO exposure presents human health hazards, it set out to determine whether the health hazard is significant, as required by *Benzene,* 448 U.S. at 639 (plurality opinion). If the agency finds the risk significant, it must then design a standard reasonably necessary and appropriate to remedying that risk, if possible. See 29 U.S.C. §652(8) (1982). To make both of these determinations, OSHA endeavored to quantify the risk allowed by the current OSHA EtO standard and the risk allowed by the proposed standard. OSHA employs a mathematical model to accomplish these tasks. . . .

1. USE OF ANIMAL STUDIES FOR THE DATABASE

In order to construct a set of data for its mathematical model, OSHA reviewed the results of the study that produced the most data: the Bushy Run study. In that study, researchers exposed rats to EtO gas at levels of 100, 33, and 10 ppm. OSHA plotted the levels of health effects to rats at each of these exposure rates and derived a dose-response curve. The agency used this curve to extrapolate expected health effects resulting from exposure to levels of EtO that had not been tested in the experiment.

AEOU asserts that any animal study of EtO effects is unreliable for extrapolation to human risk. Petitioner AEOU Brief at 19. AEOU relies on the conclusion of EPA's Carcinogen Assessment Group (CAG), which in examining the health effects of EtO, noted: "[G]iven the limited data available from animal bioassays, especially at the high dosage levels required for testing, almost nothing can be known about the true shape of the dose-response curve at low environmental levels." Environmental Protection Agency, Health Assessment Document for Ethylene Oxide, Final Report 9-145 (1985) [hereinafter cited as EPA HAD]. AEOU asserts that OSHA's reliance on animal data contravenes the weight of scientific thought, which recognizes the multiple uncertainties involved in translating animal data to human terms. See Interdisciplinary Panel on Carcinogenicity, Criteria for Evidence of Chemical Carcinogenicity, 225 Science 682, 685-86 (1984).

At the outset, we note that the validity of EPA's assessment is not before us. Rather, we consider only OSHA's decisions and the evidence supporting them. It is nevertheless instructive to review the entirety of EPA's conclusions:

> [T]he uncertainty of present estimations of cancer risks to humans at low levels of exposure should be recognized. The CAG feels that, given the limited data available from animal bioassays, especially at the high dosage levels required for testing, almost nothing can be known about the true shape of the dose-response curve at low environmental levels. At best, the linear extrapolation model used here provides a rough but plausible estimate of the upper limit of risk; i.e., it is not likely that the true risk is appreciably higher than the estimated risk, but it could very well be considerably lower. . . . *The methods used by the CAG for quantitative assessment are consistently conservative in that they tend to result in high estimates of risk.*

[EPA HAD,] supra, at 9-145 (emphasis added). In our view, this added context greatly illuminates the portion selectively quoted by AEOU. EPA's position appears to be substantially similar to OSHA's view: while nothing can be *known* (in the sense of scientific certainty) at this time about the precise biological responses at low exposure levels, estimation techniques can provide a reasonable prediction. That is, estimates based on linear extrapolation are the "best available evidence" that science can currently provide of health risks at low exposure levels.

The Supreme Court plurality in the *Benzene* case explicitly approved the use of conservative assumptions, 448 U.S. at 656 ("so long as they are supported by a body of reputable scientific thought, the Agency is free to use conservative assumptions in interpreting the data"), and implicitly accepted the use of animal studies in the substantial risk determination, 448 U.S. at 657 n.64 ("In other proceedings, the Agency has had a good deal of data from animal experiments on which it could base a conclusion of the significance of the risk.").

Moreover, Congress has impliedly approved estimation techniques when evidence is unavailable to "prove" the harmful health effects posed by toxins. In the OSH Act, Congress expressly allowed OSHA to rely on the "best *available* evidence," 29 U.S.C. §655(b)(5) (1982) (emphasis added) and to consider "the *latest available* scientific information in the field," id. (emphasis added). Indeed, Congress did "not [intend] that the Secretary be paralyzed by debate surrounding diverse medical opinions." H.R. Rep. No. 91-1291, 91st Cong., 2d Sess. 18 (1970), reprinted in Legislative History of the Occupational Safety and Health Act of 1970 at 848 (1971).

We must grant OSHA some "leeway" when it regulates on the frontiers of current knowledge. See *Benzene*, 448 U.S. at 656 (plurality opinion). We demand no more than that the agency arrive at a reasonable conclusion based on all the evidence before it.

We find that OSHA has developed substantial evidence to support its reliance on the animal studies for the establishment of a database. OSHA did not state that animal studies translate perfectly into human terms. Rather, the agency admitted it was dealing in an area of uncertainty. Moreover, OSHA did not blindly choose to rely on animal data in the face of unified scientific opposition. A number of commenters agreed that in light of the available but incomplete evidence, which suggests that EtO is truly dangerous, the agency could rely only on the animal data. See 49 Fed. Reg. at 24,756 (citing submissions of EOIC and Dr. Kenny S. Crump). Given this record support for using the experimental data, OSHA chose the Bushy Run study because it was the best controlled animal study and the study most susceptible of analysis. We find this a reasonable course to take under the circumstances. AEOU's position amounts to no more than the argument so clearly rejected by the Supreme Court in *Benzene:* the agency need not wait until deaths occur to regulate EtO. See *Benzene,* 448 U.S. at 656 & n.63 (plurality); id. at 690-91(Marshall, J., dissenting).

2. THE MODEL'S ASSUMPTIONS

OSHA models EtO's health effects by plotting a curve through known points and extrapolating into areas as yet untested. See generally Proposed Rule and Notice of Hearing, 48 Fed. Reg. 17,284, 17,292-96 (1983) (describing OSHA's risk estimation approach). The model employs several assumptions about the relationship between EtO exposure and biological response. For example, OSHA chose to employ a linear, no-threshold model similar to that used by EPA's Carcinogen Assessment Group. See EPA's HAD supra, at 9-145. This approach assumes that EtO exposure and biological response vary proportionately, and that there is no threshold level below which EtO exposure produces no adverse health effects.

AEOU challenges OSHA's model on two grounds. First, AEOU asserts that the model unlawfully assumes that there is no threshold level of EtO exposure. This assumption, AEOU argues, contravenes the teaching of the *Benzene* case. Second, AEOU claims that the model improperly translates breathing rates for rats into equivalent human terms.

a. Threshold Exposure Level

In 29 C.F.R. §1990 (1985) et seq., OSHA provides a framework for rulemaking treatment of occupational carcinogens. The regulations allow OSHA to infer a carcinogenic hazard from one or more positive human or animal studies. 29 C.F.R. §1990.143 (1985). The regulations also provide that: "No determination will be made that a 'threshold' or 'no-effect' level of exposure can be established for a human population exposed to carcinogens in general, or to any specific substance." 29 C.F.R. §1990.143(h) (1985).

AEOU presents a two-pronged attack on the threshold issue. First, AEOU charges that the no-threshold assumption violates the *Benzene* rule because it improperly assumes that EtO is harmful at low doses. Second, AEOU charges that OSHA improperly ignored evidence in the record that demonstrates that EtO does indeed have a threshold level. We treat these contentions in turn.

1. The Significance of *Benzene* for the No-Threshold Model

In the *Benzene* case, 448 U.S. 607 (1980), the Supreme Court rejected OSHA's benzene standard on two related grounds. The Court first ruled that the OSH Act requires the agency to find that its proposed standard will remedy a "significant" occupational risk. See supra, pages 1482-1484. The Court then held that no substantial evidence supported OSHA's assumption that benzene presents a risk of "significant" harm at all possible exposure levels. In fact, "OSHA did not even attempt to carry its burden of proof." 448 U.S. at 653 (plurality opinion). OSHA had made no effort whatsoever to estimate the risk presented by low levels of benzene exposure. See, e.g., id. at 631, 632 n.33. In fact the agency did not even attempt to construct a dose-responsive curve. The Court simply could not find substantial evidence for a bald assertion devoid of record support. See United Steelworkers v. Marshall, 647 F.2d 1189, 1246-47 (D.C. Cir. 1980), cert. denied, 453 U.S. 913 (1981).

AEOU asserts that OSHA's threshold position in this case is equivalent to OSHA's position on significant risk in the *Benzene* case, which the Supreme Court invalidated. In particular, AEOU argues that "[t]he Supreme Court squarely rejected OSHA standard-setting based on 'probable' or 'suspected' risks." AEOU's implied assertion is that OSHA must *unequivocally prove* the scientific validity of each and every assumption it employs.

To the extent this argument asserts that OSHA cannot make any assumptions, even if they are supported by scientific thought, Congress has clearly come to the opposite conclusion. If Congress had intended to require the agency to "prove" all of its assumptions, Congress would not have allowed the agency to rely on the "best available evidence" and the "latest available scientific information." 29 U.S.C. §655(b)(5) (1982).

Moreover, AEOU simply misconstrues the *Benzene* opinion. In that case, the Court carefully explained that, although OSHA may not act without some record basis, the agency also must be given leeway when regulatory subject matter is not subject to strict proof one way or the other. 448 U.S. at 656. The reason for this approach is clear: requiring strict proof would fatally cripple all of OSHA's regulatory efforts and run counter to the legislative branch's express delegation of hybrid rule-making power to OSHA. See Industrial Union Department, AFL-CIO v. Hodgson, 499 F.2d 467, 472-74 (D.C. Cir. 1974). Accordingly, in a passage critical to our inquiry here, the *Benzene* plurality stated: "[S]o long as they are supported by a body of reputable scientific thought, the Agency is free to use conservative assumptions in interpreting the data with respect to carcinogens, risking error on the side of overprotection rather than underprotection." Id.

In the context of this case, *Benzene* only requires that OSHA find the EtO exposure presents a substantial risk of harm on the basis of record evidence. In the instant case, OSHA has done exactly what the Supreme Court chastised the agency for not doing in *Benzene:*

> OSHA did not discuss whether it was possible to make a rough estimate, based on the more complete epidemiological and animal studies done at higher exposure levels, of the significance of the risks attributable to those levels, nor did it discuss whether it was possible to extrapolate from such estimates to derive a risk estimate for low-level exposures.

448 U.S. at 632 n.33. OSHA has most assuredly rectified that failure in the instant case. The agency has gone to great lengths to calculate, within the bounds of available scientific data, the significance of the risk presented by EtO. The EtO proceeding thus stands in stark contrast to the agency's actions in regulating benzene exposure.

We think it clear from the above-quoted portion of the *Benzene* case that the Supreme Court intended to permit the very estimates that AEOU so vigorously attacks. Indeed, it would be anomalous for the Court to have required the agency to provide more than it has provided in regulating EtO. See American Textile Manufacturers Institute, Inc. v. Donovan, 452 U.S. 490, 528 n.52 (1981) ("the agency's candor in confessing its own inability to achieve a more precise estimate should not precipitate a judicial review that nonetheless demands what the congressionally delegated 'expert' says it cannot provide").

Benzene's basic teaching is that courts must weigh OSHA's scientific assumptions under the substantial evidence issue. AEOU attacks OSHA on this score as well, arguing that there is no substantial evidence for OSHA's decision to use a no-threshold model.

2. Evidentiary Support for the No-Threshold Model

AEOU points to one commenter who supports an EtO threshold. Dr. Thomas Darby theorized that "[w]ith ethylene oxide, like most substances, there appears to be a 'no effect dose.' . . . ." Dr. Darby further assumed that human metabolism can detoxify many chemicals by removing them from the body. According to Darby, the human body can rapidly clear itself of EtO. Building on these assumptions, Darby reached the rather tepid conclusion that "it seems reasonable to believe that a safe level for ethylene oxide exists."

AEOU argues that the Ethylene Oxide Industry Council (EOIC) supported Darby's position. EOIC stated that "no adverse health effect has been readily demonstrated in man following exposure to 10 ppm . . ." AEOU also notes that OSHA admitted that the record contains "no direct evidence of an excess risk of cancer at chronic exposure levels below 14 ppm. . . ."

We find neither Dr. Darby's nor EOIC's comments sufficient to refute OSHA's no-threshold model. Although Dr. Darby advocated the threshold concept, his conclusion was less than forceful. Moreover, contrary to AEOU's assertion, EOIC's cited comments do not unhesitatingly support Dr. Darby. EOIC stated that no effects have been reliably demonstrated at levels below 10 ppm. The context of this statement, however, reveals EOIC's uncertainty with an EtO threshold. In discussing the possible methods of quantifying the risk presented by EtO exposure, EOIC hypothesized three exposure zones. The first zone presents "increased probability" of adverse health effects in man. This zone "perhaps extend[s] down to levels above 10 ppm—even though no adverse health effect has been reliably demonstrated in man following exposure to 10 ppm [EtO]." The second zone "is a zone of uncertain consequences, which may exist for [exposures] within the range of 5-10 ppm, 3-10 ppm, or perhaps 1-10 ppm." Id. The third zone "is considered to involve insignificant exposure, with no apparent hazard being present by levels at or below 1 ppm." This discussion supports no more than the proposition that there may be a threshold exposure level at or near 1 ppm. EOIC's comments hardly support an attack on a PEL that sets the exposure limit at the threshold because by definition, exposure above the threshold presents a health risk.

Indeed, a number of participants (including OSHA) joined EOIC in calculating the risk presented by low EtO exposures. Many participants assessed health risks down to exposure levels at 1 ppm and below. See 49 Fed. Reg. at 25,756-63.

By citing only the Darby and EOIC comments, AEOU presents only one side of the debate. Moreover, as we have just discussed, even the side of the story presented by AEOU is incomplete. We find AEOU's citation to contrary authority insufficient to assail OSHA's position. The exercise of a dispute in the scientific community does not allow this court to choose a particular side as the "right" one. We have no special skills to aid in the resolution of these technical questions. Rather our role is only to demand that OSHA review all sides of the issue and reasonably resolve the matter. OSHA has the expertise we lack and it has exercised that expertise by carefully reviewing the scientific data. Unlike the *Benzene* case, OSHA here expressly found risk at the 1 ppm level based on evidence submitted by a significant portion of the scientific community. We find the no-threshold assumption to be supported by substantial evidence. See also Asarco, Inc. v. OSHA, 746 F.2d 483, 492-93 (9th Cir. 1984) (no-threshold assumption upheld).

NOTES AND QUESTIONS

1. The court rejected the argument by industry scientists that there may be a safe threshold level of exposure to EtO. How much and what kind of evidence do you think these scientists would have to present before a reviewing court would be willing to invalidate a regulation based on a no-threshold model?

2. As in many other cases, the court's rejection of AEOU's arguments in favor of the existence of a safe threshold of exposure was based in large part on deference accorded the administrative agency in the face of scientific uncertainty. Suppose that OSHA, under a new administration some time in the future, decides to reject the no-threshold assumption and to assume that a safe threshold exists even for carcinogens. Could such a decision be successfully challenged in court? Would it make any difference whether or not the decision was supported by new scientific evidence different from that which existed when the *Ethylene Oxide* decision was rendered?

3. The *Ethylene Oxide* court carefully reviewed the criticisms made by industry petitioners of the various bioassays and epidemiological studies. The court noted that although flaws could be found in many of them, their cumulative impact supported OSHA's decision. The court noted that "AEOU attacks each piece of evidence, suggesting that no individual piece proves a relationship between EtO exposure and various adverse health effects. This approach disregards the marginal contribution that each piece of evidence makes to the total picture. While some of OSHA's evidence suffers from shortcomings, such incomplete proof is inevitable when the Agency regulates on the frontiers of scientific knowledge." 796 F.2d at 1495. The court then quoted from its landmark decision upholding EPA's regulation of lead additives in gasoline in Ethyl Corp. v. EPA, 541 F.2d 1, 37 (D.C. Cir.) (en banc), cert. denied, 426 U.S. 941 (1976):

Contrary to the apparent suggestion of some of the petitioners, we need not seek a single dispositive study that fully supports the Administrator's determination. Science does not work that way; nor, for that matter, does adjudicatory factfinding. Rather, the Administrator's decision may be fully supportable if it is based, as it is, on the inconclusive but suggestive results of numerous studies. By its nature, scientific evidence is cumulative: the more supporting, albeit inconclusive, evidence available, the more likely the accuracy of the conclusion.

The court then noted that this "demonstrates why OSHA need not 'prove' its assertions in the manner AEOU demands, and indeed, why it cannot. Rather OSHA need only gather evidence from which it can reasonably draw the conclusion it has reached." 796 F.2d at 1495.

4. In 1980, Justice Marshall's dissent in the *Benzene* decision contained these words:

> In this case, the Secretary found that exposure to benzene at levels above 1 ppm posed a definite, albeit unquantifiable, risk of chromosomal damage, nonmalignant blood disorders, and leukemia. The existing evidence was sufficient to justify the conclusion that such a risk was presented, but it did not permit even rough quantification of that risk. . . .
>
> In these circumstances it seems clear that the Secretary found a risk that is "significant" in the sense that the word is normally used. . . . The plurality's extraordinarily searching scrutiny of this factual record reveals no basis for a conclusion that quantification is, on the basis of 'the best available evidence,' possible at the present time. If the Secretary decided to wait until definitive information was available, American workers would be subjected for the indefinite future to a possibly substantial risk of benzene-induced leukemia and other illnesses. It is unsurprising, at least to me, that he concluded that the statute authorized him to take regulatory action now.
>
> . . . [If the plurality means that the Administrator cannot regulate until he can quantify risk], the adoption of such a test would subject American workers to a continuing risk of cancer and other serious diseases; it would disable the Secretary from regulating a wide variety of carcinogens for which quantification simply cannot be undertaken at the present time. . . .
>
> To require a quantitative showing of a 'significant' risk, therefore, would either paralyze the Secretary into inaction or force him to deceive the public by acting on the basis of assumptions that must be considered too speculative to support any realistic assessment of the relevant risk. [448 U.S. at 713, 714, 716 (Marshall, J., dissenting).]

In 1986, Judge McGowan's opinion in the Ethylene Oxide decision concluded:

> EPA's position appears to be substantially similar to OSHA's view: while nothing can be *known* (in the sense of scientific certainty) at this time about the precise biological responses at low exposure levels, estimation techniques can provide a reasonable prediction. That is, estimates based on linear extrapolation are the "best available evidence" that science can currently provide of health risks at low exposure levels. [769 F.2d 1479, 1497 (D.C. Cir. 1986).]

These two statements evidence different approaches to the policy problem of risk assessment. Of the two, which view comports more easily with the approaches taken in *Reserve* and *Ethyl Corp.*, where quantification of risk was not seen as a necessary step in the regulatory process?

5. Are the differences between *Ethylene Oxide* and the *Benzene* dissent best explained as the differences between two different individuals' perceptions of the strengths and weaknesses of quantitative risk assessment, or do they represent more generalizable attitude shifts? In support of the latter thesis, numerous signs of increased reliance on quantification can be seen within the policymaking circles of the early 1980s. In 1981, the Administrative Conference of the United States, a federally established group dedicated to studying and improving the regulatory process, undertook a major study of the federal regulation of cancer-causing chemicals. In its recommendations, adopted June 18, 1982, it concluded that "the extent of the hazard [from cancer-causing chemicals] can often be expressed in quantitative terms," and it urged that "to the extent permitted by law, priorities should be set by agencies with the objective of maximizing the net benefits to society of agency action." Noting that critics doubt the reliability of quantitative methods, it nevertheless concluded that "quantitative risk estimation has an appeal for both analysts and decisionmakers," recommending that "to the extent regulatory statutes allow and available data permit [!], agencies should attempt to estimate and describe the magnitude of the risk posed by prevailing levels of exposure to substances considered for regulation." Administrative Conference of the United States, Recommendation 82-5, Federal Regulation of Cancer-Causing Chemicals, June 18, 1982. Perhaps the Conference might be faulted for begging the crucial question here, but its recommendations were received as an important endorsement of quantitative methods. A year earlier, President Reagan had signed E.O. 12,291, which likewise endorsed and, to the extent permitted by law, mandated cost-benefit methods to be applied to all major regulations, thus further underwriting an insistence on quantification. See Chapter 5B2.

6. If the shift toward quantification as representing the "best available evidence" of risks is a generalizable one—albeit one that is by no means without its present-day critics—has it been beneficial on the whole? Or has it produced or exacerbated the very problems Justice Marshall prophesied: disabling regulatory action on the one hand, because the agency has to work through the persistent uncertainties that attend risk assessments before it can arrive at a number that it is willing to defend, while deceiving the public on the other hand, because the numbers produced inevitably acquire an aura of certainty far beyond their scientific justifications? Keep your eye on these questions as you read the remainder of this chapter. We will return to this question again at the end.

3.   Hazard Identification and Toxicity Testing

In theory, the risk assessment process can be used to characterize the probability and severity of a variety of kinds of harm including cancer, noncancer health effects, ecological damage, and damage to public welfare (economic damage). In practice, quantitative risk assessment has been used almost entirely for the characterization of cancer risks. This stems in part from the fact that such risks have a common, life-threatening endpoint: cancer (though some cancers are more life-threatening than others), while other health effects have diverse endpoints (e.g., neurological damage, damage to the immune system, and cardiovascular damage) that are conceptually difficult to compare. Scientists also have had more experience with models of cancer risks, which are better suited to risk assessment than other environmental risks because they are probabilistic in nature.

The increased emphasis on quantitative risk assessment following the *Benzene* decision may have subtly distorted regulatory priorities by making it easier for regulators to address substances that pose cancer risks than those that pose other types of harm. Some scientists have argued that the noncancer health effects of toxic substances are more widespread and may be even more threatening than their carcinogenic risk, see, for example, Weiss, Neurobehavioral Toxicity as a Basis for Risk Assessment, 9 Trends in Pharmacological Sci. 59 (1988). Yet risk assessments of carcinogens often fail to incorporate noncancer health risks because cancer risks are assumed to override other health risks that are thought to require higher thresholds of exposure before they threaten harm.

One of the greatest obstacles to regulation of toxic substances has been the lack of meaningful toxicity data for a wide spectrum of chemicals. The Toxic Substances Control Act (TSCA) was designed to deal with this problem (see TSCA §2(b)(1)) by authorizing EPA to require toxicity testing (see TSCA §4) and by requiring that EPA be notified prior to the manufacture of new chemicals (see TSCA §5). However, EPA has not required manufacturers to conduct toxicity testing prior to submitting premanufacture notices (PMNs). Manufacturers are only required to supply whatever health or environmental data are available to them when they submit their PMNs to EPA. Fewer than half of all PMNs contain test data, and no toxicity information is available for more than three-quarters of all existing chemicals, including chemicals produced in large volumes, as indicated in Figure 4.7.

A.   IDENTIFYING CARCINOGENS

Carcinogenicity testing by the federal government expanded significantly beginning in the late 1960s. In 1978, Congress required the

FIGURE 4.7
Comparison of Available Toxicity Test Data for TSCA Existing Chemicals Versus PMN Chemicals

	Existing chemicals			PMN chemicals		
	Reported production volume					
	>10^6 lb./yr.	*<10^6 lb./yr.*	*Not available*	*All cases*	*Non-polymers*	*Polymers*
Sample Size	259	136	136	3,985	2,351	1,634
TEST TYPE	(PERCENTAGES OF CHEMICALS)			(PERCENTAGES OF CHEMICALS)		
Acute	20 (15-25)	22 (15-29)	15 (9-21)	40	51	24
Subchronic	10 (7-14)	8 (5-13)	7 (3-11)	11	16	5
Chronic	4 (3-7)	3 (2-6)	3 (0-6)	<1	<1	<1
Reproductive/ developmental	6 (3-9)	4 (2-7)	7 (3-12)	<1	<1	<1
Mutagenicity	9 (6-13)	10 (5-15)	8 (4-13)	13	19	5
Minimal toxicity information	22 (18-26)	24 (18-30)	18 (12-24)	42	54	25
No toxicity information	78 (73-84)	76 (69-83)	82 (76-89)	54	42	70

Source: Auer and Gould, Carcinogenicity Assessment and the Role of Structure Activity Relationship (SAR) Analysis Under TSCA Section 5, 5 J. Env. Sci. & Health 29 (1987).

Department of Health, Education, and Welfare (the predecessor of the current Department of Health and Human Services) to publish an annual report identifying all substances to which a significant number of people are exposed that are either known to be carcinogens or that may reasonably be anticipated to be carcinogens. The report is prepared by an interagency committee consisting of representatives of federal regulatory and research agencies (FDA, EPA, CPSC, OSHA, NIOSH, the National Cancer Institute (NCI), the National Institute of Environmental Health Sciences (NIEHS), and the National Library of Medicine). Decisions by this committee are based on reviews of chemicals identified as carcinogens by the International Agency for Research on Cancer (IARC) and the results of animal tests performed by the National Toxicology Program (NTP).

The NTP was created to coordinate toxicity testing by federal health agencies. Funded largely by NIEHS, the NTP is managed by representatives of federal research and regulatory agencies. The director of the NIEHS is the director of the NTP. Decisions about what chemicals the NTP will test are made, after solicitation of public comments, by an executive committee consisting of the Assistant Secretary for Health of the Department of Health and Human Services, the heads of EPA, FDA, OSHA, and the CPSC, and the directors of the NIH, NCI, NIEHS, and NIOSH. It generally takes more than two years before a nominated chemical is selected for testing. Actual chemical testing takes even longer, because it requires preliminary studies, a two-year dosing regimen, and peer review of preliminary technical reports on the results. Chemicals are usually tested in both sexes of mice and rats. The results of these experiments are characterized based on the strength of the evidence of carcinogenicity, if any, that they present (clear evidence, some evidence, equivocal evidence, no evidence, or inadequate test). OTA, Identifying and Regulating Carcinogens 18 (Nov. 1987).

Although techniques for identifying and assessing carcinogenic hazards now are widely accepted, there is room for considerable debate concerning the relevance of animal bioassays and the appropriate slope of the dose-response curve in extrapolating to low doses. As noted above, risk assessments can reach widely varying results even when using the same experimental data, depending on the assumptions that are used to extrapolate from the data. The commonly used assumption of a no-threshold, one-hit linear extrapolation model for cancer produces risk assessments that are much higher than they would be if a carcinogenic substance is assumed to have a nonzero no-effects threshold. See Figure 4.6, above.

In Synthetic Organic Chemical Manufacturers Assn. v. Secretary, Department of Health & Human Services, 720 F. Supp. 1244 (W.D. Cal. 1989), a trade association representing chemical manufacturers sued the Secretary of HHS in an effort to prevent the listing of certain chemicals as known or suspected carcinogens in the HHS Annual Report. The trade association argued that these chemicals should not be considered to be carcinogens despite positive results in animal tests because data on pharmacokinetics and mechanisms of action raised doubts that the chemicals actually would produce cancer in humans. The court rejected this challenge to procedures for identifying cancer risks, emphasizing that the Annual Report was only "the first step in hazard identification . . . to determine whether a substance is known or may reasonably be anticipated to be a human carcinogen." For this purpose, the court stated that it

> accepts the validity of the reliance on animal testing. There is broad consensus in the scientific community that animal evidence can and should be used to predict human carcinogenicity. The International Agency for Research on Cancer has stated that "[i]n the absence of adequate data on humans, it is biologically plausible and prudent to regard agents for which there is 'sufficient evidence' of carcinogenicity in animals as if they presented a carcinogenic risk to humans." In addition, it is widely accepted that chemicals found to have no evidence of carcinogenicity in adequate studies in experimental animals present little to no carcinogenic hazard to humans.
>
> There is broad agreement in the scientific community with IARC's recommendation in this regard. Two lines of evidence support this presumption. First, all chemicals known to cause cancer in humans which have been studied under adequate test conditions have been shown to cause cancer in laboratory animals. Second, for a number of compounds where both human and animal data are available, there is good agreement between risks observed in humans and risks calculated from high-dose animal experiments. [720 F. Supp. at 1256.]

Although plaintiffs cited the legislative history indicating that HHS was "to bear the primary responsibility for evaluating the total body of available data regarding carcinogenesis," the court held that Congress had not intended the Secretary to analyze pharmacokinetics and mechanisms of action data in preparing the Annual Report.

> Pharmacokinetics studies are performed to learn how a living organism (e.g., experimental animal) handles a foreign substance like cancer, i.e., the rate of uptake, distribution and excretion of the substance, and the metabolites formed in the organism following exposure. Mechanisms of action studies are performed in an effort to ascertain the mechanism (at a cellular and subcellular level) by which a chemical produces a toxic effect like cancer. In other words, once a toxic effect is present, mechanisms studies attempt to determine how it became present.
>
> Pharmacokinetics and mechanisms of action data are not relevant to determining the first step, threshold question of whether a substance is a potential human carcinogen. [720 F. Supp. at 1257.]

The court stated that the "purpose of the Annual Reports is to provide the public and regulators with an alert that a particular substance is a known or potential human carcinogen and to stimulate further evaluation by researchers and regulators." Id. Thus, it concluded that the "analysis of pharmacokinetics and mechanisms of action data is beyond the purview of the Annual Reports." Id.

NOTES AND QUESTIONS

1. Suppose that HHS had agreed to consider pharmacokinetics and mechanisms of action data proffered by the Synthetic Organic Chemical Manufacturers Association prior to listing chemicals in the Annual Report. What impact would this have on the listing process? Would environmental or public health groups have any basis for challenging such a decision?

2. The chemical manufacturers sought to require the Secretary of HHS, prior to listing a chemical in the NTP, to use a "weight of the evidence" approach in which all data that is pertinent to risk assessment is evaluated. Why do you think HHS refused to use this approach? Had the court required the Secretary to use a "weight of the evidence" approach, what effect would this have had on the listing of chemicals in the Annual Report in the future?

3. Does it necessarily follow that consideration of additional data will always improve the quality of decision-making? Scientists have noted that because of the uncertainty that typically surrounds estimates of each of parameters of a risk assessment model, the more complicated the models are, the less precise their results are likely to be. Portier and Kaplan, The Variability of Safe Dose Estimates When Using Complicated Models of the Carcinogenic Process, 13 Fundamental and Applied Toxicology 533 (1989). Thus, efforts to require incorporation of pharmacokinetic and mechanisms-of-action data in risk assessments may actually increase the uncertainty that surrounds their results.

Pharmacokinetics and Mechanisms of Action

Some scientists challenge the current model of risk assessment used by EPA. They believe that many substances may indeed have a threshold below which there is zero carcinogenic risk, and that we should not regulate substances below this level. Bruce Ames of Berkeley is a leading proponent of this school of thought. His basic contention is that we must pay attention to the mechanism of carcinogenesis in order to assess risk appropriately and that current rodent bioassay methods are skewed, and therefore frequently invalid, because they do not do so. Ames's views rely on studies of pharmacokinetics, which analyzes how an organism processes a toxic substance—rate of uptake, distribution within the body, excretion, metabolites formed in response—and mechanisms of action, which analyze on the cellular and subcellular levels how a toxin acts to produce an adverse effect.

According to some students of pharmacokinetics and mechanisms of action, rodent testing methods are skewed because exposure at the maximum tolerated dose (MTD) will frequently induce mitogenesis, or cell proliferation, at a more-rapid-than-normal rate. Ames contends that mitogenesis is a key step in carcinogenesis, because "a dividing cell is much more at risk of mutating than a quiescent cell." See Ames and Gold, Too Many Rodent Carcinogens: Mitogenesis Increases Mutagenesis, 249 Science 970 (1990). Thus higher levels of mitogenesis lead to greater likelihood of cell mutations, which in turn lead to tumor formation. Abnormal mitogenesis, Ames contends, results from the extremely high levels of exposure to substances experienced during bioassay testing. The MTD is a dose just below the level of toxicity (toxicity being a dose that would cause severe weight loss or other signs of life-threatening illness) and is generally much higher than typical human exposure to the chemical. Ames contends that exposure at the high levels of rodent testing induces mitogenesis, leading to mutagenesis and ultimately carcinogenesis. He arrives at this conclusion in part due to the high proportion—about half—of chemicals that rodent testing indicates are carcinogenic. "You wouldn't predict that so many would be positive," he says. Marx, Animal Carcinogen Testing Challenged, 250 Science 743 (1990). Ames believes that increased cell proliferation often will not occur at lower levels of exposure. Thus, he concludes that the current regulatory regime often focuses on insignificant or nonexistent risks. Moreover, focusing on chemicals that produce carcinogenic responses at MTD levels is inappropriate; it leads to regulation of substances that, at lower and more typical levels of exposure, present little or no risk. In other words, Ames is saying that many chemicals may have a threshold below which there is no risk, and therefore there is no need to ban a chemical if exposure is below the threshold. (Ames also points out that current testing focuses on synthetic chemicals, while humans consume far more natural chemicals. Natural chemicals show about as many carcinogenic tendencies as synthetic ones; thus he claims that natural chemicals, though unassessed and unregulated, present a more significant risk than synthetic chemicals.)

Of course, there are many who dispute Ames's assertions. At least one study disputes the connection Ames advances between toxicity (leading to mitogenesis) induced by MTD exposure and the appearance of tumors. See id. at 744. The study did not find a strong correlation between toxicity indicators and tumor formation; but neither did it address Ames's contention that cell proliferation caused by MTD exposure is the critical element in assessing cancer risk. Others, however, do respond to this contention by saying cell proliferation is only part of the carcinogenesis mechanism, not necessarily the most crucial step. Carcinogenesis is a complex process that takes place in stages. Id. at 748. It involves not only cell proliferation, but also progressive mutations and reproduction of those mutations. Moreover, since cell proliferation takes place continuously in the skin (and quite rapidly during fetal development) there is doubt that cell proliferation is the most important element of carcinogenesis. Responding more directly to Ames's charge of rodent testing's invalidity, critics also point out that over 90 percent of the chemicals having carcinogenic effects in MTD rodent studies are also found to have carcinogenic effects in low-dose studies. Moreover, they answer Ames's charge of disproportionate positive test results for carcinogenesis by stating that many chemicals chosen for testing are selected because they are suspected carcinogens. For a more detailed account of the debate, see also Weinstein, Mitogenesis Is Only One Factor in Carcinogenesis, 252 Science 387-388 (1991); Carcinogens and Human Health: Part 2, 252 Science 10-13 (1991) (letter by David Rall, retired director of the National Institute of Environmental Health Sciences and the National Toxicology Program, and response by Bruce Ames and Lois Gold); Carcinogens and Human Health: Part 1, 251 Science 1644-1646 (1990) (letter by Frederica P. Perera of Columbia and response by Bruce Ames and Lois Gold).

B. TOXICITY TESTING REQUIREMENTS

Although section 5 of TSCA requires that EPA be notified 90 days in advance of the manufacture of new chemicals, EPA has not required that any toxicity testing be undertaken prior to the submission of PMNs. Section 4 of TSCA does give EPA the authority to require manufacturers to test their chemicals if the Agency determines that such testing is necessary to determine whether the chemicals present unreasonable risks. This authority has been used sparingly by EPA.

In Chemical Manufacturers Assn. v. EPA, 859 F.2d 977 (D.C. Cir. 1988) (the EHA case), the court addressed the question of how much evidence of potential harm is necessary before EPA can require companies to perform toxicity tests on existing chemicals. In upholding an EPA rule requiring testing of 2-ethylhexanoic acid (EHA), the court stated:

> EPA is empowered to issue a test rule where, in light of the evidence before it, the existence of an "unreasonable risk of injury to health" is a substantial (i.e., more than theoretical) probability. Since "unreasonable risk of injury to health" is a function of toxicity and exposure, this standard can be restated as follows: A test rule is warranted when there is a more-than-

> theoretical basis for suspecting that some amount of exposure occurs and that the substance is sufficiently toxic at that exposure level to present an "unreasonable risk of injury to health."

Even though the only exposure to the chemical at issue in the case occurred in rare instances in which workers failed to wear gloves, the court rejected the chemical manufacturers' argument that only recurrent exposures would warrant a test rule. Because EPA was concerned that even a one-time exposure could cause harm, the court upheld the test rule.

The question of how to set priorities for testing existing chemicals is a challenging one. Section 4(e) of TSCA establishes the Interagency Testing Committee (ITC), a group composed of representatives from eight federal agencies. The ITC is required to designate semiannually chemicals whose potential risks to health or the environment make them priority candidates for testing under section 4 of TSCA. Although section 4(e) of TSCA lists a number of factors for the ITC to consider in designating existing chemicals for priority testing, it does not specify how much weight each of these factors is to be given. The ITC often lacks basic data, such as data on the extent of human exposure, that are critical for establishing testing priorities.

Within one year of a chemical's designation by the ITC, EPA is required either to initiate rulemaking proceedings under section 4 of TSCA or to publish a statement in the Federal Register explaining why it has not chosen to do so. Beginning in late 1981, EPA announced that it would seek to implement ITC recommendations by negotiating voluntary testing programs with the manufacturers of priority chemicals designated by ITC. 47 Fed. Reg. 335 (1982). EPA argued that voluntary testing agreements would result in more rapid development of test data than would rulemaking proceedings to issue section 4 test rules. In Natural Resources Defense Council v. EPA, 595 F. Supp. 1255 (S.D.N.Y. 1984), an environmental group challenged EPA's practice and won. The court ruled that voluntary testing agreements were no substitute for test rules legally enforceable under TSCA. As a result of this decision, EPA agreed to incorporate future test agreements into consent agreements that will "be enforceable on the same basis as test rules." 51 Fed. Reg. 23,706, 23,708 (1986). Violation of consent agreements will constitute a "prohibited act" in violation of section 15(1) of TSCA. If negotiations between EPA, the chemical industry, and other interested parties do not produce a consent agreement by a specified date, EPA will commence rulemaking under section 4 of TSCA, as it did with respect to EHA.

In 1990 the General Accounting Office (GAO) issued a report blasting EPA's test program for making "little progress." The report noted that in 1980 EPA and the ITC had identified 2,226 chemicals that they believed might be harmful. Yet, the report said, "EPA has compiled complete test data for only six chemicals since the enactment of TSCA and has not finished assessing any of them." The ITC has designated 386 chemicals for testing since 1977, but EPA has been slow to issue test rules. It usually takes companies two to five years to complete testing of chemicals. The GAO report noted that EPA's test program "lacks overall objectives and a strategy for achieving them." GAO, EPA's Chemical Testing Program Has Made Little Progress 3 (April 1990).

The test rule at issue in the *EHA* case involved a chemical already on the market. Section 5 of TSCA requires that EPA be notified prior to the manufacture of new chemicals. Between 1979 and 1987 EPA received 10,842 premanufacture notifications (PMNs) and requests for PMN exemptions. Although 183 PMNs were withdrawn in the face of regulatory action, only 4 PMNs resulted in prohibitions' or restrictions' actually being put into effect by EPA. EPA agreed to accept voluntary testing in response to EPA concerns in an additional 149 cases and voluntary control actions by submitters in 45 cases. EPA, Environmental Progress and Challenges: EPA's Update 126 (Aug. 1988).

One of the problems with the premanufacture review process has been that EPA's review of PMNs has been based on the uses that a manufacturer intends for a chemical when it is introduced. Once the chemical has gone into production, it could be put to additional uses without EPA review unless EPA intervened. EPA has tried to develop a more efficient mechanism for reviewing significant new uses of chemicals by adopting a generic approach defining "new uses" for a category of chemicals and requiring notification of EPA prior to a significant new use of any chemical in the category.

The European Economic Community (EEC) has adopted a directive requiring that a comprehensive battery of toxicity tests be performed prior to the introduction of new chemicals. A range of tests is performed in an effort to detect most of the major kinds of toxicological effects. Sixth Amendment to the Directive on Classification, Packaging, and Labeling of Dangerous Substances. During the 1970s the United States had supported efforts by the Organization for Economic Cooperation and Development (OECD) to develop an international consensus on what would constitute a minimum package of data (MPD) to accompany PMNs for new chemicals. However, the Reagan Administration abruptly reversed this position and opposed any MPDs. R. Brickman, S. Jasanoff, and T. Ilgen, Controlling Chemicals: The Politics of Regulation in Europe and the U.S. 284 (1985). The chemical industry argues that EPA has no authority under TSCA to require a minimum data set.

One problem with the battery approach for testing chemicals is the difficulty of making the tests comprehensive enough to test for each toxicological endpoint (e.g., carcinogenicity, mutagenicity, teratogenicity, neurotoxicity, immunotoxicity, reproductive toxicity, cardiovascular toxicity, pulmonary toxicity) while remaining inexpensive and easy enough to be used as a screening device. An alternative approach would be to use a tiered system of testing akin to that used by the Food and Drug Administration for testing food additives. The tiered approach divides tests into sequential patterns that increase in specificity as the chemical progresses through each tier. If a chemical passes the first tier without positive findings, then no further testing need be done. If positive findings for a toxic endpoint are made in the first tier, then the manufacturer may withdraw the chemical or submit it for more specific testing in a second level of tests. While the tiered approach ultimately can employ many more tests than the battery approach, for most chemicals only a few of the tests would be necessary. For a tiered approach to be an effective screening device, it is critical that entry level tests have a much greater probability of finding false positives than false negatives.

EPA has used section 4 of TSCA to require testing of 30 chemicals identified as constituents of hazardous waste. The rule was issued primarily to obtain information to assist EPA in regulating hazardous wastes. It has been proposed that EPA should require PMNs to include information not only about the characteristics of new chemicals but also about the nature of waste streams and emissions generated in their manufacture, use, and disposal. This information would assist the RCRA program in determining whether or not to list new waste streams as hazardous, and it ultimately could be used to assist waste reduction efforts.

EPA has been criticized for placing undue reliance on structure-activity relationships for predicting toxicity. Most chemists and toxicologists agree that structure-activity relationship methods are available for assessing only mutagenicity and carcinogenicity and not other important toxic effects (e.g., neurotoxicity, reproductive toxicity). Toxicologists are working to develop better techniques, including the use of biological markers, for assessing a more complete range of toxic effects more efficiently.

NOTES AND QUESTIONS

1. The test rule at issue in the *EHA* case involved a substance to which humans rarely were exposed but which was structurally similar to chemicals known to cause cancer in test animals. Suppose that instead the situation were reversed and millions of persons had recurrent exposure to a chemical for which there was no toxicity data and no such structural similarity. What would EPA need to show in order to be able to issue a test rule for such a substance? Consider section 4(a)(1)(B) of TSCA. Could testing be justified solely on the basis of the numbers of persons exposed to the chemical, or would EPA also have to show some evidence that these exposures were likely to pose some risk?

2. How should the large number of chemicals for which there are

insufficient data to make even educated guesses about health risks be treated? Should the highest priority for testing be assigned to those chemicals actually detected in human tissues, with the next highest priority assigned to those detected in environmental media with which humans are in direct contact?

3. Do you agree with the chemical manufacturers' claim that EPA has no authority under TSCA to require a minimum set of test data for new chemicals? Consider section 5(b)(2)(A) of TSCA, which requires the submission of data defined in section 5(b)(2)(B) as data which the submitter believes show that the chemical will not present an unreasonable risk. Consider also section 5(e) of TSCA, which allows EPA to prohibit the manufacture of chemicals for which there are insufficient data to permit a reasonable evaluation of their effects. Could the EPA administrator use these provisions to bar the manufacture of chemicals for which no toxicity data were available?

4. Does EPA have the authority under section 4 of TSCA to require testing to assist the RCRA program? Note that section 4(a) authorizes testing to assess the risks of "disposal" as well as the risks of distribution, processing, and use of a chemical substance.

PRINCIPAL PROVISIONS OF THE TOXIC SUBSTANCES CONTROL ACT

Section 4 authorizes the EPA administrator to require the testing of any chemical substance or mixture on finding that such testing is necessary because there are insufficient data from which the chemical's effects can be predicted and the chemical either "may present an unreasonable risk of injury to health or the environment" or the chemical is produced in substantial quantities or may result in substantial human exposure.

Section 5 prohibits any person from manufacturing any new chemical substance or from processing any chemical substance for a significant new use unless the person notifies the EPA administrator at least 90 days in advance and submits data that the person believes show that the chemical will not present an unreasonable risk. The EPA administrator may prohibit or limit the manufacturing, processing, distribution, use, or disposal of any chemical if he or she determines that the information is insufficient to permit a reasoned evaluation of the effects of the chemical and that it either may present an unreasonable risk or that it may result in significant human exposure.

Section 6 authorizes the EPA administrator, to the extent

necessary to protect adequately against such risk using the least burdensome requirements, to prohibit the manufacture, processing, or distribution in commerce of a chemical substance; to limit the amounts, concentrations, or uses of it; to require labeling or recordkeeping concerning it; or to prohibit or otherwise regulate any manner or method of disposal of it, on a finding that there is a reasonable basis to conclude that the chemical "presents or will present an unreasonable risk of injury to health or the environment."

Section 7 authorizes the EPA administrator to sue to seize or to obtain other relief to protect against imminently hazardous chemical substances.

Section 8 authorizes the EPA administrator to require recordkeeping or the submission of reports concerning the manufacture or processing of chemical substances.

Section 9 requires the EPA administrator to refer chemicals to other federal agencies for regulation or to use other laws administered by EPA to regulate the chemical if he or she determines that the risks posed by the chemical may be sufficiently prevented or reduced by action taken under other laws.

Section 19 authorizes judicial review of EPA regulations issued under TSCA.

Section 20 authorizes citizen suits against any person alleged to be in violation of TSCA or against the EPA administrator for failure to perform nondiscretionary duties.

Section 21 authorizes citizen petitions for the commencement of rulemaking proceedings.

REGULATION OF TOXIC SUBSTANCES: A PATHFINDER

A wide variety of *statutory authorities* are available for regulating toxic substances, many of them administered by agencies other than EPA. Although the Toxic Substances Control Act (TSCA), 15 U.S.C. §2601 et seq., provides the most comprehensive authority to EPA, its jurisdictional reach does not extend to substances regulated by EPA under the Federal Insecticide, Fungicide, and Rodenticide Act (FIFRA) or to food, drugs, or cosmetics regulated by the Food and Drug Administration. The Occupational Safety and Health Administration (OSHA) is responsible for protecting workers from exposure to toxics under the Occupational Safety and Health

Act, 29 U.S.C. §651 et seq. The Consumer Product Safety Commission (CPSC) is responsible for protecting consumers from unreasonably dangerous products pursuant to the Consumer Product Safety Act.

Regulations implementing TSCA are found at 40 C.F.R. pts. 700-799. FIFRA regulations appear at 40 C.F.R. pts. 150-189, and regulations implementing EPCRTKA are at 40 C.F.R. pts. 355-372. FDA regulations appear in Title 21 of the C.F.R.; OSHA health and safety regulations can be found at 29 C.F.R. pt. 1910.

The most influential report on the use of risk assessment by federal agencies is the National Research Council's classic 1983 study, Risk Assessment in the Federal Government: Managing the Process. A useful introduction to risk assessment and risk regulation for nonscientists is the Conservation Foundation's superb 1985 monograph, Risk Assessment and Control. An anthology that includes a great deal of the policy debate on risk regulation is Readings in Risk (T. S. Glickman and M. Gough, eds. 1990).

Most federal regulation of toxic substances has focused on controlling cancer risks. A report by the Office of Technology Assessment in November 1987 entitled Identifying and Regulating Carcinogens provides comprehensive background information on the regulatory policies employed by a variety of federal agencies. Another useful work is F. Cross, Environmentally Induced Cancer and the Law (1989).

A comprehensive *treatise* on toxic substance regulation that also covers hazardous waste issues is D. W. Stever, Law of Chemical Regulation and Hazardous Waste (published by Clark Boardman).

D. HOW SAFE IS "SAFE"?

Up to this point, we have been primarily examining the issues involved in risk assessment. We turn now to issues of risk management.

Bear in mind that this separation is for analytical purposes only. The National Academy of Sciences report on risk regulation urged federal agencies to segregate these two activities as much as possible, assigning the resolution of risk assessment issues to science panels and the resolution of risk management issues to the regulatory agencies. National Research Council, Risk Assessment in the Federal Government: Managing the Process 5-8 (1983). Both the feasibility and the desirability of accomplishing this separation have been subjects of considerable debate in the legal and scientific communities. As you have already seen, many policy decisions must be made internally to the risk assessment methodology itself: which dose-response curve to employ, how to characterize the risk information, whether animal studies will be accepted as indicative of human health effects, the weight to be accorded different kinds of information—all are matters about which consensus science has limited amounts to say, and so policy considerations inevitably enter into the picture. The NAS report acknowledges this; it describes some 50 points in the risk *assessment* process at which a choice is required "among several scientifically plausible options" before that process can continue. Calling such points "inferential bridges," it urges explicit identification of the inference options available at each juncture so that the policymakers can address those questions, transmitting decisions to the expert risk assessors as needed. However, critics have doubted that such complete explicitness can ever be achieved in practice; thus, isolating the risk assessment process from the policymaking process inevitably will result in some, possibly important, policy decisions' being made by scientists and other "experts" without public scrutiny. See Latin, Good Science, Bad Regulations, and Toxic Risk Assessment, 5 Yale J. on Reg. 89 (1988).

Still, the question of how we ought to manage risk raises issues that amply deserve separate attention. So long as constitutional limits are not exceeded, the issue of how federal agencies should manage risk once a decision has been made to regulate is for the Congress in the first instance. Congressional approaches to risk management can be collected under three general headings: balancing approaches, health-based approaches, and technology-based approaches. Figure 4.1, above, summarizes a number of federal regulatory provisions according to these three categories. In this section we examine the different regulatory schemes in further detail, in order to gain some appreciation for how they operate in practice, and to provide some bases for appraising their relative desirability.

1. Risk-Benefit Balancing

A. INTRODUCTION

Risk-benefit balancing is simply cost-benefit analysis applied to policy decisions involving risks.* Risk-benefit analysis requires quantitative

---

*While the terms "risk-benefit balancing" and "cost-benefit balancing" can

FIGURE 4.8

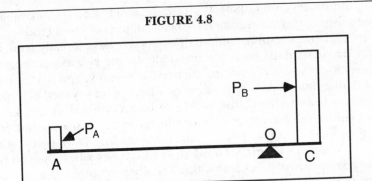

risk assessment techniques to produce numerical characterizations of risk that are then compared to the benefits society receives from the activities producing those risks. If the reductions in risks that regulation would achieve (the benefits of regulation) outweigh the benefits of not regulating it (the costs of regulation), a balancing approach to risk management urges that the risk be reduced, ideally to the point at which risks and benefits (or benefits and costs) just balance.

Talbot Page originally employed his seesaw imagery to analyze the regulatory strategy of risk-benefit balancing. Figure 4.8 shows how the concept works. In it we have depicted a risk-benefit balancing decision involving a substance (A) with potential adverse effects (OA) greatly in excess of the benefits derived from using the substance (OC). The probability (P) of realizing those benefits if the use is continued are fairly substantial, approaching 1.0, because we can fairly confidently predict them, perhaps based on past uses. Conversely, we are rather uncertain whether the adverse effects will materialize, so P_A (adverse effects) is small compared to P_B (benefits). Notice that in this figure we have replaced the "threshold finding" found in the previous figures with representations of benefits and their probabilities. That is because risks must exceed benefits before regulation is appropriate under a risk-benefit balancing regime. In risk-benefit balancing, the ideas of threshold finding and risk management decision tend to merge, because a regulator

almost be used interchangeably, it is easy to get confused by them because they place the word "benefit" on different sides of the balancing equation—the "benefits" in "risk-benefit balancing" are the benefits provided by the substance to be regulated (which are the "costs" in "cost-benefit balancing"); the "benefits" in "cost-benefit balancing" are the gains to health or the environment from regulating the risks (the "risk" in "risk-benefit balancing").

needs to make a threshold finding that risks outweigh benefits before regulating, and then the same considerations suggest that the way such risk should be managed is by placing risks and benefits in balance.

As this picture suggests, and as Page argues, a risk-benefit balancing strategy might lead to the regulation of substances with fairly low probabilities of great harm; in other words, it might lead to a policy that produced more false positives than false negatives. It all depends on the relationship between costs and benefits and their respective probabilities.

Crucial to this analysis is the assumption that we can "weigh" risks against benefits. Doing this quantitatively requires expressing risks and benefits in a common measure. Characteristically, risk-benefit advocates suggest that this be done by expressing both risks and benefits in dollars. Not all "balancing" of risks and benefits has to be done this way, but the expression "risk-benefit" balancing has taken on the connotation of a fully quantified, or monetized, assessment of both risks and benefits. We have already examined some of the forces pushing toward quantification on the risk assessment side. Similar forces have been at work promoting risk-benefit balancing.

In an effort to increase the use of cost-benefit analysis in environmental decision-making, President Reagan signed Executive Order 12,291 in 1981. Still in effect, that Order requires federal agencies to analyze "the need for and consequences of proposed government action" in order to design regulatory measures that, to the extent permitted by law, "maximize net benefits to society." The Order dictates that, "to the extent permitted by law, . . . regulatory action shall not be undertaken unless the potential benefits to society for the regulation outweigh the potential costs to society." The Office of Management and Budget (OMB), part of the Executive Office of the President, is responsible for ensuring compliance with the Order. One effect of the Order has been to force agencies to undertake explicit comparison of the risks and benefits associated with activities that are candidates for regulation. While the Order nowhere defines "costs" and "benefits," it requires that agencies prepare detailed cost-benefit analyses, called Regulatory Impact Analyses (RIAs), for all major rules, which are defined as regulations likely to have an effect on the economy of $100 million or more annually. Agencies are directed "to the extent permitted by law" to consider such cost-benefit analyses when making regulatory decisions.

The Executive Order has been characterized as establishing "a convenient and workable means of assuring that regulatory decisions are controlled by the President or by officials who are more likely to share his views than the career bureaucrats in the various federal agencies." Sunstein, Cost-Benefit Analysis and the Separation of Powers, 23 Ariz. L. Rev. 1267 (1981). It turns out that OMB has used risk assessment and cost-benefit analyses, as well as its ability to block regulatory action under the Executive Order, to increase centralized control of federal policymaking. The implementation of Executive Order 12,291 and its impact on the regulatory process is discussed in detail in Chapter 5.

For illustrative purposes, Figure 4.9 shows OMB's estimates of the cost per statistical life saved (in millions of dollars) for selected regulations. OMB, Regulatory Program of the United States Government, April 1, 1986-March 31, 1987, at xxi (1986). Notice that this table of risk-cost comparisons does not render a judgment on whether any particular regulatory initiative is risk-benefit *justified*. To do so would require making *explicit* some benchmark for how much society is prepared to pay to prevent the (statistical) loss of life. Instead, the table records certain regulatory actions, evaluates the costs associated with the regulation, divides these by the number of lives estimated to have been saved (this is the contribution of risk assessment), and thus determines what OMB estimates to be the *implicit* cost per life saved for each regulation.

While the ban on DES in cattle feed may look expensive at $132 million per life saved, OMB believes that a 1990 EPA rule listing waste from wood preserving operations as hazardous under RCRA now takes

---

FIGURE 4.9
Risk-Cost Tradeoffs for Selected Regulations

Regulation	Agency	Year issued	Cost per statistical life saved ($ millions)
1. Unvented space heaters	CPSC	1980	$ 0.07
2. Servicing wheel rims	OSHA	1984	0.25
3. Fuel system integrity	NHTSA	1975	0.29
4. Uranium mill tailings (active)	EPA	1983	53.00
5. Ethylene oxide	OSHA	1984	60.00
6. DES ban in cattlefeed	FDA	1979	132.00

NOTE—In 1984 dollars, discounted at 10 percent. Each nonfatal accident requiring hospitalization is treated as equivalent to one-fiftieth of a fatality. This relationship was selected as representative of the willingness-to-pay values for fatality risks relative to injury risks found by research studies. Cancer is counted as a fatality. Cancer latency periods were assumed to be 15 years for lung cancer associated with uranium mill tailings and 10 years for the leukemia and breast cancer associated with ethylene oxide and DES, respectively.

Discounting benefits and costs at 4 percent instead of 10 percent does not affect the conclusion that there are extremely wide variations in cost per statistical life saved between these regulations, nor does it affect the cost-effectiveness rankings. Discounted at 4 percent, banning DES in cattlefeed still costs 1,500 times more per statistical life than regulating unvented space heaters.

---

the cake—it costs $7.2 trillion per case of cancer prevented. "If the entire budget of the U.S. government was invested in cancer prevention efforts of this caliber, only one-sixth of one random case of cancer would be prevented," complains James B. MacRae, acting administrator of OMB's Office of Information and Regulatory Affairs. 21 Env. Rep. 1555 (1990). While EPA had estimated that the regulation could prevent 140 cases of cancer over the next 300 years, OMB's estimate discounted these benefits heavily because EPA's model predicted that the first case of cancer prevented would not occur for 110 years.

B. COST BENEFIT ANALYSIS

i. Introduction

The economics perspective (discussed in Chapter 1) views environmental problems as arising from two factors: (1) environmental amenities such as clean air and water are scarce (that is, valuable) and (2) markets do not exist through which that value can be registered by consumers. As Baumol and Oates stated it, we are afflicted with "an institutional arrangement under which a number of society's resources are given away free," page 41, above. Economists frequently call this affliction "market failure." In this case, the consequence of market failure is that environmental amenities are overconsumed or underproduced.

If environmental amenities could be traded in well-functioning markets (review Baumol and Oates for the reasons why these markets do not exist and are frequently difficult to create), then those amenities would move from less valued uses to more highly valued uses, measured by people's willingness to pay. When such markets do not exist, welfare economics suggests that government can sometimes legitimately intervene to achieve such a change from less valued uses to more highly valued uses directly. The result would be an improvement in total social welfare, measured by the difference between the higher value and the lower value. In order to test whether any proposed governmental policy actually accomplishes such a welfare improvement, welfare economics recommends that such policy be subjected to a cost-benefit analysis (CBA), which seeks to compare the "social benefit" of the policy to its "opportunity cost—the social value foregone when the resources in question are moved away from alternative economic activities into the specific project" contemplated by the policy. E. J. Mishan, Cost-Benefit Analysis xii (1976). Both costs and benefits often are estimated by examining people's willingness to pay for them.

As noted above, Executive Order 12,291 mandates cost-benefit analyses of all major agency rules, including those of the Environmental Protection Agency. The 1990 Clean Air Act Amendments require EPA to perform an analysis of the overall costs and benefits of the rules EPA must issue under the Amendments. Such analyses have become a standard part of environmental policy debates. Notwithstanding their prevalence, the methods employed in such analyses and the relevance of their results for environmental policymaking continue to be controversial. In the example below we provide a simplified overview of cost-benefit analytical techniques followed by a brief introduction to some of the controversies surrounding their use.

ii. An Example: EPA's Lead Phasedown Decision

Prior to its 1985 decision to reduce the lead content of gasoline substantially (see pages 450 to 451), EPA prepared a preliminary cost-benefit analysis of its options. Eventually it focused on two alternatives: a "low-lead" option, in which gasoline with a low lead content (.10 grams per gallon) would continue to be marketed to ease fears that older cars would suffer valve damage from unleaded gasoline, and a "no lead" option, which would ban all lead additives in gasoline by 1988. The results of its calculation of costs and benefits for each option are shown in Figure 4.10.

iii. Methodological Issues

1. Estimating Costs. Cost-benefit analysis attempts to assess the social impact of a proposal by comparing its benefits and costs. In environmental policy, a major component of costs typically will be the costs of compliance by regulated firms. These are designated "manufacturing costs" in the lead phasedown analysis. These costs can sometimes be quite speculative, especially when the proposal involves employing new technologies. When a proposal succeeds in forcing the development of new technology, compliance cost estimates made before the proposal is enacted can be substantially different from actual compliance costs after the technology is employed. See the discussion of technology forcing, Chapter 2B3. Whether or not technology forcing is involved, estimates of compliance costs rely heavily on industry information, which raises concern among proponents of stringent environmental protection that cost estimates may be inflated.

2. Monetizing Costs. In some situations, costs will include elements that present other difficulties in translation to dollar estimates. When considering a proposal to dam a river, for example, one of the costs of the dam is the value of lost recreation opportunities for people who fish, raft, kayak, or hike. People rarely pay for these activities, however, so it is not possible to ascertain the value of them as directly as one can ascertain the cost of constructing a scrubber for a power

FIGURE 4.10
Costs and Benefits of Reducing Lead in Gasoline
(Figures in 1983 dollars)

COSTS	Low-lead	No-lead
Manufacturing costs	$503 million	$691 million
Nonmonetized valve damage to engines	$0	D
TOTAL COSTS	$503 million	$691 million + D
BENEFITS		
Maintenance benefits	$660 million	$755 million
Environmental and health benefits		
Conventional Pollutants		
Reduced damage by eliminating misfueling	$404 million	$404 million
Nonmonetized health benefits	H1	H1
Lead		
Reduced medical care costs	$41 million	$43 million
Reduced cognitive damage	$184 million	$193 million
Nonmonetized health benefits	H2	H3
TOTAL BENEFITS	$1.289 billion + H1 + H2	$1.395 billion + H1 + H3
NET BENEFITS	$786 million + H1 + H2	$704 million + H1 + H3 − D

Source: EPA, Costs and Benefits of Reducing Lead in Gasoline (Mar. 1984).

plant's smokestack, or of reconfiguring oil refineries to produce low-lead or no-lead gasoline, or of purchasing more expensive lead substitutes. In such cases, analysts must develop "shadow prices" for these opportunity costs, looking for ways to estimate the prices people would be willing to pay for the recreational benefits if necessary. The main techniques for estimating shadow prices for use in environmental decision-making are summarized in D. Pearce and R. Turner, Economics of Natural Resources and the Environment 141-158 (1990).

Some cost-benefit analyses do not try to monetize all costs and benefits, but instead seek to identify elements of cost or benefit and present them in a descriptive fashion. Although this is better than simply ignoring such items, there remains a concern that such nonquantifiable elements will be given insufficient weight. As Pearce and Turner put it, when environmental benefits or costs "tend to be less 'concrete,' and more 'soft' than market-place benefits [or costs,] [t]he temptation is to downgrade them by comparison." Id. at 123. (Sometimes elements of cost or benefits are not monetized because doing so is impossible or unnecessary. In the lead phasedown CBA, engine valve damage was not given a dollar value estimate because of great uncertainty concerning the true effects of unleaded gasoline on engine valves.

3. Estimating Benefits.   Analogous concerns about shadow prices and monetizing values that are not traded in markets can arise on the benefits side of environmental CBAs. Such concerns frequently arise with regard to estimating the value of not degrading the environment, because payoffs in terms of environmental and public health are unlikely to have reliable market prices. When the status quo is environmentally superior to the proposal, as tends to be the case in development or construction projects, degrading the environment is a cost of the project. When the proposal is environmentally superior to the status quo, as tends to be the case in proposals to reduce pollution, removing environmental degradation is a benefit of the proposal.

These are generalities, of course. One of the requirements of a sound CBA is that it consider all relevant costs and benefits, and some benefits of environmental protection measures present fewer shadow pricing problems than others. For instance, in the lead phasedown CBA the largest monetized benefit of either option comes from reduced maintenance associated with lower-lead gasoline. These savings arise because lead and the agents added to gasoline to scavenge it from cylinder walls degrade the performance of parts of the engine and exhaust systems. For the low-lead case, EPA estimated that reduced lead would lengthen the life of exhaust systems and of spark plugs and would permit drivers to go longer between oil changes. The cost savings associated with these benefits were $341 million, $80 million, and $239 million, respectively. The difficulties in estimates such as these arise not because there are no markets for exhaust systems, mufflers, spark plugs, and motor oil, but rather because of uncertainty concerning the effect low-lead gasoline will have on extending the lives of these products.

4. Monetizing Benefits: Putting a Value on Human Life and Health.   Perhaps no aspect of CBA is more controversial than monetizing the improvements to human health and to increased life span associated with environmental proposals. Substantial ethical or normative questions can be raised here, particularly when decisions to reduce or eliminate life-threatening agents are being debated. Here we discuss some of the methodological issues, which are largely special instances of the general disagreements over shadow pricing.

Prior to the 1980s, economists and government regulators employed several different methods for calculating the dollar value of health-enhancing proposals, including estimates of increased earnings associated with better health (the human capital method) and of medical expenses saved because of better health (avoided cost method). However, these were recognized to be inconsistent with the otherwise standard assumption of CBA that all factor values should be evaluated on the basis of society's willingness to pay (WTP). Under the Reagan Administration, it became official policy to estimate the monetary value of all benefits not traded directly in the marketplace using the willingness-to-pay principle, "because the amount that people are willing to pay for a good or service is the best measure of its value to them." Executive Office of the President, Regulatory Program of the United States xix (1987).

One method used for determining WTP for health-enhancing proposals is the wage-rate differential method. Analysts look for job situations in which some job classifications are riskier than others. They calculate the risk differential between the job classifications and also the wage rate differential between them. These figures permit a calculation of the value being placed on risk in the labor market, on the assumption that the wage differential constitutes the compensation employees feel is necessary to offset the higher risk, thus indicating how much bearing that increased risk is worth to them. Studies conducted in this way have produced a range of estimates of how much people are willing to pay to save a human life, from a low of $200,000 to a high of $7 million. For a review of the studies and commentary on the methodology, see W. K. Viscusi, Strategic and Ethical Issues in the Valuation of Life, in R. Zeckhauser, Strategy and Choice (1991).

Various criticisms have been leveled against the general use of the values obtained from such studies. Workers may not understand their workplace risks; if they do not, the WTP figures would not be accurate. WTP for a human life may well vary by the type of death being avoided (violent and painful versus peaceful); it may also vary depending on the quality of life being preserved—we might pay more to prevent a kidney failure than to maintain a life on dialysis after kidney failure had occurred. See generally S. Rhoads, Valuing Life (1979). Studies in cognitive psychology also indicate people are far more willing to accept voluntary risks than involuntary risks of the same magnitude. See pages 607-608, below.

5. Monetizing Benefits: Nonfatal Health Effects. In the lead phasedown CBA, EPA monetized two types of health-related benefits: medical care expenses avoided because children would be exposed to less airborne lead and would therefore need less medical care, and improvements in cognitive ability because of reduced neurological damage from lead exposure. Neither of these involve life-threatening health effects, so the problem peculiar to the value-to-life debate did not arise in this CBA. Other issues did, however.

With respect to medical care expenses, EPA noted that since 1975 the Centers for Disease Control had considered blood lead concentrations greater than 30 micrograms per deciliter to require medical attention and monitoring. CDC recommended six follow-up checkups and a home visit to investigate sources of lead exposure. EPA calculated the costs of tests, physicians' time, and the home inspection to be $950 per child. It then estimated that of the children currently experiencing blood lead levels above the CDC "action level" of 30 µg/dl, some 45,000 would be placed below the action level by the no-lead option. This would produce total medical cost savings of $43 million (45,000 × $950).

EPA acknowledged that very few children actually are treated in the way CDC recommended, but concluded that "children with blood lead levels greater than 30 micrograms/deciliter who go untreated bear a burden which we valued equal to the cost of follow-up and/or treatment." Is the $950 figure a reliable estimate of willingness to pay for the children who in fact were treated according to CDC guidelines? For the children who were not so treated?

Notice how sensitive this benefits calculation is to the CDC action level. Were CDC to have an action level of 25 micrograms, the no-lead option would move 150,000 children from above to below the action level, tripling the medical cost benefits. In fact, in late 1985 CDC did lower its action level to 25 micrograms. In 1991 it lowered it further, to 10 micrograms (see Figure 4.14, below).

To monetize the value of reduced cognitive damage, EPA calculated the costs of 3 years of compensatory education (the cognitive effects of lead levels above the 30 µg/dl level were estimated to persist for three years) sufficient "to bring their school performance back to what it otherwise would have been." Using a Department of Education estimate of approximately $4,000 per child, this produced an estimate of the value of cognitive improvement of $193 million for the no-lead case. Again, what relationship does this calculation have to willingness to pay? Is EPA in effect here adopting a "social willingness to pay" approach on the supposition that society would have been prepared to provide three years' compensatory education for such children? That is not consistent with WTP as applied by CBA, however, because the relevant question is how much an individual is willing to pay for a benefit he or she will receive. Moreover, long-term follow-up studies of persons exposed to lead as children indicate that the damage persists, Needleman and Gatsonis, Low-Level Lead Exposure and the IQ of Children, 263 J.A.M.A. 673 (1990), suggesting that compensatory education may not compensate for the damage.

6. *Monetizing Benefits: Nonconsumptive Benefits.* On the other hand, perhaps all taxpaying members of society would be willing to pay for compensatory education. In principle, CBA ought to be prepared to include in net costs and benefits whatever benefits or costs third parties will experience from the proposal (and that are not reflected already in other factor prices). Members of society may sympathize with small chil-

dren sufficiently to be willing to pay $4,000 per year to prevent them from experiencing cognitive problems. This brand of altruistic behavior is relevant to CBA as long as individual altruists are willing to pay for it.

Two other categories of nonconsumptive external effects that can affect environmental CBAs are called "option value" and "existence value." Option value arises when individuals are prepared to pay some sum to ensure the future availability of an environmental amenity that they may be interested in enjoying in the future. Existence value arises when individuals positively value an environmental good regardless of any actual or potential use of the good. Although this might seem like an odd value for an economist to acknowledge, it is simply CBA's way of recognizing the reality that the world is populated by at least some individuals who share the sorts of environmentalist values discussed in Chapter 1. While altruism, option values, and existence values can be theoretically incorporated into CBA, problems of measurement are considerable, to say the least.

7. *The Discount Rate.* A dollar promised to you ten years from now is worth less to you than a dollar given to you today. Assuming you could place money given to you today in an account earning 10 percent per year, you would only have to deposit 38.5 cents in the account for it to be worth a dollar in ten years, so 38.5 cents is the present value of that dollar ten years down the road. Many environmental proposals involve a stream of costs and benefits extending years into the future. In order to express these costs and benefits as totals, CBA must reduce the out-year value estimates of costs and benefits to their present value.

Doing that requires employing a discount rate—sort of an interest rate in reverse—to future costs and benefits. The choice of the discount rate is tremendously important to the ultimate CBA verdict for many proposals. For instance, a benefit of $1 million to be received in 40 years has a present value of only $22,000 with a 10 percent discount rate and a value of $208,000 with a 4 percent discount rate. The Department of the Interior employed a 10 percent discount rate in formulating its initial guidelines on the recovery of natural resources damages. See State of Ohio v. Department of the Interior, 880 F.2d 432 (D.C. Cir. 1989), pages 351-363, above.

The higher the discount rate, the smaller the significance of costs and benefits that accrue in the future. Many environmental protection proposals are characterized by costs biased toward the present and benefits biased toward the future. Control of carcinogens, for instance, can be quite expensive immediately, but the health benefits of reducing exposure may only occur 20 or 30 years later, because some substances cause cancers with a latency period that long. Although preservation proposals are supported by a desire to keep areas pristine for future generations, the benefits to generations far in the future will be minuscule under almost any discount rate.

The discount rate cannot be entirely resolved by appeal to scientific or economic analysis (although there are technical debates about whether current interest rates truly reflect the marginal productivity of capital, which is theoretically the appropriate basis for discount rates respecting private investments). How much one individual would accept today instead of a dollar ten years from now is a question of rational personal budgeting, but how much our present society should spend to provide benefits to people other than ourselves—future generations, for example—has important ethical and political dimensions, as well.

8. Behavioral Assumptions. The second largest monetized benefit from low-lead gasoline arose because EPA calculated that 12 percent of the cars on the road in the early 1980s that were supposed to be using only unleaded gasoline were being fueled with leaded gasoline. Such "misfueling" was damaging the catalytic converters installed on vehicles in order to reduce emissions of hydrocarbons, carbon monoxide, and oxides of nitrogen. Both low-lead and no-lead gasolines would reduce or eliminate misfueling, resulting in improved catalytic converter performance. In order to calculate the monetary size of this benefit, EPA first had to calculate the prevalence of misfueling, the quantity of conventional pollutants that would not be emitted when misfueling ceased, and the monetary value of all the positive effects of reducing conventional pollutant levels. The result was the $404 million estimate in the CBA.

This highlights the significance of citizen responses to government regulations in determining their ultimate costs and benefits. If a CBA had been done on the initial decision to employ catalytic converters to combat conventional pollutants, and it had not anticipated 12 percent misfueling, it would have overestimated the benefits of that action by $404 million. Similarly, if the EPA had failed to study actual car owners' refueling habits, it would not have identified the misfueling phenomenon and would have underestimated the benefits of the lead phasedown by $404 million.

When EPA adopted the lead phasedown regulation in 1985, the Agency prepared a final cost-benefit analysis that sought to monetize factors not quantified in its previous analysis. Figure 4.11 summarizes EPA's estimates. Note the enormous benefits from reducing adult blood pressure, a health benefit not monetized in EPA's proposal because it had only recently been discovered through epidemiological data. Because of uncertainty concerning the blood pressure studies (the epidemiological data were strong, but scientists did not understand the precise mechanism by which lead affects blood pressure), the final cost-benefit analysis also calculated net benefits excluding blood pressure.

FIGURE 4.11

Year-by-Year Costs and Monetized Benefits of Lead Regulation, Assuming Partial Misfueling, 1985-1992

(millions of 1984 dollars)

Benefit category	1985	1986	1987	1988	1989	1990	1991	1992
	$	$	$	$	$	$	$	$
Children's health effects	232	623	568	521	470	430	383	372
Adult blood pressure	1,790	6,124	5,893	5,657	5,387	5,157	4,862	4,872
Conventional pollutants	0	231	231	233	235	239	248	258
Maintenance	106	949	892	849	818	797	783	779
Fuel economy	36	194	177	117	139	144	179	170
Total monetized benefits	2,164	8,121	7,761	7,377	7,049	6,767	6,455	6,449
Total refining costs	100	631	579	552	523	489	461	458
Net benefits	2,065	7,490	7,181	6,825	6,526	6,278	5,994	5,991
Net benefits excluding blood pressure	274	1,366	1,288	1,168	1,139	1,121	1,132	1,119

Source: Office of Policy Analysis, Environmental Protection Agency, Costs and Benefits of Reducing Lead in Gasoline, Report no. EPA-230-05-85-006 (Feb. 1985), p. E-12. Reprinted from: P. Portney, Air Pollution Policy, in Public Policies for Environmental Protection 64 (P. Portney, ed. 1990).

iv. Normative Issues

CBA is a technique for implementing the economic conception of environmental problems. All the objections that other strands of environmentalism raise against that conception can therefore be raised against it. Many of these were discussed in Chapter 1 and will not be repeated at length here. Three specific issues warrant recapitulation, however.

1. Politics as a Forum for Expressing Public Values.   When we use CBA as a necessary and sufficient condition for governmental decisions, we are accepting a controversial political premise: The sole proper role of government is to maximize the satisfaction of citizens' private preferences for goods and services, including environmental amenities. An opposing view is that public political debate provides an occasion for individuals to express citizen values instead of merely consumer values, to deliberate on the kind of society we want collectively to become.

> In this conceptual framework, government is not simply a corrective instrument at the margins of economic markets but [a] . . . central arena in which the members of society choose and legitimize . . . their collective values. The principal purposes of legislative action are to weigh and affirm social values and to define and enforce the rights and duties of members of the society, through representative democracy. The purpose of administrative action is to put into effect these affirmations by the legislature, not to rebalance them by the criteria of economic theory. [R. Andrews, Cost-Benefit Analysis as Regulatory Reform, in Cost Benefit Analysis and Environmental Regulations: Politics, Ethics, and Methods 107, 112 (D. Swartzman, R. Liroff, and K. Croke, eds. 1982).]

As Daniel Farber argues:

> [C]ost-benefit analysis is misused to provide technocratic solutions to fundamentally political questions. . . . There is no magic formula for determining how much whales are worth or how safe our drinking water should be. These issues can only be resolved through a political process which is always imperfect, but which at least aspires to identify the public interest. [Farber, Environmentalism, Economics and the Public Interest, 41 Stan. L. Rev. 1021, 1943 (1989).]

2. Willingness to Pay or Willingness to Accept?   Most CBAs of proposals to improve the environment estimate how much the beneficiaries of the proposal would be willing to pay to acquire it. Critics point out that there is no necessary reason to treat environmental improvements as things that need to be purchased. CBA could just as easily be based on willingness of people to accept (WTA) payment for degrading the environment. Using WTA would effectively give citizens an entitlement to a clean environment, which polluters are permitted to purchase from them; using WTP implicitly gives industrial sources an entitlement to operate at the existing levels of pollution, which sufferers of pollution are permitted to purchase from them.

In some situations, the choice of WTP or WTA should make little difference to the CBA outcome. The value of your willingness to pay money for a $.50 candy bar is probably not much different from the value of your willingness to accept money for the same candy bar once you own it. At other times, it will matter a great deal. Imagine John Muir being asked how much he would accept as payment for converting Yosemite National Park into an amusement park. Now imagine how much he would be willing to pay to prevent that from occurring. While the latter amount would probably be substantial in Muir's case, it would also quite likely be far less than the first sum (if he were willing to price the matter at all).

One reason discrepancies between WTA and WTP can arise is that implicitly assigning the entitlement to one side or the other affects people's wealth. The entitlements have value, and this value contributes to individual wealth. When this wealth effect is substantial, WTA is likely to be much higher than WTP, simply because the individual owning the entitlement is now wealthy enough to have environmental amenity plus everything else he or she currently consumes, rather than having to purchase that environmental amenity at the cost of being unable to consume something else he or she is now enjoying.

There is a substantial legal literature on the WTA/WTP problem, where it is often called the "offer/asking" problem. See, e.g., Kelman, Choice and Utility, 1979 Wisc. L. Rev. 769; Kelman, Consumption Theory, Production Theory, and Ideology in the Coase Theorem, 52 S. Cal. L. Rev. 669 (1979); Kennedy, Cost-Benefit Analysis of Entitlement Problems: A Critique, 33 Stan. L. Rev. 387 (1981). Empirical studies confirm that WTA is higher than WTP in many situations involving environmental decision-making. For a review, see D. Pearce and R. Turner, Economics of Natural Resources and the Environment 141-158 (1990). Do you think that using WTA to evaluate the benefits of reduced cognitive damage for lead would have produced a figure higher than $950 per child? Bear in mind that many of the children at risk of lead-related cognitive impairment are poor, inner-city children. Might it be that they would be willing to accept such a sum?

3. Distributional and Other Social Values. This last question raises another objection sometimes leveled against CBA as a decisionmaking device: Important issues of wealth distribution, as well as other sensitive social values (such as a commitment to nondiscrimination), may need to influence an ultimate governmental decision, and these typically are ignored in the standard CBA.

Even staunch supporters of CBA acknowledge this point; thus CBA

is seldom promoted as a universally applicable decision tool. In the words
of two proponents:

> Few important social decisions cannot and should not be informed by cost-
> benefit analysis. But we would not promote cost-benefit analysis as the
> final arbiter of social decisions. Some issues are of such great social concern
> that no analysis can override them. . . . [H. Leonard and R. Zeckhauser,
> Cost-Benefit Analysis Applied to Risks: Its Philosophy and Legitimacy, in
> Values at Risk 31, 42-43 (D. Maclean, ed. 1986).]

4. *In Defense of CBA.*   There are, of course, many defenders of
CBA. Leonard and Zeckhauser summarize its virtues in the context of
decisions regarding risks to human life:

> Since many important risks cannot be exchanged on a voluntary basis, it
> is essential to have a centralized decision process that will regulate or
> determine their levels. In choosing among alternative projects that create
> different levels of risk, the government (or other responsible decision
> makers) should seek the outcomes that fully informed individuals would
> choose for themselves if voluntary exchange were feasible. Risks are not
> different in principle from other commodities, such as park services, public
> transit, or housing. [Id. at 33.]

Others suggest that CBA is valuable because "[o]nly this approach
recognizes the full range of implications that may result from government control of [environmental risks.] And regardless of whether cost
considerations should drive policy decisions, most citizens would consider costs or other disadvantages to regulation to be a relevant concern
of government." F. Cross, Environmentally Induced Cancer and the Law
89 (1989).

C.   Is Risk-Benefit (or Cost-Benefit) Balancing Presumptively Correct?

Although the approach federal agencies take to risk management
is for Congress to decide in the first instance, proponents of risk-benefit
balancing have frequently urged that this approach is the presumptively
correct, or rational, or commonsense approach to the regulation of risky
substances. By and large, proponents have not argued that risk-benefit
balancing is constitutionally mandated; rather, they have seized on any
plausible language in specific statutes as a basis for asserting that Congress either meant to impose risk-benefit balancing or that Congress
should be taken to have meant risk-benefit balancing unless it clearly
states the contrary. From time to time, proponents have drawn some

solace from judicial opinions, as when Justice Powell, concurring in the *Benzene* decision, expressed the view that the OSH Act required that there be a "reasonable relationship" between the economic effects of a regulation and its expected benefits. 448 U.S. at 667.

Can the president mandate that cost-benefit balancing be used? Notice that Executive Order 12,291 directs EPA and other agencies to consider cost-benefit analyses "to the extent permitted by law." To what extent is this? Consider the following cases, in which courts were presented with arguments that provisions of the Clean Water Act and the OSH Act should be interpreted to require cost-benefit balancing.

|| ***Weyerhaeuser Co. v. Costle*** ||
|| **590 F.2d 1011 (D.C. Cir. 1978)** ||

Before MCGOWAN, TAMM, Circuit Judges and RICHEY, U.S. District Judge.

[At issue was the validity of water effluent discharge standards issued by EPA under the Clean Water Act of 1977. Section 301(b) authorizes EPA to issue one set of standards based on "the best practicable control technology currently available (BPCTCA)." BPCTCA is defined in §304(b)(1)(B) of the Act, which instructs EPA to "include consideration of the total cost of application of technology in relation to the effluent reduction benefits to be achieved from such application" and to "also take into account the age of the equipment and facilities involved, the process employed, the engineering aspects of the application of various types of control techniques, process changes, non-water quality environmental impacts (including energy requirements), and such other factors as the Administrator deems appropriate." EPA issued BPCTCA for the pulp and paper industry. The industry then brought several lawsuits, including this one, challenging the industry-wide standards. Industry representatives raised a number of challenges; the one dealt with in the following excerpt was pressed especially by Pacific Coast pulp mills, who claimed that the standards applied to them should be more lenient than those applied elsewhere because their discharges were causing less harm.] MCGOWAN, Circuit Judge:

Some of the paper mills that must meet the effluent limitations under review discharge their effluents into the Pacific Ocean. Petitioners contend that the ocean can dilute or naturally treat effluent, and that EPA must take this capacity of the ocean ("receiving water capacity") into account in a variety of ways. They urge what they term "common sense," i.e., that because the amounts of pollutant involved are small in comparison to bodies of water as vast as Puget Sound or the Pacific Ocean, they should not have to spend heavily on treatment equipment, or to increase their energy requirements and sludge levels, in order to treat wastes that the ocean could dilute or absorb.[41]

EPA's secondary response to this claim was that pollution is far from harmless, even when disposed of in the largest bodies of water. As congressional testimony indicated, the Great Lakes, Puget Sound, and even areas of the Atlantic Ocean have been seriously injured by water pollution. Even if the ocean can handle ordinary wastes, ocean life may be vulnerable to toxic compounds that typically accompany those wastes. In the main, however, EPA simply asserted that the issue of receiving water capacity could not be raised in setting effluent limitations because Congress had ruled it out. We have examined the previous legislation in this area, and the 1972 Act's wording, legislative history, and policies, as underscored by its 1977 amendments. These sources . . . support EPA's construction of the Act. They make clear that based on long experience, and aware of the limits of technological knowledge and administrative flexibility, Congress made the deliberate decision to rule out arguments based on receiving water capacity. . . .

Moreover, by eliminating the issue of the capacity of particular bodies of receiving water, Congress made nationwide uniformity of effluent regulation possible. Congress considered uniformity vital to free the states from the temptation of relaxing local limitations in order to woo or keep industrial facilities. . . .

More fundamentally, the new approach implemented changing views as to the relative rights of the public and of industrial polluters. Hitherto, the right of the polluter was pre-eminent, unless the damage caused by pollution could be proved. Henceforth, the right of the public to a clean environment would be pre-eminent, unless pollution treatment was impractical or unachievable. . . . This new view of relative rights was based in part on the hard-nosed assessment of our scientific ignorance: "we know so little about the ultimate consequences of injection of new matter into water that [the Act requires] a presumption of pollution. . . ." [Legislative History] at 1332 (remarks of Senator Buckley). It also was based on the widely shared conviction that the nation's quality

---

41. Apart from this simple "common sense" version of the argument, there is a more sophisticated economic version called the "optimal pollution" theory. This economic theory contends that there is a level or type of pollution that, while technologically capable of being controlled, is uneconomic to treat because the benefit from treatment is small and the cost of treatment is large. See generally W. Baxter, People or Penguins: The Case for Optimal Pollution (1974). . . . These economic theories are premised on a view that we have both adequate information about the effects of pollution to set an optimal test, and adequate political and administrative flexibility to keep polluters at that level once we allow any pollution to go untreated. As discussed in this section, it appears that Congress doubted these premises.

of life depended on its natural bounty, and that it was worth incurring heavy cost to preserve that bounty for future generations. . . .

[Petitioners also challenged the way EPA had interpreted its responsibility to "include consideration of the total cost of application of technology in relation to the effluent reduction benefits to be achieved from such application" in formulating its nationally uniform BPCTCA standards.] They contend that the Agency should have more carefully balanced costs versus the effluent reduction benefits of the regulations. . . .

. . . EPA must compare: total costs versus effluent reduction benefits. We shall call these the "comparison factors." . . .

Based on our examination of the statutory language and the legislative history, we conclude that Congress mandated a particular structure and weight for the . . . comparison factors, that is to say, a "limited balancing" test.[52]

[The court then summarized the "limited" cost-benefit analysis that the industry challenged.] The Agency assessed the costs of internal and external effluent treatment measures, not only for the industry, but also for each subcategory. This included a separate cost assessment for the sulfite subcategories [the only specific cost-benefit assessment challenged by industry]. An economic analysis was prepared to determine the impact of the costs on the industry. . . . It found that the industry as a whole would readily absorb the cost of compliance with the [BPCTCA] standards, estimated at $1.6 billion. Out of 270 mills employing 120,000 people, eight mills would likely be closed and 1800 people laid off. The Agency noted that the impact on the three heavily polluting sulfite subcategories would be the greatest. Of less than 30 sulfite mills, three would probably close, resulting in 550 people being laid off.

Against these costs, EPA balanced the main effluent reduction benefit: overall 5,000 fewer tons per day of BOD [biochemical oxygen de-

---

52. Senator Muskie described the "limited" balancing test:

The modification of subsection 304(b)(1) is intended to clarify what is meant by the term "practicable." *The balancing test between total cost and effluent reduction benefits* is intended to limit the application of technology only where the additional degree of effluent reduction is *wholly out of proportion* to the costs of achieving such marginal level of reduction for any class or category of sources.

The Conferees agreed upon this limited cost-benefit analysis in order to maintain uniformity within a class and category of point sources subject to effluent limitations, and to avoid imposing on the Administrator any requirement to consider the location of sources within a category or to ascertain water quality impact of effluent controls, or to determine the economic impact of controls on any individual plant in a single community.

Legislative History, at 170 (emphasis added).

mand] discharged into the nation's waters. EPA refined this balance by calculating the cost per pound of BOD removed for each subcategory. . . . Although sulfite mills must make large investments in waste treatment facilities, the cost-benefit balance is favorable for the limitations on these mills, because of the large volume of waste they produce and thus the greater treatment efficiency.

[The court upheld EPA's cost-benefit analysis against all industry challenges.]

NOTES AND QUESTIONS

1. Do you agree with the industry's conception of "common sense"?

2. Exactly how would you describe the EPA's cost-benefit analysis? What was compared with what in performing the "limited" balancing?

3. Some commentators have suggested that the Clean Water Act's success can be traced largely to the fact that it does not rely largely on risk-benefit balancing. Ronald Outen notes that unlike the Toxic Substance Control Act, "which uses the most rational and economically sensitive decision criterion," the Clean Water Act

> requires removal of pollutants just because it is technologically and economically possible to do so. It is a classic case of treatment for treatment's sake, but it is the one law you can point to that actually has removed large quantities of pollutants from waste streams. Never mind that some of these pollutants merely have been transferred from one medium to another. The fact is, most people view the Clean Water Act as a major success story. [R. B. Outen, Environmental Pollution Laws and the Architecture of Tobacco Road, in National Research Council, Multimedia Approaches to Pollution Control 142 (1987).]

4. In an earlier case addressing the validity of issuing national uniform effluent standards on an industry-by-industry basis, the Supreme Court had stated that some procedure whereby an industry member could obtain a variance from the uniform standards must be part of the regulatory scheme. du Pont v. Train, 430 U.S. 112 (1977). The *Weyerhaeuser* case included an industry challenge that the EPA's variance procedures were too strict. In ruling on that challenge, the court held that

> the [provision for obtaining a variance from the BPCTCA standards] must at minimum allow a petitioning mill operator to seek a dispensation from any limitation that, as a whole, demands more of him than section 301(b) . . . allows EPA to demand of the industry as a whole. . . . [I]ndividual [mill] operators [must be allowed] to argue that, given the overall impact of an effluent limitation on their operations, they are faced with *stricter*

requirements than the Act authorizes EPA to place on the industry as a whole.

More specifically, section 301(b)(1)(A), as interpreted by *du Pont*, requires the application of [BPCTCA] for each industrial subcategory. . . . Under *du Pont*, therefore, a variance provision should allow . . . EPA to excuse mill operators from making more than the maximum use of technology practicably available to them. Pursuant to section 304(b)(1)(B), the outlines of practicability in each case depend upon "the local cost [to the operator] of application of technology in relation to the effluent reduction benefits to be achieved." . . . The precise interrelationship of these factors in making variance decisions, moreover, basically should track the scope and interrelationship that we have assigned them in developing the general, industry-wide limitations. [590 F.2d at 1035-1036.]

Why, then, cannot the Pacific Coast mill operators raise the receiving water issue through a variance proceeding? Aren't they entitled to an individualized, albeit limited, cost-benefit balancing in such a proceeding, and wouldn't such a cost-benefit balance favor them? *Weyerhaeuser*'s interpretation of the variance requirements under the Clean Water Act were sustained by the Supreme Court in EPA v. National Crushed Stone Assn., 449 U.S. 64 (1980).

5. Another case in which the industry litigants promoted their version of "common sense" involved the Occupational Safety and Health Act. It reached the Supreme Court in 1981 after the D.C. Circuit had rejected the industry's argument that OSHA was required to perform a cost-benefit analysis prior to establishing permissible exposure limits under the OSH Act. The case was argued on January 21, 1981, the day after the Reagan Administration assumed office. After oral argument, but before the case had been decided, OSHA asked the Court to remand the case for reconsideration in light of the new administration's emphasis on cost-benefit analysis. The Court refused and ultimately issued the following interpretation of the OSH Act.

American Textile Manufacturers Institute, Inc. v. Donovan
452 U.S. 490 (1981) (the Cotton Dust case)

[This case involved a disease called byssinosis, more commonly known as "brown lung" disease. It primarily affects textile workers, because it is caused by the inhalation of cotton dust. One study showed that over 25 percent of the sample of cotton workers suffered at least some form of the disease, while 35,000 workers suffer from the most disabling form. OSHA established a permissible exposure limit (PEL)

for cotton dust in the workplace, which the industry challenged.]
Justice BRENNAN delivered the opinion of the Court:

. . . The principal question presented in these cases is whether the Occupational Safety and Health Act requires the Secretary, in promulgating a standard pursuant to §6(b)(5) of the Act, to determine that the costs of the standard bear a reasonable relationship to its benefits. Relying on §§6(b)(5) and 3(8) of the Act, . . . petitioners urge not only that OSHA must show that a standard addresses a significant risk of material health impairment, but also that OSHA must demonstrate that the reduction in risk of material health impairment is significant in light of the costs of attaining that reduction. Respondents on the other hand contend that the Act requires OSHA to promulgate standards that eliminate or reduce such risks "to the extent such protection is technologically and economically feasible." . . .

The starting point of our analysis is the language of the statute itself. Section 6(b)(5) of the Act provides:

> The Secretary, in promulgating standards dealing with toxic materials or harmful physical agents under this subsection, shall set the standard which most adequately assures, *to the extent feasible*, on the basis of the best available evidence, that no employee will suffer material impairment of health or functional capacity even if such employee has regular exposure to the hazard dealt with by such standard for the period of his working life.

Although their interpretations differ, all parties agree that the phrase "to the extent feasible" contains the critical language in §6(b)(5) for purposes of this case.

The plain meaning of the word "feasible" supports respondents' interpretation of the statute. According to Webster's Third New International Dictionary of the English Language 831 (1976), "feasible" means "capable of being done, executed, or effected." Accord, The Oxford English Dictionary 116 (1933) ("Capable of being done, accomplished or carried out"); Funk & Wagnalls New "Standard" Dictionary of the English Language 903 (1957) ("That may be done, performed or effected"). Thus, §6(b)(5) directs the Secretary to issue the standard that "most adequately assures . . . that no employee will suffer material impairment of health," limited only by the extent to which this is "capable of being done." In effect then, as the Court of Appeals held, Congress itself defined the basic relationship between costs and benefits, by placing the "benefit" of worker health above all other considerations save those making attainment of this "benefit" unachieveable. Any standard based on a balancing of costs and benefits by the Secretary that strikes a different balance than that struck by Congress would be inconsistent with the command set forth in §6(b)(5). Thus, cost-benefit analysis by OSHA is not required by the statute because feasibility analysis is. . . . .

Even though the plain language of §6(b)(5) supports this construction, we must still decide whether §3(8), the general definition of an occupational safety and health standard, either alone or in tandem with §6(b)(5), incorporates a cost-benefit requirement for standards dealing with toxic materials or harmful physical agents. Section 3(8) of the Act provides:

> The term "occupational safety and health standard" means a standard which requires conditions, or the adoption or use of one or more practices, means, methods, operations, or processes, *reasonably necessary or appropriate* to provide safe or healthful employment and places of employment.

Taken alone, the phrase "reasonably necessary or appropriate" might be construed to contemplate some balancing of the costs and benefits of a standard. Petitioners urge that, so construed, §3(8) engrafts a cost-benefit analysis requirement on the issuance of §6(b)(5) standards, even if §6(b)(5) itself does not authorize such analysis. We need not decide whether §3(8), standing alone, would contemplate some form of cost-benefit analysis. For even if it does, Congress specifically chose in §6(b)(5) to impose separate and additional requirements for issuance of a subcategory of occupational safety and health standards dealing with toxic materials and harmful physical agents; it required that those standards be issued to prevent material impairment of health *to the extent feasible.* Congress could reasonably have concluded that health standards should be subject to different criteria than *safety* standards because of the special problems presented in regulating them.

Agreement with petitioners' argument that §3(8) imposes an additional and overriding requirement of cost-benefit analysis on the issuance of §6(b)(5) standards would eviscerate the "to the extent feasible" requirement. Standards would inevitably be set at the level indicated by cost-benefit analysis, and not at the level specified by §6(b)(5). For example, if cost-benefit analysis indicated a protective standard of 1000 $\mu g/m^3$ PEL, while feasibility analysis indicated a 500 $\mu g/m^3$ PEL, the agency would be forced by the cost-benefit requirement to choose the less stringent point. We cannot believe that Congress intended the general terms of §3(8) to countermand the specific feasibility requirement of §6(b)(5). Adoption of petitioners' interpretation would effectively write §6(b)(5) out of the Act. We decline to render Congress' decision to include a feasibility requirement nugatory, thereby offending the well-settled rule that all parts of a statute, if possible, are to be given effect. Congress did not contemplate any further balancing by the agency for toxic material and harmful physical agents standards, and we should not "impute to Congress a purpose to paralyze with one hand what it sought to promote with the other."

NOTES AND QUESTIONS

1. From the perspective of an environmentalist or a person concerned about workers' health, is the result in the *Cotton Dust* case an unambiguous victory? The Court refers to a hypothetical case in which risk-benefit balancing would indicate a PEL of 1,000 micrograms per cubic meter, while feasibility analysis would dictate a PEL of 500 micrograms per cubic meter. Is it clear that the feasibility standard will always be the more stringent? Can you think of any factors that might result in its being less stringent? Recall that when OSHA promulgated what it deemed to be the most stringent feasible PEL for asbestos, the Agency conceded that workers would still be subject to significant risks (cancer risks of 7 in 1,000). 51 Fed. Reg. 22,612 (1986). Yet EPA, applying risk-benefit analysis under TSCA, later banned most uses of asbestos when it found that they present unreasonable risks to health. 54 Fed. Reg. 24,960 (1989). Which type of standard do you think most frequently will produce the more stringent regulations—the feasibility standard or risk-benefit balancing?

2. In the *Cotton Dust* case, the Supreme Court held that OSHA was not required to do risk-benefit balancing in implementing the OSH Act. Recall, however, the Supreme Court in the *Benzene* decision had earlier held that OSHA had to perform some kind of assessment of risk before it could regulate a toxic chemical in the workplace. Industrial Union Department v. American Petroleum Institute, 448 U.S. 607 (1980), above. A "safe" workplace environment, the Court said, was not a "risk-free" environment. Thus, while it is true that OSHA was not instructed to balance risks against benefits in the way preferred by cost-benefit analysts, it was told to "assess risk" before it acted. The Supreme Court did not define "significant risk" in terms of some explicit numerical level of risk, but under its mandate OSHA now engages in *quantitative risk assessment* before regulating toxics. See, e.g., its regulation of arsenic, 48 Fed. Reg. 1864 (1983).

3. Many other environmental statutes similarly direct the agency to focus its attention on the hazards posed by chemicals and other potential disease-causing or environment-damaging substances. (Section 112 of the Clean Air Act, for example, requires EPA to regulate toxic chemicals in the atmosphere so as to "protect human health" with "an ample margin of safety.") The *Benzene* decision's pronouncement that "safe" does not mean "risk-free" and its corollary that an agency must determine that a risk is "significant" before taking regulatory action have resulted in agencies' performing more and more quantitative risk assessments. Thus even where the use of risk-benefit balancing to set standards, as called for under Executive Order 12,291, is not required by law, agencies are performing quantitative risk assessments before taking action.

4. Some argue that it is presumptively necessary to perform a form of risk-benefit balancing even to implement purely health-based mandates. This argument, which has been identified with the phrase "richer is safer," maintains that the costs regulation imposes on society also affect health adversely by making us poorer and less able to afford health care. Thus, at some point regulations designed to protect public health actually may be so costly that they result in more deaths than they prevent. Consider how this argument is used in the following case, which involved a challenge to an OSHA regulation designed to protect workers not from exposure to toxic chemicals, but rather from injury by industrial equipment.

International Union, UAW v. OSHA
938 F.2d 1310 (D.C. Cir. 1991)
(Lockout/Tagout)

Before WILLIAMS, HENDERSON and RANDOLPH, Circuit Judges.
STEPHEN F. WILLIAMS, Circuit Judge:

[OSHA had promulgated a regulation requiring the placement of locks or tags on certain industrial equipment to prevent it from operating unexpectedly and to alert workers to such dangers. This "lockout/tagout" rule was challenged by the National Association of Manufacturers (NAM). NAM argued that because the rule was not a health standard promulgated under §6(b)(5), which requires protection of worker health "to the extent feasible" against "toxic materials or harmful physical agents," OSHA should be required to base its decision on cost-benefit analysis. OSHA maintained that it could impose any restriction it chose so long as it was feasible. NAM argued that this interpretation would result in a delegation of legislative authority to OSHA that was unconstitutionally overbroad. After focusing on the "reasonably necessary or appropriate" language of §3(8), which had inspired the Supreme Court's Benzene Decision, the court considered whether this could be construed to require cost-benefit analysis.]

II . . .

B

The NAM argues (as a fallback to its nondelegation claim) that Congress's use of "reasonably necessary or appropriate" in §3(8) contemplates "cost-benefit" analysis. See NAM Brief at 24-25. Under this interpretation, in imposing standards under §6(b) but outside the realm of toxics, OSHA may adopt a safety standard if its benefits outweigh its costs, and not otherwise.

Cost-benefit analysis is certainly consistent with the language of §3(8). "Reasonableness" has long been associated with the balancing of costs and benefits. The "reasonable" person of tort fame is one who takes a precaution if the gravity of the injuries averted, adjusted for their probability, exceeds the precaution's burden. United States v. Carroll Towing Co., 159 F.2d 169, 173 (2d Cir. 1947).

And while the legislative history is almost blank on the subject, it suggests concern with market failures, see, e.g., S. Rep. No. 1282, supra, at 4, reprinted in Leg. Hist. at 144, and properly conducted cost-benefit analysis should yield a solution approximating that of a market undistorted by market failures. Application of cost-benefit analysis to safety standards also gives effect to Congress's distinction between slow-acting hazards and others, with its "particular concern for health hazards of 'unprecedented complexity' that had resulted from chemicals whose toxic effects 'are only now being discovered.' " *Benzene*, 448 U.S. at 692 (Marshall, J., dissenting).

Moreover, courts have often taken the word "reasonable" in a statute to require that burdens be justified by the resulting benefits. For example, in Consolidated Rail Corp. v. ICC, 646 F.2d 642 (D.C. Cir. 1981), this court reviewed an Interstate Commerce Commission adjudication of some shippers' claims that a rate based on the expense of certain safety precautions was not "reasonable," as required by the controlling statute, because the precautions themselves were excessive and therefore unreasonable. We read the statutory criterion as requiring cost-benefit analysis for such costs, which we defined with considerable care:

> The safety measures for which expenditures are made must be reasonable ones, which means first, that they produce an expected safety benefit commensurate to their cost; and second, that when compared with other possible safety measures, they represent an economical means of achieving the expected safety benefit.

Id. at 648.

Similarly, where Congress authorized the Consumer Product Safety Commission to regulate hazards that create "an unreasonable risk" of consumer injury, we understood it to invoke the balancing test of negligence law and to authorize regulation only where the severity of the injury (adjusted for likelihood) offset the harm that the regulation would impose on manufacturers and consumers. . . .

We briefly note the Fifth Circuit's reading of §3(8), parts of which appear to agree with our own. It has stated that §3(8) requires "a specie [sic] of cost-benefit justification." National Grain & Feed Ass'n v. OSHA, 866 F.2d 717, 733 (5th Cir. 1989). At first glance, *National Grain* appears to contemplate an insistence that costs not outweigh benefits, see, e.g.,

Asbestos Information Ass'n v. OSHA, 727 F.2d 415, 423 (5th Cir. 1984), which accords with our understanding of cost-benefit analysis.

But the Fifth Circuit approach seemingly advocates consideration of costs exclusively in terms of impact on the regulated firms (as opposed to workers and consumers). Thus the court said in *Asbestos Information Ass'n*, "The protection afforded to workers should *outweigh* the economic consequences to the regulated industry." Id. (emphasis added). Evidently explicating that thought, it seemed to approve the idea that where "the cost of compliance is less than one cent per dollar [of industry sales]," and the danger is "grave," the agency has met its burden. Id. at 424. The court never explains the exclusive focus on firms. In an industry providing a good for which there are no close substitutes (i.e., facing an inelastic demand curve), firms would be scarcely affected at all: their reactions would be some combination of avoiding the costs by substituting equipment for labor, passing the costs back to labor in the form of reduced cash wages, and passing them forward to their consumers in the form of higher prices. We do not understand why one should call an analysis "cost-benefit" if it disregards costs borne by workers and consumers. The exclusion seems especially odd for application of a worker-protection statute; consumers are, after all, mostly workers.

As there appear to be many confusions about cost-benefit analysis, it may be important to make clear what we are *not* saying when we identify it as a reasonable interpretation of §3(8) as applied outside the §6(b)(5) realm. Cost-benefit analysis requires identifying values for lost years of human life and for suffering and other losses from non-fatal injuries. Nothing we say here should be taken as confining the discretion of OSHA to choose among reasonable evaluation methods. While critics of cost-benefit analysis argue that any such valuation is impossible, that is so only in the sense that pin-point figures are necessarily arbitrary, so that the decisionmaker is effectively limited to considering some range of values. In fact, we make implicit life and safety valuations each day when we decide, for example, whether to travel by train or car, the former being more costly (at least if several family members are traveling together) but safer per passenger-mile. Where government makes decisions for others, it may reasonably be expected to make the trade-offs somewhat more explicitly than individuals choosing for themselves. The difficulty of securing agreement even on a range of values hardly justifies making decisions on the basis of a pretense that resources are not scarce. In any event, OSHA has an existing obligation under Executive Order No. 12,291, 46 Fed. Reg. 13,193 (1981), to complete a cost-benefit analysis for each major rulemaking, so use of such a standard not only is doable in the qualified sense of which we have spoken but can be done without additional regulatory resources.

Thus, cost-benefit analysis entails only a systematic weighing of pros and cons, or what Benjamin Franklin referred to as a "moral or prudential algebra." Writing to a friend who was perplexed by a difficult decision, he explained his own approach:

> When those difficult cases occur, they are difficult, chiefly because while we have them under consideration, all the reasons pro and con are not present to the mind at the same time. . . . To get over this, my way is to divide half a sheet of paper by a line into two columns; writing over the one Pro, and over the other Con. Then, during three or four days consideration, I put down under the different heads short hints of the different motives, that at different times occur to me, for or against the measure. When I have thus got them all together in one view, I endeavor to estimate their respective weights. . . . And, though the weight of reasons cannot be taken with the precision of algebraic quantities, yet when each is thus considered, separately and comparatively, and the whole lies before me, I think I can judge better, and am less liable to make a rash step, and in fact I have found great advantage from this kind of equation, in what may be called moral or prudential algebra.

Reprinted in Edward M. Gramlich, Benefit-Cost Analysis of Government Programs 1-2 (1981).

As we accept the NAM's contention that §3(8)'s "reasonably necessary or appropriate" criterion can reasonably be read as requiring cost-benefit analysis, we must reject its nondelegation claim.

We hold only that cost-benefit is a *permissible* interpretation of §3(8). Given the ambiguity inherent in that section, there may be other interpretations that conform to nondelegation principles. Accordingly we remand to OSHA, noting that its treatment of some of the parties' other claims, discussed below, will likely turn on its decision. . . .

[The court then turned to NAM's challenges to OSHA's findings of "significant risk."]

III . . .

A

The Court in *Benzene* construed §3(8) of the Act to require that OSHA, before issuing any permanent standard, determine the existence of a "significant risk" to health or safety. 448 U.S. at 639. The NAM argues that there is not enough evidence in the record to support OSHA's finding of significant risk. Although it does not question OSHA's finding that the lockout regulation could prevent 122 fatalities and 28,400 lost workday injuries annually, see 54 Fed. Reg. at 36,652/3, it objects to the agency's failure to disaggregate the data industry by industry, even in the face of uncontested data showing that the variations are great, with injuries declining to zero in many industries.

How much risk is "significant" may well depend on the relevant substantive standard. *Benzene's* insistence on significant risk arose explicitly from the Court's concern that insignificant risks should not be allowed to "justify pervasive regulation limited only by the constraint of feasibility." 448 U.S. at 645. For regulations under §6(b)(5), the logic of *Benzene* thus calls for a fairly high standard of significance. For regulations outside of §6(b)(5) and constrained only by §3(8), however, *if* the standard for such regulations is indeed cost-benefit, even a slight risk might be considered significant if it could be reduced or eliminated at a cost (including costs of enforcement and compliance) less than the resulting benefits.

Uncontrolled energy unquestionably poses greater risks in some industries than in others. Even among the manufacturing industries that OSHA classifies as "high impact" for purposes of the lockout regulation, a report by OSHA's consultants shows a nearly 20-fold difference between the high and low injury rates. And the observed injury rate was zero in many of the "low impact" and "negligible impact" industries covered by the lockout regulation. Id.

OSHA nowhere explains its logic. Just because paper mill equipment (which was already subject to a lockout requirement) poses a significant hazard does not mean that sewing machines do. While we have recognized OSHA's need to avoid "minuscule industry subcategories" for administrative convenience, see Building & Construction Trades Dept. v. Brock, 838 F.2d at 1272-73, there are no obvious barriers to disaggregation here. In fact, OSHA has in past years promulgated a wide variety of industry and equipment-specific lockout standards. As we have insisted that OSHA explain its refusal to disaggregate at the behest of unions claiming that reliance on overbroad categories denied them adequate protection, id., we similarly remand for it to explain how its aggregated approach here conforms to its interpretation of the Act.

[The court remanded the case to OSHA "to address 'significant risk' in terms of whatever substantive meaning it lawfully assigns to §3(8), and particularly to explain its decision to impose lockout/tagout even where the risk appears to be diminutive or zero." However, the court did not immediately vacate the rule pending the outcome of the remand, noting that parts of it "may well have genuine life-saving effects and are highly likely to survive re-examination."] . . .

STEPHEN F. WILLIAMS, Circuit Judge, concurring:
I write separately to address the UAW's apparent assumption that application of the significant risk/feasibility analysis associated with §6(b)(5) is necessarily more protective of health and safety than a cost-benefit criterion. This is not self-evidently true.

First, if OSHA applies cost-benefit analysis, then more risks seem likely to qualify as "significant" within the meaning of *Benzene;* many risks that may seem insignificant if their discovery triggers regulatory burdens limited only by feasibility, as under §6(b)(5), may be significant if the consequence is cost-justified corrective measures. Cf. Cass R. Sunstein, After the Rights Revolution 196 (1990) (explaining *Benzene*'s significant risk requirement as an artificial device for handling the unlimited character of the regulatory burden).

Second, even where the application of cost-benefit analysis would result in less stringent regulation, the reduced stringency is not necessarily adverse to health or safety. More regulation means some combination of reduced value of firms, higher product prices, fewer jobs in the regulated industry, and lower cash wages. All the latter three stretch workers' budgets tighter (as does the first to the extent that the firms' stock is held in workers' pension trusts). And larger incomes enable people to lead safer lives. One study finds a 1 percent increase in income associated with a mortality reduction of about 0.05 percent. Jack Hadley & Anthony Osei, "Does Income Affect Mortality?," 20 Medical Care 901, 913 (September 1982). Another suggests that each $7.5 million of costs generated by regulation may, under certain assumptions, induce one fatality. Ralph L. Keeney, "Mortality Risks Induced by Economic Expenditures," 10 Risk Analysis 147, 155 (1990) (relying on E. M. Kitagawa & P. M. Hauser, Differential Mortality in the United States of America: A Study of Socioeconomic Epidemiology (1973)). Larger incomes can produce health by enlarging a person's access to better diet, preventive medical care, safer cars, greater leisure, etc. See Aaron Wildavsky, Searching for Safety 59-71 (1988).

Of course, other causal relations may be at work too. Healthier people may be able to earn higher income, and characteristics and advantages that facilitate high earnings (e.g., work ethic, education) may also lead to better health. Compare C. P. Wen, et al., "Anatomy of the Healthy Worker Effect: A Critical Review," 25 J. of Occupation Medicine 283 (1983). Nonetheless, higher income can secure better health, and there is no basis for a causal assumption that more stringent regulation will always save lives.

It follows that while officials involved in health or safety regulation may naturally be hesitant to set any kind of numerical value on human life,[1] undue squeamishness may be deadly. Incremental safety regulation

---

1. Preference-based techniques are a commonly used approach, but are subject to such pitfalls as wealth bias, age bias and inconsistency. See, e.g., Lewis A. Kornhauser, "The Value of Life," 38 Clev. St. L. Rev. 209 (1990). For example, if estimates of the benefit of reducing risks are based on the affected workers' willingness to pay for risk reduction, low-paid workers will receive less protection than better paid ones. See id. at 221. There are, however, solutions. The wealth bias problem, for example, could be avoided by estimating the willingness to pay of persons of median or mean wealth. See id. at 221-22.

reduces incomes and thus may exact a cost in human lives. For example, if analysis showed that "an individual life was lost for every $12 million taken from individuals [as a result of the regulation], this would be a guide to a reasonable value tradeoff for many programs designed to save lives." Keeney, "Mortality Risks Induced by Economic Expenditures," 10 Risk Analysis at 158. Such a figure could serve as a ceiling for value-of-life calculated by other means, since regulation causing greater expenditures per life expected to be saved would, everything else being equal, result in a net *loss* of life.

NOTES AND QUESTIONS

1. Is the court's conclusion that the OSH Act requires some limiting principle—such as cost-benefit analysis—to avoid an unconstitutional delegation of legislative authority to OSHA consistent with the Supreme Court's rejection of Justice Rehnquist's opinion in the *Benzene* decision? The D.C. Circuit here interprets the lockout-tagout rule as not falling within the rubric of section 6(b)(5)'s standards for worker protection against toxic materials or harmful physical agents.

2. Is Judge Williams's conclusion that it is permissible to interpret section 3(8) of the OSH Act as authorizing cost-benefit analysis consistent with the Supreme Court's *Cotton Dust* decision?

3. The *Lockout/Tagout* decision raises the question of how far agencies should go in attempting to trace all the side effects of regulation. Cf. Metropolitan Edison Co. v. People Against Nuclear Energy, 460 U.S. 766 (1983) (NRC need not consider psychological impact of restarting companion nuclear power plant at Three Mile Island in performing environmental impact assessment). Judge Williams argues that costs borne by consumers should be considered as well. Do you agree? Is it reasonable to assume that regulation also might have *beneficial* side effects not taken into account in conventional cost-benefit analyses (e.g., preventing deaths of workers might reduce emotional and economic damage to families and friends)? Judge Henderson did not join the portion of the majority opinion that discussed the use of cost-benefit analysis, and Judge Williams wrote alone in articulating the "richer is safer" rationale in his unusual concurrence to his own majority opinion.

4. How does Judge Williams respond to critics of cost-benefit analysis who argue that it is impossible to place a valuation on all relevant benefits of regulation?

5. Does the "richer is safer" argument articulated in Judge Williams's concurrence suggest that cost-benefit analysis should be used even to implement a purely health-based regulatory statute? How could such an analysis be performed? See Anderson, Hazards of Risk Assessment, 351 Nature 176 (1991).

6. In March 1992 OMB cited Judge Williams's "richer is safer" argument in blocking OSHA from proposing a regulation. Noting Judge Williams's suggestion that every $7.5 million in reduced income could cause an additional death, OMB argued that a regulation costing $163 million per year actually would cause 22 additional deaths, rather than saving the 8 to 13 lives that OSHA had estimated. Swoboda, OMB's Logic: Less Protection Saves Lives, Wash. Post, Mar. 17, 1992, at A15. After this incident was publicized, OMB agreed to let OSHA propose the regulations, though it insists that the "richer is safer" issue be addressed in the rulemaking.

D. TSCA AND RISK-BENEFIT BALANCING: WHERE SHOULD THE BALANCE BE STRUCK?

The Toxic Substances Control Act is a classic example of a risk-benefit balancing statute. In fact, the term "unreasonable risk" appears 35 times in 33 pages of the statute. Rodgers, The Lesson of the Owls and the Crows: The Role of Deception in the Evolution of the Environmental Statutes, 4 J. Land Use & Envtl. L. 377, 379 (1989). TSCA grants EPA broad authority to regulate the manufacture, processing, distribution, use, or disposal of any chemical substance on a finding that there is a "reasonable basis to conclude" that such an activity "presents or will present an unreasonable risk of injury to health or the environment," TSCA §6(a), 15 U.S.C. §2605(a). In determining whether a substance poses an "unreasonable risk," TSCA explicitly requires EPA to make findings concerning not only health and environmental effects, but also the benefits of various uses of the substance, the availability of substitutes for it, and "the reasonably ascertainable economic consequences" of regulation. TSCA §6(c)(1), 15 U.S.C. §2605(c)(1).

Although TSCA does not specify how this risk-benefit balancing is to be performed, it directs EPA to regulate "to the extent necessary to protect adequately against such risk using the least burdensome requirements." TSCA §6(a), 15 U.S.C. §2605(a). This suggests that EPA is to determine what balance between risks and benefits is adequately protective and then to determine the least burdensome means of achieving it. While TSCA explicitly requires EPA to consider the economic impact of regulation and the benefits of the substance to be regulated, EPA has not established any firm guidelines for determining when the cost of regulation would render a risk reasonable. The legislative history of TSCA indicates that Congress did not envision that EPA would have to perform formal cost-benefit analyses. The House Committee report on the legislation explained that the balancing required by section 6 "does not require a formal benefit-cost analysis" because "such an analysis would not be very useful" given the difficulty of assigning monetary values to benefits and costs of chemical regulation. Toxic Substances Control Act, Report by the Comm. on Interstate and Foreign Commerce, U.S. House of Representatives, H.R. Rep. 94-1341, 94th Cong., 2d Sess. 14 (1976). The Senate Committee report emphasized that while section 6(c) required some balancing, "it is not feasible to reach a decision just on the basis of quantitative comparisons" because "[i]n comparing risks, costs, and benefits . . . one is weighing noncommensurates." It stressed that EPA also must give "full consideration" to the extraordinary "burdens of human suffering and premature death." Toxic Substances Control Act, Report of the Senate Comm. on Commerce, S. Rep. 94-698, 94th Cong., 2d Sess. 13 (1976).

The best illustration of how EPA performs risk-benefit analysis is the story of the Agency's efforts to regulate asbestos risks under section 6 of TSCA. Acutely aware of the enormous difficulty of protecting the public from asbestos in schools and buildings, EPA announced in 1979 that it would consider banning all remaining uses of asbestos. 44 Fed. Reg. 60,061 (1979). It took EPA nearly ten years to promulgate such a rule, after developing a 45,000-page record. EPA's rationale for the rule is described in the following excerpt from the Federal Register notice that accompanied it.

EPA, Asbestos: Manufacture, Importation, Processing, and Distribution in Commerce Prohibitions
54 Fed. Reg. 29,460 (1989)

EPA is issuing this final rule under section 6 of the Toxic Substance Control Act (TSCA) to prohibit, at staged intervals, the future manufacture, importation, processing, and distribution in commerce of asbestos in almost all products, as identified in this rule. EPA is issuing this rule to reduce the unreasonable risks presented to human health by exposure to asbestos during activities involving these products. . . .

Section 6 of TSCA authorizes EPA to promulgate a rule prohibiting or limiting the amount of a chemical substance that may be manufactured, processed, or distributed in commerce in the U.S. if EPA finds that there is a reasonable basis to conclude that the manufacture, processing, distribution in commerce, use, or disposal of the chemical substance, or any combination of these activities, presents or will present an unreasonable risk of injury to human health or the environment. . . .

To determine whether a risk from activities involving asbestos-containing products presents an unreasonable risk, EPA must balance the probability that harm will occur from the activities against the effects of the proposed regulatory action on the availability to society of the benefits of asbestos. EPA has considered these factors in conjunction with the extensive record gathered in the development of this rule. EPA has concluded that the continued manufacture, importation, processing, and distribution in commerce of most asbestos-containing products poses an unreasonable risk to human health. This conclusion is based on information summarized [below].

EPA has concluded that exposure to asbestos during the life cycles of many asbestos-containing products poses an unreasonable risk of injury to human health. EPA has also concluded that section 6 of TSCA is the ideal statutory authority to regulate the risks posed by asbestos exposure. This rule's pollution prevention actions under TSCA are both the preferable and the least burdensome means of controlling the exposure risks posed throughout the life cycle of asbestos-containing products. Findings supporting this conclusion include the following:

1. Exposure to asbestos causes many painful, premature deaths due to mesothelioma and lung, gastrointestinal, and other cancers, as well as asbestosis and other diseases. Risks attributable to asbestos exposure and addressed by this rule are serious and are calculated for this rule using direct evidence from numerous human epidemiological studies. Studies show that asbestos is a highly potent carcinogen and that severe health effects occur after even short-term, high-level or longer-term, low-level exposures to asbestos. Asbestos exposure is compatible with a linear, no-threshold dose-response model for lung cancer. In addition, there is no undisputed evidence of quantitative differences in potency based on fiber size or type.

For the quantitative risk assessment performed as part of this rule-making, EPA used dose-response constants for lung cancer and mesothelioma that were the geometric means of the "best estimates" from a number of epidemiological studies. If EPA had instead used an upper bound estimate, as is normally done by the scientific community and in EPA regulatory risk assessment when only data from animal studies is available to extrapolate human health risk, predicted lung cancer deaths could increase by a factor of 10 and mesothelioma deaths could increase by a factor of 20.

2. People are frequently unknowingly exposed to asbestos and are rarely in a position to protect themselves. Asbestos is generally invisible, odorless, very durable, and highly aerodynamic. It can travel long distances and exist in the environment for extended periods. Therefore, exposure can take place long after the release of asbestos and at a distant location from the source of the release.

3. Additions to the current stock of asbestos-containing products would contribute to the environmental loading of asbestos. This poses the potential for an increased risk to the general population of asbestos-related disease and an increased risk to future generations because of asbestos' longevity.

4. Asbestos fibers are released to the air at many stages of the

commercial life of the products that are subject to this rule. Activities that might lead to the release of asbestos include mining of the substance, processing asbestos fibers into products, and transport, installation, use, maintainance, repair, removal, and disposal of asbestos-containing products. EPA has found that the occupational and nonoccupational exposure existing over the entire life cycles of each of the banned asbestos-containing products poses a high level of individual risk. EPA has determined that thousands of persons involved in the manufacture, processing, transport, installation, use, repair, removal, and disposal of the asbestos-containing products affected by this rule are exposed to a serious lifetime asbestos exposure risk, despite OSHA's relatively low workplace PEL. In addition, according to the EPA Asbestos Modeling Study, millions of members of the general U.S. population are exposed to elevated levels of lifetime risk due to asbestos released throughout the life cycle of asbestos-containing products. EPA believes that the exposures quantified for the analyses supporting this rule represent an understatement of actual exposure.

5. Release of asbestos fibers from many products during life cycle activities can be substantial. OSHA stated in setting its PEL of 0.2 f/cc that remaining exposures pose a serious risk because of limitations on available control technologies. Even with OSHA's controls, thousands of workers involved in the manufacture and processing of asbestos-containing products are exposed to a lifetime risk of 1 in 1,000 of developing cancer. Many other exposures addressed by this rule are not affected by engineering controls required by OSHA's PEL or by other government regulation. Because asbestos is a highly potent carcinogen, the uncontrolled high peak episodic exposures that are faced by large populations pose a significant risk.

6. Because of the life cycle or "cradle-to-grave" nature of the risk posed by asbestos, attempts by OSHA, the Consumer Product Safety Commission (CPSC), and other EPA offices to regulate the continued commercial use of asbestos still leave many persons unprotected from the hazards of asbestos exposure. Technological limitations inhibit the effectiveness of existing or possible exposure control actions under non-TSCA authorities. Many routes of asbestos exposure posed by the products subject to this rule are outside the jurisdiction of regulatory authorities other than TSCA. EPA has determined that the residual exposure to asbestos that exists despite the actions taken under other authorities poses a serious health risk throughout the life cycle of many asbestos-containing products. This residual exposure can only be adequately controlled by the exposure prevention actions taken in this rule.

7. Despite the proven risks of asbestos exposure and the current or imminent existence of suitable substitutes for most uses of asbestos, asbestos continues to be used in large quantities in the U.S. in the manufacture or processing of a wide variety of commercial products. Total

annual U.S. consumption of asbestos dropped from a 1984 total of about 240,000 metric tons to less than 85,000 metric tons in 1987, according to the U.S. Department of Interior, Bureau of Mines data. This change suggests that the use of substitutes has increased markedly since the proposal. However, the 1987 consumption total indicates that significant exposure due to the commercial use of asbestos and the resultant risks would continue for the foreseeable future absent the actions taken in this rule.

Evidence supports the conclusion that substitutes already exist or will soon exist for each of the products that are subject to the rule's bans. In scheduling products for the different stages of the bans, EPA has analyzed the probable availability of non-asbestos substitutes. In the rule, the various asbestos products are scheduled to be banned at times when it is likely that suitable non-asbestos substitutes will be available. However, the rule also includes an exemption provision to account for instances in which technology might not have advanced sufficiently by the time of a ban to produce substitutes for certain specialized or limited uses of asbestos.

8. EPA has calculated that the product bans in this rule will result in the avoidance of 202 quantifiable cancer cases, if benefits are not discounted, and 148 cases, if benefits are discounted at 3 percent. The figures decrease to 164 cases, if benefits are not discounted, and 120 cases, if benefits are discounted at 3 percent, if analogous exposures are not included in the analysis. In all likelihood, the rule will result in the avoidance of a large number of other cancer cases that cannot be quantified, as well as many cases of asbestos-related diseases. Estimates of benefits resulting from the action taken in this rule are limited to mesothelioma and lung and gastrointestinal cancer cases avoided, and do not include cases of asbestosis and other diseases avoided and avoided costs from treating asbestos diseases, lost productivity, or other factors.

EPA has estimated that the cost of this rule, for the 13-year period of the analyses performed, will be approximately $456.89 million, or $806.51 million if a 1 percent annual decline in the price of substitutes is not assumed. This cost will be spread over time and a large population so that the cost to any person is likely to be negligible. In addition, the rule's exemption provision is a qualitative factor that supports the actions taken in this rule. EPA has concluded that the quantifiable and unquantifiable benefits of the rule's staged-ban of the identified asbestos-containing products will outweigh the resultant economic consequences to consumers, producers, and users of the products.

9. EPA has determined that, within the findings required by section 6 of TSCA, only the staged-ban approach employed in this final rule will adequately control the asbestos exposure risk posed by the product categories affected by this rule. Other options either fail to address significant portions of the life cycle risk posed by products subject to the

rule or are unreasonably burdensome. EPA has, therefore, concluded that the actions taken in this rule represent the least burdensome means of reducing the risk posed by exposure to asbestos during the life cycles of the products that are subject to the bans.

10. Based on the reasons summarized in this preamble, this rule bans most asbestos-containing products in the U.S. because they pose an unreasonable risk to human health. These banned products account for approximately 94 percent of U.S. asbestos consumption, based on 1985 consumption figures. The actions taken will result in a substantial reduction in the unreasonable risk caused by asbestos exposure in the U.S.

The asbestos industry challenged EPA's asbestos ban in the following action.

Corrosion Proof Fittings v. EPA
947 F.2d 1201 (5th Cir. 1991)

JERRY E. SMITH, Circuit Judge:

The Environmental Protection Agency (EPA) issued a final rule under section 6 of the Toxic Substances Control Act (TSCA) to prohibit the future manufacture, importation, processing, and distribution of asbestos in almost all products. Petitioners claim that the EPA's rule-making procedure was flawed and that the rule was not promulgated on the basis of substantial evidence. . . .

[The court recited the facts and procedural history of the rule-making and disposed of several procedural issues, including a challenge to the standing of several of the petitioners. It then proceeded to analyze the statutory requirements that the administrator have a "reasonable basis" to conclude that asbestos presents an "unreasonable risk" and that he or she choose the "least burdensome" regulations "to protect adequately against such risk." TSCA §6(a).]

1. LEAST BURDENSOME AND REASONABLE

TSCA requires that the EPA use the least burdensome regulation to achieve its goals of minimum reasonable risk. This statutory requirement can create problems in evaluating just what is a "reasonable risk." Congress's rejection of a no-risk policy, however, also means that in certain cases, the least burdensome yet still adequate solution may entail somewhat more risk than would other, known regulations that are far more burdensome on the industry and the economy. The very language of TSCA requires that the EPA, once it has determined what an acceptable level of non-zero risk is, choose the least burdensome method of reaching that level.

In this case, the EPA banned, for all practical purposes, all present and future uses of asbestos—a position the petitioners characterize as the "death penalty alternative," as this is the *most* burdensome of all possible alternatives listed as open to the EPA under TSCA. TSCA not only provides the EPA with a list of alternative actions, but also provides those alternatives in order of how burdensome they are. [TSCA §6(a)(1)-(7); 15 U.S.C. §2605a(1)-(7).] Total bans head the list as the most burdensome regulatory option.

By choosing the harshest remedy given to it under TSCA, the EPA assigned to itself the toughest burden in satisfying TSCA's requirement that its alternative be the least burdensome of all those offered to it. . . . [T]he EPA's regulation cannot stand if there is any other regulation that would achieve an acceptable level of risk as mandated by TSCA. . . .

The EPA considered, and rejected, such options as labeling asbestos products, thereby warning users and workers involved in the manufacture of asbestos-containing products of the chemical's dangers, and stricter workplace rules. EPA also rejected controlled use of asbestos in the workplace and deferral to other government agencies charged with worker and consumer exposure to industrial and product hazards, such as OSHA, the CPSC, and the Mine Safety and Health Administration (MSHA). The EPA determined that deferral to these other agencies was inappropriate because no one other authority could address all the risks posed "throughout the life cycle" by asbestos, and any action by one or more of the other agencies still would leave an unacceptable residual risk.

Much of the EPA's analysis is correct, and the EPA's basic decision to use TSCA as a comprehensive statute designed to fight a multi-industry problem was a proper one that we uphold today on review. What concerns us, however, is the manner in which the EPA conducted some of its analysis. TSCA requires the EPA to consider, along with the effects of toxic substances on human health and the environment, "the benefits of such substance[s] or mixture[s] for various uses and the availability of substitutes for such uses," as well as "the reasonably ascertainable economic consequences of the rule, after consideration for the effect on the national economy, small business, technological innovation, the environment, and public health." Id. §2605(c)(1)(C-D).

The EPA presented two comparisons in the record: a world with no further regulation under TSCA, and a world in which no manufacture of asbestos takes place. The EPA rejected calculating how many lives a less burdensome regulation would save, and at what cost. Furthermore the EPA, when calculating the benefits of its ban, explicitly refused to compare it to an improved workplace in which currently available control technology is utilized. See 54 Fed. Reg. at 29,474. This decision artificially inflated the purported benefits of the rule by using a baseline comparison substantially lower than what currently available technology could yield. . . .

This comparison of two static worlds is insufficient to satisfy the dictates of TSCA. While the EPA may have shown that a world with a complete ban of asbestos might be preferable to one in which there is only the current amount of regulation, the EPA has failed to show that there is not some intermediate state of regulation that would be superior to both the currently-regulated and the completely-banned world. Without showing that asbestos regulation would be ineffective, the EPA cannot discharge its TSCA burden of showing that its regulation is the least burdensome available to it.

Upon an initial showing of product danger, the proper course for the EPA to follow is to consider each regulatory option, beginning with the least burdensome, and the costs and benefits of regulation under each option. The EPA cannot simply skip several rungs, as it did in this case, for in doing so, it may skip a less-burdensome alternative mandated by TSCA. Here, although the EPA mentions the problems posed by intermediate levels of regulation, it takes no steps to calculate the costs and benefits of these intermediate levels. See 54 Fed. Reg. at 29,462, 29,474. Without doing this it is impossible, both for the EPA and for this court on review, to know that none of these alternatives was less burdensome than the ban in fact chosen by the agency. . . .

2. THE EPA'S CALCULATIONS

Furthermore, we are concerned about some of the methodology employed by the EPA in making various of the calculations that it did perform. In order to aid the EPA's reconsideration of this and other cases, we present our concerns here.

First, we note that there was some dispute in the record regarding the appropriateness of discounting the perceived benefits of the EPA's rule. . . .

Although various commentators dispute whether it ever is appropriate to discount benefits when they are measured in human lives, we note that it would skew the results to discount only costs without according similar treatment to the benefits side of the equation. Adopting the position of the commentators who advocate not discounting benefits would force the EPA similarly not to calculate costs in present discounted real terms, making comparisons difficult. Furthermore, in evaluating situations in which different options incur costs at varying time intervals, the EPA would not be able to take into account that soon-to-be-incurred costs are more harmful than postponable costs. Because the EPA must discount costs to perform its evaluations properly, the EPA also should discount benefits to preserve an apples-to-apples comparison, even if this entails discounting benefits of a non-monetary nature. See What Price Posterity?, The Economist, March 23, 1991, at 73 (explaining use of discount rates for non-monetary goods). . . .

Of more concern to us is the failure of the EPA to compute the costs and benefits of its proposed rule past the year 2000, and its double-counting of the costs of asbestos use. In performing its calculus, the EPA only included the number of lives saved over the next thirteen years, and counted any additional lives saved as simply "unquantified benefits." 54 Fed. Reg. at 29,486. The EPA and intervenors now seek to use these unquantified lives saved to justify calculations as to which the benefits seem far outweighed by the astronomical costs. For example, the EPA plans to save about three lives with its ban of asbestos pipe, at a cost of $128-227 million (i.e., approximately $43-76 million per life saved). Although the EPA admits that the price tag is high, it claims that the lives saved past the year 2000 justify the price. See generally id. at 29,473 (explaining use of unquantified benefits).

Such calculations not only lessen the value of the EPA's cost analysis, but also make any meaningful judicial review impossible. While TSCA contemplates a useful place for unquantified benefits beyond the EPA's calculation, unquantified benefits never were intended as a trump card allowing the EPA to justify any cost calculus, no matter how high.

The concept of unquantified benefits, rather, is intended to allow the EPA to provide a rightful place for any remaining benefits that are impossible to quantify after the EPA's best attempt, but which still are of some concern. But the allowance for unquantified costs is not intended to allow the EPA to perform its calculations over an arbitrarily short period so as to preserve a large unquantified portion.

Unquantified benefits can, at times, permissibly tip the balance in close cases. They cannot, however, be used to effect a wholesale shift on the balance beam. Such a use makes a mockery of the requirements of TSCA that the EPA weigh the costs of its actions before it chooses the least burdensome alternative.[20]

We do not today determine what an appropriate period for the EPA's calculations would be, as this is a matter better left for agency discretion. See Motor Vehicle Mfrs. Ass'n, 463 U.S. at 53. We do note, however, that the choice of a thirteen-year period is so short as to make

---

20. . . . By not using such concerns in its quantitative analysis, even where doing so was not difficult, and reserving them as additional factors to buttress the ban, the EPA improperly transformed permissible considerations into determinative factors.

the unquantified period so unreasonably large that any EPA reliance upon it must be displaced. . . .

3. REASONABLE BASIS

In addition to showing that its regulation is the least burdensome one necessary to protect the environment adequately, the EPA also must show that it has a reasonable basis for the regulation. 15 U.S.C. §2605(a). . . .

Most problematical to us is the EPA's ban of products for which no substitutes presently are available. In these cases, the EPA bears a tough burden indeed to show that under TSCA a ban is the least burdensome alternative, as TSCA explicitly instructs the EPA to consider "the benefits of such substance or mixture for various uses and the availability of substitutes for such uses." [15 U.S.C. §2605(c)(1)(C).] These words are particularly appropriate where the EPA actually has decided to ban a product, rather than simply restrict its use, for it is in these cases that the lack of an adequate substitute is most troubling under TSCA.

As the EPA itself states, "[w]hen no information is available for a product indicating that cost-effective substitutes exist, the estimated cost of a product ban is very high." 54 Fed. Reg. at 29,468. Because of this, the EPA did not ban certain uses of asbestos, such as its use in rocket engines and battery separators. The EPA, however, in several other instances, ignores its own arguments and attempts to justify its ban by stating that the ban itself will cause the development of low-cost, adequate substitute products.

As a general matter, we agree with the EPA that a product ban can lead to great innovation, and it is true that an agency under TSCA, as under other regulatory statutes, "is empowered to issue safety standards which require improvements in existing technology or which require the development of new technology." Chrysler Corp. v. Department of Transp., 472 F.2d 659, 673 (6th Cir. 1972). As even the EPA acknowledges, however, when no adequate substitutes currently exist, the EPA cannot fail to consider this lack when formulating its own guidelines. Under TSCA, therefore, the EPA must present a stronger case to justify the ban, as opposed to regulation, of products with no substitutes.

We note that the EPA does provide a waiver provision for industries where the hoped-for substitutes fail to materialize in time. See 54 Fed. Reg. at 29,464. Under this provision, if no adequate substitutes develop, the EPA temporarily may extend the planned phase-out.

The EPA uses this provision to argue that it can ban any product, regardless of whether it has an adequate substitute, because inventive companies soon will develop good substitutes. The EPA contends that if they do not, the waiver provision will allow the continued use of asbestos in these areas, just as if the ban had not occurred at all.

The EPA errs, however, in asserting that the waiver provision will allow a continuation of the status quo in those cases in which no substitutes materialize. By its own terms, the exemption shifts the burden onto the waiver proponent to convince the EPA that the waiver is justified. See id. As even the EPA acknowledges, the waiver only "may be granted by [the] EPA in very limited circumstances." Id. at 29,460.

The EPA thus cannot use the waiver provision to lessen its burden when justifying banning products without existing substitutes. . . .

We also are concerned with the EPA's evaluation of substitutes even in those instances in which the record shows that they are available. The EPA explicitly rejects considering the harm that may flow from the increased use of products designed to substitute for asbestos, even where the probable substitutes themselves are known carcinogens. Id. at 29,481-83. The EPA justifies this by stating that it has "more concern about the continued use and exposure to asbestos than it has for the future replacement of asbestos in the products subject to this rule with other fibrous substitutes." Id. at 29,481. The agency thus concludes that any "[r]egulatory decisions about asbestos[,] which poses well-recognized, serious risks[,] should not be delayed until the risks of all replacement materials are fully quantified." Id. at 29,483.

This presents two problems. First, TSCA instructs the EPA to consider the relative merits of its ban, as compared to the economic effects of its actions. The EPA cannot make this calculation if it fails to consider the effects that alternate substitutes will pose after a ban.

Second, the EPA cannot say with any assurance that its regulation will increase workplace safety when it refuses to evaluate the harm that will result from the increased use of substitute products. While the EPA may be correct in its conclusion that the alternate materials pose less risk than asbestos, we cannot say with any more assurance than that flowing from an educated guess that this conclusion is true.

Considering that many of the substitutes that the EPA itself concedes will be used in the place of asbestos have known carcinogenic effects, the EPA not only cannot assure this court that it has taken the least burdensome alternative, but cannot even prove that its regulations will increase workplace safety. Eager to douse the dangers of asbestos, the agency inadvertently actually may increase the risk of injury Americans face. The EPA's explicit failure to consider the toxicity of likely substitutes thus deprives its order of a reasonable basis. Cf. American Petroleum Inst. v. OSHA, 581 F.2d 493, 504 (5th Cir. 1978) (An agency is required to "regulate on the basis of knowledge rather than the unknown.").

Our opinion should not be construed to state that the EPA has an affirmative duty to seek out and test every workplace substitute for any product it seeks to regulate. TSCA does not place such a burden upon the agency. We do not think it unreasonable, however, once interested parties introduce credible studies and evidence showing the toxicity of workplace substitutes, or the decreased effectiveness of safety alternatives such as non-asbestos brakes, that the EPA then consider whether its regulations are even increasing workplace safety, and whether the increased risk occasioned by dangerous substitutes makes the proposed regulation no longer reasonable. In the words of the EPA's own release that initiated the asbestos rulemaking, we direct that the agency consider the adverse health effects of asbestos substitutes "for comparison with the known hazards of asbestos," so that it can conduct, as it promised in 1979, a "balanced consideration of the environmental, economic, and social impact of any action taken by the agency." 44 Fed. Reg. at 60,065 (1979).

In short, a death is a death, whether occasioned by asbestos or by a toxic substitute product, and the EPA's decision not to evaluate the toxicity of known carcinogenic substitutes is not a reasonable action under TSCA. Once an interested party brings forth credible evidence suggesting the toxicity of the probable or only alternatives to a substance, the EPA must consider the comparative toxic costs of each. Its failure to do so in this case thus deprived its regulation of a reasonable basis, at least in regard to those products as to which petitioners introduced credible evidence of the dangers of the likely substitutes.[22]

4. UNREASONABLE RISK OF INJURY

The final requirement the EPA must satisfy before engaging in any TSCA rulemaking is that it only take steps designed to prevent "unreasonable" risks. . . .

That the EPA must balance the costs of its regulations against their benefits further is reinforced by the requirement that it seek the least burdensome regulation. While Congress did not dictate that the EPA engage in an exhaustive, full-scale cost-benefit analysis, it did require

---

22. We note that at least part of the EPA's arguments rest on the assumption that regulation will not work because the federal government will not adequately enforce any workplace standards that the EPA might promulgate. This is an improper assumption. The EPA should assume reasonable efforts by the government to implement its own regulations. A governmental agency cannot point to how poorly the government will implement regulations as a reason to reject regulation. Rather, the solution to poor enforcement of regulations is better enforcement, not more burdensome alternative solutions under TSCA.

the EPA to consider both sides of the regulatory equation, and it rejected the notion that the EPA should pursue the reduction of workplace risk at any cost. See American Textile Mfrs. Inst., 452 U.S. at 510 n.30 ("unreasonable risk" statutes require "a generalized balancing of costs and benefits" (citing Aqua Slide, 569 F.2d at 839)). Thus, "Congress also plainly intended the EPA to consider the economic impact of any actions taken by it under . . . TSCA." Chemical Mfrs. Ass'n, 899 F.2d at 348.

Even taking all of the EPA's figures as true, and evaluating them in the light most favorable to the agency's decision, . . . the agency's analysis results in figures as high as $74 million per life saved. For example, the EPA states that its ban of asbestos pipe will save three lives over the next thirteen years, at a cost of $128-227 million ($43-76 million per life saved), depending upon the price of substitutes; that its ban of asbestos shingles will cost $23-34 million to save 0.32 statistical lives ($72-106 million per life saved); that its ban of asbestos coatings will cost $46-181 million to save 3.33 lives ($14-54 million per life saved); and that its ban of asbestos paper products will save 0.60 lives at a cost of $4-5 million ($7-8 million per life saved). See 54 Fed. Reg. at 29,484-85. . . .

While we do not sit as a regulatory agency that must make the difficult decision as to what an appropriate expenditure is to prevent someone from incurring the risk of an asbestos-related death, we do note that the EPA, in its zeal to ban any and all asbestos products, basically ignored the cost side of the TSCA equation. The EPA would have this court believe that Congress, when it enacted its requirement that the EPA consider the economic impacts of its regulations, thought that spending $200-300 million to save approximately seven lives (approximately $30-40 million per life) over thirteen years is reasonable.

As we stated in the OSHA context, until an agency "can provide substantial evidence that the benefits to be achieved by [a regulation] bear a reasonable relationship to the costs imposed by the reduction, it cannot show that the standard is reasonably necessary to provide safe or healthful workplaces." American Petroleum Inst., 581 F.2d at 504. Although the OSHA statute differs in major respects from TSCA, the statute does require substantial evidence to support the EPA's contentions that its regulations both have a reasonable basis and are the least burdensome means to a reasonably safe workplace.

The EPA's willingness to argue that spending $23.7 million to save less than one-third of a life reveals that its economic review of its regulations, as required by TSCA, was meaningless. As the petitioners' brief and our review of EPA caselaw reveals, such high costs are rarely, if ever, used to support a safety regulation.

[The court then reviewed each of four subcategories of product bans included in the rulemaking—friction products (where EPA had determined that three-fourths of the anticipated asbestos-related cancer benefits would be achieved); asbestos-cement pipe products; gaskets, roofing, shingles, and paper products; and products produced outside the United States—and found each of them legally unjustified, in each case substantially on the basis of the general deficiencies reviewed in the first part of the opinion. However, the court upheld EPA's decision to ban products that once were, but no longer are, being produced in the United States, noting that "sections 5 and 6 of TSCA allow the EPA to ban a product 'that presents or *will present*' a significant risk" (emphasis the court's).]

We regret that this matter must continue to take up the valuable time of the agency, parties and, undoubtedly, future courts. The requirements of TSCA, however, are plain, and the EPA cannot deviate from them to reach its desired result. We therefore GRANT the petition for review, VACATE the EPA's proposed regulation, and REMAND to the EPA for further proceedings in light of this opinion.

NOTES AND QUESTIONS

1. TSCA and Multimedia Regulation. Why did the court strike down the asbestos ban? What impact will the court's decision have on EPA's ability to use TSCA as a comprehensive approach for reducing multimedia exposures to highly toxic substances? Note that the court states that "EPA's basic decision to use TSCA as a comprehensive statute designed to fight a multi-industry problem was a proper one that we uphold today on review." What then was wrong with EPA's decision to ban asbestos?

2. Sufficiency of Evidence. The court held that EPA had presented insufficient evidence to justify its asbestos ban. In what respects was EPA's evidence lacking? Note that EPA's decision to ban asbestos had not been undertaken lightly. It was the product of ten years of Agency activity that included an advance notice of proposed rulemaking in 1979 and a data collection rule promulgated under section 8(a) of TSCA in 1982. EPA had held 22 days of public hearings, taken thousands of pages of testimony, and received 13,000 pages of comments from more than 250 interested parties. The Agency and its contractors had prepared ten major regulatory analysis documents in support of the rule. What additional information would EPA need and what additional analysis would it have to undertake to justify an asbestos ban?

3. The "Least Burdensome" Requirement. Why did EPA believe that a ban was the "least burdensome" means "to protect adequately against" the risks posed throughout the life cycle of asbestos use? How does the court interpret section 6(a)(1)'s "least burdensome" requirement? What findings must EPA make before banning a product under the court's interpretation?

4. Reasonableness of Risk.   Did the court believe that the risks posed by asbestos were not unreasonable in light of the cost of the asbestos ban? EPA had estimated that the quantifiable benefits from the rule included the prevention of at least 202 cases of cancer at a total cost of $459 million over 13 years. 54 Fed. Reg. 29,484-29,485 (1989). Did the court think that this was too much for society to "spend" to prevent asbestos risks, did it simply disagree with EPA's calculations of costs and benefits, or both? Do you think that a risk that costs more than $2 million per life saved to eliminate is reasonable?

5. How Much Is a Life Worth?   Cost-benefit balancing is often criticized by those who find it repugnant to attempt to place a dollar value on human life. Yet decisions concerning regulation to prevent harm to public health often require, at least implicitly, some judgment concerning how much it is worth to prevent fatalities. The Administrative Conference has recommended that, except where costs and benefits are "highly conjectural" or unquantifiable, agencies "should disclose the dollar value per statistical life" used to reach determinations that the costs of regulations are justified. Administrative Conference of the United States, Valuation of Human Life in Regulatory Decisionmaking, 1 C.F.R. §305.88-7.

A study performed for the Administrative Conference reported in July 1988 that federal agencies had used widely varying values for the worth of human life in performing cost-benefit analyses, with the variance depending in part on the voluntariness and immediacy of the risk. EPA had used figures ranging between $400,000 and $7 million. The Nuclear Regulatory Commission evaluated the worth of proposed regulations by assigning a value of $1,000 per person-rem of radiation, which has been calculated to be roughly $7.4 million per fatality averted. C. Gilette and T. Hopkins, Federal Agency Valuations of Human Life 1-2 (1988). In studying wage differentials in occupations with varying levels of risk, economists have found implicit valuations of human life ranging from $200,000 to $7 million, K. Viscusi, The Valuation of Risks to Life and Health: Guidelines for Policy Analysis, in Benefits Assessment: The State of the Art 201-202 n.5 (J. Bentkover et al., eds. 1986), and from $1.6 million to $8.5 million, Fisher, Chestnut, and Violette, The Value of Reducing Risks of Death: A Note on New Evidence (1989).

While the Fifth Circuit did not specify what dollar value it would place on preventing deaths from asbestos exposure, the court noted in a footnote that

> the EPA regularly rejects, as unjustified, regulations that would save more lives at less cost. For example, over the next 13 years, we can expect more

than a dozen deaths from ingested *toothpicks*—a death toll more than twice what the EPA predicts will flow from the quarter-billion-dollar bans of asbestos pipe, shingles, and roof coatings. See L. Budnick, Toothpick-Related Injuries in the United States, 1979 Through 1982, 252 J. Am. Med. Ass'n, Aug. 10, 1984, at 796 (study showing that toothpick-related deaths average approximately one per year). [947 F.2d at 1223 n.23 (emphasis in original).]

What is the relevance of the toothpick data?

6. Comparing Costs and Benefits. EPA estimated that the most likely costs of its decision were $459 million and its quantified benefits were estimated at 202 deaths avoided (148 if benefits are discounted). That is between $2.4 and 3.1 million per death avoided. Yet the court finds that EPA's rule would result in figures as high as $74 million per death avoided. How do you explain this discrepancy?

7. The Discount Rate. In another footnote the court found that EPA's use of a 3 percent discount rate was reasonable. 947 F.2d at 1218 n.19. For years, the Office of Management and Budget and EPA had disagreed over various aspects of the asbestos ban rule. For one thing, OMB had urged that a ten percent discount rate be applied to asbestos-related cancers. The dispute is documented in EPA's Asbestos Regulations, Report of the Subcomm. on Oversight and Investigations of the House Comm. on Energy and Commerce, 99th Cong., 1st Sess. 78-82 (Oct. 1985). Congress's oversight of EPA's asbestos rule is discussed further in Chapter 5, pages 714-715.

8. Discounting Lives. The debate over whether benefits of health and safety regulation should be discounted when those benefits include saving lives is considerably more intense, with many more twists and turns, than the court's treatment suggests. Among other arguments, those opposed to discounting argue that the obligation to save life is a moral obligation owed equally to everyone, including future generations, so that a life saved 20, 40, or 100 years from now should be as highly valued as a life saved tomorrow. Some also argue that the avoidance of an irreversible course of events that culminates in death should be considered a present benefit.

Those favoring discounting remind us that dollars expended today to save a life in the future are actually more expensive than dollars expended to save a life tomorrow, because by spending now for future benefits we are deprived of the stream of benefits that would otherwise flow from those dollars between now and the future time when they will save a life. In that period of time, we might find ways to prevent the future loss of life more cheaply. For more on the discounting controversy, see C. Gillette and T. Hopkins, Federal Agency Valuations of Human Life 54-67 (1988).

In addition to employing a 3 percent discount rate, EPA discounted benefits from the date of exposure rather than the date of illness. What impact did this decision have on the apparent reasonableness of the asbestos ban? Was EPA justified in making that decision? The court did not think so: "[EPA] chose an unreasonable time upon which to base its discount calculation. . . . The EPA's approach implicitly assumes that the day on which the risk of injury occurs is the same day the injury actually occurs." Do you agree? On remand, what impact will this aspect of the court's decision have on the reasonableness of the asbestos ban? (In its comments on EPA's Regulatory Impact Analysis, OMB had observed that "a life saved 40 years from now [the latency period for asbestos-related cancers is 30-40 years] is worth roughly only one forty-fifth as much as a life saved this year.") An outraged congressional oversight committee calculated that such discounting would mean that it would be worth only $22,094.93 to OMB to save a life in these circumstances. EPA's Asbestos Regulations, Report of the Subcomm. on Oversight and Investigations of the House Comm. on Energy and Commerce, 99th Cong., 1st Sess. 79 (Oct. 1985).

9. Nonquantified Benefits. EPA's benefit estimates did not attempt to quantify certain benefits including the prevention of asbestosis and certain other diseases and the avoided costs of treating asbestos diseases and lost productivity. EPA also stated that if it had followed the normal practice of using "upper bound" estimates, its risk assessment could have projected 10 times more lung cancer deaths and 20 times more mesothelioma deaths due to asbestos exposure. Recall the concern that cost-benefit analysis exhibits a tendency to "downgrade" unquantified benefits. See page 528, above. How does the court of appeals treat the unquantified benefits of EPA's ban? Is its treatment appropriate? Do you believe that unquantified benefits should only be used as a "tie-breaker" in cost-benefit analyses?

10. The Risks of Substitutes. The data available to EPA concerning the health risks posed by asbestos are far better than the data available for virtually any other toxic substance. Unlike many other substances, scientific understanding of the dangers of asbestos is based on the results of numerous epidemiological studies that have documented scores of thousands of deaths from asbestos exposure. The court faulted EPA for not giving more serious consideration to the potential risks posed by other substances that might be substituted for asbestos. For example, vinyl chloride is used to make PVC pipe, a likely substitute for asbestos-cement pipe. Under what circumstances did the court think EPA must assess the risk of substitutes? How extensively must EPA analyze such products?

11. Technology-forcing Regulation. The court criticized EPA's assumption that the availability of a waiver would reduce the costs of replacing products for which no adequate substitutes for asbestos currently were available. Is the court suggesting that EPA should not be able to use TSCA to force the development of safer technology? Would a better approach for forcing technology be to impose a tax on asbestos products that increases over time?

12. Marginal Analysis. The court appears to require that EPA calulate the costs and benefits of the product ban compared to the costs and benefits of the next less burdensome regulatory alternative. In this way, the Agency can assess the incremental, or marginal, costs and benefits of the final regulatory step. Suppose the next less burdensome alternative were found to save 128 (discounted) lives at a cost of $125 million. Then the incremental benefits and costs of the product ban would be 20 lives and $334 million. If the Agency had made such a determination as this, would TSCA permit it to go ahead with the product ban?

13. Analysis of Subcategories. EPA had found that 102 (or 144, if benefits are not discounted) of the deaths avoided came from its ban of asbestos in friction products—primarily brake drums. The cost of this ban was estimated to be between $31 million and $85 million. The court indicated that it might have been inclined to uphold this part of the decision to ban if that had been the only part of the rule challenged, "even in the face of petitioners' arguments that workplace exposure . . . could be decreased as much as ninety percent using stricter workplace controls. . . ."

As long as the court was remanding, however, it found that it was "impossible to ignore" EPA's failure to study the effect of nonasbestos brakes on automotive safety, "despite credible evidence that non-asbestos brakes could increase significantly the number of highway fatalities." Was EPA's failure to conduct further study of the highway fatality issue justified?

14. "Clean-up" Ban on Future Products. The one aspect of the asbestos ban that the court upheld was a ban on asbestos products not currently being produced. How could EPA determine that the benefits of such a ban would outweigh its costs? Such products pose no current risks. The court stated that although "EPA cannot possibly evaluate the costs and benefits of banning unknown, uninvented products, we hold that the nebulousness of these future products, combined with TSCA's language authorizing the EPA to ban products that 'will' create a public risk, allows the EPA to ban future uses of asbestos even in products not yet on the market."

2. *Feasibility-Limited Regulation*

Next, we examine several feasibility-limited approaches to risk management. These statutes direct regulators to protect against certain health risks to the extent feasible. They can be considered to be a species of technology-based approaches because the state of existing technology plays a major role in determining the limits of feasibility.

Not all technology-based approaches to regulation impose pollution controls that are as stringent as those required by a strict feasibility-limited standard. For example, the "best practicable technology" controls at issue in *Weyerhaeuser* are less stringent than standards that require control of health risks to the limits of feasibility. Because of the nature of the adverse health effects associated with toxics, when Congress employs a technology-based approach to risk management, it generally mandates that technology be used up to the point at which it becomes infeasible to reduce emissions any further. At least, that is the theory. This type of technology approach, which we refer to as "feasibility-limited," bases the level of control on the capabilities of technology rather than on the degree of risk or the results of risk-benefit balancing. The degree of risk is not entirely irrelevant to these approaches, for they require that some threshold determination be made that health risks require regulation, as we saw in the *Benzene* case. If health can be sufficiently protected without stretching controls to the limit of feasibility, some of these approaches do not require that controls be so stretched. Thus, they can be more properly understood as feasibility-limited, health-based approaches to regulation.

Feasibility has two components: the technological and the economic. Something may be strictly possible given the current state of technology, e.g., a trip to the moon or to Mars, but so expensive that it could force an entire industry to shut down if mandated by regulators. Yet most feasibility-limited regulation is so limited precisely to avoid causing such massive dislocations. Thus, regulatory authorities implementing feasibility-limited standards have had to give consideration to both technological and economic factors, as we will see below.

A. EXAMPLE: THE OSH ACT

You have already encountered three decisions dealing with one feasibility-limited, health-based regime: the OSH Act. The *Benzene, Cot-*

ton Dust, and *Ethylene Oxide* decisions in this chapter illustrate how standards are set under that Act. One of the most influential early decisions concerning the meaning of "feasibility" under the OSH Act is United Steelworkers of America v. Marshall, 647 F.2d 1189 (D.C. Cir. 1980), cert. denied, 453 U.S. 913 (1981). This case arose after OSHA promulgated a 50 μg/m³ PEL for airborne lead. Reviewing the arguments by a number of industry groups that the standard was infeasible, the court outlined what remains the basic standard for determining feasibility under the OSH Act.

United Steelworkers of America v. Marshall
647 F.2d 1189 (D.C. Cir. 1980)

J. SKELLY WRIGHT, Chief Judge . . .

The Meaning of Feasibility. The judicial history at least establishes that there are two types of feasibility—technological and economic. . . .

The oft-stated view of technological feasibility under the OSH Act is that Congress meant the statute to be "technology-forcing," AFL-CIO v. Brennan, 530 F.2d 109, 121 (3d Cir. 1975). This view means, at the very least, that OSHA can impose a standard which only the most technologically advanced plants in an industry have been able to achieve—even if only in some of their operations some of the time. But under this view OSHA can also force industry to develop and diffuse new technology. Society of Plastics Industries, Inc. v. OSHA, 509 F.2d 1301, 1309 (2d Cir. 1975). At least where the agency gives industry a reasonable time to develop new technology, OSHA is not bound to the technological status quo. So long as it presents substantial evidence that companies acting vigorously and in good faith can develop the technology, OSHA can require industry to meet PELs never attained anywhere.

The most useful general judicial criteri[on] for economic feasibility comes from Judge McGowan's opinion in Industrial Union Dep't, AFL-CIO v. Hodgson. A standard is not infeasible simply because it is financially burdensome, 499 F.2d at 478, or even because it threatens the survival of some companies within an industry:

> Nor does the concept of economic feasibility necessarily guarantee the continued existence of individual employers. It would appear to be consistent with the purposes of the Act to envisage the economic demise of an employer who has lagged behind the rest of the industry in protecting the health and safety of employees and is consequently financially unable to comply with new standards as quickly as other employers. . . .

Id. A standard is feasible if it does not threaten "massive dislocation" to, AFL-CIO v. Brennan, 530 F.2d at 123, or imperil the existence of,

American Iron & Steel Institute v. OSHA, 577 F.2d at 836, the industry. No matter how initially frightening the projected total or annual costs of compliance appear, a court must examine those costs in relation to the financial health and profitability of the industry and the likely effect of such costs on unit consumer prices. Id. More specifically, Industrial Union Dep't, AFL-CIO v. Hodgson teaches us that the practical question is whether the standard threatens the competitive stability of an industry, 499 F.2d at 478, or whether any intra-industry or inter-industry discrimination in the standard might wreck such stability or lead to undue concentration. Id. at 478, 481. Granting companies reasonable time to comply with new PELs might not only enhance economic feasibility generally, but, where the agency makes compliance deadlines uniform for competing segments of industry, can also prevent such injury to competition. . . .

[The court then addressed the question of how OSHA could meet its burden of demonstrating that a PEL was feasible. The court noted that in previous cases courts had emphasized the availability of variances to find that standards were generally feasible. Concerned that this could lead to a circular definition of feasibility, the court interpreted these cases as "creating a general *presumption* of feasibility for an industry" that could be rebutted by firms in enforcement proceedings. The court then outlined what OSHA had to show to survive pre-enforcement review.]

When affected parties petition for pre-enforcement review of an OSHA standard, the standard must pass a preliminary test of general feasibility. First, within the limits of the best available evidence, and subject to the court's search for substantial evidence, OSHA must prove a reasonable possibility that the typical firm will be able to develop and install engineering and work practice controls that can meet the PEL in most of its operations. OSHA can do so by pointing to technology that is either already in use or has been conceived and is reasonably capable of experimental refinement and distribution within the standard's deadlines. The effect of such proof is to establish a presumption that industry can meet the PEL without relying on respirators, a presumption which firms will have to overcome to obtain relief in any secondary inquiry into feasibility . . . Insufficient proof of technological feasibility for a few isolated operations within an industry, or even OSHA's concession that respirators will be necessary in a few such operations, will not undermine this general presumption in favor of feasibility. Rather, in such operations firms will remain responsible for installing engineering and work practice controls to the extent feasible, and for using them to reduce lead exposure as far as these controls can do so. In any proceeding to obtain relief from an impractical standard for such operations, however, the insufficient proof or conceded lack of proof will *reduce* the strength of the presumption a firm will have to overcome in justifying its use of respirators.

Second, as for economic feasibility, OSHA must construct a reasonable estimate of compliance costs and demonstrate a reasonable likelihood that these costs will not threaten the existence or competitive structure of an industry, even if it does portend disaster for some marginal firms. To protect industry from the risk of wasteful guesses about the best means of compliance, we can also expect OSHA to show that new technology, even if it might fall short of meeting the PEL, will nevertheless significantly reduce lead exposure.

Such a standard of review for feasibility, of course, in no way ensures that all companies at all times can meet OSHA's demands—and as we have seen, OSHA readily concedes this. Moreover, under a "technology-forcing statute," with proof to a certainty impossible, there always remains the chance that an OSHA standard, after appearing generally feasible on review of the rulemaking, will ultimately prove generally infeasible. But we present this standard of review in the reassuring context of a scheme of devices by which employers can gain relief from such problems in the future, and by all of which devices employers can revert to respirators as a means of compliance when engineering and work practice controls prove insufficient.

[The court then generally upheld OSHA's 50 $\mu g/m^3$ PEL for lead while remanding OSHA's findings of economic feasibility for 38 industries subject to the standard. The court stayed the requirement that these industries meet the PEL through engineering and work practice controls alone, authorizing the use of respirators to meet the PEL pending further proceedings.]

NOTES AND QUESTIONS

1. Note that the court actually describes the OSH Act as a "technology-forcing statute." What do you think the court means by this statement? As a practical matter, OSHA has not sought to force technology in determining what engineering and work practice controls are feasible.

2. Some U.S. industries are in economic decline as a result of market forces or a failure to invest in research and development and capital improvements. If investments in modern engineering controls to protect workers from exposure to toxic substances are far more economically damaging to declining industries, does feasibility-limited regulation imply that workers in such industries must be exposed to greater risks?

3. Other industries are growing rapidly due to market forces but face stiff foreign competition (e.g., the nickel cadmium industry, which is growing rapidly but in which Japanese producers are making substantial inroads). They argue that requirements that they invest in expensive engineering controls will cause them substantial economic harm.

How would you respond to these concerns in the context of the OSH Act's definition of feasibility?

4. One of the major difficulties with implementing feasibility-based regulation is that it can require complicated engineering assessments that are difficult and expensive to make, particularly when most relevant information is controlled by the regulated industry. OSHA notes that it "spends an average of $500,000 and takes one year of study to determine the lowest feasible level for a *single* substance" and that it "does not have the resources to engage in that kind of analysis for more than a few substances." 54 Fed. Reg. 2,363 (1989).

5. Industry has a clear incentive to engage in strategic behavior to convince OSHA that stringent standards are infeasible. Because industry has better access to cost data, it sometimes has convinced OSHA that certain standards are far more expensive than they actually prove to be. For example:

> OSHA predicted the cotton dust standard would cost $500 million in 1977 dollars whereas industry predicted twice the cost and anticipated substantial technical problems. As a matter of fact, a later detailed study indicated that the standard cost only $250 million in 1983 dollars, improved industry competitiveness and productivity as well, and improved health more than predicted. See 50 FR 51121, 51164-67 (Dec. 13, 1985).
>
> OSHA's contractor predicted that the OSHA vinyl chloride standard could not generally be achieved with engineering controls and the attempt would cost $1.5 billion. As a matter of fact, compliance was achieved within three years at a cost of less than 10% of that predicted. See 49 FR 5001, 5253 (Jan. 22, 1980). [54 Fed. Reg. 2,366 (1989).]

Should this evidence of strategic behavior by industry lead regulatory agencies in the future to discount industry cost estimates by some factor?

6. One of the primary drawbacks of feasibility-limited approaches to regulation is that they imply that even hazards that pose significant risks must be tolerated if the technology to abate them is currently unavailable. Although at least one court has hinted that OSHA might be able to ban an activity in circumstances where there are no technologically feasible means of abating a hazard, AFL-CIO v. Brennan, 530 F.2d 109, 121 (3d Cir. 1975), OSHA has never claimed such authority.

7. In December 1981, OSHA amended the lead standard to permit certain employers who lowered workplace lead levels as far as feasible through engineering and work practice controls to rely on respirators to meet the 50 $\mu g/m^3$ level. But OSHA required that all employers meet the preexisting 200 $\mu g/m^3$ PEL through engineering and work practice controls alone. After further proceedings, OSHA determined in January 1990 that the 50 $\mu g/m^3$ PEL was technologically, but not economically, feasible for small nonferrous foundries (those with fewer than 20 employees). Thus, OSHA promulgated a bifurcated PEL requiring small

foundries to meet a 75 $\mu g/m^3$ PEL, while reaffirming the 50 $\mu g/m^3$ PEL for all other industries. 55 Fed. Reg. 3,146. In July 1991, the D.C. Circuit upheld OSHA's findings except for the finding that it was economically feasible for the brass and bronze ingot industry to comply with the 50 $\mu g/m^3$ PEL. American Iron and Steel Institute v. OSHA, 939 F.2d 975 (D.C. Cir. 1991). The court found that the data OSHA had relied on in determining economic feasibility did not sufficiently disaggregate these firms from other firms in a broad SIC classification.

8. The question of how disaggregated feasibility analysis must be was addressed by the D.C. Circuit in reviewing a challenge to OSHA's revised PEL for asbestos. OSHA had rejected a union's request to lower the PEL for asbestos to 0.1 f/cc on the ground that 0.2 f/cc was the lowest feasible level for most industries. When the union cited data showing that the automotive brake and repair industry had estimated average exposures to be 0.06 f/cc, OSHA replied that there was little reason to give weight to such evidence because the operation would not be affected by a lower PEL. The D.C. Circuit mandated that OSHA reconsider this aspect of its standard, noting that OSHA's "argument turns feasibility analysis inside out: sectors where compliance with a given PEL is easy become arguments, in effect, for a less stringent PEL. The consequence is to deny OSHA protection to those in the automotive repair sector who work in shops with higher-than-average exposure levels." Building and Contruction Trades Dept. v. Brock, 838 F.2d 1258, 1272 (D.C. Cir. 1988).

B. EXAMPLE: THE SAFE DRINKING WATER ACT

The Safe Drinking Water Act authorizes EPA to limit contaminants in public drinking water supply systems that have at least 15 service connections or that regularly serve at least 25 individuals. The principal provisions of the Act are described below. EPA is directed to limit contaminants in the drinking water provided by such systems by feasibility-limited, health-based regulation. EPA establishes health-protective goals called maximum contaminant level goals (MCLGs). These are to be set at the level at which "no known or anticipated adverse effects on the health of persons occur and which allows an adequate margin of safety." EPA determines the levels to which contamination actually is to be reduced by establishing national primary drinking water regulations that specify maximum contaminant levels (MCLs). MCLs are to be set as close "as is feasible" to the levels of the MCLGs. 42 U.S.C. §300g-1(b)(4).

The Act defines "feasible" to mean "feasible with the use of the best technology, treatment techniques and other means which the Administrator finds, after examination for efficacy under field conditions and not solely under laboratory conditions, are available (taking cost into consideration)." 42 U.S.C. §300g-1(b)(5). Thus, although EPA is not directed to balance the benefits of regulation against the cost of controls, cost considerations may determine how far EPA can go before reaching a level of control that would be deemed infeasible.

Although the Safe Drinking Water Act was enacted in 1974, EPA was slow to implement its provisions. The original Act directed EPA to establish national interim primary drinking water regulations within 90 days of its enactment. EPA established such standards for 16 chemicals and microbial contaminants based on recommendations of the U.S. Public Health Service in a 1962 study. The Act required EPA to revise these interim standards after the National Academy of Sciences completed a study recommending maximum contaminant levels for various substances. The NAS study was required to make these recommendations after consideration of the effect of contaminants on individuals more susceptible to adverse health effects than normal healthy persons, the synergistic effects of contaminants, body burdens of contaminants in exposed persons, and exposure to contaminants in other media. In 1977 NAS issued a report, Drinking Water and Health, which provided a list of chemicals that might have an adverse effect on health at various levels of contamination. Although EPA proposed in 1978 to require water systems to use generic treatment techniques rather than to monitor for individual contaminants, it eventually abandoned this approach and returned to a contaminant-by-contaminant approach to regulation.

When the Safe Drinking Water Act (SDWA) was amended in 1986, EPA had proposed final MCLs for only 8 chemicals, all volatile organic compounds (VOCs). Dissatisfied with the slow pace of EPA's implementation of the Act, Congress required EPA to regulate 83 chemicals by 1989 and to add 25 chemicals to the list every 3 years after 1989. Although the 83 chemicals listed by Congress included the chemicals EPA had identified as candidates for regulation in previous ANPRMs, it also included many substances EPA had not otherwise intended to regulate. OTA, Identifying and Regulating Carcinogens 117 (Nov. 1987). The 1986 Amendments, which require EPA to propose MCLs at the same time as MCLGs, specify that MCLs should be set at least as low as the levels that would be achieved using granulated activated carbon for the control of synthetic organic chemicals. Thus, the SDWA embodies a combination of health-based goals and rather specific technology-based standards.

PRINCIPAL PROVISIONS OF THE SAFE DRINKING WATER ACT

Section 300g-1 requires EPA to promulgate national drinking water regulations (MCLGs and MCLs) for public water systems. Regulations are to be issued for each contaminant that may have any adverse effect on health and that is known or anticipated to occur in such systems. MCLGs are to be set "at the level at which no known or anticipated adverse effects on the health of persons occur and which allows an adequate margin of safety." MCLs are to be set as close to the MCLGs "as is feasible."

Section 300g-2 authorizes states to assume primary enforcement responsibility under the Act.

Section 300g-3 requires EPA to notify states of violations of national primary drinking water regulations and to take enforcement action against public water systems if the states fail to do so. Owners or operators of public water systems are required to notify customers of violations.

Sections 300g-4 & 5 authorize states to grant variances and exemptions under certain conditions.

Section 300g-6 prohibits the use of lead in pipes, solder, or flux in public water systems or in plumbing used to provide water for human consumption that is connected to such a system.

Section 300h-1 requires EPA to establish minimum requirements for state underground injection control programs.

Section 300i grants EPA emergency powers to act against contamination of drinking water that may present an imminent and substantial endangerment to public health.

Section 300j-4 directs EPA to promulgate regulations requiring monitoring of drinking water and authorizes EPA to establish recordkeeping requirements.

Section 300j-7 authorizes judicial review of national primary drinking water regulations in the D.C. Circuit and of any other EPA action under the Act in the U.S. Courts of Appeal where the petitioner resides or transacts business.

Section 300j-8 authorizes citizen suits against any person alleged to be in violation of the Act and against the EPA administrator for failure to perform any nondiscretionary duty.

Sections 300j-21 to 26 codify the Lead Contamination Control Act of 1988, which requires recall of drinking water coolers with lead-lined tanks.

Although the 1986 Amendments to the SDWA required EPA to establish MCLs for 83 additional substances by June 1989, the EPA had promulgated MCLs for only 34 by the end of 1990. EPA promulgated new regulations for 33 contaminants in January 1991, and the Agency has pledged to set new standards for 108 contaminants by 1995. 56 Fed. Reg. 3526, 3528 (1991).

Like the OSH Act, the SDWA requires feasibility-limited reductions in risk. In implementing these statutes, costs must be given some consideration in determining the limits of feasibility. For example, in 1991 EPA promulgated standards for controlling lead in drinking water. 56 Fed. Reg. 26,460 (1991). Because of its potentially severe health effects at even low levels of exposure, EPA established an MCLG of zero for lead. In order to promulgate the MCL for lead, EPA had to determine how close to zero the standard could feasibly be set. Although the use of lead pipes and lead solder in drinking water systems was prohibited in the 1986 Amendments to the SDWA, an enormous number of homes have such plumbing or are served by water distribution systems with such plumbing. While it would be technologically possible to reduce levels of lead in drinking water to "safe" levels, it could costs tens of billions of dollars to remove all lead service pipes.

Although the SDWA appears to require EPA to establish MCLs if "it is economically and technologically feasible to ascertain the level" of contaminants in water, §300f(1)(C), 42 U.S.C. §1401(1)(C), EPA decided not to promulgate an MCL for lead. The Agency argued that Congress had not anticipated the problem of drinking water contamination occurring as a byproduct of pipe corrosion and that public water systems should not be responsible for contamination from portions of the distribution system beyond their control. 56 Fed. Reg. 26,460, 26,476 (1991). Instead, EPA adopted a "treatment technique" approach that requires water suppliers to employ corrosion control measures if more than 10 percent of water samples exceed 15 ppb lead at the tap. Corrosion control requirements take effect between 1996 and 1999 depending on the size of the water supply system. If corrosion control fails to reduce the percentage of samples exceeding this action level, water suppliers eventually may have to replace lead service lines on a schedule that stretches to the year 2014.

EPA's lead regulations have been attacked by environmental groups as well as state and local officials. Environmentalists argue that the absence of an MCL, the 90th percentile action level approach, and the lengthy compliance deadlines make the regulations virtually impossible to enforce while leaving hundreds of thousands of children exposed to high levels of lead in drinking water. Arguing that section 300f(1)(C) required EPA to establish an MCL because it is feasible to measure lead levels in water, environmental groups have sued EPA. Yet California officials maintain that they cannot afford to implement the new regulations, despite state legislation imposing fees on water suppliers to defray the costs of regulation. California Says 'No' to New Lead Rules, Calls Cost Too High for State to Implement, 22 Env. Rep. 2052 (1991).

Financially strapped localities are also expressing concern that they lack the resources to implement other SDWA regulations that are beginning to take effect. EPA regulations now require thousands of communities with unfiltered drinking water to install filtration systems unless EPA approves an alternative watershed protection program. EPA estimates that about one-half of all such communities will have to install filtration. New York City officials claim that a filtration system would cost the city $4 billion, while Boston officials estimate the cost to their city at $300 million. Both cities are pursuing alternative watershed protection programs.

Enforcement of the SDWA has been a chronic problem, particularly because the Act's regulatory targets usually are agencies of state and local government. James Elder, director of EPA's Office of Ground Water and Drinking Water, notes that "[m]any states are adopting regulations, but few are implementing them." Id. at 2053. The director of EPA's enforcement division for the SDWA program attributes widespread noncompliance with the Act's notification requirements to a lack of state and local resources.

3. Health-based (Zero, Significant, or De Minimis) Risk

A third approach to the "how safe is safe" conundrum is provided by statutes requiring that regulations be based solely on assessments of public health effects. We refer to these statutes as requiring health-based standards although not all of them employ the same methodology for establishing them. Other statutes, like the Safe Drinking Water Act, while eschewing purely health-based approaches to standard-setting, require that purely health-based goals be established as an initial matter.

A. COPING WITH UNCERTAINTY IN SETTING HEALTH-BASED GOALS

The SDWA requires that health-based goals (MCLGs) be established based solely on what is necessary to prevent adverse effects on health. EPA has had no trouble setting MCLGs at zero for known or probable carcinogens, although it has established nonzero levels for some chemicals for which evidence of carcinogenicity is considered to be rather weak. For example, in November 1985 EPA established final recommended maximum contaminant levels (the term for MCLGs prior to the 1986 Amendments) for eight volatile organic compounds. While EPA established zero as the health-based goal for those compounds that were known or probable carcinogens, it established a nonzero goal for vinylidene chloride because the evidence of its carcinogenicity was weak. To

take into account the possibility that vinylidene chloride was a carcinogen, EPA reduced the level of its nonzero health-based goal by a factor
of ten from the level that it would have set based solely on consideration
of noncancer health effects. This approach was upheld in NRDC v. EPA,
824 F.2d 1211 (D.C. Cir. 1987). The court described EPA's decision to
compromise in the face of uncertainty as "neither an unreasonable interpretation of the statute nor an unwise choice of policy." The court rejected the argument that EPA had violated its obligation to resolve
uncertainty on the side of protecting public health with the following
explanation:

> If the evidence established, for example, a 40% probability that a com-
> pound was carcinogenic, the agency's decision not to regulate would be
> difficult to square with the Drinking Water Act's instruction to the agency
> to establish a recommended level for each contaminant which, in its judg-
> ment, may have any adverse effect on health. Such a decision might well
> constitute an abuse of the discretion the agency is granted under the
> Drinking Water Act. But that situation in no way describes the instant
> case, and certainly there is no indication in the final rule that the agency
> has adopted a general policy not to establish a recommended level for a
> VOC unless a preponderance of the evidence demonstrates that it is a
> carcinogen. NRDC perhaps has taken too much to heart the agency's use
> of the word "possible" in its categorization of different VOCs. Although
> that label on its face could augur a preponderance-of-the-evidence test,
> the agency's explication of the Category II—compounds for which there
> is *some equivocal evidence* of carcinogenicity—makes it clear that the EPA
> has no such test in mind. Nor does the EPA's treatment of vinylidene
> chloride suggest that the agency employed a threshold preponderance-of-
> the-evidence test. The EPA here reasonably concluded that the evidence
> of vinylidene chloride's carcinogenicity was not even close to being in
> equipoise. The agency pointed out that no fewer than a dozen long-term
> animal studies had not demonstrated that vinylidene chloride has any
> carcinogenic effect. See 50 Fed. Reg. 46,888. Against this data EPA weighed
> two studies that revealed a possibility of carcinogenic or protocarcinogenic
> effects, and it noted that the results in both of these studies had limitations
> that made their applicability to humans highly questionable. The agency
> therefore had adequate support for its conclusion that the evidence of
> TCE's carcinogenicity was sparse and equivocal. [824 F.2d at 1217 (em-
> phasis in original).]

The court also rejected industry arguments that EPA had improperly assumed that a goal of zero was necessary for all known or probable
carcinogens. Industry had argued that the *Benzene* decision required
EPA first to determine that the risks were significant at all nonzero levels
before adopting zero as a goal. The court rejected this argument by
noting that Congress had expressly directed EPA to regulate these sub-

stances in the 1986 Amendments to the SDWA and that the *Benzene* decision therefore did not apply in this different statutory context.

B. THE DELANEY CLAUSES AND DE MINIMIS RISK

In most environmental statutes Congress has not explicitly endorsed cost-benefit or risk-benefit balancing in setting standards to control pollution or to protect public health. Rather, it has instructed agencies to control potentially dangerous substances by using "best practicable technology" (as in parts of the Clean Water Act—see *Weyerhaeuser*, above), or to regulate up to the point at which further reductions in exposures are no longer "feasible" (as in the OSH Act, see the *Cotton Dust* case, above), or sometimes simply to regulate so as to "protect the public health," often with a "margin of safety" requirement thrown in (as in the Clean Air Act, which requires provision of an "adequate margin of safety" from conventional air pollutants, CAA §109, and an "ample margin of safety" from hazardous air pollutants, CAA §112).

Suppose that a particular application of any of these instructions resulted in extremely low levels of remaining risk, so low as to be in some sense almost unnoticeable, and that relaxing the regulations somewhat would still result in extremely low risk. Even if risk-benefit balancing is not required by statute, should the agencies relax regulations in such cases? Achieving the final small degrees of pollution reduction is often very expensive, so that substantial economic consequences can turn on whether the agency imposes the strict demands of a statute or whether it recognizes this new version of regulatory "common sense"— that an activity poses risks "too small to be regulated."

In a number of regulatory settings, the regulated community has promoted the notion that regulators should recognize the concept of a de minimis risk level in establishing health-based standards. As just indicated, the idea of de minimis risk differs from risk-benefit balancing because risks are not compared with benefits. Instead, an activity's risks are compared with some regulatory cutoff, the de minimis level, below which the activity will be spared some regulatory action and above which further action will be forthcoming. That further action might be a risk-benefit balance; it might be a prohibition; it might be some other sort of regulatory attention.

How small is too small to be regulated? The typical argument for setting a de minimis level emerges from a process of *comparative risk assessment*. By quantifying the risk associated with socially acceptable activities, one can develop a range of risk levels. For example, Figure 4.12 lists OMB's estimates of the risks of various activities expressed in terms of *regulation risk*, here the total fatalities in a population of one million individuals exposed to the risk. It is often argued that the de minimis

FIGURE 4.12
Risks of Various Activities

Activity or cause	Annual fatality risk for every 1 million exposed individuals
1. Smoking (all causes)	3,000
2. Motor vehicle accidents	243
3. Work (all industries)	113
4. Alcohol	50
*5. Using unvented space heater	27
*6. Working with ethylene oxide	26
7. Swimming	22
*8. Servicing single-piece wheel rims	14
9. Aflatoxin (corn)	9
10. Football	6
11. Saccharin	5
*12. Fuel system in automobiles	5
13. Lightning	0.5
*14. DES in cattlefeed	0.3
*15. Uranium mill tailings (active sites)	0.02
From all causes in U.S.	8,695
From cancer in U.S.	1,833

*Indicates that the risk was regulated by the Federal government in the last 10 years. For these activities or causes, the risks in the table are estimates of risk prior to Federal regulation.

Source: Executive Office of the President, The Regulatory Program of the United States Government xx (1986).

level for regulatory purposes should correspond to, or be slightly lower than, the risk associated with some common activity commonly thought to be "safe" (or at least thought to pose trivial risks). De minimis determinations at EPA and the Nuclear Regulatory Commission have been described this way:

EPA and the Nuclear Regulatory Commission (NRC) . . . have proposed to set federal radiation standards using as a yardstick the fatality rates prevalent in industries commonly considered to be relatively safe. In its radiation protection proposal, EPA noted that "the risk of job-related accidental death in the safest of all major occupational categories, retail trades, [was] an annual death rate [of] 60 per million workers in 1975." This risk equates to a 45-year worklife risk of 2.7 in 1,000. The Agency based its proposed radiation protection guidelines on its finding that radiation risks of a magnitude similar to 3 in 1,000 "do not appear unreasonably high" because "they are comparable to risk of accidental death in the least hazardous occupations." In a similar vein, NRC's recent radiation protection proposal follows the approach recommended by the International Commission on Radiological Protection[,] . . . which developed its guidelines by "comparing [radiation] risk with that of workers in industries . . . which are recognized as having high standards of safety." As NRC pointed out, "in such '[s]afe' industries . . . average annual mortality due to occupational hazards does not exceed 10^{-4}. . . ." This annual rate amounts to a 45-year lifetime risk in excess of 4 in 1,000. Like EPA, NRC proposed standards on the basis that occupational mortality risks due to radiation are "acceptable" if kept at or below this "safe industry" risk level. [Rodricks, et al., Significant Risk Decisions in Federal Regulatory Agencies, 7 Regulatory Toxicol. and Pharmacol. 307 (1987).]

The following case concerns the relevance of de minimis risk levels in one regulatory setting, that of color additives to food.

Public Citizen v. Young
831 F.2d 1108 (D.C. Cir. 1987)

[A color additive may be used only after the Food and Drug Administration has listed the additive as safe. Among the requirements for determining safety is one of the so-called Delaney Clauses, named after the Congressman who introduced them. The Delaney Clause at issue here prohibits FDA from listing a color additive as safe if it is "found . . . to induce cancer in man or animal." 21 U.S.C. §376(b)(5)(B). Public Citizen, a public interest lobbying and monitoring group, brought this suit after the FDA used a quantitative risk assessment of two color additives, Orange No. 17 and Red No. 19, to determine that both pose at most "de minimis risks" to human health and, because of this determination, to list them as safe despite the Delaney Clause. The case required the court to determine whether the Delaney Clause permitted a "de minimis" exception.]

WILLIAMS, Circuit Judge:

I. THE DELANEY CLAUSE AND "DE MINIMIS" EXCEPTIONS

A. Factual Background

The FDA listed Orange No. 17 and Red No. 19 for use in externally applied cosmetics on August 7, 1986. See 21 C.F.R. §§74.1267, 74.2267 (1987) (Orange No. 17); id. §§74.1319, 74.2319 (Red No. 19). In the listing notices, it carefully explained the testing processes for both dyes and praised the processes as "current state-of-the-art toxicological testing." 51 Fed. Reg. 28,331, 28,334 (Aug. 7, 1986) (Orange No. 17); id.

at 28,346, 28,349 (Red No. 19). In both notices it specifically rejected industry arguments that the Delaney Clause did not apply because the tests were inappropriate for evaluation of the dyes. 51 Fed. Reg. at 28,342; id. at 38,358-59. It thus concluded that the studies established that the substances caused cancer in the test animals. Id. at 28,334-36, 28,341 (Orange No. 17 "induces cancer when tested in laboratory animals"); id. at 28,349-52, 28,357 (Red No. 19 "induces cancer when tested in laboratory animals").

The notices then went on to describe two quantitative risk assessments of the dyes, one by the Cosmetic, Toiletry and Fragrance Association ("CTFA," an intervenor here and the industry proponent of both dyes) and one by a special scientific review panel made up of Public Health Service scientists. Such assessments seek to define the extent of health effects of exposures to particular hazards. As described by the National Research Council, they generally involve four steps: (1) hazard identification, or the determination of whether a substance is causally linked to a health effect; (2) dose-response assessment, or determination of the relation between exposure levels and health effects; (3) exposure assessment, or determination of human exposure; and (4) risk characterization, or description of the nature and magnitude of the risk. See National Research Council, Risk Assessment in the Federal Government: Managing the Process 3 (National Academy Press 1983) ("Risk Assessment"). All agree that gaps exist in the available information and that the risk estimator must use assumptions to fill those gaps. See, e.g., Report of the Color Additive Scientific Review Panel (Sept. 1985), Joint Appendix ("J.A.") in No. 86-1548, at 139-40, 167. The choice among possible assumptions is inevitably a matter of policy to some degree. See Risk Assessment at 3.

The assessments considered the risk to humans from the substances when used in various cosmetics—lipsticks, face powders and rouges, hair cosmetics, nail products, bathwater products, and wash-off products. The scientific review panel found the life-time cancer risks of the substances extremely small: for Orange No. 17, it calculated them as one in 19 billion at worst, and for Red No. 19 one in nine million at worst. The FDA explained that the panel had used conservative assumptions in deriving these figures, and it characterized the risks as "so trivial as to be effectively no risk." It concluded that the two dyes were safe. 51 Fed. Reg. at 28,344, 28,360.

The FDA candidly acknowledged that its safety findings represented a departure from past agency practice: "In the past, because the data and information show that D & C Orange No. 17 is a carcinogen when ingested by laboratory animals, FDA in all likelihood would have terminated the provisional listing and denied CTFA's petition for the externally applied uses . . . without any further discussion." Id. at 28,341; accord id. at 28,357 (same for Red No. 19). It also acknowledged that "[a] strictly literal application of the Delaney Clause would prohibit FDA from finding [both dyes] safe, and therefore, prohibit FDA from permanently listing [them]. . . ." Id. at 28,341; id. at 28,356. Because the risks presented by these dyes were so small, however, the agency declared that it had "inherent authority" under the de minimis doctrine to list them for use in spite of this language. Id. at 28,341; id. at 28,358. It indicated that as a general matter any risk lower than a one-in-one-million lifetime risk would meet the requirements for a de minimis exception to the Delaney Clause. Id. at 28,344; id. at 28,362.

Assuming that the quantitative risk assessments are accurate, as we do for these purposes, it seems altogether correct to characterize these risks as trivial. For example, CTFA notes that a consumer would run a one-in-a-million lifetime risk of cancer if he or she ate *one* peanut with the FDA-permitted level of aflatoxins once every *250* days (liver cancer). See J.A. 529, citing FDA Bureau of Foods, Assessment of Estimated Risk Resulting From Aflatoxins in Consumer Peanut Products and Other Food Commodities (1978). Another activity posing a one-in-a-million lifetime risk is spending 1,000 minutes (less than 17 hours) every year in the city of Denver—with its high elevation and cosmic radiation levels— rather than in the District of Columbia. Most of us would not regard these as high-risk activities. Those who indulge in them can hardly be thought of as living dangerously. Indeed, they are risks taken without a second thought by persons whose economic position allows them a broad range of choice.

According to the risk assessments here, the riskier dye poses one ninth as much risk as the peanut or Colorado hypothetical; the less risky one poses only one 19,000th as much.

It may help put the one-in-a-million lifetime risk in perspective to compare it with a concededly dangerous activity, in which millions nonetheless engage, cigarette smoking. Each one-in-a-million risk amounts to less than one *200,000th* the lifetime risk incurred by the average male smoker. J.A. 536, citing E. Crouch & R. Wilson, "Inter-Risk Comparisons," in J. Rodricks & R. Tardiff, eds., Assessment and Management of Chemical Risks 97, 105, 108 (1984). Thus, a person would have to be exposed to more than 2,000 chemicals bearing the one-in-a-million lifetime risk, at the rates assumed in the risk assessment, in order to reach 100th the risk involved in smoking. To reach that level of risk with chemicals equivalent to the less risky dye (Orange No. 17), he would have to be exposed to more than 40 million such chemicals.

B. Plain Language and the De Minimis Doctrine

The Delaney Clause of the Color Additive Amendments provides as follows:

[A] color additive . . . (ii) shall be deemed unsafe, and shall not be listed, for any use which will not result in ingestion of any part of such additive, if, after tests which are appropriate for the evaluation of the safety of additives for such use, or after other relevant exposure of man or animal to such additive, it is found by the Secretary to induce cancer in man or animal. . . .

21 U.S.C. §376(b)(5)(B).

The natural—almost inescapable—reading of this language is that if the Secretary finds the additive to "induce" cancer in animals, he must deny listing. Here, of course, the agency made precisely the finding that Orange No. 17 and Red No. 19 "induce[ ] cancer when tested in laboratory animals." (Below we address later agency pronouncements appearing to back away from these statements.)

The setting of the clause supports this strict reading. Adjacent to it is a section governing safety generally and directing the FDA to consider a variety of factors, including probable exposure, cumulative effects, and detection difficulties. 21 U.S.C. §376(b)(5)(A). The contrast in approach seems to us significant. For all safety hazards other than carcinogens, Congress made safety the issue, and authorized the agency to pursue a multifaceted inquiry in arriving at an evaluation. For carcinogens, however, it framed the issue in the simple form, "If A [finding that cancer is induced in man or animals], then B [no listing]." There is language inviting administrative discretion, but it relates only to the process leading to the finding of carcinogenicity: "appropriate" tests or "other relevant exposure," and the agency's "evaluation" of such data. Once the finding is made, the dye "shall be deemed unsafe, and shall not be listed." 21 U.S.C. §367(b)(5)(B).

Courts (and agencies) are not, of course, helpless slaves to literalism. One escape hatch, invoked by the government and CTFA here, is the de minimis doctrine, shorthand for *de minimis non curat lex* ("the law does not concern itself with trifles"). The doctrine—articulated in recent times in a series of decisions by Judge Leventhal—serves a number of purposes. One is to spare agency resources for more important matters. See Alabama Power Co. v. Costle, 636 F.2d 323, 360 (D.C. Cir. 1979). But that is a goal of dubious relevance here. The finding of trivial risk necessarily followed not only the elaborate animal testing, but also the quantitative risk assessment process itself; indeed, application of the doctrine required additional expenditure of agency resources.

More relevant is the concept that "notwithstanding the 'plain meaning' of a statute, a court must look beyond the words to the purpose of the act where its literal terms lead to 'absurd or futile results.' " *Alabama Power*, 636 F.2d at 360 n.89 (quoting United States v. American Trucking Ass'ns, 310 U.S. 534 (1939)). Imposition of pointless burdens on regulated entities is obviously to be avoided if possible, see *Alabama Power*,

636 F.2d at 360-61, especially as burdens on them almost invariably entail losses for their customers: here, obviously, loss of access to the colors made possible by a broad range of dyes.

We have employed the concept in construing the Clean Air Act's mandate to the Environmental Protection Agency to set standards providing "an ample margin of safety to protect the public health," 42 U.S.C. §7412(b)(1) (1982). That does not, we said, require limits assuring a "risk-free" environment. Rather, the agency must decide "what risks are acceptable in the world in which we live" and set limits accordingly. See Natural Resources Defense Council, Inc. v. EPA, 824 F.2d 1146, 1164-65 (D.C. Cir. 1987) (citing Industrial Union Dep't, AFL-CIO v. American Petroleum Inst., 448 U.S. 607, 642 (1980)). Assuming as always the validity of the risk assessments, we believe that the risks posed by the two dyes would have to be characterized as "acceptable." Accordingly, if the statute were to permit a de minimis exception, this would appear to be a case for its application.

Moreover, failure to employ a de minimis doctrine may lead to regulation that not only is "absurd or futile" in some general cost-benefit sense but also is directly contrary to the *primary* legislative goal. See id. at 360 (de minimis doctrine a "tool to be used in implementing the legislative design"). In a certain sense, precisely that may be the effect here. The primary goal of the Act is human safety, but literal application of the Delaney Clause may in some instances increase risk. No one contends that the color additive Amendments impose a zero-risk standard for noncarcinogenic substances; if they did, the number of dyes passing muster might prove minuscule. As a result, makers of drugs and cosmetics who are barred from using a carcinogenic dye carrying a one-in-20-million lifetime risk may use instead a noncarcinogenic, but toxic, dye carrying, say, a one-in-10-million lifetime risk. The substitution appears to be a clear loss for safety.

Judge Leventhal articulated the standard for application of de minimis as virtually a presumption in its favor: "Unless Congress has been extraordinarily rigid, there is likely a basis for an implication of de minimis authority to provide [an] exemption when the burdens of regulation yield a gain of trivial or no value." *Alabama Power*, 636 F.2d at 360-361. But the doctrine obviously is not available to thwart a statutory command; it must be interpreted with a view to "implementing the legislative design." Id. at 360. Nor is an agency to apply it on a finding merely that regulatory costs exceed regulatory benefits. Id. at 361.

Here, we cannot find that exemption of exceedingly small (but measurable) risks tends to implement the legislative design of the color additive Delaney Clause. The language itself is rigid; the context—an alternative design admitting administrative discretion for all risks other than carcinogens—tends to confirm that rigidity. Below we consider first the legislative history; rather than offering any hint of softening, this only strengthens the inference. Second, we consider a number of factors that make Congress's apparent decision at least a comprehensible policy choice.

1. Legislative History

[After a detailed review of the legislative history, the court concluded that Congress meant the Delaney prohibition to be rigid and absolute.] . . .

2. Possible Explanations for an Absolute Rule

Like all legislative history, this is hardly conclusive. But short of an explicit declaration in the statute barring use of a de minimis exception, this is perhaps as strong as it is likely to get. Facing the explicit claim that the Clause was "extraordinarily rigid," a claim well supported by the Clause's language in contrast with the bill's grants of discretion elsewhere, Congress persevered.

Moreover, our reading of the legislative history suggests some possible explanations for Congress's apparent rigidity. One is that Congress, and the nation in general (at least as perceived by Congress), appear to have been truly alarmed about the risks of cancer. House Report at 11; Color Additive Hearings at 327 (statement of Rep. Oren Harris, Chairman); id. at 491 (statement of Dr. Zavon) (Delaney Clause "tends to highlight the current hysteria regarding cancer"). This concern resulted in a close focus on substances increasing cancer threats and a willingness to take extreme steps to lessen even small risks. Congress hoped to reduce the incidence of cancer by banning carcinogenic dyes, and may also have hoped to lessen public fears by demonstrating strong resolve.

A second possible explanation for Congress's failure to authorize greater administrative discretion is that it perceived color additives as lacking any great value. For example, Congressman Delaney remarked, "Some food additives serve a useful purpose. . . . However, color additives provide no nutrient value. They have no value at all, except so-called eye appeal." Color Additives Hearings at 108. Representative Sullivan said, "we like the bright and light [lipstick] shades but if they cannot safely be produced, then we prefer to do without these particular shades." Id. at 114. And Representative King: "The colors which go into our foods and cosmetics are in no way essential to the public interest or the national security. . . . [C]onsumers will easily get along without [carcinogenic colors]." Id. at 246-47.

It is true that the legislation as a whole implicitly recognizes that colors additives are of value, since one of its purposes was to allow tolerances for certain dyes—harmful but not carcinogenic—that would have been banned under the former law. See House Report at 8-9; S. Rep. No. 795, 86th Cong., lst Sess. 1-2 (1959). There was also testimony pointing out that in some uses color additives advance health: they can help identify medications and prevent misapplications where a patient must take several. See Color Additives Hearings at 255 (statement of representative of Pharmaceutical Manufacturers Association). Nevertheless, there is evidence that Congress thought the public could get along without carcinogenic colors, especially in view of the existence of safer substitutes. Thus the legislators may have estimated the costs of an overly protective rule as trivial.

So far as we can determine, no one drew the legislators' attention to the way in which the Delaney Clause, interacting with the flexible standard for determining safety of noncarcinogens, might cause manufacturers to substitute more dangerous toxic chemicals for less dangerous carcinogens. . . . But the obviously more stringent standard for carcinogens may rest on a view that cancer deaths are in some way more to be feared than others.

Finally, as we have already noted, the House committee (or its amanuenses) considered the possibility that its no-threshold assumption might prove false and contemplated a solution: renewed consideration by Congress.

Considering these circumstances—great concern over a specific health risk, the apparently low cost of protection, and the possibility of remedying any mistakes—Congress's enactment of an absolute rule seems less surprising. . . .

CONCLUSION

In sum, we hold that the agency's de minimis interpretation of the Delaney Clause of the Color Additive Amendments is contrary to law. The listing decisions for Orange No. 17 and Red No. 19 based on that interpretation must therefore be corrected.

NOTES AND QUESTIONS

1. Is the de minimis risk version of "common sense"—we should not use scarce resources to eliminate extremely low levels of risk—more or less compelling than the optimal pollution version of common sense addressed in *Weyerhaeuser*?

2. The FDA's de minimis policy is but one of a variety of measures that the Agency has taken through the years to breathe some flexibility into an extremely rigid piece of legislation. Richard Merrill has depicted the policy as part of the "FDA's decade-long efforts to reconcile Con-

gress's language with circumstances Congress may not have foreseen and for which it surely did not provide." He summarizes the factors that have induced FDA to seek escape from Delaney's literal meaning:

> Improvements in analytic chemistry have enlarged the universe of compounds that FDA regulates as food (and color) additives. More extensive testing of chemicals and more sensitive protocols have enhanced toxicologists' ability to identify substances capable of producing tumors, including several substances adopted for food use years ago [e.g., saccharin, which had been in use since the early 1900s, but was not found to be carcinogenic in animals until the early 1970s]. Some of these substances gained market acceptance long before their carcinogenicity was discovered. In addition to these science-driven pressures on regulators, the public health community's concerns about the relationship between diet and cancer have shifted focus. A consensus has emerged that dietary patterns influence cancer incidence. Investigators have also revealed that the human food supply is full of substances (most occurring naturally) that have been, or may be, shown to cause cancer in laboratory animals. [Merrill, FDA's Implementation of the Delaney Clause: Repudiation of Congressional Choice or Reasoned Adaptation to Scientific Progress?, 5 Yale J. on Reg. 1, 2-3 (1988).]

3. What is the relevance of the last two points Professor Merrill makes? On these points, see also Ames, Dietary Carcinogens and Anticarcinogens: Oxygen Radicals and Degenerative Diseases, 221 Science 1256 (1983); Committee on Diet, Nutrition, and Cancer, Commission on Life Sciences, National Research Council, National Academy of Sciences, Diet, Nutrition and Cancer: Directions for Research (1982). Professor Bruce Ames has argued that it is a serious mistake to focus regulatory attention and economic resources on removing extremely low risks of cancer associated with manmade chemicals because humans are exposed to much greater cancer risks from their dietary patterns and the consumption of natural carcinogens and anticarcinogens. See page 513; see also Ames, Ranking Possible Carcinogenic Hazards, 236 Science 271 (1987). Did such comparative risk considerations arise in the Public Citizen v. Young litigation? How did the court address them?

4. Ames's suggestion that naturally occurring substances are consistently riskier than manmade substances has been challenged by some researchers. Two researchers from the Columbia University School of Public Health reexamined Ames's data by including allegedly more representative examples of synthetic chemicals and more consistent measures of exposure. Their results suggest that risks ranging from large to small are presented by both natural and synthetic substances. See Perera and Boffetta, Perspectives of Comparing Risks of Environmental Carcinogens, 80 J. Natl. Cancer Inst. 1282 (1988). They argue that few natural substances have been tested for carcinogenesis and that Ames

has exaggerated the risks of exposure to naturally occurring carcinogens.

5. The court's decision dealt only with the Delaney Clause applicable to color additives in section 706 of the FDCA, 21 U.S.C. §376(B)(5)(B), and not with the separate Delaney Clause applicable to food additives in section 409, 21 U.S.C. 348(c)(3)(A). The court noted that while "the clauses have almost identical wording, the context is clearly different" given the potentially greater social costs of banning certain food additives. 831 F.2d at 1117. Do you agree? Citing this statement, EPA has interpreted the food additives Delaney Clause to permit a de minimis exception when it establishes tolerances for pesticide residues on processed foods under section 409. 56 Fed. Reg. 7750 (1991). EPA argues that since FIFRA contains no Delaney Clause and no Delaney Clause applies to pesticide residues on nonprocessed foods under section 408 of the FDCA, it would be irrational to apply the Clause strictly to processed foods. EPA's position is currently being reviewed by the U.S. Court of Appeals for the Ninth Circuit. Les v. EPA, No. 91-70234 (9th Cir.).

6. Putting aside the jurisprudential question of whether a court ought to be the institution that recognizes a de minimis exception to Delaney (and by extension a fair number of other seemingly absolute statutes), do you think it is wise policy to do so? If your answer is yes, why do you suppose Congress, which has had this issue brought to it in various ways more than once, has refused to do so?

7. In addition to the de minimis argument to which the court devoted most of its attention in Public Citizen v. Young, the Justice Department also argued that the two color additives did not "induce cancer within the meaning of the Delaney Clause," despite the FDA's previous finding to the contrary. This position, which "is difficult to reconcile with FDA's historical view, shared by other agencies, that high-dose animal tests are a reliable means for identifying human cancer hazards," Merrill, FDA's Implementation of the Delaney Clause: Repudiation of Congressional Choice or Reasoned Adaptation to Scientific Progress?, 5 Yale J. on Reg. 1, 85 (1988), was not taken seriously by the court.

C. SECTION 112 OF THE CLEAN AIR ACT

The Delaney Clauses administered by the FDA are the only instances of a purely "zero-risk" regulatory scheme under current environmental laws. Until the Clean Air Act was amended in 1990, the section of the Clean Air Act regulating hazardous air pollutants, section 112, had been interpreted by some to be another example of a zero-risk statute because it required EPA to provide an "ample margin of safety to protect the public health." The history of EPA's interpretation of section 112 is told in Chapter 6, pages 855-859. You may wish to read that now.

In Natural Resources Defense Council v. EPA, 824 F.2d 1146 (D.C. Cir. 1987) (Vinyl Chloride), a unanimous U.S. Court of Appeals sitting en banc addressed the meaning of section 112. It held that to determine what constitutes an "ample margin of safety" the EPA "Administrator [must] make an intitial determination of what is 'safe.' This determination must be based exclusively upon the Administrator's determination of the risk to health at a particular emission level." The court emphasized that "the Administrator's decision does not require a finding that 'safe' means 'risk-free,'" citing Justice Stevens's observation in the *Benzene* decision that few people consider many daily activities that entail risk (such as driving a car or breathing city air) to be unsafe. Instead, the court found only that "the Administrator's decision must be based upon an expert judgment with regard to the level of emission that will result in an 'acceptable' risk to health" and that "[t]his determination must be based solely upon the risk to health."

The *Vinyl Chloride* case indicated that EPA must decide what constitutes an "ample margin of safety" through a two-step process. In the first step, EPA must determine what is a safe level of emissions without considering costs or technological feasibility. In the second step, EPA may then consider costs and feasibility in determining how far to go beyond mere "safety" in providing an "ample margin" of same.

The D.C. Circuit's *Vinyl Chloride* decision confronted EPA with the need to develop a methodology for deciding when a risk is "acceptable." (An unacceptable risk is sometimes also called a "significant risk.") As a result of the court's decision, EPA had to withdraw two other NESHAPs that had been challenged—a standard for radionuclides promulgated only after EPA had been held in contempt of court and a standard for benzene emissions. EPA's first opportunity to respond to the *Vinyl Chloride* decision came when it reproposed the benzene NESHAP in July 1988.

EPA proposed four approaches for determining what is an acceptable risk in response to the *Vinyl Chloride* decision. 53 Fed. Reg. 28,496 (1988). Approach A, called the "Case-by-Case Approach," proposed to base acceptable risk decisions on case-by-case consideration of levels of individual risk (probability of an exposed individual's getting cancer), population risk (number of predicted cases of cancer when average individual risk is multiplied by the number of exposed individuals), the distribution of risks among exposed populations, and the uncertainties involved, without establishing any hard-and-fast rules. Approach B, called the "Incidence" or "Population Risk" Approach, would deem acceptable one case of cancer per year per source category. Approach C would deem an individual risk of 1 in 10,000 to be acceptable, while Approach D would accept an individual risk of 1 in 1 million.

Three of these four approaches are represented in Figure 4.13, which is adapted from a figure in EPA's Federal Register notice. The

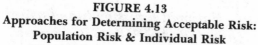

FIGURE 4.13
Approaches for Determining Acceptable Risk:
Population Risk & Individual Risk

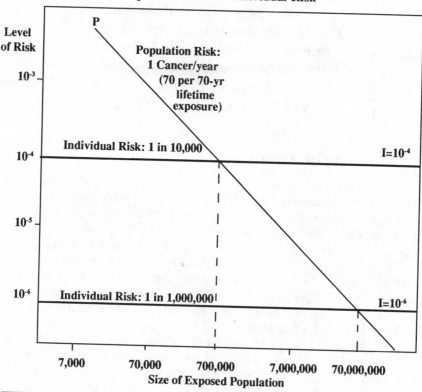

x-axis represents the size of the exposed population (ranging from 1 to 10 million); levels of individual risk (ranging from 1 in 1 million to 1) appear on the y-axis. The one-cancer-per-year "Incidence" or "Population Risk" approach (Approach B) appears as the line descending from left to right, while the "Individual Risk" approaches of 1 in 10,000 (Approach C) and 1 in 1 million (Approach D) appear as the horizontal lines.

In 1989 EPA reached a final decision on its proposed standards for controlling benzene emissions under section 112, which it announced in the following Federal Register notice. The General Counsel of EPA at the time described the contents of the final rule as representing the state-of-the-art thinking on how to determine acceptable or significant risk. What follows is an excerpt from EPA's final rule.

EPA, National Emission Standards for
Hazardous Air Pollutants; Benzene
Emissions from Maleic Anhydride
Plants, Ethylbenzene/Styrene Plants,
Benzene Storage Vessels, Benzene
Equipment Leaks, and Coke By-Product
Recovery Plants
54 Fed. Reg. 38,044 (1989)

SELECTION OF APPROACH

Based on the comments and the record developed in the rule-making, EPA has selected an approach, based on Approaches A and C but also incorporating consideration of incidence from Approach B and consideration of health protection for the general population on the order of 1 in 1 million from Approach D. Thus, in the first step of the *Vinyl Chloride* inquiry, EPA will consider the extent of the estimated risk were an individual exposed to the maximum level of a pollutant for a lifetime ("MIR"). The EPA will generally presume that if the risk to that individual is no higher than approximately 1 in 10 thousand, that risk level is considered acceptable and EPA then considers the other health and risk factors to complete an overall judgment on acceptability. The presumptive level provides a benchmark for judging the acceptability of maximum individual risk ("MIR"), but does not constitute a rigid line for making that determination.

The Agency recognizes that consideration of maximum individual risk ("MIR")—the estimated risk of contracting cancer following a life-time exposure at the maximum, modeled long-term ambient concentration of a pollutant—must take into account the strengths and weaknesses of this measure of risk. It is an estimate of the upperbound of risk based on conservative assumptions, such as continuous exposure for 24 hours per day for 70 years. As such, it does not necessarily reflect the true risk, but displays a conservative risk level which is an upperbound that is unlikely to be exceeded. The Administrator believes that an MIR of approximately 1 in 10 thousand should ordinarily be the upper end of the range of acceptability. As risks increase above this benchmark, they become presumptively less acceptable under section 112, and would be weighed with the other health risk measures and information in making an overall judgment on acceptability. Or, the Agency may find, in a particular case, that a risk that includes MIR less than the presumptively acceptable level is unacceptable in the light of other health risk factors.

In establishing a presumption for MIR, rather than a rigid line for acceptability, the Agency intends to weigh it with a series of other health measures and factors. These include the overall incidence of cancer or other serious health effects within the exposed population, the numbers of persons exposed within each individual lifetime risk range and associated incidence within, typically, a 50 km exposure radius around facilities, the science policy assumptions and estimation uncertainties associated with the risk measures, weight of the scientific evidence for human health effects, other quantified or unquantified health effects, effects due to co-location of facilities, and co-emission of pollutants.

The EPA also considers incidence (the numbers of persons estimated to suffer cancer or other serious health effects as a result of exposure to a pollutant) to be an important measure of the health risk to the exposed population. Incidence measures the extent of health risk to the exposed population as a whole, by providing an estimate of the occurrence of cancer or other serious health effects in the exposed population. The EPA believes that even if the MIR is low, the overall risk may be unacceptable if significant numbers of persons are exposed to a hazardous air pollutant, resulting in a significant estimated incidence. Consideration of this factor would not be reduced to a specific limit or range, such as the 1 case/year limit included in proposed Approach B, but estimated incidence would be weighed along with other health risk information in judging acceptability.

The limitations of MIR and incidence are put into perspective by considering how these risks are distributed within the exposed population. This information includes both individual risk, including the number of persons exposed within each risk range, as well as the incidence associated with the persons exposed within each risk range. In this manner, the distribution provides an array of information on individual risk and incidence for the exposed population.

Particular attention will also be accorded to the weight of evidence presented in the risk assessment of potential human carcinogenicity or other health effects of a pollutant. While the same numerical risk may be estimated for an exposure to a pollutant judged to be a known human carcinogen, and to a pollutant considered a possible human carcinogen based on limited animal test data, the same weight cannot be accorded to both estimates. In considering the potential public health effects of the two pollutants, the Agency's judgment on acceptability, including the MIR, will be influenced by the greater weight of evidence for the known human carcinogen.

In the *Vinyl Chloride* decision, the Administrator is directed to determine a "safe" or "acceptable" risk level, based on a judgment of "what risks are acceptable in the world in which we live." 824 F.2d at 1165. To aid in this inquiry, the Agency compiled and presented a "Survey of Societal Risk" in its July 1988 proposal (53 FR 28512-28513). As described there, the survey developed information to place risk estimates in perspective, and to provide background and context for the Administrator's judgment on the acceptability of risks "in the world in which we live." Individual risk levels in the survey ranged from 10^{-1} to 10^{-7} (that is, the lifetime risk of premature death ranged from 1 in 10 to 1 in 10 million), and incidence levels ranged from less than 1 case/year to estimates as high as 5,000 to 20,000 cases/year. The EPA concluded from the survey that no specific factor in isolation could be identified as defining acceptability under all circumstances, and that the acceptability of a risk depends on consideration of a variety of factors and conditions. However, the presumptive levels established for MIR of approximately 1 in 10 thousand is within the range for individual risk in the survey, and provides health protection at a level lower than many other risks common "in the world in which we live." And, this presumptive level also comports with many previous health risk decisions by EPA premised on controlling maximum individual risks to approximately 1 in 10 thousand and below.

In today's decision, EPA has selected an approach based on the judgment that the first step judgment on acceptability cannot be reduced to any single factor. The EPA believes that the level of the MIR, the distribution of risks in the exposed population, incidence, the science policy assumptions and uncertainties associated with the risk measures, and the weight of evidence that a pollutant is harmful to health are all important factors to be considered in the acceptability judgment. The EPA concludes that the approach selected best incorporates all of this vital health information, and enables it to weigh them appropriately in making a judgment. In contrast, the single measure Approaches B, C and D, while providing simple decisionmaking criteria, provide an incomplete set of health information for decisions under section 112. The Administrator believes that the acceptability of risk under section 112 is best judged on the basis of a broad set of health risk measures and information. As applied in practice, the EPA's approach is more protective of public health than any single factor approach. In the case of the benzene sources regulated here, more than 99 percent of the population living within 50 km would be exposed to risks no greater than approximately 1 in 1 million; and, the total number of cases of death or disease estimated to result would be kept low.

Under the two-step process specified in the *Vinyl Chloride* decision, the second step determines an "ample margin of safety," the level at which the standard is set. This is the important step of the standard-setting process of which the actual level of public health protection is established. The first step consideration of acceptability is only a starting point for the analysis, in which a floor for the ultimate standard is set. The standard set at the second step is the legally enforceable limit that must be met by a regulated facility.

Even though the risks judged "acceptable" by EPA in the first step of the *Vinyl Chloride* inquiry are already low, the second step of the inquiry, determining an "ample margin of safety," again includes consideration of all of the health factors, and whether to reduce the risks even further. In the second step, EPA strives to provide protection to the greatest number of persons possible to an individual lifetime risk level no higher than approximately 1 in 1 million. In the ample margin decision, the Agency again considers all of the health risk and other health information considered in the first step. Beyond that information, additional factors relating to the appropriate level of control will also be considered, including costs and economic impacts of controls, technological feasibility, uncertainties, and any other relevant factors. Considering all of these factors, the Agency will establish the standard at a level that provides an ample margin of safety to protect the public health, as required by section 112.

NOTES AND QUESTIONS

1. Recall the four approaches to answering the "how safe is safe" question that EPA initially had proposed. Which of these approaches do you think the public favored? Which approach would be favored by industry? By regulators? Why?

2. One result of employing the Incidence Approach (Approach B) would be that the level of protection for any individual would depend on how densely populated the surrounding area is. As can be seen from Figure 4.13, very high levels of individual risk (e.g., 1 in 1,000) could be tolerated for rural populations (e.g., a community of 1,000) while far lower levels (e.g., less than 1 in million) would be required in large metropolitan areas (e.g., New York City). Would this approach unfairly discriminate against individuals living in rural areas?

3. Why do you think EPA chose a combination of the four approaches for making "ample margin of safety" determinations rather than adhering to a single approach? Does EPA's new policy provide adequate guidance concerning how the Agency will make ample margin of safety determinations in the future, or does its simply confirm existing ad hoc practices? Would it be desirable for EPA to follow a less flexible, but more certain, policy for making such decisions?

4. How flexible do you think EPA will be in determining what levels of individual risk constitute an "ample margin of safety"? In applying its new approach to regulation of benzene source categories, EPA determined not to tighten controls on ethylbenzene-styrene process vents. EPA's decision left some individuals exposed to a maximum individual risk of 1 in 50,000 from this source, because the total numbers of such people were small enough that the incidence of cancer produced by this source category was estimated to be 1 case of cancer every 300 years. 54

Fed. Reg. 38,046. EPA decided to reduce emissions from benzene storage vessels by 20 to 60 percent to lower the estimated maximum individual risk from this source from a range of 1 in 2,500 to 1 in 25,000 to a level of 1 in 33,000, reducing the estimated incidence of cancer from this source from 1 case every 10 to 20 years to 1 case every 25 years. Id. at 38,047. For coke by-product recovery plants, EPA promulgated a standard that it estimated would reduce benzene emissions from this source by 97 percent. However, even at this reduced level the maximum individual risk would be 1 in 5,000, a risk greater than the 1 in 10,000 benchmark of EPA's overall approach. EPA sought to justify this decision by noting that it reflected a significant reduction in MIR from current levels and by stressing uncertainties in emissions estimates. EPA noted that the standard for coke by-product recovery plants would reduce MIR from an estimated current level of 7 in 1,000 (which is estimated to be responsible for 2 cases of cancer per year) to 1 in 5,000 and a cancer incidence of 1 case every 20 years. The Agency described this as "comparable" to the 1 in 10,000 benchmark in light of "estimating uncertainties in this case," which it believed to have resulted in an overestimation of actual levels of benzene emissions from this source. Id. EPA also determined not to tighten controls on benzene equipment leaks, despite previous estimates that emissions from this source category presented a MIR of 6 in 10,000 and 1 case of cancer every five years. EPA concluded that actual emissions levels were substantially lower than its previous estimates. Although the Agency was not able to calculate actual emissions levels, it expressed the view that "the resulting MIR would be comparable to the benchmark of approximately 1 in 10,000." Id. at 38,048.

5. EPA's decisions about regulation of benzene source categories suggest that under EPA's new approach for making "ample margin of safety" decisions the 1 in 10,000 benchmark is not a hard-and-fast maximum level of individual risk that will be tolerated. Actual levels of individual risk that will be tolerated will depend in part on the number of persons exposed. Thus, EPA will tolerate greater MIRs for small exposed populations. For example, EPA estimates that 100 people will be exposed to individual risks greater than 1 in 10,000 due to emissions from coke by-product recovery plants, but the Agency notes that because of the small population exposed at this level, it will cause only 1 cancer every 5,000 years. Will EPA's approach provide less protection for persons in sparsely populated areas than for persons living in cities?

6. More recently, when EPA interpreted the food additives Delaney Clause of section 409 of the FDCA to contain a de minimis exception, see page 591, the Agency stated that it would consider three factors in deciding what constitutes a "trivial risk": "the weight of the evidence regarding carcinogenicity, the size of the population exposed to the risk,

and the level of the risk." 56 Fed. Reg. 7750, 7754 (1991). EPA stated that "the risk comparisons most relevant to such an exercise are the prior decisions of the regulatory agencies" because they are the products of a public process. Id. at 7757. After reviewing how the "how safe is safe" issue has been addressed in other contexts, EPA concluded that when the entire U.S. population is exposed to a probable human carcinogen, "the agency consensus appears to be that risks less than 1 in 1 million generally can be found to be acceptable without consideration of other factors while risks greater than that level require further analysis as to their acceptability." Id. Is this approach consistent with the policy articulated in EPA's NESHAP for benzene?

7. In 1990 Congress substantially revised section 112. What is the relevance of EPA's rule after the Clean Air Act Amendments of 1990? See Chapter 6I and section 112 as amended.

8. EPA's track record in implementing health-based standards is not encouraging. EPA promulgated national emissions standards for only seven hazardous air pollutants (NESHAPs) in more than two decades since enactment of section 112. One interpretation of this history is that EPA's difficulties were the result of its reluctance to implement an unreasonably stringent statutory standard. EPA argues that some balancing of cost and economic considerations against protection of public health is inevitable in making regulatory decisions for controlling toxic substances.

While EPA would prefer statutory authorities that permit a more explicit balancing of risks against costs, EPA's track record for implementing TSCA, which requires such balancing, is no better than its record for implementing section 112. EPA has regulated even fewer toxic substances under section 6 of TSCA than under section 112 of the Clean Air Act. EPA's most comprehensive regulation under section 6 of TSCA—the phaseout of commercial uses of asbestos—took a decade for EPA to complete and then was struck down by the Fifth Circuit in *Corrosion Proof Fittings.*

9. Why has EPA had such a dismal track record in implementing statutes to control toxic substances? Does the problem lie with the way EPA's statutory authorities are structured, or is it simply a result of the way EPA has chosen to implement these authorities? Do the statutes that EPA must implement place impossible informational demands on the Agency?

10. Health-based standards are largely a product of the notion that life is too precious to compromise for economic gain. When Senator Mitchell articulated this principle during the debate on the 1990 Clean Air Act Amendments, George Will wrote a column describing it as "useful nonsense." Will explains that "[i]t is useful to talk that way, thereby inclining our minds to place high value on life, precisely because we

constantly must act in ways that cause that value to be jostled and com-promised by competing values." George Will, Suddenly: The American Idea Abroad and at Home, 1986-1990 206 (1990).

PROBLEM EXERCISE: REGULATION OF TOXIC SUBSTANCES

Assume that the U.S. Department of Health and Human Services determines on the basis of the results of animal bioassays that chemical X is a probable human carcinogen. HHS lists the chemical as a substance reasonably anticipated to be a carcinogen in its Annual Report on Car-cinogens.

Question One. Under what statutory authority could chemical X be regulated when it is used as: (a) an industrial solvent, (b) a pesticide, (c) a food or color additive, (d) a contaminant in drinking water, and (e) an air pollutant?

Question Two. What additional information, if any, would EPA, OSHA, or FDA need in order to be able to regulate chemical X under each of the statutes that authorize regulation of it for each of the five uses listed above? Why?

Question Three. How stringently could chemical X be regulated under each of the statutes that authorize regulation of it?

4. Risk Assessment as a Policy Paradigm

In the past decade, the use of quantitative risk assessment has grown so dramatically that it now has become a kind of institutional paradigm for organizing environmental policymaking. Quantitative risk assessment plays a variety of roles in regulatory decision-making, even under statutes that do not mandate risk-benefit balancing. Risk assessments are used not only to establish that risks are significant enough to warrant regu-lation under the OSH Act, but also to compare one risk to another. These comparisons can be used for two distinct purposes, one of which you already have seen. A chart similar to Figure 4.13, above, might be used to argue that risks falling below those posed by some generally accepted activity or some natural occurrence thought to be highly un-likely (such as being struck by lightning) ought to be considered insig-nificant and probably not worth regulating. A second purpose is to use rankings of as-yet-unregulated risks to establish priorities for an agency's agenda. We discuss priority setting separately in Chapter 5. This use of quantitative risk assessment has seemed almost self-evidently rational to many people, for as Paul Portney, vice president of Resources for the Future, has said, "If we don't try to make quantitative risk assessments, how do we decide what to regulate—by rolling dice?"

In fact, a host of objections have been raised against the use of quantitative risk assessments. Some, those based on the high degree of uncertainty that infects the process, have been discussed previously. Others question whether the kind of comparisons among risks implied by employing quantitative risk assessments are appropriate comparisons on which to base public risk reduction policy. Environmentalists initially were very critical of risk assessment because they believed it would reduce the ability of the public to influence regulatory policy while facilitating the use of risk-benefit balancing schemes that trade lives for economic gain. Now that risk assessments increasingly are being used to support regulatory decisions, the regulated community has been more critical of risk assessment than environmentalists. The Office of Management and Budget maintains that the use of conservative assumptions in risk assessments biases environmental policy toward unreasonably stringent regulation.

This section provides a brief sketch of some of these objections. We begin with excerpts from a famous article by then-EPA administrator William Ruckelshaus that is still one of the most thoughtful explanations by a public official of his attitudes toward quantitative risk assessment and its appropriate role in public policy.

Ruckelshaus, Risk in a Free Society
14 Envtl. L. Rep. 10190 (1984)

[Ruckelshaus begins by stating that, "needless to say, EPA's primary mission is the reduction of risk." He then reminds us of the accusations made against EPA in the early 1980s that risk assessments were being manipulated "so as to make the risks seem less than they were and [thus to] excuse the Agency from taking action." Therefore, when he became administrator, one primary problem he faced was that of restoring the public's trust in EPA. To accomplish this, he advocated a sharp demarcation between "the assessment of risk" and "the management of risk." "Risk assessment is the use of a base of scientific research to define the probability of some harm coming to an individual or a population as a result of exposure to a substance or situation. Risk management, in contrast, is the public process of deciding what to do where risk has been determined to exist. It includes integrating risk assessment with considerations of engineering feasibility and figuring out how to exercise our imperative to reduce risk in the light of social, economic and political factors." Ruckelshaus acknowledges the uncertainties of risk assessment that have already been noted—extrapolating from animals to humans and from high to low doses, limited data on actual exposures—all of which contribute to the wide variability of risk assessments depending on assumptions or judgments made at each stage of the assessment. "Such choices are influenced by values . . . which are supposed to be safely sequestered in risk management, [but which] also appear as important influences on the outcome of risk assessments." One approach to making such judgments is to be relentlessly conservative at every turn. He described this as EPA's historical approach. However, given the "serious economic and social effects" of regulations of carcinogens, for example, Ruckelshaus argues that such an approach is unsatisfactory.]

[What I require is some knowledge of] how likely *real* damage is to occur in the uncontrolled and partially controlled and fully controlled cases. Only then can I apply the balancing judgments that are the essence of my job. This, of course, tends to insert the policymaker back into the guts of risk assessment, which we had concluded is less than wise.

This is a real quandary. I now believe that the main road out of it lies through a marked improvement in the way we communicate the realities of risk analysis to the public. The goal is public understanding. We will only retain the administrative flexibility we need to effectively protect the public health and welfare if the public believes we are trying to act in the public interest. . . .

How then do we encourage [public] confidence [that we are trying to act in the public interest]? Generally speaking there are two ways to do it. First, we could assign guardianship of the Agency's integrity—its risk assessment task—to a group of disinterested experts who are above reproach in the public eye. This is the quasi-judicial, blue ribbon panel approach. . . .

Alternatively, we could all become a lot smarter about risk. The Agency could put much more effort into explaining what it is doing and what it does, and does not, know. . . . We have to expose the assumptions that go into risk assessments. We have to admit our uncertainties and confront the public with the complex nature of decisions about risk.

Living in a technological society is like riding a bucking bronco. I do not believe we can afford to get off, and I doubt that someone will magically appear who can lead it about on a leash. The question is: how do we become better bronco busters? I think a great part of the answer is to bring about a major improvement in the quality of public debate on environmental risk.

This will not be easy. Risk assessment is a probabilistic calculation, but people do not respond to risks "as they should" if such calculations were the sole criterion of rationality. . . .

We have research that points out that people tend to overestimate the probability of unfamiliar, catastrophic and well-publicized events and underestimate the probability of unspectacular or familiar events that claim one victim at a time. Many people are afraid to fly commercial airlines, but practically nobody is afraid of driving in cars, a victory of subjectivity over actuarial statistics.

In general, response to risk is most negative when the degree of risk is unknown and the consequences are particularly dreaded. Expert assessment does not seem to help here. People will fight like fury to keep a hazardous waste facility out of their neighborhood, despite expert assurances that it is safe, while people living under high dams located on earthquake faults pay scant attention to expert warnings.

Other hazard characteristics influence public perceptions of risk. For example, the voluntary or involuntary nature of the risks is important. . . . People also take into consideration whether the risk is distributed generally throughout the population or affects only a small identifiable group. . . .

The way risks and options are presented also influences perceptions. You might be worried if you heard that occupational exposure at your job doubled your risk of some serious disease; you might be less worried if you heard that it had increased from one-in-a-million to two-in-a-million. . . .

Many people interested in environmental protection, having observed this mess, conclude that considerations of risk lead to nothing useful. After all, if the numbers are no good and the whole issue is so confusing, why not just eliminate all exposure to toxics to the extent that technology allows? The problem with such thinking is that, even setting aside what I have just said about the necessity for improving the national debate on the subject, risk estimates are the only way we have of directing the attention of risk management agencies toward significant problems.

[Ruckelshaus then described a recent experience of EPA's in trying to provide the people of Tacoma, Washington with better risk assessment information about arsenic emissions from a copper smelter in their town. Arsenic is a human carcinogen, and best available technology controls would not reduce the risk "to levels the public might find acceptable. In fact, it looked as if reducing to acceptable levels of risk might only be possible if the plant closed." EPA organized a series of workshops to inform the citizens of the trade-offs between health risk and the possibility of the plant closing. Ruckelshaus was convinced that those who attended the workshops gained a better understanding of "the anatomy of environmental decisions, and local groups were able to come up with options that increased protection while allowing the plant to remain open, options well worth considering. . . ." He concluded his article by proposing some principles for more reasonable discussion about risk.]

First, we must insist on risk calculations being expressed as distributions of estimates and not as magic numbers that can be manipulated without regard to what they really mean. We must try to display more realistic estimates of risk to show a range of probabilities. To help do this we need new tools for quantifying and ordering sources of uncertainty and for putting them in perspective.

Second, we must expose to public scrutiny the assumptions that underlie our analysis and management of risk. If we have made a series of conservative assumptions within the risk assessment, so that it represents an upper bound estimate of risk, we should try to communicate this and explain why we did it. Although public health protection is our primary value, any particular action to control a pollutant may have effects on other values, such as community stability, employment, natural resources, or the integrity of the ecosystem. We have to get away from the idea that we do quantitative analysis to find the "right" decision, which we will then be obliged to make if we want to call ourselves rational beings. But we are not clockwork mandarins. The point of such analysis is, in fact, the orderly exposition of the values we hold, and the reasoning that travels from some set of values and measurements to a decision.

Third, we must demonstrate that reduction of risk is our main concern and that we are not driven by narrow cost-benefit considerations. Of course cost is a factor, because we are obliged to be efficient with our resources and those of society in general. Where we decline to control some risk at present, we should do so only because there are better targets; we are really balancing risk against risk, aiming to get at the greatest first.

Finally, we should understand the limits of quantification; there are some cherished values that will resist being squeezed into a benefits column, but are no less real because of it. Walter Lippman once pointed out that in a democracy "the people" as in "We the People," refers not only to the working majority that actually makes current decisions, and not only to the whole living population, but to those who came before us, who provided our traditions and our physical patrimony as a nation, and to those who will come after us, and inherit. Many of the major decisions we make on environmental affairs touch on this broader sense of public responsibility.

I suppose that the ultimate goal of this effort is to get the American people to understand the difference between a safe world and a zero-risk world with respect to environmental pollutants. We have to define what safe means in light of our increasing ability to detect minute quantities of substances in the environment and to associate carcinogenesis with an enormous variety of substances in common use. According to Bruce Ames, the biochemist and cancer expert, the human diet is loaded with toxics of all kinds, including many carcinogens, mutagens and teratogens. Among them are such foodstuffs as black pepper, mushrooms, celery, parsnips, peanut butter, figs, parsley, potatoes, rhubarb, coffee, tea, fats, browned meat, and alfalfa sprouts. The list goes on; my point is that it would be hard to find a diet that would support life and at the same time impose no risk on the consumer.

So what is safe? Are we all safe at this instant? Most of us agree that we are, although we are subjected to calculable risks of various sorts of catastrophes that can happen to people listening to lectures in buildings. We might be able to reduce some of them by additional effort, but in general we consider that we have (to coin a phrase) an "adequate margin of safety" sitting in a structure that is, for example, protected against lightning bolts but exposed to meteorites.

I think we can get people to start making those judgments of safety about the arcane products of modern technology. I do not think we are ever going to get agreement about values; a continuing debate about values is the essence of a democratic policy. But I think we must do better in showing how different values lead rationally to different policy outcomes. And we can only do that if we are able to build up a reservoir of trust, if people believe that we have presented fairly what facts we have, that we have exposed our values to their view, and that we have respected their values, whether or not such values can be incorporated finally in our decisions. We have, I hope, begun to build that sort of trust at EPA.

A Note on Objections to Quantitative Risk Assessment

Environmentalists initially were quite hostile to risk assessment. In a response to Administrator Ruckelshaus, David Doniger of the Natural Resources Defense Council expressed a number of reservations about the use of quantitative risk assessments (QRAs) by EPA. See Doniger, The Gospel of Risk Management: Should We Be Converted?, 14 Envtl. L. Rep. 10222 (June 1984). Using Doniger's article as a starting point and supplementing it with arguments raised by others, this note summarizes some of the recurring reservations.

QRA Techniques Are Unproved. "The current techniques for estimating the size of cancer risks are . . . too uncertain and fragile to be a rational basis for the 'risk management' decisions the Administrator wishes to make," Doniger writes. "The Agency does not have the support even for its contention that its estimates are confidently conservative; a variety of factors not taken into account can lead to significant underestimates of risk. . . . Administrator Ruckelshaus would admit that you wouldn't try to send a man into orbit on the strength of [risk assessment] equations. As he wrote in these pages, 'We simply do not know what [the] shape of the dose-response curve is at low doses, in the sense that we know, let us say, what the orbit of a satellite will be when we shoot it off.' These numbers are no more reliable for protecting public health."

The Risk-Benefit Tradeoffs Enabled by QRA Are Unjustifiable.
"When the Administrator urges the American people to accept a philosophy of deliberately trading off lives and health against the economic
costs of pollution controls ("risk management"), he is both disregarding
the requirements of the Clean Air Act and swimming against the strong
tide of public opinion. [W]hen lives and health are on the line, the general
public will not accept a philosophy which abandons that goal and legiti-
mizes such trade-offs. This philosophical and moral rejection of the
Administrator's policy is not going to change, for such trade-offs are
deeply repugnant to most people."

Doniger here is invoking a substantial line of criticism against treating health, safety, and the environment, on the one hand, and economic
costs, on the other hand, as if they could be expressed in the same
currency. Many people view environmental laws as dealing with incommensurables—a stretch of wild river versus the completion of an interstate highway, the logging of old-growth forest versus the protection of
the spotted owl, the economic viability of a business and the economic
welfare of its employees versus human lives at risk from carcinogens.
While it may be inevitable that these competing values must be judged
against each other, viewing what is at stake in such trade-offs as reducible
to a common measuring stick, typically dollars, oversimplifies and distorts the issues. One source of objections such as these draws on processes
of democratic deliberation to provide alternative decision mechanisms.
Such deliberation may be particularly apt in cases of conflict among
incommensurables, Mark Sagoff argues, because what counts on such
occasions is the case one makes for one's beliefs and convictions, not how
much one is willing to pay for them. "When a person advocates a policy
as being right or appropriate for society as a whole . . . the intensity of
the desire [which is measured by cost-benefit analysis's reliance on people's willingness to pay for environmental regulation] is no longer relevant. Rather, advocates must present arguments that convince the public
or its representatives to adopt a policy. . . . These policymakers may
consider economic factors, but they should not use the economic method
to evaluate competing beliefs." Sagoff, Economic Theory and Environmental Law, 79 Mich. L. Rev. 1392 (1982). See also Sagoff, The Economy
of the Earth (1988), and two reviews of Sagoff's book: Rose, Environmental Faust Succumbs to Temptations of Economic Mephistopheles,
or, Value by Any Other Name Is Preference, 87 Mich. L. Rev. 1631
(1989) and Farber, Environmentalism, Economics and the Public Interest, 41 Stan. L. Rev. 1022 (1989).

A second source of objection against risk-benefit balancing is the
value of human autonomy, the capacity we desire to be authors of our
own lives. Mark Sagoff has written on this subject as well. "The principal
value informing public law for the workplace and the environment—as

well as private behavior—may be autonomy, not efficiency. Public policy
. . . may represent our attempt . . . to control the conditions under
which we pursue happiness—the conditions under which we lead our
lives." Sagoff, On Markets for Risks, 41 Md. L. Rev. 755, 761 (1982).

QRA Ignores Differences Among Risks. These ethical suggestions
have been reinforced in recent years by findings by cognitive psychologists that individuals perceive or process risks in a much more complicated fashion than may be implied by QRA. People take account of
more characteristics of risk than simply the probability of harm and the
magnitude of that harm. Among the distinctions found by cognitive
psychologists are the following:

Voluntary versus involuntary risk. Individuals apparently are willing to accept greater degrees of risk for risks that they can choose to
avoid (voluntary risks) than for risks that they have little or no choice
about (involuntary risks).

Dispersed versus concentrated risk. Some studies suggest that people
perceive widely dispersed risks as less risky than highly concentrated
risks, even though the total population risk in both cases is identical. A
chance that 1 person will die in each of 100 neighborhoods, each with
100 inhabitants, is perceived as a more acceptable risk than the same
chance that one of the neighborhoods will be wiped out entirely, the
other 99 remaining untouched.

Recent versus remote risks. People tend to overestimate the magnitude of danger from rare events, such as earthquakes and floods, when
they are aware of one that has occurred recently. They tend to underestimate the magnitude when they lack a ready mental reference to such
an event in the past. (This is one explanation, by the way, for why so
many environmental laws have been enacted on the heels of some highly
visible environmental catastrophe, such as the Santa Barbara oil spill,
Love Canal, or Bhopal.)

The richer, the more multi-factored our perceptions of risk, the
more difficult becomes the exercise of comparing risks to one another.
If more than one risk characteristic is acknowledged to be germane to
policy formation, for example, then the construction of simple one-factor
rankings of the kind shown in Figure 4.13 becomes impossible.

Are These Differences Relevant for Public Policy? EPA seems to
have acknowledged that some of these distinctions are germane for policy formation. EPA's policy on hazardous air pollutants, pages 594-597
above, for instance, considers both MIR and population risk in setting
acceptable risk levels. Isn't this acknowledging the distinction between
concentrated and dispersed risk? At some point, concern about concentrated risk (high MIR) seems to warrant action even if overall population
risk is quite low. See Raynor and Canoter, How Fair Is Fair Enough?

The Cultural Approach to Societal Technology Choice, 7 Risk Analysis 3 (Mar. 1987). On the other hand, couldn't exclusive attention to high MIR, if this implied more lax treatment of low but widely dispersed risk, actually increase instances of disease or death? See Goldstein, The Maximally Exposed Individual, 6 Envtl. Forum 13 (Nov.-Dec. 1989).

Likewise, the voluntary-involuntary distinction has seemed relevant to many commentators, some of whom urge that regulators secure the consent of individuals exposed to risk or else ensure that adequate compensation be provided to those injured. E.g., Brooks, The Resolution of Technically Intensive Public Policy Disputes, 9 Sci., Tech. & Hum. Values 39 (Winter 1984).

Based on the persistent findings of cognitive psychologists that these and other distinctions matter to people, Peter Sandman has proposed redefining terms. "To the experts, risk means expected annual mortality. But to the public . . . risk means much more than that. Let's redefine terms. Call [population risk] 'hazard.' Call all the other factors, collectively, 'outrage.' Risk, then, is the sum of hazard and outrage. . . . We have two decades of data indicating the voluntariness, control, fairness, and the rest are important components of our society's definition of risk. When a risk manager continues to ignore these factors—and continues to be surprised by the public's response of outrage—it is worth asking whose behavior is irrational." P. Sandman, Risk Communication: Facing Public Outrage, EPA J. 21-22 (Nov. 1987).

Should Risk Decisions Be Made Democratically, Not Technically?

Other commentators stress a theme mentioned earlier: that QRA cedes too much decisionmaking authority to technicians and should be subject to more democratic and open processes. Even if such decisions cannot routinely be made by plebiscite, the perception of trustworthiness in regulatory agencies may be as important to the public's acceptance of such decisions as are risk assessments. " 'Tolerable' risk level issues are inextricably linked with the process by which the risk was allocated or imposed." Kasperson, Six Propositions on Public Participation and Their Relevance for Risk Communication, 6 Risk Analysis 275, 280 (Sept. 1986). Maintaining public trust appears to require that agencies organize themselves so that the public and interested parties can communicate their concerns, assumptions, and choices and that ultimate decisions be seen in some sense as responsive to those inputs. See, e.g., Fiorino, Environmental Risk and Democratic Process: A Critical Review, 14 Colum. J. Envtl. L. 501 (1989); McGarity, Risk and Trust: The Role of Regulatory Agencies, 14 Envtl. L. Rptr. 10198 (Aug. 1986); Brooks, above. Two excellent analyses of the implications of the results of cognitive psychology for democratic policy are Hornstein, Reclaiming Environmental Law: A Normative Critique of Comparative Risk Analysis, 92 Colum. L. Rev. — (1992); Krier and Gillette, Risk, Courts, and Agencies, 138 U.

Pa. L. Rev. 1027 (1990). Hornstein's article also is a thoughtful review of the pros and cons of comparative risk assessment.

Reservations from the Regulated Community: Is Risk Assessment Too Conservative?

While environmentalists have become more comfortable with risk assessment, some continue to object to it. A Greenpeace representative told a congressional committee in 1991 that risk assessment "endangers the environment, public health and the democratic process" and is used "to justify pollution." House Panel Rejects Late EPA Testimony, Hears Discussion of Risk Assessment Practices, 22 Env. Rep. 225 (1991). But risk assessment is now more frequently coming under attack from the regulated community, particularly when it is used to support environmental regulation. Industries facing more stringent regulations are now seeking to revisit assumptions or methodologies employed in the risk assessments used by regulators. See, e.g., Roberts, Dioxin Risks Revisited, 251 Science 624 (1991); Roberts, Flap Erupts Over Dioxin Meeting, 251 Science 866 (1991). Scientists are being asked to take a second look at the risks of substances long ago deemed extremely hazardous based on new and supposedly more refined data. Abelson, Excessive Fear of PCBs, 253 Science 361 (1991); Stone, No Meeting of Minds on Asbestos, 254 Science 928 (1991).

The regulated community's most consistent criticism of risk assessment is the notion that it employs assumptions that are too conservative, resulting in unreasonably stringent regulation. This argument has been made most vociferously by the Office of Management and Budget. OMB makes three general arguments:

1. The continued reliance on conservative (worst-case) assumptions distorts risk assessment, yielding estimates that may overstate likely risks by several orders of magnitude. . . .
2. Conservative biases embedded in risk assessment impart a substantial "margin of safety." The choice of an appropriate margin of safety should remain the province of responsible risk-management officials, and should not be preempted through biased risk assessments. . . .
3. Conservatism in risk assessment distorts the regulatory priorities of the Federal Government, directing societal resources to reduce what are often trivial carcinogenic risks while failing to address more substantial threats to life and health. [OMB, Regulatory Program of the United States Government for Fiscal Year 1991 14 (1990).]

After reviewing OMB's critique, the Center for Risk Analysis at the Harvard School of Public Health concluded that it "does not present a balanced, accurate critique" of actual risk assessment practices by federal agencies. They note that although OMB emphasizes the use of "worst case" assumptions, it does not mention the many factors that may cause risk assessments to seriously underestimate actual risks. Most risk assessments do not consider all exposure pathways, all hazard endpoints, or the possible synergistic effects of the multiple pollutants to which humans are exposed. Some human subpopulations may be more sensitive to the toxic effects of certain substances than the animal species typically tested in bioassays. Moreover, in arguing for the use of "most likely" estimates of risk, the OMB report confuses this concept with "expected value" estimates, which generally are not equivalent. Center for Risk Analysis, Comments on OMB, Current Regulatory Issues in Risk Assessment and Management (Dec. 17, 1990).

The notion that risk assessment is inherently too cautious has been contradicted in several instances by discoveries that certain substances pose substantially greater risks than originally thought. For example, as indicated in Figure 4.14, scientists' definition of lead poisoning has been ratcheted downward substantially over the last two decades as new information has revealed that levels previously thought to be safe posed significant risks to health. Moreover, because individual variability in susceptibility to risks is high, if risks associated with chemical exposure are relative, rather than simply additive, as data suggest for radiation-induced tumors, Storer, Mitchell, and Mitchell, Extrapolation of the Relative Risk of Radiogenic Neoplasms Across Mouse Strains to Man, 114 Radiation Res. 331 (1988), then susceptible individuals face much greater additional risks from chemical exposure than are reflected in current risk assessments. Hoel, A Balanced Approach to Risk Assessment, 7 Toxicology & Indus. Health 305, 310 (1991).

Ironically, conservative assumptions are far more useful in justifying decisions *not* to regulate because they increase the decisionmaker's confidence that the risks are no greater than a certain level. As William Ruckelshaus explains:

> This conservative approach is fine when the risks projected are vanishingly small; it is always nice to learn that some chemical is *not* a national crisis. But when the risks estimated through such assessments are substantial, so that some action may be in the offing, . . . I need to know how likely *real* damage is to occur in the uncontrolled and partially controlled and fully controlled cases. Only then can I apply the balancing judgments that are the essence of my job. [Ruckelshaus, Risk in a Free Society, 14 Envtl. L. Rep. 10190, 10191 (1984).]

Thus, before EPA adopts stringent regulations, such as its decision to phase out virtually all remaining uses of asbestos, the agency may employ assumptions that it believes will substantially underestimate the risk. 54 Fed. Reg. 29,460 (1990).

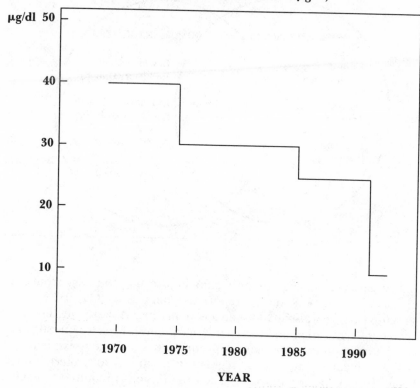

FIGURE 4.14
The Changing Definition of Childhood Lead Poisoning
(based on levels of lead in blood in μg/dl)

Because of pervasive uncertainty, scientists must employ some form of default assumptions if they are to perform quantitative risk assessments. Risk management considerations inevitably will influence these choices. Thus, rather than conceiving of the process as one sharply divided between risk assessment and risk management, the two inevitably overlap when risk characterization decisions must be made. As reflected in Figure 4.15, the process of risk characterization inevitably will be influenced in some ways by the purpose for which risks are being assessed, just as risk management decisions inevitably are influenced by economic factors, regardless of underlying statutory directives.

While risk assessment has become a pervasive feature of environmental regulation, efforts to improve how it is used, and to defuse the controversy that surrounds it, continue. In the 1990 Clean Air Act Amendments, Congress directed the National Academy of Sciences to

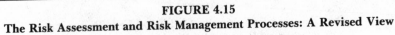

FIGURE 4.15
The Risk Assessment and Risk Management Processes: A Revised View

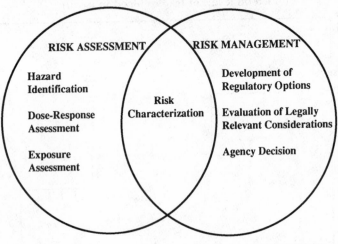

review the methodology used by EPA in assessing the risks from hazardous air pollutants and to report to Congress by May 1993. CAA §112(o). Congress also established a national Risk Assessment and Management Commission and directed it to conduct a broader investigation of "the policy implications and appropriate uses of risk assessment and risk management" in federal regulatory programs to protect human health from exposure to toxics. The Commission is required to issue a report containing recommendations for legislation or administrative action by November 1994.

E. ALTERNATIVES TO CONVENTIONAL REGULATORY APPROACHES

1. Informational and Burden-Shifting Approaches

People voluntarily engage in many activities—driving a car, skiing, mountainclimbing—that subject them to risks, sometimes significant ones. Yet people resent being exposed involuntarily to even relatively modest risks and demand that society act to minimize such exposure. See Sagoff, On Markets for Risk, 41 Md. L. Rev. 755 (1982). If the goal of toxic substance regulation is to minimize involuntary exposure to risks, it can be pursued not only by regulations that reduce toxic emissions, but also by providing individuals with information that will enable them to choose to avoid certain risks.

Informational approaches can help reduce exposure to toxics by informing consumers of risks they can choose to avoid or by generating support for further action to reduce involuntary exposures to risk. The distinction between risks borne voluntarily and those borne involuntarily is not always an easy one to make. Some risks are easier to avoid than others, and some individuals are more capable than others of taking steps to avoid risks. We have no choice about breathing, although in theory we could all wear space suits that filter toxic pollutants out of the air we breathe. But few would be comfortable with the notion that this makes such exposures a risk that we bear voluntarily, even if we were provided with comprehensive information about what pollutants were in each batch of air we encounter. Opportunities for voluntary avoidance of risks are greater when the risks involve products that informed consumers can choose not to purchase. Thus, as discussed in Chapter 2, when individuals are informed and have choices, market forces can serve as a powerful complement to regulation to prevent environmental damage.

But it is not easy to keep consumers with limited attention spans informed of the risks they may choose to avoid. Information is not gathered and distributed without cost. Yet approaches that inform consumers of risks may often be far cheaper than traditional regulatory approaches for controlling risks. The latter often place significant burdens on regulators to demonstrate that certain substances or activities pose risks worth regulating in the face of scientific uncertainty. Thus, considerable effort is being devoted to develop new informational approaches to regulation as well as approaches that shift the burden of gathering information to respond to uncertainty.

Some federal environmental regulations already require the disclosure of risk information to workers and consumers. For example, OSHA has required that workers be informed of the presence of hazardous chemicals in the workplace through a regulation called the hazard communication standard. As a result of a decision by the U.S. Court of Appeals for the Third Circuit, OSHA has expanded its initial hazard communication standard to cover all industries it regulates. United Steelworkers of America v. Auchter, 763 F.2d 728 (3d Cir. 1985). The federal Emergency Planning and Community Right-to-Know Act, discussed below, is designed to provide the public with information on the presence of toxic chemicals in their communities. It requires that companies publicly disclose their annual emissions of more than 300 different toxic chemicals and that local authorities be notified about hazardous substances stored or used by the companies.

Informational approaches also may assist in the enforcement of environmental laws. For example, the Safe Drinking Water Act requires that public water suppliers inform their customers when they violate the Act either by failing to monitor drinking water or by detecting contaminants in it at levels that exceed the maximum contaminant levels promulgated under the Act. By requiring that potential victims be informed of violations, this kind of informational regulation can contribute to public pressure to correct violations. For example, the editor of a small newspaper in Washington, North Carolina became curious when he noticed a cryptic sentence on the back of his water bill. When he inquired further he discovered information that led to his writing a Pulitzer Prize-winning series of articles. The articles revealed that for eight years local authorities had sought to conceal the fact that enormously high levels of carcinogenic chemicals had contaminated the town's drinking water. Within a month of the first article informing residents of the danger, the town's water supply system was shut down and the incumbent mayor was defeated in a bid for reelection. A new filtration system ultimately was installed to remove the chemicals from the drinking water. Pitt, City Gets Clean Water; Its Paper Gets a Pulitzer, N.Y. Times, April 16, 1990, at A10.

Informational regulations have not always proved successful. In 1983, EPA decided an informational approach was the best way to respond to the widespread presence of asbestos hazards in schools. Rather than issuing regulations requiring that asbestos hazards be abated, EPA required school authorities to undertake a one-time inspection of their buildings to determine if friable asbestos was present and to inform parents and school employees if such materials were found. EPA officials believed that if parents were informed that their children were exposed to a potential hazard, they would ensure that action would promptly be taken to abate it. The regulation, however, proved to have unfortunate consequences. Despite EPA's efforts to provide guidance, school officials generally had a poor understanding of asbestos hazards and the proper means for abating them. Many inspections were poorly performed. Discoveries of asbestos often produced panicked reactions from parents and school authorities that actually may have exacerbated the risks to children. In 1987, Congress responded to this debacle by requiring EPA to issue regulations requiring periodic inspections for asbestos and specifying abatement actions that must be undertaken when asbestos hazards are found.

As concern for protection of health grows, private industry has become more interested in providing consumers with information that will assist them in purchasing safe products. For example, a number of supermarket chains have agreed to conduct testing programs to ensure that the fruits and vegetables they carry are free from pesticides. Schneider, Grocery Chains Testing for Pesticides, N.Y. Times, Oct. 20, 1987. Ironically, regulatory authorities have been critical of such programs on the ground that the government, and not the private sector, should be responsible for determining the safety of the food supply. Concern over misleading information supplied by vendors of food products resulted in enactment of the Nutrition Labeling and Education Act of 1990, 104 Stat. 2353. The Act limits health claims that can be made in advertising food products to four that are viewed as supported by broad scientific consensus. The legislation also requires that food products be labeled with certain uniform nutritional information to assist consumers in purchasing healthy products.

While informational approaches to regulation are generally considered to be less burdensome on industry than other forms of regulation, the Office of Management and Budget has voiced concern over the growing use of informational strategies for regulation. OMB acknowledges that informational approaches can be valuable alternatives to traditional regulation in some circumstances, but it implies that private markets can do a better job of producing and disseminating the optimal level of information than existing regulations. In OMB's view, the OSHA Hazard Communication standard is too comprehensive because it attempts to inform employees of all potential safety or health risks from chemicals regardless of their magnitude. OMB believes that this cannot be justified in economic terms unless there is "a systematic market failure across virtually all potentially hazardous chemicals." OMB, Regulatory Program of the U.S. Government April 1, 1990-March 31, 1991, at 29 (1990). OMB notes that regulations implementing EPA's Emergency Planning and Community Right-to-Know Act were developed without determing how much information would be economically optimal and that they duplicate informational requirements imposed on owners of underground storage tanks. Id. at 30. The application of "right-to-know" legislation to food labeling would constitute an unfair subsidy of the rich by the poor, OMB argues. Because the costs of providing information will be passed on to all consumers, poor people who do not care about risk information will have to pay for ensuring that wealthier people who are more likely to value such information are kept informed, according to OMB. Id. Do you agree with these criticisms?

As we have seen, a critical issue environmental regulation attempts to address is how to respond to uncertainty. Regulations that increase incentives for gathering and disseminating information may help improve society's response to environmental risk by reducing uncertainties concerning the presence and significance of risks. While regulatory authorities generally bear the burden of proving that risks are significant enough to warrant regulation, some new approaches to regulation have sought to shift this burden by requiring persons who generate risks to demonstrate that the risks are insignificant enough to warrant regulation. Licensing schemes such as FIFRA and the Food, Drug, and Cosmetic Act already shift the burden to the manufacturers of pesticides, therapeutic drugs, and food additives to demonstrate the safety of their products. But society generally has not required that manufacturers of other products or dischargers of toxic pollutants make similar demonstrations, perhaps because they would be deemed too burdensome. A California citizens' initiative called Proposition 65, which was adopted in 1986, represents the most innovative effort to change the traditional burden of proof in a manner that would generate incentives for reducing public exposure to involuntary risk.

A. CALIFORNIA'S PROPOSITION 65: A BURDEN-SHIFTING APPROACH TO THE INFORMATION PROBLEM

On November 4, 1986, California voters overwhelmingly approved an innovative new approach to regulation of toxic substances. The law, adopted as voter initiative Proposition 65, is titled the "Safe Drinking Water and Toxic Enforcement Act of 1986." It combines a duty-to-warn approach with a shifting of the burden of demonstrating the safety of emissions of carcinogens and reproductive toxins. The simple concept articulated in Proposition 65 is that no one should knowingly expose another without warning to chemicals known to cause cancer or reproductive toxicity unless the discharger can demonstrate that the risk is not significant. This concept had so much political appeal that the initiative's opponents thought it could be defeated only by convincing voters that it had too many loopholes. Noting that Proposition 65 did not apply to pollution from government agencies, oil companies and agribusinesses waged a $5.7 million advertising campaign against the initiative with the official slogan: "No on 65. It's Full of Exemptions." Proponents responded that they would be happy to work to remove any loopholes after Proposition 65 was approved. Voters approved the initiative by nearly a 2-1 margin. (Ironically, a subsequent voter initiative to extend Proposition 65 to government agencies was narrowly defeated in 1990 after fierce opposition from local governments concerned that it would require extensive warnings about drinking water contamination.)

The operative provisions of Proposition 65 are remarkably simple. First, the law prohibits the discharge into sources of drinking water of any chemical that is a carcinogen or reproductive toxin except in amounts that the discharger can prove are insignificant. The law states:

> No person in the course of doing business shall knowingly discharge or release a chemical known to the state to cause cancer or reproductive toxicity into water or onto or into land where such chemical passes or probably will pass into any source of drinking water, notwithstanding any other provisions of authorization of law except as provided in Section 25249.9. [Ch. 6.6 Cal. Health & Safety Code §25249.5.]

Section 25249.9 exempts discharges that the discharger shows "will not cause any significant amount of the discharged or released chemical to enter any source of drinking water" and that also are in compliance with all applicable regulations.

The second major provision of Proposition 65 is a prohibition on exposing anyone to carcinogens or reproductive toxins without warning unless the person responsible for the exposure can show that it poses no significant risk assuming lifetime exposure. The law provides:

> No person in the course of doing business shall knowingly and intentionally expose any individual to a chemical known to the state to cause cancer or reproductive toxicity without first giving a clear and reasonable warning to such individual, except as provided in Section 25249.10. [Ch. 6.6 Cal. Health & Safety Code §25249.6.]

Section 25249.10 exempts both exposures "for which federal law governs warning in a manner that preempts state authority" and:

> [a]n exposure for which the person responsible can show that the exposure poses no significant risk assuming lifetime exposure at the level in question for substances known to the state to cause cancer, and that the exposure will have no observable effect assuming exposure at one thousand (1,000) times the level in question for substances known to the state to cause reproductive toxicity, based on evidence and standards of comparable scientific validity to the evidence and standards which form the scientific basis for the listing of such chemical [as a substance known to cause cancer or reproductive toxicity]. [Ch. 6.6 Cal. Health & Safety Code §25249.10.]

Proposition 65 attempts to overcome some of the problems that have plagued chemical-by-chemical regulation of toxic substances by shifting the burden to dischargers of carcinogens and reproductive toxins to show that their discharges pose no significant risk. It avoids the problem of making government agencies determine how to control emissions by leaving that up to the discharger, who has the option of warning exposed individuals about emissions that the discharger is unwilling to control (unless the discharges are into a source of drinking water). To facilitate enforcement, the law authorizes enforcement actions by any citizen, as well as state and local officials, and it permits citizen plaintiffs to retain a portion of the civil penalties assessed against violators.

Not surprisingly, the initial implementation of Proposition 65 created considerable controversy. Bowing to industry pressure, California governor George Deukmejian placed only substances that had been demonstrated to cause cancer and reproductive toxicity in *humans* on the list of chemicals "known to the state to cause cancer." Thus, the state's original list of carcinogens and reproductive toxins subject to the law contained only 29 substances. Arguing that the law also required the listing of all substances that cause cancer or reproductive damage in animal tests, the supporters of Proposition 65 sued the governor. In AFL-CIO v. Deukmejian, 260 Cal. Rptr. 479 (Cal. App. 1989), the California Court of Appeals held that chemicals found to be carcinogens or reproductive toxins as a result of animal testing had to be included in the minimum list of chemicals "known to the state to cause cancer or reproductive toxicity" as defined by Proposition 65.

Following the decision in AFL-CIO v. Deukmejian, the list of chemicals known to the state of California to cause cancer or reproductive toxicity has been substantially expanded beyond the governor's initial list. By the end of 1991, 480 chemicals were on the list. Some products containing these substances have been exempted by regulation.

In response to a petition from the Grocery Manufacturers of America, the California Health and Welfare Agency, the agency designated by the governor to implement Proposition 65, exempted food products containing naturally occurring carcinogens and reproductive toxins from the requirements of the legislation. The exemption applies to chemicals that are natural constituents of food or that can be shown to be present "solely as a result of absorption or accumulation of the chemical" from "the environment in which the food is raised, or grown, or obtained." 22 Cal. Code Regs. §12501. However, producers and distributors of food are required to use quality control measures that reduce natural chemical contaminants to the "lowest level currently feasible." In Nicolle-Wagner v. Deukmejian, 230 Cal. App. 3d 652, 281 Cal. Rptr. 494 (1991), this exemption was upheld by a California court of appeals, which found that Proposition 65 was directed at controlling exposure to toxics added to the environment by human activity.

While Proposition 65 does not specify what constitutes a "significant risk" for purposes of exposure to substances subject to the law, the law authorizes the California Health and Welfare Agency to issue regulations implementing its provisions. Because Proposition 65 placed the burden of disproving that a risk was significant on the discharger, California businesses discharging listed substances pressed for swift enactment of regulations specifying what exposure levels posed "significant risk." The shift in the burden of proof reversed the normal incentive for the regulated community to seek delay in the issuance of implementing regulations. Toxicologists from all over the country swarmed to California to participate in regulatory proceedings implementing the Act. Acting far more rapidly than federal regulators ever had, the Health and Welfare Agency issued regulations covering hundreds of toxic substances. The regulations define "significant risk" for carcinogens as a risk greater than 1 in 100,000. For reproductive toxins, Proposition 65 specifies that exposure at a level of one-thousandth the no-observed-effects level or above constitutes a "significant risk."

The key to its rapid and comprehensive regulatory implementation was that Proposition 65 reversed the usual incentive for industry to prolong the regulatory process with endless debates over "how safe is safe." As David Roe, a co-author of the law, observes, "California managed to draw bright lines for more chemicals in the first twelve months of the Proposition 65 era than the federal government had managed to accomplish, under the supposedly omnibus Toxic Substances Control Act, in the previous twelve years." Roe notes that "much of the scientific information on which the California lines were based came directly from federal regulatory agencies, which had long since completed their assessment of the relevant research results; the difference was that, for once, there was a premium on getting to the bottom line." Roe, An Incentive-Conscious Approach to Toxic Chemical Controls, 3 Econ. Dev. Q. 179, 181 (1989).

Businesses that discharge a listed substance at levels in excess of those defined to constitute a "significant risk" can escape liability (unless the substance passes into a source of drinking water) by providing a "clear and reasonable warning" to persons exposed. The question of what constitutes such a warning has been a subject of some dispute. A trade association of grocers initially responded to Proposition 65 by establishing a toll-free telephone number that consumers could call to find out if certain products contained carcinogens or reproductive toxins in significant amounts. Callers were not permitted to request a list of products containing carcinogens or reproductive toxins, but were warned if they happened to ask about a specific product that did. Although the hotline received 28,000 calls in the first 14 months, only 488 warning messages were issued. Grocers maintained that the availability of the toll-free number made it unnecessary for warning labels to be displayed in their stores. Proponents of Proposition 65, who dubbed the system "800-BALONEY," filed suit, maintaining that the toll-free number was an attempt to circumvent the law. In August 1989 a California Superior Court ruled that the toll-free number "does not provide clear and reasonable warnings" as required by the law.

Regulations implementing Proposition 65 initially created a safe harbor for companies discharging airborne carcinogens if they took out a small newspaper ad stating: "WARNING: This area contains a chemical known to the state of California to cause cancer." 22 Cal. Code Reg. §12601. After a successful court challenge to this regulation, a new warning requirement was proposed that would include signs stating: "WARNING: Emissions or effluents from this facility will expose you to chemicals known to the state of California to cause cancer, including the following. . . ." Pease, Chemical Hazards and the Public's Right to Know: How Effective Is California's Proposition 65?, 33 Environment 13 (Dec. 1991).

Business interests opposed to Proposition 65 vigorously lobbied the Reagan Administration to preempt it. They argued that Proposition 65 creates barriers to interstate commerce by requiring warning labels on their products, sold in a state with 15 percent of the national market. The Reagan Administration rejected these requests. Claims that Proposition 65 is preempted by FIFRA in its application to pesticides or by the Federal Hazardous Substances Act, 15 U.S.C. §1261, which authorizes the Consumer Product Safety Commission to regulate hazardous consumer products, have been rejected by courts. D-Con v. Allenby, 728 F. Supp. 605 (N.D. Cal. 1989); Chemical Specialties Manufacturers Association v. Allenby, 744 F. Supp. 934 (N.D. Cal. 1990).

Shortly after enactment of Proposition 65, the chairman of the Chemical Manufacturers' Association predicted that the law would have "a significant and detrimental effect on the agricultural and manufacturing business in the state." CMA Chairman Urges Renewal of Clean Air Act, Voluntary Steps on Air Toxics by Industry, 17 Env. Rep. 220 (1986). Yet little evidence has developed to suggest that the Act has had such an impact. Fear of adverse consumer reactions to warning labels has encouraged some manufacturers to reformulate their products to remove carcinogens and reproductive toxins. Kiwi Brands, Inc., a division of Sara Lee, removed a carcinogenic chemical from its Kiwi waterproofing spray for shoes. Pet Inc. accelerated the removal of lead solder from cans used for several of its products including Old El Paso tamale/chili gravy and Progresso tomatoes. It is impossible to tell how frequently products are being reformulated. While some companies are releasing products with "new formulas they can now tout as safer—and sometimes even more effective, . . . [o]ther companies are reformulating quietly to avoid calling attention to chemicals in their old products." Smith, California Spurs Reformulated Products, Wall St. J., Nov. 1, 1990, at B1. Sears, Roebuck and Company reports that several of its suppliers have reformulated scores of products including carburetor cleaners and car wax.

A study of the impact of Proposition 65 notes that since 1987 California companies subject to the reporting provisions of the federal Emergency Planning and Community Right-to-Know Act no longer report discharging six of the listed chemicals. Pease, above, at 16. The study noted that as of 1991 only 13 legal actions had been initiated under Proposition 65 for exposure to airborne toxics. Six were initiated by environmental groups and seven by the California attorney general. Id. at 19-20. Some of these actions have produced notable results. Five of eight companies discharging ethylene oxide have agreed either to eliminate its use or to reduce emissions by 99 percent and to pay penalties that range from $125,000 to $1.1 million. In response to a private lawsuit, the California wine industry agreed to discontinue the use of lead foil wrappers for wine bottles starting January 1, 1992.

One concern voiced by critics of Proposition 65 is that products containing weak carcinogens will be replaced with more dangerous substances that have not been identified as carcinogens or reproductive toxins because they have not been fully tested. When threatened with a lawsuit in September 1989, the Gillette Company removed Liquid Paper correction fluid from the California market because it contained trichloroethylene (TCE), a carcinogenic substance. Four months later it introduced a "New Improved" Liquid Paper reformulated with the solvent 1,1,1-trichloroethane (TCA) instead of TCE. Yet an official of the Consumer Product Safety Commission has expressed "great concern" that TCA could be carcinogenic because of its structural similarity to the solvents it replaced. Smith, above, at B7. In fact, Liquid Paper's leading competitor, Wite-Out Products, Inc., which originally had switched to TCA, has introduced a new correction fluid without TCA because of concern that TCA is toxic and likely to be banned as an ozone-depleting chemical.

NOTES AND QUESTIONS

1. Apparently Proposition 65 is not having nearly the dire economic impact forecast by the business interests who opposed its adoption. Does this suggest that companies can readily find noncarcinogenic substitutes for substances subject to the Act, or does it indicate that the legislation has had little impact on actual exposure?

2. How do the levels that define "significant risk" for purposes of Proposition 65 compare with EPA's answer to the "how safe is safe" question under section 112 of the Clean Air Act?

3. An unusual provision of the law is section 25180.7, which requires government employees to report within 72 hours to local health officers and to the local Board of Supervisors any information they receive about the illegal discharge of hazardous waste that is likely to cause injury to public health. Why do you think such a provision was included in the law?

4. Should Proposition 65 be preempted? What if it were found to have a significant impact on the production practices of national manufacturers? The Reagan and Bush Administrations have stressed that respect for state autonomy is important to federalism. Indeed, Executive Order 12,612, 3 C.F.R. 252 (1987), requires federal agencies to defer to state standard-setting wherever possible. Would federal intervention to preempt Proposition 65 be consistent with these principles?

5. Critics of Proposition 65 note that it does not distinguish between the relative levels of risk posed by different products that contain substances subject to the law. Concerns have been expressed that Proposition 65 will saturate consumers with warnings about a bewildering array of relatively minor risks, overwarning consumers to the point that they will abandon risk-avoidance efforts. Proposition 65's impact could be severely

diluted if industry groups include warning labels on virtually all products to avoid any potential liability under Proposition 65. How realistic is this fear?

6. Now that the California wine industry has agreed to discontinue the use of lead foil wrappers, if lead continues to be found in wine will the industry have any reason to fear liability under Proposition 65?

B.   THE EMERGENCY PLANNING AND COMMUNITY RIGHT-TO-KNOW ACT

In December 1984 an accidental release of methyl isocynate at a chemical plant owned by the Union Carbide Corporation in Bhopal, India killed more than 3,000 people and severely injured scores of thousands of others. In response to this tragedy, several bills were introduced into Congress to strengthen regulation of toxic air pollutants. While arguing that a similar accident could not happen in the United States, the chemical industry pledged to reexamine its safety practices. On August 11, 1985, an accidental release of aldicarb oxime at a Union Carbide plant in Institute, West Virginia resulted in the brief hospitalization of scores of residents, severely damaging the credibility of the industry shortly after it had assured the public that such accidents could not happen here.

Congress ultimately responded not by enacting new controls on toxic emissions, but rather by adopting legislation requiring comprehensive emergency planning and the reporting of chemical releases. This legislation, which was adopted at the same time as the Superfund Amendments and Reauthorization Act of 1986, is known as the Emergency Planning and Community Right-to-Know Act of 1986 (EPCRTKA), Pub. L. 99-499, 100 Stat. 1613 (1986), 42 U.S.C. §§11001-11050. The principal provisions of the Act are outlined below. Section 301 of EPCRTKA requires the establishment of state emergency response commissions and local emergency planning committees, which must develop comprehensive emergency response plans required by section 303. Section 304 of EPCRTKA requires companies to notify these officials if any chemicals placed by EPA on a list of extremely hazardous substances pursuant to section 302 are released in amounts greater than certain designated thresholds.

PRINCIPAL PROVISIONS OF THE EMERGENCY PLANNING AND COMMUNITY RIGHT-TO-KNOW ACT

Section 301 requires the establishment of state emergency response commissions and local emergency planning committees.

Section 302 requires EPA to publish a list of extremely hazardous substances and threshold planning quantities for these substances. Requires facilities where substances on the list are present in an amount in excess of the threshold quantities to notify the state emergency response commission and the local emergency planning committees.

Section 303 requires local emergency planning committees to prepare a comprehensive emergency response plan and specifies minimum requirements for such plans.

Section 304 requires owners and operators of facilities to notify community emergency response coordinators of releases of extremely hazardous substances.

Sections 311 and 312 require owners and operators of facilities required by OSHA to prepare material safety data sheets (MSDSs) to submit MSDSs and an emergency and hazardous chemical inventory form to the local emergency planning committee, the state emergency response commission, and the local fire department.

Section 313 requires owners and operators of facilities that have ten or more full-time employees and that are in SIC Codes 20 through 39 as of July 1, 1985 to complete a toxic chemical release form reporting the releases of each of more than 300 toxic chemicals used in quantities that exceed established threshold quantities during the preceding calendar year. These forms must be submitted to EPA and state officials by July 1 of each year to report data reflecting releases during the preceding calendar year. EPA is required to establish and maintain in a computer database a national toxic release inventory (TRI), based on data submitted on these forms, which must be accessible by the public through computer telecommunication.

Section 325 provides for civil, administrative, and criminal penalties for certain violations of the Act and authorizes enforcement actions by EPA.

Section 326 authorizes citizen suits against owners and operators of facilities that fail to comply with the Act and against the EPA administrator and state officials for failure to perform certain duties required by the Act.

To facilitate emergency planning, sections 311 and 312 of EPCRTKA require companies to report annually to local emergency planning authorities information concerning the identities, locations, and amounts of hazardous chemicals used at the facilities. Perhaps the most significant new requirement added by EPCRTKA is contained in section 313, which requires for the first time annual reporting of releases of toxic chemicals. This provision covers companies that employ ten or more full-time employees in a wide variety of industries if they manufacture, process, or otherwise use more than certain threshold quantities of listed chemicals. These companies must file Toxic Chemical Release Forms or Emissions Inventories with EPA and the states by July 1 of every year. The reports must include estimates of the "annual quantity of the toxic chemicals entering each environmental medium." The reports are to be based on readily ascertainable data; no additional monitoring or measurement requirements are imposed. Citizen suits can be brought under section 326 of EPCRTKA against companies that fail to comply with the reporting requirements imposed by the legislation.

The information generated by EPCRTKA's reporting requirements must be made available to the public through a national computerized database accessible through personal computers. Congress anticipated that the availability of information about releases of toxic chemicals would enable the public to put substantial pressure on companies to reduce emissions. Early returns suggest that the law is having this impact.

Results of the first Toxic Release Inventory (TRI) were summarized at the beginning of this chapter. EPA was shocked by the large volume of reported releases. Community organizations and environmental groups used the data to support calls for stronger regulation. During the first week after the TRI became available through the National Library of Medicine, the Library received 225 requests for subscriptions, most from community groups and ordinary citizens. Suro, Grass-Roots Groups Show Power Battling Pollution Close to Home, N.Y. Times, July 2, 1989, at 1. On August 1, 1989, USA Today published a two-page list of "The Toxic 500," the U.S. counties with the most pollution from industrial chemicals as reported in the TRI. The National Wildlife Federation published a book identifying the 500 largest dischargers, who released more than 7.5 billion pounds of toxics, including 39 known or probable carcinogens. See G. Poje, The Toxic 500 (1988). NRDC used the data to prepare "A Who's Who of American Toxic Air Polluters" identifying more than 1,500 major sources of toxic air emissions. Subsequent updates of the TRI have continued to receive wide publicity, Holusha, The Nation's Pollution: Who Emits What, and Where, N.Y. Times, Oct. 13, 1991, at F10 (see Figure 4.16), and many community groups have used the TRI to issue reports publicizing local polluters. Schneider, For Communities, Knowledge of Polluters Is Power, N.Y. Times, Mar. 14, 1991, at D5.

As a result of publicity concerning their toxic releases, many companies have pledged to make voluntary reductions. Officials of some companies stated that they were shocked to discover that they were releasing such large quantities of toxic substances. The Monsanto Cor-

FIGURE 4.16
Toxic Air and Water Emissions by State

Where the Water Is Tainted

Pounds per square mile in each state.

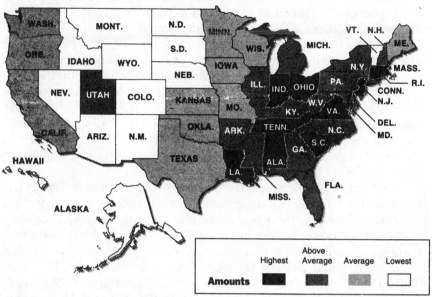

Amounts — Highest | Above Average | Average | Lowest

Where the Air is Bad

Pounds per square mile in each state.

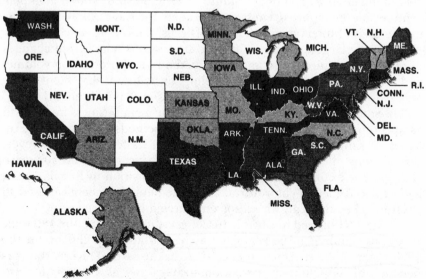

Source: Holusha, The Nation's Polluters—Who Emits What, and Where, N.Y. Times, Oct. 13, 1991, at F10.

625

poration, for example, found that its 35 plants released more than 374 million pounds of toxic substances, more than 20 million pounds of it into the air. As a result, Monsanto's chairman pledged to reduce air emissions of hazardous chemicals by 90 percent by the end of 1992. Elkins, Toxic Chemicals, the Right Response, N.Y. Times, Nov. 13, 1988, at F3; Shabecoff, The Early Returns of a Toxic Poll, N.Y. Times, Nov. 20, 1988, at F10. AT&T has established a goal of eliminating all its toxic air emissions by the year 2000. Representatives of the Chemical Manufacturers Association concede that current levels of toxic emissions are too high and that public disclosure will spur companies to find ways to reduce releases. Section 313 Reports of Toxic Emissions Said to Reveal Need for Pollution Prevention, 19 Env. Rep. 154, 155 (1989). Some financial advisers have even begun to use the TRI data to screen companies for investors based on the belief that large dischargers of toxics are not efficient producers. Holusha, The Nation's Pollution: Who Emits What, and Where, N.Y. Times, Oct. 13, 1991, at F10.

A study of the ways eight companies have responded to EPCRTKA found that the TRI data have generated new corporate waste reduction initiatives. Ironically, the study noted that while these companies were motivated by fears of common law liability, adverse publicity, and new regulatory requirements, these fears probably were not well-founded because the public has not yet taken full advantage of the TRI data. Tufts University Center for Environmental Management, Managing Chemical Risks: Corporate Response to SARA Title III (July 1990). Analyzing the data filed by 29 companies responsible for nearly 23 percent of emissions, a National Wildlife Federation study found a 39 percent decline in reported emissions between 1987 and 1988. However, on the basis of interviews with plant officials, the report concluded that "most of the largest decreases in toxic emissions resulted from changes in reporting requirements, analytical methods, and production volume, and not from source reduction, recycling, or pollution abatement." Poje and Horowitz, Phantom Reductions: Tracking Toxic Trends 1 (Aug. 1990). Some companies had reclassified their main business in order to escape reporting requirements, used new methods for estimating releases, or simply stopped reporting on certain waste streams. However, several companies *had* changed production practices to reduce toxic discharges. For example, the Unocal Chemicals Division in Kenai, Alaska had replaced methyl chloroform, an ozone-depleting chemical used to clean metal equipment, with a solvent derived from citrus peel.

The TRI proved invaluable to Congress in specifying the 189 toxic chemicals required to be regulated as hazardous air pollutants in the 1990 Clean Air Act Amendments. EPA has used the TRI as the cornerstone of its pollution prevention strategy and as a means for improving the effectiveness of existing regulatory programs. Based on data from the TRI, EPA has asked 600 dischargers to reduce voluntarily their emissions of 17 of the most dangerous toxics by 1995. The TRI has helped EPA adjust its regulatory priorities by revealing that some chemicals are released in far greater quantities than the Agency had anticipated. For example, epichlorohydrin, a chemical used in the production of epoxy resins, solvents, plastics, and other products, is classified as a probable human carcinogen, but EPA had not considered regulating it until the TRI revealed that 70 facilities in 24 states discharged 363,000 pounds of it in 1987. EPA previously had only been aware of 20 sources of epichlorohydrin emissions. Elkins, EPA Has Varied Plans for Use of Toxic Release Inventory Database, Hazardous Waste Management 42 (Aug. 1989). Congress subsequently placed this chemical on the list of 189 substances that must be regulated as hazardous air pollutants. EPA's Water Office has used the TRI data to identify potential violations of NPDES permits, to help in reviewing permit requests, and to establish water quality standards. The Agency's Office of Toxic Substances has screened TRI data to determine what existing chemicals should be subjected to regulatory investigations and to verify production estimates for regulated chemicals.

NOTES AND QUESTIONS

1. The TRI is by no means a complete listing of all releases of toxic chemicals. Federal facilities, as well as major nonmanufacturing operations that release large quantities of toxics (such as incinerators, electric utilities, TSDs, the transportation industry, and mining operations), are exempt from the Act's reporting requirements. EPA also has exempted toxics sent to recycling facilities, even though substantial releases may occur from recycling operations. Shenkman, Right-to-Know More, 1990 Envtl. Forum 21, 23-25 (July-Aug. 1990). Is there any justification for not extending EPCRTKA's requirements to facilities that discharge more than certain threshold quantities of toxics?

2. EPCRTKA does not require that any warning labels be placed on products or that the public be informed prior to toxics discharges. Data on toxic releases are reported once a year, after the releases have occurred. Thus, unlike Proposition 65, which has the potential to mobilize the market forces of consumer purchasing decisions, EPCRTKA's effectiveness will turn on the extent to which the public uses the TRI to lobby for emissions reductions. Which approach do you think will be more effective in reducing exposures to toxics, Proposition 65 or EPCRTKA—or are the two approaches more properly viewed as complementary? How could the TRI data help plaintiffs seeking to enforce Proposition 65's requirements?

3. NRDC has criticized EPA's pollution prevention strategy for focusing on reducing toxic *releases* rather than reducing the *generation*

of toxic wastes. The group has recommened that EPCRTKA's reporting requirements be expanded to require accounting for quantities of chemicals used, produced, or generated as waste per unit of production. This would enable authorities to develop more effective source reduction strategies that focus on inefficient users and producers of toxics. NRDC Proposes Strategy to Reduce Inefficient Use of Toxic Chemicals, 22 Env. Rep. 2055 (1991).

4. Inspired by the apparent success of EPA's program, England, Australia, and Canada have begun to develop programs similar to the TRI. American companies subject to the reporting requirements are recommending that they be extended to their international competitors as well. This proposal is likely to be discussed at the "Earth Summit" in Rio de Janeiro in June 1992.

5. Concerned that many companies had failed to comply with EPCRTKA's reporting requirements, EPA announced that it would inspect 800 facilities per year by coupling EPCRTKA compliance inspections with those made under TSCA and FIFRA. Final Compliance Monitoring Strategy for EPCRTKA Section 313 Issued by Agency, 19 Env. Rep. 611 (1988). An EPA contractor who conducted a pilot study of 25 facilities that had filed TRI reports determined that approximately 80 percent of the estimates of toxic releases were in close agreement with the contractor's assessment. Estimates of Toxic Chemical Releases Seem Fairly Accurate, Pilot Study Finds, 19 Env. Rep. 2701 (1989).

2. Common Law Liability

As noted in Chapter 2, common law liability can be viewed as a system for regulating the production of environmental harms and, as such, an alternative to centralized command-and-control regulation. Because common law liability serves not only to compensate individuals after damage has occurred but also to create incentives to prevent future damage and thus to avoid further liability, it can result in reductions in environmentally harmful behavior. See the discussion of the relationship between tort liability and safety regulation, page 34.

The idea that common law liability might substitute for statutory controls gains some credence when you realize that many of the environmental harms that the environmental statutes are designed to reduce have been clearly cognizable at common law for centuries. "Under settled principles in the law of nuisance, trespass, and personal injury tort, actors can be held liable for the injuries they cause to the person or property of another. Polluters were never an exception to this rule. . . ." C. Schroeder, The Evolution of Federal Regulation of Toxic Substances, in Government and Environmental Politics 263, 277-278 (M. Lacey, ed. 1989).

Furthermore, many people are dissatisfied with the relatively slow progress under the federal statutes as well as with other characteristics of the statutory system. Some have grown so dissatisfied with the workings of centralized command-and-control regulation that they would urge as much reliance on the common law liability system as possible, and would correspondingly dismantle much of the statutory system that presently exists.

According to Havender and Wilson,

> It is likely that when the actors in the economy are operating under rules that unambiguously assign responsibility (subject to the incentives and constraints of possible loss of markets, potential liability, and insurance oversight), simply letting those [forces] loose will result in a better balance between the public's need for innovation and its competing need for safety than the practice of boundless "prudence" that has taken form in our current law and regulatory customs. [Havender and Wilson, Cancer's Uncertainty and Public Policy, 2 Cato J. 543, 564 (1982).]

In contrast, others think the prospects for the private law of tort, nuisance, and trespass adequately to handle many of the problems posed by environmental harms are actually rather dim, and that the common law's inadequacies are, indeed, one of the explanations and justifications for the development of statutory regulation of the environment. See, e.g., Schroeder, above; Abraham, Individual Action and Collective Responsibility: The Dilemma of Mass Tort Reform, 73 Va. L. Rev. 845 (1987).

Perhaps the fairest assessment is somewhere in between: The common law may be able to substitute for centralized regulation in some situations, and it may be a valuable supplement to such regulation (which typically does not provide compensation for victims) in others.

Toxic tort litigation has been dominated by the massive numbers of lawsuits brought by workers exposed to asbestos. It is estimated that more than 21 million Americans have experienced occupational exposures to asbestos and that at least 200,000 of them will die by the end of the century from cancers caused by asbestos. I. Selikoff, Disability Compensation for Asbestos-Associated Disease in the United States (June 1981). When all diseases caused by asbestos are considered, it is estimated that 265,000 people in the United States will have died as a result of asbestos-related diseases by the year 2015. P. MacAvoy, The Economic Consequences of Asbestos-Related Disease (1982).

Paul Brodeur provides a dramatic account of the history of the asbestos litigation in his book Outrageous Misconduct. He describes how the legal strategy set in motion by a few small-town lawyers eventually overcame the concerted efforts of manufacturers of asbestos products and their insurers to conceal evidence demonstrating that the companies were aware that asbestos was killing workers on a vast scale. The asbestos industry maintained that they were unaware of the dangers of exposure to asbestos at the levels workers encountered until an influential study performed by Dr. Irving Selikoff was released in 1965. The key legal victory overturning this "state-of-the-art" defense occurred in Borel v. Fibreboard Paper Products Corp., 493 F.2d 1076 (5th Cir. 1973), cert. denied, 419 U.S. 869 (1974).

Despite workers' compensation laws that bar suits by workers against their employers, asbestos litigation mushroomed after courts recognized the right of workers to sue the suppliers of asbestos for failure to warn of its risks. As the Fifth Circuit subsequently observed in Jackson v. Johns-Manville Sales Corp., 750 F.2d 1314, 1335-1336 (5th Cir. 1985) (en banc), "No other category of tort litigation has ever approached, either qualitatively or quantitatively, the magnitude of the claims premised on asbestos exposure." By 1982 the costs to industry of the asbestos litigation had reached $1 billion and the litigation had precipitated the bankruptcy of a major U.S. corporation, the Manville Corporation. Estimates of the cost of future liability range from $8 to $87 billion over the next 25 years. While it is now clear that the victims of asbestos exposure will never receive adequate compensation, a reviewer of Brodeur's account concludes that the primary lesson of the history of the asbestos tragedy is that "the tort system emerged as *the* uniquely effective means of exposing and defeating the asbestos conspiracy, providing compensation to victims and deterring future malfeasance." Rosenberg, The Dusting of America: A Story of Asbestos—Carnage, Cover-up and Litigation, 99 Harv. L. Rev. 1693, 1695 (1986).

While a handful of other industries may face massive tort liability (e.g., lead paint manufacturers), there are formidable obstacles to the use of tort litigation to redress environmental exposures to toxics. See, e.g., Santiago v. Sherwin-Williams, — F. Supp. — (D. Mass. 1992) (rejecting market share liability theory in lawsuit against lead paint manufacturers because of the absence of signature injuries). In order to introduce you to the possibilities and the limitations of common law liability as an environmental regulatory tool, in this section we review some of the major stumbling blocks it faces with respect to the regulation of toxic substances, as well as some of the efforts to surmount those obstacles.

A. CAUSATION

Certainly the most intractable obstacle to recovery at common law for toxic discharges is proving causation. The common law standard requires that the plaintiff prove that but for the defendant's conduct plaintiff's injury would not have occurred. This requirement has been called "the most pervasive and enduring requirement of tort liability over the centuries." Wright, Actual Causation v. Probabilistic Linkage: The Bane of Economic Analysis, 14 J. Legal. Stud. 435, 435 (1985). Meeting it is frequently beyond the capacities of scientific knowledge. In some circumstances, science will simply be unable to establish that exposure to a particular chemical is capable of causing the kind of harm of which the plaintiff complains. Even when science can establish a causal link between toxic agent and harm, that link will be limited to statistical correlation.

Phillip Harter explains that the concept of medical causation turns on statistical associations between categories of events rather than individual cases. After two events are determined to be associated statistically, several criteria must be employed to assess whether they are "causally" related. These include: (1) the strength of the association between exposure and disease, (2) its consistency over populations and circumstances, (3) its timing (does exposure antedate the disease?), (4) its specificity, (5) whether the frequency and severity of the disease varies with the length and strength of exposure, (6) the biological plausibility of the causal relationship, and (7) the prevalence of the disease among exposed and unexposed populations.

> These criteria are then used to determine whether members of an exposed population are more likely to develop a disease than those who were not. Since these relationships are statistical correlations among categories of populations, causation is therefore expressed in terms of a probability of incurring the disease following an exposure. Only rarely can it be scientifically determined that someone who has a disease contracted it because of an exposure to a particular agent. [P. Harter, The Dilemma of Causation in Toxic Torts i-iii (1986).]

Compounding the problems with statistical evidence is the fact that plaintiffs frequently can prove so little about the specific circumstances leading up to their illness that medical causation evidence cannot be easily applied to their individual cases. The exact amount of the plaintiff's exposure to the toxic is frequently unknown; often it occurred years ago. The plaintiff also has no way of conclusively establishing his or her exposure to other agents that might be the cause of his or her harm, so the relative contribution of the toxic is a further unknown. Only in the case of so-called signature diseases, diseases uniquely caused by exposure to a specific chemical—such as asbestosis—will medical science be able to establish but-for cause. For more discussion of medical and scientific causation, see Brennan, Causal Chains and Statistical Links: The Role of Scientific Uncertainty in Hazardous Substances Litigation, 73 Cornell L. Rev. 469 (1988); Brennan, Helping Courts with Toxic Torts, 51 U. Pitt. L. Rev. 1 (1989).

Very often, therefore, toxic torts plaintiffs will be unable to satisfy the cause-in-fact requirement. However, systematically absolving defendants of all liability when we know that their activity is statistically linked to serious harm will result in potentially significant underdeterrence. Suppose a defendant's toxic releases from its plant are estimated to increase the risk of cancer among its 1,000 neighbors by 10 percent. If we would expect 10 cancers within such a population in the normal course of things, the increased risk associated with the defendant's toxic releases means that we ought now to expect 11, one of which is properly attributable to the defendant's activities. If but-for causation is an essential condition of liability, this defendant, and all similar ones, will escape liability entirely, thus externalizing a cost, in terms of excess cancers, that ought to be reflected in its production and pollution control decisions. Too many toxic discharges will occur. For a review of the internalization argument, see Shavell, An Analysis of Causation and the Scope of Liability in the Law of Torts, 9 J. Legal Stud. 463, 475-485 (1985).

On the other hand, loosening or liberalizing the causation standard threatens to hold individuals liable for harms they did not cause. Not only would we not normally think such defendants ought to be responsible for such losses, but finding liability in such cases also might result in overdeterrence; indeed, it might discourage activity that is not environmentally harmful in the sense pertinent to the lawsuit.

The difficulty of recovering damages in toxic tort litigation is also illustrated by the litigation brought by persons exposed to atmospheric nuclear testing in Nevada prior to the 1963 Test Ban Treaty.

Allen v. United States
588 F. Supp. 247 (D. Utah), revd. on other grounds, 816 F.2d 1417 (10th Cir. 1987)

JENKINS, District Judge.

[Plaintiffs were residents of Nevada and Utah who had been exposed to radioactive fallout from atmospheric tests of U.S. nuclear weapons over the Nevada Test Site prior to the 1963 Test Ban Treaty. They exhibited various diseases, including leukemia, breast cancer, and thyroid cancer. Some had died. Medical evidence introduced at the trial established that exposure to ionizing radiation from the atmospheric tests increased the risk of these diseases.

Judge Jenkins concluded that the government had breached the duty it owed to the plaintiffs in failing to monitor fallout so as to be able to measure the risks of long-term, chronic effects—such as the injuries complained of by the plaintiffs—on those near the test site and in failing to warn those nearby of the possible risks. He then proceeded to discuss causation.]

THE QUESTION OF CAUSATION

Before any findings as to duty or negligent breach of duty may be applied to determine the question of liability, each plaintiff must show that he has suffered injury as a result of the defendant's conduct, at least in part. . . . In most cases, the factual connection between defendant's conduct and plaintiff's injury is not genuinely in dispute. Often, the cause-and-effect relationship is obvious: A's vehicle strikes B, injuring him; a bottle of A's product explodes, injuring B; water impounded on A's property flows onto B's land, causing immediate damage. . . .

Determination of the cause-in-fact, or factual connection, issue is complicated by the nature of the injuries suffered (various forms of cancer and leukemia), the nature of the causation mechanism alleged (ionizing radiation from nuclear fallout, as opposed to ionizing radiation from other sources, or other carcinogenic mechanisms), the extraordinary time factors and other variables involved in tracing any causal relationship between the two.

. . . In this case, the factual connection singling out the defendant as the source of the plaintiffs' injuries and deaths is very much in genuine dispute. . . .

Ionizing radiation—or other carcinogens—seem to add to the number of cancers already occurring in people, rather than producing new, distinct varieties of cancer. . . . The intrinsic nature of the alleged injury itself thus restricts the ability of the plaintiffs to demonstrate through evidence a direct cause-in-fact relationship between radiation from any source and their own cancers or leukemia. At least within the scope of our present knowledge, the injury is not specifically traceable to the asserted cause on an injury-by-injury basis.

This does not, however, end the inquiry. That the court cannot now peer into the damaged cells of a plaintiff to determine that the cancer or leukemia was radiation-induced does *not* mean (1) that the damage was not in fact caused by radiation; (2) that the radiation damage involved did not result from the defendant's conduct; or (3) that a satisfactory factual connection can never be established between plaintiff's injury and defendant's conduct for purposes of determining liability. Experience and the evidence in the record indicate that indeed it can.

[In the absence of cause-in-fact, the plaintiff should seek to establish] the most exclusive factual connection that he can between his injury and the defendant. . . . The more exclusive the factual connections that may be established by evidence, the stronger the rational basis for focusing the tools of legal analysis upon a specific defendant's conduct. . . .

That the defendant has engaged in risk-creating conduct of a particular type, and plaintiff's injuries are consistent with the kind of harm that is predicted and observed when such risks are created, makes the factual connection seem more exclusive—exclusive of other defendants, other connections, other "causes."

Whether any of these factual connections will lead to liability is, as Professor Thode reminds us, "an issue involving *the scope of the legal system's protection afforded to plaintiff* and not an issue of factual causation." 1977 Utah L. Rev. at 6 (emphasis added).

[After analyzing a number of cases allowing the plaintiff to recover despite an inability to prove cause-in-fact, Judge Jenkins ruled:]

Where a defendant who negligently creates a radiological hazard which puts an identifiable population group at increased risk, and a member of that group at risk develops a biological condition which is consistent with having been caused by the hazard to which he has been negligently subjected, such consistency having been demonstrated by substantial, appropriate, persuasive and connecting factors, a fact finder *may* reasonably conclude that the hazard caused the condition absent persuasive proof to the contrary offered by the defendant.

In this case, such factors shall include, among others: (1) the probability that plaintiff was exposed to ionizing radiation due to nuclear fallout from atmospheric testing at the Nevada Test Site at rates in excess of natural background radiation; (2) that plaintiff's injury is of a type consistent with those known to be caused by exposure to radiation; and (3) that plaintiff resided in geographical proximity to the Nevada Test Site for some time between 1951 and 1962. Other factual connections may include but are not limited to such things as time and extent of exposure to fallout, radiation sensitivity factors such as age or special sensitivities of the afflicted organ or tissue, retroactive internal or external dose estimation by current researchers, a latency period consistent with a radiation etiology, or an observed statistical incidence of the alleged injury greater than the expected incidence in the same population.

[Examining the evidence for each of the 24 plaintiffs, the court found in favor of 10 of them.]

NOTES AND QUESTIONS

1. Allen on Appeal. The court ruled that the fallout was a substantial factor in causing 8 cases of leukemia, 1 case of breast cancer, and 1 case of thyroid cancer experienced by 10 of the 24 plaintiffs. The district court decision subsequently was reversed by the U.S. Court of Appeals for the Tenth Circuit, Allen v. United States, 816 F.2d 1417

(10th Cir. 1987), cert. denied, 484 U.S. 1004 (1988), on the ground that the government's actions involved policy judgments protected by the discretionary function exception to the Federal Tort Claims Act. The Ninth Circuit had used the same rationale to dismiss tort claims by miners injured by radiation while mining uranium for the government's nuclear weapons program. Begay v. United States, 768 F.2d 1059 (9th Cir. 1985). The compelling stories of the individuals involved in the fallout litigation are described in P. L. Fradkin, Fallout: An American Nuclear Tragedy (1989).

2. *Is Cause-in-Fact Necessary?* Do you agree that once substantial factual connections are established between the defendant and the plaintiff—even though those "connections" do not include the fact that the defendant caused the plaintiff's injury—that the legal system can decide that the "scope" of the plaintiff's protection entitles him to recover against the defendant? Or do you think cause in fact is a necessary, minimum condition to such recovery?

3. *The Substantial Factor Test.* The Restatement (Second) of Torts attempted to circumvent some of the confusion created by the distinction between cause in fact and proximate cause by stating that liability depends on an actor's conduct being the "legal cause" of harm, a test that is satisfied if the actor's conduct is "a substantial factor in bringing about the harm." Restatement (Second) of Torts §§430, 431. The "substantial factor" formulation is now widely cited in tort decisions. Occasionally, courts have followed *Allen*'s lead and interpreted that test as dispensing with the need for the plaintiff to show that the defendant's conduct was more than likely a but-for cause of the harm. A Missouri court of appeals did so when the neighbors of a chemical plant sued the plant and its manager for chemically induced illnesses. Elam v. Alcolac, 765 S.W.2d 42 (Mo. App. 1988). Citing *Allen,* the court rejected defendants' argument that finding liability required finding that defendants' conduct was a but-for cause of the plaintiffs' injuries. In so ruling, the court said:

> The traditional and foremost policy of the tort law is to deter harmful conduct and to ensure that innocent victims of that conduct will have redress. Cognate principles of equity and economic efficiency also inform that policy: that the costs of the pervasive injury which result from mass exposure to toxic chemicals shall be borne by those who can control the danger and make equitable distribution of the losses, rather than by those who are powerless to protect themselves. [765 S.W.2d at 176.]

4. *Reasonable Medical Certainty.* However, the Restatement's drafters apparently thought that but-for causation was to continue to play a role in most tort situations. The substantial factor formulation

was apparently motivated by situations in which two or more independently sufficient causes produced the plaintiff's injury, as when a fire set by the defendant and a natural fire converge on the plaintiff's house. In such-cases the but-for requirement would absolve the defendant, but that result was thought unjustified. In reviewing the existing cases, the Restatement captured the idea that a defendant could be and had been held liable in such situations by explaining that the defendant's conduct could be found a substantial factor in the plaintiff's injury. §432(b), comment d and illustrations. In other situations, §432(a) provides that an actor's conduct "is not a substantial factor in bringing about harm to another if the harm would have been sustained even if the actor had not [acted]." In the toxic tort situation, the holding in Sterling v. Velsicol Chemical Corp., 855 F.2d 1189 (6th Cir. 1988) is more representative of courts' treatment of the causation issue than is *Elam*.

> To the extent that the plaintiffs seek damages for their bodily injuries, they must prove to a "reasonable medical certainty," though they need not use that specific terminology, that their ingestion of the contaminated water caused each of their particular injuries. This standard implicates the qualifications of the witnesses testifying, the acceptance in the scientific community of their theories, and the degree of certainty as to their conclusions. This standard is of particular importance when dealing with injuries or diseases of a type that may inflict society at random, often with no known specific origin. On numerous occasions, the Tennessee Supreme Court has addressed the degree of certainty of medical testimony required to establish a causal connection between a plaintiff's injuries and a defendant's tortious conduct. Whereas numerous jurisdictions have rejected medical experts' conclusions based upon a "probability," a "likelihood," and an opinion that something is "more likely than not" as insufficient medical proof, the Tennessee courts have adopted a far less stringent standard of proof and have required only that the plaintiffs prove a causal connection between their injuries and the defendant's tortious conduct by a preponderance of the evidence. While, in accordance with Tennessee common law, plaintiffs' proof by a reasonable medical certainty requires them only to establish that their particular injuries more likely than not were caused by ingesting the contaminated water, their proofs may be neither speculative nor conjectural. Medical testimony that ingesting the contaminated water "possibly," "may have," "might have," or "could have" caused the plaintiffs' presently ascertainable or anticipated injuries does not constitute the same level of proof as a conclusion by a reasonable medical certainty. Although it is argued that a lesser standard of proof allocates loss on a socially acceptable basis, it is the province of the state legislatures to make such changes as they have done in some areas by establishing "no-fault" or other alternate systems. [855 F.2d at 1200-1201.]

5. The Agent Orange Litigation.   A similar result was reached in In Re Agent Orange Product Liability Litigation, 597 F. Supp. 740

(E.D.N.Y. 1984), affd., 818 F.2d 145 (2d Cir. 1987). This was a class action on behalf of Vietnam veterans exposed to the defoliant Agent Orange, which frequently contained high levels of dioxin. After reviewing the developing law of causation in toxic torts, Judge Weinstein concluded that "even if the class could prove that they were injured by Agent Orange, no individual class members would be able to prove that his or her injuries were caused by Agent Orange," because doing so would require showing that it was "more likely than not" that an individual's cancer "is attributable to Agent Orange rather than being part of the 'background' level of cancer in the population as a whole." Id. at 833-834. The Agent Orange litigation ultimately was settled in May 1984 when seven chemical companies that manufactured Agent Orange agreed to create a $180 million fund for veterans who were totally disabled and for the families of veterans whose deaths were believed to have been associated with exposure to Agent Orange. Judge Weinstein's discussion of the causation problem was made in connection with his approval of the settlement agreement, a decision that was affirmed by the Second Circuit. In re "Agent Orange" Product Liability Litigation, 818 F.2d 145 (2d Cir. 1987).

6. *Legal Versus Scientific Causation.* Harter notes that the causation problem stems in large part from the different purposes for which law and science employ concepts of causation. While "the scientific inquiry is to determine the relationship between the disease and its causes," which often is expressed in statistical terms, "law, on the other hand, must make a decision regarding a particular individual," and thus seeks proof that a particular case of a disease was produced by a particular exposure. Law requires that some judgment be made concerning causation even in the face of scientific uncertainty. "Thus, law and science may well reach quite different answers as to the 'cause' of a disease." P. Harter, The Dilemma of Causation in Toxic Torts vi (1986).

7. *Administrative Compensation Schemes.* When CERCLA was amended in 1986, a proposal to establish an administrative compensation scheme for victims of exposure to toxic waste was narrowly defeated, in part because of concerns that relaxation of causation requirements would generate massive numbers of unfounded claims. A more popular approach to the problem has been to specify certain categories of persons exposed to toxic substances who would be compensated without individualized proof of causation. For example, in 1984, Congress enacted the Veterans' Dioxin and Radiation Exposure Compensation Standards Act, 38 U.S.C. §353, which sought to allow veterans exposed to Agent Orange to recover disability benefits for diseases deemed to be service-connected. Rather than requiring veterans to prove in individual adjudicatory proceedings that their disabilities were caused by exposure to

Agent Orange, the Act directs the Veterans Administration to determine what diseases could be deemed sufficiently related to exposure to Agent Orange to permit compensation to be paid without individualized proof of causation. The Act requires the VA to appoint a committee of scientific experts to advise it and to make its decisions based on "sound scientific and medical evidence." After consulting the committee, the VA decided that "sound scientific and medical evidence does not establish a cause and effect relationship between dioxin exposure" and any disease other than chloracne, a skin rash. This decision was overturned in Nehmer v. Veterans Administration, 712 F. Supp. 1404 (N.D. Cal. 1989) as inconsistent with Congress's intent *not* to require rigorous proof of causation. The court held that Congress had intended only to require a significant "statistical association" between dioxin exposure and a particular disease before it could be deemed service-connected, while the VA essentially had required proof of a causal relationship. Due to this decision and further pressure from Congress, the VA has gradually expanded the list of diseases it deems sufficiently service-connected to permit compensation.

In October 1990 Congress established another administrative compensation program, the Radiation Exposure Compensation Act, 42 U.S.C. §2210, note. The Act creates a trust fund to provide compensation to persons with specified diseases associated with radiation exposure who failed to recover in *Allen* and *Begay*. Congress intervened after these decisions protected the government from tort liability despite evidence that officials deliberately concealed radiation dangers to avoid jeopardizing nuclear weapons tests. Compensation is available under the Act for persons who mined uranium for the federal atomic testing program or who were exposed to fallout from the Nevada test site or from weapons tests in the South Pacific. Under the legislation, persons with specific diseases may receive payments of up to $100,000 for each uranium miner, and up to $50,000 for residents near the Nevada test site, without showing individual proof of causation. The Bush Administration's proposed fiscal year 1993 budget provides $171 million for the trust fund.

While the federal programs are limited responses to specific incidents of past exposure, California and Minnesota have established broader administrative compensation schemes. California Hazardous Substance Compensation Program, Cal. Health & Safety Code §§25300-25611; Minnesota Harmful Substance Compensation Program, Minn. Stat. §115B.25-115B.37. These programs create administrative boards that may award compensation for injuries caused by exposure to hazardous substances when recovery cannot be obtained from private parties. However, due to familiar problems with proof of causation, they have not been widely used. Between 1983 and 1991, California's program made only 5 awards (totaling $47,641); the 230 awards (totaling $240,000) made under Minnesota's program have been limited to compensation for property damage.

B. ACCRUAL OF THE CAUSE OF ACTION AND THE STATUTES OF LIMITATIONS

Until recently, even toxic torts plaintiffs who could show cause in fact, or substantial factor, as the case might be, might have found themselves facing an obstacle posed by the statutes of limitations. A tort plaintiff has a limited time within which to bring suit. The time period begins when the cause of action accrues, or becomes sufficiently concrete that the court will hear the case, and it ends after the period of years defined in the statutes governing periods of limitations for the kind of action being brought. Typically, causes of action for personal injury tort, damage to property (nuisance), and trespass have different limitations periods. Their case

If the plaintiff's cause of action accrued before the plaintiff became aware that she had a claim to bring, the long latency periods associated with many toxic exposures might result in the statute of limitation's running out before she acquired such knowledge. Thus, when her injury eventually materializes, her cause of action would be barred by the limitations period. Strange as this may seem, the principles governing accrual of tort causes of action in a number of jurisdictions permitted this result. For example, some states provided that the cause of action accrued when the defendant completed the last act within his control that caused the plaintiff injury. See, e.g., Askey v. Occidental Chemical Corp., 102 A.D. 2d 130, 477 N.Y.S.2d 242 (1984). An alternative rule of accrual more favorable to toxic tort plaintiffs is some version of the discovery rule. Under one such version, a cause of action does not accrue until the plaintiff knows, or should reasonably have come to know, facts sufficient to inform her that she has been injured and that such injury may be actionable. Advocates of toxic tort victims put considerable pressure on state legislatures and state courts in the late 1970s and early 1980s promoting the discovery rule, and by 1986 a considerable number of states had adopted some version of it, either by statute or by judicial interpretation.

In 1986 the SARA amendments added section 309 to CERCLA, which provides that a cause of action brought "under State law for personal injury, or property damages, which are caused or contributed to by exposure to any hazardous substance, or pollutant or contaminant, released into the environment from a facility" shall accrue on "the date the plaintiff knew (or reasonably should have known) that the personal injury or property damages . . . were caused or contributed to by the

hazardous substance or pollutant or contaminant concerned." 42 U.S.C.
§§9658(a)(1), (b)(4)(A). CERCLA further extends the statute of limitations for minors or incompetent plaintiffs to the date they had legal
representatives appointed. 42 U.S.C. §9658(A)(4)(B). This provision was
adopted by Congress as an outgrowth of a study, authorized by the
original CERCLA legislation in 1980, that found that common law remedies were inadequate to ensure compensation of victims of toxic releases. Conf. Rep. No. 962, 99th Cong., 2d Sess. 261 (1986).

C. INJURY

While the increasingly widespread acceptance of the discovery rule
eliminates one obstacle in the path of toxic tort plaintiffs, the cause-in-
fact requirement remains a considerable obstacle to plaintiffs' recovering
for an injury, disease, or other adverse health condition when they can
only show a less than 50 percent statistical likelihood that the defendant's
actions caused their conditions. This has not deterred all toxic tort litigation, however. In addition to continuing to challenge the cause-in-fact
requirement, tort lawyers have been actively exploring nontraditional
theories of injury. They are bringing cases that concede the application
of the cause in fact requirement but in which they raise new kinds of
injuries that can be shown to have been caused by the defendant's conduct. This section contains cases raising three such theories: cancerphobia and the fear of cancer; medical monitoring; and increased risk of
disease.

Hagerty v. L&L Marine Services
788 F.2d 315 (5th Cir. 1986)

REAVLEY, Circuit Judge:
[While in the defendant's employ, the plaintiff was engaged in
loading a barge with chemicals at a Union Carbide plant in Puerto Rico.
Allegedly as a result of faulty equipment, plaintiff was completely
drenched with dripolene, a chemical containing benzene, toluene, and
xylene. His shoes were ruined and he suffered brief dizziness followed
by leg cramps. The next day he had a stinging sensation in his lower
extremities. "Because of these symptoms, the extent of his immersion
in the chemical, and his understanding of the carcinogenic effect of that
chemical, he is now fearful that he will in time contract the disease." He
had no manifestations of cancer at the time of the litigation.
In the course of reversing the trial court's erroneous dismissal of
Hagerty's case, the circuit court commented on the plaintiff's claim that
he be allowed to recover for his "cancerphobia."]
Upon trial the plaintiff is entitled to recover damages for all of his

past, present and probable future harm attributable to the defendant's tortious conduct. Those damages include pain and suffering and mental anguish. The present fear or anxiety due to the possibility of contracting cancer constitutes a present fact of mental anguish and may be included in recoverable damages. . . . *Ruled in his favor*

CANCERPHOBIA

Defendants contend that a plaintiff's cancerphobia should not be considered a present injury unless accompanied by "physical manifestations." Only a physical injury requirement, they argue, will ensure against the proliferation of "unworthy claims." It would also deny worthy claims, perhaps that of Hagerty. We believe the courts have better devices with which to choose between the worthy and the unworthy.

Cancerphobia is merely a specific type of mental anguish or emotional distress. See, e.g., Gale & Goyer, Recovery for Cancerphobia and Increased Risk of Cancer, 15 Cum. L. Rev. 723, 725 (1985). Courts have long allowed plaintiffs to recover for psychic and emotional harm in Federal Employers Liability Act or Jones Act/maritime cases. . . .

The physical injury requirement, like its counterpart, the physical impact requirement, was developed to provide courts with an objective means of ensuring that the alleged mental injury is not feigned. W. Prosser, The Law of Torts §54, at 330-33 (4th ed. 1971). We believe that notion to be unrealistic. It is doubtful that the trier of fact is any less able to decide the fact or extent of mental suffering in the event of physical injury or impact. With or without physical injury or impact, a plaintiff is entitled to recover damages for serious mental distress arising from fear of developing cancer where his fear is reasonable and causally related to the defendant's negligence. The circumstances surrounding the fear-inducing occurrence may themselves supply sufficient indicia of genuineness. It is for the jury to decide questions such as the existence, severity and reasonableness of the fear.

Here, Hagerty has testified that he studied the characteristics of the chemicals he dealt with and thus knew before his exposure that dripolene was a carcinogen. In addition, he felt physical effects after dousing; having previously watched benzene absorb into his finger, these effects triggered anxiety because he realized that his entire body had absorbed the chemical. He further testified that he saw a doctor after the exposure and advised his co-worker to do the same. His doctor advised him to undergo periodic medical testing for cancer. In addition to doing so, he subsequently left his job as tankerman out of concern for future accidents. From this evidence, we conclude that Hagerty has presented sufficient indicia of genuineness so as to make summary judgment of his cancerphobia claim improper.

Known Carcinogen

Tests $ cost

NOTES AND QUESTIONS

1. Spurious Claims. As the *Hagerty* court indicates, courts sometimes justified physical injury as a precondition to recovery for emotional distress as a means of separating genuine claims from spurious ones. Do you agree with the court that the physical injury requirement does a poor job in this regard? How does the court propose to police the distinction between genuine and false claims of cancerphobia? Is its proposal adequate to the task? What, exactly, is the difference between a genuine and a false claim? Presumably, false claims include situations in which the plaintiff subjectively is experiencing no fear of cancer, but says she is in order to recover. What about situations in which the plaintiff was experiencing no fear of cancer until, after the exposure, she began reading literature on the pervasiveness of toxic chemicals in our society and on the need for citizens to take whatever actions they could to shut down the chemical industry? Is a fear of cancer from toxics exposure genuine if the plaintiff is a smoker, and thus arguably subjecting himself to much greater cancer risk from that source?

2. Physical Injury Requirement. Should plaintiffs be able to recover compensation for exposure to toxic substances even before any physical injury is manifest? It is well-known that exposure to certain substances increases the risk of certain diseases that may occur only after a long latency period. Should plaintiffs be able to recover for the increased risk of disease associated with such exposure? When suing for damages rather than an injunction, the normal rule is that plaintiffs must furnish sufficient evidence to enable damages to be determined without resort to speculation or conjecture. In cases of exposure to risk of harm, what would those damages be? There are two distinct problems here. The first is the conceptual one of whether exposing someone to the risk of harm damages that person. Is the risk of harm itself a harm? The second ties risk assessment into the burden of proof difficulty: how can the court assess the risk associated with exposure confidently enough to make it the basis of a damage award? In Anderson v. W. R. Grace & Co., 628 F. Supp. 1219 (D. Mass. 1986), a federal district court dismissed claims for damages based on enhanced risk due to exposure to drinking water contaminated by toxic wastes in Woburn, Massachusetts. Applying Massachusetts law, the court held that "recovery depends on establishing a 'reasonable probability' that the harm will occur" and that plaintiffs had not quantified the magnitude of their enhanced risk. 628 F. Supp. at 1231. The court expressed concern over a flood of speculative lawsuits and the "inevitable inequity" of undercompensating those who actually develop cancer while providing a windfall to those who do not. While most courts have agreed with this result, see, e.g., Ayers v. Township of Jackson, 25 E.R.C. 1956 (N.J. Sup. Ct. 1987), others have recognized a cause of action for enhanced risk while requiring that proof of future injury be reasonably certain, see, e.g., Hagerty v. L&L Marine Services, 788 F.2d 315 (5th Cir. 1986); Wilson v. Johns-Manville Sales Corp., 684 F.2d 111 (D.C. Cir. 1982), or that plaintiffs exhibit some present manifestation of disease, see, e.g., Jackson v. Johns-Manville Sales Corp., 781 F.2d 394 (5th Cir. 1986), cert. denied, 478 U.S. 1022 (1986); Brafford v. Susquehanna Corp., 586 F. Supp. 14 (D. Colo. 1984).

|| ### In re Paoli Railroad Yard PCB Litigation
916 F.2d 829 (3d Cir. 1990) ||

BECKER, Circuit Judge.

This is a toxic tort case brought by some thirty-eight persons who have either worked in or lived adjacent to the Paoli railyard, an electric railcar maintenance facility at the western terminus of the noted Paoli Local, which serves the Philadelphia Main Line. The plaintiffs' primary claim is that they have contracted a variety of illnesses as the result of exposure to polychlorinated biphenyls, better known as PCBs. PCBs are toxic substances which, as the result of decades of PCB use in the Paoli railcar transformers, can be found in extremely high concentration at the railyard and in the ambient air and soil.

[The district court granted summary judgment in favor of all defendants on all claims, except those for property damage and response costs under CERCLA. The plaintiffs appealed, challenging especially several evidentiary rulings that excluded plaintiff's medical experts from offering certain testimony. In the course of addressing the appeal, the court analyzed plaintiffs' claim for medical monitoring expenses.]

MEDICAL MONITORING

Because it bears on the question of what evidence is admissible, we turn first to the viability of certain plaintiffs' "medical surveillance," or "medical monitoring," claims, by which plaintiffs sought to recover the costs of periodic medical examinations that they contend are medically necessary to protect against the exacerbation of latent diseases brought about by exposure to PCBs. Neither the Pennsylvania Supreme Court nor the Pennsylvania Superior Court has decided whether a demonstrated need for medical monitoring creates a valid cause of action. Therefore, sitting in diversity, we must predict whether the Pennsylvania Supreme Court would recognize a claim for medical monitoring under the substantive law of Pennsylvania and, if so, what its elements are. See Erie R.R. Co. v. Tompkins, 304 U.S. 64 (1938).

Medical monitoring is one of a growing number of non-traditional torts that have developed in the common law to compensate plaintiffs who have been exposed to various toxic substances. Often, the diseases or injuries caused by this exposure are latent. This latency leads to problems when the claims are analyzed under traditional common law tort doctrine because, traditionally, injury needed to be manifest before it could be compensable. Thus, plaintiffs have encountered barriers to recovery which "arise from the failure of toxic torts to conform with the common law conception of an injury." Note, Medical Surveillance Damages, [note 22], at 852.

Nonetheless, in an effort to accommodate a society with an increasing awareness of the danger and potential injury caused by the widespread use of toxic substances, courts have begun to recognize claims like medical monitoring, which can allow plaintiffs some relief even absent present manifestations of physical injury. More specifically, in the toxic tort context, courts have allowed plaintiffs to recover for emotional distress suffered because of the fear of contracting a toxic exposure disease, the increased risk of future harm, . . . and the reasonable costs of medical monitoring or surveillance.

It is easy to confuse the distinctions between these various non-traditional torts. However, the torts just mentioned involve fundamentally different kinds of injury and compensation. Thus, an action for medical monitoring seeks to recover only the quantifiable costs of periodic medical examinations necessary to detect the onset of physical harm, whereas an enhanced risk claim seeks compensation for the anticipated harm itself, proportionately reduced to reflect the chance that it will not occur. We think that this distinction is particularly important because the Pennsylvania Supreme Court has expressed some reluctance to recognize claims for enhanced risk of harm. In Martin v. Johns-Manville Corp., 508 Pa. 154, 494 A.2d 1088 (1985), the court made clear that a plaintiff in an enhanced risk suit must prove that future consequences of an injury are reasonably probable, not just possible. Id. at 165 n.5, 494 A.2d at 1094 n.5.

Martin does not lead us to believe that Pennsylvania would not recognize a claim for medical monitoring, however. First, the injury that the court was worried about finding with reasonable probability in Martin is different from the injury involved here. The injury in an enhanced risk claim is the anticipated harm itself. The injury in a medical monitoring claim is the cost of the medical care that will, one hopes, detect that injury. The former is inherently speculative because courts are forced to anticipate the probability of future injury. The latter is much less speculative because the issue for the jury is the less conjectural question of whether the plaintiff needs medical surveillance. Second, the Pennsylvania Supreme Court's concerns about the degree of certainty required can easily be accommodated by requiring that a jury be able reasonably to determine that medical monitoring is probably, not just possibly, necessary.

Defining injury in this way is not novel. In Friends for All Children, Inc. v. Lockheed Aircraft Corp., 746 F.2d 816 (D.C. Cir. 1984), the court, in recognizing a claim for medical monitoring damages for children exposed to the depressurization of an airplane cabin, noted that "[i]t is difficult to dispute that an individual has an interest in avoiding expensive diagnostic examinations just as he or she has an interest in avoiding physical injury." Id. at 826. See also Laxton v. Orkin Exterminating Co., 639 S.W.2d 431 (Tenn. 1982) (ingestion of contaminated water requiring testing held to be injury in itself, even though ingestion found to be harmless).

Similarly, in Askey v. Occidental Chemical Corp., 102 A.D.2d 130, 477 N.Y.S.2d 242 (1984), the court analyzed the issue as follows:

> Damages for the prospective consequences of a tortious injury are recoverable only if the prospective consequences may with reasonable probability be expected to flow from the past harm. Consequences which are contingent, speculative, or merely possible are not properly considered in ascertaining damages. If a plaintiff seeks future medical expenses as an element of consequential damage, he must establish with a degree of reasonable medical certainty through expert testimony that such expenses will be incurred. In light of the foregoing, it would appear that under the proof offered here persons exposed to toxic chemicals emanating from the landfill have an increased risk of invisible genetic damage and a present cause of action for their injury, and may recover all "reasonably anticipated" consequential damages. The future expense of medical monitoring could be a recoverable consequential damage provided that plaintiffs can establish with a reasonable degree of medical certainty that such expenditures are "reasonably anticipated" to be incurred by reason of their exposure.

Id. at 136-37, 477 N.Y.S.2d at 247.

Thus, the appropriate inquiry is not whether it is reasonably probable that plaintiffs will suffer harm in the future, but rather whether medical monitoring is, to a reasonable degree of medical certainty, necessary in order to diagnose properly the warning signs of disease.

Federal district courts, sitting in diversity, have addressed the medical monitoring issue under Pennsylvania law. In Villari v. Terminix International, Inc., 663 F. Supp. 727 (E.D. Pa. 1987), the court allowed plaintiffs, who had presented sufficient medical evidence of present physical injuries resulting from exposure to an allegedly carcinogenic pesticide, to recover the costs of future medical surveillance. Id. at 735. The court required a showing of present physical injury and expressly refused to follow Ayers, which it characterized as holding that "the cost of future medical monitoring is a proper element of damages whenever medical testimony establishes the need for future monitoring." Id. at 735 n.5. However, because the plaintiffs in *Villari* had demonstrated sufficient physical injury, the question whether the cause of action could be sustained without it was not squarely raised.

Villari's putative physical injury requirement was rejected in Merry v. Westinghouse Electric Corp., 684 F. Supp. 847 (M.D. Pa. 1988). In *Merry*, property owners whose wells had been contaminated by toxic substances sought recovery for, inter alia, the cost of medical surveillance. In denying defendant's motion for summary judgment, the court agreed with *Villari* that "a plaintiff need not exhibit symptoms of a disease before medical surveillance is sought," id. at 849, but disagreed to the extent that *Villari* required "*physical* injury before a claim for future medical monitoring can be maintained." Id. (emphasis in original). Consequently, *Merry* suggested that a medical monitoring action could be premised upon proof of exposure to hazardous substances resulting in the potential for injury and the need for early detection and treatment. Id. at 850.

We agree with *Merry*, and predict that the Supreme Court of Pennsylvania would follow the weight of authority and recognize a cause of action for medical monitoring established by proving that:

1.   Plaintiff was significantly exposed to a proven hazardous substance through the negligent actions of the defendant.
2.   As a proximate result of exposure, plaintiff suffers a significantly increased risk of contracting a serious latent disease.
3.   That increased risk makes periodic diagnostic medical examinations reasonably necessary.
4.   Monitoring and testing procedures exist which make the early detection and treatment of the disease possible and beneficial.

These factors would, of course, be proven by competent expert testimony. . . .

The policy reasons for recognizing this tort are obvious. Medical monitoring claims acknowledge that, in a toxic age, significant harm can be done to an individual by a tortfeasor, notwithstanding latent manifestation of that harm. Moreover, as we have explained, recognizing this tort does not require courts to speculate about the probability of future injury. It merely requires courts to ascertain the probability that the far less costly remedy of medical supervision is appropriate. Allowing plaintiffs to recover the cost of this care deters irresponsible discharge of toxic chemicals by defendants and encourages plaintiffs to detect and treat their injuries as soon as possible. These are conventional goals of the tort system as it has long existed in Pennsylvania. . . .

For all of the foregoing reasons, the summary judgment will be reversed, and the case remanded to the district court for further proceedings consistent with this opinion.

NOTES AND QUESTIONS

1. Splitting a Cause of Action, Plus More on the Accrual of a Cause of Action. Before a plaintiff can sue in tort, she must have suffered an injury. Jurisdictions that refused to follow the discovery rule in cases of latent illness were sometimes criticized for countenancing a situation in which a plaintiff could not sue immediately after exposure, because she had as yet suffered no injury, and also could not sue when the injury became manifest, because the statute of limitations had run. One response to this dilemma, of course, is to adopt the discovery rule. Another is to interpret "injury" very expansively, so that a plaintiff could sue on the event of exposure itself. This latter approach was taken by the *Askey* court, relied on in the principal case. *Askey*, in turn, relied on an earlier New York Court of Appeals decision, Schmidt v. Merchants Despatch Transportation Co., 270 N.Y. 287, 200 N.E. 824 (1936), which it described as follows:

> In that case, a plaintiff sued his former employer more than three years after the termination of employment to recover for a lung disease caused by the inhalation of dust negligently allowed to accumulate in the air. The decision is the source of the rule, reaffirmed many times since, that the applicable three-year period of limitations in cases such as this begins to run from the date of the last exposure to the foreign substance and not from the date on which the disease caused by that substance was or could have been discovered. . . . The Court of Appeals said . . . that a cause of action accrues when the forces wrongfully put in motion produce injury by the wrongful invasion of personal or property rights, and that the "injury to the plaintiff [in that case] was complete when the alleged negligence of the defendant caused the plaintiff to inhale the deleterious dust."
>
> The theory of liability grows out of the invasion of the body by the foreign substance, with the assumption being that the substance acts immediately upon the body setting in motion the forces which eventually result in disease. . . . [Askey v. Occidental Chemical Corp., 102 A.D.2d 130, 135-136, 477 N.Y.S.2d 242, 246-247 (1984).]

Having permitted the plaintiff to sue as soon as a toxic particle makes contact with the plaintiff's body, the court was then confronted with the normal requirement that a plaintiff bring in one lawsuit all of his or her damages claims arising out of the same incident. This is the rule against "splitting a cause of action." Thus,

> [i]n deciding the Statute of Limitations issue, the Court of Appeals . . . grappled with the problem which confronts us here, i.e., whether plaintiffs

have a claim for injuries not yet present, or as Special Term phrased it, whether plaintiffs have a claim for "potential injuries which they may be afflicted with in the future." The apparent answer given by the Court of Appeals is "Yes," provided that the proper medical proof is adduced. In *Schmidt* the Court of Appeals recognized that a plaintiff has a cause of action immediately on exposure to a foreign substance and can recover all damages which he can show resulted or "would result therefrom," even though at the time the action is commenced no serious damage to the plaintiff has developed. [102 A.D.2d at 136, 477 N.Y.S.2d at 246-247.]

2. Out of the Frying Pan and into the Fire? Cases like *Hagerty* and *In re Paoli* permit plaintiffs to sue in advance of any latent disease's materializing by permitting medical monitoring expenses or cancerphobia to count as "injuries." Under the discovery rule, then, the statute of limitations will begin to run when the plaintiff discovers that he is suffering from fear of cancer or that he needs medical monitoring. Is this always an unmitigated advantage for the plaintiff? What advice would you give a client who has been exposed to toxic chemicals and wants to know whether bringing a lawsuit now will bar him from suing later for cancer, should cancer materialize 20 years hence? Suppose the client can afford his own medical monitoring but cannot afford medical expenses for cancer. Can he wait to sue until later on? For more on suits for medical monitoring generally, see Gara, Medical Surveillance Damages: Using Common Sense and the Common Law to Mitigate the Dangers Posed by Environmental Hazards, 12 Harv. Envtl. L. Rev. 265 (1988).

3. Medical Monitoring and Superfund. The costs of sampling for and monitoring underground water contamination levels, ground contamination levels, and the like are recoverable as "response costs" under Superfund. Should the costs of medical monitoring for individuals exposed to the release or threat of release of a hazardous substance from a Superfund facility also be recoverable as response costs? See Williams v. Allied Automotive, 704 F. Supp. 782 (N.D. Ohio 1988); Brewer v. Ravan, 689 F. Supp. 1176 (M.D. Tenn. 1988); Ambrogi v. Gould Inc., 750 F. Supp. 1233 (M.D. Pa. 1990).

One additional sort of injury a plaintiff might claim is the injury of suffering an increased risk of becoming ill with cancer. Consider the next case.

|| **Sterling v. Velsicol Chemical Corp.** ||
855 F.2d 1188 (6th Cir. 1988)

GUY, Circuit Judge, on rehearing. . . .

FACTS

In August, 1964, the defendant, Velsicol Chemical Corporation (Velsicol), acquired 242 acres of rural land in Hardeman County, Tennessee. The defendant used the site as a landfill for by-products from the production of chlorinated hydrocarbon pesticides at its Memphis, Tennessee, chemical manufacturing facility. Before Velsicol purchased the landfill site and commenced depositing any chemicals into the ground, it neither conducted hydrogeological studies to assess the soil composition underneath the site, the water flow direction, and the location of the local water aquifer, nor drilled a monitoring well to detect and record any ongoing contamination. From October, 1964, to June, 1973, the defendant deposited a total of 300,000 55-gallon steel drums containing ultrahazardous liquid chemical waste and hundreds of fiber board cartons containing ultrahazardous dry chemical waste in the landfill. . . .

[Commencing in 1967, public health officials and local residents became concerned about underground contamination from the site. Several reports showed the underground aquifer to be highly contaminated, and nearby residents were advised to stop using their well water for any purpose. In 1973, the site was shut by state order.]

In 1978, forty-two plaintiffs sued Velsicol in the Circuit Court of Hardeman County, Tennessee, on behalf of themselves and all others similarly situated for damages and injunctive relief. The complaint sought $1.5 billion in compensatory damages and $1 billion in punitive damages. . . . The complaint sought relief for involuntary exposure to certain chemical substances known to cause cancer, affect the central nervous system and permanently damage other organs of the human body, and for loss of value to their real property in the region affected by the chemicals. Additionally, seven individual civil actions involving fourteen plaintiffs were instituted against Velsicol alleging that the defendant negligently disposed of toxic chemical wastes. . . .

After a bench trial of the five claims, the district court found Velsicol liable to the plaintiffs on legal theories of strict liability, common law negligence, trespass, and nuisance. The court concluded that the defendant's hazardous chemicals, which escaped from its landfill and contaminated plaintiffs' well water, were the proximate cause of the representative plaintiffs' injuries. The district court awarded the five individuals compensatory damages totalling $5,273,492.50 for their respective injuries, plus prejudgment interest dating back to July, 1965, of $8,964,973.25. All damages, except for $48,492.50 to one plaintiff for property damage claims, were awarded for personal injuries. The district court also awarded $7,500,000 in punitive damages to the class as a whole. . . .

On appeal, the defendant argues that . . . the district court erred in finding that the plaintiffs were exposed to its chemicals and that there was a causal connection between their exposure, if any, and their resultant injuries. Accordingly, the defendant asserts the district court improperly awarded compensatory damages to the plaintiffs for their alleged injuries.

[The individual plaintiffs sought recovery for a variety of present injuries, including headaches, loss of balance, fatigue, nausea, vomiting, numbness, nervousness, skin irritation, coughing, partial loss of eyesight, kidney damage, and liver damage.] . . .

The main thrust of Velsicol's argument on appeal is that there was insufficient evidence to support a finding of causation between its disposal of toxic chemicals and plaintiffs' injuries.

[The trial] court, as is appropriate in this type of mass tort class action litigation, divided its causation analysis into two parts. It was first established that Velsicol was responsible for the contamination and that the particular contaminants were *capable* of producing injuries of the types allegedly suffered by the plaintiffs. Up to this point in the proceeding, the five representative plaintiffs were acting primarily in their representative capacity to the class as a whole. This enabled the court to determine a kind of generic causation—whether the combination of the chemical contaminants and the plaintiffs' exposure to them had the capacity to cause the harm alleged. This still left the matter of *individual* proximate cause to be determined. Although such generic and individual causation may appear to be inextricably intertwined, the procedural device of the class action permitted the court initially to assess the defendant's potential liability for its conduct without regard to the individual components of each plaintiff's injuries. However, from this point forward, it became the responsibility of each individual plaintiff to show that his or her specific injuries or damages were proximately caused by ingestion or otherwise using the contaminated water. We cannot emphasize this point strongly enough because generalized proofs will not suffice to prove individual damages. The main problem on review stems from a failure to differentiate between the general and the particular. This is an understandably easy trap to fall into in mass tort litigation. Although many common issues of fact and law will be capable of resolution on a group basis, individual particularized damages still must be proved on an individual basis.

[The appellate court thereupon examined in detail the evidence with respect to the specific alleged injuries.] . . . .

INCREASED RISK OF CANCER AND OTHER DISEASES

Plaintiffs sought to recover damages for the prospect that cancer and other diseases may materialize as a result of their exposure. The district court awarded the five representative plaintiffs damages predicated upon their being at risk for, or susceptible to, future disease.

Where the basis for awarding damages is the potential risk of susceptibility to future disease, the predicted future-disease must be medically reasonably certain to follow from the existing present injury. While it is unnecessary that the medical evidence conclusively establish with absolute certainty that the future disease or condition will occur, mere conjecture or even possibility does not justify the court awarding damages for a future disability which may never materialize. Tennessee law requires that the plaintiff prove there is a reasonable medical certainty that the anticipated harm will result in order to recover for a future injury. Therefore, the mere increased risk of a future disease or condition resulting from an initial injury is not compensable. While neither the Tennessee courts, nor this court, has specifically addressed damage awards for increased risk or susceptibility to cancer and kidney and liver diseases, numerous courts have denied recovery where plaintiffs alleged they might suffer from these future diseases or conditions as a result of existing injuries.

For example, in Ayers v. Jackson, 189 N.J. Super. 561, 461 A.2d 184 (1983), 325 county residents alleged that toxic wastes leaked through the municipal landfill and contaminated their well water. Plaintiffs' experts testified the ground water was contaminated with numerous known carcinogenic chemicals including benzene, acetone, and chloroform. Plaintiffs argued they suffered from a present condition of enhanced risk of kidney and liver disease and cancer from ingesting the contaminated well water. The *Ayers* court held that damages were not recoverable for such prospective consequences where the plaintiffs' proofs did not establish that they would in the future, to a reasonable medical certainty, suffer from such injury. The court observed that all individuals who were exposed to the well water contamination were at an increased risk of developing cancer and liver and kidney damage. However, the court noted that because plaintiffs' experts could not formulate a quantitative measure to a reasonable medical certainty of excess kidney, liver, and cancer risk, it was left to speculation as to possible consequences of the ingestion of the alleged carcinogens on the future health of each plaintiff. Similarly, in Hagerty v. L&L Marine Services, Inc., 788 F.2d 315 (5th Cir.), reconsideration denied, 797 F.2d 256 (5th Cir. 1986) (en banc), a plaintiff who was accidentally drenched with chemicals containing known carcinogens, sued for damages including compensation for the increased risk that he would develop cancer in the future as a result of his exposure. The court concluded that because he did not allege with medical certainty that he would develop cancer in the future, he did not state a claim. The court reasoned that plaintiff's increased risk of cancer was not presently compensable because he could not show that the toxic exposure would more probably than not lead to cancer. . . .

In the instant case, the district court found an increased risk for susceptibility to cancer and other diseases of only twenty-five to thirty percent. This does not constitute a reasonable medical certainty, but rather a mere possibility or speculation. Indeed, no expert witnesses ever testified during the course of trial that the five representative plaintiffs had even a probability—i.e., more than a fifty percent chance—of developing cancer and kidney or liver disease as a result of their exposure to defendant's chemicals. . . .

For the foregoing reasons, we affirm in part, reverse in part, and remand for recalculation of damages.

NOTES AND QUESTIONS

1. *Liability for Increased Risk.* Under one theory, allowing recovery for increased risk would match tort recovery to the evidence of causation that medical science is capable of providing: Both the cause of action and the medical evidence would rely on statistical evidence of probabilities rather than on any determination that the defendant's action caused the specific malady of which the plaintiff might later complain. As Professor Robinson has argued, allowing recovery for increased risk "does not entail changing the standards for defining what activities (risks) are tortious," Robinson, Probabilistic Causation and Compensation for Tortious Risk, 14 J. Legal Stud. 779, 782 (1985), and the theory of recovery would be brought into line with traditional doctrine not by abandoning the cause-in-fact requirement but by "redefin[ing] compensable 'injury' to make 'tortious' risk a basis of liability—adjusting compensation according to a probabilistic measure of anticipated loss." Id. at 783.

2. *Liability for Future Consequences of Present Injury.* Professor Robinson's approach to liability for increased risk treats increased risk of cancer as a present invasion of a legally protected interest, to wit, the interest in being free from exposure to increased risk. As such, it is actionable regardless of any manifestations of any other present injury, because the increased risk of future harm is itself a harm. An alternative theory of recovery for increased risk treats the prospect of future injury resulting from the increased risk as additional consequences of a separate, present, harm. As such, some independently identifiable injury is a necessary predicate for the cause of action. Once such an injury is shown, the law permits testimony about future consequences because of its rule against splitting a cause of action—because of that rule, it must permit the plaintiff to bring all her cognizable claims for damages in the present lawsuit. Under the rules governing accrual and splitting of causes

of action, plaintiffs must be allowed to recover all damages that can be made reasonably certain in the present lawsuit.

Which theory of recovery for increased risk does the *Velsicol* opinion discuss? Would the plaintiffs' prospects for recovery have been better had they presented the other theory? Which theory does the court in *In re Paoli* adopt? Under the approach of *Velsicol* or *In re Paoli*, if a plaintiff shows that defendant's conduct constituted 51 percent of the total risk he faces for contracting cancer, would the court allow him to recover all his cancer damages from the defendant? Might this lead to overdeterrence of defendant's activities?

3. Proportionate Liability. If the plaintiffs in *Sterling* had been allowed to recover for increased risk of cancer under the first theory— risk of harm is itself a harm—presumably so would everyone who had been exposed to Velsicol's chemicals, regardless of whether they ever developed cancer. Using the facts of the example on page 632, above, the defendant would be liable for the increased risk of all 1,000 neighbors. Alternatively, commentators have suggested that the courts wait until cancer cases materialize in the exposed population, and then permit recovery under a theory of proportionate liability. Under this approach, the defendant would pay for 1/11 of the damages associated with any cancer case that materialized among the 1,000 exposed neighbors. Whereas liability for increased risk nominally satisfies the cause-in-fact requirement while changing the definition of compensable injury, this proposal is usually treated as dispensing with the cause-in-fact requirement and substituting a rule of liability based on proportionate contribution to risk. Does anything substantial turn on this particular distinction?

Proportionate liability has been extensively discussed, with almost universal approval, in the theoretical literature. See, e.g., Delgado, Beyond Sindell: Relaxation of Cause-in-Fact Rules for Indeterminate Plaintiffs, 70 Calif. L. Rev. 881 (1982); Rosenberg, The Causal Connection in Mass Exposure Cases: A Public Law Vision of the Tort System, 97 Harv. L. Rev. 849 (1984). But see Abraham, Individual Action and Collective Responsibility: The Dilemma of Mass Tort Reform, 73 Va. L. Rev. 845 (1987); Elliott, Why Courts? Comment on Robinson, 14 J. Legal Stud. 799 (1985). Professor Dan Farber agrees that the no-recovery result that seems required under standard cause-in-fact analysis in cases where only statistical evidence of causation is required is mistaken, but has proposed that the injured parties whose injuries were most likely caused by the defendant's conduct get full recovery, while those least likely to have been injured by the defendant receive nothing. See Farber, Toxic Causation, 71 Minn. L. Rev. 1219 (1987). Why might one prefer this most likely victim (MLV) approach over proportionate liability? What circumstances must obtain for it to be applicable? How does it apply to the example just given?

4. Comparing the Approaches of Tort Law and Administrative Agencies to the Use of Risk Assessment. To date, common law judges have been very reluctant to permit recoveries on the basis of evidence that defendant's activity has increased the risk of harm occurring. As we have seen, regulatory agencies routinely regulate toxic discharges, licensing of toxic products, and the production of toxic products on the basis of assessments of increased risks. In fact, they rely increasingly on quantitative assessments of risk. While acknowledging the uncertainties of QRA, agencies themselves as well as courts reviewing administrative action are prepared to accept QRAs as the "best available evidence that science can currently provide of health risks at low exposure levels." The *Ethylene Oxide* case, page 498, above. If risk assessment generally and QRAs specifically are good enough to form the basis for regulatory action, why are they treated as "speculative" by the common law courts? Can you explain the difference on the ground that courts are asked to order the transfer of money from a particular defendant to a plaintiff? Would the payment of money damages invariably be more costly to a defendant than regulatory actions taken against it? Isn't the goal of compensating victims actually a compelling reason for the courts to act in toxic torts cases rather than an argument against their doing so?

Alternatively, is it the courts' skepticism about QRAs that represents the more sound approach? Should we rethink the decision not to send the regulatory agencies down the road represented by *Ethyl Corp.*, page 444, above, in which regulators would seek to reduce risks as much as possible once they had been qualitatively identified as material, rather than consume resources in pursuing questionable quantification of risk and then seeking an ever-more-precise balancing of quantified risk against quantified costs?

5. Admission of Expert Testimony. Toxic torts cases frequently become battles of experts presenting testimony on complex scientific issues. Once the giver is qualified as an expert, opinion testimony may be offered on causation that can be based on evidence that is not itself admissible. Courts increasingly have considered whether to restrict certain kinds of testimony out of fear that juries will give it unwarranted credence. Some commentators have suggested that the court appoint its own independent expert to provide the jury with an assessment of the scientific validity of testimony on either side. Elliot, Toward Incentive-Based Procedure: Three Approaches for Regulating Scientific Evidence, 69 B.U.L. Rev. 487 (1989). This is in part a reaction to the liberalization of evidentiary rules that has permitted the admission of testimony that many believe to be of questionable scientific validity (e.g., testimony of "clinical ecologists").

6. Impact of the Jury System. The operation of the jury system has helped victims of exposure to toxic substances to overcome some of the barriers to recovery that the common law has erected. As Phillip Harter notes, such cases

> will usually be decided in a court by a lay jury that is congenitally unable to resolve the competing technical claims. Thus, the jury will necessarily reflect its policy views of the matter—which carries with it a societal belief in the allocation of liability. As a result of that, there are undoubtedly more negotiations and settlements over toxic tort issues than there would have been a decade ago. That is because under rigorous rules the plaintiff may well not be able to mount the burden of proof, but if the case is submitted to the jury, it may not insist on rigorous application of the rules. Indeed, once the plaintiff presents *some* evidence on causation, the court is more likely to submit the case to the jury than was formerly the case. The jury, in turn, may create an informal presumption that necessitates the defendant to disprove causation (or, as the technical term has it, the burden of going forward shifts to the defendant). While not particularly reflected in the law itself, to the extent that does happen—and it appears that it does with some frequency—it is a major change. [P. Harter, The Dilemma of Causation in Toxic Torts v-vi (1986) (emphasis in original).]

PROBLEM EXERCISE: TOXIC TORTS

Suppose a group of neighbors brings suit against a company that owns and operates a local chemical manufacturing plant. Sufficient evidence is adduced at trial to support the following findings:

1. Normal background risk of leukemia suggests that one could expect somewhere between two and four cases of leukemia among the neighborhood population.
2. The chemical plant discharged substantial quantities of a toxic substance known to cause leukemia into both the air and the water for a period of ten years that ended four years ago.
3. The discharges were the result of negligence on the part of the managers of the chemical plant.
4. Best estimates are that the plant's discharges increased the risk of leukemia to exposed persons by something between 33⅓ percent and 66⅔ percent above the normal background risk.
5. Five neighbors (all of whom are plaintiffs) who live near the plant have now been diagnosed as having leukemia.

Question One. Under the but-for causation requirement, what decision would the court reach concerning whether the company is liable to the five plaintiffs who have leukemia? Under the substantial factor requirement?

Question Two. Suppose that the state has a three-year statute of limitations that runs from the date of exposure rather than from the date a disease is discovered. Would the plaintiffs' action be barred by such a statute of limitations?

Question Three. Can other neighbors who were exposed to the toxic discharges but who have not yet contracted leukemia bring suit? For what injuries, if any, can they recover?

=5=

‖ *The Regulatory Process* ‖

Since the issues in this proceeding were joined . . . we have
had several lawsuits, almost four years of substantive and procedural
maneuvering before the EPA, and now this extended Court challenge. . . .

Cases like this highlight the critical responsibilities Congress
has entrusted to the courts in proceedings of such length, complexity
and disorder. Conflicting interests play fiercely for enormous stakes,
advocates are prolific and agile, obfuscation runs high, common
sense correspondingly low, the public interest is often obscured.

We cannot redo the agency's job. . . . So in the end we can
only make our best effort to understand, to see if the result makes
sense, and to assure that nothing unlawful or irrational has taken
place.

—Sierra Club v. Costle,
657 F.2d 298, 410 (D.C. Cir. 1981)

Regulatory policy is the product of fierce competition between a
variety of public and private interests in legislative bodies, administrative
agencies, and the courts. A thorough understanding of how regulations
are developed, interpreted, and enforced requires more than mere
knowledge of "black letter" administrative law; it also demands an appreciation of the complex, and often highly political, processes by which
law affects policy. Nowhere are those processes more influential in shaping regulatory policy than in the environmental area.

Most environmental legislation delegates to administrative agencies
the unenviable task of translating the laws into workable regulatory programs. By increasing the authority of administrative agencies, the rapid
growth of such regulatory legislation has helped transform "the system
of shared powers created by the constitution" into "a system of shared
influence over bureaucratic decisionmaking." Strauss, Legislative Theory and the Rule of Law, 89 Colum. L. Rev. 427, 428 (1989), quoting
M. McCabbins and T. Sullivan, eds., Congress: Structure and Policy 403
(1987). A wide range of interests seek to influence how agencies implement the environmental statutes, including environmental groups, regulated industries, powerful congressional committees, and the Executive

657

Office of the President. The umpire lurking in the background is the judiciary, whose intervention routinely is sought by parties disappointed by agency decisions. Despite today's more deferential climate of judicial review, the threat of judicial intervention continues to have substantial influence on administrative decisions.

While the environmental statutes increasingly contain highly detailed instructions, the sheer complexity of the regulatory task inevitably dictates that agencies retain considerable discretion. The Administrative Procedure Act and the environmental statutes establish some procedural ground rules governing the exercise of that discretion. This chapter explores how the regulatory process operates, the forces that influence agency decisions, and evolving institutional mechanisms for controlling agency action. After examining how agencies establish regulatory priorities, we focus on the rulemaking process and the competition between Congress and the president for control of environmental policy-making. We conclude by discussing the role of the judiciary in the regulatory process, a major factor in the early development of environmental law that retains considerable importance today.

A.   ESTABLISHING REGULATORY PRIORITIES

The rapid growth of environmental law has expanded administrative responsibilities far more rapidly than agency resources. Faced with limited resources and multiple regulatory responsibilities, environmental agencies have been forced to confront the increasingly important question of how regulatory priorities should be set. Widespread dissatisfaction with EPA's implementation of the environmental laws has inspired increasingly specific statutory directives, often coupled with action-forcing provisions (e.g., statutory deadlines coupled with citizen suit provisions). Frustrated by these constraints, EPA has argued that it could provide more environmental protection if it had the flexibility to concentrate its limited resources where the greatest reductions in risk can be achieved.

1. Reducing Risk as a Method for Setting Priorities

Most regulatory agencies do not employ any systematic method for establishing regulatory priorities. They respond to problems in a largely ad hoc fashion in response to pressure from public and private interests. Such an ad hoc approach to priority-setting may have political advantages, but it also can reduce agency productivity. See Shapiro and

McGarity, Reorienting OSHA: Regulatory Alternatives and Legislative Reform, 6 Yale J. on Reg. 1, 20-21 (1989).

Data limitations have been a persistent barrier to comprehensive priority-setting by agencies. EPA has been particularly handicapped by a lack of systematic environmental monitoring networks. The radon problem, estimated to cause thousands of lung cancer deaths, was discovered by accident when Stanley Watras, a worker at a nuclear power plant, set off the plant's radiation alarms on *arriving* at work. Efforts to find the source of the radiation were unavailing until his home was discovered to have radon levels that exposed him to risks equivalent to those of smoking more than 200 packs of cigarettes per day.

The internal organizational structure of an agency also can have a significant impact on how priorities are set. EPA was created by executive order in 1970 to consolidate in one agency programs that had been scattered among several agencies. While it was thought that this would facilitate a comprehensive, multimedia attack on pollution, the growth of medium-specific divisions within EPA (air and radiation, water, solid waste and emergency response, and pesticides and toxic substances) has made it difficult for the Agency to establish priorities on a cross-media basis. See Marcus, EPA's Organizational Structure, 54 Law & Contemp. Probs. 5, 39 (Autumn 1991). Only rarely has EPA been able to undertake significant regulatory initiatives on its own. For a description of one of the rare exceptions see Alm, The Multimedia Approach to Pollution Control: An Impossible Dream?, in National Research Council, Multimedia Approaches to Pollution Control: Symposium Proceedings 114, 115 (1987) (describing EPA's 1984 initiative to slash levels of lead in gasoline.)

The notion that regulatory agencies should use a more systematic method for setting priorities that relies on the results of risk assessments is gaining considerable support. Proponents of risk assessment argue that it can be used to ensure that agencies focus their limited resources on the most serious problems first. If, for example, risk assessments indicate that greater reductions in overall societal risk can be obtained by spending money on radon control than by cleaning up a Superfund site, proponents of this approach would advocate allocating more funds to radon control programs and less to Superfund.

In 1987 EPA embarked on a major initiative to examine the consequences of using comparative risk assessment as the central principle to govern agency priority-setting. Seventy-five EPA staff members examined how the Agency's priorities would differ if it simply concentrated on the problems believed to pose the greatest risks. After nine months of study, they produced a report entitled Unfinished Business: A Comparative Assessment of Environmental Problems. The study attempted to rank the 31 environmental problems listed in Chapter 1 on the basis of their relative risks.

Although the use of quantitative risk assessment techniques has been confined mainly to assessment of cancer risks, the EPA study attempted also to consider noncancer health effects, ecological damage, and adverse economic effects of environmental problems. While the study found that it was virtually impossible to perform any rigorous quantitative assessments of risks other than cancer, it attempted to provide rough qualitative rankings of all four categories of risks. EPA found that data were simply inadequate to perform rigorous risk assessments of most existing problems and that even rough rank-orderings were virtually impossible for new activities (such as biotechnology) and new toxic chemicals. The study found serious conceptual difficulties in comparing risks that are fundamentally different in character (e.g., comparing ecological risks to risks of cancer or risks of damage to developmental, immunological, reproductive, or respiratory systems). The Agency found that there is no general methodology for assessing noncancer risks or ecological risks and that environmental exposure data were surprisingly poor.

Despite all these difficulties, the Unfinished Business report concluded that the problems risk assessment identified as posing the greatest risks did not correspond well with the Agency's current program priorities.

> Areas of relatively high risk but low EPA effort include: indoor radon; indoor air pollution; stratospheric ozone depletion; global warming; non-point sources; discharges to estuaries, coastal waters, and oceans; other pesticide risks; accidental releases of toxics; consumer products; and worker exposures. Areas of high EPA effort but relatively medium or low risks include: RCRA sites; Superfund; underground storage tanks; and municipal nonhazardous waste sites. [EPA, Unfinished Business: A Comparative Assessment of Environmental Problems xv (1987).]

The study concluded that "EPA's priorities appear more closely aligned with public opinion" than with the results of its risk assessments. The Agency noted that national opinion polls showed high public concern over chemical waste disposal, water pollution, chemical plant accidents, and outdoor air pollution and relatively low concern over indoor air pollution, consumer products, genetic engineering, and global warming.

As a result of this study, EPA endorsed the concept of using comparative risk reduction as a basis for setting Agency priorities. Unfinished Business found that EPA's priorities could be organized around "the fundamental goal of reducing risks" and that "the concept appears compelling."

The EPA subsequently asked its Science Advisory Board (SAB), a group of scientists from outside the Agency, to review the conclusions of Unfinished Business. In response to EPA's request, the SAB appointed a committee of 39 distinguished scientists and other experts. This group reviewed Unfinished Business and prepared a followup report, entitled Reducing Risk, that included their own comparative risk assessment of environmental problems. EPA Science Advisory Board, Reducing Risk: Setting Priorities and Strategies for Environmental Protection (1990).

Most of the outside experts who prepared Reducing Risk enthusiastically endorsed the notion that EPA should use environmental risk to set priorities. But they also acknowledged the difficulties involved in performing comparative assessments of environmental risks. The SAB found that even defining categories of environmental problems was fraught with difficulty. They noted that the categories employed in Unfinished Business grouped some problems on the basis of the types of pollution involved, others on the basis of sources of pollutants, and others on the basis of receptors of pollutants. The SAB deemed this to be unsatisfactory for purposes of comparative risk assessment because the categories lacked a consistent basis for comparison. They also noted that Unfinished Business omitted some very serious problems such as habitat destruction and the decline in genetic diversity. The SAB emphasized that the rankings produced by Unfinished Business in many cases were subjective and "cannot be supported fully by existing data" in large part because of the absence of good data to assess certain risks. Moreover, they questioned some of the assumptions and conclusions made in the prior report.

After independently reviewing data on relative risks, the SAB generally agreed with the most striking finding of Unfinished Business: that regulatory priorities are more closely aligned with the public's perception of risks than with the experts'. They concluded that "the remaining and emerging environmental risks considered most serious by the general public today are different from those considered most serious by the technical professionals charged with reducing environmental risks." EPA Science Advisory Board, Reducing Risk 12 (1990). For example, the Reducing Risk task force concluded that ecological risks were not getting the attention they deserved and that EPA should consider them to be as important as human health risks because ecosystems are essential to human health and long-term economic growth and "are intrinsically valuable in their own right." Recognizing that the methodology for ecological risk assessment is primitive, the study focused on factors such as the size of the area affected by such risks and how long-lasting ecological damage could be. The SAB found that some risks that the public is very concerned about, such as oil spills, radioactive materials, and groundwater pollution, actually posed relatively low risks to human health and the environment. (Figure 5.1 compares EPA's assessment of the top environmental concerns with the public's ranking based on a March 1990 public opinion poll.)

FIGURE 5.1
EPA's Assessment of Top Environmental Concerns and the Public's Ranking

EPA'S TOP CONCERNS
(not in rank order)*

Ecological risks

Global climate change
Stratospheric ozone depletion
Habitat alteration
Species extinction and loss of
  biodiversity

Health risks

Criteria air pollutants (e.g.,
  smog)
Toxic air pollutants (e.g.,
  benzene)
Radon
Indoor air pollution
Drinking water contamination
Occupational exposure to
  chemicals
Application of pesticides
Stratospheric ozone depletion

PUBLIC'S TOP CONCERNS
(in rank order)**

1. Active hazardous waste sites (67%)
2. Abandoned hazardous waste sites (65%)
3. Water pollution from industrial wastes (63%)
4. Occupational exposure to toxic chemicals (63%)
5. Oil spills (60%)
6. Destruction of ozone layer (60%)
7. Nuclear power plant accidents (60%)
8. Industrial accidents releasing pollutants (58%)
9. Radiation from radioactive wastes (58%)
10. Air pollution from factories (56%)
11. Leaking underground storage tanks (55%)
12. Coastal water contamination (54%)
13. Solid waste and litter (53%)
14. Pesticide risk to farm workers (52%)
15. Water pollution from agricultural runoff (51%)
16. Water pollution from sewage plants (50%)
17. Air pollution from vehicles (50%)
18. Pesticide residues in foods (49%)
19. Greenhouse effect (48%)
20. Drinking water contamination (46%)
21. Destruction of wetlands (42%)
22. Acid rain (40%)
23. Water pollution from city runoff (35%)
24. Nonhazardous waste sites (31%)
25. Biotechnology (30%)
26. Indoor air pollution (22%)
27. Radiation from x-rays (21%)
28. Radon in homes (17%)
29. Radiation from microwave ovens (13%)

*EPA Science Advisory Board, Reducing Risk (1990)
**March 1990 Roper Poll (% rating each problem "very serious")
Source: Counting on Science at EPA, 249 Science 616 (1990).

Reducing Risk endorsed the notion that "EPA should target its environmental protection efforts on the basis of opportunities for the greatest risk reduction." Id. at 6. It recommended that EPA incorporate risk-based priorities into the Agency's strategic planning and budget processes while making efforts to improve data and analytical methodologies to support comparative risk assessment. EPA has enthusiastically endorsed these recommendations and has taken steps to implement them.

NOTES AND QUESTIONS

1. Reducing Risk criticizes the approach used in Unfinished Business to classify environmental problems into discrete categories. The 31 categories used in the prior report are listed in Figure 1.1, page 9. Categories of problems deemed most important in Reducing Risk are shown in the left column of Figure 5.1. Which set of categories is more useful for purposes of comparing environmental risks? Where would you include the lead poisoning problem in performing such comparisons?

2. EPA found that its current priorities appear to be more in line with the public's ranking of risk than with the results of its experts' comparative risk assessment. Figure 5.1 illustrates these results. How would you rank the importance of these problems in relative terms? Do your rankings correspond more closely to EPA's current priorities or to the results of EPA's experts' study? Would you have expected EPA's current priorities to be more closely aligned with its experts' assessments of relative risks or with the public's? What factors could explain the apparent divergence between EPA's actual priorities and the experts' assessment of risks? Who do you think should set EPA's priorities: "experts" or the public? Which approach to priority-setting would be more efficient in economic terms? Which approach would be more consistent with democratic values? Which would result in more environmental protection? Why?

3. In deciding what priority you would like EPA to give an environmental problem, which is more important to you, the magnitude of the risk you face as an individual or the aggregate level of risk to society as a whole? During a Senate hearing that considered the conclusions of Reducing Risk, Senator Howard Metzenbaum remarked: "People who I know who live near toxic waste sites in Ohio would not be happy to hear that . . . problems at toxic waste sites, for instance, are relatively low risk, . . . especially if they believed EPA would be using a ranking system as an excuse to devote less resources to the cleanup of such sites in the future." How would you respond to this concern?

4. For which of the following purposes, if any, do you think EPA

should use comparative risk assessments: Establishing an Agency budget? Making legislative proposals to Congress? Educating and informing the public concerning the risks they face? Setting Agency priorities for the issuance of regulations? Setting Agency priorities for enforcement of existing regulations? Suppose that a party responsible for cleanup costs at a Superfund site can demonstrate through a risk assessment that a greater reduction in environmental risk could be obtained if the cleanup money was spent on something else, such as a program to educate the public about the dangers of radon. Should the money be shifted elsewhere instead of being used to clean up the site?

5. Would you favor replacing the existing environmental statutes with a single comprehensive law that gives EPA discretion to concentrate on what it deems to be the most serious risks? One proposal would replace existing laws with a single statute that authorizes regulation on the basis of "unreasonable risk" and that would require a single permit for each major facility that emits pollutants instead of separate permits under the different statutes. What advantages would this approach have? What disadvantages? Why do you think many consider this idea to be politically naive?

6. EPA has received many favorable comments on the recommendations contained in Reducing Risk. The president's budget for Fiscal Year 1992 endorsed the concept of shifting the Agency's spending priorities to the areas of largest risk. EPA cites the administration's request for more money to protect the Great Lakes and the Chesapeake Bay as indicative of the Agency's greater emphasis on ecological risks. Yet the largest reductions made by OMB in EPA's 1992 budget request involved grants to combat nonpoint source pollution, which was ranked as one of the most serious water pollution problems. The Agency has discovered that its existing budgetary priorities are so tightly controlled by statute that it cannot reallocate any more than a tiny portion of its budget to programs that it concludes deserve higher priority. Agency officials are attempting to convince Congress to give EPA more flexibility. We consider next the many ways in which EPA's discretion has been constrained by statute and the mechanisms that are available to force regulatory action under the environmental laws.

2. Agency-Forcing Mechanisms

Dissatisfied with administrative implementation of the environmental laws, Congress has incorporated increasingly detailed regulatory directives into the environmental laws, coupled with provisions designed to force agencies to act. The classic agency-forcing device is a provision that authorizes a citizen suit against agency officials who fail to take certain action. Virtually all of the major federal environmental laws expressly authorize suits by citizens against agency officials who fail to perform "nondiscretionary duties." When coupled with a statutory deadline requiring an agency to initiate or complete an action by a specific date, citizen suits can be a means of enlisting judicial help in influencing agency priorities. The proliferation of these and other devices for controlling agency discretion follows some general patterns described below.

A. MODELS OF AGENCY-FORCING MECHANISMS

Based on a comprehensive review of modern regulatory statutes, Sidney Shapiro and Robert Glicksman describe three general models employed by Congress to control agency discretion: *the coercive model,* under which the agency's discretion concerning whether to regulate is removed while the agency is permitted to choose the appropriate method of regulation; *the prescriptive model,* under which the agency retains its regulatory discretion but, if it chooses to regulate, it must regulate in accordance with relatively detailed substantive criteria; and *the ministerial model,* which couples a deadline with a detailed substantive standard defining the appropriate manner of regulation. Shapiro and Glicksman, Congress, the Supreme Court, and the Quiet Revolution in Administrative Law, 1988 Duke L.J. 819.

Most of the environmental legislation adopted by Congress from 1984 to the present employs the coercive model by specifying regulations EPA must issue by specified deadlines. The 1984 Amendments to RCRA, the 1986 Amendments to CERCLA, and the 1990 Clean Air Act Amendments require EPA to undertake scores of regulatory actions, with statutory deadlines attached to virtually every significant task required by the legislation. These deadlines facilitate congressional oversight while increasing EPA's ability to resist outside pressures for delaying or avoiding decisions. However, they do not ensure that the substance of the Agency's decision will be of high quality.

The prescriptive model for controlling agency discretion (giving the agency discretion as to whether or not to regulate, while providing detailed instructions concerning the substance of regulation) is rarely used by Congress in part because prescriptive statutes may deter agencies from deciding to regulate. As Shapiro and Glicksman note, Congress instead has favored a ministerial model by limiting agency discretion over both whether to regulate and how to do so. Recent environmental statutes have even contained "hammer" provisions that specify regulatory outcomes that will take effect automatically if an agency fails to act by a certain deadline. Others specify regulations that take effect unless and until the agency acts to change them. Shapiro and Glicksman note that these innovations "address some of the key deficiencies in the coercive and prescriptive models" by giving the agency powerful incentives to perform its statutory duties.

Not surprisingly, Congress's efforts to control more closely the exercise of discretion by environmental agencies have not been warmly received by executive branch officials. Former EPA administrator William Ruckelshaus has criticized the trend toward increasingly specific legislation, noting that "You cannot squeeze the complexity inherent in managing environmental risks between the pages of a statute." Another EPA official has argued that "unrealistic deadlines, especially when coupled with 'citizen suit' provisions that encourage litigation to enforce those deadlines, impinge upon the constitutional authority of the executive branch to establish and implement its own regulatory agenda." Habicht, Responses to Justice Antonin Scalia, 24 Houston L. Rev. 111, 116 (1987). J. William Futrell, president of the Environmental Law Institute, describes federal hazardous waste legislation as becoming much like the tax code, where as a result of interest group politics the "administrative discretion of the Internal Revenue Service (IRS) is severely proscribed by hundreds of specific congressional directives that mandate special treatment of favored localities and certain industries," 24 Houston L. Rev. 125, 133 (1987).

Despite these complaints, the trend toward increasing legislative specificity and proliferating deadlines continued in the Clean Air Act Amendments of 1990. The Amendments dramatically expand the number of regulations EPA must issue under statutory deadlines. While constraining EPA discretion in many respects, the Amendments also give EPA unprecedented authority by vastly expanding the scope of regulatory targets and by creating a national permit program governing air emissions.

B. CITIZEN SUITS AND STATUTORY DEADLINES

Virtually all of the major federal environmental statutes authorize citizens to bring action-forcing litigation against EPA when the EPA administrator has failed to perform a nondiscretionary duty. Most citizen suit provisions are patterned on section 304(a)(2) of the Clean Air Act, which authorizes "any person" to sue the administrator of EPA "where there is alleged a failure of the Administrator to perform any act or duty under this chapter which is not discretionary with the Administrator." 42 U.S.C. §7604(a)(2). Virtually identical provisions are contained in the Clean Water Act (§504(a)(2)), 33 U.S.C. §1365, the Resource Conservation and Recovery Act (§7002(a)(2)), 42 U.S.C. §6972(a)(2), the Safe Drinking Water Act (§1449), 42 U.S.C. §300j-8, the Toxic Substances Control Act (§20(a)(2)), 15 U.S.C. §2619, the Comprehensive Environmental Response, Compensation, and Liability Act (§310), 42 U.S.C. §9654, and other statutes. Because these statutes also authorize court awards of attorneys' fees to prevailing parties, plaintiffs can recover their legal costs when they successfully sue officials who fail to act.

In cases where EPA has failed to act, the principal issue often is whether EPA's alleged duty was nondiscretionary or not.[7] The allegedly nondiscretionary duty usually is some form of rulemaking action. While debate over the extent to which a statute makes some actions nondiscretionary is frequently possible, see, e.g., Natural Resources Defense Council, Inc. v. Train, 545 F.2d 320 (2d Cir. 1976), if a statutory deadline has been attached to the duty, the nondiscretionary nature of the duty can hardly be questioned, and the principal issue is the nature of the relief the court should order. Deadline suits usually result in a court-ordered schedule for completion of the rulemaking action, but courts generally cannot dictate to the agency what the substance of the rules will be.

As statutory deadlines have proliferated in recent years, "deadline suits" have become a common form of environmental litigation. After statutory deadlines have been missed, plaintiffs routinely have been successful in obtaining court orders directing agency officials to act on a court-supervised schedule. Recent environmental legislation has sought to provide greater incentives for agencies to meet deadlines by incorporating "hammer" provisions, which specify the content of regulations that will take effect automatically if deadlines are missed.

The 1984 Hazardous and Solid Waste Amendments to RCRA are frequently cited by critics of agency-forcing directives. See, e.g., Futrell, 24 Houston L. Rev. 125, 134 (1987) (calling them a "classic example of intergovernmental distrust" because they are "lengthy and unparalleled in their level of detail, intrusion into EPA's management practices, and prescription of new regulatory practices"). The history that led to adoption of these provisions provides useful insight into the reasons why Congress employs action-forcing mechanisms. In 1976 Congress enacted RCRA and required EPA to promulgate regulations governing hazardous waste management by April 1978. When the deadline expired, EPA had not even issued proposed regulations and was unable to indicate when it would do so.

In September 1978 several environmental organizations brought a "deadline suit" against EPA. The federal district court in Washington ordered EPA to promulgate the regulations by December 1979, a date suggested by EPA itself. EPA later sought and obtained from the court an extension of this deadline to enable it to stretch out promulgation of the regulations in stages until the fall of 1980. Although this schedule was met, EPA failed to promulgate the important permitting standards for land disposal facilities by the deadline. In October 1981 EPA requested an additional two years' time to promulgate the regulations; the court ordered EPA to promulgate them by February 1, 1982. After EPA appealed that ruling, the D.C. Circuit ordered EPA to issue the regulations by July 15, 1982. Although the agency met that deadline, by the time RCRA was reauthorized in 1984 only 5 land disposal facilities and

17 hazardous waste incinerators had received RCRA permits. More than 1,500 other land disposal facilities and 17 incinerators were operating under "interim status" with minimal controls. Thus Congress determined to establish new deadlines for many aspects of the RCRA program that "were negotiated with EPA, and modified at EPA's behest." R. Fortuna and D. Lennett, Hazardous Waste Regulation: The New Era 16 (1987).

How well have the new RCRA deadlines worked? In July 1988, the General Accounting Office reported that 66 of the 76 new deadlines had passed. Of these deadlines, EPA had met 3 of the 4 statutory deadlines with hammer provisions but only 24 (or 39 percent) of the 62 deadlines without hammer provisions. EPA maintained that the principal reason why it missed so many of the deadlines was a lack of resources.

EPA's failure to meet many of the deadlines imposed by the 1984 Amendments to RCRA resulted in a comprehensive "megadeadline" suit by the Environmental Defense Fund. Environmental Defense Fund v. Reilly, Civ. No. 89-0598 (D.D.C. Mar. 8, 1989). In response to this lawsuit, EPA proposed a schedule for completing the various rulemakings required by these deadlines. RCRA requires that these rulemakings be completed by deadlines that extend to November 1992. Under EPA's proposed schedule, it would not complete the last of these actions (final permit determination for storage facilities) until December 2004.

In determining what is an appropriate schedule for completion of such a rulemaking, representations by EPA officials about the amount of time necessary to complete the rulemaking usually carry considerable weight with the court. Consider the following statements (from an affidavit by the director of EPA's Office of Solid Waste) about the amount of time required for EPA to complete the RCRA rulemakings subject to the deadline litigation mentioned above:

> The timetable for development and completion of a typical regulatory action under RCRA, exclusive of preliminary data-gathering and analysis, is approximately 31 months. . . . Minor regulatory amendments will take less time, and rulemakings with significant economic impact (e.g., those with economic impacts of more than $100 million and thus requiring additional regulatory analysis under Executive Order 12291) will take more. This time period encompasses development of a proposal, public comment periods, and development of the final rule. The timetable for a proposal (approximately 17 months) includes the internal agency review and approval of a planned regulatory action (the "development plan"); the formation of, deliberations by, and decision on the action by the Agency-wide workgroup assigned to the rule; the review of the rule by senior management at EPA ("red border review"); any necessary redrafting of the rule; review of the Agency-approved regulatory action by the Office of Management and Budget under Executive Order 12291 and the Paperwork Reduction Act; and submission of the proposal to the Federal Register for

publication. Data-gathering and analysis by the EPA office responsible for the rule continues during most phases of this process.

Public comment periods for most RCRA rules are at least 60 days. However, a longer or subsequent comment period is often necessary to provide members of the public sufficient time to review, analyze and prepare comments on, technically complex or controversial RCRA rules with substantial but complex impacts on a diverse regulated community.

Following the public comment period, development of the final rule will take approximately one year. This period includes the time necessary to analyze public comments, raise significant policy issues for decision by appropriate senior management, redrafting of the rule, review and approval by the Agency workgroup, red border review, Office of Management and Budget review, any redrafting necessary to address reviewers' comments, and submission of the final rule to the Federal Register for publication. [Declaration of Sylvia K. Lowrance in Environmental Defense Fund v. Reilly, Civ. No. 89-0598 (D.D.C. Mar. 8, 1989).]

This summary of the various stages in EPA's current rulemaking procedures provides some indication of why it takes so long for the Agency to take regulatory action. After nearly a year of negotiations, the parties eventually settled the RCRA deadline by agreeing to a comprehensive schedule for future RCRA rulemakings.

There is no clear consensus concerning the impact of statutory deadlines on agency performance. While they have been widely criticized, they are increasingly popular with Congress, which seems to view them as indispensible tools for stimulating agency action. The popularity of deadlines may stem in part from the reluctance of courts to get involved in agency priority-setting in their absence. Although section 706 of the APA authorizes courts to "compel agency action unlawfully withheld or unreasonably delayed," reviewing courts have been loath to second-guess agency priorities even in cases of lengthy rulemaking delays. Sierra Club v. Thomas, 828 F.2d 783 (D.C. Cir. 1987); United Steelworkers of America v. Rubber Manufacturing Assn., 783 F.2d 1117 (D.C. Cir. 1986) (refusal to order OSHA to expedite benzene rulemaking).

In an effort to explore the impact of deadlines in a more systematic way, EPA commissioned a study of its own experience with statutory deadlines. The study found that between 1970 and 1980 a total of 328 deadlines had been inserted by Congress into 15 environmental laws. Of these deadlines, 86 percent were directed at EPA, 22 percent at the states, and 7 percent at regulated industries. More than one-third of the deadlines required the promulgation of regulations, and another one-third required the completion of reports or studies. Only 14 percent of the deadlines were met. Environmental and Energy Study Institute, Statutory Deadlines in Environmental Legislation: Necessary But Need Improvement 12 (1985).

The study found that, despite the fact that so many deadlines had been missed, deadlines have been a valuable tool in speeding action by EPA, the states, and the regulated community. The study found that deadlines serve to mobilize the attention of agency management, although they are not sufficient by themselves to speed agency action (as indicated by the fact that deadlines that are attached to actions that EPA deems to be unwise or unpopular seldom result in faster action by EPA). See, for example, the deadline suit that ultimately resulted in EPA administrator William Ruckelshaus's being held in contempt of court for failure to promulgate radionuclide standards, Sierra Club v. Ruckelshaus, 602 F. Supp. 892 (N.D. Cal. 1984), as described in Beers, 24 Houston L. Rev. 148 (1987). In response to the contempt order, EPA promulgated standards that required no additional controls on the mill tailing sites. 49 Fed. Reg. 43,909 (1984), although the Agency later agreed to reconsider this standard.

Despite the concern frequently expressed by agencies that deadlines compromise the quality of agency action, the study found little evidence to support this assertion. The study noted that Congress imposes many unrealistic deadlines on EPA, which dilutes their effectiveness, but that Congress is becoming more sophisticated in crafting deadlines and in attaching significant consequences for noncompliance. The study essentially found that deadlines are a necessary evil for stimulating action by administrative agencies. The report recommended that Congress improve its use of deadlines by applying them only to the most important tasks, by using more realistic deadlines, by establishing interim deadlines for major, long-term undertakings, and by paying more attention to the appropriations process to ensure that adequate resources are made available to agencies to perform regulatory tasks.

These thoughtful recommendations have not defused the controversy surrounding statutory deadlines. For example, the 1986 Amendments to CERCLA required EPA to begin remedial action at 175 NPL sites by October 17, 1989. Although EPA announced that it had met the deadline by commencing 178 remedial actions, an inspector general's audit subsequently charged that EPA counted dozens of sites at which cleanups had not actually started. The IG alleged that as the deadline drew near, EPA focused on commencing action on the least contaminated sites in order to boost its numbers, rather than addressing the worst sites first as Congress had intended. EPA Overstated 1989 Site Cleanup Count, Misled Congress, Inspector General Finds, 22 Env. Rep. 220 (1991). EPA vigorously denied these charges.

Deadlines are now routinely inserted into the environmental laws whenever they are amended; they also are routinely missed. For example, the 1990 Clean Air Act Amendments imposed statutory deadlines on virtually every significant regulatory action they require EPA to take. Despite having announced elaborate plans for adhering to this schedule, by February 1992 EPA had missed 19 deadlines for significant rulemaking actions covering most of the Act's key regulatory programs. Subcomm. on Health and the Environment, House Comm. on Energy & Commerce, Clean Air Left in the Lurch 2 (1992). For 11 of these missed deadlines, EPA had been unable to meet even its own revised timetable, presented to Congress only three months earlier. Id. at 3.

Deadlines are widely viewed as a kind of necessary evil—necessary to ensure that agencies eventually perform their duties, but not always sufficient to ensure that they are performed as rapidly as Congress would like. Courts only intervene after deadlines have been missed and a lawsuit brought, and their intervention is usually confined to incorporating the agency's "new" schedule into a court order. This may prevent further slippage in the agency's schedule, although the agency already may have succeeded in "gaming" the court by building such slippage into the schedule it presents.

C. Petitions to Initiate Rulemaking

"Deadline" litigation is not the only avenue for persuading agencies to initiate regulatory proceedings. Section 553(e) of the Administrative Procedure Act and most federal environmental laws require agencies to give citizens the right to petition for the initiation of rulemaking proceedings. A study performed for the Administrative Conference of the United States found that citizen petitions are used relatively infrequently. Most administrative practitioners indicated that there "were more effective ways to influence agency action, such as informal contacts or litigation, and that they would be loath to file a petition for rulemaking because of the delay they expect in the final disposition of their requests." Luneberg, Petitions for Rulemaking: Federal Agency Practice and Recommendations for Improvement 140 (1986). The Administrative Conference found that "few agencies have established sound practices in dealing with petitions or responding promptly to such petitions." Recommendation No. 86-6, Petitions for Rulemaking, 1 C.F.R. §305.86-6, Preamble. It recommended that agencies adopt new procedures to rectify these problems including maintenance of a public petition file and prompt provision of notice to petitioners of the disposition of petitions.

Although agencies generally are not required to respond to citizen petitions by a certain date, one unusual exception to this rule is provided by section 21 of the Toxic Substances Control Act, 15 U.S.C. §2620. Section 21 of TSCA requires EPA within 90 days to grant or deny citizen petitions to initiate rulemaking actions under TSCA to control chemicals that may present "unreasonable risks" to public health or the environment. If EPA fails to act on such a petition within 90 days, or denies the petition, the petitioners may file suit in federal district court seeking de novo review of such failure or denial. If a court determines that the action sought by the petition meets the requisite statutory standard, "the court shall order the [EPA] Administrator to initiate the action requested by the petitioner." 15 U.S.C. §2620(b)(4)(B). The combination of a tight deadline for EPA to respond to petitions and a cause of action to challenge petition denials in court provides petitioners with a potentially significant tool to stimulate agency action.

While the 90-day response deadline and the possibility of citizen suits have ensured that EPA pays attention to section 21 petitions, they cannot force EPA to adopt final rules. For example, in December 1978 the Environmental Defense Fund (EDF) filed a section 21 petition asking EPA to conduct a rulemaking to require abatement of asbestos hazards in schools. Noting that asbestos is present in approximately 31,000 elementary and secondary schools attended by 15 million children, EDF's petition maintained that abatement standards were necessary to redress an "unreasonable risk." While conceding that "a problem exists," EPA Administrator Douglas Costle denied EDF's petition in March 1979, concluding that regulations were not necessary because EPA could address the problem more effectively through a "nonregulatory program of cooperation with and assistance to state and local (including school) authorities." 44 Fed. Reg. 20,290 (1979). After EDF sued EPA pursuant to section 21(b)(4) of TSCA, Environmental Defense Fund v. Costle, No. 79-1360 (D.D.C. May 18, 1979), EPA reversed its position and announced that it would grant EDF's petition. 44 Fed. Reg. 40,900 (1979). EDF dismissed its lawsuit after EPA pledged "to have a complete regulatory program by the school summer vacation of 1980." 44 Fed. Reg. 54,676 (1979). This commitment was never honored, although EPA did require a one-time inspection of schools to determine if friable asbestos is present and to require notification of parents if such asbestos were found. 47 Fed. Reg. 23,360 (1982).

A subsequent section 21 petition filed by the Service Employees International Union (SEIU) in November 1983 again forced EPA to pay attention to the asbestos-in-schools problem. After announcing that it would "partially grant" SEIU's petition for asbestos abatement rules, EPA refused to commence a rulemaking, a decision found to be inconsistent with section 21's requirements in Service Employees International Union v. Thomas, No. 84-2790 (D.D.C. 1987), 1987 W.L. 14598. In October 1986 Congress intervened and enacted legislation requiring EPA to establish standards for abatement of asbestos hazards in schools by tight deadlines coupled with hammer provisions. Asbestos Hazard Emergency Response Act (AHERA), codified as Title II of TSCA, §§201 et seq., 15 U.S.C. §§2641 et seq. Final rules implementing AHERA were promulgated by EPA on October 17, 1987. 52 Fed. Reg. 41,826 (1987).

Arguing that the 90 days provided for EPA to respond to a section 21 petition is inadequate to allow the Agency to determine whether or not to issue a proposed rule, EPA subsequently amended its procedural rules to reaffirm its position that petitions filed under section 21 of TSCA may be granted without the Agency's making a commitment to commence rulemaking. 54 Fed. Reg. 21,623 (1989). As amended, EPA's TSCA regulations now provide that petitions can be granted by issuance of an advance notice of proposed rulemaking, a notice of some other action (such as "a formal regulatory investigation designed to lead to issuance of rules within a reasonable time"), or issuance of a proposed rule. 40 C.F.R. §750.2(a).

The history of the asbestos-in-schools standards illustrates how difficult it can be to force a reluctant agency to initiate rulemaking proceedings. A variety of tools may be needed to stimulate agency action; citizen petitions, citizen suits, congressional oversight, and legislation. The asbestos abatement regulations ultimately were promulgated only after Congress adopted legislation specifically requiring EPA to adopt such rules and specifying alternative regulations that would take effect automatically if statutory deadlines are missed.

NOTES AND QUESTIONS

1. Consider carefully the provisions of TSCA section 21(b)(4). Suppose EPA, instead of denying a section 21 petition, simply ignores it. What legal action can the petitioner take, and what relief can be sought? What must the petitioner prove in order to be entitled to such relief?

2. The D.C. Circuit has held that EPA's response to a section 21 petition is not subject to judicial review under section 706 of the APA because section 21 provides its own independent standard of de novo review. Environmental Defense Fund v. Reilly, 909 F.2d 1497 (D.C.C. 1990).

3. When it grants a section 21 petition, is EPA under any legal compulsion to promulgate a final rule? What legal action, if any, could a petitioner take if EPA announced that it was "granting" a section 21 petition and then issued a proposed rule on which it never took final action? Consider 5 U.S.C. §706(1), the section of the Administrative Procedure Act that authorizes courts to "compel agency action unlawfully withheld or unreasonably delayed." Does section 21 of TSCA establish any deadline for EPA to take final action on a proposed rule issued in response to a section 21 petition? If EPA takes final action by withdrawing the proposed rule, what legal action may the petitioner take?

B.   THE RULEMAKING PROCESS AND REGULATORY OVERSIGHT

Even after an agency has decided to initiate regulatory action, numerous procedural hurdles must be overcome before regulations are promulgated. In the absence of some legal (or political) action-forcing mechanism, proposed regulations often languish for long periods of time as agencies respond to more immediate priorities. For example, in response to a congressional inquiry, the Food and Drug Administration discovered in 1991 that it had no idea how many regulations it had proposed but never acted on. After conducting a search of "card files, the Federal Register, . . . and the memories of senior staff members," the Agency estimated that 400 proposed regulations had been left indefinitely in regulatory limbo. Hilts, Under Revamping, FDA to Review Many Dormant Proposals on Safety, N.Y. Times, June 10, 1991, at A15. Controversial regulations are particularly likely to be sidetracked in the face of opposition from interest groups, the Executive Office of the President, or Congress.

1.   *The Rulemaking Process*

A.   RULEMAKING PROCEDURES

In the late 1960s, when the fledgling environmental movement launched an assault on the use of DDT, formal adjudicatory hearings played a more prominent role in decision-making by regulatory agencies. In 1971, when environmentalists finally succeeded in forcing EPA to consider cancelling the registration of DDT, an adjudicatory hearing was held. The hearing took more than 7 months and produced more than 9,000 pages of testimony from 125 expert witnesses. After environmental concerns stimulated an avalanche of federal environmental legislation in the early 1970s, agencies relied increasingly on informal rulemaking proceedings to make regulatory decisions. Today most environmental regulations are promulgated through informal rulemaking, although pesticide cancellation proceedings under FIFRA still involve formal adjudicatory hearings.

The procedural requirements for informal rulemaking are relatively straightforward. Informal rulemaking proceedings are governed by section 4 of the Administrative Procedure Act (APA), 5 U.S.C. §553, which requires that agencies provide (1) public notice in the Federal Register of proposed rulemaking actions, (2) an opportunity for the public to submit written comments, and (3) publication of final rules in the Federal Register accompanied by a concise statement of their basis and purpose. Agencies are permitted to formulate rules through informal rulemaking unless an enabling statute requires that hearings be conducted on the record.

Agencies undertake to develop rulemaking proposals prior to issuing a notice of proposed rulemaking. In some cases agencies may publish an advance notice of proposed rulemaking (ANPR) to solicit input from the public when the agency need not act quickly or to defuse pressure for faster action by indicating that the agency is considering the issue.

For EPA rulemaking proceedings, draft rulemaking documents usually are prepared by a work group of EPA staff who represent offices likely to be affected by the initiative. Draft notices of proposed rulemaking and supporting documents, which may be prepared with the help of outside consulting firms in more complex rulemakings, generally are reviewed by a steering committee composed of representatives from the major EPA offices. The final step in EPA's internal review procedures is "red border" review by top-level management and the EPA administrator.

An influential article by an EPA attorney describes the rulemaking development process that prevailed during EPA's early history. Pederson, Formal Records and Informal Rulemaking, 85 Yale L.J. 38 (1975). Its recommendations for more regularized procedures for maintaining rulemaking dockets to facilitate judicial review have generally been adopted by the Agency. The article identifies important aspects of the practical politics of the rulemaking process within a large agency: the difficulties of obtaining support for innovative rulemaking initiatives, the problems of distilling complex issues based on highly technical information into briefing materials for agency managers, and bureaucratic timidity that is seemingly institutionalized in the internal review process. Pederson describes the too-frequent product of the internal review process as follows:

> The bureaucratic weight and inertia and the relatively coarse mesh of the review process have two adverse (and seemingly contrary) effects on those who develop regulations. First, stiff or problematical regulations may simply not be pushed because too much bureaucratic counterpressure will be generated. (The impulse for strict regulations must be present at the working group level if there is to be any hope that strict regulations will be issued—the upper levels of review by nature tend to water down regulations in light of other factors.) Second, regulations that do get pushed may still be arbitrary to some degree, particularly in the direction from which opposition is unlikely. The upper levels of review cannot be thorough enough to catch the technical errors or errors of detail on which the legality and, indeed, the wisdom of the regulations may depend. [Id. at 59.]

Some of the federal environmental laws specify additional rule-making procedures, but these procedures generally are consistent with those of the informal rulemaking model. For example, section 307(d) of the Clean Air Act, 42 U.S.C. §7607(d), provides extensive require-ments for maintenance of a rulemaking docket by EPA for rulemakings under the Clean Air Act. It also specifies a standard for judicial review of agency action, which generally tracks the judicial review provisions of APA section 706 (although it provides that courts may invalidate rules for procedural errors only if the errors were so serious that "there is a substantial likelihood that the rule would have been significantly changed if such errors had not been made").

Other environmental statutes require that public hearings be held before certain major regulatory decisions are made (see, e.g., §§3001(a) and 3004(a) of RCRA, 42 U.S.C. §§6921(a) and §6924(a), which also require "consultation with appropriate Federal and State agencies"). Sec-tion 6(c) of the Toxic Substances Control Act, 15 U.S.C. §2605(c), spec-ifies detailed procedures for informal rulemaking under section 6(a) of TSCA. It requires that EPA provide an opportunity for oral testimony and authorizes the submission of rebuttal testimony and cross-exami-nation if the EPA administrator determines that it is necessary to resolve disputed issues of material fact. The Occupational Safety and Health Act also requires OSHA to hold a public hearing if written objections are filed to a proposed rule by any interested parties, and it gives such parties the right to conduct cross-examination when it conducts hearings on proposed rules.

THE REGULATORY PROCESS: A PATHFINDER

The Administrative Procedure Act (APA), 5 U.S.C. §551 et seq., establishes the basic procedural requirements agencies must follow in conducting informal rulemaking. Its basic re-quirements—that agencies provide public notice and an op-portunity to comment prior to promulgating regulations—are implemented through notices published daily in the Fed-eral Register describing agency actions and how to comment on them. Public comments and background documentation for agency actions are usually kept in rulemaking dockets referenced in the Federal Register notices. Information con-cerning the location, content, and hours of operation of EPA's nine rulemaking dockets is contained in EPA, Access EPA: Major EPA Dockets (1991 ed.), available from EPA.

Some environmental statutes supplement the APA by specifying additional procedures agencies must follow before taking certain actions. See, e.g., §6(c) of TSCA or §307(d) of the Clean Air Act. The Negotiated Rulemaking Act of 1990 generally codifies agency practices for conducting negotiated rulemaking. The Freedom of Information Act, 5 U.S.C. §552, provides an important tool for obtaining information from agencies that may assist citizens in participating in rulemaking proceedings.

Other statutes require agencies to consider certain factors when undertaking rulemaking. For instance, the National Environmental Policy Act requires consideration of environmental impacts before major federal actions are taken, and the Regulatory Flexibility Act requires consideration of the impact of regulation on small businesses. The Paperwork Reduction Act requires OMB clearance before agencies can submit information collection requests to the public.

Executive Order 12,291 requires agencies to submit virtually all proposed and final rules for review by OMB's Office of Information and Regulatory Affairs (OIRA) prior to publication in the Federal Register. Executive Order 12,498 requires agencies to submit significant regulatory initiatives for review by OMB a year in advance.

Since 1985 regulatory initiatives approved by OMB have been published in the annual Regulatory Program of the United States Government, which provides a wealth of information about significant regulatory activities by federal agencies as well as statistics on regulatory review by OMB. This publication, which generally has been released by OMB in late summer (except for 1989, when it was not published), usually includes an appendix with copies of the executive orders and guidance documents governing regulatory review. More detailed information on the plans of individual agencies is contained in the biannual Regulatory Agendas published by each agency in the Federal Register in late April and October. The Regulatory Agendas indicate the status of all pending and planned rulemaking actions by executive agencies, although the timelines they contain for agency action are notoriously optimistic.

A useful introduction to the regulatory process is provided by a publication of the Administrative Conference of the United States entitled A Guide to Federal Agency Rulemaking (2d ed. 1991). It surveys the rulemaking process and judicial review in comprehensive fashion, highlighting important legal and procedural issues.

B. ESTABLISHING REGULATORY STANDARDS

Agencies charged with implementing the environmental, health, and safety statutes of the 1970s soon discovered that it was an unenviable task. They found that the broad authority and sweeping aspirational commands contained in many of the statutes frequently were qualified by vague and sometimes contradictory directives. The complex judgments these required and the sheer volume of new responsibilities delegated to agencies placed unprecedented demands on their limited resources. Moreover, the prospect of high compliance costs virtually guaranteed fierce resistance from the regulated community to the implementation of the statutes.

Thus, it is not surprising that rulemaking proceedings often became complex, protracted battles that served as the opening acts for equally protracted litigation. As a result of these and other factors, the progress of EPA and OSHA in implementing statutory directives has disappointed many in the environmental, labor, and public health communities. In 1988 John Mendeloff summarized their complaints:

> After fifteen years, despite the urgings of the Natural Resources Defense Council, the EPA has issued final rules for only five toxic substances under section 112 of the Clean Air Act, which addresses hazardous air pollutants such as asbestos and benzene.
>
> After fifteen years, OSHA has established new workplace exposure limits for only ten health hazards. During the same period, the private standard setting organization, which OSHA was designed to supplant, has recommended lower exposure limits for hundreds of chemicals.
>
> Dissatisfaction with the slow pace of EPA's reregistration program for existing pesticides led Congress, in 1978, to try to streamline the process by calling for standards for six hundred active ingredients of each of the tens of thousands of pesticide products. Although the task was projected to take ten years to complete, by 1985 standards had been set for fewer than a dozen ingredients.
>
> Advocates claimed that the Toxic Substances Control Act (TSCA) of 1976 would provide a comprehensive framework for the regulation of toxic chemicals. By the end of 1984, controls had been placed on only four so-called old chemicals (those on the market before 1979). And although the EPA officials in charge of TSCA had identified forty-one additional chemicals for which additional testing would be required, no testing regulations had been adopted. [J. Mendeloff, The Dilemma of Toxic Substance Regulation 2 (1988).]

Figure 5.2 shows how long various steps in OSHA's rulemaking process have taken. As the chart indicates, years may elapse between the initiation of a rulemaking proceeding and the time a final regulation takes effect. Although OSHA rulemakings involve more formalized hearing procedures than EPA's, the time periods reflected in the chart probably are not substantially longer than for significant EPA rulemakings.

Why have administrative agencies taken so long to promulgate so

FIGURE 5.2
Time Elapsed for Components of OSHA Rulemaking

Standards	Hearing	Decisionmaking	Judicial review	Total
Asbestos	3 days	4 months	21 months	25 months
14 Carcinogens	3 days	11 months	10 months	21 months
Vinyl Chloride	6 days	85 months	2 months	7 months
Coke Ovens	75 days	63 months	16 months	79 months
Benzene	22 days	21 months	28 months	49 months
DBCP	2 days	6 months	none	6 months
Arsenic	12 days	51 months	34 months	85 months
Lead	49 days	69 months	20 months	89 months
Cotton Fiber Dust	7 days	44 months	35 months	79 months
Acrylonitrile	11 days	18 months	none	18 months
Noise	24 days	100 months	46 months	146 months

Source: Shapiro and McGarity, Reorienting OSHA: Regulatory Alternatives and Legislative Reform, 6 Yale J. on Reg. 1, 6-7 (1989).

few regulations? Agencies face several constraints on their ability to complete complex rulemakings efficiently and expeditiously. These include budgets that rarely provide sufficient resources to conduct more than a handful of major rulemakings in any given year, frequent turnover of technical staff, and the difficulty of obtaining critical information that typically is more readily available to the regulated community than to the regulators. Shapiro and McGarity describe some of the constraints currently facing regulatory agencies in the following terms:

Because agencies have a relatively small number of scientists, engineers, and economists to undertake rigorous scientific and policy analysis, only a few chemicals or products can be considered for regulation at any one time. The growth in government spending on regulatory activities slowed considerably in the first five years of the Reagan Administration, and overall staffing by regulatory agencies fell by eleven percent in the same period. Under these parsimonious conditions, government has had difficulty attracting and retaining qualified staff. Agencies' attempts to compensate by creating advisory committees and hiring consultants to carry out their regulatory missions have created problems of accountability and coordination. Finally, upper-level management at regulatory agencies turns over at a surprisingly high rate. [Shapiro and McGarity, Reorienting OSHA: Regulatory Alternatives and Legislative Reform, 6 Yale J. on Reg. 1, 6-7 (1989).]

As a result of these and other constraints, "[n]o health and safety agency has been able to promulgate regulations for more than three controversial chemicals in any given year." Id. at 3.

When agencies administer licensing provisions in statutes such as the Food, Drug, and Cosmetic Act (for new drugs) or FIFRA (for pesticides) the burden is on prospective applicants to demonstrate the safety of their products. But in setting regulatory standards, agencies bear the burden of justifying the standards. In the face of severely limited resources, these agencies often need complicated economic and technical analyses to support their standards. This increases their dependence on the regulated community (and on outside contractors) for information. Yet the regulated community often has considerable incentive to resist providing information to regulators to delay standard-setting in order to postpone its attendant compliance costs.

A rare empirical study of the regulatory process examined EPA's development of effluent standards specifying "best practicable technology" (BPT) for controlling discharges of water pollutants under the Clean Water Act. The study noted that EPA has an advantage over OSHA and the Consumer Product Safety Commission (CPSC) because both the Clean Water Act (§308) and the Clean Air Act (§114) give EPA authority to require regulated companies to submit data, authority that OSHA and the CPSC lack. However, the study found that each of the three agencies had to rely heavily on outside consultants to gather virtually all of their technical and economic information and to develop initial recommendations concerning what the regulations should be. W. Magat, A. Krupnick, and W. Harrington, Rules in the Making 23 (1986). Nearly all the information obtained by EPA during the rulemaking came from the regulated community. Virtually all comments EPA received were complaints from industry that the proposed regulations were too stringent. Labor unions and consumer groups were found to be somewhat more active in the OSHA and CPSC proceedings.

There are good reasons to expect the regulated community to participate in the rulemaking process more actively than public interest groups. As James Q. Wilson notes in The Politics of Regulation (1980), environmental and other public interest regulations impose concentrated costs on industry in return for widely dispersed benefits to the public. Summarizing the extensive literature on regulatory failures, Cass Sunstein notes that because environmental statutes "involve diffuse and numerous beneficiaries and well-organized regulated classes," they are particularly prone to inadequate implementation and enforcement. C. R. Sunstein, After the Rights Revolution 102 (1990). While the growth of powerful environmental groups has helped counteract this tendency, the concentrated costs of complying with regulation ensure that the regulated community will participate more extensively in the regulatory process than environmental groups, who are likely to focus only on regulations that have national impact. Congress has responded to this problem by writing increasingly detailed statutes in an effort to prevent

EPA policy-making from being captured by the regulated community or the Agency's own bureaucracy. See, e.g., Lazarus, The Tragedy of Distrust in the Implementation of Federal Environmental Law, 54 Law & Contemp. Probs. 311, 316-317 (Autumn 1991).

Figure 5.3 outlines the process used by EPA in setting the BPT effluent standards for industrial facilities. As the chart indicates, EPA's contractors had to perform detailed economic analyses of the impact of various levels of pollution control on dozens of industries. This required EPA and its contractors to define industry subcategories based on examination of their production processes, to characterize their wastewater and treatment technology options, and to analyze their costs, energy use, and nonwater quality impacts. Even though EPA had the legal authority under section 308 of the Clean Water Act to inspect industrial facilities, time constraints often made such forced data collection efforts unworkable. As Magat et al. note:

> Even when industry did provide EPA with all the data it requested, often the real problem was understanding what the data meant. Industry was capable of manipulating the rulemaking process by withholding data on costly, but effective, abatement technologies and by supplying excessive and confusing data. [W. Magat, A. Krupnick, and W. Harrington, Rules in the Making 36 (1986).]

What factors influence agency decisions? Magat et al. tried to gather data to answer this question by comparing the stringency of the BPT effluent standards EPA had proposed with the stringency of the standards EPA ultimately adopted for each industry. The study found no relationship between the stringency of EPA's effluent standards and the degree of active participation by firms in the rulemaking process (as measured by the frequency of filing written comments). However, the study did find that trade association budgets, estimated industry compliance costs, and the quality of the information available to EPA were significantly related to the stringency of the standards—the less stringent the standards, the higher the trade association budgets, the greater the projected compliance costs, and the poorer the quality of the information available to EPA. The influence of trade association budgets appeared greatest at the contracting stage of the rulemaking, suggesting that EPA's contractors may have proposed less stringent standards for industries known to be well-represented in the rulemaking.

C. PROPOSALS FOR RULEMAKING REFORM

The slow pace and contentious nature of the rulemaking process have stimulated many suggestions for reform. As Congress continues to expand the regulatory responsibilities of agencies, the need for agencies

682

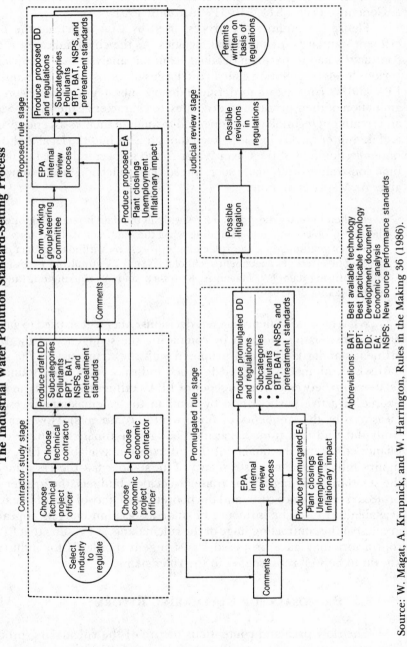

FIGURE 5.3

The Industrial Water Pollution Standard-Setting Process

Abbreviations: BAT: Best available technology
               BPT: Best practicable technology
               DD: Development document
               EA: Economic analysis
               NSPS: New source performance standards

Source: W. Magat, A. Krupnick, and W. Harrington, Rules in the Making 36 (1986).

to develop more efficient rulemaking procedures is growing more urgent. With the enactment of the Clean Air Act Amendments of 1990, EPA is now required to issue far more regulations much faster than ever before. The Amendments require EPA to issue 50 major and 30 minor regulations on air pollution alone during the first 2 years—this for an agency that has averaged only about 7 or 8 major regulations per year. Lavelle, Talking About Air, 1991 Natl. L.J. 1, 30 (June 10, 1991). EPA failed to meet many of the Amendments' first-year deadlines for issuing major rules and guidelines. See Subcomm. on Health & the Environment, U.S. House Energy and Commerce Comm., Inauspicious Beginnings: A Review of the First Year of Implementation of the Clean Air Act of 1990 (1991). It missed 19 of the deadlines that expired in the first 14 months, Subcomm. on Health & the Environment, House Comm. on Energy & Commerce, Clean Air Left in the Lurch 2 (1992), despite early recognition that some fundamental changes had to be made in the Agency's rulemaking procedures. Bush Signs Clean Air Act Amendments, Predicts Benefits for All U.S. Citizens, 21 Env. Rep. 1387 (1990).

i. Negotiated Rulemaking

Negotiated rulemaking has become increasingly popular in recent years. In 1982 the Administrative Conference of the United States recommended that federal agencies experiment with negotiated rulemaking procedures. Congress explicitly endorsed negotiated rulemaking in 1990 when it adopted the Negotiated Rulemaking Act, Pub. L. No. 101-648, 104 Stat. 4969, 5 U.S.C. §581. The Act confirms federal agencies' authority to conduct negotiated rulemaking, but does not require that it be employed.

In a negotiated rulemaking, the major private groups interested in a prospective rulemaking action attempt to resolve their differences through negotiations prior to issuance of a proposed rule. Pursuant to the Federal Advisory Committee Act, the participants in a negotiated rulemaking are appointed to a negotiating committee by the agency responsible for the rule. Negotiations among the interest groups then take place with the assistance of an agency-appointed mediator. Agency staff responsible for developing the proposed rule also may participate. If the negotiations are successful, the parties agree on the substance of a proposed rule, which is then issued by the agency for public comment. The agency then follows the standard notice-and-comment procedures of informal rulemaking and the parties to the negotiation participate in the rulemaking.

If successful, negotiated rulemaking should reduce the chances that conflicts among interest groups will result in legal challenges to the regulation ultimately adopted. Once a consensus rule has been proposed, the rulemaking should be able to proceed relatively quickly because contentious issues presumably will have been resolved during the pre-proposal negotiations.

Not all rules are good candidates for negotiated rulemaking. Indeed, the procedure probably works well only in certain narrowly defined circumstances. Philip Harter has identified certain criteria for a successful regulatory negotiation. These include the following:

(1) The parties should have power to affect the decision and an incentive to bargain.

(2) The number of parties should be small enough to permit bargaining.

(3) The issue must be ready for decision and a firm deadline for decision should be set.

(4) Negotiation must have the potential to benefit all parties.

(5) The issue should not center on a fundamental value conflict between parties.

(6) More than one issue should be involved to allow trade-offs across issues.

(7) The agency should commit to propose the product of the negotiations.

Harter, Negotiating Regulations: A Cure for Malaise, 71 Geo. L.J. 1 (1982).

The Negotiated Rulemaking Act of 1990 endorses some of these criteria, as reflected in the factors that it requires agencies to consider before embarking on a negotiated rulemaking. The Act specifies that agencies should consider whether there are a limited number of significantly affected interests that can be adequately represented in a negotiation and whether there is a reasonable likelihood of reaching consensus within a fixed period of time. The Act essentially codifies what had been existing agency procedures for conducting negotiated rulemakings.

Regulatory negotiation is becoming an accepted alternative for developing proposed rules, although it is doubtful that it can be used successfully in the most controversial rulemakings, which rarely will meet the criteria outlined above. Only regulations that involve a small number of issues, that affect a limited number of interests, and that have firm deadlines requiring that some action be taken are likely to be successful candidates for regulatory negotiation. While the regulations mandated by the tight deadlines in the Clean Air Act Amendments satisfy the latter condition, many will affect so many diverse interests as to make regulatory negotiation infeasible. For such regulations, like those governing the new permits to be issued under the Clean Air Act, EPA has convened informal roundtables to gain early input from affected interests rather than employing the full negotiated rulemaking procedures. For other regulations, like the new controls on emissions of nitrogen oxide that primarily affect power plants, EPA is using negotiated rulemaking. La-velle, Talking About Air, 1991 Natl. L.J. 1 (June 10, 1991). In August 1991 regulatory negotiations produced an agreement among oil com-panies, environmentalists, and state officials on proposed rules for re-formulated gasoline required by the Clean Air Act Amendments.

EPA's Regulatory Negotiation Pilot Project has chalked up some successes in similar circumstances in the past, including negotiations involving nonconformance penalties for heavy duty trucks and emissions limits for wood stoves. OSHA's initial attempt at regulatory negotiation, negotiation of a permissible exposure limit for benzene, did not result in consensus. Nor did EPA's negotiations over a standard for protecting farm workers from exposure to pesticides.

Even when complete consensus is not reached, the negotiations may assist the agency in developing an acceptable standard. EPA's ne-gotiated rulemaking to develop regulations requiring the inspection and abatement of asbestos hazards in schools pursuant to the Asbestos Haz-ard Emergency Response Act did not reach complete consensus. How-ever, the negotiations were instrumental in developing regulations that withstood a court challenge from one of the principal parties to the negotiations. In Safe Buildings Alliance v. Environmental Protection Agency, 846 F.2d 79 (D.C. Cir. 1988), EPA's regulations were upheld by the D.C. Circuit without discussion of the fact that the petitioners had participated in the development of the proposed regulations. The Negotiated Rulemaking Act now specifies that rules that are the product of negotiated rulemaking "shall not be accorded any greater deference by a court than a rule which is the product of other rulemaking pro-cedures." 5 U.S.C. §590.

It is not clear whether expanded use of negotiated rulemaking procedures would accelerate the pace of the rulemaking process. Ne-gotiations may take considerable time, in some cases more time than the agency would have spent in developing its own notice of proposed rule-making. The need to make a decision by a realistic deadline is often cited as a prerequisite for a successful negotiation. Thus, negotiated rulemaking is most useful in circumstances where agencies already are under some compulsion to act.

ii. Generic Approaches to Rulemaking

Agencies have tried several alternative approaches for speeding up the glacial progress of standard-setting. One approach has been to per-mit agencies to adopt interim standards based on substantially reduced information thresholds while the agency gathers the necessary data to determine at what levels final standards should be set. When OSHA was created, Congress realized that the Agency faced a mammoth task in promulgating regulations to protect workers from exposure to a plethora of workplace hazards. To ensure that workers rapidly were provided with at least a modicum of protection, Congress directed OSHA to adopt as interim standards, without conducting rulemaking under the Administrative Procedure Act, national consensus standards already established by a national standard-setting organization or any health or safety standards already adopted by other federal agencies. 5 U.S.C. §655(a). In 1971 OSHA adopted exposure limits for approximately 400 chemicals based largely on the Threshold Limit Values (TLVs) adopted by the American Conference of Governmental Industrial Hygienists (ACGIH) in 1968.

While this approach allowed OSHA to promulgate relatively comprehensive regulations rapidly, it did not address the problem the Agency would face in enforcing such standards. Moreover, "interim" standards have a way of acquiring a life of their own. Although Congress contemplated that OSHA would revise the interim standards to provide more protection to workers through normal rulemaking proceedings, OSHA did not revise the standards to keep them up to date with changes in the ACGIH TLVs until 1989, long after the TLVs had been lowered for hundreds of the chemicals. When it finally got around to updating the standards, OSHA employed a generic rulemaking approach that considered health, risk, and feasibility evidence for 428 substances in one massive rulemaking. On June 7, 1988, OSHA proposed to amend the permissible exposure limits (PELs) covering air contaminants and to add new PELs to address substances not previously regulated. OSHA adopted a final regulation in January 1989. The 650-page final rule occupied an entire volume of the Federal Register. It strengthened 212 permissible exposure limits (PELs) while setting new PELs for 164 substances that had not been regulated by OSHA. 54 Fed. Reg. 2,332 (1989). OSHA officials have expressed a desire to revise and update these standards on a regular basis, while using substance-specific proceedings only where additional protection is required. For a discussion of the advantages and disadvantages of alternatives to OSHA's current standard-setting procedures, see GAO, Options for Improving Safety and Health in the Workplace 24-28 (1990).

While the approach of borrowing standards established by another body offers the prospect of economies in rulemaking, it may come at the expense of public health protection. OSHA's reliance on the TLVs adopted by the ACGIH has come under fire from public health professionals. The TLVs are purported to represent "airborne concentrations of substances . . . under which it is believed that nearly all workers may be repeatedly exposed day after day without adverse effect." However, a comprehensive study of the data supporting the TLVs found that they were set at levels that were poorly correlated with actual threshold levels for reported health effects in workers. Roach and Rappaport found that the levels of the TLVs were closely correlated with the actual exposures typically reported by industry. They concluded that the levels of the TLVs were not based purely on health considerations; rather, they "appear to reflect the levels of exposure which were perceived at the time to be achievable in industry." Roach and Rappaport, But They Are Not Thresholds: A Critical Analysis of the Documentation of Threshold Limit Values, 17 Am. J. Industrial Medicine 727 (1990).

Another approach has been to set standards on a generic basis for groups of similar regulatory targets. In 1974 OSHA embarked on a Standards Completion Project designed to promulgate groups of standards for 400 chemicals over a period of two years. But the Agency eventually shelved the project, in part because of the realization that the task was too immense given the amount of evidence that would have to be marshalled to justify the standards.

In 1977 OSHA embarked on a rulemaking to establish a generic policy for regulating carcinogens in an effort to speed up the rulemaking process. The idea behind the cancer policy proposal was to resolve on a generic basis many of the controversies surrounding the identification and assessment of carcinogens and to create rebuttable presumptions that would make it more difficult for parties to challenge OSHA's basic methodology during rulemakings focusing on individual substances. The generic rulemaking itself consumed enormous resources, and the policy finally issued in 1980 was promptly reconsidered when the Reagan Administration took office. Although efforts to repeal the policy have been unsuccessful, the product, which is similar to EPA's generic risk assessment guidelines, has not produced dramatic economies in rulemaking procedures.

Regulations are not the only means available for inducing changes in industrial health and safety practices. General duty clauses written into statutes can establish a standard of conduct that can be enforced even in the absence of implementing regulations. For example, section 5 of the OSH Act provides that each employer has a general duty to furnish to workers a workplace "free from recognized hazards that are causing or are likely to cause death or serious physical harm," 29 U.S.C. §654. The Clean Air Act Amendments of 1990 have added new section 112(r), which imposes a general duty on stationary sources to prevent accidental releases of hazardous substances. This presumably will permit EPA to take enforcement action when accidental releases occur without having to promulgate new regulations. See Mounteer, The "General Duty" Under the Clean Air Act to Prevent Accidental Releases of Extremely Hazardous Substances, 22 Env. Rep. 141 (1991).

Another explanation for the slow pace of the regulatory process is offered by those who argue that it is a product of unreasonably stringent statutory requirements. John Mendeloff has popularized this explanation by coining the catchy phrase "overregulation causes underregulation." According to his thesis, because EPA and OSHA must set regulatory standards too strictly, the agencies are reluctant to regulate more than a handful of the hundreds of toxic substances that deserve to be regulated. The example most frequently offered to support this is EPA's experience in implementing section 112 of the Clean Air Act, which requires that hazardous air pollutants be regulated to provide an "ample margin of safety." Concern over the potential impact of implementing this provision strictly may explain why between 1970 and 1984 EPA regulated only five pollutants under section 112, all of them as a result of a court order or the threat of a court order. See J. Mendeloff, The Dilemma of Toxic Substance Regulation 134-137 (1988). While this thesis may capture much of the explanation for the failure of section 112, it does not necessarily follow that less stringent statutory standards will result in any more comprehensive regulation. EPA has regulated only a handful of toxic substances under the Toxic Substance Control Act's seemingly more reasonable "unreasonable risk" standard, and it has done so largely as a result of congressional pressure, including an amendment mandating a ban on PCBs.

Thus, while a substantial relaxation of regulatory standards might encourage somewhat more extensive regulation, it would not reduce the opportunities for delay inherent in the rulemaking process. Moreover, it is doubtful that such a proposal would be politically feasible except perhaps as the product of unprecedented industry-wide bargaining among major interest groups, which itself would be subject to the same constraints that apply to regulatory negotiation.

2. Presidential Oversight of Rulemaking

When decisions are being made about environmental regulations that affect important constituencies, few government officials are purely disinterested observers of the rulemaking process. No official has more clout with executive agencies than the president, who appoints agency officials who serve at the president's pleasure. In the exercise of this "clout" over executive agencies, the president is supposed to be guided by a constitutional duty to "take Care that the Laws be faithfully executed." U.S. Const., art. II, §3.

Presidents have long sought to assert greater control over regulatory decisions. These efforts accelerated with the growth of regulatory legislation in the early 1970s. When he created EPA by executive order in 1970 President Nixon cited the importance of having a single-mission agency that would be independent of political pressures. But when the new agency's actions alarmed business leaders, he acted quickly to assert oversight authority. In June 1971 President Nixon established a program of "Quality of Life" review that required EPA to submit significant rulemaking proposals to the Office of Management and Budget (OMB) before publishing them in the Federal Register. OMB distributed the proposals to other federal agencies for comment and attempted to resolve disagreements between agencies. With the assistance of the National Industrial Pollution Control Council, a group of 63 corporate executives appointed to provide input on environmental regulations, the Secretary of Commerce and OMB battled EPA to scale back its plans for regulation. As early as 1972, environmentalists were complaining bitterly to Congress that OMB "is reviewing in secrecy every major action of the Environmental Protection Agency," that other federal "agencies, acting as spokesmen for industrial interests, have effective power to veto EPA's actions," and that these forces were "gelding implementation of the new Clean Air Act." Implementation of the Clean Air Act Amendments of 1970, Hearings Before the Subcomm. on Air and Water Pollution of the Senate Comm. on Public Works, 92d Cong., 2d Sess. at 4 (1972) (testimony of Richard Ayres of the Natural Resources Defense Council). Despite vigorous pressure from the White House in several regulatory disputes, EPA's first two administrators, William Ruckelshaus and Russell Train, were able to retain considerable independence because of the political popularity of environmental causes and the Watergate scandal, which ultimately resulted in President Nixon's resignation.

President Ford continued the QOL review program and established a Council on Wage and Price Stability to review the inflationary impact of regulatory proposals. EPA officials continued to complain that the process was being used to pressure EPA to weaken regulations, but the pressure also stimulated EPA to improve its own analytical capabilities and to create an internal clearance process for regulations. QOL review was abandoned by the Carter Administration in favor of a more selective process, the Regulatory Analysis Review Group (RARG), that reviewed a few of the most significant rulemaking proposals during the public comment period. Efforts by RARG's mission-oriented economists to apply cost-benefit analysis to regulatory proposals produced some highly publicized attempts at presidential intervention in rulemaking involving OSHA's cotton dust standard, EPA's relaxation of the national ambient air quality standard for ozone, and promulgation of a new source performance standard for coal-fired power plants. After protests from Congress, President Carter pledged not to compromise environmental standards for economic gain in the future.

A. REGULATORY REVIEW UNDER EXECUTIVE ORDER 12,291

i. The Regulatory Review Process

The Reagan Administration revolutionized regulatory review by establishing a program of unprecedented scope inspired by a deep ideological hostility toward regulation. Having "declare[d] war on government overregulation" in its 1980 campaign platform, the administration appointed a Task Force on Regulatory Relief chaired by Vice President George Bush. Determined to make good on promises of regulatory "relief," the Task Force sent a letter to hundreds of businesses and trade associations inviting them to nominate regulations that should be relaxed or eliminated. From the responses to this invitation the Task Force eventually created a "hit list" of 119 regulations, including many prominent environmental standards, which it directed agencies to reconsider. Asserting that federal environmental regulations would cost the country more than $500 billion over the next decade, the Task Force pledged to provide relief from unnecessarily burdensome regulations.

On February 17, 1981, President Reagan issued Executive Order 12,291, 3 C.F.R. 127 (1981), which established the basic structure of the regulatory review program that remains in effect today. The Order centralized unprecedented regulatory review power in the Office of Management and Budget and placed a temporary freeze on new regulations. EO 12,291 directed agencies, before proposing significant regulations, to perform detailed cost-benefit analyses and not to regulate unless benefits outweighed costs. To enforce these directives agencies were required to submit all proposed and final rules to OMB for review prior to publication. Agencies were directed not to publish proposed or final rules until OMB had completed its review. Portions of EO 12,291 are reproduced below.

|| *Executive Order No. 12,291* ||
|| **3 C.F.R. 127 (1981)** ||

By the authority vested in me as President by the Constitution and laws of the United States of America, and in order to reduce the burdens of existing and future regulations, increase agency accountability for regulatory actions, provide for presidential oversight of the regulatory process, minimize duplication and conflict of regulations, and insure well-reasoned regulations, it is hereby ordered as follows: . . .

Sec. 2 General Requirements. In promulgating new regulation, reviewing existing regulation, and developing legislative proposals concerning regulation, all agencies, to the extent permitted by law, shall adhere to the following requirements:

(a) Administrative decisions shall be based on adequate information concerning the need for and consequences of proposed government action;

(b) Regulatory action shall not be undertaken unless the potential benefits to society for the regulation outweigh the potential costs to society;

(c) Regulatory objectives shall be chosen to maximize the net benefits to society;

(d) Among alternative approaches to any given regulatory objective, the alternative involving the least net cost to society shall be chosen; and

(e) Agencies shall set regulatory priorities with the aim of maximizing the aggregate net benefits to society, taking into account the condition of the particular industries affected by the regulations, the condition of the national economy, and other regulatory actions contemplated for the future.

Sec. 3 *Regulatory Impact Analysis and Review*

(a) In order to implement Section 2 of this Order, each agency shall, in connection with every major rule [defined as a rule with an annual effect on the economy of $100 million or more], prepare, and to the extent permitted by law consider, a Regulatory Impact Analysis. . . .

(c) Except as provided in Section 8 of this Order, agencies shall prepare Regulatory Impact Analyses of major rules and transmit them, along with all notices of proposed rulemaking and all final rules, to the Director as follows:

(1) If no notice of proposed rulemaking is to be published for a proposed major rule that is not an emergency rule, the agency shall prepare only a final Regulatory Impact Analysis, which shall be transmitted, along with the proposed rule, to the Director at least 60 days prior to the publication of the major rule as a final rule;

(2) With respect to all other major rules, the agency shall prepare a preliminary Regulatory Impact Analysis which shall be transmitted, along with a notice of proposed rulemaking, to the Director at least 60 days prior to the publication of a notice of proposed rulemaking, and a final Regulatory Impact Analysis, which shall be transmitted along with the final rule at least 30 days prior to the publication of the major rule as a final rule;

(3) For all rules other than major rules, agencies shall submit to the Director, at least 10 days prior to publication, every notice of proposed rulemaking and final rule.

(d) To permit each proposed major rule to be analyzed in light of the requirements stated in Section 2 of this Order, each preliminary and final Regulatory Impact Analysis shall contain the following information:

(1) A description of the potential benefits of the rule, including any beneficial effects that cannot be quantified in monetary terms, and the identification of those likely to receive the benefits;

(2) A description of the potential costs of the rule, including

any adverse effects that cannot be quantified in monetary terms, and the identification of those likely to bear the costs;

(3) A determination of the potential net benefits of the rule, including an evaluation of effects that cannot be quantified in monetary terms;

(4) A description of alternative approaches that could substantially achieve the same regulatory goal at lower cost, together with an analysis of this potential benefit and costs and a brief explanation of the legal reasons why such alternatives, if proposed, could not be adopted; and

(5) Unless covered by the description required under paragraph (4) of this subsection, an explanation of any legal reasons why the rule cannot be based on the requirements set forth in Section 2 of this Order.

(e)(1) The Director, subject to the direction of the Task Force, which shall resolve any issues raised under this Order or ensure that they are presented to the President, is authorized to review any preliminary or final Regulatory Impact Analysis, notice of proposed rulemaking, or final rule based on the requirements of this Order.

(2) The Director shall be deemed to have concluded review unless the Director advises an agency to the contrary under subsection (f) of this Section:

(A) Within 60 days of a submission under subsection (c)(1) or a submission of a preliminary Regulatory Impact Analysis or notice of proposed rulemaking under subsection (c)(2);

(B) Within 30 days of the submission of a final Regulatory Impact Analysis and a final rule under subsection (c)(2); and

(C) Within 10 days of the submission of a notice of proposed rulemaking or final rule under subsection (c)(3).

(f)(1) Upon the request of the Director, an agency shall consult with the Director concerning the review of a preliminary Regulatory Impact Analysis or notice of proposed rulemaking under this Order, and shall, subject to Section 8(a)(2) of this Order, refrain from publishing its preliminary Regulatory Impact Analysis or notice of proposed rulemaking until such review is concluded.

(2) Upon receiving notice that the Director intends to submit views with respect to any final Regulatory Impact Analysis or final rule, the agency shall, subject to Section 8(a)(2) of this Order, refrain from publishing its final Regulatory Impact Analysis or final rule until the agency has responded to the Director's views, and incorporated those views and the agency's response in the rulemaking file.

(3) Nothing in this subsection shall be construed as displacing the agencies' responsibilities delegated by law. . . .

Sec. 8. Exemptions

(a) The procedures prescribed by this Order shall not apply to:

(1) Any regulation that responds to an emergency situation, *provided that,* any such regulation shall be reported to the Director as soon as it is practicable, the agency shall publish in the Federal Register a statement of the reasons why it is impracticable for the agency to follow the procedures of this Order with respect to such a rule, and the agency shall prepare and transmit as soon as is practicable a Regulatory Impact Analysis of any such major rule; and

(2) Any regulation for which consideration or reconsideration under the terms of this Order would conflict with deadlines imposed by statute or by judicial order, *provided that,* any such regulation shall be reported to the Director together with a brief explanation of the conflict, the agency shall publish in the Federal Register a statement of the reasons why it is impracticable for the agency to follow the procedures of this Order with respect to such a rule, and the agency, in consultation with the Director, shall adhere to the requirements of this Order to the extent permitted by statutory or judicial deadlines.

NOTES AND QUESTIONS

1. Consider the goals identified in section 2 of EO 12,291. Sections 2(b) and (c) provide that "[r]egulatory action shall not be undertaken unless the potential benefits to society for the regulation outweigh the potential costs to society" and that "[r]egulatory objectives shall be chosen to maximize the net benefits to society." Are these principles consistent with the standards for regulatory action specified in some of the statutes we have examined? Consider, for example, the workplace exposure standard for cotton dust under the Occupational Safety and Health Act as reviewed in American Textile Manufacturers Institute, Inc. v. Donovan, 452 U.S. 490 (1981), the Delaney Clause of the Food, Drug, and Cosmetic Act as interpreted in Public Citizen v. Young, 831 F.2d 1108 (D.C. Cir. 1987), or the effluent discharge standards of the Clean Water Act as interpreted in Weyerhaeuser Company v. Costle, 590 F.2d 1011 (D.C. Cir. 1978), all of which are discussed in Chapter 4. If they are not consistent, which standard should the agency employ?

2. Consider the review process and regulatory impact analysis requirements outlined in section 3. What must EPA do before publishing a proposed regulation? Suppose OMB disagrees with a regulation EPA wants to propose. OMB believes that the proposed regulation is far too costly. EPA believes that the regulation is necessary to protect human

health and that costs should not be considered in such circumstances. What can OMB do to change EPA's mind? What can EPA do if it is not convinced by OMB's arguments? What impact is OMB review likely to have on EPA's ability to complete rulemaking actions?

3. Throughout the Order, the words "to the extent permitted by law" qualify the Order's directives (§§2, 3(a), 6(a), 7(e)), and section 3(f)(3) provides that nothing in the Order "shall be construed as displacing the agencies' responsibilities delegated by law." What does this mean? Who should decide the extent to which compliance with the terms of the Order are "permitted by law," the agencies or OMB?

4. Suppose that EPA is required to promulgate a regulation by a statutory deadline that is approaching rapidly. What effect, if any, should that have on OMB review under the Order? See §8(a)(2).

5. Should OMB have the power to dictate the substance of agency decisions? Would it make a difference to your answer if the director of OMB were a passionate environmentalist dealing with an EPA administrator like Anne Gorsuch Burford?

6. In reviewing regulations under EO 12,291, OMB frequently was frustrated by the fact that its review took place only at the eleventh hour, when proposed or final rules were about to be published. To give OMB a chance to review regulations further in advance of publication, a second executive order, Executive Order 12,498, 3 C.F.R. 323 (1985), was promulgated on January 4, 1985. This Order requires agencies to submit to OMB annually a draft regulatory program describing significant regulatory actions planned for the upcoming year. OMB reviews agency submissions to determine whether or not to include them in an annual publication, The Regulatory Program of the U.S. Government. Agencies are directed to refrain from undertaking initiatives not approved by OMB as part of the Regulatory Program. Figure 5.4 outlines the major steps in the regulatory review process required by EO 12,291 and EO 12,498.

ii. The Impact of Regulatory Review

Two years after EO 12,291 was promulgated, the Task Force on Regulatory Relief announced that the new regulatory review procedures had been an unqualified success in reducing "the regulatory burden of Federal regulation on the American public" and "sharply curtailing . . . the proliferation of new Federal regulations." The Task Force claimed that it had prevented "unnecessary costs totaling $9 to $11 billion for one-time capital expenditures and $6 billion in recurring annual costs." OMB, Executive Order 12,291 on Federal Regulation: Progress During 1982 (April 1983), at 4. These claims of savings, however, did not consider any of the *benefits* of regulations that were relaxed or repealed. OMB officials had admitted that their previous savings estimates "were

FIGURE 5.4
The Regulatory Management Process

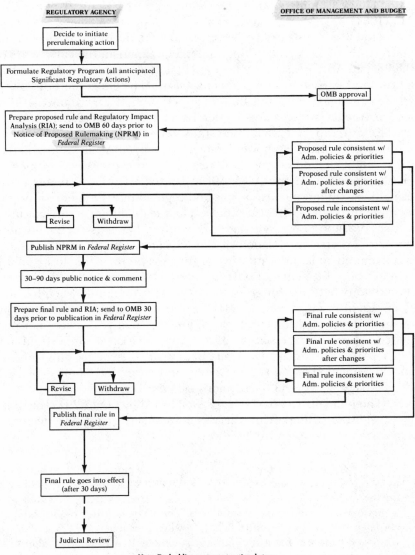

Note: Dashed lines represent optional steps

Source: National Academy of Public Administration, *Presidential Management of Rulemaking in Regulatory Agencies* 12 (1987).

mainly from industry sources" and that it was "conceivable" that the program may actually have saved nothing or had net costs. Role of OMB in Regulation: Hearings of the Oversight and Investigations Subcomm. of the House Comm. on Energy & Commerce, 97th Cong., 1st Sess. 114-115 (1981).

How has regulatory review affected EPA decision-making? A detailed study of EPA rulemaking under EO 12,291 in the early years of the Reagan Administration concluded that the Executive Order had had a profound impact on EPA decisions. Olson, The Quiet Shift of Power: Office of Management and Budget Supervision of Environmental Protection Agency Rulemaking Under Executive Order 12,291, 4 Va. J. Nat. Resources L. 1 (1984). The study found that OMB not only had exercised "de facto veto power" to block certain EPA rules, but also that it had employed other, more subtle, and "more pervasive" influences on EPA decisions. As one OMB official boasted: "The Government works using three things: money, people and regulations; the agency must get all three through OMB." Id. at 6. Despite the qualifiers in the Executive Order, the study observed that "OMB often bases its review on nonstatutory criteria, in violation of the Executive Order, and sometimes serves merely to launder industry arguments on their way to EPA." Id. at 40. Former EPA chief of staff John Daniel confirmed this observation in testimony before a congressional oversight committee when he cited examples of instances when OMB "kept urging upon us considerations of the costs through certain types of analyses that really were not permitted . . . under the statute." EPA: Investigation of Superfund and Agency Abuses (Part 3): Hearings Before the Subcomm. on Oversight and Investigation of the House Comm. on Energy and Commerce, 98th Cong., 1st Sess. 81 (1983) (testimony of John Daniel).

The regulatory review process established by EO 12,291 clearly has had a substantial impact on the way EPA makes regulatory decisions. The Olson study noted the following:

> First, a more rigorous internal review has developed. EPA has beefed up its economic analyses; in fact, by May 1983 EPA had spent $2.45 million on the still-uncompleted Regulatory Impact Analysis (RIA) for RCRA owner/operator land disposal standards. The Reagan Order requires that considerable analysis be undertaken; however, in general, EPA staff interviewed believed that a full-blown cost-benefit RIA is of little value to EPA decisionmakers and is essentially a waste of EPA's scarce resources.
>
> EPA's more rigorous internal review has increased significantly the time it takes to issue some rules. The drafting of the RIA's for two major rules, for example, has taken in excess of two years. In 1982, General Accounting Office (GAO) investigators found in general that "the knowledge that all regulations must be reviewed by OMB may indirectly cause delay" due to intensified internal review within the agency. A more recent GAO study concluded that while cost-benefit analyses may be time-

consuming, costly and flawed by significant data gaps, in some cases these analyses have aided EPA decisionmakers.

A more subtle and consequential internal EPA development induced by OMB review is a "guessing game" in which EPA attempts to draft rules it believes will clear OMB. As one EPA official put it, "we are practicing the art of the possible." The agency staff starts with reduced expectations, and drafts initially a proposal that will clear both the EPA hierarchy and OMB.

The Executive Order has effectively institutionalized OMB input, especially where OMB has a strong policy interest. Of course, most rules receive little OMB attention. It is, however, OMB's goal to induce in EPA staff the understanding that rules in certain form will never clear OMB, and therefore should not even be sent there for review. This goal seems to have been at least in part achieved. [Olson, The Quiet Shift of Power: Office of Management and Budget Supervision of Environmental Protection Agency Rulemaking Under Executive Order 12291, 4 Va. J. Nat. Resources L. 1, 49-50 (1984).]

Four principal objections have been raised to the way in which regulatory review has been conducted. First, it is argued that rather than simply performing an advisory and consultative role, OMB has used the regulatory review process to displace agency decision-making by dictating substantive changes in regulations, often in ways that are inconsistent with statutory standards. Second, it is argued that by requiring already overburdened agencies to perform complicated and costly economic analyses to justify their regulations during an extended review process, OMB review has reduced the capacity of agencies to regulate and has created further delays in already overdue regulatory action. Third, it is argued that because OMB cloaks its actions in secrecy, it undermines public confidence in the rulemaking process and facilitates OMB actions that effectively serve as a conduit for regulated industries. Fourth, it is argued that because OMB's desk officers have less technical expertise than the agencies whose regulations they review, OMB is less capable of making regulatory judgments than the agencies. OMB vigorously denies these charges.

What does seem evident is that regulatory review has been used exclusively to promote less stringent regulation rather than to increase the net benefits of regulation. OMB review focuses almost exclusively on reducing the *cost* of regulation rather than on increasing its *net benefits*. For example, the Executive Order requires that detailed cost-benefit analyses (which it called "regulatory impact analyses," or RIAs) be performed for major rules (rules having an "annual effect on the economy of $100 million or more"). However, OMB does not interpret this provision as requiring RIAs for actions repealing or relaxing regulations. Thus, when the Task Force on Regulatory Relief directed EPA to propose repealing limitations on the amount of lead in gasoline, EPA did not perform any cost-benefit analysis of this proposal. Two years after the effort to repeal the lead limits was thwarted, EPA performed a cost-benefit analysis that found that virtually eliminating lead additives from gasoline would produce billions of dollars' worth of net benefits to society. EPA, Costs and Benefits of Reducing Lead in Gasoline (Feb. 1985). See Figure 4.11 on page 533. As a result, EPA later slashed the maximum permissible level of lead in gasoline to one-eleventh of previous levels.

The controversy over OMB's regulatory review program highlights a larger and more fundamental question: Who ultimately should be responsible for making environmental policy decisions? The environmental laws direct the EPA administrator to make various regulatory decisions, but because the administrator serves at the pleasure of the president, should the president be able to dictate how these decisions are made? The Executive Orders attempt to avoid this issue by characterizing OMB's review as "advisory and consultative," but OMB's "advice" often is viewed as binding by EPA. Indeed, few examples can be found of an agency declining to accept OMB's "advice." In August 1983 OMB officials could not cite a single instance in which a rule disapproved by OMB had been promulgated by an agency. Id. at 44. Three years later OMB was able to cite only six such instances. In four of them the agency had acted under the compulsion of a judicial deadline. In the other two the agency had successfully appealed to the White House. See Percival, Checks Without Balance: Executive Office Oversight of the Environmental Protection Agency, 54 Law & Contemp. Probs. 127, 150-151 (Autumn 1991).

Another important issue is the impact of OMB review on the openness of the rulemaking process. If OMB is able to dictate in secret the substance of rulemaking decisions, OMB review may effectively supplant the APA model of open, participatory informal rulemaking proceedings. In response to a congressional initiative to deny appropriations to the OMB unit that conducts regulatory reviews, in 1986 OMB announced a new disclosure policy that authorized disclosure, after final regulations have been promulgated, of drafts of the regulatory proposals submitted to OMB for review.

The criticisms of OMB review are debated in Morrison, OMB Interference with Agency Rulemaking: The Wrong Way to Write a Regulation, 99 Harv. L. Rev. 1059 (1986), in which public interest lawyer Alan Morrison questions neither the *concept* of presidential supervision of rulemaking nor the need for ensuring better coordination and planning of regulatory policy, but sharply criticizes the way OMB has abused the regulatory review process; and DeMuth and Ginsburg, White House Review of Agency Rulemaking, 99 Harv. L. Rev. 1075 (1986), in which Christopher DeMuth and Douglas Ginsburg, two former OMB officials (one of whom is now a judge on the D.C. Circuit), argue that OMB should be able to pressure EPA into changing regulatory decisions be-

FIGURE 5.5

How Government Regulations Are Made

699

cause it is necessary to restrain EPA from "spending" too much of society's resources on pollution control. Recommendations for improving presidential oversight of rulemaking are contained in National Academy of Public Administration, Presidential Management of Rulemaking in Regulatory Agencies (1987).

Presidential efforts to control agency decision-making have not ended with Executive Orders 12,291 and 12,498. In October 1987 Executive Order 12,612, 3 C.F.R. 252 (1987), entitled "Federalism," was issued. This Order directs federal regulatory agencies, to the maximum extent possible, to refrain from establishing uniform national standards, to defer to the states to establish standards when possible, and to grant states the maximum administrative discretion possible. In May 1988 President Reagan issued Executive Order 12,630, 3 C.F.R. 554 (1988), which requires federal agencies to conduct a "takings" analysis before adopting regulations that may deprive private parties of the value of their property. EPA's general counsel protested that the Order was "hopelessly vague and dangerously overbroad" and that it conceivably could cover "all EPA regulatory actions, including thousands of local permit decisions as well as every other governmental regulatory activity." New White House "Takings" Order May Weaken EPA Rules, Chill Enforcement, Inside EPA, May 20, 1988, at 8. Proposed legislation to codify this Executive Order and to require environmental regulations to undergo "takings" review and clearance by the Justice Department narrowly failed in 1991 when an amendment to transportation legislation that had been adopted by the Senate was dropped during conference committee.

The Bush Administration has continued the Reagan Administration's regulatory review program. Its most significant contribution has been the creation of a Council on Competitiveness chaired by Vice President Dan Quayle, which is designed to serve as the successor to the Reagan Administration's Task Force on Regulatory Relief. The six permanent members of the Council on Competitiveness are the director of OMB, the secretaries of Commerce and the Treasury, the chair of the President's Council of Economic Advisers, the White House chief of staff, and the attorney general. The Council is responsible for coordinating regulatory policy and for hearing appeals of regulatory review disputes between OMB and the agencies under Executive Order 12,291.

In its first major regulatory decision, the Council on Competitiveness in December 1990 effectively vetoed EPA's proposal to adopt a new source performance standard banning incineration of lead acid batteries and requiring recycling of 25 percent of the waste stream sent to municipal incinerators. Congressional oversight hearings subsequently revealed that the Council has played a broad and active role in blocking and weakening EPA regulations, including regulations implementing the requirements of the amended Clean Air Act. For example, at the behest of the Competitiveness Council, EPA in May 1991 proposed permit regulations that would allow sources of air pollution to amend their permits to increase emissions without public notice or comment if a state failed to object within seven days. In August 1991 EPA's general counsel, just prior to leaving the Agency, wrote a memorandum stating that it is "highly unlikely that a reviewing court would uphold the [permit] regulation upon judicial review" if adopted in the form proposed. When EPA sought to delete this provision from the final rule, the Competetiveness Council blocked the regulation, causing EPA to miss the November 15, 1991 statutory deadline for promulgating the permit rule. Vice President Quayle, chair of the Council, reportedly stated that "the administration was sending a message to 'overzealous' regulators. 'You have met the enemy,' the vice president said. 'It's called the Competitiveness Council.' " Davis and Gutfeld, New EPA Rule on Air Pollution Blocked by Bush, Wall St. J., Jan. 31, 1992, at A3. Several states and environmental groups have brought a lawsuit seeking to force issuance of the permit rules. In the section that follows we consider what legal limits should govern regulatory review of EPA actions.

B.   Legal Bounds on Executive Oversight

An early decision that delighted the authors of EO 12,291 actually involved a challenge to President Carter's intervention in an EPA rulemaking. In Sierra Club v. Costle, 657 F.2d 298 (D.C. Cir. 1981), decided just after the Reagan Administration took office, the D.C. Circuit was faced with a challenge to EPA's promulgation of new source performance standards for coal-fired power plants. The court rejected a variety of challenges to the regulation from utilities and environmental groups. An important procedural question in the case centered around the environmentalists' claim that the standards had been weakened significantly at the eleventh hour due to the personal intervention of the president and the White House staff. As you read this excerpt you may wish to refer to section 307(d) of the Clean Air Act, which outlines certain procedures to be followed in rulemakings under the Act.

|| *Sierra Club v. Costle* ||
|| **657 F.2d 298 (D.C. Cir. 1981)** ||

Wald, Circuit Judge:

We have already held that a blanket prohibition against meetings during the post-comment period with individuals outside EPA is unwarranted, and this perforce applies to meetings with White House officials. We have not yet addressed, however, the issue whether such oral communications with White House staff, or the President himself, must be docketed on the rulemaking record, and we now turn to that issue. The facts, as noted earlier, present us with a single undocketed meeting held on April 30, 1979, at 10:00 A.M., attended by the President, White House staff, other high ranking members of the Executive Branch, as well as EPA officials, and which concerned the issues and options presented by the rulemaking.

We note initially that section 307 makes specific provision for including in the rulemaking docket "written comments" of other executive agencies along with accompanying documents on any proposed draft rules circulated in advance of the rulemaking proceeding. Drafts of the final rule submitted to an executive review process prior to promulgation, as well as all "written comments," "documents," and "written responses" resulting from such interagency review process, are also to be put in the docket prior to promulgation. This specific requirement does not mention informal meetings or conversations concerning the rule which are not part of the initial or final review processes, nor does it refer to oral comments of any sort. Yet it is hard to believe Congress was unaware that intra-executive meetings and oral comments would occur throughout the rulemaking process. We assume, therefore, that unless expressly forbidden by Congress, such intra-executive contacts may take place, both during and after the public comment period; the only real issue is whether they must be noted and summarized in the docket.

The court recognizes the basic need of the President and his White House staff to monitor the consistency of executive agency regulations with Administration policy. He and his White House advisers surely must be briefed fully and frequently about rules in the making, and their contributions to policymaking considered. The executive power under our Constitution, after all, is not shared—it rests exclusively with the President. The idea of a "plural executive," or a President with a council of state, was considered and rejected by the Constitutional Convention. Instead the Founders chose to risk the potential for tyranny inherent in placing power in one person, in order to gain the advantages of accountability fixed on a single source. To ensure the President's control and supervision over the Executive Branch, the Constitution—and its judicial gloss—vests him with the powers of appointment and removal, the power to demand written opinions from executive officers, and the right to invoke executive privilege to protect consultative privacy. In the particular case of EPA, Presidential authority is clear since it has never been considered an "independent agency" but always part of the Executive Branch.

The authority of the President to control and supervise executive policymaking is derived from the Constitution; the desirability of such control is demonstrable from the practical realities of administrative rulemaking. Regulations such as those involved here demand a careful weighing of cost, environmental, and energy considerations. They also have broad implications for national economic policy. Our form of government simply could not function effectively or rationally if key executive policymakers were isolated from each other and from the Chief Executive. Single mission agencies do not always have the answers to complex regulatory problems. An overworked administrator exposed on a 24-hour basis to a dedicated but zealous staff needs to know the arguments and ideas of policymakers in other agencies as well as in the White House.

We recognize, however, that there may be instances where the docketing of conversations between the President or his staff and other Executive Branch officers or rulemakers may be necessary to ensure due process. This may be true, for example, where such conversations directly concern the outcome of adjudications or quasi-adjudicatory proceedings; there is no inherent executive power to control the rights of individuals in such settings. Docketing may also be necessary in some circumstances where a statute like this one *specifically requires* that essential "information or data" upon which a rule is based be docketed. But in the absence of any further Congressional requirements, we hold that it was not unlawful in this case for EPA not to docket a face-to-face policy session involving the President and EPA officials during the post-comment period, since EPA makes no effort to base the rule on any "information or data" arising from that meeting. Where the President himself is directly involved in oral communications with Executive Branch officials, Article II considerations—combined with the strictures of *Vermont Yankee* [where the Supreme Court held that courts may not require agencies to employ additional rulemaking procedures not required by Congress]— require that courts tread with extraordinary caution in mandating disclosure beyond that already required by statute.

The purposes of full-record review which underlie the need for disclosing ex parte conversations in some settings do not require that courts know the details of every White House contact, including a Presidential one, in this informal rulemaking setting. After all, any rule issued here with or without White House assistance must have the requisite *factual support* in the rulemaking record, and under this particular statute the Administrator may not base the rule in whole or in part on any *"information or data"* which is not in the record, no matter what the source. The courts will monitor all this, but they need not be omniscient to perform their role effectively. Of course, it is always possible that undisclosed Presidential prodding may direct an outcome that *is* factually based on the record, but different from the outcome that would have obtained in the absence of Presidential involvement. In such a case, it would be true that the political process did affect the outcome in a way the courts could not police. But we do not believe that Congress intended that the courts convert informal rulemaking into a rarified technocratic process, unaffected by political considerations or the presence of Presidential power. In sum, we find that the existence of intra-Executive Branch meetings during the post-comment period, and the failure to docket one such meeting involving the President, violated neither the procedures mandated by the Clean Air Act nor due process.

NOTES AND QUESTIONS

1. Does Sierra Club v. Costle lay to rest any questions concerning the legality of regulatory review under the Executive Orders? Does it suggest that the president can lawfully dictate to an agency head the substance of a regulatory decision Congress has directed the agency to make?

2. In subsequent litigation, plaintiffs have argued that OMB unlawfully usurped decisionmaking authority delegated by Congress to executive agencies. In Public Citizen Health Research Group v. Tyson, 796 F.2d 1479 (D.C. Cir. 1986), Public Citizen charged that OMB had illegally forced OSHA to delete a short-term exposure limit (STEL) from regulations controlling occupational exposures to ethylene oxide (EtO). Faced with vigorous OMB opposition to a STEL and a court-ordered deadline for promulgating the EtO standard, OSHA had simply crossed out all reference to the STEL in the final regulation that was sent to the Federal Register for publication. The regulations were then published without any explanation of why the STEL had been deleted. The chairs of five congressional committees supported Public Citizen's claim that OMB had acted illegally by filing an amicus brief that broadly challenged the legality of OMB review under the Executive Orders. In response, the Justice Department defended the legality of OMB review, characterizing OMB's actions as "advisory and consultative" and arguing that the ultimate decision to delete the STEL was made by OSHA and not OMB. The D.C. Circuit struck down the decision to delete the STEL as unsupported by the administrative record. The court noted that "OMB's participation in the EtO rulemaking presents difficult constitutional questions concerning the executive's proper role in administrative proceedings and the appropriate scope of delegated power from Congress to certain executive agencies." However, the court found it unnecessary to reach this issue in light of its decision that deletion of the STEL was unsupported by the record.

3. The result in Public Citizen Health Research Group v. Tyson confirms that, regardless of who ultimately is responsible for an administrative decision, that decision must conform to applicable requirements of the underlying regulatory statute and the Administrative Procedure Act in order to withstand judicial review. If OMB directs agencies to make decisions arbitrarily or capriciously or to base them on factors inconsistent with the requirements of the underlying regulatory statute,

such decisions are likely to be reversed. Suppose, however, that the administrative record and the appropriate statutory criteria would support *either* a decision favored by the agency or a different decision favored by OMB. Does Sierra Club v. Costle suggest that a decision directed by the president might be upheld in these circumstances even if it differs from that which the agency would have reached independent of presidential input? Would this present the "difficult constitutional questions" to which the *Public Citizen* court referred?

4. In National Grain & Feed Association v. OSHA, 866 F.2d 717 (5th Cir. 1989), the Fifth Circuit rejected a challenge to an OSHA regulation premised in part on the notion that OMB had coerced OSHA into changing the standard. While noting that the union had provided the court with a "colorful tale of 'the behind-the-scenes evolution of the OSHA standard,' " the court found that the rulemaking record indicated that most of OMB's recommendations had been rejected prior to OSHA's publication of a proposed rule. Finding no merit in the claim that "off-the-record coercion of OSHA" had obstructed judicial review, the court stated that OSHA's "final rule must stand or fall on the basis of the record before the agency, not on the basis of some 'secret record' of OMB's." 866 F.2d 717, 729 n.22.

5. As noted above, the Competitiveness Council vetoed EPA's efforts to prohibit incineration of lead acid batteries and to require recycling of 25 percent of the waste sent to municipal incinerators shortly before EPA promulgated the incinerator NSPS. While the Clean Air Act does not specifically impose a recycling requirement, EPA believed that it had the legal authority to require it and vigorously fought for its inclusion until meeting with the Council on December 19, 1990. NRDC has sought judicial review of EPA's decision, New York v. Reilly, No. 91-1168 (D.C. Cir. filed April 10, 1991), arguing that the Council rejected the requirement on the basis of considerations not relevant under the statute. The only public record of the Council's actions is a press release it issued that cited "federalism concerns" as a ground for opposing the proposals. What would NRDC need to show in order to establish that rejection of the recycling requirement was illegal?

6. The veto of EPA's proposed recycling requirement by the Council on Competitiveness is described in Victor, Quayle's Quiet Coup, 1991 Natl. J. (July 6, 1991). The article notes that lobbyists representing municipal and county governments "called the White House, sent follow-up letters, and even met several times with White House aides" in their successful effort to quash the recycling requirement. Even though her organization ultimately prevailed, one of these lobbyists, Barbara Paley, associate legislative director at the National Association of Counties, expressed misgivings about the process:

> This is not the way you want to go, because you don't want to turn these things into political power battles devoid of the issue. . . .

> It's nice that we got in, but I guess that there may be times when we will be concerned about an organization like the Competitiveness Council, which nobody knows a whole lot about and nobody knows who does what to whom there. We don't think that you should have to go around the back door to groups that are not out there in the open and who do not function in a substantive area to achieve this kind of objective. [Id. at 1680.]

Does the behind-closed-doors process employed by the Council on Competitiveness raise any legal concerns under the Administrative Procedure Act? What procedures could the Council adopt to respond to such concerns?

7. Members of Congress upset over OMB's alleged abuses of its regulatory review powers under the Executive Orders have proposed to enact limits on OMB's authority. In 1986 Congress threatened to take away funds from OMB's Office of Information and Regulatory Affairs (OIRA), the OMB division that conducts regulatory reviews. This action inspired OMB to promulgate a new disclosure policy that makes available drafts of proposed regulations sent to OMB after final regulatory action has been taken. However, regulations that never clear OMB are not subject to disclosure, and the public cannot use the Freedom of Information Act (FOIA) to learn which regulations were sent to OMB and when. Wolfe v. Department of Health and Human Services, 839 F.2d 768 (D.C. Cir. 1988) (en banc) (holding that information concerning the status of regulations is exempt from disclosure under FOIA because it is deliberative rather than factual since it "will generally disclose the recommended outcome of the consultative process at each stage of the process, as well as the source of any decision not to regulate"). The Competitiveness Council has refused to be bound by OMB's disclosure policies, and it even has refused to disclose the identities of private persons or parties with whom it meets or the nature of the discussions. The Council argues that it is not required by law to disclose such information and that as an arm of the Executive Office its activities are protected by executive privilege. Do you agree? See United States v. Nixon, 418 U.S. 683 (1974).

8. Some other statutory limits on executive oversight may be inferred from the environmental statutes themselves. For example, the Executive Orders purport to recognize that OMB review cannot countermand statutory or judicial deadlines for agency action. However, because OMB routinely ignored such deadlines, conflict was virtually inevitable. Courts generally are reluctant to umpire disputes between the executive and legislative branches. But in cases of clear conflict between statutory directives and executive action (or inaction) the judiciary may enter the fray, although it usually treads lightly when it does so, as illustrated by the following case.

‖ *Environmental Defense Fund v. Thomas* ‖
‖ 627 F. Supp. 566 (D.D.C. 1986) ‖

FLANNERY, District Judge:

In November of 1984, Congress enacted the Hazardous and Solid Waste Amendments of 1984 ("1984 Amendments"), Pub. L. 98-616 (Nov. 8, 1984), which amended the Resource Conservation and Recovery Act ("RCRA"), 42 U.S.C. §6924. RCRA is a comprehensive statute designed to regulate the management of hazardous and solid wastes. One of the new amendments, Section 3004(w) of RCRA, 42 U.S.C. §6924(w), provides that "(n)ot later than March 1, 1985, the (Environmental Protection Agency or "EPA") Administrator shall promulgate final permitting standards under this section for underground tanks that cannot be entered for inspection."

This deadline was not met. . . .

OMB commenced its review of the proposed permitting standards on March 4, 1985. Since these were not "major rules" under the meaning of EO 12291, EPA anticipated that OMB would complete its review within 10 days. On March 15, 1985, EPA staff briefed OMB staff on the proposed regulations. OMB refused to clear the regulations and on March 25, 1985, notified EPA that it was extending its review of the proposed regulations. OMB apparently wanted EPA to gather additional information prior to promulgating the regulations even though it would delay the process. By April 10, 1985, EPA had still not received any formal comments from OMB.

By April 12, 1985, it was clear that OMB had serious differences with EPA over what regulations to propose. At a meeting of April 16, 1985 between OMB and EPA staff members, OMB sought significant changes in the proposed regulations in four areas. The idea, apparently, was to shift the goal of the regulations away from EPA's philosophy of containing all leaks of waste disposals to OMB's philosophy of preventing only leaks of waste that can be demonstrated by risk analysis to threaten harm to human health.

Internal disagreement within OMB further delayed OMB's consideration of the regulations. Some OMB staff members apparently felt that OMB should not be dictating substantive policy decisions to EPA while others felt the precedent being set an important one for OMB review of other RCRA regulations.

After this suit was filed on May 30, 1985, OMB continued to seek specific changes in EPA's proposed regulations as well as changes not previously discussed. After various negotiations regarding the substance of the regulations, OMB completed its review and cleared the proposed regulations on June 12, 1985. The EPA Administrator signed them June

14, 1985 and the proposed regulations were published in the Federal
Register on June 26, 1985, 50 Fed. Reg. 26444, after OMB approved
some last-minute stylistic changes made by EPA staff. . . .

OMB's Interference with the Promulgation Process

From the discussion above, it seems clear that OMB did contribute
to the delay in the promulgation of the regulations by insisting on certain
substantive changes. The released documents show that EPA was ready
to announce proposed regulations in the Federal Register as early as
March 31, 1985, but due to OMB it did not happen until three months
later.

A certain degree of deference must be given to the authority of
the President to control and supervise executive policymaking. Sierra
Club v. Costle, 657 F.2d 298, 405 (D.C. Cir. 1981) (regarding whether
oral communications between EPA and the White House must be docketed on the rulemaking record when EPA revises Clean Air Act provisions). Yet, the use of EO 12291 to create delays and to impose substantive
changes raises some constitutional concerns. Congress enacts environmental legislation after years of study and deliberation, and then delegates to the expert judgment of the EPA Administrator the authority to
issue regulations carrying out the aims of the law. Under EO 12291, if
used improperly, OMB could withhold approval until the acceptance of
certain content in the promulgation of any new EPA regulation, thereby
encroaching upon the independence and expertise of EPA. Further,
unsuccessful executive lobbying on Capitol Hill can still be pursued administratively by delaying the enactment of regulations beyond the date
of a statutory deadline.

This is incompatible with the will of Congress and cannot be sustained as a valid exercise of the President's Article II powers.

Such concerns were noted by Congress when EO 12291 was passed.
In order to ensure the legality of the operation of EO 12291, James C.
Miller III, now the director but then the administrator of OMB's Office
of Information and Regulatory Affairs ("OIRA"), appeared before a
congressional committee and stressed the importance of construing narrowly the authority granted to OMB. Mr. Miller testified:

> President Reagan's Executive order imposes on the agencies only "to the
> extent permitted by law" and only to the extent that its terms would not
> "conflict with deadlines imposed by statute or by judicial order." The
> limited application of [EO 12291] is a crucial point, one that insures [its]
> legality and the legality of actions pursuant to [it]. . . . If a statute or a
> court order establishes a date for a rulemaking action, the Executive Order
> 12291 cannot delay that action.

Testimony of James C. Miller III, in Role of OMB in Regulation: Hearing Before the Subcomm. on Oversight and Investigation of House Comm. on Energy & Commerce, 97th Cong., 1st Sess. 46 (1981).

The Justice Department has also emphasized that EO 12,291 must be construed narrowly to survive legal challenge.

> [I]t is clear that the President's exercise of supervisory powers must conform to legislation enacted by Congress. In issuing directives to govern the Executive Branch, the President may not, as a general proposition, require or permit agencies to transgress boundaries set by Congress.

U.S. Department of Justice, Office of Legal Counsel Opinion on EO 12291, February 13, 1981.

This court has previously found that in certain egregious situations, statutory delay caused by OMB review is in contravention to applicable law under Section 8(a)(2) of EO 12291 and therefore that no further OMB review could occur. NRDC v. Ruckelshaus, 13 ELR 20817, 10818 (D.D.C. 1984). In *Ruckelshaus*, however, by the time the court order issued, EPA was six years past the deadline set by Congress. In the case at bar, enjoining OMB from interacting at all with EPA simply because OMB *might* cause delay past the new judicial deadline is premature and an unwarranted intrusion into discretionary executive consultations.

There is, however, some credence in plaintiffs' fear that the regulations due June 30, 1986, may still be delayed by OMB. . . .

Through answers to interrogatories, plaintiffs show that EPA submitted 169 regulations to OMB which were subject to statutory or judicial deadlines, and on 86 occasions OMB extended its review beyond the time periods outlined in EO 12291. OMB's propensity to extend review has become so great that EPA keeps a running record of the number of its rulemaking actions under extended review by OMB and the resulting delays. The average delay per regulation is 91 days; total delays were more than 311 weeks. Apparently Section 8(a)(2) of EO 12291 is simply ignored.

Congress clearly is concerned with OMB's use of EO 12291 with regard to the deadlines set within the 1984 Amendments. The House Committee report that accompanied the 1984 Amendments states:

> The Committee is extremely concerned that EPA has not been able to comply with past statutory mandates and timetables, not just for RCRA, but for virtually all its programs. . . . The Administrator's ability to meet this deadline (for publishing a schedule for land disposal ban decisions), as with all other deadlines in this bill, shall not be impaired in any way whatsoever by Executive Order 12291.

Hazardous Waste Control and Enforcement Act of 1983, Report of House Comm. on Energy and Commerce, 98th Cong., 1st Sess., May

17, 1983, at 34. 35, 1984 U.S. Code Cong. & Admin. News 5576, 5593-94.

The Hazardous and Solid Waste Amendments of 1984 added at least 44 new deadlines to RCRA, 29 of which must be satisfied within the next 20 months.

This court declares that OMB has no authority to use its regulatory review under EO 12291 to delay promulgation of EPA regulations arising from the 1984 Amendments of the RCRA beyond the date of a statutory deadline. Thus, if a deadline already has expired, OMB has no authority to delay regulations subject to the deadline in order to review them under the executive order. If the deadline is about to expire, OMB may review the regulations only until the time at which OMB review will result in the deadline being missed. From its tracking system, EPA can determine when further delay due to OMB review will result in a deadline being missed.

While this may be an intrusion into the degree of flexibility the executive agencies have in taking their time about promulgating these regulations, this is simply a judicial recognition of law as passed by Congress and of the method for dealing with deadlines laid down by the President himself. Such a recognition is not new. See NRDC v. Gorsuch, 17 ERC 2013, 2016 (D.D.C. 1982). Indeed, OMB itself admits that it cannot prevent an agency from complying with statutory requirements. Yet declaratory relief is necessary to ensure compliance with the clearly expressed will of Congress. This is not an inappropriate interference with the interaction of executive agencies; all such interaction may continue absent a "conflict with deadlines imposed by statute or by judicial order." Sec. 8, EO 12291.

NOTES AND QUESTIONS

1. In the deadline litigation above, the court ultimately imposed on EPA the schedule it had proposed rather than the deadline proposed by the plaintiffs. EPA had asked the court to give it until June 30, 1986 to promulgate the regulations in final form, while plaintiffs sought a deadline of April 25, 1986. The court noted that "[p]romulgation of regulations 16 months after a Congressional deadline is highly irresponsible," but it concluded that "[n]ow that the damage is done," it should accept EPA's revised schedule as long as the Agency was proceeding in good faith.

2. The court found that it had jurisdiction over OMB and it declared that OMB had no authority to delay the promulgation of regulations beyond the date of statutory deadlines. What is the significance of such regulatory relief? Why do you suppose that the court declined to grant an injunction against OMB?

3. What impact do you think this decision will have on OMB review of EPA regulations in future cases in which EPA has missed a statutory deadline? Can EPA effectively circumvent OMB review by delaying action on controversial regulations until after a statutory deadline has passed?

4. The Supreme Court addressed the question of OMB's regulatory review authority for the first time in Dole v. United Steelworkers of America, 494 U.S. 26 (1990). The Paperwork Reduction Act, which requires federal agencies to obtain OMB approval for information collection requests, 44 U.S.C. §3507(a)(3), is the sole source of *statutory* authority for OMB review. The Court considered whether the Act gives OMB the authority to bar OSHA from expanding its hazard communication standard.

OSHA's hazard communication standard requires companies to provide information to workers about toxic chemicals used in the workplace. After having been withdrawn when the Reagan Administration took office, the standard was reissued by OSHA in 1983, with the support of businesses eager for federal preemption of more stringent state right-to-know laws. A union persuaded the Third Circuit that the standard was inadequate because it applied only to manufacturing companies, and the court held that the standard must be broadened to apply to all workers covered by the OSH Act. The court twice ordered OSHA to issue a new standard, but OMB directed OSHA not to do so because it disapproved of the standard. OMB argued that it had the authority to block the regulation because the Paperwork Reduction Act requires it to approve any "information collection requests" by a federal agency. "Collection of information" is defined by the Act as "the obtaining or soliciting of facts or opinions by an agency through the use of written report forms, application forms, schedules, questionnaires, reporting or recordkeeping requirements, or other similar methods. . . ." OMB argued that OSHA was "soliciting facts" when it required someone to communicate certain data to a third party. The Third Circuit ruled that "OMB cannot in the guise of reducing paperwork substitute its judgment for that of any agency having substantive rulemaking responsibility." Associated Builders and Contractors, Inc. v. Brock, 862 F.2d 63 (3d Cir. 1989). The Supreme Court affirmed the Third Circuit's decision in Dole v. United Steelworkers of America, 494 U.S. 26 (1990). The Court explained that a disclosure rule was not an information collection request because

[D]isclosure rules do not result in information being made available for agency personnel to use. The promulgation of a disclosure rule is a final agency action that represents a substantive regulatory choice. An agency charged with protecting employees from hazardous chemicals has a variety of regulatory weapons from which to choose: It can ban the chemical altogether; it can mandate specified safety measures, such as gloves or goggles; or it can require labels or other warnings alerting users to dangers and recommended precautions. An agency chooses to impose a warning requirement because it believes that such a requirement is the least intrusive measure that will sufficiently protect the public, not because the measure is a means of acquiring information useful in performing some other agency function. [Id. at 33-34.]

The Court noted that OMB's rationale for disapproving the rules was that "the mandated disclosures would be of little benefit to the employees OSHA sought to protect." But it concluded that "there is no indication in the Paperwork Reduction Act that OMB is authorized to determine the usefulness of agency-adopted warning requirements to those being warned" because "Congress focused exclusively on the utility of the information to the agency." Thus, it concluded that OMB had exceeded its authority.

5. The decision in Dole v. United Steelworkers turns on an interpretation of OMB's authority under the Paperwork Reduction Act, and not Executive Order 12,291. What relevance, if any, do you think the decision has for the legality of OMB's review of environmental regulations under EO 12,291? Can OMB block EPA regulations that impose disclosure requirements on industry?

6. The Paperwork Reduction Act does not purport to give OMB authority to review anything other than agency information collection requests. OMB has been eager to obtain legislative endorsement for regulatory review under EO 12,291. At one point the Agency had been willing to support the enactment of new disclosure requirements in return for legislation giving it statutory authority for regulatory review, but efforts to fashion a legislative compromise have broken down. Reauthorization of the Paperwork Reduction Act has been delayed indefinitely. The congressional committee handling the reauthorization process had reached an agreement with the White House that new time limits on OMB review would be incorporated into the statute, but the White House backed away from this agreement. Congress is threatening to impose additional restrictions on OMB as the tug-of-war for control of regulatory oversight continues.

7. In his 1992 State of the Union Message, President Bush announced a 90-day moratorium on the issuance of any proposed or final regulations by federal agencies. In a memorandum to agency heads the president explained that this action was being taken in order to permit agencies to "weed out unnecessary and burdensome regulations, which impose needless costs on consumers and substantially impede economic growth." The memorandum qualified the moratorium by instructing agency heads not to "postpone any regulation that is subject to a statutory

or judicial deadline that falls during the review period." Memorandum for Certain Department and Agency Heads, Reducing the Burden of Government Regulation 3 (Jan. 28, 1992). Does the president have the legal authority to stop agencies from issuing regulations? At the time the moratorium was issued, EPA already had missed 19 deadlines for the issuance of regulations required by the 1990 Clean Air Act Amendments. Does the moratorium apply to these regulations? Can it be applied to them without violating the legal principles articulated in EDF v. Thomas?

3. Congressional Oversight of Rulemaking

The president is not the only source of pressure exerted on agencies. Its lawmaking and appropriations powers give Congress formidable tools for influencing agency decision-making. Although the Supreme Court's decision in INS v. Chadha, 462 U.S. 919 (1983), removed the "legislative veto" from Congress's arsenal, Congress has not hesitated to exercise other oversight authority to influence agency action and to contest presidential efforts to exert greater control over regulatory decisions. As noted above, congressional dissatisfaction with EPA's performance has resulted in the enactment of increasingly specific statutory directives designed to serve as agency-forcing mechanisms. These provisions effectively dictate what agency priorities should be and establish timetables for agency action enforceable in court.

Congress has been far more than a disinterested observer of the regulatory process. Members of Congress often seek to influence agency decisions, and congressional pressure can have a significant impact on agency decision-making. A study of congressional oversight by the National Academy of Public Administration noted that congressional oversight can serve several purposes:

> First, oversight seeks to assure that the intent of Congress is followed. . . .
> Second, oversight can assure that programs are implemented efficiently and that administrative waste, fraud and abuse are exposed. . . .
> A third purpose of oversight is to collect information to be used in reauthorizing or amending the statutes under which agencies operate. . . .
> Fourth, oversight may also be designed to evaluate the effectiveness of an agency's pursuit of a particular policy and to consider ways to increase the agency's ability to accomplish its tasks. . . .
> Fifth, oversight may be used to protect congressional prerogatives and powers against executive branch usurpation. . . .
> Sixth, oversight activities may be used by members of Congress to advocate programs of interest to them. . . .

A final purpose of oversight is to permit members of Congress to respond to perceived criticisms, crises, and complaints about agencies. Members focus political attention and public scrutiny on administrative actions to reverse directions that may be seen as unpopular, misguided, or illegal. They may serve the public interest, as they see it, and their individual political interests as well.

National Academy of Public Administration, Congressional Oversight of Regulatory Agencies: The Need to Strike a Balance and Focus on Performance 7-9 (1989).

In recent years congressional committees have devoted considerable effort to reviewing the operations of EPA and other agencies charged with implementing environmental and public health legislation. The NAPA study found that a total of 34 Senate committees and 56 House committees have some jurisdiction over EPA activities. EPA officials made 56 appearances before such committees in 1984, 79 in 1985, and 63 in 1986. Id. at 19-23. Former EPA administrator Lee Thomas has complained that Congress subjected EPA to too much, and the wrong kind of, oversight, which he termed "I gotcha oversight," that "is motivated, sometimes to a large extent, by an overzealous staff, sometimes by a member who is particularly interested in publicity, and sometimes by members and staff who feel that the way to get their direction on something is through intimidation." Id. at 27.

Some have argued that this fragmented oversight structure inhibits unified priority-setting at EPA. See Lazarus, The Neglected Question of Congressional Oversight of EPA: Quis Custodiat Ipsos Custodes, 54 Law & Contemp. Probs. 205 (Autumn 1991).

Congressional pressure has caused the replacement of virtually all the original Reagan Administration appointees to EPA, including Administrator Anne Gorsuch Burford. Congressional oversight also has played an important role in helping EPA resist pressure from the Executive Office of the President to weaken or block regulatory proposals. For example, after EPA announced in February 1985 that it would not propose an asbestos ban under section 6(a) of TSCA but rather would refer the matter to OSHA pursuant to section 9 of TSCA, the revelation in congressional hearings that EPA had caved into pressure from OMB helped persuade the Agency to reverse its decision. EPA's Asbestos Regulations, Hearings Before the Subcomm. on Oversight & Investigations of the House Comm. on Energy & Commerce, 99th Cong., 1st Sess. (April 16, 1985); EPA's Asbestos Regulations: Report on a Case Study of OMB Interference in Agency Rulemaking, Subcomm. on Oversight & Investigations, House Comm. on Energy & Commerce, 99th Cong., 1st Sess. (Oct. 1985). OMB sought to have EPA refer the matter to OSHA because it believed that this would effectively kill the proposal. As a result of pressure from the congressional committee, EPA reversed itself and eventually promulgated the asbestos ban in July 1989.

Members of Congress do not always champion environmental protection and public health causes when they seek to influence agency decisions. Indeed, one of the issues considered by the D.C. Circuit in another portion of its Sierra Club v. Costle opinion was the charge by environmentalists that improper congressional pressure had caused EPA to weaken the new source performance standards for coal-fired power plants. The court noted that two conditions must be met before congressional pressure would be grounds for overturning an agency's decision: (1) the content of the pressure must be designed to force the agency to base its decision on factors not relevant under the applicable regulatory statute, and (2) the decision must be affected by those extraneous considerations. Sierra Club v. Costle, 657 F.2d 298, 409 (D.C. Cir. 1981). The court found that Senator Byrd's meeting with EPA administrator Costle to express his strongly held views about the impact of the standards on the coal industry did not satisfy these criteria. Alan Morrison observes that congressional oversight can benefit the regulated community because some members of Congress "are very comfortable passing broad, remedial legislation, but are also willing to bend to the desire of powerful regulated industries by ensuring that rules needed to carry out such legislation are never effectively implemented, or at most impose minimal burdens on the industries." Morrison, OMB Interference with Agency Rulemaking: The Wrong Way to Write a Regulation, 99 Harv. L. Rev. 1059, 1071 (1986).

C.   JUDICIAL REVIEW AND THE REGULATORY PROCESS

As noted in Chapter 2, one of the key developments in the early growth of environmental law was the opening up of the courts to citizens seeking review of agency actions. While the early cases relied largely on the judicial review provisions of the Administrative Procedure Act, today most of the major federal environmental statutes expressly provide their own private rights of action to facilitate judicial review of agency action taken pursuant to them. The statutes supplement the judicial review provisions of APA section 706, often by specifying the types of agency actions that are reviewable as well as where and when review may be obtained. See, e.g., RCRA §7006(a), 42 U.S.C. §6976; TSCA §19, 15 U.S.C. §2618; CWA §509(b), 33 U.S.C. §1369(b); CAA §307(b), 42 U.S.C. §7607(b). Access to the courts is rarely problematic for environmental interests today, though the question of whether a party has standing to obtain review is occasionally controversial. The scope of judicial review has been a key battleground as the pendulum has swung from the "hard look" doctrine to a highly deferential position after Chevron U.S.A. v. Natural Resources Defense Council, 467 U.S. 837 (1984), with courts now instructed to defer to agencies' interpretations of statutory authority in cases of statutory ambiguity.

One of the most important early precedents for using the courts to require agencies to respond to environmental concerns was Scenic Hudson Preservation Conference v. Federal Power Commission, 354 F.2d 608 (2d Cir. 1965), cert. denied, 384 U.S. 941 (1966). *Scenic Hudson* involved a challenge to a decision by the old Federal Power Commission to grant a construction license for a hydroelectric power plant at Storm King Mountain on the Hudson River. The Commission had refused to consider the impact of the project on fisheries, and it had sharply limited the kinds of issues that could be raised by environmentalists, who sought to show that there were better alternatives than construction of the plant. The United States Court of Appeals instructed the agency in no uncertain terms that it had an obligation to consider the project's impact on the environment when making licensing decisions.

Robert Rabin concludes that *Scenic Hudson,* "more than any other single judicial decision, marked the birth of the environmental movement." Rabin, Federal Regulation in Historical Perspective, 38 Stan. L. Rev. 1189, 1298 (1986). Not only did it lead to the founding of the Natural Resources Defense Council, but it also "posed a direct challenge to every agency whose developmental mandate threatened environmental interests." Id. at 1298-1299. By requiring mission-oriented agencies to hear environmental concerns, the decision opened the door not only to changes in agency decision-making, but also to participation in regulatory proceedings by a wider class of interests. Because *Scenic Hudson* made judgments concerning intangible environmental impacts important, it spurred more rigorous judicial review by courts whose "suspicion about the good faith of mission-oriented agencies converged with doubts about the regulators' special competence to assess" these values. Id. at 1300. The enactment of NEPA gave environmental interests a revolutionary new tool for forcing agencies to consider their concerns. Combined with the Supreme Court's signal in Citizens to Preserve Overton Park, Inc. v. Volpe, 401 U.S. 402 (1971), that reviewing courts would no longer accept pat explanations for agency decisions, the new environmental statutes fueled a movement to conscript federal agencies into the environmental crusade.

1. STANDING AND ACCESS TO THE COURTS

Although the environmental laws encourage broad public participation in the development and enforcement of environmental regulations, access to courts remains limited by constitutional and prudential considerations to persons with a particular stake in a controversy. The question of what persons are sufficiently affected by a challenged action to have standing to sue was addressed in the following classic Supreme Court decision.

Sierra Club v. Morton
405 U.S. 727 (1972)

Mr. Justice STEWART delivered the opinion of the Court.

The Mineral King Valley is an area of great natural beauty nestled in the Sierra Nevada Mountains in Tulare County, California, adjacent to Sequoia National Park. It has been part of the Sequoia National Forest since 1926, and is designated as a national game refuge by special Act of Congress. Though once the site of extensive mining activity, Mineral King is now used almost exclusively for recreational purposes. Its relative inaccessibility and lack of development have limited the number of visitors each year, and at the same time have preserved the valley's quality as a quasi-wilderness area largely uncluttered by the products of civilization.

The United States Forest Service, which is entrusted with the maintenance and administration of national forests, began in the late 1940s to give consideration to Mineral King as a potential site for recreational development. Prodded by a rapidly increasing demand for skiing facilities, the Forest Service published a prospectus in 1965, inviting bids from private developers for the construction and operation of a ski resort that would also serve as a summer recreation area. The proposal of Walt Disney Enterprises, Inc., was chosen from those of six bidders, and Disney received a three-year permit to conduct surveys and explorations in the valley in connection with its preparation of a complete master plan for the resort.

The final Disney plan, approved by the Forest Service in January 1969, outlines a $35 million complex of motels, restaurants, swimming pools, parking lots, and other structures designed to accommodate 14,000 visitors daily. This complex is to be constructed on 80 acres of the valley floor under a 30-year use permit from the Forest Service. Other facilities, including ski lifts, ski trails, a cog-assisted railway, and utility installations, are to be constructed on the mountain slopes and in other parts of the valley under a revocable special-use permit. To provide access to the resort, the State of California proposes to construct a highway 20 miles in length. A section of this road would traverse Sequoia National Park, as would a proposed high-voltage power line needed to provide electricity for the resort. Both the highway and the power line require the approval of the Department of the Interior, which is entrusted with the preservation and maintenance of the national parks.

Representatives of the Sierra Club, who favor maintaining Mineral King largely in its present state, followed the progress of recreational planning for the valley with close attention and increasing dismay. They unsuccessfully sought a public hearing on the proposed development in 1965, and in subsequent correspondence with officials of the Forest Service and the Department of the Interior, they expressed the Club's objections to Disney's plan as a whole and to particular features included in it. In June 1969 the Club filed the present suit in the United States District Court for the Northern District of California, seeking a declaratory judgment that various aspects of the proposed development contravene federal laws and regulations governing the preservation of national parks, forests, and game refuges, and also seeking preliminary and permanent injunctions restraining the federal officials involved from granting their approval or issuing permits in connection with the Mineral King project. The petitioner Sierra Club sued as a membership corporation with "a special interest in the conservation and the sound maintenance of the national parks, game refuges and forests of the country," and invoked the judicial-review provisions of the Administrative Procedure Act, 5 U.S.C. §701 et seq.

After two days of hearings, the District Court granted the requested preliminary injunction. It rejected the respondents' challenge to the Sierra Club's standing to sue, and determined that the hearing had raised questions "concerning possible excess of statutory authority, sufficiently substantial and serious to justify a preliminary injunction. . . ." The respondents appealed, and the Court of Appeals for the Ninth Circuit reversed. 433 F.2d 24. With respect to the petitioner's standing, the court noted that there was "no allegation in the complaint that members of the Sierra Club would be affected by the actions of [the respondents] other than the fact that the actions are personally displeasing or distasteful to them," id., at 33, and concluded:

> We do not believe such club concern without a showing of more direct interest can constitute standing in the legal sense sufficient to challenge the exercise of responsibilities on behalf of all the citizens by two cabinet level officials of the government acting under Congressional and Constitutional authority. Id., at 30.

Alternatively, the Court of Appeals held that the Sierra Club had not made an adequate showing of irreparable injury and likelihood of success on the merits to justify issuance of a preliminary injunction. The court thus vacated the injunction. The Sierra Club filed a petition for a writ of certiorari which we granted, 401 U.S. 907, to review the questions of federal law presented.

The first question presented is whether the Sierra Club has alleged facts that entitle it to obtain judicial review of the challenged action.

Whether a party has a sufficient stake in an otherwise justiciable controversy to obtain judicial resolution of that controversy is what has traditionally been referred to as the question of standing to sue. Where the party does not rely on any specific statute authorizing invocation of the judicial process, the question of standing depends upon whether the party has alleged such a "personal stake in the outcome of the controversy," Baker v. Carr, 369 U.S. 186, 204, as to ensure that "the dispute sought to be adjudicated will be presented in an adversary context and in a form historically viewed as capable of judicial resolution." Flast v. Cohen, 392 U.S. 83, 101. Where, however, Congress has authorized public officials to perform certain functions according to law, and has provided by statute for judicial review of those actions under certain circumstances, the inquiry as to standing must begin with a determination of whether the statute in question authorizes review at the behest of the plaintiff.

The Sierra Club relies upon §10 of the Administrative Procedure Act (APA), 5 U.S.C. §702, which provides:

> A person suffering legal wrong because of agency action, or adversely affected or aggrieved by agency action within the meaning of a relevant statute, is entitled to judicial review thereof.

Early decisions under this statute interpreted the language as adopting the various formulations of "legal interest" and "legal wrong" then prevailing as constitutional requirements of standing. But, in Data Processing Service v. Camp, 397 U.S. 150, and Barlow v. Collins, 397 U.S. 159, decided the same day, we held more broadly that persons had standing to obtain judicial review of federal agency action under §10 of the APA where they had alleged that the challenged action had caused them "injury in fact," and where the alleged injury was to an interest "arguably within the zone of interests to be protected or regulated" by the statutes that the agencies were claimed to have violated.

In *Data Processing,* the injury claimed by the petitioners consisted of harm to their competitive position in the computer-servicing market through a ruling by the Comptroller of the Currency that national banks might perform data-processing services for their customers. In *Barlow,* the petitioners were tenant farmers who claimed that certain regulations of the Secretary of Agriculture adversely affected their economic position vis-a-vis their landlords. These palpable economic injuries have long been recognized as sufficient to lay the basis for standing, with or without a specific statutory provision for judicial review. Thus, neither *Data Processing* nor *Barlow* addressed itself to the question, which has arisen with increasing frequency in federal courts in recent years, as to what must be alleged by persons who claim injury of a noneconomic nature to interests that are widely shared. That question is presented in this case.

The injury alleged by the Sierra Club will be incurred entirely by reason of the change in the uses to which Mineral King will be put, and the attendant change in the aesthetics and ecology of the area. Thus, in referring to the road to be built through Sequoia National Park, the complaint alleged that the development "would destroy or otherwise adversely affect the scenery, natural and historic objects and wildlife of the park and would impair the enjoyment of the park for future generations." We do not question that the type of harm may amount to an "injury in fact" sufficient to lay the basis for standing under §10 of the APA. Aesthetic and environmental well-being, like economic well-being, are important ingredients of the quality of life in our society, and the fact that particular environmental interests are shared by the many rather than the few does not make them less deserving of legal protection through the judicial process. But the "injury in fact" test requires more than an injury to a cognizable interest. It requires that the party seeking review be himself among the injured.

The impact of the proposed changes in the environment of Mineral King will not fall indiscriminately upon every citizen. The alleged injury will be felt directly only by those who use Mineral King and Sequoia National Park, and for whom the aesthetic and recreational values of the area will be lessened by the highway and ski resort. The Sierra Club failed to allege that it or its members would be affected in any of their activities or pastimes by the Disney development. Nowhere in the pleadings or affidavits did the Club state that its members use Mineral King for any purpose, much less that they use it in any way that would be significantly affected by the proposed actions of the respondents. . . .

The trend of cases arising under the APA and other statutes authorizing judicial review of federal agency action has been toward recognizing that injuries other than economic harm are sufficient to bring a person within the meaning of the statutory language, and toward discarding the notion that an injury that is widely shared is ipso facto not an injury sufficient to provide the basis for judicial review. We noted this development with approval in *Data Processing*, 397 U.S., at 154, in saying that the interest alleged to have been injured "may reflect 'aesthetic, conservational, and recreational' as well as economic values." But broadening the categories of injury that may be alleged in support of standing is a different matter from abandoning the requirement that the party seeking review must himself have suffered an injury.

Some courts have indicated a willingness to take this latter step by conferring standing upon organizations that have demonstrated "an organizational interest in the problem" of environmental or consumer protection. Environmental Defense Fund v. Hardin, 138 U.S. App. D.C. 391, 395, 428 F.2d 1093, 1097. It is clear that an organization whose members are injured may represent those members in a proceeding for judicial review. See, e.g., NAACP v. Button, 371 U.S. 415, 428. But a mere "interest in a problem," no matter how longstanding the interest and no matter how qualified the organization is in evaluating the problem, is not sufficient by itself to render the organization "adversely affected" or "aggrieved" within the meaning of the APA. The Sierra Club is a large and long-established organization, with a historic commitment to the cause of protecting our Nation's natural heritage from man's depredations. But if a "special interest" in this subject were enough to entitle the Sierra Club to commence this litigation, there would appear to be no objective basis upon which to disallow a suit by any other bona fide "special interest" organization, however small or short-lived. And if any group with a bona fide "special interest" could initiate such litigation, it is difficult to perceive why any individual citizen with the same bona fide special interest would not also be entitled to do so.

The requirement that a party seeking review must allege facts showing that he is himself adversely affected does not insulate executive action from judicial review, nor does it prevent any public interests from being protected through the judicial process. It does serve as at least a rough attempt to put the decision as to whether review will be sought in the hands of those who have a direct stake in the outcome. That goal would be undermined were we to construe the APA to authorize judicial review at the behest of organizations or individuals who seek to do no more than vindicate their own value preferences through the judicial process. The principle that the Sierra Club would have us establish in this case would do just that.

As we conclude that the Court of Appeals was correct in its holding that the Sierra Club lacked standing to maintain this action, we do not reach any other questions presented in the petition, and we intimate no view on the merits of the complaint. The judgment is affirmed.

Mr. Justice POWELL and Mr. Justice REHNQUIST took no part in the consideration or decision of this case.

Mr. Justice DOUGLAS, dissenting.

I share the view of my Brother Blackmun and would reverse the judgment below.

The critical question of "standing" would be simplified and also put neatly in focus if we fashioned a federal rule that allowed environmental issues to be litigated before federal agencies or federal courts in the name of the inanimate object about to be despoiled, defaced, or invaded by roads and bulldozers and where injury is the subject of public outrage. Contemporary public concern for protecting nature's ecological equilibrium should lead to the conferral of standing upon environmental objects to sue for their own preservation. See Stone, Should Trees Have Standing?—Toward Legal Rights for Natural Objects, 45 S. Cal. L. Rev.

450 (1972). This suit would therefore be more properly labeled as Mineral King v. Morton.

Inanimate objects are sometimes parties in litigation. A ship has a legal personality, a fiction found useful for maritime purposes. The corporation sole—a creature of ecclesiastical law—is an acceptable adversary and large fortunes ride on its cases. The ordinary corporation is a "person" for purposes of the adjudicatory processes, whether it represents proprietary, spiritual, aesthetic, or charitable causes.

So it should be as respects valleys, alpine meadows, rivers, lakes, estuaries, beaches, ridges, groves of trees, swampland, or even air that feels the destructive pressures of modern technology and modern life. The river, for example, is the living symbol of all the life it sustains or nourishes—fish, aquatic insects, water ouzels, otter, fisher, deer, elk, bear, and all other animals, including man, who are dependent on it or who enjoy it for its sight, its sound, or its life. The river as plaintiff speaks for the ecological unit of life that is part of it. Those people who have a meaningful relation to that body of water—whether it be a fisherman, a canoeist, a zoologist, or a logger—must be able to speak for the values which the river represents and which are threatened with destruction. . . .

The voice of the inanimate object, therefore, should not be stilled. That does not mean that the judiciary takes over the managerial functions from the federal agency. It merely means that before these priceless bits of Americana (such as a valley, an alpine meadow, a river, or a lake) are forever lost or are so transformed as to be reduced to the eventual rubble of our urban environment, the voice of the existing beneficiaries of these environmental wonders should be heard.

NOTES AND QUESTIONS

1. The Sierra Club's complaint contained the following allegations concerning the Club's interest in the dispute:

> Plaintiff Sierra Club is a non-profit corporation organized and operating under the laws of the State of California, with its principal place of business in San Francisco, California since 1892. Membership of the club is approximately 78,000 nationally, with approximately 27,000 members residing in the San Francisco Bay Area. For many years the Sierra Club by its activities and conduct has exhibited a special interest in the conservation and the sound maintenance of the national parks, game refuges and forests of the country, regularly serving as a responsible representative of persons similarly situated. One of the principal purposes of the Sierra Club is to protect and conserve the national resources of the Sierra Nevada Mountains. Its interests would be vitally affected by the acts hereinafter described

and would be aggrieved by those acts of the defendants as hereinafter more fully appears.

Why was this allegation insufficient to establish the Sierra Club's standing? What would they have had to allege concerning their interests and activities in order to have had standing to bring their action?

2. The government argued before the Supreme Court that if the Sierra Club had standing on the basis of their allegation, then "anyone who asserts an interest in a controversy has standing." Do you agree?

3. While Sierra Club v. Morton was before the Supreme Court, the Wilderness Society and other environmental groups filed an amicus brief that described in more detail the specific nature of the Sierra Club's interest in Mineral King. It recited the Club's long efforts to include the area in Sequoia National Park, that the Club regularly conducted camping trips in the area, and that its individual members used the area for recreational purposes and would be damaged by its development. In its reply brief, however, the Sierra Club expressly declined to rely on this as a basis for standing. Why, do you think, did they refuse to do so?

4. Although he did not join in Justice Douglas's very personal dissent, Justice Blackmun also dissented. Noting that the case involved "significant aspects of a wide, growing, and disturbing problem, that is, the nation's and the world's deteriorating environment," Justice Blackmun questioned whether the law must "be so rigid and our procedure so inflexible that we render ourselves helpless when the existing methods and the traditional concepts . . . do not prove to be entirely adequate for new issues." Both Justice Douglas and Justice Blackmun felt so strongly about their dissents that they took the unusual step of reading them from the bench when the decision was announced.

5. A great deal of additional, and fascinating, background information about the history of Mineral King and Sierra Club v. Morton is provided in Turner, Who Speaks for the Future?, 1990 Sierra 30 (July-Aug. 1990), an article that includes extensive photographs of the Mineral King area. The article reports that the area is known as Mineral King because of a brief silver mining boom that in 1879 led 300 miners into the area. The boom went bust by 1882, but it left a sufficient residue of development to keep the area from being included in Sequoia National Park when the park was created in 1890. In 1908, John Muir and the Sierra Club launched a major campaign to expand Sequoia National Park to include Mineral King. After a lengthy struggle, Mineral King was again left out of the park when the park was doubled in size in 1926, although Mineral King did become part of the Sequoia National Game Refuge.

Ironically, the Board of Directors of the Sierra Club had endorsed the development of a ski resort in the area in 1949 when the Forest Service first called for bids to develop a small hotel and two ski lifts. (The area has spectacular natural attractions for skiers—"high bowls that border the valley on three sides, deep powder snow, spectacular views.") No bids were forthcoming then because of the high cost of making the remote area accessible to skiers. After the Forest Service issued a new request for bids in 1965, the Disney plan was selected. The Disney plan was for a development ten times larger and more expensive than contemplated in the Forest Service's request for bids. The Sierra Club decided to oppose the project only after a year of rancorous internal debate. When the Club asked for a public hearing, the Forest Service replied that no hearing was necessary because one had been held more than a decade earlier.

6. The Sierra Club had three substantial legal arguments against the project—that it violated Forest Service regulations concerning the size and duration of leases to private parties, that it violated Interior Department regulations concerning road building in national parks, and that it was inconsistent with the area's status as a wildlife refuge. Yet the Club was unable to get a public hearing from any government agency. Why did the government choose to challenge the Club's standing rather than focusing its defense on the substance of the case? Was this a wise strategy?

7. The Disney organization never became a party to the litigation. In its public statements on the controversy, it took positions supportive of the notion that citizens should be able to use the courts to challenge the legality of government actions. A decade before the litigation, the Sierra Club had made Walt Disney an honorary life member of the organization as a tribute to Disney's wildlife films.

8. The Supreme Court's recognition that injury to aesthetic and environmental values may be sufficient to confer standing even if the injury is shared by many remains the case's most significant legacy. While the Court ruled against the Sierra Club on the standing issue, it noted in a footnote that the decision did not bar the Sierra Club from seeking to amend its complaint when the case returned to the district court. On remand, the Sierra Club amended its complaint to allege that its members used the area and it added as coplaintiffs nine individuals who regularly visited Mineral King and a group that owns property nearby. The Club also added a new claim that the National Environmental Policy Act, which had been enacted after the original lawsuit had been filed, required the preparation of an environmental impact statement (EIS). The draft EIS was released in January 1975. By then Mineral King had become a national environmental *cause celebre*. When the final EIS was released in 1976, the Mineral King project had essentially died a natural death. The EIS found severe environmental impacts from the proposed development and recommended that the project be scaled down significantly. The ski resort was never built. The Sierra Club's lawsuit eventually was dismissed without prejudice in 1977. Mineral King was made part of Sequoia National Park in October 1978.

Standing Doctrine in Environmental Cases After Sierra Club v. Morton

Sierra Club confirmed a shift in standing logic. Previously, standing doctrine in effect conceived of the government as being just like a private party, and standing could be determined by the following test. Hypothetically substitute "Jones" for the government agency as defendant in the case. If the complaint stated a cause of action in tort, or for breach of contract, or for violation of a property right against Jones, the plaintiff had standing. This became known as the "legal wrong" test of standing. The government agency could then invoke its alleged statutory authority for the action, and thus the issue of the validity of the statute or the propriety of the action under the statute would be joined.

This legal wrong test, which has also been termed a "private law" model of standing, was modified somewhat as the regulatory state expanded. The Supreme Court began to acknowledge standing in situations where specific statutory language suggested that Congress had intended to give additional parties the right to sue. For instance, in FCC v. Sanders Brothers Radio Station, 309 U.S. 470 (1940), the Court permitted a competitor of an FCC licensee to sue on the basis of the competitor's alleged economic injury, even though the common law did not protect against competitively caused economic loss, because the Federal Communications Act allows anyone "aggrieved or whose interests are adversely affected" to seek judicial review, 47 U.S.C. §402(b)(6), and the competitor had suffered a traditionally recognized type of injury, economic damage.

When the Administrative Procedure Act was passed in 1946, it provided that "a person suffering legal wrong because of agency action, or adversely affected or aggrieved by agency action within the meaning of a relevant statute, is entitled to judicial review thereof." 5 U.S.C. §702. In his influential manual on the APA, the attorney general stated that this language codified then-existing law.

In the 1960s, lower courts pushed standing doctrine to the limits of section 702, largely under the influence of citizen and environmental groups—the presumed beneficiaries of many of the statutes Congress had enacted—who were dissatisfied with agency interpretations and actions. The details of these doctrinal developments are told in Stewart, The Reformation of American Administrative Law, 88 Harv. L. Rev. 1669 (1975); Sunstein, Standing and the Privatization of Public Law, 88 Colum. L. Rev. 1432 (1988).

Sierra Club and contemporary cases seemed to recognize a general right of citizens to challenge government action as long as they had suffered "injury in fact" and raised claims "arguably" within the "zone of interests" that Congress sought to protect. *Sierra Club* was followed in the Court's next term by United States v. Students Challenging Reg-

ulatory Agency Proceedings, 412 U.S. 669 (1973) (SCRAP). Plaintiffs
were law students challenging the ICC's approval of a freight rate they
alleged would discourage the use of recycled materials. As injury-in-fact,
they alleged that the rate change would lead to increased litter, as well
as an increase in consumption of natural resources, in the forests, parks,
and mountain areas around Washington, D.C., which the students used
for hiking, fishing, and backpacking. Although the Court thought this
an "attenuated line of causation," it held the plaintiffs' allegations sufficient for standing.

SCRAP was a high-water mark for environmental standing. Although it has never overruled *SCRAP*, the Court has issued decisions
suggesting that it has drawn back from it. This is especially so in one
recurring pattern of cases in which the plaintiff's injury is not directly
caused by the complained-of agency action, but is mediated by the actions
of third parties. In such cases, the Court has expressed concern over
whether a ruling in the plaintiff's favor will actually redress the plaintiff's
injury; otherwise, it has said, "exercise of its power . . . would be gratuitous and thus inconsistent with the Art. III limitation" limiting federal
jurisdiction to "cases and controversies." Simon v. Eastern Kentucky
Welfare Rights Organization, 426 U.S. 26, 38 (1976) (EKWRO).

In *EKWRO*, the Court denied the standing of a representative of
indigent patients to challenge an IRS rule allowing hospitals to retain
charitable tax-exempt status regardless of their treatment of indigent
patients—allegedly in violation of federal law. The decision to treat such
patients was made by the hospital board of directors; plaintiffs had not
convincingly shown that the change in tax policy would lead to the
directors' decision to change hospital treatment policy.

In Allen v. Wright, 468 U.S. 737 (1984), plaintiffs, representatives
of minority children, challenged tax-exempt treatment of discriminatory
private schools, alleging that this treatment interfered with desegrega-
tion of public schools by siphoning white students away from the public
school system. The Court denied standing, finding "[t]he links in the
chain of causation between the challenged Government conduct and the
asserted injury are far too weak for the chain as a whole to sustain
respondents' standing." See also Linda R.S. v. Richard D., 410 U.S. 614
(1973) (mother of illegitimate child lacked standing to challenge state
attorney general's nonenforcement of child-support laws, as criminal
prosecution might well not result in payment of support); Warth v.
Seldin, 422 U.S. 490 (1975) (exclusionary zoning ordinance could not
be challenged by low-income groups injured by lack of low-income housing, as absence of such housing may be due to economic factors as well
as the ordinance).

In recent years, the Court has articulated the requirements of
standing as consisting of four parts. To have standing to sue, a plaintiff
must allege:

(1)   that the challenged action will cause plaintiff some actual or
      threatened injury-in-fact;
(2)   that the injury is fairly traceable to the challenged action;
(3)   that the injury is redressable by judicial action; and
(4)   that the injury is to an interest arguably within the zone of
      interests to be protected by the statute alleged to have been
      violated.

It has also stated that the first three requirements are constitutional,
based on Art. III, while the fourth is "prudential," and thus can be
altered by Congress. (Congress could, for example, grant standing to
everyone in the world who satisfied the first three requirements, thus
eliminating the fourth part entirely.) See, e.g., Valley Forge Christian
College v. Americans United for Separation of Church and State, 454
U.S. 464 (1982).

NOTES AND QUESTIONS

1. Individuals who reside in the flood plain of the Glover Creek
sue to challenge the Secretary of the Interior's designation of the leopard
darter as an endangered species. They allege that the designation blocks
federal funding of flood control projects on the Glover. On a challenge
to standing, what result? See Glover River Organization v. Department
of the Interior, 675 F.2d 251 (10th Cir. 1982). For more on the Endangered Species Act, see Chapter 8C.

2. Organizations have standing to assert the interests of their members as long as (1) the organizations' members themselves would have
standing to sue and (2) the interests the organization seeks to protect
are "germane to the organization's purposes." Automobile Workers v.
Brock, 477 U.S. 274 (1986).

3. An animal rights organization challenges a government decision
not to ban the import of South African seal skins. Does the organization
have standing? See Animal Welfare Institute v. Kreps, 561 F.2d 1002
(D.C. Cir. 1977). The Secretary of the Interior decides that the Endangered Species Act's requirement that agencies consult with Interior before undertaking a project that destroys habitat critical to an endangered
species does not apply to federal agencies' funding of projects on foreign
soil. An animal rights organization sues. One member had visited an
A.I.D.-funded project in Sri Lanka, where he observed that at least eight
endangered species were found in the project area. Does the organization have standing? See Defenders of Wildlife v. Interior Department,
851 F.2d 1035 (8th Cir. 1988); Defenders of Wildlife v. Lujan, 911 F.2d
117 (8th Cir. 1990), cert. granted, 111 S. Ct. 2008 (1991).

4. A consumer organization sues the National Highway Transpor-

tation and Safety Administration (NHTSA), alleging that NHTSA's failure to promulgate stringent fuel efficiency regulations deprives its members of the opportunity to purchase fuel-efficient cars. The operative statute provides for fines against manufacturers whose autos fail to meet the statutory standards. Standing? Would the argument for standing be stronger if Congress determined that enforcing the fuel efficiency standards is an "effective means" to compel the production of more fuel-efficient cars? The D.C. Circuit has wrestled with the relevance of such congressional determinations, thus far inconclusively. Compare Center for Auto Safety v. NHTSA, 793 F.2d 1322 (D.C. Cir. 1986); Center for Auto Safety v. Thomas, 806 F.2d 1071 (D.C. Cir. 1986), rehg. en banc granted, judgment vacated, 810 F.2d 301 (D.C. Cir. 1987); Center for Auto Safety v. Thomas, 847 F.2d 843 (D.C. Cir. 1988); Dellums v. NRC, 863 F.2d 968 (D.C. Cir. 1988).

Sierra Club's basic holding that a "user" of public lands has standing to challenge federal actions affecting those lands has remained intact. Lately, however, questions have arisen as to what exactly plaintiffs must allege and prove to establish user standing. In one case, a national environmental organization challenged Interior's decision to lift protective restrictions on 180 million acres of public land. After years of preliminary skirmishing, including entry of a preliminary injunction, the trial court granted the government's challenge to the organization's standing.

Plaintiff had submitted affidavits from two of its members, one of whom stated that she used and enjoyed federal lands, "particularly those in the vicinity of South Pass-Green Mountain, Wyoming," an area of some two million acres, only 4,500 of which were affected by Interior's decision. The district court determined the affidavits insufficient to allege "use and enjoyment." The D.C. Circuit reversed, and the government appealed. The Supreme Court's decision follows.

Lujan v. National Wildlife Federation
110 S. Ct. 3177 (1990)

JUSTICE SCALIA delivered the opinion of the Court.

In this case we must decide whether respondent, the National Wildlife Federation (hereinafter respondent), is a proper party to challenge actions of the Federal Government relating to certain public lands.

Respondent filed this action in 1985 in the United States District Court for the District of Columbia against petitioners the United States Department of the Interior, and the Director of the Bureau of Land Management (BLM), an agency within the Department. In its amended complaint, respondent alleged that petitioners had violated the Federal Land Policy and Management Act of 1976 (FLPMA), 90 Stat. 2744, 43 U.S.C. §1701 et seq. (1982 ed.), the National Environmental Policy Act of 1969 (NEPA), 83 Stat. 852, 42 U.S.C. §4321 et seq., and §10(e) of the Administrative Procedure Act (APA), 5 U.S.C. §706, in the course of administering what the complaint called the "land withdrawal review program" of the BLM. . . .

In its complaint, respondent averred generally that the reclassification of some withdrawn lands and the return of others to the public domain would open the lands up to mining activities, thereby destroying their natural beauty. . . . Appended to the amended complaint was a schedule of specific land status determinations, which the complaint stated had been "taken by defendants since January 1, 1981"; each was identified by a listing in the Federal Register. . . .

III

A

We first address respondent's claims that the Peterson and Erdman affidavits alone suffice to establish respondent's right to judicial review of petitioner's actions. Respondent does not contend that either the FLMPA or NEPA provides a private right of action for violations of its provisions. Rather, respondent claims a right to judicial review under §10(a) of the APA, which provides:

> A person suffering legal wrong because of agency action, or adversely affected or aggrieved by agency action within the meaning of a relevant statute, is entitled to judicial review thereof. 5 U.S.C. §702.

This provision contains two separate requirements. First, the person claiming a right to sue must identify some "agency action" that affects him in the specified fashion; it is judicial review "thereof" to which he is entitled. . . . When, as here, review is sought not pursuant to specific authorization in the substantive statute, but only under the general review provisions of the APA, the "agency action" in question must be "final agency action." See 5 U.S.C. §704. . . .

Second, the party seeking review under §702 must show that he has "suffer[ed] legal wrong" because of the challenged agency action, or is "adversely affected or aggrieved" by that action "within the meaning of a relevant statute." Respondent does not assert that it has suffered "legal wrong," so we need only discuss the meaning of "adversely affected or aggrieved . . . within the meaning of a relevant statute." . . . [T]o be "adversely affected or aggrieved . . . within the meaning" of a statute, the plaintiff must establish that the injury he complains of (*his* aggrievement, or the adverse effect *upon him*) falls within the "zone of interests" sought to be protected by the statutory provision whose violation forms the legal basis for his complaint. Thus, for example, the failure of an agency to comply with a statutory provision requiring "on the record" hearing would assuredly have an adverse effect upon the company that has the contract to record and transcribe the agency's proceedings; but since the provision was obviously enacted to protect the interests of the parties to the proceedings and not those of the reporters, that company would not be "adversely affected within the meaning" of the statute. . . .

C

We turn, then, to whether the specific facts alleged in the two affidavits considered by the District Court raised a genuine issue of fact as to whether an "agency action" taken by petitioners caused respondent to be "adversely affected or aggrieved . . . within the meaning of the relevant statute." We assume, since it has been uncontested, that the allegedly affected interests set forth in the affidavits—"recreational use and aesthetic enjoyment"—are sufficiently related to the purposes of respondent association that respondent meets the requirements of §702 if any of its members do. . . .

We also think that whatever "adverse effect" or "aggrievement" is established by the affidavits was "within the meaning of the relevant statute"—i.e., met the "zone of interests" test. The relevant statute, of course, is the statute whose violation is the gravamen of the complaint— both the FLPMA and NEPA. We have no doubt that "recreational use and aesthetic enjoyment" are among the *sorts* of interests those statutes were specifically designed to protect. The only issue, then, is whether the facts alleged in the affidavits showed that those interests of *Peterson* and *Erman* were actually affected.

The Peterson affidavit averred:

> My recreational use and aesethic enjoyment of federal lands, particularly those in the vicinity of South Pass-Green Mountain, Wyoming have been and continue to be adversely affected in fact by the unlawful actions of the Bureau and the Department. In particular, the South Pass-Green Mountain area of Wyoming has been opened to the staking of mining claims and oil and gas leasing, an action which threatens the aesthetic beauty and wildlife habitate potential of these lands. App. to Pet. for Cert. 191a.

Erman's affidavit was substantially the same as Peterson's, with respect to all except the area involved; he claimed use of land "in the vicinity of Grand Canyon National Park, the Arizona Strip (Kanab Plateau), and the Kaibab National Forest." Id., at 187a.

The District Court found the Peterson affidavit inadequate for the following reasons:

Peterson . . . claims that she uses federal lands *in the vicinity* of the South Pass-Green Mountain area of Wyoming for recreational and aesthetic enjoyment and that her recreational and aesthetic enjoyment has been and continues to be adversely affected as a result of the decision of BLM to open it to the staking of mining claims and oil and gas leasing. . . . This decision opened up to mining approximately 4500 acres within a two million acre area, the balance of which, with the exception of 2000 acres, has always been open to mineral leasing and mining. . . . There is no showing that Peterson's recreational use and enjoyment extends to the particular 4500 acres covered by the decision to terminate classification of the remainder of the two million acres affected by this termination. All she claims is that she uses lands "in the vicinity." The affidavit on its face contains only a bare allegation of injury, and fails to show specific facts supporting the affiant's allegation. 699 F. Supp., at 331.

The Court of Appeals disagreed with the District Court's assessment as to the Peterson affidavit (and thus found it unnecessary to consider the Erman affidavit) for the following reason:

If Peterson was not referring to lands in this 4500-acre affected area, her allegation of impairment to her use and enjoyment would be meaningless, or perjurious. . . . [T]he trial court overlooks the fact that unless Peterson's language is read to refer to the lands affected by the Program, the affidavit is, at best, a meaningless document.

At a minimum, Peterson's affidavit is ambiguous regarding whether the adversely affected lands are the ones she uses. When presented with ambiguity on a motion for summary judgment, a District Court must resolve any factual issues of controversy in favor of the non-moving party. . . . This means that the District Court was obliged to resolve any factual ambiguity in favor of NWF, and would have had to assume, for the purposes of summary judgment, that Peterson used the 4500 affected acres. 278 U.S. App. D.C., at 329, 878 F.2d, at 431.

That is not the law. In ruling upon a Rule 56 motion, "a District Court must resolve any factual issues of controversy in favor of the non-moving party" only in the sense that, where the facts specifically averred by that party contradict facts specifically averred by the movant, the motion must be denied. That is a world apart from "assuming" that general averments embrace the "specific facts" needed to sustain the complaint. As set forth above, Rule 56(e) provides that judgment "shall be entered" against the nonmoving party unless affidavits or other evidence "set forth specific facts showing that there is a genuine issue for trial." . . .

At the margins there is some room for debate as to how "specific" must be the "specific facts" that Rule 56(e) requires in a particular case. But where the fact in question is the one put in issue by the §702 challenge here—whether one of respondent's members has been, or is threatened to be, "adversely affected or aggrieved" by Government action—Rule 56(e) is assuredly not satisfied by averments which state only that one of respondent's members uses unspecified portions of an immense tract of territory, on some portions of which mining activity has occurred or probably will occur by virtue of the governmental action. It will not do to "presume" the missing facts because without them the affidavits would not establish the injury that they generally allege. That converts the operation of Rule 56 to a circular promenade: plaintiff's complaint makes general allegation of injury; defendant contests through Rule 56 existence of specific facts to support injury; plaintiff responds with affidavit containing general allegation of injury, which must be deemed to constitute averment of requisite specific facts since otherwise allegation of injury would be unsupported (which is precisely what defendant claims it is).

Respondent places great reliance, as did the Court of Appeals, upon our decision in United States v. Students Challenging Regulatory Agency Procedures (*SCRAP*), 412 U.S. 669 (1973). The *SCRAP* opinion, whose expansive expression of what would suffice for §702 review under its particular facts has never since been emulated by this Court, is of no relevance here, since it involved not a Rule 56 motion for summary judgment but a Rule 12(b) motion to dismiss on the pleadings. The latter, unlike the former, presumes that general allegations embrace those specific facts that are necessary to support the claim. Conley v. Gibson, 355 U.S. 41, 45-46 (1957).

IV

We turn next to the Court of Appeals' alternative holding that the four additional member affidavits proffered by respondent in response to the District Court's briefing order established its rights to §702 review of agency action.

A

It is impossible that the affidavits would suffice, as the Court of Appeals held, to enable respondent to challenge the entirety of petitioners' so-called "land withdrawal review program." That is not an "agency action" within the meaning of §702, much less a "final agency action" within the meaning of §704. The term "land withdrawal review program" (which as far as we know is not derived from any authoritative text) does not refer to a single BLM order or regulation, or even to a completed universe of particular BLM orders and regulations. It is simply the name by which petitioners have occasionally referred to the continuing (and thus constantly changing) operations of the BLM in reviewing withdrawal revocation applications and the classifications of public lands and developing land use plans as required by the FLPMA. It is no more an identifiable "agency action"—much less a "final agency action"—than a "weapons procurement program" of the Department of Defense or a "drug interdiction program" of the Drug Enforcement Administration. As the District Court explained, the "land withdrawal review program" extends to, currently at least, "1250 or so individual classification terminations and withdrawal revocations." 699 F. Supp., at 322.[2]

Respondent alleges that violation of the law is rampant within this program—failure to revise land use plans in proper fashion, failure to submit certain recommendations to Congress, failure to consider multiple use, inordinate focus upon mineral exploitation, failure to provide required public notice, failure to provide adequate environmental impact statements. Perhaps so. But respondent cannot seek *wholesale* improvement of this program by court decree, rather than in the offices of the Department or the hall of Congress, where programmatic improvements are normally made. Under the terms of the APA, respondent must direct its attack against some particular "agency action" that causes it harm. Some statutes permit broad regulations to serve as the "agency action," and thus to be the object of judicial review directly, even before the concrete effects normally required for APA review are felt. Absent such a provision, however, a regulation is not ordinarily considered the type of agency action "ripe" for judicial review under the APA until the scope of the controversy has been reduced to more manageable proportions, and its factual components fleshed out, by some concrete action applying the regulation to the claimant's situation in a fashion that harms or threatens to harm him. (The major exception, of course, is a substantive

---

2. Contrary to the apparent understanding of the dissent, we do not contend that no "land withdrawal review program" exists, any more than we would contend that no weapons procurement program exists. We merely assert that it is not an identifiable "final agency action" for purposes of the APA. If there is in fact some specific order or regulation, applying some particular measure across-the-board to all individual classification terminations and withdrawal revocations, and if that order or regulation is final, and has become ripe for review in the manner we discuss subsequently in the text, it can of course be challenged under the APA by a person adversely affected—and the entire "land withdrawal review program" insofar as the content of that particular action is concerned, would thereby be affected. But that is quite different from permitting a generic challenge to all aspects of the "land withdrawal review program," as though that itself constituted a final agency action.

rule which as a practical matter requires the plaintiff to adjust his conduct immediately. Such agency action is "ripe" for review at once, whether or not explicit statutory review apart from the APA is provided.)

In the present case, the individual actions of the BLM identified in the six affidavits can be regarded as rules of general applicability (a "rule" is defined in the APA as agency action of "general or particular applicability *and future effect*," 5 U.S.C. §551(4)) (emphasis added) announcing, with respect to vast expanses of territory that they cover, the agency's intent to grant requisite permission for certain activities, to decline to interfere with other activities, and to take other particular action if requested. It may well be, then, that even those individual actions will not be ripe for challenge until some further agency action or inaction more immediately harming the plaintiff occurs.[3] But it is at least entirely certain that the flaws in the entire "program"—consisting principally of the many individual actions referenced in the complaint, and presumably actions yet to be taken as well—cannot be laid before the courts for wholesale correction under the APA, simply because one of them that is ripe for review adversely affects one of respondent's members.

The case-by-case approach that this requires is understandably frustrating to an organization such as respondent, which has as its objective across-the-board protection of our Nation's wildlife and the streams and forests that support it. But this is the traditional, and remains the normal, mode of operation of the courts. Except where Congress explicitly provides for our correction of the administrative process at a higher level of generality, we intervene in the administration of the laws only when, and to the extent that, a specific "final agency action" has an actual or immediately threatened effect. *Toilet Goods Assn.*, 387 U.S., at 164-166. Such an intervention may ultimately have the effect of requiring a regulation, a series of regulations, or even a whole "program" to be revised by the agency in order to avoid the unlawful result that the court discerns. But it is assuredly not as swift or as immediately far-reaching a corrective process as those interested in systemic improvement would desire. Until confided to us, however, more sweeping actions are for the other Branches.

Justice BLACKMUN, with whom Justice BRENNAN, Justice MARSHALL, and Justice STEVENS, join, dissenting.

---

3. Under the Secretary's regulations, any person seeking to conduct mining operations that will "cause a cumulative surface disturbance" of 5 acres or more must first obtain approval of a plan of operations. Mining operations that cause surface disturbance of less than 5 acres do not require prior approval, but prior notice must be given to the district office of the BLM. . . . Thus, before any mining use ordinarily involving more than "negligible disturbance" can take place, there must occur either agency action in response to a submitted plan or agency inaction in response to a submitted notice.

In my view, the affidavits of Peggy Kay Peterson and Richard Loren Erman, in conjunction with other record evidence before the District Court on the motions for summary judgment, were sufficient to establish the standing of the National Wildlife Federation (Federal or NWF) to bring this suit. . . .

. . . [T]he allegations contained in the Peterson and Erman affidavits, in the context of the record as a whole, were adequate to defeat a motion for summary judgment. These affidavits, as the majority acknowledges, were at least sufficiently precise to enable Bureau of Land Management (BLM) officials to identify the particular termination orders to which the affiants referred. And the affiants averred that their "recreational use and aesthetic enjoyment of federal lands . . . have been and continue to be adversely affected in fact by the unlawful actions of the Bureau and the Department." The question, it should be emphasized, is not whether the NWF has *proved* that it has standing to bring this action, but simply whether the materials before the District Court established "that there is a genuine issue for trial," see Rule 56(e), concerning the Federation's standing. In light of the principle that "[o]n summary judgment the inferences to be drawn from the underlying facts contained in [evidentiary] materials must be viewed in the light most favorable to the party opposing the motion," United States v. Diebold, Inc., 369 U.S. 654, 655 (1962), I believe that the evidence before the District Court raised a genuine factual issue as to NWF's standing to sue. . . .

In part IV-A, ante, the majority sets forth a long and abstract discussion of the scope of relief that might have been awarded had the Federation made a sufficient showing of injury from environmental damage to a particular tract of land. Since the majority concludes in other portions of its opinion that the Federation lacks standing to challenge *any* of the land-use decisions at issue here, it is not clear to me why the Court engages in the hypothetical inquiry contained in Part IV-A. In any event, I agree with much of the Court's discussion, at least in its general outline. The Administrative Procedure Act permits suits to be brought by any person "adversely affected or aggrieved by agency action." 5 U.S.C. §702. In some cases the "agency action" will consist of a rule of broad applicability; and if the plaintiff prevails, the result is that the rule is invalidated, not simply that the court forbids its application to a particular individual. Under these circumstances a single plaintiff, so long as he is injured by the rule, may obtain "programmatic" relief that affects the rights of parties not before the court. On the other hand, if a generally lawful policy is applied in an illegal manner on a particular occasion, one who is injured is not thereby entitled to challenge other applications of the rule.

Application of these principles to the instant case does not turn on whether, or how often, the Bureau's land management policies have been described as a "program." In one sense, of course, there is no question that a "program" exists. Everyone associated with this lawsuit recognizes that the BLM, over the past decade, has attempted to develop and implement a comprehensive scheme for the termination of classifications and withdrawals. The real issue is whether the actions and omissions NWF contends are illegal are themselves part of a plan or policy. For example: if the agency had published a regulation stating that an Environmental Impact Statement should never be developed prior to the termination of a classification or withdrawal, NWF could challenge the regulation (which would constitute an "agency action"). If the reviewing court then held that the statute required a pre-termination EIS, the relief (invalidation of the rule) would directly affect tracts other than the ones used by individual affiants. At the other extreme, if the applicable BLM regulation stated that an EIS *must* be developed, and NWF alleged that the administrator in charge of South Pass/Green Mountain had inexplicably failed to develop one, NWF should not be allowed (on the basis of the Peterson affidavit) to challenge a termination in Florida on the ground that an administrator there made the same mistake.

NOTES AND QUESTIONS

1. Does the decision in Lujan v. National Wildlife Federation change the nature or character of the injury that must be alleged in order for a plaintiff to have standing to object to decisions concerning the disposition of public lands? Does it make any difference in this case that NEPA does not create its own private right of action to seek judicial review?

2. How specific must the allegation of injury be in order for an environmental plaintiff to have standing in cases of this sort? How specific must it be to be able to survive a motion for summary judgment? Is it necessary for the plaintiff to be able to prove that one of its members has used the precise parcel of land that has been opened to development activity? Could standing be defeated by subdividing parcels subject to reclassification into small pieces and pledging not to develop the specific parcels used by plaintiffs? Does *Lujan* imply that plaintiffs suing for violations of air pollution permits may have to demonstrate that they inhale the offending molecules that exceed permissible limits?

3. Who do you think would suffer more direct harm, the students in *SCRAP*, the Sierra Club members in Sierra Club v. Morton, or the National Wildlife Federation's members in Lujan v. National Wildlife Federation? What explains the different results in these cases? Does *Lujan* call into question the result in *SCRAP*?

4. Justice Scalia suggests that the BLM's "land withdrawal review program" did not constitute final agency action ripe for review. Why not? What would have to happen first in Justice Scalia's view for the action to be reviewable? Why is this typically not a problem in cases involving judicial review of agency rulemaking actions? Curiously, the government had argued in the district court that NWF's claims were barred by laches, arguing that "the Federation offers no explanation why, despite its detailed knowledge of BLM's revocation and termination activities, it has waited so long to institute litigation." 110 S. Ct. at 3202 n.16 (Brennan, J., dissenting).

5. In Conservation Law Foundation v. Reilly, 950 F.2d 38 (1st Cir. 1991), an environmental organization based in Boston whose members reside in New England sued to compel EPA to conduct a preliminary assessment of all federal facilities on the Federal Agency Hazardous Waste Compliance Docket pursuant to section 120(d) of CERCLA, 42 U.S.C. §9620(d), which gave the Agency until April 1988 to do so. The Agency conceded it had failed to assess 225 of the 840 sites originally placed on the list. A panel of the First Circuit reversed a district court decision that had upheld the plaintiff's standing. Although it stated that *Lujan* was not controlling, the First Circuit's ruling was apparently influenced by that decision. In its view, plaintiffs lacked standing to seek an injunction applicable to all the sites (a nationwide injunction) because members of the organization had alleged that its members lived, worked, or carried out recreational activities near only a few of the facilities.

Consult the citizen suit provision of CERCLA, 42 U.S.C. §9659(a). Is the result in *Conservation Law Foundation* consistent with congressional intent? Is it a correct application of the principles in *Lujan*?

Recall that national environmental organizations monitor EPA performance largely through litigation involving nationwide, nondiscretionary duties. See pages 666-671, above. What impact will *Conservation Law Foundation* have on such monitoring?

6. Preservationists have long argued that there is value in preserving natural areas in a pristine state, unmarked by human impact. Economists have recognized that such preservation of natural areas has economic value, a concept they call "existence value," because humans value the knowledge that pristine areas exist. See discussion of cost-benefit analysis in Chapter 4. However, in cases involving challenges to the development of wilderness areas, the courts have required environmental plaintiffs to demonstrate that they regularly visit or use such areas. Who would have standing to protest the development of an area from which humans have been excluded? Can the concept of standing be reconciled with preservationist impulses?

7. Professor Cass Sunstein rejects the notion that standing doctrine should be constitutionally based. He argues that

[t]he problem of concreteness has nothing to do with the question of standing. Whether a plaintiff is able to point to an injury peculiar to him is a question independent of the concreteness or abstraction of the dispute. For example, the dispute in Sierra Club v. Morton—the principal modern example of a case denying standing on injury-in-fact grounds—was hardly hypothetical or remote. Standing limitations are also said to be a way of ensuring sincere or effective advocacy. But institutional litigants not having injury in fact are particularly likely to be strong advocates. It is expensive to initiate a lawsuit, and those who do so without meeting the standing requirements are especially committed. [Sunstein, Standing and the Privatization of Public Law, 88 Colum. L. Rev. 1432, 1448 (1988).]

In the absence of the injury-in-fact requirement, what would limit the class of parties who could be plaintiffs in environmental litigation? An excellent analysis of standing is Fletcher, The Structure of Standing, 98 Yale L.J. 221 (1988).

8. Further developments are likely in the evolution of standing doctrine. The Supreme Court has granted certiorari in Defenders of Wildlife v. Lujan, 911 F.2d 117 (8th Cir. 1990), cert. granted, 111 S. Ct. 2008 (1991), page 728, above. (Defenders eventually prevailed on the merits of its claim that the Endangered Species Act requires agency consultation with respect to foreign projects.) The Supreme Court's decision could further develop the traceability-redressability aspects of standing doctrine. It may also examine the role of congressional determinations of traceability-redressability because the Eighth Circuit relied on such determinations in ruling on standing.

The Zone of Interests Test and Standing for Business Interests

The "zone of interests" requirement for standing has been an issue in a few recent cases. Because environmental regulation is rapidly creating a market for pollution control products and for environmental cleanup technologies, firms that develop and market such products or services have an economic stake in the implementation of laws that require pollution control and environmental cleanup. One trade association that has been particularly active in lobbying for the implementation of RCRA's hazardous waste regulations is the Hazardous Waste Treatment Council (HWTC), which represents more than 60 hazardous waste treatment firms and manufacturers of treatment technology. In Hazardous Waste Treatment Council v. EPA, 861 F.2d 277 (D.C. Cir. 1988), cert. denied, 490 U.S. 1106 (1989) (*HWTC I*), the Treatment Council sought judicial review of EPA's rules concerning the burning of hazardous wastes as fuel on the ground that the rules were not stringent enough.

Concerned by "the apparent anomaly of regulated entities demanding stricter regulation," the D.C. Circuit asked for briefing on the question of the Treatment Council's standing, which EPA had not challenged. The court subsequently concluded that the Treatment Council's interest in more stringent RCRA regulations was economic and not environmental. Thus, the court held that the Treatment Council did not fall within the zone of interests protected by RCRA. In its opinion denying the Treatment Council standing in *HWTC I,* the court argued that "judicial intervention may defeat statutory goals if it proceeds at the behest of interests that coincide only accidentally with those goals." The court observed that the Treatment Council's economic interests might lead it to advocate regulations that are so stringent that they would boomerang and increase illegal dumping, resulting in net harm to the environment.

The Treatment Council then sought to reestablish its standing in another pending case by adding individuals who lived near hazardous waste treatment and disposal facilities as members of its organization. However, another panel of the D.C. Circuit rejected this effort as untimely because the individuals had not been members of the Treatment Council when it filed its petition for review. Petro-Chem Processing, Inc. v. EPA, 866 F.2d 433 (D.C. Cir. 1989) (*HWTC II*).

In Portland Audubon Society v. Hodel, 866 F.2d 302 (9th Cir. 1989), the Northwest Forest Resource Council, a timber industry group, attempted to intervene in a suit by an environmental group challenging the adequacy of an environmental impact statement for timber sales in Oregon. The district court's denial of intervention was upheld by the Ninth Circuit. The court held that the timber industry group's economic interest in timber sales had no direct relation to the interest intended to be protected by the National Environmental Policy Act. The court held that it was permissible to refuse intervention to a group that did not have an interest directly protected by the statute. Despite the industry group's argument that NEPA requires balancing of environmental and economic interests, the court held that because NEPA protects only environmental interests, intervention in NEPA suits must be permitted only on behalf of environmental interests. See also Cross-Sound Ferry Services, Inc. v. Interstate Commerce Commission, 873 F.2d 395 (D.C. Cir. 1989) (holding that a ferry service did not have standing to complain about the environmental impact of a proposed competing operation); Competitive Enterprise Institute v. National Highway Safety Administration, 901 F.2d 107 (D.C. Cir. 1990) (holding that a nonprofit group representing business interests fell within the zone of interests of the Energy Policy and Conservation Act by alleging the adverse effect of fuel economy standards on the safety of vehicle occupants, but not within the zone of interests protect by NEPA); Allied Signal, Inc. v. Lujan, 736 F. Supp. 1558 (N.D. Cal. 1990) (holding that a potentially responsible party under CERCLA does not have standing to challenge a cleanup plan as a violation of the Endangered Species Act because the company's injury does not flow from the challenged conduct).

NOTES AND QUESTIONS

1. Do you agree with the D.C. Circuit's justification for denying standing to the Hazardous Waste Treatment Council? Is the fear that an industry group's economic interest in stricter environmental regulations might actually harm environmental interests in other contexts a realistic one? Can *HWTC* be distinguished from cases such as *Portland Audubon Society* or Allied Signal v. Lujan, where corporate plaintiffs also sought to use environmental statutes to advance their interests? In future cases what can the Treatment Council do to ensure its standing to challenge regulations that it deems to be too lax?

2. Corporations potentially could play an important role in enforcing the environmental laws by using the laws' citizen suit provisions against unscrupulous competitors who violate the law. In Sierra Club v. Morton the Supreme Court confirmed that economic injury is not required for individuals to establish standing to sue; aesthetic injuries also may qualify. Should a corporation have standing to sue for aesthetic harm? Suppose a shopping center alleges that it has suffered aesthetic injury due to the unlawful pollution of a nearby stream "because the area in which the [center] is situated has become less pleasant and attractive." Would the corporate owner of the shopping center have standing to sue? See Citizens Coordinating Committee v. Washington Metropolitan Area Transit Authority, 765 F.2d 1169 (D.C. Cir. 1985).

3. The problem below gives you an opportunity to digest many of the lessons of this chapter concerning action-forcing litigation, standing, and judicial review. Although the regulations at issue in the problem have finally been promulgated by EPA (four years after expiration of the deadline), for purposes of the problem assume the facts are as stated therein.

PROBLEM EXERCISE: ACTION-FORCING
LITIGATION, STANDING, AND
JUDICIAL REVIEW

Like most of the major federal environmental statutes, the Resource Conservation and Recovery Act contains both a citizen suit provision and a provision for judicial review of agency action. The citizen suit provision is contained in section 7002 of RCRA, 42 U.S.C. §6972, and the judicial review provision is section 7006, 42 U.S.C. §6976. These provisions, which are very similar to those contained in the other major federal environmental statutes, serve as the basis for the following problem.

Section 3004(n) of RCRA, 42 U.S.C. §6924(n), required the EPA administrator to promulgate regulations for the monitoring and control of air emissions at hazardous waste treatment, storage, and disposal facilities by May 8, 1987. EPA failed to meet this deadline. Suppose that you have now graduated from law school and have just passed the bar. You have been assured by your new law firm that you will be allowed to do pro bono work as long as you bill 2,000 hours each year to paying clients. You have told a friend of yours working at a national environmental group that you would like to volunteer to perform some legal work for them. The friend, who is extremely busy fighting for new environmental legislation, tells you that his group is upset by EPA's failure to regulate air emissions from hazardous waste facilities. He asks you to represent the group in a lawsuit against EPA for the Agency's failure to comply with section 3004(n) of RCRA.

You inform the managing partner at your law firm that you would like to represent the environmental group. After checking for potential conflicts of interests with the firm's existing clients, the managing partner reports to you that he is surprised to discover that there are none. You agree to file a lawsuit against EPA on behalf of the environmental group.

Question One.   What portion of the citizen suit provision of section 7002 of RCRA authorizes the environmental group to sue EPA? In which federal court could you file the action? What are the procedural prerequisites to filing such an action? Consider section 7002(c). How would you establish the environmental group's standing to sue? Consider each of the four elements of standing doctrine.

Question Two.   Prior to filing the lawsuit against EPA, the national environmental group you represent is contacted by a citizens' group based in a small rural community. The rural group states that its members who live nearby a hazardous waste landfill have suddenly become seriously ill as a result of fumes from the facility. They want to join the national group in filing a lawsuit to stop the fumes as soon as possible. Would the rural group have standing to sue EPA? For what? Consider elements of standing doctrine and Conservation Law Foundation v. Reilly. Could the groups sue the owner of the landfill under section 7002(a)(1)(B) of RCRA? What would the national group need to show in order to have organizational standing in such a suit? What are the procedural prerequisities to filing the lawsuit? Consider section 7002(b)(2)(A). When~could the lawsuit be filed?

Question Three.   Suppose the national environmental group is approached by a company that sells devices used to control air emissions for waste disposal facilities. The company wants to join the group as a coplaintiff in the suit against EPA. What would the company need to allege in order to have standing?

Question Four. Suppose EPA has actually just proposed regulations to implement section 3004(n). What impact, if any, will this have on your lawsuit against EPA? What would you advise your clients concerning participation in the rulemaking proceedings? What can they do to influence the Agency to adopt strong regulations?

Question Five. Suppose that after you have filed your lawsuit against EPA, EPA concedes that it has missed the statutory deadline for promulgating the section 3004(n) regulations. EPA and your client negotiate a new schedule for promulgating the section 3004(n) regulations that is placed in a consent decree approved by the court in settlement of the litigation. Your managing partner approaches you and asks if you are going to apply for a court award of attorneys' fees pursuant to section 7002(e) of RCRA. How would you respond? Are you entitled to recover attorneys' fees? See §7002(e) of RCRA and Maher v. Gagne, 448 U.S. 122 (1980). If fees were awarded, at what rate would they be calculated— the hourly rate your firm charges for your services ($100 per hour) or the hourly rate at which you charged the environmental group for your services ($0 per hour)? See Save Our Cumberland Mountains, Inc. v. Hodel, 857 F.2d 1516 (D.C. Cir. 1988); Student Public Interest Group of N.J. v. Monsanto Co., 721 F. Supp. 604 (D.N.J. 1989), affd., 891 F.2d 283 (3d Cir. 1989).

Question Six. Suppose that EPA complies with the terms of the consent decree and promulgates the regulations required by section 3004(n) by the new deadline you negotiated with the Agency. You call your friend at the environmental group to share the good news, but discover that he is very upset because the regulations are so weak. He tells you that EPA rejected all the recommendations his group made during the informal rulemaking proceeding and adopted regulations that will do little to protect human health and the environment. He notes that under the new EPA regulations the air emissions that caused severe illness to the rural group would not even be regulated. What legal action can his group take to challenge EPA's regulations? Consider section 7006 of RCRA. In what court can such an action be filed? When can such an action be filed? What will you have to establish in order to get the court to overturn EPA's regulations? See Administrative Procedure Act, 5 U.S.C. §706.

2. The Scope of Judicial Review

When the Supreme Court in Citizens to Preserve Overton Park v. Volpe, 401 U.S. 402 (1971), reversed a decision to authorize the expenditure of federal funds to build an interstate highway through a park, the decision was a surprise for two reasons: It indicated that courts were willing to review a wider range of agency actions and to scrutinize more carefully the rationale behind agency decisions. The plaintiffs in *Overton Park* alleged that the Secretary of Transportation had violated a provision of the Department of Transportation Act of 1966 that prohibited him from approving any project that required public parkland unless he determined that no feasible and prudent alternative to the use of the land existed and that all possible planning had been done to minimize harm to the park from such use. Relying on the judicial review provisions of section 706 of the APA, the plaintiffs argued that the Secretary's decision was an abuse of discretion and contrary to law.

In response to the lawsuit, the government argued that the Secretary's decision was not reviewable by a court because it was "committed to agency discretion by law" and thus exempt from review pursuant to the judicial review provisions of the APA, 5 U.S.C. §701(a). Because the Secretary had not made any specific findings at the time he made the decision, the Agency submitted affidavits to the court to support the Secretary's claim that he had indeed balanced the cost of other routes and safety considerations against the environmental impacts of the project. Although the court held that the Secretary did not need to make formal findings, it remanded the case to the district court for review based on reconstruction of the record actually before the Secretary at the time the decision was made. The court indicated that the Secretary had an obligation under the statute to do more than simply articulate a universally applicable rationale (i.e., that considerations of costs, the directness of the route, and community disruption favor use of the parkland) and that courts had an obligation to ensure that agency officials exercise their discretion properly.

With the enactment of the National Environmental Policy Act, which declared the importance of environmental values in national policy and required agencies to prepare environmental impact statements, environmentalists gained a powerful tool for challenging agency decisions. Courts began a period of greater scrutiny of agency actions characterized as the "hard look" doctrine, as Judge Leventhal referred to it in Greater Boston Television Corp. v. FCC, 444 F.2d 841, 851 (D.C. Cir. 1970), cert. denied, 403 U.S. 923 (1971).

This burst of judicial activism featured greater scrutiny of agency actions not only at the behest of environmentalists, but also in response to challenges by regulated industries. The courts struck down several EPA regulations in response to lawsuits by affected industries, even after the Agency began to develop detailed administrative records to support its rules. See, e.g., Kennecott Copper Corp. v. EPA, 462 F.2d 846 (D.C. Cir. 1972) (national secondary air quality standard for sulfur dioxide struck down as inadequately justified by agency); International Harvester Co. v. Ruckelshaus, 478 F.2d 615 (D.C. Cir. 1973) (denial of waiver for new motor vehicle emissions reduction standards invalidated); Portland Cement Association v. Ruckelshaus, 486 F.2d 375 (D.C. Cir. 1973) (new source performance standard for Portland cement plants struck down).

The movement by reviewing courts to require agencies to go beyond the minimum procedures required by the APA was brought to an abrupt halt by the Supreme Court in Vermont Yankee Nuclear Power Corp. v. Natural Resources Defense Council, 435 U.S. 519 (1978). *Vermont Yankee* involved a challenge to a decision by the Atomic Energy Commission to grant a license to a nuclear power plant. Although the license had been granted only after extensive licensing hearings, the hearings did not consider the environmental effects of the uranium fuel cycle, deferring that issue for a subsequent informal rulemaking proceeding. NRDC argued that NEPA required the AEC to employ additional factfinding procedures when considering the environmental impact of nuclear waste disposal. The D.C. Circuit agreed and held that such issues must be considered in individual licensing proceedings employing more formalized factfinding procedures. Natural Resources Defense Council v. Nuclear Regulatory Commission, 547 F.2d 633, 653 (D.C. Cir. 1976). The Supreme Court then reversed.

In an opinion by Justice Rehnquist, the Court held that the APA "established the maximum procedural requirements which Congress was willing to have the courts impose upon agencies in conducting rulemaking procedures." While noting that "[a]gencies are free to grant additional procedural rights in the exercise of their discretion," the Court held that "reviewing courts are generally not free to impose them if the agencies have not chosen to grant them." Vermont Yankee Nuclear Power Corp. v. Natural Resources Defense Council, 435 U.S. 519 (1978). Sternly admonishing the lower courts that "our cases could hardly be more explicit in this regard," Justice Rehnquist warned:

[I]f courts continually review agency proceedings to determine whether the agency employed procedures which were, in the court's opinion, perfectly tailored to reach what the court perceives to be the "best" or "correct" result, judicial review would be totally unpredictable. And the agencies, operating under this vague injunction to employ the "best" procedures and facing the threat of reversal if they did not, would undoubtedly adopt full adjudicatory procedures in every instance. Not only would this totally disrupt the statutory scheme, through which Congress enacted "a formula upon which opposing social and political forces have come to rest," Wong

Yang Sung v. McGrath, 339 U.S., at 40, but all the inherent advantages of informal rulemaking would be totally lost. [435 U.S. at 546-547.]

Vermont Yankee repudiated attempts by reviewing courts to require agencies to provide more complete rulemaking records encompassing a wider range of issues that might be deemed relevant on judicial review. The decision had important implications for judicial review of agency compliance with the procedural obligations established by the National Environmental Policy Act (NEPA), an issue we will examine when we study NEPA in Chapter 8. But it had even broader implications, sending the lower courts a message that they should be more deferential to agency rulemaking procedures.

As Robert Rabin notes, *Vermont Yankee* marked a watershed between competing approaches to judicial review. Prior to *Vermont Yankee* the D.C. Circuit and other courts "were pressing toward a decisionmaking methodology that would closely resemble the adversarial search for truth so congenial to the judicial mind—a methodology that demanded joinder of issue, elaborate articulation of all contending values, impartiality of perspective, and a carefully reasoned decision." Instead of this approach, which he characterizes as the "Right Answer" approach, the Court, reluctant to eliminate all checks on agency decisions, adopted what Rabin calls the "Best Efforts" approach: "[t]aking into account that the agency's statutory mission might appropriately create a political tilt, and recognizing the quasi-legislative character of agency rulemaking, the Court sought assurance of good faith consideration of the issues by the regulator rather than demanding a pristine search for truth." Rabin, Federal Regulation in Historic Perspective, 38 Stan. L. Rev. 1189, 1311-1312 (1986).

While *Vermont Yankee* mandated greater judicial deference to agency procedural decisions, the Court did not abandon judicial review as a check on the substance of agency decisions. Even though the APA specifies a relatively deferential standard of review (section 706 provides that courts are to overturn agency action only if it is "arbitrary, capricious, an abuse of discretion, or otherwise not in accordance with law"), the Court has not made the standard a toothless one. In Motor Vehicle Manufacturers Association v. State Farm Mutual Auto Insurance Co., 463 U.S. 29 (1983), the Supreme Court affirmed a D.C. Circuit decision striking down the Reagan Administration's rescission of a regulation requiring automobile manufacturers to install passive restraint systems in cars. The Court held that the agency had failed to offer an adequate explanation of its decision in light of the extensive evidence in the record that passive restraint systems could prevent substantial numbers of deaths in automobile accidents.

Shortly after the *State Farm* decision, the Supreme Court substantially expanded judicial deference to agency decisions in the case that follows. The case involved a challenge to another agency effort to change policy abruptly.

Chevron U.S.A. v. Natural Resources Defense Council
467 U.S. 837 (1984)

Justice STEVENS delivered the opinion of the Court.

In the Clean Air Act Amendments of 1977, Pub. L. 95-95, 91 Stat. 685, Congress enacted certain requirements applicable to States that had not achieved the national air quality standards established by the Environmental Protection Agency (EPA) pursuant to earlier legislation. The amended Clean Air Act required these "nonattainment" States to establish a permit program regulating "new or modified major stationary sources" of air pollution. Generally, a permit may not be issued for a new or modified major stationary source unless several stringent conditions are met. The EPA regulation promulgated to implement this permit requirement allows a State to adopt a plantwide definition of the term "stationary source." Under this definition, an existing plant that contains several pollution-emitting devices may install or modify one piece of equipment without meeting the permit conditions if the alternative will not increase the total emissions from the plant. The question presented by these cases is whether EPA's decision to allow States to treat all of the pollution-emitting devices within the same industrial grouping as though they were encased within a single "bubble" is based on a reasonable construction of the statutory term "stationary source."

The EPA regulations containing the plantwide definition of the term stationary source were promulgated on October 14, 1981. 46 Fed. Reg. 50766. Respondents filed a timely petition for review in the United States Court of Appeals for the District of Columbia Circuit pursuant to 42 U.S.C. §7607(b)(1). The Court of Appeals set aside the regulations. National Resources Defense Council, Inc. v. Gorsuch, 222 U.S. App. D.C. 268, 685 F.2d 718 (1982).

The court observed that the relevant part of the amended Clean Air Act "does not explicitly define what Congress envisioned as a 'stationary source,' to which the permit program . . . should apply," and further stated that the precise issue was not "squarely addressed in the legislative history." Id., at 273, 685 F.2d, at 723. In light of its conclusion that the legislative history bearing on the question was "at best contradictory," it reasoned that "the purposes of the nonattainment program should guide our decision here." Id., at 276, n.39, 685 F.2d, at 726, n.39. Based on two of its precedents concerning the applicability of the bubble concept to certain Clean Air Act programs, the court stated that the bubble concept was "mandatory" in programs designed merely to maintain existing air quality, but held that it was "inappropriate" in programs enacted to improve air quality. Id., at 276, 685 F.2d, at 726. Since the purpose of the permit program—its "raison d'etre," in the court's view—was to improve air quality, the court held that the bubble concept was inapplicable in these cases under its prior precedents. Ibid. It therefore set aside the regulations embodying the bubble concept as contrary to law. We granted certiorari to review that judgment, 461 U.S. 956 (1983), and we now reverse.

The basic legal error of the Court of Appeals was to adopt a static judicial definition of the term "stationary source" when it had decided that Congress itself had not commanded that definition. Respondents do not defend the legal reasoning of the Court of Appeals. Nevertheless, since this Court reviews judgments, not opinions, we must determine whether the Court of Appeals' legal error resulted in an erroneous judgment on the validity of the regulations.

When a court reviews an agency's construction of the statute which it administers, it is confronted with two questions. First, always, is the question whether Congress has directly spoken to the precise question at issue. If the intent of Congress is clear, that is the end of the matter; for the court as well as the agency must give effect to the unambiguously expressed intent of Congress. If, however, the court determines Congress has not directly addressed the precise question at issue, the court does not simply impose its own construction on the statute, as would be necessary in the absence of an administrative interpretation. Rather, if the statute is silent or ambiguous with respect to the specific issue, the question for the court is whether the agency's answer is based on a permissible construction of the statute.

"The power of an administrative agency to administer a congressionally created . . . program necessarily requires the formulation of policy and the making of rules to fill any gap left, implicitly or explicitly, by Congress." Morton v. Ruiz, 415 U.S. 199 (1974). If Congress has explicitly left a gap for the agency to fill, there is an express delegation of authority to the agency to elucidate a specific provision of the statute by regulation. Such legislative regulations are given controlling weight unless they are arbitrary, capricious, or manifestly contrary to the statute. Sometimes the legislative delegation to an agency on a particular question is implicit rather than explicit. In such a case, a court may not substitute its own construction of a statutory provision for a reasonable interpretation made by the administrator of an agency.

We have long recognized that considerable weight should be accorded to an executive department's construction of a statutory scheme it is entrusted to administer, and the principle of deference to administrative interpretations has been consistently followed by this Court whenever decision as to the meaning or reach of a statute has involved reconciling conflicting policies, and a full understanding of the force of the statutory policy in the given situation has depended upon more than ordinary knowledge respecting the matters subjected to agency regulations. See, e.g., National Broadcasting Co. v. United States, 319 U.S. 190; Labor Board v. Hearst Publications, Inc., 322 U.S. 111; Republic Aviation Corp. v. Labor Board, 324 U.S. 793; Securities & Exchange Comm'n v. Chenery Corp., 332 U.S. 194; Labor Board v. Seven-Up Bottling Co., 344 U.S. 344.

. . . If this choice represents a reasonable accommodation of conflicting policies that were committed to the agency's care by the statute, we should not disturb it unless it appears from the statute or its legislative history that the accommodation is not one that Congress would have sanctioned. United States v. Shimer, 367 U.S. 374, 382, 383 (1961). Accord Capital Cities Cable, Inc. v. Crisp, 467 U.S. 691, 699-700 (1984).

In light of these well-settled principles it is clear that the Court of Appeals misconceived the nature of its role in reviewing the regulations at issue. Once it determined, after its own examination of the legislation, that Congress did not actually have an intent regarding the applicability of the bubble concept to the permit program, the question before it was not whether in its view the concept is "inappropriate" in the general context of a program designed to improve air quality, but whether the Administrator's view that it is appropriate in the context of this particular program is a reasonable one. Based on the examination of the legislation and its history, which follows, we agree with the Court of Appeals that Congress did not have a specific intention on the applicability of the bubble concept in these cases, and conclude that the EPA's use of that concept here is a reasonable policy choice for the agency to make. . . .

Our review of the EPA's varying interpretations of the word "source"—both before and after the 1977 Amendments—convinces us that the agency primarily responsible for administering this important legislation has consistently interpreted it flexibly—not in a sterile textual vacuum, but in the context of implementing policy decisions in a technical and complex arena. The fact that the agency has from time to time changed its interpretation of the term "source" does not, as respondents argue, lead us to conclude that no deference should be accorded the agency's interpretation of the statute. An initial agency interpretation is not instantly carved in stone. On the contrary, the agency, to engage in informed rulemaking, must consider varying interpretations and the wisdom of its policy on a continuing basis. Moreover, the fact that the agency has adopted different definitions in different contexts adds force to the argument that the definition itself is flexible, particularly since Congress has never indicated any disapproval of a flexible reading of the statute.

Significantly, it was not the agency in 1980, but rather the Court of Appeals that read the statute inflexibly to command a plantwide definition for programs designed to maintain clean air and to forbid such a definition for programs designed to improve air quality. The distinction the court drew may well be a sensible one, but our labored review of the problem has surely disclosed that it is not a distinction that Congress ever articulated itself, or one that the EPA found in the statute before the courts began to review the legislative work product. We conclude that it was the Court of Appeals, rather than Congress or any of the decisionmakers who are authorized by Congress to administer this legislation, that was primarily responsible for the 1980 position taken by the agency.

POLICY

The arguments over policy that are advanced in the parties' briefs create the impression that respondents are now waging in a judicial forum a specific policy battle which they ultimately lost in the agency and in the 32 jurisdictions opting for the "bubble concept," but one which was never waged in the Congress. Such policy arguments are more properly addressed to legislators or administrators, not to judges.

In these cases, the Administrator's interpretation represents a reasonable accommodation of manifestly competing interests and is entitled to deference: the regulatory scheme is technical and complex, the agency considered the matter in a detailed and reasoned fashion, and the decision involves reconciling conflicting policies. Congress intended to accommodate both interests, but did not do so itself on the level of specificity presented by these cases. Perhaps that body consciously desired the Administrator to strike the balance at this level, thinking that those with great expertise and charged with responsibility for administering the provision would be in a better position to do so; perhaps it simply did not consider the question at this level; and perhaps Congress was unable to forge a coalition on either side of the question, and those on each side decided to take their chances with the scheme devised by the agency. For judicial purposes, it matters not which of these things occurred.

Judges are not experts in the field, and are not part of either political branch of the Government. Courts must, in some cases, reconcile competing political interests, but not on the basis of the judges' personal policy preferences. In contrast, an agency to which Congress has delegated policymaking responsibilities may, within the limits of that delegation, properly rely upon the incumbent administration's views of wise policy to inform its judgments. While agencies are not directly accountable to the people, the Chief Executive is, and it is entirely appropriate for this political branch of the Government to make such policy choices— resolving the competing interests which Congress itself either inadvert-

ently did not resolve, or intentionally left to be resolved by the agency
charged with the administration of the statute in light of everyday realities.

When a challenge to an agency construction of a statutory provision, fairly conceptualized, really centers on the wisdom of the agency's
policy, rather than whether it is a reasonable choice within a gap left
open by Congress, the challenge must fail. In such a case, federal judges—
who have no constituency—have a duty to respect legitimate policy choices
made by those who do. The responsibilities for assessing the wisdom of
such policy choices and resolving the struggle between competing views
of the public interest are not judicial ones: "Our Constitution vests such
responsibilities in the political branches." TVA v. Hill, 437 U.S. 153, 195
(1978).

We hold that the EPA's definition of the term "source" is a permissible construction of the statute which seeks to accommodate progress
in reducing air pollution with economic growth. "The Regulations which
the Administrator has adopted provide what the agency could allowably
view as . . . [an] effective reconciliation of these twofold ends. . . ."
United States v. Shimer, 367 U.S., at 383.

The judgment of the Court of Appeals is reversed.

NOTES AND QUESTIONS

1. The judicial review provisions of the Administrative Procedure
Act provide that reviewing courts are to "decide all relevant questions
of law, interpret constitutional and statutory provisions, and determine
the meaning or applicability of the terms of an agency action." 5 U.S.C.
§706. Is this consistent with the notion that courts should defer to agency
interpretations of statutes?

2. Judicial deference to the decisions of administrative agencies
stems in part from notions of agency expertise. To what extent are such
notions relevant when the agency is not making complicated technical
or scientific judgments, but rather is engaging in statutory interpretation? Who should be more "expert" at divining the intent of Congress—
courts or agencies?

3. *Chevron* was decided by a unanimous Supreme Court, though
only six justices participated in the decision. The decision's two-step
analytical framework appears to have been endorsed by all the Justices,
although there continue to be disagreements as to its precise meaning
and its application. However, in order to apply this analysis, courts still
must determine whether a statute is ambiguous (Step 1)—and statutory
ambiguity often is in the eye of the beholder, as decisions subsequent to
Chevron make clear. In Chemical Manufacturers Association v. Natural
Resources Defense Council, 470 U.S. 116 (1985), the Supreme Court

split 5-4 on the question whether or not the word "modified" in the Clean Water Act was ambiguous. In Board of Governors v. Dimension Financial Corp., 474 U.S. 361 (1986), the Supreme Court unanimously rejected the Federal Reserve Board's interpretation of the term "bank" by concluding that the term was clear and unambiguous.

4. Recall the D.C. Circuit's decision in American Mining Congress v. EPA, 824 F.2d 1177 (D.C. Cir. 1987), which dealt with EPA's complicated definition of the term "solid waste" in the Resource Conservation and Recovery Act. In that case, the D.C. Circuit rejected the Agency's interpretation of the statutory language. How do you think the D.C. Circuit dealt with *Chevron* in deciding the *American Mining Congress* case? The author of the *American Mining Congress* decision, former judge and now Solicitor General Kenneth W. Starr, made the following comments about *Chevron* shortly before hearing the *American Mining Congress* case:

> One is thus brought to wonder if there can be, other than in banking regulation, a clear and unambiguous statute. Is the world really filled with . . . "quiche" that is subject to regulation by [a] National Quiche Commission, even though the NQC is regulating what all of us, outside of administrative law at least, would think of as pizzas and frisbees? After all, no lesser light than Chief Justice Hughes found the term "foreign country" to be inherently ambiguous. And in a relativistic age where one still hears an occasional jeremiad against cultural imperialism, whatever that is, perhaps nothing does have clear meaning other than the word "bank." [Judicial Review of Administrative Action in a Conservative Era, 39 Admin. L. Rev. 353, 362 (1987).]

In light of these sentiments, what do you think accounts for Judge Starr's subsequent decision not to defer to EPA's interpretation of the meaning of the term "solid waste" in RCRA, as discussed in Chapter 3? Should it make a difference for purposes of applying the *Chevron* test whether the agency interpretation primarily implicates the agency's managerial or regulatory judgment as opposed to the agency's core powers?

5. While *Chevron* appears to be popular with judges, academicians have been more critical of it. Professor Sunstein and others have argued that *Chevron* not only will promote confusion, but it also threatens to undermine separation of powers principles. Professor Sunstein argues that

> those who are limited in their authority by law should not be the judge of those limits. Administrative agencies are constrained by statute, that is, law, and the mere fact that the statute is ambiguous shouldn't give the agency, of all people, the authority to decide on the meaning of the limitation. The cute way in which it's sometimes put is that foxes shouldn't guard henhouses. If *Chevron* is taken to mean that agencies judge the scope of their own authority, then one has precisely that problem. [Id.]

Professor Sunstein notes that there are differences between "pure questions of law, questions that turn only on the meaning of statutes, and mixed questions of law and fact, as to which agency expertise is far more relevant." Deference to agencies is more appropriate in dealing with mixed questions of law and fact than it is in deciding pure questions of law, according to Professor Sunstein. Into which of these categories would you place the question of the proper definition of the statutory term "solid waste"?

6. In Dole v. United Steelworkers, Justice White, joined by Chief Justice Rehnquist, expressly rejected the "foxes guarding the chicken coop" criticism of *Chevron*. Justice White argued that the Court has never accepted that argument and cited Justice Scalia's concurrence in Mississippi Power & Light Co. v. Mississippi ex rel. Moore, 487 U.S. 354, 377 (1988), as an excellent explanation of the reasons for rejecting it. Moreover, he noted a number of decisions subsequent to *Chevron* in which the Court had deferred to agency interpretations of their jurisdictional authority including Massachusetts v. Morash, 490 U.S. 107, 116-118 (1989); K Mart Corp. v. Cartier, Inc., 486 U.S. 281, 292-293 (1988); EEOC v. Commercial Office Products Co., 486 U.S. 107, 114-116 (1988); NLRB v. Food & Commercial Workers, 484 U.S. 112, 123-128 (1987); Japan Whaling Association v. American Cetacean Society, 478 U.S. 221, 233 (1986); Commodity Futures Trading Commission v. Schor, 478 U.S. 833, 845 (1986); and Chemical Manufacturers Assn. v. Natural Resources Defense Council, Inc., 470 U.S. 116, 125-126 (1985). Dole v. United Steelworkers, 494 U.S. 26, 54-55 (1990) (White, J., dissenting). In Dole v. United Steelworkers Justice Scalia joined the majority opinion finding that the Paperwork Reduction Act unambiguously did not authorize OMB review of OSHA's hazard communication standard.

7. How, if at all, do you think *Chevron* has affected judicial review of decisions by administrative agencies? *Chevron* must be the most frequently cited decision in administrative law cases. Shortly after its sixth birthday *Chevron* had been cited more than 1,000 times, with the number of citations to it continuing to increase rapidly. Sunstein, Law and Administration After *Chevron*, 90 Colum. L. Rev. 2071, 2074-2075 (1990). Yet one must be careful about casually assuming that its popularity as a point of reference for judicial opinions is a true measure of its impact. *Chevron* does not seem to have insulated agency interpretations of statutes from effective judicial review. In the first four years after *Chevron* was decided, the Supreme Court rejected an administrative agency's interpretation of a statutory provision in six cases. In addition to striking down the Federal Reserve Board interpretation of the term "bank" in *Dimension Financial*, the Court in Immigration and Naturalization Service v. Cardoza-Fonseca, 408 U.S. 421 (1988), rejected INS's interpretation of the term "well founded fear" of persecution for purposes of determining when asylum may be granted to refugees. In doing so, the Court

suggested that agencies may be entitled to less deference when their decisions are based on pure questions of statutory interpretation (such as whether the "well founded fear" standard of the Refugee Act is the same as in the Immigration and Nationality Act) than with respect to questions of interpretation that arise in the application of the statute to a particular set of facts.

8. Empirical studies of the impact of *Chevron* provide some interesting data. Peter Schuck and Donald Elliott found a pronounced increase in agency affirmances by the federal courts of appeal in the immediate aftermath of *Chevron*. Their data showed that in the six-month period of 1984 immediately prior to the *Chevron* decision, agency decisions were affirmed by reviewing courts in 70.9 percent of cases, while 14.4 percent were reversed and 14.4 percent were remanded to the agencies. In a six-month period in 1985 after *Chevron*, affirmances jumped to 81.3 percent of all cases, while reversals dropped to 8.2 percent and remands to 9.3 percent. Schuck and Elliott, To the *Chevron* Station: An Empirical Study of Federal Administrative Law, 1990 Duke L.J. 984. In order to test whether these changes persisted, particularly after *Cardoza-Fonseca,* Schuck and Elliot examined a sample of cases in March and April 1988. They found that the affirmance rate had receded to 75 percent, while reversals had held steady at 8.2 percent and remands had risen to 17.0 percent. While Schuck and Elliot note that this result "suggests the tantalizing hypothesis that the results of judicial review over large numbers of cases may be far more sensitive to subtle changes in legal doctrine than we had anticipated," they conclude that it is not possible to exclude other factors that may have changed over time. A more striking change was observed by Schuck and Elliot when the data were analyzed by agency groupings. They found that the rate of reversals and remands for health, safety, and environmental agencies (EPA, NRC, FDA, OSHA, and the Federal Mine Safety and Health Review Commission) had declined from 28 percent to 6 percent.

In a more recent study of the Supreme Court's use of *Chevron,* Thomas Merrill finds it "clear that *Chevron* is often ignored by the Supreme Court." Merrill, Judicial Deference to Executive Precedent, 101 Yale L.J. 969, 970 (1992). Statistics compiled by Professor Merrill indicate that *Chevron*'s two-step framework has been used in only about half of the cases in which the Court has recognized that a question of deference to an agency interpretation is presented. Surprisingly, he finds that "in recent Terms the application of *Chevron* has resulted in *less* deference to executive interpretations than was the case in the pre-*Chevron* era." Id. Merrill attributes that result to "the Court's reluctance to embrace the draconian implications of the doctrine for the balance of power among the branches, and to practical problems generated by its all-or-nothing approach to the deference question." Id.

9. Noting that "*Chevron* has altered the distribution of national

powers among courts, Congress, and administrative agencies" in an extraordinarily broad range of areas, Professor Sunstein views *Chevron* as "one of the very few defining cases in the last twenty years of American public law." He argues that *Chevron*, along with *Vermont Yankee* and recent efforts to revive serious limits on standing, is representative of a revival of the old notion that law and administration are incompatible. Sunstein, Law and Administration After *Chevron*, 90 Colum. L. Rev. 2071, 2075 (1990). Professor Sunstein maintains that *Chevron* should only apply in cases where Congress has delegated law-making authority to agencies, and thus it should not serve as a broad mandate for automatic deference to agency interpretations in many contexts.

10. *Chevron* does not guarantee that agencies will prevail when regulations are challenged. Courts continue to remand agency rules on a variety of grounds. Consider *Corrosion Proof Fittings*, page 557; see also Competitive Enterprise Institute v. NHTSA, — F.2d — (D.C. Cir. 1992) (NHTSA failed to explain why lowering the corporate average fuel economy standard would not save lives, invoking the rationale of *State Farm*, page 745)). In Shell Oil v. EPA, 950 F.2d 741 (D.C. Cir. 1991), a 13-year-old procedural violation (inadequate notice and opportunity for comment when rules were proposed) is requiring reconsideration of a major part of the RCRA regulatory program. Agencies also have been found to transgress even *Chevron*'s generous bounds of interpretation. See the *Lockout/Tagout* decision, page 545; and *American Mining Congress*, page 229. Coupled with a renewed threat to invalidate environmental regulations as "takings," see pages 962-963, these cases have led some to conclude that the federal courts are becoming increasingly hostile to environmental regulation. See, e.g., Schneider, Courthouse Is a Citadel No Longer: U.S. Judges Curb Environmentalists, N.Y. Times, Mar. 22, 1992, at B7.

=6=
‖ *Air Pollution Control* ‖

[T]he clean air bill . . . is an unwise, ill-advised patchwork of legislation that should not be enacted. The cost of the bill will be very high: a report for the Business Roundtable places the cost at more than $50 billion a year, while a vice president at Resources for the Future estimates each American household could spend an additional $300 to $400 annually. Yet, there is little evidence that these new regulations would actually improve the quality of the air. . . . The Clean Air Act's unduly stringent and extremely costly provisions could seriously threaten this nation's economic expansion. . . . [N]ow is not the time to enact legislation with questionable benefits but certain and serious economic costs.

> —*Letter to President Bush from seven prominent economists,*
> *October 1990*

This restores America's place as a world leader in environmental protection. . . . For the first time, we've moved away from the red tape, bureaucratic approach of the past. . . . [The new Clean Air Act] offers incentives, choice, and flexibility for industry to find the best solutions, all in the context of continued economic growth.

> —*George Bush**

Efforts to control air pollution have in many respects been the most difficult and long-standing environmental struggle in the United States. As discussed in Chapter 2, early in this century the United States Supreme Court was writing its own injunction to limit sulfur dioxide emissions that crossed state lines. Local air pollution regulations are among the oldest environmental laws, and the Clean Air Act of 1970 was the first of the modern-era federal regulatory statutes. Much of EPA's early history revolved around efforts to implement the Act, which greatly influenced other environmental legislation that followed.

---

*Remarks on signing the Clean Air Act Amendments of 1990 (Nov. 15, 1990).

Despite nearly 20 years of regulatory experience and several hundred billion dollars' worth of pollution control expenditures, air quality problems remain near the top of the environmental agenda. More than 74 million people—nearly one-third of the population of the United States—live in areas that failed to meet air quality standards during 1990. Perhaps no problem more directly confronts the way we live; today's cars each emit much less pollution than those of 1970, but the number of vehicle-miles traveled has increased by 55 percent. Air pollution in Los Angeles has become so pervasive that one government proposal to achieve compliance with air quality standards features a ban on gasoline-powered vehicles (including lawnmowers) by the year 2007, limits on car ownership, a prohibition on free parking, and other drastic measures to force people out of their cars.

After more than a decade of legislative gridlock Congress adopted the Clean Air Act Amendments of 1990, the most far-reaching environmental legislation in history. Congress approved these Amendments by overwhelming bipartisan majorities in the midst of an international crisis that ultimately led to war and despite warnings by economists that the measure would cost the economy more than $50 billion per year. The more than 700 pages of language enacted into law include measures that dictate fundamental changes in the products we use, the cars we drive, and the fuels they burn. The Amendments subject hundreds of thousands of small businesses to regulation for the first time. They require unprecedented regulatory activity by EPA, posing an immense challenge to conventional regulatory procedures. The results of this experience will have enormous influence in shaping the future of environmental regulation.

The 1990 Amendments represent the culmination of a bitter decade-long struggle that pitted region against region, industry against industry, and federal authority against state authority. Rich lessons can be derived from this legislative struggle and from the decades of experience with the former law. The complex balance of authority between federal and state governments on which the Act relies can provide important insights into issues of federalism. The development of the Act's emissions trading provisions illuminates the battle over the use of economic incentives in environmental regulation. The Act's technology-forcing provisions have important lessons for regulatory policy and for the role of government in our mixed economy. Before exploring these issues, we first consider the nature of the air pollution problem and the structure of the Clean Air Act.

A. THE AIR POLLUTION PROBLEM

Controlling air pollution is a multidimensional challenge. The number of potentially harmful residuals that can be discharged as air pollutants is extremely large. Some of these pollutants are highly mobile; others are chemically interactive. Each individual source can emit many different pollutants, and some of the residuals of concern are produced in vast quantities by numerous sources and diverse types of sources. Each of these characteristics of the air pollution problem creates difficulties for a regulatory regime.

A useful starting point for analysis of the air pollution problem is to consider the problems that air pollutants can cause and where these pollutants originate. The Clean Air Act distinguishes among several different kinds of pollutants. Here we provide a brief overview of the problems presented by what might be considered the conventional air pollutants, those that have been studied for the longest period of time: carbon monoxide, sulfur dioxide, oxides of nitrogen, volatile organic compounds, particulates, and lead. Today these are all regulated under sections 108 and 109 of the Act, either as so-called criteria pollutants or as precursors to such pollutants. See section 6C1, below. Hazardous air pollutants are examined in section I, the problems associated with acid deposition in section F, and pollutants that affect the upper atmosphere in Chapter 9.

The following general summary of the effects of air pollutants, written in 1977 by Alfred Kneese, is still valid today:

> The direct and observable effects of these [pollutants] on people (and other forms of life) range in severity from the lethal to the merely annoying. Except for extreme air pollution episodes, fatalities are not, as a rule, directly traceable individually to deterioration in air quality. Instead, air pollution is an environmental stress that, in conjunction with a number of other environmental stresses, tends to increase the incidence and seriousness of a variety of diseases, including lung cancer, emphysema, tuberculosis, pneumonia, bronchitis, asthma, and even the common cold. Acute episodes of poor air quality, that is, short periods of high concentrations of residuals, have been correlated with increased death rates and increased rates of hospital admissions. . . . But the most important health effects appear to be associated with chronic exposure, that is, exposure of relatively low concentrations for long periods of time, conditions that exist in most large cities. [A. Kneese, Economics and the Environment 33-34 (1977).]

While fatalities or severe health problems caused by air pollution are rarely obvious, acute episodes of severe exposures have brought them to public attention. For example, on October 26, 1948, residents of

Donora, Pennsylvania awoke to find that a blanket of warm air above a cool air mass had trapped the pollutants emitted from the town's factories. The deadly inversion lasted for four days. Within two days, visibility had been sharply reduced and the town's doctors were flooded with people with breathing difficulties. Twenty people and numerous animals died; more than half of the town's 12,000 residents became ill. W. A. Andrews, ed., Environmental Pollution 135 (1972).

Such episodes have become rare in the United States, but acute exposures are a serious problem in a growing number of developing countries. More than two-thirds of the global urban population, mostly in developing countries, breathes air that has unhealthy levels of particulate matter at least part of the year, and major cities outside the United States experience very high average concentrations, with peak levels higher still. Tehran and Calcutta, for example, averaged particulate levels nearly 10 times higher than those of New York City during a four-year period (1976-1980) studied by the United Nations. Conditions in some of the major cities of Eastern Europe are also extremely poor. See World Resources Institute, World Resources 1990-91, at 201-216. See also French, Eastern Europe's Clean Break with the Past, 1991 World Watch 21-27 (Mar.-April 1991); J. Russell, Environmental Issues in Eastern Europe: Setting an Agenda (Royal Institute of International Affairs, 1990); United Nations Environment Programme and World Health Organization, Monitoring the Environment: An Assessment of Urban Air Quality, 31 Environment 6 (1989).

Even the lower levels of air pollution routinely experienced in the United States still contribute to premature mortality. Joel Schwartz, an EPA scientist, has discovered a striking correlation between particulate levels in urban areas and deaths from respiratory and cardiovascular diseases. What is striking about this data is that the correlation holds even for particulate levels well below the existing national standard. On the basis of this data, Schwartz estimates that particulates are responsible for three percent of all deaths in the United States, or 60,000 deaths each year. Airborne Particulates Greatly Contribute to About 60,000 Deaths Annually, Study Says, 22 Env. Rep. 131 (May 17, 1991); Schwartz, Particulate Air Pollution and Daily Mortality in Detroit, 56 Env. Res. 204 (1991); Schwartz and Marcus, Mortality and Air Pollution in London: A Time Series Analysis, 131 Am. J. Epid. 185 (1990).

Some of the other major adverse health effects associated with the criteria pollutants and the hazardous air pollutants initially regulated by EPA are summarized in Figure 6.1. In addition to those effects listed, carbon monoxide can impair mental functions, sulfur oxides can cause damage to vegetation and exterior paints, nitrogen oxides can reduce growth in plants, and various particulates can cause serious damage to animals and crops. Volatile organic compounds (VOCs) are not themselves identified on the chart. These compounds, a subset of the hydro-

FIGURE 6.1
Health Effects of the Regulated Air Pollutants

Criteria pollutants	*Health concerns*
Ozone	Respiratory tract problems such as difficult breathing and reduced lung function. Asthma, eye irritation, nasal congestion, reduced resistance to infection, and possibly premature aging of lung tissue
Particulate matter	Eye and throat irritation, bronchitis, lung damage, and impaired visibility
Carbon monoxide	Ability of blood to carry oxygen impaired. Cardiovascular, nervous, and pulmonary systems affected
Sulfur dioxide	Respiratory tract problems; permanent harm to lung tissue
Lead	Retardation and brain damage, especially in children
Nitrogen dioxide	Respiratory illness and lung damage
Hazardous air pollutants	
Asbestos	A variety of lung diseases, particularly lung cancer
Beryllium	Primary lung disease, although also affects liver, spleen, kidneys, and lymph glands
Mercury	Several areas of the brain as well as the kidneys and bowels affected
Vinyl chloride	Lung and liver cancer
Arsenic	Cancer
Radionuclides	Cancer
Benzene	Leukemia
Coke oven emissions	Respiratory cancer

carbons contained in gasoline, are of concern because in the atmosphere they react with oxides of nitrogen to produce photochemical smog. Ozone, one of the criteria pollutants, is used as the indicator for such smog.

Addressing these health effects, which are associated with chronic exposures, presents problems for regulators attempting to achieve air pollution levels that will protect the "public health." Populations move, air pollutants interact, and levels of pollution are not constant. Factors other than chronic exposure to air pollution also are associated with many of the health effects, especially the respiratory diseases. Lifestyle factors, particularly smoking, are strong contributors. In such circumstances it is difficult to determine how to establish air pollution controls sufficient to protect the public health.

Four of the conventional pollutants—carbon monoxide, volatile organic compounds, oxides of nitrogen, and lead—are produced by the internal combustion engines that drive cars and trucks. Such engines are the primary sources of carbon monoxide, although all fossil fuel combustion processes, including utility and other industrial boilers, produce it to some extent as carbon from the fuels bonds with single oxygen atoms. Oxides of nitrogen are produced by combustion because nitrogen in the air is oxidized by the heat produced during combustion. Unburned as well as partially unburned VOCs escape from internal combustion engines and from oil refineries and chemical plants, as well as from evaporation in gasoline stations and fuel storage areas, dry cleaners, oil-based paint applications, and gas tanks. As auto emission controls have gone into effect, sources other than the internal combustion engine have become the major sources of VOCs.

The major sources of sulfur oxides are coal combustion (and to a lesser extent oil combustion), and the major locations for such combustion are utility power plants, although industrial boilers and residential heating also contribute to emissions. Particulates also originate from these sources, but in certain locations agricultural operations can discharge significant quantities of particulates, as can forest fires. Fugitive dust from mining sites, construction sites, and the like also can be a significant localized source of particulate matter.

The reduction of lead emissions is the singular success story in air pollution control. Through its authority to regulate gasoline additives, EPA has drastically reduced airborne lead in the United States in the last decade. For details on lead emissions and their control, see Chapter 4C1 and 2 and Chapter 4D1.

B.   THE CLEAN AIR ACT: ORIGINS AND PRINCIPLES

The principal statutory authorities for controlling air pollution are contained in the Clean Air Act. While other federal environmental laws can be used to address some aspects of air pollution (e.g., air emissions from hazardous waste disposal facilities are regulated under RCRA, air contaminants in the workplace are regulated under the OSH Act, and the Emergency Planning and Community Right to Know Act requires reporting of toxic air emissions), the Clean Air Act establishes comprehensive sets of measures to control outdoor air pollution throughout the nation.

The Clean Air Act of 1970 was the first of the comprehensive, medium-based, federal regulatory programs created in the 1970s to protect the environment. Because most of these laws emerged from the same congressional committees, the concepts and language adopted in the Clean Air Act provided important precedents for much of the environmental legislation that followed. Before beginning our examination of the Act, however, a brief historical review is in order.

1. Historical Perspective: Pre-1970 Developments

With the industrial growth of the late nineteenth century, air pollution became a serious local problem in many areas. The Georgia v. Tennessee Copper Co. litigation, discussed in Chapter 2, illustrates how virtually uncontrolled emissions from industrial facilities caused such substantial environmental damage that equitable remedies were imposed in common law nuisance actions. Municipal smoke abatement ordinances were among the first environmental regulations adopted in the United States. Chicago, Cincinnati, New York, and Pittsburgh were among the first cities to adopt such regulations in the 1880s and 1890s. A few states also adopted regulations in the nineteenth century, but it was not until 1952 that the first state air pollution control agency was created, by Oregon. EPA, Environmental Progress and Challenges 13 (1988); S. Edelman, The Law of Air Pollution Control (1970). Because of the enormous smog problem created by California's love affair with the automobile, in 1959 California enacted legislation requiring the state Department of Public Health to establish air quality standards and to determine what controls on vehicle emissions would be necessary to comply with them.

The federal government made its first foray into the field with the Air Pollution Control Act of 1955, ch. 360, 69 Stat. 322 (1955). The Act provided for research and technical assistance and authorized the Secretary of Health, Education, and Welfare (HEW) to work toward a better understanding of the causes and effects of air pollution. The Motor Vehicle Act of 1960, 74 Stat. 162 (1960), expanded federal research support to address pollution from motor vehicles. See T. Jorling, The Federal Law of Air Pollution Control, Federal Environmental Law (E. Golgin and T. Guilbert, eds. 1974).

Federal air pollution regulation began with the Clean Air Act of 1963, 42 U.S.C. §§1857-1857l (1964). The Act empowered the Secretary of HEW to define air quality criteria based on scientific studies. The criteria were advisory, but the Secretary could convene a conference of state and local pollution officials in cases where interstate pollution endangered health or welfare. In theory, the conference procedure could provide the basis for a federal abatement action and a cease and desist order. However, by 1970 there had been less than a dozen conferences and only a single enforcement action. J. Esposito, Vanishing Air 118-151 (1970).

Congress first provided for direct regulation of air pollution in the

Motor Vehicle Air Pollution Control Act of 1965. HEW was directed to establish auto emissions standards "giving appropriate consideration to technological feasibility and economic costs." The Agency established standards for model year 1970 that required roughly a 50 percent reduction in hydrocarbons and carbon monoxide. These standards became the baseline for further reductions mandated by Congress in 1970.

The final federal clean air law prior to 1970 was the Air Quality Act of 1967. This Act created a comprehensive federal program for the first time. HEW was directed to define "air quality control regions" reflecting the meteorological and topographical factors that govern air quality. Federal funding was available for states willing to create regional commissions, necessary where air quality regions crossed state boundaries, but none were formed. States were required to adopt ambient air quality standards (typically expressed in terms of a maximum quantity of pollution per unit of time) consistent with the federal criteria of the 1963 Act. The next step was state adoption of implementation plans to meet the standards, subject to HEW approval. The only mechanism for federal enforcement was the conference procedure created in 1963.

AIR POLLUTION CONTROL: A PATHFINDER

The federal Clean Air Act is the principal source of statutory authority for controlling air pollution. Originally enacted in 1963 and amended in 1967, the Act did not provide for comprehensive national regulation until the Clean Air Act Amendments of 1970 were adopted. The 1970 Amendments established the basic program for controlling air pollution that remains in effect today. The Clean Air Act was amended in comprehensive fashion in 1977, and, after a long legislative struggle, again in 1990.

Although they are the product of more than a decade of legislative debate, the massive Clean Air Act Amendments of 1990 generated remarkably little formal legislative history. Because the conference committee did not complete its work until just before adjournment, Congress simply ran out of time to prepare an elaborate conference report. While the Amendments occupy nearly 100 pages of tiny print in the October 26, 1990 Congressional Record (pp. H13101-13197), the Joint Explanatory Statement of the Committee of Conference occupies less than 7 pages (H13197-13203). A more detailed explanation of the legislation was inserted into the October 27, 1990 Congressional Record by Senator Baucus, the floor manager of the legislation (S16969-16983).

A useful guide to the 1990 Amendments is J. Quarles

and W. H. Lewis, Jr., The NEW Clean Air Act: A Guide to the Clean Air Program as Amended in 1990 (1990), available from the Washington, D.C. office of Morgan, Lewis & Bockius. The guide contains checklists for compliance planning and appendices listing likely nonattainment areas for various pollutants, relevant guidance documents, the 189 hazardous air pollutants, and the potential source categories to be regulated under amended section 112.

EPA has prepared materials and has hosted video teleconferences to educate the public about the provisions of the new Clean Air Act Amendments. The resource materials for these teleconferences include a 24-page summary of the new amendments. EPA, Legal Winds of Change: Business and the New Clean Air Act (Videoconference Resource Materials, Nov. 28, 1990).

EPA regulations implementing the Clean Air Act, which are likely to expand dramatically in coming years, are found at 40 C.F.R. parts 50-87.

To understand why the Clean Air Act has become such a complex beast, it is important to appreciate its historical background. A useful survey of how the federal role in air pollution control evolved is contained in J. Krier and E. Ursin, Pollution and Policy (1977). An early history of the Act that emphasizes the many institutional actors that influenced its implementation is R. Shep Melnick, Regulation and the Courts: The Case of the Clean Air Act (Brookings 1983). William Pederson's classic article, Why the Clean Air Act Works Badly, 199 U. Pa. L. Rev. 1059 (1981), spurred interest in the development of the kind of permit program now incorporated in the 1990 Amendments. Craig Oren has provided the most detailed guide to the impenetrable PSD provisions of the Act. Oren, Prevention of Significant Deterioration: Control-Compelling Versus Site-Shifting, 74 Iowa L. Rev. 1 (1988); Oren, Detail and Delegation: A Study in Statutory Specificity, 15 Colum. J. Envtl. L. 143 (1990).

2. The Clean Air Act: 1970 to 1990

Notwithstanding the clear influence of earlier statutes, the Clean Air Act of 1970 marked a major change in priorities, emphasis, and approach. The slow pace of federal enforcement had become an embarrassment publicized by Ralph Nader and echoed in political campaign speeches. The Act replaced the system of state air quality standards based on HEW health criteria with provisions mandating uniform, national standards based on the criteria documents. States were left with the responsibility to issue implementation plans, but the newly created EPA was required to promulgate a plan if the one proposed by a state was found to be inadequate. EPA was also directed to set nationally uniform emissions limits for major new stationary sources. Finally, the discretionary process for control of vehicle emissions was drastically limited; Congress required a 90 percent reduction in existing auto pollutant levels by the 1976 model year, subject only to the possibility of a one-year extension.

Why did Congress depart so markedly from its prior approach? No doubt political considerations played a major role. The Democratically controlled Congress stood to benefit, and Senator Muskie, the Act's principal author, was considered the leading candidate to oppose President Nixon, a Republican, in the 1972 elections. The difficulties associated with implementing the law were Nixon's problem. On the other hand, there was less opposition to federal standards than one might have expected. While the automobile industry was not happy with stringent regulation, it preferred a preemptive federal law to the possibility of inconsistent state regulations.

Interestingly, another contributing factor may have been the *absence* of strong environmental lobbying groups. That absence may have made Muskie and Nixon face a "politicians' dilemma" (a kind of prisoners' dilemma—see page 47, above) that created incentives for them "to pursue a less than ideal outcome in order to avoid an even less desirable result." Elliott, Ackerman, and Millian, Toward a Theory of Statutory Evolution: The Federalization of Environmental Law, 1 J. L. Econ. & Org. 313 (1985). In this instance, Nixon and Muskie were arguably "prisoners" to a bargaining situation in which neither could afford to take the risk of being viewed as weak on the environment with the approach of a presidential race. Without a strong environmental group to sanction a "reasonable" bill, Elliott et al. argue that the two candidates could only show strength by proposing tougher and tougher legislation.

In 1977 Congress amended the Act to address the many areas of the country that had failed to come into compliance with the national ambient air quality standards. In Part D of Title I of the Act Congress imposed a host of new measures designed to ensure that nonattainment areas would soon come into compliance with the national standards. The failure of these provisions to achieve this goal, which eventually led to comprehensive revisions in the 1990 Amendments, is considered in section E below. Congress also adopted the prevention of significant deterioration (PSD) program in Part C of Title I of the Act. The PSD provisions impose a complicated set of additional requirements applicable to limit air pollution in areas with air quality better than the NAAQS. The operation of these provisions is taken up below in section H. Can you imagine why it was necessary to adopt additional regulations for areas *cleaner* than required by federal standards?

After enactment of the 1977 Amendments, 13 years passed before the Clean Air Act again was amended in comprehensive fashion. As the new deadlines set by the 1977 Amendments came and went, experience with the existing Act made the most convincing case for new legislation. However, the Reagan Administration's ideological opposition to regulation combined with severe regional splits within Congress over acid rain controls produced legislative gridlock. It took a new administration and key leadership changes in Congress to finally break the deadlock with the enactment of the Clean Air Act Amendments of 1990.

A fascinating account of the political jockeying that ultimately produced the Clean Air Act Amendments of 1990 is provided in J. Edelson, A Win for Clean Air, 1991 Envtl. Forum 10-17 (Jan.-Feb. 1991). Key events in this saga included the following: In the summer of 1989, President Bush delivered on his campaign pledge to send comprehensive clean air legislation to Congress. The Bush Administration proposal included many far-reaching provisions, including a 10-million-ton-per-year reduction in sulfur dioxide emissions to combat acid rain, provisions to reduce emissions of hazardous air pollutants by 85 percent, and a clean fuels program that shocked many industry lobbyists. With the leadership in Congress committed to enacting a new law (Robert Byrd of West Virgina, who had opposed acid rain controls for fear of harming his state's coal industry, had been replaced as Senate Majority Leader by George Mitchell of Maine), the prospects for a new Clean Air Act had improved to the point that industry no longer believed that it could block the legislation.

The Senate Environment and Public Works Committee acted quickly in the fall of 1989. Dominated by environmentally minded senators, the committee reported out a bill with provisions for dealing with ozone nonattainment, acid rain, and hazardous air pollutants that were far more stringent than the administration's bill. Facing the threat of a filibuster by conservative Republicans, Senator Mitchell began six weeks of marathon closed-door negotiations with the administration and a group of senators called the Group of 15. Both industry and environmental lobbyists were excluded from the negotiations, which produced an agreement on a more moderate bill that the participants agreed not to amend on the Senate floor.

During House committee markup in September 1989 a bitter battle broke out between Detroit-area congressman John Dingell, the powerful chairman of the House Energy and Commerce Committee and an auto industry ally, and Los Angeles area congressman Henry Waxman, chairman of that committee's Health and Environment subcommittee and a champion of strict air pollution controls. A compromise ultimately was reached that provided for stringent new auto emission standards but delayed their implementation. However, a dispute concerning how to ease the burden of new acid rain controls on Midwestern utilities blocked the legislation's progress for several months.

After narrowly defeating an amendment to relax provisions establishing a national permit program for sources of air pollution, the Senate overwhelmingly approved its bill on April 3, 1990. The House approved its version of the bill by an overwhelming margin on May 23, 1990. A conference committee of seven senators and 140 House members then began months of negotiations to agree on a single bill. For the most part the negotiations took place behind closed doors. As one of the negotiators noted, "The legislation was so intricate, so complicated, so divided on geographic, political, and economic levels, it would have been nearly impossible to publicly debate all the issues." Id. at 14. By the time Congress recessed in August 1990, the conferees had only succeeded in reaching agreement on one relatively uncontroversial topic—phasing out ozone-depleting chlorofluorocarbons.

Thus in the end the resolution of more than a decade of intense debate turned on political maneuvering in a conference committee sometimes holding all-night meetings throughout the last eight weeks of the session. Facing a drop-dead deadline, the conference committee met until 5:00 A.M. on October 22, 1990. The result was a massive body of complicated legislation for which there is virtually no formal legislative history because there was no time to prepare a conference report. The House approved the conference bill by a vote of 401-25 on October 26. The Senate concurred by a vote of 89-10 on October 27. President Bush signed the legislation on November 15, 1990.

The 1990 Amendments address several important deficiencies in the prior Act by imposing new requirements for areas out of compliance with air quality standards, a new program to control hazardous air pollutants, an acid rain control program, and new controls on mobile sources and the fuels they burn. The 700-page bill that resulted has been termed "one of the most complex pieces of regulatory legislation . . . ever adopted, and one of the most impenetrable." Nickel, Now, the Race to Regulate, 1991 Envtl. Forum 18-22 (Jan.-Feb. 1991). The Amendments imply another round of federal regulation, state implementation, and source compliance with potential for litigation in each state. The Environmental Protection Agency is mandated to complete more than 100 rulemakings within two years, including the creation of a new permit program for existing stationary sources. One important amendment created a clean fuels program for mobile sources. For a useful overview, see J. Quarles and W. Lewis, The NEW Clean Air Act: A Guide to the Clean Air Program as Amended in 1990 (1990). The Amendments continue the "leapfrog" relationship of the federal environmental statutes, in which the experience gained from one statute is subsequently incorporated in others. Jorling, The Federal Law of Air Pollution Control, in Federal Environmental Law 1058, 1060 (E. Dolgin and T. Guilbert, eds. 1974).

MAJOR PROVISIONS OF THE CLEAN AIR ACT

TITLE I Section 108: requires EPA to identify "air pollutants" anticipated to endanger public health or welfare and to publish air quality criteria.

Section 109: requires EPA to adopt nationally uniform ambient air quality standards (NAAQSs) for criteria air pollutants. *1° + 2°*

Section 110: requires states to develop and submit to EPA for approval state implementation plans (SIPs) specifying measures to assure that air quality within each state meets the NAAQS. *can sell emissions right* *§14 monitoring*

Section 111: requires EPA to establish nationally uniform, technology-based standards for major new stationary sources of air pollution—New Source Performance Standards (NSPSs).

Section 112: mandates technology-based standards to reduce listed hazardous air emissions from major sources in designated industrial categories, with additional regulation possible if necessary to protect public health with an "ample margin of safety." *§751 stat* *855 this book* *-look at health not environment §(2) p.749 stat*

Part C (Sections 160-169A): specifies requirements to prevent significant deterioration of air quality (PSD) for areas with air quality that exceeds the NAAQSs.

Part D (Sections 171-178): specifies requirements for areas that fail to meet the NAAQSs (nonattainment areas).

TITLE II (Sections 202-216): requires EPA to establish nationally uniform emissions standards for automobiles and light trucks that manufacturers must meet by strict deadlines.

TITLE III Section 304: authorizes citizen suits against violators of emissions standards and against the EPA administrator for failure to perform nondiscretionary duties.

Section 307: authorizes judicial review of nationally applicable EPA actions exclusively in the U.S. Court of Appeals for the District of Columbia.

TITLE IV (Sections 401-416): creates a system of marketable allowances for sulfur dioxide emissions from power plants and major industrial sources to reduce acid precipitation.

TITLE V (Sections 501-507): requires permits for all major industrial sources with state administration and federal oversight.

TITLE VI (Sections 601-617): establishes a program for controlling substances that contribute to depletion of stratospheric ozone.

3.   *The Clean Air Act Today*

As originally enacted, the Clean Air Act of 1970 was a complicated piece of legislation. It has become more so as a result of subsequent amendments, including the major amendments of 1977 and of 1990. Before delving into the details, you would do well to have in mind the general structure of the statute, which has remained relatively stable throughout.

In 1970 the federal government assumed responsibility for setting four major types of standards. EPA was directed to: (1) establish *nationally uniform ambient air quality standards* (NAAQSs) for pollutants that EPA determined came from numerous or diverse sources and that "may reasonably be anticipated to endanger public health or welfare" (these are called the "criteria pollutants" because they satisfy the criteria identified in section 108 of the Act) (§§108, 109); (2) establish *new source performance standards* for categories of pollution sources that contribute significantly to health- or welfare-endangering air pollution (§111); (3) control mobile sources—automobiles, buses, and trucks (§§202-234)—by establishing *vehicle emissions standards* and by regulating *fuel content* (in some instances, Congress itself has enacted the exact numerical limitations for mobile source emissions and fuel content); and (4) establish *national emission standards* for existing sources of hazardous air pollutants, pollutants thought to pose a particularly acute danger to public health (§112).

The major responsibility delegated to—or left with—the states is the responsibility to figure out precisely how to achieve the NAAQSs. Section 110 of the Act requires states to prepare, and to update, a State Implementation Plan (SIP) that is adequate to assure that each air quality control region within the state will come into compliance with the NAAQSs by a specified date. If a state fails to prepare a satisfactory plan, the EPA is instructed to prepare one for it, as a last resort.

The most significant addition of the 1977 Amendments was the statutory separation of the country into areas that were not yet achieving the NAAQSs ("nonattainment areas") and those in which air quality was better than the ambient standards ("PSD" areas, for "prevention of significant deterioration").

Regions may be nonattainment for one of the criteria pollutants but not others, and frequently are. The significance of being designated nonattainment under the 1977 Amendments is that the state is required to enact a SIP that imposes strict limitations on the construction of new or modified sources that would affect air quality in the region and also to retrofit Reasonably Available Control Technology (RACT) (as well as any other pollution controls needed to attain the NAAQSs) on existing sources. New sources must meet the toughest of all standards, those requiring Lowest Achievable Emission Rate (LAER), must show that any other sources owned by the new source owner comply with the existing SIP, and must offset new pollution from the source by ensuring reductions of pollution from existing sources (§§171-178).

PSD regions are classified into one of three subclasses, each of which places limits on the permissible increases in pollution, over a baseline that is to be determined when the first PSD permit is received by the state. Major new sources must employ Best Available Control Technology (BACT) and supply advance verification, typically through the use of computer modeling, that the added pollution will not exceed the allowable increase, or increment (§§161-169).

In addition, the 1977 Amendments added certain visibility protections in national parks and other federal areas where visibility is found to have special value (§169A).

The 1990 Amendments add further complications. The Amendments adjust existing mobile source standards, make significant changes in the nonattainment and PSD programs, and fundamentally alter the design of the hazardous air pollutants program. In addition, the Amendments add a new program for the reduction of acid rain (Title IV) and initiate an air emissions permitting program for major sources (Title V). They also expand EPA's authority to impose administrative penalties for minor violations, stiffen potential criminal penalties, and expand the grounds for citizen suits.

The 1990 Amendments also reflect several potentially significant conceptual adjustments. One involves an expanded deployment of incentive-based regulatory techniques, most notably the acid rain reduction program. A second involves the recognition that end-of-the-pipe controls, whether they be at the end of an automobile tailpipe or at the end of a factory's smokestack, are going to be inadequate to achieve the NAAQSs in some major population centers. So, for example, Title I of the Amendments requires some nonattainment areas to implement work-related vehicle trip reduction programs (such as car and van pooling), to participate in a clean fuels program, or to require utilities to switch to low-pollution fuels. Likewise, Title II, in addition to making changes in existing emissions standards for new vehicles, also implements a clean fuels program to ensure the availability of alternative fuels for new production vehicles, as well as instituting a program to encourage the development of low-emissions vehicles.

C. NATIONAL AMBIENT AIR QUALITY STANDARDS

In the next three sections we examine the goal that has been at the heart of the Clean Air Act since 1970: achieving air quality levels throughout the country that protect the public health and welfare, the principal regulatory mechanism that was to achieve this goal, the state implementation plans, and, finally, the subsequent struggles of EPA and the Congress to cope with failure—deciding what to do about areas of the country that have not yet attained the required air quality levels.

The idea of setting national ambient air quality standards (NAAQSs) and then having the states decide how to control local pollution sources so as to meet those standards is deceptively simple. As you study the following materials, try to appreciate how complicated each step in this process actually is. Should Congress have anticipated the difficulties and written legislation that would have coped with them better? Do the difficulties suggest that these simple ideas are conceptually flawed and should be abandoned? If so, what principles should guide the nation's air pollution policies? Keep your eye on these questions as you are introduced into the intricacies of the Clean Air Act.

Establishing NAAQSs

Section 109 of the Clean Air Act requires the EPA administrator to set primary NAAQSs at the level "which in the judgment of the Administrator, based on [the ambient air quality] criteria and allowing an adequate margin of safety, are requisite to protect the public health." The air quality criteria are supposed to "accurately reflect the latest scientific knowledge useful in indicating the kind and extent of all identifiable effects on public health or welfare which may be expected from the presence of such pollutant in the ambient air," CAA §108(a)(2).

Each step in this process is difficult and controversial. Scientific data are often lacking or inconsistent. EPA often has to interpret very limited evidence of adverse health effects based on data drawn from a tiny portion of the population exposed to certain pollutants. These health effects may vary depending on both the magnitude and the duration of exposures. The very idea of a health effect is also not fixed. Is a "health effect" any detectable change in blood chemistry, or only changes proved to have an adverse effect on bodily functions? What populations should be used as the measure of effects, given that small children and the elderly may be more susceptible to effects of air pollution? Should it matter that most human exposure to a particular air pollutant is from non-air sources? What constitutes a margin of safety if there is no known threshold for a particular pollutant?

The answer to each of these questions is crucial, because the ambient air quality standards serve as the basis for both short-term and longer-term exposure limits applicable to the entire nation, with potentially billions of dollars in industry control costs dependent on the outcome.

The regulatory burden involved in establishing a NAAQS is so demanding that EPA has strong incentives to avoid making frequent changes in such standards, much less to promulgate new ones. Once EPA promulgates an ambient standard, every SIP must be amended and reviewed. At the time of enactment of the Act in 1970, air quality criteria already had been promulgated for five major pollutants: sulfur oxides, particulates, carbon monoxide, hydrocarbons, and photochemical oxidants. A sixth, nitrogen oxides, was added by EPA in 1971. Only one other pollutant, lead, has been added since then, as a result of a citizen suit. NRDC v. Train, 545 F.2d 320 (2d Cir. 1976). Lead was a unique case because EPA had formally recognized the health risk of airborne lead when it promulgated regulations under section 211 to limit lead in gasoline. In this situation, the court concluded that EPA had a nondiscretionary duty to set national ambient standards. More recent litigation suggests some uncertainty as to the specific actions necessary to trigger nondiscretionary duties. See, e.g., Thomas v. New York, 802 F.2d 1443 (D.C. Cir. 1986). The existing NAAQSs are listed in Figure 6.2.

Although the NAAQSs are rarely changed, they are almost always under review as new scientific evidence appears. We consider an example of this administrative review process below. As of 1992, evidence was under review indicating the possible need for alternate averaging times for ozone and its effects on health; new evidence on health effects of carbon monoxide was being considered showing cardiac and fetal effects; changes in the nitrogen oxide standard were under review to address ecological effects; the lead standard was under review to reflect new evidence concerning the impact of lead on blood pressure and neurological and reproductive damage at exposure levels previously thought to be safe; changes in the sulfur dioxide standard were still under consideration based on comments received on the April 1988 proposal (see below); and EPA was considering whether to adopt a secondary standard for fine particulate matter to control visibility impairment (the existing secondary standard is designed to protect public welfare only against soiling and nuisance).

The leading case interpreting sections 108 and 109 is Lead Industries Association v. EPA, 647 F.2d 1130 (D.C. Cir. 1980). After EPA issued its ambient air quality standards for lead, they were challenged by a trade association representing lead producers and users, as well as by several companies. In affirming EPA's standards, the court, in

FIGURE 6.2
National Ambient Air Quality Standards

Pollutant	Primary (health related)		Secondary (welfare related)	
	Averaging time	Concentration	Averaging time	Concentration
Particulates	Annual arithmetic means	50 µg/m³	Annual arithmetic means	50 µg/m³
	24-hour	150 µg/m³	24-hour	150 µg/m³
Sulfur dioxide	Annual arithmetic means	80 µg/m³ (0.03 ppm)	3-hour	1300 µg/m³ (0.50 ppm)
	24-hour	365 µg/m³ (0.14 ppm)		
Carbon monoxide	8-hour	9 ppm (10 µg/m³)	No secondary standard	
	1-hour	35 ppm (40 µg/m³)	No secondary standard	
Nitrogen oxide	Annual arithmetic mean	0.053 ppm (100 µg/m³)	Same as primary	
Ozone	Maximum daily 1-hour average	0.12 ppm (235 µg/m³)	Same as primary	
Lead	Maximum quarterly average	1.5 µg/m³	Same as primary	

an opinion written by Judge Skelly Wright, established several propositions concerning the interpretation of EPA's authority.

First, "the legislative history of the Act . . . shows the Administrator may not consider economic and technological feasibility in setting air quality standards; the absence of any provision requiring consideration of these factors was no accident; it was the result of a deliberate decision by Congress to subordinate such concerns to the achievement of health goals." 647 F.2d at 1149. In the court's view, this interpretation was consistent with the "technology-forcing" nature of the Act.

Second, the court quoted the Senate report accompanying the Act to the effect that the goal in setting standards was to ensure "an absence of adverse effects" and that protecting "the most sensitive groups within the population" was to be a "major consideration" in determining where to set the ambient air standards.

Third, the determination of what constitutes an "adverse effect" was left by Congress to the adminstrator's discretion in the first instance; in exercising that discretion "Congress directed the Adminstrator to err on the side of caution in making the necessary decisions." Specifically, EPA was not limited to protecting against effects that were *clearly* harmful or *clearly* adverse, as the industry petitioners had urged; nor did it have to wait until a "medical consensus" had formed concerning whether an effect was adverse. To require this would be inconsistent with the statute's "precautionary nature." In reaching this conclusion, the court emphasized Congress's use of the "margin of safety" requirement, finding it

> significant that Congress has recently acknowledged that more often than not the "margins of safety" that are incorporated into air quality standards turn out to be very modest or nonexistent, as new information reveals adverse health effects at pollution levels once thought to be harmless. . . . Congress' directive . . . to allow an "adequate margin of safety" alone plainly refutes any suggestion that the Administrator is only authorized to set primary air quality standards which are designed to protect against health effects that are known to be clearly harmful. [Id. at 1154-1155.]

In setting the primary standard at 1.5 $\mu g/m^3$, EPA had based the standard in part on experiments showing that children and women experience increased levels of erythrocyte protoporphyrin, or EP, in their blood at low levels of exposure to lead. EP at sufficiently high levels interferes with the ability of the blood's hemoglobin to secure oxygen in the lungs for distribution to the body, thus causing anemia. However, at the low levels studied in the relevant experiments, the EP-elevation was a "sub-clinical" effect of exposure to lead. That is, it was an effect that could only be detected by laboratory blood tests, because it was not sufficiently high to cause observable ("clinical") symptoms. EPA also based the standard on the "action levels" for blood lead levels already

established by the Centers for Disease Control. These action levels were
the concentrations at which the CDC advised that some intervention
occur to reduce blood lead levels in children.

NOTES AND QUESTIONS

1. In setting the standard for airborne lead, the administrator was
concerned about lowering the levels of lead in the blood of the sensitive
population. After studying the problem and making some simplifying
assumptions, EPA judged that non-air sources of lead (e.g., lead-based
paint, lead from canned foods and pipes) contributed 12 μg/dl to the
target population, on average. In order to achieve its stated goal of
lowering 99.5 percent of the target population to blood lead levels below
30 μg/dl—CDC's action level at the time—EPA calculated that the average total blood lead level in that population would have to be 15 μg/
dl. Figuring—also on the basis of studies coupled with assumptions—
that the ratio of airborne lead to blood lead levels was 1:2, the Agency
set the primary air standard at 1.5 μg/m^3.

EPA justified its standard by arguing that "the maximum safe individual blood lead level should be no higher than the blood lead level
used by [CDC] in screening children for lead poisoning." 647 F.2d at
1144. Subsequent to this decision, CDC lowered the screening level to
25 μg/dl, and in 1991 it lowered the level again, to 10 μg/dl. What impact,
if any, should this have on the level of the NAAQS? What if it were
impossible to get 99.5 percent of the childrens' blood lead levels below
the CDC level, due to their exposure to other sources of lead?

2. Suppose EPA could be convinced that it would be much cheaper
to lower blood lead levels to the target population mean level of 15 μg/
dl by controlling non-air contributions to those levels? Specifically, suppose that a campaign to eliminate peeling lead-based paint in urban
dwellings would attain that result at one-tenth the cost of additional air
pollution controls. Would this provide a basis for EPA either (1) to refuse
to promulgate an ambient standard for lead; or (2) to promulgate a
lesser standard, perhaps with a recommendation to the Department of
Housing and Urban Development that it accelerate its program of lead
paint removal? (See §§108, 109.)

3. In Chapter 2, we introduced the trade-off between regulatory
strategies that are inflexible but relatively easy to administer and more
complex but more flexible strategies. There, the contrast was between
nationally uniform technology-based standards and cost-benefit balancing standards. See pages 160-162, above. Proponents of greater flexibility
have criticized the nationally uniform ambient standards of the Clean
Air Act as well. In an early article, Professor Krier argued that uniform
standards are a "fundamentally mistaken end":

To justify uniform standards as efficient in cost-minimization terms one would have to assume that the costs of a given level of pollution and a given level of control are the same across the nation. This assumption, however, is manifestly not valid. For example, aesthetic costs and materials losses will be functions of the varying resource endowments, degree of development, and human attitudes that exist in different regions. Even health costs—which were of the greatest concern to Congress in passing the 1970 legislation—vary from place to place. Since such costs represent the aggregate of individual health effects, and since population varies significantly by region, so too will total health costs. If one believes that per capita and not aggregate health costs should be the relevant factor, efficiency considerations would still suggest some variation in air quality levels. This is because the costs of pollution control will also vary, depending upon population, density and nature of development, and meteorological and topographical conditions in any particular region. In short, since the costs of pollution and the costs of control vary across the country, it is difficult to see how a uniform standard can begin to take the varying costs into account. The standard that minimizes total costs for a region in Iowa is hardly likely to do so for all the regions of California or New York or Colorado as well. To require adherence to the same stringent standard everywhere will in many areas result in the imposition of control costs which are much larger than the pollution costs avoided. [Krier, The Irrational National Air Quality Standards: Macro- and Micro-Mistakes, 22 UCLA L. Rev. 323, 336-337 (1974).]

What exactly is Professor Krier proposing as an alternative to nationally uniform ambient standards?

Krier contends that the only defensible rationale for nationally uniform standards is that it is simply too costly to set regional standards. In light of his criticisms, why do you suppose that Congress chose the nationally uniform approach?

At the time Professor Krier wrote the quoted article, states had just barely begun to implement their SIPs. Subsequently, it has become apparent that the SIP-writing process provides an occasion for states to take into account variations in pollution abatement costs in allocating emission controls among industries. For instance, a study of the paper industry has found that the stringency of pollution controls in SIPs tends to vary with differences in costs and benefits. R. Luken, Efficiency in Environmental Regulation: A Benefit-Cost Analysis of Alternative Approaches (1990).

4. Other criticism of the Clean Air Act's simplified approach to ambient standards focuses on its exclusive reliance on adverse health and welfare effects as the determinants of the proper standard. It is argued that this approach neglects the need to consider costs in setting ambient levels. While it might be conceptually possible to ignore costs in cases of air pollutants that easily can be reduced to no-effect threshold levels, critics of the Act argue that it is conceptually impossible to do so

for pollutants for which no safe threshold exists. In such cases, the administrator seems barred by Congress from considering costs (see *Lead Industries Association*), and yet seemingly must trade off costs against benefits to arrive at some non-zero level of control. Do you agree?

According to this view, a major problem with the NAAQS approach is the obstacle it creates to candid public debate about air quality goals because the EPA cannot explicitly discuss its considerations of costs. See, e.g., M. Landy, M. Roberts, and S. Thomas, The Environmental Protection Agency: Asking the Wrong Questions, ch. 3 (1990); Eads, The Confusion of Goals and Instruments: The Explicit Consideration of Costs in Setting National Ambient Air Quality Standards, in To Breathe Fresh Air (M. Gibson, ed., 1985).

EPA confronted the no-threshold problem when deciding whether to revise the original NAAQS for carbon monoxide. In its Notice of Proposed Rulemaking, EPA remarked that "the criteria document supports the conclusion that a clear threshold of adverse health effects cannot be identified with certainty for CO. . . . (This does not necessarily mean that there is no threshold, other than zero, for CO; it simply means that no clear threshold can be identified with certainty based on existing medical evidence.)" 45 Fed. Reg. 55,066, 55,071 (1980).

After receiving extensive comments, as well as reassessments of the scientific information by staff and the Clean Air Scientific Advisory Committee, the administrator decided not to revise the standard. 50 Fed. Reg. 37,484 (1985). The administrator continued to maintain that the health effects of carbon monoxide were a continuum, exhibiting no clear no-effects threshold. In such circumstances, he said, "setting a standard with an adequate margin of safety is necessarily a public health policy judgment that must take into account . . . the known continuum of effects, understanding of the underlying biological mechanisms of effects, and any gaps and uncertainties in the existing scientific data base." 50 Fed. Reg. 37,484, 37,488 (1985).

The administrator summarized his rationale as follows:

> Given the uncertainties in the existing data base and the possibility that the results of the new studies in progress might warrant further revisions within a few years, the Administrator has concluded that it would not be prudent to promulgate the proposed revisions at this time, particularly when they would alter the manner in which attainment is determined.
>
> In short, the Administrator has concluded that it would not be prudent to defer a decision on the CO standards pending the results of the new research mentioned above, that the standards should provide approximately the same level of protection as that afforded by the current standards, and that disruption of ongoing control programs should be minimized. Given these considerations, the Administrator has concluded that the best course of action is not to revise the CO primary standards at this time. [Id. at 37,494.]

In what sense is this rationale a "public health judgment"? Is the administrator implicitly taking costs into account in making his determination? If so, would a candid discussion of costs and benefits have been preferable? Is the administrator's decision consistent with *Lead Industries Association*?

5. Efforts to force EPA to give some consideration to costs in promulgating NAAQSs were emphatically rejected by the D.C. Circuit in NRDC v. EPA, 902 F.2d 962 (D.C. Cir. 1990). In upholding the NAAQS for particulates, the court deemed "entirely without merit" the claim that EPA had erred in not considering "the health consequences of unemployment" potentially caused by the standard. Citing the language of section 108(a)(2), which requires air quality criteria to reflect health effects "which may be expected from the presence of such pollutant in the ambient air," the court concluded that "[c]onsideration of costs associated with alleged health risks from unemployment would be flatly inconsistent with the statute, legislative history and case law on this point." 902 F.2d at 973. Is this consistent with Judge Williams's observation in International Union, UAW v. OSHA, 938 F.2d 1310 (D.C. Cir. 1991), discussed in Chapter 4D1a, that stricter regulation may cost lives because of its effect on the income of workers and consumers?

6. Some of the political considerations implicated by national ambient air quality standards are evident from EPA's 1979 revision of ozone standards. EPA relaxed the NAAQS for ozone from 0.08 to 0.12 ppm. This decision was affirmed despite substantial evidence of political pressure influencing the final rules. American Petroleum Institute v. Costle, 665 F.2d 1176 (D.C. Cir. 1981). EPA also calculated the expected cost savings ($2.7 billion per year) attributable to the relaxation, arguing that benefits and costs could be taken into account when choosing a margin of safety. The episode is recounted in detail in M. Landy, M. Roberts, and S. Thomas, The Environmental Protection Agency: Asking the Wrong Questions 49-88 (1990). Studies have indicated that ozone levels of 0.12 ppm, the current standard, double the likelihood of asthma attacks in exposed populations. See, e.g., Zamel et al., Effect of Low Concentrations of Ozone on Inhaled Allergen Responses in Asthmatic Subjects, 338 Lancet 221 (1991). The rate of hospitalizations for asthma in the United States has nearly tripled since 1970; the rate for children under 15 rose 43 percent between 1979 and 1987, an increase that cannot be accounted for solely by better diagnosis. Link Between Asthma and "Safe" Ozone Levels Is Studied, N.Y. Times, Aug. 8, 1991, at C3. Alleging that the 0.12 ppm ozone standard is inadequate to protect public health, a coalition of states and health and environmental groups filed a suit against EPA in 1991.

7. Further insight into EPA's approach to evaluating public health risks in the context of revising NAAQSs is provided by the following excerpt from a proposed decision not to revise the NAAQS for sulfur

oxides. The current standards do not regulate exposures for periods of less than 3 hours although sensitive populations (asthmatics) may experience measurable changes in respiratory function during exposures as brief as five to ten minutes. As you read the following, consider how EPA dealt with evidence concerning the size of the affected population, the likelihood of exposure, the relative contribution of airborne sulfur dioxide, and other determinants of total risk.

EPA, Ambient Air Quality Standards for Sulfur Oxides
53 Fed. Reg. 14,926, 14,931-14,934 (1988)

SUMMARY: As a result of its review and revision of the health and welfare criteria, EPA proposes not to revise [the existing standards for SO_2, which are a primary standard of 0.14 parts per million (ppm) (365 micrograms per cubic meter ($\mu g/m^3$)), averaged over a period of 24 hours and not to be exceeded more than once per year, with a 0.03 ppm (80 $\mu g/m^3$) annual arithmetic mean, and a secondary standard of 0.5 ppm (1300 $\mu g/m^3$), averaged over a period of 3 hours and not to be exceeded more than once per year]. The Administrator also solicits comments on an alternative of adding a 1-hour primary standard of 0.4 ppm. . . .

CONSIDERATION OF SHORT-TERM (1-HOUR) PRIMARY STANDARD

As discussed above, the assessment of available scientific evidence and recommendations of staff and CASAC [Clean Air Scientific Advisory Committee] have led the Administrator to conclude that the current primary and secondary SO_2 standards are adequate to protect the public health and welfare from the effects associated with 24-hour, annual, and 3-hour average concentrations of SO_2 in the atmosphere. This recent assessment of the scientific literature included a review of the potential effects on asthmatics and other sensitive individuals associated with short-term (1-hour or less) exposures to SO_2. While the Administrator is inclined to conclude that this information does not warrant setting a new short-term primary standard, there has been considerable discussion on whether such a standard is needed to protect against such exposures. For reasons outlined in the staff assessment, 1-hour is an appropriate averaging time to consider for such a possible new standard. The discussion below summarizes the basis for such consideration and assesses the protection afforded by the present standards against short-term exposures.

1. Short-Term Health Effects

The basis for considering the possible addition of a new 1-hour standard rests largely on the staff and CASAC assessment of the results of several relatively recent controlled human exposure studies. The major effects observed in these studies are measurable changes in respiratory function in asthmatics and atopics exposed for short periods (as little as 5-10 minutes up to 1-hour) to 0.4 ppm SO_2 or more. [For example, 25 percent of exercising asthmatic subjects, whose respiratory ventilation was increased by exercise or by hyperventilation and who were not using preventive medication at the time, experienced a doubling (or more) in airway resistance when breathing a 0.5 ppm concentration for 10 minutes. Other subjects experienced] shortness of breath, wheezing and coughing. The fraction of asthmatic subjects experiencing changes in lung function and symptoms increased with concentration over the range of 0.4 to 0.75 ppm.

While mindful of the guidance in the criteria document that "caution should be employed in regard to any attempted extrapolation of these observed quantitative exposure-effect relationships to what might be expected under ambient conditions," the staff and CASAC concluded that consideration should be given to a new short-term standard to address these effects. Based on practical considerations relating to monitoring, modeling, data manipulation and storage, and implementation, the staff recommended using a 1-hour averaging time for any such standard. As explained below, the relationship between 1-hour average concentrations and shorter-term concentrations would allow the use of a 1-hour standard, set at an appropriate level, to control shorter-term peaks. Staff and CASAC identified a number of factors that should be considered in decisionmaking concerning a 1-hour standard.

a. Significance of Effects. The functional changes and symptoms observed in the controlled studies appear to be transient and reversible, and, at lower concentrations [less than 0.75 ppm] and exercise levels, they are within the range of day-to-day variations that most asthmatics typically experience from exercise or other stimuli. They are, in general, not equivalent to the more severe responses that accompany an asthma "attack." Finally, because medications already widely used by asthmatics can prevent or ameliorate reaction to SO_2, an asthmatic who is already medicated due to other stimuli will likely not experience a response to an exposure. The scientific community is divided as to whether and to what extent these effects at lower concentrations should be considered "adverse" or "clinically significant."

b. Relative Effect of SO_2 Compared to Other Stimuli. Exercise alone, without pollutant exposure, is among a number of stimuli that commonly induce bronchoconstriction in asthmatics. Cold and/or dry air exacerbates the effects of exercise even in the absence of SO_2. It is likely that the incidence of bronchoconstriction induced by SO_2 is very small compared with that induced by factors unrelated to pollution.

   c. Sensitive Population.   Diagnosed asthmatics make up approximately 4 percent of the total U.S. population (about 10 million individuals) while atopics constitute roughly 8 percent. Some additional percentage of the population not diagnosed as atopic or asthmatic may also display hyperreactive airway responses to SO_2. Asthmatics appear to be at greater risk than atopics. Studies to date have shown a wide distribution of sensitivity among asthmatics and atopics tested. . . . The consequences of a functional change are of greater concern in more severe asthmatics, but such individuals may be somewhat protected from SO_2 because they routinely use medication due to their susceptibility to responses from other stimuli and the reduced chance that they would experience sustained levels of moderate to high exercise.

   d. Variance About the 1-Hour Average.   The available studies indicate that SO_2 effects occur within 5 to 10 minutes but do not necessarily worsen with continued exposure over an hour. Concentrations averaged over 5 or 10 minutes vary about the 1-hour mean, reaching peak values that are clearly higher than the 1-hour value. Analyses of recent data indicate that at higher concentrations near large point sources, these peaks are likely to be within a factor of 2 of the mean. Thus, the maximum 5 to 10 minute peak associated with a 1-hour value of 0.5 ppm is probably less than 1 ppm.

   e. Probability of Exposure.   The staff assessment found that given current air quality levels, peak SO_2 concentrations in the 0.4 to 0.75 ppm range for 5 to 10 minutes are very infrequent and limited in extent to the vicinity of certain large sources. Given low indoor levels and the limited time individuals spend in moderate to high activity, the probability that any individual asthmatic would experience any effects of SO_2 is low. This issue has been examined in the quantitative analyses discussed in the following section.

   ## 2.   Protection Afforded by Current Standards
   ##   Against Short-Term Effects

   In determining whether to revise the present standards by the addition of a 1-hour primary standard, it is particularly important to evaluate: (1) the extent to which implementation of the current standards protects against potential very short-term effects, and (2) the relative increase in protection that would be afforded by the addition of a possible 1-hour primary standard. The first point is addressed in this section while the second point is addressed in the following section.

(a) Air Quality and Exposure Analyses. [The staff analyzed the predicted frequency of 1-hour exceedances of 0.5 ppm if the current standards are met.] This concentration (0.5 ppm) was the lowest short-term (5-minute to 1-hour) level found to produce changes in respiratory function and symptoms in the controlled studies of exercising "mild" asthmatics included in the 1982 staff paper. . . .

Although the analyses are uncertain, the available results permit the following tentative conclusions:

(1) Based on current U.S. monitored air quality data and reasonable estimates of ratios of 5-minute peaks to 1-hour means, 5-minute concentrations and exposures to 0.5 ppm or more are expected primarily in the vicinity (usually less than 20 km) of major point sources such as utilities and smelters. Approximately 10 to 40 percent of the sensitive population (asthmatics) in the U.S. are estimated to live in the vicinity of utilities, with a much smaller percentage living near smelters.

(2) Based on modeled air quality and exposures for several large utility power plants, the current standards (24-hour and 3-hour) place substantial limits on exceedances of, and exposures to, 1-hour concentrations in excess of 0.5 ppm.

(3) Of those asthmatics living in the vicinity (roughly 10-25 km) of the four power plants studied at their current emissions, the percentage estimated to be exposed once per year to a 5-minute SO_2 concentration of 0.5 ppm while at exercise varied from 1 percent to 14 percent depending on the plant. A rough extrapolation to all of the power plants in the country suggests that approximately 100,000 individual asthmatics or about 1 percent of the national asthmatic population, will experience at least one such exposure of concern per year. The vast majority of these 1 percent would experience only one such exposure per year.

(4) Because not all of the exposures to 0.5 ppm resulted in measurable effects in controlled studies, fewer than 25 percent of the asthmatics exposed are likely to experience even moderate pulmonary function changes and symptoms. It is possible that individual asthmatics substantially more sensitive than those studied might experience larger or comparable effects at even lower levels. However, CASAC has pointed out that there is no evidence to refute or support this possibility. Moreover, severe asthmatics may be protected because they less often achieve elevated activity levels and often are already medicated to alleviate the effect of other environmental stimuli commmonly encountered. . . .

3.   1-Hour Standard Alternative

. . . EPA staff and CASAC recommended a range of potential
1-hour standards for the Administrator's consideration. This range, based
on the updated staff assessment is 0.2 to 0.5 ppm (520 to 1300 μg/m³).
Considering typical 5-minute peak to 1-hour mean ratios of 2 to 1, the
lower bound (0.2 ppm) represents a 1-hour level for which the maximum
5 to 10 minute peak exposures are not likely to exceed 0.4 ppm. This
is the lowest level where responses of potential clinical significance in
free breathing "mild to moderate" asthmatics have been reported in the
literature cited in the criteria document addendum. A 1-hour standard
at the upper bound of the range (0.5 ppm) would maintain maximum
hourly values in the vicinity of the lowest concentrations (0.4 to 0.5 ppm)
producing significant responses in the available studies summarized above.
It would afford somewhat greater protection against short-term peaks
than that now provided by the current standards. Based on the preliminary analysis of exposure near large point sources discussed above, it
appears that under such a standard, 1 to 4 percent of the asthmatics
residing in the vicinity of the point sources analyzed, or between 200 to
1400 individuals per plant, would be annually exposed while at exercise
to 5-minute peaks at or above 0.5 ppm. On a national level, fewer than
1 percent of all asthmatics would experience such exposures. Nevertheless, a 0.5 ppm level would not completely preclude 5 to 10 minute
exposures on the order of 1 ppm.

Considering typical 5-minute peak to 1 hour mean ratios of 2 to 1
or lower, 1-hour standard alternatives of 0.3 to 0.4 ppm could result in
5-minute peaks on the order of 0.6 to 0.8 ppm. Several CASAC members
supported a 1-hour standard in this portion of the overall range. If a
1-hour ambient standard of 0.4 ppm were implemented at the four
power plants studied in the exposure analysis discussed above, the percentage of the asthmatics living in the vicinity of those plants who would
be exposed once per year to a 5-minute SO_2 concentration of 0.5 ppm
while at exercise would be less than 1 to 2 percent.

After considering the views of CASAC, the Administrator is inclined to conclude that a 1-hour primary ambient standard to protect
exercising asthmatics and atopics from short-term exposures to SO_2 is
not warranted. As explained above, this inclination is based on, among
other things, the uncertain significance of the health effects involved
and on the infrequence of inducement of such effects by SO_2. However,
the Administrator solicits comments on the alternative of a 1-hour standard at the level of 0.4 ppm.

NOTES AND QUESTIONS

1. The Clean Air Scientific Advisory Committee (CASAC) is one of several advisory bodies that provide EPA with advice on scientific and technical matters. The composition of such groups is sometimes controversial, since many of the experts are employed by the industries that could be regulated. On the other hand, such bodies can provide an important service by improving the quality of EPA analysis. See S. Jasanoff, The Fifth Branch: Science Advisors as Policymakers 101-122 (1990).

2. EPA compares a proposed change in the *primary* standard with the existing *secondary* standard. What difference is there between the two? See §§109, 110.

3. Why did EPA limit its analysis to a one-hour standard? Isn't it likely that there would be an effect associated with a higher concentration for, say, 30 minutes?

4. How does EPA take into account the fact that the effect is treatable by medication? Does this suggest a principle of broader application? For instance, might the adverse effects of ozone be mitigated by staying inside and not exercising?

5. What significance is attached to the fact that exercise and "other stimuli" can produce the same form of bronchoconstriction associated with SO_2? If smoking produces comparable or more serious health effects than smog, is that relevant to the standard for ozone?

6. How does EPA define the potentially affected population? According to EPA there are ten million asthmatics plus some percentage of the 20 million atopics potentially at risk, but EPA argues that only about 100,000 might experience (and fewer than 25 percent of these are *likely* to experience) moderate pulmonary function changes. How does EPA reach this result? In October 1990 medical authorities reported that there had been a sharp increase in deaths among asthmatics. Should this have any impact on EPA's decision?

7. How does the "adequate margin of safety" required by section 109 figure in the proposal?

8. The pressures to avoid amending the NAAQS also apply when EPA might have reason to consider weakening the standards. For example, EPA has in one instance reaffirmed a standard even after the science on which it was based has arguably been discredited. Oren, Prevention of Significant Deterioration: Control-Compelling Versus Site-Shifting, 74 Iowa L. Rev. 64-67 (1988).

PROBLEM EXERCISE: THE BIRTH
OF A NAAQS

The ambient lead standard is the only identification of a new criteria air pollutant in the history of the Clean Air Act. The burdens triggered by section 109 (see the section that follows on state implementation plans) have effectively deterred EPA from the exercise of this authority. EPA believes that it has more flexible authority to address new problems in other ways.

EPA has recently identified air emissions from solid waste landfills as a potential subject for regulation. 56 Fed. Reg. 24,468 (1991). Gas forms as solid waste decays. Emissions consist primarily of methane and carbon dioxide, both of which release trace amounts of over 100 other organic compounds. Landfill gases cause odors and can be a fire hazard; they also contribute to ozone formation. Some of the compounds emitted also qualify as hazardous air pollutants.

Question One. EPA has proposed regulating some compounds in landfill gases by the promulgation of a "standard of performance" under section 111. What pollutants are covered by this section? What is the rationale for regulation of pollutants that are neither criteria pollutants nor hazardous air pollutants?

Question Two. EPA has not proposed regulating the methane fraction of landfill gas although it is a potent contributor to the "greenhouse effect" responsible for global warming and it also causes fires. Are these effects, as opposed to more common health impacts, sufficient to justify regulation under the Act? See section 302(h).

Question Three. Section 111(a)(1) requires that EPA consider the cost of control and "any nonair quality health and environmental impact and energy requirements" when setting a standard of performance. Could EPA require landfills to collect methane and sell it for use as a fuel for generating electricity if the resultant revenue would substantially offset control costs? Does it permit or require EPA to assign some value to reductions in the buildup of greenhouse gases? See EPA, Regulatory Impact Analysis of Air Pollutant Emission Standards and Guidelines for Municipal Solid Waste Landfills 12-4 (Mar. 1991) (quantitative estimates presented only for reductions in VOCs).

Question Four. Assume EPA establishes a standard for landfill gas under section 111. Are the findings made pursuant to this rulemaking likely to support a subsequent petition for an ambient air quality standard? Consider the requirements of section 109. See also NRDC v. Train, 545 F.2d 320 (2d Cir. 1976) and Thomas v. New York, 802 F.2d 1443 (D.C. Cir. 1986), cert. denied, 482 U.S. 919 (1987).

D. STATE IMPLEMENTATION PLANS

The NAAQSs are only the beginning. The NAAQSs define the level of air quality to be achieved throughout the nation for the criteria air pollutants. The centerpiece of the regulatory process is the state implementation plan (SIP), which dictates how the ambient air quality standards are to be achieved. As the term implies, SIPs are established at the state level, although EPA is required to review and approve plans to assure they will achieve the NAAQSs. Most of all, the SIP was intended to result in a plan for achieving air quality goals:

> It is supposed to assign specific emission limitations to individual sources and establish timetables for compliance by those sources; set up procedures to review new sources; establish systems to monitor air quality; and provide for enforcement. Section 110 requires a detailed demonstration that the state has the necessary laws and administrative capacity to assure that the standards are met by the combined efforts of individual source owners. A citizen should be able to pick up a plan, read it, and understand that if company X meets the obligations and timetables there prescribed it will have done its share to assure that health and environmental damage from the criteria air pollutants will be an unfortunate memory of the past within that air quality region and state. This is not a fairy tale. It is the conception and purpose of the law. [W. Rodgers, Environmental Law: Air and Water Pollution 254 (1986).]

The geographic basis for SIPs under the 1970 Act was air quality control regions, originally defined in the 1967 Act as areas with serious air quality problems, but extended so that all areas are covered. Regions may cross state lines, in which case EPA was to mesh the submissions from each affected state. T. Jorling, The Federal Law of Air Pollution Control, in Federal Environmental Law 1058, 1067 (E. Dolgin and T. Guilbert, eds. 1973).

The SIP is the focal point for defining controls on existing sources. As originally enacted, the Clean Air Act required nationally uniform emission limits only for *new* stationary sources, in contrast with the Clean Water Act, adopted two years later, which contained such requirements for all sources. (Why might Congress have made such a distinction between air and water?) Thus, one state may impose severe requirements on power plants while another may choose to emphasize transportation controls. States were also left some freedom to choose the means of regulation, including economic incentives. (The distinction between new and existing sources has been eroded by requirements applicable to areas that fail to meet the NAAQS, as discussed in section E below, and by requirements for older fossil fuel burning power plants, as discussed in section F below.) Detailed procedural and substantive requirements for

SIP formulation and approval are set forth in section 110 of the Act, including a demonstration of adequate provisions for monitoring, enforcement, staffing, and periodic review and revision.

The Act also outlined a process for defining the measures necessary to achieve air quality goals. The first step was to inventory emissions and project expected growth to establish the extent of the problem. Since detailed studies of emissions had not been done—especially for the thousands of smaller sources—this required much estimation.

The second step was to choose control strategies for reducing emissions. New sources had to be addressed with a permit system, as discussed below. Mobile sources were subject to federal standards, discussed in section G. States had the most discretion in their approach to existing stationary sources, but most adopted some form of categorical emission limitations based on criteria similar to those required for new sources—a judgment about what is technically achievable and economically affordable. SIPs also may incorporate more flexible regulatory approaches, such as "bubbles." (See §110(a)(2)(A).) The methods chosen had to be legally enforceable. In some states this has required legislative action.

The third step was to demonstrate that the measures proposed would be adequate to achieve the NAAQSs, a process requiring air quality models that are themselves controversial. "Some might argue . . . that modeling is more sorcery than science. Computer modeling is an extremely complex and imprecise tool whose accuracy diminishes with the number of sources, the distance between source and monitor, and the variation in the terrain." Reed, State Implementation Plans, in Law of Environmental Protection 11-28 (S. Novick, ed., 1988). Modeling is nevertheless required, and it plays a key part in the regulatory process. See Note 4, page 788 below.

The states' role in planning is only half the story. A key feature of the SIP process is the complex interaction between federal and state authorities. States are largely free to adopt their own procedures, as long as they include notice and public hearings. EPA must determine whether the plan will achieve the NAAQSs. Revisions are frequently necessary in response to changes by individual sources or information indicating inadequate progress. EPA originally had four months to approve or disapprove SIPs and proposed SIP revisions. Because the Agency frequently failed to meet this deadline and sometimes approved most but not all of a proposed plan, considerable confusion and litigation occurred. EPA was given greater flexibility and more time for plan review in the 1990 Amendments. See §110(k).

An approved SIP is promulgated as a federal rule and becomes enforceable by the public. EPA may promulgate and enforce a substitute rule if it finds the state proposal inadequate. The end result has been aptly described as "extremely cumbersome. . . . This procedural duplication, intended to safeguard the Act's national goals from too much federalist diversity, sometimes afflicted the SIP process with procedural rigidity bordering on rigor mortis." Reed, in id. at 11-30.

PROBLEM EXERCISE: STATE IMPLEMENTATION PLANS AND POLITICAL CHOICES

One of the most sensitive issues arising under the Clean Air Act is whether measures to limit or discourage the use of automobiles should be employed to reduce emissions. The provisions of the Act reflect the political sensitivity of such choices.

Question One. What forms of restrictions on the use of cars are permitted or excluded from consideration in the SIP process? See §§110(a)(5), 110(c)(2)(B)-(E) and 110(c)(5). What policy considerations help explain the distinction made in these provisions? See also Council of Commuter Organizations v. Thomas, 799 F.2d 879 (2d Cir. 1986) (legislation permitting the elimination of bridge tolls in New York City does not require improvements in mass transit).

Question Two. What can EPA do if states fail to comply with the requirements for formulating and implementing SIPs? See section 179(b). Prior to the 1990 Amendments, EPA also had authority to impose a moratorium on construction of new sources. Section 110(a)(2)(I), as amended by Pub. L. No. 101-549, §101(b) (Nov. 15, 1990). Why would Congress remove this sanction while also seeking to continue pressures on states to attain ambient air quality standards? (We examine new requirements for "reasonable further progress" below, pages 810-814.) One concern has been the legality and appropriateness of federal regulation of land use decisions. By comparison, how intrusive are the transportation choices required of states as identified in Question One?

NOTES AND QUESTIONS

1. It should be evident that the concept of a state implementation "plan" is misleading. The SIP is in reality a dynamic process. SIPs may be partially or conditionally approved. Sources may close down or change their emissions. New sources may be found, meteorological data may improve, and mathematical models are periodically refined. All of these events imply changes in the SIP, and under the Act all require both state and EPA approval and usually two sets of notice and comment. Each decision to approve or disapprove is potentially subject to litigation (see section 307(b)); more than 100 cases were brought by mid-1973. The

result is a process that demands constant revision but that makes changes procedurally very difficult. See Pedersen, Why the Clean Air Act Works Badly, 129 U. Pa. L. Rev. 1059 (1981).

2. Section 110 creates a complex balance between state and federal authority that leaves many unanswered questions. States have substantial discretion to set individual limits and to allocate the allowable pollution among sources, but EPA is ultimately responsible for assuring that the state plan will attain the NAAQSs. In Train v. NRDC, 421 U.S. 60 (1975), the Supreme Court addressed one of the basic questions concerning this balance: Was EPA required to review every variance from a SIP, or only those that would result in extending the deadline for compliance with the NAAQSs? The Court accepted EPA's reading of the Act and required federal review only where attainment of the NAAQSs is at issue. Why do you suppose EPA adopted this view, which constrained its authority? See also Reed, above.

3. Why not permit compliance by "cutting emissions only when meteorological conditions likely will . . . concentrate [pollution] under a temperature inversion"? As long as the end result is to meet the standards, why should controls be required? See §123.

4. Models, rather than empirical measurements, are the principal means for testing the adequacy of a SIP proposal. Why is this the case? While the courts have generally supported EPA's choice of computer models, there have been exceptions. In Ohio v. EPA, 784 F.2d 226 (6th Cir. 1986), the Sixth Circuit rejected EPA's use of a model, citing the absence of empirical validation of the model's results. Noting that studies at other sites had produced "unimpressive" results, the court concluded that "[i]n the absence of a record supporting the trustworthiness of agency decision-making tools as they were applied, we cannot uphold [EPA methods]." Compare Connecticut v. EPA, 696 F.2d 147 (2d Cir. 1982) (burden on petitioners to demonstrate availability of better model).

5. The cumbersome bureaucratic procedures associated with the SIP process had left most observers convinced there must be a better way. William Pederson proposed greater reliance on individual permits akin to the system created by the Clean Water Act. Pedersen, Why the Clean Air Act Works Badly, 129 U. Pa. L. Rev. 1059 (1981). Will the use of thousands of individual permits improve the SIP process? Why? Recall Professor Rodgers's contention that a citizen should be able to "pick up a plan, read it, and understand that if company X meets the obligations and timetables there prescribed" it will be doing its part to assure attainment of air quality goals. Pedersen argues that this has simply not been true in practice due to ambiguities in the SIP process and the need for constant revision. Pedersen's suggestions have been adopted in large measure in the new permit provisions of the 1990 Amendments.

6. When it first proposed the new permit program during the debate on the 1990 Amendments, EPA thought that it would be popular with industry. The Agency noted that the program would provide greater certainty to industrial sources by consolidating in a single permit all the various requirements of the Act that are applicable to the source. Moreover, the permit program would provide sources with some assurance that requirements would not change during the length of the permit's life. And permits could be modified more easily and flexibly than SIPs. However, much to the Agency's surprise, industry lobbyists vigorously opposed EPA's permit program. Why?

7. If states are free to decide whether and how much to "force technology," what opportunity does a discharger have to present defenses based on cost or technological impossibility? The Supreme Court addressed this basic issue in Union Electric v. EPA, 427 U.S. 246 (1976). An electric utility company had been notified by EPA that sulfur dioxide emissions from its plants violated the emissions limitations contained in Missouri's state implementation plan. The company argued that it would be forced to shut down because it could not comply with the SIP's restrictions on sulfur dioxide emissions. It argued that EPA should have disapproved Missouri's SIP because it included restrictions that were economically and technologically infeasible. EPA argued that it did not have the authority under the Clean Air Act to reject a SIP on the grounds of economic or technological infeasibility.

The *Union Electric* Court accepted EPA's argument, holding that claims of infeasibility are "wholly foreign to the Administrator's consideration of a state implementation plan." Union Electric had premised its argument on the notion that section 110(a)(2)'s requirement that the primary air quality standards be met "as expeditiously as practicable but . . . in no case later than three years" required EPA to determine whether a proposed SIP's provisions actually can be achieved. The Court, however, emphasized the technology-forcing character of the Act, which is "expressly designed to force regulated sources to develop pollution control devices that might at the time appear to be economically or technologically infeasible." Thus it concluded that "the Administrator must approve a plan that provides for attainment of the primary standards in three years even if attainment does not appear feasible." Besides,

. . . Congress plainly left with the States, so long as the national standards were met, the power to determine which sources would be burdened by regulation and to what extent. Technology forcing is a concept somewhat new to our national experience and it necessarily entails certain risks. But Congress considered those risks in passing the 1970 Amendments and decided that the dangers posed by uncontrolled air pollution made them worth taking. Petitioner's theory would render that considered legislative judgment a nullity, and that is a result we refuse to reach. [427 U.S. at 269.]

8. The Court in *Union Electric* emphasized that companies were free to present claims of infeasibility to the state agency formulating the implementation plan and to obtain variances from the state that could be submitted to EPA as revisions to the SIP. "So long as the national standards are met, the State may select whatever mix of control devices it desires, and industries with particular economic or technological problems may seek special treatment in the plan itself." 427 U.S. at 266. The Court also noted that the Clean Air Act did provide some escape valves for states with sources that could not comply with the NAAQSs. Under section 110(e) of the Act (subsequently repealed by the 1990 Amendments), a governor could request EPA to grant a two-year extension of the three-year deadline for attainment of the primary air quality standards on a finding that it is technologically infeasible for a source to comply. Under section 110(f) (also repealed in 1990), a governor could request a one-year postponement of any compliance date in an implementation plan if compliance is technologically infeasible and "the continued operation of [the emissions source] is essential to national security or to the public health or welfare. . . ." The Court also noted that "[c]laims of technological or economic infeasibility . . . are relevant to fashioning an appropriate compliance order under §113(a)(4)," which provides that such orders "must specify a 'reasonable' time for compliance with the relevant standard, taking into account the seriousness of the violation and 'any good faith efforts to comply with applicable requirements.'"

9. In addition to its authority to issue compliance orders under section 113(a), EPA may seek civil penalties and injunctive relief against a source violating a SIP under section 113(b), and the Act prescribes criminal penalties for knowing violations in section 113(c). Citizen suits also may be brought under section 304 to obtain injunctions against violators when the government has failed to take enforcement action. The *Union Electric* decision left open the possibility of raising economic and technological defenses in the context of fashioning relief in response to an enforcement action. Is this conclusion based on a reading of the statute or on broader due process principles? In either case, is flexibility in the enforcement stage consistent with the absolutist interpretation of the SIP process itself? Perhaps in response to this dilemma, Congress added section 120 to the Clean Air Act in 1977, which authorizes EPA to impose civil penalties on sources violating the Act in amounts equal to the savings enjoyed by the source as a result of its noncompliance. This provision was designed to remove any economic incentive for sources to delay compliance with the Act.

10. A chronic problem with the SIP process has been the frequent need for states to revise their SIPs and the cumbersome and time-consuming procedures for obtaining EPA approval for those revisions. In General Motors Corp. v. United States, 496 U.S. 530 (1990), the

Supreme Court addressed the question whether EPA can enforce an existing SIP if it has failed to complete its review of a proposed SIP revision in a timely manner. A General Motors plant had sought an extension of a compliance deadline for installation of emissions controls imposed by an existing SIP. Massachusetts authorities had approved the extension and submitted it to EPA as a proposed SIP revision one day before the existing SIP compliance deadline. Twenty months later, while the proposed SIP revision was still pending at EPA, the Agency filed an enforcement action under section 113(b), alleging violations of the existing SIP's deadline. A year later, EPA finally decided to reject the proposed SIP revision. Noting that section 110(a)(2) of the Act required EPA to approve or disapprove a state's initial SIP within four months of its submission, GM argued that a four-month deadline also should apply to SIP revisions. A district court agreed and held that EPA should be precluded from penalizing the company for noncompliance with an existing SIP when the Agency has failed to act within four months of submission of a proposed SIP revision.

The First Circuit reversed the district court, and its judgment was upheld by the Supreme Court. The Court held that the four-month deadline applied only to EPA's review of state's initial SIP submissions. While noting that the Administrative Procedure Act requires agencies to conclude matters "within a reasonable time," 5 U.S.C. §555(b), the Court held that EPA was not barred from enforcing an existing SIP even if the Agency had delayed unreasonably in acting on a proposed SIP revision. Is this result fair? If the district court's decision had been upheld instead, what impact would it have had on EPA's ability to enforce SIP provisions? A provision in the Clean Air Act Amendments of 1990, section 110(k), now mandates that EPA act within 12 months of the submission of proposed SIP revisions, unless the submission contains insufficient information, in which case the state is treated as if it had not made a submission.

A Note on the Clean Air Act's New National Permit System

The 1990 Amendments added numerous requirements for measures to address areas as yet unable to come into compliance with the NAAQSs. Many SIP revisions will be necessary, requiring substantial effort by states and EPA. The changes dealing with nonattainment areas are described below. Another important set of amendments incorporated in Title V creates the Clean Air Act's first national permit system for all major sources of air pollution. These requirements will further complicate the SIP process but will also eventually add much greater specificity for permitees, regulators, and concerned citizens.

Permits will be required of all major sources, including any source subject to new source requirements. EPA also was given broad authority to expand the categories of industries subject to permit requirements. States will administer permits but must meet minimum requirements for staffing, collection of fees, and procedures. One desirable feature of permits from industry's point of view is some measure of certainty that the permittee is in compliance with the Act if in compliance with the permit. However, permits with terms of three years or more are subject to revision to reflect subsequently promulgated requirements. Industry is generally concerned about the administrative delays and costs that may result from defining and implementing a new bureaucratic requirement. See, e.g., J. Quarles and W. Lewis, The NEW Clean Air Act 47-51 (1990).

The new permit program requires permittees to pay fees based on the size of their emissions, which will provide an additional economic incentive for pollution reduction. The fees are designed to offset the administrative costs incurred by states in implementing the permit program. To be approved, permit programs must require permittees to pay fees sufficient to cover all "reasonable (direct and indirect) costs" associated with development and administration of the program, including preparation of regulations as well as monitoring and modeling of emissions. The fee program generally must collect in the aggregate at least $25 per ton of regulated pollutant, but a state need not count emissions of any pollutant from any one source in excess of 4,000 tons per year. All fees must be used solely to support the program. See §502(b). Fees may be reduced for small businesses. §507(f).

The permit fee is based on administrative costs and not environmental damage. However, because the fee varies with the amount of emissions, it is consistent with economic notions of providing incentives for efficient pollution control.

E. THE NONATTAINMENT PROBLEM

1. Nonattainment: A Clean Air Act Report Card

In light of the country's continued population growth and economic expansion and the steady increase in the use of motor vehicles since 1970, any improvement in air quality should probably be taken as a measure of some success. In fact, we have a number of indications of improvement, although they are not uniform.

As an initial matter, you should be aware that it is harder to assess changes in air quality than might be supposed. "First, air quality can be described in a variety of ways—for instance, by average pollutant concentrations, frequency of violations of the NAAQS, extremely hazardous incidents, and so on. . . . Second, it is a bit heroic to think of air quality in national terms. Inevitably, some areas will improve while others stay the same or worsen, regardless of the measures used. . . . Third, the air quality monitoring network upon which a trends analysis must be based is simply inadequate. . . . [A] country spending as much for air pollution control as the United States should be ashamed of the thinness of its monitoring efforts." Portney, Air Pollution Policy, in Public Policies for Environmental Protection 27, 40 (P. Portney, ed. 1990).

One measure of air quality trends is the total emissions for the major ambient pollutants. These trends are shown in Figure 6.3. In addition to total emissions, EPA also makes estimates by sector of the economy. These are summarized in Figure 6.4.

A second measure of trends is provided by calculating national ambient concentration averages, relying on the monitoring network to which Portney refers. As he suggests, it is a surprisingly limited network, consisting of 1,726 sites nationwide for total suspended particulates (TSP), 347 for SO_2, 274 for ozone, 198 for CO, 94 for lead, and only 84 for NOx. Averages from these sites indicate varying degrees of improvement. In the period 1975 to 1989, ambient concentrations fell by 45 percent for sulfur dioxide and carbon monoxide, with the decreases for SO_2 due to a combination of pollution control devices and use of lower

FIGURE 6.3
Trends in Total U.S. Emissions of Major Ambient Pollutants, 1970-89

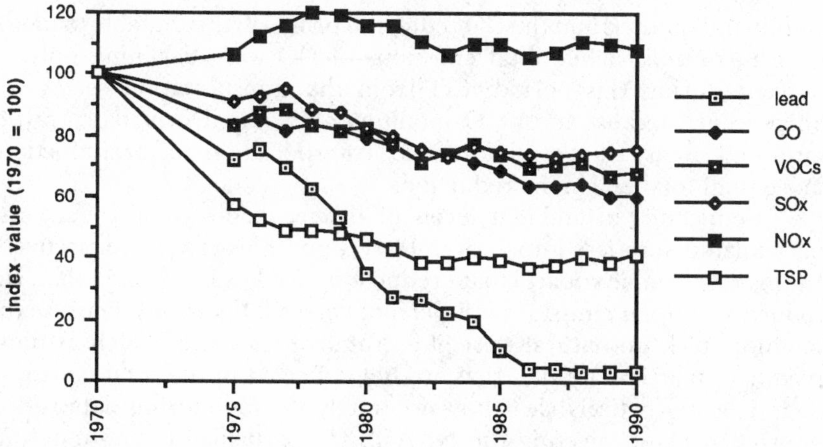

Sources: Council on Environmental Quality, 21st Annual Report, Table 39 (1991).
EPA, National Air Quality & Emissions Trends Report, 1990 (1991).

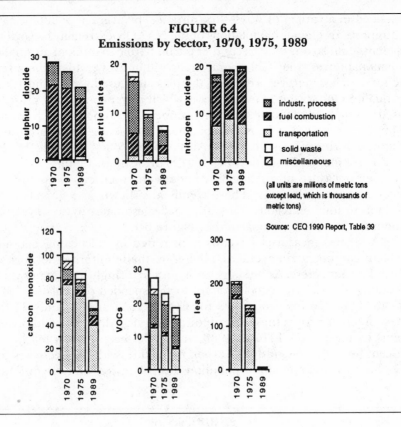

FIGURE 6.4
Emissions by Sector, 1970, 1975, 1989

sulfur content fuels and the CO reduction primarily attributable to motor vehicle controls. While total emissions of CO were declining only 23 percent during this period, CO from the transportation sector fell 38 percent. Because most CO monitors are located in urban, traffic-saturated areas, they tend to reflect transportation sector reductions more than total emissions reductions.

Reductions in ambient levels of ozone, oxides of nitrogen, and particulates were less impressive: 13, 17, and 18 percent, respectively. In this case, ambient particulate reductions are less impressive than the reduction in total emissions (18 percent versus 29 percent), because the monitors pick up natural dust plus "fugitive emissions," such as those from construction activity, that are not reflected in the total emissions data. It is not entirely clear how accurately the monitoring data reflect improvements in meeting the NAAQS for particulates. The monitors measure particulates up to 45 microns in diameter, but in 1987 EPA revised the particulate NAAQS so that it would apply only to particles 10 microns or less in diameter to reflect the fact that smaller particles present a far greater health danger than larger ones. Because of this change, the particulate standard is now sometimes referred to as the PM-10 standard. See 52 Fed. Reg. 24,634 (1987).

The undeniable success story in air quality control is the reduction in airborne lead—it has fallen by 92 percent since 1975, almost entirely because of EPA's program to phase out lead in gasoline.

2. Nonattainment: The Historical Background

The Clean Air Act was initially adopted with high hopes that ambient air quality standards would be met by 1975. The *Union Electric* decision reflected the simplistic expectation that existing sources would do whatever it takes to meet the standards, or be closed down. Congress did not devote much attention to dealing with areas unable to comply by 1975, other than the extreme sanction of a ban on all new sources.

One mechanism for ensuring compliance was the EPA's authority to write federal implementation plans for states that refused to promulgate adequate SIPs. However, early EPA efforts here proved disastrous for the Agency. In one notorious case, EPA proposed gasoline-rationing regulations for southern California that would have reduced vehicle travel by 82 percent. After a firestorm of protest, the Agency abandoned the proposal, see Santa Rosa v. EPA, 534 F.2d 150 (9th Cir. 1976), and in 1977 Congress sharply limited EPA's authority to include transportation control elements in a FIP. §§110(c)(3)(A-E), (4), partially repealed by the 1990 Amendments. Pub. L. 101-549, §101(d).

Reluctant to shoulder the burden of drafting implementation plans, the Agency eventually approved some SIPs that offered no realistic chance of attaining compliance with the NAAQSs. It also approved SIPs that contained lax variance procedures, producing state variances that were virtually unreviewable.

The *Union Electric* decision also had not completely closed the door on the consideration of feasibility, declaring that such consideration is "relevant to fashioning an appropriate compliance order under section 113(a)(4)," 427 U.S. at 268, so that delayed compliance orders based on feasibility became another escape valve in the statutory scheme.

A final significant reason for the difficulty in meeting the ambient standards was the enormous technical and economic challenge they presented. An estimated 200,000 stationary sources, plus the automobile industry, were given three years to comply with costly and sometimes technically difficult requirements. The procedural and legal difficulties mentioned above were to a considerable degree reflective of the underlying technological and economic difficulties involved.

Prior to the 1977 Amendments, EPA had responded to SIP inadequacy by developing a compromise strategy. Rather than banning all new source construction until the standards were attained, EPA imposed two conditions on new sources in areas that had not met the deadlines for achieving compliance with the NAAQSs: adoption of the most stringent possible controls, possibly even more stringent than for new sources elsewhere, and a requirement that a new source offset its projected additional emissions by reducing emissions from existing sources by a greater amount. 40 C.F.R. pt. 51, App. 5 (1977).

Congress recognized and responded to the reality of extensive noncompliance when it overhauled the Clean Air Act in 1977. The new requirements for nonattainment areas were incorporated in part D of title I, sections 171-178. §§107(d), 171 "Nonattainment areas" were officially recognized in the statute. (Note that air quality control regions could be partially in compliance under the 1977 Amendments, in which case only the noncomplying area was subject to part D. Areas also could be in compliance for some pollutants and not others—indeed, this is typical—in which case part D applied only to emissions of the pollutants not meeting the NAAQSs.)

The 1977 Amendments extended the compliance date for nonattainment areas to December 31, 1982, §172(a)(1), and authorized further extensions for the pollutants proving most difficult to control—ozone and carbon monoxide—up to December 31, 1987. Twenty-nine states found it necessary to request an extension to 1987.

The 1977 Amendments also ratified the concept of EPA's extemporized offset program, while supplying a number of new statutory details. In their turn, the 1990 Amendments add further refinements, which we describe after examining the nonattainment offset program in more detail.

3. Use of Offsets and Bubbles to Promote Attainment

As the two oldest pieces of federal pollution control legislation, the Clean Air Act and the Clean Water Act have been the focal points of ongoing debates over the most appropriate regulatory strategies for solving problems of environmental pollution. The Air Act has been the major forum for one important aspect of that debate: the pros and cons of command-and-control regulation versus market-oriented or incentive-based regulation.

Under the command-and-control approach, government authorities issue specific pollution control commands to regulated firms and then monitor the firms to ensure that the commands are followed. In its original design, the Clean Air Act of 1970 epitomized this approach to regulation, and the overall structure of the Act is still dominated by it.

Still, from the very beginning, critics urged that more flexible regulatory strategies be adopted, especially strategies that would create situations in which the self-interest of regulated firms would motivate *them* to achieve pollution reductions in the most cost-effective manner possible. Government, under this approach, concentrates on determining how much pollution reduction is the appropriate goal, taking into account public health and welfare considerations, other national priorities, international considerations, the overall social costs of achieving pollution reduction, or whatever other factors the political system determines to be germane. As discussed in Chapter 2, pages 173-177, more flexible regulation such as this theoretically offers substantial advantages over a command-and-control approach, primarily through reduced compliance costs, but also by providing greater incentives for technological innovation and perhaps by reducing administrative costs.

Incentives for firms to meet the established goal can take a variety of forms, but the engine driving all incentive-based methods is firms' financial incentives to reduce pollution. In the late 1960s and early 1970s the method most discussed by policy analysts and theorists was a pollution tax. Interest has subsequently shifted to market-based systems, which allow firms to trade emissions allowances with one another or among plants owned by a single firm.

In all instances the argument for incentive-based regulation is that it can achieve almost any desired level of pollution reduction more cost-effectively than command-and-control can, because the costs of complying with government pollution commands almost always vary from plant to plant. "Indeed, the cost of controlling a unit of a given pollutant may vary by a factor of 100 or more among sources depending upon the age and location of plants and the available technologies. Any given aggregate pollution level can be met at minimum aggregate control cost if, and only if, firms control at the same *marginal cost,* as opposed to the same emission or control *level.*" Hahn and Stavins, Incentive Based Environmental Regulation, 18 Ecology L.Q. 1, 16 (1991).

Furthermore, the control costs of firms will tend to converge on the same marginal cost if firms are allowed to trade the obligation to reduce pollution among themselves. Suppose that firm *A* has an obligation to reduce a pollutant by 1 ton and that it will cost it $1,000 to do so. Firm *B*, on the other hand, has the capability of reducing the pollutant from its stacks by 1 ton for a cost of only $500. If firms can trade their obligations, *A* will be able to shop around for firms like *B* and they will be able to contract with one another to reach the 1 ton reduction, with *A* paying *B* a sum of money for *B* to assume the obligation to reduce. How much will *A* end up paying to *B*? Regardless of the amount, the real costs to society of reducing the pollutant by 1 ton will only be $500, whereas under command-and-control, *A* would have expended $1,000 in real costs to achieve the same end. Eventually, these opportunities to trade should produce a situation in which all firms are expending roughly the same marginal cost to eliminate pollution.

EPA's first significant experiment with incentive-based regulation arose through its efforts to accommodate industrial growth in areas of the country that were not in compliance with the NAAQSs. The Agency's approach included both the offset concept and a related idea, the "bubble."

The two procedures have distinct regulatory definitions and purposes, although they arguably serve similar functions. In the nonattain-

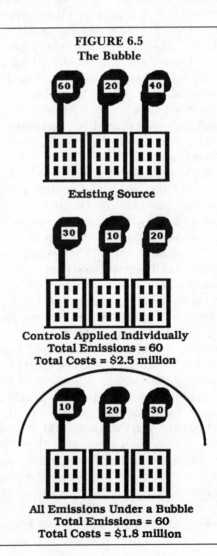

FIGURE 6.5
The Bubble

Existing Source

Controls Applied Individually
Total Emissions = 60
Total Costs = $2.5 million

All Emissions Under a Bubble
Total Emissions = 60
Total Costs = $1.8 million

ment context, allowing a firm to apply a bubble to a single site can enable it to reduce existing emissions at the site sufficiently so that a planned addition to or modification of the facility will not add additional net emissions to the area, thus avoiding new source review under part D entirely.

In general, the supposition behind the bubble, and its primary attraction, is that plant managers will know better how to achieve any stipulated amount of emissions reduction than regulators will, so some cost savings will occur if they are allowed the flexibility to find least-cost approaches. The potential for doing so exists because sizable industrial facilities typically have a fair number of discrete sources of air emissions—smokestacks from a number of boilers, vents, engines that drive machinery, sources of evaporative emissions, and so on. Under the most extreme form of command-and-control regulation, regulators would write emissions standards for each individual source. The bubble policy permits a firm to place all such sources at a single facility under an imaginary regulatory bubble. As long as the facility produces emissions less than some total amount for the entire facility (the total might simply be the sum of the requirements for individual sources), a regulator using the bubble policy will be indifferent to where within the plant the individual emissions occur.

A number of studies of existing facilities and existing control technologies have been done indicating that this is not just theory. Du Pont conducted a study of various bubble proposals, both on a plant-specific basis and nationwide, and the results of its study have played a prominent role in the debate over bubbling. As an example of its findings, du Pont calculated the impact of a bubble covering the emission of volatile organic compounds (VOCs) at its Deepwater, New Jersey Chambers Works facility. Du Pont estimated that complying with EPA's and New Jersey's emission point-by-emission point command-and-control regulations would cost $15 million in capital expenditures. The bubble du Pont proposed would reduce emissions at some of its major points by 99.9 percent, in excess of EPA's requirements, while reducing emissions much less elsewhere. The net result was that du Pont proposed to beat the overall plant emissions that would have resulted from command-and-control regulation (2,769 tons per year) by 84 percent, emitting only 438 tons per year, while saving over $10 million in capital costs.

Offsetting requires two or more sources. Under the nonattainment program of part D of the Air Act, new sources are required to offset new emissions by obtaining reductions in emissions elsewhere. Offsets may occur within the same company, or on a contractual basis between companies, or between a company and another entity such as a governmental unit. The offset policy therefore envisions the possibility of creating an emissions trading market, with firms that are building new plants or expanding existing plants purchasing pollution reductions—

and hence acquiring rights to pollute—from existing facilities. In principle, will the offset program result in least-cost emissions reductions as the bubble is supposed to do?

The 1990 Amendments create another emissions trading program, this one to implement the new acid rain controls. Before considering that program, work your way through the following problem. (For further reading on the concepts involved in incentive-based or market-based regulation, see Hahn and Stavins, Incentive Based Environmental Regulation, 18 Ecology L.Q. 1 (1991), and the works cited there; see also D. Pearce and R. Turner, Economics of Natural Resources and the Environment, chs. 5-8 (1990).)

PROBLEM EXERCISE: INCENTIVE-BASED APPROACHES TO AIR POLLUTION CONTROL

One measure of air quality involves calculating how much of a particular pollutant is present in a specified volume of air. Under the Air Act, the typical unit of measure is micrograms per cubic liter (μg/

FIGURE 6.6
Offsetting

Existing Source

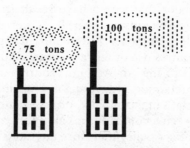

Old Source Plus a New Source

l³). This is a measure of ambient air quality. For sulfur dioxide, for example, the law requires that the annual arithmetic mean for the ambient concentration of sulfur dioxide in the air not exceed 80 μg/l³.

For any specific measurement point, the ambient concentration of sulfur dioxide is contributed to by every source of sulfur dioxide pollution close enough that the pollution plume from that source reaches the measurement point. Furthermore, a single source, A, might contribute a great deal to the ambient levels at measurement point #1, relatively close to the source, while contributing only minimally at measurement point #2, some distance away. A second source, B, close to point #2 and far from point #1, might have the opposite relative effects.

Now suppose that ambient levels are in excess of the ambient air quality standard at point #1, but the level at point #2 is in compliance with the standard. You are the official in charge of achieving the ambient air quality standard at both points. As part of that effort, you have ordered source A to remove a pound of sulfur dioxide from its stack gases.

The owners of sources B and A approach you. They claim that it is much cheaper to remove a pound of pollution from source B than it is from source A and that they have worked out a deal between them whereby source A would pay source B enough money to cover B's abatement costs, plus a little profit, if B would remove the pound from its stack gases. The money A is offering is still less than the cost to A if A had to remove the pollution from its own stack gases. They want you to approve this "trade."

Question One. From the point of view of someone interested in achieving compliance at *both* points, should you be interested in this arrangement? Why? Is a pound of pollution removed by source B more or less valuable than a pound removed by source A? Why? Should it make any difference how far away source B is from source A?

From here on, this Problem builds on some of the facts of the Selecting an Air Pollution Control Strategy, pages 155-159, above, except that the current Clean Air Act applies. You should reread the introductory material as well as "Act Two" of that problem. For present purposes, the pollutant being regulated is sulfur dioxide, *not* a carcinogen as in the earlier problem.

POLLUTCO now owns only one facility, located in the rural area. POLLUTCO's factory was regulated when the Clean Air Act was originally enacted, and it is currently permitted to emit 36,000 tons of pollutant per year. It has installed Technology One on its factory.

NEWCO is investigating the possibility of locating at a site in the urban area, in NAP's neighborhood. When it turns to air pollution problems, it discovers that the applicable law permits it to locate there if it offsets its additional pollution by obtaining reductions from other sources in the area. Reductions have to be greater than one-to-one, so that the net effect of the additional source is actually a reduction in total emissions. The state has said this requirement is satisfied if the offsets are 1.5 to 1. As a new source, NEWCO's plant will have to comply with new source performance standards as well. (Under the CAA nonattainment program, the requirement for new sources is that they be controlled to the "lowest achievable emissions rate," or LAER, which can be stricter than NSPS.) EPA has determined that NSPS be based on Technology Two, operating at the 96 percent level. The facility NEWCO is planning would be identical in size and operating characteristics to the urban facility in the earlier problem: without controls, it would emit 60 tons per hour of pollutant and would operate 2,000 hours per year, on average.

Question Two. NEWCO approaches POLLUTCO to see if POLLUTCO would be interested in engaging in an offset transaction. NEWCO proposes to pay POLLUTCO a sum of money to reduce its pollution enough that their combined emissions will be less than POLLUTCO's current levels. How much will POLLUTCO have to reduce emissions to offset NEWCO? How much should POLLUTCO be willing to accept as payment for doing this?

Question Three. Assume POLLUTCO and NEWCO strike a deal. Should NAP object to the offset scheme? What grounds for complaint might it have?

Question Four. NAP does some investigating and discovers that POLLUTCO has actually been operating its facility at reduced capacity for the past three years. (The facility is getting old, and POLLUTCO has been switching its production to other, newer facilities.) During that time it has never emitted more than 27,000 tons of pollutants per year, and it apparently has no plans to increase output there. Why might NAP complain now? How should STAFF respond to NAP's complaint? From the point of view of the objectives of the offset program, should this offset trade be permissible? If the amount of offset credit were limited to reductions in actual, rather than permissible, emissions, would POLLUTCO be free to choose the base year for purposes of measuring reductions? See Citizens Against the Refinery's Effects v. EPA, 643 F.2d 183 (4th Cir. 1981).

Question Five. Suppose that POLLUTCO's facility is actually operating at its 36,000-tons-per-year allowance. It is, however, still an old facility, and POLLUTCO's central management has plans to shut it down. Suppose POLLUTCO is deciding whether to shut down the rural plant, and its analysts tell management that it is likely 4 facilities of roughly the same pollution capabilities as NEWCO's will move into the region in the next 12 to 18 months. Should this information have any impact on the timing of the decision to shut down? Why? If POLLUTCO were to sell all of its current pollution allowance and then shut down, should environmental groups protest these sales? Could POLLUTCO claim offsets even if environmental groups could show that it would have shut down anyway?

In contrast to ambient air quality levels at specific locations, another possible measure of air pollution is total pollution loading: the regulatory authority could simply calculate the sum of all contributions to sulfur dioxide emissions from all sources. In 1980, for instance, the total annual sulfur dioxide loading nationwide was approximately 18.9 million tons. Then, the regulatory authority could mandate that this total loading be reduced by some amount within a stipulated period of time.

The acid rain provisions of the 1990 Clean Air Act Amendments adopt this approach by prescribing a national ceiling of approximately 8.9 million tons of sulfur dioxide emissions by the year 2000. The method for achieving this reduction will include EPA's distribution of annual "allowances," or permits, to emit sulfur dioxide. The total face value of all of the allowances will be 8.9 million tons. Emitters may buy and sell allowances. The Act also sets up means for emitters to obtain extra allowances for taking steps that the Act seeks to encourage, like early compliance with some provisions of the Act. Because the allowances are marketable, emitters will have an incentive to take such steps.

Question Six. Why might an air pollution control strategy try to control total loading of a pollutant rather than to achieve uniform ambient pollution levels throughout some geographical area? Is the use of an incentive-based approach more or less acceptable when the objective is to control total loading than when the objective is to achieve uniform ambient levels? Why?

Question Seven. Is there reason to be concerned about the misuse of offsets and bubbles in nonattainment areas? Congress has restricted the part D offset program to allay certain fears of abuse. Unfortunately, the stringency of part D requirements also creates enormous incentives to push the limits of permissible trading. There is another problem with strict rules. On the one hand, critics of trading argue that "unless the rules governing trading are fairly strict, they will only enable industries to 'game' regulators. That is, industries will use trading opportunities to exploit weaknesses in state plans." R. Liroff, Reforming Air Pollution Regulation: The Toil and Trouble of EPA's Bubble 11 (1986). On the other hand, the more strict the rules and the supervision to assure trading is not abused, the less valuable the trading program becomes to the applicant.

4.   The 1990 Amendments

The 1990 Amendments included several provisions designed to improve the integrity of the program.

a.   Offset Area.   A source needing to offset emissions under the 1990 Amendments can do so only within the same attainment area in which it wishes to locate; however, it can go outside that area if (1) the other area is of an equal or higher classification as the siting area and (2) emissions from the other area contribute to a violation of the NAAQS in the siting area.

b.   Permissible Offsets.   Can a new source offset emissions from an existing source that are allowed under an existing SIP but which the existing source is in fact not emitting (perhaps because it has downsized its plant, or perhaps because the control requirements for it are relatively lax), or must the offsetting emissions represent reductions from actual operating levels? Assuming that an applicant should be allowed to offset from allowable emissions, should this still be permitted when the underlying SIP, which establishes the allowable levels, is suspected or proved to be inadequate to achieve the NAAQSs? How do the 1990 Amendments address these issues? See §173.

c.   Growth Allowances.   Under the 1977 Amendments, some states chose to provide for new growth in nonattainment areas by creating a "growth allowance" in their SIPs that they could then allocate to new sources without requiring the new sources to obtain offsets. Under the 1990 Amendments, so-called old growth allowances (allowances for new growth under the old Act) cannot be used as a basis for permit approval if the SIP establishing them has been found by the administrator to be "substantially inadequate."

5.   Fine-Tuning SIPs

America's unabated love affair with the automobile has unquestionably been the single greatest obstacle to meeting air quality goals. For example, vehicle-miles traveled in the Washington, D.C. metropolitan area increased by about 70 percent from 1968 to 1985, and there is no end in sight. Since emissions standards for automobiles were set by the federal government (but for the California waiver), the 1970 Act left states with only politically unpopular strategies to reduce vehicle miles traveled (parking bans, car pooling incentives, and so on) or less effective programs to improve maintenance of older cars and reduce emissions released during fueling.

While the 1977 Amendments imposed much more stringent requirements for SIPs in nonattainment areas, Congress further undermined the integrity of the SIP process by creating several special-interest exemptions and related provisions designed to promote nonenvironmental objectives. Section 118(b) allowed a variance for federal facilities. Section 119 authorized the same for primary nonferrous smelters, a term which has in practice encompassed copper, lead, and zinc smelters. Congress added section 110(a)(3)(C) in order to assure that other dischargers would not be subject to more stringent requirements as a result of these waivers. (What is the operational result of this provision? How can it be justified?) Yet another exemption was made available for new health or educational institutions in clean air areas. §169(1).

The large number of nonattainment areas, tight deadlines, and complicated procedures for SIP revisions resulted in considerable confusion and litigation concerning implementation of the nonattainment provisions of the 1977 Amendments. For example, section 110(c)(l) contemplated approval of nonattainment-area SIPs and the imposition of a ban on construction of new sources in areas without such approvals no later than July 1, 1979. When this proved impractical, EPA proposed "partial" and "conditional" approvals. With some qualifications, this approach was largely upheld in City of Seabrook v. EPA, 659 F.2d 1349 (5th Cir. 1981). But see Connecticut Fund for the Environment v. EPA, 696 F.2d 147 (2d Cir. 1982) (allowing conditional approvals but finding them insufficient to allow the state to avoid a construction ban).

Conditional approval allowed extended negotiations between EPA and states unable or unwilling to produce adequate plans. A different set of issues arose in states that found themselves unable to fully implement approved SIPs. For example, in American Lung Association v. Kean, 670 F. Supp. 1285 (D.N.J. 1987), New Jersey admitted it had failed to implement seven strategies for VOC reduction identified in its SIP, asserting that the state had only committed to study their feasibility. New Jersey lost, a victim of what has been described as "a perverse kind of reward system. . . . [S]tates doing little to develop meaningful SIPs . . . are protected because they never did much of anything that could be used against them. States who played the game, producing stern SIPs with clear commitments, cannot slip away from enforcement obligations nearly so easily." W. Rodgers, Environmental Law: Air and Water Pollution, sec. 3.10 at 261 (1986).

As the 1987 deadline for attainment provided in the 1977 Amendments approached and it became apparent that many regions would not achieve complete attainment, EPA again found itself in a difficult position. In November 1987 EPA proposed a policy providing for further extensions beyond the statutory deadlines, together with requirements for gradual reductions in emissions while awaiting congressional direction. 52 Fed. Reg. 45,044 (1987). In the meantime environmentalists had challenged the Agency's approval of air pollution control measures for southern California without any showing that such measures would be adequate to meet the December 1987 deadline. In Abramowitz v. EPA, 832 F.2d 1071 (9th Cir. 1987), the court found the Act's deadlines, whether feasible or not, clear and unambiguous. Emphasizing the statutory language, the court found that "[i]n the case of ozone and carbon monoxide standards, each SIP must contain enforceable measures to assure attainment of the applicable standard not later than December 31, 1987. 42 U.S.C. §7502(c) (1982)." Yet the court noted that neither EPA nor the state had made an effort to develop such measures; rather, "[w]hat the record does reveal is EPA's desire to seek legislative relief." The court concluded:

> Because we find the language of the Act clear and unambiguous, we do not believe that EPA has the discretion to ignore the statutory deadline. We are informed by counsel for both sides of their expectation that Congress will extend the deadline once again in the near future, but we must apply the law as it now stands, not as it may become. As one commentator has noted, the Clean Air Act has been "a potpourri of postponements, revisions, extensions and suspensions." Rodgers, §3.13 at 289. Until the Clean Air Act is further considered, however, the Agency must "give effect to the unambiguously expressed intent of Congress." Chevron, 467 U.S. at 843. Although the Agency's task may be difficult, it must nevertheless comply with its legislative mandate. Placed between the express intent of Congress and the recalcitrance of the Agency, the proper role of the court in this case must be to remind the Agency that its duty is to apply the existing law. [832 F.2d at 1079.]

Finding that EPA had exceeded its authority by approving the South Coast carbon monoxide and ozone control measures without requiring a demonstration of attainment before December 31, 1987, the court ordered EPA to disapprove the relevant SIP provisions.

Following this and the expiration of the attainment deadline, EPA was confronted with promulgating its own federal implementation plan (FIP) for the area. Recognizing that the Los Angeles region has the worst urban air pollution in the United States, EPA was faced with a choice between development of a FIP that would cause massive economic and social dislocation in an attempt to achieve attainment rapidly or a FIP that would authorize decades of noncompliance. While EPA hoped that the issue would be resolved by the enactment of comprehensive amendments to the Clean Air Act for the first time since 1977, legislative gridlock prevailed in Congress. Faced with a court order to promulgate a FIP, EPA described the impossible position in which it found itself when it solicited public comments on the issue in the following Federal Register notice.

EPA, Approval and Promulgation of Implementation Plans; California— South Coast Air Basin; Ozone and Carbon Monoxide Plans
53 Fed. Reg. 49,494 (1988)

In the course of administering the Clean Air Act, EPA often has been called upon to interpret the law where Congress has left a gap that must be filled. But few of EPA's prior determinations have been so difficult, or threatened such upheaval, as the judgment we must now make about the ozone and carbon monoxide problems in the South Coast Basin that surrounds Los Angeles.

Ozone is a pollutant with serious health effects that, as we are increasingly becoming aware, may cause permanent long-term damage if breathed at certain concentrations. The effects are unmistakable at levels commonly encountered in the Los Angeles area, which has the worst ozone problem in the United States, suffering from both the highest levels and the most frequent violations of the national ozone standard.

CO reduces the amount of oxygen delivered to all tissues of the body, and, at certain levels, poses a threat to human health. The Basin frequently violates the federal air quality standards for CO.

EPA wants to—and must—do something constructive to remedy this unacceptable public health threat. But, in its present form, the law intended to address the problem cannot deal with it effectively. This is because the last statutory deadline for a plan to meet the standard—December 31, 1987—has now passed, and Congress has given EPA no instructions as to what to do under these circumstances.

EPA has acknowledged a duty under the Clean Air Act to develop a federal implementation plan (FIP) to help the South Coast Basin attain the primary national ambient air quality standard (NAAQS) for ozone and carbon monoxide (CO). But the Act does not specify the date by which such a plan must project attainment. Since the deadline has passed, and Congress has not extended it, must an EPA plan require immediate attainment? Or should it call for attainment within a period (three to five years) analogous to the relevant previous rounds of planning required by the statute (specifically, section 110(a) and (e), and the second round of planning for areas that received attainment date extensions from 1982 to 1987 under Section 172(a)(2))? Attainment of the ozone NAAQS appears to require, in the case of the South Coast Basin, extreme restrictions on the use of fossil fuels and the reactive hydrocarbons that are now essential components of many industrial, commercial, and consumer products and activities. It is for this reason that an immediate or a near-term attainment FIP for the South Coast, if determined to be statutorily required, would raise serious questions of enforceability and potential conflicts with other statutes. As a practical matter, immediate attainment is impossible and a five-year plan would impose requirements so draconian as to remake life in the South Coast Basin.

The South Coast authorities estimate that an 80 to 90 percent reduction in volatile organic compound ("VOC") emissions is necessary to attain the ozone standard. Thus a plan that provides for attainment in the South Coast immediately or even within five years would have to prohibit most traffic, shut down major business activity, curtail the use of important consumer goods, and dramatically restrict all aspects of social and economic life. Implementation and enforcement of such drastic measures may well be impossible, and could prevent satisfaction of the basic necessities of life—including food, shelter, and medical services. Such a plan would effectively usurp many state and local government functions and would radically restrict individual opportunity. Indeed, an immediate or a near-term attainment FIP for ozone would destroy the economy of the South Coast, so that most of the population would be forced to resettle elsewhere. Similar drastic consequences would flow from a short-term plan to attain the CO standard.

Given these consequences of short-term plans, should EPA instead allow a longer term for attainment—one that supports local efforts in making progress over a period such as the twenty years provided for in the plan under consideration by the South Coast Air Quality Management District (SCAQMD)? Such a course appeals to common sense, but is without precedent in the Act.

A long-term FIP might appear to offer a more realistic (though still exceedingly difficult) path to attainment, and would complement ongoing state and local efforts to develop a SIP. But it also raises significant issues. Such a FIP would require EPA to make difficult legislative-type decisions about the projected pace and direction of technological and life-style change, over a long period of time. A long-term plan would have more gradual and less dislocating impacts than a short-term FIP but would still have profound implications for much of the local economy, for some national and foreign industries, and for the entire way of life in the South Coast Basin. Moreover, in either circumstance, EPA arguably must to some extent exercise legislative-type powers that, while perhaps permitted by the courts (see Chevron, U.S.A., Inc. v. NRDC, 467 U.S. 837 (1984)), are more appropriately exercised by Congress. Nonetheless, in the absence of legislative direction, EPA believes it may need to resolve several fundamental issues of legislative scope to comply with its legal obligation to develop a FIP for the South Coast.

The Agency believes that, in fulfilling this obligation, it should seek to act consistently with at least the key principles underlying the statute, while minimizing the extent to which EPA performs legislative-type decisionmaking. As discussed in detail below, this is a very difficult task. EPA officials have repeatedly urged the 100th Congress to come to grips with this issue and to amend and extend the Clean Air Act. Their failure to do so leaves EPA with no course other than to press on and try to discern, as best the Agency can, what the prior enacting Congress would have intended us to do. . . .

EPA here finds itself confronted by a most painful dilemma—one that clearly needs a Congressional solution. Absent action by Congress, however, EPA must do its best to achieve a result most consistent with the language, history, and purposes of the Clean Air Act.

If EPA interprets the Act to permit a FIP attainment deadline significantly beyond 1987, it may stretch the boundaries of the statute in an unprecedented way, and arguably assume legislative-type authority to direct the pace of technological, economic, and environmental change in the South Coast. The scope of any plan attempting to address the pollution problem in the South Coast must be equal to the enormity of that problem. Should EPA determine to prepare a long-term FIP for the South Coast, it would no doubt encounter great practical difficulties in developing and implementing such a massive plan.

But EPA would also face serious legal and practical problems if it undertook a plan requiring immediate and short-term attainment. The immediate and short-term FIP interpretations are arguably more in keeping with the original lapsed deadline, and with Congress'[s] expressions of intent to be the provider of relief if deadlines proved too harsh. But these interpretations, if imposed here, would wreak a level of economic and social disruption that is likely beyond anything Congress would have imagined would be imposed without some mitigation.

Thus, there appears to be no easy solution to the problem before us.

NOTES AND QUESTIONS

1. How would you have sought to resolve the "most painful dilemma" described by EPA? Should EPA have promulgated a FIP that did not provide for compliance until decades after the 1987 deadline, or should it have opted for a plan requiring immediate, short-term attainment with its attendant social dislocation?

2. The *Abramowitz* litigation that placed EPA in such a difficult position exemplified the need for congressional clarification. This was finally achieved in the 1990 Amendments, which are described below. The Court of Appeals decision was only the latest round in a lengthy

and sometimes bitter struggle fought by a small band of citizen activists in Los Angeles. Their story is a classic example of the impact a few persistent citizens can have on a recalcitrant bureaucracy. Mark Abramowitz, the named plaintiff, was then a 29-year-old resident of Santa Monica holding a graduate degree in environmental science who drove a battered Volkswagen with personalized license plates reading "FGT SMOG." Abramowitz and the local Coalition for Clean Air had battled the South Coast Air Quality Management District for over a decade. After EPA approved the SIP for Los Angeles in 1984, Abramowitz filed suit pro se. "A few weeks later, his phone rang. It was the EPA calling to inquire if he might consider an out-of-court settlement. 'I'm a reasonable sort of fella,' Abramowitz replied. What were his terms? 'Clean air.'" Russel, L.A. Air, 10 Amicus Journal 10 (Summer 1988). After indicating its willingness to consider the adoption of more stringent SIP provisions in a settlement, EPA later allowed the issue to go to court.

3. Attaining the NAAQSs in southern California presents substantial difficulties. Because of its infamous traffic congestion, topography, and climate, Los Angeles suffers from more air quality violations than any other urban area in America; violations occur as many as two days out of three, sometimes by as much as 300 percent. The pollution problem is a major policy issue in the air basin, which has its own governmental entity, the South Coast Air Quality Management District (SCAQMD) responsible for it. The SCAQMD has over 1,000 employees, its own inspection and compliance staff, and an extensive research and development program. Its policies are determined by a 12-member governing board representing the Governor, the State Assembly and Senate, and the county and city governments.

4. After developing the most stringent air quality control plan in the country, SCAQMD, Air Quality Management Plan (1989), the SCAQMD has shifted abruptly to an approach that relies on market forces to produce dramatic reductions in emissions. Companies will be allowed to buy and sell pollution credits in an open market to ease the burden of meeting strict emission reduction quotas. Stevenson, Trying a Market Approach to Smog, N.Y. Times, Mar. 25, 1992, at D1.

The Nonattainment Problem and the 1990 Amendments

The net result of almost 20 years of seeking compliance with the NAAQSs was that, from 1987 to 1989, 96 areas had some violation of the ozone standard, 41 areas violated standards for carbon monoxide, and another 58 did not meet the particulate standards. In some areas violations were the exception, but in the dirtiest cities they remained all too frequent. It was apparent that additional strategies, not simply more time, were essential to achieve air quality goals.

In addition to making changes in the overall program for nonattainment, the 1990 Amendments impose additional responsibilities on nonattainment areas depending on how severe is their nonattainment problem. First, the overall changes:

a. Refining the Concept of Reasonable Further Progress. The 1977 version of the nonattainment program required nonattainment areas to have in place plans that would achieve "reasonable further progress" (RFP) toward the NAAQS, §172(b)(3), amended by Pub. L. No. 101-549. RFP was vaguely defined to mean "annual incremental reductions in emissions," which satisfied the administrator, but exactly how much was required was never clearly specified by EPA. §171(1). The 1990 Amendments authorize the administrator to "require" annual incremental reductions in specified numerical amounts. They also establish by statute specific incremental reductions for certain of the nonattainment regions referred to above. For example, an area classified moderate for ozone has to submit a plan that ensures a 15 percent reduction in VOC emissions by 1996.

b. Adjusting the Areas Classified Nonattainment. For the automobile pollutants—ozone and carbon monoxide—the 1990 Amendments state that if a nonattainment area classified as serious, severe, or extreme is located within an urban area (a metropolitan statistical area or a consolidated metropolitan statistical area), then the entire area generally is so classified. This is done for two reasons: First, under the old law, only new sources locating "in" a nonattainment area were subject to new source review under the strict nonattainment program. Encompassing entire urban areas means that all sources located in the expanded areas will be subject to such review. Second, the serious, severe, or extreme areas are subject to various transportation and fuel control measures (for instance, inspection and maintenance programs) that will more effectively reduce the automobile pollutants if applied areawide. EPA's initial classification and designation of areas for air quality planning purposes appears at 56 Fed. Reg. 56,694 (1991).

c. Regulating Smaller Sources. New source review currently applies to sources emitting more than 100 tons per year. The 1990 Amendments reduce the threshold for ozone-producing pollutants to 50 tons for serious areas, 25 tons for severe areas, and 10 tons for extreme areas. These revisions recognize the significant contributions to air quality made by relatively small sources.

d. Guidance on RACT. The current law requires that existing sources in nonattainment areas install reasonably available control technology. States have made slow progress here, and they have complained of a lack of guidance from EPA in defining RACT. The 1990 Amendments require EPA to issue Control Technique Guidelines (CTGs) for volatile organic compounds, proceeding industry by industry on a priority basis.

  e. Attainment Dates. Nonattainment areas are to be in compliance with the NAAQSs "as expeditiously as possible," but no later than certain prescribed dates. The statute provides different compliance dates for specific areas:

Ozone	marginal	1993
	moderate	1996
	serious	1999
	severe-15	2005
	severe-17	2007 (see §181(a)(2))
	extreme	2010
Carbon monoxide	moderate-1	1995
	moderate-2	1995
	serious	2000
Particulates	moderate	1994
	serious	2001

The exact compliance date for carbon monoxide and particulates is December 31 of the years indicated; for ozone, it is November 15 of the years indicated.

  Turn now to the requirements for particular nonattainment classifications.

  a. Ozone Areas. The main participants in the production of ozone, or urban smog, are nitrogen oxides and volatile organic compounds, or VOCs. VOCs are emitted from automobiles as well as from stationary sources. In general, the 1990 Amendments aimed at ozone reflect the conviction that the ozone problem cannot be adequately addressed through end-of-the-pipe controls on automobiles, trucks, and buses alone (although these are tightened, too, in title II). Since the 1970 law was enacted, vehicle-miles traveled have increased 55 percent and continue to grow at the rate of nearly 3 percent per year. Cold starts and idling in congested traffic contribute disproportionately to the ozone problem; thus the type of driving involved in daily commuting is the worst type with respect to the ozone problem. Reflecting this analysis, the 1990 Amendments turn to two types of automobile-related measures in addition to end-of-the-pipe measures. They adopt measures designed to produce cleaner fuels and they require transportation controls of various types.

  The 1990 Amendments require a series of pollution reduction

measures that expand as you move from less seriously nonattaining areas to the more serious nonattainment problems:

i. Marginal areas. These areas must submit to EPA data on actual emissions from all sources; they must fix any vehicle inspection and maintenance (I&M) program they were required to have under the 1977 Amendments to ensure that cars on the road comply with emissions requirements; and they must submit inventories of emissions sources every three years, conduct new source reviews, and fix RACT rules.

ii. Moderate areas. These areas must comply with requirements for Marginals and also within 6 years reduce VOCs by 15 percent; implement RACT for most VOC sources covered by a CTG issued before November 1990 and for major sources that will not be covered by any CTG; require gas stations to install vapor recovery systems; implement a basic I&M program; and make a basic attainment demonstration.

iii. Serious areas. These must comply with requirements for Moderates and also must provide a special demonstration to EPA (using modeling techniques) that the plan will attain the NAAQS; achieve 3 percent emissions reduction each year, averaged over consecutive three-year periods; implement an enhanced I&M program, including enforcement through the denial of vehicle registration; use transportation control measures in areas where projections of vehicle mileage, emissions, and congestion exceed levels projected as necessary for attainment; and implement a clean fuels program (providing that gasoline sold in the area will be reformulated gasoline, gasoline that has been blended so as to reduce the production of VOCs on combustion [ethanol or MTBE blends, for example], see discussion of the mobile sources provisions, section G).

iv. Severe areas. These areas must comply with requirements for Serious areas and also adopt measures to ensure that any growth in vehicle emissions is offset elsewhere and require major employers to implement programs to reduce work-related vehicle trips and mileage.

v. Extreme areas. These areas must comply with requirements for Severe areas and also must require utilities and industrial and commercial boilers emitting more than 25 tons per year of nitrogen oxide to burn natural gas, methanol or ethanol, or some other low-polluting fuel, or use advanced control technology to catch nitrogen oxide emissions; and enact traffic control measures during heavy traffic hours.

The 1990 Amendments also specify the amount of offset emissions required before a new source permit can be approved. That amount varies according to the area's classification: for extreme areas, 1.5 to 1; for severe areas, 1.3 to 1; for serious areas, 1.2 to 1; for moderate areas, 1.15 to 1; and for marginal areas, 1.1 to 1.

b. Carbon Monoxide Areas. This is the other major automobile pollutant. The 1990 Amendments establish two general sub-classifications for this pollutant, moderate and serious.

i. Moderate areas. Reporting requirements generally parallel those for ozone. In addition, Moderate-2 areas (those with carbon monoxide concentrations greater than 12.7 ppm) must submit a forecast of vehicle miles traveled and they must have an enhanced I&M program.

ii. Serious areas. These areas must comply with Moderate requirements and also establish a clean fuels program for times of the year when carbon monoxide levels are the highest; establish the same sort of transportation control measures as required of areas that are severe for ozone; study stationary source contributions to carbon monoxide and produce a plan to reduce their emissions; and demonstrate by March 31, 1996 that emission reductions equivalent to those required by December 31, 1995 have in fact been met, under penalty of further transportation controls and economic measures for noncompliance.

c. Particulate Areas. There are just two sub-classifications, moderate and serious. Because particulates can have significant nonanthropogenic sources, the administrator can waive some of the requirements for Serious areas on a determination that anthropogenic sources are not significant contributors to exceedances. The administrator is also required to issue control measures for urban fugitive dust and emissions from residential wood stoves and planned agricultural and silvicultural burns, as well as to explore other categories of sources contributing to nonattainment for particulates and to issue control measures accordingly.

i. Moderate areas. These areas must implement a permit program for new and modified sources; conduct a demonstration of whether attainment by the end of 1994 is feasible; implement RACT and other "reasonably available control measures" (RACM) for particulates; and include quantitative milestones in the revised SIP.

ii. Serious areas. These must comply with requirements for Moderate areas and apply the "best available control measures" (BACM); also, a Serious area failing to meet a milestone must then operate under a plan achieving annual 5 percent reductions in particulates calculated from the most recent source inventory.

Improving Air Quality in Nonattainment Areas: Is It Worth the Cost?

Air pollution controls have been expensive, and some question whether attainment of the national air quality standards is worth the cost, particularly the high cost of meeting the ozone standard. In 1988 the Office of Technology Assessment (OTA) estimated that it would cost $6-7 billion a year for cities with high ozone levels to implement the range of currently available technologies for controlling ozone formation and that full implementation of such measures would only achieve half the reduction needed to bring all cities into compliance. OTA, Urban Ozone and the Clean Air Act: Problems and Proposals for Change (1988). A subsequent OTA report found that two-thirds of the reductions in ozone levels needed to meet the NAAQS could be achieved using existing technologies at an annual cost of $4-8 billion in the mid-1990s and $9-13 billion during the next century. OTA, Catching Our Breath: Next Steps for Reducing Urban Ozone (July 1989).

Some economists have argued that the costs of attaining the NAAQSs are greatly in excess of any likely benefits. See, e.g., R. Crandall et al., Regulating the Automobile (1986). Yet estimates of both benefits and costs are uncertain. One study of Los Angeles concluded that the value of missed work days and shortened life spans due to air pollution in that region alone exceeds $10 billion a year. Weisman, LA Fights for Breath, N.Y. Times Magazine, July 30, 1989, at 33. Other studies suggest that the agricultural benefits of reducing ozone by one-half could be as much as $5 billion per year. J. MacKenzie and M. El-Ashry, Ill Winds: Airborne Pollution's Toll on Trees and Crops 10 (1988).

Two economists from Resources for the Future estimate that achieving compliance with the NAAQSs in the Los Angeles area could cost between $10 to $13 billion annually while providing only about $4 billion in annual benefits. Krupnick and Portney, Controlling Urban Air Pollution: A Benefit-Cost Assessment, 252 Science 522 (1991). Examination of how these estimates were derived illuminates the uncertainties that plague cost-benefit analysis. Krupnick and Portney concede that it is extremely difficult to estimate benefits because it is difficult to determine the precise relationships between specific pollutants in Los Angeles's chemical soup and specific health effects. They based their health effects estimates on epidemiological data linking sulfate particles to premature deaths in the region and on clinical data showing how individuals respond in laboratory experiments to various levels of ozone exposure. To assess the value of avoiding these adverse health effects, Krupnick and Portney turned to surveys of how much people are willing to pay to avoid them. This produced benefit estimates of $2 billion for reduced premature mortality risk (valued at $1,000 for each reduction of 0.001 in annual mortality risk), $300 million for reduced respiratory ailments (valued at $25 per asthma attack prevented, $20 per reduced activity day, and $5 per day of occasional coughing), $700 million for reduced particulate-related morbidity, and $1 billion for reduced materials damage.

These estimates provoked sharp criticism. Two researchers whose work was cited by Krupnick and Portney (Frederick W. Lipfert and Samuel C. Morris of the Brookhaven National Laboratory) criticized the study for considering only the effects of sulfate aerosols and for valuing each premature death avoided at only $1 million, a figure far less than that used in other studies. Lipfert and Morris, Air Pollution Benefit-Cost Assessment, 253 Science 606 (1991). Robert Friedman, the project director of the 1989 OTA study, argues that Krupnick and Portney are far too confident that costs exceed benefits. Friedman, Air Pollution Benefit-Cost Assessment, 253 Science 607 (1991). Noting that 20 million people are exposed to ozone levels in excess of the NAAQS for an average of about 9 hours per year, Friedman argues that averting acute coughing and painful breathing alone is "likely to be worth several billion dollars per year." He emphasizes that the medical community is even more concerned about chronic health effects not considered in the Krupnick-Portney analysis in light of evidence suggesting that air pollution in Los Angeles may cause permanent damage to lung function. Another economist suggests that the study is of little relevance to the debate over air pollution controls because it did not focus on damage to forests, visibility, agricultural damage, and lake acidification, which are greater problems than coughing. Chapman, Air Pollution Benefit-Cost Assessment, 253 Science 608 (1991).

The executive officer of the South Coast Air Quality Management District, James M. Lents, argues that Krupnick and Portney overestimated the costs of controlling air pollution in Los Angeles by using old estimates that have been contradicted by experience. Lents, Air Pollution Benefit-Cost Assessment, 253 Science 607 (1991). He notes that as pollution control "measures have been implemented, costs have fallen by almost half, largely because of rapid advances in technology, such as new and cleaner paints and materials that have eliminated the need for expensive retrofit controls" and that some "measures will actually save money by conserving on energy and materials." Lents argues that the total benefits of controlling air pollution in Los Angeles could easily approach $19 billion per year, and he criticizes Krupnick and Portney's study for "its stark avoidance of moral principle" by tolerating continued poisoning of the air. He concludes that "despite what the economic studies say, I defy the authors to look an asthmatic straight in the eye and tell them that [avoiding] their last life-threatening asthma attack could be valued at $25." Id. at 608.

While acknowledging uncertainties in their estimates of benefits and costs, Krupnick and Portney maintain that their study was based on the best evidence available concerning the health effects of air pollution. Krupnick and Portney, Air Pollution Benefit-Cost Assessment, 253 Science 608 (1991). They concede, however, that if evidence of chronic impairment of lung function is "substantiated, and *if* this loss in lung function is significant enough to affect the way people live or the time at which they die, all bets are off on our estimates of the benefits." Id. at 609 (emphasis in original). Noting that "values like $25 per avoided asthma attack come from questionnaires administered to ordinary citizens, *including asthmatics*," Krupnick and Portney respond to Lents's moral argument in the following manner:

> [A]t a time when so many households in Los Angeles and in the nation suffer from hunger, crime, poor health, homelessness, addiction, illiteracy, and other problems, can it *really* be wrong to ask whether the best use of society's next million, billion, or ten billion dollars lies in reducing urban ozone concentrations? [Id. (emphasis in original).]

Opponents of the 1990 Clean Air Act Amendments frequently cited another study in which Portney found that the Amendments would cost between $29-36 billion per year by the year 2005, while providing annual benefits ranging from "$6-25 billion ($2-9 billion for acid rain, $4-12 billion for urban air quality, and $0-4 billion for hazardous air pollutants)." Portney, Economics and the Clean Air Act, reprinted in 136 Cong. Rec. H12916, 12918 (Oct. 26, 1990). During the final stages of the legislative debate, Portney questioned why "Congress and the President are about to shake hands on a landmark piece of environmental law for which costs may exceed benefits by a considerable margin." While conceding that innovation could cause control costs to decline over time and that individuals may value reduced health and ecological risks more than economists think they do, Portney thought the real explanation was that the public simply did not appreciate the Amendments' true costs. Id. Robert Friedman of OTA counters that Congress considered Portney's analysis, which is cited in the committee reports, but that it simply "reached a different conclusion" concerning costs and benefits:

> [The Members] substituted their own judgments about the value of avoiding acute respiratory symptoms for those obtained from the economics literature. Moreover, they made judgments about the value of avoiding potential, but unproved, chronic health risks. I find this quite reasonable. The four valuation studies used by Krupnick and Portney used mail or telephone surveys of between 40 and 400 adults each, asking participants how much they would be willing to pay to avoid specific respiratory symptoms. The results of these studies provide useful information to Congress, but do we really want these studies to supersede the judgment of our elected representatives? In the end, it is the responsibility of the Congress to be the arbiter of our nation's collective values and to make the tough, yet necessary, judgment calls when our scientific and technical "crystal ball" is cloudy. [Friedman, Air Pollution Benefit-Cost Assessment, 253 Science 607 (1991).]

NOTES AND QUESTIONS

1. Whose estimates of the costs and benefits of air pollution control do you find to be the most reasonable? On what do you base your

assessment? What role, if any, should cost-benefit analysis play in the development of air pollution control regulations? Should Congress give EPA the discretion to balance economic, environmental, and other considerations in establishing NAAQSs?

2. Do you agree that Congress made an implicit cost-benefit judgment when it adopted the 1990 Clean Air Act Amendments? Is the economists' real complaint with the way Congress has struck the balance, or is it with the process by which legislative judgments are made?

3. Money invested in environmental controls "does not vanish into thin air," as one economist notes, but rather represents a wealth transfer from polluting industries to companies that provide pollution control services. Gutfeld, For Each Dollar Spent on Clean Air Someone Stands to Make a Buck, Wall St. J., Oct. 29, 1990, at 1. Should cost-benefit analyses take into account the economic benefits of such investments?

4. The debate over cost-benefit analyses of air pollution control once again reflects a clash between the moral outrage and cool analysis perspectives. Would you raise any further issues not brought out in this particular exchange? See the discussion of cost-benefit analysis, Chapter 4D1b, pages 525-536.

F. INTERSTATE AIR POLLUTION

In terms of historical understandings of the relationship between federal and state authority, the control of interstate air pollution provides an easy rationale for federal regulation of air pollution. EPA's authority in the 1965 Act to convene an interstate conference to address such problems, albeit weak and unsuccessful, marked the first federal attempt to control emissions sources directly.

Despite this, the construction of a detailed regulatory program to address interstate air pollution has lagged significantly behind other developments under the Air Act, and the control of such pollution would still have to be considered an unfulfilled promise. At times this lack of attention has produced new and substantial air pollution problems. For example, utility companies in the 1970s responded to increasingly stringent control of local air pollution by building tall stacks that could project pollution plumes into the upper atmosphere, sending the pollution long distances. More than 175 stacks higher than 500 feet were constructed after enactment of the 1970 Act. This practice was terminated by section 123 of the 1977 Amendments, but not before utility companies had constructed the 111 "big dirties" that are the primary sources of acid rain in the eastern United States.

As you read the following abbreviated account of the regulation of interstate air pollution, ask yourself why this aspect of the air pollution problem has been so neglected.

1. The Evolving Federal Response to Interstate Air Pollution

Until congressional enactment of an acid rain program in the 1990 Clean Air Amendments, the only provisions in the Act addressed to interstate air pollution were in the SIP process. As originally enacted, section 110(a)(2)(E) required SIPs to include "adequate provisions for intergovernmental cooperation, including measures necessary to insure" noninterference with other states' attainment or maintenance of air quality standards. EPA construed this language to require only an exchange of information, and this interpretation was upheld. NRDC v. EPA, 483 F.2d 690 (8th Cir. 1973).

The first mandatory provisions were included in the 1977 Amendments. Section 110(a)(2)(E) required that states regulate emissions that will significantly interfere with the attainment of NAAQS or PSD requirements in another state. (See §110(a)(2)(D) today.) Section 126 created a process by which a state could petition EPA to restrict sources responsible for violating section 110.

Because the prohibitions in sections 110 and 126 have been narrowly applied, they have been almost entirely ineffective. See, e.g., Connecticut v. EPA, 696 F.2d 147 (2d Cir. 1982) (source must be responsible for five percent of total emissions in an area in violation of an ambient air quality standard); Air Pollution Control District v. EPA, 739 F.2d 1071 (6th Cir. 1984) (interstate emissions cannot violate a PSD program until there is an application that triggers the PSD baseline). Why would EPA tend to adopt a narrow reading of these provisions? One factor has to do with the limitations of applying air quality modeling to long-range pollution. For example, acid rain involves the chemical transformation of sulfur to sulfates over distances of hundreds of miles. See generally S. Novick, Law of Environmental Protection, sec. 11.02(5)[d] (1988).

The 1977 Amendments also included section 115, dealing with international air pollution. This section gives EPA discretion to require modifications of a SIP in response to evidence from another country that air pollution from the United States is causing harmful pollution in the complaining country. Once such a finding has been made, the administrator has a nondiscretionary duty to provide a remedy if the foreign country offers the same rights to the United States. New York and Canada unsuccessfully sought relief under this section. Thomas v. New York, 802 F.2d 1443 (D.C. Cir. 1986), cert. denied, 482 U.S. 919

(1987) (letter by Administrator Costle did not trigger section 115 because it was not subject to notice and comment rulemaking).

2. Control of Acid Deposition

A. THE ACID DEPOSITION PROBLEM

Acid deposition in both its dry and wet forms has become a major environmental concern in the last decade. The acidification of precipitation in large parts of the eastern United States and Canada is proven, and the damaging effects of acidity on lakes, forests, and crops is also increasingly evident. However, the Clean Air Act had been ineffective as a means of responding to the problem prior to enactment of the 1990 Amendments. The materials that follow serve to introduce the problem and highlight some of the obstacles to solving it.

Several points should be kept in mind. First, acid deposition is primarily associated with sulfur emissions, which are in turn attributable mainly to large, coal-burning power plants built prior to the imposition of stringent new source controls in 1974. One of the more controversial aspects of the 1977 Clean Air Act Amendments concerned provisions adopted for regulating new coal-burning power plants. Once the decision was made to restrict the use of tall stacks, utility companies could comply with the new source performance standards only by using low-sulfur western coal or installing expensive sulfur removal technology, the so-called scrubbers. Because coal-switching generally was cheaper than scrubbers, many companies were likely to shift their coal purchases away from high-sulfur eastern coal, hurting the politically influential mining industry. A political compromise ultimately dictated that all new coal-burning power plants install scrubbers; this eliminated the incentive to shift to western coal. This saga is the subject of Bruce Ackerman and William Hassler's book Clean Coal/Dirty Air (1981), criticized in Latin, Ideal Versus Real Regulatory Efficiency: Implementation of Uniform Standards and Fine-Tuning Regulatory Reforms, 37 Stan. L. Rev. 1267 (1985). Much of the politics of acid rain therefore revolved around the balance of interests between high-sulfur coal midwestern states and eastern states suffering from the combined effects of acid deposition and soils without effective acid-buffering capacity. Canada has also joined in legal actions seeking further controls on U.S. sulfur emissions.

The causes and effects of acid deposition are, however, still subject to considerable debate. The process occurs over a large area and involves numerous reactions by both manmade and naturally occurring chemicals. Automobile emissions and other sources of fossil fuel combustion also contribute to the problem. Forest dieback may be due to multiple stresses that similarly defy isolation of precise contributing factors. See generally Mohnen, The Challenge of Acid Rain, 259 Scientific American 30 (August 1988). Despite the uncertainties, the National Commission on Air Quality (created by the 1977 Amendments to the Clean Air Act) recommended significant reductions of sulfur oxide emissions in the eastern United States in its 1981 report, To Breathe Clean Air.

In response to the scientific uncertainty and potential economic implications of an acid rain program, Congress created the National Acid Precipitation Assessment Program (NAPAP) in 1980. The NAPAP experience represents a fascinating case study in the use of scientific research as the basis for answering policy questions. NAPAP spent ten years and over half a billion dollars and involved several thousand scientists in an effort to establish the risks of acid precipitation and the most effective way to control it. Yet when Congress finally adopted an acid rain program in the 1990 Amendments, this effort was ignored.

The conclusions to be drawn from the NAPAP story are the subject of considerable debate. See generally, Learning From an Acid Rain Program, 251 Science 1302 (1991); Learning From the Acid Rain Program, 252 Science 1474 (1991). One view is that the process became so absorbed in pure science that it lost sight of the need to answer policy questions. For example, economic issues were largely overlooked while considerable resources were devoted to constructing a computer model of the atmosphere with much greater resolution than was necessary for policy purposes.

A related problem was that despite a decade of work, NAPAP did not complete a final report with clear conclusions. A 26-page document titled "Draft Assessment Highlights" attempted to summarize 27 volumes totaling more than 6,000 pages. This allowed for a serious debate about the study's most relevant conclusions. According to some of the affected industries (and the television program "60 Minutes") the NAPAP analysis proves that the problem had been overstated. Singer, The Answers to Acid Rain Fall on Deaf Ears, Wall St. J., Mar. 6, 1990. Others read the same material and found a compelling case for the opposite conclusion. Moore, Acid Truths, 16 Outside 17-18 (June 1991). Still others argue that NAPAP did help to shape understanding of the issues and define the debate, at least in its early years.

Virtually all observers agree that changing politics rather than new scientific information was primarily responsible for the adoption of an acid rain control program in 1990. The election of a new president who had pledged during the campaign to become an "environmental president" and new Senate leadership more favorably disposed to environmental concerns effectively assured that an acid rain control program would be enacted in some form.

Opposition to mandating reductions in sulfur emissions had been based on concerns common to most environmental regulation. The arguments most frequently voiced were based on scientific uncertainties, the cost and economic impact of controls, and the potential benefits of delaying regulation pending further research. More specifically, it was said the cost of achieving reductions, estimated to be several billion dollars annually, might translate into large increases in electricity prices and adverse economic impacts. It was argued that the relative effectiveness of proposed control strategies was poorly understood; and, conversely, that substantially improved knowledge might result from awaiting the results of ongoing research. Progress had been made in reducing sulfur emissions under the existing laws. Further reductions in sulfur dioxide were likely since the government had committed to research and development of "clean coal technologies" in cooperation with the government of Canada. Finally, it was argued that public health already was adequately protected by the ambient air quality standards. See, e.g., testimony of Lee Thomas, EPA administrator, before the Senate Committee on Environment and Public Works, April 22, 1987; Edison Electric Institute, Acid Raid and the Clean Air Act (1988).

Why was it so difficult to work out a political compromise on acid rain? One important factor was the intense regional divisions created by the issue: It was feared that the costs would fall disproportionately on one region and the benefits on another (although there was some evidence that acid deposition was becoming a problem outside the northeast, e.g., P. Roth, et al., The American West's Acid Rain Test (1985)). When asked by members of the public why EPA had not taken more vigorous action to combat acid rain, EPA Administrator William Ruckelshaus was fond of asking the questioner, "Where are you from?" and then arguing that only Congress could address the seemingly intractable regional conflicts the problem posed. Despite an agressive litigation strategy, those seeking more stringent controls were generally unsuccessful in using the courts to obtain any leverage from the interstate pollution provisions of the Clean Air Act. As discussed below, lawsuits based on many different legal theories were unsuccessful in forcing EPA to require greater reductions in sulfur dioxide emissions.

The courts initially facilitated EPA's reluctance to recognize an acid rain problem, and they also were quick to view congressional inaction as acceptance of the status quo. Writing separately in New York v. EPA, 852 F.2d 574 (D.C. Cir. 1988), Judge Ruth Ginsburg noted that

> the EPA has taken *no* action against sources of interstate air pollution under either §126(b) or §110(a)(2)(E) in the decade-plus since those provisions were enacted. Congress, when it is so minded, is fully capable of instructing the EPA to address particular matters promptly. . . . Congress did not supply such direction in this instance; instead, it allowed and has left unchecked the EPA's current approach to interstate air pollution. The judiciary, therefore, is not the proper place in which to urge alteration of the Agency's course. [Id. at 581.]

Thus, in marked contrast to the judicial role in the evolution of the program for Prevention of Significant Deterioration, discussed in section H below, the judiciary adamantly refused to venture where Congress feared to tread, despite potential legal avenues for forcing action to control acid deposition. With the election of 1988, the stage finally was set for action.

Although reauthorization of the Clean Air Act had faced legislative gridlock throughout the Reagan Administration, the situation changed dramatically after President Bush took office in 1989. Senator Robert Byrd of West Virginia, who had fought vigorously against any acid rain control program for fear of hurting high-sulfur coal interests in his state, was replaced as Senate majority leader by George Mitchell of Maine, a strong supporter of environmental protection measures from a state victimized by acid rain. President Bush and the leadership of both houses of Congress made legislative action on the Clean Air Act reauthorization a top priority. In June 1989 President Bush proposed comprehensive amendments to the Clean Air Act including significant steps to reduce emissions of sulfur dioxide. Under the administration's plan the 107 dirtiest power plants in 19 states would be required to reduce sulfur dioxide emissions by 10 million tons per year and nitrogen oxide emissions by 2 million tons per year by the year 2000, with half of the reductions to be achieved by the end of 1995. Utilities would be given the flexibility to meet their emission reduction targets through emissions trading, fuel switching, or other means of their choosing. The administration estimated compliance costs at $700 million annually the first five years and $3.8 billion annually over the second five years. Industry lobbyists hoped to delay action by urging more careful consideration of the economic impact of a strengthened Clean Air Act. Yet once the Bush Administration and the congressional leadership had made a commitment to adopt an acid rain control program, the forces were set in motion that resulted in adoption of the 1990 Amendments.

One of the more hotly debated provisions in the Amendments was a program of training and benefits for workers laid off as a consequence of compliance with the Clean Air Act. This program was aggressively sought by eastern coal state representatives concerned by potential job loss among miners. The administration strongly opposed the program due to its potential cost and at one point even threatened a veto over this provision. Yet Senator Byrd successfully championed the program. The program authorizes a total of $250 million for displaced workers over five years, to be administered under the Job Training Partnership Act. Benefits will be available to workers in an approved training program after exhausting unemployment compensation, and only if their total family income falls below a "lower living standard."

B. EMISSIONS TRADING AND THE 1990 AMENDMENTS' ACID RAIN CONTROL PROGRAM

One difficulty with allowing trading for most conventional air pollutants is that the location and timing of emissions determines the severity of pollution; trading must be confined to identical pollutants within a single airshed or additional adjustments must be made to account for concentration and other measures of impact. T. Tietenberg, Emissions Trading: An Exercise in Reforming Pollution Policy (1985); Levin and Elman, The Case for Environmental Incentives, Envtl. Forum 7-11 (Jan.-Feb. 1990). In contrast, acid rain offers a problem well suited to a trading approach, since emissions reductions are of relatively constant value over time and space. Dudek and Palmisano, Emissions Trading: Why Is This Thoroughbred Hobbled?, 13 Colum. J. Envtl. L. 217 (1988).

A closely related problem is the need for sufficient trades to assure permits are available on competitive terms. This may not occur if the relevant "market" is small, for example, a pollutant emitted by only a few sources in an airshed, or if firms choose to hoard their emissions rights to assure a future supply or freeze out competitors. The large size of the national market for acid rain trades lessens these concerns, and several provisions were included in the program specifically to promote the evolution of a competitive market.

In recent years "economic incentive approaches for enhancing environmental quality have moved to center stage in Washington," Hahn and Stavins, Incentive Based Environmental Regulation, 18 Ecology L.Q. 20 (1991). The Bush Administration has actively sought opportunities for incorporating market-based policies into the Air Act, a bipartisan group chaired by Senator Wirth and the late Senator Heinz endorsed this strategy, as did the Environmental Defense Fund. While Congress previously had enacted a tax on emissions of chlorofluorocarbons as part of the strategy for protection of the ozone layer, discussed in Chapter 9, the acid rain control program incorporated in title IV of the 1990 Amendments arguably provides the first robust test of market-based policies.

i. The Acid Rain Control Program

The acid rain program begins with a nationwide cap on emissions: Sulfur dioxide emissions from fossil fuel-fired electric power plants must be reduced by 10 million tons per year from 1980 levels by the year 2000. Nitrogen oxide emissions also must be reduced by approximately 2 million tons per year below 1980 levels. All sources within the defined category are covered, including existing and future sources.

Reductions are to be achieved in two phases. The first phase takes effect in 1995 and applies to 111 large existing power plants in 21 states (the "big dirties"); the second phase begins January 1, 2000 and applies to all power plants within the 48 contiguous states and the District of Columbia. Compliance with the program is also enhanced by continuous monitoring requirements and stiff penalties for violations.

The potential for trading is created by allocating to utilities pollution allowances based on their past emissions and fuel consumption. An allowance permits the holder to emit one ton of sulfur dioxide during or after the calendar year of issuance. To assure that the post-2000 cap is achieved, allowances will be limited to 8.95 million tons annually. Allowances may be reallocated within a company to cover multiple units, transferred to another owner, or even transferred to a later year.

ii. Trading Allowances: An Example of How They Can Work

The value of excess allowances to individual utilities is that they can be sold to others who need them. The excess allowances, whether obtained by an affected unit's abating more than required by law or by taking advantage of conservation incentive plans, could be quite substantial. Consider the potential advantages to a unit of "overcomplying," that is, reducing emissions beyond the required amounts. Contemporary scrubbers are capable of removing 99 percent of sulfur dioxide from a power plant's stack emissions. Unabated sulfur dioxide emissions vary depending on the sulfur content and heat value of the coal being used. Illustrative values for power plants in Illinois and Indiana could be on the order of 2.5 percent sulfur content, by weight, in coal that contains 12,000 Btu/lb. Assuming that 95 percent of the sulfur content of the coal goes to the stacks, a power plant using such a coal input would produce about 4 pounds of sulfur dioxide per million Btu. If that unit employed scrubbers that eliminated 99 percent of those emissions, its net emissions would be .04 lbs./mBtu. Under one of the incentive provisions of the 1990 Amendments, the difference between .04 and 1.2 lbs./mBtu, multiplied by the unit's baseline and divided by 2,000, would be available to the unit as incentive allowances that the unit's owner could then sell or reallocate among its other units. §404(d)(6).

To know how many allowances this might make available to the utility company operating this mythical power plant, you need to know the plant's baseline. For existing plants, the baseline equals the historical average fuel consumption of the unit, in millions of British Thermal Units (mmBtu). See §402(4)(A). For simplicity, assume that we are dealing with a 600 megawatt (MW) unit that has operated at a 60 percent utilization rate (.60) in recent years. Over the course of a year (1 year = 8,760 hours), that unit will produce 3.15 billion kilowatt-hours of electricity (600 megawatts = 600,000 kilowatts × 8,760 × .6). Coal-fired power plants require approximately 10,000 Btu (.01 mmBtu) to generate a kilowatt-hour of electricity. Therefore, the amount of fuel required to run this plant for a year equals 31,500,000 mmBtu.

This incentive plan thus would provide a maximum benefit to the utility of $(1.2 - 0.4) \times 31,500,000/2,000 = 12,600$ extra allowances. (This is a maximum, because getting bonus allowances is subject to availability. See §404(d)(6).) The utility company could: (a) allocate some or all of these to other units within the same utility system, (b) sell them to others, or (c) bank them for succeeding years.

In order to satisfy additional political objectives and operational concerns, the statute includes a number of provisions for "bonus" allowances and EPA direct sales and auctions. In addition, bonus allowances can be obtained in Phase I by:

- units that install "scrubbers" and need an additional two years' delay;
- units that emit less than a specified amount of sulfur dioxide per unit of energy prior to 1995 receive two-for-one allowances, not to exceed 3.5 million allocated on a first-come, first-served basis;
- units that reduce emissions through the use of conservation or renewable energy and meet other related conditions can obtain bonuses from a pool of 300,000 allowances; and
- a pool of 200,000 allowances for each year of Phase I is available to utilities in Indiana, Ohio, and Illinois.

A different set of extensions and bonus opportunities is provided in Phase II for "clean coal" technology, conservation and renewable energy, ten midwestern states, and "clean states"—states that had achieved low emission levels by 1985. Why was each of these provisions included? See Markey and Moorhead, The Clean Air Act and Bonus Allowances, Public Utilities Fortnightly, May 15, 1991, at 30-34.

To further complicate matters, industrial units can be brought into the program. This can occur by voluntary "opt in" (why would an industry want to do this?) or by regulation, should EPA determine that industrial emissions are expected to exceed 5.6 million tons per year on the basis of a 20-year forecast. Finally, in order to promote the creation of a market and the availability of allowances, EPA will withhold 2.8 percent of each unit's allowance allocation for sale and auction.

The implementation of the acid rain program will require numerous EPA regulations and administrative interpretations. No wonder the law quickly spawned a small industry of conferences, papers, and specialized newsletters with names like "Emissions Trader."

The most important consequence of the trading program may be a change in the attitude of regulated industries that are now encouraged to look for business opportunities associated with emissions reductions rather than simply looking for loopholes or extensions. As an official with the utility-funded Electric Power Research Institute stated,

> The new amendments will create a nationwide market for [emission allowances], which revolutionizes the nature of utility compliance planning. . . . [C]ompliance planning is no longer a one-time engineering challenge. It is an ongoing financial planning question. It requires a broader-based planning effort involving a wide spectrum of expertise.
> The legislation calls for utilities to understand the market in a way they haven't had to before. . . . They need to know what their neighbors are doing to comply with the legislation. And they need to get a good overall picture of what the industry is doing. It's a bit like playing Wall Street or the Chicago Commodity Exchange. [Responding to the Clean Air Challenge, EPRI J., April-May 1991, at 23-23.]

The article that follows describes how one of the utilities most affected by the new sulfur dioxide emissions limits is responding to the trading system.

Lippman, Clean Air Law Forces Choices
Wash. Post, Nov. 27, 1990, at D1, D4

James E. Rogers Jr. seems pretty cheerful for a man whose company expects to take a $1.6 billion hit under the new Clean Air Act and faces painful, high-risk decisions about its business. "It's chaotic, but the wonderful thing about chaos is that's where the opportunities are," he said. "It's going to be interesting." Rogers is chairman of PSI Energy Inc., an electric utility in Indiana. The company generates nearly all of its output by burning high-sulfur coal, emitting the sulfur dioxide that causes acid rain.

According to Rogers, PSI is the utility most affected by the Clean Air Act signed by President Bush on Nov. 15, which requires that the emissions be curtailed beginning in 1995. PSI executives have calculated that it will cost the utility $1.4 billion in this decade to meet the acid rain limits of the new law and another $200 million to cut nitrous oxide emissions. Those are serious numbers for a company that was brought to the brink of bankruptcy by the cost of writing off an uncompleted nuclear plant in 1984 and that has a book value of $2.8 billion. What Rogers wants to do is engineer a combination of legislative support, regulatory approval and technological change that will allow the company to recoup the costs of clean air compliance and make money in the process.

Industry analysts say polluting utilities such as PSI have a limited number of ways to meet the new requirements. They can switch to low-sulfur coal, which is more expensive, generates less electricity per ton and requires new combustion equipment; add emission-cutting "scrubbers" to their generating units, at a cost of at least $125 million each; or install new technologies such as "co-firing" burners that use a mixture of coal and natural gas. But Rogers said in an interview that PSI's options are more limited: PSI cannot just abandon high-sulfur coal. Of the 13 million tons of coal the utility burns each year, he said, half comes from Indiana mines that are within PSI's service area. "Some of the coal companies are our largest customers," he said. "Because of the politics of the state, because of who we serve, we have to comply with clean air [regulations] and continue to use high-sulfur coal. Our strategy is driven by that objective."

While PSI's compliance plan won't be completed until the Environmental Protection Agency issues regulations for implementing the new law, Rogers said the company is considering several moves:

- Purchase a portion of a nuclear plant owned by another utility in nearby Illinois, run a 19-mile transmission line to link the two systems and mothball one of PSI's coal plants, using the nuclear power to make up the difference. PSI already has links to 10 neighboring utilities, and it recently won the approval of federal regulators to sell surplus power to them at an unregulated price. A link to the Illinois nuclear plant would fit in with Roger's long-term strategy of using PSI's transmission lines as a source of cash by allowing other generators of power to use them as conduits—for a fee.
- Install on one plant a new type of coal converter that turns coal into a synthetic gas that meets the new emissions requirements. PSI has announced an agreement with Destec Energy Inc., a subsidiary of Dow Chemical Co., to install a Destec coal gasification unit at one of its plants, to produce 230 megawatts of power from a burner that meets the new federal standards.
- Add scrubbers to its remaining coal-fired units. Here is where Rogers hopes to take advantage of a provision of the new law to convert expenditures into opportunity. Under the new law, utilities that reduce acid rain emissions earn credits, or allowances, that they can sell to other utilities that are not in compliance. "Maybe I'll over-comply early" by adding scrubbers as soon as possible, instead of waiting, Rogers said. "I'll generate all these allowances and maximize my burn of Indiana coal."

By "over-compliance," a strategy several utilities are reportedly contemplating, PSI would acquire allowances it could sell to help defray the cost of the scrubbers. But what is the value of the allowances in the marketplace? No one knows, because the market has never been tested.

So Rogers faces the problem of convincing Indiana regulators that the cost of adding the expensive scrubbers now is justified by the potential return, so the regulators will approve the expense and allow it to be passed along to PSI's consumers.

In the electric utility business, one of the favorite jargon words is CWIP (pronounced quip), an acronym for construction work in progress. Some states permit utilities to bill their customers for CWIP projects— that is, get some of the cost back before the work is finished. Indiana does not permit CWIP billing for power plants, but it does permit CWIP billing for pollution-control equipment, Rogers said. "To the extent we invest in scrubbers, we have the ability to collect before the facilities are completed," he said. "That means the ratepayers (customers) pay for the scrubbers, so they should benefit from the allowances they create"— that is, get reduced rates if the scrubbers they pay for allow PSI to earn money from selling its credits.

What Rogers does not want to do is invest in scrubbers, the Destec project and other compliance strategies only to have state regulators reject the plan after the fact and disapprove rate increases. Using his commitment to Indiana coal as leverage, he said, he plans to ask the state legislature for a law that would require the Indiana Public Service Commission to approve PSI's acid rain compliance plan in advance. "I want to get the commission to hold hands with me," he said. "I want to over-comply early and generate these credits and use them to offset our costs and attract business" with reduced rates. "But we're going to have to gamble together on what the credits will be worth," Rogers said.

NOTES AND QUESTIONS

1. How was the objective of reducing sulfur dioxide emissions by 10 million tons per year chosen? One factor may have been a study of the costs per ton of emissions reduction by the Congressional Budget Office (CBO). The CBO estimated that costs would be $270 per ton for an 8-million-ton-per-year program, $360 per ton in a 10-million-ton-per-year program, and $720 per ton in a 12-million-ton-per-year program. CBO, Curbing Acid Rain: Cost, Budget, and Coal-Market Effect, xix (1986).

2. What is the legal status of allowances? The Act states they are not "property" rights but rather "limited authorizations." EPA can, for example, reduce their value by ratcheting down Phase II allowances pro rata if necessary to stay within the 8.95-million-ton-per-year cap.

3. What is the relationship between the allowances and other regulatory requirements, including the ambient air quality standards for sulfur dioxide and the new source standards for power plants? If trading stimulates technological innovation (as economists predict), will this trig-

ger more stringent technology-based requirements for new sources, and
if so, will this undermine the value of allowances? A related issue arises
from EPA's treatment of utility investments to extend the life of old
power plants by replacing boilers. In Wisconsin Electric Power Co. v.
EPA, 893 F.2d 901 (7th Cir. 1990), the court held that such investments
would trigger new source requirements. This resulted in intense lobbying
by the utility industry, which argued that it substantially limited their
flexibility. After failing to win legislative relief in the 1990 Amendments,
the industry sought help from the Department of Energy and the Competitiveness Council. In a highly unusual action, the Department of Energy actually drafted large portions of a "WEPCO fix" later proposed
by EPA. 56 Fed. Reg. 27,630 (1991).

4. Since utility investments are subject to state regulation, utilities
may have incentives quite different from those of other businesses. For
example, because they have long planning horizons they may prefer to
hold on to allowances in order to ensure an adequate supply in the
future, unless an effective options market develops. They may also question the value of selling allowances if state regulators demand that most
of the earnings obtained be passed on to the customers who paid for
the pollution control measures earlier through higher rates. Utilities that
share power regionally through power pools also will have to establish
rules governing whether allowances can be pooled.

5. Notice that the chairman of PSI expresses the view that the
company must continue to use high-sulfur coal in any event. What reason
does he offer? If the utility could comply with Clean Air Act regulations
more cheaply by shifting to low-sulfur coal, isn't it costing its ratepayers
more money by refusing to make such a switch? Does this policy make
economic sense for the utility?

6. Why should existing sources be given allowances? Doesn't this
policy discriminate against new sources and reward utilities for their past
pollution? Consider other ways in which emission rights might have been
distributed. What explains the distribution chosen by Congress?

7. If trading offers such large opportunities for cost reductions,
why hasn't it received more support? One study suggests that the only
constituency for efficiency has been economists. See S. Kelman, What
Price Incentives? Economists and the Environment (1981). Others suggest a variety of factors. Some environmentalists express moral outrage
at the notion of "rights to pollute"; they also may resent industry profits
from trades. Many fear that trading systems will be difficult to police
effectively, resulting in higher levels of emissions than otherwise would
be the case. Regulators and industry may prefer the system they know,
and the latter also may be concerned by the prospects of additional costs
for the acquisition of permits. See generally Hahn and Stavins, above;
Hanley, Hallet, and Moffatt, Why Is More Notice Not Taken of Econ-

omists' Prescriptions for the Control of Pollution?, 22 Env. and Planning 1241 (1990).

8. Can trading schemes, even if they are policed rigorously, result in increased pollution? One result of the use of trading mechanisms may be that companies whose emissions otherwise would be below legal limits will acquire pollution rights to sell to other companies. By ensuring that companies in the aggregate discharge the maximum levels of pollution permitted by law, allowance trading may increase emissions. Of course, the overall levels of allowable pollution permitted could always be ratcheted downward to counteract this tendency.

9. Recall the offset provisions of the Clean Air Act that govern new sources in nonattainment areas. The Minnesota Mining and Manufacturing Company (3M), a pioneer in source reduction, has a corporate policy that it will neither use nor sell offset allowances it acquires by voluntarily reducing emissions of chemicals. "Top management felt if we sold credits all we would have done is transfer emissions, not reduce them," explains a company spokesman. 3M has returned credits (reportedly worth more than $1 million) that otherwise would have allowed emissions of more than 1,000 pounds of organic solvents per day in the Los Angeles area. Holusha, Hutchinson No Longer Holds Its Nose, N.Y. Times, Feb. 3, 1991, at C1. Is such a decision economically rational? (The company does take a tax deduction for the value of the credits.) Should such voluntary emissions reductions be taken into account in determining the amount by which other sources must reduce emissions? According to a company spokesman, 3M more recently made an exception to its policy to sell some emissions credits to a Procter & Gamble facility in Camareo, California in order to prevent job losses. 3M donated the proceeds of the sale to an environmental group.

10. The Chicago Board of Trade has voted to create a new futures contract in rights to emit sulfur dioxide. Under the plan proposed by the Board, beginning in 1993 investors could purchase "cash forward" contracts to deliver rights to emit sulfur dioxide in 25-ton allotments up to three years in advance. (The rights themselves will be issued starting in 1995.) Passell, A New Commodity to Be Traded: Government Permits for Pollution, N.Y. Times, July 17, 1991, at A1. For example, a utility could guarantee itself the right to emit an additional 2,500 tons of sulfur dioxide in the year 1996 by purchasing 100 futures contracts due in 1996. These rights could be purchased from another utility planning to shut down an old coal plant in that year or from an investor who thinks the price of the allowances will fall. Id. at A14. A managing director of Kidder, Peabody & Company "estimates that the contracts will initially trade at about $400 a ton and will fluctuate with factors ranging from the demand for electricity to the state of scrubber technology." Id. He notes that the price of such contracts is not likely to exceed $2,000

because utilities have the option of exceeding their emissions limit on payment of a $2,000-per-ton fine. Is the value of the future contracts likely to be affected by how strictly EPA enforces the law? If so, will this produce a marketplace measure of how effective environmental enforcement is? Are investors who own futures contracts in pollution rights likely to demand more vigorous environmental enforcement to preserve or enhance the value of their investments? Would this interest give such investors standing to sue? Groups such as the Nature Conservancy currently buy up natural areas to preserve them from development. Would it be possible for such a group in effect to purchase away pollution by buying a futures contract in pollution rights, taking delivery of the rights, and then not exercising them?

G. MOBILE SOURCE CONTROLS: A TECHNOLOGY-FORCING VENTURE

Emissions from automobiles and other "mobile sources" were the first forms of air pollution subjected to national regulation. Mobile sources of air pollution are regulated by Title II of the Clean Air Act. The mobile source control program combines emissions standards with regulations to control fuel additives. The emissions standards imposed by Title II have been one of the most successful but controversial aspects of efforts to control air pollution. The approach Congress employed to deal with vehicle emissions differs considerably from the regulations applied to stationary sources. As discussed in Chapter 2, pages 168-173, Congress simply required that automakers install the technology necessary to achieve specific reductions in vehicle emissions by certain deadlines. In doing so, it embarked on a grand experiment in technology forcing in the face of claims by manufacturers that the requisite technology could not be developed so quickly. (Compare the RCRA land disposal ban, discussed in Chapter 3.)

Congress's efforts to force the development of auto emissions control technology confronted a powerful tension aptly characterized by Judge Leventhal's observation in International Harvester v. Ruckelshaus, 478 F.2d 615 (D.C. Cir. 1973): "The automobile is an essential pillar of the American economy . . . [that] has had a devastating impact on the American environment." That fundamental tension persists today, and it no longer involves only the auto industry and the government. The 1990 Clean Air Act Amendments adopt even tighter emissions control requirements, and they broaden the focus of technology forcing to embrace the development of cleaner-burning gasoline and cars that use alternative fuels. As a result, major oil companies have now been drawn into the controversy, which has aligned them against the auto industry, EPA, the states, and even one another.

1. History and Background

In the late 1950s it became apparent that automobile emissions were contributing to increased air pollution. At the time little was known about the composition of auto emissions or their environmental consequences. In his influential book Unsafe at Any Speed, Ralph Nader criticized the attitude of auto industry executives who stated that because they *felt* there was no problem with vehicle emissions, there was no need to conduct research on their environmental effects. R. Nader, Unsafe at Any Speed 147 (1965). To find out more, Congress in 1960 enacted the Schenck Act, which directed the Surgeon General to study the impact of motor vehicle emissions on human health.

California, where the problem was most acute, became the first state to require emissions controls. Recognizing that the technology to control emissions would have to be developed, California attempted to force technology through regulation. In 1960 California enacted its own Motor Vehicle Pollution Control Act, which established a state board to oversee the development of emissions control devices. The board was charged with establishing criteria for approving emissions control devices and with testing and certifying them. An interesting feature of the California legislation is that the deadlines it established for installation of emissions controls ran from the date when officials certified that *two* satisfactory control devices had been developed. After the state board issued such a certification, emissions controls had to be installed on all new and used cars sold in the state. The law was to be enforced by prohibiting the registration of vehicles that lacked such devices. By November 1962 the California board had accepted seven emissions control devices for testing despite fierce opposition from auto manufacturers. The first emissions control requirements on California automobiles took effect in 1965.

In 1965 Congress enacted the Motor Vehicle Air Pollution Control Act, which authorized the Secretary of HEW to establish auto emissions standards after considering their costs and "technological feasibility." Congress had acted in part in response to charges that the major auto manufacturers had been colluding to impede the development of emissions controls. The first federal controls on automobile emissions of carbon monoxide and hydrocarbons took effect in the 1968 model year. In the 1967 Air Quality Act, Congress provided that the federal emissions control standards would apply in all states except for California, which was authorized to adopt its own more stringent standards.

In a special message to Congress on the environment in 1970,

President Nixon endorsed even tighter controls on vehicle emissions based on estimates of the lowest emissions levels attainable with developing technology. Yet he recognized that even such stringent controls eventually would be insufficient because growth of the vehicle fleet could cancel out progress from emissions controls. Thus, he proposed the development of clean alternatives to the internal combustion engine:

> Our responsibility now is also to look beyond the Seventies, and the prospects then are uncertain. Based on present trends, it is quite possible that by 1980 the increase in the sheer number of cars in densely populated areas will begin outrunning the technological limits of our capacity to reduce pollution from the internal combustion engine. . . . [U]nless vehicles with an alternative, low-pollution power source are available, vehicle-caused pollution will once again begin an inexorable increase. Therefore, prudence dictates that we move now to ensure that such a vehicle will be available if needed. [R. Nixon, Public Papers of the President 101 (1970).]

President Nixon ordered federal agencies to begin research and development for unconventional vehicles. As an incentive to the private sector to develop such vehicles, he pledged that federal agencies would purchase them even if they cost more than conventional vehicles.

In the 1970 Clean Air Act Congress imposed "strong medicine" on automobile manufacturers to force the development of greatly improved emissions control technology. In what one senator described as perhaps the "biggest industrial judgment that has been made in the U.S. in this century," 116 Cong. Rec. 33085 (1970) (remarks of Sen. Baker), Congress directed automotive manufacturers to curtail emissions of hydrocarbons and carbon monoxide from new vehicles by 90 percent within five years. Manufacturers were given one additional year to achieve a similar reduction in emissions of nitrogen oxide. Congress decided on a 90-percent reduction by relying on the simple notion that since air pollution levels in major cities were approximately five times the expected levels of the NAAQSs, emissions would need to be reduced by at least 80 percent, with an additional 10 percent necessary to provide for growing vehicle use. S. Rep. No. 91-1196, 91st Cong., 2d Sess. at 25 (1970). A committee staff member involved in the legislative drafting process recently described the 90-percent rollback requirements as "a back of the envelope calculation. . . . We didn't have any particular methodology. We just picked what sounded like a good goal." Easterbrook, Cleaning Up, Newsweek, July 24, 1989, at 29. President Nixon had proposed a 1980 deadline, but after Senator Nelson proposed banning the internal combustion engine by 1975, Senator Muskie fashioned a "compromise" appending the earlier deadline to the Administration's bill.

The mobile source regulations present a classic example of the technology-forcing concept introduced in Chapter 2. Congress adopted the rollback requirements with full knowledge that the technology to meet them did not yet exist, might not be available by the deadline, and had an unknown cost. The legislation gave EPA the power, at least in theory, to shut down the entire automobile industry if it failed to comply. The "statute was, indeed, deliberately designed as 'shock treatment' to the industry." International Harvester v. Ruckelshaus, 478 F.2d 615, 648 (D.C. Cir. 1973). The auto companies began a battle in the courts, the Congress, and the media that continues to this day.

Concerned that auto manufacturers might not be able to meet the deadline, Congress had provided the EPA administrator with limited discretion to grant the automobile companies a one-year extension, if the administrator determined that (i) such an extension was essential to the public interest or the public health and welfare, (ii) the auto companies had made all good-faith efforts to comply, (iii) the company petitioning for the extension had established that effective control technology was not available to meet the standards, and (iv) a study conducted by the National Academy of Sciences was consistent with the company's claim. §205(b)(5)(D).

Faced with such a petition, Administrator Ruckelshaus denied an extension on the ground that the companies had not met their burden with respect to requirement (iii). The administrator's conclusions depended heavily on EPA's own extrapolations from limited laboratory experiments with one design of the catalytic converter. The Agency reasoned that, although the technology had not yet been demonstrated (in 1972, when the petition was filed) to be able to meet the standards over a 50,000-mile vehicle life as required under the Act, anticipated continued development of the technology would result in 1975 model year cars' being able to meet the standards. Hence, in EPA's judgment, the technology was "available."

In International Harvester v. Ruckelshaus, 478 F.2d 615 (D.C. Cir. 1973), the D.C. Circuit overturned EPA's decision not to extend the deadline. Reasoning that the risks associated with an erroneous denial of the extension were much greater than those associated with an erroneous grant, the court placed the burden of rebutting the companies' initial showing of nonavailability on EPA and found that the Agency had not met that burden.

This was not the last extension the auto industry received. EPA also granted a one-year extension of the 1976 deadline for nitrogen oxide controls. Congress amended the Clean Air Act in 1977 to grant the auto industry further extensions. As a result of these extensions, the original hydrocarbon and carbon monoxide standards did not take effect until 1980 and 1981 respectively, the very dates the industry originally had forecast that it could meet. The final nitrogen oxide standard was relaxed and the deadline extended to 1981.

FIGURE 6.7

Assessments of the mobile source experience are mixed. Some believe it confirms the notion that "there is a certain comfort in being asked for the impossible: you know you will not actually have to do it." Margolis, The Politics of Auto Emissions, 49 Pub. Interest 3, 13 (1977). Others liken it to the fairy tale Rumpelstiltskin, wherein a maiden is ordered to weave straw into gold, a seemingly impossible task that she miraculously accomplishes. D. Currie, Air Pollution: Federal Law and Analysis (1981). It seems clear that emissions control technology would not have developed as quickly as it did without the regulations. Only a few months after the *International Harvester* remand General Motors announced that it would install catalytic converters in all its 1975 model year cars that would last the life of the car while permitting improved fuel economy. See Ditlow, Federal Regulation of Motor Vehicle Emissions Under the Clean Air Amendments of 1970, 4 Ecology L.Q. 495, 514-516 (1975). Most vehicles failed to comply with even the revised standards, however, due to differences between test results for prototypes and actual performance on the road. Nevertheless, emissions controls ultimately produced dramatic reductions in vehicle emissions. As Currie notes, even though the industry knew EPA would not shut it down, perhaps "the cosmetic efforts industry felt compelled to make in order to establish its good faith could not, given the resourcefulness of its engineers, but have produced some improvement." D. Currie, above, at 2-114. Others argue that emissions controls were not a good investment, particularly since they encouraged consumers to keep older cars longer. R. Crandall, H. Gruenspecht, T. Keeler, and L. Lave, Regulating the Automobile 115-116 (1986).

Technology forcing and technology forecasting may be to some extent inherently at odds. If the nature of the solution were evident, "forcing" would not be necessary. David Doniger, an NRDC attorney, argues that "before a regulation exists, industry has little incentive to invent effective controls. Invariably industry later finds better and cheaper ways to cut emissions, so actual costs are nowhere near the dire predictions." Easterbrook, above, at 32.

NOTES AND QUESTIONS

1. Who should be responsible for developing improved emissions control technology—the auto manufacturers, the government, or independent entrepreneurs? California's initial program was premised on the notion that technology-forcing regulation would encourage entrepreneurs to develop technology, although auto manufacturers were reluctant to use devices developed by others. In 1969 the federal government sued the four largest auto manufacturers, alleging that they had conspired to delay the development of emissions control devices. The suit was settled by consent decree. United States v. Automobile Manufacturers Association, 307 F. Supp. 617 (C.D. Calif. 1969), affd. sub nom. City of New York v. United States, 397 U.S. 248 (1970). Why would California's initial program premise the deadline for installing emissions control devices on certification that at least *two* such devices existed?

2. Professor Currie notes that it was never likely that EPA would seek to shut down the automobile industry. Why, then, was the law effective at all? Why didn't the manufacturers simply ignore the law and call EPA's bluff? See sections 203(a)(1) and 205. Do these sections provide an adequate answer?

3. A major challenge faced by technology-forcing regulation is the question of what combination of carrots and sticks to use to provide an incentive for the development of new technology. The Clean Air Act's imposition of a deadline, coupled with the escape hatch of an extension, provided the auto industry with considerable incentives to maintain that the deadline could not be met and to lobby for extensions. In effect, the

auto industry and EPA were engaged in a high-stakes game of chicken. Can you think of any alternative approaches to technology forcing that would avoid the all-or-nothing character of an absolute deadline while providing incentives for companies to develop control technology? Could a scheme of escalating taxes imposed on manufacturers of nonconforming vehicles guarantee the attainment of emissions control goals? Could tradeable emissions rights work for auto manufacturers?

4. Crandall notes the problem created by giving people an incentive to retain older cars longer and thereby avoid the expense of emissions controls and energy efficiency standards. In 1969, 12 percent of cars in the United States were 10 years old or older. By 1987 the figure had increased to 29 percent. States could regulate pre-Clean Air Act vehicles if they chose to do so. See T. Jorling, The Federal Law of Air Pollution Control, in Federal Environmental Law 1128-1130 (E. Dolgin and T. Guilbert, eds. 1974). Oil companies have argued that emissions reductions could be obtained more cheaply by providing "bounties" to encourage consumers to scrap old cars rather than by reformulating gasoline. In a demonstration program, Unocal spent $6 million to buy and scrap 8,400 cars, some of which emitted 67 times more pollution than new cars. Wald, For Cleaner Air, Scrap Dirty Cars, Firm Says, N.Y. Times, Oct. 24, 1991, at A20. Oil industry consultants propose that the government offer $700 each to buy 9 million cars dating from 1967 to 1978. In March 1992 the Bush Administration announced that it would give pollution credits to companies that purchase and scrap old cars. Davis and Harwood, Bush Plans to Offer Pollution Credits to Firms That Buy, Then Junk Old Cars, Wall St. J., Mar. 9, 1992, at A3.

2. The 1990 Amendments and the Future of Technology-Forcing Regulation

The Clean Air Act's mobile source controls have kept air pollution far lower than it otherwise would have been. But as the vehicle fleet has turned over, most of the emissions reductions to be obtained from the initial controls have been realized. With further increases projected in the number of vehicle miles travelled, mobile source pollution would increase unless new controls were adopted. Thus, when Congress considered the 1990 Clean Air Act Amendments, mobile source controls were a subject of great controversy. Auto companies maintained that they had done all that they could to reduce emissions through tailpipe controls and that Congress should now find other targets such as oil companies, who could be required to make cleaner-burning fuels. Congress ultimately chose to expand the scope of mobile source controls through an even broader effort at technology forcing. The 1990 Amendments seek to force development not only of better tailpipe controls but also of cleaner fuels and cleaner engines, as discussed below.

The 1990 Amendments: A Plan for Progress?

Title II of the 1990 Amendments addresses mobile sources. It contains four different types of provisions: (1) emissions standards for various classes of vehicles, including heavy-duty trucks, light-duty trucks, light-duty vehicles (e.g., cars) and diesel engines; (2) numerous supporting provisions that define conditions under which such vehicles are to be tested, how the tests are to be conducted, enforcement provisions, manufacturers' responsibilities, and so forth; (3) a set of definitions for alternatives to standard gasoline as fuel for mobile sources; (4) provisions for employing such alternatives under various circumstances. Thus, like Title I, Title II reflects the judgment that alternatives to end-of-the-pipe controls (which are expected to achieve the emissions standards) must be employed if further progress on auto-related pollution problems is going to be made.

1. Emissions Standards.   We limit discussion to the new standards for light-duty vehicles only. The 1990 Amendments mandate the following emissions limitations (in grams per mile):

CO	3.4 gpm	(no change)
NOx	0.4 gpm	(currently 1.0 gpm)
HC	.25 gpm	(currently .41 gpm)

These standards are to be phased in over a period of years beginning with model year 1994, meaning that an increasing percentage of a manufacturer's sales must comply with the requirements each year after that model year.

The Amendments require the administrator to consider further tightening of the emissions standard for light-duty vehicles and trucks and to report these findings to the Congress no later than June 1, 1997. Stricter Tier II standards effective after January 1, 2003 are to be imposed at the administrator's discretion after consideration of the need for tighter controls to achieve NAAQSs, the cost-effectiveness of further controls, and the availability of technology to meet further reductions.

2. Clean Fuels Programs.   The Amendments define reformulated gasoline, oxygenated gasoline, and clean fuels, giving detailed performance specifications for each definition.

a. Reformulated gasoline.   This must have an oxygen content of not less than 2.0 percent, a benzene content of not more than 1 percent, and nitrogen oxide emissions no worse than "baseline gasoline." This gas would have an oxygen content higher than that of baseline gasoline and would improve combustion, reducing carbon monoxide and hydrocarbon emissions. Reformulated gasoline can currently be achieved by blending gasoline with ethanol or methyl-tertiary-butyl ether (MTBE). Reformulated gasoline must be used in the 9 urban areas that have the worst ozone conditions, beginning in 1995 and phased in over a five-year period. Other cities can join the reformulated gasoline program voluntarily. The bill contains provisions designed to ensure a sufficient supply of reformulated gasoline in the participating areas. Reformulated gasoline must also meet certain standards for toxic emissions.

b. Oxygenated fuels. These must have an oxygen content of not less than 2.7 percent. Oxygenated fuels must be the fuels exclusively sold in areas that are nonattainment for carbon monoxide and during the time period that the administrator determines is the peak time for carbon monoxide pollution (which must be not less than four months of the year). (This provision and the requirement of reformulated gasoline for ozone nonattainment areas are implemented by making them required components of the relevant state implementation plans.)

c. Alternative fuel vehicles. There are two mandatory clean vehicle programs in the new amendments.

i. In areas that are Extreme, Severe, or Serious for ozone or that are Serious for carbon monoxide and have a population greater than 250,000: 30 percent of passenger car and light-duty truck "fleets" must meet the California standards for low emissions vehicles (LEV) by 1998, 50 percent by 1999, and 70 percent by 2000. A "fleet" consists of any group of 10 vehicles or more employed by a single operator and capable of being fueled in a central location. The emission standard for hydrocarbons for such vehicles is .075 gpm, compared to .25 gpm for conventional cars. The Amendments also contain fleet requirements for heavy-duty trucks.

ii. Beginning in 1996, 150,000 clean-fuel vehicles must be manufactured for general sale in California. Other states may opt into the program. Clean-fuel vehicles must meet a transitional LEV standard until the year 2000, when they must meet the LEV standard.

d. Urban buses. The Amendments strike a compromise between those who wanted to ban diesel engines in urban buses entirely and those who wished to permit them by requiring the administrator to perform an in-use evaluation of diesel engines in 1993. If diesels cannot meet fairly stringent performance characteristics, the administrator must mandate alternative fuels.

NOTES AND QUESTIONS

1. The clean fuels program as originally proposed by the Bush Administration was far more ambitious, mandating production of alternative-fuel vehicles in 1995 and the sale of at least one million such vehicles a year in the nine smoggiest cities by 1997. The concept of reformulated, less-polluting gasoline was introduced as a compromise by oil industry interests. The natural gas and grain industries also had interests at stake as potential sellers of new fuels. The negotiation process took on the character of a large, high-stakes poker game as deals were repeatedly cut and broken. For example, the gas industry early on agreed to limit the role for clean fuels to vehicle fleets and to support less restrictive standards for passenger cars as the basis for an alliance with the auto industry. The agreement was included in the House bill, scrapped in conference but revived at the last minute as a compromise. Edelson, A Win for Clean Air, 8 Envtl. Forum 10, 16 (1991).

The potential future role for alternative fuels is a complex and controversial subject with significant implications for the future of the automobile and petroleum industries. Each fuel has relative advantages and disadvantages, and it appears that the worldwide automobile industry may be entering a period of multiple, competing fuels. For example, compressed natural gas (CNG) results in emission of substantially less carbon monoxide but slightly more nitrogen oxide; ethanol produces less nitrogen oxide but about the same levels of carbon monoxide. The prospect of widespread reliance on natural gas raises supply and security concerns, while the use of ethanol may disrupt food supplies and cause environmental damage to farms. Emerging concerns about global warming also favor certain fuels more than others: reformulated gasoline results in a slight increase in emissions of carbon dioxide, while CNG and ethanol can reduce carbon dioxide. Other countries have adopted aggressive alternative fuels programs and have accumulated substantial experience. For example, Brazil relies heavily on ethanol, while New Zealand has used CNG. The United States encouraged alternative fuels development in several ways prior to the Clean Air Act Amendments, including granting credits applicable to the fuel economy standards, federal purchases of alternatively fueled vehicles, and tax credits for ethanol. See generally D. Gordon, Transportation, Energy, and the Environment (1991); National Energy Strategy: Powerful Ideas for America 67-71 (1991); and D. Sperling, New Transportation Fuels: A Strategic Approach to Technological Change (1988).

2. During the debate on the Clean Air Act Amendments of 1990, oil company lobbyists argued that the legislation was imposing impossible requirements for the development of cleaner-burning fuels. William Rosenberg, EPA assistant administrator for air, described what happened when Congress called their bluff in the following terms: "Three

days before the conference committee finished its work, representatives from the oil industry said they couldn't make reformulated gas to meet the standard. Three days after they finished, Amoco started selling it on Pennsylvania Avenue." Bush Signs Clean Air Act Amendments, Predicts Benefits for all U.S. Citizens, 21 Env. Rep. 1387 (Nov. 23, 1990). Reportedly one of the reasons why the companies quickly changed their tune was the discovery that a company marketing a cleaner-burning fuel in southern California was rapidly gaining market share at the expense of its competitors. Eight months after the Amendments were signed into law, Arco announced that it had developed a new gasoline that reduces emissions by about one-third—almost as much as methanol blends. While cheaper than methanol, the fuel is estimated to cost between 15 and 20 percent more than unleaded gasoline. As a result, Arco announced that it would not produce the new gasoline unless it was required to do so. Matthew L. Wald, Gasoline as Clean as Methanol Is Developed to Cut Pollution, N.Y. Times, July 11, 1991, at A1. Why do you think Arco announced that it will not produce the fuel unless it is required to do so? Michael Bradley, director of Northeast States for Coordinated Air Use Management, maintains that oil companies are " 'all of a sudden doing some very amazing refinements to gasoline,' because they were faced with the possibility that methanol or other alternative fuels would be mandated." Id. Arco's technological advance was the product of an unconventional research strategy spurred by the fear that California regulators eventually would require an alcohol-fuel blend for cars unless an equally clean gasoline alternative was developed. Rose, Atlantic Richfield Co. Is Winning the West by Breaking the Mold, Wall St. J., Aug. 7, 1991, at A1.

3. Several key compromises went into the new mobile source provisions. Congressman Henry Waxman agreed to roll back to two years or 24,000 miles the required warranty for many emissions control parts in return for an agreement to extend to 8 years or 80,000 miles the required warranty for the three most costly emissions control devices. This agreement won the support of independent auto repair shops, who estimated that they were losing $5 billion a year in business to auto dealers. Weisskopf, Industries Dance with the Devil on Cleaner Air, Wash. Post, Dec. 24, 1990, at A13. The Amendments also won support from manufacturers of nonroad vehicles by prohibiting the imposition of emissions standards under consideration in California for new nonroad (e.g., construction and farm vehicles) engines smaller than 175 horsepower, a source of emissions projected to equal that from 21 million light-duty cars and trucks. Moore, The 1990 Clean Air Act Amendments (1991).

There are many promising technologies that, despite past progress, could achieve substantial further reductions in emissions. For example, a substantial fraction of emissions occur in the first minutes after starting the engine, because the catalytic converter is only effective after being heated. Prototypes of electrically heated catalysts have reduced emissions as much as 90 percent from current levels, and still further reductions occur when the technology is used together with reformulated gasoline. Walsh, Car Lines—1990: The Year in Review, Dec. 1990, at 35-36.

4. Environmental and energy regulation may be partly responsible for the trend toward the switch from automobiles to light-duty trucks, as the latter are subject to less stringent regulation. Light trucks and vans, which average only 20 miles per gallon, now account for one-third of light-duty vehicle sales and 15 percent of commuter trips. R. Heavenrich, J. Murrell, and K. Hellman, Light-Duty Automotive Technology and Fuel Economy Trends Through 1991 (1991); J. MacKenzie and M. Walsh, Driving Forces: Motor Vehicle Trends and Their Implications for Global Warming, Energy Strategies, and Transportation Planning (1991). What forms of flexible regulatory alternatives might help address this problem? A bill passed by the California legislature but vetoed by the governor would have created a fee-rebate system for taxing emissions from new cars; purchasers of cleaner cars would be given a rebate paid for from revenues collected from buyers of dirtier, less efficient models. The same concept is incorporated in bills that would promote fuel economy now being considered in several states. Gordon, above, at 182.

Aside from the unintended impact of regulation, it has been argued that much of the reason for the American love affair with the automobile has to do with a wide range of direct and indirect subsidies. For example, 90 percent of people who drive to work park for free, a benefit employers can provide as an untaxed fringe benefit. In contrast, employers are only permitted a tax-free transit subsidy of up to $15 per month. Also, during the past decade federal highway spending increased 85 percent while transit support dropped 5 percent. "We drive and drive not because of a collective memory of the Western frontier but because we have piled subsidy on top of subsidy to encourage the use of automobiles over every other form of transportation. . . . We are behaving like the most rational possible economic beings. Offered generous bonuses— hidden and direct—to drive, that's exactly what we do." Mathews, The Myth of the American Car Cult, Wash. Post, Mar. 31, 1991, at B7.

5. In recent years, technology that could have been applied to improve fuel economy and reduce emissions has instead gone into increasing automobile power and performance. Average engine horsepower reached a minimum for cars in 1981-1982 and has risen steadily since, equalling 1975 highs, while average car weight has declined by 900 pounds. R. Heavinrich et al., above, at 15. Should Congress consider limits on vehicle performance if necessary to achieve energy and environmental goals?

6. The standards and policies of the United States have had a considerable impact on the global automobile industry. About 40 percent

of all the registered vehicles in the world are in North America, while another 40 percent are in Europe. About 50 million new vehicles are manufactured each year, a figure about equal to the total world stock of vehicles in 1950. Motor vehicles are now responsible for about 14 percent of global emissions of carbon dioxide, the principal greenhouse gas, and all indications are that such emission will continue to increase rapidly barring substantial improvements in efficiency and a switch to nonfossil fuels. See generally J. MacKenzie and M. Walsh, above.

PROBLEM EXERCISE: THE CALIFORNIA STANDARDS OPTION

The desire of automobile manufacturers to avoid having to comply with numerous, conflicting state vehicle emissions standards was an important factor in the enactment of national vehicle emissions controls in the Clean Air Act of 1970. That Act preempted more stringent state vehicle emissions standards except for California's standards, which already were more stringent than the requirements embodied in the 1970 legislation. As a result, vehicles sold in California have had to meet more stringent emission standards than vehicles sold in the rest of the country.

During the debate on the 1990 Amendments, a provision authorizing other states to adopt the more stringent California standards was proposed, in part to forestall the adoption of a more stringent national standard.

Question One. What position are you likely to take on this proposal if you represent: (1) a national automobile manufacturer, (2) a state air pollution control agency, (3) a national oil company, (4) EPA, (5) a national environmental group, (6) a local auto dealer, or (7) a local factory owner who does not do business with the auto industry? Why?

The proposal ultimately was adopted in section 177 of the Clean Air Act, which now gives states with nonattainment areas the option of adopting vehicle emissions standards identical to California's more stringent standards. Any state that chooses to adopt the California standards must do so at least two years before the commencement of the model year to which they will be applicable.

Question Two. Suppose that a small state on the East Coast is considering whether or not to opt for the California standards. What position do you think each of the seven groups listed above is likely to take on this question? Do you think it likely that any state would opt for the California standards? Why or why not?

In July 1991, 12 contiguous East Coast states (every state from Virginia to Maine) and the District of Columbia signed a memorandum of understanding pledging to consider adoption of the California standards. Automobile manufacturers were shocked by this development.

Question Three.   What factors would explain the tentative agreement of the East Coast states to adopt the California standards? Compare this situation with the prisoners' dilemma, discussed in Chapter 1.

H. PREVENTION OF SIGNIFICANT DETERIORATION

The 1970 Clean Air Act did not mention "prevention of significant deterioration," or PSD, now one of the most complex of the Act's regulatory programs. The origins of the PSD program rest in the simple statement in section 101 that one purpose of the Act is to "protect and enhance" air quality. Armed with this single phrase and some supportive legislative and administrative history, the Sierra Club filed a lawsuit that ultimately spawned the PSD program. See T. Jorling, The Federal Law of Air Pollution Control, in Federal Environmental Law 1058, 1077-1082 (E. Dolgin and T. Guilbert, eds. 1974); Hines, A Decade of Nondegradation Policy in Congress and the Courts: The Erratic Pursuit of Clean Air and Clean Water, 62 Iowa L. Rev. 643 (1977). In Sierra Club v. Ruckelshaus, 344 F. Supp. 253 (D.D.C. 1972), affd. on the opinion below, 2 ELR 20656 (D.C. Cir. 1972), affd. by an equally divided court, 412 U.S. 541 (1973), a district court enjoined EPA from approving SIPs insofar as they allowed air quality to deteriorate to the level of the NAAQSs. The Court provided no indication of how this goal was to be accomplished. EPA therefore was forced to develop an entirely new regulatory program applicable to areas with air quality better than the NAAQSs. Congress largely codified EPA's program when it added part C to Title I of the Clean Air Act in the 1977 Amendments. The PSD program was then shaped by an unusual court decision, Alabama Power v. Costle, 636 F.2d 323 (D.C. Cir. 1979), that constituted a kind of judicial rulemaking proceeding requiring comprehensive and highly detailed revisions in EPA's regulations. R. Melnick, Regulation and the Courts: The Case of the Clean Air Act 75 (1983).

The PSD program is designed to ensure that air quality does not deteriorate in areas that meet or exceed the NAAQSs. Because it applies only to areas already in attainment with the NAAQS, the PSD program cannot be a product of a desire to protect health, if one assumes that the primary NAAQSs have been set at proper levels. Rather, it is founded on a desire to enhance and maintain clean air for the values and benefits it represents and to ensure that regulation does not simply shift air pollution from dirty to clean air areas. The PSD program reduces the air quality impacts of new sources while preventing harms not adequately captured by the NAAQSs.

The PSD program today is a complex counterpart to the nonattainment program, complete with its own list of acronyms, missed deadlines, and shared federal-state responsibilities. Its complexity is a product of unusual statutory and judicial specificity that has been found to carry "a dual message: that complex legislative schemes can frequently outstrip the capacities of Congress, agency and courts without resolving key policy issues; and that the flaws of complexity cannot readily be remedied by carving out areas of administrative discretion within an intricate scheme." Oren, Detail and Delegation: A Study in Statutory Specificity, 15 Colum. J. Envtl. L. 143, 150 (1990).

The PSD program employs two principal strategies for preventing deterioration of air quality: (1) a requirement that covered sources obtain a permit after demonstrating that their emissions will not cause air quality to deteriorate beyond specified numerical increments, and (2) a requirement that they install the "best available control technology" (BACT). Craig Oren, who has studied the PSD program extensively, explains what sources are covered by its program and how these requirements are applied to them in the article that follows.

Oren, Prevention of Significant Deterioration: Control-Compelling Versus Site-Shifting
74 Iowa L. Rev. 1, 13-26 (1988)

WHAT SOURCES ARE COVERED?

The PSD program applies to the construction or modification of a "major emitting facility"—a stationary source, such as a power plant or industrial boiler, which emits substantial amounts of air pollution even with the installation of pollution controls.[62] A permit is needed either to

---

62. The term "major emitting facility" is defined in §169(1), 42 U.S.C. §7479 (1982). If a source is in one of 28 specified categories (e.g., chemical process plants), it is covered if it emits or has the "potential to emit" more than 100 tons annually of any air pollutant; if not, it is covered if it has the "potential to emit" more than 250 tons annually. . . .

Numerous complexities exist in defining the term "major emitting facility." . . .

(1) What is "potential to emit"? In its pre-*Alabama Power* regulations, EPA ruled that emission controls should not be taken into account in judging whether a source has the necessary potential to emit more than the 100/250 threshold. 43 Fed. Reg. 26,388, 26,391-92 (June 19, 1978). This interpretation, while having

build such a facility, or to modify an existing major emitting facility through a physical change (be it the addition of a new operation, or the replacement of an old piece of equipment) that increases the facility's overall emissions by more than de minimis amounts.[63] Because the def-

---

considerable support in the legislative history, was rejected in Alabama Power Co. v. Costle, 636 F.2d 323, 352-55 (D.C. Cir. 1979), which held that the Act obligated EPA to take emissions controls into account in determining potential to emit.

. . . EPA adopted this view in its 1980 regulations. Thus a source may avoid the PSD permit requirement by accepting a state permit that contains sufficient emission control requirements and[/or] restrictions on hours of operation to bring overall emissions below the 100/250 ton threshold. . . .

(2) What pollutants are covered? The literal terms of the Act extend coverage to a source that exceeds the 100/250 threshold for any air pollutant, not just an air pollutant regulated by the Act. See Alabama Power Co. v. Costle, 636 F.2d 323, 352 (D.C. Cir. 1979); Currie, Nondegradation and Visibility Under the Clean Air Act, 68 Calif. L. Rev. 38, 56-57 (1980). Without explanation, the agency chose in its regulations to cover only emissions of regulated pollutants. 40 C.F.R. §§51.166(b), 52.21(b) (1987). This decision has not been challenged.

63. Many of the issues raised in the preceding note relating to the calculation of the 100/250 threshold are also important in determining whether there has been a modification. . . . There are, though, some additional complexities:

(1) How large must an increase be to constitute a modification? In its pre-Alabama Power regulations, EPA elected to use the same 100/250 ton threshold for modifications as for construction. 40 C.F.R. §§51.24(b)(2), 52.21(b)(2) (1978). Thus, just as a new source with the potential to emit 90 tons of sulfur dioxide would escape coverage, so too would an existing major emitting facility that wanted to add 90 tons of emissions potential.

This interpretation, though, was rejected in Alabama Power Co. v. Costle, 636 F.2d 323, 399-400 (D.C. Cir. 1979). The court pointed out that §165(a), 42 U.S.C. §7475(a)(1982), establishes permit requirements that apply to the "construction" of a major emitting facility, and that §169(2)(C), 42 U.S.C. §7479(2)(C) (1982), defines "construction" as including a "modification" within the meaning of §111(a), 42 U.S.C. §7411(a) (1982). This latter section is thus the key to the definition of "modification." Section 111(a)(4) does not mention the 100/250 ton threshold, but instead defines a "modification" as any physical change which increases the amount of any air pollutant. Thus the court concluded that physical changes that increase emissions by less than the 100/250 threshold constitute modifications; in fact, a physical change constitutes a modification even if the addition does not raise emissions over the 100/250 threshold for the increased pollutant. See 45 Fed. Reg. 52,712 (Aug. 7, 1980) (example 6); 40 C.F.R. §§51.166(b)(2), 52.21(b)(2) (1987) (definition of "major modification" as a net increase in any air pollutant).

The court did, however, allow EPA to exempt from the permit requirement increases that are "truly de minimis." Alabama Power, 636 F.2d at 400. EPA has since defined "de minimis" thresholds, ranging from 100 to 0.0004 tons, for each of the pollutants regulated under the Act. 40 C.F.R. §§51.166(b)(23)(i), 52.21(b)(23)(i) (1987). Increases above these levels are considered "significant," and thus require a permit.

(2) What kinds of increases are covered? Under §111(a)(4), 42 U.S.C. §7411(a)(4)

inition of a major emitting facility is broad enough to include a plant
with many emission points, it is possible for a plant owner to "net out"
of the permit requirement for an increase at one point in the plant by
"contemporaneously" lowering emissions at another point so that there
is less than a de minimis increase from the plant as a whole. Similarly,
modernizations of individual points that do not cause a net increase in
emissions of more than de minimis amounts are exempt.[64]

By the terms of the statute, the program applies only to facilities
located in an attainment area: that is, an area that either meets any of
the ambient standards, or for which insufficient information exists to
say whether it meets the standard. Since, though, every part of the
country meets at least one ambient standard, the program's coverage is
nationwide.

Under this broad definition of an attainment area, an area is subject
to the PSD program if it is in attainment for one criteria pollutant though
in nonattainment for all others. But the program will apply only to
emissions of pollutants for which the area is in attainment. Suppose, for
instance, that a permit is sought for a source that would emit both sulfur
dioxide and hydrocarbons, and that the source would be located in an
area that is classified as nonattainment for ozone. The sulfur dioxide
emissions would be covered by PSD, but the hydrocarbon emissions
would be exempt; instead, because hydrocarbons contribute to ozone
formation, these emissions would be covered by the new source review
program for "nonattainment areas" established by part D of the Act.
Alternatively, these emissions may be barred by section 110(a)(2)(I)'s

---

(1982), only a "physical change" or a "change in the method of a source's operation" can be a modification. For instance, it has been held that shutting off
a pollution control system constitutes a change in the method of operation and
is therefore covered by PSD. See United States v. Chevron U.S.A., Inc., 639 F.
Supp. 770, 778 (W.D. Tex. 1985); cf. National-Southwire Aluminum v. EPA,
838 F.2d 835, 840-41 (6th Cir.) (same conclusion reached in the context of the
NSPS program), cert. denied, 109 S. Ct. 390 (1988).

64. Some of the principal issues raised by "netting" are the following:

(1) What time constraints exist on netting? In determining whether an increase
in emission has occurred, only "contemporaneous" increases and decreases in
emissions are considered. 40 C.F.R. §§51.166(b)(3)(i), 51.2.21(b)(3)(i) (1987). . . .
Thus a reduction in 1989 may be used to offset an increase occurring no later
than 1994. If the state is running the program, it may define "contemporaneous"
in any "reasonable" way it chooses. 40 C.F.R. §51.166(b)(3) (1987). In any case,
a reduction may be used only once and a source may not take credit for decreases
that are required by law. 45 Fed. Reg. 52,698-701 (Aug. 7, 1980). . . .

(2) Must offsetting reductions be "equivalent"? EPA's regulations do not allow
netting among different pollutants; that is, an increase in particulate matters
may not be offset by a decrease in sulfur dioxide. Even when a single pollutant
is concerned, EPA takes the view that a reduction may be credited against an
increase only if the health and welfare impacts of the changes are equivalent.
40 C.F.R. §§51.166(b)(3)(vi)(c), 52.21(b)(3)(vi)(c) (1987).

construction ban if the nonattainment area has not submitted a SIP that meets the requirements of the Act.

WHAT MUST COVERED SOURCES DO?

According to the latest published data, about one hundred projects, three-quarters of them modifications, pass through the PSD permitting process each year. Each of these projects must obtain, prior to construction, a permit from either EPA or the state in which the source will be located, depending on whether EPA has approved the PSD provisions of the state's SIP or has otherwise delegated the program to the state. Construction without a permit is punishable by civil penalty and injunction.

There are in practice two major requirements for obtaining a permit. First, the facility must install the "best available control technology" (BACT) for every pollutant regulated under the Clean Air Act whose emissions it will increase by more than de minimis amounts.[75] Unlike

---

75. . . . The scope of the BACT requirement raises issues similar to those encountered in defining "major emitting facility," and "modification." The major questions are the following:

(1) What pollutants are subject to BACT? Under §165(a)(4), the BACT requirement applies to all pollutants regulated under the Act, not just those for which ambient standards are set. 42 U.S.C. §7475(a)(4) (1982). . . . [The 1990 Amendments now exempt hazardous air pollutants from the PSD program. See §112(b)(6).—ED.] Similarly, chlorofluorocarbons (CFCs)—chemicals that are suspected of depleting stratospheric ozone concentrations—appear to be subject to PSD now that EPA has promulgated regulations under the Act controlling their use. 53 Fed. Reg. 30,566 (Aug. 12, 1988) (to be codified at 40 C.F.R. §82). . . .

(2) How great must emissions of a pollutant be for BACT to apply? In its pre-*Alabama Power* regulations, EPA ruled that the BACT requirement applied only to pollutants for which the source exceeded the 100/250 ton threshold. Thus, if a source had the potential to emit 255 tons of sulfur dioxide and 30 tons of particulate matter, BACT would only apply to sulfur dioxide. See, e.g., 40 C.F.R. §51.24(i)(1) (1978), reprinted in 43 Fed. Reg. 26,385 (June 19, 1978). *Alabama Power* reversed the agency, noting that §165(a)(4), 42 U.S.C. §7475(a)(4), expressly requires BACT "for each pollutant" without any mention of the 100/250 threshold. Alabama Power Co. v. Costle, 636 F.2d 323, 403-05 (D.C. Cir. 1979). As with modifications, though, the court gave the agency discretion to exempt from BACT pollutants that are emitted in de minimis amounts, id., at 405, and the agency has responded by promulgating the same de minimis test for BACT as for modifications. See 40 C.F.R. §§51.166(b)(23), 52.21(b)(23) (1987). . . . Since the de minimis level for particulate matter is 25 tons, the source cited above would therefore need BACT for both pollutants. By contrast, a source emitting 90 tons each of both pollutants would be exempt from BACT because it would not cross the 100/250 threshold for any pollutant, and would therefore not be a "major emitting facility."

NSPS, which are category-wide, BACT is set by the permitting authority on a case-by-case basis for each individual facility. BACT must reflect the maximum achievable degree of emission reduction, taking into account energy, environmental, and economic impacts, and other costs. If there is an NSPS for the facility's category, BACT must be defined at least as stringently. . . .

Second, the source must show that it will not cause any air quality "increment" to be exceeded. These increments are numerical limits on the maximum permissible increases in the concentrations in clean air areas of sulfur dioxide or particulate matter, or, as a result of recent EPA action, nitrogen oxides. For instance, the permissible increase in the annual average concentration of sulfur dioxide is limited to . . . two, twenty, or forty micrograms, depending on the area's classification. The increments restrict, in general, increases occurring after the "baseline date"—the date when the first application is submitted in the area for a PSD permit. The pre-existing "baseline" concentrations of pollution are irrelevant, unless the source would cause a violation of the ambient standards. For example, if the baseline is seventy, the annual average concentration of sulfur dioxide will be held to the primary standard of eighty micrograms regardless of the increments. But Class II areas with a baseline of forty and ten would be limited to sixty and thirty micrograms, respectively.

The size of the increments is determined by whether the area is Class I, Class II, or Class III; Class I has the most restrictive increments and Class III the least restrictive. There is no particular air quality significance to the size of the increments for each class: this is not surprising, since there is no air quality effect that is caused by new emissions rather than old emissions. Rather, the increments for each class were chosen as a rough measure of whether an area should be kept at its present air quality, or whether moderate or greater growth is appropriate.

Nor is there any special significance to the selection of the pollutants covered by the increment scheme. EPA and Congress originally confined the increments to sulfur dioxide and particulate matter because they were the two pollutants for which an increment scheme was judged to be technically workable. In fact, the codification requires EPA to devise increments or an equally effective scheme for the other existing, as well as future, criteria pollutants. The recently promulgated nitrogen oxide increments are the result of litigation by environmental groups to enforce this requirement. In addition, as a result of the revision of the particulate matter standard to cover only respirable particles, the agency is planning to promulgate increments for these particles and cease enforcement of the present particulate matter increments established in the statute. There is, though, no indication of when other criteria pollutants will be covered by the increment scheme or an alternative.

In the 1977 PSD codification, Congress classified almost all areas

Class II and gave the states and Indian tribes the power to redesignate areas. There are important exceptions, though, to this rule. Many national parklands were designated as Class I areas not subject to redesignation; there are known as mandatory Class I areas. Other parklands are in the intermediate category of "Class II floor areas"; these are initially classified Class II, but may not be redesignated Class III.

These initial classifications have assumed special importance. The sponsors of PSD envisioned that states and tribes would redesignate areas promptly. In fact, there have been no redesignations, except for several Indian tribes in Montana that have redesignated their reservations from Class II to Class I. There is therefore no area carrying the Class III designation, and only one reported instance of an area seriously considering this classification. Thus, except for the mandatory Class I parks, the entire Nation, from the pristine reaches of Alaska to the smoggy skies of Los Angeles, is Class II.

NOTES AND QUESTIONS

1. Professor Oren suggests that the PSD program functions through two related but different strategies, "control compelling," or the additional level of technology forcing required by BACT review, and "site-shifting," preventing or discouraging even well-controlled sources from locating in areas considered inappropriate. Why aren't NSPSs adequate to meet the first objective? One reason is that BACT applies to some sources for which there is no applicable NSPS, such as lumber and wood products. A second reason is that the PSD program applies to pollutants not covered by the category's NSPS. In addition, BACT generally is far more stringent than most NSPSs for sources covered by both. Professor Oren notes that BACT review is case-by-case and constantly updated; categorical rules are more likely to be watered down by worst-case factors.

According to Oren, the impact of the PSD program on site choice is less demonstrable. Large emitters seeking to locate in Class II areas may consume the entire growth increment, particularly if located in inappropriate terrain (e.g., where the pollution will be trapped by nearby hills). However, permissible sites are probably available close by, and other Class II regions would have the same problem. Most sources have their greatest impact within a short distance, and emissions may be permitted even within close proximity if they occur at different times or if they are subject to different wind patterns. Thus, the effect of increments may be to provide additional pressure for technology forcing, so that increments would only rarely be violated. However, whether or not it is good policy to force more stringent controls on the basis of site categorization is debatable. Moreover, where development is mainly associated with new facilities rather than replacement of old ones, states eventually will exhaust their increments. Oren, above, at 30-40.

2. Another reason BACT has been more stringent than many NSPSs is that EPA has used a "top-down" approach to BACT determinations that considers first the most effective technology for controlling emissions. Less effective control technology is only considered if the most effective controls are found not to be achievable after considering the factors outlined in section 169(3). This approach has been challenged by industry. See Foote and Wyckoff, New Source Review, in Law of Environmental Protection 11.05[3][b][iii] [D] (S. Novick, et al., eds. 1991).

3. An alternative to Oren's conception of the PSD program's impact maintains that it is an "un-program" whose primary impact is to encourage measures to avoid PSD requirements. The vast majority of modified sources avoid the PSD program by investing in controls or by agreeing to operational restrictions that make it possible to avoid PSD requirements through plantwide netting.

4. For modified sources, a key issue has been whether EPA should use the source's actual emissions or its potential emissions to determine if the modification is sufficiently major to trigger new source review (NSR). EPA had used an "actual-to-potential" approach that compared the old unit's actual emissions with the modified unit's potential to emit. Compare Puerto Rican Cement Co. v. EPA, 889 F.2d 272 (1st Cir. 1989), with Wisconsin Electric Co. v. Reilly, 893 F.2d 901 (7th Cir. 1990). As a result of White House pressure, EPA has proposed adopting an "actual-to-future actual" approach that compares the old unit's actual emissions with the modified unit's future actual emissions. 56 Fed. Reg. 27,630 (1991). This may reduce the impact of the PSD program in encouraging plantwide netting.

5. The PSD program has assumed considerable importance in the effort to protect western national parks from encroachment by development in nearby areas. Because of their distance from urban centers and the ability to move electricity long distances efficiently, these areas are attractive for construction of power plants. However, for numerous reasons the PSD program has not been an effective means of addressing the problem. Oren, The Protection of Parklands from Increased Air Pollution: A Look at Current Policy, 13 Harv. Envtl. L. Rev. 313 (1989).

6. Voting records on the PSD program show substantial support from representatives of the Sunbelt, the region most likely to suffer any growth restrictions. Oren, Prevention of Significant Deterioration, 74 Iowa L. Rev. 1, 111-112 (1988). Does it make sense to invest a higher value in the loss of existing clean air than in the improvement of dirty air (assuming the Act is effective in shifting the location of new facilities to the areas possessing the latter)? As one authority notes, the effect is that "the highest air pollution concentrations are permitted in those areas where the most people live, while remote areas are afforded extra pro-

tection!" P. Portney, Air Pollution Policy, in Public Policies for Environmental Protection 78 (P. Portney, ed. 1990). Professor Oren suggests that the consequences of this preference may be considerable; for example, it may create a subtle disincentive to tighten ambient air quality standards, since the cost of attainment will increase if sources are more concentrated. Another effect may be to weaken political support for improving air quality in urban areas. Oren, Prevention of Significant Deterioration, at 78-81.

7. The calculation of increments, like the evaluation of SIPs in general, is based on atmospheric models. Section 165(e)(2). Modeling results are least likely to be accurate when addressing multiple sources and complex terrain, arguably the situations when precision is most needed. Monitoring is required (see §165(e)(2)) but cannot account for the effect of statutory exclusions and modifications of actual emissions, and in any event is itself too subject to variation to be the basis for reliable judgments. Id. at 40-44. To further complicate matters, Congress excluded emissions from certain sources in defining the unused increment; emissions from sources outside the United States (important in the Southwest), tall stacks, and plants that converted from oil or gas to coal in response to other federal laws are simply not counted. §163(c)(1).

8. One consequence of the increment concept is that new sources will over time use up the allowed opportunity for growth. Indeed, there is arguably an incentive to get in early if it appears the increment may be exhausted. See, e.g., Citizens Against the Refinery's Effects v. EPA, 643 F.2d 178 (4th Cir. 1981) (choice between two applicants in the same PSD area filing on the same day). How can areas in this situation make room for further growth?

9. The PSD provisions of the Act establish specific maximum allowable increases (ambient air quality increments) for sulfur dioxide and total suspended particulates, so-called Set I pollutants. §163. EPA was given greater latitude to establish regulations for other pollutants under section 166. In particular, regulations for "Set II" pollutants need not include an area classification system. Section 166(c) of the Clean Air Act requires that the Set II regulations "provide specific numerical measures against which permit applications may be evaluated" and "fulfill the goals and purposes" of the Clean Air Act and PSD program. Section 166(d) also requires that the Set II regulations "provide specific measures at least as effective as the increments" established in the Set I rules. §§166(c), (d). EPA failed to meet a 1979 deadline for promulgating Set II regulations and was put under a court-ordered schedule in April 1987. Sierra Club v. Thomas, 658 F. Supp. 165 (N.D. Cal. 1987).

10. EPA has now issued regulations for one Set II pollutant—nitrogen dioxide. In its Set II regulations, EPA generally followed the approach Congress had adopted for the Set I pollutants. EPA used the same three-tiered classification scheme for protected areas (though no

Class III areas have been established to date), and it again used the approach of establishing ambient air quality increments, while indicating that states could adopt alternative strategies if they could demonstrate that they were as effective as the increment approach. EPA set the permissible increments for nitrogen dioxide by reference to the national ambient air quality standards. The permissible increments were defined by using the same percentage of the nitrogen dioxide ambient standard as the percentage that the Set I increments were of their annual ambient standards. The D.C. Circuit has recently remanded the Set II regulations to EPA. The court held that while EPA's approach complied with section 166(d)'s requirement that the regulations be at least as effective as the Set I rules, EPA had failed to consider whether the goals of the PSD program required an even more stringent standard, as required by section 166(c). The court noted that the PSD program

> emphasizes special considerations, such as national wilderness areas and their "natural, recreational, scenic, or historic value[s]." Thus a pollutant that has only mild public health effects but severe effects on wilderness areas might demand a lower increment (measured as a percentage of its ambient standards) than one with severe health effects but only mild effects on wilderness areas. [Environmental Defense Fund v. EPA, 898 F.2d 183, 190 (D.C. Cir. 1990).]

A Note on PSD and the 1990 Amendments

The 1990 Amendments made only technical changes in the PSD program. Hazardous air pollutants were exempted. §112(b)(6). The creation of permit requirements for new sources will add to the administrative complexity associated with implementing the PSD program. One result may be even greater efforts by industry to avoid regulation by contesting EPA's administrative interpretations of "major modification." J. Quarles and W. Lewis, The NEW Clean Air Act 72-76 (1990).

I. AIR TOXICS

In many respects, the original Clean Air and Clean Water Acts were quite different, as your study of this chapter and the next will reveal. However, one respect in which they were initially very similar was in their approach to the problem of toxic emissions. Under both the CAA of 1970 and the FWPCA of 1972, the Environmental Protection Agency was under orders to control toxic emissions on the basis of what was necessary to protect health, without regard to costs or technological feasibility.

Ever since these toxic control provisions were enacted, EPA has been trying to change them. Through creative lawyering, the consent of major environmental litigants, the interest and devotion of a single federal district court judge, and the ex post facto agreement of the Congress, the basic design of the water toxics provisions was transmuted from health-based standards to technology-based standards soon after their enactment. In the next chapter, we recount in more detail the relatively early success EPA had in making changes in the FWPCA.

In contrast, the history of section 112 of the CAA had until 1990 been one of paralysis and frustration. Prior to the 1990 Amendments, section 112(a)(1) defined a "hazardous" air pollutant as "an air pollutant to which no ambient air quality standard is applicable and which in the judgment of the Administrator causes, or contributes to, air pollution which may reasonably be anticipated to result in an increase in serious irreversible, or incapacitating reversible, illness." Once the administrator determined a pollutant to be hazardous, the administrator was to set allowable emissions standards "at the level which in his judgment provides an ample margin of safety to protect the public health." §112(b)(1)(B). This system for regulating hazardous air pollutants differed from that for ambient air quality pollutants, regulated under sections 108-110, in several major respects. Most important, hazardous air pollutant regulation bypassed the federalism-sensitive structure of the state implementation plan process entirely, in that EPA directly regulates the sources of those pollutants. Why do you suppose Congress chose to do this?

Section 112 originally gave the administrator 90 days to identify the hazardous pollutants, 6 months after that to propose standards, and 6 months after that to issue final regulations. These deadlines were viewed as hopelessly unrealistic by EPA, which thought that it would take 3 to 7 years to complete a health assessment adequate to support a final emissions standard for a substance. See Dwyer, The Pathology of Symbolic Legislation, 17 Ecology L.Q. 233, 238 (1990).

Aside from its unrealistic deadlines, section 112 inspired fear in EPA because the generally accepted no-safe-threshold assumption for carcinogens led many to conclude that the only level of carcinogenic emissions that would provide "an ample margin of safety" was zero. EPA was extremely reluctant to accept this interpretation because literal application of a zero-emissions standard would require the shutdown of important parts of the American economy, including the steel industry, chemical manufacturing, and petroleum refining.

Accordingly, regulation under section 112 proceeded slowly between 1970 and 1976, with EPA proposing standards for only four pollutants: asbestos, beryllium, mercury, and vinyl chloride. All of these proposed standards were issued only under compulsion of court action initiated by the Environmental Defense Fund. Vinyl chloride received regulatory attention only after several workers at a polyvinyl chloride plant died of an extremely rare form of cancer, angiosarcoma of the liver. Doniger, Federal Regulation of Vinyl Chloride: A Short Course in the Law and Policy of Toxic Substances Control, 7 Ecology L.Q. 497 (1978).

Asbestos and vinyl chloride were the first carcinogens regulated under section 112. Though EPA considered banning the production, processing, and use of asbestos, as well as prohibiting its emission, it eventually rejected both options on grounds of enforcement difficulties and adverse economic consequences. (Was the Agency justified in taking these considerations into account?) The Agency was unable to identify a nonharmful, nonzero amount of asbestos emissions. While the Agency theorized that "there are levels of asbestos exposure that will not be associated with any *detectable* risk," it concluded that "these levels are not known." 38 Fed. Reg. 8,820, 8,820 (1973). Instead of setting quantitative emissions levels, the Agency decided to limit visible emissions and to establish requirements for certain production procedures. Environmental groups chose not to litigate the EPA's failure to ban asbestos emissions even though quantitative standards were never established due to the difficulty of measuring asbestos emissions.

The EPA took a different position in its regulation of vinyl chloride, saying that "for carcinogens there may be no atmospheric concentration which poses absolutely no public health risk." 40 Fed. Reg. 59,532, 59,533 (1975). However, it was reluctant to propose a zero-emissions rule for vinyl chloride because doing so would apparently result in shutting down major segments of American industry. Environmental groups recommended that EPA ban all vinyl chloride products for which alternate products were currently available and to gradually phase out all other vinyl products as substitutes became available. 41 Fed. Reg. 46,560, 46,561-46,562 (1976). The Agency considered this approach, which might be called "zero emissions as soon as feasible," as well as one proposed by the vinyl industry. The vinyl industry suggested that emissions standards should be established on the basis of plant-by-plant cost-benefit analyses. Id. at 46,562.

The EPA rejected both of these proposals in favor of an approach that sought to reduce vinyl chloride emissions to the "lowest level achievable by the use of the best available technology" (BAT). EPA maintained that this standard would reduce vinyl chloride emissions by 95 percent. The Agency predicted that this would reduce cancers caused by such emissions from 20 per year to 1 per year among the 4.6 million persons living near vinyl chloride plants. "Zero emissions as soon as possible" was ruled out because the available alternatives lacked the positive qualities of vinyl chloride (e.g., nonflammability) and because of the unknown health and environmental risks the substitutes may pose. The cost-benefit approach was rejected because section 112 did not allow for an extensive consideration of costs.

The Environmental Defense Fund filed a lawsuit against EPA on the ground that the BAT standard was too permissive, but the parties reached an out-of-court settlement, with EPA agreeing to reconsider its approach and to issue more stringent regulations. In 1977, EPA proposed to adopt zero emissions as the long-term goal of its regulatory strategy. 42 Fed. Reg. 28,154 (1977). In accordance with normal procedures under the Administrative Procedure Act, EPA took comments from the public on the proposal. No final action was taken until 1985, when EPA withdrew its 1977 proposal and reaffirmed its original BAT-based regulations, with minor changes. 50 Fed. Reg. 1,182 (1985).

This time the Natural Resources Defense Council sued EPA, arguing that section 112 did not allow BAT regulations specifically, and the consideration of costs and feasibility generally, to be considered in the formulation of emissions standards. This litigation resulted in two decisions by the Court of Appeals for the District of Columbia Circuit, a 2-1 panel decision subsequently superseded by a unanimous en banc decision. NRDC v. EPA, 824 F.2d 1146 (D.C. Cir. 1987) (en banc), revg. 804 F.2d 710 (D.C. Cir. 1986) (*Vinyl Chloride*).

The panel's majority decision affirmed the EPA's interpretation of the statute. In light of the absence of conclusive evidence that vinyl chloride emissions caused adverse health effects at all nonzero levels, it ruled that EPA had acted reasonably in considering economic and technological feasibility:

> Since the Administrator has no way of knowing health effects in the range of uncertainty, such considerations as technological and economic feasibility seem natural, perhaps inevitable, choices to inform the Administrator's decision whether he has amply provided for a reasonable degree of safety from the unknown. By emphasizing available technology, the EPA has ensured the maximum regulation against uncertainty without the economic and social displacements that would accompany the closing of an industry or any substantial part of an industry. By ensuring that costs do not become grossly disproportionate to the level of reduction achieved, the EPA guarantees that the consuming public does not pay an excessive price for the marginal benefits of increasing increments of protection against the unknown. [NRDC v. EPA, 804 F.2d 710, 722 (D.C. Cir. 1986).]

[handwritten: opinion written by Bork]

The majority rejected the argument that the apparent lack of a safe threshold for vinyl chloride necessarily required a zero emissions level if the "ample margin of safety" language was to be met. In its view, this argument

> confuses a "non-threshold pollutant" with an "apparent non-threshold pollutant." The former poses a known hazard at all non-zero levels. The

latter may appear to pose a risk at all levels, but, by definition, sufficient
data are not available to establish the hazard to public health. We believe
that this is precisely the type of uncertainty for which the Administrator
was vested with discretion, and even though the Administrator may assume
that some risk to health is probable at all concentrations, it is still up to
him to decide what constitutes a reasonable degree of protection given
that uncertainty that does exist. [804 F.2d 710 n.7.]

The en banc court reversed the panel's ruling, finding EPA's approach to be unreasonable and remanding for further action by the
Agency. The court first determined that, although the Congress had not
defined "ample margin of safety," guidance could be gained from the
Senate Report's explanation that "margin of safety" under section 109
of the Act was meant to afford "a reasonable degree of protection . . .
against hazards which research has not yet identified." S. Rep. No. 1196,
91st Cong., 2d Sess. 10 (1970). It also determined that Congress's use
of the word "safety" "is significant evidence that [Congress] did not
intend to require the Administrator to prohibit all emissions of non-
threshold pollutants. As the Supreme Court has recently held, 'safe' does
not mean 'risk free.' Industrial Union Dep't, AFL-CIO v. American
Petroleum Inst., 448 U.S. at 642. Instead, something is 'unsafe' only
when it threatens humans with 'a significant risk of harm.'" Id.

The en banc court found that EPA's attempt to rely primarily on
BAT technology was unsupported by the statute. Instead,

[w]e find that the congressional mandate to provide "an ample margin of
safety" "to protect the public health" requires the Administrator to make
an initial determination of what is "safe." This determination must be based
exclusively upon the Administrator's determination of the risk to health
at a particular emission level. Because the Administrator in this case did
not make any finding of the risk to health the question of how that determination is to be made is not before us. We do wish to note, however,
that the Administrator's decision does not require a finding that "safe"
means "risk-free," see Industrial Union Dep't, 448 U.S. at 642, or a finding
that the determination is free from uncertainty. Instead, we find only that
the Administrator's decision must be based upon an expert judgment with
regard to the level of emission that will result in an "acceptable" risk to
health. Environmental Defense Fund, 598 F.2d at 83-84. In this regard, the
Administrator must determine what inferences should be drawn from
available scientific data and decide what risks are acceptable in the world
in which we live. See Industrial Union Dep't, 448 U.S. at 642 ("There are
many activities that we engage in every day—such as driving a car or even
breathing city air—that entail some risk of accident or material health
impairment; nevertheless, few people would consider those activities 'unsafe.'"); Alabama Power Co. v. Costle, 636 F.2d 323, 360-361 (D.C. Cir.
1979). This determination must be based solely upon the risk to health.
The Administrator cannot under any circumstances consider cost and

technological feasibility at this stage of the analysis. The latter factors have no relevance to the preliminary determination of what is safe. Of course, if the Administrator cannot find that there is an acceptable risk at any level, then the Administrator must set the level at zero.

Congress, however, recognized in section 112 that the determination of what is "safe" will always be marked by scientific uncertainty and thus exhorted the Administrator to set emission standards that will provide an "ample margin" of safety. This language permits the Administrator to take into account scientific uncertainty and to use expert discretion to determine what action should be taken in light of that uncertainty. See *Environmental Defense Fund,* 598 F.2d at 83 ("by requiring EPA to set standards providing an 'ample margin of safety,' Congress authorized and, indeed, required EPA to protect against dangers before their extent is conclusively ascertained"); *Hercules,* 598 F.2d at 104 ("Under the 'ample margin of safety' directive, EPA's standards must protect against incompletely understood dangers to public health and the environment, in addition to well-known ← risks."). In determining what is an "ample margin" the Administrator may, and perhaps must, take into account the inherent limitations of risk assessment and the limited scientific knowledge of the effects of exposure to carcinogens at various levels, and may therefore decide to set the level below that previously determined to be "safe." This is especially true when a straight line extrapolation from known risks is used to estimate risks to health at levels of exposure for which no data is available. This method, which is based upon results of exposure at fairly high levels of the hazardous pollutants, will show some risk at every level because of the rules of arithmetic rather than because of any knowledge. In fact the risk at a certain point on the extrapolated line may have no relationship to reality; there is no particular reason to think that the actual line of the incidence of harm is represented by a straight line. Thus, by its nature the finding of risk is uncertain and the Administrator must use his discretion to meet the statutory mandate. It is only at this point of the regulatory process that the Administrator may set the emission standard at the lowest level that is technologically feasible. In fact, this is, we believe, precisely the type of policy choice that Congress envisioned when it directed the Administrator to provide an "ample margin of safety." Once "safety" is assured, the Administrator should be free to diminish as much of the statistically determined risk as possible by setting the standard at the lowest feasible level. Because consideration of these factors at this stage is clearly intended "to protect the public health," it is fully consistent with the Administrator's mandate under section 112. [NRDC v. EPA, 824 F.2d at 1164-1165.]

NOTES AND QUESTIONS

1. In the initial panel opinion the majority attempted to distinguish between an "apparent non-threshold pollutant" and a "non-threshold pollutant." What is the difference between the two, according to panel majority? Can you think of any carcinogens that would be "non-threshold

pollutants" under this definition? The en banc decision, authored by the same judge as the panel majority, no longer speaks of apparent non-threshold pollutants. Why did the court abandon this distinction?

2. What role, if any, can uncertainty play in the determination of "how safe is safe" under the en banc decision? Why does the en banc decision reject NRDC's argument that EPA automatically must set a zero level of emissions in order to provide an "ample margin of safety" against nonthreshold carcinogens? If "ample margin of safety" does not mean "risk free," how much risk can EPA tolerate? The decision quotes Justice Stevens's comment in the *Benzene* decision that few people would consider many daily activities such as driving a car or breathing city air to be unsafe. Does this mean that an ample margin of safety need not provide any greater level of safety than existing automobile safety or air pollution control laws? How should EPA go about determining what constitutes an "ample margin of safety"?

3. In the court's view, EPA was allowed to take technological and economic considerations into account only after deciding what is an acceptable level of risk. What factors may EPA consider in this first step of determining what constitutes a "safe" level of emissions? Can "safe" mean zero risk?

4. EPA may subsequently consider costs and technological feasibility in determining how far to go beyond mere "safety" in providing an "ample margin" of safety. Is it realistic to think that EPA's initial judgment about what constitutes safety can be divorced entirely from considerations of cost or feasibility? What if EPA knows that it is not feasible to reduce certain types of emissions to levels that it otherwise would consider to be "safe"?

5. How should EPA implement the first step of this two-step process—determining what constitutes an acceptable level of risk? Should EPA consider what other risks people voluntarily accept in determining "how safe is safe"? It has been argued that society should concentrate on regulating its "portfolio of risks" in descending order of their seriousness. Does this mean that EPA should concentrate first on reducing levels of cigarette smoking before regulating hazardous air pollutants that pose less serious risks?

6. Note that the alternative approach agreed to by EPA in its 1977 settlement agreement with EDF sought to force the development of better emissions control technology. It attempted to do so by establishing an ultimate "goal" of zero emissions to be achieved over time through progressively more stringent standards. To what extent would the D.C. Circuit's interpretation of section 112 require, or permit, technology-forcing regulation? EPA's response to the *Vinyl Chloride* decision is discussed in Chapter 4, pages 593-597.

The 1990 Amendments and Air Toxics

This is how matters stood when Congress took up amendments to the Clean Air Act in 1989 and 1990: The one constant throughout the first 20 years of section 112 had been its very disappointing record in addressing the problems of toxic air pollutants. By 1989, EPA had still only regulated 7 toxic air pollutants (the previously named four plus benzene, radionuclides, and inorganic arsenic—coke oven emissions had been named as a section 112 pollutant, but no emissions standards had been set). Although EPA had been pressured at various times to do more under the NESHAPS program, momentum for change had increased dramatically in 1987, when EPA released the results of the first Toxic Release Inventory mandated under SARA's right-to-know provisions. (See the discussion of EPCRTKA, pages 622-628, above.) The initial TRI data indicated that more than 2.7 billion pounds of toxic air pollutants are emitted annually in the United States. Risk assessment estimates by EPA, based on just a subset of all toxic air pollutants, indicated that exposure to toxic air pollutants likely was resulting in 1,000 to 3,000 cancer deaths each year.

When Congress revised section 112, it turned to the technology-based strategy that EPA had been haltingly attempting to apply. As revised, section 112 now requires EPA to issue "maximum achievable control technology" (MACT) standards for each source category on a list to be published by EPA by November 1991. That list must include both major sources (defined as sources emitting either 10 tons per year of any single toxic air pollutant or 25 tons per year of any combination of such pollutants) and area sources (defined as "any stationary source . . . that is not a major source," a provision designed to identify small toxic emitters such as dry cleaners). Eight years after issuing MACT controls, EPA must determine whether additional controls are necessary to ensure "an ample margin of safety," as that phrase was understood prior to the 1990 Amendments. For carcinogens, the statute requires the establishment of standards to control residual risks if the most exposed individual is exposed to more than a one-in-one-million lifetime cancer risk from any regulated source following implementation of MACT. §112(f)(2)(A). Sources that voluntarily reduce emissions by 90 percent prior to implementation of MACT standards can gain a six-year extension for compliance with technology-based controls.

The new toxics provisions also contain a list of 189 named toxic air pollutants that constitute the initial substances to be controlled under section 112. §112(b)(1). EPA may add to or delete from the list in accordance with prescribed procedures. §112(b)(2).

These amendments once again bring the federal approach to air toxics and water toxics into remarkable agreement, albeit on very different terms than their initial congruence some 20 years ago. Both are now primarily technology-based, with backup provisions to address situations in which application of BAT or MACT leaves unacceptably high residual risk. Both now include statutorily enumerated lists of toxics to be regulated by EPA, 126 in the Clean Water Act, 189 in the Clean Air Act. There are important differences of detail, but we will leave exploration of those for the next chapter.

For more on the history of carcinogen regulation under section 112, see F. Cross, Environmentally Induced Cancer and the Law 104-107 (1989); Graham, The Failure of Agency-Forcing: The Regulation of Airborne Carcinogens Under Section 112 of the Clean Air Act, 1985 Duke L.J. 100 (1985).

Incentives for Early Reduction

In keeping with their attention to incentive-based devices of various kinds, the 1990 Amendments revised the air toxics program to include a provision that will grant sources a six-year extension of compliance with the MACT standards if they voluntarily reduce emissions by 90 percent or more before MACT standards are proposed. See §112(i)(5). Once a source satisfies the Agency that such a reduction will be achieved, the source's actual reductions become an "alternative emission limitation" (that is, an alternative to otherwise applicable MACT) that is fully enforceable as an emissions limitation. §112(i)(5)(B).

Why was Congress willing to trade a six-year compliance extension for early reductions? Will it reduce industry compliance costs? Will it provide greater protection during the next few years to persons living near sources that opt to make early reductions? What about future years? See the table below, which compares emissions under MACT and the early reduction scenario, based on the assumption that MACT requires a 98 percent reduction in emissions. Is it desirable to trade greater protection in the four years before the MACT requirement otherwise would become effective for lesser protection in years 5 through 10?

Emissions Under Early Reductions v. MACT

Time (years)	MACT scenario	Early reduction scenario
Year 1	100	10
Year 2	100	10
Year 3	100	10
Year 4	100	10
Year 5	2	10
Year 6	2	10
Year 7	2	10
Year 8	2	10

		Early reduction
Time (years)	MACT scenario	scenario
Year 9	2	10
Year 10	2	10
Totals	412	100

Source: 56 Fed. Reg. 27,338, 27,339 (1991).

What should a source be required to do to qualify for this extension? The Amendments enumerate 189 hazardous air pollutants. Should a source be required to reduce by 90 percent existing emissions of each and every such pollutant that it currently emits? MACT technology under section 112 applies source by source, not pollutant by pollutant, and EPA has interpreted the 90-percent requirement to mean 90 percent of total emissions. Hazardous pollutants vary in their toxicity, however, and Congress instructed EPA to "limit the use of offsetting reductions" of low-risk pollutants in situations where the source is emitting "high-risk pollutants." §112(i)(5)(E).

EPA has now proposed to implement the early reduction program by using a hazard-weighting factor for pollutants. The Agency has identified 35 high-risk pollutants and assigned them weights varying from 100,000 for dioxin, 1,000 for benzidene, and 100 for asbestos down to 10 for the majority of carcinogens and all the noncarcinogens on its list. Under the Agency's proposal, hazardous pollutants not on the high-risk list carry a weight of one. 56 Fed. Reg. 27,338, 27,354 (1991).

EPA proposes that a source must satisfy two tests to qualify for the early reduction program: (1) it must show a 90 percent total hazardous air pollutant reduction; and (2) it must show a 90 percent reduction in its weighted total emissions. Id. at 25,355.

EPA's proposal incorporates elements of the early compliance bonus allowance program under the acid rain title (§404(d)(6) and of the bubble policy. How would you evaluate EPA's proposal? Does it make sense to permit a source of hazardous air pollutants to delay installing available control technology? Could the early reductions program unfairly benefit sources who failed to control their emissions prior to enactment of the 1990 Amendments to the detriment of competitors who already had invested in controls? Should sources be required to achieve emissions reductions of 90 percent or more for each hazardous air pollutant they emit? As far as its "bubble" aspects go, is it sound policy for EPA to permit inter-pollutant trading under such a regulatory bubble given uncertainty concerning the relative risks of different pollutants to diverse exposed populations? Should trades be permitted between carcinogens and noncarcinogens?

EPA's assistant administrator for air and radiation programs cites the toxics trading system in the early reductions program as one of the reasons why EPA now estimates that the costs of implementing the 1990 Amendments will be $2 billion less than originally estimated. Rosenberg, At EPA, We Avoid Penny-Wise Regulation, Wall St. J., Mar. 5, 1992, at A15.

= 7 =

‖ *Water Pollution Control* ‖

[I]n 1972, Congress was under the impression that BAT would largely solve the pollution control problem. Water quality upgrading would remain as a backup system for those rare exceptions in which water required it. Whatever the reason, the exceptions have swallowed the rule. Nonpoint pollution grows, sewage treatment barely holds its own, and even industrial BAT has proven to be less stringent than anticipated—indeed, it is often little more stringent than the interim 1977 standard of best practicable technology (BPT)—all of which puts more pressure on water quality upgrading to do the job. The estuaries have been left with a safety net that in the past, for excellent reasons, has caught nothing at all.

—*Oliver Houck**

Warts and all, the Clean Water Act's NPDES program is America's most successful pollution control program to date . . . for a mix of reasons that include its (impossible) goals, its reliance on action-forcing technological standards, and its watch-dogging and enforcement by citizen organizations.

—*Oliver Houck***

The evolution of the nation's water pollution control program followed a path strikingly similar to that of air pollution control. Despite severe interstate pollution problems that spawned some early common law nuisance actions, regulation was left almost entirely to state and local authorities until after World War II. After efforts to use federal financial assistance failed to induce states to adopt effective controls on air and water pollution, comprehensive federal regulatory programs were adopted in the early 1970s.

Two years after creating a national air pollution control program,

---

*Ending the War: A Strategy to Save America's Coastal Zone, 47 Md. L. Rev. 358, 389-390 (1988).

**Recent Developments Under the Clean Water Act NPDES Program (Feb. 5, 1991).

Congress adopted an even more comprehensive program of water pollution controls in the Federal Water Pollution Control Act Amendments
of 1972 (FWPCA). This program represented a substantial departure
from the approach incorporated in the Clean Air Act in three respects.
First, Congress largely rejected ambient environmental quality as the
basis for standard-setting in favor of uniform, technology-based limits
on dischargers. Second, to ensure that effluent limits were applied to
all point source dischargers, Congress created a national permit program
and prohibited all unpermitted discharges of water pollutants. Third,
the FWPCA provided a massive infusion of federal funds to accelerate
the construction of sewage treatment facilities.

Like the experience with the Clean Air Act, implementation of
national controls on water pollution has been a chronic disappointment
when measured against Congress's expectations. Two decades after enactment of the FWPCA, the successes and failures of this program offer
important lessons for regulatory policy. This chapter examines those
lessons, expanding on some familiar themes—the problem of defining
regulatory targets, the tension between uniformity and flexibility, and
the pros and cons of alternative regulatory approaches. It explores why
nonpoint sources of water pollution have escaped effective regulation
and it examines efforts to slow the destruction of wetlands. The chapter
concludes by discussing how environmental regulations are enforced.

Before examining the regulatory program, it is important to consider briefly the nature and sources of water pollution problems. As you
read the materials that follow, consider in what respects water pollution
problems are similar to, and different from, air pollution problems. What
relevance should these similarities and differences have for designing
effective regulatory responses to each?

A.   THE WATER POLLUTION PROBLEM

While a great deal is known about individual pollutants and sources
of water pollution, our knowledge of the overall impact of water pollution remains surprisingly limited in many respects. Water quality data
cannot be aggregated in any effective fashion because the data have so
many parameters and are collected in a largely decentralized fashion by
states using widely varying data collection practices. In December 1990,
EPA candidly admitted that water quality data are so poor that no objective, overall answer can be provided to the question whether the nation's
water quality is getting better or worse. EPA, Meeting the Environmental
Challenge 3 (1990). Many examples of specific water quality improve-

ments can be given, but counter-examples also are available, and many new problems are discovered as more data are gathered.

Most authorities agree that, despite enormous expenditures on water pollution controls, the record of water quality improvement is mixed at best, particularly with respect to toxic pollutants and pollution from nonpoint sources. When it conducted a comprehensive review of environmental trends in 1987, the Conservation Foundation offered the following assessment of the results of spending over $300 billion on water pollution control:

> [T]he water quality in many streams and lakes has improved, sometimes dramatically. But in most cases little more has been done than to prevent further degradation—although this is not a trivial accomplishment in view of the increases in industrial production, agricultural output, and population that have occurred over the intervening decade and a half. In some cases, however, even this fight has been lost, and water quality has gotten worse. [Substantial progress has been made in reducing] "conventional" pollutants such as organic matter, sediment, nutrients, salts, and bacteria from point sources—industries and municipal wastewater treatment plants that discharge their wastes through sewer pipes. . . . At the same time, however, it is becoming clear that these conventional pollutants are not the only point-source pollutants of concern. Furthermore, point-source polluters are not the only cause of degradation of U.S. waters. Toxic pollutants can continue to cause serious water quality problems after most of the conventional discharges are cleaned up. These toxic substances come predominantly from industries and municipal wastewater treatment plants releases but can also come from nonpoint sources such as urban runoff, agricultural practices, abandoned mining operations, and atmospheric fallout. Such nonpoint sources are increasingly recognized as contributing substantial amounts of both conventional and toxic pollutants to surface waters . . .
>
> [E]xisting pollution control programs have done little to protect groundwater quality. Contamination is widespread, threatening drinking water supplies for millions of Americans. The sources of contamination are diverse, ranging from septic tanks to hazardous waste dumps, and from fertilizers applied on farms and lawns to leaking storage tanks. [Conservation Foundation, State of the Environment: A View Toward the Nineties 87-88 (1987).]

This mixed record of success is also reflected in the conclusions of another reviewer that while there has been "some improvement in water quality since 1972 . . . [i]n terms of aggregate measures or national averages, it has not been dramatic." Some "local success stories of substantial cleanup in what had been seriously polluted water bodies" must be balanced against other areas where "water bodies show trends of declining water quality." A. Freeman, Water Pollution Policy, in Public Policies for Environmental Protection 120 (P. Portney, ed. 1990).

1. Types of Pollutants

Efforts to control water pollution are complicated by the many chemical, biological, and physical processes that affect water quality and by the varying natural characteristics of water bodies. Because the presence of oxygen in water is necessary for aquatic life, an important focus of pollution control has been to restrict pollutants that deplete oxygen, such as organic wastes and chemicals that consume oxygen when they decompose. Biochemical oxygen demand (BOD), a measure of a substance's oxygen-depleting capacity, is an important parameter for determining the impact of pollutants on dissolved oxygen levels. Pollutants that change a water body's temperature also will affect levels of dissolved oxygen because they alter the solubility of oxygen in water.

Pollutants that contribute bacteria to water, such as fecal coliform and fecal streptococcus bacteria that come from human and animal wastes, also are a focus of concern. The National Oceanic and Atmospheric Administration reported in 1990 that more than 35 percent of all shellfish beds in the United States had been closed or restricted because of pollution, often due to the presence of high levels of bacteria.

Suspended solids added to water bodies by soil erosion and other runoff can cause significant harm to aquatic resources by carrying harmful substances and by blocking sunlight necessary for the development of submerged aquatic vegetation. While much erosion is the product of natural forces, development activities accelerate erosion, increasing substantially the presence of suspended solids in water. Other solids that dissolve in water (typically measured together as total dissolved solids, or TDS) can harm aquatic organisms and impair the fitness of water for human use. Discharges of nitrogen and phosphorous can have a severe impact on water quality by contributing to algae blooms through nutrient overenrichment.

A wide array of toxic substances and heavy metals are added to water bodies through industrial activity, nonpoint source runoff, and atmospheric deposition. Significant sources of toxics include hazardous wastes discharged into sewers (recall RCRA's domestic sewage exemption) and pesticide runoff. A national water quality inventory found that in 1990 water quality was impaired in more than 28,000 miles of streams by heavy metals, in more than 20,000 miles of streams by pesticides, and in nearly 250,000 acres of lakes and reservoirs by toxic organics. EPA, National Water Quality Inventory: 1990 Report to Congress (1992).

2. Sources of Pollution

As we will see below, distinctions between sources of water pollution—point versus nonpoint sources, industrial sources versus publicly owned treatment works—have considerable significance for regulatory purposes. Putting aside for the moment the regulatory significance of these distinctions, consider the major sources of water pollution problems. Figure 7.1 lists the major sources of water pollution and the types of pollutants associated with each.

Municipal sewage is a major source of water pollutants. As illustrated in Figure 7.2, because many cities have combined sewer and stormwater runoff systems, large quantities of untreated sewage often bypass treat-

FIGURE 7.1
Pollutants and Their Sources

	BOD	Bacteria	Nutrients	Ammonia	Turbidity	TDS	Acids	Toxics
Point Sources								
Municipal Sewage Treatment Plants	●	●	●	●				●
Industrial Facilities	●							●
Combined Sewer Overflows	●	●	●	●	●	●		●
Nonpoint Sources								
Agricultural Runoff	●	●	●		●	●		●
Urban Runoff	●	●	●		●	●		●
Construction Runoff			●		●			●
Mining Runoff					●	●	●	●
Septic Systems	●	●	●					●
Landfills/Spills	●							●
Silviculture Runoff	●		●		●			●

Source: Modified from 1986 305(b) National Report.
Abbreviations: Biological Oxygen Demand, BOD; Total Dissolved Solids, TDS.

FIGURE 7.2
Typical Combined Sewer Collection Network During a Storm

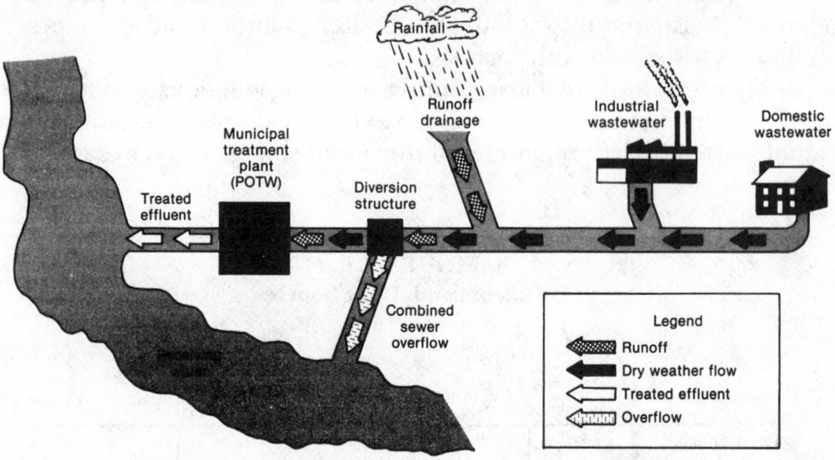

The capacity of municipal sewage treatment plants is usually not adequate to handle the large volumes of combined wastewaters (domestic wastewater, industrial wastewater, and storm water runoff) that may result during storms. In such situations, the wastewater that cannot be handled by the plant is not treated and is diverted to the receiving waters. This diversion is known as a combined sewer overflow.

Source: After U.S. Environmental Protection Agency, Office of Water, Combined Sewer Overflow Toxic Pollutant Study, EPA 440/1-84/304 (April 1984).

ment plants and are discharged into surface waters when sewers overflow after storms. EPA has estimated that it would cost cities more than $15.2 billion to correct the *combined sewer overflow* problem.

Enormous quantities of toxic substances also flow through municipal treatment plants, in part because industries have an incentive to discharge into publicly owned treatment works (POTWs) to escape more stringent limits on direct discharges to surface waters. An EPA contractor found that these discharges are so substantial that

> even if the receiving waters were completely pure, large numbers of municipal treatment plants would be exceeding water quality standards for many of the toxic chemicals investigated—65 percent for cadmium, 47 percent for silver, 35 percent for lead, 33 percent for copper, 30 percent for cyanide, and 4 to 10 percent for mercury, zinc, chromium, and nickel. [Conservation Foundation, State of the Environment: A View Toward the Nineties 103 (1987).]

The rate of water quality violations is even higher when toxics already are present in the receiving waters and when discharges occur during periods of low stream flow.

Sewage treatment technologies are treated in Figure 7.3. While

FIGURE 7.3

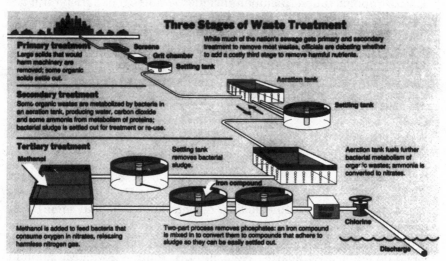

Source: N.Y. Times, Sept. 13, 1988, at C4.

considerable progress has been made in constructing wastewater treatment plants (between 1972 and 1988, the number of people served by sewage treatment plants with at least secondary treatment technology rose from 85 million to 144 million), many cities have not installed secondary treatment technology. EPA estimated in 1988 that it would cost $88 billion to complete construction of wastewater treatment facilities to ensure at least secondary treatment. EPA, Meeting the Environmental Challenge 2 (1990). Moreover, even plants that employ secondary treatment typically discharge harmful nutrients, leading authorities to question whether tertiary treatment should be required.

Industrial facilities, which have received the greatest amount of regulatory attention, contribute to pollution directly through discharges to surface waters or indirectly through atmospheric deposition of industrial air pollutants or through pollution discharged into sewers that flows through municipal treatment plants. The more than 22,000 facilities that filed reports under the Emergency Planning and Community Right-to-Know Act reported that they discharged 189 million pounds of toxic chemicals into rivers, lakes, and streams in 1989. A total of 1.2 billion pounds of toxics were injected into underground wells in 1989. Releases of Toxic Chemicals in 1989 Reached 5.7 Billion Pounds, EPA Reports, 22 Env. Rep. 223 (1991).

EPA believes that *nonpoint sources* of water pollution are perhaps the most important sources of the nation's remaining water quality problems. Nonpoint source pollution includes runoff from agricultural activities, urban areas, and construction sites; mines; timber cutting; and land disposal of waste. Approximately 76 percent of the lakes, 65 percent of the streams, and 45 percent of the estuaries that do not meet water quality standards fail to do so largely due to pollution from nonpoint sources. GAO, Greater EPA Leadership Needed to Reduce Nonpoint Source Pollution 8 (Oct. 1990).

NOTES AND QUESTIONS

1. How does water pollution differ from air pollution, and what regulatory differences might you therefore expect? Compare the measures of air quality (sulfur dioxide, carbon monoxide, and so on) with those for water quality (dissolved oxygen, dissolved solids, and so on). Which might be more difficult to use as the basis for a regulatory system based on ambient standards? Note also that there is a wide variation in the quality of unpolluted waters. Freshwaters vary in character due to natural erosion and the resulting sediment loads; not all rivers can be trout streams. Coastal estuaries are naturally saline. How might you expect this difference to be reflected in regulatory objectives?

2. Another difference between air and water pollution is the important role played by publicly owned treatment works, most municipally owned and operated, which treat substantial amounts of industrial waste and household refuse. Why might such sources be more difficult to regulate than industrial dischargers?

3. Reviews of the progress of water pollution control efforts inevitably emphasize deficiencies in the basic data necessary to evaluate water quality. Why should this problem persist? Wouldn't you expect that both industry and environmentalists would agree on the importance of detailed information on water pollution problems so that the billions of dollars going into pollution control would be spent where they can do the most good? Reform proposals have been advanced periodically. See, e.g., Portney, Reforming Environmental Regulations: Three Modest Proposals, 4 Issues in Sci. and Tech. 74 (1988). Part of the problem is that federal law has made water quality largely irrelevant to the regulatory system, eliminating much of the incentive for collecting such data. See Pedersen, Turning the Tide on Water Quality, 15 Ecology L.Q. 69 (1988).

B. STATUTORY AUTHORITIES FOR CONTROLLING WATER POLLUTION

1. Water Pollution Control: A Historical Perspective

The shift to waterborne methods of human waste disposal made water pollution a major concern of large cities in the nineteenth century. Typhoid outbreaks were not uncommon in areas where raw sewage was dumped into sources of drinking water. The discovery that disease was transmitted by germs exacerbated public concern over sewage disposal practices. As noted in Chapter 2, these practices spawned early common law nuisance actions between states. Missouri v. Illinois, 200 U.S. 496 (1906); New York v. New Jersey, 256 U.S. 296 (1921).

Even though states asked the Supreme Court to umpire interstate sewage disposal disputes, water pollution control was considered largely a local responsibility. When Congress enacted the Rivers and Harbors Act of 1899, which barred unpermitted discharges of refuse into navigable waters, its aim was not to protect water quality but to prevent interferences with navigation, the lifeblood of American commerce then. After major U.S. cities began chlorinating their drinking water, typhoid outbreaks were virtually eliminated by 1930. V. Tschinkel, The Rise and Fall of Environmental Expertise, in Technology and the Environment 160 (J. Ausabel and H. Sladovich, eds. 1989). Public concern over water pollution shifted to its impact on recreation and aquatic life. See, e.g., New Jersey v. City of New York, 284 U.S. 585 (1931).

After World War II water pollution problems intensified as industrial activity accelerated. Congress initially responded by funding research and by providing federal grants for state water pollution control programs in the Water Quality Act of 1948. Federal funding was expanded in the Federal Water Pollution Control Act of 1956, enacted despite President Eisenhower's opposition to direct federal aid for the construction of municipal sewage treatment facilities.

Like the legislation that preceded enactment of the 1970 Clean Air Act, the Federal Water Pollution Control Act in theory authorized the federal government to act against interstate pollution through a cumbersome procedure of abatement conferences. In the Water Quality Act of 1965, Congress strengthened these provisions by requiring states to adopt water quality standards for interstate waters subject to the approval of a new agency, the Federal Water Pollution Control Administration. If a state did not adopt water quality standards within two years the federal government in theory could intervene and adopt its own standards, after a long and cumbersome procedure. States also were required to promulgate state implementation plans, though federal officials could not impose an implementation plan if a state failed to act. As a result, even when water quality standards were adopted, there was no effective mechanism to translate them into workable requirements on individual dischargers, and the federal government had no meaningful enforcement authority. Barry, The Evolution of the Enforcement Provisions of the Federal Water Pollution Control Act: A Study of the Difficulty in Developing Effective Legislation, 86 Mich. L. Rev. 1103 (1970). Thus, it is not surprising that the 1965 Act produced only slow progress. By 1972 only about one-half of the states had water quality standards, and the Senate Committee on Public Works (chaired by Senator Muskie) issued a report concluding that "the Federal water pollution program . . . has been inadequate in every vital aspect."

Despite amendments gradually expanding and strengthening federal authorities, the modern era of comprehensive federal regulation of water pollution was not born until enactment of the Federal Water Pollution Control Act of 1972. An unlikely catalyst for this legislation was the revival of the long-dormant Rivers and Harbors Act of 1899, or, as it came to be known, the Refuse Act. To protect navigation, section 13 of the Act prohibited discharges into navigable waters of the United States of "any refuse matter of any kind or description whatever other than that flowing from streets and sewers and passing therefrom in a liquid state." Exceptions were to be made only with the permission of the Secretary of the Army. The Act had not been considered a pollution control law until two Supreme Court decisions in the 1960s construed the Act to encompass discharges of industrial wastes, whether or not they threatened navigation. United States v. Republic Steel Corp., 362 U.S. 482 (1960); United States v. Standard Oil Co., 384 U.S. 224 (1966).

The discharges at issue in those cases could have been found in virtually any waterway around the country. In 1970 Congressman Reuss of Wisconsin, chairman of the House Subcommittee on Conservation and Natural Resources, saw the Refuse Act's promise as a tool for dramatic action against the growing water pollution problem. His subcommittee issued a report publicizing the Act's *qui tam* provisions, a common law remedy allowing citizens to prosecute crimes and keep half of the fines paid. Reuss cleverly decided to test these provisions by compiling a list of 270 Wisconsin companies discharging wastes without a permit. Suits were brought against four companies, and the Congressman sent his share of the resulting fines back to the state Department of Natural Resources to help fund construction of sewage treatment plants. See Comment, Discharging New Wine into Old Wineskins: The Metamorphosis of the Rivers and Harbors Act of 1899, 33 U. Pitt. L. Rev. 483 (1972). Several hundred suits ultimately were filed under the Refuse Act, though the average fine collected was only about $2,000. R. Zener, The Federal Law of Water Pollution Control, in Federal Environmental Law 785-786 (E. Dolgin and T. Guilbert, eds. 1974).

The Refuse Act experience illustrates the capacity of different in-stitutional actors to influence the evolution of environmental policy as issues move between the courts, the executive branch, and the Congress. Congressman Reuss's role illustrates one of the unique features of Amer-ican environmental law—the fact that one person can make an enormous difference by looking for laws applicable to new problems and by using the courts to demand that they be enforced. His actions helped change the political dynamic by creating an immediate demand among dis-chargers for some form of permit program to protect them from law-suits. In December 1970, while legislation was being debated in Congress, President Nixon by executive order created a permit program (to be administered by the Army Corps of Engineers and EPA). After the administration announced that it would not take enforcement action against any discharger that had applied for a permit, more than 23,000 permit applications were filed. Ironically, the permit program faltered when a court enjoined its operation for failure to comply with the en-vironmental impact statement requirement of the new National Envi-ronmental Policy Act (NEPA). Kalur v. Resor, 335 F. Supp. 1 (D.D.C. 1971). Before that decision could be appealed, Congress acted.

2. Statutory Authorities

Spurred by the Refuse Act experience and growing concern over the demonstrated inadequacies of state water pollution controls, Congress in October 1972 adopted the Federal Water Pollution Control Act Amendments (FWPCA), or, as now called, the Clean Water Act. Pub. L. 92-500, 33 U.S.C. §1251 et seq. The FWPCA was enacted when Congress overrode a veto by President Nixon, who opposed its massive increase in federal funds for sewage treatment. (Nixon's subsequent effort to impound half of the funds authorized resulted in the enactment of the Congressional Budget and Impoundment Act of 1974.)

In order "to restore and maintain the chemical, physical, and biological integrity of the Nation's waters," the FWPCA broke new ground in three important areas. First, it mandated the imposition of technology-based discharge limits that "facilitate enforcement by making it unnec-essary to work backward from an overpolluted body of water to deter-mine which point sources are responsible and which must be abated." EPA v. California ex rel. State Water Resources Control Board, 426 U.S. 200, 204 (1976). Second, as a result of experience with the Refuse Act, Congress imposed a nationwide permit system on point source discharg-ers while retaining the previously required water quality standards. This served "to transform generally applicable effluent limitations and other standards—including those based on water quality—into the obligations (including a timetable for compliance) of the individual discharger." 426

U.S. at 204-205. Finally, Congress substantially expanded the federal role in financing construction of municipal treatment facilities.

The FWPCA, which was renamed the Clean Water Act when amended in 1977, remains the principal federal statute regulating water pollution. As indicated on the following page, the Clean Water Act is not the only federal statute that addresses water pollution problems. In 1972 Congress also enacted the Marine Protection, Research, and Sanctuaries Act, known as the Ocean Dumping Act, and the Coastal Zone Management Act.

The Ocean Dumping Act prohibits all dumping of wastes in the ocean except where permits are issued by EPA (for nondredged materials) or by the U.S. Army Corps of Engineers (for dredged materials). Permits are conditioned on a showing that the dumping will not "unreasonably degrade" the environment. A major motivation for the Act was to prevent dischargers from evading the Clean Water Act's permit requirements by simply dumping wastes into the ocean. While EPA's stated policy since 1973 has been to phase out all ocean dumping, Congress eventually had to amend the Ocean Dumping Act to establish deadlines for phasing out dumping of industrial waste and municipal sewage sludge. After New York City won an extension of the deadline for ending ocean dumping of sewage sludge in City of New York v. EPA, 543 F. Supp. 1084 (S.D.N.Y. 1981), the Act was amended in 1988 to impose escalating disposal fees (increasing over time from $100 to $200 per ton), culminating in a ban on such dumping in 1992.

The Coastal Zone Management Act provides financial assistance to encourage states to adopt federally approved coastal management plans. The Act requires certification that activities affecting land or water use in a coastal zone conform to such plans before federal permits can be issued. Legislation to require *all* states to develop land use control plans had passed the Senate in 1972 but ultimately failed to win adoption despite President Nixon's support for establishing a national land use policy. In 1990 Congress amended the Coastal Zone Management Act to require states with approved plans to adopt measures to control nonpoint source pollution consistent with minimum federal guidelines promulgated by EPA. By 1992, coastal management plans had been approved for 29 states and territories, covering nearly 95 percent of the U.S. coastline and the shores of the Great Lakes. CEQ, Environmental Quality—22nd Annual Report 38 (1992).

In addition to the statutes listed below, RCRA and CERCLA have considerable relevance for groundwater protection and remediation, as discussed in Chapter 3. Many states also have adopted their own groundwater protection legislation. This chapter focuses primarily on the regulatory programs established under the federal Clean Water Act to control pollution of surface waters and to encourage states to develop programs to address nonpoint sources.

PRINCIPAL FEDERAL STATUTES THAT REGULATE WATER POLLUTION

The Clean Water Act prohibits all unpermitted discharges into the waters of the United States (including the territorial sea) of pollutants from point sources, imposes effluent limitations on dischargers, and requires statewide planning for control of pollution from nonpoint sources.

The Ocean Dumping Act prohibits in the area seaward of the inner boundary of the U.S. territorial sea the transportation of wastes for dumping and the dumping of wastes unless a permit has been obtained. EPA is responsible for issuing permits for all materials except for dredged materials, for which permits must be obtained from the U.S. Army Corps of Engineers.

The Oil Pollution Act makes owners of vessels discharging oil liable for costs of cleanup; establishes an Oil Spill Liability Trust Fund to pay response costs; imposes minimum design standards to prevent spills by vessels operating in U.S. waters.

The Coastal Zone Management Act offers federal financial assistance to states that adopt federally approved coastal management plans and requires federal actions in coastal areas to be consistent with state programs. Amended in 1990 to require states to adopt programs to control nonpoint sources of coastal water pollution.

The Safe Drinking Water Act regulates contaminants in drinking water supplied by public water systems, establishes a permit program regulating the underground injection of hazardous waste, and restricts activities that threaten sole-source aquifers.

3. The Structure of the Clean Water Act

The Clean Water Act is the most comprehensive source of federal regulatory authority to control water pollution. To assist you in developing an understanding of the structure of the Clean Water Act, the major provisions of the Act are outlined below. Following a brief description of these provisions, their operation and implementation is discussed in more detail in the sections that follow.

MAJOR PROVISIONS OF THE CLEAN WATER ACT

§101 Goals. Declares national goals of fishable/swimmable waters by 1983 and the elimination of pollutant discharges into navigable waters by 1985.

§§201-219 Construction Grants Program. Provided federal grants for the construction of wastewater treatment plants, a program phased out in favor of a revolving loan fund by the 1987 Amendments. §208 = BMPs

§301 Effluent Limitations. Prohibits "the discharge of any pollutant" (defined in §502(12) as the addition of any pollutant to navigable waters from any point source or to the waters of the ocean or contiguous zone from any point source other than a vessel) except those made in compliance with the terms of the Act, including the permit requirements of section 402. Imposes multitiered effluent limitations on existing sources whose stringency and timing depends on the nature of the pollutant discharged and whether the outfall is directed to a water body or a publicly owned treatment works (POTW).

§302 Water Quality Related Effluent Limitations. Authorizes the imposition of more stringent effluent limitations when necessary to prevent interference with the attainment or maintenance of desired water quality.

§303 Water Quality Standards. Requires states to adopt and to review triennially water quality criteria and standards subject to EPA approval and to identify areas where effluent limits are insufficient to achieve such standards. x TMDLs "water qual. limited segments"

§304 Federal Water Quality Criteria and Guidelines. Requires EPA to adopt water quality criteria and guidelines for effluent limitations, pretreatment programs, and administration of the NPDES permit program.

§306 New Source Performance Standards. Requires EPA to promulgate new source performance standards reflecting best demonstrated control technology.

§307 Toxic and Pretreatment Effluent Standards. Requires dischargers of toxic pollutants to meet effluent limits reflecting the best available technology economically achievable. Requires EPA to establish pretreatment standards to prevent discharges from interfering with POTWs.

§309 Enforcement Authorities. Authorizes compliance orders and administrative, civil, and criminal penalties for violations of the Act.

§319 Nonpoint Source Management Programs. States must identify waters that cannot meet water quality standards

due to nonpoint sources, identify the activities responsible for the problem, and prepare management plans identifying controls and programs for specific sources.

§402 NPDES Permit Program. Establishes a national permit program, the pollution discharge elimination system (NPDES), that may be administered by EPA or by the states under delegated authority from EPA.

§404 Dredge and Fill Operations. Requires a permit from the Army Corps of Engineers for the disposal of dredged or fill material into navigable waters with the concurrence of EPA unless associated with "normal" farming.

§505 Citizen Suits. Authorizes citizen suits against any person who violates an effluent standard or order, or against EPA for failure to perform a nondiscretionary duty.

§509 Judicial Review. Authorizes judicial review of certain EPA rulemaking actions in the U.S. Courts of Appeals.

The Clean Water Act adopts breathtakingly ambitious goals in section 101(a) ("that the discharge of pollutants into the navigable waters be eliminated by 1985," §101(a)(1), and that fishable/swimmable waters be achieved "wherever attainable" by July 1, 1983, §101(a)(2)) that suggest a virtually cost-blind determination to control water pollution. While the Act concentrates its regulatory firepower on pollution from point sources, in 1987 Congress added section 101(a)(7), which articulates a new goal of developing and implementing "programs for the control of nonpoint sources of pollution," §101(a)(7).

The construction grants program of Title II of the Act, sections 201-219, played an important role in federal-state interactions until 1987, when it was replaced by a revolving loan fund. The program often had produced a tug-of-war between federal and local officials, with the latter seeking to use federal funds to encourage development by extending their sewer systems and the former bent on ensuring that treatment works were constructed at the end of the sewer line.

The heart of the Clean Water Act is section 301's requirement for nationally uniform, technology-based limits on point source discharges administered through a national permit program required by section 402. CEQ explained the rational for this approach as follows:

Perhaps the predominant influence on the law was the universal recognition that basing compliance and enforcement efforts on a case-by-case judgment of a particular facility's impacts on ambient water quality is both scientifically and administratively difficult. To minimize the difficulties in

relating discharges to ambient water quality, the law requires minimum
effluent limitations for each category of discharger, based on technological
and economic feasibility, regardless of receiving water requirements. [CEQ,
Environmental Quality—1973, at 171 (1973).]

Congress mandated that standards be uniform by industrial category,
recognizing that industries varied in their capabilities for reducing pollution. Existing dischargers were to employ "best practicable" control
technology (BPT) by 1977 and "best available" technology (BAT) by
1983. New dischargers were required by section 306 to meet BAT-based
requirements.

　　Implementation of these requirements, like implementation of the
Clean Air Act, has featured missed deadlines, lawsuits, court orders,
and, ultimately, statutory extensions. Congress in 1977 adopted major
amendments to the Clean Water Act that extended the deadlines for
compliance with the technology-based effluent limitations and that adjusted the requirements for certain dischargers. The BAT deadline was
extended to July 1, 1984 for dischargers of toxic pollutants. For dischargers of "conventional pollutants"—BOD, fecal coliform, suspended
solids, and pH—BAT requirements were relaxed. Instead of BAT, they
were required to achieve "best conventional" technology (BCT) by July
1, 1984 if the incremental benefit of such upgrading exceeded the costs.
§304(b)(4). In 1987 these deadlines again were extended because it had
taken EPA far longer to establish effluent limitations than anticipated.

　　The 1972 Act required POTWs to provide secondary treatment by
1977 and advanced treatment by 1983. Congress later extended the
secondary treatment deadline to July 1988 and eliminated the advanced
treatment requirement. POTWs also were required to obtain permits
for sludge disposal. Industrial dischargers into POTWs were required
by section 307(b) to obtain pretreatment permits to assure that their
waste discharges do not interfere with the treatment process. In 1987
Congress allowed POTWs discharging into "marine waters" to receive
a waiver from secondary treatment requirements if there is no interference with water quality standards. §301(h). Effluent limits on point source
discharges are discussed in section C, below. A summary of how they
have changed over time is presented in Figure 7.4.

　　The system of ambient water quality standards that Congress had
initiated in the 1965 Act was retained primarily to be used as a backup
when effluent limitations proved insufficient to protect water quality.
States must designate uses for which the water bodies within their jurisdiction are to be protected subject to EPA review of their adequacy
to "protect the public health or welfare, enhance the quality of water,
and serve the purposes of this Act." §303(c)(2). Permits for point sources
must incorporate any more stringent conditions necessary to meet water
quality standards, which may be modified for conventional pollutants

FIGURE 7.4
Technology-Based Effluent Limits and Deadlines for Compliance

Source	1972 Act	1977 Amendments	1981 Amendments	1987 Amendments
INDUSTRIAL FACILITIES	BPT by 1977 BAT by 1983	For toxics BAT by 1984 or within 3 years For conventional pollutants BCT by 1984		BAT as soon as possible, within 3 years and no later than 3/31/89
POTWs	Secondary treatment by 1977 Advanced treatment by 1983		Secondary treatment by 1988 Advanced treatment requirement eliminated	

only if EPA finds the added costs bear no reasonable relationship to the benefits. §302(a). In 1987 Congress in section 304(l) required states to identify water impaired by toxic pollutants and to establish individual control strategies for sources of such pollutants. Water quality-based controls are discussed in section D, below.

Nonpoint sources of water pollution are not subject to permit requirements. While section 208 of the Act has long required states to engage in areawide planning that can encompass measures to control nonpoint source pollution, this program has been ineffective. In 1987 Congress added section 319, which requires states to identify waters impaired by nonpoint source pollution and the sources of such pollution and to prepare management plans for controlling it, subject to EPA approval. See section E, below.

Section 404 establishes a permit requirement for disposal of dredged and fill material into navigable waters. As discussed in section F, this permit program, which is administered jointly by the Army Corps of Engineers and EPA, plays an important role in efforts to protect wetlands.

The National Pollutant Discharge Elimination System (NPDES), created in section 402, is the administrative system for issuance of permits to the thousands of individual point source dischargers. States meeting minimum federal requirements may assume primary responsibility for issuance of permits. In states that decline to do so, EPA is required to administer the permit program. EPA retains oversight authority over state permit decisions as well as independent enforcement authority. The Act provides several enforcement options, including administrative compliance orders, administrative penalties, and civil and criminal fines in government actions taken under section 309. Citizen enforcement suits are authorized by section 505(a). Enforcement problems are discussed in section G below, which compares the Clean Water Act's enforcement authorities with those contained in other federal environmental laws.

NOTES AND QUESTIONS

1. The "zero discharge" and "fishable/swimmable" goals contained in section 101(a) have been widely condemned by economists, who question the logic of even articulating an aspirational standard that appears so expensive and infeasible. Why would Congress adopt such a seemingly unrealistic goal? One clue may be found in Senator Muskie's statement during the debates prior to enactment that "[w]hat we need to produce the technology required by the bill is a national commitment to what we want to achieve—come up with modern technology, new and changed. . . ."

2. Consider the principal types of pollution control regulations mandated by the Clean Water Act: (1) a general prohibition on point source discharges except as authorized by permits requiring (a) compliance with technology-based effluent limitations or (b) more stringent effluent limitations when necessary to protect the quality of receiving waters; (2) pretreatment requirements for dischargers to POTWs; and (3) permit requirements for dredge and fill operations. Is the range of controls available under the Clean Water Act more extensive or less extensive than that available under the Clean Air Act? Which Act employs the requirements most likely to force technology?

3. Economists have been extremely critical of the Clean Water Act's use of nationally uniform effluent standards for classes and categories of industries. They note that a discharge may be insignificant in one water body (e.g., the Mississippi) but catastrophic in another (a small trout stream or a lake that supplies a town's water supply). Consequently, the benefits of control will vary geographically. Moreover, a focus on the technology available to each industry may result in inefficient allocation of costs *among* industries that may have different costs for controlling the same pollution. Pedersen, Turning the Tide on Water Quality, 15 Ecology L.Q. 69, 83 (1988).

You may recall similar concerns in the context of the Clean Air Act. Is the case for uniformity any different in the context of water quality? Cf. Currie, Congress, the Court, and Water Pollution, 1977 Sup. Ct. Rev. 39 (uniformity can lead to overexpenditure but use-based regulation assumes greater knowledge than is practical, is inadequate to allow for growth, does not deal with high concentrations in mixing zones, and does not address aesthetic concerns).

4. A. Myrick Freeman III estimates that the costs of federal water pollution control policy in 1985 ranged from $25 to $30 billion, while the range of estimated benefits was only $6 to $28 billion. Freeman, Water Pollution Policy, in Public Policies for Environmental Protection 125-126 (P. Portney, ed. 1990). While Freeman notes that these estimates probably understate benefits (by excluding the benefits of controls on toxic effluents) and overestimate costs (because engineering estimates fail to reflect cost-reducing technological innovation), he deems it likely that costs outweigh benefits in the aggregate. Freeman argues that the Clean Water Act's current approach should be replaced with "the principle that pollution control policies should be designed to maximize the net benefits from pollution control activities." Id. at 127. Do you agree? Freeman would set water quality standards for each segment of a water body at the point where the "marginal benefits of raising water quality to that point would just equal the marginal cost of doing so," and effluent reduction requirements would vary across dischargers even within the same industrial category. Why do you think Congress eschewed Freeman's approach to pollution control?

5. The distinction between water quality standards and effluent limitations is critical. Water quality standards describe tolerable limits for particular uses (e.g., water suitable for swimming may be limited to no more than 200 fecal coliform bacteria per 100 milliliters). Effluent standards describe an amount of pollution discharged in a time period (e.g., 1 pound of x pollutant per day) or more typically a maximum amount per unit of production (e.g., 1 pound of x pollutant per ton of steel). Which type of system is more responsive to considerations of economic efficiency? Which is more responsive to equity concerns?

Water quality standards are roughly comparable to ambient air quality standards. Why was Congress willing to adopt a regulatory scheme for air quality based on ambient standards at almost the same time it was coming to the conclusion that such a system had been a failure in the context of water pollution? Some authorities advocate reconsideration of the water quality standards approach; e.g., Pedersen, above. Based on the Air Act experience, how could such a system be employed effectively?

C. EFFLUENT LIMITATIONS ON POINT SOURCE DISCHARGES

Building on the Refuse Act's simple strategy of requiring a permit for all discharges to navigable waters, section 301 of the Clean Water Act flatly declares that "the discharge of any pollutant by any person shall be unlawful," except in compliance with certain sections of the Act. The most important of these sections are section 402 (permit requirements) and section 301 (effluent limitations). Thus, on its face the Act appears to be both remarkably simple and comprehensive: It prohibits all pollutant discharges unless the discharger has a permit that incorporates effluent limitations—restrictions on the quantities of pollutants that may be discharged.

As with so many other areas of environmental regulation, the definition of "regulatory targets" under the Clean Water Act becomes more complicated the closer one looks. Thus, before discussing effluent limitations, it is important to examine the Act's key jurisdictional terms more closely.

Section 502(12) of the Act defines "discharge of a pollutant" to include "any addition of any pollutant to navigable waters from any point source" or "to the waters of the contiguous zone or the ocean from any point source other than a vessel or other floating craft." This language indicates that the Act's permit requirements do not cover *all* pollutant discharges, but rather only discharges from point sources. Thus the definition of "point source" will have important jurisdictional consequences, along with the definition of "navigable waters" and even "addition of a pollutant."

The term "navigable waters" is defined in section 502(7) to mean "the waters of the United States." Based on legislative history indicating that Congress sought to extend federal regulation as broadly as possible under its constitutional authority to regulate interstate commerce, courts have interpreted "waters of the United States" to include virtually any surface waters, whether navigable or not, as we will see in section F. United States v. Riverside Bayview Homes, 474 U.S. 121 (1985). While a few early decisions suggested that discharges to groundwater or deep well injection also could be regulated under the Clean Water Act in order to protect surface waters, United States v. GAF Corp., 389 F. Supp. 1379 (S.D. Tex. 1975), United States Steel Corp. v. Train, 556 F.2d 822 (7th Cir. 1977), following a contrary decision in Exxon Corp. v. Train, 554 F.2d 1310 (5th Cir. 1977), EPA determined to use the Clean Water Act only to regulate discharges to surface waters. Thus, it is useful to think of the Act's permit requirements as encompassing all discharges to surface waters from point sources.

1. Defining "Point Sources" Subject to Permit Requirements

Why would Congress have chosen to focus federal water pollution control efforts almost exclusively on point source discharges? Congress was aware that nonpoint sources made a considerable contribution to water pollution, though it may not have fully appreciated their importance. But it recognized that point sources are easier to control, both politically and administratively, particularly when pollution control technology emphasized end-of-the-pipe solutions. Control of nonpoint source pollution requires some form of land use control, which has been politically unpopular, even at the state level, as we will see in section F. Thus, it was not until the Clean Water Act was amended in 1987 that Congress explicitly identified control of nonpoint source pollution as a goal of the Act.

Even limited to point source dischargers, implementation of a national permit program posed major administrative challenges for EPA. Recognizing the enormous task it faced, EPA announced that it would focus first on processing permit applications from major dischargers in areas where water pollution was the worst. Fearing that it would have to process millions of permit applications, the Agency also issued regulations exempting certain categories of point sources from the Act's permit requirements on the ground of administrative infeasibility. An environmental group challenged EPA's decision in the case that follows.

|| *NRDC v. Costle* ||
|| 568 F.2d 1369 (D.C. Cir. 1977) ||

LEVENTHAL, Circuit Judge:

In 1973 the EPA Administrator issued regulations that exempted certain categories of "point sources" of pollution from the permit requirements of §402. The Administrator's purported authority to make such exemptions turns on the proper interpretation of §402.

A "point source" is defined in §502(14) as "any discernible, confined and discrete conveyance, including but not limited to any pipe, ditch, channel, tunnel, conduit, well, discrete fissure, container, rolling stock, concentrated animal feeding operation, or vessel or other floating craft, from which pollutants are or may be discharged."

The 1973 regulations exempted discharges from a number of classes of point sources from the permit requirements of §402, including all silvicultural point sources; all confined animal feeding operations below a certain size; all irrigation return flows from areas of less than 3,000 contiguous acres or 3,000 noncontiguous acres that use the same drainage system; all nonfeedlot, nonirrigation agricultural point sources; and separate storm sewers containing only storm runoff uncontaminated by any industrial or commercial activity. The EPA's rationale for these exemptions is that in order to conserve the Agency's enforcement resources for more significant point sources of pollution, it is necessary to exclude these smaller sources of pollutant discharges from the permit program.

The National Resources Defense Council, Inc. (NRDC) sought a declaratory judgment that the regulations are unlawful under the FWPCA. Specifically, NRDC contended that the Administrator does not have authority to exempt any class of point source from the permit requirements of §402. It argued that Congress in enacting §§301, 402 of the FWPCA intended to prohibit the discharge of pollutants from *all* point sources unless a permit had been issued to the discharger under §402 or unless the point source was explicitly exempted from the permit requirements by statute. The District Court granted NRDC's motion for summary judgment. It held that the FWPCA does not authorize the Administrator to exclude any class of point sources from the permit program. NRDC v. Train, 396 F. Supp. 1393 (D.D.C. 1975). The EPA has appealed to this court. . . .

I. LEGISLATIVE HISTORY . . .

The NPDES permit program established by §402 is central to the enforcement of the FWPCA. It translates general effluent limitations into the specific obligations of a discharger. . . .

The appellants argue that §402 not only gives the Administrator the discretion to grant or refuse a permit, but also gives him the authority to exempt classes of point sources from the permit requirements entirely. They argue that this interpretation is supported by the legislative history of §402 and the fact that the unavailability of this exemption power would place an unmanageable administrative burden on EPA. . . .

Under the EPA's interpretation the Administrator would have broad discretion to exempt large classes of point sources from any or all requirements of the FWPCA. This is a result that the legislators did not intend. Rather they stressed that the FWPCA was a tough law that relied on explicit mandates to a degree uncommon in legislation of this type. . . .

There are innumerable references in the legislative history to the effect that the Act is founded on the "basic premise that a discharge of pollutants without a permit is unlawful and that discharges not in compliance with the limitations and conditions for a permit are unlawful." Even when infeasibility arguments were squarely raised, the legislature declined to abandon the permit requirement. . . .

The wording of the statute, legislative history, and precedents are clear: the EPA Administrator does not have the authority to exempt categories of point sources from the permit requirements of §402. . . .

II. Administrative Infeasibility

The appellants have stressed in briefs and at oral argument the extraordinary burden on the EPA that will be imposed by the above interpretation of the scope of the NPDES program. The spectre of millions of applications for permits is evoked both as part of appellants' legislative history argument—that Congress could not have intended to impose such burdens on the EPA—and as an invitation to this court to uphold the regulations as deviations from the literal terms of the FWPCA necessary to permit the agency to realize the general objectives of that act. . . .

A. Uniform National Effluent Limitations

EPA argues that the regulatory scheme intended under Titles III and IV of the FWPCA requires, first, that the Administrator establish national effluent limitations and, second, that these limitations be incorporated in the individual permits of dischargers. EPA argues that the establishment of such limitations is simply not possible with the type of point sources involved in the 1973 regulations, which essentially involve the discharge of runoff—i.e., wastewaters generated by rainfall that

drain over terrain into navigable waters, picking up pollutants along the
way. . . .

EPA contends that certain characteristics of runoff pollution make
it difficult to promulgate effluent limitations for most of the point sources
exempted by the 1973 regulations:

> The major characteristic of the pollution problem which is generated
> by runoff . . . is that the owner of the discharge point . . . has no control
> over the quantity of the flow or the nature and amounts of the pollutants
> picked up by the runoff. The amount of flow obviously is unpredictable
> because it results from the duration and intensity of the rainfall event, the
> topography, the type of ground cover and the saturation point of the land
> due to any previous rainfall. Similar factors affect the types of pollutants
> which will be picked up by that runoff, including the type of farming
> practices employed, the rate and type of pesticide and fertilizer application,
> and the conservation practices employed. . . .
>
> An effluent limitation must be a precise number in order for it to
> be an effective regulatory tool; both the discharger and the regulatory
> agency need to have an identifiable standard upon which to determine
> whether the facility is in compliance. That was the principle of the passage
> of the 1972 Amendments.

Implicit in EPA's contentions is the premise that there must be a uniform
effluent limitation prior to issuing a permit. That is not our understanding of the law. . . .

As noted in NRDC v. Train, [510 F.2d 692 (D.C. Cir. 1975),] the
primary purpose of the effluent limitations and guidelines was to provide
uniformity among the federal and state jurisdictions enforcing the NPDES
program and prevent the "Tragedy of the Commons" that might result
if jurisdictions can compete for industry and development by providing
more liberal limitations than their neighboring states. 510 F.2d at 709.
The effluent limitations were intended to create floors that had to be
respected by state permit programs.

But in NRDC v. Train it was also recognized that permits could be
issued before national effluent limitations were promulgated and that
permits issued subsequent to promulgation of uniform effluent limitations could be modified to take account of special characteristics of subcategories of point sources. . . .

In [Train] this court fully appreciated that technological and administrative constraints might prevent the Administrator from developing guidelines and corresponding uniform numeric effluent limitations
for certain point sources anytime in the near future. The Administrator
was deemed to have the burden of demonstrating that the failure to
develop the guidelines on schedule was due to administrative or technological infeasibility. 510 F.2d at 713. Yet the underlying teaching was
that technological or administrative infeasibility was a reason for ad-

justing court mandates to the minimum extent necessary to realize the general objectives of the Act. It is a number of steps again to suggest that these problems afford the Administrator the authority to exempt categories of point sources from the NPDES program entirely.

With time, experience, and technological development, more point sources in the categories that EPA has now classed as exempt may be amenable to national effluent limitations achieved through end-of-pipe technology or other means of pollution control. . . .

In sum, we conclude that the existence of uniform national effluent limitations is not a necessary precondition for incorporating into the NPDES program pollution from agricultural, silvicultural, and storm water runoff point sources. The technological or administrative infeasibility of such limitations may result in adjustments in the permit programs, as will be seen, but it does not authorize the Administrator to exclude the relevant point source from the NPDES program.

B. *Alternative Permit Conditions Under §402(a)*

EPA contends that even if it is possible to issue permits without national effluent limitations, the special characteristics of point sources of runoff pollution make it infeasible to develop restrictions on a case-by-case basis. EPA's implicit premise is that whether limitations are promulgated on a class or individual source basis, it is still necessary to articulate any limitation in terms of a numerical effluent standard. That is not our understanding.

Section 402 provides that a permit may be issued upon condition "that such discharge will meet either all applicable requirements under sections 301, 302, 306, 307, 308 and 403 of this Act, *or prior to taking of necessary implementing actions relating to all such requirements, such conditions as the Administrator determines are necessary to carry out the provisions of this Act.*" 33 U.S.C. §1342(a) (Supp. V 1975) (emphasis added). This provision gives EPA considerable flexibility in framing the permit to achieve a desired reduction in pollutant discharges. The permit may proscribe industry practices that aggravate the problem of point source pollution. . . .

[W]hen numerical effluent limitations are infeasible, EPA may issue permits with conditions designed to reduce the level of effluent discharges to acceptable levels. This may well mean opting for a gross reduction in pollutant discharge rather than the fine-tuning suggested by numerical limitations. But this ambitious statute is not hospitable to the concept that the appropriate response to a difficult pollution problem is not to try at all.

It may be appropriate in certain circumstances for the EPA to require a permittee simply to monitor and report effluent levels; EPA manifestly has this authority. Such permit conditions might be desirable where the full extent of the pollution problem is not known.

C. General Permits

Finally, EPA argues that the number of permits involved in the absence of an exemption authority will simply overwhelm the Agency. Affidavits filed with the District Court indicate, for example, that the number of silviculture point sources may be over 300,000 and that there are approximately 100,000 separate storm sewer point sources. We are and must be sensitive to EPA's concerns of an intolerable permit load. But the District Court and the various parties have suggested devices to mitigate the burden—to accommodate within a practical regulatory scheme Congress's clear mandate that all point sources have permits. All that is required is that EPA make full use of its interpretational authority. The existence of a variety of options belies EPA's infeasibility arguments.

Section 402 does not explicitly describe the necessary scope of a NPDES permit. The most significant requirement is that the permit be in compliance with limitation sections of the Act described above. As a result NRDC and the District Court have suggested the use of area or general permits. The Act allows such techniques. Area-wide regulation is one well-established means of coping with administrative exigency. An instance is area pricing for natural gas producers, which the Supreme Court upheld in Permian Basin Area Rate Cases, 390 U.S. 747 (1968). A more dramatic example is the administrative search warrant which may be issued on an area basis despite the normal Fourth Amendment requirement of probable cause for searching specific premises. Camara v. Municipal Court, 387 U.S. 523 (1967).

In response to the District Court's order, EPA promulgated regulations that make use of the general permit device. 42 Fed. Reg. 6846-53 (Feb. 4, 1977). The general permit is addressed to a class of point source dischargers, subject to notice and opportunity for public hearing in the geographical area covered by the permit. Although we do not pass on the validity of the February, 1977 regulations, they serve to dilute an objection of wholesale infeasibility.

Our approach is not fairly subject to the criticism that it elevates form over substance [such] that the end result will look very much like EPA's categorical exemption. It is the function of the courts to require agencies to comply with legislative intent when that intent is clear, and to leave it to the legislature to make adjustments when the result is counterproductive. At the same time, where intent on an issue is unclear, we are instructed to afford the administering agency the flexibility necessary to achieve the general objectives of the Act. . . . These lines of authority conjoin in our approach. We insist, as the Act insists, that a permit is necessary; the Administrator has no authority to exempt point sources from the NPDES program. But we concede necessary flexibility in the shaping of the permits that is not inconsistent with the clear terms of the Act.

There is also a very practical difference between a general permit and an exemption. An exemption tends to become indefinite: the problem drops out of sight, into a pool of inertia, unlikely to be recalled in the absence of crisis or a strong political protagonist. In contrast, the general or area permit approach forces the Agency to focus on the problems of specific regions and requires that the problems of the region be reconsidered at least every five years, the maximum duration of a permit. . . .

NOTES AND QUESTIONS

1. In general, the more comprehensive a regulatory program is, the greater is the administrative burden on the agency that must implement it. At some point the universe of regulatory targets becomes so large that it simply is not feasible to apply the same standards to all. Rather than requiring that *all* point sources be regulated, would it make more sense to give EPA the authority to require permits for whatever sources (point or nonpoint) that it determines pose the greatest problems? If EPA had the authority to issue permits authorizing discharges, why did it not have the authority to exempt point sources from permit requirements?

2. The court offers several suggestions for easing the administrative burden of permitting the sources EPA sought to exempt, including the use of general permits and other alternatives to numerical effluent limitations. Is there any "very practical difference" between a general or area-wide permit and an exemption, and if so, how could a general permit contribute to achieving the objectives of the Act?

3. Is it clear that all of the sources EPA sought to exempt from permit requirements were indeed point sources? Industry intervenors had argued that some of them were not. Does the court ever specify what a point source is? Would EPA have been more likely to prevail in court if it had determined that irrigation return flows were not encompassed within the definition of "point sources" rather than seeking simply to exempt them from permit requirements? Would such an interpretation by EPA be entitled to judicial deference under the *Chevron* doctrine?

4. Under what circumstances should pollutant discharges that occur due to weather conditions be considered discharges from point sources? The American Iron and Steel Institute had argued that only "volitional

flows" that add pollutants to navigable waters should be considered point source discharges. Would this interpretation be more sensible because it would exempt from permit requirements natural runoff that happens to flow through a discrete conveyance? Or should it depend on whether or not the conveyance usually collects pollution? Why not simply abandon the point-nonpoint source distinction in favor of one that turns on whether the discharge is caused by human activities or naturally occurring ones? Would this be an easy distinction to make? Should the determination of point source status depend instead on how amenable the discharge is to control?

5. Consider whether or not the following activities involve discharges from point sources that require an NPDES permit. Is an NPDES permit required for a city-owned culvert that carries runoff from a nearby landfill into a stream? See Dague v. City of Burlington, 732 F. Supp. 458 (D. Vt. 1989) (finding the culvert to be a point source). Are individuals whose homes are hooked up to a defective private septic system from which raw sewage flows through a pipe into a river required to obtain permits for the discharge of their human waste? See Friends of the Sakonnet v. Dutra, 738 F. Supp. 623 (D.R.I. 1990) (noting EPA's position that users of private treatment works may be point sources, but finding it unnecessary to decide). Is a dam that discharges water whose oxygen content has been reduced by the dam's presence required to obtain an NPDES permit? See National Wildlife Federation v. Gorsuch, 693 F.2d 156 (D.C. Cir. 1982) (EPA properly determined that Congress did not intend to require dams to obtain NPDES permits). Does the discharge of dead fish from a hydroelectric plant's penstocks require a permit? See National Wildlife Federation v. Consumers Power Co., 862 F.2d 580 (6th Cir. 1988) (no permit required, following holding in NWF v. Gorsuch). If an operation processing gold ore uses a settling pond that overflows during a sudden snowmelt, discharging toxic materials into a nearby stream, is a permit required? See United States v. Earth Sciences, Inc., 599 F.2d 368 (10th Cir. 1979) (permit required because Congress defined "point source" to embrace "the broadest possible definition of any identifiable conveyance from which pollutants might enter the waters of the United States"); see also Sierra Club v. Abston Construction Co., 620 F.2d 41 (5th Cir. 1980) (surface runoff from strip mine a point source when spoil piles are designed so that it is reasonably likely that pollutants will be discharged through ditches or other discrete conveyances); compare section 402(l) (1987 amendment exempting from permit requirements discharges of stormwater runoff from oil, gas, and mining operations that do not come into contact with products or waste material).

6. Note that section 502(12)'s definition of "discharge" refers to the "*addition* of any pollutant *from* any point source" (emphasis supplied). If the party responsible for the addition of pollutants is different from the

party responsible for the point source through which it travels, who, if anyone, must obtain a permit for the discharge? See Friends of the Sakkonet v. Dutra, above. Part of the rationale of the decisions holding dams to be exempt from NPDES permit requirements is the notion that they do not *add* any pollutants to the water that passes through them. See National Wildlife Federation v. Consumers Power Co., above. Some dischargers have argued that pollutants not actually added by their activities should not be regulated. For example, if a company uses contaminated water for noncontact cooling water and returns it unaltered to the water body from which it came, must it obtain a permit? While EPA has not exempted such discharges from NPDES permit requirements, it has issued regulations, called the "net/gross" policy, that allow limited adjustments to otherwise applicable effluent limits in such circumstances if dischargers can demonstrate that they meet certain criteria. 40 C.F.R. §122.45(g).

7. Examine the current statutory definition of "point source," which is contained in §502(14). Note that the definition is the same as that quoted in NRDC v. Costle, except that Congress has added a sentence exempting "agricultural stormwater discharges and return flows from irrigated agriculture." Return flows from irrigated agriculture were exempted in the 1977 Amendments in response to NRDC v. Costle. This exemption has generated considerable criticism because agricultural irrigation has created severe pollution problems in some areas, as illustrated by the problem at California's Kesterson National Wildlife Refuge, where return flows have produced a buildup of naturally occurring selenium in concentrations toxic to wildlife.

8. In the 1987 Amendments, Congress required NPDES permits for storm water discharges associated with industrial activity and those from municipal separate storm sewer systems serving a population of 100,000 or more. §402(p). Congress confirmed that permits for industrial storm water discharges must meet all applicable provisions of section 301 and section 402 including BAT/BCT, §402(p)(3)(A), and it required that municipal permits prohibit non-storm water discharges into storm sewers while requiring controls to reduce pollutant discharges "to the maximum extent practicable." §402(p)(3)(B). Faced with permit requirements applicable to 114,000 industrial facilities and 220 cities, 55 Fed. Reg. 47,990 (1990), EPA belatedly issued permit application regulations under court order in October 1990. In April 1992, EPA adopted a four-tiered approach to industrial storm water permitting that relies on general permits for most dischargers. 57 Fed. Reg. 11,394 (1992). If storm water discharges in particular watersheds, or from certain industries or specific facilities, are found to contribute to water quality problems, watershed-, industry-, or facility-specific permits may be required. Is this a sensible approach to the dilemma between flexibility and administrative complexity?

2. Effluent Limitations on Industrial Dischargers

At the heart of the Clean Water Act are technology-based effluent limitations applicable to all point source dischargers and implemented through enforceable permits. Congress intended that the effluent limits be uniform throughout the nation for "similar point sources with similar characteristics," in part to prevent geographic competition for industry from undermining water pollution control standards. As noted above, this approach is criticized by economists who favor standards that would base controls on individualized assessments of costs and benefits. Consider whether more flexible standards realistically could be implemented by EPA as you learn about the Agency's difficulties in implementing the existing technology-based approach.

A. The Evolution of a Regulatory Program

The 1972 Act sought to force existing dischargers to employ progressively more stringent pollution control technology in two phases. Section 301(b)(1) originally required existing sources to employ the "best practicable control technology currently available" (BPT) by July 1, 1977, followed by the "best available technology economically achievable for each category or class" (BAT) by July 1, 1983. New sources were required by section 306 to meet a more stringent standard that would reduce their effluents to the greatest degree "achievable through application of the best available demonstrated control technology" (BADT), which could include process changes and a zero-discharge standard.

EPA faced a formidable task in determining how to translate technology-based standards into enforceable limits on industrial source categories. Section 304(b) of the FWPCA gave EPA one year to publish guidelines identifying the degree of effluent reduction attainable through the application of the levels of technology required by the Act. Swift action was crucial because Congress had given EPA and the states only two years to implement the new NPDES permit program. The Act specified that a discharger would not be considered in violation of the Act for the first two years after enactment if it had applied for a permit within six months of enactment. Congress had contemplated that the states would shoulder most of the actual burden of issuing permits (permits may be issued either by EPA or by states with programs approved by EPA), and it had required EPA to issue procedural guidelines to govern state operation of the NPDES permit program within two months after enactment of the Act.

Six months after enactment of the Clean Water Act, EPA had received nearly 33,000 applications for NPDES permits. By mid-1974 EPA had received 65,000 applications, but only 15 states had taken over responsibility for permit issuance. It soon became apparent that EPA would have to write more than 50,000 permits and define the range of technologically possible effluent limits for dozens of different industries, an enormous technical and administrative burden. The process of writing permits had already begun due to the Refuse Act experience, but without the detailed, industry-based assessment of technology dictated by section 304. Moreover, the section 304 process was supposed to be completed in only 12 months. Recall, too, that EPA was then a new agency with equally substantial tasks under the Clean Air Act.

EPA recognized that it would be unable to meet the one-year deadline in section 304(b)(1)(A) for promulgating effluent guidelines for classes and categories of point sources. The Agency announced that instead it would publish the guidelines in three groups over a two-year period, concentrating first on the 27 industry categories identified by section 306(b)(1)(A) as targets for new source performance standards. NRDC then sued EPA for failure to meet the deadline for issuing the guidelines, and EPA was placed on a court-ordered schedule requiring issuance of guidelines for all point source effluent discharges by December 31, 1974. NRDC v. Train, 510 F.2d 692 (D.C. Cir. 1975).

To further complicate matters, it soon became apparent that the Act was ambiguous concerning a crucial point: were effluent limits intended to be uniform by industry, or individually determined with reference to the industry effluent guidelines required by section 304? Section 304(b) required EPA to "publish regulations providing guidelines for effluent limitations," but EPA had not issued such guidelines when it adopted effluent limits for existing sources under section 301(b) and for new sources under section 306. EPA needed to issue regulations rapidly to give industries subject to them time to meet the 1977 deadline for installing certain levels of pollution control technology.

EPA determined that it would issue industry-wide effluent limitations under section 301 without waiting to promulgate guidelines under section 304(b). It proceeded to set numerical limits for various pollutants that were to be applied to different industries based on analyses of the capabilities of alternative pollution control technologies. Dischargers argued that effluent limits should be determined in individual permit proceedings and that issuance of the guidelines was a prerequisite to issuance of individual permits. Had this argument prevailed, final permit issuance would have been delayed for years, and industry would have been afforded many more opportunities to seek plant-specific adjustments in effluent limits during permit proceedings.

After six different United States Courts of Appeals reached varying opinions on this question, the Supreme Court finally resolved the issue in du Pont v. Train, 430 U.S. 112 (1977). The Court agreed with EPA that section 301 limitations "are to be adopted by the Administrator, . . . they are to be based primarily on classes and categories, and . . .

they are to take the form of regulations." 430 U.S. at 129. The Court noted that the Act's BAT requirement provided expressly for regulation by "categories and classes" of dischargers, language difficult to reconcile with case-by-case permits. 430 U.S. at 126. While the Act's BPT requirement did not contain similar language, the Court held that industry-wide BPT regulation was permissible "so long as some allowance is made for variations in individual plants as EPA has done by including a variance clause in its 1977 limitations." 430 U.S. at 128. The Court noted the "impossible burden" that would be imposed on EPA were it to be required to determine BPT in tens of thousands of individual permits proceedings sufficiently in advance of the 1977 compliance deadline. Id. at 132-133.

The *du Pont* decision established the validity of EPA's basic approach. What remained was the task of defining, implementing, and defending effluent limitations for every industrial category. Because the BPT effluent limitations had not been issued at the time most of the first round of discharge permits were issued, most permits did not contain categorical limits on discharges but rather incorporated individually negotiated limits based on the permit writer's "best professional judgment." Thus, the imposition of nationally uniform, categorical effluent limits was deferred long beyond the initial deadlines.

B. THE DEVELOPMENT OF EFFLUENT LIMITATIONS

The task of implementing sections 301 and 304 required an enormous administrative effort. EPA discovered that it was even more complicated than expected. While only 27 industrial categories were identified in the Act, EPA identified 180 industrial subcategories and 45 other classifications for which it believed distinct effluent standards were needed. CEQ, Environmental Quality—1974, at 141 (1974). Relying heavily on outside contractors for analysis of treatment technologies and industrial processes, EPA promulgated effluent guidelines for 30 industries by July 1974. The BPT guidelines, reflecting the performance of technology to be employed by 1977, relied largely on end-of-the-pipe treatment technologies for common pollutants and their parameters (e.g., biochemical oxygen demand, metals, pH, total suspended solids). The BAT guidelines, to be achieved by 1983, emphasized not only control technology but also process changes that for a few industries could result in attainment of the "no discharge" goal. Id. at 142.

EPA's effluent standards were invariably challenged in court. By 1977, more than 200 lawsuits had been filed. While this litigation delayed implementation of the effluent limits, judicial decisions helped clarify the requirements of the Act. As discussed in Chapter 4, claims that the condition of receiving waters should be taken into account in establishing effluent limitations were rejected in Weyerhaeuser Co. v. Costle, 590 F.2d 101 (D.C. Cir. 1978). In EPA v. National Crushed Stone Association, 449 U.S. 64 (1980) the Supreme Court held that firms could be required to comply with technology-based effluent limits that would force some firms in an industry subcategory to go out of business. In many other cases courts reviewed industry claims that the technology was not available to comply with EPA's standards. By 1989, United States Courts of Appeals had decided at least 27 cases challenging the validity of effluent guidelines. See Chemical Manufacturers Association v. EPA, 870 F.2d 177, 198 n.39 (5th Cir. 1989).

Examination of how EPA develops effluent standards for industry subcategories illustrates why technology-based standards are difficult to implement. Technology-based standards require the implementing agency to acquire a detailed understanding of the production processes and control technologies available for each industry subcategory. A study of how EPA developed effluent standards for the corn wet milling industry (a subcategory of the grain mills industry) found that the acquisition of substantial technical data is not an adequate substitute for detailed understanding of an industry. S. Gaines, Decision Making Procedures at the Environmental Protection Agency, 62 Iowa L. Rev. 839 (1977). Corn wet milling is the process for refining whole corn into corn oil, corn syrup, corn starch, and a variety of other by-products used in paper, adhesive, and textile manufacturing. While this rulemaking was an early example of a process which has evolved and improved in many respects, most of the basic elements of the process remain much the same today.

Gaines notes that EPA relied heavily on an engineering consulting firm to acquire data to support development of the corn wet milling standards. Six months after it was hired, the consulting firm provided EPA with a study of the industry, its wastes, and its treatment technologies that served as the basis for the standards adopted by EPA nine months later. The new source performance standards were then challenged in the Eighth Circuit, which twice struck them down as insufficiently supported in the record. CPC International, Inc. v. Train, 515 F.2d 1032 (8th Cir. 1975), CPC International, Inc. v. Train, 540 F.2d 1329 (8th Cir. 1976). A district court invalidated the standards for existing sources on similar grounds. Grain Processing Corp. v. Train, 407 F. Supp. 96 (S.D. Iowa 1976).

Gaines does not fault EPA's consultant for failing to gather sufficient raw data on which to base the standards, but rather for a failure to appreciate what the data meant and other key errors that stemmed from a lack of intimate knowledge of the industry. For instance, the consultant's report failed to appreciate that *average* data on the mills' observed effluents masked substantial variations between firms and over time. Other errors compounded the problems (e.g., the report analyzed pollutant concentrations expressed in milligrams per liter, a function of the volume of water used in processing that is highly variable from plant to plant, while the guidelines were to be expressed in terms of the amount of pollutant per unit of production). A graph in the contractor's report (that was reproduced in EPA's guidelines) erroneously indicated that 25,000 to 35,000 bushels of corn can be processed each day in a corn wet mill with no raw wastewater discharges. Remarkably, even though the EPA work group responsible for drafting the regulations had identified some of these problems, they were repeated in the final guidelines.

Recognizing that EPA's lack of familiarity with the industry could impede development of the effluent standards, industry representatives were not eager to assist EPA by providing data. Yet Gaines found that they also failed to provide an effective critique of EPA's proposal. As Gaines notes:

> Curiously, industry's comments [to the rulemaking] do not illuminate the critical problems with the rulemaking. Instead, they are a combination of very specific but inconsequential comments and sweeping unsupported statements. . . . The vagueness of the industry's comments on the substantive issues causes one to suspect . . . that because the industry lacked firm data with which to rebut the rulemaking proposal, it sought to badger the agency with a series of unsubstantiated allegations about the impossibility of compliance with the rule. Given the industry's earlier refusal to provide EPA with all of the relevant information about the industry and its processes, the Agency's perception that the industry was unable to argue against the proposed rule on its merits is readily understandable. [Gaines, Decision Making Procedures at the Environmental Protection Agency, 62 Iowa L. Rev. 839, 856-857 (1977).]

Section 308 of the Clean Water Act gives EPA data collection authority to assist in the development of effluent guidelines. This authority includes the right to impose record-keeping, sampling, and reporting requirements on point sources and a right of entry to inspect and gather data on the premises of such sources. A study of the guidelines development process found that this authority had not been of much help to EPA in developing BPT standards because legal challenges by industry delayed data gathering and "forced data collection through Section 308 authority created or worsened an adversarial relationship between EPA and an industry." W. Magat, A. Krupnick, and W. Harrington, Rules in the Making 36 (1986). As a result, "[i]ndustry was capable of manipulating the rulemaking process by withholding data on costly, but effective, abatement technologies and by supplying excessive and confusing data." Id.

The process used by EPA to develop effluent standards for industrial dischargers is illustrated in Figure 5.3, page 682. As EPA has acquired more experience in promulgating effluent standards, the process has improved somewhat, though it remains extraordinarily cumbersome and data-intensive. EPA staff may take as many as 20 samples of waste water at a plant and analyze each for 100 different pollutants in order to contribute to development of a data base to support effluent guidelines. Settlement with NRDC Puts EPA on Schedule to Issue Effluent Guidelines for 20 Industries, 22 Env. Rep. 2323, 2324 (1992).

William Pedersen views the process of establishing effluent guidelines to be a wasteful exercise that leads to standards that quickly become out-of-date:

> Each guideline has required a major and expensive rulemaking. Most of the effort was spent on exploring, for EPA's education, details of the costs and achievable reductions for various technologies in the industry under consideration at the time the guideline was being developed. That knowledge had only short-term value; it quickly became outdated with economic changes and the advance of technology. Moreover, the process demanded that EPA develop expertise in an impossibly wide variety of fields, duplicating knowledge already acquired by the industries involved. [Pedersen, Turning the Tide on Water Quality, 15 Ecology L.Q. 69, 85 (1988).]

Pedersen maintains that the fundamental flaw in the effluent standards is their technology-based approach, which "makes environmental performance irrelevant" while bringing costs to center stage. The result "has been a slight and variable willingness to cut back unduly strict requirements, coupled with a complete inability to strengthen unduly lenient standards." Id. at 87.

NOTES AND QUESTIONS

1. Magat, Krupnick, and Harrington found that, aside from OMB's growing influence, the process of formulating effluent standards has not changed in any fundamental manner. EPA has gained considerable experience in preparing (and defending) standards, and its performance has improved from what it was when the corn wet milling standard was issued. In Weyerhaeuser v. Costle, 590 F.2d 1011, 1026 (D.C. Cir. 1978), the court noted that "EPA has taken its responsibility quite seriously, employing no less than three highly qualified private consulting firms to augment its own technological expertise. Accordingly, we must not be too quick to draw conclusions, differing from those of the Agency, in this necessarily imprecise area of knowledge."

2. Consultants play a major role in the preparation of almost all EPA rules. As a practical matter, it would be impossible for EPA to fulfill its obligations without them due to staff restrictions and shifting requirements for expertise. To assist in the development of the corn wet milling standard, EPA chose a contractor with substantial experience

designing new mills. Would EPA have done better choosing a contractor with more general experience designing pollution control equipment?

3. Gaines found that environmental groups had not submitted comments during corn wet milling rulemaking. This is not unusual. Dozens of rules are promulgated every year; environmental groups lack the resources to comment on more than a few. Such groups are also more likely to comment on issues of general applicability or rules affecting the largest sources of pollution.

4. The rulemaking process has been substantially altered by the emphasis now given to OMB review as discussed in Chapter 5. Economic impacts are now addressed much more formally within the Agency and during interagency review. However, usually such review is limited to broader policy questions that would not necessarily identify the type of analytical problems described by Gaines.

C.   Effluent Standards for Toxic Water Pollutants

Ironically, Congress turned to technology-based effluent standards because of wide agreement that water quality-based approaches were far more difficult to implement. In the one area where Congress initially sought to retain a water quality-based approach—control of toxic pollutants—EPA soon agreed to substitute a technology-based approach as well. Deficiencies in this approach resulted in yet another shift in regulatory emphasis when the 1987 Amendments placed renewed emphasis on a water quality-based approach for controlling toxics, as we will see in section D.

i.   The Initial Section 307(a) Program

The 1972 Act reflected congressional concern that discharges of toxic pollutants posed potentially serious health risks. Thus, Congress created a regulatory scheme for toxics very different from the technology-based program otherwise applicable to point sources. To implement section 101(a)(3)'s ambitious goal that there be no discharge of "toxic pollutants in toxic amounts," section 307(a) of the 1972 Act required EPA to establish a list of toxic water pollutants and to set health-based standards for controlling them within 90 days. Unlike the technology-based standards, in which cost considerations could play a limited role, these regulations were to be strictly health-based and were to be established without regard to cost, technological feasibility, or economic impact. After being sued for failure to implement section 307(a), EPA proposed standards for nine toxic pollutants in the spring of 1974. What happened next is described below.

> ## Hall, The Evolution and Implementation of EPA's Regulatory Program to Control the Discharge of Toxic Pollutants to the Nation's Waters
> ### 10 Nat. Resources Law. 507 (1978)

In requiring EPA to publish within ninety days of passage of the Act a list of toxic pollutants to be regulated under this section, Congress apparently assumed the existence of a substantial body of data on the toxicity and persistence of pollutants, the identity of the dischargers thereof, and the feasibility of effective control. In fact, very little of this type of information existed for more than a few toxic pollutants, given the overall size of the field. Moreover, the task of assembling and evaluating these data, and filling gaps when they were discovered, proved to be far more than a 90-day exercise. The preparation must be especially thorough in light of the formal, "trial-type" rulemaking hearings as distinct from the informal "legislative" or "information-gathering" hearings which are conducted in establishing these standards (this is the only section of the Act which requires formal rulemaking hearings available in establishing pretreatment standards under Section 307(b), or under various provisions of the Toxic Substances Control Act).

Immediately environmental groups wanted the Agency to set 307(a) standards for a large number of substances, applicable to all sources of discharge. When the Agency missed the 90-day deadlines, the Natural Resources Defense Council ("NRDC") sued to force action. The Agency thereupon published a list of nine toxic pollutants, and on December 27, 1973, proposed standards for each. The nine pollutants were aldrin/dieldrin, benzidine, cadmium, cyanide, DDT (DDD, DDE), endrin, mercury, polychlorinated biphenyls (PCBs), and toxaphene. A thirty-day evidentiary hearing was held on these standards in April and May, 1974.

During these hearings, industry objectors introduced evidence which raised problems in the following areas: analytical and monitoring technology, hydrological assumptions contained in the proposed standards (which varied depending on the character and flow rate of the receiving waters), availability of control technology, impact of the proposed standards on important segments of the nation's economy, and identity of point source discharges. The gaps in the data base were of sufficient concern that at the conclusion of the hearing the Agency decided that responsible and defensible standards could not and therefore should not be promulgated on that record. It was decided to gather additional data and repropose new standards at a later date. The new proposal, however, was not to be forthcoming until June of 1976, and then only for a more limited number of pollutants.

Meanwhile on December 7, 1973, NRDC sued EPA to compel it to regulate substantially more than nine compounds under Section 307(a). [After EPA declined to promulgate any of the proposed standards, two additional lawsuits were brought against it and a fourth suit was filed to compel EPA to promulgate pretreatment standards for 35 industries under section 307(a).]

As these four cases made their way along the dockets of three different federal judges in the United States District Court for the District of Columbia in the fall of 1975, individuals within EPA were becoming increasingly aware of both the need for and the desirability of an integrated strategy for the control of toxic pollutants—a strategy which would make full use of all of the relevant sections of the Act at the Administrator's disposal. This approach would at a minimum utilize effluent limitations guidelines (Sections 301 and 304), new source performance standards (Section 306), toxic pollutant effluent standards (Section 307(a)), and pretreatment standards (Sections 307(b) and (c)), and perhaps other authorities as well.

[EPA believed that the BAT effluent limitations offered the best hope for implementing such a strategy, which it was reluctant to pursue until the four lawsuits were settled.]

During the 1974 hearings on the Agency's proposed toxic effluent standards, one of the most persistent criticisms from industry was that regulation under Section 307(a) confronted them with a moving target. They feared that EPA would become a "pollutant-of-the-month club," issuing different standards for different pollutants over an indefinite period of time with no regard for the availability or compatibility of various control technologies. It would thus become impossible for corporate decision-makers to plan their technology installations, since these plans could be interrupted and revised at any time by a new toxic pollutant effluent standard. In addition, it would be extremely difficult to estimate long term costs.

These problems would be substantially alleviated, it was said, by an industry-by-industry, rather than pollutant-by-pollutant approach. This way, the Agency could develop a single regulatory package consisting of effluent limitations guidelines, new source performance standards, and pretreatment standards applicable to all of the problem pollutants in the discharge of the particular industry. Industry could then proceed to implement the program, committing resources in the reasonable belief that the chances of being disrupted and redirected in midstream would be minimal.

Since Sections 301, 304, 306, and 307(b) and (c) contemplate industry-by-industry regulation and 307(a) does not, the former sections are naturally more adaptable to this strategy. Moreover, Sections 301, 304, and 306 expressly require consideration of technology, and offer a longer compliance time (by July 1, 1983, in the case of BAT) than the one-year period required under 307(a).

The approach outlined above also offers substantial benefits to the environment, and hence was attractive to the plaintiff environmental groups. By focusing the full spectrum of the foregoing sections on the control of toxics, it appeared highly likely that a larger number of harmful pollutants could be controlled in the discharges of a larger number of plants than if Section 307(a) alone were relied upon, even though the implementation time would be longer.

Finally, the regulation of pollutants on an industry-by-industry basis offers administrative efficiencies to EPA as well. Data on effluent content and control technology can be gathered at one time, for all pollutants, instead of in repeated plant visits and industry surveys each time a new pollutant is added to the list.

Under this strategy, Section 307(a) would be utilized in those relatively few cases when the toxicity of the pollutant is so serious that stringent controls and the one-year compliance time are desired regardless of the availability of control technology. Where process or other controls are not available to achieve compliance, a shutdown of operations would be the likely result. While substantial expenditures or even shutdowns may be justified to avert the serious adverse effects of chronic or acute exposure to toxic pollutants, it would seem to be the more prudent regulatory course to gather at least a reasonable amount of this information before a pollutant is put on the 307(a) list, rather than after. This element of early data gathering was reflected in the toxics strategy as it began to take shape within the Agency in the fall of 1975.

---

ii. The Settlement Agreement and the "Flannery Decree"

After lengthy negotiations between EPA and the environmental groups and several meetings with industry intervenors, a comprehensive settlement agreement was reached. Incorporated into a consent decree, called the "Flannery Decree" after the judge who approved it, the settlement committed EPA to a schedule for promulgating effluent guidelines, pretreatment standards, and new source performance standards for 65 toxic pollutants and 21 industries. The agreement established tight deadlines for issuance of standards in order to give industrial dischargers at least three years to meet compliance deadlines.

This unique settlement was possible because all sides perceived it as providing benefits. As an NRDC attorney explained:

EPA was off the scientific hook, at least temporarily. The environmental groups would not obtain the stringent effluent standards prescribed by

Congress, but they would see far more comprehensive regulations issued
much sooner than if they had persisted in the litigation. Even the regulated
industries were glad to substitute a one-time, complete set of regulatory
requirements for the old "pollutant-of-the-month" approach that appeared to require a never-ending series of improvements as EPA added
new chemicals to the list and developed toxic effluent standards. [J. Banks,
Dumping into Surface Waters: The Making and Demise of Toxic Discharge
Regulations, in Beyond Dumping 41-42 (B. Piasecki, ed. 1984).]

When he approved the settlement, Judge Flannery noted that it
did not preclude any party from challenging the regulations that ultimately were issued to implement the decree. Some industry groups subsequently challenged the legality of the consent decree, but it was upheld
by a divided D.C. Circuit panel in Citizens for a Better Environment v.
Gorsuch, 718 F.2d 1117 (1983). The Flannery Decree was subsequently
ratified, amended in some details, and incorporated in section 301 of
the Act by the 1977 Amendments. A statement by the House conferees
noted that the approach in section 307(a) had failed primarily due to
"the formal, cumbersome rulemaking process."
    Although the Flannery Decree originally required EPA to establish
technology-based standards for 65 toxic pollutants discharged by 21
primary industries, it was subsequently redefined to cover 126 pollutants
from 34 industrial categories. These 126 pollutants, which by no means
include all significant toxic pollutants of concern today, became known
as "priority pollutants."

NOTES AND QUESTIONS

1. Why did lawyers for environmental groups agree to a regulatory
approach that permitted consideration of economic impact, when the
original program did not? See Hall, The Control of Toxic Pollutants
Under the Federal Water Pollution Control Act Amendments of 1972,
63 Iowa L. Rev. 609 (1978). Is a technology-based approach for controlling toxic discharges necessarily easier to implement than an approach that sets standards in an effort to achieve health-based levels of
water quality?
    2. The D.C. Circuit subsequently upheld three of the six toxic
effluent standards EPA had promulgated under section 307 in decisions
confirming the authority of EPA to regulate toxics in the face of enormous uncertainty even at the price of severe economic impacts. Environmental Defense Fund v. EPA, 598 F.2d 62 (D.C. Cir. 1978) (zero
discharge standard for PCBs upheld); Hercules, Inc. v. EPA, 598 F.2d
91 (D.C. Cir. 1978) (standards for endrin and toxaphene upheld). But
as Oliver Houck notes, "§307 had for all practical purposes expired by

the time these opinions were written," because EPA was "paralyzed" by the difficulties of implementing a health-based standard. Houck, The Regulation of Toxic Pollutants Under the Clean Water Act, 21 Envtl. L. Rep. 10528 (Sept. 1991).

3. The process for issuing effluent standards has been so cumbersome that some have argued in favor of using negotiated rulemaking. As noted in Chapter 5, regulatory negotiation sometimes can resolve issues more quickly and with a greater likelihood of finality. Negotiated settlements resolved challenges to EPA's effluent guidelines for two important industrial categories, steel and petroleum refineries. See Miller, Steel Industry Effluent Limitations: Success at the Negotiating Table, 13 Envtl. L. Rep. 10094 (1983).

4. Dissenting in Citizens for a Better Environment v. Gorsuch, Judge Wilkey decried "government by consent decree" and argued that the Flannery Decree had infringed impermissibly on EPA's discretion. He reasoned that judicial enforcement of the consent decree would reduce the ability of the public to monitor or influence agency actions, giving greater powers to special interest groups. To preclude future Flannery Decrees, in March 1986 the Reagan Administration's Justice Department promulgated a "Policy Regarding Consent Decrees and Settlement Agreements" designed to restrict the circumstances under which executive agencies will enter into consent decrees. The policy prohibits executive agencies from entering into any consent decree "that divests a [government official] of discretion" or "that converts into a mandatory duty the otherwise discretionary authority of [an official] to revise, amend, or promulgate regulations." See Percival, The Bounds of Consent: Consent Decrees, Settlements and Federal Environmental Policy Making, 1987 U. Chi. Legal Forum 327. What, if anything, gives EPA the authority to make a legally binding policy commitment in a consent decree that may extend over a period of several years?

5. EPA's implementation of the Flannery Decree disappointed environmental groups, particularly when the Reagan Administration sought relief from its requirements. After failing to convince the court that it should be relieved of its obligations under the decree, EPA promulgated relatively weak standards, described by an NRDC lawyer as follows:

> Many require absolutely no progress beyond BPT cleanup levels achieved by industrial sources in 1977. Others require only marginal progress because they are based on end-of-pipe treatment systems rather than in-plant changes that can reduce specific constituents more effectively in a portion of the plant's discharge. In all, the final regulations are considerably weaker than the proposed versions published several years ago by the Carter administration. [J. Banks, Dumping into Surface Waters: The Making and Demise of Toxic Discharge Regulations, in Beyond Dumping 46 (B. Piasecki, ed. 1984).]

6. The Chemical Manufacturers Association lobbied the Reagan Administration to replace the nationally uniform, technology-based controls in the Clean Water Act with more flexible controls that would not require dischargers to employ BAT as long as their discharges did not result in violations of state ambient water quality standards. What advantages would this approach have? What disadvantages?

7. Proponents of more flexible environmental controls generally favor decentralizing authority so that state and local governments can tailor regulations to local needs. They maintain that decentralization generally results in less stringent controls because state and local governments are less capable of resisting pressure from industries that they are competing to keep or attract. Local authorities also may have fewer resources to implement regulatory programs. For example, the Reagan Administration reduced financial assistance for state water pollution control programs by 56 percent, even as it argued for greater state control of these programs. Id. at 49.

D. PROVIDING FLEXIBILITY THROUGH VARIANCES

The trade-off between flexibility and complexity is well illustrated by efforts to fine-tune national effluent standards. Standards established for industrial categories containing as many as 100 or more dischargers may be inappropriate for individual plants with special circumstances not easily taken into account in a national standard. For example, a plant may have a shortage of land on which to build additional waste treatment capacity, or air quality controls may prevent the use of certain treatment processes. How should EPA take such factors into account without either defeating the goal of nationally uniform standards or hopelessly complicating the standard-setting process?

The 1972 Act did not explicitly address this issue other than to allow EPA flexibility to define additional industry subcategories. In its early regulations, EPA devised an alternative approach allowing individual permit applicants an opportunity to request a variance for factors "fundamentally different" from those considered by EPA. As noted above, in the *du Pont* decision, the Supreme Court strongly endorsed this "FDF variance" for BPT, although it later held in EPA v. National Crushed Stone Association, 449 U.S. 64 (1980), that EPA need not consider an individual firm's ability to afford BPT requirements.

While Congress authorized some modifications of effluent standards in sections 301(c) and 301(g), the 1977 Amendments added section 301(*l*), which prohibited modification of any requirements applicable to toxic pollutants. In Chemical Manufacturers Association v. NRDC, 470 U.S. 116 (1985), the Supreme Court reviewed a Third Circuit decision holding that FDF variances could not be granted for discharges of toxics into sewage treatment systems, which are known as "indirect" discharges and governed by the pretreatment program. The Court had to decide whether an FDF variance was a "modification" in the sense used by section 301(*l*).

Chemical Manufacturers Association
v. NRDC
470 U.S. 116 (1985)

Justice WHITE delivered the opinion of the Court.

Section 301(*l*) states that EPA may not "modify" any requirement of §301 insofar as toxic materials are concerned. EPA insists that §301(*l*) prohibits only those modifications expressly permitted by other provisions of §301, namely, those that §301(c) and §301(g) would allow on economic or water-quality grounds. Section 301(*l*), it is urged, does not address the very different issue of FDF variances. . . .

A

NRDC insists that the language of §301(*l*) is itself enough to require affirmance of the Court of Appeals, since on its face it forbids any modifications of the effluent limitations that EPA must promulgate for toxic pollutants. If the word "modify" in §301(*l*) is read in its broadest sense, that is, to encompass any change or alteration in the standards, NRDC is correct. But it makes little sense to construe the section to forbid EPA to amend its own standards, even to correct an error or to impose stricter requirements. . . . As NRDC does and must concede, §301(*l*) cannot be read to forbid every change in the toxic waste standards. The word "modify" thus has no plain meaning as used in §301(*l*), and is the proper subject of construction by EPA and the courts. . . . We should defer to [EPA's] view unless the legislative history or the purpose and structure of the statute clearly reveal a contrary intent on the part of Congress. NRDC submits that the legislative materials evinces such a contrary intent. We disagree. . . .

[Based on an examination of the legislative history of section 301(*l*), the Court concludes that Congress intended for it to bar only waivers based on the economic capability of dischargers under section 301(c) or on water quality considerations under section 301(g).]

After examining the wording and legislative history of the statute, we agree with EPA and CMA that the legislative history itself does not evince an unambiguous congressional intention to forbid all FDF waivers with respect to toxic materials.

C

Neither are we convinced that FDF variances threaten to frustrate the goals and operation of the statutory scheme set up by Congress. The nature of FDF variances has been spelled out both by this Court and by the Agency itself. The regulation explains that its purpose is to remedy categories which were not accurately drawn because information was either not available to or not considered by the Administrator in setting the original categories and limitations. An FDF variance does not excuse compliance with a correct requirement, but instead represents an acknowledgement that not all relevant factors were taken sufficiently into account in framing that requirement originally, and that those relevant factors, properly considered, would have justified—indeed, required— the creation of a subcategory for the discharger in question. As we have recognized, the FDF variance is a laudable corrective mechanism, "an acknowledgment that the uniform . . . limitation was set without reference to the full range of current practices, to which the Administrator was to refer." EPA v. National Crushed Stone Assn., 449 U.S. 64, 77-78 (1980). It is, essentially, not an exception to the standard-setting process, but rather a more fine-tuned application of it.

We are not persuaded by NRDC's argument that granting FDF variances is inconsistent with the goal of uniform effluent limitations under the Act. . . .

NRDC concedes that EPA could promulgate rules under §307 of the Act creating a subcategory for each source which is fundamentally different from the rest of the class under the factors the EPA must consider in drawing categories. The same result is produced by the issuance of an FDF variance for the same failure properly to subdivide a broad category. Since the dispute is therefore reduced to an argument over the means used by EPA to define subcategories of indirect dischargers in order to achieve the goals of the Act, these are particularly persuasive cases for deference to the Agency's interpretation.

NRDC argues, echoing the concern of the Court of Appeals below, that allowing FDF variances will render meaningless the §301(*l*) prohibition against modifications on the basis of economic and water quality factors. That argument ignores the clear difference between the purpose of FDF waivers and that of §301(c) and (g) modifications, a difference we explained in *National Crushed Stone*. A discharger that satisfies the requirements of §301(c) qualifies for a variance "simply because [it] could not afford a compliance cost that is not fundamentally different from those the Administrator has already considered" in creating a category and setting an effluent limitation. 449 U.S., at 78. A §301(c) modification forces "a displacement of calculations already performed, not because those calculations were incomplete or had unexpected effects, but only because the costs happened to fall on one particular operator, rather than on another who might be economically better off." Ibid. FDF variances are specifically unavailable for the grounds that would justify the statutory modifications. Both a source's inability to pay the foreseen costs, grounds for a §301(c) modification, and the lack of a significant impact on water quality, grounds for a §301(g) modification, are irrelevant under FDF variance procedures.

EPA and CMA point out that the availability of FDF variances makes bearable the enormous burden faced by EPA in promulgating categories of sources and setting effluent limitations. Acting under stringent timetables, EPA must collect and analyze large amounts of technical information concerning complex industrial categories. Understandably, EPA may not be apprised of and will fail to consider unique factors applicable to atypical plants during the categorical rulemaking process, and it is thus important that EPA's nationally binding categorical pretreatment standards for indirect dischargers be tempered with the flexibility that the FDF variance mechanism offers, a mechanism repugnant to neither the goals nor the operation of the Act.

III

Viewed in its entirety, neither the language nor the legislative history of the Act demonstrates a clear congressional intent to forbid EPA's sensible variance mechanism for tailoring the categories it promulgates. In the absence of a congressional directive to the contrary, we accept EPA's conclusion that §301(*l*) does not prohibit FDF variances.

JUSTICE MARSHALL, . . . dissenting.
. . . EPA's argument that §301(*l*) proscribes only those modifications otherwise authorized by §§301(c) and (g) . . . is clearly inconsistent with congressional intent; the plain meaning of the statute and its legislative history show a clear congressional intent to ban all "modifications." . . .

If these two modifications are the only ones now prohibited, the result is wholly counterintuitive. EPA is in effect contending that economic and water-quality factors present the most compelling case for modification of the standard in the nontoxic context—as they are explicitly authorized by statute—but the least compelling case for modification in the toxic context—as they are the only modifications prohibited by §301(*l*). As might be expected, EPA does not present any theory, much less a logical argument, for evidence in the legislative history, to support this extremely inconsistent result. . . .

EPA's second construction of the statutory scheme is, on the surface, a more plausible one. EPA argues that FDF variances do not excuse compliance with the correct standards, but instead provide a means for setting more appropriate standards. It is clear that, pursuant to §307(b)(2), EPA can "revise" the pretreatment standards, as long as it does so "following the procedure established . . . for the promulgation of such standards." The statute contemplates that the standards will be set and revised through notice-and-comment rulemaking and will be applicable to categories of sources. EPA argues that such a "revision," which is clearly not proscribed by §301(*l*), would be substantively indistinguishable from an FDF variance. . . .

To support its argument, EPA points out that the factors that may justify an FDF variance are the same factors that may be taken into account in setting and revising the national pretreatment standards. . . . EPA acknowledges that the statute requires that the national pretreatment standards be established—and therefore revised—for "categories" of dischargers and not on a case-by-case basis. It argues, however, that nothing in the Clean Water Act precludes EPA from defining a subcategory that has only one discharger.

The logic of EPA's position is superficially powerful. If EPA can, through rulemaking, define a subcategory that includes only one discharger, why should it not be able to do so through a variance procedure? In fact, if rulemaking and the variance procedure were alternative means to the same end, I might have no quarrel with EPA's position, which the Court has accepted. . . .

However, the Agency's position does not withstand more than superficial analysis. An examination of the legislative history of the 1972 amendments to the Clean Water Act—the relevance of which both the Court and EPA ignore—reveals that Congress attached great *substantive* significance to the method used for establishing pollution control requirements.

The Conference Committee Report directed EPA to "make the determination of the economic impact of an effluent limitation on the basis of classes and categories of point sources, *as distinguished from a plant by plant determination.*" 1972 Leg. Hist. 304 (emphasis added). . . .

The legislative history also makes clear why Congress found it so important that the standards be set for "categories" of dischargers, and not for individual dischargers. Congress intended to use the standards as a means to "force" the introduction of more effective pollution control technology. . . . By requiring that the standards be set by reference to either the "average of the best" or very "best" technology, the Act seeks to foster technological innovation. . . .

Unlike the statutory revision mechanism of §307(b), FDF variances are set not by reference to a category of dischargers, but instead by reference to a single discharger. In evaluating an application for a variance, EPA does not look at the group of dischargers in the same position as the applicant, but instead focuses solely on the characteristics of the applicant itself. Under the FDF program, there is no mechanism for

EPA to ascertain whether there are any other dischargers in that position. Moreover, there is no mechanism for EPA to group together similarly situated dischargers. Quite to the contrary, a scheme in which the initial screening may be done by the individual States, at times determined by when the variance application is filed, is unlikely to lead to the identification of new subcategories. . . .

In the aggregate, if EPA defines a new pretreatment subcategory through rulemaking, the BAT-level pollution control requirement of each discharger would be determined by reference to the capability of the "best" performer. In contrast, if EPA provides individual variances to each plant in this group, only one discharger would have a requirement based on the capability of the best performer—the best performer itself. The others would necessarily be subject to less stringent standards. . . .

It is true, of course, that even the statutory revision procedure might identify a subcategory with only one discharger. That procedure, however, will have established that this discharger is uniquely situated. In contrast, an FDF variance sets an individual requirement even where there may be similarly situated dischargers.

NOTES AND QUESTIONS

1. How do the majority and the dissent differ in their characterizations of the purpose of FDF variances? To what extent do these differences reflect different conceptions of the role of the effluent standards in forcing the development of improved pollution control technology?

2. As of July 1985 EPA headquarters had received 58 applications for FDF variances and granted only four. There may have been some additional requests denied by states or EPA regional offices. Pedersen, Turning the Tide on Water Quality, 15 Ecology L.Q. 69, 86 n.81 (1988). Given the small number of favorable applications for variances, why do you think there has been so much litigation concerning them? What impact is the availability of FDF variances likely to have on the administrative costs of implementing effluent limitations?

3. Note that BAT regulations are only now coming into effect for many industries, and more applications for FDF variances are being received. Because these applications generally require EPA to assess plant-specific technical data on production processes and control technologies, EPA has been slow to rule on such applications, taking an average of three years to process them. To expedite the FDF process, the 1987 Amendments required EPA to rule on FDF variance applications within 180 days of submission, a deadline that EPA has found to be difficult to meet. EPA's failure to meet this deadline has been held not to stay a discharger's obligation to comply with the effluent limits that are the

subject of the application. See Chemical Manufacturers Association v. EPA, 870 F.2d 177 (5th Cir. 1989) (citing §505(a)(2)).

4. The 1987 CWA Amendments specifically address the FDF variance for the first time. A new section 301(n) sets out permissible grounds for FDF variances for toxic pollutants. Could the FDF variance provision ever be used to justify more *stringent* conditions on a discharger? What circumstances might justify such action, and how might it come about? EPA's regulations allow for the possibility. Does section 301(n)?

3. Effluent Limitations: The State of the Art

The process of implementing the Clean Water Act's technology-based approach to water pollution control has been laborious, technically complex, and marked by repeated delays and missed deadlines. Having "shifted our faith from science to engineering," Houck, The Regulation of Toxic Pollutants Under the Clean Water Act, 21 Envtl. L. Rep. 10528, 10536 (1991), the Act and the Flannery Decree forced EPA to make engineering judgments based on detailed studies of production processes and pollution control technologies on an industry subcategory-by-subcategory basis. Many effluent guidelines have taken five or more years to develop. 55 Fed. Reg. 80, 81 (1990). When ultimately implemented, "BAT had lost its bite," though it "has probably been the most effective pollution control program in the world in terms of producing identifiable abatement—short of outright bans—if only because alternative programs have proven equally burdensome and so much less effective." Houck, above, at 10538, 10541.

The Flannery Decree ultimately produced numerous effluent guidelines, but it did not ensure comprehensive coverage of industrial dischargers. By 1990 EPA had promulgated effluent guidelines and standards covering 51 categories of dischargers and had completed all but one of the rulemakings required under the Flannery Decree. Despite this progress, EPA's effluent guidelines remain far from comprehensive. Nearly 80 percent of existing industrial dischargers of toxics (59,338 of 74,525) still are not covered by BAT standards. Natural Resources Defense Council v. Reilly, 32 ERC (BNA) 1969, 1972 n.25 (D.D.C. 1991). Moreover, the guidelines that have been issued by EPA often fail to cover significant substances or are based on data that are woefully outdated. As a result, even though all dischargers must have a permit, large quantities of toxics are being discharged because they are uncontrolled or poorly controlled in existing permits.

When it amended the Clean Water Act in 1987, Congress expressly required EPA to strengthen, expand, and revise existing technology-based controls to ensure that significant sources of discharges did not escape regulation. Congress added section 304(m) of the Act, which requires EPA by set deadlines to establish a schedule for the annual review and revision of existing effluent guidelines, to promulgate revisions to them, to identify classes of sources discharging toxics or unconventional pollutants for which categorical effluent limitations and new source performance standards have not been issued, to establish a schedule for promulgating such limits and standards, and to promulgate them.

EPA missed all of the deadlines in section 304(m), although it belatedly identified six industries as candidates for new or revised effluent guidelines. Arguing that EPA had failed to comply with the requirements of section 304(m), NRDC sued EPA. In Natural Resources Defense Council v. Reilly, 32 ERC (BNA) 1969 (D.D.C. 1991), a federal district court rejected EPA's arguments that the deadlines in section 304(m) should be considered to be unenforceable "targets" because of the enormity of the task EPA faced. The court held that section 304(m) requires EPA to identify all industries currently discharging toxics or unconventional pollutants in significant amounts not covered by existing guidelines. "Surely the Congress which passed §304(m) out of frustration with the agency's sluggishness did not intend to confer upon the agency discretion to limit the scope and set the pace of effluent guidelines preparation simply by refraining from 'identifying known polluters.' " 32 ERC at 1975. Nine months after the court's decision, NRDC and EPA agreed on a new timetable for issuance of effluent guidelines for more than 20 industries. Embodied in a consent decree, the agreement establishes a detailed schedule for EPA to propose and to promulgate effluent guidelines for various source categories. The decree specifies four new source categories for which effluent guidelines are to be established, and it requires EPA to identify eight additional source categories to regulate on a timetable running to the year 2003. It also requires EPA to study 11 other source categories in order to determine whether effluent guidelines should be promulgated for them. Representatives of the chemical industry are supporting the consent decree, which expressly does not resolve the question whether EPA has the discretion to refuse to promulgate effluent guidelines for a particular source category. Settlement with NRDC Puts EPA on Schedule to Issue Effluent Guidelines for 20 Industries, 22 Env. Rep. 2323 (1992).

Because Congress established March 31, 1989 as the final date for compliance with technology-based effluent limits, EPA's belated promulgation of guidelines has reduced (or eliminated) the lead time for certain industries to install controls. In Chemical Manufacturers Association v. EPA, 870 F.2d 177 (5th Cir. 1989), several companies in the organic chemicals, plastics, and synthetic fiber (OCPSF) industries argued that this denied them due process and should change the kinds of technology that should be considered "available" in promulgating BAT standards. Noting that Congress had been aware of EPA's delay in prom-

ulgating the BAT limitations when it enacted the deadline, the Fifth
Circuit rejected both arguments. The court observed that companies
that missed the deadline would be subject to EPA enforcement under
section 309 of the Act, guided by EPA's post-deadline enforcement policy. Section 309 provides for the issuance of administrative orders specifying a "reasonable" time for compliance depending on the seriousness
of the violation "and any good faith efforts to comply with applicable
requirements." EPA's enforcement policy provides that noncompliance
resulting from EPA's delay in issuing effluent limitations will result in
orders specifying a new compliance schedule. The court rejected the
notion that reliance on EPA's exercise of prosecutorial discretion was an
inadequate remedy, noting that EPA enforcement actions are subject to
judicial review. Rejecting the industry's argument that the availability of
BAT should depend on the amount of lead time available to install
technology, the court concluded that Congress had intended instead for
EPA to base BAT determinations on "available model technology," without considering the lead time available to individual plants.

In the same case NRDC also had challenged EPA's NSPS for the
OCPSF industries because the Agency had failed to consider recycling
technologies that could eliminate discharges. The court agreed with
NRDC that the NSPS was insufficiently stringent. Noting that 36 plants
in the industry already achieve zero discharge through recycling, the
court held that it was arbitrary and capricious for EPA to adopt a NSPS
no more stringent than the effluent guidelines for existing sources without considering recycling technology. The court remanded the NSPS to
EPA "for consideration of whether zero discharge limits would be appropriate for new plants" due to the availability of recycling.

The litigation over the organic chemicals effluent standards illustrates how cumbersome and complex the process of developing industry-
wide effluent limitations continues to be. The administrative record
developed by EPA in the course of promulgating the standards totaled
more than 600,000 pages. Briefs in the Fifth Circuit litigation consumed
more than 3,000 pages, with a 9,000-page appendix. Several months
after the initial Fifth Circuit decision rejecting all challenges by industry
petitioners to the OCPSF standard, the court modified its decision to
remand standards for 20 pollutants for further consideration by EPA.
The court found that EPA had failed "to demonstrate a reasonable basis
for its conclusion that in-plant treatment can eliminate pollutants as
effectively as end-of-the-pipe systems" on which biological treatment is
used. In October 1991, EPA announced that it would not complete action
on the issues remanded by the Fifth Circuit in October 1989 until at
least May 1993. 56 Fed. Reg. 54,040 (1991).

NOTES AND QUESTIONS

1. Why is the chemical industry supporting the new consent decree between EPA and NRDC?

2. Oliver Houck concludes that EPA has promulgated technology-based standards whose stringency often varies with an industry's relative political clout:

> It is an astonishing but commonplace fact that when a BAT-limited industry is required to reduce *x* further—due to water quality, health, public relations, or other considerations—it finds the ability to do so. In this regard, BAT appears to be more a problem of lead time and amortization of costs than a problem of engineering. BAT remains as driven by the most an industry will accept as by the most it can do.
>
> This conclusion is reinforced by the equally disturbing fact that discharge standards have emerged unevenly, with a heavy "zero discharge" hand on such unfortunates as seafood canners and placer mine operators, and a remarkably blind eye to available closed-cycle systems for some of the nation's highest-volume dischargers of broad-spectrum toxins. The disparities in these standards reflect nothing more starkly than a disparity in clout. These disparities are amplified by the fact that, for the decade of the 1980s, EPA only worked with any intensity on that limited group of industries and that limited set of toxic compounds mandated by the 1976 decree. [Houck, The Regulation of Toxic Pollutants Under the Clean Water Act, 21 Envtl. L. Rep. 10528, 10539 (Sept. 1991).]

Does this experience suggest that a technology-*forcing* approach to regulation should be employed more extensively? Would industries with little political clout be any better off under alternative approaches to regulation?

3. Delays in issuing effluent guidelines effectively have postponed investment in pollution control technology for many industries. Despite its concern about having sufficient lead time to comply with the guidelines, the OCPSF industries did not seek to accelerate their issuance but rather to postpone the ultimate compliance date. By contrast, even though NRDC argued that the regulations were too weak, it asked the court to let them take effect until more stringent standards could be adopted. Can you think of any way to reverse the incentives favoring delay in these circumstances? Given the Fifth Circuit's decision on the compliance deadline problem, how would you advise dischargers concerned that they will be unable to meet the standards?

4. POTWs and the Pretreatment Program

Publicly owned wastewater treatment works (POTWs) are substantial point source dischargers whose effluent contains by-products of municipal sewage and industrial discharges subject to the pretreatment program. Sludge is the potentially hazardous byproduct of the treatment process, which POTWs must manage in large quantities. Most sludge is disposed on land; it no longer may legally be dumped into the ocean as New York City and some of its neighbors in New Jersey have done for years. The 1987 Amendments added section 405 to the Clean Water Act, which requires EPA to develop standards for disposal of sewage sludge to be implemented through the NPDES permits issued to POTWs.

POTWs are regulated separately from industrial point source dischargers under the Clean Water Act, which applies a separate set of effluent limits to them under section 301(b)(1)(B) of the Act. POTWs may administer the section 307 pretreatment program applicable to industrial facilities discharging into their system. Because POTWs are publicly owned, their compliance problems have been aggravated by cutbacks in public funding for investments in treatment technology.

A. Sewage Treatment

Sewage disposal became a water pollution problem in the late nineteenth century when urban areas turned to sewer systems for disposing of human waste. The percentage of the U.S. population served by sewer systems rose from 3 percent in 1860 to 33 percent in 1900 and 50 percent in 1930. Council on Environmental Quality, Environmental Quality—1974, at 144 (1974). Sewer systems improved sanitary conditions in cities by collecting waste and transporting it downstream. While it was widely assumed that rivers and streams could easily assimilate wastes, growing volumes of raw sewage eventually created problems so severe that water pollution became a national concern. By 1910, 38 percent of the nation's population was served by sewer systems, but only 4 percent was served by sewage treatment plants. Id. (The sewage treatment process is illustrated in Figure 7.3, page 871).

Municipalities were often reluctant to invest in expensive treatment facilities that would primarily benefit downstream populations. Beginning in 1956, the federal government sought to overcome this resistance by providing federal funds for the construction of sewage treatment plants. More than $75 billion in federal, state, and local funds has been invested in the construction of thousands of sewage treatment plants, which now serve 144 million people with at least secondary treatment systems. However, the continued expansion of sewer systems has outpaced the expansion of treatment capacity in some areas, such as New York City. Gold, Despite Decades of Spending, Sewage Plants Are Full Up, N.Y. Times, Aug. 18, 1991, at E16.

In 1972 Congress required POTWs to achieve at least secondary treatment levels by 1977 and an even more advanced level of treatment by 1983. The latter requirement was eliminated in 1981, though limits more stringent than secondary treatment limits may still be imposed if necessary to meet applicable water quality standards. §301(b)(1)(C). Congress also relaxed treatment requirements in 1977 when it added section 301(h), which authorizes POTWs discharging directly into marine waters to waive secondary treatment requirements in certain circumstances.

Despite the relaxation of treatment requirements, many POTWs remain out of compliance. Boston's notorious sewage problems, a prominent topic in the 1988 presidential campaign, resulted in a ban on new sewer hookups in the area until new treatment facilities were sited. Even with a $6.8 billion budget, officials acknowledge that Boston's sewage may not be treated adequately until the next century. With the phaseout of federal construction grants mandated by the 1987 Amendments, hard-pressed local governments are going to find it even more difficult to upgrade sewage treatment capacity. Chronic enforcement problems with POTWs are likely to persist because of funding problems and the difficulty of imposing effective sanctions on publicly owned entities.

Not all sewage discharges pass through to POTWs. Investigators have found clandestine sewage discharge pipes that bypass treatment works. A systematic survey of New York City's shoreline in 1991 found 171 pipes discharging 4.5 million gallons of untreated sewage per day. The survey was conducted by sending inspectors out in boats at low tide over a two-and-one-half year period. When environmental officials investigated further, they discovered that two-thirds of the pipes were owned by city agencies. The remaining one-third were owned by state agencies, the U.S. Army, and private businesses and homes. Gold, New Sewage Culprits in New York Found in Public Sector, N.Y. Times, July 10, 1991, at A1. The sewage discharged through these pipes, however, was only one-quarter of 1 percent of the 1.8 billion gallons processed daily by New York's 14 sewage treatment plants.

B.   THE PRETREATMENT PROGRAM

As controls on toxic discharges into surface waters have been strengthened, more pressure has been placed on a particularly weak link in the Clean Water Act's system of controls: the pretreatment program. Many industrial sources have chosen to avoid the NPDES permit process and to escape RCRA standards by discharging toxics and hazardous waste into sewers. These indirect dischargers are exempt from NPDES permit requirements. (Remember that the NPDES requirements apply only to point sources that discharge into surface waters and that domestic sewage is exempt from regulation as a hazardous waste under RCRA.) The Office of Technology Assessment reported in 1987 that more than 160,000 industrial facilities discharge more than one trillion gallons of wastewater containing RCRA hazardous wastes into municipal sewers each year. If not treated at industrial facilities, these "indirect" waste discharges would contain 160,000 metric tons of hazardous components, including 62,000 metric tons of metals that are priority pollutants, 40,000 tons of organic chemicals that are priority pollutants, and 64,000 tons of other hazardous organic chemicals. OTA, Wastes in Marine Environments 212 (1987).

The rationale for exempting indirect dischargers from the NPDES program was that it would be redundant to require controls on discharges that already would be subject to treatment in POTWs. To prevent indirect discharges from interfering with the operation of POTWs, section 307 of the Clean Water Act requires pretreatment of such discharges to control pollutants that are not susceptible to treatment by POTWs. EPA has promulgated general pretreatment regulations that prohibit the discharge of pollutants that might interfere with or pass through POTWs and that require the development of local pretreatment programs. In Arkansas Poultry Federation v. EPA, 852 F.2d 324 (8th Cir. 1988), the Eighth Circuit upheld EPA's definitions of "interference" and "pass through," which provide that indirect dischargers may only be penalized for discharges that actually cause permit violations at POTWs. EPA is promulgating technologically based pretreatment requirements on an industry-wide basis ("categorical pretreatment requirements"). Individual POTWs also are authorized to impose local limits.

Some of the problems encountered in implementing the pretreatment program are described in the following excerpt.

Houck, *Ending the War: A Strategy to Save America's Coastal Zone*
47 Md. L. Rev. 358, 384-388 (1988)

Pretreatment is one of those efficiency-based concepts that sounds plausible in a course in "Economics and the Environment." It is unnecessary to require industry to remove wastes and sewage that the local municipal plant is going to be treating anyway. Efficiencies of scale should allow industries to discharge their wastes into municipal systems with a credit for the municipal treatment. Congress, which bought this argument from the start, has directed the EPA to develop separate "pretreatment" standards for industrial discharges into POTWs. The standards are of two types: (1) "categorical" standards for a limited number of industries and for a somewhat larger number of toxics; and (2) general standards that, in essence, prohibit the introduction of substances that would harm the POTW system itself. The standards are implemented not by the EPA or the states, but by participating POTWs themselves.

The federal standards have been a nightmare to develop. Local imple- *great*
mentation is approaching, even at this late date, a state of chaos.

The EPA has labored at length on pretreatment standards. Fifteen
years after the passage of the CWA, with litigation at every turn, the
Agency has finally promulgated for twenty-seven industries categorical
standards which regulate (but, of course, do not prohibit) the discharge
of one hundred twenty-six toxic substances. The first shortcoming is
obvious: any unlisted industries and toxics, which include a wide range
of nasty substances, are essentially uncovered. Also, after considerable
trial and error, as well as judicial review, the EPA has promulgated its
"prohibited" standards designed to prevent "interference" with POTW
systems. The basic shortcoming of this approach is that a POTW will
rarely be able to locate the sources of "interference" (i.e., who is putting
what into its system and causing what impact). The POTW system is
treated, in effect, as a receiving basin. Abatement of these effects is
subject to the same kind of "I'm not the one who is causing the problem"
arguments and difficulties of proof that plagued the pre-1972 efforts
at water pollution control.

Notwithstanding the difficulties with the standards noted above,
their implementation presents an even larger problem. First, only major
POTWs, which are defined as POTWs with a daily flow of more than
five million gallons and others with significant industrial inputs, are
required to have pretreatment programs. Thus, of the more than 15,000
POTWs in the United States about 1,500 have pretreatment programs,
which receive an estimated 82 percent of the total industrial wastewater
entering POTWs. The remaining 18 percent escape the program and
any pretreatment at all. Adding to this loophole is the fact that implementation of the program is left to the local POTW, whose responsibility
it is to identify the industries that are discharging wastewater into its
system, to permit those discharges, and to monitor compliance. Needless
to say, even if the purpose of a *national* discharge program were to offset
the political pressures placed on states to relax their programs, those
same pressures are even more formidable at the local level, producing
a wide variety of standards and levels of compliance among the local
municipal systems. The only federal monitoring requirements for categorical industries and their discharges to local systems are a *semi-annual*
report on these discharges and notification of any additional loads that
would interfere with the POTW. The EPA guidance manual also recommends random sampling of industrial effluent and on-site inspections, but these recommendations are not mandatory.

At the end of the treatment process, the POTWs are left with a
mountain of sludge that has been rendered useless, indeed hazardous,
by the introduction of industrial wastes. These contaminants prevent
the most obvious and beneficial uses of sewage sludges, while creating

considerable pressure for other disposal methods such as incineration and ocean dumping that produce additional environmental hazards. Of course, those toxics that are not "treated" and retained in the sludge are passed through to the receiving waters which turn out to be, in large part, the Nation's estuaries. No less than 37 percent of the toxics entering our Nation's waters and estuaries pass from industries through POTWs.

Virtually every review of the pretreatment program has rated it a failure. A 1980 Oversight Subcommittee report to the House Public Works Committee concluded that "[a]fter eight years of trying, EPA has been almost totally unsuccessful in implementing this requirement of the law." The hearings left the subcommittee "with considerable doubt" about the workability of the program. A 1982 report by the General Accounting Office found the program "undefined," resulting in "costly, inequitable and/or redundant treatment that may not address toxic pollution problems" and would "drain . . . scarce Federal, State and local pollution control resources." A 1987 Office of Technology Assessment report identified major, continuing shortcomings with the pretreatment program, none of them susceptible to any easy solution.

These findings speak for themselves. In 1987 Congress struck a glancing blow at the pretreatment program from the opposite end—the sludges. The EPA now must identify the toxics present in sewage sludge and specify numerical limits for them. The burden apparently will remain on the POTW, however, to work a reduction in toxic inputs from the sources. I wish them well. I am not holding my breath.

There comes a time in The Emperor's New Clothes when a village boy points out that the emperor, in fact, is not wearing any clothes at all. That boy was taking a fresh look. Similarly, it is difficult for us to take a fresh look at pretreatment and municipal treatment as a whole. Even the staunchest defender of the municipal treatment program, however, has to blanch at the introduction of industrial pollution into its municipal sewer systems. Even the most vigorous defender of federalism has to blush at a program that turns the responsibility for regulating nearly half of the toxic pollution discharged in this country over to 15,000 disparate, local POTWs. Notwithstanding the notions of "efficiency" that motivated this program, it has produced one set of categorical standards for those industries that discharge into POTWs, another set for those that do not, and an entirely new bureaucracy to implement and enforce these standards. In the name of "efficiency" we have doubled the number of pollution standards, multiplied the number of regulatory agencies by about a hundredfold, and managed, in the end, to so poison our sewage sludges that they have become, in reality, hazardous wastes.

As was once said of the American involvement in Vietnam, it is time to declare this program a victory and get out.

NOTES AND QUESTIONS

1. In another portion of his article Houck questions the basic premise of our nation's sewage disposal policy—the use of our waterways for sewage disposal, which he terms "a little barbaric." Noting that alternative technology exists, he decries "the illogic of first putting human wastes into our water and then building ever more expensive plants to take them out." Yet now that hundreds of billions of dollars have been invested in an infrastructure centered around waterborne sewage disposal, he appears to recognize, at least in the short term, the futility of his complaint. Id. at 381-383.

2. A 1989 study conducted by the Chesapeake Bay Foundation of the implementation of pretreatment programs by POTWs in the Chesapeake Bay watershed found "pervasive, substantial and longstanding violations of the law." The study found that none of the POTWs had complied with the requirement of EPA's general pretreatment standards that a minimum of ten local limits be set on discharges of toxic substances. Although POTWs are required to have NPDES permits for their discharges to surface waters, the study found that none of the permits issued to plants in the Chesapeake Bay area contained any limits on discharges of specific toxics, despite known toxic pollution problems in the area. The report did find that where pretreatment programs had been implemented properly, as in Hampton Roads, Virginia, they had resulted in dramatic improvements in the quality of discharges from POTWs. Chesapeake Bay Study Alleges Serious Flaws in Region's Industrial Pre-treatment Program, 19 Env. Rep. 2341 (1989).

3. Is the delegation of program authority to hundreds of local entities who subject to intense local political pressure from dischargers a basic flaw in the pretreatment program? Why doesn't support for a clean environment effectively counterbalance local political pressures? Many federal environmental programs are delegated to the states subject to EPA supervision. EPA must approve POTWs' pretreatment programs. Could the system of program delegation be improved, or is the concept fundamentally flawed? Is the basic problem that indirect dischargers are too numerous and mobile to be subject to effective enforcement action?

4. EPA estimated in 1989 that one-third of the 1,500 cities with pretreatment programs were not in compliance with federal requirements. Calling the pretreatment program "the weak link for removal of toxic pollution from our nation's waterways," EPA and the Justice Department launched a major pretreatment enforcement initiative in October 1989. EPA, DOJ Escalates Enforcement Actions Against Cities Lax on Industry Discharges, 20 Env. Rep. 1051 (1989). Major enforcement actions were brought against several cities (including Detroit, Phoenix,

El Paso, San Antonio, and Los Angeles) and numerous industrial dischargers for violating pretreatment requirements.

5. One reason why so many toxic materials are discharged into sewers is the domestic sewage exclusion to RCRA. RCRA's definition of "solid waste" expressly exempts "solid or dissolved materials in domestic sewage . . . or industrial discharges which are point sources subject to permits under section [402 of the Clean Water Act]," RCRA §1004(27). Thus, facilities can escape RCRA regulation by discharging hazardous waste into surface waters subject to NPDES permits, and they can escape the NPDES permit process by discharging such waste into sewers. Should the domestic sewage exclusion apply to hazardous waste mixed with sewage from an industrial plant rather than from residences? In Comite Pro Rescate de la Salud v. Puerto Rico Aqueduct and Sewer Authority, 888 F.2d 180 (1st Cir. 1989), the First Circuit said no.

6. The pretreatment program was supposed to prevent the domestic sewage exclusion from causing harm. When Congress amended RCRA in 1984, it required EPA to undertake a comprehensive study of the impact of the domestic sewage exclusion. RCRA §3018. EPA completed the Domestic Sewage Study in February 1986. The study found that many significant hazardous waste discharges are not covered by existing pretreatment regulations because they involve chemicals that, while hazardous, are not among the 126 priority pollutants covered by the Flannery Decree. The study noted that pretreatment standards for certain industries "do not specifically regulate nonpriority organics, despite the fact that many of these pollutants are discharged in significant concentrations and/or loadings." More than 38.3 million pounds of toxic pollutants discharged annually are not covered by effluent limits under the Flannery Decree, and more than 7.2 million pounds of hazardous metals and between 81 and 132 million pounds of priority hazardous organic constituents are discharged to POTWs even after implementation of categorical pretreatment standards. EPA, Report to Congress on the Discharge of Hazardous Wastes to Publicly Owned Treatment Works 7-9 (Feb. 1986).

7. In response to its Domestic Sewage Study, EPA in 1990 revised its pretreatment regulations. 55 Fed. Reg. 30,082 (1990). While the new regulations place numerical limits on discharges of ignitable waste, restrictions on discharges of toxic or corrosive waste are left largely to individual POTWs because of the variability of waste streams. The regulations require discharges of trucked or hauled waste to be made only at specific discharge points designated by POTWs. POTWs are required to use permits or an equivalent mechanism to control discharges by significant industrial users, who must file semiannual reports on their discharges. See Hogeland, EPA's Pretreatment Regulation Amendments: Forcing Enforcement, 20 Env. Rep. 889 (1990).

8. In a 1991 report to Congress, EPA reaffirmed its faith in the

pretreatment program, which it found had reduced discharges of metals by 95 percent and discharges of toxic organics by 40 to 75 percent. The report noted that data from the Toxic Release Inventory indicated that at least 680 million pounds of toxics were discharged to 1,700 POTWs in 1988. While the report found that two-thirds of POTWs had not established local limits for dischargers, it maintained that the flexibility afforded to POTWs by the program was necessary because of wide variations in local circumstances. EPA, Report to Congress on the National Pretreatment Program (1991).

WATER POLLUTION CONTROL: A PATHFINDER

The national regulatory program to control water pollution dates from enactment of the Federal Water Pollution Control Act of 1972, now known as the Clean Water Act, codified at 33 U.S.C. §§1251-1387. Significant amendments to the Act were adopted in 1977, 1981, and 1987, and its reauthorization is now under consideration by Congress. Other federal statutory authorities for controlling water pollution are outlined on page 877. The interface between these authorities is explored in Office of Technology Assessment, Wastes in Marine Environments (1987).

Data on the condition of the nation's waters are contained in the biennial water quality inventory that section 305 of the Act requires states to conduct. These data are summarized in EPA, National Water Quality Inventory: 1990 Report to Congress (1992). EPA regulations implementing the Clean Water Act are found at 40 C.F.R. pts. 100-140. Effluent guidelines and standards and general pretreatment regulations are at 40 C.F.R. pts. 400-471. EPA's section 404 regulations are at 40 C.F.R. pts. 230-233; the Army Corps of Engineers's section 404 and ocean dumping regulations are found at 33 C.F.R. pts. 323-330. EPA's ocean dumping regulations are at 40 C.F.R. pts. 220-229.

D. WATER QUALITY-BASED CONTROLS: THE REGULATORY "SAFETY NET"?

The enactment of the Clean Water Act in 1972 reflected a fundamental shift away from a water quality-based approach to pollution control toward an approach that emphasized technology-based effluent limitations. This shift was a result of a broad consensus that previous water quality-based control efforts had been a dismal failure. Congress recognized that ambient water quality standards were ineffective because of "the character of the standards themselves, which focused on the tolerable effects rather than the preventable causes of water pollution," EPA v. California State Water Resources Board, 426 U.S. 200, 202 (1976). To ensure that reductions were required in pollutant discharges, Congress required the use of certain technology-based levels of control regardless of the conditions of the receiving waters, as illustrated by Weyerhaeuser v. Costle, discussed in Chapter 4.

1. Water Quality Standards

Despite the Act's new emphasis on a technology-based approach, Congress did not entirely abandon water quality-based controls; rather, it retained them as a "safety net" to back up the technology-based controls on which the Act primarily relies. Section 301(b)(1)(C) requires that NPDES permits include any more stringent limits that are necessary to ensure compliance with water quality standards the states must adopt pursuant to section 303. To implement this requirement, section 303(d) directs states to identify waters with insufficient controls and to calculate limits on pollutant loadings necessary for such waters to achieve water quality standards with a margin of safety. For reasons discussed below, these provisions have not been widely implemented, though they are likely to be used more frequently in the future.

Section 302 provides another vehicle for water quality-based controls by dictating that they be used to prevent discharges from interfering with "attainment or maintenance" of desired levels of water quality. EPA has not used this provision because it also authorizes modifications of effluent limits if a discharger demonstrates that there is no reasonable relationship between their costs and benefits. §302(b)(2)(A).

Water quality standards have two components: (1) designated uses and (2) water quality criteria. "Designated uses" represent the purposes for which each water segment is to be protected (e.g., public water supplies, propagation of fish and wildlife, recreational purposes, agriculture). "Water quality criteria" reflect judgments concerning the degree of protection from individual pollutants that is necessary to attain designated uses. When combined with designated uses, water quality criteria yield what are called "water quality standards," limits on ambient concentrations of pollutants in particular classes of waters. States must review and revise their water quality standards every three years (a "triennial review") and they must submit such standards to EPA for review and approval. §303(c). EPA can modify state standards that fail to meet the requirements of the Act. §303(c)(4).

A. DESIGNATED USES AND ANTIDEGRADATION

While states have some flexibility in establishing designated uses for water segments, section 303(c)(2)(A) directs states in vague terms to "protect the public health or welfare, enhance the quality of water and serve the purposes" of the Act. States are directed to consider the use and value of their waters "for public water supplies, propagation of fish and wildlife, recreational purposes, and agricultural, industrial, and other purposes," including navigation. This ambiguous language has been interpreted by EPA to require at a minimum that water quality standards meet the "fishable/swimmable" goal of section 101(a)(2) unless that would result in "substantial and widespread economic and social impact." EPA also has required states to establish antidegradation policies designed to protect existing uses of water segments and to prevent deterioration of waters that exceed the purity necessary to meet the fishable/swimmable goal unless "necessary to accommodate important economic or social development." 40 C.F.R. §131.12(a)(2).

B. WATER QUALITY CRITERIA

States must adopt water quality criteria that specify maximum ambient levels of pollutants that will ensure that waters can be used for their designated purposes. EPA is directed by section 304(a) of the Act to develop water quality criteria, which can be used as a point of reference for states promulgating their own criteria. EPA's regulations do not specify for what pollutants criteria must be adopted by the states. Rather, they simply require that sufficient criteria be adopted "to protect the designated use."

The section 304(a) criteria are scientific recommendations that EPA develops for states to consider in adopting regulatory criteria under section 303(c). EPA's initial approach to issuing criteria was to conduct reviews of the scientific literature, which resulted in a series of water quality criteria documents, known as the 1968 "Green Book," the 1973 "Blue Book," and the 1976 "Red Book." The Agency subsequently adopted more formal procedures for developing water quality criteria, and it promulgated guidelines for developing criteria to protect aquatic life and human health when it published criteria for 64 toxic pollutants in November 1980. 45 Fed. Reg. 79,318. Additional criteria were adopted later, as summarized in the 1986 "Gold Book," called Quality Criteria for Water 1986.

EPA's criteria did not receive an enthusiastic response from the states. Four years after publication of the 1980 criteria, one observer noted:

> Fewer than 20 states have any numerical standards for toxics. Those that do usually cover only a handful of heavy metals, and almost never consider chronic effects or exposures through the food chain. Only 16 states have quantitative standards for lead, cyanide, and cadmium; fewer than 15 have a PCB standard. Most of these standards are less stringent than EPA's national criteria, and the range of values (for any given pollutant) across the states is considerable. [Banks, Dumping into Surface Waters: The Making and Demise of Toxic Discharge Regulations, in Beyond Dumping 47 (B. Piasecki, ed. 1984).]

The Reagan Administration contributed to the problem by expressing the view that EPA's criteria were scientifically flawed and should not be relied on by states.

In light of the uneven record of the states in adopting water quality criteria, the 1987 Amendments added a requirement that states adopt criteria for toxic pollutants "the discharge or presence of which could reasonably be expected to interfere with those designated uses adopted by the states." Because of the difficulty in determining what levels of pollutants are safe for attaining designated uses, some states adopted "narrative criteria" (e.g., "free from toxicity") that do not specify numerical limits on the ambient concentration of pollutants but that could form the basis for whole effluent toxicity testing. In the absence of numeric criteria for specific chemicals, however, it is virtually impossible to employ water quality standards to impose additional limitations on discharges to a water body. The 1987 Amendments addressed this problem by requiring that numerical criteria be adopted for toxic pollutants, section 303(c)(2)(B), though they also expressly endorse the use of biological assessment criteria when numerical criteria are not available.

Water Quality Criteria: Sources of Scientific Uncertainty

Over the years EPA has developed water quality criteria for many toxics and conventional pollutants, though the quality of the data supporting such criteria frequently has criticized. These criticisms reflect in part uncertainty about the impacts of a bewildering mix of toxic pollutants on aquatic organisms. Consider the enormous range of variables that aquatic toxicologists confront.

Only a small fraction of the tens of thousands of commonly used chemicals have been tested for toxicity to aquatic organisms. Moreover, many significant toxic pollutants (e.g., organotins) are not even on EPA's list of priority pollutants. Acquiring thorough test data concerning the effects of even a few hundred toxic substances would be a vast under-taking. Scientists necessarily must rely on certain simplified reference points for acute and chronic toxicity. Most testing has focused on acute toxicity because it is faster and easier to perform such tests. Thus, our knowledge of chronic effects is quite limited even though they may be more serious than acute effects.

Pollutants have different impacts on different organisms. Scientists typically select surrogate species of aquatic organisms, usually a crusta-cean, a fish, and an alga, for use in testing. But we know very little concerning the relative sensitivity of the hundreds of significant species of aquatic organisms in relation to surrogate species. Aquatic toxicity testing traditionally has had gross lethality as its endpoint of concern, rather than sublethal effects of toxics on the growth and development of aquatic organisms. Such testing may make scientists reasonably con-fident that they know what dose of a given chemical will kill half of the species within a given period of time (the LD50, for lethal dose for 50 percent of the test organisms), but it does not necessarily reveal much about the full range of effects of chemicals on complex ecosystems. Moreover, tests of specific substances on isolated species do not reflect actual conditions in a water body where organisms encounter complex mixtures of chemical compounds and are affected by ecosystem pro-cesses as well as interactions with other organisms.

The impacts of toxics vary with the characteristics of receiving waters. While EPA has issued water quality criteria for both freshwater and marine environments, in estuaries like the Chesapeake Bay, where freshwater rivers and streams meet the ocean, salinity fluctuates dra-matically over the seasons. Yet no water quality criteria have been issued by EPA for estuaries.

Water quality criteria generally are based on concern for protecting human health or aquatic life from concentrations of pollutants in the water. Yet scientists have discovered that concentrations of pollutants on the surface, or microlayer, of a water body often are very different from concentrations below. In such circumstances, compliance with water quality criteria in the water column may not be sufficient to protect the health of aquatic organisms, particularly those for whom the microlayer is unusually important. Similarly, many toxic pollutants accumulate in sediments in concentrations different from those in the water. They may become resuspended in the water when sediments are disturbed, and they may have severe impacts on benthic organisms. While there is vo-luminous research on contamination of aquatic sediments, EPA has not promulgated any sediment quality criteria, though some states have be-gun to do so. See Marcus, Managing Contaminated Sediments in Aquatic Environments: Identification, Regulation, and Remediation, 21 Envtl. L. Rep. 10020 (1991). EPA has been developing sediment quality criteria that are likely to be controversial because of their potential impact on the disposal of contaminated sediments disturbed during dredging operations.

There also are practical obstacles to implementing water quality-based approaches, including difficulties in detecting and measuring reliably the presence of certain substances in environmental media and the absence of low-cost screening techniques for scanning large numbers of samples. It can be difficult to measure with precision levels of individual pollutants in effluent discharges; it is even more difficult to determine how pollutant flows mix with receiving waters in order to assess the impact of individual discharges on overall water quality.

These factors greatly complicate the task of implementing water quality-based approaches to regulation. While scientists are working to develop improved toxicity testing procedures (the development of biomarkers that focus on cellular and biological responses in aquatic organisms eventually may enable scientists to develop a better early warning system), they simply are unable, given current knowledge, to predict reliably the impact of specific contaminants on specific aquatic resources. Uncertainty seems destined to dominate debates over the significance of changes in water quality for years to come.

2. The Impact of Water Quality Standards on Permit Limits

While section 301(b)(1)(c) of the Act provides that NPDES permits must include limits that will ensure that water quality standards are not violated, water quality standards rarely have resulted in the imposition of more stringent controls on dischargers. Professor Oliver Houck explains that water quality-based controls have "rarely worked" because of "almost insurmountable difficulties" in determining:

> (1) the desired "use" of a stream, which would determine its water quality, given the competing desire to attract industrial growth; (2) the actual water quality of a stream in all of its constituents; (3) the effects of a single discharge, as well as the cumulative and synergistic effects of multiple discharges, on this water quality; (4) the cause of any particular drop in water quality; and (5) an appropriate "allocation" of reductions among diverse causes, each of whom is legitimately pointing a finger at somebody else.

Professor Houck notes that in Louisiana, with almost one-fifth of its water areas identified as "water quality limited" (i.e., polluted), water quality upgrading has yet to lead to the revision of a single NPDES permit. Houck, Ending the War: A Strategy to Save America's Coastal Zone, 47 Md. L. Rev. 358, 389-390 (1988).

The process of translating water quality standards into more stringent controls on dischargers is conceptually daunting. Section 303(d) of the Clean Water Act requires states to identify those waters for which effluent limitations for nontoxic pollutants are not stringent enough to achieve water quality standards. In order to translate the water quality standards into more stringent controls on discharges for such waters, the Act requires states to establish total maximum daily loadings (TMDLs) of these pollutants, subject to EPA review and approval. §303(d).

TMDLs have rarely been employed in the past because of many of the same data and informational problems that have plagued water quality criteria. Courts have been reluctant to order EPA to promulgate TMDLs when states have failed to act. See Environmental Defense Fund v. Costle, 657 F.2d 275 (D.C. Cir. 1981); but see Scott v. City of Hammond, 741 F.2d 992 (7th Cir. 1984). Yet interest in TMDLs appears to be growing as gains from technology-based effluent limits are being exhausted. TMDLs are also of interest to those concerned about the contribution of nonpoint sources to water quality problems. As the General Accounting Office noted, the TMDL process

> [p]rovides a comprehensive approach to identifying and resolving water pollution problems regardless of the sources of pollution. If implemented, the TMDL process can provide EPA and the states with a complete listing of key water pollutants, the source of the pollutants, information on the amount of pollutants that need to be reduced, options between point and/or nonpoint approaches, costs to clean up, and situations where it may not be feasible to meet water quality standards. [GAO, Water Pollution— More EPA Action Needed to Improve the Quality of Heavily Polluted Waters 34-35 (1989).]

EPA reported that its regional offices approved more than 300 TMDLs in 1989, with more than half of the TMDLs being approved by Region IV (based in Atlanta) and none in three other regions. Alaska Center for the Environment v. Reilly, 762 F. Supp. 1422, 1425 (W.D. Wash. 1991). Oregon is developing 40 TMDLs as a result of a consent decree. Employing the TMDL approach to regulate dioxin in the Columbia River, Oregon denied a discharge permit to a proposed paper mill while tightening standards on existing dischargers. In *Alaska Center for the Environment* an environmental group sought to require EPA to issue federal TMDLs when the state of Alaska failed to do so. Alaska had not submitted a single TMDL to EPA, although it had told EPA in its biennial section 305(b) report that several hundred water segments were "impaired" or "threatened" by pollution. Finding it "highly unlikely that Congress intended an important aspect of the federal water pollution control scheme to be frustrated by the failure of a state to act," the court held that Alaska's failure to submit TMDLs for 11 years constituted the constructive equivalent of a determination that no TMDLs were necessary, thus triggering EPA's review obligations. 762 F. Supp. at 1428. While EPA argued that section 303(d)(2)'s 30-day deadline for EPA to promulgate a TMDL was wholly unrealistic, particularly given the absence of state data, the court indicated that EPA should not be absolved of responsibility for at least initiating a factfinding process.

Translating a TMDL into permit limits for individual dischargers is scientifically and politically difficult. To estimate the impact of specific discharges on water quality under varying flow conditions, states apply dilution factors and mixing zones that vary wildly, often reflecting political rather than scientific judgments. Houck, The Regulation of Toxic Pollutants Under the Clean Water Act, 21 Envtl. L. Rep. 10528, 10546 (1991). Moreover, while "EPA has unhelpfully offered several alternative methods for making TMDL allocations, ranging from even to uneven percentage reductions among sources," these do not "even begin to resolve the [political] difficulties of whether a state regulatory agency wishes to place its head into the jaws of a public utility, a chemical plant, or local farmer" in establishing permit limits. Id. When pollution crosses state boundaries, downstream states are eager to require dischargers in upstream states to bear the brunt of reductions required to meet water quality standards. In the case that follows, Oklahoma sought to prevent the issuance of an NPDES permit to an Arkansas wastewater treatment plant by arguing that the plant's discharges would contribute to violations of Oklahoma's water quality standards. After the Tenth Circuit overturned EPA's issuance of the permit, the Supreme Court granted review.

|| *Arkansas v. Oklahoma* ||
|| 112 S. Ct. 1046 (1992) ||

JUSTICE STEVENS delivered the opinion for a unanimous Court.

I

In 1985, the City of Fayetteville, Arkansas, applied to the EPA, seeking a permit for the City's new sewage treatment plant under the National Pollution Discharge Elimination System (NPDES). After the appropriate procedures, the EPA, pursuant to §402(a)(1) of the Act, 33 U.S.C. §1342(a)(1), issued a permit authorizing the plant to discharge up to half of its effluent (to a limit of 6.1 million gallons per day) into an unnamed stream in northwestern Arkansas. That flow passes through a series of three creeks for about 17 miles, and then enters the Illinois River at a point 22 miles upstream from the Arkansas-Oklahoma Border.

The permit imposed specific limitations on the quantity, content, and character of the discharge and also included a number of special conditions, including a provision that if a study then underway indicated that more stringent limitations were necessary to ensure compliance with Oklahoma's water quality standards, the permit would be modified to incorporate those limits.

Respondents challenged this permit before the EPA, alleging, inter alia, that the discharge violated the Oklahoma water quality standards. Those standards provide that "no degradation [of water quality] shall be allowed" in the upper Illinois River, including the portion of the River immediately downstream from the state line.

Following a hearing, the Administrative Law Judge (ALJ) concluded that the Oklahoma standards would not be implicated unless the contested discharge had something more than a "mere de minimis impact" on the State's waters. He found that the discharge would not have an "undue impact" on Oklahoma's waters and, accordingly, affirmed the issuance of the permit.

On a petition for review, the EPA's Chief Judicial Officer first ruled that §301(b)(1)(C) of the Clean Water Act requires an NPDES permit to impose any effluent limitations necessary to comply with applicable state water quality standards. He then held that the Act and EPA regulations offered greater protection for the downstream state than the ALJ's "undue impact" standard suggested. He explained the proper standard as follows:

[A] mere theoretical impairment of Oklahoma's water quality standards— i.e., an infinitesimal impairment predicted through modeling but not expected to be actually detectable or measurable—should not by itself block the issuance of the permit. In this case, the permit should be upheld if the record shows by a preponderance of the evidence that the authorized discharges would not cause an actual *detectable* violation of Oklahoma's water quality standards. Id., at 117a (emphasis in original).

On remand, the ALJ made detailed findings of fact and concluded that the City had satisfied the standard set forth by the Chief Judicial Officer. Specifically, the ALJ found that there would be no detectable violation of any of the components of Oklahoma's water quality standards. The Chief Judicial Officer sustained the issuance of the permit.

Both the petitioners (collectively Arkansas) and the respondents in this litigation sought judicial review. Arkansas argued that the Clean Water Act did not require an Arkansas point source to comply with Oklahoma's water quality standards. Oklahoma challenged the EPA's determination that the Fayetteville discharge would not produce a detectable violation of the Oklahoma standards.

The Court of Appeals did not accept either of these arguments. The court agreed with the EPA that the statute required compliance with Oklahoma's water quality standards, see 908 F.2d 595, 602-615 (CA10 1990), and did not disagree with the Agency's determination that the discharges from the Fayetteville plant would not produce a detectable violation of those standards. Id., at 631-633. Nevertheless, relying on a theory that neither party had advanced, the Court of Appeals reversed the Agency's issuance of the Fayetteville permit. The court first ruled that the statute requires that "where a proposed source would discharge effluents that would contribute to conditions currently constituting a violation of applicable water quality standards, such [a] proposed source may not be permitted." Id., at 620. Then the court found that the Illinois River in Oklahoma was already degraded, that the Fayetteville effluent would reach the Illinois River in Oklahoma, and that that effluent could "be expected to contribute to the ongoing deterioration of the scenic [Illinois R]iver" in Oklahoma even though it would not detectably affect the River's water quality. . . .

II

. . . In Milwaukee v. Illinois, 451 U.S. 304 (1981) (*Milwaukee II*), we held that the 1972 Amendments to the Federal Water Pollution Control Act [preempted the federal common law of nuisance]. In addressing Illinois' claim that Milwaukee's discharges into Lake Michigan constituted a nuisance, we held that the comprehensive regulatory regime created by the 1972 Amendments preempted Illinois' federal common law remedy. We observed that Congress had addressed many of the problems we had identified in *Milwaukee I* by providing a downstream State with an opportunity for a hearing before the source State's permitting agency, by requiring the latter to explain its failure to accept any recommendations offered by the downstream State, and by authorizing the EPA, in its discretion, to veto a source State's issuance of any permit if the waters of another State may be affected. *Milwaukee II,* 451 U.S., 325-326.

In *Milwaukee II,* the Court did not address whether the 1972 Amendments had supplanted *state* common law remedies as well as the federal common law remedy. See id., at 310, n.4. On remand, Illinois argued that §510 of the Clean Water Act, 33 U.S.C. §1370, expressly preserved the State's right to adopt and enforce rules that are more stringent than federal standards. The Court of Appeals accepted Illinois' reading of §510, but held that that section did no more than to save the right and jurisdiction of a state to regulate activity occurring within the confines of its boundary waters. Illinois v. Milwaukee, 731 F.2d 403, 413 (CA7 1984), cert. denied, 469 U.S. 1196 (1985).

This Court subsequently endorsed that analysis in International Paper Co. v. Ouellette, 479 U.S. 481 (1987), in which Vermont property owners claimed that the pollution discharged into Lake Champlain by a paper company located in New York constituted a nuisance under Vermont law. The Court held the Clean Water Act taken "as a whole, its purposes and its history" preempted an action based on the law of the affected State and that the only state law applicable to an interstate discharge is the "law of the State in which the point source is located." Id., at 493, 487. Moreover, in reviewing §402(b) of the Act, the Court pointed out that when a new permit is being issued by the source State's permit-granting agency, the downstream state

> does not have the authority to block the issuance of the permit if it is dissatisfied with the proposed standards. An affected State's only recourse is to apply to the EPA Administrator, who then has the discretion to disapprove the permit if he concludes that the discharges will have an undue impact on interstate waters. §1342(d)(2). . . . Thus the Act makes it clear that affected States occupy a subordinate position to source States in the federal regulatory program.

Id., at 490-491.

Unlike the foregoing cases, this litigation involves not a State-issued permit, but a federally issued permit. . . .

III

. . . Section 402(b) authorizes each State to establish "its own permit program for discharges into navigable waters within its jurisdiction." 33 U.S.C. §1342(b). Among the requirements the state program must satisfy are the procedural protections for downstream States discussed in *Ouellette* and *Milwaukee II*. See 33 U.S.C. §§1342(b)(3), (5). Although these provisions do not authorize the downstream State to veto the issuance of a permit for a new point source in another State, the Administrator retains authority to block the issuance of any state-issued permit that "is outside the guidelines and requirements of the Act." 33 U.S.C. §1342(d)(2).

In the absence of an approved state program, the EPA may issue an NPDES permit under §402(a) of the Act. (In this case, for example, because Arkansas had not been authorized to issue NPDES permits when the Fayetteville plant was completed, the permit was issued by the EPA itself.) The EPA's permit program is subject to the "same terms, conditions, requirements" as a state permit program. 33 U.S.C. §1342(a)(3). Notwithstanding this general symmetry, the EPA has construed the Act as requiring that EPA-issued NPDES permits also comply with §401(a). That section, which predates §402 and the NPDES, applies to a broad category of federal licenses, and sets forth requirements for "[a]ny applicant for a Federal license or permit to conduct any activity including, but not limited to, the construction or operation of facilities, which may result in any discharge into the navigable waters." 33 U.S.C. §1341(a). Section 401(a)(2) appears to prohibit the issuance of any federal license or permit over the objection of an affected State unless compliance with the affected State's water quality requirements can be insured.

IV

The parties have argued three analytically distinct questions concerning the interpretation of the Clean Water Act. First, does the Act require the EPA, in crafting and issuing a permit to a point source in one State, to apply the water quality standards of downstream States? Second, even if the Act does not *require* as much, does the Agency have the statutory authority to mandate such compliance? Third, does the Act provide, as the Court of Appeals held, that once a body of water fails to meet water quality standards no discharge that yields effluent that reach[es] the degraded waters will be permitted?

In this case, it is neither necessary nor prudent for us to resolve the first of these questions. In issuing the Fayetteville permit, the EPA assumed it was obligated by both the Act and its own regulations to ensure that the Fayetteville discharge would not violate Oklahoma's standards. As we discuss below, this assumption was permissible and reasonable and therefore there is no need for us to address whether the Act requires as much. Moreover, much of the analysis and argument in the briefs of the parties relies on statutory provisions that govern not only federal permits issued pursuant to §§401(a) and 402(a), but also state permits issued under §402(b). It seems unwise to evaluate those arguments in a case such as this one, which only involves a federal permit.

Our decision not to determine at this time the scope of the Agency's statutory *obligations* does not affect our resolution of the second question, which concerns the Agency's statutory *authority*. Even if the Clean Water Act itself does not require the Fayetteville discharge to comply with Oklahoma's water quality standards, the statute clearly does not limit the EPA's authority to mandate such compliance.

Since 1973, EPA regulations have provided that an NPDES permit shall not be issued "[w]hen the imposition of conditions cannot ensure compliance with the applicable water quality requirements of all affected States." 40 CFR §122.4(d) (1991); see also 38 Fed. Reg. 13533 (1973); 40 CFR §122.44(d) (1991). Those regulations—relied upon by the EPA in the issuance of the Fayetteville permit—constitute a reasonable exercise of the Agency's statutory authority.

Congress has vested in the Administrator broad discretion to establish conditions for NPDES permits. Section 402(a)(2) provides that for EPA-issued permits "[t]he Administrator shall prescribe conditions for such permits to assure compliance with the requirements of [§402(a)(1)] and *such other requirements as he deems appropriate.*" 33 U.S.C. §1342(a)(2) (emphasis supplied). Similarly, Congress preserved for the Administrator broad authority to oversee state permit programs:

> No permit shall issue . . . if the Administrator . . . objects in writing to the issuance of such permit as being outside the guidelines and requirements of this chapter.

33 U.S.C. §1342(d)(2).

The regulations relied on by the EPA were a perfectly reasonable exercise of the Agency's statutory discretion. The application of state water quality standards in the interstate context is wholly consistent with the Act's broad purpose, "to restore and maintain the chemical, physical, and biological integrity of the Nation's waters." 33 U.S.C. §1251(a). Moreover, as noted above, §301(b)(1)(C) expressly identifies the achievement of state water quality standards as one of the Act's central objectives. The Agency's regulations conditioning NPDES permits are a well-tailored means of achieving this goal.

Notwithstanding this apparent reasonableness, Arkansas argues that our description in *Ouellette* of the role of affected States in the permit process and our characterization of the affected States' position as "subordinate," see 479 U.S., at 490-491, indicates that the EPA's application of the Oklahoma standards was error. We disagree. Our statement in *Ouellette* concerned only an affected State's input into the permit process; that input is clearly limited by the plain language of §402(b). Limits on an affected State's direct participation in permitting decisions, however, do not in any way constrain the *EPA's* authority to require a point source to comply with downstream water quality standards.

Arkansas also argues that regulations requiring compliance with downstream standards are at odds with the legislative history of the Act and with the statutory scheme established by the Act. Although we agree with Arkansas that the Act's legislative history indicates that Congress intended to grant the Administrator discretion in his oversight of the issuance of NPDES permits, we find nothing in that history to indicate that Congress intended to preclude the EPA from establishing a general requirement that such permits be conditioned to ensure compliance with downstream water quality standards.

Similarly, we agree with Arkansas that in the Clean Water Act Congress struck a careful balance among competing policies and interests, but do not find the EPA regulations concerning the application of downstream water quality standards at all incompatible with that balance. Congress, in crafting the Act, protected certain sovereign interests of the States; for example, §510 allows States to adopt more demanding pollution-control standards than those established under the Act. Arkansas emphasizes that §510 preserves such state authority only as it is applied to the waters of the regulating State. Even assuming Arkansas's construction of §510 is correct, cf. id., at 493, that section only concerns *state* authority and does not constrain the *EPA's* authority to promulgate reasonable regulations requiring point sources in one State to comply with water quality standards in downstream States.

For these reasons, we find the EPA's requirement that the Fayetteville discharge comply with Oklahoma's water quality standards to be a reasonable exercise of the Agency's substantial statutory discretion. Cf. Chevron U.S.A., Inc. v. Natural Resources Defense Council, Inc., 467 U.S. 837, 842-845 (1984).

V

The Court of Appeals construed the Clean Water Act to prohibit any discharge of effluent that would reach waters already in violation of existing water quality standards. We find nothing in the Act to support this reading.

The interpretation of the statute adopted by the court had not been advanced by any party during the agency or court proceedings. Moreover, the Court of Appeals candidly acknowledged that its theory "has apparently never before been addressed by a federal court." 908 F.2d, at 620, n.39. The only statutory provision the court cited to support its legal analysis was §402(h), see id., at 633, which merely authorizes the EPA (or a state permit program) to prohibit a publicly owned treatment plant that is violating a condition of its NPDES permit from accepting any additional pollutants for treatment until the ongoing violation has been corrected. See 33 U.S.C. §1342(h).

Although the Act contains several provisions directing compliance with state water quality standards, see, e.g., 33 U.S.C. §1311(b)(1)(C), the parties have pointed to nothing that mandates a complete ban on discharges into a waterway that is in violation of those standards. The statute does, however, contain provisions designed to remedy existing water quality violations and to allocate the burden of reducing undesirable discharges between existing sources and new sources. See, e.g., 33 U.S.C. §1313(d). Thus, rather than establishing the categorical ban announced by the Court of Appeals—which might frustrate the construction of new plants that would improve existing conditions—the Clean Water Act vests in the EPA and States broad authority to develop long-range, area-wide programs to alleviate and eliminate existing pollution. See, e.g., 33 U.S.C. §1288(b)(2).

To the extent that the Court of Appeals relied on its interpretation of the Act to reverse the EPA's permitting decision, that reliance was misplaced.

VI

The Court of Appeals also concluded that the EPA's issuance of the Fayetteville permit was arbitrary and capricious because the Agency misinterpreted Oklahoma's water quality standards. The primary difference between the court's and the Agency's interpretation of the standards derives from the court's construction of the Act. Contrary to the EPA's interpretation of the Oklahoma standards, the Court of Appeals read those standards as containing the same categorical ban on new discharges that the court had found in the Clean Water Act itself. Although we do not believe the text of the Oklahoma standards supports the court's reading (indeed, we note that Oklahoma itself had not advanced that interpretation in its briefs in the Court of Appeals), we reject it for a more fundamental reason—namely, that the Court of Appeals exceeded the legitimate scope of judicial review of an agency adjudication. . . .

As discussed above, EPA regulations require an NPDES permit to comply "with the applicable water quality requirements of all affected States." 40 CFR §122.4(d) (1991). This regulation effectively incorporates into federal law those state law standards the Agency reasonably determines to be applicable. In such a situation, then, state water quality standards—promulgated by the States with substantial guidance from the EPA and approved by the Agency—are part of the federal law of water pollution control.

Two features of the body of law governing water pollution support this conclusion. First, as discussed more thoroughly above, we have long recognized that interstate water pollution is controlled by *federal* law. Recognizing that the system of federally approved state standards as applied in the interstate context constitutes federal law is wholly consistent with this principle. Second, treating state standards in interstate controversies as federal law accords with the Act's purpose of authorizing the EPA to create and manage a uniform system of interstate water pollution regulation.

Because we recognize that, at least insofar as they affect the issuance of a permit in another State, the Oklahoma standards have a federal character, the EPA's reasonable, consistently held interpretation of those standards is entitled to substantial deference. In this case, the Chief Judicial Officer ruled that the Oklahoma standards—which require that there be "no degradation" of the upper Illinois River—would only be violated if the discharge effected an "actually detectable or measurable" change in water quality.

This interpretation of the Oklahoma standards is certainly reasonable and consistent with the purposes and principles of the Clean Water Act. As the Chief Judicial Officer noted, "unless there is some method for measuring compliance, there is no way to ensure compliance." Moreover, this interpretation of the Oklahoma standards makes eminent sense in the interstate context: if every discharge that had some theoretical impact on a downstream State were interpreted as "degrading" the downstream waters, downstream States might wield an effective veto over upstream discharges.

The EPA's application of those standards in this case was also sound. On remand, the ALJ scrutinized the record and made explicit factual findings regarding four primary measures of water quality under the Oklahoma standards: eutrophication, aesthetics, dissolved oxygen, and metals. In each case, the ALJ found that the Fayetteville discharge would not lead to a detectable change in water quality. He therefore concluded that the Fayetteville discharge would not violate the Oklahoma water quality standards. Because we agree with the Agency's Chief Judicial Officer that these findings are supported by substantial evidence, we conclude that the Court of Appeals should have affirmed both the EPA's construction of the regulations and the issuance of the Fayetteville permit. . . .

The court incorrectly concluded that the EPA's decision was arbitrary and capricious. This error is derivative of the court's first two errors. Having substituted its reading of the governing law for the Agency's, and having made its own factual findings, the Court of Appeals concluded that the EPA erred in not considering an important and relevant fact—namely, that the upper Illinois River was (by the court's assessment) already degraded.

As we have often recognized, an agency ruling is "arbitrary and capricious if the agency has . . . entirely failed to consider an important aspect of the problem." Motor Vehicle Mfrs. Assn. of United States, Inc. v. State Farm Mutual Automobile Insurance Co., 463 U.S. 29, 43 (1983). However, in this case, the degraded status of the River is only an "important aspect" because of the Court of Appeals' novel and erroneous interpretation of the controlling law. Under the EPA's interpretation of that law, what matters is not the River's current status, but rather whether the proposed discharge will have a detectable effect on that status. If the Court of Appeals had been properly respectful of the Agency's permissible reading of the Act and the Oklahoma standards, the court would not have adjudged the Agency's decision arbitrary and capricious for this reason.

In sum, the Court of Appeals made a policy choice that it was not authorized to make. Arguably, as that court suggested, it might be wise to prohibit any discharge into the Illinois River, even if that discharge would have no adverse impact on water quality. But it was surely not arbitrary for the EPA to conclude—given the benefits to the River from

the increased flow of relatively clean water and the benefits achieved in
Arkansas by allowing the new plant to operate as designed—that allow-
ing the discharge would be even wiser. It is not our role, or that of the
Court of Appeals, to decide which policy choice is the better one, for it
is clear that Congress has entrusted such decisions to the Environmental
Protection Agency.

Accordingly, the judgment of the Court of Appeals is Reversed.

NOTES AND QUESTIONS

1. Does the Court's decision effectively make EPA the umpire of
interstate water pollution disputes? EPA issued the permit challenged
in this case only because Arkansas had not been delegated the authority
to operate the NPDES program. If Arkansas had been delegated such
authority and had issued the permit, how, if at all, would Oklahoma's
ability to challenge the permit have been affected?

2. The Court declined to decide whether EPA was required to apply
the water quality standards of the downstream state, holding only that
it was permissible for EPA to do so. Suppose that in another case an
upstream state's discharges did cause "an actually detectable or measurable change in water quality" in violation of a downstream state's standards. Could EPA legally issue a permit for such discharges?

3. How did Arkansas interpret *Ouellette*? How does the Court distinguish it from the instant case? Could Oklahoma file a common law
nuisance action against the Arkansas plant? In light of *Ouellette*, what
law would apply to such an action?

4. Arkansas argued that it would be chaotic to require dischargers
to comply with the water quality standards of all downstream states
because some rivers flow through numerous states (e.g., the Mississippi).
Is this a valid concern? Could a downstream state effectively dictate the
terms of NPDES permits in upstream states by adopting very stringent
water quality standards? What checks exist to prevent downstream states
from adopting unreasonably stringent water quality standards?

5. What would Oklahoma need to show in order to convince EPA
to deny issuance of the permit? In light of the Court's decision, do the
existing violations of Oklahoma's water quality standards have any significance for dischargers in upstream states?

3. The "Toxic Hot Spots" Program: A Return to a Water Quality Approach

Having largely abandoned the water quality-based approach to pollution
control in 1972, Congress in 1987 sought to resuscitate it as a supplementary mechanism for controlling toxic water pollutants. The 1987

Amendments added section 304(*l*) to the Clean Water Act, which directs EPA and the states to identify waters with toxic problems and to impose new controls on sources of discharges to them. Recognizing that eventual compliance with BAT standards will be insufficient in some waters to meet water quality standards for toxics, Congress required states to identify such waters and to develop "individual control strategies" for reducing toxic discharges to them.

Section 304(*l*)(1) requires all states to submit three lists of waters to EPA: (A) waters that "cannot reasonably be anticipated to attain or maintain (i) water quality standards for such waters . . . due to toxic pollutants" (the A(i) list), "or (ii) that water quality which shall assure protection of public health, public water supplies, agricultural and industrial uses, and the protection and propagation of a balanced population of shellfish, fish and wildlife, and allow recreational activities in and on the water" (the A(ii) list), and (B) waters not expected to meet water quality standards even after application of BAT due entirely or substantially to toxic pollution from point sources (the B list). Note that the A(i) list is considerably broader than the B list because it apparently includes waters not expected to meet water quality standards due to toxic pollution from nonpoint sources. The A(ii) list is the broadest because it includes even some waters that comply with state water quality standards if they are not expected to meet the water quality goals of the Act.

For each water segment "included on such lists," states are required to determine "the specific point sources discharging any such toxic pollutant which is believed to be preventing or impairing such water quality and the amount of each such toxic pollutant discharged by each such source," §304(*l*)(1)(C). Although EPA initially interpreted this requirement as applicable only to waters on the B list, in Natural Resources Defense Council v. EPA, 915 F.2d 1314, 1319 (9th Cir. 1990), the Ninth Circuit held that the reference to "lists" made it applicable to waters on any of the three lists. Thus, states must identify point sources contributing to waters whose impairment is not primarily a product of point source pollution. The court reserved judgment on the question of whether individual control strategies had to be applied to waters on each of these lists.

Section 304(*l*)(1)(D) requires each state to develop "an individual control strategy which . . . will produce a reduction in the discharge of toxic pollutants from point sources identified by the State, . . . which reduction is sufficient, in combination with existing controls on point and nonpoint sources of pollution, to achieve the applicable water quality standard as soon as possible, but not later than 3 years after the date of the establishment of such strategy." §304(*l*)(1)(D). "The effect of the individual control strategies is simply to expedite the imposition of water-quality-based limitations on polluters—limitations which otherwise would have had to be imposed when the polluters' NPDES permits expired."

Natural Resources Defense Council v. EPA, 915 F.2d 1314, 1319 (9th Cir. 1990). Because the states were given until June 1989 to submit their lists to EPA, the control strategies are supposed to produce achievement of water quality standards by June 1992.

Implementation of section 304(*l*)'s water quality-based "regulatory safety net" has been hampered by the same informational and conceptual obstacles that traditionally have bedeviled such approaches to pollution control. Monitoring data are sparse, and few states have adopted comprehensive water quality criteria for toxics. Many state standards for toxics are expressed in narrative, rather than numerical, form and are difficult to translate into individual controls. Section 303(c)(2) requires states to adopt numerical water quality criteria for all priority pollutants that could reasonably be expected to interfere with the state's designated uses for which EPA has published water quality criteria under 304(a). By February 1990 only six states had established criteria for toxic pollutants fully acceptable to EPA. By November 1991 EPA determined that 35 states had complied with §303(c)(2). But the Agency found it necessary to propose to adopt its own numeric criteria for priority toxic pollutants in 22 states. 56 Fed. Reg. 58,240 (1991).

States varied considerably in the thoroughness of their section 304(*l*) lists of affected waters and dischargers. In the initial lists submitted in February 1989 some states listed dozens of affected water segments while others listed none. (The number of dischargers included in the states' lists ranged from zero to 180.) Much of the variation in state responses stemmed from differences in the quantity and quality of toxics monitoring data as well as differences in the thoroughness with which existing data sources were reviewed. Few states have adequate toxics monitoring programs; some responded to perceived data inadequacies with a "what-you-don't-know-won't-hurt-you" approach, incorporating only a few waters or dischargers for which the data were clearest. Many failed to consult additional data sources including the Toxics Release Inventory established by the Emergency Planning and Community Right-to-Know Act. Although EPA had encouraged states to include waters affected by any toxic pollutant, rather than just the 126 priority pollutants, few states did so. Yet Connecticut found that nearly one-half of the facilities causing toxic pollution problems in the state's waters were discharging non-priority pollutants such as biocides, water conditioning agents, and oxidative treatment chemicals. Surface Water "Toxic Hot Spots" Program Criticized as Inadequate at Senate Hearing, 20 Envtl. Rep. 466 (1989).

In June 1989 EPA released a list of 595 water segments and 879 dischargers that the states, supplemented by EPA, had determined to be subject to the requirements of section 304(*l*). Id. Several environmental and citizen groups have petitioned EPA to add certain water segments and dischargers to the lists. Petitions by Environmental Groups Could Add Many Industries to 304(*l*) List, 20 Env. Rep. 627 (1989). EPA has advised the states that it interprets the section 304(*l*) requirements to be part of a continuing process and that the section 304(*l*) lists should be reviewed and updated periodically as additional data about toxic pollution become available. Some states disagree, arguing that the statutory language indicates that it should be a one-time process.

EPA's regulations provide that an individual control strategy (ICS) should be incorporated into a final NPDES permit and be supported by documentation indicating that the permit's effluent limits are sufficient to meet applicable water quality standards. 40 C.F.R. §123.46(c). EPA is required to approve or disapprove ICSs submitted by states. If EPA disapproves a state's control strategy, or if the state fails to submit one, EPA must develop and implement its own control strategy. While section 509(b)(1) makes EPA's promulgation of any individual control strategy reviewable in the United States Courts of Appeals, at least three circuits have held that it does not authorize such review of EPA decisions to *approve* state ICSs. Borough of St. Marys v. EPA, 945 F.2d 67 (3d Cir. 1991); Roll Coater, Inc. v. Reilly, 932 F.2d 668 (7th Cir. 1991); Boise Cascade Corp. v. EPA, 942 F.2d 1427 (9th Cir. 1991).

Lack of comprehensive monitoring data continues to be a major obstacle to implementation of the section 304(*l*) program. While the National Water Quality Inventory indicates that one-third of monitored waters have elevated levels of toxics, EPA reports that only one-third of all river miles and less than one-half of all lake acres have even been evaluated to determine if they attain their designated uses. Many of the evaluations "did not include the chemical-specific information necessary to identify the priority toxic pollutants which pose a threat to designated uses." 56 Fed. Reg. 58,420, 54,431 (1991). The monitoring data that do exist in each state usually are not kept in any consistent format or in any central location.

Although initially pessimistic about the prospects for success with section 304(*l*) because of its water quality-based approach, Houck, Ending the War: A Strategy to Save America's Coastal Zone, 47 Md. L. Rev. 358, 390-391 (1988), Professor Houck now reserves judgment, noting that 520 ICSs had been approved by May 1991. Houck, Regulation of Toxic Pollutants Under the Clean Water Act, 21 Envtl. L. Rep. 10528, 10548 (1991). While he notes that ICSs, like TMDLs, rely on easily manipulable calculations relating ambient pollution levels back to effluent limits, Professor Houck acknowledges that section 304(*l*) has at least accelerated this process.

NOTES AND QUESTIONS

1. EPA has been far more aggressive in implementing the requirements of section 304(*l*) for reviewing ICSs and state submissions of lists

of waters affected by toxics than it has been in developing the additional effluent limits required by section 304(m). What might explain this apparent difference in attitude?

2. While 45 states have adopted aquatic life criteria for the priority pollutants, the criteria vary dramatically in stringency from state to state. Fewer than one-third of the aquatic life criteria use numbers derived from EPA's guidance. "The most striking feature of the toxic criteria that have been adopted—aside from the delay in their adoption—is their variation from state to state." Houck, above, at 10543. Why would Congress and EPA tolerate substantial variations among the states in the stringency of their water quality standards? Will this allow state governments to compete against each other to attract industry by promising looser regulation?

WATER POLLUTION CONTROL: A PROBLEM EXERCISE

For nearly 60 years a gun manufacturer has owned a skeet shooting club on a point overlooking a river. It is estimated that 4 million pounds of lead shot and 11 million pounds of clay targets have fallen into the river from the club's 12 shooting ranges. Neither the gun manufacturer nor the club (nor any of the club's patrons) has ever had an NPDES permit authorizing them to discharge lead shot or clay targets into the river. Sediment samples taken from the riverbed have found high levels (up to 640,000 parts per million) of lead, a priority toxic pollutant under the Clean Water Act, and tests on shellfish and waterfowl in the area have found elevated levels of lead in their tissues and blood that the U.S. Fish and Wildlife Service believes to be acutely toxic.

Question One. Has the club or any of its patrons violated the Clean Water Act by discharging pollutants into surface waters without an NPDES permit? See §§502(12), 502(14) and Romero-Barcelo v. Brown, 643 F.2d 835 (1st Cir. 1981), revd. on other grounds sub nom. Weinberger v. Romero-Barcelo, 456 U.S. 305 (1982). What, if anything, would you advise the club to do to ensure that neither it nor its patrons violates the law?

Question Two. Suppose that an NPDES permit were required in these circumstances, and that an existing, industry-wide effluent standard has been promulgated for the firearms manufacturing industry. Should this standard be incorporated into the club's permit? Could the club obtain a variance from this standard? How? What alternative limits could be incorporated into the club's permit to reduce lead contamination of the river?

Question Three. Suppose that the state has adopted water quality criteria for lead to protect aquatic life and human health based on measurements of the presence of lead in the water column. If levels of lead in the water column are higher than permissible under these criteria, how, if at all, could section 303(d) or section 304(*l*) of the Clean Water Act be used to place additional restrictions on the club's discharges?

Question Four. Suppose that, despite the high concentration of lead in the sediment, lead levels in the water column do not exceed the criteria, although benthic organisms have accumulated dangerous levels of lead, apparently due to feeding on material in the sediment. Could the state be required to adopt sediment quality criteria under section 303(c)(2)(B)?

Question Five. If lead levels in the river violate the existing water quality standard for lead, can a foundry in another state located upstream from the club obtain an NPDES permit to discharge lead into the same river?

E. CONTROL OF POLLUTION FROM NONPOINT SOURCES

In many parts of the country, pollution from nonpoint sources has become an even more serious problem than discharges from industrial facilities and municipal sewage systems. Indeed, as we have achieved some success in controlling point sources, multiple, diffuse emissions of runoff from streets, farms, mines, and other areas have become a severe problem, accounting for nearly 100 percent of sediment, 82 percent of nitrogen, and 84 percent of phosphorous reaching the nation's surface waters. Conservation Foundation, State of the Environment: A View Toward the Nineties (1987). The pollutants contributed by these so-called nonpoint sources can be every bit as damaging as point source discharges. Nonpoint sources contribute not only sediment and nutrients, but also oil and gasoline that run off city streets, pesticides and toxic chemicals that wash off farmlands, and heavy metals, bacteria, and oxygen-demanding substances contributed by other sources. EPA estimates that nonpoint sources account for 65 percent of the contamination in polluted rivers, 76 percent in impaired lakes, and 45 percent in damaged estuaries. EPA, Environmental Progress and Challenges: EPA's Update 46 (1988). Most states identify nonpoint sources as the primary reason why water quality in their state is insufficient to support designated uses.

1. Federal Programs Encouraging Control of Nonpoint Sources

The severe impact of nonpoint sources on the water pollution problem has been recognized for decades. Yet nonpoint sources have largely escaped federal regulation because of political, administrative, and technical difficulties. Effective controls on nonpoint sources may require changes in land use management practices that are fiercely resisted by local authorities. Land use regulation is traditionally a local function, but so was waste disposal and sewage treatment until Congress recognized an overriding national interest. In fact, Congress came very close to requiring a national land use program in the early 1970s. President Nixon proposed legislation that would have required all states to develop land use control programs as a condition for obtaining federal funds for highway, airport, and recreation projects. Although the legislation passed the Senate, it ultimately failed to win enactment due to resistance to federal involvement in an area traditionally left to local decision-making. Congress largely abandoned efforts to mandate land use controls as a means for protecting the environment. Congress sought to encourage areawide planning in section 208 of the FWPCA, but it exempted nonpoint sources from the NPDES permit program created in 1972. The 1977 Amendments to the Clean Air Act expressly prohibited EPA from demanding regulation of parking and siting of buildings that attract large numbers of vehicles as a strategy for controlling air pollution.

Controls on nonpoint sources are also difficult to develop and administer. Recall that EPA initially deemed it infeasible to regulate pollution generated by runoff even when conveyed through a point source and argued that it could not "instruct each individual farmer on his farming practices." Natural Resources Defense Council v. Costle, 568 F.2d 1369, 1380 (D.C. Cir. 1977). Although the development of measures to control nonpoint pollution continues, examples of successful control efforts remain rare. Senate Panel Told Examples of Success Rare in Efforts to Limit Non-Point Source Pollution, 22 Env. Rep. 651 (1991). As the problem grows, Congress is adopting an increasingly aggressive federal posture toward nonpoint controls, though states are finding it difficult to adopt new programs without additional resources. The history of federal efforts is described below.

A. SECTION 208 OF THE CLEAN WATER ACT

The federal Clean Water Act has relied on a largely ineffective planning process to address nonpoint sources of water pollution. Section

208 requires states to develop areawide waste treatment management
plans that are to include a process for identifying nonpoint sources and
establishing feasible control measures. Plans prepared under section 208
are to be submitted to EPA in return for receiving federal financial
assistance for the planning process. Decisions concerning NPDES permits and section 404 permits are supposed to be consistent with the
section 208 plans.

In 1977 Congress added section 208(j), which authorized the Department of Agriculture to share the costs of "best management practices" adopted by farmers to control nonpoint pollution. This program
has not been widely embraced by farmers. William Rodgers argues that
"[p]aying half of the cleanup costs of practices not otherwise commend-
ing themselves to the users is an unlikely way to provoke a steady raid
on the treasury. Altruism, discounted by fifty percent, has yet to win its
first political campaign." Rodgers, Environmental Law—Air and Water
141 (1986). See also Note, State and Federal Land Use Regulation: An
Application to Groundwater and Nonpoint Source Pollution Control, 95
Yale L.J. 1433 (1986).

The section 208 planning process also is widely viewed as a failure.
While many states have some form of areawide planning, section 208
did not stimulate significant new programs. EPA eventually stopped
providing financial assistance to states under section 208.

B. THE FOOD SECURITY ACT OF 1985

In 1985 Congress adopted a farm bill that addressed agriculture's
contribution to nonpoint pollution. The Food Security Act of 1985 (FSA),
16 U.S.C. §§3811-3813, requires farmers on highly erodible lands to
adopt conservation plans employing "best management practices" to control runoff and to implement those plans by 1995 on penalty of loss of
federal farm subsidies. Because of the importance of such subsidies, this
provision has been described as "so severe as to make the plans tanta-
mount to a regulatory requirement." Rosenthol, Going with the Flow:
USDA's Dubious Commitment to Water Quality, 5 Envtl. Forum 15, 16
(Sept.-Oct. 1988). The FSA also denies federal farm subsidies to those
who plant on wetlands converted to cropland after December 23, 1985.
See Tripp and Dudek, The Swampbuster Provisions of the Food Security
Act of 1985: Stronger Wetland Conservation if Properly Implemented
and Enforced, 16 Envtl. L. Rep. 10120 (1986).

Despite publicly embracing protection of water quality as a major
new goal, the Soil Conservation Service has yet to take this mission to
heart. It abandoned its initial proposal to adopt minimum performance
requirements for erosion control and authorized farmers to exempt
themselves from practices they deem too expensive. Conservation plans

are now routinely approved, to the chagrin of competing farmers who took the early requirements seriously. Enforcement of the "swamp buster" provisions has not been vigorous—only five farmers lost benefits during the first three years of the program. Rosenthol, above, at 16. See also Malone, A Historical Essay on the Conservation Provisions of the 1985 Farm Bill: Sodbusting, Swampbusting, and the Conservation Reserve, 34 U. Kan. L. Rev. 577 (1986).

C.   SECTION 319 OF THE CLEAN WATER ACT

When it amended the Clean Water Act in 1987, Congress added control of nonpoint sources to the declaration of national goals in section 101 of the Act and adopted more aggressive measures to encourage the adoption of such controls. Congress mandated that controls on runoff that passes through municipal and industrial storm sewers be strengthened by requiring EPA to bring storm water discharges into the NPDES permit program pursuant to section 402(p). These permits are to prohibit non-storm-water discharges into storm sewers and to include "controls to reduce the discharge of pollutants to the maximum extent practicable."

The most significant provision in the 1987 Amendments that addresses control of nonpoint sources is the addition of section 319. In a pattern similar to that used in section 304(*l*) for controlling toxic hot spots, section 319 requires states to prepare "state assessment reports" that identify waters that cannot reasonably be expected to meet water quality standards because of nonpoint pollution and significant sources of that pollution for each affected water segment. §319(a)(1). States also are required to develop "state management programs" that include identification and implementation of best management practices to control nonpoint pollution from significant sources of it. The management programs must contain schedules for implementation of best management practices, certification that sufficient state authority exists to implement the program, and identification of sources of financial support.

The state assessments reports and management programs are submitted to EPA for review and approval. States with approved programs are eligible for federal financial assistance to implement their programs. By 1992 EPA had approved assessment reports for all states and management programs for 44 states. EPA, Managing Nonpoint Pollution: Final Report to Congress on section 319 (1992). Section 319(g) attempts to address the problem of interstate nonpoint source pollution by authorizing states to petition EPA to convene interstate management conferences to develop interstate agreements for controlling nonpoint source pollution. Interstate agreements reached at management conferences are to be incorporated in the respective states' management programs.

The 1987 Amendments generated early enthusiasm for the section 319 program by authorizing $400 million for grants to state programs. However, only a small portion of these funds actually were appropriated, and only $40 million in grants was distributed during the next three years. Noting that 47 states already had some kind of program for addressing nonpoint sources, Oliver Houck argued that "[a]t best, the new federal funding will encourage more specificity in these plans. More likely, it will produce a second round of paperwork comparable to that generated in the early 1970s by the hauntingly similar section 208 program." Houck, Ending the War: A Strategy to Save America's Coastal Zone, 47 Md. L. Rev. 358, 377 (1988). Houck may well have been prescient. While EPA maintains that it is too early to tell whether the section 319 program has made a difference to water quality, the administration's fiscal year 1993 budget proposes a 50 percent further reduction in funding for the program.

While continuing its efforts to encourage the development of nonpoint source controls, EPA views decisions concerning the adoption of control measures as the responsibility of state and local governments. When it reported on its strategy for controlling nonpoint source pollution in 1989, EPA described its role as "to support and reinforce States and local governments as they make difficult decisions that affect water quality, to improve their knowledge of sound land use practices, and to provide the scientific basis on which they make these public policy decisions." EPA, National NPS Agenda 5 (1989). Measures to control nonpoint sources are widely considered to be a key issue in reauthorization of the Clean Water Act.

D. SECTION 1455b OF THE COASTAL ZONE MANAGEMENT ACT

The pattern of increasing federal encouragement for nonpoint source control programs continued in November 1990 when Congress added section 1455b to the Coastal Zone Management Act, 16 U.S.C. §1455b. This amendment requires states with federally approved coastal zone management programs to develop a Coastal Nonpoint Pollution Control Program subject to review and approval by EPA and NOAA. While the addition of yet another planning requirement to federal law is not in itself of any great significance, section 1455b of the CZMA requires far more specificity in nonpoint source management planning than ever before. States must identify land uses that contribute to degradation of threatened or impaired coastal waters and critical areas adjacent to them and provide for the implementation of additional management measures to achieve water quality standards. "Management measures" are defined in section 1455b(g)(5) as "economically achievable measures for the control of" nonpoint sources "which reflect the greatest degree of pollutant reduction achievable through the application of the best available nonpoint pollution control practices, technologies, processes, siting criteria, operating methods, or other alternatives."

The state programs must conform to guidance EPA is required to issue by May 1992. Six minimum requirements for such guidance are outlined in section 1455b(g)(2), which reflects an effort to require as much specificity as possible in the description of control measures, regulatory targets, pollutants to be controlled, costs, effects of controls, and monitoring. EPA issued proposed guidance in June 1991, 56 Fed. Reg. 27,618 (1991), which it described as emphasizing pollution prevention measures (e.g., siting requirements for marinas, a ban on the use of pressure-treated wood below water) and management systems for reducing nonpoint pollution. State programs must be submitted to EPA and NOAA for approval by November 1995.

Representatives of coastal states are not convinced that these new requirements will stimulate states to adopt significant new control measures. Kerry Kehoe of the Coastal States Organization argues that states simply do not have the resources to implement new programs. Comment Period for Non-Point Source Guidance Extended as Industry, States Question Feasibility, 22 Env. Rep. 1795 (1991). Congress appropriated only $2 million of the $6 million it authorized for the program. States Express Concern About Lack of Funds Needed to Carry Out New Non-Point Guidance, 22 Env. Rep. 1347 (1991). State officials think this would provide most states only enough money for "a nice slide slow" and that even punitive sanctions would have little impact on state programs.

NOTES AND QUESTIONS

1. Why have the various federal programs that address nonpoint pollution not been more successful in controlling the problem? Is it a product of their largely nonregulatory approach, which seeks to encourage states voluntarily to adopt control measures? Is the problem primarily one of inadequate state resources to invest in control measures? Or is it a lack of technical information concerning what control measures actually work?

2. Are nonpoint sources so numerous and diverse that a regulatory program is simply infeasible? While there are hundreds of thousands of farmers, the Soil Conservation Service (SCS) has an army of 13,000 employees who are charged with providing technical advice and support to them. The SCS and others maintain that only a voluntary approach will induce change in agricultural practices because farmers resist any program that smacks of regulation. Note that the FSA's requirements apply to farmers who wish to continue to receive federal subsidies. Could

this be a sufficient "carrot" to permit the SCS to implement an aggressive "best management practices" program?

3. Experience with implementation of the Food Security Act of 1985 illustrates how difficult it can be to effect change in mission-oriented agencies. It is not surprising that the U.S. Department of Agriculture and the SCS have failed to implement aggressively the environmental measures in the FSA, because to a large extent their traditional missions have been at odds with environmental goals. The General Accounting Office noted in a 1990 report that "[t]he conflict is especially true for USDA because some of its most significant programs and activities in-volve—and even promote—activities that can lead to increased nonpoint source pollution," including farm commodity price supports and timber harvesting programs. GAO, Greater EPA Leadership Needed to Reduce Nonpoint Source Pollution 15 (1990). What could be done to make these agencies more sympathetic to environmental concerns? Consider the federal consistency provisions in section 319(k) of the Clean Water Act, which one commentator has recommended that EPA use to insist that SCS alter its policies to incorporate water quality concerns. Rosenthol, Going with the Flow: USDA's Dubious Commitment to Water Quality, 5 Envtl. Forum 15, 18 (Sept.-Oct. 1988). What would be required to implement this suggestion?

4. The 1987 Amendments to the Clean Water Act were described by President Reagan in the message accompanying his unsuccessful veto as potentially "the ultimate whip hand for Federal regulators." Do you agree? Examine the provisions of section 402(p) for controlling urban nonpoint pollution and the provisions of section 319 for controlling nonpoint pollution generally. To what extent do these impose pollution control requirements enforceable by citizen suit? Past efforts to control nonpoint sources sought to create incentives for state action, without much effect. How do the provisions of section 319 differ from those of section 208?

5. Nonpoint sources are significant contributors of toxic pollutants. A study of the Hudson River found that nonpoint sources added more than 6,000 times the PCBs, 700 times the lead, cadmium, and mercury, and 23 times the oil and grease than did point sources. Non-point Sources Found by INFORM to Be Major Contributors of Toxics to Hudson River, 18 Env. Rep. 1263 (1987). Compare the approach to nonpoint source control embodied in section 319 with the new program for controlling toxic pollution contained in section 304(*l*). How do the two programs relate to one another? Does the toxic hot spots program created by section 304(*l*) of the 1987 Amendments require the application of in-dividual control strategies for nonpoint sources of toxic pollution? EPA initially said no, but a federal appeals court has required the Agency to reconsider this decision. Natural Resources Defense Council v. EPA, 915

F.2d 1314 (9th Cir. 1990). Can toxic pollutants be controlled effectively without some form of regulation of nonpoint sources?

6. Airborne pollution is another significant source of water pollution in some areas. For example, according to some studies airborne sources may amount to one-fourth or more of pollutants going into the Chesapeake Bay. Tripp and Oppenheimer, Restoration of the Chesapeake Bay: A Multi-State Institutional Challenge, 47 Md. L. Rev. 425 (1988). Is there any existing authority for imposing more stringent requirements on air polluters in order to protect water quality?

7. Can TMDLs be used to require the adoption of controls on nonpoint sources? In the few instances in which they have been used in the past, most TMDLs have been applied to impose controls only on point sources. NRDC staffers have argued that TMDLs should be used to require reductions in nonpoint source contributions. They cite Oregon's use of TMDLs to require cities and three counties to adopt watershed management plans to control runoff into the Tualatin River. Thompson, Poison Runoff!, 6 Envtl. Forum 10 (July-Aug. 1989).

8. Section 319(m)(1) of the Clean Water Act requires EPA to report to Congress on progress toward reducing pollution from nonpoint sources. In its first report implementing this provision, EPA noted a significant increase in state initiatives to control nonpoint sources. EPA, Activities and Programs Implemented Under Section 319 of the Clean Water Act as Amended by the Water Quality Act of 1987 (Dec. 1987). Some of the examples cited by EPA include: user fees on fertilizers and chemicals in Iowa to finance research and implementation of controls to protect water quality; development and use of a Lake Vulnerability Index for evaluation of large construction projects in Maine; implementation of a land retirement program for erodible croplands in Minnesota; and implementation of highly effective animal waste management systems in Utah.

2.   State Land Use Controls and Water Quality

Despite a strong tradition of local control over land use decisions, many states have adopted legislation to protect sensitive resources and to manage development. In 1972 Florida adopted an Environmental Land and Water Management Act that seeks to control development and to protect critical areas through a state planning system and a state land acquisition program. See Reed, Keynote Address: Florida's Environmental Future: Issues '88 Conference, 3 J. Land Use & Envtl. L. 305 (1987). In 1973, Oregon imposed the toughest statewide controls on development and created a state agency, the Department of Land Conservation and Development, to oversee their implementation. For two decades Vermont has required significant development projects to be reviewed by regional boards to determine their conformance with environmental and land use regulations. Hawaii has planning requirements that attempt to preserve prime agricultural land from development.

While early land use legislation was a product of diverse concerns about growth management, new programs have been directed more specifically at control of nonpoint sources of water pollution. In 1984 Maryland adopted a Critical Areas Act designed to protect the Chesapeake Bay from nonpoint pollution through statewide controls on development in a 1,000-foot buffer zone around the Bay. Like Oregon's program, Maryland's law authorizes a state commission to adopt strict criteria governing development, and localities are directed to conform their land use decisions to the statewide criteria. These laws seek to balance environmental values with strong constituencies for growth and development and private control of property. The ultimate effectiveness of these laws depends on strong public support and political leadership. The complex political forces that affect their implementation are explored in the excerpt that follows from Robert Liberty of 1000 Friends of Oregon. Liberty provides some unusually revealing insights into the politics of land use controls based on experience with Oregon's program.

> ## Liberty, The Oregon Planning Experience: Repeating the Success and Avoiding the Mistakes
> ### 1 Md. Pol. Stud. 45, 46-55 (1988)

PRESSURES WORKING AGAINST THE IMPLEMENTATION OF STATE LAND USE POLICIES

A. Unnatural Selection Favoring the Spineless: The Loss of Will Within the Administering Commission and Agency

Franklin Roosevelt observed that new agencies lose their value after a few years as a sense of mission is replaced by a bureaucratic preoccupation with self-preservation. This was confirmed by Oregon's experience during the implementation phase with respect to both the appointed commission and its staff.

By 1982, nine years after the creation of the Land Conservation and Development Commission (LCDC), a majority of its members no longer seemed to care whether the law was enforced or even understood the law they were supposed to administer. The Commission and its staff, the Department of Land Conservation and Development (DLCD), began to bow to political pressures against full implementation of the state's land use policies ("Goals"). . . .

B. Guardian Foxes: The Politics of Local Plan Administration

After the adoption of legislation, many advocates of the new state role in Oregon seemed to forget one of the reasons for the state planning legislation: the failure of local governments to regulate land development so that the resulting land uses served the public as well as private interests. The endlessly repeated cries of outrage over the loss of purely local control over land use decisions dulled memories of what was obvious at the time of adoption: As measured against the broader public interest, purely "local control" didn't work.

Furthermore, the advocates of local control succeeded in casting the system of local decision-making as the epitome of grassroots democracy. Local control was said to be desirable because it reflected local policy preferences and benefitted from local residents' knowledge of local conditions. But that is not how "local control" has expressed itself in reality in Oregon during the administration phase. Consider one citizen's experience with his county's planning commission:

> On the surface, the process appears straightforward. I received timely notices of hearings once the county was aware of my testimony. Decisions appeared to be reached in public and in an unbiased manner.
>
> Much more, however, was going on below the surface. For instance, the developer freely admitted in an open hearing that he engaged in ex parte contacts by providing private tours of the development site for planning commission members before the vote was taken.
>
> The effect of that activity may have been profound. For instance, the Commission chairman tried to prevent me from testifying at the Stage III hearing. When that failed, he did not pay attention when I presented my testimony. My integrity was questioned and a concerted effort was made to humiliate me personally. It was apparent from the outset that the planning commission had its mind closed to any possible alternative but that the development should be approved. . . .

Experience showed that the foxes did not make good guards for the henhouse. The state stepped in to discipline the foxes by adopting a planning process and state policies to guide local decisions toward the greater good. But the enactment of these programs did not transform the foxes into guardian angels—they are still foxes and they still get hungry.

Subversion Through Facilitation: Why Local Government Planners Don't Administer Local Plans so as to Implement State Policy

To understand why a new planning law can be undercut in the implementation and administration phases, it is necessary to understand the forces acting on planners employed by local governments. Those forces result in a bias to favor approval of applications, rather than denial. This is a serious problem with respect to geographic areas where conservation is the chief objective. These forces are a mix of the professional, psychological and political. . . .

[E]nforcement of the law is actually [planners'] most important role. Planners' attitude toward substantive planning laws, as far as I can determine, is one of mild irritation and sometimes contempt because these laws, drafted by nonplanners, constrain the exercise of their professional discretion.

Sometimes planners seem unacquainted with the very concept of legally binding substantive planning. They do not appear to understand that where the law mandates a particular result the mediation of a compromise is in fact a negotiated violation of the law. Instead of acting to carry out the will of the people as expressed by the legislature, many local government planners blithely overrule the legislature in order to "facilitate" an outcome desired by an individual applicant, an outcome which is often at the expense of public policy.

The professional orientation of planners as "facilitators" is reflected in their treatment of applicants as clients. This seems to have its roots in professional training and the psychology of relationships. When a person appears before the front desk, it is natural and appropriate for the planner to provide assistance. Giving people the unpleasant news that you cannot issue them a permit for their house or other development can be emotionally taxing. The planner's anxiety level is even higher when he or she has been lectured by the elected official about the need to accommodate the public. When the planner has been specifically told to approve all applications that are not opposed by someone, then there will be little doubt as to the outcome. . . .

At least in Oregon, because of the tendency to approve projects, appeals tend to come from opponents. Thus planners come to identify the unpleasantness of appeals with opponents of projects.

Oregon's state land use policies were subject to public hearings before a wide audience and repeatedly debated by the state commission and the legislature. The resulting Goals were a set of compromises reflecting and articulating the public interest. But the local plans intended to implement those Goals are rarely applied in a public arena. Instead they are applied in the peace and quiet of local planning department offices. In this setting the effects of professional training, interpersonal dynamics and political pressure can have free play, at the expense of the public interest so painstakingly debated and articulated before the state legislature and state commission.

THE VIRTUES OF INFLEXIBILITY AND PETTIFOGGING: HOW AMBIGUITY IN STATE CRITERIA AND LOCAL LAND USE PLANS ERODES STATE POLICY

"Flexibility" has been the rallying cry of critics of Oregon's planning law. The rhetorical justifications for "flexibility" are (1) to allow more creative planning approaches which will achieve the same objectives or (2) because some state criterion does not fit local conditions. Early in the planning program, flexibility is also demanded to allow deviation from state policy so as to accommodate differing local policy preferences. Those are the formal justifications for flexibility. Whether those justifications are disingenuous efforts to subvert the state policies is an important political question. But "flexibility" can be criticized based on its results independently from the underlying political motivations.

Let us compare the implementation of two important policy objectives in the Oregon planning program. The first example concerns the interpretation of the statute which strictly limits houses and land divisions in exclusive farm use ("EFU") zones. The statute allows "dwellings customarily provided in conjunction with farm use." My organization, 1000 Friends of Oregon, reads this to mean "farmers' houses." A "farmer" is someone who makes all or most of his income from farming. This simple proposition has been so fiercely resisted by counties that it has resulted in years of litigation, repeated efforts at clarification in LCDC rule-making, and pitched battles in the legislature. In the implementation phase almost all counties resisted adopting numeric gross income criteria to define "farm" or "farmer" for purposes of implementing the statutory criteria. As a result, almost anything can qualify as a "farm dwelling." . . .

Clarity of expression is critical during the administration phase. All the high ideals and consensus on concepts expressed by the state commission are worthless at the time of administration of the plans. The only thing which counts is what is printed in the plans. Those regulatory words are themselves the embodiment of the state's policy. They must be clear and strong enough that they will work to safeguard those policies, even in the absence of a powerful human advocate. They will not be effective without a painstaking attention to detail that the less experienced will denounce as "pettifogging." A little pettifogging at the outset can provide a great deal of clarity later.

ALL THE NEWS PRINTED TO GIVE YOU FITS:
THE DECLINE IN FAVORABLE PRESS COVERAGE DURING
THE POST-ADOPTION PHASES

The political basis for planning tends to be eroded during the
implementation and administration phases because the press coverage
during this period tends to be less favorable.

Let us consider a pair of stories about the adoption and then the
implementation of the legislation creating the Columbia River Gorge
National Scenic Area. The first article appeared in the Portland Oregonian in November 1986 when President Reagan signed the bill creating the Columbia Gorge National Scenic Area:

> WASHINGTON—President Reagan Monday signed a bill to protect
> the scenic wonders of the Columbia Gorge, climaxing a lengthy effort in
> Congress to protect the spectacular river canyon that beckoned Oregon
> trail pioneers. . . .
> "After nearly 30 years of effort, I'm ecstatic that we have secured
> protection for a gem of God's creation," [Senator Mark] Hatfield said
> moments after learning from high-ranking White House officials that
> Reagan probably would sign the measure.
> "It has been an uphill battle, won only by consensus, compromise
> and commitment," he said. "The obvious winners are the thousands of
> residents of the gorge—who will no longer be subjected to political turmoil
> and indecision—and the tens of thousands of Americans and people the
> world over who will forever be able to view this beautiful area."

The second article appeared in the Oregonian seventeen months
later. It describes the effort to apply the standards in the statute prohibiting new commercial uses in the Gorge to a couple wishing to establish
a bed-and-breakfast in their house:

Business Dream Now Political Nightmare

> BRIDAL VEIL—Laurel Slater's dream of turning her family's Co-
> lumbia River Gorge homestead into a bed-and-breakfast business has turned
> into a bitter lesson on Columbia River Gorge politics.
> Slater's yearlong effort to win approval for her business has sparked
> a heated political battle involving the U.S. Forest Service, the Multnomah
> County Planning Commission and the Friends of the Gorge.
> The Friends of the Gorge, an organization that was instrumental in
> the creation of the Columbia River Gorge National Scenic Area, is fighting
> to block Slater's plans. . . .
> "My idea was to share my historical traditions with my 2 year-old
> son, Timothy, and my husband," she said. "Then I encountered so many
> roadblocks and felt like I was a ping-pong ball for the governmental agen-

cies and the Friends of the Gorge. I soon learned that there are so many chances for a dream to be shot down."

These articles are representative of similar changes in the tone of newspaper stories about Oregon's planning effort between the mid-1970's to the early 1980's.

The political repercussions of the latter type of articles are obvious: The erosion of public support for a program which is perceived as a heartless bureaucracy operating to destroy the simple aspirations of plain folks like the readers. . . .

RESISTING THE PRESSURES: CRAFTING COUNTERBALANCING FORCES

Oregon's experience should become a basis for the development of forces, legal, administrative or political, which counterbalance the pressures to erode or evade state policies.

With regard to the loss of zeal in the administering staff, the use of planning benchmarks could provide the necessary resurgence of public support for the conservation (and other) objectives in the planning program. The benchmarks are measures or standards for evaluating its success (e.g., numeric standards on the water quality of Chesapeake Bay or a reduction in the rate of conversion of farmland). Outside consultants would then periodically measure the degree to which the benchmarks are being met and report the results to the governor, the state commission, the legislature and the public. The discussion over the failings identified in the reports could provide the political support needed to make changes in the staffing and policies of the commission.

There is little which can be done to correct the problems associated with local administration of state conservation policies, short of stripping local governments of these powers and having the conservation policies administered by state employees who would not be subject to the same kinds or levels of pressure to grant permits.

Local governments need to be reminded that their role in land use decisions is derived from the legislature and is not a divine right. It is appropriate to caution them that the retention of their remaining land use planning powers is contingent on the quality of their performance.

The problem with local government planners' orientation toward applicants could be addressed in part through the adoption or amendment of a code of ethics for planners. This code should include a statement regarding local government and state agency planners' responsibility to administer the state law and local plans as intended and to remain strictly impartial between parties in the planning process. In addition, the state commission's staff should provide periodic education programs for local planners, explaining the purposes of the legislation and their role in achieving those objectives. Finally, planners could be made personally liable to any project applicant or opponent who is damaged as a result of private assurances made by planners which were clearly contrary to state and local land use regulations.

To prevent destructive ambiguities in local plans, the state commission could adopt a rule requiring all local plans to contain "clear and objective" standards for all, or most, of the critical program components. At the local level, lawyers and planners could be recruited to conduct mock appeal hearings on hypothetical applications for developments under key plan provisions. These hearings would be designed to explore the extent to which proposed wording can be read to authorize developments clearly not within the intent of the state criteria or the local board. As an alternative to simulation, the state commission should be able to require revisions to local plan standards whenever actual litigation reveals these standards inadequate as tools for implementing the state policies.

NOTES AND QUESTIONS

1. How generalizable are Liberty's conclusions? To what extent are the implementation problems he identifies illustrations of more general problems of regulatory policy we have discussed, for example, the difficulty of defining regulatory targets, trade-offs between local flexibility and uniformly vigorous implementation of controls, and regulation creating incentives for strategic behavior by winners and losers?

2. What can other states learn from the Oregon experience? Are the same political obstacles to implementation of land use controls likely to be present in most states? How practical are the reform proposals advanced by Liberty? Could citizen suit provisions help counter the loss of political will? Consider who would be the likely plaintiffs and defendants and whether state and local governments would be likely to support such provisions.

3. Are the forces that operated to resist implementation in Oregon also influences at the national level? Does a combination of shared federal and state authority increase or diminish the factors Liberty describes?

4. State land use controls inevitably generate political controversy. Oregon's program has survived several vigorous repeal initiatives. Vermont's program also has been controversial, though it now is widely credited with having spared the state from the national crisis in the banking industry. Vermont is the only New England state not to experience a bank failure. Many attribute this to the long review process required by the state land use control program, which discouraged developers who were poorly capitalized. Feder, Vermont Development Laws

May Have Saved Its Banks, N.Y. Times, Mar. 4, 1991, at D1. Not only were fewer projects developed in Vermont, but the ones that were built "ended up being more marketable because they were more environmentally attractive." Id. at D3. By contrast, banks in New Hampshire, where development has been left largely unregulated, have experienced severe financial problems, having more than twice the rate of nonperforming loans than Vermont.

5. Because land use controls affect property values, any time a group can succeed in changing the rules, windfall gains and losses may accrue to developers and property owners. Studies of the economic impact of land use controls have found that restrictions on development increased the value of existing residential developments while reducing the return to holders of undeveloped property and agricultural lands. Beaton, Living by the Shore: The Impact of Zoning on Housing Costs, 1 Md. Poly. Stud. 57 (1988). Thus, there are always economic incentives encouraging efforts to change such laws. Could these incentives be countered effectively by tax policies that seek to recoup some of the gains and to compensate for the losses generated by such programs?

6. Some state and local governments allow a form of trading to offset the economic impact of land use regulation. Development rights taken from one area or building can be applied to another. Is this approach less subject to the implementation problems described by Liberty? Another approach that has been suggested is to provide for trading of discharge rights within a watershed between point and nonpoint sources. For example, farmers agreeing to reduce their runoff could sell nitrogen discharge rights to municipal sewage treatment plants. Economists argue that this would be a more efficient approach to controlling water pollution because it allows the market to allocate controls where they are the least costly. Do you see any problems with a program authorizing trading between point and nonpoint sources of water pollution?

3. Land Use Controls and the Takings Clause

Efforts to control nonpoint source pollution through land use controls often collide with the expectations of property owners who wish to develop their land. Some property owners argue that restrictions on development constitute a "taking" of private property rights for which the government is required by the Constitution to provide compensation. The Fifth Amendment to the U.S. Constitution provides that "private property [shall not] be taken for public use, without just compensation." While judicial interpretations of the takings clause have followed a tortuous and often confusing course, the federal courts recently have been more sympathetic to takings claims in a manner that many believe threatens land use controls.

Takings disputes raise fundamental questions concerning the meaning of property and the relationship between individuals and the state in our constitutional system. They have been a prominent part of challenges to environmental regulation since long before current controversies arose. In 1973 the Council on Environmental Quality conducted a comprehensive study of the takings issue and devoted an entire chapter of its fourth annual report to it. CEQ observed that the rise of environmental regulation was spurring the development of a new conception of property rights that views land as a scarce resource that society has an interest in protecting for future generations. CEQ, Environmental Quality 149-150 (1973).

A. THE EVOLUTION OF TAKINGS DOCTRINE

The original understanding of the scope of the takings clause appears to have been more limited than subsequent judicial interpretations of it. There is evidence indicating that the framers of the Constitution envisioned the takings clause as applying only to actual physical invasions of property. Note, The Origins and Original Significance of the Just Compensation Clause, 94 Yale L.J. 694 (1985). In early cases, government actions that caused a physical invasion of property were considered takings, Pumpelly v. Green Bay Co., 80 U.S. 166 (1871) (construction of dam that flooded private property), while regulations that severely affected the value of property were not. Mugler v. Kansas, 123 U.S. 623 (1887) (compensation not required to brewery owners for ban on production and sale of alcoholic beverages), Hadacheck v. Sebastian, 239 U.S. 394 (1915) (upholding ordinance banning use of brick kilns in neighborhood where brick manufacturer operates).

The notion that regulation could constitute a taking if it destroyed the value of property even if it did not involve a direct physical invasion was endorsed by the Supreme Court in Pennsylvania Coal Co. v. Mahon, 260 U.S. 393 (1922). A statute prohibiting the mining of coal in a manner that could cause the subsidence of homes on the surface was held to be a taking because it effectively abolished the value of underlying mineral rights. Justice Holmes declared that "while property may be regulated to a certain extent, if regulation goes too far it will be recognized as a taking." 260 U.S. at 415. While noting that "[g]overnment hardly could go on if to some extent values incident to property could not be diminished without paying for every such change in general law," Holmes argued that damage to a private residence was not the kind of public nuisance that must yield to the state's police power. In dissent, Justice Brandeis argued that the regulation was not a taking, but rather "merely the prohibition of a noxious use."

Six years after deciding *Pennsylvania Coal*, the Supreme Court upheld a Virginia law that had been used to require that a tree on private land be destroyed in order to prevent the spread of infection to trees owned by others. In Miller v. Schoene, 276 U.S. 272 (1928), the Supreme Court stated that "[w]here the public interest is involved, preferment of that interest over the property interest of the individual, to the extent even of its destruction, is one of the distinguishing characteristics of every exercise of the policy power which affects property." 276 U.S. at 280. This decision, which did not even cite *Pennsylvania Coal*, suggests that even regulations that result in the destruction of property will not be viewed as takings if they are designed to protect against at least some kinds of harm.

In subsequent decisions the Court has had a difficult time articulating a coherent rationale for determining when regulation "goes too far" in reducing the value of property. As Justice Brandeis pointed out in his dissent in *Pennsylvania Coal*, the results of a diminution-in-value approach to takings can be manipulated depending on how broadly one defines the property from which the reduction in value is calculated (e.g., the particular coal subject to the regulation or all property owned by the mining company). The economic effect of a regulation that reduces by one-tenth the value of ten identical lots owned by a private party is the same as one that entirely destroys the value of one such parcel.

In Penn Central Transportation Co. v. City of New York, 438 U.S. 104 (1978), the Court conceded that it had been unable to develop any single formula for determining when a taking had occurred. It listed a series of factors to be considered, including the economic impact of the regulation on "distinct, investment-backed expectations" and the nature and purpose of the interference with property. Upholding an ordinance that barred development of air rights above a railroad terminal against a takings challenge, the Court indicated that transferable development rights might be applied to offset economic losses otherwise sufficient to constitute a taking.

In the early 1980s the Supreme Court continued to recognize that physical invasions of property can constitute takings, Loretto v. Teleprompter Corp., 458 U.S. 419 (1982), but it was reluctant to define under what circumstances a regulation so diminished the value of property as to constitute a taking. In a series of decisions, the Court avoided confronting this question by holding that before plaintiffs could pursue takings claims, they had to apply for variances and exhaust state remedies. Agins v. Tiburon, 447 U.S. 255 (1980); McDonald, Sommer & Frates v. County of Yolo, 477 U.S. 340 (1986). When it finally confronted the regulatory takings question, it was sharply divided.

In Keystone Bituminous Coal Association v. DeBenedictis, 480 U.S. 470 (1987), the Court held, by a 5-4 margin, on facts virtually identical to those of *Pennsylvania Coal Co.*, that a restriction on the exercise of mineral rights was not a taking because it was designed to protect public health and safety by minimizing damage to surface areas. Justice Rehnquist argued in dissent that the law's purposes were too broad to fall within the nuisance exception, which has never before been allowed to completely extinguish the value of property. In two other decisions that term the Court gave a sympathetic reception to takings claims. In Nollan v. California Coastal Commission, 483 U.S. 825 (1987), the Court held that the California Coastal Commission could not require a landowner to grant an easement over beachfront property as a condition for approving a building permit without providing compensation. In First English Evangelical Lutheran Church v. County of Los Angeles, 482 U.S. 304 (1987), the Court held that a damages remedy was available if a prohibition on rebuilding in a flood plain constituted a "temporary taking."

B. Land Use Regulation and Takings Disputes Today

As we have seen, environmental regulation tends to create winners and losers because neither pollution nor environmental regulation is evenhanded in its impact. Takings jurisprudence today can be viewed as a judicial effort to make largely ad hoc assessments of the fairness of government regulation based on its impact on individual property owners. In this sense, it represents a constitutional check on regulations whose impact is unusually concentrated on certain "losers." Yet, mindful of Justice Holmes's admonition that government "hardly could go on" if it had to provide compensation for every change in property value it induces, courts continue to be reluctant to find regulatory takings. Even environmental regulations that severely affect property values generally are upheld as necessary to prevent harm to the commons. When the *First English* case, which had been dismissed prior to trial, was remanded from the Supreme Court, a California appeals court had little trouble finding that no taking was involved because the prohibition on building in a flood plain protected public safety. First English Evangelical Lutheran Church v. County of Los Angeles, 210 Cal. App. 3d 1353 (1989).

With encouragement from a more conservative Supreme Court, takings claims are being pressed more aggressively as environmental regulation expands. In some cases, federal courts have found that land use regulations resulted in regulatory takings, basing their findings on a more liberal application of the diminution-in-value approach and a more restrictive view of the public nuisance exemption.

In Whitney Benefits, Inc. v. United States, 926 F.2d 1169 (Fed. Cir.), cert. denied, 112 S. Ct. 406 (1991), the Federal Circuit found that a ban on the mining of alluvial valley floors imposed by the Surface Mining Control and Reclamation Act constituted a taking because it deprived two mining companies of all economic use of their coal deposits. Noting that the Act permitted other companies to mine coal, the court found that it could not fit within the nuisance exception and awarded more than $140 million in compensation to the two companies. The Supreme Court denied the government's request for review, which had been premised on the argument that the companies never had been denied a mining permit and could have exchanged the land for other federal land with minerals that could have been mined.

In Loveladies Harbor, Inc. v. United States, 21 Cl. Ct. 153 (1990), the Court of Claims found that the denial of a permit to develop wetlands constituted a taking because it deprived owners of undeveloped beach-front property of all economically viable use. While the government had argued that the property, even in undeveloped form, could still be used for recreational activities such as hunting and birdwatching, the court found that the permit denial had reduced the value of the property by 99 percent. Finding no substantial countervailing interest in preventing development, the court held that a taking had occurred. In Florida Rock Industries, Inc. v. United States, 21 Cl. Ct. 161 (1990), the Claims Court held that a denial of a permit for mining limestone constituted a taking despite government arguments that such mining would create a nuisance. The court found that limestone mining was not generally considered a nuisance in the area and that the plaintiff, who had purchased the property with the intention of mining it, could not "recoup its investment" in any other way. The court found that the value of the property had been reduced by 95 percent by the denial of the permit and awarded more than $1 million in compensation.

Although it denied review in *Whitney Benefits,* the Supreme Court has agreed to review a decision by South Carolina's highest court, which rejected a takings claim. In Lucas v. South Carolina Coastal Council, 404 S.E.2d 895 (S.C. 1991), cert. granted, 112 S. Ct. 436, the Supreme Court is reviewing a takings challenge to regulations that prohibited a landowner from building a home on undeveloped beachfront property. The plaintiff in the case paid $975,000 to purchase two beachfront lots in 1986, two years before South Carolina enacted a coastal protection law prohibiting development of the property. The South Carolina Supreme Court held that the regulation did not constitute a taking because it was enacted to prevent "serious public harm." The landowner argues that even if the court recognizes a nuisance exception to the takings clause, construction of a house should not be considered to be a nuisance. The Justice Department is supporting the landowner in an amicus brief before the Supreme Court that urges a narrow construction of the nuisance exception to takings doctrine. But the brief does not urge the Court to overrule *Keystone Bituminous Coal,* as had an earlier draft. Barrett and Gutfeld, Administration to Urge Broader Limits on Health, Safety, Environmental Rules, Wall St. J., Jan. 3, 1992, at A8.

C.   Evolving (and Diverging) Conceptions of Property Rights and Environmental Harm

The continuing controversy over the takings clause reflects competing conceptions of the meaning of private property rights that are founded on different notions of individual responsibility for environmental protection. As environmental regulation developed, Joseph Sax and others articulated a new vision of property rights that emphasized the subordination of private rights to public trusts for the protection of natural resources. Sax, Takings, Private Property and Public Rights, 81 Yale L.J. 149 (1971). This concept was articulated by the Wisconsin Supreme Court in Just v. Marinette County, 201 N.W.2d 761 (1972), when it stated that "[a]n owner of land has no absolute and unlimited right to change the essential natural character of his land so as to use it for a purpose for which it was unsuited in its natural state and which injures the rights of others."

Richard Epstein takes sharp exception to this view and argues that compensation should be required for a broad array of government actions that reduce the economic value of private property. R. Epstein, Takings (1985). Professor Epstein appears to reject the application of the nuisance exception in cases of nonpoint source pollution by arguing that land use controls do not redress a physical invasion of the property of another but rather pollution of one's own property. Id. at 123. Ironically, Epstein does not appear to be suggesting that government conversely should recoup *increases* in property values that are the products of its activities.

These competing conceptions of property rights reflect evolving (and diverging) notions of fairness as well as changes in our understanding of how environmental harm is caused. Lord Holt's ancient maxim that "every man must so use his own as not to damnify another" acquires new meaning once it is understood that actions long recognized as incident to property rights (e.g., the building of a home) may contribute to severe environmental damage by causing nonpoint source pollution. Yet environmentalists who decry the unfairness of any individual's involuntary exposure to risk should also be concerned about the fairness of visiting disproportionate economic losses on an individual in the name of environmental protection. The CEQ's observation nearly two decades ago remains accurate today:

> [D]espite the criticisms that have been aimed at various judicial formulations, it may well be that no single formula is either possible or desirable. In the final analysis, all such formulae seem to be attempts to extrapolate from what is at base an ethical judgment about the fairness of alternative means of distributing the costs of protecting certain land-related values that yield positive net benefits to society. In most cases that judgment has traditionally suggested that the proper balance between the interests of

private landowners and the public is maintained by requiring compensation when land use regulations do not leave the landowner with any "reasonable" use of his property. Increasingly, as new concepts of property have become more firmly established and recognition of the value of land as a scarce resource has mounted, the definition of reasonable use has changed. [CEQ, Environmental Quality 150 (1973).]

Reconciling notions of fairness to individuals with the need to prevent formerly commonplace activities from contributing to serious environmental problems will remain an important challenge facing environmental law.

NOTES AND QUESTIONS

1. Individuals are constantly subject to the possibility of suffering substantial economic losses as a result of changes in conditions in the marketplace. In our mixed economy, the government now plays an important role in the marketplace. Why are economic losses suffered due to government action considered more objectionable than losses incurred as a result of Adam Smith's "invisible hand"?

2. Are new approaches that make compensation more affordable a possible answer to the takings problem? Note the Supreme Court's observation in *Penn Central* that transferable development rights might help offset losses that otherwise would give rise to takings claims. Approaches that provide some compensation could be theoretically attractive because they reduce the incentives for rent-seeking behavior that place land use controls under constant pressure from developers seeking to profit from relaxation of regulation.

3. Suppose EPA decided to abolish the emissions allowances it has established under Title IV of the Clean Air Act after concluding that it needs to reduce sulfur dioxide emissions more rapidly than specified in the Act. Would that constitute a taking of private property by entirely destroying the economic value of the allowances?

4. Would Professor Epstein's approach require as a matter of constitutional law that residents opposed to the siting of landfills be compensated for the economic consequences of their perceived exposure to increased environmental risk?

F.   WETLANDS PROTECTION AND THE SECTION 404 PERMIT PROGRAM

While they can be areas of great beauty, to the untrained eye wetlands often appear as undesirable swamps that could only be improved by development. They were long viewed as "wastelands, sources of mosquitos and impediments to development and travel," J. Kusler, Our National Wetland Heritage 1 (1983), whose draining and filling was a sign of progress, often subsidized by government. But scientists now realize that wetlands are among the most vital and productive of all ecosystems. Wetlands serve as feeding and breeding grounds for fish and waterfowl, as filters for pollution, and as mechanisms for flood control. They are a particularly critical link in the ecological chain whose environmental importance is not reflected in their market price. EPA has described the value of wetlands in the following terms:

> Wetlands are habitats for many forms of fish and wildlife. Approximately two-thirds of this nation's major commercial fisheries use estuaries and coastal marshes as nurseries or spawning grounds. Migratory waterfowl and other birds also depend on wetlands, some spending their entire lives in wetlands and others using them primarily as nesting, feeding or resting grounds. The role of wetlands in improving and maintaining water quality in adjacent water bodies is increasingly being recognized in the scientific literature. Wetlands remove nutrients such as nitrogen and phosphorus, and thus help prevent over-enrichment of waters (eutrophication). Also, they filter harmful chemicals, such as pesticides and heavy metals, and trap suspended sediments, which otherwise would produce turbidity (cloudiness) in water. This function is particularly important as a natural buffer for nonpoint pollution sources.
>
> Wetlands also have socioeconomic values. They play an important role in flood control by absorbing peak flows and releasing water slowly. Along the coast, they buffer land against storm surges resulting from hurricanes and tropical storms. Wetlands vegetation can reduce shoreline erosion by absorbing and dissipating wave energy and encouraging the deposition of suspended sediments. Also, wetlands contribute $20 billion to $40 billion annually to the nation's economy, for example, through recreational and commercial fishing, hunting of waterfowl, and the production of cash crops such as wild rice and cranberries. [EPA, Environmental Progress and Challenges: EPA's Update 60 (1988).]

Wetlands often are attractive sites for development, in part due to humans' love for proximity to water. As a result, a precious part of the nation's ecological heritage has been lost. Scientists estimate that wetland acreage in the original 48 states has declined from more than 200 million to less than 90 million acres. Wetlands that remain are under relentless assault. Nearly half a million acres are disappearing each year, due largely to agricultural and urban development.

1. The Structure of the Section 404 Program

The most visible (and controversial) wetlands protection program is a product of section 404 of the Clean Water Act. When it adopted the

FWPCA in 1972, Congress established a separate permit program, in addition to the NPDES, to govern discharges of dredge and fill material. Section 404 of the Act, whose importance was not immediately appreciated, requires all dischargers of dredge and fill to the waters of the United States to obtain a permit from the U.S. Army Corps of Engineers. The Corps administers the section 404 permit program in cooperation with EPA.

The definition of dredge and fill material determines whether a permit must be obtained from the Corps under section 404 or from EPA under section 402 of the Clean Water Act, which covers all discharges of pollutants from point sources. The section 404 permit program covers discharges of dredge and fill materials. The former are defined by EPA and the Corps as "material that is excavated or dredged from the waters of the United States." 40 C.F.R. §232.2(g); 33 C.F.R. §323.2(c). Material not excavated from such waters is subject to the section 404 permit program if it is used as fill material. The Corps defines "fill material" as "material used for the primary purpose of replacing an aquatic area with dry land or of changing the bottom elevation of a waterbody," 33 C.F.R. §323.2(k), while EPA considers any pollutant that has such an effect to be fill. 40 C.F.R. §232.2(i).

Note that the language of section 404 only refers to discharges of dredge and fill material. It does not encompass a great many other activities that contribute to the destruction of wetlands. But see Save Our Community v. United States Environmental Protection Agency, 741 F. Supp. 605 (N.D. Tex. 1990) (section 404 permit requirement cannot be circumvented by draining wetland). As a result, less than 20 percent of all wetland losses are due to activities subject to the section 404 program. Moreover, because of exemptions and general permit provisions, of the 70,000 development activities each year that are covered by section 404, only about 15,000 are required to obtain individual permits. Swamp Gas, 8 Envtl. Forum 10 (July-Aug. 1991). The vast majority of permit applications are approved; fewer than 500 are denied each year.

Permit issuance decisions are governed by guidelines developed jointly by EPA and the Corps pursuant to section 404(b)(1). The section 404(b)(1) guidelines, 40 C.F.R. pt. 230, emphasize consideration of alternatives to mitigate the adverse environmental impact of discharges. Permits are not to be issued unless four conditions are satisfied: (1) there is no practicable alternative that will have a less adverse impact on the aquatic ecosystem, (2) no statutory violations will occur, (3) there will be no significant adverse impacts, and (4) all reasonable mitigation measures are employed.

While the Corps makes the initial determination concerning permitting, EPA is authorized by section 404(c) to veto any permit if it determines that the discharge "will have an unacceptable adverse effect on aquatic resources, wildlife, drinking water, or recreation." This authority has been rarely used. Between 1972 and 1983 EPA vetoed only one permit under section 404(c). In the next five years it vetoed five.

The Clean Water Act is not the only source of federal authority for protecting wetlands. Congress also has provided funds for wetlands acquisition supplemented by revenues obtained from the sale of duck stamps to waterfowl hunters. Funding for this program was expanded in the Emergency Wetlands Resources Act of 1986, which requires the Secretary of the Interior to develop a plan establishing priorities for wetlands acquisition in consultation with EPA and other federal and state agencies. Other federal laws, such as the "Swampbuster" provisions of the Food Security Act of 1985 (which bar federal farm subsidies to persons producing crops on land converted from wetlands) and the Coastal Barriers Resource Act of 1982 (which prohibits most new federal spending for development of designated barrier islands), also help to preserve wetland resources. Many states also have wetland protection programs, though few of these protect nontidal wetlands.

2.   The Scope of the Section 404 Program and Wetlands Delineation

Because of their diversity and seasonal variability, defining what constitutes a wetland for regulatory purposes is a difficult challenge. While section 404 of the Act does not use the term "wetland" ("wetlands" *are* mentioned in section 208(i)(2)), the Act's legislative history clearly indicates that Congress intended to protect wetlands. How broadly the section 404 program protects wetlands depends on how broadly the Act's jurisdictional definition of "navigable waters" is interpreted. If "navigable waters" were interpreted to limit the Act's jurisdiction only to waters that are truly navigable, few wetlands would be protected.

Section 502(7) of the Act defines "navigable waters" broadly to include "waters of the United States, including the territorial seas." Yet the Army Corps of Engineers initially interpreted the Act as extending federal jurisdiction only to waters actually, potentially, or historically navigable, an interpretation that covered few wetland areas. This interpretation was deemed too restrictive in Natural Resources Defense Council v. Calloway, 392 F. Supp. 685 (D.D.C. 1975), which held that Congress had intended to extend federal regulatory authority to the limits of its Commerce Clause powers. Because these powers potentially are so vast, see, e.g., Wickard v. Filburn, 317 U.S. 111 (1942), the Corps still had to determine how far to go in broadening section 404's application to wetlands. Another interpretation adopted by the Corps was challenged in the case that follows.

United States v. Riverside Bayview Homes, Inc.
474 U.S. 121 (1985)

WHITE, J., delivered the opinion for a unanimous Court.

This case presents the question whether the Clean Water Act, together with certain regulations promulgated under its authority by the Army Corps of Engineers, authorizes the Corps to require landowners to obtain permits from the Corps before discharging fill material into wetlands adjacent to navigable bodies of water and their tributaries.

The relevant provisions of the Clean Water Act originated in the Federal Water Pollution Control Act Amendments of 1972 and have remained essentially unchanged since that time. Under §§301 and 502 of the Act, any discharge of dredged or fill materials into "navigable waters"—defined as the "waters of the United States"—is forbidden unless authorized by a permit issued by the Corps of Engineers pursuant to §404. After initially construing the Act to cover only waters navigable in fact, in 1975 the Corps issued interim final regulations redefining "the waters of the United States" to include not only actually navigable waters but also tributaries of such waters, interstate waters and their tributaries, and nonnavigable intrastate waters whose use or misuse could affect interstate commerce. 40 Fed. Reg. 31320 (1975). More importantly for present purposes, the Corps construed the Act to cover all "fresh-water wetlands" that were adjacent to other covered waters. A "fresh-water wetland" was defined as an area that is "periodically inundated" and is "normally characterized by the prevalence of vegetation that requires saturated soil conditions for growth and reproduction." 33 C.F.R. §209.120(d)(2)(h) (1976). In 1977 the Corps refined its definition of wetlands by eliminating the reference to periodic inundation and making other minor changes. The 1977 definition reads as follows:

> The term "wetlands" means those areas that are inundated or saturated by surface or ground water at a frequency and duration sufficient to support, and that under normal circumstances do support, a prevalence of vegetation typically adapted for life in saturated soil conditions. Wetlands generally include swamps, marshes, bogs and similar areas. 33 CFR §323.2(c) (1978).

In 1982, the 1977 regulations were replaced by substantively identical regulations that remain in force today. See 33 CFR §323.2 (1985).

Respondent Riverside Bayview Homes, Inc. (hereafter respondent), owns 80 acres of low-lying, marshy land near the shores of Lake St. Clair in Macomb County, Michigan. In 1976, respondent began to place fill materials on its property as part of its preparations for construction of a housing development. The Corps of Engineers, believing that the property was an "adjacent Wetland" under the 1975 regulation defining "waters of the United States," filed suit in the United States District Court for the Eastern District of Michigan, seeking to enjoin respondent from filling the property without the permission of the Corps.

The District Court held that the portion of respondent's property lying below 575.5 feet above sea level was a covered wetland and enjoined respondent from filling it without a permit. Respondent appealed, and the Court of Appeals remanded for consideration of the effect of the intervening 1977 amendments to the regulation. On remand, the District Court again held the property to be a wetland subject to the Corps' permit authority.

Respondent again appealed, and the Sixth Circuit reversed. 729 F.2d 391 (1984). The court construed the Corps' regulations to exclude from the category of adjacent wetlands—and hence from that of "waters of the United States"—wetlands that were not subject to flooding by adjacent navigable waters at a frequency sufficient to support the growth of aquatic vegetation. . . . Under the court's reading of the regulations, respondent's property was not within the Corps' jurisdiction, because its semi-aquatic characteristics were not the result of frequent flooding by the nearby navigable waters. Respondent was therefore free to fill the property without obtaining a permit.

We granted certiorari to consider the proper interpretation of the Corps' regulations defining "waters of the United States" and the scope of the Corps' jurisdiction under the Clean Water Act, both of which were called into question by the Sixth Circuit's ruling. We now reverse.

[The Court rejected the Sixth Circuit's interpretation of the Corps' regulations and held that they do not require frequent flooding by navigable waters. Rather, "saturation by either surface or ground water is sufficient to bring an area within the category of wetlands, provided that the saturation is sufficient to and does support wetland vegetation." This interpretation "plainly bring[s respondent's] property within the category of wetlands as defined by the current regulations."] Hence, it is part of the "waters of the United States" as defined by 33 C.F.R. §323.2 (1985), and if the regulation itself is valid as a construction of the term "waters of the United States" as used in the Clean Water Act, a question which we now address, the property falls within the scope of the Corps' jurisdiction over "navigable waters" under §404 of the Act.

An agency's construction of a statute it is charged with enforcing is entitled to deference if it is reasonable and not in conflict with the expressed intent of Congress. Accordingly, our review is limited to the question whether it is reasonable, in light of the language, policies, and legislative history of the Act for the Corps to exercise jurisdiction over wetlands adjacent to but not regularly flooded by rivers, streams, and other hydrographic features more conventionally identifiable as "waters."

On a purely linguistic level, it may appear unreasonable to classify "lands," wet or otherwise, as "waters." Such a simplistic response, however, does justice neither to the problem faced by the Corps in defining the scope of its authority under §404(a) nor to the realities of the problem of water pollution that the Clean Water Act was intended to combat. In determining the limits of its power to regulate discharges under the Act, the Corps must necessarily choose some point at which water ends and land begins. Our common experience tells us that this is often no easy task: the transition from water to solid ground is not necessarily or even typically an abrupt one. Rather, between open waters and dry land may lie shallows, marshes, mudflats, swamps, bogs—in short, a huge array of areas that are not wholly aquatic but nevertheless fall far short of being dry land. Where on this continuum to find the limit of "waters" is far from obvious.

Faced with such a problem of defining the bounds of its regulatory authority, an agency may appropriately look to the legislative history and underlying policies of its statutory grants of authority. Neither of these sources provides unambiguous guidance for the Corps in this case, but together they do support the reasonableness of the Corps' approach of defining adjacent wetlands as "waters" within the meaning of §404(a). Section 404 originated as part of the Federal Water Pollution Control Act Amendments of 1972, which constituted a comprehensive legislative attempt "to restore and maintain the chemical, physical, and biological integrity of the Nation's waters." CWA §101. This objective incorporated a broad, systemic view of the goal of maintaining and improving water quality: as the House Report on the legislation put it, "the word 'integrity' . . . refers to a condition in which the natural structure and function of ecosystems is [sic] maintained." H.R. Rep. No. 92-911, p. 76 (1972). Protection of aquatic ecosystems, Congress recognized, demanded broad federal authority to control pollution, for "[w]ater moves in hydrologic cycles and it is essential that discharge of pollutants be controlled at the source." S. Rep. No. 92-414, p. 77 (1972).

In keeping with these views, Congress chose to define the waters covered by the Act broadly. Although the Act prohibits discharges into "navigable waters," the Act's definition of "navigable waters" as "the waters of the United States" makes it clear that the term "navigable" as used in the Act is of limited import. In adopting this definition of "navigable waters," Congress evidently intended to repudiate limits that had been placed on federal regulation by earlier water pollution control statutes and to exercise its powers under the Commerce Clause to regulate at least some waters that would not be deemed "navigable" under the classical understanding of that term.

Of course, it is one thing to recognize that Congress intended to allow regulation of waters that might not satisfy traditional tests of navigability; it is another to assert that Congress intended to abandon traditional notions of "waters" and include in that term "wetlands" as well. Nonetheless, the evident breadth of congressional concern for protection of water quality and aquatic ecosystems suggests that it is reasonable for the Corps to interpret the term "waters" to encompass wetlands adjacent to waters as more conventionally defined. Following the lead of the Environmental Protection Agency, the Corps has determined that wetlands adjacent to navigable waters do as a general matter play a key role in protecting and enhancing water quality:

> The regulation of activities that cause water pollution cannot rely on . . . artificial lines . . . but must focus on all waters that together form the entire aquatic system. Water moves in hydrologic cycles, and the pollution of this part of the aquatic system, regardless of whether it is above or below an ordinary high water mark, or mean high tide line, will affect the water quality of the other waters within that aquatic system.
>
> For this reason, the landward limit of Federal jurisdiction under Section 404 must include any adjacent wetlands that form the border of or are in reasonable proximity to other waters of the United States, as these wetlands are part of this aquatic system. 42 Fed. Reg. 37128 (1977).

We cannot say that the Corps' conclusion that adjacent wetlands are inseparably bound up with the "waters" of the United States—based as it is on the Corps' and EPA's technical expertise—is unreasonable. In view of the breadth of federal regulatory authority contemplated by the Act itself and the inherent difficulties of defining precise bounds to regulable waters, the Corps' ecological judgment about the relationship between waters and their adjacent wetlands provides an adequate basis for a legal judgment that adjacent wetlands may be defined as waters under the Act.

This holds true even for wetlands that are not the result of flooding or permeation by water having its source in adjacent bodies of open water. The Corps has concluded that wetlands may affect the water quality of adjacent lakes, rivers, and streams even when the waters of those bodies do not actually inundate the wetlands. . . . Again, we cannot say that the Corps' judgment in these matters is unreasonable, and we therefore conclude that a definition of "waters of the United States" encompassing all wetlands adjacent to other bodies of water over which the Corps has jurisdiction is a permissible interpretation of the Act. Because respondent's property is part of a wetland that actually abuts on a navigable waterway, respondent was required to have a permit in this case. . . .

NOTES AND QUESTIONS

1. Acknowledging the difficulty of defining jurisdictional boundaries with precision, the Court in *Riverside Bayview* appears to endorse

a functional approach that interprets the jurisdictional reach of section 404 expansively to promote the goals of the Act. The decision reflects concern that a more restrictive interpretation of regulatory authority could undermine the congressional goal of providing comprehensive protection to water quality. Could EPA and the Corps expand their jurisdictional reach even further? If wetlands are "waters," could the Clean Water Act be used to regulate discharges to groundwater as well as to surface waters? Is the test purely functional, requiring a showing that groundwaters "do as a general matter play a key role in protecting and enhancing water quality"? Compare United States Steel Corp. v. Train, 556 F.2d 822 (7th Cir. 1977) (EPA may regulate groundwater discharges by sources subject to surface water permitting) with Exxon Corp. v. Train, 554 F.2d 1310 (5th Cir. 1977) and Kelly v. United States, 23 E.R.C. 1494 (W.D. Mich. 1985) (EPA may not regulate groundwater discharges under the Clean Water Act).

2. The section 404 program has been controversial because it extends the reach of federal regulation more broadly and in a manner that potentially affects more individuals than most other federal environmental programs. Yet the expansive jurisdictional reach of "waters of the United States" has been tempered in significant ways. Section 404(f)(1) exempts discharges from normal farming, forestry, and ranching operations, although section 404(f)(2) qualifies this exemption by refusing to extend it to discharges incidental to activities designed to convert a wetland area "into a use to which it was not previously subject." The Corps also has exercised its general permit authority under section 404(e) to obviate the need for individual permit applications in many instances, and the Corps' regulations allow de minimis dischargers to escape regulation. Environmentalists argue that these exemptions have been abused and that section 404(f)(2) should be enforced more aggressively in order to regulate currently exempt activities that effectively cause changes in water use. See Tripp and Herz, Wetland Preservation and Restoration, 7 Va. J. Nat. Resources L. 221 (1988).

3. The Supreme Court also addressed the takings issue in another part of *Riverside Bayview* not reproduced above. The Sixth Circuit had held that a narrow construction of the Corps' regulations was necessary because a broader construction might result in the taking of private property without just compensation. The Supreme Court acknowledged that section 404 could produce such a result, but "[o]nly when a permit is denied and the effect of the denial is to prevent 'economically viable' use of the land in question can it be said that a taking has occurred." The Court concluded that this theoretical possibility was not grounds for a narrowing construction of the Corps' regulations. Rather, the proper remedy would be simply to provide compensation. As noted above, it has been very difficult to establish that section 404 results in a taking, see, e.g., Deltona Corp. v. United States, 657 F.2d 1184 (Ct. Cl. 1981), until recent decisions apparently employing a more expansive view of

what constitutes denial of "economically viable" use. Loveladies Harbor, Inc. v. United States, 21 Cl. Ct. 153 (1990); Florida Rock Industries, Inc. v. United States, 21 Cl. Ct. 161 (1990).

4. Congress rejected efforts by development interests to narrow the reach of section 404 when it adopted the 1977 Amendments. With reauthorization of the Clean Water Act before Congress once again, a new and more vigorous lobbying campaign has been launched by a group that includes developers, agricultural interests, and oil and mining companies. Using a logo that shows a duck flying over cattails, the group calls itself the National Wetlands Coalition. It is promoting legislation that would remove millions of acres of wetlands from section 404, strip EPA of any role in the permit process, and relax controls on remaining wetlands by dividing them into categories subject to varying levels of protection. Much of the renewed attack on section 404 has featured hyperbolic anecdotes offered to demonstrate its "regulatory overkill." Compare Bush's Swamp Thing, Wall St. J., July 25, 1991, with Wetlands: Knee-Deep in Tall Tales, Wall St. J., Sept. 12, 1991, at A19.

Wetlands Identification and Delineation

Defining what constitutes a wetland has been extremely difficult. While the regulatory definitions adopted by EPA, 40 C.F.R. 230.3(t), and the Corps, 33 C.F.R. 328.3(b), in 1977 are the same, each agency followed different procedures for identifying and delineating wetlands. To provide more uniform standards for identification of wetlands, an interagency task force from EPA, the Corps, the Soil Conservation Service, and the Fish and Wildlife Service published the Federal Manual for Identifying and Delineating Jurisdictional Wetlands in 1989. The manual focused on three conditions—hydrology, soils, and vegetation—and specified the parameters of each necessary to make an area a jurisdictional wetland. The Delineation Manual caused considerable controversy, in part because it was adopted as a technical guidance document that was not subject to notice-and-comment procedures. After complaints from oil and agricultural interests and intervention from the Bush Administration's Competitiveness Council, EPA and the Corps proposed in August 1991 to revise the wetlands delineation manual. 56 Fed. Reg. 40,446 (1991). Their proposal would drastically reduce the wetland acreage subject to protection under section 404. The proposal has come under intense criticism from scientists, environmental groups, and state officials. See Searchinger & Rader, Bush's Cynical Attack on Wetlands, N.Y. Times, Aug. 19, 1991, at A15 (environmentalists call it "probably the largest weakening of an environmental regulation in U.S. history"). They argue that the proposed changes are not based on scientifically valid criteria, would reduce protected wetland acreage by 30 percent (including almost one-half of the Everglades), and would make the identification process difficult, if not unworkable.

3. The Section 404 Permit Process

The permit process established by section 404 has produced bitter confrontations between developers and environmental groups, each of whom has been highly critical of the process. Development interests argue that the process is too cumbersome and takes too long. Environmentalists argue that the Corps has been far too lenient in granting permits to development interests and that EPA has been too willing to defer to the Corps. Oliver Houck describes section 404 as an "open wound across the body of environmental law, one of the simplest statutes to describe and one of the most painful to apply." Houck, Hard Choices: The Analysis of Alternatives Under Section 404 of the Clean Water Act and Similar Environmental Laws, 60 Colo. L. Rev. 773 (1989).

Decisions concerning permit applications under section 404 turn largely on an analysis of alternatives to a proposed project. Alternatives analysis is a central feature of several environmental laws, most notably section 102 of the National Environmental Policy Act (NEPA), which requires the preparation of environmental impact statements on major federal actions; section 4(f) of the Department of Transportation Act, which prohibits the construction of federal highways in parklands unless there is no "feasible and prudent alternative"; and section 7 of the Endangered Species Act, which prohibits federal actions that threaten endangered species unless there are no alternatives, the benefits of the proposal outweigh the benefits from alternatives, and the action is of regional or national significance. NEPA and the Endangered Species Act are discussed in Chapter 8.

The section 404(b)(1) guidelines provide that "no discharge of dredged or fill material shall be permitted if there is a practicable alternative . . . which would have less adverse impact on the aquatic ecosystem. . . ." 40 C.F.R. §230.10(a). The guidelines define an alternative as "practicable" if it is "available" and "capable of being done after taking into consideration cost, existing technology, and logistics in light of overall project purposes." Thus, the guidelines employ a kind of feasibility-limited approach to regulation that is supposed to tolerate environmental damage only if no alternative is available. If alternatives are available, the permit is to be denied without further inquiry into the suitability of the site and the environmental impact of the discharge.

The guidelines are designed to place a heavy burden on developers who seek approval to locate in wetland areas projects that do not "require access or proximity" to the water. For such non-water-dependent projects, the guidelines presume that a less damaging alternative is available "unless clearly demonstrated otherwise." The developer bears the burden of proving that no alternative is available, which under the guidelines includes demonstrating that no other property could "reasonably" be obtained to fulfill the "basic purpose of the proposed activity." 40 C.F.R. §230.10(a)(2). In the case below the Second Circuit addressed the question whether the "availability" of alternative property should be assessed at the time a project commences or at the time of permit application. EPA had vetoed the issuance of a section 404 permit for a shopping mall because it deemed a nonwetland site that subsequently had been purchased by another developer to have been available to the permit-seeking developer at the time it had commenced the project.

> ## Bersani v. Robichaud
> ### 850 F.2d 36 (2d Cir. 1988)

Before TIMBERS, PRATT, and MINER, Circuit Judges.

TIMBERS, Circuit Judge:

This case arises out of [the Pyramid Companies'] attempt to build a shopping mall on certain wetlands in Massachusetts known as Sweedens Swamp. Acting under the Clean Water Act, 33 U.S.C. §1251 et seq. (1982), EPA vetoed the approval by the Corps of a permit to build the mall because EPA found that an alternative site had been available to Pyramid at the time it entered the market to search for a site for the mall. The alternative site was purchased later by another developer and arguably became unavailable by the time Pyramid applied for a permit to build the mall.

On appeal, the thrust of Pyramid's argument is a challenge to what it calls EPA's "market entry" theory, i.e., the interpretation by EPA of the relevant regulation, which led EPA to consider the availability of alternative sites at the time Pyramid entered the market for a site, instead of at the time it applied for a permit. . . .

Sweedens Swamp is a 49.5 acre wetland which is part of an 80 acre site near Interstate 95 in South Attleboro, Massachusetts. . . .

The effort to build a mall on Sweedens Swamp was initiated by Pyramid's predecessor, the Edward J. DeBartolo Corporation ("De-Bartolo"). DeBartolo purchased the Swamp some time before April 1982. At the time of this purchase an alternative site was available in North Attleboro (the "North Attleboro site"). Since Massachusetts requires state approval (in addition to federal approval) for projects that would fill wetlands, DeBartolo applied to the Massachusetts Department of Environmental Quality Engineering ("DEQE") for permission to build on Sweedens Swamp. . . . .

One of the key issues in dispute in the instant case is just when did Pyramid begin searching for a suitable site for its mall. EPA asserts that

Pyramid began to search in the Spring of 1983. Pyramid asserts that it began to search several months later, in September 1983. The difference is crucial because on July 1, 1983—a date between the starting dates claimed by EPA and Pyramid—a competitor of Pyramid, the New England Development Co. ("NED"), purchased options to buy the North Attleboro site. This site was located upland and could have served as a "practicable alternative" to Sweedens Swamp, *if* it had been "available" at the relevant time. Thus, if the relevant time to determine whether an alternative is "available" is the time the applicant is searching for a site (an issue that is hotly disputed), and if Pyramid began to search at a time *before* NED acquired options on the North Attleboro site, there definitely would have been a "practicable alternative" to Sweedens Swamp, and Pyramid's application should have been denied. On the other hand, if Pyramid did not begin its search until *after* NED acquired options on the North Attleboro site, then the site arguably was not "available" and the permit should have been granted. Of course it also is possible that the North Attleboro site remained "available" after NED's acquisition of the options, since Pyramid arguably could have purchased the options from NED. Moreover, since the North Attleboro site indisputably was "available" when Pyramid's predecessor, DeBartolo, purchased Sweedens Swamp, one might argue, as EPA does, that Pyramid should be held to stand in its predecessor's shoes. The district court apparently agreed with Pyramid on the issue of when Pyramid entered the market, stating that "Pyramid initially became interested in developing a shopping mall in the Attleboro area in September 1983." Bersani v. EPA, supra, 674 F. Supp. at 409.

In December 1983, Pyramid purchased Sweedens Swamp from DeBartolo. In August 1984, Pyramid applied under §404(a) to the New England regional division of the Corps (the "NE Corps") for a permit. It sought to fill or alter 32 of the 49.6 acres of the Swamp; to excavate nine acres of uplands to create artificial wetlands; and to alter 13.3 acres of existing wetlands to improve its environmental quality. Later Pyramid proposed to mitigate the adverse impact on the wetlands by creating 36 acres of replacement wetlands in an off-site gravel pit. . . .

[Despite recommendations by EPA, the U.S. Fish and Wildlife Service, and the regional office of the Army Corps of Engineers that the permit be denied, Corps headquarters decided to issue the permit. EPA then initiated a review of the permit issuance decision under section 404(c).]

On May 13, 1986, EPA issued its final determination, which prohibited Pyramid from using Sweedens Swamp. It found (1) that the filling of the Swamp would adversely affect wildlife; (2) that the North Attleboro site could have been available to Pyramid at the time Pyramid investigated the area to search for a site; (3) that considering Pyramid's failure or unwillingness to provide further materials about its investigation of alternative sites, it was uncontested that, at best, Pyramid never checked the availability of the North Attleboro site as an alternative; (4) that the North Attleboro site was feasible and would have a less adverse impact on the wetland environment; and (5) that the mitigation proposal did not make the project preferable to other alternatives because of scientific uncertainty of success. In the second of these findings, EPA used what Pyramid calls the "market entry" approach. [Pyramid then sued EPA in federal district court. After EPA was granted summary judgment, Pyramid appealed.]

One of Pyramid's principal contentions is that the market entry approach is inconsistent with both the language of the 404(b)(1) guidelines and the past practice of the Corps and EPA. . . .

As EPA has pointed out, the preamble to the 404(b)(1) guidelines states that the purpose of the "practicable alternatives" analysis is "to recognize the special value of wetlands and to avoid their unnecessary destruction, particularly where practicable alternatives *were* available in non-aquatic areas to achieve the basic purpose of the proposal." 45 Fed. Reg. 85,338 (1980) (emphasis added). In other words, the purpose is to create an incentive for developers to avoid choosing wetlands when they could choose an alternative upland site. Pyramid's reading of the regulations would thwart this purpose because it would remove the incentive for a developer to search for an alternative site at the time such an incentive is needed, i.e., at the time it is making the decision to select a particular site. If the practicable alternatives analysis were applied to the time of the application for a permit, the developer would have little incentive to search for alternatives, especially if it were confident that alternatives soon would disappear. Conversely, in a case in which alternatives were not available at the time the developer made its selection, but became available by the time of application, the developer's application would be denied even though it could not have explored the alternative site at the time of its decision.

Pyramid attacks this reasoning by arguing that few developers would take the risk that an available alternative site would become unavailable and the EPA's reading improperly considers the motives and subjective state of mind of the applicant. These arguments are wide of the mark. Whether most real-life developers would take such a risk is irrelevant. The point is that Pyramid's time-of-application theory is completely at odds with the expressed intent of the regulations to provide an incentive to avoid choosing wetlands. Similarly, EPA's interpretation does not require courts to investigate the subjective state of mind of a developer. EPA discusses state-of-mind issues only because it is discussing the *purpose* behind the regulations, which is concerned with incentives, and thus in fact is indirectly concerned with the developer's state of mind.

In short, we conclude that a common-sense reading of the statute can lead only to the use of the market entry approach used by EPA. . . .

[W]e believe the extensive administrative record supports a finding that the North Attleboro site was available to Pyramid when it entered the market. Even if Pyramid were found not to have entered the market until September 1983, after NED had acquired options to purchase the North Attleboro site, it does not necessarily follow that the site was unavailable. Aside from the fact that NED did not acquire all the options for the North Attleboro site until June 1984, it also was possible for Pyramid to attempt to purchase the options from NED. The record shows no such attempts to purchase the site, or even to investigate its availability. Alternatively, even though the district court apparently was not persuaded by it, there also is evidence in the record to show that Pyramid actually entered the market in the Spring of 1983, before NED had purchased its options. Finally, the evidence shows that the North Attleboro site had been available to DeBartolo, Pyramid's predecessor. EPA could reasonably have determined that Pyramid should be held to "stand in the shoes" of DeBartolo, especially since it was able to obtain state approval of the project under the less-stringent state standards that had originally applied to DeBartolo. . . .

PRATT, Circuit Judge, dissenting:

In this case I have no problem with EPA's basic approach. It conscientiously attempted to weigh the economic advantages against the ecological disadvantages of developing Sweedens Swamp and, in approaching this determination, it properly looked to alternate available sites. However, EPA went wrong—seriously wrong—when it adopted the market entry theory to decide whether an alternate site was available. By focusing on the decisionmaking techniques and tactics of a particular developer, instead of the actual alternatives to disturbing the wetland, EPA ignored the statute's central purposes.

The market entry theory in effect taints a particular developer with respect to a particular site, while ignoring the crucial question of whether the site itself should be preserved. Under the market entry theory, developer *A* would be denied a permit on a specific site because when he entered the market alternatives were available, but latecomer developer *B*, who entered the market after those alternatives had become unavailable, would be entitled to a permit for developing the same site. In such a case, the theory no longer protects the land, but instead becomes a distorted punitive device: it punishes developer *A* by denying him a permit, but grants developer *B* a permit for the same property—and the only difference between them is when they "entered the market."

The market entry theory has further problems. In this case, for example, if a Donald Trump had "entered the market" after NED took the option on the North Attleboro site and made it unavailable, under EPA's approach he apparently would have been entitled to a permit to develop Sweedens Swamp. But after obtaining the permit and the land, could Trump then sell the package to Pyramid to develop? Or could he build the mall and then sell the developed site to Pyramid? If, on the one hand, the answer to these questions is "yes," then the market entry theory is no more than a troublesome mirage that could easily be circumvented by Pyramid's using a second party to buy the land and obtain the permit. If, on the other hand, the answer is "no," then Pyramid is forever tainted, forever prohibited—somewhat like a bill of attainder—from owning this particular site, and only because at some time in the past it had "entered the market" while an alternative was still available.

Furthermore, in a business that needs as much predictability as possible, the market entry theory will regrettably inject exquisite vagueness. When does a developer enter the market? When he first contemplates a development in the area? If so, in what area—the neighborhood, the village, the town, the state or the region? Does he enter the market when he first takes some affirmative action? If so, is that when he instructs his staff to research possible sites, when he commits money for more intensive study of those sites, when he contacts a real estate broker, when he first visits a site, or when he makes his first offer to purchase? Without answers to these questions a developer can never know whether to proceed through the expense of contracts, zoning proceedings, and EPA applications. Such a vague standard as "market entry" falls far short of the requirement that an agency articulate its standards with sufficient clarity so that the affected community may know what those standards are.

Even more important, the result reached by EPA and the majority is contrary to what Congress sought to achieve when it passed §1344. Pyramid has been "punished" for beginning its quest when the North Attleboro site was still available; but Sweedens Swamp nevertheless could be destroyed through an identical application by some other developer who happened to enter the market after that alternate site became unavailable. And this would be so even if another, better-suited site should become available after the second developer enters the market, because the "common sense" market entry theory looks only, and blindly, to the alternatives available at the time the applicant "entered the market."

THE PROPER THEORY FOR DETERMINING WHETHER AN ALTERNATE SITE IS AVAILABLE

Since Congress delegated to EPA the responsibility for striking a difficult and sensitive balance among economic and ecological concerns, EPA should do so only after considering the circumstances which exist, not when the developer first conceived of his idea, nor when he entered the market, nor even when he submitted his application; rather, EPA, like a court of equity, should have the full benefit of, and should be

required to consider, the circumstances which exist at the time it makes
its decision. This is the only method which would allow EPA to make a
fully informed decision—as Congress intended—based on whether at
the moment, there is available a site which can provide needed economic
and social benefits to the public, without unnecessarily disturbing valuable wetlands.

NOTES AND QUESTIONS

1. What impact is the "market theory" approach to determining
availability likely to have on developers' future choices of sites for non-
water-dependent activities? How would you respond to Judge Pratt's
criticism of the market entry theory? Is he right that another developer
who had not previously entered the market subsequently could use the
market entry theory to obtain a section 404 permit for developing Sweedens Swamp? Or would EPA require an applicant to show that no practicable alternative existed both when it entered the market *and* when it
applied for the permit?

2. Pyramid had rejected the North Attleboro site because of poor
road access and strong community resistance to previous development
efforts there. A consultant hired by the Corps' regional office had reported that it was feasible to develop either the Sweedens Swamp site
or the North Attleboro site but that "from a commercial standpoint only
one mall could survive in the area." 850 F.2d at 42. Pyramid subsequently
entered into a joint venture with the owner of the North Attleboro site
and built a shopping mall there that opened in September 1989.

3. The Corps has been criticized in the past for giving disproportionate weight to the interests of developers when performing alternatives analysis. For example, the Corps frequently has found that
alternatives that substantially reduce a developer's profit are not practicable (citing the section 404(b)(1) regulations' directive to consider "cost")
without considering the magnitude of environmental losses. See Comment, Bersani v. EPA: Toward a Plausible Interpretation of the §404(b)(1)
Guidelines for Evaluating Permit Applications for Wetland Development, 15 Colum. J. Envtl. L. 99, 104 (1990). The Corps initially subsumed
its section 404(b)(1) review within the "public interest" review the Corps
had performed under the old Rivers and Harbors Act, which emphasized
nonenvironmental values. 33 C.F.R. §320.4(a)(1). See Houck, Hard
Choices: The Analysis of Alternatives Under Section 404 of the Clean
Water Act and Similar Environmental Laws, 60 U. Colo. L. Rev. 773,
779 (1989). However, after a lawsuit by environmentalists, National Wildlife Federation v. Marsh, 14 E.L.R. 20262, 20264 (D.D.C. 1984), the
Corps agreed that EPA's section 404(b)(1) guidelines take precedence
and a permit may not be issued if it would not comply with the guidelines.

4. The Reagan Administration was particularly hostile to the section 404 program. The administration expanded the use of general permits and sought to expedite the issuance of individual permits. The Corps responded by issuing numerous permits over the objections of EPA and the Fish and Wildlife Service, as in the *Bersani* case. The Bush Administration at first was far more supportive of the section 404 program following President Bush's endorsement of a national goal of "no net loss" of wetlands during the 1988 presidential campaign. In April 1989 the Corps of Engineers issued interim guidance described by Professor Houck as "one of the most astonishing about-faces in the history of federal environmental law." Houck, above, at 795. The guidance, issued in the context of an application to develop a waterfront resort in Louisiana called Plantation Landing, acknowledges that section 404 is designed to discourage development in wetlands. It establishes that cost savings alone cannot justify a permit, because development in wetlands usually is less expensive, and that the relative size of adverse impacts also cannot justify a permit, since the Act is designed to avoid cumulative losses.

5. Professor Houck recommends abandoning the alternatives test and restricting permits in wetland areas to water-dependent activities— activities that must be located there, such as a pier. He would allow only two exceptions: the first for the rare circumstance in which a wetland location is less harmful than an upland alternative as provided in section 404(b)(1), the second for discharges demonstrating "fundamentally different factors" that justify a finding that the applicant is in effect water-dependent. See Houck, above, at 829-830.

6. While EPA has exercised its veto authority under section 404(c) fewer than two dozen times, it appears to have become more aggressive in recent years. In November 1990 it vetoed a massive water project called the Two Forks Dam that was designed to expand metropolitan Denver's water supply. EPA based its veto on an assessment of the project's environmental impact and a finding that less damaging alternatives were available to supplement the city's water supply. EPA Blocks Permit for Two Forks Dam; Less Damaging Alternatives said Available, 21 Env. Rep. 1483 (1990). In 1991 an EPA regional office began the veto process for a permit authorizing the filling of 76 acres of wetlands for a New Jersey housing development despite a mitigation plan for enhancing 155 acres of existing wetlands. Region II Administrator Begins Process to Veto Permit to Fill Wetlands in New Jersey, 22 Env. Rep. 304 (1991).

7. An important emerging issue in the administration of the section 404 program is the possibility of mitigation through the creation of new wetlands or enhancement of areas already degraded. In *Bersani* the developer had promised to turn an abandoned gravel pit into new wetlands that would cover a larger area than the wetlands the project would fill. While the Corps had argued that this proposal would reduce adverse

impact to the point at which the nonwetland site was no longer a less damaging alternative, EPA refused to accept this conclusion. Why not allow this land use equivalent of emissions trading? Professor Houck suggests several problems: such a policy would make it too easy to justify loss of wetlands; the areas lost almost always outweigh those gained; and the productivity of the new areas is much less, sometimes failing altogether. He proposes that such trades be a last resort and then only accepted in a ratio of three to one. EPA and the Corps have subsequently entered into a Memorandum of Agreement that establishes that mitigation measures should be used to minimize unavoidable adverse impacts rather than to offset avoidable ones when a practicable alternative is available. The Memorandum also endorses a "no net loss" of wetlands approach in specifying mitigation required to offset unavoidable impacts.

New Approaches to Wetlands Protection

Section 404 continues to be the focus of intense controversy, both in the courts and in Congress. As noted above, section 404 applies to only a small fraction (generally estimated to be 15 to 20 percent) of all activities that contribute to wetlands losses—the losses caused by discharge of dredged or fill material.

In recent years many leaders, including the National Governors' Association and President Bush, have called for a more aggressive effort to conserve wetlands, citing a goal of "no net loss." This goal was first proposed by the National Wetlands Policy Forum—a group of developers, farmers, oil executives, conservationists, and public officials convened by The Conservation Foundation and chaired by then-governor Thomas Kean of New Jersey. At a time when losses continue at a rate of 300,000 to 500,000 acres per year, "no net loss" is an ambitious objective. More important, it has focussed attention on the need for a much broader conservation strategy.

A goal of no net loss requires a systematic approach to wetlands conservation. The wetlands resource must be inventoried, losses identified, and a strategy devised to reduce losses to a minimum and compensate for those that continue. The Forum suggested that regulatory programs would have to be both more effective—broader in scope and more aggressive in application—and more efficient. It also emphasized the need for nonregulatory tools to encourage wetlands conservation. For example, crop support payments and other subsidies could be tied to wetlands conservation (as has been attempted by the 1985 Farm Bill), and property tax incentives could be created to encourage stewardship. Land use planning could take more considered account of wetlands resources so that development can be shaped and directed to avoid conflicts. Ambitious public programs to acquire, restore, and preserve valuable wetlands areas would also be essential, especially in areas such as the Louisiana coast where huge losses (40 to 50 square miles per year) are caused by natural erosion and the continuing effects of river channelization and diversion projects and oil exploration.

A panel of scientists appointed by the National Research Council recommended in 1991 that the nation embark on an aggressive effort to restore 10 million acres of wetlands by the year 2010. Noting that mitigation projects have often failed when undertaken by developers, the panel recommended that a National Aquatic Ecosystem Restoration Trust Fund be established to fund restoration efforts by federal and state·agencies. The agencies would offer financial incentives to private landowners to restore wetlands in cooperation with volunteer efforts. The panel also recommended that restoration efforts be undertaken for 2 million acres of polluted lakes and 400,000 miles of rivers and streams. Stevens, Panel Urges Big Wetlands Restoration Project, N.Y. Times, Dec. 12, 1991, at B16.

So far, there have been only scattered efforts to implement "no net loss" at the federal level. Indeed, political uproar over section 404, both in Congress and in the administration, threatens much of that program in the pending reauthorization of the Clean Water Act. See Pub. L. No. 102-104, 105 Stat. 510, 518 (1991) (barring the Corps from using its appropriations to identify or to delineate wetlands under the 1989 Delineation Manual). In the long term, a broader approach is clearly necessary if wetlands conservation efforts are to be effective.

G. ENVIRONMENTAL ENFORCEMENT: THE CASE OF THE CLEAN WATER ACT

To be effective, regulation must induce compliance. Thus it is critical that regulation incorporate enforcement provisions that create strong incentives for compliance. While the environmental statutes provide broad enforcement authorities, compliance problems have been widespread for several reasons. The vast number and diversity of regulatory targets can make monitoring and enforcement difficult. Regulations are not always written in a manner that facilitates proof of violations. Government agencies, which include some of the most notorious polluters, often lack the resources necessary for compliance and do not fear enforcement sanctions. Enforcement resources are inadequate to target all violators, and enforcement against the most serious violators can be costly because the procedural protections afforded defendants increase with the stringency of potential penalties.

Because enforcement issues have received the most attention in connection with the Clean Water Act, we explore them here to illustrate problems that are applicable to enforcement of environmental regulation generally. After focusing on the problem of how to monitor compliance by regulatory targets, we consider the various mechanisms available for taking enforcement action when noncompliance is discovered. We then explore the growth of criminal enforcement and the controversy engendered by citizen enforcement actions. We conclude by focusing on problems of enforcement delegation to state and local authorities.

1. Monitoring and Detecting Violations

Serious enforcement difficulties can be avoided if regulatory programs are designed to facilitate compliance monitoring. Establishing objective means for measuring and monitoring compliance can be enormously difficult given the vast number, variety, and complexity of pollutants and dischargers subject to environmental regulation. The Clean Water Act regulates more than 66,000 point sources discharging hundreds of different pollutants. Yet the Act's permit provisions have become a model for other enforcement programs, including the Clean Air Act's new national permit program. Permits embody a written record of the controls applicable to each source that can be compared with the results of monitoring to determine if violations have occurred.

Determining whether or not a discharger is in compliance with permit limits is not as easy as one might think. Inspectors cannot simply walk into a plant and insert "some perfectly accurate meter into the wastewater or smoke stack emission stream" and obtain "a constant rate-of-discharge result that could be expressed equally well in any time unit, from per second to per year." C. Russell, W. Harrington, and W. Vaughan, Enforcing Pollution Control Laws 10 (1986). Inspectors first have to gain access to a plant, which usually involves announcing inspections in advance, giving the plant operator an opportunity to conceal violations. Sampling is costly and time-consuming and may yield results with large margins of error.

> [E]ven when the source is trying to comply with the permit terms it will have fluctuating discharges. These fluctuations may have both periodic elements due to production patterns, boiler soot-blowing, or other routine causes as well as random components ultimately traceable to human or machine failure, fluctuations in ambient conditions such as temperature, or random startup and shutdown decisions. Thus, the stream being measured is not constant, and measurements at one time can be applied only to broader compliance questions through statistical inference with associated probabilities of errors of two types—that a violation will be found

where none exists or that true violations will be missed. To further complicate matters, the measurement instruments have their own errors that must be accounted for in the inference procedure. The perfect instrument does not exist. [Id.]

Faced with these difficulties, environmental enforcement authorities rely heavily on self-monitoring and self-reporting requirements as a means for detecting violations. The pollution control statutes generally authorize EPA to impose monitoring, recordkeeping, and reporting requirements (e.g., CWA §308(a)(A), CAA §114) on dischargers. Because reliance on regulatory targets to report their own violations has obvious drawbacks, the statutes also generally give enforcement officials the right to conduct inspections. However, EPA needs a warrant before it can inspect a business without the consent of the owner. Marshall v. Barlow's, Inc., 436 U.S. 307 (1978).

Although it is not widely known, most of the major federal environmental statutes have provisions that protect employees who report violations by their employers. These provisions prohibit an employer from discharging or discriminating against any employee who reports environmental violations (e.g., CWA §507, CAA §322, OSHA §660(c), RCRA §7001, CERCLA §110, SDWA §1450(i), TSCA §23). Regulations implementing these statutes appear at 29 C.F.R. §24.1 et seq. Whistleblowers may seek a hearing before an administrative law judge in the Department of Labor who may award them back pay, reinstatement, or other relief, subject to judicial review and civil judicial enforcement. These provisions have not been used extensively. Robert Devore of the Department of Labor reports that between 1983 and 1991, 490 whistleblower complaints were heard by the Department; 92 employees won judgments, which totaled $822,900. Most cases have involved the provisions of section 210 of the Energy Reorganization Act, which protects workers at nuclear power plants.

When it amended the Clean Air Act in 1990, Congress sought to improve compliance monitoring and the reporting of violations. To help enforcement authorities acquire evidence of violations, Congress added a bounty provision in section 113(f) of the Act that authorizes EPA to pay a reward of up to $10,000 to anyone who provides information that leads to a criminal conviction or civil penalty under the Act. Similar provisions are included in CERCLA §109(d). Congress also required utilities subject to Title IV of the Clean Air Act to install continuous emissions monitoring systems or their equivalent. CAA §412(a), 42 U.S.C. §7651k(a). Monitoring equipment is subject to tampering, which may result in criminal prosecutions when detected. See, e.g., Schneider, Coal Company Admits Safety Test Fraud, N.Y. Times, Jan. 19, 1991, at A14 (since 1980 six mining companies have been convicted for tampering with device that monitors levels of coal dust in mines). Congress has directed EPA in section 412(d) of the Clean Air Act to issue regulations specifying the consequences of breakdowns in monitoring equipment. To provide an incentive for utilities to keep monitors operating properly (and to prevent them from turning off monitors to conceal high levels of emissions), EPA has proposed to assume that emissions are at the highest possible levels throughout any period for which monitoring data are unavailable. Arguing that this will overstate true emissions, the utility industry has appealed to the Competitiveness Council in an effort to force EPA to change this proposal.

2. Enforcement Authorities and Policies

Even when violations of environmental regulations are discovered, enforcement can be time-consuming and expensive and its outcome uncertain. Defendants enjoy procedural protections that can be used to make it more costly for authorities to discharge their burden of proving violations. To facilitate enforcement, the environmental laws provide a menu of enforcement options—criminal, civil, and administrative—whose procedural requirements vary with the severity of potential sanctions. They also authorize citizens to sue violators when government authorities have failed to take enforcement action.

The enforcement provisions of the Clean Water Act, which are typical of those found in the major federal environmental laws, are outlined below. As these provisions illustrate, the statutes provide a broad range of penalties for violators. Criminal violations can result in imprisonment and heavy fines; civil suits can result in injunctive relief and substantial monetary penalties, and lesser monetary penalties may be imposed administratively. In addition, violators may be barred from receiving federal contracts or loans.

ENFORCEMENT PROVISIONS OF THE CLEAN WATER ACT

§308 authorizes monitoring and reporting requirements and inspections by authorities.

§309(a) authorizes issuance of administrative compliance orders.

§309(b) authorizes civil enforcement actions for injunctive relief.

§309(c) provides criminal penalties for negligent violations (fines of $2,500 to $25,000 per day and up to 1 year in prison), knowing violations (fines of $5,000 to $50,000 per day of violation and up to 3 years in prison with doubled

penalties for repeat violations), knowing endangerment of another (fines of up to $250,000 and 15 years in prison), and false statements (fines of up to $10,000 and 2 years in prison).

§309(d) provides civil penalties of up to $25,000 per day for each violation.

§309(e) & (f) require EPA to join states as defendants in suits against municipalities and authorizes suits against treatment works and dischargers for violations of pretreatment regulations.

§309(g) authorizes administrative penalties (up to $10,000 per violation with a $25,000 maximum for violations heard without an adjudicatory hearing—"Class I penalties"—and up to $10,000 per day with a $125,000 maximum for violations subject to adjudicatory hearings—"Class II penalties") and gives citizens the right to comment on them.

§402(h) authorizes ban on new sewer hookups to publicly owned treatment works violating their discharge permits.

§504 authorizes EPA to sue to restrain any source contributing to pollution "presenting an imminent or substantial endangerment" to public health or welfare.

§505 authorizes citizen suits for injunctive relief and civil penalties against any person violating an effluent standard or order and provides for awards of attorneys' fees to prevailing parties.

§508 gives EPA authority to blacklist violators, barring them from all federal contracts and loans.

Virtually every time it has reauthorized the major environmental statutes, Congress has expanded and strengthened their enforcement authorities. For example, when the Clean Water Act was amended in 1987, Congress substantially increased the maximum civil and criminal penalties and gave EPA administrative enforcement authority under the Act for the first time. In 1990 Congress added even stronger and more detailed enforcement provisions to the Clean Air Act. See CAA §113.

Because judicial enforcement actions generally are more formal and more expensive, environmental authorities usually go to court only to prosecute the most egregious violations. A former assistant attorney general responsible for environmental enforcement has noted, "[t]he simple truth is that we cannot bring . . . even a significant number of these [enforcement] actions to court." Dinkins, Shall We Fight or Will We Finish: Environmental Dispute Resolution in a Litigious Society, 14 Envtl. L. Rep. 10398 (1984). While defendants do not have a constitutional right to a jury trial in suits that seek exclusively equitable relief, the Supreme Court has held that the Seventh Amendment's right to a jury trial applies in suits for civil penalties under the environmental laws. Tull v. United States, 481 U.S. 412 (1987). Trials are expensive and time-consuming; thus, more than 95 percent of environmental enforcement cases are resolved through settlements. Settlements often include negotiated penalties incorporated into consent decrees approved by a court.

Resources devoted to federal environmental enforcement effort have increased substantially since the early days of the Reagan Administration. By the end of 1987, 140 Justice Department attorneys were assigned to environmental cases, compared with only 25 in January 1983. In fiscal year 1991, EPA referred a record 474 civil and criminal cases to the Department of Justice for prosecution, more than three and one-half times the number referred in 1982. Criminal enforcement actions were rare until recently (only 25 criminal cases were prosecuted in the 1970s); between 1983 and 1987, 339 federal criminal indictments were returned in environmental cases. Habicht, The Federal Perspective on Environmental Criminal Enforcement: How to Remain on the Civil Side, 17 Envtl. L. Rep. 10478, 10479 (1987). Between 1988 and 1990, 292 defendants were charged with criminal violations; of these 177 were convicted and sentenced to a combined total of more than 111 years in prison. EPA, Enforcement Accomplishments Report—FY 1990 (1991).

Despite the steady increase in judicial enforcement, the vast majority of environmental enforcement actions never see the courthouse door. More than 90 percent are handled through administrative enforcement procedures, which are procedurally simpler but provide less stringent penalties. In fiscal year 1990 EPA initiated 3,804 administrative enforcement actions and referred 440 cases to the Department of Justice for judicial enforcement; state authorities initiated 10,105 administrative actions, referring only 649 cases for judicial enforcement. Id. at 3-1 to 3-5. Figures 7.5 and 7.6 illustrate the changing subject matter of administrative and civil enforcement actions from 1977 to 1990.

Administrative enforcement actions may involve the issuance of administrative orders and the assessment of civil penalties. Most environmental statutes authorize EPA to issue administrative orders (see, e.g., CWA §309(g), RCRA §3008(a)), which give officials flexibility to specify remedial action that must be taken by a certain date. If, after notice and an opportunity for a hearing, the action specified in the administrative order is not taken, environmental authorities can go to court to seek its enforcement. The environmental laws also authorize EPA to assess administrative civil penalties, which may be contested in hearings before an administrative law judge whose decisions are subject to judicial review based on the administrative record. Nearly all administrative cases ultimately are settled; fewer than 5 percent proceed to hearings before an administrative law judge.

Minor violations also can be handled by sending a notice of vio-

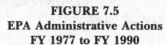

FIGURE 7.5
EPA Administrative Actions
FY 1977 to FY 1990

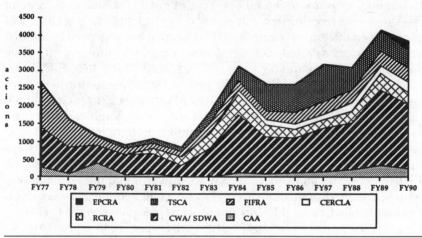

FIGURE 7.6
EPA Civil Referrals to DOJ
FY 1977 to FY 1990

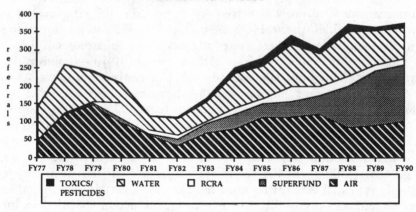

lation, which requires the recipient to correct a technical violation without assessing a penalty. Notices of violation may be used by federal enforcement officials to give state authorities operating delegated programs an opportunity to take enforcement action prior to the initiation of federal enforcement proceedings. The 1990 Clean Air Act Amendments also authorize EPA to issue field citations, akin to traffic tickets but with penalties of up to $5,000 per day of violation. CAA §113(d)(3).

Government enforcement authorities enjoy considerable discretion in deciding whether or not to initiate enforcement proceedings (see Heckler v. Chaney, 470 U.S. 821 (1985)) and in choosing the type of enforcement action to initiate. While "bean-counting" can give a misleading picture of overall enforcement activity, statistical data on enforcement actions suggest some overall patterns. As illustrated by Figures 7.5 and 7.6, the number of EPA enforcement actions dropped significantly in the early years of the Reagan Administration, confirming the widespread impression that the federal enforcement effort slackened substantially during that period. Since 1983 the number of enforcement actions has grown steadily and significantly. EPA enforcement has concentrated on violations of the Clean Water Act and the Clean Air Act, with CERCLA (Superfund) enforcement actions recently increasing in importance.

By contrast, the Safe Drinking Water Act has received little enforcement emphasis. While 101,588 violations of the Safe Drinking Water Act were reported in fiscal year 1987, states took enforcement action for only 2,544 of these violations; EPA brought only 50 enforcement actions. Provisions requiring water suppliers to notify their customers of violations were widely ignored; the public was notified of violations in only 5,269 cases. National Wildlife Federation, Danger on Tap (Oct. 1988). A 1990 report by the General Accounting Office found a continuing failure by states and water suppliers to test for, and to report, violations of drinking water standards.

The enormous number and diversity of regulatory targets makes the development of effective enforcement policy a particular challenge in the environmental area. EPA has pledged to increase cross-media enforcement actions and to emphasize pollution prevention programs. The Agency believes that it can better target violations involving the most significant risks to human health and the environment by focusing on specific industries and pollutants where compliance histories are poor. The trend of the early to mid-1980s for EPA to transfer greater enforcement authority to regional offices is now being reversed. EPA is using its enforcement authorities to encourage companies to incorporate environmental compliance concerns into management structures. Companies that violate environmental laws increasingly are being asked to adopt environmental auditing procedures to alert management to additional compliance problems and to ensure the existing problems do not recur. Requirements for environmental audits have been incorporated in some settlements, and EPA is also asking some companies to adopt pollution prevention programs as a condition for settlement.

Enforcement officials also are acting to improve the deterrent effect of enforcement actions by publicizing enforcement actions more ƒ widely and by increasing penalties. EPA has developed a "Policy on Civil Penalties" designed to ensure that penalties imposed on violators are sufficient to recoup the economic benefit of violations and to encourage future compliance. Under this policy civil penalties are calculated based on the economic benefit of delayed compliance (as calculated by a computer program developed by EPA staff), the gravity of the offense (based on its actual and potential impact on public health and the environment and its effect on EPA's ability to perform its regulatory functions), the wilfulness of the offense, and the violator's past compliance and cooperation with enforcement authorities. Debarment of violators from government contracts also is being used as a sanction.

The expense and risk of enforcement proceedings create substantial incentives for settlement. As a result, administrative penalties assessed against environmental violators often are reduced substantially when cases are settled. EPA's inspector general has criticized the Agency as a "paper tiger" that routinely agrees to large reductions in civil penalties without adequate justification. Enforcement Lax, U.S. Auditors Say, N.Y. Times, Oct. 4, 1989, at A21. The inspector general's report cited numerous cases in which proposed fines and penalties were reduced by up to 96 percent without any supporting documentation justifying the reductions. EPA has pledged to correct this problem. Habicht Promises Management Review of EPA Enforcement Program, Seeks Improvement, 19 Env. Rep. 1337 (1989).

NOTES AND QUESTIONS

1. How can incentives for gathering and reporting compliance data in an accurate and timely manner be improved? As noted above, EPA has proposed to adopt a presumption that emissions are at the highest possible levels when monitoring data are unavailable. What impact would this have on incentives for companies to keep their monitors operating properly? Is the utility industry correct in arguing that EPA's proposal is likely to overstate actual emissions? Even if that is so, does it necessarily follow that the proposal should be rejected?

2. As noted above, government officials enjoy considerable discretion in making decisions to initiate enforcement proceedings. The enforcement provisions of the Safe Drinking Water Act, however, purport to *require* EPA to take enforcement action in certain circumstances. Consider the language of section 1414(a) of the Safe Drinking Water Act, 42 U.S.C. §300g-3. Does it require EPA to take enforcement action in all cases where a state has failed to act 30 days after EPA finds that a public water supply system has violated national primary drinking water regulations? Is it realistic to expect that enforcement action be taken for

every violation? Is it legally possible to eliminate enforcement discretion by requiring an agency by statute to take enforcement action?

3. Efforts to limit enforcement discretion cut both ways. EPA is developing regulations to implement the new national permit program required by the Clean Air Act Amendments of 1990. At the behest of the Motor Vehicle Manufacturers Association, the Competitiveness Council has directed EPA to propose regulations stating that enforcement action will not be undertaken against violators of Clean Air Act permits unless the violation "is endangering or causing damage to public health or the environment." What impact would this have on EPA's ability to enforce the Clean Air Act?

3. Criminal Enforcement

While criminal penalties for environmental violations are found in the Refuse Act of 1899, criminal prosecutions have not played a significant role in environmental enforcement until recently. Criminal penalties were included in the major federal environmental statutes enacted in the 1970s. As these acts have been reauthorized, Congress has expanded the range of violations for which criminal penalties apply while increasing substantially the size of the penalties.

Virtually all the federal environmental laws now provide criminal penalties for "knowing" or "wilful" violations of environmental regulations. See, e.g., Clean Air Act §113(c); Clean Water Act §309(c); CERCLA §§103(b), (c), and (d)(2); RCRA §§3008(d) and (e); TSCA §§15 and 16; FIFRA §14(b). The Clean Air Act Amendments of 1990 make virtually all knowing violations of any requirement of the Act a felony, including violations of recordkeeping and reporting requirements. Both the Clean Water Act and Clean Air Act also impose criminal penalties for certain negligent acts that violate the statutes. CWA §309(c)(1), Apex Oil Co. v. United States, 530 F.2d 1291 (8th Cir.), cert. denied, 429 U.S. 827 (1976); United States v. Frezzo Brothers, Inc., 703 F.2d 62 (3d Cir.), cert. denied, 464 U.S. 829 (1983); CAA §113(c)(4).

Courts have long drawn a distinction between regulatory statutes to protect public health or safety and common law crimes in addressing what needs to be proved to establish a criminal violation. In United States v. Dotterweich, 320 U.S. 277 (1943) and United States v. Park, 421 U.S. 658 (1975), the Supreme Court indicated that responsible corporate officials can be held criminally liable for violating health or safety regulations without requiring proof of evil intent. Although there is very little case law interpreting some of the criminal provisions of the environmental laws, courts have built on these decisions by allowing juries to infer that acts are "knowing" or "wilful" from evidence demonstrating that a defendant should have known that an act is a violation. See, e.g.,

United States v. Sellers, 926 F.2d 410 (5th Cir. 1991) ("knowingly" in RCRA does not require knowledge that materials were regulated as hazardous wastes, but rather only that defendant knew that materials had potential to cause harm); United States v. McDonald & Watson Waste Oil Co., 933 F.2d 35 (1st Cir. 1991); United States v. Buckley, 934 F.2d 84 (6th Cir. 1991).

The environmental laws generally make both corporate officers and employees who make corporate decisions personally liable. United States v. Northeastern Pharmaceutical & Chemical Co., 810 F.2d 726, 745 (8th Cir. 1986). The Clean Water Act and Clean Air Act both expressly provide that "any responsible corporate officer" may be held liable for criminal acts. CWA §309(c)(6); CAA §113(c)(6). Employees can be held criminally liable if they knew or should have known that their employer failed to comply with applicable regulations. United States v. Johnson & Towers, 741 F.2d 662, 663 (3d Cir. 1984), cert. denied, 469 U.S. 1208 (1985) (RCRA). Even federal contractors have been found criminally liable. In United States v. Dee, 912 F.2d 741 (4th Cir. 1990), three civilian managers at the U.S. Army's Aberdeen Proving Ground were convicted of knowingly managing hazardous wastes without a permit in violation of RCRA.

The development of mandatory sentencing guidelines has the potential to increase substantially the sentences received by defendants convicted of criminal violations of the environmental laws. Guidelines adopted by the United States Sentencing Commission on November 1, 1987 abolished parole and severely restricted the use of probation for environmental crimes. Marzulla and Kappel, Nowhere to Run, Nowhere to Hide: Criminal Liability for Violations of Environmental Statutes in the 1990s, 16 Colum. J. Envtl. L. 201, 213 (1991). As a result, a defendant convicted of an environmental crime is now likely to receive two years in prison and a five-figure fine. Id.

How to provide an effective criminal sanction against a corporation responsible for an environmental disaster remains an open question following the *Exxon Valdez* oil spill. Although Exxon ultimately pled guilty to four misdemeanors and paid a criminal fine of $125 million and civil penalties and restitution exceeding $1 billion, the corporation's chairman previously had boasted that similar penalties would not have a material effect on Exxon's multibillion dollar annual business. After an outcry from the business community, the Sentencing Commission excluded environmental crimes from stiff new recommended guidelines for sentencing corporations that were submitted to Congress on May 1, 1991.

In an effort to encourage corporations to perform environmental audits the Justice Department issued guidelines in 1991 that offer leniency, but not complete immunity, to companies that discover and report violations promptly to regulators. Congress rejected a proposal to establish a "safe harbor" in the Clean Air Act that would preclude prosecutions for violations discovered and corrected following environmental audits due to fears that corporations could abuse the audit process to insulate themselves from prosecution for serious violations. California's Corporate Criminal Liability Act, Calif. Penal Code §387, uses a stick, rather than a carrot, to encourage disclosure by making nondisclosure of "a serious concealed danger" a felony punishable by up to three years in prison and a fine of up to $1 million.

Criminal prosecutions under the environmental laws have increased in recent years, though they remain only a tiny portion of all environmental enforcement cases. In 1982 the Justice Department established an environmental crimes unit to prosecute criminal violations of the environmental laws. EPA now has more than 60 criminal investigators, who have been given the right to carry firearms and to make arrests. A total of 104 defendants were charged in federal criminal cases involving environmental violations in fiscal year 1991. Most federal criminal prosecutions involved violations of RCRA's hazardous waste regulations or violations of the Clean Water Act. In fiscal year 1991, 72 defendants were convicted (45 individuals and 27 organizations) in 48 criminal cases. Enforcement Actions at EPA Continue to Climb in Civil, Criminal Cases, Penalty Assessments, 22 Env. Rep. 1832 (1991). A total of $14.1 million in fines was levied, a figure that will increase at least ninefold (due to the *Exxon Valdez* fine) when fiscal year 1992 data become available. Criminal enforcement is likely to continue to increase as more resources are devoted to the enforcement effort. The Pollution Prosecution Act of 1990 will quadruple the number of federal special agents and support staff devoted to criminal enforcement by 1995.

4. Citizen Suits to Enforce Environmental Regulations

Prior to enactment of the Clean Air Act Amendments of 1970, Congress considered proposals to enact legislation with burden-shifting provisions to make it easier for citizens to obtain judicial relief in common law actions. These proposals, which foreshadowed the approach employed today by California's Proposition 65, were not adopted. Instead, beginning in 1970 with the Clean Air Act, Congress included citizen suit provisions in virtually all the major environmental statutes it adopted (except for FIFRA). See, e.g., CAA §304, CWA §505, ESA §11(g), RCRA §7002, TSCA §18, CERCLA §310. These provisions were designed to enlist citizens as "private attorneys general," as under the Refuse Act, to supplement government enforcement.

The citizen suit provisions of the environmental laws generally authorize "any person" to commence an action against "any person" alleged to be in violation of the laws. They require citizens to notify the alleged violator and federal and state authorities prior to filing suit. Sixty days' notice usually is required, although the amount of notice can vary for certain violations (e.g., section 505(b) of the Clean Water Act authorizes suits alleging violations of NSPS requirements or toxic effluent standards to be brought immediately after notice, as does section 7002(b)(1)(A) of RCRA for violations of RCRA subtitle C). The citizen suit provisions usually specify that if federal or state authorities are diligently prosecuting an action to require compliance, filing of a citizen suit is barred, though citizens are authorized to intervene in federal enforcement actions as of right (e.g., CWA §505(b)(1)(B), CAA §304(b)(1)(B)).

While federal agencies and officials are among the "persons" who can be sued for violating environmental regulations, the statutes also generally authorize suits to force officials to perform their mandatory duties. For example, the Clean Water Act provides that the EPA administrator may be sued by citizens "where there is alleged a failure of the Administrator to perform any act or duty . . . which is not discretionary," 33 U.S.C. §1365(a)(1)(2). (The citizen suit provisions in the other statutes contain virtually identical language.) As discussed in Chapter 5, this has been an action-forcing device that has played a critical role in ensuring that EPA issues regulations implementating the environmental statutes.

While action-forcing litigation against EPA played a major role in the development of environmental law during the 1970s, citizen suits were rarely filed during this period against private parties who violated environmental regulations. This changed in 1982 due to concern over a dramatic decline in governmental enforcement effort during the early days of the Reagan Administration. The Natural Resources Defense Council initiated a national project to use citizen suits to fill the enforcement void.

The citizen suit project focused on enforcement of the Clean Water Act because it was easy to prove violations. Dischargers are required to file discharge monitoring reports (DMRs), which are available to the public and can serve as prima facie evidence of NPDES permit violations. Joined by local environmental groups, NRDC systematically scrutinized DMRs and sent 60-day notice letters to dischargers who reported violations of permit limits. Notice letters were then followed by citizen suits. As a result of this project, the total number of citizen suits brought under the Clean Water Act increased from 6 in 1981 to 62 in 1983, surpassing the 56 Clean Water Act cases referred by EPA to the Justice Department for prosecution that year. Miller, Private Enforcement of Federal Pollution Control Laws, 14 Envtl. L. Rep. 10407, 10424 (1984).

Based on self-reported violations contained in the DMRs, citizen suits became relatively easy to win, particularly after several courts rejected efforts to create new defenses to such suits (including claims that discharge monitoring reports prepared by defendants were too unreliable to serve as the basis for violations or that they violated the Fifth Amendment privilege against self-incrimination). After complaints from dischargers (the general counsel of the Chemical Manufacturers Association complained that his members would have contested permit provisions more aggressively if they had known that their permits were going to be enforced), EPA commissioned a comprehensive study of citizen suits in 1984. The study found that citizen suits generally had been operating in a manner consistent with the goals of the environmental statutes by both stimulating and supplementing government enforcement. Environmental Law Institute, Citizen Suits: An Analysis of Citizen Enforcement Actions Under EPA-Administered Statutes (1984). The study found no evidence that citizen suits had interfered with government enforcement efforts or that they had focused on trivial violations.

After courts rejected repeated efforts by dischargers to create new defenses to citizen suits, dischargers finally discovered a more successful strategy by focusing on the language of section 505 of the Clean Water Act, which authorizes suits against any person "alleged to be *in violation*" of the Act. Defendants argued that this language meant that citizen plaintiffs had to prove that dischargers were in violation of the Act at the moment a suit was filed and could not simply rely on past monitoring reports in order to prevail. This argument received a mixed reception in the U.S. Courts of Appeals, culminating in the following Supreme Court decision.

Gwaltney of Smithfield v. Chesapeake Bay Foundation
484 U.S. 49 (1987)

JUSTICE MARSHALL delivered the opinion of the Court.

In this case, we must decide whether §505(a) of the Clean Water Act, 33 U.S.C. §1365(a), confers federal jurisdiction over citizen suits for wholly past violations. . . .

The holder of a federal NPDES permit is subject to enforcement action by the Administrator for failure to comply with the conditions of the permit. The Administrator's enforcement arsenal includes administrative, civil, and criminal sanctions. §1319. The holder of a state NPDES permit is subject to both federal and state enforcement action for failure to comply. §§1319, 1342(b)(7). In the absence of federal or state enforcement, private citizens may commence civil actions against any person "alleged to be in violation of" the conditions of either a federal or state NPDES permit. §1365(a)(1). If the citizen prevails in such an action, the court may order injunctive relief and/or impose civil penalties payable to the United States Treasury. §1365(a).

The Commonwealth of Virginia established a federally approved state NPDES program administered by the Virginia State Water Control Board (Board). Va. Code §§62.1-44 et seq. (1950). In 1974, the Board issued a NPDES permit to ITT-Gwaltney authorizing the discharge of seven pollutants from the company's meat-packing plant on the Pagan River in Smithfield, Virginia. The permit, which was reissued in 1979 and modified in 1980, established effluent limitations, monitoring requirements, and other conditions of discharge. In 1981, petitioner Gwaltney of Smithfield acquired the assets of ITT-Gwaltney and assumed obligations under the permit.

Between 1981 and 1984, petitioner repeatedly violated the conditions of the permit by exceeding effluent limitations on five of the seven pollutants covered. These violations are chronicled in the Discharge Monitoring Reports (DMRs) that the permit required petitioner to maintain. The most substantial of the violations concerned the pollutants fecal coliform, chlorine, and total Kjeldahl nitrogen (TKN). Between October 27, 1981, and August 30, 1984, petitioner violated its TKN limitation 87 times, its chlorine limitation 34 times, and its fecal coliform limitation 31 times. Petitioner installed new equipment to improve its chlorination system in March 1982, and its last reported chlorine violation occurred in October 1982. The new chlorination system also helped to control the discharge of fecal coliform, and the last recorded fecal coliform violation occurred in February 1984. Petitioner installed an upgraded wastewater treatment system in October 1983, and its last reported TKN violation occurred on May 15, 1984.

Respondents Chesapeake Bay Foundation and Natural Resources Defense Council, two nonprofit corporations dedicated to the protection of natural resources, sent notice in February 1984, to Gwaltney, the Administrator of EPA, and the Virginia State Water Control Board, indicating respondents' intention to commence a citizen suit under the Act based on petitioner's violations of its permit conditions. Respondents proceeded to file this suit in June 1984, alleging that petitioner "has violated . . . [and] will continue to violate its NPDES permit." Respondents requested that the District Court provide declaratory and injunctive relief, impose civil penalties, and award attorney's fees and costs. The District Court granted partial summary judgment for respondents in August 1984, declaring Gwaltney "to have violated and to be in violation" of the Act. The District Court then held a trial to determine the appropriate remedy.

Before the District Court reached a decision, Gwaltney moved in May 1985 for dismissal of the action for want of subject-matter jurisdiction under the Act. Gwaltney argued that the language of §505(a), which permits private citizens to bring suit against any person "alleged to be in violation" of the Act, requires that a defendant be violating the Act at the time of suit. Gwaltney urged the District Court to adopt the analysis of the Fifth Circuit in Hamker v. Diamond Shamrock Chemical

Co., 756 F.2d 392 (1985), which held that "a complaint brought under [§505] must allege a violation occurring at the time the complaint is filed." Id., at 395. Gwaltney contended that because its last recorded violation occurred several weeks before respondents filed their complaint, the District Court lacked subject-matter jurisdiction over respondents' action.

The District Court rejected Gwaltney's argument concluding that §505 authorizes citizens to bring enforcement actions on the basis of wholly past violations. [It] found that "[t]he words 'to be in violation' may reasonably be read as comprehending unlawful conduct that occurred solely prior to the filing of the lawsuit as well as unlawful conduct that continues into the present." 611 F. Supp. 1542, 1547 (E.D. Va. 1985). In the District Court's view, this construction of the statutory language was supported by the legislative history and the underlying policy goals of the Act. Id., at 1550. The District Court held in the alternative that respondents satisfied the jurisdictional requirements of §505 because their complaint alleged in good faith that Gwaltney was continuing to violate its permit at the time the suit was filed. Id., at 1549, n.8.

The Court of Appeals affirmed, expressly rejecting the Fifth Circuit's approach in *Hamker* and holding that §505 "can be read to comprehend unlawful conduct that occurred only prior to the filing of a lawsuit as well as unlawful conduct that continues into the present." 791 F.2d 304, 309 (CA4 1986). The Court of Appeals concluded that its reading of §505 was consistent with the Act's structure, legislative history, and purpose. Although it observed that "[a] very sound argument can be made that [respondents'] allegations of continuing violations were made in good faith," the Court of Appeals declined to rule on the District Court's alternative holding, finding it unnecessary to the disposition of the case. Id., at 308, n.9.

Subsequent to the issuance of the Fourth Circuit's opinion, the First Circuit also had occasion to construe §505. It took a position different from that of either the Fourth or the Fifth Circuit, holding that jurisdiction lies under §505 when "the citizen-plaintiff fairly alleges a continuing likelihood that the defendant, if not enjoined, will again proceed to violate the Act." Pawtuxet Cove Marina, Inc. v. Ciba-Geigy Corp., 807 F.2d 1089, 1094 (1986). The First Circuit's approach precludes suit based on wholly past violations, but permits suit when there is a pattern of intermittent violations, even if there is no violation at the moment suit is filed. We granted certiorari to resolve this three-way conflict in the Circuits. . . .

It is well settled that "the starting point for interpreting a statute is the language of the statute itself." Consumer Product Safety Comm'n v. GTE Sylvania, Inc., 447 U.S. 102, 108 (1980). The Court of Appeals concluded that the "to be in violation" language of §505 is ambiguous, whereas petitioner asserts that it plainly precludes the construction adopted below. We must agree with the Court of Appeals that §505 is not a provision in which Congress' limpid prose puts an end to all dispute. But to acknowledge ambiguity is not to conclude that all interpretations are equally plausible. The most natural reading of "to be in violation" is a requirement that citizen-plaintiffs allege a state of either continuous or intermittent violation—that is, a reasonable likelihood that a past polluter will continue to pollute in the future. Congress could have phrased its requirement in language that looked to the past ("to have violated"), but it did not choose this readily available option.

Respondents urge that the choice of the phrase "to be in violation," rather than phrasing more clearly directed to the past, is a "careless accident," the result of a "debatable lapse of syntactical precision." But the prospective orientation of that phrase could not have escaped Congress' attention. Congress used identical language in the citizen suit provisions of several other environmental statutes that authorize only prospective relief. See, e.g., Clean Air Act, 42 U.S.C. §7604; Resource Conservation and Recovery Act of 1976, 42 U.S.C. §6972 (1982 ed. and Supp. III); Toxic Substances Control Act, 15 U.S.C. §2619 (1982 ed. and Supp. IV). Moreover, Congress has demonstrated in yet other statutory provisions that it knows how to avoid this prospective implication by using language that explicitly targets wholly past violations. . . .

Our reading of the "to be in violation" language of §505(a) is bolstered by the language and structure of the rest of the citizen suit provisions in §505 of the Act. These provisions together make plain that the interest of the citizen-plaintiff is primarily forward-looking.

One of the most striking indicia of the prospective orientation of the citizen suit is the pervasive use of the present tense throughout §505. A citizen suit may be brought only for violation of a permit limitation "which is in effect" under the Act. 33 U.S.C. §1365(f). Citizen-plaintiffs must give notice to the alleged violator, the Administrator of EPA, and the State in which the alleged violation "occurs." §1365(b)(1)(A). A Governor of a State may sue as a citizen when the Administrator fails to enforce an effluent limitation "the violation of which is occurring in another State and is causing an adverse effect on the public health or welfare in his State." §1365(h). The most telling use of the present tense is in the definition of "citizen" as "a person . . . having an interest which is or may be adversely affected" by the defendant's violations of the Act. §1365(g). This definition makes plain what the undeviating use of the present tense strongly suggests: the harm sought to be addressed by the citizen suit lies in the present or the future, not in the past.

Any other conclusion would render incomprehensible §505's notice provision, which requires citizens to give 60 days notice of their intent to sue to the alleged violator as well as to the Administrator and the State. §1365(b)(1)(A). If the Administrator or the State commences enforcement action within that 60 day period, the citizen suit is barred, presumably because governmental action has rendered it unnecessary. §1365(b)(1)(B). It follows logically that the purpose of notice to the alleged violator is to give it an opportunity to bring itself into complete compliance with the Act and thus likewise render unnecessary a citizen suit. If we assume, as respondents urge, that citizen suits may target wholly past violations, the requirement of notice to the alleged violator becomes gratuitous. Indeed, respondents, in propounding their interpretation of the Act, can think of no reason for Congress to require such notice other than that "it seemed right" to inform an alleged violator that it was about to be sued.

Adopting respondents' interpretation of §505's jurisdictional grant would create a second and even more disturbing anomaly. The bar on citizen suits when governmental enforcement action is under way suggests that the citizen suit is meant to supplement rather than to supplant governmental action. The legislative history of the Act reinforces this view of the role of the citizen suit. The Senate Report noted that "[t]he Committee intends the great volume of enforcement actions [to] be brought by the State," and that citizen suits are proper only "if the Federal, State, and local agencies fail to exercise their enforcement responsibility." S. Rep. No. 92-414, p. 64 (1971), reprinted in 2 A Legislative History of the Water Pollution Control Act Amendments of 1972, p. 1482 (1973) (hereinafter Leg. Hist.). Permitting citizen suits for wholly past violations of the Act could undermine the supplementary role envisioned for the citizen suit. This danger is best illustrated by an example. Suppose that the Administrator identified a violator of the Act and issued a compliance order under §309(a). Suppose further that the Administrator agreed not to assess or otherwise seek civil penalties on the condition that the violator take some extreme corrective action, such as to install particularly effective but expensive machinery, that it otherwise would not be obliged to take. If citizens could file suit, months or years later, in order to seek the civil penalties that the Administrator chose to forgo, then the Administrator's discretion to enforce the Act in the public interest would be curtailed considerably. The same might be said of the discretion of state enforcement authorities. Respondents' interpretation of the scope of the citizen suit would change the nature of the citizens' role from interstitial to potentially intrusive. We cannot agree that Congress intended such a result. . . .

Our conclusion that §505 does not permit citizen suits for wholly past violations does not necessarily dispose of this lawsuit, as both lower courts recognized. The District Court found persuasive the fact that "[respondents'] allegation in the complaint, that Gwaltney was continuing to violate its NPDES permit when plaintiffs filed suits, appears to have been made fully in good faith." 611 F. Supp., at 1549, n.8. On this basis, the District Court explicitly held, albeit in a footnote, that "even if Gwaltney were correct that a district court has no jurisdiction over citizen suits based entirely on unlawful conduct that occurred entirely in the past, the Court would still have jurisdiction here." Ibid. The Court of Appeals acknowledged, also in a footnote, that "[a] very sound argument can be made that [respondents'] allegations of continuing violations were made in good faith," 791 F.2d, at 308, n.9, but expressly declined to rule on this alternative holding. Because we agree that §505 confers jurisdiction over citizen suits when the citizen-plaintiffs make a good-faith allegation of continuous or intermittent violation, we remand the case to the Court of Appeals for further consideration.

Petitioner argues that citizen-plaintiffs must prove their allegations of ongoing noncompliance before jurisdiction attaches under §505. We cannot agree. The statute does not require that a defendant "be in violation" of the Act at the commencement of suit; rather, the statute requires that a defendant be "*alleged* to be in violation." Petitioner's construction of the Act reads the word "alleged" out of §505. As petitioner itself is quick to note in other contexts, there is no reason to believe that Congress' drafting of §505 was sloppy or haphazard. We agree with the Solicitor General that "Congress's use of the phrase 'alleged to be in violation' reflects a conscious sensitivity to the practical difficulties of detecting and proving chronic episodic violations of environmental standards." Our acknowledgment that Congress intended a good-faith allegation to suffice for jurisdictional purposes, however, does not give litigants license to flood the courts with suits premised on baseless allegations. Rule 11 of the Federal Rules of Civil Procedure, which requires pleadings to be based on a good-faith belief, formed after reasonable inquiry, that they are "well grounded in fact," adequately protects defendants from frivolous allegations.

Petitioner contends that failure to require proof of allegations under §505 would permit plaintiffs whose allegations of ongoing violation are reasonable but untrue to maintain suit in federal court even though they lack constitutional standing. Petitioner reasons that if a defendant is in complete compliance with the Act at the time of suit, plaintiffs have suffered no injury remediable by the citizen suit provisions of the Act. Petitioner, however, fails to recognize that our standing cases uniformly recognize that allegations of injury are sufficient to invoke the jurisdiction of the court. In Warth v. Seldin, 422 U.S. 490, 501 (1975), for example, we made clear that a suit will not be dismissed for lack of standing if there are sufficient "allegations of fact"—not proof—in the complaint or supporting affidavits. This is not to say, however, that such allegations may not be challenged. In United States v. SCRAP, 412 U.S. 669, 689 (1973), we noted that if the plaintiffs' "allegations [of standing] were in fact untrue, then the [defendants] should have moved for summary judgment on the standing issue and demonstrated to the District Court that the allegations were sham and raised no genuine issue of fact." If the defendant fails to make such a showing after the plaintiff offers evidence to support the allegation, the case proceeds to trial on the merits, where the plaintiff must prove the allegations in order to prevail. But the Constitution does not require that the plaintiff offer this proof as a threshold matter in order to invoke the District Court's jurisdiction.

Petitioner also worries that our construction of §505 would permit citizen-plaintiffs, if their allegations of ongoing non-compliance become false at some later point in the litigation because the defendant begins to comply with the Act, to continue nonetheless to press their suit to conclusion. According to petitioner, such a result would contravene both the prospective purpose of the citizen suit provisions and the "case or controversy" requirement of Article III. Longstanding principles of mootness, however, prevent the maintenance of suit when " 'there is no reasonable expectation that the wrong will be repeated.' " United States v. W. T. Grant Co., 345 U.S. 629, 633 (1953) (quoting United States v. Aluminum Co. of America, 148 F.2d 416, 448 (CA2 1945)). In seeking to have a case dismissed as moot, however, the defendant's burden "is a heavy one." 345 U.S., at 633. The defendant must demonstrate that it is *absolutely clear* that the alleged wrongful behavior could not reasonably be expected to recur." United States v. Phosphate Export Assn., Inc., 393 U.S. 199, 203 (1968) (emphasis added). Mootness doctrine thus protects defendants from the maintenance of suit under the Clean Water Act based solely on violations wholly unconnected to any present or future wrongdoing, while it also protects plaintiffs from defendants who seek to evade sanction by predictable "protestations of repentance and reform." United States v. Oregon State Medical Society, 343 U.S. 326, 333 (1952).

Because the court below erroneously concluded that respondents could maintain an action based on wholly past violations of the Act, it declined to decide whether respondents' complaint contained a good-faith allegation of ongoing violation by petitioner. We therefore remand the case for consideration of this question. The judgment of the Court of Appeals is vacated, and the case is remanded for further proceedings consistent with this opinion.

Justice SCALIA, with whom Justice STEVENS and Justice O'CONNOR join, concurring in part and concurring in the judgment.

I join Parts I and II of the Court's opinion [holding that section 505 does not authorize suits for a wholly past violation]. I cannot join Part III [holding that section 505 authorizes suits by plaintiffs who make a good-faith allegation of a continuous or intermittent violation] because I believe it misreads the statute to create a peculiar new form of subject-matter jurisdiction.

The Court concludes that subject-matter jurisdiction exists under §505 if there is a good-faith allegation that the defendant is "in violation."

Thereafter, according to the Court's interpretation, the plaintiff can never be called on to prove that jurisdictional allegation. This creates a regime that is not only extraordinary, but to my knowledge utterly unique. I can think of no other context in which, in order to carry a lawsuit to judgment, allegations are necessary but proof of those allegations (if they are contested) is not. The Court thinks it necessary to find that Congress produced this jurisprudential anomaly because any other conclusion, in its view, would read the word "alleged" out of §505. It seems to me that, quite to the contrary, it is the Court's interpretation that ignores the words of the statute.

Section 505(a) states that "any citizen may *commence* a civil action on his own behalf . . . against any person . . . who is alleged to be in violation . . ." (emphasis added). There is of course nothing unusual in the proposition that only an allegation is required to *commence* a lawsuit. Proof is never required, and could not practicably be required, at that stage. From this clear and unexceptionable language of the statute, one of two further inferences can be made: (1) The inference the Court chooses, that the requirement for commencing a suit is the same as the requirement for maintaining it, or (2) the inference that, in order to maintain a suit the allegations that are required to commence it must, if contested, be proven. It seems to me that to favor the first inference over the second is to prefer the eccentric to the routine. It is well ingrained in the law that subject-matter jurisdiction can be called into question *either* by challenging the sufficiency of the allegation *or* by challenging the accuracy of the jurisdictional facts alleged. Had Congress intended us to eliminate the second form of challenge, and to create an extraordinary regime in which the jurisdictional fact consists of a good-faith belief, it seems to me it would have delivered those instructions in more clear fashion than merely specifying how a lawsuit can be commenced.

In my view, therefore, the issue to be resolved by the Court of Appeals on remand of this suit is not whether the allegation of a continuing violation on the day suit was brought was made in good faith after reasonable inquiry, but whether the petitioner was in fact "in violation" on the date suit was brought. The phrase in §505(a), "to be in violation," unlike the phrase "to be violating" or "to have committed a violation," suggests a state rather than an act—the opposite of a state of compliance. A good or lucky day is not a state of compliance. Nor is the dubious state in which a past effluent problem is not recurring at the moment but the cause of that problem has not been completely and clearly eradicated. When a company has violated an effluent standard or limitation, it remains, for purposes of §505(a), "in violation" of that standard or limitation so long as it has not put in place remedial measures that clearly eliminate the cause of the violation. It does not suffice to defeat subject-matter jurisdiction that the success of the attempted remedies becomes clear months or even weeks after the suit is filed. Subject-matter jurisdiction "depends on the state of things at the time of the action brought"; if it existed when the suit was brought, "subsequent events" cannot "oust" the court of jurisdiction. It is this requirement of clarity of cure for a past violation, contained in the phrase "to be in violation," rather than a novel theory of subject-matter jurisdiction by good-faith allegation, that meets the Court's concern for " 'the practical difficulties of detecting and proving chronic episodic violations,' " quoting Brief for the United States as Amicus Curiae 18.

Thus, I think the question on remand should be whether petitioner had taken remedial steps that had clearly achieved the effect of curing all past violations by the time suit was brought. I cannot claim that the Court's standard and mine would differ greatly in their practical application. They would, for example, almost certainly produce identical results in this lawsuit. See 611 F. Supp. 1542, 1549, n.8 (ED Va. 1985) (District Court, in stating that allegation of continuing violation was in good faith, relied entirely on post-complaint uncertainty as to whether cause of TKN violation was cured). This practical insignificance, however, makes all the more puzzling the Court's willingness to impute to Congress creation of an unprecedented scheme where that which must be alleged need not be proved.

Even if the Court were correct that no evidence of a state of noncompliance has to be produced to survive a motion for dismissal on grounds of subject-matter jurisdiction, such evidence would still be required in order to establish the plaintiff's standing. While Gwaltney did not seek certiorari (or even appeal to the Court of Appeals) on the denial of its motion to dismiss for lack of standing, it did raise the standing issue before us here and we in any event have an independent obligation to inquire into standing where it is doubtful. If it is undisputed that the defendant was in a state of compliance when this suit was filed, the plaintiff would have been suffering no remediable injury in fact that would support suit. The constitutional requirement for such injury is reflected in the statue itself, which defines "citizen" as one who has "an interest which is or may be adversely affected." 33 U.S.C. §1365(g).

Accordingly, even on the Court's theory of this case it seems to me that the remand should require the lower court to consider not just good-faith allegation of a state of violation but its actual existence. . . . Of course that disposition would call attention to the fact that we have interpreted the statute to confer subject-matter jurisdiction over a class of cases in which, by the terms of the statute itself, there cannot possibly be standing to sue.

NOTES AND QUESTIONS

1. After *Gwaltney*, under what circumstances can a citizen suit be maintained in light of the "in violation" language of section 505? What

must a plaintiff allege about the violation in order to be authorized to sue? Can a plaintiff be required to prove at trial that this allegation is true?

2. The Court's decision is premised on the notion that citizen suits can only be used to address present or future harms. Is Justice Marshall correct that "[a]ny other conclusion would render incomprehensible" the 60-day notice requirement? Could a notice requirement be useful even if citizen suits could be brought against wholly past violations?

3. As noted above, the Clean Water Act had been the most popular vehicle for citizen suits because it was easy to prove that a violation had occurred using defendants' own discharge monitoring reports (DMRs). After *Gwaltney*, citizens must be prepared to prove the likelihood of ongoing violations. What constitutes an "ongoing" or "continuing" violation? Can a citizen prove an ongoing violation solely by reference to the DMRs? The Court did not accept Gwaltney's argument that the "in violation" language required plaintiffs to prove that the violation was occurring at the moment suit was filed. Note Justice Scalia's comment that neither a "good or lucky day" nor "the dubious state in which a past effluent problem is not recurring at the moment but the cause of that problem has not been completely and clearly eradicated" was sufficient to place a discharger in a state of compliance. Can a one-shot discharge be considered an "ongoing" violation if its harmful effects still linger?

4. How does Justice Marshall answer the question of what happens if a good-faith allegation of a continuing violation proves to be untrue? Do you agree with Justice Scalia's view that if a violation had been corrected the plaintiff would not have standing because there would be "no remediable injury in fact that could support the suit"? After a defendant has voluntarily corrected a violation is it really no longer possible to provide judicial redress? Wouldn't the possibility of a subsequent penalty provide some redress, not only by deterring future violations but also by reducing the likelihood that the past violation would ever have occurred? Has the Supreme Court construed the purpose of citizen suits too narrowly as abatement rather than deterrence, thus undermining efforts to use citizen suits to encourage pollution prevention?

5. Does *Gwaltney* make it possible for defendants to defeat any citizen suit for readily correctable violations? If so, will citizen suits only be able to deter violations that are the most difficult for defendants to avoid? The result in *Gwaltney* is a particularly ironic contrast to the Justice Department's 1970 policy for suits under the Refuse Act, which encouraged suits "to punish or prevent significant discharges which are either accidental or infrequent, but which are not of a continuing nature resulting from the ordinary operations of a manufacturing plant." United States Department of Justice, Guidelines for Litigation Under the Refuse Act §11 (1970). Can *Gwaltney* be reconciled with this policy?

6. One commentator notes that the *Gwaltney* decision "has provided a great incentive for defense counsel to raise every issue and use any

means available to delay trial as long as possible." He notes that "[i]f trial can be delayed long enough for the defendant to come into compliance, it can escape from the suit and avoid any penalty." Miller, Gwaltney of Smithfield, Ltd. v. Chesapeake Bay Foundation: Invitation to the Dance of Litigation, 18 Envtl. L. Rep. 10098, 10103 (1988). Is this what you would advise your client to do if you were defending a citizen suit? Is such a result desirable from an environmental standpoint?

7. The Court rejects the Chesapeake Bay Foundation's explanation that the phrase "to be in violation" was a "careless accident" by observing that Congress used identical language in the citizen suit provisions contained in other environmental laws. Yet isn't it reasonable to assume that Congress simply borrowed the same language whenever it wanted to include a citizen suit provision in subsequent legislation, thus buttressing CBF's argument?

The Congressional Response to *Gwaltney*

Gwaltney's impact is potentially broad precisely because the "to be in violation" language was repeated in the citizen suit provisions of other federal environmental statutes. However, since the *Gwaltney* controversy Congress has been more careful in its choice of words. The citizen suit provision included in the Emergency Planning and Community Right-to-Know Act, EPCRTKA §326, 42 U.S.C. §11046, authorizes any person to sue an owner or operator of a facility "for *failure to do*" any of four enumerated requirements (e.g., submitting a toxic chemical release form required by section 313). When Congress amended the Clean Air Act in 1990 it provided that after November 15, 1992 the language "alleged to be in violation" would be replaced with the phrase "alleged to have violated (if there is evidence that the alleged violation has been repeated) or to be in violation." CAA §707(g), 42 U.S.C. §7604(g) (1993). Similar amendments are under consideration as Congress considers reauthorization of the Clean Water Act.

How should these provisions be interpreted? Do they authorize citizen suits for wholly past violations? Note that both section 326 of EPCRTKA and section 707(g) of the CAA retain the 60-day notice requirement that the Court found to be a striking sign of section 505's "prospective orientation." Do these amendments reflect a larger pattern of greater congressional specificity in response to narrow interpretations of public law by the Supreme Court? See Eskridge, Overriding Supreme Court Statutory Interpretation Decisions, 101 Yale L.J. 331 (1991).

The *Gwaltney* Remand

On remand, the Fourth Circuit interpreted the *Gwaltney* decision to authorize citizens to file suit based on "a good faith allegation of ongoing violation" but to require proof of such a violation at trial. Chesapeake Bay Foundation v. Gwaltney of Smithfield, Ltd., 844 F.2d 170 (4th Cir. 1988). The court noted that this could be accomplished either "(1) by proving violations that continue on or after the date the complaint is filed, or (2) by adducing evidence from which a reasonable trier of fact could find a continuing likelihood of a recurrence in intermittent or sporadic violations." The district court then reinstated the entire judgment. The judge found that although the violations had not continued, when the suit was filed "there existed a very real danger and likelihood of further violation" because witnesses had expressed doubt that the upgraded wastewater treatment system would cure all nitrogen discharge violations. Chesapeake Bay Foundation v. Gwaltney of Smithfield, Ltd., 688 F. Supp. 1078, 1079 (E.D. Va. 1988). Gwaltney then appealed to the Fourth Circuit.

The Fourth Circuit affirmed the district court's conclusion that a penalty could be imposed even though the violations did not recur and rejected Gwaltney's claims of mootness and lack of standing. Chesapeake Bay Foundation v. Gwaltney of Smithfield, Ltd., 890 F.2d 690 (4th Cir. 1989). The court held that the plaintiffs did not lack standing because judicial redress could be provided to them through the deterrent effect of civil penalties. The court held that the case was not moot, regardless of subsequent events, because there was an ongoing violation when the suit was filed and "a suit seeking penalties is intrinsically incapable of being rendered moot by the polluter's corrective actions." 890 F.2d at 696. However, the court held that "for purposes both of determining ongoing violations and of assessing penalties" it must consider separately each permit parameter alleged to have been violated. 890 F.2d at 698. The court affirmed the $289,822 penalty for nitrogen (TKN) discharge violations by holding that even though the last violation occurred prior to filing of the lawsuit a "reasonable trier of fact could find a continuing likelihood of a recurrence in intermittent or sporadic violations" of the permit's TKN limits. But the court reversed the $995,500 penalty for chlorine violations by holding that no reasonable person could allege in good faith an ongoing violation of the permit's chlorine limits.

Citizen Suits in the Aftermath of *Gwaltney*

Questions raised by *Gwaltney* have been addressed by the lower federal courts in numerous subsequent cases as defendants have sought to block citizen suits. The post-*Gwaltney* cases generally indicate that: (1) determinations concerning whether or not a violation is ongoing are to be made as of the time the complaint is filed, Atlantic States Legal Foundation, Inc. v. Tyson Foods, Inc., 897 F.2d 1128 (11th Cir. 1990); (2) a violation is not ongoing if remedial measures ensure that there is no reasonable prospect for recurrence, Chesapeake Bay Foundation v. Gwaltney of Smithfield, Ltd., 844 F.2d 170 (4th Cir. 1988) (*Gwaltney II*); (3) plaintiffs need only make a good-faith allegation of an ongoing violation in order to be able to file suit, Sierra Club v. Union Oil of California, 853 F.2d 667 (9th Cir. 1988), but they must be able to prove it to prevail at trial, *Gwaltney II;* Carr v. Alta Verde Industries, 924 F.2d 558 (5th Cir. 1991); and (4) courts are divided on whether a parameter-by-parameter assessment of violations must be made in determining whether a violation is ongoing. Compare *Gwaltney II* with NRDC v. Texaco Refining and Marketing, 719 F. Supp. 281 (C.D. Del. 1989), affd., 31 ERC 1605 (3d Cir. 1990). See also Unterberger, Citizen Enforcement Suits: Putting *Gwaltney* to Rest and Setting Sights on the Clean Air Act, 21 Env. Rep. 1631 (1991); Smith, The Viability of Citizens' Suits Under the Clean Water Act After Gwaltney of Smithfield, Ltd. v. Chesapeake Bay Foundation, 40 Case W. Res. L. Rev. 1 (1989-1990).

In *Gwaltney* the Supreme Court warned against changing "the nature of the citizens' role from interstitial to potentially intrusive" for fear that citizen suits could infringe on the exercise of enforcement discretion by federal and state authorities. Courts in subsequent cases have wrestled with the question whether a properly commenced citizen suit may continue after the defendant reaches a settlement agreement with government officials. In Atlantic States Legal Foundation v. Eastman Kodak Co., 933 F.2d 124 (2d Cir. 1991), the Second Circuit held that as long as the settlement reasonably assures that the violations alleged in the citizen suit have ceased and will not recur, then the citizen suit cannot proceed even though the state did not initiate enforcement proceedings during the 60-day statutory notice period. However, the court held that plaintiffs could seek an attorneys' fees recovery because they had motivated the settlement agreement. In EPA v. City of Green Forest, 921 F.2d 1394 (8th Cir. 1990), cert. pending, the Eighth Circuit reached a similar decision, holding that a consent decree filed by EPA after a properly commenced citizen suit could bar the citizen action. Even though the plaintiffs had been precluded from participating in the consent decree negotiations, the court noted that their role as private attorneys general was fully served by the EPA. While noting that "there may be some cases in which it would be appropriate to let a citizens' action go forward in the wake of a subsequently-filed government enforcement action," the court emphasized that EPA must be afforded a preeminent role in enforcing CWA violations. 921 F.2d at 1404. Other courts have stressed that the government enforcement cannot bar a previously filed citizen suit unless it addresses the claims made in the citizen suit. See Hudson River Fishermen's Association v. County of Westchester, 686 F. Supp. 1044 (S.D.N.Y. 1988).

Prior to the 1987 Amendments, the language of the Clean Water Act's citizen suit provision provided that the only government enforcement action that barred a citizen suit was "a civil or criminal action in a court of the United States," §505(b)(1)(B). Administrative enforcement actions were not held to bar citizen suits because they were limited to small penalties assessed in proceedings in which citizens could not intervene. Friends of the Earth v. Consolidated Rail Corp., 768 F.2d 57 (2d Cir. 1985). When it gave EPA administrative enforcement authority in the 1987 Amendments, Congress added a provision precluding citizens from obtaining civil penalties in citizen suits if EPA had filed an administrative enforcement action or if "a State has commenced and is diligently prosecuting an action under a State law comparable to [§309(g)]." §309(g)(6)(A). However, Congress required that citizens be given an opportunity to comment on proposed administrative penalties, §309 (g)(4)(A), and to seek a hearing, §309(g)(4)(B), and judicial review to contest penalty assessments, §309(g)(8). In light of these provisions, courts are wrestling with how to determine the comparability of state administrative enforcement proceedings. See Connecticut Coastal Fishermen's Association v. Remington Arms Co., 777 F. Supp. 173 (D. Conn. Sept. 11, 1991) (state need only have authority to assess civil penalties, but need not exercise it for state regulatory scheme to be comparable); North and South Rivers Watershed Association v. Town of Scituate, 755 F. Supp. 484 (D. Mass. 1991) (while administrative order issued under state law that does not authorize civil penalties, overall state regulatory scheme is comparable because it contains penalty assessment provisions equivalent to those of CWA); Atlantic States Legal Foundation v. Universal Tool & Stamping, 735 F. Supp. 1404, 1415 (N.D. Ind. 1990) (Indiana law not comparable because it does not provide for public notice and participation, penalty assessment, judicial review, and other matters provided by section 309(g)).

     While subsequent government enforcement action may bar properly commenced citizen suits, corrective action by the violator generally has not. The Fourth and Eleventh Circuits have recognized that post-complaint corrective actions can moot claims for injunctive relief, but not claims for civil penalties for both pre- and post-complaint violations. See Atlantic State Legal Foundation v. Tyson Foods, 897 F.2d 1128 (11th Cir. 1990); Chesapeake Bay Foundation v. Gwaltney of Smithfield, 890 F.2d 690, 696-697 (4th Cir. 1989). In *Tyson Foods*, the district court had stayed the proceedings in order to allow the violator to come into compliance and then had dismissed the citizen suit. The Eleventh Circuit reversed, holding that if a plaintiff proved that the alleged violations were "ongoing" at the time the complaint was filed, even if subsequent actions of the violator completely remedied the violations, claims for injunctive relief may be moot, but claims for civil penalties for pre- and post-complaint violations were not moot. The court emphasized the role civil penalties play in deterring violations and noted that the district court's decision would defeat the purpose of citizen suits as a tool for supplementing governmental action. 897 F.2d at 1136-1137.

Implementation of the permit provisions of the Clean Air Act Amendments of 1990 eventually may produce a new wave of citizen suits. Section 504 of the Clean Air Act mandates new monitoring and reporting requirements that will facilitate citizen suits for permit violations. The 1990 Amendments specifically authorize the imposition of "appropriate civil penalties" in citizen suits, §304(a), and they direct that such penalties either be deposited into a special fund "to finance air compliance and enforcement activities," §304(g)(1), or "be used in beneficial mitigation projects" (limited to $100,000 per action) consistent with the Act to "enhance the public health or the environment." §304(g)(2).

5. Enforcement Against Federal Facilities

Enforcement remains an area of potential friction between federal and state authorities. Although most federal environmental legislation is the product of concern over the inadequacy of decentralized regulatory approaches, most federal environmental laws rely heavily on state authorities to administer and enforce the national programs, subject to federal supervision. Enforcement against federal facilities has been particularly problematic.

Many of the environmental laws specify that their provisions are applicable to facilities owned or operated by federal agencies. For example, section 313(a) of the Clean Water Act provides that the federal government, its officers, agents, and employees "shall be subject to, and comply with, all Federal, State, interstate, and local requirements, administrative authority, and process and sanctions respecting the control and abatement of water pollution in the same manner, and to the same extent as any nongovernmental entity including the payment of reasonable service charges." Section 6001 of RCRA has virtually identical language. But federal agencies are not necessarily subject to the same sanctions as other violators of the environmental laws. Section 313(a) of the Clean Water Act provides that "the United States shall be liable only for those civil penalties arising under Federal law or imposed by a State or local court to enforce an order or the process of such court." RCRA section 6001 waives only federal immunity from sanctions for the enforcement of injunctive relief. EPA generally has been precluded from taking direct enforcement action against sister federal agencies, while states have been handicapped in recovering penalties from federal agencies due to narrow interpretations of waivers of sovereign immunity in the environmental laws. See Stever, Perspectives on the Problem of Federal Facility Liability for Environmental Contamination, 17 Envtl. L. Rep. 10114 (1987).

The Congressional Budget Office has found that the federal government now spends more money trying to bring its own facilities into compliance with the environmental laws than it does in administering the laws. CBO, Federal Liabilities Under Hazardous Waste Laws (May 1990). However, insufficient funding for environmental compliance and the absence of effective enforcement have helped make some facilities owned or operated by federal agencies among the most persistent violators of the environmental laws. In July 1988 the U.S. Department of Energy estimated that environmental cleanup at federal nuclear weapons facilities could cost between $66 to $100 billion. Department of Energy, Environmental, Safety, and Health Report for the Department of Energy Defense Complex (July 1, 1988). In 1988, 32 federal land disposal facilities were on EPA's list of significant noncompliers with RCRA.

The Justice Department refuses to allow EPA to sue federal facilities, on the ground that it would violate constitutional principles of separation of powers to allow one executive agency to sue another. These arguments are criticized in Herz, United States v. United States: When Can the Federal Government Sue Itself?, 32 Wm. & Mary L. Rev. 893 (1991). EPA efforts to obtain administrative consent orders or enforceable compliance agreements with the 16 of these facilities for which it is the lead enforcement agency have been largely unsuccessful, Department of Defense and Department of Energy Compliance with Hazardous Waste Laws, Memorandum from Subcomm. on Oversight & Investigations, House Comm. on Energy & Commerce (June 3, 1988), though one DOE facility has agreed to pay an administrative penalty levied by EPA for repeated violations of a previous consent agreement. Even if federal environmental authorities began levying civil penalties against the contractors that operate these plants, most of the contractors would be entitled to automatic reimbursement of such fines pursuant to their contracts with the government. Catch 22 Language in Weapons Plant Contracts Impedes Safety Penalties, Baltimore Sun, Sept. 26, 1989, at 18A.

In United States v. Dee, 912 F.2d 741 (4th Cir. 1990), cert. denied, 111 S. Ct. 1307 (1991), federal employees were convicted of criminal violations of RCRA for the first time. The defendants were engineers working for federal contractors who were convicted for knowing violations of RCRA's TSD standards. The Fourth Circuit rejected the argument that sovereign immunity barred the prosecution, stating that while "federal officers enjoy a degree of immunity for a particular sphere of official actions, there is no general immunity from criminal prosecution." Criminal prosecutions of federal officials may be the only effective sanction if states are not permitted to impose civil penalties on federal facilities. However, there are substantial barriers to states' conducting such prosecutions, including the fact that most environmental crimes at such facilities occur on federal land. Smith, Shields for the King's Men: Official Immunity and Other Obstacles to Effective Prosecution of Federal Officials for Environmental Crimes, 16 Colum. J. Envtl. L. 1 (1991).

Justice Department officials have argued that states should not be able to impose civil penalties for environmental violations by federal agencies because it would be a convenient means for states to line their coffers at federal expense while disrupting federal priorities for environmental compliance. Stewart Reflects on DOJ's Status, Limits in Environmental Enforcement, Litigation, 21 Env. Rep. 1564 (1990). Legislation is pending in Congress that would explicitly confirm that states and EPA may fine federal facilities for violations of environmental laws. The Department of Energy has argued against such legislation on the ground that its facilities produce so many diverse hazardous waste streams that compliance with RCRA is extremely difficult. In United States Department of Energy v. Ohio, — S. Ct. — (1992), the Supreme Court held that federal agencies are immune from civil penalties for violations of the Clean Water Act and RCRA. Emphasizing that waivers of sovereign immunity must be unequivocal, the Court held that federal agencies are liable only for fines designed to induce them to comply with judicial orders to modify their behavior prospectively, and not for fines imposed as penalties for past violations. In dissent, Justice White complained that the Court's decision "deprives the states of a powerful weapon in combatting federal agencies that persist in despoiling the environment." Congress may soon restore that weapon. Until it does, what incentives do federal agencies have to obey the Clean Water Act and RCRA? Ohio has argued that civil penalties are an essential component of the regulatory scheme because they are necessary to deter illegal activity at federal facilities.

6. State and Local Enforcement Problems: Case Studies

Federal environmental officials rely heavily on state authorities for enforcement of most of the major federal environmental laws. Unlike TSCA, which is exclusively a federal program, the Clean Water Act, the Safe Drinking Water Act, and RCRA authorize EPA to delegate authority to administer and enforce environmental programs to states that meet minimum federal requirements.

Despite an impressive arsenal of enforcement tools, enforcement problems persist, particularly in delegated state programs that are subject to local political pressure from influential industries. While EPA oversight is supposed to operate to ensure that state programs meet minimum federal standards, EPA has not exercised its oversight authority aggressively in part because its primary sanction—withdrawal of state delegation—would only increase the Agency's workload without providing substantial additional resources to implement it.

A. BETHLEHEM STEEL'S SPARROWS POINT PLANT

Several notorious examples of noncompliance with the environmental laws can be traced to enforcement problems with delegated state programs. For example, in February 1987, the Bethlehem Steel Corporation was found to have violated the Clean Water Act more than 700 times between 1978 and 1983 by discharging large quantities of toxic chemicals from its plant at Sparrows Point, Maryland. Lax federal and state enforcement that had tolerated these violations for years was exposed largely due to a citizen suit eventually settled for $1.5 million. The case is described in detail in Oppenheimer, Humpty Dumpty, 1988 Amicus J. 14-23 (Winter 1988). Bethlehem Steel had repeatedly avoided imposition of stricter permit limits that were to have gone into effect in 1978 through careful negotiation and litigation that extended over six years. The plant's outdated permit limits authorized daily discharges of: "11,860 pounds of oil and grease; 1,230 pounds of iron; 990 pounds of zinc; 44 pounds of free cyanide; 51,900 pounds of unspecified solids; and 454 pounds of chromium." Id. Yet the plant frequently discharged two to three times these amounts of pollutants. The plant reported violations of the Clean Water Act to authorities in every month but one between 1979 and 1983.

> "The company had many expenses to make," said Henry H. von Spreckelsen, Bethlehem's communications manager, in a comment typical of those heard from almost any company that violates the law, as well as from government officials who let them do it. "There's a lot of things we did do. We spent millions and millions of dollars on pollution control. But there's just so many dollars to go around." [Id.]

The NRDC lawyer who ultimately brought the citizen suit against Bethlehem Steel attributed enforcement problems to the cozy relationship large companies develop with state regulators. "[T]he regulatory agency's staff become more absorbed with the challenge of solving the plant's operational problems, which are the source of pollution, than in guaranteeing that the law will be met." Id. Permit negotiations extend for years as companies object to proposed conditions, appeal them, and negotiate. Although federal audits raised doubts about the reliability of industry self-monitoring, enforcement authorities conducting inspections often do little more than "quick tours of plants and cursory examination of company records." Id.

B. AVTEX FIBERS, INC.

Another notorious example of enforcement problems is the Avtex Fibers Inc. plant in Front Royal, Virginia, 70 miles west of Washington, D.C., which is now a Superfund site. The plant, originally owned by American Viscose Corporation, was used to produce rayon beginning in 1940. After causing fish kills in the formerly pristine South Fork of the Shenandoah River, state authorities ordered the plant in 1948 to install a wastewater treatment system to neutralize sulfuric acid discharges. In 1959 pollution from the plant caused a major fish kill along 35 miles of the river. FMC Corporation purchased the plant from American Viscose in 1963. In 1976, Avtex Fibers Inc. bought the plant from FMC, which retained ownership of the wastewater treatment plant. EPA, "Avtex Fibers Site," Superfund Update #1 (July 1991).

Toxic waste generated in large quantities by the plant was stored on-site in 23 unlined surface impoundments, which were first found by EPA to be causing contamination in 1980. In 1982, carbon disulfide was found to have leached into groundwater, contaminating wells used by residents across the river from the plant. In 1983 and 1984 Avtex purchased 23 residential properties with contaminated wells and installed groundwater pumping systems. Carbon disulfide, cadmium, lead, hydrogen sulfide, and arsenic were found in the groundwater. In 1986 Avtex signed an administrative order with EPA, agreeing to conduct a remedial investigation/feasibility study of the contamination pursuant to CERCLA.

Despite frightening pollution problems, Avtex had become the sole supplier of rayon fabric to the U.S. space program, which used the material in rocket nozzles. It also had become a politically influential local employer, with more than 1,300 workers employed at the plant. In the meantime, Avtex violated its NPDES permit more than 1,700 times, discharged PCBs into the Shenandoah River, and emitted more than 770 times the allowable levels of carbon disulfide into the air. Yet it was not until after the company announced on October 31, 1988 that it intended to close that state authorities filed an enforcement action seeking $19.7 million in penalties for NPDES permit violations. Officials Cite Communications Lapses Causing Enforcement Problems at Avtex Cite, 21 Env. Rep. 422 (1990). One week after the suit was filed, Avtex announced that it had obtained a new three-year $38-million contract from NASA to reopen the plant, having underbid its only competitor, a company that did not have a similar history of environmental violations.

In December 1988 Avtex reached agreement with the state to drop the enforcement action in return for the company's pledge to spend $5.7 million on cleanup measures and to pay a $2 million civil penalty over six years. In January 1989 this agreement was incorporated into a consent decree. However, by April 1989 additional violations and PCB contamination were discovered. In June 1989 EPA issued an administrative order under section 106 of CERCLA directing Avtex and FMC to begin remedial activities within 60 days. In July 1989 the company was fined $990,000 in state court for continuing water pollution violations, but avoided an injunction against further operations and avoided payment of the previously imposed $2 million civil penalty by pledging to spend $9.3 million on cleanup. After initially agreeing to comply with EPA's section 106 order, Avtex notified EPA in November 1989 that it could not do so. The State Water Control Board then convened a formal hearing and on November 9, 1989 revoked the plant's NPDES permit. The company then shut down and an EPA Emergency Response Team was dispatched to the site, which was in a "highly unstable" condition due to corrosion of an acid reclamation structure.

In February 1990 the company filed for Chapter 11 bankruptcy. EPA then ordered FMC to continue to operate the wastewater treatment system at the site. FMC sued the federal government, alleging that the government was responsible for much of the contamination because it had required the facility to produce rayon during World War II. In February 1992 a district court held that the federal government's involvement in directing operations at the facility during World War II was sufficient to hold the government liable under CERCLA. FMC Corp. v. United States Department of Commerce, — F. Supp. — (E.D. Pa. 1992).

The Avtex saga is frequently cited as an illustration of how a politically influential local employer that produces a product viewed as important by the government can avoid effective enforcement action, despite early and repeated evidence of environmental violations. While federal and state enforcement officials blame one another for failure to bring the problem to each other's attention, today more than 32 miles of the Shenadoah River are contaminated with PCBs, acid spillage at the plant has eaten holes in the earth, and a surrounding residential area has been devastated by groundwater contamination. The owners of the plant repeatedly avoided significant penalties for environmental violations through threats of closure and job loss coupled with promises of future cleanup.

C. MIDNIGHT DUMPING BY METAL PLATERS

Enforcement problems may even be greater at the local level because municipalities charged with enforcement of pretreatment programs have even less experience with environmental enforcement than states do. Problems with enforcement of pretreatment regulations against small metal plating operations are described in Nelson, Dump-n-Duck Polluters Give EPA the Slip, Chicago Sun-Times, Sept. 17, 1989, at 1.

The article reports estimates that two-thirds of the 400 metal plating operations in the Chicago area deliberately violate pretreatment regulations by dumping untreated toxic wastes into the sewer system. In one incident "10,000 fish died after someone poured two tons of cyanide-laced plating chemicals into city sewers that empty into the Chicago River." While EPA attributes the problem to lax local enforcement, local authorities maintain that it is extremely difficult to catch the metal platers "because they are so transient, numerous and clever in dodging authorities" and "they often simply abandon their plants" when caught.

> Plating companies coat objects—from printed circuit boards to locomotive engines—with substances such as chromium, zinc or cadmium. In the process, the object gets a caustic bath to remove oils and an acid bath to remove rust. It then is plated with a metal mixture. The metal often is mixed with cyanide for its shiny finish. A simple plating operation requires only running water, electricity and a few large vats for the chemical baths. Any warehouse—in a rundown industrial area of Chicago or in a new industrial park in the suburbs—will do. Companies that plate tiny printed circuit boards "can put a profitable plating shop in a 20-by-20 room," [Richard] Sustich [, an enforcement official for the Chicago water district,] said. "All they need is a source of electricity, water and a drain." When district inspectors walked into one storefront "research lab" in a suburban shopping center, he said, they found a circuit board plating operation with a simple solution to getting rid of toxic waste: flush it down the toilet. [Id.]

While some metal platers simply do not understand the law that requires them to treat their waste prior to disposal, it is estimated that one-third of the operations deliberately seek to evade it. Local authorities issued 2,132 notices of violation to companies in 1988, but only 15 companies were sued. When companies are finally caught, they often simply abandon their operations, leaving authorities to clean up the mess. Or they may sell the company to a relative or employee who disclaims all responsibility for violations.

In some cases, even large, established companies have been caught engaging in deliberate violations. For example:

> District inspectors sampled discharge from each of the industries in the Centex industrial park in Elk Grove Village. All had pollutant levels at or below the legal limit. But when the inspectors sampled the waste water in the sewer downstream from the park, it exceeded the legal limits. Something didn't add up. Sure enough, when they sneaked back after hours and retested the companies' sewer discharges, they found numerous violations. . . . [A company had] periodically exceeded the standards, so the district installed a permanent sampling apparatus at the plant. The device automatically measures the pollution level of the plant's discharge at random intervals. It is locked in a fiberglass hut to prevent tampering. The district in April charged that [the company] had found a way to beat

even that state-of-the-art system. A district surveillance team found an
employee standing with his ear against the hut listening for the apparatus
to turn on and off, Sustich said. At his signal, the plant would discharge
a tidal wave of toxic waste water into the sewers. [Id.]

NOTES AND QUESTIONS

1. How many different reasons are given in the above case studies
to explain why the environmental laws were violated? Why don't competing companies who are complying with the regulations bring citizen
suits against the violators?

2. Suppose you discovered a metal plater dumping toxic pollutants
illegally as described in the article above. Would the *Gwaltney* decision
cause any problems for a citizen who wishes to file an enforcement action
against such a company?

PROBLEM EXERCISE: CITIZEN ENFORCEMENT
OF THE CLEAN WATER ACT

On August 22 a volunteer for a local environmental group you
represent informs you that a fish kill has been discovered in a nearby
stream 500 yards downriver from an outfall pipe at a manufacturing
plant. The plant has an NPDES permit issued by the state that limits the
amount of phosphorus, nitrogen, and total suspended solids in discharges from its outfall. A friend who works at the plant subsequently
informs you in confidence that an accident occurred at the plant on
August 15 that caused a large quantity of toxic chemicals to spill into a
holding tank. He tells you that similar accidents have occurred twice
before during the five years he has worked at the plant. Although your
friend does not know what happened to the chemicals, he notes that
when he checked the holding tank on August 24, he discovered that it
had been emptied.

On November 15 the environmental group checks with the state
environmental agency to review the discharge monitoring report (DMR)
the plant was required to file for August. After discovering that the
plant failed to file a DMR for August, the environmental group asks
you to file a citizen suit on their behalf. On November 25 you send a
letter to the owner of the plant, the state environmental agency, and
EPA informing them that you plan to file a citizen suit against the plant
owner for failure to file a DMR for August and for discharging pollutants
in violation of the plant's permit.

On March 25 you file a citizen suit against the owner of the plant,
alleging that he has violated the Act by failing to file a DMR and by

discharging pollutants in violation of the plant's NPDES permit. On April 7 the plant owner belatedly submits to the state environmental agency a DMR reporting no violations of the plant's permit during August.

Question One. Suppose that defense counsel, citing *Gwaltney,* files motions to dismiss and for summary judgment arguing that there is no ongoing violation because the missing DMR has now been filed, that the case is now moot, and that you lack standing since there is no relief available that would redress any injury to you. How would you respond? Is your case likely to survive the motion to dismiss? See Sierra Club v. Simkins Industries, 847 F.2d 1109 (4th Cir. 1988), cert. denied, 491 U.S. 904 (1989).

Question Two. Suppose that after your lawsuit is filed the state environmental agency assesses a $1,000 administrative penalty against the owner of the plant for failing to file a DMR in timely fashion. The owner agrees to pay the penalty in return for the state's agreement not to pursue further investigation into the fish kill. Although you are outraged by what you perceive to be a sweetheart settlement, state law does not permit you to challenge it in court. Defense counsel renews his motion to dismiss, arguing that the penalty should bar your citizen suit because it is now moot and that you lack standing since there is no relief available that would redress your alleged injury. How would you respond? Who is likely to prevail on this issue? Would it make any difference if the administrative settlement included a pledge by the company not to violate its permit terms in the future? Would it make any difference if the state had commenced its adminstrative enforcement action on March 20? See §309(g)(6). Is there any way for you to challenge the administrative settlement outside of state court? See §§309(g)(4) and (6).

Question Three. Your friend who works at the plant reports that the employee responsible for preparing DMRs was told by the plant manager that the plant would be closed and he would lose his job if the company lost the citizen suit. Your friend is reluctant to testify at trial because he is certain he would be fired. Without your friend's testimony it will be impossible to link the plant to the fish kill. What protection is available to your friend under section 507 of the Clean Water Act?

Question Four. Suppose that the court reserves judgment on the motion to dismiss and the case proceeds to trial. With Perry Mason as your co-counsel, you succeed in having the employee responsible for preparing the DMR break down on the stand and confess that he falsified it to cover up deliberate discharge of the toxics. Under section 309 of the Clean Water Act, what is the potential criminal liability of the following persons for the filing of the false DMR or the deliberate discharge of the toxics: (1) the employee who prepared the DMR, (2) the plant manager, (3) the owner of the company?

Question Five.   Citing its tough policy of not tolerating violations of the environmental laws by its employees, the company then fires the employee who broke down on the stand and blames him for any violations. Is he entitled to protection under section 507? See §507(d). If plant employees do not testify, what is the likely outcome of your citizen suit? If you win, what relief can the court grant and what penalties can be imposed on the company?

=8=

Protection of Public Resources

It may seem curious to some that the survival of a relatively small number of three-inch fish among all the countless millions of species extant would require the permanent halting of a virtually completed dam for which Congress has expended more than $100 million. . . . We conclude, however, that the explicit provisions of the Endangered Species Act require precisely that result.

TVA v. Hill, 437 U.S. 153, 172-173 (1978)

The first rule of the tinkerer, Aldo Leopold reminds us, is to keep all the pieces.

—*E. O. Wilson*

Measures to protect public resources were the first, and some of the most significant, environmental laws. These include the National Environmental Policy Act, the Endangered Species Act, and the many statutes that govern management of public lands. These statutes seek to protect the environment not by regulating pollution but by controlling activities that have unacceptable environmental effects in order to preserve public resources for future generations. The laws governing public lands and resources cover an immense field that is worthy of separate study. See Public Land and Resource Law: A Pathfinder, page 1125.

This chapter focuses on NEPA and the Endangered Species Act, statutes with broad application that reflect with unusual clarity the tension between the "moral outrage" and "cool analysis" perspectives introduced in Chapter 1. While NEPA's goals include statements of moral concern for the environment, the Act's operative provisions are the epitomy of the cool analysis perspective. Their morality is to affirm the value of analysis by requiring that environmental impacts be considered without imposing substantive judgments concerning their worth. In sharp contrast, "moral outrage" runs throughout the provisions of the Endangered Species Act. The Act's seemingly absolutist proscription of activities that threaten the continued existence of even the humblest plants

1021

and animals reflects extraordinary devotion to the value of biological diversity.

PROTECTION OF PUBLIC RESOURCES: A PATHFINDER

The National Environmental Policy Act is codified at 42 U.S.C. §§4321-4370. The general regulations governing implementation of NEPA, promulgated by the Council on Environmental Quality, are the most helpful elaboration on the bare requirements of the statute; they can be found at 40 C.F.R. pts. 1500-1517. Each federal agency also has regulations, typically published in the Code of Federal Regulations or in internal manuals, that spell out in greater detail their policies for compliance with NEPA.

The principal treatises on environmental law, particularly S. Rodgers, Environmental Law and S. Novick, Law of Environmental Protection, are useful references for questions concerning NEPA. A comprehensive treatise on NEPA is D. Mandelker, NEPA Law and Litigation, published by Callaghan. Leading analyses of NEPA's early history include F. Anderson and R. Daniels, NEPA in the Courts: A Legal Analysis of the National Environmental Policy Act (1973) and R. Liroff, A National Policy for the Environment: NEPA and Its Aftermath (1976). The annual report of the Council on Environmental Quality typically provides a good review of current implementation of the Act.

Countless monographs and law review articles have analyzed NEPA and its case law. NEPA's twentieth anniversary in 1990 spawned several retrospectives. See Symposium on NEPA at Twenty, 20 Envtl. L. 447-810 (1990). For a broader international perspective, see the Environmental Impact Assessment Review, published by Elsevier Scientific Publishing Company.

The Endangered Species Act is codified at 16 U.S.C. §§1531-1544. The Secretaries of Interior and Commerce have jointly promulgated regulations to govern implementation of the Act, in 50 C.F.R. pt. 402. The lists of endangered and threatened species can be found in 50 C.F.R. pt. 17.

Far and away the most thorough and definitive treatise on the ESA and other wildlife statutes is M. Bean's The Evolution of National Wildlife Law (2d ed. 1983), published by Praeger. Bean provides a thorough analysis of the evolution of the Act, its implementation by the agencies, and its interpretation by the courts. An update on developments under the three key provisions of the Act (sections 4, 7, and 9), is provided by J. Kilbourne in The Endangered Species Act Under the Microscope: A Closeup Look from a Litigator's Perspective, 21 Envtl. L. 499-586 (1991). For a history of American policies toward wildlife, see P. Matthiessen's classic, Wildlife in America (1987), published by Viking, and T. Lund, American Wildlife Law (1980), published by University of California Press. The leading treatise on protection of wildlife under *international* law is Simon Lyster's International Wildlife Law (1985), published by Grotius.

Current information on new species listings and other actions or issues under the ESA can be found in the Endangered Species Update, published by the University of Michigan, and the Endangered Species Technical Bulletin, published by the Department of the Interior.

The conservation of endangered species rests, of course, on science. Perhaps the best introductions are E. O. Wilson's Biodiversity (1986), published by National Academy Press, and his forthcoming book, The Diversity of Life. Current scholarship can be found in two leading journals: Conservation Biology and BioScience.

A. THE NATIONAL ENVIRONMENTAL POLICY ACT

1. *Overview*

On January 1, 1970, President Richard Nixon inaugurated what would come to be known as "the environmental decade" by signing into law the National Environmental Policy Act (Pub. L. 91-190, codified at 42 U.S.C. §§4321-4370a). The Act, usually referred to as "NEPA," set forth broad principles and goals for the nation's environmental policy. It established as "the continuing policy of the Federal Government . . . to use all practicable means and measures . . . to create and maintain conditions under which man and nature can exist in productive harmony, and fulfill the social, economic and other requirements of present and future generations of Americans." §101(a), 42 U.S.C. §4331(a).

NEPA adopted an unusual strategy to pursue this ambitious goal. Rather than erecting an elaborate regulatory scheme applicable to business and industry, NEPA instead mandated a significant change in the decisionmaking procedures used by federal agencies. The Act required all federal agencies to consider the likely environmental effects of their activities. Specifically, section 102 of NEPA requires that all federal agencies

> include in every recommendation or report on proposals for legislation and other major federal actions significantly affecting the quality of the human environment, a detailed statement by the responsible official on—
>
> (i) the environmental impact of the proposed action, (ii) any adverse environmental effects which cannot be avoided should the proposal be implemented, (iii) alternatives to the proposed action, (iv) the relationship between local short-term uses of man's environment and the maintenance and enhancement of long-term productivity, and (v) any irreversible and irretrievable commitments of resources which would be involved in the proposed action should it be implemented. [42 U.S.C. §4332(C).]

The remarkably simple structure of NEPA is outlined below.

STRUCTURE OF THE NATIONAL ENVIRONMENTAL POLICY ACT

§101 establishes as the continuing policy of the Federal Government the use of all practicable means to create and maintain conditions under which man and nature can exist in productive harmony.

§102 requires all federal agencies to prepare an environmental impact statement (EIS) on major federal actions significantly affecting the quality of the environment. The EIS must include a detailed statement of environmental impacts, alternatives to the proposed action and any irretrievable commitments of resources involved.

§103 requires all federal agencies to propose measures to bring their policies into conformity with NEPA.

§201 requires the president to submit to Congress an annual Environmental Quality Report.

§202 establishes three-member Council on Environmental Quality (CEQ) in the Executive Office of the President.

§204 outlines duties and functions of CEQ including annual reporting on the condition of the environment, information gathering, investigation and appraisal of changes in the natural environment and review and appraisal of federal programs and activities.

Reviewing federal agency actions for compliance with NEPA, the courts quickly established that section 102's obligations were substantial. The "detailed statement" required (known as an "environmental impact statement," or EIS) has become, through judicial and administrative interpretations, an often massive undertaking. While federal regulations provide that an EIS generally should not exceed 150 pages in length, many are far longer: the EIS on an offshore oil lease sale is likely to be several hundred pages, while the EIS for licensing of a nuclear power plant may reach several thousand.

Each federal agency is made responsible for implementing NEPA, but Congress also created a central agency, the Council on Environmental Quality (CEQ), to coordinate agencies' compliance with NEPA. CEQ developed guidelines for NEPA implementation and, in 1978, armed with an executive order from President Carter, CEQ promulgated regulations on NEPA implementation that are binding on all federal agencies. 40 C.F.R. pt. 1500. These regulations, which reflect much of the case law that had developed under the statute, are the first recourse for analysis of any NEPA problem. They spell out many of the details of the NEPA process, and they receive considerable deference from the courts.

The principal arbiters of NEPA's requirements, however, have been the federal courts. Hundreds of judicial decisions have examined and elaborated on NEPA's requirements. The following case was the first major decision to examine the Act and to explain the duties it imposes on federal agencies.

Calvert Cliffs Coordinating Committee v. United States Atomic Energy Commission
449 F.2d 1109 (D.C. Cir. 1971)

Before WRIGHT, TAMM and ROBINSON, Circuit Judges.

J. SKELLY WRIGHT, Circuit Judge:

These cases are only the beginning of what promises to become a flood of new litigation—litigation seeking judicial assistance in protecting our natural environment. Several recently enacted statutes attest to the commitment of the Government to control, at long last, the destructive engine of material "progress." But it remains to be seen whether the promise of this legislation will become a reality. Therein lies the judicial role. In these cases, we must for the first time interpret the broadest and perhaps most important of the recent statutes: the National Environmental Policy Act of 1969 (NEPA). We must assess claims that one of the agencies charged with its administration has failed to live up to the congressional mandate. Our duty, in short, is to see that important legislative purposes, heralded in the halls of Congress, are not lost or misdirected in the vast hallways of the federal bureaucracy.

NEPA, like so much other reform legislation of the last 40 years, is cast in terms of a general mandate and broad delegation of authority to new and old administrative agencies. It takes the major step of requiring all federal agencies to consider values of environmental preservation in their spheres of activity, and it prescribes certain procedural measures to ensure that those values are in fact fully respected. Petitioners argue that rules recently adopted by the Atomic Energy Commission to govern consideration of environmental matters fail to satisfy the rigor demanded by NEPA. The Commission, on the other hand, contends that the vagueness of the NEPA mandate and delegation leaves much room for discretion and that the rules challenged by petitioners fall well within the broad scope of the Act. . . .

I

We begin our analysis with an examination of NEPA's structure and approach and of the Atomic Energy Commission rules which are said to conflict with the requirements of the Act. The relevant portion of NEPA is Title I, consisting of five sections. Section 101 sets forth the Act's basic substantive policy: that the federal government "use all practicable means and measures" to protect environmental values. Congress did not establish environmental protection as an exclusive goal; rather, it desired a reordering of priorities, so that environmental costs and benefits will assume their proper place along with other considerations. In Section 101(b), imposing an explicit duty on federal officials, the Act provides that "it is the continuing responsibility of the Federal Government to use all practicable means, consistent with other essential considerations of national policy," to avoid environmental degradation, preserve "historic, cultural, and natural" resources, and promote "the widest range of beneficial uses of the environment without . . . undesirable and unintended consequences."

Thus the general substantive policy of the Act is a flexible one. It leaves room for a responsible exercise of discretion and may not require particular substantive results in particular problematic instances. However, the Act also contains very important "procedural" provisions—provisions which are designed to see that all federal agencies do in fact exercise the substantive discretion given them. These provisions are not highly flexible. Indeed, they establish a strict standard of compliance. . . .

. . . Section 102(2)(C) requires that responsible officials of all agencies prepare a "detailed statement" covering the impact of particular actions on the environment, the environmental costs which might be avoided, and alternative measures which might alter the cost-benefit equation. The apparent purpose of the "detailed statement" is to aid in the agencies' own decisionmaking process and to advise other interested agencies and the public of the environmental consequences of planned federal action. Beyond the "detailed statement," Section [102(2)(E)] requires all agencies specifically to "study, develop, and describe appropriate alternatives to recommended courses of action in any proposal which involves unresolved conflicts concerning alternative uses of available resources." This requirement, like the "detailed statement" requirement, seeks to ensure that each agency decision maker has before him and takes into proper account all possible approaches to a particular project (including total abandonment of the project) which would alter the environmental impact and the cost-benefit balance. Only in that fashion is it likely that the most intelligent, optimally beneficial decision will ultimately be made. Moreover, by compelling a formal "detailed statement" and a description of alternatives, NEPA provides evidence that the mandated decision making process has in fact taken place and, most importantly, allows those removed from the initial process to evaluate and balance the factors on their own.

Of course, all of these Section 102 duties are qualified by the phrase "to the fullest extent possible." We must stress as forcefully as possible that this language does not provide an escape hatch for footdragging agencies; it does not make NEPA's procedural requirements somehow "discretionary." Congress did not intend the Act to be such a paper tiger. Indeed, the requirement of environmental consideration "to the fullest extent possible" sets a high standard for the agencies, a standard which must be rigorously enforced by the reviewing courts. . . .

. . . [T]he Section 102 duties are not inherently flexible. They must be complied with to the fullest extent, unless there is a clear conflict of *statutory* authority. Considerations of administrative difficulty, delay or economic cost will not suffice to strip the section of its fundamental importance.

We conclude, then, that Section 102 of NEPA mandates a particular sort of careful and informed decisionmaking process and creates judicially enforceable duties. The reviewing courts probably cannot reverse a substantive decision on its merits, under Section 101, unless it be shown that the actual balance of costs and benefits that was struck was arbitrary or clearly gave insufficient weight to environmental values. But if the decision was reached procedurally without individualized consideration and balancing of environmental factors—conducted fully and in good faith—it is the responsibility of the courts to reverse. As one District Court has said of Section 102 requirements: "It is hard to imagine a clearer or stronger mandate to the Courts."

In the cases before us now, we do not have to review a particular decision by the Atomic Energy Commission granting a construction permit or an operating license. Rather, we must review the Commission's recently promulgated rules which govern consideration of environmental values in all such individual decisions. The rules were devised strictly in order to comply with the NEPA procedural requirements—but petitioners argue that they fall far short of the congressional mandate. [The rules provided that an applicant seeking permission to build and operate a nuclear power plant must prepare an "environmental report" assessing the likely impacts of the facility and possible alternatives. On the basis of the report, Commission staff would then prepare its own "detailed statement." The report and the detailed statement would accompany the application through the review process. However, they would not be considered by the licensing board (which decides the application), or received into evidence, unless environmental issues were raised by a party to the proceeding.] . . .

The question here is whether the Commission is correct in thinking that its NEPA responsibilities may "be carried out in toto outside the hearing process"—whether it is enough that environmental data and evaluations merely "accompany" an application through the review process, but receive no consideration whatever from the hearing board.

We believe that the Commission's crabbed interpretation of NEPA makes a mockery of the Act. What possible purpose could there be in the Section 102(2)(C) requirement (that the "detailed statement" accompany proposals through agency review processes) if "accompany" means no more than physical proximity—mandating no more than the physical act of passing certain folders and papers, unopened, to reviewing officials along with other folders and papers? What possible purpose could there be in requiring the "detailed statement" to be before hearing boards, if the boards are free to ignore entirely the contents of the statement? NEPA was meant to do more than regulate the flow of papers in the federal bureaucracy. The word "accompany" in Section 102(2)(C) must not be read so narrowly as to make the Act ludicrous. It must, rather, be read to indicate a congressional intent that environmental factors, as compiled in the "detailed statement," be *considered* through agency review processes.

Beyond Section 102(2)(C), NEPA requires that agencies consider the environmental impact of their actions "to the fullest extent possible." The Act is addressed to agencies as a whole, not only to their professional staffs. Compliance to the *"fullest"* possible extent would seem to demand that environmental issues be considered at every important stage in the decision making process concerning a particular action—at every stage where an overall balancing of environmental and nonenvironmental factors is appropriate and where alterations might be made in the proposed action to minimize environmental costs. . . .

NEPA mandates a case-by-case balancing judgment on the part of federal agencies. In each individual case, the particular economic and technical benefits of planned action must be assessed and then weighed against the environmental costs; alternatives must be considered which would affect the balance of values. The magnitude of possible benefits and possible costs may lie anywhere on a broad spectrum. Much will depend on the particular magnitudes involved in particular cases. In some cases, the benefits will be great enough to justify a certain quantum of environmental costs; in other cases, they will not be so great and the proposed action may have to be abandoned or significantly altered so as to bring the benefits and costs into a proper balance. The point of the individualized balancing analysis is to ensure that, with possible alterations, the optimally beneficial action is finally taken.

Certification by another agency that its own environmental standards are satisfied involves an entirely different kind of judgment. Such agencies, without overall responsibility for the particular federal action in question, attend only to one aspect of the problem: the magnitude of certain environmental costs. They simply determine whether those costs extend an allowable amount. Their certification does not mean that they found no environmental damage whatever. In fact, there may be significant environmental damage (e.g., water pollution), but not quite enough to violate applicable (e.g., water quality) standards. Certifying agencies do not attempt to weigh that damage against the opposing benefits. Thus the balancing analysis remains to be done. It may be that the environmental costs, though passing prescribed standards, are nonetheless great enough to outweigh the particular economic and technical benefits involved in the planned action. The only agency in a position to make such a judgment is the agency with overall responsibility for the proposed federal action—the agency to which NEPA is specifically directed. . . .

NEPA requires that an agency must—to the *fullest* extent possible under its other statutory obligations—consider alternatives to its actions which would reduce environmental damage. That principle establishes that consideration of environmental matters must be more than a *pro forma* ritual. Clearly, it is pointless to "consider" environmental costs without also seriously considering action to avoid them. Such a full exercise of substantive discretion is required at every important, appropriate and nonduplicative stage of an agency's proceedings.

NOTES AND QUESTIONS

1. How did the AEC interpret the "detailed statement" requirement of NEPA section 102? What role did the AEC provide for such a statement? What more ambitious process does the court envision?

2. The AEC argued that it need not consider air and water pollution caused by a proposed plant because those effects already are subject to

EPA regulation. Is that position unreasonable? Is it supported by NEPA? Why does the court reject it? How would such a rule affect the nature and scope of the review envisioned by the court? Does the court's formulation make NEPA review redundant of reviews under other environmental laws?

3. As he elaborates on NEPA's requirements, is Judge Wright drawing on "moral outrage" or is he relying on "cool analysis"?

4. One issue raised by Judge Wright in *Calvert Cliffs* is whether NEPA imposes enforceable *substantive* obligations on federal agencies. That issue was confronted by the Supreme Court several years later in the following case, which it decided summarily without hearing oral argument.

Strycker's Bay Neighborhood Council, Inc. v. Karlen
444 U.S. 223 (1980)

[Plaintiffs sought to enjoin construction of a low-income housing project on the Upper West Side of Manhattan. They challenged the approval of the project by the U.S. Department of Housing and Urban Development. In the first round of litigation, the Second Circuit had held that NEPA required consideration of alternatives to the proposed project, even though NEPA did *not* require preparation of an EIS. Following the Second Circuit's decisions, the case was remanded to HUD.]

PER CURIAM.

On remand, HUD prepared a lengthy report entitled Special Environmental Clearance (1977). After marshaling the data, the report asserted that, "while the choice of Site 30 for development as a 100 percent low-income project has raised valid questions about the potential social environmental impacts involved, the problems associated with the impact on social fabric and community structures are not considered so serious as to require that this component be rated as unacceptable." Special Environmental Clearance Report 42. The last portion of the report incorporated a study wherein the Commission evaluated nine alternative locations for the project and found none of them acceptable. While HUD's report conceded that this study may not have considered all possible alternatives, it credited the Commission's conclusion that any relocation of the units would entail an unacceptable delay of two years or more. According to HUD, "[m]easured against the environmental costs associated with the minimum two-year delay, the benefits seem insufficient to justify a mandated substitution of sites." Id., at 54.

After soliciting the parties' comments on HUD's report, the District Court again entered judgment in favor of petitioners. See Trinity Episcopal School Corp. v. Harris, 445 F. Supp. 204 (1978). The court was "impressed with [HUD's analysis] as being thorough and exhaustive," id., at 209-210, and found that "HUD's consideration of the alternatives was neither arbitrary nor capricious"; on the contrary, "[i]t was done in good faith and in full accordance with the law." Id. at 220.

On appeal, the Second Circuit vacated and remanded again. Karlen v. Harris, 590 F.2d 39 (1978). The appellate court focused upon that part of HUD's report where the agency considered and rejected alternative sites, and in particular upon HUD's reliance on the delay such a relocation would entail. The Court of Appeals purported to recognize that its role in reviewing HUD's decision was defined by the Administrative Procedure Act (APA), 5 U.S.C. §706(2)(A), which provides that agency actions should be set aside if found to be "arbitrary, capricious, an abuse of discretion, or otherwise not in accordance with law. . . ." Additionally, however, the Court of Appeals looked to "[t]he provisions of NEPA" for "the substantive standards necessary to review the merits of agency decisions. . . ." 590 F.2d, at 43. The Court of Appeals conceded that HUD had "given 'consideration' to alternatives" to redesignating the site. Id., at 44. Nevertheless, the court believed that " 'consideration' is not an end in itself." Ibid. Concentrating on HUD's finding that development of an alternative location would entail an unacceptable delay, the appellate court held that such delay could not be "an overriding factor" in HUD's decision to proceed with the development. Ibid. According to the court, when HUD considers such projects, "environmental factors, such as crowding low-income housing into a concentrated area, should be given determinative weight." Ibid. The Court of Appeals therefore remanded the case to the District Court, instructing HUD to attack the shortage of low-income housing in a manner that would avoid the "concentration" of such housing on Site 30. Id., at 45.

In Vermont Yankee Nuclear Power Corp. v. NRDC, 435 U.S. 519, 558 (1978), we stated that NEPA, while establishing "significant substantive goals for the Nation," imposes upon agencies duties that are "essentially procedural." As we stressed in that case, NEPA was designed "to insure a fully informed and well-considered decision," but not necessarily "a decision the judges of the Court of Appeals or of this Court would have reached had they been members of the decisionmaking unit of the agency." Ibid. Vermont Yankee cuts sharply against the Court of Appeals' conclusion that an agency, in selecting a course of action, must elevate environmental concerns over other appropriate considerations. On the contrary, once an agency has made a decision subject to NEPA's procedural requirements, the only role for a court is to insure that the agency has considered the environmental consequences; it cannot " 'interject itself within the area of discretion of the executive as to the choice of the action to be taken.' " Kleppe v. Sierra Club, 437 U.S. 390, 410, n.21 (1976). See also FPC v. Transcontinental Gas Pipe Line Corp., 423 U.S. 326 (1976).

In the present litigation there is no doubt that HUD considered the environmental consequences of its decision to redesignate the proposed site for low-income housing. NEPA requires no more. The petitions for certiorari are granted, and the judgment of the Court of Appeals is therefore reversed.

Mr. Justice MARSHALL, dissenting.

The issue raised by these cases is far more difficult than the *per curiam* opinion suggests. . . .

The issue before the Court of Appeals . . . was whether HUD was free under NEPA to reject an alternative acknowledged to be environmentally preferable solely on the ground that any change in sites would cause delay. This was hardly a "peripheral issue" in the case. Whether NEPA, which sets forth "significant substantive goals," Vermont Yankee Nuclear Power Corp. v. NRDC, supra, at 558, permits a projected 2-year time difference to be controlling over environmental superiority is by no means clear. Resolution of the issue, however, is certainly within the normal scope of review of agency action to determine if it is arbitrary, capricious, or an abuse of discretion. The question whether HUD can make delay the paramount concern over environmental superiority is essentially a restatement of the question whether HUD in considering the environmental consequences of its proposed action gave those consequences a "hard look," which is exactly the proper question for the reviewing court to ask. Kleppe v. Sierra Club, supra, at 410, n.21.

The issue of whether the Secretary's decision was arbitrary or capricious is sufficiently difficult and important to merit plenary consideration in this Court. Further, I do not subscribe to the Court's apparent suggestion that *Vermont Yankee* limits the reviewing court to the essentially mindless task of determining whether an agency "considered" environmental factors even if that agency may have effectively decided to ignore those factors in reaching its conclusion. Indeed, I cannot believe that the Court would adhere to that position in a different factual setting. Our cases establish that the arbitrary-or-capricious standard prescribes a "searching and careful" judicial inquiry designed to ensure that the agency has not exercised its discretion in an unreasonable manner. Citizens to Preserve Overton Park, Inc. v. Volpe, 401 U.S. 402, 416 (1971). Believing that today's summary reversal represents a departure from that principle, I respectfully dissent.

NOTES AND QUESTIONS

1. In *Strycker's Bay* the Supreme Court states that "once an agency has made a decision subject to NEPA's procedural requirements, the only role for a court is to insure that the agency has considered the environmental consequences." If an agency has "considered" environmental consequences in an EIS, can it then give *no* weight to those factors in its final decision? Consider Justice Marshall's argument in dissent. Consider also Judge Wright's suggestion in *Calvert Cliffs* that a court could "reverse a substantive decision on its merits, under Section 101, [if] the actual balance of costs and benefits that was struck was arbitrary or clearly gave insufficient weight to environmental values." Does the Supreme Court reject that interpretation in *Strycker's Bay*? What "weight" had the Second Circuit required HUD to give to environmental values?

2. Two major sets of issues arise frequently in NEPA litigation: (1) questions concerning the circumstances under which agencies are required to prepare EISs, and (2) questions concerning the adequacy of the EIS. In cases where an agency has not prepared an EIS, courts must determine whether an EIS is required and, if not, whether the agency has complied with NEPA's other requirements. Where the agency has prepared an EIS, judicial review often focuses on the adequacy of that document. We consider these two fundamental sets of questions in turn.

2. Under What Circumstances Must an Environmental Impact Statement Be Prepared?

The threshold for the EIS requirement is set out in the statute: An EIS must be prepared for "proposals for legislation and other major Federal actions significantly affecting the quality of the human environment." To determine the scope and timing of NEPA's obligations, the courts have parsed these statutory words and looked to the congressional purposes that lie behind them. To define the boundaries of the inquiry, courts have focused on the first clause: There must be a "proposal" either for "legislation" or for "major Federal action." Within these boundaries the crucial question then becomes whether the action's effects on the "human environment" will be "significant."

A. "PROPOSALS FOR LEGISLATION AND OTHER MAJOR FEDERAL ACTIONS"

By its terms, NEPA applies both to proposals for "legislation" and to proposals for "other major Federal actions." While the courts have occasionally grappled with the application of NEPA to "legislation" (see

Andrus v. Sierra Club, 442 U.S. 347 (1979), holding that agency requests to Congress for appropriations are not "proposals for legislation"), by far the lion's share of litigation has centered around the application of NEPA to "other" actions. Our discussion, therefore, will focus on cases arising under that clause.

i. "Major Federal Action"

It is now well-settled that the term "major Federal actions" is not confined to projects that the federal government is funding or carrying out. The courts have found that the term also includes private projects that require federal approval as well as federal programs, policies, and rules. The case law is summarized in the CEQ Regulations contained in 40 C.F.R. §1508.18. These regulations define "major Federal action" to include "actions with effects that may be major and which are potentially subject to Federal control and responsibility." Id. The CEQ regulations specify that such action may include a failure to act by responsible officials if that failure would be reviewable under the Administrative Procedure Act or other applicable law as agency action.

Under CEQ's interpretation, major federal actions include "projects and programs entirely or partly financed, assisted, conducted, regulated, or approved by federal agencies" as well as "new or revised agency rules, regulations, plans, policies, or procedures." Id. Enforcement actions taken by federal agencies are not included within CEQ's definition of major federal action. The CEQ regulations note that federal actions generally fall within one of the following categories:

(1)   Adoption of official policy, such as rules, regulations, and interpretations adopted pursuant to the Administrative Procedure Act, 5 U.S.C. §551 et seq.; treaties and international conventions or agreements; formal documents establishing an agency's policies which will result in or substantially alter agency programs.

(2)   Adoption of formal plans, such as official documents prepared or approved by federal agencies which guide or prescribe alternative uses of federal resources, upon which future agency actions will be based.

(3)   Adoption of programs, such as a group of concerted actions to implement a specific policy or plan; systematic and connected agency decisions allocating agency resources to implement a specific statutory program or executive directive.

(4)   Approval of specific projects, such as construction or management activities located in a defined geographic area. Projects include actions approved by permit or other regulatory

decision as well as federal and federally assisted activities. (40 C.F.R. §1508.18(b).)

Difficult questions about the extent of NEPA's application to a private project arise when only a small but integral part of the project requires federal approval. This occasionally occurs in cases involving "segmentation" of a highway project. In those cases, courts have held that, in approving a proposed highway project, the Federal Highway Administration must consider the effects of possible future highway construction that will be made possible by the instant proposal, unless the proposed segment has "logical termini" and "independent utility." See, e.g., Lange v. Brinegar, 625 F.2d 812 (9th Cir. 1980); Swain v. Brinegar, 542 F.2d 364 (7th Cir. 1976). A somewhat similar issue arose in Winnebago Tribe of Nebraska v. Ray, 621 F.2d 269 (8th Cir. 1980). In that case an Indian tribe argued that because construction of a proposed power line required a permit to cross the Missouri River from the Army Corps of Engineers, the Corps was required to prepare an EIS covering the impact of the entire transmission line. The Eighth Circuit rejected this argument and held that the Corps could restrict its consideration to the impact on the area in and around the navigable waters in determining whether the action required an EIS.

ii. Problems of Timing and Scope

The most difficult and persistent questions in determining whether there is a "proposal for . . . major Federal action" have been the appropriate timing and scope of the review that NEPA requires. As several cases have illustrated, these two questions are bound up together.

The interplay of timing and scope is perhaps most pronounced in federal resource management programs. Thorough review in an EIS may serve useful functions at several stages in the development and implementation of such a program. Choosing the proper time and scope for EIS review thus requires hard choices: Should the agency prepare an EIS for its formulation of national policy so that it may consider the environmental consequences of the fundamental policy choices made at that stage? Should it prepare an EIS for each region of the country before the national program is implemented, so that the particular characteristics, needs, and problems of the region can be considered? Should it prepare an EIS for each action taken in implementing the program in the field (each timber sale, grazing lease, or mining permit approved), so that it can evaluate environmental consequences on the basis of the concrete information that only becomes available when one has a proposal for specific action at a specific site? Should it prepare an EIS at every one of these stages, at the risk of drowning itself, and the public, in paper?

In the case that follows, the Sierra Club argued that the Department of the Interior could not allow further development of federal coal reserves in a four-state area of the Northern Great Plains without preparing a comprehensive EIS on the entire region. Interior had conducted three studies of potential coal development in the region and had prepared a national "Coal Programmatic EIS" for the Department's coal leasing program throughout the country. The D.C. Circuit held that four factors should govern when a programmatic EIS must be commenced: (1) the likelihood and imminence of a program's coming to fruition, (2) the extent of information available on the effects of a program, (3) the extent to which irretrievable resource commitments are being made, and (4) the potential severity of environmental effects. After finding that factors (2) and (4) already made an EIS ripe, the court remanded the case to Interior, which obtained Supreme Court review in the case that follows.

|| *Kleppe v. Sierra Club* ||
|| **427 U.S. 390 (1976)** ||

MR. JUSTICE POWELL delivered the opinion of the Court. . . .

The major issue remains the one with which the suit began: whether NEPA requires petitioners to prepare an environmental impact statement on the entire Northern Great Plains region. Petitioners, arguing the negative, rely squarely upon the facts of the case and the language of §102(2)(C) of NEPA. We find their reliance well placed.

. . . [Section] 102(2)(C) requires an impact statement "in every recommendation or report on proposals for legislation and other major Federal actions significantly affecting the quality of the human environment." Since no one has suggested that petitioners have proposed legislation on respondents' region, the controlling phrase in this section of the Act, for this case, is "major Federal actions." Respondents can prevail only if there has been a report or recommendation on a proposal for major federal action with respect to the Northern Great Plains region. . . . [T]he relevant facts show[] there has been none; instead, all proposals are for actions of either local or national scope. The local actions are the decisions by the various petitioners to issue a lease, approve a mining plan, issue a right-of-way permit, or take other action to allow private activity at some point within the region identified by respondents. Several Courts of Appeals have held that an impact statement must be included in the report of recommendation on a proposal for such action if the private activity to be permitted is one "significantly affecting the quality of the human environment" within the meaning of §102(2)(C). The petitioners do not dispute this requirement in this case, and indeed have prepared impact statements on several proposed actions of this type in the Northern Great Plains during the course of this litigation. Similarly, the federal petitioners agreed at oral argument that §102(2)(C) required the Coal Programmatic EIS that was prepared in tandem with the new national coal-leasing program and included as part of the final report on the proposal for adoption of that program. Their admission is well made, for the new leasing program is a coherent plan of national scope, and its adoption surely has significant environmental consequences.

But there is no evidence in the record of an action or a proposal for an action of regional scope. The District Court, in fact, expressly found that there was no existing or proposed plan or program on the part of the Federal Government for the regional development of the area described in respondents' complaint. It found also that the three studies initiated by the Department in areas either included within or inclusive of respondents' region—that is, the Montana-Wyoming Aqueducts Study, the North Central Power Study, and the NGPRP [Northern Great Plains Resources Program]—were not parts of any plan or program to develop or encourage development of the Northern Great Plains. That court found no evidence that the individual coal development projects undertaken or proposed by private industry and public utilities in that part of the country are integrated into a plan or otherwise interrelated. These findings were not disturbed by the Court of Appeals, and they remain fully supported by the record in this Court. . . .

IV . . .

Even had the record justified a finding that a regional program was contemplated by the petitioners, the legal conclusion drawn by the Court of Appeals cannot be squared with the Act. The court recognized that the mere "contemplation" of certain action is not sufficient to require an impact statement. But it believed the statute nevertheless empowers a court to require the preparation of an impact statement to begin at some point prior to the formal recommendation or report on a proposal. The Court of Appeals accordingly devised its own four-part "balancing" test for determining when, during the contemplation of a plan or other type of federal action, an agency must begin a statement. . . .

The Court's reasoning and action find no support in the language or legislative history of NEPA. The statute clearly states when an impact statement is required, and mentions nothing about a balancing of factors. Rather, as we noted last Term, under the first sentence of §102(2)(C) the moment at which an agency must have a final statement ready "is the time at which it makes a recommendation or report on a *proposal* for federal action." Aberdeen & Rockfish R. Co. v. SCRAP, 422 U.S.

289, 320 (1975) *(SCRAP II)* (emphasis in original). The procedural duty imposed upon agencies by this section is quite precise, and the role of the courts in enforcing that duty is similarly precise. A court has no authority to depart from the statutory language and, by a balancing of court-devised factors, determine a point during the germination process of a potential proposal at which an impact statement *should be prepared.* Such an assertion of judicial authority would leave the agencies uncertain as to their procedural duties under NEPA, would invite judicial involvement in the day-to-day decisionmaking process of the agencies, and would invite litigation. As the contemplation of a project and the accompanying study thereof do not necessarily result in a proposal for major federal action, it may be assumed that the balancing process devised by the Court of Appeals also would result in the preparation of a good many unnecessary impact statements. . . .

V

Our discussion thus far has been addressed primarily to the decision of the Court of Appeals. It remains, however, to consider the contention now urged by respondents. They have not attempted to support the Court of Appeals' decision. Instead, respondents renew an argument they appear to have made to the Court of Appeals, but which that court did not reach. Respondents insist that, even without a comprehensive federal plan for the development of the Northern Great Plains, a "regional" impact statement nevertheless is required on all coal-related projects in the region because they are intimately related. . . .

. . . [Section]102(2)(C) may require a comprehensive impact statement in certain situations where several proposed actions are pending at the same time. NEPA announced a national policy of environmental protection and placed a responsibility upon the Federal Government to further specific environmental goals by "all practicable means, consistent with other essential considerations of national policy." §101(b), 42 U.S.C. §4331(b). Section 102(2)(C) is one of the "action-forcing" provisions intended as a directive to "all agencies to assure consideration of the environmental impact of their actions in decisionmaking." Conference Report on NEPA, 115 Cong. Rec. 40416 (1969). By requiring an impact statement Congress intended to assure such consideration during the development of a proposal or—as in this case—during the formulation of a position on a proposal submitted by private parties. A comprehensive impact statement may be necessary in some cases for an agency to meet this duty. Thus, when several proposals for coal-related actions that will have cumulative or synergistic environmental impact upon a region are pending concurrently before an agency, their environmental consequences must be considered together. Only through comprehensive consideration of pending proposals can the agency evaluate different courses of action.

Agreement to this extent with respondents' premise, however, does not require acceptance of their conclusion that all proposed coal-related actions in the Northern Great Plains region are so "related" as to require their analysis in a single comprehensive impact statement. . . .

. . . Cumulative environmental impacts are, indeed, what require a comprehensive impact statement. But determination of the extent and effect of these factors, and particularly identification of the geographic area within which they may occur, is a task assigned to the special competency of the appropriate agencies. Petitioners dispute respondents' contentions that the interrelationship of environmental impacts is regionwide and, as respondents' own submissions indicate, petitioners appear to have determined that the appropriate scope of comprehensive statements should be based on basins, drainage areas, and other factors. We cannot say that petitioners' choices are arbitrary. Even if environmental interrelationships could be shown conclusively to extend across basins and drainage areas, practical considerations of feasibility might well necessitate restricting the scope of comprehensive statements.

In sum, respondents' contention as to the relationships between all proposed coal-related projects in the Northern Great Plains region does not require that petitioners prepare one comprehensive impact statement covering all before proceeding to approve specific pending applications. As we already determined that there exists no proposal for regionwide action that could require a regional impact statement, the judgment of the Court of Appeals must be reversed, and the judgment of the District Court reinstated and affirmed. . . .

MR. JUSTICE MARSHALL, with whom MR. JUSTICE BRENNAN joins, concurring in part and dissenting in part.

While I agree with much of the Court's opinion, I must dissent from Part IV, which holds that the federal courts may not remedy violations of the National Environmental Policy Act of 1969 (NEPA), 83 Stat. 852, 42 U.S.C. §4321 et seq.—no matter how blatant—until it is too late for an adequate remedy to be formulated. As the Court today recognizes, NEPA contemplates agency consideration of environmental factors throughout the decisionmaking process. Since NEPA's enactment, however, litigation has been brought primarily at the end of that process—challenging agency decisions to act made without adequate environmental impact statements or without any statements at all. In such situations, the courts have had to content themselves with the largely unsatisfactory remedy of enjoining the proposed federal action and ordering the preparation of an adequate impact statement. This remedy is insufficient because, except by deterrence, it does nothing to further early consideration of environmental factors. And, as with all after-the-fact remedies, a remand for preparation of an impact statement after the basic decision to act has been made invites post hoc rationalizations, cf. Citizens to Preserve Overton Park v. Volpe, 401 U.S. 402, 419-420 (1971), rather than the candid and balanced environmental assessments envisioned by NEPA. Moreover, the remedy is wasteful of resources and time, causing fully developed plans for action to be laid aside while an impact statement is prepared.

Nonetheless, until this lawsuit, such belated remedies were all the federal courts had had the opportunity to impose under NEPA. In this case, confronted with a situation in which, according to respondents' allegations, federal agencies were violating NEPA prior to their basic decision to act, the Court of Appeals for the District of Columbia Circuit seized the opportunity to devise a different and effective remedy. It recognized a narrow class of cases—essentially those where both the likelihood of eventual agency action and the danger posed by nonpreparation of an environmental impact statement were great—in which it would allow judicial intervention prior to the time at which an impact statement must be ready. The Court today loses sight of the inadequacy of other remedies and the narrowness of the category constructed by the Court of Appeals, and construes NEPA so as to preclude a court from ever intervening prior to a formal agency proposal. This decision, which unnecessarily limits the ability of the federal courts to effectuate the intent of NEPA, is mandated neither by the statute nor by the various equitable considerations upon which the Court relies.

NOTES AND QUESTIONS

1. What environmental reviews had the Secretary undertaken or agreed to undertake? Why did the Sierra Club want more?

2. Consider the question of *timing*. The majority seem to agree that an EIS must be completed by the time of the agency's "recommendation or report on a proposal" for action. What is the debate? What earlier obligations has the Court of Appeals imposed on the agencies? Why does Justice Marshall believe the lower court's approach is necessary? Why did the Sierra Club abandon this approach on appeal?

3. The majority in *Kleppe* relied largely on the interpretation of the statutory term "proposal" in deciding the timing of NEPA's obligations. Two years after *Kleppe*, CEQ defined "proposal" in its regulations as existing "at that stage in the development of an action when an agency subject to the Act has a goal and is actively preparing to make a decision on one or more alternative means of accomplishing that goal and the effects can be meaningfully evaluated." 40 C.F.R. §1508.23. The CEQ reaffirmed that preparation of an EIS should be completed in time for inclusion in any recommendation or report on the proposal. Does this

CEQ regulation depart from the Supreme Court's decision in *Kleppe*? The CEQ also issued more general guidance on the issue of "timing," which is contained in 40 C.F.R. §1502.5.

4. Consider also the question of *scope*. The Sierra Club argued that an EIS must be prepared for actions that are "intimately related." Did the Supreme Court reject this interpretation? What would the Sierra Club have to show to persuade a court to compel preparation of a regional EIS? What difficulties does that showing pose for environmental plaintiffs? Might the Sierra Club fare better under the CEQ's post-*Kleppe* regulations contained in 40 C.F.R. §1508.25? These regulations direct agencies to determine the scope of EISs by considering three types of actions (connected actions, cumulative actions, and similar actions), three types of alternatives, and three types of impacts (direct, indirect, and cumulative). Consider the impact and application of these regulations in the following cases.

Thomas v. Peterson
753 F.2d 754 (9th Cir. 1985)

[The Forest Service planned construction of a gravel road to service timber harvesting in an area known as "Jersey Jack." The Service concluded that the road would not have "significant" effects on the environment and therefore approved construction without preparing an EIS. The Service subsequently approved two timber sales in the area, also without preparing an EIS. Conservation groups brought this action to enjoin construction of the road, alleging violations of the National Forest Management Act, the Endangered Species Act, and NEPA.]

Before WRIGHT, SNEED, and ALARCON, Circuit Judges.

SNEED, Circuit Judge.

THE NEPA CLAIM

The central question that plaintiffs' NEPA claim presents is whether the road and the timber sales are sufficiently related so as to require combined treatment in a single EIS that covers the cumulative effects of the road and the sales. If so, the Forest Service has proceeded improperly. An EIS must be prepared and considered by the Forest Service before the road can be approved. If not, the Forest Service may go ahead with the road, and later consider the environmental impacts of the timber sales.

Section 102(2)(C) of NEPA requires an EIS for "major Federal actions significantly affecting the quality of the human environment." 42 U.S.C. §4332(2)(C) (1982). While it is true that administrative agencies must be given considerable discretion in defining the scope of environmental impact statements, see Kleppe v. Sierra Club, 427 U.S. 390, 412-415 (1976), there are situations in which an agency is required to consider several related actions in a single EIS, see id. at 409-410. Not to require this would permit dividing a project into multiple "actions," each of which individually has an insignificant environmental impact, but which collectively have a substantial impact.

Since the Supreme Court decided the *Kleppe* case, the Council on Environmental Quality (CEQ) has issued regulations that define the circumstances under which multiple related actions must be covered by a single EIS. The regulations are made binding on federal administrative agencies by Executive Order. See Exec. Order No. 11991, 3 C.F.R. 1977 Comp. 123 (1978); Andrus v. Sierra Club, 442 U.S. 347, 357-358 (1979). The CEQ regulations and this court's precedents both require the Forest Service to prepare an EIS analyzing the combined environmental impacts of the road and the timber sales.

A.   CEQ Regulations

1.   Connected Actions

The CEQ regulations require "connected actions" to be considered together in a single EIS. See 40 C.F.R. §1508.25(a)(1) (1984). "Connected actions" are defined as actions that "(i) Automatically trigger other actions which may require environmental impact statements. (ii) Cannot or will not proceed unless other actions are taken previously or simultaneously. (iii) Are interdependent parts of a larger action and depend on the larger action for their justification." Id.

The construction of the road and the sale of the timber in the Jersey Jack area meet the second and third, as well as perhaps the first, of these criteria. It is clear that the timber sales cannot proceed without the road, and the road would not be built but for the contemplated timber sales. This much is revealed by the Forest Service's characterization of the road as a "logging road," and by the first page of the environmental assessment for the road, which states that "[t]he need for a transportation route in the assessment area is to access the timber lands to be developed over the next twenty years." Moreover, the environmental assessment for the road rejected a "no action" alternative because that alternative would not provide the needed timber access. The Forest Service's cost-benefit analysis of the road considered the timber to be the benefit of the road, and while the Service has stated that the road will yield other benefits, it does not claim that such other benefits would justify the road in the absence of the timber sales. Finally, the close interdependence of the road and the timber sales is indicated by an

August 1981 letter in the record from the Regional Forester to the Forest Supervisor. It states, "We understand that sales in the immediate future will be dependent on the early completion of portions of the Jersey Jack Road. It would be advisable to divide the road into segments and establish separate completion dates for those portions to be used for those sales."

We conclude, therefore, that the road construction and the contemplated timber sales are inextricably intertwined, and that they are "connected actions" within the meaning of the CEQ regulations.

2. Cumulative Actions

The CEQ regulations also require that "cumulative actions" be considered together in a single EIS. 40 C.F.R. §1508.25(a)(2). "Cumulative actions" are defined as actions "which when viewed with other proposed actions have cumulatively significant impacts." Id. The record in this case contains considerable evidence to suggest that the road and the timber sales will have cumulatively significant impacts. The U.S. Fish & Wildlife Service, the Environmental Protection Agency, and the Idaho Department of Fish & Game have asserted that the road and the timber sales will have significant cumulative effects that should be considered in an EIS. The primary cumulative effects, according to these agencies, are the deposit of sediments in the Salmon River to the detriment of that river's population of salmon and steelhead trout, and the destruction of critical habitat for the endangered Rocky Mountain Gray Wolf. These agencies have criticized the Forest Service for not producing an EIS that considers the cumulative impacts of the Jersey Jack road and the timber sales. For example, the Fish & Wildlife Service has written, "Separate documentation of related and cumulative potential impacts may be leading to aquatic habitat degradation unaccounted for in individual EA's (i.e., undocumented cumulative effects). . . . Lack of an overall effort to document cumulative impacts could be having present and future detrimental effects on wolf recovery potential." These comments are sufficient to raise "substantial questions" as to whether the road and the timber sales will have significant cumulative environmental effects. Therefore, on this basis also, the Forest Service is required to prepare an EIS analyzing such effects. . . .

C. Timing of the EIS

The Forest Service argues that the cumulative environmental effects of the road and the timber sales will be adequately analyzed and considered in the EA's and/or EIS's that it will prepare on the individual timber sales. The EA or EIS on each action, it contends, will document the cumulative impacts of that action and all previous actions.

We believe that consideration of cumulative impacts after the road has already been approved is insufficient to fulfill the mandate of NEPA. A central purpose of an EIS is to force the consideration of environmental impacts in the decisionmaking process. That purpose requires that the NEPA process be integrated with agency planning "at the earliest possible time," 40 C.F.R. §1501.2, and the purpose cannot be fully served if consideration of the cumulative effects of successive, interdependent steps is delayed until the first step has already been taken.

The location, the timing, or other aspects of the timber sales, or even the decision whether to sell any timber at all, affects the location, routing, construction techniques, and other aspects of the road, or even the need for its construction. But the consideration of cumulative impacts will serve little purpose if the road has already been built. Building the road swings the balance decidedly in favor of timber sales even if such sales would have been disfavored had road and sales been considered together before the road was built. Only by selling timber can the bulk of the expense of building the road be recovered. Not to sell timber after building the road constitutes the "irrational" result that *Trout Unlimited's* standard is intended to avoid [Trout Unlimited v. Morton, 509 F.2d 1276 (9th Cir. 1974)]. Therefore, the cumulative environmental impacts of the road and the timber sales must be assessed before the road is approved.

The Forest Service argues that the sales are too uncertain and too far in the future for their impacts to be analyzed along with that of the road. This comes close to saying that building the road now is itself irrational. We decline to accept that conclusion. Rather, we believe that if the sales are sufficiently certain to justify construction of the road, then they are sufficiently certain for their environmental impacts to be analyzed along with those of the road. Cf. City of Davis v. Coleman, 521 F.2d 661, 667-676 (9th Cir. 1975) (EIS for a road must analyze the impacts of industrial development that the road is designed to accommodate). Where agency actions are sufficiently related so as to be "connected" within the meaning of the CEQ regulations, the agency may not escape compliance with the regulations by proceeding with one action while characterizing the others as remote or speculative.

Sierra Club v. Peterson
717 F.2d 1409 (D.C. Cir. 1983)

Before WRIGHT and SCALIA, Circuit Judges, and MACKINNON, Senior Circuit Judge.

MACKINNON, Senior Circuit Judge:

In proceedings in the district court, the Sierra Club challenged the decision by the United States Forest Service (Forest Service) and the Department of the Interior (Department) to issue oil and gas leases on lands within the Targhee and Bridger-Teton National Forests of Idaho and Wyoming. The plaintiff alleged that the leasing program violated the National Environmental Policy Act (NEPA), 42 U.S.C. §4321 et seq. (1976), because no Environment Impact Statement (EIS) was prepared prior to the action. On cross-motion for summary judgment the district court upheld the decision to issue the leases without preparing an EIS. . . .

In 1980, the Forest Service received applications for oil and gas leases in the Palisades Further Planning Area. After conducting an Environmental Assessment (EA), the Forest Service recommended granting the lease applications, but with various stipulations attached to the leases. Because the Forest Service determined that issuance of the leases with the recommended stipulations would not result in significant adverse impacts to the environment, it decided that, with respect to the *entire* area, no Environmental Impact Statement was required at the leasing stage.

The leasing program approved by the Forest Service divides the land within the Palisades Further Planning Area into two categories— "highly environmentally sensitive" lands and non-highly environmentally sensitive lands. The stipulations attached to each lease are determined by the particular character of the land. All of the leases for the Palisades contain "standard" and "special" stipulations. These stipulations require the lessee to obtain approval from the Interior Department before undertaking any surface disturbing activity on the lease, but do not authorize the Department to *preclude* any activities which the lessee might propose. The Department can only impose conditions upon the lessee's use of the leased land.

In addition, a No Surface Occupancy Stipulation (NSO Stipulation) is attached to the leases for lands designated as "highly environmentally sensitive." This NSO Stipulation *precludes* surface occupancy unless and until such activity is specifically approved by the Forest Service.

For leases *without* a[n NSO] Stipulation, the lessee must file an application for a permit to drill prior to initiating exploratory drilling activities. The application must contain a surface use and operating plan which details the proposed operations including access roads, well site locations, and other planned facilities. On land leased without a[n NSO] Stipulation the Department *cannot* deny the permit to drill; it can only impose "reasonable" conditions which are designed to mitigate the environmental impacts of the drilling operations. [Eighty percent of the leases issued in the Palisades contained NSO stipulations. The Sierra Club appealed the district court's judgment only with respect to those lands leased without an NSO stipulation.] . . .

III

The National Environmental Policy Act (NEPA) requires preparation of an Environmental Impact Statement whenever a proposed major federal action will significantly affect the quality of the human environment. 42 U.S.C. §4332(2)(C) (1976). To determine the nature of the environmental impact from a proposed action and whether an EIS will be required, federal agencies prepare an environmental assessment. 40 C.F.R. §1501.4(b) & (c) (1982). If on the basis of the Environmental Assessment the agency finds that the proposed action will produce "no significant impact" on the environment, then an EIS need not be prepared. Id. at §1501.4(e).

An agency's finding of "no significant impact" and consequent decision not to prepare an EIS can only be overturned if the decision was arbitrary, capricious, or an abuse of discretion. Judicial review of an agency's finding of "no significant impact" is not, however, merely perfunctory as the court must insure that the agency took a "hard look" at the environmental consequences of its decision.

Cases in this circuit have employed a four-part test to scrutinize an agency's finding of "no significant impact." The court ascertains

(1) whether the agency took a "hard look" at the problem;

(2) whether the agency identified the relevant areas of environmental concern;

(3) as to the problems studied and identified, whether the agency made a convincing case that the impact was insignificant; and

(4) if there was an impact of true significance, whether the agency convincingly established that changes in the project sufficiently reduced it to a minimum.

Applying the foregoing test to this agency decision, we are satisfied that the agency has taken the requisite "hard look" and has "identified the relevant areas of environmental concern." However, in our opinion, the finding that "no significant impact" will occur as a result of granting leases *without* an NSO Stipulation is not supportable on this record.

The finding of "no significant impact" is premised upon the conclusion that the lease stipulations will prevent any significant environmental impacts until a site-specific plan for exploration and development is submitted by the lessee. At that time, the federal appellees explain, an appropriate environmental analysis, either an Environmental Assessment or an EIS, will be prepared. In bifurcating its environmental analysis, however, the agency has taken a foreshortened view of the impacts which could result from the act of *leasing*. The agency has essentially assumed that leasing is a discrete transition which will not result in any "physical or biological impacts." The Environmental Assessment concludes

> that there will be no significant adverse effects on the human environment due to oil and gas lease issuance. Therefore, no environmental impact statement will be prepared. The determination was based upon consideration of the following factors . . . (a) few issued leases result in active exploration operations and still fewer result in discovery or production of oil or gas; (b) the act of issuing a lease involves no physical or biological impacts; (c) the cumulative environmental effect of lease issuance on an area-wide basis is very small; (d) effects of lease activities once permitted will be mitigated to protect areas of critical environmental concern by appropriate stipulations including no-surface occupancy; (e) if unacceptable environmental impacts cannot be corrected, activities will not be permitted; and (f) the action will not have a significant effect on the human environment.

The conclusion that no significant impact will occur is improperly based on a prophecy that exploration activity on these lands will be insignificant and generally fruitless.

While it may well be true that the majority of these leases will never reach the drilling stage and that the environmental impacts of exploration are dependent upon the nature of the activity, nevertheless NEPA requires that federal agencies determine at the outset whether their major actions can result in "significant" environmental impacts. Here, the Forest Service concluded that any impacts which might result from the act of leasing would either be insignificant or, if significant, could be mitigated by exercising the controls provided in the lease stipulations.

Even assuming, arguendo, that all lease stipulations are fully enforceable, once the land is leased the Department no longer has the authority to *preclude* surface disturbing activities even if the environmental impact of such activity is significant. The Department can only impose "mitigation" measures upon a lessee who pursues surface disturbing exploration and/or drilling activities. None of the stipulations expressly provides that the Department or the Forest Service can *prevent* a lessee from conducting surface disturbing activities. Thus, with respect to the smaller area with which we are here concerned, the decision to allow surface disturbing activities has been made at the *leasing stage* and, under NEPA, this is the point at which the environmental impacts of such activities must be evaluated.

NEPA requires an agency to evaluate the environmental effects of its action at the point of commitment. The purpose of an EIS is to insure that the agency considers all possible courses of action and assesses the environmental consequences of each proposed action. The EIS is a decision-making tool intended to "insure that . . . environmental amenities and values may be given appropriate consideration in decision-making. . . ." 42 U.S.C. §4332(2)(B). Therefore, the appropriate time for preparing an EIS is *prior* to a decision, when the decisionmaker retains a maximum range of options. Environmental Defense Fund v. Andrus, 596 F.2d 848, 852-853 (9th Cir. 1979). Accord, Port of Astoria v. Hodel, 595 F.2d 467, 478 (9th Cir. 1979) (NEPA requires that an EIS be prepared "at an early stage when alternative courses of action are still possible . . ."); Scientists' Inst. for Public Information, Inc. v. Atomic Energy Comm'n, 481 F.2d 1079, 1094 (D.C. Cir. 1973) (In determining *when* to prepare an EIS the agency must ascertain to what extent its decision embodies an "irretrievable commitment" of resources which precludes the exercise of future "options."). An EIS is required when the "critical agency decision" is made which results in "irreversible and irretrievable commitments of resources" to an action which will affect the environment. On the facts of this case, that "critical time," insofar as lands leased without a[n] NSO Stipulation are concerned, occurred at the point of leasing.

Notwithstanding the assurance that a later site-specific environmental analysis will be made, in issuing these leases the Department made an irrevocable commitment to allow *some* surface disturbing activities, including drilling and roadbuilding. While theoretically the proposed two-stage environmental analysis may be acceptable, in this situation the Department has not complied with NEPA because it has sanctioned activities which have the potential for disturbing the environment without fully assessing the possible environmental consequences.

The Department asserts that it cannot accurately evaluate the consequences of drilling and other surface disturbing activities until site-specific plans are submitted. If, however, the Department is in fact concerned that it cannot foresee and evaluate the environmental consequences of leasing without site-specific proposals, then it may delay preparation of an EIS provided that it reserves both the authority to *preclude* all activities pending submission of site-specific proposals and the authority to *prevent* proposed activities if the environmental consequences are unacceptable. If the Department chooses not to retain the authority to *preclude* all surface disturbing activities, then an EIS assessing the full environmental consequences of leasing must be prepared at the point of commitment—when the leases are issued. The Department can decide, in the first instance, by which route it will proceed.

NOTES AND QUESTIONS

1. Is the Ninth Circuit's decision in *Thomas* consistent with the Supreme Court's decision in *Kleppe*? How have the new CEQ regulations changed the analysis of timing and scope?

2. In Sierra Club v. Peterson, the court focuses its review on the

Forest Service's determination that the effects of its action will not be "significant." We will discuss that question later. For now, consider the question of timing: Why must the Forest Service prepare an EIS at the leasing stage? The Forest Service had argued that preparation of an EIS should not be required at this stage because "any impacts which might result from the act of leasing would either be insignificant or, if significant, could be mitigated by exercising the controls provided in the lease stipulations." Why does that argument fail? What could the Forest Service do differently in future leasing decisions to avoid the EIS requirement?

3. In Conner v. Burford, 605 F. Supp. 107 (D. Mont. 1985), affd. in part and revd. in part, 848 F.2d 1441 (9th Cir. 1988), cert. denied, 489 U.S. 1012 (1989), the plaintiffs pressed the question whether the Forest Service could ignore the possible impacts of oil exploration, development, and production when deciding to issue leases with no surface occupancy (NSO) stipulations. At issue was a Forest Service decision to lease 1.3 million acres of the Gallatin and Flathead National Forests in Montana. Placing NSO stipulations in more than 500 of the 700 leases to be issued, the Forest Service issued a "finding of no significant impact" for the sale, arguing that "the sale of an NSO lease has *no* effect on the environment, let alone a significant one." 848 F.2d at 1447 (emphasis in original). The District Court held that the Forest Service had violated NEPA:

> To use the NSO stipulation as a mechanism to avoid an EIS when issuing numerous leases on potential wilderness areas circumvents the spirit of NEPA. Subsequent site-specific analysis, prompted by a proposal from a lessee of one tract, may result in a finding of no significant environmental impact. Obviously, a comprehensive analysis of cumulative impacts of several oil and gas development activities must be done before any single activity can proceed. Otherwise, a piecemeal invasion of the forests would occur, followed by realization of a significant and irreversible impact. [605 F. Supp. at 108-109.]

On appeal, the Ninth Circuit reversed. The court held that NEPA would apply to subsequent decisions to remove an NSO stipulation and that "piecemeal invasion of the forests will be avoided because . . . government evaluation of surface-disturbing activity on NSO leases must include consideration of the potential for further connected development and cumulative impacts from all oil and gas development activities pursuant to the federal leases." 848 F.2d at 1448. Is that reasoning persuasive? Is lease-by-lease review a good substitute for comprehensive review of the entire 1.3-million-acre sale? If the Forest Service is reviewing one lease at a time, what is the likely form of its review—full environmental impact statement, or environmental assessment? If the Service considers the potential cumulative impacts of related development in reviewing a single lease, what options does it have to address those impacts? How would its options be different if it were reviewing the entire sale?

B. "SIGNIFICANTLY AFFECTING THE QUALITY OF THE HUMAN ENVIRONMENT"

The crucial threshold question for NEPA's EIS requirement is whether a proposed action is likely to significantly affect the quality of the human environment. It is this question that is typically the focus of an agency's analysis of its obligations under NEPA. And it is this question that is most troublesome for the courts in enforcing those obligations. This is illustrated by the following early case, which involved the question whether an EIS had to be prepared for the construction of a jail and related facilities as an annex to the federal courthouse in Manhattan. After residents and businesses in the surrounding area filed suit under NEPA, a federal district court held that no EIS was required because the project would not significantly affect the quality of the environment. The Second Circuit affirmed as to an office building that was part of the project but reversed with respect to the detention center. Hanly v. Mitchell, 460 F.2d 640 (2d Cir. 1972) (*Hanly I*). The court required the General Services Administration (GSA) to evaluate more fully the effects of the detention center (e.g., the possibility of disturbances that would cause noise, the impact of an outpatient treatment center on crime in the neighborhood, and possible traffic and parking problems) before determining that an EIS was unnecessary. On remand, GSA prepared a 25-page "Assessment of the Environmental Impact" that considered these factors in more detail. On the basis of this assessment GSA decided that the detention center would not have a significant effect on the environment. After the district court denied an injunction, the case was again appealed to the Second Circuit, which issued the decision that follows.

Hanly v. Kleindienst
471 F.2d 823 (2d Cir. 1972)

Before FRIENDLY, Chief Judge, and MANSFIELD and TIMBERS, Circuit Judges.

MANSFIELD, Circuit Judge: . . .

. . . [W]e believe that the appropriate criterion in the present case is the "arbitrary, capricious" standard established by the Administrative Procedure Act, since the meaning of the term "significantly" as used in §102(2)(C) of NEPA can be isolated as a question of law. . . .

Upon attempting, according to the foregoing standard, to interpret the amorphous term "significantly," as it is used in §102(2)(C), we are faced with the fact that almost every major federal action, no matter how limited in scope, has *some* adverse effect on the human environment. It is equally clear that an action which is environmentally important to one neighbor may be of no consequence to another. Congress could have decided that every major federal action must therefore be the subject of a detailed impact statement prepared according to the procedure prescribed by §102(2)(C). By adding the word "significantly," however, it demonstrated that before the agency in charge triggered that procedure, it should conclude that a greater environmental impact would result than from "any major federal action." Yet the limits of the key term have not been adequately defined by Congress or by guidelines issued by the CEQ and other responsible federal agencies vested with broad discretionary powers under NEPA. Congress apparently was willing to depend principally upon the agency's good faith determination as to what conduct would be sufficiently serious from an ecological standpoint to require use of the full-scale procedure.

Guidelines issued by the CEQ, which are echoed in rules for implementation published by the Public Buildings Service, the branch of GSA concerned with the construction of the MCC, suggest that a formal impact statement should be prepared with respect to "proposed actions, the environmental impact of which is likely to be highly controversial." See Council on Environmental Quality, Statements on Proposed Federal Actions Affecting the Environment, Guidelines §5(b), 36 Fed. Reg. 7724 (April 23, 1971). However, the term "controversial" apparently refers to cases where a substantial dispute exists as to the size, nature or effect of the major federal action rather than to the existence of opposition to a use, the effect of which is relatively undisputed. This court in *Hanly I*, for instance, did not require a formal impact statement with respect to the office building portion of the Annex despite the existence of neighborhood opposition to it. The suggestion that "controversial" must be equated with neighborhood opposition has also been rejected by others.

In the absence of any Congressional or administrative interpretation of the term, we are persuaded that in deciding whether a major federal action will "significantly" affect the quality of the human environment the agency in charge, although vested with broad discretion, should normally be required to review the proposed action in the light of at least two relevant factors: (1) the extent to which the action will cause adverse environmental effects in excess of those created by existing uses in the area affected by it, and (2) the absolute quantitative adverse environmental effects of the action itself, including the cumulative harm that results from its contribution to existing adverse conditions or uses in the affected area. Where conduct conforms to existing uses, its adverse consequences will usually be less significant than when it represents a radical change. Absent some showing that an entire neighborhood is in

the process of redevelopment, its existing environment, though frequently below an ideal standard, represents a norm that cannot be ignored. For instance, one more highway in an area honeycombed with
roads usually has less of an adverse impact than if it were constructed
through a roadless public park. See, e.g., Citizens to Preserve Overton
Park v. Volpe, 401 U.S. 402 (1971).

Although the existing environment of the area which is the site of
a major federal action constitutes one criterion to be considered, it must
be recognized that even a slight increase in adverse conditions that form
an existing environmental milieu may sometimes threaten harm that is
significant. One more factory polluting air and water in an area zoned
for industrial use may represent the straw that breaks the back of the
environmental camel. Hence the absolute, as well as comparative, effects
of a major federal action must be considered. . . .

. . . Rather than encourage agencies to dispense with impact statements, we believe that application of the foregoing objective standards,
coupled with compliance with minimum procedural requirements (specified below), which are designed to assure consideration of relevant facts,
will lead agencies in doubtful cases (so-called "grey" areas) to obtain
impact statements rather than to risk the delay and expense of protracted
litigation. . . .

Appellants further contend that they have never been given an
opportunity to discuss the MCC with any governmental agency prior to
GSA's submission of its Assessment, which raises the question whether
the agency acted "without observance of procedure required by law,"
see Citizens to Preserve Overton Park v. Volpe, 401 U.S. 402. We do not
share the Government's view that the procedural mandates of §102(A),
(B), and (D), 42 U.S.C. §4332(2)(A), (B) and (D), apply only to actions
found by the agency itself to have a significant environmental effect.
While these sections are somewhat opaque, they are not expressly limited
to "major Federal actions significantly affecting the quality of the human
environment." Indeed if they were so limited §102(D), which requires
the agency to develop appropriate alternatives to the recommended
course of action, would be duplicative since §102(C), which does apply
to actions "significantly affecting" the environment, specifies that the
detailed impact statement must deal with "alternatives to the proposed
action." 42 U.S.C. §4332(2)(C)(iii). However, in our view the Assessment
does, in fact, satisfy the requirement of §102(2)(A) that an interdisciplinary approach taking into account the "natural and social sciences
and the environmental design arts" be used. The GSA has retained
architects familiar with the design requirements of the Civic Center and
consulted with the Office of Lower Manhattan Development in an effort
to harmonize the MCC with the Civic Center. The Assessment scrupu-
lously takes into account the aesthetics and the tangible factors involved
the designing and planning of the MCC. Furthermore, we find that

§102 (2)(D) was complied with insofar as the GSA specifically considered the alternatives to continuing operation at the present facility at West Street and evaluated the selected site as compared with other specified possibilities. Although the assessment of the alternative sites was not as intensive as we might hope, its failure to analyze them in further detail does not warrant reversal.

A more serious question is raised by the GSA's failure to comply with §102(2)(B), which requires the agency to "identify and develop methods and procedures . . . which will insure that presently unquantified environmental amenities and values may be given appropriate consideration in decisionmaking along with economic and technical considerations." 42 U.S.C. §4332(2)(B). Since an agency, in making a threshold determination as to the "significance" of an action, is called upon to review in a general fashion the same factors that would be studied in depth for preparation of a detailed environmental impact statement, §102(2)(B) requires that some rudimentary procedures be designed to assure a fair and informed preliminary decision. Otherwise the agency, lacking essential information, might frustrate the purpose of NEPA by a threshold determination that an impact statement is unnecessary. Furthermore, an adequate record serves to preclude later changes in use without consideration of their environmental significance as required by NEPA.

Where a proposed major federal action may affect the sensibilities of a neighborhood, the prudent course would be for the agency in charge, before making a threshold decision, to give notice to the community of the contemplated action and to accept all pertinent information proffered by concerned citizens with respect to it. Furthermore, in line with the procedure usually followed in zoning disputes, particularly where emotions are likely to be aroused by fears, or rumors of misinformation, a public hearing serves the dual purpose of enabling the agency to obtain all relevant data and to satisfy the community that its views are being considered. However, neither NEPA nor any other federal statute mandates the specific type of procedure to be followed by federal agencies. . . .

Notwithstanding the absence of statutory or administrative provisions on the subject, this court has already held in *Hanly I* at 647 that federal agencies must "affirmatively develop a reviewable environmental record . . . even for purposes of a threshold section 102(2)(C) determination." We now go further and hold that before a preliminary or threshold determination of significance is made the responsible agency must give notice to the public of the proposed major federal action and an opportunity to submit relevant facts which might bear upon the agency's threshold decision. We do not suggest that a full-fledged formal hearing must be provided before each such determination is made, although it should be apparent that in many cases such a hearing would be advisable for reasons already indicated. The necessity for a hearing will depend greatly upon the circumstances surrounding the particular proposed action and upon the likelihood that a hearing will be more effective than other methods in developing relevant information and an understanding of the proposed action. The precise procedural steps to be adopted are better left to the agency, which should be in a better position than the court to determine whether solution of the problems faced with respect to a specific major federal action can better be achieved through a hearing or by informal acceptance of relevant data. . . .

FRIENDLY, Chief Judge (dissenting):

The learned opinion of my brother Mansfield gives these plaintiffs . . . both too little and too much. It gives too little because it raises the floor of what constitutes "major Federal actions significantly affecting the quality of the human environment," 42 U.S.C. §4332(2)(C), higher than I believe Congress intended. It gives too much because it requires that before making a threshold determination that no impact statement is demanded, the agency must go through procedures which I think are needed only when an impact statement must be made. The upshot is that a threshold determination that a proposal does not constitute major Federal action significantly affecting the quality of the human environment becomes a kind of mini-impact statement. The preparation of such a statement under the conditions laid down by the majority is unduly burdensome when the action is truly minor or insignificant. On the other hand, there is a danger that if the threshold determination is this elaborate, it may come to replace the impact statement in the grey area between actions which, though "major" in a monetary sense, are obviously insignificant (such as the construction of the proposed office building) and actions that are obviously significant (such as the construction of an atomic power plant). We would better serve the purposes of Congress by keeping the threshold low enough to insure that impact statements are prepared for actions in this grey area and thus to permit the determination that no statement is required to be made quite informally in cases of true insignificance. . . .

It is not readily conceivable that Congress meant to allow agencies to avoid [the EIS] requirement by reading "significant" to mean only "important," "momentous," or the like. One of the purposes of the impact statement is to insure that the relevant environmental data are before the agency and considered by it prior to the decision to commit Federal resources to the project; the statute must not be construed so as to allow the agency to make its decision in a doubtful case without the relevant data or a detailed study of it. This is particularly clear because of the absence from the statute of any procedural requirement upon an agency in making the threshold determination that an impact statement is not demanded, although the majority has managed to contrive one. What

Congress was trying to say was "You don't need to make an impact statement, with the consequent expense and delay, when there is no sensible reason for making one." I thus agree with Judge J. Skelly Wright's view that "a statement is required whenever the action *arguably* will have an adverse environmental impact," Students Challenging Regulatory Agency Procedures (S.C.R.A.P.) v. United States, 346 F. Supp. 189, 201 (D.D.C. 1972) (three-judge court) (emphasis in original), prob. juris. noted, 409 U.S. 1073, with the qualification, doubtless intended, that the matter must be *fairly* arguable. . . .

[The CEQ Guidelines] provide that "if there is *potential* that the environment may be significantly affected, the statement is to be prepared." Guidelines §5(b), 36 Fed. Reg. 7724 (1971) (emphasis added). And they state further, in a remark highly relevant to this case:

> Proposed actions, the environmental impact of which is likely to be highly controversial, should be covered in all cases.

Id. This Guideline has been expressly adopted by the GSA in its own regulations, GSA Public Buildings Service Order 1095.1A, Attachment B, §1(a)(5) (Dec. 2, 1971). With respect, I see no basis for reading this as limited to cases where there is a dispute over what the environmental effects actually will be. Rather, I would think it clear that this includes action which the agency should know is likely to arouse intense opposition, even if the actual environmental impact is readily apparent. Apart from the former being the natural meaning of the words, the CEQ may well have had in mind that when action having some environmental impact "is likely to be highly controversial," an agency assessment that the action does not constitute major Federal action significantly affecting the environment is almost certain to evoke challenge in the courts. The CEQ could well have believed that rather than to incur the delay incident to such a suit, and the further delay if a court sustains the challenge— both vividly illustrated in this case where nearly two years have elapsed since the initial assessment that an impact statement was not required and a further remand is being directed—the agency would do better to prepare an impact statement in the first instance. In addition to possibly providing new information making reconsideration or modification of the project appropriate, such a policy has the added benefits of allowing opponents to blow off steam and giving them a sense that their objections have been considered—an important purpose of NEPA, as it is of the British statutory inquiry. . . .

. . . The energies my brothers would require GSA to devote to still a third assessment designed to show that an impact statement is not needed would better be devoted to making one.

I would reverse and direct the issuance of an injunction until a reasonable period after the making of an impact statement.

NOTES AND QUESTIONS

1. As the court's debate in *Hanly* makes clear, the threshold determination required by NEPA presents difficult questions of both substance and procedure: What does "significantly" mean and how should significance be determined? What answers does the majority provide to these questions? How helpful are its formulations? Does Judge Friendly offer a more workable approach?

2. In another portion of his dissent, Judge Friendly notes that the "action agencies" that are responsible for implementation of NEPA often have "missions" (such as highway or jail construction) that NEPA only serves to impede. Should this influence the degree of deference courts afford to these agencies' interpretation of NEPA?

3. The amorphous and subjective character of the "significance" test continues to plague the agencies and the courts, as discussed below. However, there is much stronger consensus today on the procedure by which this determination must be made.

i. Procedure for Determining Whether or Not to Prepare an EIS

In the *Hanly* litigation and other early cases, the courts demanded that agencies "affirmatively develop a reviewable environmental record" to support determinations that their actions would not "significantly affect the quality of the human environment." This "reviewable environmental record" has become what is now called an "environmental assessment." The CEQ regulations reflect these decisions in setting out the process by which agencies determine whether an EIS is required. Section 1501.4 of the CEQ regulations directs agencies to determine whether the proposal is one that "(1) [n]ormally requires an environmental impact statement, or (2) [n]ormally does not require either an environmental impact statement or an environmental assessment (categorical exclusion)." Actions in the first category presumptively require preparation of an EIS; actions in the second category presumptively do not. If the proposed action falls in neither of these two categories, agencies are directed to prepare an environmental assessment and to make the determination of whether or not to prepare an EIS on the basis of the results of that assessment. If an agency determines on the basis of the environmental assessment not to prepare an EIS, the agency must make the finding of no significant impact available to the affected public as specified in §1506.6 of the CEQ regulations. In cases where the proposed action is without precedent or is very similar to one that normally requires preparation of an EIS, the CEQ regulations direct the agency to make a proposed finding of no significant impact available for public review for 30 days before the agency makes its final determination whether or not to prepare an EIS.

The CEQ regulations specify that an environmental assessment should include "brief discussions of the need for the proposal, of alternatives as required by section 102(2)(E), of the environmental impacts of the proposed action and alternatives, and a listing of agencies and persons consulted," in short, a kind of mini-EIS. 40 C.F.R. §1508.9. Under the CEQ regulations the "environmental assessment" serves two purposes. First, it provides the basis for the agency's determination whether to prepare an EIS. Second, when the agency concludes that an EIS is not required, the environmental assessment is the vehicle for the agency's compliance with NEPA's other requirements. Most important, in many cases, under section 102(2)(E), an agency must study alternatives to the proposed action, whether or not it is required to prepare an EIS.

ii. Determining the "Significance" of Action

In its 1978 regulations, the CEQ made its own attempt to elaborate on how to interpret the term "significantly" in NEPA. 40 C.F.R. §1508.27. The CEQ advised that "significantly" as used in NEPA requires consideration of both context and intensity:

(a) Context. This means that the significance of an action must be analyzed in several contexts such as society as a whole (human, national), the affected region, the affected interests, and the locality. Significance varies with the setting of the proposed action. For instance, in the case of a site-specific action, significance would usually depend upon the effects in the locale rather than in the world as a whole. Both short- and long-term effects are relevant.

(b) Intensity. This refers to the severity of impact. Responsible officials must bear in mind that more than one agency may make decisions about partial aspects of a major action. The following should be considered in evaluating intensity:

(1) Impact that may be both beneficial and adverse. A significant effect may exist even if the Federal agency believes that on balance the effect will be beneficial.

(2) The degree to which the proposed action affects public health or safety.

(3) Unique characteristics of the geographic area such as proximity to historic or cultural resources, parklands, prime farmlands, wetlands, wild and scenic rivers, or ecologically critical areas.

(4) The degree to which the effects on the quality of the human environment are likely to be highly controversial.

(5) The degree to which the possible effects on the human environment are highly uncertain or involve unique or unknown risks.

(6) The degree to which the action may establish a precedent for future actions with significant effects or represents a decision in principle about a future consideration.

(7) Whether the action is related to other actions with individually insignificant but cumulatively significant impacts. Significance exists if it is reasonable to anticipate a cumulatively significant impact on the environment. Significance cannot be avoided by terming an action temporary or by breaking it down into small component parts.

(8) The degree to which the action may adversely affect districts, sites, highways, structures, or objects listed in or eligible for listing in the National Register of Historic Places or may cause loss or destruction of significant scientific, cultural, or historical resources.

(9) The degree to which the action may adversely affect an endangered or threatened species or its habitat that has been determined to be critical under the Endangered Species Act of 1973.

(10) Whether the action threatens a violation of Federal, State, or local law or requirements imposed for the protection of the environment. [43 Fed. Reg. 56,005 (1978); 44 Fed. Reg. 874 (1979).]

In determining whether the effects of an action are "significant," one must, of course, make some judgments about what "effects" must be considered. NEPA demands consideration of effects "on the human environment." The CEQ Regulation defining "effects," 40 C.F.R. §1508.8, provides the following explanation:

> Effects and impacts as used in these regulations are synonymous. Effects includes ecological (such as the effects on natural resources and on the components, structures, and functioning of affected ecosystems), aesthetic, historic, cultural, economic, social, or health, whether direct, indirect, or cumulative. Effects may also include those resulting from actions which may have both beneficial and detrimental effects, even if on balance the agency believes that the effect will be beneficial.

NOTES AND QUESTIONS

1. The question of what "effects" are cognizable under NEPA was addressed by the Supreme Court in Metropolitan Edison Co. v. People Against Nuclear Energy (*PANE*), 460 U.S. 766 (1983). In *PANE* the Court held that NEPA did not require agencies to evaluate the risk that restart of a nuclear power plant that is a companion to the damaged Three Mile Island reactor would harm the psychological health of the surrounding community. The court concluded that regardless of the gravity of the harm alleged, NEPA does not apply unless the harm has a sufficiently close connection to the physical environment. The court deemed the physical effects of the past nuclear mishap to be irrelevant to the claim that the psychological impact of restarting the companion reactor required preparation of an EIS. Is this a tenable distinction?

2. In *Hanly*, the majority was uncertain "whether psychological and

sociological effects upon neighbors constitute the type of factors that may be considered in making a determination [whether or not to perform an EIS] since they do not lend themselves to measurement." 471 F.2d at 833. Judge Friendly disagreed in his dissent, noting that NEPA speaks of "the overall welfare and development of man," 42 U.S.C. §4331(a), and requires federal agencies to act to "assure for all Americans safe, healthful, productive and esthetically and culturally pleasing surroundings." Id. §4331(b)(2). Is Judge Friendly's view consistent with the Supreme Court's decision in *PANE*?

3. The Circuits split over the question of what standard of review should be applied to a decision not to prepare an EIS. The D.C. Circuit, for example, held that such decisions were to be reviewed under the "arbitrary and capricious" standard of review. See, e.g., Sierra Club v. Peterson, discussed above at pages 1044-1048. The Fifth and Ninth Circuits applied the purportedly more rigorous standard of "reasonableness." See, e.g., Foundation for North American Wild Sheep v. United States Department of Agriculture, 681 F.2d 1172 (9th Cir. 1982). But which is the stricter standard? Refer back to Sierra Club v. Peterson. What kind of review does the court undertake in deciding whether the Forest Service decision is "arbitrary and capricious"?

4. The Supreme Court seems to have resolved the debate over standards of review in Marsh v. Oregon Natural Resources Council, discussed at pages 1074-1078, infra. The Court adopted the "arbitrary and capricious" standard for review of decisions not to prepare a supplemental EIS. The Court emphasized, however, that "courts should not automatically defer to the agency's express reliance on an interest in finality without carefully reviewing the record and satisfying themselves that the agency has made a reasoned decision based on its evaluation of the significance—or lack of significance—of the new information." The Court's decision presumably extends to review of all agency decisions not to prepare an EIS.

Judgments about whether an EIS is required are necessarily fact-intensive. Some of the challenges in making such judgments are illustrated by the following problem.

PROBLEM EXERCISE: THE NATIONAL ENVIRONMENTAL POLICY ACT

The Development Company owns a 500-acre parcel of land in northern New Jersey. The land is all wetlands that are breeding grounds for several dozen species of birds and for fish of the Hudson River. Users of the marsh reportedly include an occasional peregrine falcon (a listed endangered species). Under the Clean Water Act, Development must obtain a permit from the U.S. Army Corps of Engineers before undertaking any activity that would involve filling the wetlands.

Initially, Development proposed to use the entire parcel in an "integrated" development project that would include a residential area, office towers, and a large shopping center. The economic feasibility study prepared for Development concluded that the project could be commercially successful if all three elements were built. The economic viability of each element, however, depends largely on its proximity to the others. For example, the residential area would be attractive largely because it would be close to shopping and offices; the shopping center and offices would be attractive largely because they would be close to each other and to the residential area.

Development is now seeking a permit from the Army Corps of Engineers to fill 40 acres of wetlands for the construction of the shopping center. Development has argued that no environmental impact statement (EIS) needs to be prepared for this project because the shopping center would have only modest effects on the environment and, with proposed mitigation, would cause no net harm.

Assume that you are counsel to the Corps of Engineers. The District Engineer has asked you to advise him as to his responsibilities under the National Environmental Policy Act. (Endangered Species Act issues have been assigned to another attorney.) Must the District Engineer order preparation of an EIS before issuing a permit for construction of the shopping center?

3.   Is the EIS Adequate?

When an agency has prepared an EIS for its proposed action, the focus of judicial review naturally shifts to the adequacy of that document. The CEQ Regulations describe the basic structure and content of the EIS. 40 C.F.R. §§1502.10-1502.18. Each EIS must include: a summary (to facilitate public review); an explanation of the purpose of and need for the proposed action; a description and comparative assessment of alternatives; a description of the environment that will be affected by the action; and an analysis of the environmental consequences of the proposal and alternatives. Id. Litigation centers on the adequacy of the agency's assessment of alternatives and the scope and detail of its analysis of environmental consequences.

A.   ALTERNATIVES

NEPA requires that agencies assess and consider alternatives to proposed actions. These requirements are contained both in section

102(2)(C)(iii)'s description of the elements of an environmental impact statement ("a detailed statement by the responsible official on . . . alternatives to the proposed action") and in what is now section 102(2)(E)'s independent requirement that agencies must "study, develop, and describe appropriate alternatives to recommended courses of action in any proposal which involves unresolved conflicts concerning alternative uses of available resources."

Analysis of alternatives is arguably the most important part of NEPA. The question of the adequacy of an agency's assessment of alternatives arose in the early stages of the litigation that culminated in the Strycker's Bay v. Karlen decision discussed above. In Trinity Episcopal School Corp. v. Romney, 523 F.2d 88 (2d Cir. 1975), plaintiffs challenged the decision by the Department of Housing and Urban Development (HUD) to fund construction of low-income public housing on a site in New York City. They argued that HUD was required by NEPA to do more than simply accept the New York City Housing Authority's unsupported conclusion that there were no alternative sites for the public housing project because of the scarcity of land. The Second Circuit agreed. It held that what is now section 102(2)(E) required HUD to study alternatives to the project even though HUD was not obliged to prepare an EIS subject to section 102(2)(C)(iii). On remand, HUD prepared a study of alternatives, but rejected them all. HUD's decision was challenged again, culminating in the *Strycker's Bay* decision by the Supreme Court.

The Supreme Court had an opportunity to interpret directly NEPA's requirement for analysis of alternatives in Vermont Yankee Nuclear Power Corp. v. NRDC (a different portion of which is discussed in Chapter 5). Recall that the case involved an Atomic Energy Commission licensing proceeding (a function now performed by the Nuclear Regulatory Commission) for a nuclear power plant being built by Consumers Power. Under the Commission's licensing procedures, when a utility applied for a permit to construct a nuclear power plant, Commission staff were responsible for preparing draft and final environmental impact statements. A public adjudicatory hearing was then held by the Atomic Safety and Licensing Board. In *Vermont Yankee* the Court considered whether NEPA required the Commission to reopen the proceeding to consider energy conservation measures as an alternative to construction of the plant. In the late 1960s and early 1970s environmentalists had opposed the construction of nuclear power plants on the grounds that they were unsafe and unneeded. Following the energy crises of the early 1970s, environmentalists increasingly turned to arguments that energy conservation measures could supply the equivalent power more cheaply. After the D.C. Circuit held that the Commission was required to address the conservation alternative, the Supreme Court granted review.

Vermont Yankee Nuclear Power Corp.
v. NRDC
435 U.S. 519 (1978)

MR. JUSTICE REHNQUIST delivered the opinion of the Court. . . .

With respect to the permit to Consumers Power, the court first held that the environmental impact statement for construction of the Midland reactors was fatally defective for failure to examine energy conservation as an alternative to a plant of this size. . . .

The Court of Appeals ruled that the Commission's "threshold test" for the presentation of energy conservation contentions was inconsistent with NEPA's basic mandate to the Commission. The Commission, the court reasoned, is something more than an umpire who sits back and resolves adversary contentions at the hearing stage. And when an intervenor's comments "bring 'sufficient attention to the issue to stimulate the Commission's consideration of it,' " the Commission must "undertake its own preliminary investigation of the proffered alternative sufficient to reach a rational judgment whether it is worthy of detailed consideration in the EIS. Moreover, the Commission must explain the basis for each conclusion that further consideration of a suggested alternative is unwarranted." 547 F.2d, at 628, quoting from Indiana & Michigan Electric Co. v. FPC, 502 F.2d 336, 339 (1974), cert. denied, 420 U.S. 946 (1975).

While the court's rationale is not entirely unappealing as an abstract proposition, as applied to this case we think it basically misconceives not only the scope of the agency's statutory responsibility, but also the nature of the administrative process, the thrust of the agency's decision, and the type of issues the intervenors were trying to raise.

There is little doubt that under the Atomic Energy Act of 1954, state public utility commissions or similar bodies are empowered to make the initial decision regarding the need for power. 42 U.S.C. §2021(k). The Commission's prime area of concern in the licensing context, on the other hand, is national security, public health, and safety. §§2132, 2133, 2201. And it is clear that the need, as that term is conventionally used, for the power was thoroughly explored in the hearings. Even the Federal Power Commission, which regulates sales in interstate commerce, 16 U.S.C. §824 et seq. (1976 ed.), agreed with Consumers Power's analysis of projected need.

NEPA, of course, has altered slightly the statutory balance, requiring "a detailed statement by the responsible official on . . . alternatives to the proposed action." 42 U.S.C. §4332(C). But, as should be obvious even upon a moment's reflection, the term "alternatives" is not self-defining. To make an impact statement something more than an exercise in frivolous boilerplate the concept of alternatives must be bounded by some notion of feasibility. As the Court of Appeals for the District of Columbia Circuit has itself recognized:

> There is reason for concluding that NEPA was not meant to require detailed discussion of the environmental effects of "alternatives" put forward in comments when these effects cannot be readily ascertained and the alternatives are deemed only remote and speculative possibilities, in view of basic changes required in statutes and policies of other agencies—making them available, if at all, only after protracted debate and litigation not meaningfully compatible with the time-frame of the needs to which the underlying proposal is addressed. National Resources Defense Council v. Morton, 458 F.2d 827, 837-838 (1972).

Common sense also teaches us that the "detailed statement of alternatives" cannot be found wanting simply because the agency failed to include every alternative device and thought conceivable by the mind of man. Time and resources are simply too limited to hold that an impact statement fails because the agency failed to ferret out every possible alternative, regardless of how uncommon or unknown that alternative may have been at the time the project was approved.

With these principles in mind we now turn to the notion of "energy conservation," an alternative the omission of which was thought by the Court of Appeals to have been "forcefully pointed out by [intervenor] Saginaw in its comments on the draft EIS." Again, as the Commission pointed out, "the phrase 'energy conservation' has a deceptively simply ring in this context. Taken literally, the phrase suggests a virtually limitless range of possible actions and developments that might, in one way or another, ultimately reduce projected demands for electricity from a particular proposed plant." Moreover, as a practical matter, it is hard to dispute the observation that it is largely the events of recent years that have emphasized not only the need but also a large variety of alternatives for energy conservation. Prior to the drastic oil shortages incurred by the United States in 1973, there was little serious thought in most Government circles of energy conservation alternatives. Indeed, the Council on Environmental Quality did not promulgate regulations which even remotely suggested the need to consider energy conservation in impact statements until August 1, 1973. See 40 CFR §1500.8(a)(4) (1977); 38 Fed. Reg. 20554 (1973). And even then the guidelines were not made applicable to draft and final statements filed with the Council before January 28, 1974. Id., at 20557, 21265. The Federal Power Commission likewise did not require consideration of energy conservation in applications to build hydroelectric facilities until June 19, 1973. 18 CFR pt. 2, App. A., §8.2 (1977); 38 Fed. Reg. 15946, 15949 (1973). And these regulations were not made retroactive either. Id., at 15946. All this occurred over a year and a half after the draft environmental statement for Midland had been prepared, and over a year after the final environmental statement had been prepared and the hearings completed.

We think these facts amply demonstrate that the concept of "alternatives" is an evolving one, requiring the agency to explore more or fewer alternatives as they become better known and understood. This was well understood by the Commission, which, unlike the Court of Appeals, recognized that the Licensing Board's decision had to be judged by the information then available to it. And judged in that light we have little doubt the Board's actions were well within the proper bounds of its statutory authority. Not only did the record before the agency give every indication that the project was actually needed, but also there was nothing before the Board to indicate to the contrary.

We also think the court's criticism of the Commission's "threshold test" displays a lack of understanding of the historical setting within which the agency action took place and of the nature of the test itself. In the first place, while it is true that NEPA places upon an agency the obligation to consider every significant aspect of the environmental impact of a proposed action, it is still incumbent upon intervenors who wish to participate to structure their participation so that it is meaningful, so that it alerts the agency to the intervenors' position and contentions. This is especially true when the intervenors are requesting the agency to embark upon an exploration of uncharted territory, as was the question of energy conservation in the late 1960's and early 1970's.

> [C]omments must be significant enough to step over a threshold requirement of materiality before any lack of agency response or consideration becomes of concern. The comment cannot merely state that a particular mistake was made . . .; it must show [why] the mistake was of possible significance in the results . . . Portland Cement Assn. v. Ruckelshaus, 486 F.2d 375, 394 (1973), cert. denied sub nom. Portland Cement Corp. v. Administrator, EPA, 417 U.S. 921 (1974).

Indeed, administrative proceedings should not be a game or a forum to engage in unjustified obstructionism by making cryptic and obscure reference to matters that "ought to be" considered and then, after failing to do more to bring the matter to the agency's attention, seeking to have that agency determination vacated on the ground that the agency failed to consider matters "forcefully presented." In fact, here the agency continually invited further clarification of Saginaw's contentions. Even without such clarification it indicated a willingness to receive evidence on the matters. But not only did Saginaw decline to further focus its contentions, it virtually declined to participate, indicating that it had "no conventional findings of fact to set forth" and that it had not "chosen to search the record and respond to this proceeding by submitting citations of matter which we believe were proved or disproved."

We also think the court seriously mischaracterized the Commission's "threshold test" as placing "heavy substantive burdens . . . on intervenors . . ." 547 F.2d, at 627, and n.11. On the contrary, the Commission explicitly stated:

> We do not equate this burden with the civil litigation concept of a prima facie case, an unduly heavy burden in this setting. But the showing should be sufficient to require reasonable minds to inquire further. App. 344 n.27.

We think this sort of agency procedure well within the agency's discretion.

. . . Nuclear energy may some day be a cheap, safe source of power or it may not. But Congress has made a choice to at least try nuclear energy, establishing a reasonable review process in which courts are to play only a limited role. The fundamental policy questions appropriately resolved in Congress and in the state legislatures are *not* subject to reexamination in the federal courts under the guise of judicial review of agency action. Time may prove wrong the decision to develop nuclear energy, but it is Congress or the States with their appropriate agencies which must eventually make that judgment. In the meantime courts should perform their appointed function. NEPA does set forth significant substantive goals for the Nation, but its mandate to the agencies is essentially procedural. See 42 U.S.C. §4332. It is to insure a fully informed and well-considered decision, not necessarily a decision the judges of the Court of Appeals or of this Court would have reached had they been members of the decisionmaking unit of the agency. Administrative decisions should be set aside in this context, as in every other, only for substantial procedural or substantive reasons as mandated by statute, not simply because the court is unhappy with the result reached. And a single alleged oversight on a peripheral issue, urged by parties who never fully cooperated or indeed raised the issue below, must not be made the basis for overturning a decision properly made after an otherwise exhaustive proceeding.

NOTES AND QUESTIONS

1. What does *Vermont Yankee* tell us about the scope of the agency's duty to consider alternatives? What duty had the Commission conceded? Why does the Court refuse to require it to consider the alternatives suggested by intervenor Saginaw? What should Saginaw have done differently? Was their basic problem a failure to present their arguments to the Commission in a timely fashion, a failure to present sufficiently extensive evidence to bolster their arguments, or both?

2. The Court observes that "the concept of 'alternatives' is an evolving one, requiring the agency to explore more or fewer alternatives as they become better known and understood." What result do you think the Court would reach if the licensing proceeding occurred today and the Commission refused to consider energy conservation as an alternative to construction of the plant?

3. How obvious must an alternative be before it must be considered in an EIS? Can an agency be required to consider alternatives that employ technology that, while not currently available, could be developed in the future?

4. In some cases the number of possible alternatives is virtually infinite. In such situations, the courts have required that agencies consider an array of alternatives that represents the range of possibilities. The Ninth Circuit addressed this problem in California v. Block, 690 F.2d 735 (9th Cir. 1982). The U.S. Forest Service had prepared an EIS on a national management plan for 62 million acres of "roadless areas" in the National Forest System. The Forest Service project, called the "Roadless Area Review and Evaluation II" (RARE II), inventoried all roadless areas and allocated them among three planning categories: wilderness, nonwilderness, and further planning. For the final EIS, the Forest Service used an elaborate set of decision criteria to develop 11 alternative allocations. These included 3 extremes (all wilderness, no wilderness, and no action), which served only as points of reference and were not seriously considered. Of the 8 alternatives given serious consideration *none* allocated more than 33 percent of the roadless area to wilderness. The State of California challenged the EIS, arguing that the Forest Service had violated NEPA by unreasonably restricting the range of alternatives considered. The Ninth Circuit agreed, holding that while the Service's "decision criteria" were diverse, the resulting alternatives were not. The Forest Service was required to consider an alternative that allocated more than a third of the acreage to wilderness.

5. In its Regulation on the "scope" of an EIS, CEQ requires agencies to consider three types of alternatives: (1) no action, (2) other reasonable courses of action, and (3) mitigation measures not already included in the proposed action. 40 C.F.R. §1508.25. The CEQ Regulations refer to this analysis of alternatives as "the heart of the environmental impact statement," which is designed to define the issues sharply and to provide "a clear basis for choice among options by the decisionmaker and the public." See 40 C.F.R. §1502.14.

6. In *Vermont Yankee* Justice Rehnquist eschews Judge Wright's suggestion in *Calvert Cliffs* that NEPA imposes substantive obligations enforceable in court. He notes that "NEPA does set forth significant substantive goals for the Nation, but its mandate to the agencies is essentially procedural." Lynton Caldwell criticizes this as a "crabbed interpretation of NEPA" because it views the substantive mandate of section

101(b) as "largely rhetorical, imposing no mandate upon the agencies cognizable by the courts." Caldwell, NEPA Revisited: A Call for a Constitutional Amendment, Envtl. Forum 18 (Nov.-Dec. 1989). Yet the question whether an agency has adequately complied with NEPA's procedural requirements often requires courts to perform some assessment of the quality of an agency's analysis, as explored below.

B.   ANALYSIS

Each EIS must include a detailed assessment of the environmental consequences of the proposed action and the alternatives. The CEQ Regulations, 40 C.F.R. §1502.16, specify that this assessment must include discussions of:

(a)   Direct effects and their significance.
(b)   Indirect effects and their significance.
(c)   Possible conflicts between the proposed action and the objectives of Federal, regional, State, and local (and, in the case of a reservation, Indian tribe) land use plans, policies, and controls for the area concerned.
(d)   The environmental effects of alternatives, including the proposed action. . . .
(e)   Energy requirements and conservation potential of various alternatives and mitigation measures.
(f)   Natural or depletable resource requirements and conservation potential of various alternatives and mitigation measures.
(g)   Urban quality, historic and cultural resources, and the design of the built environment, including the reuse and conservation potential of various alternatives and mitigation measures.
(h)   Means to mitigate adverse environmental impacts. [43 Fed. Reg. 55,996 (1978); 44 Fed. Reg. 873 (1979).]

Plaintiffs have identified a nearly infinite variety of flaws in agencies' analyses of "environmental consequences." We consider here three of the most important areas of attack: the quality of the analysis; problems in scope and timing; and assessment of unknown or uncertain effects.

i.   Quality of the Analysis in an EIS

As one might expect, courts often are reluctant to judge the quality of analysis in an EIS. In a few cases, however, plaintiffs have been able to demonstrate shortcomings sufficient to persuade a court that an EIS is inadequate.

The Second Circuit's decision in Sierra Club v. United States Army

Corps of Engineers, 701 F.2d 1011 (2d Cir. 1983), was the culmination of litigation brought by the Sierra Club to enjoin the construction of a highway (known as the Westway) along the west side of Manhattan. The Sierra Club challenged both the Federal Highway Administration's (FHWA) decision to fund the project and the Army Corps of Engineers's decision to issue a permit allowing discharge of fill material into the Hudson River for the construction. The focus of the NEPA dispute was the effect of the construction on fish populations in the river.

An EIS had been prepared by the New York State Department of Transportation (NYSDOT) for the FHWA. A Draft EIS (DEIS) was released for public comment in 1974, and the Final EIS (FEIS) was published in 1977. In finding that there would be no adverse impacts on fish, the FEIS relied on a technical report on water quality impacts (Water Report), which characterized the "interpier" area to be filled as a "biological wasteland."

When the FEIS was released, FHWA announced its decision to fund the project. It was then that the proponents sought a permit from the Corps. Three federal agencies, the Environmental Protection Agency (EPA), the National Marine Fisheries Service (Fisheries Service), and the Fish and Wildlife Service (Wildlife Service), who had objected unsuccessfully to the EIS, then objected to the permit. The analysis of fisheries impacts in the draft and final EISs had relied on data on fish populations that were collected in 1973. The three agencies argued that those data were inaccurate and demanded further study. In 1978, NYSDOT agreed to commission an additional study of the fish populations in the area to be filled. This study, known as the Lawler Study, found that the populations were much richer than previously thought. Nonetheless, FHWA and the Corps decided not to prepare a supplemental EIS to address the issues raised by these new data.

The district court held a trial, taking testimony from many of the government officials and consultants who participated in preparation of the EIS. The district court enjoined the project pending preparation of a supplemental EIS and appointed a Special Master to supervise the agencies' compliance with the court's order. The district court's decision was appealed to the Second Circuit, which rendered the following decision.

Sierra Club v. United States Army Corps of Engineers
701 F.2d 1011 (2d Cir. 1983)

Before OAKES, MESKILL and KEARSE, Circuit Judges.
KEARSE, Circuit Judge:

A. NEPA

As the Supreme Court has stated repeatedly, although NEPA established " 'significant substantive goals for the Nation,' the balancing of the substantive environmental issues is consigned to the judgement of the executive agencies involved, and the judicially reviewable duties that are imposed on the agencies are 'essentially procedural.' " Strycker's Bay Neighborhood Council, Inc. v. Karlen, 444 U.S. 223, 227 (1980) (quoting Vermont Yankee Nuclear Power Corp. v. Natural Resources Defense Council, Inc., 435 U.S. 519, 558 (1978) (*"Vermont Yankee"*)). "The only role for a court is to insure that the agency has taken a 'hard look' at environmental consequences; it cannot 'interject itself within the area of discretion of the executive as to the choice of the action to be taken.' " Kleppe v. Sierra Club, 427 U.S. 390, 410 n.21 (1976) (quoting Natural Resources Defense Council, Inc. v. Morton, 458 F.2d 827, 838 (D.C. Cir. 1972)).

The primary function of an environmental impact statement under NEPA is " 'to insure a fully informed and well-considered decision,' [although] not necessarily 'a decision the judges of the Court of Appeals or of this Court would have reached had they been members of the decisionmaking unit of the agency.' " Strycker's Bay Neighborhood Council, Inc. v. Karlen, supra, 444 U.S. at 227 (quoting *Vermont Yankee, supra,* 435 U.S. at 558). In order to fulfill its role, the EIS must set forth sufficient information for the general public to make an informed evaluation and for the decisionmaker to "consider fully the environmental factors involved and to make a reasoned decision after balancing the risks of harm to the environment against the benefits to be derived from the proposed action." County of Suffolk v. Secretary of Interior, 562 F.2d 1368, 1375 (2d Cir. 1977), cert. denied, 434 U.S. 1064 (1978). In so doing, the EIS insures the integrity of the process of decision by giving assurance that stubborn problems or serious criticisms have not been "swept under the rug." Silva v. Lynn, 482 F.2d 1282, 1285 (1st Cir. 1973). The " 'detailed statement' " required by §102(2)(C) of NEPA thus "is the outward sign that environmental values and consequences have been considered during the planning stage of agency actions." Andrus v. Sierra Club, 442 U.S. 347, 350 (1979).

Given the role of the EIS and the narrow scope of permissible judicial review, the court may not rule an EIS inadequate if the agency has made an adequate compilation of relevant information, has analyzed it reasonably, has not ignored pertinent data, and has made disclosures to the public. . . .

In the present case the district court's rulings on the merits of plaintiffs' NEPA claims were consonant with the proper scope of its review and the proper view of the obligations imposed on FHWA and the Corps. With respect to the fisheries issues, the court found, inter alia, that the FEIS contained false statements depicting the interpier region as "biologically impoverished" and as a "biological wasteland," when in fact the interpier area in winter harbored a concentration of juvenile striped bass. The court found that the FEIS statements regarding aquatic impact had not been compiled in "objective good faith." Notwithstanding NYSDOT's contention that "the FEIS set forth the relevant facts that were known about the interpier area and the surrounding Hudson estuary at the time it was prepared . . . ," the court's findings to the contrary are amply supported by the record.

For example, after the DEIS was issued, the Project received critical comments regarding fisheries impact from Fisheries Service, Wildlife Service, and EPA to the effect that the fish life had been underestimated and that the information provided was inadequate. Although the FEIS purported to respond to these comments, no new studies were performed, no additional information was collected, no further inquiry was made; and the FEIS essentially reiterated or adopted the statements in the DEIS. Employees of the Project and FHWA testified that they knew before getting any data from the Lawler study that the Project's 1973 sampling had been faulty in both timing and technique and that these flaws were the reason the earlier study had revealed virtually no fish in the interpier area. Yet the Water Report, prepared in the wake of comments to the DEIS and appended to the FEIS, simply relied on the 1973 data. Bridwell, who was responsible for the preparation of the FEIS's fisheries discussion, testified that he was aware that the Water Report had not attempted to make any thorough or investigative inquiry into the existence of fish in the interpier area. He stated that the Water Report had attempted to verify only the existing literature on fish life in that area. It is not clear that even this academic study was performed: the Water Report neither identified any existing literature on the subject nor stated that there was no such literature; Bridwell himself was unaware of whether any literature existed. The evidence at trial suggested that there was no literature upon which the Report could have based its conclusion that the interpier area was biologically impoverished.

Initial responsibility for the inaccurate characterization of the interpier area as a biological wasteland must be attributed to Sydec, which the court found authored the FEIS and which was under the jurisdiction of NYSDOT, 541 F. Supp. at 1371. NEPA did not prohibit FHWA's reliance on NYSDOT for preparation of the FEIS, see NEPA §102(2)(D), 42 U.S.C. §4332(2)(D) (added by Pub. L. No. 94-83, 89 Stat. 424 (1975)), but it did require FHWA to make its own independent evaluation of the FEIS, §102(2)(D)(iii), 42 U.S.C. §4332(2)(D)(iii). There was no evidence the FHWA made any independent evaluation whatever of the fisheries issues. There was no proof that it had sought to learn what comments had been received on the DEIS from other federal agencies with expertise in special environmental subjects. FHWA officials testified that they could not recall whether they had reviewed the pointed criticisms of Fisheries Services. They stated that they may simply have ignored these criticisms as unimportant in relation to other Westway concerns. While it would indeed have been within FHWA's discretion to make a substantive determination that an adverse impact on fisheries did not outweigh the benefits to be gained, this was not the evaluation that was made. Rather, FHWA ignored criticisms pointing out that FHWA lacked "sufficient information to permit a valid assessment" of marine impact.

In short, we concur in the district court's view that the FEIS did not reasonably adequately compile relevant information with respect to fisheries impact. The evidence as to the cavalier manner in which the Project had reached its conclusion that the interpier area was a biological wasteland, and as to FHWA's failure to make an independent evaluation or to react in any way to sister agencies' pointed comments that the draft EIS did not provide adequate information for a reasoned assessment of impact on fisheries, easily supports the district court's findings (1) that the FEIS's fisheries conclusions lacked a "substantial basis in fact," and (2) that a decisionmaker relying on the January 1977 EIS could not have fully considered and balanced the environmental factors. In the circumstances, we agree that FHWA's issuance of the FEIS, and the Corps' reliance on the FEIS, violated NEPA.

B. The Clean Water Act

The district court's ruling that the Corps violated §404 of the Clean Water Act, 33 U.S.C. §1344, is also supported by the record. . . .

The district court's findings suggest that the Corps's decision was arbitrary and capricious. The court found every level of the Corp's review process woefully inadequate. It found that although the district engineer did not make his decision to approve the permit application until some 2 1/2 years after the application was filed, the decision "was made without having any reliable fishery information whatever." 536 F. Supp. at 1253. Similarly, the court found that the division engineer's decision was based on so little information that it could "only be explained as resulting from an almost fixed predetermination to grant the Westway landfill permit." Id. at 1248. It found the chief of engineers' decision virtually a rubber stamp of the decisions of his subordinates: "It is clear that [the chief of engineers] sought to expedite the matter, and saw no reason to 'second guess' the decision of the Division Engineer." Id. at 1251.

These findings are supported by the record. NYSDOT's application for a permit was filed in April 1977 and formally approved by the district engineer in September 1979. There was no evidence that in the interval the Corps did anything whatever to conduct its own investigation into the fisheries questions on which it was to pass. It had announced that the FEIS was adequate for its purposes barely two weeks after receiving NYSDOT's application, hardly an indication that any critical thought had been brought to bear on the fisheries issues. The Corps then received criticisms from Fisheries Service, Wildlife Service, and EPA, indicating that there were serious inadequacies in the information provided by the SEIS. It was required to give "great weight" to the views of Fisheries Service and Wildlife Service, 33 C.F.R. §320.4(c); yet it merely passed them on to the Project and was not moved to conduct any inquiry of its own. Nor, apparently, was it interested in helping to shape the Lawler study that EPA finally prevailed upon NYSDOT to commission. Indeed, knowing that the Lawler study was underway, the district engineer decided to approve the permit without waiting for the results of the study. The division engineer's decision was at least equally flawed. By the time that decision was rendered, the Lawler report had been received, and it confirmed the criticisms of the objecting federal agencies and revealed the inaccuracy of the FEIS's conclusion that the interpier area was a biological wasteland. Nonetheless, the division engineer, like the district engineer, merely forwarded all federal agency criticisms of the FEIS to NYSDOT and FHWA, and had no independent Corps study made of the question raised. At the chief of engineers level there may have been some effort by a Corps biologist to review independently the Lawler data, but this hardly sufficed to meet the Corps's obligation under the Clean Water Act to make a reasoned decision: it resulted only in a two-page memorandum that the record does not reveal was even reviewed by the decisonmakers.

Thus the record discloses that at every level of review the Corps simply ignored the views of sister agencies that were, by law, to be accorded "great weight." The evidence amply warranted the district court's finding that the Corps never made a serious attempt to discover, or to make a decision based on, reliable fisheries information. In the face of the Lawler report and the other federal agencies' criticisms, the Corps's unquestioning reliance on the FEIS must be regarded as arbitrary and capricious. We affirm the court's ruling that the Corps violated the Clean Water Act. . . .

III. RELIEF

A. The Requirement of a Supplemental EIS on Fisheries Issues

The principal relief ordered by the district court was an injunction against any further Westway activities affecting the bed or waters of the

Hudson River unless and until a supplemental EIS has been prepared by the Corps containing adequate and accurate information with respect to the fisheries issues. . . . [W]e regard this relief as well within the proper scope of the district court's discretion in the circumstances of the present case.

. . . [T]he record revealed that the authors of the FEIS had not made an adequate compilation of fisheries data, had not compiled information in objective good faith, had paid no heed to the experts' warnings that they lacked needed information, and hence had reached the erroneous conclusion that the interpier area was a biological wasteland. This baseless and erroneous factual conclusion then became a false premise in the decisionmakers' evaluations of the overall environmental impact of Westway and their balancing of the expected benefits of the proposed action against the risks of harm to the environment. Thus, the January 1977 EIS provided no valid "outward sign that environmental values and consequences [had] been considered" with respect to fisheries issues, Andrus v. Sierra Club, supra, 442 U.S. at 350, and hence furnished no assurance that the Westway approvals had been given on a reasoned basis.

Enforcement of NEPA requires that the responsible agencies be compelled to prepare a new EIS on those issues, based on adequately compiled information, analyzed in a reasonable fashion. Only if such a document is forthcoming can the public be appropriately informed and have any confidence that the decisionmakers have in fact considered the relevant factors and not merely swept difficult problems under the rug. Accordingly, we uphold the district court's requirement that before Westway landfill may proceed, FHWA or the Corps must prepare a new EIS on fisheries issues. Whether the new statement be called an amended EIS or a supplemental EIS, as in the judgments below, NEPA requires no less.

Our ruling on this point is not, however, an expansive one. We do not intend to suggest that inaccuracies in an EIS will always, or even usually, warrant a court's ordering the preparation of a supplemental EIS. Had the January 1977 EIS contained a reasoned analysis of fisheries data reasonably adequately compiled, and merely drawn an erroneous factual conclusion, we would not believe it proper to order FHWA or the Corps to prepare a SEIS. See Hanly v. Kleindienst, 471 F.2d 823 (2d Cir. 1972), cert. denied, 412 U.S. 908 (1973). Or had reasonable investigative efforts resulted in less accurate data than later became available, the determination as to whether the later data warranted preparation of a SEIS, see 33 C.F.R. §230.11(b) (1981); see also 33 C.F.R. §209.410(g)(1) (1977); would be a matter committed to the discretion of the responsible agencies, not to the judgment of the court.

Nor do we express any view as to whether the decisionmakers' overall evaluation of the benefits and detriments of Westway was "wrong."

We hold simply that a decision made in reliance on false information, developed without an effort in objective good faith to obtain accurate information, cannot be accepted as a "reasoned" decision.

NOTES AND QUESTIONS

1. Cases concerning the adequacy of an agency's analysis in an EIS tend to be fact-intensive and fact-bound. Nonetheless, the Westway case indicates some of the possible points of attack. It also illustrates just how substantial the impact of NEPA litigation can be. Largely as a result of this decision, the Westway project has now been abandoned.

2. What legal "handles" does the Second Circuit's decision offer for potential NEPA plaintiffs? What kind of record should plaintiffs try to build for a challenge to the adequacy of analysis in an EIS? What kinds of evidence seem most persuasive to the court?

3. One recurring question in EIS challenges is what obligation agencies have to consider information that is presented after the EIS is completed. The Supreme Court addressed that question in the following case.

Marsh v. Oregon Natural Resources Council
490 U.S. 360 (1989)

Justice STEVENS delivered the opinion for a unanimous Court.

[The Army Corps of Engineers had completed an environmental impact statement for a three-dam project in Oregon's Rogue River Basin in 1971. In 1980 the Corps released its Final Environmental Impact Statement Supplement No. 1, but it subsequently refused to prepare a second supplemental EIS to review information developed after 1980. Plaintiffs argued that the Corps was required to prepare a second supplemental EIS because two memoranda prepared after 1980—one by biologists with Oregon's Department of Fish and Wildlife and another by the U.S. Soil Conservation Service—indicated that the project would have greater adverse impacts on the environment than previously thought. The district court rejected this claim, but the Ninth Circuit reversed, holding that the two documents revealed significant new information that the Corps had failed to evaluate with sufficient care.]

The subject of post-decision supplemental environmental impact statements is not expressly addressed in NEPA. Preparation of such statements, however, is at times necessary to satisfy the Act's "action-forcing" purpose. NEPA does not work by mandating that agencies achieve particular substantive environmental results. Rather, NEPA promotes its sweeping commitment to "prevent or eliminate damage to the environment and biosphere" by focusing government and public attention on the environmental effects of proposed agency action. 42 U.S.C. §4321. By so focusing agency attention, NEPA ensures that the agency will not act on incomplete information, only to regret its decision after it is too late to correct. Similarly, the broad dissemination of information mandated by NEPA permits the public and other government agencies to react to the effects of a proposed action at a meaningful time. It would be incongruous with this approach to environmental protection, and with the Act's manifest concern with preventing uninformed action, for the blinders to adverse environmental effects, once unequivocally removed, to be restored prior to the completion of agency action simply because the relevant proposal has received initial approval. As we explained in TVA v. Hill, 437 U.S. 153, 188, n.34 (1978), although "it would make sense to hold NEPA inapplicable at some point in the life of a project, because the agency would no longer have a meaningful opportunity to *weigh* the benefits of the project versus the detrimental effects on the environment," up to that point, "NEPA cases have generally required agencies to file environmental impact statements when the remaining governmental action would be environmentally 'significant.'"

This reading of the statute is supported by Council on Environmental Quality (CEQ) and Corps regulations, both of which make plain that at times supplementation is required. The CEQ regulations, which we have held are entitled to substantial deference, impose a duty on all federal agencies to prepare supplements to either draft or final EIS's if there "are significant new circumstances or information relevant to environmental concerns and bearing on the proposed action or its impacts." Similarly, the Corps' own NEPA implementing regulations require the preparation of a supplemental EIS if "new significant impact information, criteria or circumstances relevant to environmental considerations impact on the recommended plan or proposed action." . . .

. . . [A]n agency need not supplement an EIS every time new information comes to light after the EIS is finalized. To require otherwise would render agency decisionmaking intractable, always awaiting updated information only to find the new information outdated by the time a decision is made. On the other hand, and as [the Government] concede[s], NEPA does require that agencies take a "hard look" at the environmental effects of their planned action, even after a proposal has received initial approval. See Brief for Petitioners 36. Application of the "rule of reason" thus turns on the value of the new information to the still pending decisionmaking process. In this respect the decision whether to prepare a supplemental EIS is similar to the decision whether to prepare an EIS in the first instance: If there remains "major Federal actio[n]" to occur, and if the new information is sufficient to show that the remaining action will "affec[t] the quality of the human environment" in a significant manner or to a significant extent not already considered, a supplemental EIS must be prepared. Cf. 42 U.S.C. §4332(2)(C).

The parties disagree, however, on the standard that should be applied by a court that is asked to review the agency's decision. [The Government] argue[s] that the reviewing court need only decide whether the agency decision was "arbitrary and capricious," whereas respondents argue that the reviewing court must make its own determination of reasonableness to ascertain whether the agency action complied with the law. . . .

The question presented for review in this case is a classic example of a factual dispute the resolution of which implicates substantial agency expertise. Respondents' claim that the Corps' decision not to file a second supplemental EIS should be set aside primarily rests on the contentions that the new information undermines conclusions contained in the FEISS [Final Environmental Impact Statement Supplement No. 1], that the conclusions contained in the ODFW memorandum and the SCS survey are accurate, and that the Corps' expert review of the new information was incomplete, inconclusive, or inaccurate. The dispute thus does not turn on the meaning of the term "significant" or on an application of this legal standard to settled facts. Rather, resolution of this dispute involves primarily issues of fact. Because analysis of the relevant documents "requires a high level of technical expertise," we must defer to "the informed discretion of the responsible federal agencies." Kleppe v. Sierra Club, 427 U.S. 390, 412 (1976). Under these circumstances, we cannot accept respondents' supposition that review is of a legal question and that the Corps' decision "deserves no deference." Accordingly, as long as the Corps' decision not to supplement the FEISS was not "arbitrary or capricious," it should not be set aside.

. . . When specialists express conflicting views, an agency must have discretion to rely on the reasonable opinions of its own qualified experts even if, as an original matter, a court might find contrary views more persuasive. On the other hand, in the context of reviewing a decision not to supplement an EIS, courts should not automatically defer to the agency's express reliance on an interest in finality without carefully reviewing the record and satisfying themselves that the agency has made a reasoned decision based on its evaluation of the significance—or lack of significance—of the new information. A contrary approach would not simply render judicial review generally meaningless, but would be contrary to the demand that courts ensure that agency decisions are founded on a reasoned evaluation "of the relevant factors."

[Applying the standard of review outlined above, the Supreme Court reversed the Ninth Circuit and held that the Corps was not required to prepare a supplemental EIS.]

ii. Timing and Scope Revisited

Courts hearing challenges to an EIS are often asked to review the agency's judgments about the appropriate timing and scope of its analysis. They generally have responded by emphasizing that the proper scope of an EIS varies with the nature of the proposed action and its timing depends on how close the agency is to reaching a critical stage of the decisionmaking process. For example, in California v. Block, 690 F.2d 753 (9th Cir. 1982), discussed above, the State of California argued that the EIS prepared for the Forest Service's national management plan for roadless areas had failed to examine adequately site-specific impacts. The Forest Service argued that a programmatic EIS describing the first step in a multi-stage national project need not include detailed examination of the kinds of site-specific impacts normally considered in EISs for more narrowly focused projects. Noting that the "detail that NEPA requires in an EIS depends upon the nature and scope of the proposed action," the Ninth Circuit concluded that the "critical inquiry . . . is not whether the project's site-specific impact should be evaluated in detail, but when. . . ." 690 F.2d at 761. Thus, the court concluded that when preparing a programmatic EIS, "site-specific impacts need not be fully evaluated until a 'critical decision' has been made to act on site development." Id.

Applying this standard, the Ninth Circuit focused on the impact of the designation of areas as wilderness or nonwilderness. The Forest Service argued that a nonwilderness designation meant only that an area will not be considered now for inclusion in the wilderness system and that separate EISs would be prepared when specific development proposals are made concerning specific areas. The Ninth Circuit, however, found that the Forest Service had made a "critical decision" to commit these areas to nonwilderness use because the nonwilderness designation meant that the areas would not be managed as wilderness for at least the next 10 to 15 years. Thus, it held that the EIS must contain detailed site-specific analysis of the program's environmental consequences.

The Forest Service then argued that it had adequately assessed the site-specific impacts of its action by relying on two-page computer printouts for each area in the RARE II inventory. These contained information on the location and acreage of the area, its basic land-form type, its ecosystem type, the number of wilderness-associated wildlife species in the area, and a numerical rating of the area's wilderness attributes. The numerical ratings were obtained by using the Wilderness Attribute Rating System (WARS). This system employed worksheets containing a series of check boxes to indicate generic qualities of the site, and then a small space for comments, described as follows by the district court:

The comments are of a brief, and very general nature. For example, one comment under the "opportunity for solitude" attribute merely stated "good topographical variation." The type of land features or vegetation present in this area is undisclosed. Major features of an area are reduced to highly generalized descriptions such as "mountain" or "river." One can hypothesize how the Grand Canyon might be rated: "Canyon with river, little vegetation." [California v. Bergland, 483 F. Supp. 465, 486 n.22 (E.D. Cal. 1980.)]

The Ninth Circuit rejected the Forest Service's argument that any deficiencies in the EIS could be remedied simply by considering the WARS worksheets to be part of the final EIS. The court recognized that preparation of site-specific analyses for the RARE II decision would be a mammoth undertaking. However, it concluded that "[h]aving decided to allocate simultaneously millions of acres of land to nonwilderness use, the Forest Service may not rely upon forecasting difficulties or the task's magnitude to excuse the absence of a reasonably thorough site-specific analysis of the decision's environmental consequences." 690 F.2d 753, 765.

NOTES AND QUESTIONS

1. In Marsh v. Oregon Natural Resources Council, the Supreme Court upheld an agency's refusal to prepare a supplemental EIS in the face of new information. At what point can an agency simply refuse to consider new information? When an EIS has been completed? When a project has been approved? When construction has begun? When construction is completed?

2. The court in California v. Block demanded that the programmatic EIS prepared by the Forest Service include detailed analysis of every one of the hundreds of areas affected. Is that a realistic demand? If you were advising the Forest Service, what strategy would you suggest for their NEPA compliance?

3. Consider the following approach, from the CEQ Regulations:

§1508.28   Tiering

"Tiering" refers to the coverage of general matters in broader environmental impact statements (such as national program or policy statements) with subsequent narrower statements or environmental analyses (such as regional or basinwide program statements or ultimately site-specific statements) incorporating by reference the general discussions and concentrating solely on the issues specific to the statement subsequently prepared. Tiering is appropriate when the sequence of statements or analyses is:

(a) From a program, plan, or policy environmental impact statement to a program, plan, or policy statement or analysis of lesser scope or to a site-specific statement or analysis.

(b) From an environmental impact statement on a specific action at an early stage (such as need and site selection) to a supplement (which is preferred) or a subsequent statement or analysis at a later stage (such as environmental mitigation). Tiering in such cases is appropriate when it helps the lead agency to focus on the issues which are ripe for decision and exclude from consideration issues already decided or not yet ripe.

4. Many of the principles of timing and scope that are articulated in *Kleppe, Thomas,* and Sierra Club v. Peterson are relevant to assessment of the adequacy of an EIS.

iii. Analysis in Uncertainty

One of the most heated controversies concerning NEPA in recent years has been the debate over what agencies must do to assess adequately effects that are highly uncertain. In Sierra Club v. Sigler, 695 F.2d 957 (5th Cir. 1983), the Fifth Circuit considered an EIS for an oil distribution center and deepwater port in Galveston Bay. The Sierra Club argued that the Army Corps of Engineers should consider the possible effect on the Bay of a total cargo loss by a supertanker using the new port. While all agreed a total cargo loss could occur, there was considerable uncertainty about its likelihood and consequences. The court therefore required the Corps to prepare a "worst-case analysis" to assess the effects of such an accident.

In Save Our Ecosystems v. Clark, 747 F.2d 1240 (9th Cir. 1984), the Ninth Circuit considered the application of NEPA to decisions by the Bureau of Land Management (BLM) and the Forest Service to apply pesticides on lands subject to their jurisdiction. BLM and the Forest Service argued that they did not need to consider the risks associated with pesticide use as long as the pesticides had been approved for such use by the EPA. The court rejected this argument, emphasizing that the licensing of pesticides does not "reflect a conclusion that a pesticide is safe under *any* condition." Noting uncertainty about whether the pesticides were likely to cause cancer, the court held that the agencies must prepare a "worst-case analysis" to assess those risks—the agencies must estimate what the effects of pesticide use would be if the pesticides were in fact carcinogenic.

In response to *Save Our Ecosystems* and similar decisions from other courts, CEQ acted to curtail the worst-case-analysis requirement. In 1986, the CEQ rescinded a "worst-case" Regulation it had adopted in 1978 and replaced it with the following revised Regulation:

§1502.22 Incomplete or Unavailable Information

When an agency is evaluating reasonably foreseeable significant adverse effects on the human environment in an environmental impact statement and there is incomplete or unavailable information, the agency shall always make clear that such information is lacking.

(a) If the incomplete information relevant to reasonably foreseeable significant adverse impacts is essential to a reasoned choice among alternatives and the overall costs of obtaining it are not exorbitant, the agency shall include the information in the environmental impact statement.

(b) If the information relevant to reasonably foreseeable significant adverse impacts cannot be obtained because the overall costs of obtaining it are exorbitant or the means to obtain it are not known, the agency shall include within the environmental impact statement:

(1) A statement that such information is incomplete or unavailable;

(2) a statement of the relevance of the incomplete or unavailable information to evaluating reasonably foreseeable significant adverse impacts on the human environment;

(3) a summary of existing credible scientific evidence which is relevant to evaluating the reasonably foreseeable significant adverse impacts on the human environment; and

(4) the agency's evaluation of such impacts based upon theoretical approaches or research methods generally accepted in the scientific community. For the purposes of this section, "reasonably foreseeable" includes impacts which have catastrophic consequences, even if their probability of occurrence is low, provided that the analysis of the impacts is supported by credible scientific evidence, is not based on pure conjecture, and is within the rule of reason.

(c) The amended regulation will be applicable to all environmental impact statements for which a Notice of Intent (40 CFR 1508.22) is published in the FEDERAL REGISTER on or after May 27, 1986. For environmental impact statements in progress, agencies may choose to comply with the requirements of either the original or amended regulation. [51 Fed. Reg. 15,625 (1986).]

NOTES AND QUESTIONS

1. How severely has CEQ curtailed the worst-case-analysis requirement? Would this new Regulation change the result in *Sigler* or in *Save Our Ecosystems*? What analysis would you expect the Fifth Circuit to require, under this Regulation, for the Galveston deepwater port? What analysis would you expect the Ninth Circuit to require of BLM and the Forest Service before they resumed use of pesticides on their lands?

2. In Robertson v. Methow Valley Citizens Council, 490 U.S. 332 (1989), a companion case to Marsh v. Oregon Natural Resources Council, the Supreme Court reversed a decision by the Ninth Circuit holding that NEPA requires the use of worst-case analysis despite the new CEQ Regulations. The Supreme Court rejected the Ninth Circuit's conclusion

that the rescinded CEQ Regulations were "merely a codification of prior NEPA case law." Noting that the Regulations had been amended only after "considerable criticism" of the worst-case-analysis requirement, the Court held that the new Regulations were entitled to "substantial deference." 490 U.S. at 356.

4. Epilogue: Does NEPA Work?

Now that NEPA is more than two decades old, numerous assessments have been made of its impact and effectiveness. See, e.g., Symposium on NEPA at Twenty: The Past, Present and Future of the National Environmental Policy Act, 20 Envtl. L. 447-810 (1990); Caldwell, A Constitutional Law for the Environment: 20 Years with NEPA Indicates the Need, 31 Environment 10 (Dec. 1989); Parenteau, NEPA at Twenty: Shining Knight or Tilting at Windmills?, 6 Envtl. Forum 14 (Sept.-Oct. 1989). NEPA clearly has provided environmental lawyers with a strategic tool that has been used at times to slow down development projects. But it is unclear how frequently the requirement that agencies "consider" environmental effects has resulted in more environmentally responsible actions by agencies. Serge Taylor's classic study of NEPA, Making Bureaucracies Think: The Environmental Impact Statement Strategy of Administrative Reform (1984), found that when agencies allow environmental analysts to explore a wide range of alternatives, all projects tend to benefit from relatively inexpensive mitigation measures. When concerned outsiders with access to the courts also get involved, some of the worst projects—those with "the greatest environmental costs and little political support"—are eliminated. Id. at 251.

A more modest inquiry is whether NEPA assures a reliable assessment of a project's likely effects. Because NEPA entrusts the assessment of impacts to agencies that typically are project proponents, the quality of EISs often depends on the strength of outside pressures. Recall the controversy discussed in Chapter 1 concerning the report by the Fish & Wildlife Service that the environmental impact of oil development in Prudhoe Bay had been greatly underestimated. Some have suggested that projects approved under NEPA should be monitored so that unanticipated environmental consequences can be assessed and mitigated. Others have proposed that EISs be prepared by an independent agency without a vested interest in the results as is done in some of the many countries that now require EISs.

As agencies have gained more experience with NEPA, the EIS process has become more routine, fueling fewer lawsuits. Figure 8.1 illustrates that the filing of environmental impact statements declined rather steadily between 1976 and 1984 to about one-third of the 1976 level. While 1,238 NEPA lawsuits were filed between 1974 and 1983, an

FIGURE 8.1
**Impact Statements and Lawsuits Filed Under the National Environmental
Policy Act, 1974-1984**

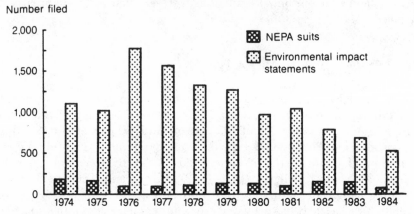

Source: Conservation Foundation, State of the Environment: A View Toward the
Nineties 39 (1987).

average of 124 per year, only 539 were filed between 1984 and 1990,
an average of only 77 per year. CEQ, Environmental Quality: 22nd
Annual Report 142-143 (1992). While correctly predicting the decline
in the numbers of NEPA cases, Serge Taylor cautioned in 1984 that it
should not be viewed as indicating a decline in NEPA's impact. "The
combination of legal risk averseness on the part of agency officials, more
technically sophisticated plaintiffs, and cases whose factual complexity
can mask and muffle the legal precedents of a judge's substantive policy
choices suggests that it will be a long time before judicial oversight of
the EIS process becomes irrelevant to [agency] choices." S. Taylor, Making Bureaucracies Think 248 (1984).

The Council on Environmental Quality reports that 456 EISs were
filed in 1991. CEQ, Environmental Quality: 22nd Annual Report 150
(1992). The Department of Agriculture filed 145 EISs, more than any
other federal agency; the Department of Transportation was second
with 87, followed by the Department of the Interior with 64 and the
Army Corps of Engineers with 45. Id. at 148-150. A total of 45 NEPA
lawsuits were filed in 1990, 27 against the Department of Transportation, 10 against the Corps, and 8 against EPA. Id. at 144. A failure to
prepare an EIS was the most frequent ground cited for litigation, followed by challenges to the adequacy of EISs and EAs. Eleven injunctions
were issued against federal agencies in NEPA cases in 1990. Id. at 143.

Assessment of the overall impact of NEPA is a complex task. Lynton

Caldwell, whose 1964 essay "Environment: A New Focus for Public Policy" was influential in the statute's enactment, finds that "NEPA is a paradoxical statute" that "has survived without strong and focused support from Congress, the executive branch, or outside interests." Caldwell, NEPA Revisited: A Call for a Constitutional Amendment, 1989 Envtl. Forum 18, 20 (Nov.-Dec. 1989). Caldwell concludes that, after initial difficulties, most agencies have improved the quality of their EISs, particularly after the issuance of the CEQ guidelines in 1978. Citing a National Science Foundation study, he notes that NEPA has provided a welcome tool for many agency personnel "to resist political importunities to pursue environmentally harmful measures." Caldwell argues that NEPA's significance extends far beyond the EIS requirement but that the failure of the executive branch to take NEPA to heart to stop environmentally destructive proposals in their early stages has limited its impact. As a result, "a provision intended to brake the free-wheeling of mission-narrow administrators became a bonanza for public-interest lawyers" as the public "turned to lawyers and litigation to stop action that the President could have stopped." Caldwell concedes that NEPA has been used to block or delay controversial projects, though such litigation is not as frequent now that agencies have improved their compliance with the law. He finds NEPA's biggest disappointments to be the judiciary's failure to link the EIS requirement to the Act's substantive precepts and presidents' failure to take the CEQ seriously.

Not content with the results of NEPA, Caldwell has proposed the adoption of a constitutional amendment embodying a "statement of basic environmental rights and duties under law." Caldwell premises his call for an environmental amendment to the Constitution on the notion that economic and political pressures for environmentally deleterious action are simply too strong. He argues that an environmental amendment would: (1) make it more difficult for a president to ignore the environment, (2) encourage courts to consider the substantive merits of environmental disputes rather than deferring to environmental agencies, and (3) enhance the credibility of the United States in international environmental protection efforts (a subject we consider in Chapter 9).

Other observers view NEPA as a mixed bag. A typical assessment is that while "NEPA's true action-forcing potential" may have been "killed" by the judiciary's "relegating [it] to a procedural statute," the NEPA process nevertheless has improved the quality of agency decision-making. Millan, Wanted: NEPA, Dead or Alive, Reward: Our Global Environment, 22 Env. Rep. 2081, 2083 (1991). Oliver Houck views NEPA as "missing the point. It is producing lots of little statements on highway segments, timber sales, and other foregone conclusions; it isn't even present, much less effective, when the major decisions on a national energy policy and a national transportation policy are made." Houck, Letter to Michael R. Deland (Feb. 19, 1991). Antonio Rossman blames the Supreme Court for many of NEPA's problems, noting that in each of the NEPA cases the Court has heard it "has never written to expand NEPA's application and has consistently narrowed or reversed generous rulings by the courts of appeals." Rossmann, NEPA: Not So Well at Twenty, 20 Envtl. L. Rep. 10174 (1990). By contrast, Daniel Mandelker declares NEPA "alive and well" because the Supreme Court has reaffirmed the statute's most important principles even while narrowing their application. Mandelker, NEPA Alive and Well: The Supreme Court Takes Two, 19 Envtl. L. Rep. 10385, 10387 (1989). All in all, NEPA has not fully realized the high hopes of its supporters, but many would agree that it has improved thousands of agency decisions that affect the quality of the environment.

B. CONSERVATION OF ENDANGERED SPECIES

Throughout this century Congress has been concerned about the need to protect certain species of wildlife in danger of extinction. But it was only in the last two decades that comprehensive programs for protection of endangered species were developed at the federal level. Beginning in 1966, federal legislation and an international convention (the Convention on International Trade in Endangered Species of Wild Fauna and Flora) established a comprehensive program that "restricts the taking of species currently in danger of extinction or likely to become so, regulates trade in them, provides authority for the acquisition of habitat needed for their survival, and mandates the consideration of impacts upon them resulting from various federal activities." M. Bean, The Evolution of National Wildlife Law 318 (1983).

In the past decade, protection of endangered species has come to be seen in its larger context—the conservation of biological diversity. Congress's Office of Technology Assessment has defined "biological diversity" as "the variety and variability among living organisms and the ecological complexes in which they occur." OTA Technologies to Maintain Biological Diversity 313 (1987). Properly understood, "biological diversity" includes not only the diversity of species, but also genetic diversity—the variation among individuals of the same species—and the diversity of ecosystems, or natural communities. It also includes the ecological and evolutionary processes on which those systems depend, such as predation, mutation, and decay.

With this broader understanding, the conservation of biological diversity poses a fundamental challenge, implicating, for example, climate change, toxic chemicals, and land use. But the Endangered Species

Act (ESA) is the cornerstone of U.S. efforts to conserve biological diversity. It is a mechanism for saving species, the diversity within them, and the natural systems on which they depend. It is, ultimately, the safety net when broader efforts fail.

In this section, we examine the principal federal program for protection of endangered species: the Endangered Species Act, 16 U.S.C. §1531 et seq. Before turning to that statute, however, it is worth considering the moral, economic, and political groundings of the conservation of species.

1. Why Should We Conserve Endangered Species?

At the beginning of this course, we considered some of the intellectual and cultural roots of environmental protection. These issues come to the fore in debates about the extinction of species. Aesthetic concerns and moral principles are often invoked in support of conservation, but conservation may also be justified by narrower concerns for human health and economic well-being. Some of these arguments are set forth in the following excerpts from the writings of Edward O. Wilson, prominent biologist and eloquent champion of biodiversity.

> ### E. O. Wilson, Toward a Lasting Conservation Ethic
> **ESA Oversight, Hearings Before the Subcomm. on Environmental Pollution of the Senate Environment and Public Works Comm., 97th Cong., 1st Sess. 366 (1981)**

In reflecting on the preservation of species and genetic diversity, it is worth remembering that a butterfly is far more complicated than any machine ever constructed by man. And because of the microorganisms living in it, a cubic inch of Virginia soil contains more structure and provides greater opportunities for scientific advance than the entire surface of Jupiter. When these comparisons are expanded to include the three to ten million species that comprise the whole biota, the magnitude of Earth's living treasury literally exceeds our imaginative capacity. Scientists have documented the vast opportunities offered by species variation for the development of new crops, drugs, and renewable energy sources. Others have demonstrated the vital role of rich, stable ecosystems in the regeneration of oxygen and its maintenance. But there is a great deal more to organic diversity than these utilitarian considerations.

cool quote

The great German zoologist Karl von Frisch once said that the honeybee is like a magic well: the more you draw from it, the more there is to draw. And so it is with any species, which is a unique configuration of genes assembled over thousands or millions of years, possessing its own biology, mysteries, and still untested uses for mankind. Only a tiny fraction of the millions of species, less than 0.01 percent, have been studied in any detail; most have not even been given a scientific name.

Last year I was . . . asked . . . to give my opinion concerning the most serious problem of the Eighties. I rephrased the question in the following form: What event likely to occur in the 1980s will our descendants most regret, even those living a thousand years from now? The relatively unconventional opinion I gave was the following. The worst thing that can happen—*will* happen—is not energy depletion, economic collapse, limited nuclear war, or conquest by a totalitarian government. As terrible as these catastrophes would be for us, they can be repaired within a few generations. The one process ongoing in the 1980s that will take millions of years to correct is the loss of genetic and species diversity by the destruction of natural habitats. This is the folly our descendants are least likely to forgive us.

The bleeding of diversity is greatest in the moist tropical forests, but it is also occurring at an unknown rate in the United States. We should keep in mind that extinction is accelerating not only in birds and mammals, but also in such forms as mosses and insects. These organisms receive little attention but are magic wells nonetheless, the importance of which may not be appreciated for generations—when it will be too late.

‖ *E. O. Wilson, Biophilia* ‖
121 (1984)

A conservative estimate of the current extinction rate is one thousand species a year, mostly from the destruction of forests and other key habitats in the tropics. By the 1990s the figure is expected to rise past ten thousand species a year (one species per hour). During the next thirty years fully one million species could be erased.

Whatever the exact figure—and the primitive state of evolutionary biology permits us only to set broad limits—the current rate is still the greatest in recent geological history. It is also much higher than the rate of production of new species by ongoing evolution, so that the net result is a steep decline in the world's standing diversity. Whole categories of organisms that emerged over the past ten million years, among them the familiar condors, rhinoceros, manatees, and gorillas, are close to the end. For most of their species, the last individuals to exist in the wild state could well be those living there today. It is a grave error to dismiss the hemorrhaging as a "Darwinian" process, in which species autonomously come and go and man is just the latest burden on the environment. Human destructiveness is something new under the sun. Perhaps it is matched by the giant meteorites thought to smash into the Earth and darken the atmosphere every hundred million years or so (the last one apparently arrived 65 million years ago and contributed to the extinction of the dinosaurs). But even that interval is ten thousand times longer than the entire history of civilization. In our own brief lifetime humanity will suffer an incomparable loss in aesthetic value, practical benefits from biological research, and worldwide biological stability. Deep mines of biological diversity will have been dug out and carelessly discarded in the course of environmental exploitation, without our even knowing fully what they contained.

By economic measure alone, the diversity of species is one of Earth's most important resources. It is also the least utilized. We have come to depend completely on less than 1 percent of living species for our existence, with the remainder waiting untested and fallow. In the course of history, according to estimates recently made by Norman Myers, people have utilized about 7,000 kinds of plants for food, with emphasis on wheat, rye, maize, and about a dozen other highly domesticated species. Yet at least 75,000 exist that are edible, and many of these are superior to the crop plants in use. The strongest of all arguments from surface ethics is a logical conclusion about this unrealized potential: the more the living world is explored and utilized, the greater will be the efficiency and reliability of the particular species chosen for economic use. Among the potential star species are these:

The winged bean (*Psophocarpus tetragonolobus*) of New Guinea has been called a one-species supermarket. It contains more protein than cassava and potato and possesses an overall nutritional value equal to that of soybean. It is among the most rapidly growing of all plants, reaching a height of fifteen feet within a few weeks. The entire plant can be eaten, tubers, seeds, leaves, flowers, stems, and all, both raw and ground into flour. A coffeelike beverage can be made from the liquefied extract. The species has already been used to improve the diet in fifty tropical countries, and a special institute has been set up in Sri Lanka to study and promote it more thoroughly.

The wax gourd (*Benincasa hispida*) of tropical Asia grows an inch every three hours over a course of four days, permitting multiple crops to be raised each year. The fruit attains a size of up to 1 by 6 feet and a weight of 80 pounds. Its crisp white flesh can be eaten at any stage, as a cooked vegetable, a base for soup, or a dessert when mixed with syrup.

The Babussa palm (*Orbigyna martiana*) is a wild tree of the Amazon rain forest known locally as the "vegetable cow." The individual fruits, which resemble small coconuts, occur in bunches of up to 600 with a collective weight of 200 pounds. Some 70 percent of the kernel mass is composed of a colorless oil, used for margarine, shortening, fatty acids, toilet soap, and detergents. A stand of 500 trees on one hectare (2.5 acres) can produce 125 barrels of oil per year. After the oil has been extracted the remaining seedcake, which is about one-fourth protein, serves as excellent animal fodder.

Even with limited programs of research, biologists have compiled an impressive list of such candidate organisms in the technical literature. The vast majority of wild plants and animals are not known well enough (certainly many have not yet been discovered) even to guess at those with the greatest economic potential. Nor is it possible to imagine all the uses to which each species can be put. Consider the case of the natural food sweeteners. Several species of plants have been identified whose chemical products can replace conventional sugar with negligible calories and no known side effects. The katemfe (*Thaumatococcus danielli*) of the West African forests contains two proteins that are 1,600 times sweeter than sucrose and is now widely marketed in Great Britain and Japan. It is outstripped by the well-named serendipity berry (*Dioscoreophyllum cumminsii*), another West African native whose fruit produces a substance 3,000 times sweeter than sucrose.

Natural products have been called the sleeping giants of the pharmaceutical industry. One in every ten plant species contains compounds with some anticancer activity. Among the leading successes from the screening conducted so far is the rosy periwinkle, a native of the West Indies. It is the very paradigm of a previously minor species, with pretty five-petaled blossoms but otherwise rather ordinary in appearance, a roadside casual, the kind of inconspicuous flowering plant that might otherwise have been unknowingly consigned to extinction by the growth of sugarcane plantations and parking lots. But it also happens to produce two alkaloids, vincristine and vinblastine, that achieve 80 percent remission from Hodgkin's disease, a cancer of the lymphatic system, as well as 99 percent remission from acute lymphocytic leukemia. Annual sales of the two drugs reached $100 million in 1980.

A second wild species responsible for a medical breakthrough is the Indian serpentine root (*Rauwolfia serpentina*). It produces reserpine, a principal source of tranquilizers used to relieve schizophrenia as well as hypertension, the generalized condition predisposing patients to stroke, heart malfunction, and kidney failure.

The natural products of plants and animals are a select group in a literal sense. They represent the defense mechanisms and growth regulators produced by evolution during uncounted generations, in which only organisms with the most potent chemicals survived to the present time. Placebos and cheap substitutes were eliminated at an early stage. Nature has done much of our work for us, making it far more efficient for the medical researcher to experiment with extracts of living tissue than to pull chemicals at random off the laboratory shelf. Very few pharmaceuticals have been invented from a knowledge of the first principles of chemistry and medicine. Most have their origin in the study of wild species and were discovered by the rapid screening of large numbers of natural products.

For the same reason, technical advances utilizing natural products have been achieved in many categories of industry and agriculture. Among the most important have been the development of phytoleum, new plant fuels to replace petroleum; waxes and oils produced from indefinitely renewing sources at more economical rates than previously thought possible; novel kinds of fibers for paper manufacture; fast-growing siliceous plants, such as bamboo and elephant grass, for economical dwellings; superior methods of nitrogen fixation and soil reclamation; and magic-bullet techniques of pest control, by which microorganisms and parasites are set loose to find and attack target species without danger to the remainder of the ecosystem. Even the most conservative extrapolation indicates that many more such discoveries will result from only a modest continuing research effort.

NOTES AND QUESTIONS

1. Why should we care about the extinction of species? What reasons does Wilson articulate? What other reasons are there? Recall the discussion in Chapter 1 of competing values and the different approaches economics and ecology employ in conceptualizing environmental problems. In what respects do arguments concerning the importance of biodiversity reflect an economic perspective?

2. The Endangered Species Act (ESA) refers to the "esthetic, ecological, educational, historical, recreational and scientific value" of species in danger of or threatened with extinction. §2(a)(3), 16 U.S.C. §1531(a)(3). Surely not all species have the same value to mankind, as the ESA implicitly recognizes by excluding from its protections insect pests determined to "present an overwhelming and overriding risk to man." Why then should all disappearing species be entitled to the same level of protection? From an economic perspective, wouldn't it make more sense to vary the level of protection on the basis of some assessment of the value of the species to mankind? How could such an assessment be done given our present knowledge?

3. To what extent does uncertainty justify strict protection for endangered species? Wilson states that we have studied in detail less than one one-hundredth of one percent of all species. If we know so little about the characteristics of species that are fast disappearing, is it reasonable to assume that what we are losing includes some valuable re-

sources? Is biodiversity inherently valuable because it is impossible to know what we are losing as species disappear?

4. Recall the discussion in Chapter 1 concerning the "new ecology's" emphasis on the inherent instability of ecological communities. If ecosystems are in constant turmoil even when undisturbed by man and many species disappear as a result of natural forces, why should we be concerned about protecting endangered species?

5. A recent example of the pharmaceutical use of rare plants is the development of a drug called Taxol that is used to treat breast cancer and ovarian cancer. The drug is made from material found only in the bark and needles of Pacific yew trees. Environmentalists are concerned that this discovery threatens to decimate the yew population because it takes six 100-year-old yews to make enough Taxol to treat a single patient. How would you resolve this controversy?

2. The Endangered Species Act: An Overview

The most significant legislation for preserving biodiversity has been the Endangered Species Act of 1973. The major provisions of the Endangered Species Act are outlined below. The Act protects species that are listed by the Secretary (under section 4) as either "endangered species" or "threatened species." Endangered species include "any species which is in danger of extinction throughout all or a significant portion of its range." Threatened species include "any species which is likely to become an endangered species within the foreseeable future throughout all or a significant portion of its range."

MAJOR PROVISIONS OF THE ENDANGERED SPECIES ACT

Section 3: Definitions
§3(6) defines "endangered species" as "any species which is in danger of extinction throughout all or a significant portion of its range."

§3(20) defines "threatened species" as "any species which is likely to become an endangered species within the foreseeable future throughout all or a significant portion of its range."

Section 4: Listing Endangered and Threatened Species
§4(a) requires the Secretary of Commerce or the Secretary of the Interior to determine whether any species is "endangered" or "threatened" and to designate critical habitat of such species.

§4(b) provides that the listing determination is to be based solely on "best scientific and commercial data available" and that the designation of critical habitat is to be based on the "best scientific data available . . . taking into consideration the economic impact, and any other relevant impact, of specifying any particular area as critical habitat."

§4(b)(3) provides that citizens may petition to force listing determination.

§4(f) requires the Secretary to develop and implement recovery plans for endangered and threatened species unless he finds they will not promote conservation of the species.

Section 7: Review of Federal Actions

§7(a) provides that all federal agencies must insure, in consultation with the Secretary of the Interior, that their actions are "not likely to jeopardize the continued existence of any endangered species or threatened species or result in the destruction or adverse modification" of such species' critical habitat.

§§7(e)-(h) provide that if action is barred by a "jeopardy" determination, its proponent may seek exemption from the Cabinet-level "Endangered Species Committee."

Section 9: Prohibitions   *applies to everyone, not just govt*

§9(a) prohibits sale, import, export, or transport of any species listed as endangered.

§9(a)(1)(B) & (C) makes it unlawful to "take" (broadly defined by section 3(19) to cover harassing, harming, killing, capturing, or collecting) any endangered *animal* species.

§9(a)(2)(B) prohibits removal or damage of endangered *plants* on federal lands or anywhere else if in knowing violation of state law.

§9 states that these prohibitions generally apply to threatened species, except as the Secretary has specified otherwise, and they apply to any "person," including any corporation or government entity.

Section 11: Enforcement and Citizen Suits

§11(a) & (b) provides civil and criminal penalties for violations of the Act.

§11(g) authorizes citizen suits against any person alleged to be in violation of the Act and against the Secretary for failure to perform any nondiscretionary duty.

While threatened species are to be protected by regulations "necessary and advisable to provide for the conservation of such species," in general, threatened species have been extended the same protections accorded species listed as endangered. Specific protections are provided in sections 7 and 9 of the Act. Section 7 of the Act requires all federal agencies to "insure that any action authorized, funded, or carried out" by them "is not likely to jeopardize the continued existence of any endangered species or threatened species or result in the destruction or adverse modification of [critical] habitat of such species," 16 U.S.C. §1536. Section 9 of the Act regulates private conduct by making it illegal for *any* person to sell, import, export, or transport any plant or animal species listed as endangered. Endangered fish or wildlife are given even greater protection by section 9(a)(1), which makes it illegal for anyone to "take" them. "Take" is broadly defined to mean "to harass, harm, pursue, hunt, shoot, wound, kill, trap, capture, or collect, or to attempt to engage in any such conduct." Section 9(a)(2)(B) makes it illegal to remove or damage endangered plants from federal lands or from any other property if it is done in knowing violation of any state law or regulation including state criminal trespass law.

In the remaining sections of this chapter, we consider the three key sections of the statute: section 4, section 7, and section 9. Any study of the Endangered Species Act must begin, however, with one of the most celebrated cases in environmental law—TVA v. Hill, 437 U.S. 153 (1978)—in which the Supreme Court resoundingly affirmed the sweeping protections that this statute provides to species on the brink of extinction.

TVA v. Hill
437 U.S. 153 (1978)

Mr. Chief Justice BURGER delivered the opinion of the Court. . . .

The Little Tennessee River originates in the mountains of northern Georgia and flows through the national forest lands of North Carolina into Tennessee, where it converges with the Big Tennessee River near Knoxville. The lower 33 miles of the Little Tennessee takes the river's clear, free-flowing waters through an area of great natural beauty. . . .

In this area of the Little Tennessee River the Tennessee Valley Authority, a wholly owned public corporation of the United States, began constructing the Tellico Dam and Reservoir Project in 1967, shortly after Congress appropriated initial funds for its development. . . . When fully operational, the dam would impound water covering some 16,500 acres—much of which represents valuable and productive farmland—

thereby converting the river's shallow, fast-flowing waters into a deep reservoir over 30 miles in length.

The Tellico Dam has never opened, however, despite the fact that construction has been virtually completed and the dam is essentially ready for operation. Although Congress has appropriated monies for Tellico every year since 1967, progress was delayed, and ultimately stopped, by a tangle of lawsuits and administrative proceedings. After unsuccessfully urging TVA to consider alternatives to damming the Little Tennessee, local citizens and national conservation groups brought suit in the District Court, claiming that the project did not conform to the requirements of the National Environmental Policy Act of 1969 (NEPA), 42 U.S.C. §4331 et seq. After finding TVA to be in violation of NEPA, the District Court enjoined the dam's completion pending the filing of an appropriate environmental impact statement. The injunction remained in effect until late 1973, when the District Court concluded that TVA's final environmental impact statement for Tellico was in compliance with the law.

A few months prior to the District Court's decision dissolving the NEPA injunction, a discovery was made in the waters of the Little Tennessee which would profoundly affect the Tellico Project. Exploring the area around Coytee Springs, which is about seven miles from the mouth of the river, a University of Tennessee ichthyologist, Dr. David A. Etnier, found a previously unknown species of perch, the snail darter, or *Percina (Imostoma) tanasi.* This three-inch, tannish-colored fish, whose numbers are estimated to be in the range of 10,000 to 15,000, would soon engage the attention of environmentalists, the TVA, the Department of the Interior, the Congress of the United States, and ultimately the federal courts, as a new and additional basis to halt construction of the dam.

Until recently the finding of a new species of animal life would hardly generate a cause celebre. This is particularly so in the case of darters, of which there are approximately 130 known species, 8 to 10 of these having been identified only in the last five years. The moving force behind the snail darter's sudden fame came some four months after its discovery, when the Congress passed the Endangered Species Act of 1973, 16 U.S.C. §1531 et seq. (1976) ("Act"). This legislation, among other things, authorizes the Secretary of the Interior to declare species of animal life "endangered" and to identify the "critical habitat" of these creatures. . . .

In January 1975, the respondents in this case and others petitioned the Secretary of the Interior to list the snail darter as an endangered species. After receiving comments from various interested parties, including TVA and the State of Tennessee, the Secretary formally listed the snail darter as an endangered species on October 8, 1975. 40 Fed. Reg. 47505-47506; see 50 C.F.R. §17.11(i) (1976). In so acting, it was noted that "the snail darter is a living entity which is genetically distinct and reproductively isolated from other fishes." 40 Fed. Reg., at 47505. More important for the purposes of this case, the Secretary determined that the snail darter apparently lives only in that portion of the Little Tennessee River which would be completely inundated by the reservoir created as a consequence of the Tellico Dam's completion. Id., at 47506. The Secretary went on to explain the significance of the dam to the habitat of the snail darter.

> [T]he snail darter occurs only in the swifter portions of shoals over clean gravel substrate in cool, low-turbidity water. Food of the snail darter is almost exclusively snails which require a clean gravel substrate for their survival. *The proposed impoundment of water behind the proposed Tellico Dam would result in total destruction of the snail darter's habitat.* Ibid. (emphasis added).

Subsequent to this determination, the Secretary declared the area of the Little Tennessee which would be affected by the Tellico Dam to be the "critical habitat" of the snail darter. 41 Fed. Reg. 13926-13928; see 50 CFR §17.81. Using these determinations as a predicate, and notwithstanding the near completion of the dam, the Secretary declared that pursuant to §7 of the Act, "all Federal agencies must take such action as is necessary to insure that actions authorized, funded, or carried out by them do not result in the destruction or modification of this critical habitat area." 41 Fed. Reg., at 13928; 50 CFR, at §17.81(b). This notice, of course, was pointedly directed at TVA and clearly aimed at halting completion or operation of the dam. . . .

In February 1976, pursuant to §11(g) of the Endangered Species Act, 16 U.S.C. §1540(g), respondents filed the case now under review, seeking to enjoin completion of the dam and impoundment of the reservoir on the ground that those actions would violate the Act by directly causing the extinction of the species *Percina (Imostoma) tanasi*. The District Court denied respondents' request for a preliminary injunction and set the matter for trial. . . .

Trial was held in the District Court on April 29 and 30, 1976, and on May 25, 1976, the court entered its memorandum opinion and order denying respondents their requested relief and dismissing the complaint. The District Court found that closure of the dam and the consequent impoundment of the reservoir would "result in the adverse modification, if not complete destruction, of the snail darter's critical habitat," making it "highly probable" that "the continued existence of the snail darter" would be "jeopardize[d]." [Hill v. Tennessee Valley Authority,] 419 F. Supp. 753, 757 (ED Tenn. [1976]). Despite these findings, the District Court declined to embrace the plaintiffs' position on the merits: that once a federal project was shown to jeopardize an endangered species, a court of equity is compelled to issue an injunction restraining violation of the Endangered Species Act. . . .

Thereafter, in the Court of Appeals, respondents argued that the District Court had abused its discretion by not issuing an injunction in the face of "a blatant statutory violation." [Hill v. Tennessee Valley Authority,] 549 F.2d 1064, 1969 (CA6 1977). The Court of Appeals agreed, and on January 31, 1977 it reversed, remanding "with instructions that a permanent injunction issue halting all activities incident to the Tellico Project which may destroy or modify the critical habitat of the snail darter." Id. at 1075. The Court of Appeals directed that the injunction "remain in effect until Congress, by appropriate legislation, exempts Tellico from compliance with the Act or the snail darter has been deleted from the list of endangered species or its critical habitat materially redefined." Ibid. . . .

One would be hard pressed to find a statutory provision whose terms were any plainer than those in §7 of the Endangered Species Act. Its very words affirmatively command all federal agencies "to *insure* that actions *authorized, funded,* or *carried out* by them do not *jeopardize* the continued existence" of an endangered species or "*result*" in the destruction or modification of habitat of such species. . . ." 16 U.S.C. §1536. (Emphasis added.) This language admits of no exception. Nonetheless, petitioner urges, as do the dissenters, that the Act cannot reasonably be interpreted as applying to a federal project which was well under way when Congress passed the Endangered Species Act of 1973. To sustain that position, however, we would be forced to ignore the ordinary meaning of plain language. It has not been shown, for example, how TVA can close the gates of the Tellico Dam without "carrying out" an action that has been "authorized" and "funded" by a federal agency. Nor can we understand how such action will "*insure*" that the snail darter's habitat is not disrupted. Accepting the Secretary's determinations, as we must, it is clear that TVA's proposed operation of the dam will have precisely the opposite effect, namely the *eradication* of an endangered species.

Concededly, this view of the Act will produce results requiring the sacrifice of the anticipated benefits of the project and of many millions of dollars in public funds. But examination of the language, history, and structure of the legislation under review here indicates beyond doubt that Congress intended endangered species to be afforded the highest of priorities. . . .

The legislative proceedings in 1973 are, in fact, replete with expressions of concern over the risk that might lie in the loss of *any* endangered species. Typifying these sentiments is the Report of the House Committee on Merchant Marine and Fisheries on H.R. 37, a bill which contained the essential features of the subsequently enacted Act of 1973; in explaining the need for the legislation, the report stated:

As we homogenize the habitats in which these plants and animals evolved, and as we increase the pressure for products that they are in a position to supply (usually unwillingly) we threaten their—and our own— genetic heritage.

The value of this genetic heritage is, quite literally, incalculable. . . .

Who knows, or can say, what potential cures for cancer or other scourges, present or future, may lie locked up in the structures of plants which may yet be undiscovered, much less analyzed? . . . Sheer self-interest impels us to be cautious.

The institutionalization of that caution lies at the heart of H.R. 37. . . .

H.R. Rep. No. 93-412, [93rd Cong., 1st Sess.] 4-5 (1973). (Emphasis added.)

As the examples cited here demonstrate, Congress was concerned about the *unknown* uses that endangered species might have and about the *unforeseeable* place such creatures may have in the chain of life on this planet. . . .

One might dispute the applicability of [this argument] to the Tellico Dam by saying that in this case the burden on the public through the loss of millions of unrecoverable dollars would greatly outweigh the loss of the snail darter. But neither the Endangered Species Act nor Art. III of the Constitution provides federal courts with authority to make such fine utilitarian calculations. On the contrary, the plain language of the Act, buttressed by its legislative history, shows clearly that Congress viewed the value of endangered species as "incalculable." Quite obviously, it would be difficult for a court to balance the loss of a sum certain—even $100 million—against a congressionally declared "incalculable" value, even assuming we had the power to engage in such a weighing process, which we emphatically do not. . . .

Having determined that there is an irreconcilable conflict between operation of the Tellico Dam and the explicit provisions of §7 of the Endangered Species Act, we must now consider what remedy, if any, is appropriate. It is correct, of course, that a federal judge sitting as a chancellor is not mechanically obligated to grant an injunction for every violation of law. This Court made plain in Hecht Co. v. Bowles, 321 U.S. 321, 329 (1944), that "[a] grant of *jurisdiction* to issue compliance orders hardly suggests an absolute duty to do so under any and all circumstances." As a general matter it may be said that "[s]ince all or almost all equitable remedies are discretionary, the balancing of equities and hardships is appropriate in almost any case as a guide to the chancellor's discretion." D. Dobbs, *Remedies* 52 (1973). . . .

But these principles take a court only so far. Our system of government is, after all, a tripartite one, with each Branch having certain defined functions delegated to it by the Constitution. While "[i]t is emphatically the province and duty of the judicial department to say what the law is," Marbury v. Madison, 5 U.S. 137 (1803), it is equally—and emphatically—the exclusive province of the Congress not only to formulate legislative policies and mandate programs and projects, but also to establish their relative priority for the Nation. Once Congress, exercising its delegated powers, has decided the order of priorities in a given area, it is for the Executive to administer the laws and for the courts to enforce them when enforcement is sought.

Here we are urged to view the Endangered Species Act "reasonably," and hence shape a remedy "that accords with some modicum of common sense and the public weal." But is that our function? We have no expert knowledge on the subject of endangered species, much less do we have a mandate from the people to strike a balance of equities on the side of the Tellico Dam. Congress has spoken in the plainest of words, making it abundantly clear that the balance has been struck in favor of affording endangered species the highest of priorities, thereby adopting a policy which it described as "institutionalized caution." . . .

We agree with the Court of Appeals that in our constitutional system the commitment to the separation of powers is too fundamental for us to pre-empt congressional action by judicially decreeing what accords with "common sense and the public weal." Our Constitution vests such responsibilities in the political branches.

Affirmed.

NOTES AND QUESTIONS

1. TVA v. Hill is one of the clearest instances of judicial repudiation of the kind of balancing approaches favored by the "cool analysis" perspective. The majority opinion relies in part on committee reports expressing the view that biodiversity's genetic legacy is of "literally incalculable" value. Is the majority's rationale for refusing to balance the equities the notion that Congress already has done so? Or is the Court simply agreeing with Congress that such balancing cannot be done because it is impossible to calculate the value of genetic diversity?

2. Proponents of the project had argued that, even if completion of the dam would violate the Endangered Species Act, the judiciary should exercise its equitable discretion to decline to issue an injunction. Why did the Supreme Court instead order that an injunction be issued? Does the Court's decision imply that courts *must* enjoin all actions that violate the Act? If an injunction had not been issued in this case, would the finding of an ESA violation have any practical impact? Are courts required to enjoin violations of other environmental laws? See Weinberger v. Romero-Barcelo, 456 U.S. 305 (1982) (Clean Water Act does not foreclose the exercise of equitable discretion to decline to enjoin violation). What type of judicial relief should be provided when agencies violate procedural requirements, for example, by failing to perform a study or to consult with a certain agency?

3. Justices Powell and Blackmun dissented on the ground that the Act should be interpreted to apply only prospectively and not to actions that are virtually complete when an endangered species is discovered. In a separate dissent, Justice Rehnquist, who had favored summary reversal, argued that the district court's refusal to issue an injunction should be upheld because it was not an abuse of discretion.

4. But for the enactment of NEPA, the dam probably would have been completed before the snail darter could bring the ESA to the rescue. The enactment of NEPA gave environmental groups, who had long opposed the dam, a new tool that blocked further construction for nearly two years until an EIS was completed. After the snail darter was discovered, what steps did the plaintiffs have to take before they could invoke the Endangered Species Act? What "action" did they seek to enjoin?

5. Following the Supreme Court's decision, Congress acted swiftly to amend the Endangered Species Act. Section 7 of the Act was extensively amended in 1978, 1979, and 1982. "From an original two sentences, the provision has been expanded to occupy nearly 10 pages of statutory text and now includes detailed procedures for its implementation, new federal duties, and a complex procedure for exempting qualified activities from its commands." M. Bean, The Evolution of National Wildlife Law 355 (1983). While these amendments qualified some of the duties imposed by section 7, "they remain stringent and highly protective" and section 7's "essential command remains intact." Id.

As amended, section 7 now includes a process for granting exemptions from its "no jeopardy" rule. Section 7 establishes a committee of high-ranking government officials, known as the "God Squad" because of their power to decide the fate of species. The committee is authorized to grant any exemption if it determines that there are no reasonable and prudent alternatives to the federal action, that the action is in the public interest on a regional or national basis, and that the benefits of the action clearly outweigh the benefits of alternatives that do not jeopardize preservation of the species.

The Tellico Dam project was the first case to come before the Committee. The Committee unanimously refused an exemption for the dam because the Committee determined that there were reasonable alternatives to the project and that the project's benefits did not clearly outweigh the benefits of the alternatives. In the 15 years since the Committee was established, it has been convened only 3 times, and it has never granted a wholesale exemption from the Act.

6. In TVA v. Hill the Supreme Court had rejected the argument that continued congressional appropriations for the Tellico Dam reflected an intent to exempt it from the ESA because courts disfavor "repeals by implication." However, in 1980 Congress expressly author-

ized completion of the dam by exempting it from the ESA through an appropriations rider.

> [T]he pork barrel proponents, in forty-two seconds, in an empty House chamber, were able to slip a rider onto an appropriations bill, repealing all protective laws as they applied to Tellico and ordering the reservoir's completion. Despite a half-hearted veto threat by President Carter and a last-minute constitutionally-based lawsuit brought by the Cherokee Indians, the TVA was ultimately able to finish the dam, close the gates, and flood the valley on November 28, 1979. [Plater, In the Wake of the Snail Darter: An Environmental Law Paradigm and Its Consequences, 19 U. Mich. J.L. Ref. 805, 813-814 (1986).]

While completion of the dam destroyed the last significant population of snail darters, small relict populations have been discovered elsewhere.

3. Which Species Are Protected: Section 4

As TVA v. Hill makes clear, the Endangered Species Act provides potentially powerful protections. These protections, however, extend only to species that have been *listed* as "endangered" or "threatened" by the Secretary of the Interior (or, for certain marine species, the Secretary of Commerce). The determination to list a species, governed by section 4, is thus the key to the entire statute.

TVA v. Hill also clearly illustrates that the determination to list a species also carries potentially enormous consequences. In the wake of the Supreme Court's decision, Congress amended the Act in 1978, imposing elaborate procedures and strict deadlines on the Secretary's listing determinations. See generally M. Bean, The Evolution of National Wildlife Law 334-341. These new requirements paralyzed the listing process. Published listing proposals for approximately 2,000 species were withdrawn because the Secretary could not meet the new deadlines. Id. at 335. Then, in 1981, OMB insisted that every listing proposal be subject to a "regulatory impact analysis" to assess its economic implications. Listings ceased almost entirely. In the first year of the Reagan Administration only two species made it through the process and onto the endangered species list: an orchid in Texas and the Hay Springs amphipod, a crustacean found only in the National Zoo in Washington, D.C.

In 1982, Congress moved to resurrect the listing process. It streamlined section 4, stripping away procedural requirements that it had added four years before and narrowing the Secretary's discretion. These new provisions were intended to ensure that listing decisions are based solely on scientific evidence concerning species' prospects for survival, to the exclusion of all other factors. This attempt to insulate listing decisions from political factors was put to the test in the fight over the northern spotted owl in the case that follows.

Northern Spotted Owl v. Hodel
716 F. Supp. 479 (W.D. Wash. 1988)

ZILLY, District Judge.

A number of environmental organizations bring this action against the United States Fish & Wildlife Service ("Service") and others, alleging that the Service's decision not to list the northern spotted owl as endangered or threatened under the Endangered Species Act of 1973, as amended, 16 U.S.C. §1531 et seq. ("ESA" or "the Act"), was arbitrary and capricious or contrary to law.

Since the 1970s the northern spotted owl has received much scientific attention, beginning with comprehensive studies of its natural history by Dr. Eric Forsman, whose most significant discovery was the close association between spotted owls and old growth forests. This discovery raised concerns because the majority of remaining old-growth owl habitat is on public land available for harvest.

In January 1987, plaintiff Greenworld, pursuant to Sec. 4(b)(3) of the ESA, 16 U.S.C. §1533(b)(3), petitioned the Service to list the northern spotted owl as endangered. In August 1987, 29 conservation organizations filed a second petition to list the owl as endangered both in the Olympic Peninsula in Washington and in the Oregon Coast Range, and as threatened throughout the rest of its range.

The ESA directs the Secretary of the Interior to determine whether any species have become endangered or threatened due to habitat destruction, overutilization, disease or predation, or other natural or manmade factors. 16. U.S.C. §1533(a)(1). The Act was amended in 1982 to ensure that the decision whether to list a species as endangered or threatened was based solely on an evaluation of the biological risks faced by the species, to the exclusion of all other factors.

The Service's role in deciding whether to list the northern spotted owl as endangered or threatened is to assess the technical and scientific data in the administrative record against the relevant listing criteria in section 4(a)(1) and then to exercise its own expert discretion in reaching its decision.

In July 1987, the Service announced that it would initiate a status review of the spotted owl and requested public comment. 52 Fed. Reg.

34396 (Sept. 11, 1987). The Service assembled a group of Service biologists, including Dr. Mark Shaffer, its staff expert on population viability, to conduct the review. The Service charged Dr. Shaffer with analyzing current scientific information on the owl. Dr. Shaffer concluded that:

> the most reasonable interpretation of current data and knowledge indicate continued old growth harvesting is likely to lead to the extinction of the subspecies in the foreseeable future which argues strongly for listing the subspecies as threatened or endangered at this time.

The Service invited a peer review of Dr. Shaffer's analysis by a number of U.S. experts on population viability, all of whom agreed with Dr. Shaffer's prognosis for the owl, although each had some criticisms of his work.

The Service's decision is contained in its 1987 Status Review of the owl ("Status Review") and summarized in its Finding on Greenworld's petition ("Finding"). The Status Review was completed on December 14, 1987, and on December 17 the Service announced that listing the owl as endangered under the Act was not warranted at that time. 52 Fed. Reg. 48552, 48554 (Dec. 23, 1987). . . .

The Status Review and the Finding to the listing petition offer little insight into how the Service found that the owl currently has a viable population. Although the Status Review cites extensive empirical data and lists various conclusions, it fails to provide any analysis. . . .

The Service's documents also lack any expert analysis supporting its conclusion. Rather, the expert opinion is entirely to the contrary.

Numerous other experts on population viability contributed to or reviewed drafts of the Status Review, or otherwise assessed spotted owl viability. Some were employed by the Service; others were independent. None concluded that the northern spotted owl is not at risk of extinction. For example, as noted above, Dr. Shaffer evaluated the current data and knowledge and determined that continued logging of old growth likely would lead to the extinction of the owl in the foreseeable future. This risk, he concluded, argued strongly for immediate listing of the subspecies as threatened or endangered.

The Service invited a peer review of Dr. Shaffer's analysis. Drs. Michael Soule, Bruce Wilcox, and Daniel Goodman, three leading U.S. experts on population viability, reviewed and agreed completely with Dr. Shaffer's prognosis for the owl. . . .

The court will reject conclusory assertions of agency "expertise" where the agency spurns unrebutted expert opinions without itself offering a credible alternative explanation. See, e.g., American Tunaboat Ass'n v. Baldrige, 738 F.2nd 1013, 1016 (9th Cir. 1984). Here, the Service disregarded all the expert opinion on population viability, including that of its own expert, that the owl is facing extinction, and instead merely asserted its expertise in support of its conclusions.

The Service has failed to provide its own or other expert analysis supporting its conclusions. Such analysis is necessary to establish a rational connection between the evidence presented and the Service's decision. Accordingly, the United States Fish and Wildlife Service's decision not to list at this time the northern spotted owl as endangered or threatened under the Endangered Species Act was arbitrary and capricious and contrary to law.

The court further finds that it is not possible from the record to determine that the Service considered the related issue of whether the northern spotted owl is a threatened species. This failure of the Service to review and make an express finding on the issue of threatened status is also arbitrary and capricious and contrary to law. . . .

In deference to the Service's expertise and its role under the Endangered Species Act, the court remands this matter to the Service, which has 90 days from the date of this order to provide an analysis for its decision that listing the northern spotted owl as threatened or endangered is not currently warranted. Further, the Service is ordered to supplement its Status Review and petition Finding consistent with this court's ruling.

NOTES AND QUESTIONS

1. This action to force the listing of the spotted owl was made possible by procedural and substantive amendments to section 4 adopted by Congress in 1982. How were the environmental groups able to compel the Secretary to consider the owl for listing? Note how the court describes the Fish and Wildlife Service's role in listing decisions: "to assess the technical and scientific data in the administrative record against the relevant listing criteria in section 4(a)(1) and then to exercise its own expert discretion in reaching its decision." What does the court's decision imply about the limits of the Service's discretion? On what grounds could the Secretary decide not to list the owl? Coupled with judicial review, does section 4 now provide an effective mechanism for insulating listing decisions from political or economic considerations?

2. The Act authorizes the Secretary to act more quickly when delay in listing would pose a significant risk to the well-being of the species in question. Such an emergency listing may be promulgated with only a detailed statement of reasons and notice to affected states. It is effective for 140 days. As one might expect, the Secretary's determinations in such circumstances receive particular deference from the courts. See City of Las Vegas v. Lujan, 891 F.2d 927 (D.C. Cir. 1989) (rejecting a challenge to the emergency listing of the desert tortoise).

3. Section 4 requires that when the Secretary lists a species as en-

dangered or threatened, he or she must also designate the species's "critical habitat," to the extent that the critical habitat can be determined and designation is prudent. These provisions were intended to ensure that listing decisions were not held up by uncertainty about critical habitat. They also provide enforceable standards. Indeed, when the Secretary on remand decided to list the northern spotted owl as "threatened," but declined to designate critical habitat, the court held that critical habitat designation may be deferred only in "extraordinary circumstances," and ordered the Secretary to propose a designation within 60 days. Northern Spotted Owl v. Lujan, 758 F. Supp. 621 (W.D. Wash. 1991).

4. There is obvious logic to Congress's decision that the Act's stringent protections should apply only to species that the Secretary has formally determined to be endangered or threatened. But consider the ramifications for the Act's effectiveness in addressing the "global crisis" described by E. O. Wilson. As of April 1992, the Secretary had listed 520 species as "endangered" in the United States (277 animals and 243 plants) and another 161 species as "threatened" (97 animals and 64 plants). Another 528 species (including 3 plants) found only outside the United States were also listed. Thus, in all, the Secretary had extended the Act's protections to only 681 species in the United States and 1209 species worldwide.

Clearly the Act is not, by itself, an adequate response to the loss of global biological diversity, which Wilson estimates is occurring at the rate of 1,000 species each year. Even if one focuses solely on the United States, however, it is clear that the listing requirement is a major hindrance to the Act's effectiveness. At current funding levels, the Secretary has been able to process only 50 listing decisions each year. Yet the Secretary has identified over 3,600 species that are likely to be in need of protection, and data collected by The Nature Conservancy suggest that there may be as many as 9,000 species that should be listed. Several species have already become extinct awaiting the Act's protections. At the current rate of 50 listings a year, many more are sure to follow.

5. Should the Secretary be required to prepare an environmental impact statement before listing a species? The Sixth Circuit has held not, on the grounds that the Secretary has no discretion to reject a listing proposal on environmental grounds and that listing serves the environmental purposes of NEPA. Pacific Legal Foundation v. Andrus, 657 F.2d 829 (6th Cir. 1981).

4.   Review of Federal Actions: Section 7

The most important protection accorded endangered and threatened species is contained in section 7, the provision made famous by TVA v. Hill. As that case explained, section 7 provides for review of all federal actions that may affect endangered species and prohibits those actions that are found to "jeopardize" the existence of any such species. Section 7 also authorizes affirmative programs to conserve listed species. The following case explains the "consultation" process that section 7 establishes and the authorities that section provides.

|| ***Thomas v. Peterson*** ||
|| **753 F.2d 754 (9th Cir. 1985)** ||

Before WRIGHT, SNEED, and ALARCON, Circuit Judges.

SNEED, Circuit Judge:

Plaintiffs sought to enjoin construction of a timber road in a former National Forest roadless area. The District Court granted summary judgment in favor of defendant R. Max Peterson, Chief of the Forest Service, and plaintiffs appealed. We affirm in part, reverse in part, and remand for further proceedings consistent with this opinion.

We conclude that: (1) The National Environmental Policy Act (NEPA) requires the Forest Service to prepare an Environmental Impact Statement (EIS) that analyzes the combined environmental impacts of the road and the timber sales that the road is designed to facilitate. (2) The National Forest Management Act (NFMA) does not forbid construction of a timber road the cost of which exceeds the value of the timber that it accesses. (3) The Endangered Species Act (ESA) requires the Forest Service to prepare a biological assessment to determine whether the road and the timber sales that the road is designed to facilitate are likely to affect the endangered Rocky Mountain Gray Wolf, and construction of the road should be enjoined pending compliance with the ESA. . . .

THE ENDANGERED SPECIES ACT CLAIM

The plaintiffs' third claim concerns the Forest Service's alleged failure to comply with the Endangered Species Act (ESA) in considering the effects of the road and timber sales on the endangered Rocky Mountain Gray Wolf.

The ESA contains both substantive and procedural provisions. Substantively, the Act prohibits the taking or importation of endangered species, see 16 U.S.C. §1538, and requires federal agencies to ensure that their actions are not "likely to jeopardize the continued existence of any endangered species or threatened species or result in the destruction or adverse modification" of critical habitat of such species, see 16 U.S.C. §1536(a)(2).

The Act prescribes a three-step process to ensure compliance with its substantive provisions by federal agencies. Each of the first two steps serves a screening function to determine if the successive steps are required. The steps are:

(1) An agency proposing to take an action must inquire of the Fish & Wildlife Service (F & WS) whether any threatened or endangered species "may be present" in the area of the proposed action. See 16 U.S.C. §1536(c)(1).

(2) If the answer is affirmative, the agency must prepare a "biological assessment" to determine whether such species "is likely to be affected" by the action. Id. The biological assessment may be part of an environmental impact statement or environmental assessment. Id.

(3) If the assessment determines that a threatened or endangered species "is likely to be affected," the agency must formally consult with the F & WS. Id. §1536(a)(2). The formal consultation results in a "biological opinion" issued by the F & WS. See id. §1536(b). If the biological opinion concludes that the proposed action would jeopardize the species or destroy or adversely modify critical habitat, see id. §1536(a)(2), then the action may not go forward unless the F & WS can suggest an alternative that avoids such jeopardization, destruction, or adverse modification. Id. §1536(b)(3)(A). If the opinion concludes that the action will not violate the Act, the F & WS may still require measures to minimize its impact. Id. §1536(b)(4)
(ii)-(iii).

Plaintiffs first allege that, with respect to the Jersey Jack road, the Forest Service did not undertake step (1), a formal request to the F & WS. The district court found that to be the case, but concluded that the procedural violation was insignificant because the Forest Service was already aware that wolves may be present in the area. The court therefore refused to enjoin the construction of the road. Plaintiffs insist, based on TVA v. Hill, 437 U.S. 153 (1978), that an injunction is mandatory once any ESA violation is found. Defendants respond, citing Village of False Pass v. Clark, 733 F.2d 605 (9th Cir. 1984), that *TVA* applies only to substantive violations of the ESA, and that a court has discretion to deny an injunction when it finds a procedural violation to be de minimis.

We need not reach this issue. The Forest Service's failure goes beyond the technical violation cited by the district court, and is not de minimis.

Once an agency is aware that an endangered species may be present in the area of its proposed action, the ESA requires it to prepare a biological assessment to determine whether the proposed action "is likely to affect" the species and therefore requires formal consultation with the F & WS. See supra. The Forest Service did not prepare such an assessment prior to its decision to build the Jersey Jack road. Without a biological assessment, it cannot be determined whether the proposed project will result in a violation of the ESA's substantive provisions. A failure to prepare a biological assessment for a project in an area in which it has been determined that an endangered species may be present cannot be considered a de minimis violation of the ESA.

The district court found that the Forest Service had "undertaken sufficient study and action to further the purposes of the ESA," Memorandum Decision at 1149, E.R. 103. Its finding was based on affidavits submitted by the Forest Service for the litigation. See Memorandum Decision at 1148, E.R. 99. These do not constitute a substitute for the preparation of the biological assessment required by the ESA.

. . . The procedural requirements of the ESA are analogous to those of NEPA: under NEPA, agencies are required to evaluate the environmental impact of federal projects "significantly affecting the quality of the human environment," 42 U.S.C. §4332(2)(C); under the ESA, agencies are required to assess the effect on endangered species of projects in areas where such species may be present. 16 U.S.C. §1536(c). A failure to prepare a biological assessment is comparable to a failure to prepare an environmental impact statement. . . .

The Forest Service argues that the procedural requirements of the ESA should be enforced less stringently than those of NEPA because, unlike NEPA, the ESA also contains substantive provisions. We acknowledge that the ESA's substantive provisions distinguish it from NEPA, but the distinction acts the other way. If anything, the strict substantive provisions of the ESA justify *more* stringent enforcement of its procedural requirements, because the procedural requirements are designed to ensure compliance with the substantive provisions. The ESA's procedural requirements call for a systematic determination of the effects of a federal project on endangered species. If a project is allowed to proceed without substantial compliance with those procedural requirements, there can be no assurance that a violation of the ESA's substantive provisions will not result. The latter, of course, is impermissible. See TVA v. Hill, 437 U.S. 153.

The district court, citing Palila v. Hawaii Dept. of Land and Natural Resources, 639 F.2d 495 (9th Cir. 1981), held that "[a] party asserting a violation of the Endangered Species Act has the burden of showing the proposed action would have some prohibited effect on an endangered species or its critical habitat," and found that the plaintiffs in this case had not met that burden. Memorandum Decision at 1149, E.R. 102. This is a misapplication of *Palila*. That case concerned the ESA's prohibition of the "taking" of an endangered species, 16 U.S.C. §1538(a)(1)(B), not the ESA's procedural requirements. Quite naturally, the court in *Palila* found that a plaintiff, in order to establish a violation of the "taking" provision, must show that such a "taking" has occurred. See 639 F.2d at 497. The holding does not apply to violations of the ESA's procedural requirements. A plaintiff's burden in establishing a procedural violation is to show that the circumstances triggering the procedural requirement exist, and that the required procedures have not been followed. The plaintiffs in this case have clearly met that burden.

. . . Congress has assigned to the agencies and to the Fish & Wildlife Service the responsibility for evaluation of the impact of agency actions on endangered species, and has prescribed procedures for such evaluation. Only by following the procedures can proper evaluation be made. It is not the responsibility of the plaintiffs to prove, nor the function of the courts to judge, the effect of a proposed action on an endangered species when proper procedures have not been followed. Cf. City of Davis v. Coleman, 521 F.2d 661, 667 (9th Cir. 1975) (under NEPA, agency, not plaintiff, is responsible for investigating the environmental effects of a proposed action).

We therefore hold that the district court erred in declining to enjoin construction of the Jersey Jack road pending compliance with the ESA.

Affirmed in part, reversed in part, and remanded.

NOTES AND QUESTIONS

1. The ESA imposes a graduated review requirement somewhat reminiscent of the categorical exclusion-environmental assessment-environmental impact statement hierarchy under NEPA. Recall that under NEPA, the proponent of an action makes each determination about what review NEPA requires. How is ESA different? How are the key determinations made? Who finally determines whether an action may go forward?

2. The consultation process established by section 7 has proved an effective mechanism for avoiding conflicts with endangered species. One analysis found that over a three-year period, 1982-1984, there were 18,670 informal and formal consultations with FWS. Only 86 consultations, or 1 in 200, resulted in jeopardy opinions. In many of those cases, the projects were able to proceed after adopting "reasonable and prudent alternatives" identified by FWS in its opinion.

3. The determination whether an action is likely to "jeopardize" the continued existence of a listed species must be based on "the best scientific and commercial data available." What is the "best . . . available"? That is the issue in the next case.

	Roosevelt Campobello International	
	Park Commission v. EPA	
	684 F.2d 1041 (1st Cir. 1982)	

COFFIN, Chief Judge.

Pittston proposes to construct an oil refinery and marine terminal in Eastport, Maine, a relatively pristine area of great natural beauty near the Canadian border. The area is known for being the foggiest on the East Coast, experiencing some 750-1000 hours of fog a year; daily tides approximate twenty feet. The plan contemplates that crude oil shipments will arrive several times a week in supertankers, or Very Large Crude Carriers (VLCCs), as long as four football fields, or slightly less than a quarter of a mile. The tankers will travel through Canadian waters around the northern tip of Campobello Island, where the Roosevelt Campobello International Park is located, see 16 U.S.C. §1101 et seq., down Head Harbor Passage to a refinery near Eastport where they will be turned and berthed. Numerous barges and small tankers will carry the refined product from Eastport to destination markets in the Northeast.

The protracted procedural history of this case begins in April 1973, when Pittston applied to the Maine Board of Environmental Protection (BEP) for permission to locate the refinery in Eastport. After public hearings, the BEP approved the proposal under the Maine Site Location of Development Law, 38 M.R.S.A. §481 et seq., subject to a number of pre-construction and pre-operation conditions designed primarily to reduce the risk of oil spills. Pittston subsequently filed an application with EPA to obtain an NPDES permit, and submitted an Environmental Assessment Report to aid EPA in its duty to prepare an Environmental Impact Statement (EIS) pursuant to NEPA. EPA promulgated a draft EIS recommending issuance of the permit as conditioned by the Maine BEP, held a joint public hearing with the Army Corps of Engineers in Eastport, and received approximately 600 responses during a public comment period. In September 1977, the Maine Department of Environmental Protection certified, under §401(a)(1) of the Clean Water Act, 33 U.S.C. §1341(a)(1), that the proposed discharge would satisfy the appropriate requirements of state and federal law. In June 1978, the final EIS was issued, again recommending that the permit be issued pursuant to the BEP conditions.

Several months later, the National Marine Fisheries Service (NMFS) of the Department of Commerce and the Fish and Wildlife Service (FWS) of the Department of Interior initiated consultations with EPA concerning the proposed refinery's impact on endangered species—the right and humpback whales, and the northern bald eagle, respectively—under §7 of the Endangered Species Act (ESA), 16 U.S.C. §1536. In November, the NMFS issued a threshold determination that there were insufficient data to conclude that the project was not likely to jeopardize the continued existence of the endangered whales. In December, the FWS concluded that the project was likely to jeopardize the bald eagle. In light of these opinions and of the value of the natural resources in the Eastport area as noted in the EIS, EPA's Region I issued a notice of determination to deny Pittston's application for an NPDES permit in January 1979.

Pittston thereafter sought an adjudicatory hearing and administrative review of this decision. . . .

The adjudicatory hearing took place over five weeks in January and February of 1980. More than fifty witnesses testified and were cross-examined; several hundred exhibits were introduced. In January 1981, the ALJ [Administrative Law Judge] rendered EPA's Initial Decision, overturning EPA Region I and ordering that the NPDES permit issue. He concluded that the EIS was adequate to comply with NEPA, and that no supplemental EIS was necessary; that the risk of oil spills was "minute" and that the refinery was therefore not likely to jeopardize any endangered species; and that the conditions imposed by the Maine BEP, and assumed by the EIS, were not required to be conditions of the federal permit. Petitioners subsequently sought review before the EPA Administrator, and also moved to reopen the record to admit a recent study showing an increased number of endangered whales in the Eastport region. Both motions were denied, and in September 1981 EPA Region I issued the NPDES permit to the Pittston Company. Petitioners now seek review in this court pursuant to §509(b)(1)(F) of the Clean Water Act, 33 U.S.C. §1369(b)(1)(F). . . .

The obligation imposed on EPA by section 7(a)(2) of the ESA, 16 U.S.C. §1536(a)(2) is to "insure that any action authorized, funded, or carried out . . . is not likely to jeopardize the continued existence of any endangered species." An action would "jeopardize" the species if it "reasonably would be expected to reduce the reproduction, numbers, or distribution of a listed species to such an extent as to appreciably reduce the likelihood of the survival and recovery of that species in the wild." 50 C.F.R. §404.02 (1980). . . .

An agency's duty to consult with the Secretary of Commerce or Interior, depending on the particular endangered species, does not divest it of discretion to make a final decision that "it has taken all necessary action to insure that its actions will not jeopardize the continued existence of an endangered species." National Wildlife Federation v. Coleman, 529 F.2d 359, 371 (5th Cir. 1976). The consultation process, however, is not merely a procedural requirement. Not only is a biological opinion required of the Secretary of Commerce or Interior, "detailing how the agency action affects the species or its critical habitat," 16 U.S.C. §1536(b), but the 1979 Amendments to ESA require that in fulfilling its consultation duty and in insuring the absence of likelihood of jeopardy "each agency shall use the best scientific and commercial data available." 16 U.S.C. §1536(a)(2). Moreover, the legislative history emphasizes that "[c]ourts have given substantial weight to these biological opinions as evidence of an agency's compliance" with the Act, that "[t]he Amendment would not alter this state of the law or lessen in any way an agency's obligation" under §7, and that a federal agency which "proceeds with [an] action in the face of inadequate knowledge or information . . . does so with the risk that it has not satisfied the standard of" §7(a)(2). H. Conf. Rep. at 12, reprinted in 1979 U.S. Code Cong. & Ad. News at 2576. See also H.R. Rep. No. 95-1625, 95th Cong., 2d Sess. 12, reprinted in 1978 U.S. Code Cong. & Ad. News 9453, 9462.

In reviewing an agency's decision after consultation our task is "to ascertain whether 'the decision was based on a consideration of the relevant factors and whether there has been a clear error of judgment.' " National Wildlife Federation v. Coleman, 529 F.2d at 372 (quoting Citizens to Preserve Overton Park, Inc. v. Volpe, 401 U.S. 402, 416 (1971)). We must also inquire into whether the ALJ "followed the necessary procedural requirements." *Overton Park*, 401 U.S. at 417. . . .

The ALJ's conclusion that the risk of a major oil spill was minute was based primarily on three items of evidence. First, the ALJ relied heavily on assurances from the Coast Guard which, after reviewing the testimony of Pittston's witnesses before the BEP and other data, wrote EPA on March 28, 1977, that the channel in Head Harbor Passage was "adequate for safe navigation by 250,000 DWT tankers" if four conditions were met. These conditions were

> (1) that the channel passage area depths, configurations and current data shown on nautical charts and surveys be confirmed by hydrographic survey, (2) provision for a navigation system wherein the existence and movement of all traffic in the area could be monitored, communicated with and scheduled, (3) provision for means to control movement of tankers in the event of steering and/or propulsion failure during transit and (4) development and strict adherence to an operating procedure for tanker passage.

In response to a request by the Council on Environmental Quality that the Coast Guard assist Pittston in carrying out "real time simulation" studies in order to ascertain the precise conditions for safe navigation prior to granting the permit, Rear Admiral Fugaro of the Coast Guard responded in August 1977 that it could not divert scarce resources until "final clearance had been granted for construction of a refinery . . . [so that] no possibility exists that these efforts may be wasted." . . .

Second, the ALJ found confirmation of the Coast Guard's assurance in the computer simulation studies of Dr. Eda, who concluded that a loaded 250,000 DWT tanker could maintain a trajectory close to a desired track in Head Harbor Passage without tug assistance in a 60 knot wind. . . .

Also cited with approval by the ALJ was a second study by Frederick R. Harris, Inc. premised on provision for a more adequate turning basin for the VLCCs than an earlier study which had approved the project subject to severe restrictions and "a high order of seamanship and prudence." This study, the ALJ found, deemed the proposed approach "satisfactory for the type and size of vessels specified providing navigational aids are installed, and providing recommended operational procedures were followed." These included tug assistance from entry into channel, lighted buoys and radar reflectors, an electronic guidance system involving land based radar and electronic range finders, confining berthing and deberthing to slack tide, limiting Head Harbor transit to daylight or clearly moonlit hours, proscribing entrance to the Passage if visibility is less than a mile, and barring tankers awaiting a berth from anchoring in Eastport waters.

Finally, the ALJ made rather minute review of testimony concerning prevailing currents and cross-currents, fog, wind, and duration of oil spill effects, concluding in general that currents were not excessive for shipping, that the expected presence of fog was not so great as to bar shipping during most of the time, that winds were in general within tolerable limits, and that the effects of large known oil spills had not been long lasting over a period of years.

We have set forth in some detail and full strength all of the strands of the decision of the ALJ because we conclude that, in light of EPA's duty to insure that the project is unlikely to jeopardize endangered whales or eagles, the ALJ's failure to require, at a minimum, that "real time simulation" studies be done to assure the low risk of an oil spill prior to granting the permit violated his duty to "use the best scientific . . . data available." Given the Supreme Court's statement that the ESA is designed to prevent the loss of any endangered species, "regardless of the cost," TVA v. Hill, 437 U.S. at 188 n.34, we cannot see how the permit can issue when real time simulation studies, which EPA, the State of Maine, and the Coast Guard all view as being necessary to a final determination of safety, are to be delayed until the Coast Guard has adequate funds to undertake them.

NOTES AND QUESTIONS

1. In *Roosevelt Campobello*, why did section 7 apply to a private construction project? What species were involved? Who decides whether the proposed project is "likely to jeopardize" those species? What process does the Act prescribe for that determination? The Act requires use of the "best data available." What is the basis for the court's determination that the data considered were inadequate? What does "available" mean under the court's interpretation?

2. In implementing section 7, agencies and courts have focused on the "no jeopardy" proscription of section 7(a)(2). But section 7 proclaims a broader, more affirmative mandate, as outlined in the next case.

Carson-Truckee Water Conservancy District v. Clark
741 F.2d 257 (9th Cir. 1984)

Before DUNIWAY, Senior Circuit Judge, PREGERSON, and NORRIS, Circuit Judges.

PREGERSON, Circuit Judge:

The Carson-Truckee Water Conservancy District and Sierra Pacific Power Company (appellants) sought a declaratory judgment that the Secretary of the Interior (Secretary) violated the Washoe Project Act, 43 U.S.C.A. §§614-614d (West 1964) and related reclamation laws in refusing to sell water from the Stampede Dam and Reservoir on the Little Truckee River for municipal and industrial (M & I) use in Reno and Sparks. In addition, Nevada sought a determination that the Secretary was required to obtain a permit from the Nevada State Engineer to operate the Stampede Dam in California. The Pyramid Lake Paiute Tribe of Indians (Tribe) intervened in support of the Secretary. We affirm in part and vacate in part.

FACTUAL BACKGROUND AND DISTRICT COURT DECISIONS

. . . The Little Truckee River flows into the Truckee River, which then flows from California into Nevada and into Pyramid Lake. Stampede Dam is located on the Little Truckee in California. The Secretary now operates Stampede Dam in a way that conserves two species of fish, the cui-ui fish and Lahontan cutthroat trout, that are protected under the Endangered Species Act (ESA), 16 U.S.C. §§1531-1543 (1982). Appellants concede that the Secretary's obligations under ESA supersede his obligations under the Washoe Project Act and related federal reclamation laws. Appellants, however, challenge the extent of the Secretary's obligations under ESA. . . .

[The District Court held that the Secretary is required to sell water from Stampede Dam not needed to fulfill his trust obligations to the Tribe and his obligations under ESA, that ESA required the Secretary to give priority to conserving the cui-ui fish and Lahontan cutthroat trout as long as they were endangered and threatened, and that the Secretary's finding that there was no excess water to sell after fulfilling those statutory obligations was not arbitrary. The appellants challenged the court's interpretation of the ESA.]

Appellants urge a reading of ESA that would lead to a result at odds with the statute's clearly stated objectives. Appellants contend that the Secretary's authority is defined solely by ESA §7(a)(2), 16 U.S.C. §1536(a)(2). Thus, they argue that the Secretary is authorized only to take actions that avoid "jeopardizing" the continued existence of a species. Appellants contend that the Secretary may not do more than that.

In addition to its §7(a)(2) "jeopardy" provision, however, ESA also directs the Secretary to conserve threatened and endangered species to the extent that they are no longer threatened or endangered. Appellants, relying solely on §7(a)(2), would have us ignore the other sections of ESA directly applicable here and relied on by the district court. *Carson-Truckee II*, 549 F. Supp. at 708-10. ESA §2(b), (c), & §3(3), 16 U.S.C. §1531(b), (c), & §1532(3). ESA §7(a)(1), moreover, specifically directs that the Secretary "shall" use programs administered by him to further the conservation purposes of ESA. 16 U.S.C. §1536(a)(1). Those sections, as the district court found, direct that the Secretary actively pursue a species conservation policy. See also Tennessee Valley Authority v. Hill, 437 U.S. 153, 184 (1978) (ESA requires the Secretary to give highest priority to the preservation of endangered species; Congress intended to "halt *and reverse* the trend toward species extinction, whatever the cost." (emphasis added)).

The purpose of ESA §7(a)(2) is to ensure that the federal government does not undertake actions, such as building a dam or highway, that incidentally jeopardize the existence of endangered or threatened species. See TVA v. Hill, 437 U.S. 153 for an example of §7(a)(2)'s application. Contrary to appellants' contention, ESA §7(a)(2) is inapplicable here because the Secretary has not undertaken a project that threatens an endangered species. Instead, following the mandate of ESA §7(a)(1), §2(b), (c), & §3(3), 16 U.S.C. §1536(a)(1), 1531(c), (b), & §1532(3), the Secretary actively seeks to conserve endangered species. Thus, the district court properly applied ESA §2(b), (c), & §3(3) rather than ESA §7(a)(2) to this case.

Applying the proper code sections to this case, the Secretary's decision is well justified. The Washoe Project Act anticipates but does not require the Secretary to sell water to recover project construction costs. See supra 741 F.2d at pp. 260-261. ESA, on the other hand, directs the Secretary to use programs under his control for conservation purposes where threatened or endangered species are involved. Following this directive, the Secretary here decided to conserve the fish and not to sell the project's water. Given these circumstances, the ESA supports the Secretary's decision to give priority to the fish until such time as they no longer need ESA's protection.

NOTES AND QUESTIONS

1. How did the court find authority for the Secretary of the Interior to allocate water to the conservation of these endangered fish? Does he

have an enforceable duty to do so? What duty or authority do *other* federal agencies have to take such actions?

2. Does the section 7 consultation requirement apply to federal agencies funding projects in foreign countries? Prior to 1981, the Departments of Interior and Commerce had agreed that the Endangered Species Act requires federal agencies to ensure that foreign projects that they fund do not threaten endangered species in other countries. After the Reagan Administration reversed the government's position, environmental groups brought suit. In Defenders of Wildlife v. Lujan, 911 F.2d 117 (8th Cir. 1990), cert. granted, 111 S. Ct. 2008 (1991), the Eighth Circuit held that the Endangered Species Act does apply overseas. The Supreme Court has agreed to review the Eighth Circuit's decision.

5.   Protection Against Private Action: Section 9

By its terms, section 7 applies only to federal actions. The Endangered Species Act also provides listed species some protection against private actions. Section 9 prohibits any "person" (including any corporation or other private entity, and any federal, state, or local government agency) from taking, selling, importing, or exporting any protected species. 16 U.S.C. §1532(13). These provisions are aimed primarily at stopping the trade in live animals, skins, and other parts that threatens the existence of many species, such as parrots, alligators, and elephants. But section 9 is broader than it appears.

For example, in Palila v. Hawaii Department of Land and Natural Resources, 471 F. Supp. 985 (D. Haw. 1979) (*Palila I*), affd., 639 F.2d 495 (1981), a federal district court used section 9 to require Hawaiian officials to remove feral sheep and goats from the critical habitat of an endangered bird. These animals were found to be harming mamane trees, on which the endangered Palila, a bird found only in a small area on the upper slopes of Mauna Kea on the island of Hawaii, depends for food. When *Palila I* was decided in 1979 it was estimated that only 1,400 to 1,600 Palila remained. In 1986, when the court was asked to consider the impact on the Palila of mouflon sheep maintained by the state for sport hunting, approximately 2,200 Palila were in existence. That controversy resulted in the following decision.

> ### Palila v. Hawaii Department of Land and Natural Resources
> **649 F. Supp. 1070 (D. Haw. 1986), affd.,**
> **852 F.2d 1106 (9th Cir. 1988)**

SAMUEL P. KING, Senior District Judge.
    In this proceeding, I face the competing interests of mouflon sheep

hunters on the slopes of Mauna Kea and of the endangered bird species Palila, which makes its home there. . . .

Under the Endangered Species Act of 1973, 16 U.S.C. §§1531-1543 (1982), the Secretary of the Interior is authorized to declare species of animal life "endangered" and to identify the "critical habitat" of these species. Once a species has been listed as endangered, section 9 of the Act makes it unlawful for any person to "take" any such species. 16 U.S.C. §1538(a)(1)(B). As defined by the Act, the term "take" means to "harass, harm, pursue, hunt, shoot, wound, kill, trap, capture, or collect or to attempt to engage in any such conduct." 16 U.S.C. §1532(19). At issue in this litigation is whether the state's maintenance of mouflon sheep on Mauna Kea "harms" the Palila so as to result in a "taking."

The Secretary of the Interior has defined "harm" to mean:

> an act which actually kills or injures wildlife. Such act may include significant habitat modification or degradation where it actually kills or injures wildlife by significantly impairing essential behavioral patterns, including breeding, feeding or sheltering. 50 C.F.R. §17.3 (1985).

I understand this to prohibit activities that significantly modify or degrade the habitat, resulting in actual injury to the wildlife species. This would include activities that significantly impair essential behavioral patterns to the extent that there is an actual negative impact or injury to the endangered species, threatening its continued existence or recovery.

The Secretary's Redefinition of Harm

The proper interpretation of the term "harm" has been disputed by the parties throughout the proceedings. In particular, defendants stress the Secretary's redefinition of the term in 1981. These amended regulations, however, did not embody a substantial change in the previous definition. Under both the original definition and the definition as amended in 1981, "harm" may include significant habitat destruction that injures protected wildlife.

Defendants argue that, following my *Palila I* decision, the Secretary redefined "harm" to stress that there must be an "actual injury" to wildlife from habitat destruction or modification. Defendants argue that a showing of "actual injury" requires plaintiff to show a present pattern of decline in the number of Palila. They argue that because the Palila population has remained static, or is perhaps slightly larger than at the time of *Palila I,* there is no evidence that the mouflon are harming Palila.

Defendants' expert witness, Dr. Mountainspring, further stressed the distinction between "actual" and "potential" harm. He argued that the mouflon are not *presently* harming Palila because the sheep eat primarily the shoots and sprouts of mamane, whereas the birds feed primarily on the seeds and pods. Thus, the sheep are not depriving Palila of their food source at present. He conceded, however, as did each expert at trial, that the mouflon sheep are presently degrading the mamane forest, that this degradation is irreversible because it is suppressing the forest's regeneration, that Palila depend on mamane for their existence, and that continued degradation could drive the Palila into extinction. Defendants maintain, though, that any effect the mouflon has on mamane and indirectly on Palila is only a "potential" injury and does not fall within the redefinition of harm.

I refuse to accept, the Secretary's final redefinition does not support, and Congress could not have intended such a shortsighted and limited interpretation of "harm." A finding of "harm" does not require death to individual members of the species; nor does it require a finding that habitat degradation is presently driving the species further toward extinction. Habitat destruction that prevents the recovery of the species by affecting essential behavioral patterns causes actual injury to the species and effects a taking under section 9 of the Act.

In passing the Endangered Species Act, it is "beyond doubt that Congress intended endangered species to be afforded the highest of priorities." Tennessee Valley Authority v. Hill, 437 U.S. 153, 175 (1978). Moreover, Congress was aware that the primary threat to endangered species was destruction of habitat. 437 U.S. at 179. Thus, one of the main purposes of the Act was conservation and preservation of the ecosystems upon which endangered species depend. 16 U.S.C. §1531(b). It is clear, then, that Congress intended to prohibit habitat destruction that harms an endangered species. . . .

In 1981, the Secretary proposed to amend the definition of "harm" to read simply "an act which injures or kills wildlife." 46 Fed. Reg. at 29,490. He reasoned that under the original definition, a showing of habitat modification alone, without any concomitant injury to wildlife, could be sufficient to invoke the criminal penalties of section 9. 46 Fed. Reg. at 29,490. Under this proposal, "harm" would require actual death or injury to individual species members.

The Secretary received 328 comments on the proposed redefinition, 262 of which were in opposition to the proposal. The Secretary thus did not adopt the original proposal, but promulgated the version that exists today. The Secretary explained that "harm" was being redefined

to mean any action, including habitat modification, which actually kills or injures wildlife, rather than the present interpretation which might be read to include habitat modification or degradation alone without further proof of death or injury. Habitat modification as injury would only be covered by the new definition if it significantly impaired essential behavioral patterns of a listed species.

The Secretary clarified his intent that the redefinition did *not* limit harm to

direct physical injury to an individual member of the wildlife species. . . .
The purpose of the redefinition was to preclude claims of a Section 9
taking for habitat modification alone without any attendant death or injury
of the protected wildlife. Death or injury, however, may be caused by
impairment of essential behavioral patterns which can have significant and
permanent effects on a listed species. 46 Fed. Reg. at 54,748.

Thus the redefinition stresses the critical link between habitat modification and injury to the species. Obviously since the purpose of the
Endangered Species Act is to protect endangered wildlife, there can be
no finding of a taking unless habitat modification or degradation has
an adverse impact on the protected species. As the Secretary explained,
however, this injury to the species does not necessitate a finding of death
to individual species members. Drawing from this, I conclude that a
showing of "harm" similarly does not require a decline in population
numbers. The Palila is hovering at or near the critical population mark;
it is both biologically and legally endangered. Until the bird has reached
a sufficiently viable population to be delisted, it should not be necessary
for it to dip closer to extinction before the prohibitions of section 9 come
into force. The key to the Secretary's definition is harm to the species
as a whole through habitat destruction or modification. If the habitat
modification prevents the population from recovering, then this causes
injury to the species and should be actionable under section 9.

Mouflon Sheep Are Harming the Palila

At the time of the *Palila I* decision, the record was clear that feral
sheep and goats had a severe negative impact on the mamane forest. By
consuming the shoots and seedlings, the animals prevented regeneration
of the forest and thus brought about the "relentless decline of the Palila's
habitat." 471 F. Supp. at 990. . . .

Now I must determine whether mouflon sheep have a similar negative impact on the mamane and on the Palila. If the mouflon sheep
are similarly "harming" the Palila, the Endangered Species Act mandates
their removal.

Impacts of Mouflon on Mamane and on Palila

Since the *Palila I* decision, Dr. Giffin has conducted extensive research into the mouflon. His findings on the mouflon feeding habits
and the corresponding impact on the ecosystem are of particular significance.

Mouflon sheep also prefer the mamane habitat. They depend on
mamane for shade, concealment, moisture, and most importantly, for
food. Unfortunately for the Palila, mamane is also the favorite food of
the mouflon sheep and is the most important item in the mouflon diet.
(The mamane is a legume and is therefore very tasty.) The mouflon eat
the leaves, stems, seedlings and basal shoots of the mamane; they also
commonly strip and eat the bark of the tree. The sheep also eat grasses
and the pukiawe shrub, although these items are of lesser importance
in the diet.

Defendants argue that mouflon do not have as deleterious [an]
effect on the mamane habitat as the feral sheep, because they do not
eat exclusively mamane. However, Giffin and others have concluded
that the mouflon's feeding habits are "essentially the same" as those of
the feral sheep. Like the feral sheep, the mouflon also overbrowse
the mamane, particularly at timberline. This feeding similarly results in
lower abundance and growth rates of mamane, poor survival of mamane
seedlings and saplings, and general destruction of the native understory. . . .

The mouflon sheep impacts are readily apparent on Mauna Kea.
Portions of the mountain, where mouflon sheep populations are, or
have been, high, are heavily damaged. In these areas, there is heavy
overgrazing, a decrease in total ground cover, a sharp browseline, many
dead mamane (snags), and little or no regeneration. The suppression of
mamane is particularly acute at treeline. Research has shown that if the
mouflon sheep were removed from these areas, regeneration would occur with time.

Thus the evidence shows that at their present level, which is approximately the number of sheep necessary to maintain a viable sport-
hunting population, mouflon sheep are having the same destructive
impact on the mamane as the feral sheep. The mamane forest in its
present state is at its peak carrying capacity. In other words, the Palila
population may be as large as it can be now, given the condition of the
mamane on the mountain. Continued grazing by mouflon will continue
to suppress mamane growth and regeneration. This in turn will harm
the Palila in one of two ways. Either the mouflon sheep will further
degrade the mamane ecosystem, thus decreasing the remaining Palila
habitat and further depressing the Palila population. Or, at best, the
mouflon will merely slow or prevent the recovery of the mamane forest,
suppressing the available food supply and nesting sites for Palila, and

thus preventing the Palila population from expanding toward recovery.

In conclusion, I find that the mouflon sheep are harming the Palila within the definition of 50 C.F.R. §17.3. The mouflon are having a significant negative impact on the mamane forest, on which the Palila is wholly dependent for breeding, feeding, and sheltering. This significant habitat degradation is *actually presently injuring* the Palila by decreasing food and nesting sites, so that the Palila population is suppressed to its currently critically endangered levels. If the mouflon continue eating the mamane, the forest will not regenerate and the Palila population will not recover to a point where it can be removed from the Endangered Species List. Thus, the presence of mouflon sheep on Mauna Kea threatens the continued existence and the recovery of the Palila species. If the Palila is to have any hope of survival, the mouflon must be removed to give the mamane forest a chance to recover and expand.

Inappropriateness of Multiple Use Approach

The State argues for multiple use on Mauna Kea, asserting that both mouflon sheep and Palila can coexist on Mauna Kea. The State's position stems from their conflicting obligations to foster sport-hunting and to protect endangered species such as the Palila. They argue, based in part on recommendations by their wildlife biologist, Jon Giffin, that with careful management and oversight, it is possible both to maintain a viable sport-hunting population of mouflon and to enhance the mamane ecosystem to encourage the survival of Palila. . . .

. . . [T]he Endangered Species Act does not allow a "balancing" approach for multiple use considerations. I have found that mouflon sheep are "harming" the Palila population within the meaning of 50 C.F.R. §17.3. Once this significant negative impact has been shown, the Act leaves no room for mixed use or other management strategies or policies. In addition, all of the experts agreed that, biologically speaking, mouflon were harming Palila—that is, mouflon sheep are basically incompatible with the mamane ecosystem which the bird needs to survive. It was only when the State's experts were faced with the competing objectives of trying to maintain viable populations of both sheep and bird, that they advocated a policy of "coexistence" with Palila. . . .

CONCLUSION

In conclusion, I find that the presence of mouflon sheep in numbers sufficient for sport-hunting purposes is harming the Palila. They degrade the mamane ecosystem to the extent that there is an actual present negative impact on the Palila population that threatens the continued existence and recovery of the species. Once this determination has been made, the Endangered Species Act leaves no room for balancing policy considerations, but rather requires me to order the removal of the mouflon sheep from Mauna Kea. . . .

NOTES AND QUESTIONS

1. Why did the Sierra Club bring this action under section 9 instead of under section 7?

2. Section 9 prohibits "taking" of an endangered species. How has the state "taken" the Palila? Must the Sierra Club produce dead or maimed Palilas to make a case? What "injury" to the Palila has the Sierra Club demonstrated?

3. What result would you expect if this case arose on private land? On federal land? See Sierra Club v. Yeutter, 926 F.2d 429 (5th Cir. 1991), discussed below.

4. What result would be reached if it were the mamane tree, and not the palila, that was endangered? See section 9(a)(2). Consider the following news report.

Ignoring Pleas of Environmentalists, Kansas Man Digs Up Virgin Prairie
N.Y. Times, Nov. 23, 1990, at B18

The largest remaining stretch of virgin prairie in northeast Kansas disappeared under the plow this week after futile attempts by the Nature Conservancy and local environmentalists to buy it. The plowing of the 80-acre Elkins Prairie was first noticed soon after sunrise on Sunday, and the news quickly spread to a community group that had worked for two years to preserve the land, one of the few remaining unspoiled pieces of the 200 million acres of tall grass prairie that once covered North America.

Environmentalists hurried to the site and pleaded with the landowner to stop his tractor. The Douglas County Commission called an emergency meeting and after negotiating half the night offered to pay the landowner $6,000 an acre within six months, the equivalent of what developers had recently paid for nearby land. But the owner, Jack Graham, rejected the offer and resumed plowing. By late Monday, only a small strip of virgin prairie remained.

"It's heart-wrenching," said Joyce Wolf, leader of a group that had hoped to buy the land for an environmental education area. "He has stolen a resource from a community." Mr. Graham, a 39-year-old businessman who bought the land five years ago, declined to comment on his action. His lawyer, Thomas Murray, said Mr. Graham and his family "simply wanted to make their property more productive," but he would not elaborate.

Only about 2 percent of the original tall-grass prairie in North America remains, and Craig Freeman, coordinator of the state's Natural Heritage Program, said the Elkins stretch, about a mile outside this booming college town, was a particularly fine example of the complex prairie ecosystem. It was home to 150 species of plants, including two threatened species, Mead's milkweed and the western prairie fringed orchid. . . .

Last year the Nature Conservancy, a national land preservation organization, offered to buy the Elkins Prairie for $3,500 an acre within a year, Ms. Wolf said, a bid that had unintended consequences. The organization's failure to offer a higher price, Mr. Murray said, convinced the Grahams that the land was not as environmentally important as many Lawrence residents believed. The Kansas director of the conservancy, Alan Pollom, defended the offer, saying it was based on an appraisal. "We can't unjustifiably enrich someone using the funds of a nonprofit organization," he said. . . .

"We had hoped to use the Elkins Prairie to teach generations of young people what this countryside looked like before we tore it up into sections and fenced lines and blacktopped roads," said Stan Herd, an artist known for creating large images by planting and plowing farmland. "This was a tiny speck of our heritage, and it's gone."

Throughout the day on Monday, people gathered on a corner across the busy two-lane highway from the Elkins Prairie, talking as they watched the tractor work its way back and forth across the land. "I question the wisdom of plowing up good prairie, but I would defend his right to do it," said Larry Warren, a farmer and neighbor. "It's his land; it's his prerogative."

But Buzz Hoagland, a biology professor at the University of Kansas, argued that individuals have a responsibility to preserve the environment, even at the expense of their own profits. "It took a couple of million years for this land to evolve to the state it is in today, and it took 48 hours to destroy it," Dr. Hoagland said. "One of the things that bothers me the most is that we get up in arms over destruction of the rain forest, when the natural habitats in North America have been all but eliminated. We don't seem to get upset about the destroying of the things in our own backyard."

NOTES AND QUESTIONS

1. The article notes that the Elkins Prairie was the home to 150 species of plants, including two threatened species, Mead's milkweed

and the western prairie fringed orchid. If threatened plants are entitled to essentially the same protections under the Endangered Species Act as are endangered plants, did Mr. Graham act legally when he plowed up the virgin prairie? Why or why not? NO

2. Suppose that a local Earth First! group had gotten wind of Mr. Graham's plans to plow up the virgin prairie. They decide to sneak onto the Elkins Prairie in the middle of the night to dig up as many Mead's milkweeds and western prairie fringed orchids as possible and to transplant them elsewhere. Would such actions violate section 9 of the Endangered Species Act?

3. Does the local environmentalists' unwillingness to pay the price Mr. Graham wanted for the Elkins Prairie demonstrate that it was not worth preserving? Do you agree with Mr. Warren that because the land belonged to Mr. Graham it was his prerogative to plow it under, or with Dr. Hoagland's argument that individuals have a responsibility to preserve the environment even at the expense of their own profits?

A Note on Incidental Taking, Private Actions, and Habitat Conservation Plans

Note that section 9 can also apply to federal agencies. In Sierra Club v. Yeutter, the Fifth Circuit held that the Forest Service had violated section 9 by authorizing clear-cutting in forests that were habitat for the endangered red-cockaded woodpecker, finding that the practice "resulted in significant habitat modification" that had "caused and accelerated the decline in the species." 926 F.2d 429, 438 (5th Cir. 1991). In Defenders of Wildlife v. Administrator, 882 F.2d 1294 (8th Cir. 1989), the Eighth Circuit held that EPA had violated section 9 when it registered pesticides containing strychnine. The court found that endangered species had been poisoned by the pesticides, which could not have been used without the EPA registration.

In *Defenders of Wildlife*, as in *Palila*, the rigid proscriptions of section 9 apply even though the "taking" is merely incidental to the activities involved. For federal actions, however, section 7 provides some flexibility. If the Secretary has concluded that an agency action, and the resulting incidental take, are not likely to jeopardize the continued existence of the species and that the impact of the taking will be minimized, she may provide the agency with a written statement authorizing the taking. 16 U.S.C. §1536(b)(4). See *Defenders of Wildlife*, supra, 882 F.2d at 1300.

For its first decade, the Act provided no similar flexibility for private actions. Any private action that would incidentally harm a protected animal was subject to criminal sanctions.

In 1982, Congress recognized this inconsistency. It provided a remedy in section 10(a), authorizing the Secretary to permit "incidental" takings associated with private actions if the actor prepares a habitat conservation plan (HCP) that minimizes the impacts of the taking and assures that the taking "will not appreciably reduce the likelihood of the survival and recovery of the species in the wild." 16 U.S.C. §1539(a)(2)(B)(iv).

When Congress adopted section 10(a) it had a specific model in mind—an HCP prepared for development on San Bruno Mountain, near San Francisco, the last bastion of the mission blue butterfly. The San Bruno HCP is the product of lengthy negotiations among the landowners, developers, conservationists, and local governments. It provides for the protection, in perpetuity, of 87 percent of the butterfly's habitat. Payments by the landowners and developers, and ultimately assessments on units within the development, provide annual revenues to support habitat management and long-term enforcement of the plan. Through active management of the habitat, controlling recreational use, and removing exotic vegetation, the butterfly's prospects for survival are actually enhanced.

Congress emphasized that it expected future HCPs to be measured against the San Bruno plan. It is perhaps an unrealistic standard. It is not often possible to allow development in a species's habitat while also enhancing its prospects for survival.

The San Bruno model is nonetheless important. At their best, as in San Bruno, HCPs can bring together the broad array of interests with a stake in the management of a species's habitat to produce a rigorous and comprehensive program for conservation of the species.

In the first decade of their use, only a handful of HCPs have been completed—FWS has never enforced section 9 against incidental takings, and so there has been little incentive for anyone to seek a permit. But with FWS showing more interest in enforcement, HCPs are on the rise. There are now two dozen in preparation. Over the coming decade, HCPs promise to be an increasingly important mechanism for reconciling development with the conservation of endangered species, and perhaps a model for resolving other, similar conflicts. For a comprehensive analysis of HCPs, see M. Bean, S. Fitzgerald, and M. O'Connell, Reconciling Conflicts Under the Endangered Species Act: The Habitat Conservation Planning Experience (1991).

To gain a greater understanding of how the Endangered Species Act operates, consider the following problem exercise.

PROBLEM EXERCISE: THE ENDANGERED SPECIES ACT

The Four Seasons motel is located on private land in the center of the town of East Yellowstone, which is just outside Yellowstone National Park and in the heart of grizzly bear territory. The fine restaurant of this motel is surrounded by picture windows that overlook its grounds. On one edge of this panorama the motel has placed an open dumpster, where it disposes of all the waste from its kitchen. The dumpster is illuminated by a spotlight.

Garbage is an easy source of food for grizzly bears, and an open dumpster will quickly draw grizzlies away from their usual foraging. So it is no surprise that grizzly bears frequent the dumpster at the Four Seasons motel. Indeed, the bears have become a major attraction for the motel.

Garbage is not known to be harmful to grizzly bears. But the principal cause of grizzly bear mortality is confrontations with humans, and when bears are drawn into town on a regular basis it is likely that a human confrontation will eventually occur. For this reason, the Audubon Society has asked the Four Seasons motel to take the simple measures necessary to ensure that bears cannot get into its dumpster. The motel has refused.

The grizzly bear is listed as a threatened species in Yellowstone and the surrounding area. Can Audubon establish that the Four Seasons motel is violating the Endangered Species Act? What should their theory be?

C. PUBLIC RESOURCE MANAGEMENT AND THE ENVIRONMENT

The role government should play in managing public resources is a subject of continuing controversy. For the first century of the republic the dominant federal role was to transfer public lands to private parties to encourage settlement and development. The focus of public resource management has now shifted. Most laws encouraging disposal of public lands have been repealed—one can no longer "homestead" on the public domain. The result is that one-third of the nation's land is now held permanently in federal ownership. Some of these public lands are protected for their natural, cultural, or scenic values—as parks, wilderness areas, or wildlife refuges. Most are entrusted to the stewardship of the Bureau of Land Management (BLM) and the Forest Service under broad mandates to manage for "multiple uses" that "will best meet the needs of the American public." Multiple Use, Sustained Yield Act, 16 U.S.C. §531(a). See the Federal Land Policy and Management Act of 1976 (FLPMA), 43 U.S.C. §1701 et seq.; the National Forest Management Act of 1976, 16 U.S.C. §1600 et seq. See generally Wilkinson and Anderson, Land and Resource Planning on the National Forests, 64 Or. L. Rev. 1 (1985). That mandate has been a recipe for controversy. See Huffman,

Public Lands Management in an Age of Deregulation and Privatization, 10 Pub. Land L. Rev. 29 (1989). The laws governing management of public lands are outlined in the Pathfinder below.

PUBLIC LAND AND RESOURCE LAW: A PATHFINDER

Public Land Management Systems. Public lands are managed in four systems: general public lands, managed by the Bureau of Land Management (BLM); National Forests, managed by the U.S. Forest Service; National Wildlife Refuges, managed by the U.S. Fish and Wildlife Service; and National Parks, managed by the National Park Service. Wilderness areas, governed by the Wilderness Act of 1964, may be designated on lands in any of the four systems.

Multiple Use. Congress has mandated that most public lands, including the 340 million acres managed by BLM and the 191 million acres in the National Forests (except for wilderness areas), be managed for "multiple use" as defined in the Federal Land Policy and Management Act (FLPMA) for BLM lands and the National Forest Management Act (NFMA) for the National Forests. Despite elaborate planning and public participation requirements, "multiple-use" management has been vulnerable to local politics, with land managers often emphasizing economic uses—grazing, logging, mineral development—over wildlife and wilderness values. Congress also has often undercut the FLPMA and NFMA by, for example, forbidding BLM from raising grazing fees or specifying the "annual cut" that must be allowed in the National Forests.

Dominant Use. For one class of lands—the National Wildlife Refuges—Congress has placed a thumb on the balance, establishing as a dominant use the conservation of wildlife. Other uses, such as grazing or motorboating, are allowed on a refuge only if "compatible" with the purposes for which the refuge was established. The National Wildlife Refuge System now includes 492 units totalling 88 million acres. Sixteen of these refuges, accounting for 77 million acres, are in Alaska and were created or expanded in the Alaska Lands Act of 1980.

Preservation. Two classes of federal lands enjoy almost absolute protection—the National Parks and the National Wilderness Areas. Congress in 1916 created the National Park Service and charged it with management of what today are 350 natural, historic, and recreational preserves covering 80 million acres "to conserve the scenery and the natural and historic objects and wild life therein and to provide for the enjoyment of the same in such manner and by such means as will leave them unimpaired for the enjoyment of future generations." 16 U.S.C. §1. Wilderness Areas must be managed under the Wilderness Act to preserve their "primeval character and influence" and "natural condition" with motorized equipment, permanent roads, and commercial enterprise generally prohibited. 16 U.S.C. §1131(c).

Public Resources. The Mining Law of 1872 guarantees citizens a right to discover, develop, and patent hardrock mineral deposits on any public lands, unless the lands have been expressly withdrawn from mineral entry. Other minerals are subject to lease by the government, principally under the Mineral Leasing Act of 1920 and, offshore, under the Outer Continental Shelf Lands Act of 1953. Congress has also acted to protect important wildlife resources through measures such as the Migratory Bird Treaty Act, the Marine Mammal Protection Act, and other laws.

1. Private Development of Public Resources

Environmentalists argue that federal resource management policies cause substantial environmental damage while subsidizing private mining, timber, and grazing interests. A particularly egregious example is the Mining Act of 1872, which gives private parties the right to develop and extract hardrock mineral deposits from public lands without payment of royalties. Twenty-acre tracts of public land on which such minerals are found may be acquired by private interests for $5, even if the land is worth millions. More than 3 million acres of public land have been patented in this manner, including land later converted to ski resorts, condominiums, and golf courses. The General Accounting Office found that public land with a market value of $47.9 million was sold for less than $4,500 between 1970 and 1988. GAO, Federal Land Management: The Mining Law of 1872 Needs Revision (1989).

Federal timber policies have been the focus of similar criticism. Some economists estimate that the government loses up to $200 million per year on timber sales from the national forests. McNeil, How Most of the Public Forests Are Sold to Loggers at a Loss, N.Y. Times, Nov. 3, 1991, at D2. They maintain that most Forest Service land is in areas unsuited for timber harvesting but that "publicly owned trees are cut because the Forest Service sells them so cheaply that loggers would be foolish to say no." The government "builds roads, pays rangers, absorbs the risks of fires and insects, then sells at a loss." Id. The Forest Service argues that its timber sales are profitable, though its calculations have been criticized for ignoring significant categories of costs while amortizing logging roads over unrealistically long periods (e.g., 1,800 years for a road in the Chugach National Forest in Alaska, "as if the current Italian Government was still paying for the Appian Way"). Id.

To encourage development in Alaska, the Forest Service has since the 1920s promoted logging in Alaska's Tongass National Forest, the largest temperate rain forest in North America. After Congress directed the Forest Service to guarantee a supply of federal timber to companies building pulp mills, federal timber worth $200 to $600 per thousand board feet was sold for only $2 per thousand board feet, which critics have likened to "selling 500-year-old trees for about the price of a cheeseburger." Forest Murder: Ours and Theirs, N.Y. Times, Sept. 20, 1989, at A26. While the logging operations provide 1,500 jobs, critics argue that "it would be cheaper just to pay each logger $36,000 a year—and it would protect the environment besides." Id. Responding to these criticisms, Congress enacted the Tongass Timber Reform Act of 1990, 104 Stat. 4435, which reduced the volume of timber to be harvested while expanding nonharvestable wilderness areas, see City of Tenakee Springs v. Franzell,—F.2d—(9th Cir. 1992). But this legislation has not silenced critics of Tongass timber harvesting. See, e.g., Why Let Chainsaws Pare the Old Forests at All?, N.Y. Times, Nov. 3, 1991, at E3.

Economists recommend that federal subsidies be replaced with a policy of charging market prices for minerals, timber, and grazing rights on public lands. Others argue that governments can never manage resources effectively and that the only way to ensure protection of the commons is to privatize public land. Communities dependent on public resources argue that federal subsidies are necessary to preserve jobs, as illustrated by the controversy over protection of the northern spotted owl and the old-growth forests of the Pacific Northwest.

2. *Preservation of Biodiversity: The Spotted Owl Controversy*

Public resources serve more than purely economic values. The ancient forests of the Pacific Northwest sustain rich biological communities that are complex and distinctive ecosystems. In addition to their aesthetic value, old-growth forests are critical and irreplaceable reservoirs of biological diversity. Containing 500-year-old evergreens towering more than 300 feet, the Northwest's old-growth forests are the habitat of the rare northern spotted owl, which has become both the symbol of the forest's ecological values and a lightning rod for controversy. Scientists estimate that thousands of acres of old-growth forest are necessary to provide an adequate food supply for one pair of these beautiful birds. As logging has reduced the habitat of the owl, its numbers have dwindled to fewer than 3,000 pairs and its continued survival is now in jeopardy.

Today only about 5 percent of the ancient forests present in colonial times remain. Since the 1950s the logging of old-growth forests has been a mainstay of the timber industry in the Northwest. Old-growth forests once covered 19 million acres on the western slope of the Cascades; there are now 2.5 to 3.5 million acres of old-growth forests left there. Parks and wilderness areas protect 900,000 acres, but on the rest logging continues to clear almost another 70,000 acres each year.

Virtually all the remaining old-growth forest is on public lands, including national forests managed by the Forest Service. The National Forest Management Act (NFMA) requires the Service to "provide for multiple use and sustained yield of goods and services from the National Forest System in a way that maximizes long term net public benefit in an environmentally sound manner." 36 C.F.R. §219.1(a). The Forest Service has promoted aggressive logging of old-growth forests. In recent years nearly one-third of all timber harvested in Oregon and Washington came from national forests.

FIGURE 8.2

A Northern Spotted Owl.
—*Kenneth R. Bevis*

Efforts to protect the spotted owl by halting logging operations in the remaining old-growth forests will accelerate job losses in the Northwest timber industry, which already is in a state of decline. Increased mechanization and greater exports of unprocessed logs to Asia contributed to the closing of 200 northwestern lumber mills in the 1980s. Ultimately, the industry's reliance on old-growth timber will end, due either to conservation measures or exhaustion of the supply. But since measures to protect the owl could speed up the painful transition occurring in the industry, they have spawned an intense struggle. Arguing that their very way of life is being jeopardized for the sake of a bird, mill owners, loggers, and their employees have battled environmentalists before agencies, Congress, and the courts.

Arguing that the spotted owl is an "indicator species" whose status reflects the health of forest ecosystems, environmental groups have pursued a variety of legal actions to stop the logging of old-growth forests. As noted above, they forced the Fish and Wildlife Service to reconsider whether to place the spotted owl under the protection of the Endangered Species Act. They also have invoked the NFMA, NEPA, and the Migratory Bird Treaty Act. The NFMA requires the Forest Service to provide sufficient habitat "to maintain viable populations of existing native and desired non-native vertebrate species" in forest planning areas. 36 C.F.R. §219.19. Charging violations of NFMA and NEPA, the Seattle Audubon Society (SAS) sued the Forest Service for its failure to protect spotted owl habitat in the national forests. In March 1989 a federal district court granted a preliminary injunction ordering that certain timber sales in Washington and Oregon be postponed. Seattle Audubon Society v. Evans, 771 F. Supp. 1081, 1084 (W.D. Wash. 1991), affd., 952 F.2d 297 (9th Cir. 1991). While this litigation was pending, the Fish and Wildlife Service announced its intention to list the owl as "threatened" under the Endangered Species Act following the decision in Northern Spotted Owl v. Hodel, 716 F. Supp. 479 (W.D. Wash. 1988), discussed at page 1100, above.

Fearful that litigation would continue to delay timber sales, the northwestern congressional delegation attached a rider to an Interior Department appropriations bill enacted in October 1989. Dubbed the "Northwest Timber Compromise Act of 1989," section 318 of the appropriations bill directed BLM and the Forest Service to offer specified quantities of timber for sale in fiscal years 1989 and 1990. To prevent further litigation from blocking timber sales, section 318 stated that Congress "determines and directs" that compliance with its provisions "is adequate consideration for the purpose of meeting the statutory requirements that are the basis for" the pending litigation. As a gesture to environmentalists, section 318 required the Forest Service to adopt a spotted owl conservation plan, and it stated that cutting of "ecologically significant old growth forest stands" should be limited to amounts necessary to meet the quotas it required. Section 318 was part of a series of nine appropriations riders adopted in the 1980s to nullify injunctions or prohibit judicial review of Forest Service and BLM actions in the Northwest.

In response to section 318, the district court in *Seattle Audubon Society* dissolved its injunction. The Audubon Society then appealed to the Ninth Circuit, which reversed. The Ninth Circuit held that section 318 was an unconstitutional legislative intrusion into the judicial realm because it attempted to dictate the outcome of pending litigation without amending the underlying substantive law. The Supreme Court then granted review and reversed. Robertson v. Seattle Audubon Society, 112 S. Ct. 1407 (1992). The Court avoided the constitutional question by finding that the appropriations rider had amended (albeit temporarily) the substantive laws covering the designated public lands. It declined to address the constitutional implications of a change in substantive law that swept no more broadly than applications at issue in pending litigation because the issue had been raised only in an amicus brief.

Following the decision to list the spotted owl as a "threatened" species, an Interagency Scientific Committee (ISC) was established by the Forest Service, BLM, the Fish and Wildlife Service (FWS), and the National Park Service to develop a habitat conservation strategy for the spotted owl. On April 2, 1990, the ISC issued its report, Report of the Interagency Scientific Committee to Address the Conservation of the Northern Spotted Owl, A Conservation Strategy for the Northern Spotted Owl (1990). The report concluded that "the owl is imperiled over significant portions of its range because of continuing losses of habitat from logging and natural disturbances" and that "delay in implementing a conservation strategy cannot be justified on the basis of inadequate knowledge." On June 22, 1990 the owl was formally listed as a threatened species under the Endangered Species Act. 55 Fed. Reg. 26,114 (1990). Four days later, however, the Bush Administration announced that it would delay adopting a habitat protection plan while it sought an amendment to relax the Act. Egan, Softening Stand on Spotted Owl, Administration Delays Protection, N.Y. Times, June 27, 1990, at A1.

Faced with renewed litigation, the Forest Service maintained that, in light of the listing of the owl as a "threatened" species, it did not need to adopt a revised habitat conservation plan as required by section 318 or the NFMA. While stating that it would manage timber sales in a manner "not inconsistent with" the ISC Report, 55 Fed. Reg. 40,413 (1990), the Forest Service argued that the ESA listing of the owl relieved it of any obligation to maintain the species under the NFMA. This argument was rejected in the case below, which held that the Forest Service's duties under the NFMA and the ESA are "concurrent." Judge Dwyer found that the Forest Service had committed "a remarkable series of violations of the environmental laws" throughout the course of litigation over the spotted owl. 771 F. Supp. at 1089. Citing testimony from Forest Service biologists that "considerable political pressure" was used to alter the conclusions of the ISC report, id., the judge found that the Secretaries of Agriculture and Interior simply decided "to drop the effort" to comply with the law. Judge Dwyer then considered whether or not to enjoin future timber sales in a portion of the opinion that follows.

Seattle Audubon Society v. Evans
771 F. Supp. 1081 (W.D. Wash. 1991), affd., 952 F.2d 297 (9th Cir. 1991)

DWYER, District Judge.

More is involved here than a simple failure by an agency to comply with its governing statute. The most recent violations of NFMA exemplifies a deliberate and systematic refusal by the Forest Service and the FWS to comply with the laws protecting wildlife. This is not the doing of the scientists, foresters, rangers, and others at the working levels of these agencies. It reflects decisions made by higher authorities in the executive branch of government. . . .

The northern spotted owl is now threatened with extinction. . . . The FWS has found that the owl is threatened *throughout* its range. 55 Fed. Reg. 26114. . . .

The Forest Service estimates that an additional 66,000 acres of spotted owl habitat would be destroyed if logging went forward to the extent permitted by the ISC Report over the next sixteen months. That would be in addition to about 400,000 acres of habitat logged in the seven years since the agency began preparing these guidelines, all without having a lawful plan or EIS for the owl's management in place. . . .

To log tens of thousands of additional acres of spotted owl habitat before a plan is adopted would foreclose options that might later prove to have been necessary. . . .

The logging of 66,000 acres of owl habitat, in the absence of a conservation plan, would itself constitute a form of irreparable harm. Old growth forests are lost for generations. No amount of money can replace the environmental loss.

While the agency's proposal would involve logging an estimated one percent of the remaining habitat, the experts agree that cumulative loss of habitat is what has put the owl in danger of extinction. There is a substantial risk that logging another 66,000 acres, before a plan is adopted, would push the species past a population threshold from which it could not recover. . . .

. . . The injunction would not prohibit the logging of existing sales, but rather the sale of additional logging rights in owl habitat areas while the Forest Service was in the process of adopting a plan. Thus, timber sale reductions do not translate directly into harvest reductions. . . .

Additional timber supplies from private lands can reasonably be expected to enter the market if the price of timber stumpage increases, as it probably will do if Forest Service sales decline. In addition, some timber now exported will probably be diverted to the domestic market. . . .

Over the past decade many timber jobs have been lost and mills closed in the Pacific Northwest. The main reasons have been modernization of physical plants, changes in product demand, and competition from elsewhere. Supply shortages have also played a part. Those least able to adapt and modernize, and those who have not gained alternative supplies, have been hardest hit by the changes. By and large, the companies with major capital resources and private timber supplies have done well; many of the smaller firms have had trouble.

Job losses in the wood products industry will continue regardless of whether the northern spotted owl is protected. A credible estimate is that over the next twenty years more than 30,000 jobs will be lost to worker-productivity increases alone.

A social cost is paid whenever an economic transformation of this nature takes place, all the more so when a largely rural industry loses sizeable numbers of jobs. Today, however, in contrast to earlier recession periods, states offer programs for dislocated workers that ease and facilitate the necessary adjustments.

Counties in timber-dependent communities derive revenues from the harvest of national forest timber. . . . Revenues from this source will decline later if harvests decline. These public entities, however, do not expect to obtain revenues from sales made in violation of law.

The timber industry no longer drives the Pacific Northwest's economy. In Oregon, for example, the level of employment in lumber and wood products declined by seventeen percent between 1979 and 1989. In the same period, Oregon's total employment increased by twenty-three percent.

The wood products industry now employs about four percent of all workers in Western Oregon, two percent in Western Washington, and six percent in Northern California. Even if some jobs in wood products were affected by protecting owl habitat in the short term, any effect on the regional economy probably would be small.

The remaining wilderness contributes to the desirability of this region as a site for new industries and their employees. The resulting economic gains, while hard to measure, are genuine and substantial. The FWS has recently noted that preservation of old growth brings economic benefits and amenities "of extremely high value." 56 Fed. Reg. 20816, 20822 (May 6, 1991). . . .

Any reduction in federal timber sales will have adverse effects on some timber industry firms and their employees, and a suspension of owl habitat sales in the national forests is no exception. But while the loss of old growth is permanent, the economic effects of an injunction are temporary and can be minimized in many ways.

To bypass the environmental laws, either briefly or permanently, would not fend off the changes transforming the timber industry. The argument that the mightiest economy on earth cannot afford to preserve old growth forests for a short time, while it reaches an overdue decision on how to manage them, is not convincing today. It would be even less so a year or a century from now.

For the reasons stated, the public interest and the balance of equities require the issuance of an injunction directing the Forest Service to comply with the requirements of NFMA by March 5, 1992, and preventing it from selling additional logging rights in spotted owl habitat until it complies with the law.

NOTES AND QUESTIONS

1. Note the sharply different ways in which the parties to the spotted owl dispute frame the issue. Loggers view it as a stark choice between their jobs and the owl, while environmental groups frame the question as whether biodiversity should be permanently sacrificed to provide a temporary subsidy. How does Judge Dwyer balance the competing interests in deciding to issue an injunction precluding further sales of old-growth timber? To what extent does his decision turn on the relative irreversibility of cutting 500-year-old trees versus the perceived temporary and compensable nature of job losses?

2. While there are many reasons to protect old-growth forests, a central concern is the conservation of biological diversity—protecting the unique collection of animal and plant species and processes that comprise the old-growth forest ecosystem. Consider the three different statutory strategies for conserving biological diversity that are represented in this case—the NFMA, the Endangered Species Act, and, somewhat less directly, NEPA. How does each of these strategies work? What are their strengths and shortcomings as tools for conserving biological diversity?

3. When Congress adopted section 318, the appropriations rider that sought to provide a temporary resolution to this conflict, members from Oregon and Washington expressed considerable frustration with the Forest Service for failure to adopt and implement forest management

plans. Why had the Forest Service failed to resolve the problem? Does it help to know that Congress in section 318 mandated sale of 7.7 billion board feet from Forest Service lands in fiscal years 1989 and 1990 and that, by the court's calculation, the Forest Service could sell only 3 to 3.6 billion board feet in fiscal years 1991 and 1992 if it adhered to the recommendations of the Interagency Scientific Committee? Are appropriations riders an appropriate vehicle for resolving such conflicts, or should Congress be required to amend the underlying environmental laws permanently if it wishes to exempt certain actions?

4. Judge Dwyer enjoined the Forest Service from offering for sale almost all remaining old-growth timber in the national forests in Oregon and Washington. He stated that the injunction would remain in effect until the Forest Service issued an EIS and adopted a plan for conservation of the owl that would ensure its continued viability. Judge Dwyer's injunction was upheld by the Ninth Circuit in December 1991. Seattle Audubon Society v. Evans, 952 F.2d 297 (9th Cir. 1991).

5. Federal policy concerning the management of public resources provides potent illustrations of how changes in government policy create winners and losers. Efforts to change resource development policies to preserve public resources threaten industries and communities that have become dependent on access to those resources. To mitigate the economic dislocations caused by measures to protect old-growth forests, Congress in 1990 banned the export of unprocessed timber from public lands in the Pacific Northwest, in hopes that such a ban would help stem the loss of jobs at local timber mills.

6. Noting that "[j]ob loss claims are always suspect," the editors of the Wall Street Journal proposed the following solution to the spotted owl controversy:

> The truth is that jobs are lost all the time in a dynamic economy, and while that can cause considerable immediate grief for those caught unprepared, most industrious people can get back on their feet soon if an economy is healthy and creating new jobs. . . .
>
> This is not to deny that the situation in the Northwest poses difficult choices for policy makers. The better solution, though, would be to use the market more creatively to find answers. . . .
>
> What that ought to mean in the Northwest, and wherever land use is in question, is (1) private property, the bedrock of market-based prosperity, is respected; and (2) where public property or resources are disputed, their proper pricing should be the goal, along with the elimination of subsidies. Translation: Privatize where possible, with perhaps some land going to groups such as the Nature Conservancy.
>
> If the body politic indeed concludes that an owl, or an ecosystem, deserves special protection (often, it appears, for merely psychic rewards) then buy off enough of the logging operations to satisfy that goal. [Logging on Protectionism, Wall St. J., Sept. 6, 1990, at A14.]

Would this be a more satisfactory resolution of public resource management problems? Should environmental groups be permitted to bid for development rights to public resources, such as offshore oil leases, in order to prevent their development? Should this approach displace environmental protection measures like the Endangered Species Act? Note that the regulatory impact of such statutes may have a substantial effect on the cost of "buying off" developers. The Nature Conservancy purchased 10,000 acres of land near Austin, Texas from the Resolution Trust Corporation to create a nature preserve for the golden-cheeked warbler. While the land had a book value of $190 million, the Conservancy acquired it for only $15.5 million because most other potential bidders were deterred by the presence of the bird, which is protected by the ESA. McCoy, A Warbler Habitat Seized from Thrifts Is Sold for a Song, Wall St. J., Sept. 9, 1991.

7. In January 1992 the Fish and Wildlife Service proposed a habitat conservation plan for the spotted owl that would restrict logging on 6.9 million acres of land owned by the federal government. The Service predicted that its plan would cost 20,700 jobs in the timber industry, based on a model assuming 10.3 jobs lost per million board feet of unsold timber. Timber industry representatives denounced the plan as "a legal lynching of an entire region by an out-of-control Federal agency." Logging Limits Proposed on 7 Million Acres, N.Y. Times, Jan. 10, 1992, at A12.

8. BLM refused to adopt the guidelines recommended by the ISC. Faced with a preliminary determination that several of its proposed sales might jeopardize the continued existence of the spotted owl, BLM refused to enter consultations with the Fish and Wildlife Service, the usual process for finding alternatives that could avoid jeopardy. Rather, in September 1991 BLM asked the Secretary of the Interior to convene the "God Squad" established by section 7(e) of the Endangered Species Act so that it could seek an exemption from the Act's restrictions as applied to 44 sales of old-growth timber. The Secretary approved the request to convene the panel. EPA, which had argued that BLM had invoked the God Squad improperly, abruptly withdrew from the panel's fact-finding hearings when they convened in January 1992. Consider the criteria for granting an exemption under section 7(h)(1)(A) of the ESA. Are the timber sales proposed by BLM likely to qualify for an exemption?

3. *Moral Outrage, Uncertainty, and Resource Management*

The tension between "moral outrage" and "cool analysis" and the problems of decision-making under uncertainty are themes that figure prominently in disputes over management of public resources and the preservation of environmental values. At first blush the Endangered Species Act appears to be rooted in the "moral outrage" perspective. While there are elements of the statute that reflect a balancing approach, such as the largely theoretical exemption process, in the end the statutory commands are essentially absolute. All federal actions affecting a protected species must be accompanied by assurance that there will be no jeopardy to its survival and recovery.

While their seemingly absolute nature may be rooted in moral concern about environmental damage, the Endangered Species Act and other efforts to preserve biodiversity are largely a response to uncertainty. In the words of Chief Justice Burger, "Congress was concerned about the *unknown* uses that endangered species might have and about the *unforeseeable* place such creatures may have in the chain of life on this planet." TVA v. Hill, 437 U.S. at 178-179 (emphasis in original). Congress seems to be saying that even if we wished to engage in "cool analysis," when it comes to protection of biodiversity, balancing of costs and benefits cannot be done with any confidence because the benefits of biodiversity essentially are unquantifiable.

The costs of species protection measures are far more visible and immediate than are the diffuse, long-term benefits of preserving biodiversity. Thus, people on whom the costs are concentrated may express moral outrage of their own, to wit, the loggers protesting outside the God Squad hearings on the spotted owl, carrying signs that read "Loggers Pay Taxes, Owls Do Not" and "We Need Jobs, Not Birds." Egan, Politics Reign at Spotted Owl Hearing, N.Y. Times, Jan. 9, 1992, at A14. A BLM lawyer at the hearings argued that it is immoral to favor animals over humans and that current policy "is far more likely to result in homeless people rather than homeless owls." Id. Alaska Congressman Don Young argues that protection of the spotted owl is a product of "imperfect 'feel good' legislation [that causes] a comfortable urbanized population to be spared the costs of their compulsions" while imposing these costs on others. Don Young, The Survival of the Fittest, 1990 Envtl. Forum, 34 (July-Aug. 1990). Young maintains that

> [w]e must acknowledge . . . that the earth is a dynamic entity. Millions of species have fought and lost the battle of evolution against predators, climate and habitat changes, and their own frail evolutionary niche. Despite all of our best intentions, it is by nature's design that the stronger will survive, sometimes at the expenses of the weak. [Id. at 35.]

Congressman Young and others argue that the ESA should be amended to require balancing the costs and benefits of protecting a species. Indeed, many environmentalists believe that BLM's request to convene the God Squad over the spotted owl is part of a political strategy to force amendments to relax the Endangered Species Act. In the article that follows, Michael Bean, an attorney with the Environmental Defense Fund, explains why he believes uncertainty makes it impossible to incorporate balancing approaches into the Endangered Species Act.

Bean, We Don't Know the Benefits Side of the Equation
1990 Envtl. Forum 30 (July-Aug. 1990)

A weed is "a plant whose virtues have not yet been discovered," wrote Ralph Waldo Emerson more than a century ago. This simple truth is at the heart of a current debate over whether the Endangered Species Act—protector of "weeds," "predators," "trash fish," and other undesirables—should be amended to permit a balancing of the benefits and the economic impacts of protecting imperiled species. The truth today is as plain as in Emerson's time; we are unable to strike any defensible balance simply because we have only the most rudimentary understanding of the benefits side of the equation—we have yet to discover the virtues of most species.

Emerson's words are more than clever musings; they have proved right time and again. Prior to the discovery of penicillin, the lowly mold from which the life-saving antibiotic was derived was, frankly, just a lowly mold. The Pacific yew, a small understory conifer routinely discarded and burned in clearcutting operations, was, until very recently, little more than a "weed." Now, however, it is recognized as the source of a chemical that has been shown to be highly effective in the treatment of ovarian cancer. The National Cancer Institute last year began ringing alarms about the short supply of the yew because it—like the better known spotted owl—occurs primarily in the quickly disappearing ancient forests of the Pacific Northwest. If, prior to these discoveries, a balance had been sought between the costs and benefits of protecting the mold or the Pacific yew, the value of the lives saved by these medicines would have been left out of the equation.

Admittedly, although not every species will be shown to harbor some compound of extraordinary medical or other economic value, it is impossible to say which one will and which will not. Nevertheless, if we were able to determine that no economic value will ever be realized from a particular species, would we then be justified to conclude that the species is of no use and is therefore expendable? I suggest not, because we lack an adequate understanding of the ecological role each species plays in Darwin's "tangled bank of life."

Like Aldo Leopold, whose understanding of ecological relationships was unparalleled, we ought to be less impressed by the extent of our knowledge than by its limits. "The last word in ignorance," wrote Leopold, "is the man who says of a plant or animal, 'What good is it?'"

The effort to devise a means of balancing the benefits of endangered species preservation against its economic impacts thus begins with the very question that Leopold dismissed as unanswerable and misguided. He went on to ask, "Who but a fool would discard seemingly useless parts? To keep every cog and wheel is the first precaution of intelligent tinkering." Indeed, the result of such a balancing exercise would simply be a self-deceiving assertion that we can safely disregard Leopold's first precaution. Finally, the addition of new balancing provisions to the ESA might be justified on the grounds that the act, as currently written, is stronger than necessary to address the problem of accelerating species loss. But that contention is belied by a mountain of evidence to the contrary: despite notable achievements for some species, the overall record is discouraging. The General Accounting Office concluded in 1988 that fully twice as many ostensibly "protected" species are declining as are recovering. At least 18 endangered species have already become extinct, triple the number that have recovered and been delisted. Others, including such prominent species as the California condor and the black-footed ferret, have been unable to survive in the wild, despite the act's nominal protection; their future depends entirely on the success of last-ditch captive propagation efforts.

NOTES AND QUESTIONS

1. Opponents of the spotted owl paint a picture of economic activity grinding to a halt because of frequent discoveries of rare and obscure creatures. Interior Secretary Lujan argues that "the way we do this thing is all wrong. . . . It is not just the spotted owl. The Delta smelt, Colorado squaw fish, the desert tortoise. There is no end to it." Egan, Politics Reign at Spotted Owl Hearing, N.Y. Times, Jan. 9, 1992, at A14. Jessica Mathews disagrees, noting that such "[c]onflicts are actually astonishingly rare. Of 10,000 yearly consultations with the Fish and Wildlife Service for various federal permits and approvals, an average of 25 are found to jeopardize a listed species, and many of these conflicts are easily resolved by modifying the project." Mathews, It's *Not* Jobs vs. Endangered Species, Wash. Post, Jan. 26, 1992, at C7. A study by World Wildlife Fund found that between 1987 and 1991 only 19 federal activities out of almost 75,000 projects were blocked because of irreconcilable conflicts with endangered species. World Wildlife Fund, For Conserving Species, Talk Is Cheaper Than We Think (1992). While more than 2,000 formal consultations between federal agencies and the Fish and Wildlife or National Marine Fisheries Service resulted in the issuance of 353 opinions holding that a project might jeopardize a protected species, in nearly every case alternatives were developed that allowed the project to go forward. Noting that 29 airplanes crashed into buildings during

this period, Nature Conservancy president John C. Sawhill states that "a developer faced a greater chance during that time of having an airplane crash into something he built than having a project stopped by the Endangered Species Act." Sawhill, Saving Endangered Species Doesn't Endanger Economy, Wall St. J., Feb. 20, 1992, at A15. Developers argue that these statistics do not reflect the full impact of the ESA because many projects are abandoned after informal consultations that do not show up in the statistics. Kenworthy, Wildlife Protection Stops Few Projects, Study Asserts, Wash. Post, Feb. 11, 1992, at A19.

2. If the Endangered Species Act were amended to permit greater balancing of interests, what factors would you balance to resolve a controversy like that surrounding the spotted owl? What weight would you give to each of those factors, and how would you incorporate uncertainty in your analysis?

3. Public opinion polls show strong support for the Endangered Species Act. A poll released in 1992 showed that voters supported the Act by 66 percent to 11 percent. When asked to choose between protecting species or saving jobs and businesses, species protection won out by a margin of 48 percent to 29 percent. Sawhill, above, at A15. What factors might explain the public's strong support for the Act?

= 9 =

Protection of the Global Environment

By the end of the next decade, the die will pretty well be cast. As the world enters the twenty-first century, the community of nations either will have rallied and turned back the threatening trends, or environmental deterioration and social disintegration will be feeding on each other. The ultimate rationale for a massive social mobilization to safeguard the earth is summed up in a bit of graffiti painted on a bridge in Rock Creek Park in Washington, D.C. It says, "Good planets are hard to find."*

Perhaps the most stunning recent development in environmental policy has been the rapid rise of international concern for the environment. Environmental problems increasingly are viewed as transcending national borders and, in some cases, posing major risks to the health of the planet that could cause worldwide economic and social dislocation. The globalization of environmental concern is having a profound impact on international trade and diplomacy, stimulating the development of new international legal regimes that will assume an increasingly important role in environmental policy in coming years.

The globalization of environmental problems is a product of many factors including rapid worldwide population growth, the increasing scale of international economic activity, and improvements in scientific understanding of mankind's impact on earth's ecosystems. The current world population of 5.3 billion is expected to more than double during the next century, with more than 90 percent of the increase occurring in the poorest countries. World Commission on Environment and Development, Our Common Future 2 (1987). As global economic activity increases from $13 trillion to $100 trillion over the next several decades, the nations of the world will become even more interdependent, both economically and ecologically. Global environmental problems are what

---

*Outlining a Global Action Plan, in L. Brown, C. Flavin, and F. Postel, State of the World 1989, at 192 (1989).

the World Commission on Environment and Development has termed "interlocking crises" spawned by the ecological impact of human activity and the need to meet basic needs of a rapidly growing world population. After introducing international environmental law, this chapter explores how these crises are stimulating new responses to ozone depletion, global warming, and environmental concerns raised by international trade and development policies.

A. INTRODUCTION TO INTERNATIONAL ENVIRONMENTAL LAW

Unlike domestic law, where common law, legislation, and constitutional provisions provide a reasonably clear framework for the operation of environmental regulation, international law depends largely on negotiations and political relationships to define the rights and responsibilities of sovereign states. For the most part, international law operates with "little procedural hierarchy" and does not give any court or agency an "accepted primacy over another." M. Janis, An Introduction to International Law 7 (1988). Litigation and adjudication are rare. International law is "soft law" that is largely the product of international diplomacy and custom and whose enforcement depends less on "legal" sanctions than on "moral" suasion or fear of diplomatic retribution. Id. at 2.

INTERNATIONAL ENVIRONMENTAL LAW: A PATHFINDER

International environmental law materials can pose difficult research challenges for students. *Treaties* to which the United States is a party are published by the U.S. State Department in United States Treaties and Other International Agreements (UST). Prior to the appearance of the bound volumes of UST, slips of such treaties were published by the U.S. Government Printing Office (GPO) as Treaties and Other International Acts (TIAS). Treaties can be shepardized through Shepard's United States Citations: Statutes. The GPO also issues an annual publication, Treaties in Force: A List of Treaties and Other International Agreements of the United States. Treaties to which the United States is not a party can be found in the United Nations publication Multilateral Treaties Deposited with the Secretary-General.

Valuable *periodicals* include the Bureau of National Affairs' weekly International Environment Reporter, the monthly Department of State Bulletin, which reports on developments in international relations and is accessible through NEXIS, Environment magazine, and the European Environmental Review. A comprehensive, up-to-date compendium of documents relevant to public and private international law (including treaties to which the United States is not a party) can be found in the American Society of International Law's bimonthly publication, ILM: International Legal Materials, which is accessible through LEXIS. The Worldwatch Institute also publishes a bimonthly magazine entitled Worldwatch. Newsletters include UNEP News, published by the U.N. Environment Programme, and the OECD Observer.

The Worldwatch Institute publishes an annual State of the World report that reviews environmental trends, as does the World Resources Institute (World Resources 1991-1992). The World Wildlife Fund's International Atlas of the Environment also provides valuable data on international environmental conditions. Greenpeace and the World Wildlife Fund are among the largest *environmental groups* active in the international arena. The Center for International Environmental Law, which has offices in Washington and London, specializes in this area. NRDC and EDF also have active international programs.

Useful references for further research include Developments in the Law—International Environmental Law, 104 Harv. L. Rev. 1484 (1991) and Schaffer, Researching International Law, 1 Geo. Intl. Envtl. L. Rev. 199 (1988).

The clearest and most significant source of international environmental law is agreements between sovereign states. International treaties or conventions are akin to contracts in that they derive their legal force from the consent of the parties. Bilateral agreements to address cross-boundary environmental problems long have been popular. As discussed in Chapter 2, the Boundary Waters Treaty of 1909 between the United States and Canada served as the basis for the *Trail Smelter* decision, and the Migratory Bird Treaty of 1916 between the same nations gave rise to the Missouri v. Holland decision. While President Theodore Roosevelt's attempt to convene a world conference on conservation of natural resources failed in 1909, multilateral agreements, like the Montreal Protocol on Substances that Deplete the Ozone Layer, are becoming a more accepted means for addressing global environmental problems. The 1990 report of the Council on Environmental Quality lists 140 international treaties and conventions relating to the environment, most of which were signed after 1970. CEQ, Environmental Quality—Twentieth Annual Report 401 (1990). The United States is a party to approximately one-third of these agreements, many of which have influenced the practices of nonsignatories. J. Sebenius, Crafting a Winning Coalition, in Greenhouse Warming: Negotiating a Global Regime 69, 70-71 (1991) (some provisions of the Law of the Sea may be effective despite U.S. refusal to ratify the Convention).

In the absence of express agreements between sovereigns, international law also can be derived from customary practices observed by nations in the course of their international relations, which give rise to reliance interests. In addition to customary law, the domestic practices of most or all states can be a source for deriving general principles of international law. The assumption is that rules observed by nearly all sovereigns are sufficiently fundamental to be deemed a component of international law. M. Janis, An Introduction to International Law 4-5 (1988).

Like domestic common law, international law has rarely dealt effectively with transboundary pollution problems. The *Trail Smelter* arbitration in 1935 relied on common law nuisance principles recognized in Missouri v. Illinois and Georgia v. Tennessee Copper to hold a Canadian smelter liable for damage caused in the United States. The decision, however, is virtually the only decision involving adjudication of a transboundary pollution dispute, and its precedential value is limited because it was founded on unusual stipulations and a bilateral agreement establishing procedures for resolving such disputes. Developments in the Law—International Environment Law, 104 Harv. L. Rev. 1484, 1500-1501 (1991). In addition to the problem of proving causal injury that has plagued the common law, there is no systematic set of legal procedures governing most international pollution disputes.

Efforts to develop general principles for resolving transboundary pollution disputes and for combating other international environmental problems have proceeded in both regional and global intergovernmental organization (IGOs). In 1972 the United Nations convened the first Conference on the Human Environment in Stockholm. The 133 nations who were represented at the conference approved the Stockholm Declaration on Human Environment, which outlines international environmental rights and responsibilities in strong, but highly general, language. Principle I of the Stockholm Declaration provides that "Man has the fundamental right to freedom, equality and adequate conditions of life, in an environment of quality that permits a life of dignity and well-being." The Declaration states that governments have a responsibility to protect and improve the environment for both present and future generations. While it recognizes that nations have "the sovereign right to exploit their own resources pursuant to their own environmental policies," it declares that they also have "the responsibility to ensure that activities within their jurisdiction or control do not cause damage to the environment of other States or of areas beyond the limits of national jurisdiction." Stockholm Declaration on the Human Environment, Principle 21.

Although it left the development of more specific principles of international environmental law to future negotiation, the Stockholm Conference was a landmark event. It launched a process of international collaboration on environmental policy and lead to creation of the United Nations Environment Programme (UNEP). International cooperation intensified after a followup conference in Nairobi, UNEP's headquarters, in 1982. The Nairobi conference led to the creation of the World Commission on Environment and Development. In 1987 the Commission issued a report, entitled Our Common Future, which proposed that the U.N. develop an international convention outlining new environmental rights and responsibilities for all nations based on principles of sustainable development. Noting that no effective mechanism exists for settling international environmental disputes through binding procedures, the Commission proposed that new procedures be established to facilitate resolution of disputes parties are unable to resolve through negotiation.

UNEP's activities, and the Stockholm and Nairobi conferences, have helped to promote international environmental agreements, such as the Montreal Protocol, that address specific environmental problems. Petsonk, The Role of the United Nations Environment Programme (UNEP) in the Development of International Environmental Law, 5 Am. U.J. Intl. L. 351 (1990). The process initiated with the 1972 Stockholm Conference continued with the 1992 United Nations Conference on Environment and Development in Rio de Janeiro. After lengthy negotiations in preparation for the Rio Conference, representatives from more than 160 nations reached agreement in April 1992 on a Declaration of Principles to be released at the Conference. Reaffirming, and building on, the 1972 Stockholm Declaration, the Declaration articulates principles to promote "a new and equitable global partnership" and to stimulate further international agreements to "protect the integrity of the global environment and developmental systems." Excerpts from the draft Declaration appear below.

United Nations Conference on Environment and Development, Draft Declaration of Principles
(1992)

The Conference on Environment and Development, . . .
Recognizing the integral and interdependent nature of the earth, our home,

Proclaims that:

Principle 1. Human beings are at the center of concerns for sustainable development. They are entitled to a healthy and productive life in harmony with nature.

Principle 2. States have, in accordance with the Charter of the United Nations and the principles of international law, the sovereign right to exploit their own resources pursuant to their own environmental and developmental policies, and the responsibility to insure that activities within their jurisdiction or control do not cause damage to the environment of other states or of areas beyond the limits of national jurisdiction.

Principle 3. The right to development must be fulfilled so as to equitably meet developmental and environmental needs of present and future generations.

Principle 4. In order to achieve sustainable development, environmental protection shall constitute an integral part of the development process and cannot be considered in isolation from it. . . .

Principle 7. States shall cooperate in a spirit of global partnership to conserve, protect and restore the health and integrity of the earth's ecosystem. In view of the different contributions to global environmental degradation, states have common but differentiated responsibilities. The developed countries acknowledge the responsibility that they bear in the international pursuit of sustainable development in view of the pressures their societies place on the global environment and of the technologies and financial resources they command.

Principle 8. To achieve sustainable development and a higher quality of life for all people, states should reduce and eliminate unsustainable patterns of production and consumption and promote appropriate demographic policies. . . .

Principle 13. States shall develop national law regarding liability and compensation for the victims of pollution and other environmental damage. States shall also cooperate in an expeditious and more determined manner to develop further international law regarding liability and compensation for adverse effects of environmental damage caused by activities within their jurisdiction or control to areas beyond their jurisdiction.

Principle 14. States should effectively cooperate to discourage or prevent the relocation and transfer to other states of any activities and substances that cause severe environmental degradation or are found to be harmful to human health.

Principle 15. In order to protect the environment, the precautionary approach shall be widely applied to states according to their capabilities. Where there are threats of serious or irreversible damage, lack of full scientific certainty shall not be used as a reason for postponing cost-effective measures to prevent environmental degradation.

Principle 16. National authorities should endeavor to promote the internalization of environmental costs and the use of economic instruments, taking into account the approach that the polluter should, in principle, bear the cost of pollution, with due regard to the public interest and without distorting international trade and investment.

NOTES AND QUESTIONS

1. What is the value of the UNCED Declaration? Does it articulate any new substantive principles of international environmental law? Does it create any new rights or provide any new remedies for addressing international environmental problems?

2. In language virtually identical to the 1972 Stockholm Declaration, the UNCED Declaration reaffirms each nation's right to exploit its own resources and its responsibility to prevent extraterritorial damage. How much guidance does the Declaration provide concerning how to balance the competing values implicated by environmental protection? Compare the Declaration's treatment of these issues with that of U.S. environmental law.

3. Tensions between developing countries and the industrialized world are reflected throughout the UNCED Declaration. Other portions of the Declaration declare eradication of poverty to be "an indispensible requirement for sustainable development" and state that the needs of developing countries "shall be given special priority." Noting that environmental "[s]tandards applied by some countries may be inappropriate and of unwarranted economic and social cost to other countries," it recommends that further measures to address "trans-boundary or global environmental problems should, as far as possible, be based on an international consensus."

4. Declarations of international principles have been of limited value in the absence of an effective mechanism for applying and enforcing them. Lang, Environmental Protection: The Challenge for International Law, 20 J. World Trade L. 489, 490 (1986). While vague norms of international liability may have some impact on the behavior of nations, international law has yet to provide meaningful relief for even the most egregious examples of transboundary pollution, such as radiation from the Chernobyl nuclear power plant accident. Handl, Paying the Piper for Transboundary Nuclear Damage: State Liability in a System of Transnational Compensation, and Goldie, Liability for Nuclear Accidents, in International Law and Pollution (D. Macgraw, ed. 1991). Proposals to apply strict liability principles in international law have made little headway, McCaffrey, International Liability and International Watercourses: The Work of the International Law Commission Relating to International Pollution, in id. at 90-119, although there is

some interest in elevating environmental protection to the status of a fundamental human right.

Most international disputes that are adjudicated are decided by domestic, rather than international, courts. M. Janis, An Introduction to International Law 6 (1988). While some international tribunals have been established (e.g., the International Court of Justice (ICJ), the European Court of Justice, and the European Court of Human Rights), sovereign states are reluctant to accede legal responsibility to a foreign tribunal. Proposals to create an international body with authority to enforce standards of environmental conduct have been opposed by nations fearful of encroachments on their sovereignty. G. Porter and J. Brown, Global Environmental Politics 152-156 (1991). Arrangements for adjudicating transboundary environmental disputes through new regional legal structures eventually may prove more effective. The European Community plans to apply uniform environmental standards through a single European Environmental Agency with enforcement available in the European Court of Justice.

5. Efforts to control international environmental problems have employed three general approaches: (1) bilateral or multilateral treaties that respond to regional or global problems (such as depletion of the ozone layer), (2) negotiations or arbitrations to resolve transboundary disputes, and (3) application of domestic law to influence extraterritorial activities (e.g., through trade sanctions or consumer boycotts). A variety of creative strategies have been employed to overcome political obstacles to the establishment and implementation of international standards. In the article that follows, Peter Sand, a senior environmental affairs officer with the U.N. Economic Commission for Europe, describes these approaches. We then examine how they have been used in efforts to protect the global atmosphere.

Sand, Lessons Learned in Global Environmental Governance
WRI Publications Brief (June 1990)

INNOVATIONS IN STANDARD-SETTING

International standards have traditionally been set through treaties. An ad hoc diplomatic conference negotiates and adopts a treaty, which takes effect after a specified number of nations ratify it. This diplomatic route has two main drawbacks: the need for consensus leads to standards set at the lowest common denominator, and the need for ratification ties implementation to the speed of the slowest boats in the convoy.

A process this antiquated and cumbersome is no match for global environmental problems that involve unforeseeable change, sometimes under crisis conditions. The capacity to track frequent, rapid change is critical to international environmental governance. Can this classical process be renovated to suit modern needs?

Asymmetry: Beating the Lowest-Common-Denominator Rule

The sway of the lowest common denominator is well documented in existing international regimes, where collective action is often limited to what the least enthusiastic party will accept. But there are several options for making ambitious—or at least better-than-minimum—standards appeal to prospective parties.

Selective incentives may persuade a reluctant party to accept standards through the familiar parliamentary practice of judiciously distributing special favors to build a coalition or a majority. A case in point is the 1987 Montreal Protocol on Substances That Deplete the Ozone Layer. Soviet factories under construction were grandfathered in, European Community nations were allowed to aggregate their national consumption limits, and developing countries allowed to postpone compliance by ten years. It is easy to criticize the Montreal Protocol as riddled with loopholes, but without them it would either have lost vital signatories or jelled at a lower level of collective commitment. Paradoxically, loopholes can raise the general level of obligation above the predictable common denominator.

Differential obligations imply a strategy that does not even pretend to treat states equally. The European Community's 1988 Directive Limiting Emissions of Atmospheric Pollutants from Large Combustion Plants deliberately skews obligations to take account of members' differing economic and technological states. This strategy is also applied to funding in the Vienna/Montreal ozone agreements, under which Singapore pays $1500 annually but has the same membership rights as the United States, which pays $300,000. Skewing is carried a step farther in the "critical loads" approach that aims at equitable rather than equal sharing, as in the 1988 Sofia Protocol Concerning the Control of Emissions of Nitrogen Oxides of Their Transboundary Fluxes.

Regional solidarity facilitates custom-built asymmetrical regimes because compensatory trade-offs are easier to devise for countries with geographic or cultural affinities. Regional marine protection agreements—say, the 1974 Helsinki and Paris Conventions for the Baltic and the North Sea—generally involve greater cooperation than global agreements do.

Over-achievement by lead countries can have a bandwagon effect that raises targets. The 1985 Helsinki Protocol was first to introduce an "upwardly mobile" target by calling for sulphur-emission reductions of "at least 30 percent." By 1988, twelve parties had already reached the 30-percent target and ten had announced that they would go on to reduce emissions by more than 50 percent. Similarly, the 1987 Montreal Protocol settled after much hard bargaining for CFC reductions of 50 percent by 1999, but in March 1989 the 12-member European Community triggered the next step by pledging 85-percent reductions "as soon as possible" and a complete phase-out of CFCs by the year 2000. While this upward revision of the bottom line was partly due to new evidence about the Antarctic ozone hole, worldwide publicity given to over-achievers also proved influential.

Fast Tracks: Beating the Slowest-Boat Rule

The most serious drawback of the treaty system is the time lag between drafting, adoption, and entry into force. The 1982 UN Convention on the Law of the Sea, for instance, took fourteen years to negotiate and has yet to take effect. Signed by 157 countries between 1982 and 1984, the treaty does not enter into force until 60 of its signatories ratify it (42 have done so).

Provisional treaty application is one way to bypass ratification delays. A classical example is the 1947 General Agreement on Tariffs and Trade (GATT), which never legally came into force, but has operated for more than forty years now under a provisional protocol. A recent environmental example is the 1989 Basel Convention on the Control of Transboundary Movements of Hazardous Wastes, which avoids anarchy associated with ratification delays by resolving that signatories shall act in accord with the convention without waiting for it to come into force.

Soft-law options allow states to forgo treaty-making altogether, through joint declaration of common rules of conduct (as opposed to the "hard law" of treaties). Soft law can take effect instantly, but the very informality that makes it an attractive short-cut also makes it inherently risky. For instance, no sooner had the West German Minister for the Environment signed the 1988 Sofia Declaration on the 30% Reduction of Nitrogen Oxide Emissions than the Secretary of State for Economic Affairs publicly questioned the declaration's legal force. UNEP's Government Council has been a prolific soft-lawmaker, issuing a whole series of declarations and "guidelines," some of which served as forerunners of treaties.

Delegated law-making is yet another way of bypassing ratification, by ceding to a specialized intergovernmental body the power to adopt and regularly amend technical standards. Among the most advanced regulatory regimes patterned along these lines are the World Health

Organization's international health regulations and the World Meteorological Organization's standard practices and procedures.

Beating both the lowest-common-denominator and slowest-boat syndromes is a tall order—but one existing institution fills it. Under the 1944 Chicago Convention on International Civil Aviation, the Council of the International Civil Aviation Organization (ICAO) has since 1981 laid down worldwide standards on aircraft noise and engine emissions. Once the Council adopts a technical annex by two-thirds majority, it becomes mandatory without ratification for all states that do not within 60 days notify the Council that they will apply different national rules, and for all air traffic over the high seas. This flexible opt-out system, specifically designed to accommodate the divergent requirements of developed and developing nations, makes it comparatively easy to adjust technical standards by majority agreement, without forcing complete uniformity. The ICAO method of standard-setting is probably the closest thing to global environmental legislation developed so far.

NOTES AND QUESTIONS

1. In what respects are the problems Sand identifies in obtaining and implementing international consensus—standards being set to accommodate the least common denominator and delays in implementation—similar to problems arising in a federal system? In what circumstances is decision-making by consensus required in domestic environmental policy (e.g., siting decisions)? Does it actually operate to produce less stringent or more stringent environmental standards? How important a factor is delay in the promulgation and implementation of domestic environmental regulations? Can you identify aspects of U.S. environmental regulation that are similar to some of the strategic responses Sand identifies?

2. U.S. environmental regulation has had an important influence on the policies of other governments as approaches developed in the United States are adapted elsewhere. For example, some version of the EIS process is now used in many parts of the world. Professor John Bonine suggests that four U.S. initiatives have been particularly influential throughout the world: the creation of national parks, the Freedom of Information Act, the EIS process, and citizen suits. Bonine, A Voice from the Wilderness, Calling Your Name, 6 Yale J. on Reg. 393 (1989). See also Developments in the Law—International Environmental Law, 104 Harv. L. Rev. 1484, 1599-1604 (1991).

3. U.S. environmental law has given U.S. citizens much greater opportunity to participate in the process of formulating and implementing environmental standards than citizens of other countries. Spurred by citizen organizations in the United States and Europe, non-

governmental organizations (NGOs) recently have become a major force in the development of international environmental law. For example, NGOs played a major role in persuading governments opposed to whaling to join the International Whaling Commission (IWC) in numbers sufficient to enact a global ban on commercial whaling. Despite the unusual powers of the IWC, Japan, South Korea, and Iceland now threaten to defy the whaling ban, a situation that illustrates the difficulty of enforcing international standards against nations who perceive economic disadvantages from them.

4. Some argue that there are inherent limits to what can be accomplished through international agreements. While participation in international agreements can improve a government's image, commitments that go beyond standards required by domestic legislation risk political trouble at home. The negotiations preparatory to the Rio Conference featured sharp differences in the positions of developed and developing countries concerning the level of assistance the developed world should provide to help developing countries invest in environmental controls. Developing countries also may resist efforts to look to international custom as a source of international law if they did not participate in the development of those customs. Id. at 1505-1506.

B.   PROTECTION OF THE GLOBAL ATMOSPHERE

The discovery that air pollutants are causing long-term, and potentially irreversible, damage to the global atmosphere has been a powerful catalyst for the development of international environmental law. Unlike transboundary pollution that primarily affects countries downwind or downriver, pollution of the Earth's atmosphere threatens serious damage to the entire planet. Mounting evidence of damage to this global commons has forced the countries of the world to join together in unprecedented efforts to develop international air pollution controls.

Ozone depletion and global warming are the two principal problems caused by pollution of the global atmosphere. The discovery in 1985 of a hole in the Earth's ozone layer over Antarctica stimulated intense intergovernmental negotiations. These negotiations culminated in a remarkable diplomatic achievement, the signing of the Montreal Protocol on Substances that Deplete the Ozone Layer in September 1987.

The Montreal Protocol's innovative approach for implementing global, technology-forcing regulation in the face of widely disparate national interests and considerable scientific and technological uncertainty has become a model for the development of international environmental controls. The sections that follow explore the complex process that led to the Montreal Protocol and efforts to use it as a model for developing an effective international response to global warming.

1. Ozone Depletion

High in the Earth's stratosphere is a layer of ozone, an unstable compound of three oxygen atoms, that is essential to the health of the planet. Because ozone absorbs certain wavelengths of ultraviolet radiation, it protects the Earth from excessive radiation that otherwise would cause millions of skin cancer deaths, widespread blindness, and other serious health problems, as well as severe damage to plants and animals.

A. Scientific Warnings

In 1974 two scientists from the University of California, Sherwood Rowland and Mario Molina, published a paper suggesting that the ozone layer could be threatened with destruction from a family of chemicals once hailed as a miracle of modern science. Chlorofluorocarbons (CFCs), chemicals used in a wide variety of industrial applications including aerosol propellants, foam blowing, air conditioning, and solvents, were discovered in the 1920s but only used widely beginning in the 1950s. Ironically, much of their attraction stemmed from their lack of other environmental risks—they are not toxic or flammable, and they have excellent insulating, cooling, and cleaning properties. Weisskopf, CFCs: Rise and Fall of Chemical "Miracle," Wash. Post, April 10, 1988.

The inventor of CFCs, Thomas Midgley, a chemist also credited with developing tetraethyl lead, created the chemical as a new coolant to facilitate mass production of refrigerators. Subsequently developed under the trade name Freon, "CFCs not only made home refrigerators safe and reliable but also facilitated a national food distribution network, redesigned comfort and shaped social habits." Id. About 2 billion pounds of CFCs were used worldwide in the late 1980s, with the value of equipment using CFCs exceeding $100 billion in the United States alone.

The remarkable stability of CFCs allows them to remain in the atmosphere for up to a century or more, unlike conventional air pollutants, which are broken down in a period of hours or days. Thus, Rowland and Molina hypothesized that CFCs would reach the upper atmosphere, where they could be broken apart by the intense energy of the sun, releasing chlorine. The chlorine would then act as a catalyst, converting ozone (O_3) to oxygen, destroying the Earth's protective ozone shield.

Rowland and Molina's study sparked considerable research that confirmed that their hypothesis was theoretically sound, though it was not possible then to prove definitively that CFCs actually were destroying the ozone layer. Testifying before a congressional committee, an executive from the E. I. du Pont de Nemours Co., a major CFC producer, argued that the "chlorine-ozone hypothesis is at this time purely speculative with no concrete evidence . . . to support it." However, he pledged that if it could be established that "chlorofluorocarbons cannot be used without a threat to health, DuPont will stop production of these compounds." Fluorocarbons: Impact on Health and Environment, Hearings before the House Comm. on Interstate & Foreign Commerce, 93d Cong., 2d Sess. 381 (1974).

In the mid-1970s the United States accounted for almost one-half of global CFC use, the majority of it used as propellants for aerosol sprays. As publicity focused on potential harm to the ozone layer, American consumers stopped buying aerosol sprays (including those without CFCs); in less than two years the market for products with such sprays dropped by two-thirds without any government regulation. Competing manufacturers began advertising that their products did not contain chemicals thought to harm the ozone layer. While disputing the notion that CFCs threatened the ozone layer, industry eventually agreed, after several states initiated regulatory proceedings, that federal regulation would be preferable to potentially conflicting state standards. R. Benedick, Ozone Diplomacy: New Directions in Safeguarding the Planet 31 (1991) (hereinafter Ozone Diplomacy); L. Dotto and H. Schiff, The Ozone War 195-197 (1978).

In March 1978 regulations were jointly issued by EPA (under TSCA), the FDA, and the CPSC to limit the use of CFCs in "nonessential" aerosol propellants (military and medical uses were exempted). (Congress also gave EPA broad authority to limit CFCs in the 1977 Clean Air Act Amendments; see part B, title I.) T. Stoel, A. Miller, and B. Milroy, Fluorocarbon Regulation: An International Comparison 218-223 (1980). While Canada, Norway, and Sweden followed suit, other European governments that were large CFC users did not. Acting through the European Community, they eventually adopted largely meaningless restrictions on aerosols and a "cap" on production that actually allowed for growth of more than 60 percent.

Pressure for companies in the United States to develop alternatives to CFCs continued to build following a further warning of the threat to the ozone layer from the National Academy of Sciences in 1979. But this pressure evaporated in the early 1980s after equivocal research results and the Reagan Administration's deregulation campaign resulted in the announcement that the United States would no longer support international controls. Convinced that further regulation was unlikely, U.S. companies shelved research to develop CFC substitutes.

Beginning in 1981, a UNEP environmental law committee began regular meetings to discuss a possible international agreement to protect the ozone layer. Initially there was some hope for an agreement in time for the tenth anniversary of the Stockholm Declaration in 1982. But it was not until 1983, after William Ruckelshaus had succeeded Anne Gorsuch Burford as EPA administrator, that the United States reversed its position and supported international controls. Not surprisingly, the United States advocated a policy based on what it had already done, that is, a worldwide ban on aerosol propellant uses of CFCs. The European governments, in turn, advocated a ban on construction of new capacity—a policy in effect in the European Community and without adverse economic consequences due to substantial excess CFC production capacity. Leaders of European industry and government "felt that the Americans had been panicked into 'over-hasty measures' . . ." R. Benedick, Ozone Diplomacy 33 (1991). Eager "to preserve market dominance and to avoid for as long as possible the costs of switching to alternative products," executives of large European chemical companies were even allowed to represent their governments on official delegations during subsequent international negotiations. Id. These executives "and their government colleagues, treated the ozone threat as trivial and were openly cynical about the objectives and prospects of the negotiations." Id. Finding agreement on regulation impossible, the parties in March 1985 approved the Vienna Convention to Protect the Ozone Layer, which established a framework to govern future scientific cooperation and negotiations.

While a major, international research effort under the auspices of the World Meteorological Organization and UNEP was under way, scientists with the British Antarctic Survey published startling findings in May 1985. Based on measurements of springtime levels of ozone in the stratosphere over Halley Bay, Antarctica, they found that seasonal ozone loss had sharply accelerated to the point where a "hole" of greatly diminished ozone levels in the stratosphere had grown to cover an area the size of the United States. These findings were so astonishing that the scientists had delayed publication of them for three years while double-checking their accuracy. Because this discovery indicated that the ozone layer was in far greater jeopardy than previously thought, it spurred more detailed investigations and intensified international negotiations. In 1987 the Airborne Antarctic Ozone Experiment, using high-altitude airplanes, ground monitors, and satellites, launched studies that eventually found even greater ozone loss and linked it to the presence of manmade chemicals in the stratosphere. See CFCs and Stratospheric Ozone, 19 Ambio (Oct. 1990) (special issue).

B. THE MONTREAL PROTOCOL

Even before international research could pinpoint the role of CFCs in ozone depletion, the discovery of the ozone "hole" had demonstrated the vulnerability of the ozone layer. This contributed to a heightened sense of urgency that spurred international negotiations based on the framework established by the Vienna Convention. Four negotiating sessions, beginning in Geneva in December 1986, culminated in the signing of the Montreal Protocol on Substances that Deplete the Ozone Layer in September 1987. The Protocol called for a freeze on production and consumption of CFCs and halons at 1986 levels, followed by a 50 percent reduction in CFC use by industrialized countries over a ten-year period. While developing countries were allowed to increase CFC consumption for ten years, trade restrictions were imposed on imports to, and exports from, nonparties to the Protocol.

The Protocol represented a remarkable diplomatic achievement given the obstacles to agreement on international environmental controls. First, the science of ozone depletion was highly uncertain throughout the entire negotiation process. S. Roan, The Ozone Crisis (1989). Year-to-year measurements of global ozone had shown no statistically significant changes. Estimates of eventual ozone loss—anticipated to occur decades later—actually had *declined* from about 18 percent in 1979 to only 3 percent in 1983. Despite the discovery of the ozone "hole," scientists were unable to link it precisely to CFCs until after the Protocol was completed (some environmentalists even had sought to delay negotiations in hopes that better evidence would become available). R. Benedick, Ozone Diplomacy 9-20 (1991).

To further challenge negotiators, CFCs had high economic value and powerful advocates in industry who argued that reasonable substitutes were unavailable for many applications. Public concern was evident in the United States, but some Europeans were skeptical of U.S. motives. At the outset of the negotiations, the United States, which already had taken unilateral action against aerosols, was virtually the only major country actively seeking CFC reductions. Moreover, developing countries maintained that it would be unfair to restrict their access to a technology that had contributed to development of the industrialized world. Finally, the concept of damage to the ozone layer was not easily translated into identifiable risks except for skin cancer, a relatively manageable disease that afflicts only a subset of the population. Id.; Mathews, Introduction and Overview, in Greenhouse Warming: Negotiating a Global Regime (J. Mathews, ed. 1991).

In the excerpt that follows, Richard Benedick, the chief U.S. negotiator, describes the factors that contributed to the success of the Protocol negotiations and the lessons they hold for future international agreements on environmental standards.

R. Benedick, Ozone Diplomacy
5-7 (1991)

The success at Montreal can be attributed to no single prime cause. Rather, a combination of planning and chance, of key factors and events, made an agreement possible. Nevertheless, certain elements . . . are particularly relevant for policymakers struggling to find viable approaches to such comparable issues as climate change.

First and foremost was the indispensable *role of science* in the ozone negotiations. Scientific theories and discoveries alone, however, were not sufficient to influence policy. The best scientists and the most advanced technological resources had to be brought together in a cooperative effort to build an international scientific consensus. Close collaboration between scientists and government officials was also crucial. Scientists were drawn out of their laboratories and into the negotiating process, and they had to assume an unaccustomed and occasionally uncomfortable shared responsibility for the policy implications of their findings. For their part, political and economic decision makers needed to understand the scientists, to fund the necessary research, and to be prepared to undertake internationally coordinated actions based on realistic and responsible assessments of risks.

Second, the *power of knowledge and of public opinion* was a formidable factor in the achievement at Montreal. A well-informed public was the prerequisite to mobilizing the political will of governments and to weakening industry's resolve to defend the chemicals. The findings of scientists had to be made accessible and disseminated. Legislative hearings helped in airing scientific opinion and policy alternatives. The media, particularly press and television, played a vital role in bringing the issue before the public and thereby stimulating political interest. Both UNEP and the U.S. government undertook major public education campaigns on ozone and CFCs, using traditional diplomatic channels as well as various communications media. These efforts, aimed at both governments and citizenries, helped influence several countries to change their initial positions on the need for regulations.

Third, because of the global scope of the issues, the *activities of a multilateral institution* were critical to the success of the negotiations. UNEP commanded respect for its commitment and its sensitivity to national interests, particularly in the developing countries. UNEP was indispensable in mobilizing data and informing world public opinion, as well as during the negotiating and implementing phases. It was UNEP—inviting, cajoling, and pressuring governments to the bargaining table—that broadened the protocol to a global dimension. UNEP also provided an objective international forum, free of the time-consuming debates on irrelevant political issues that have often marred the work of other UN bodies. . . . In sum, UNEP went far beyond a traditional secretariat function: it was a model for effective multilateral action.

Fourth, an *individual nation's policies and leadership* made a major difference. The United States undertook such leadership in achieving international agreement on ozone protection. The U.S. government set the example by being the first to take regulatory action against the suspect chemicals. Later, it developed a comprehensive global plan for protecting the ozone layer and tenaciously campaigned for its international acceptance through bilateral and multilateral initiatives. The staff of the U.S. Environmental Protection Agency (EPA) labored tirelessly to develop volumes of analyses on all aspects of the problem that gradually had an impact on skeptics both at home and abroad. A negotiating strategy devised by the U.S. Department of State not only employed customary diplomacy but also capitalized on the expertise of the EPA and the National Aeronautics and Space Administration (NASA), as well as involving Congress, environmental groups, industry, and the media.

The progressive U.S. policies on ozone, reinforced by the size and importance of the United States as the largest single producer and consumer of CFCs and halons, enabled it to play a formative central role in the drive for international controls. Other nations, however, also had a share of leadership and influence. The Federal Republic of Germany, for example, was instrumental in turning around the European Community's initially negative position. And the ozone history demonstrated that even countries with small or negligible shares of production or consumption could exert a disproportionate leverage on the course of events: Canada and Norway were consistent leaders from the very start in pushing for strong measures to protect the ozone layer, and Australia, Finland, and New Zealand played major roles in decisions to strengthen the treaty in 1990.

Fifth, *private-sector organizations*—industry and citizens' groups—participated actively, and usually with opposing objectives, in the ozone diplomacy. Environmental organizations warned the general public of the risks, pressured governments to act, and promoted research and legislation. Industrial associations and individual firms also mounted efforts to influence public and official opinion; industry's outlook and actions were crucial, since the technical solutions to the problems ultimately depended on its cooperation. Representatives of industrial and environmental groups attended the ozone negotiations as observers, offering their differing perspectives to both negotiators and media representatives.

Sixth, the *process* involved in reaching the ozone accord was itself a determining factor. Subdividing this complex problem into more manageable components during a prenegotiating phase proved invaluable. Well before the opening of formal negotiations for an ozone protocol, informal scientific and economic workshops generated creative ideas and laid the foundation for international consensus. This fact-finding process was instrumental in overcoming the arguments for delaying action. The extensive preliminary scientific and diplomatic groundwork enabled the subsequent negotiations to move forward relatively rapidly.

Finally, unlike traditional international treaties that seek to cement a status quo, the Montreal Protocol was deliberately designed as a *flexible and dynamic instrument*. Relying on periodic scientific, economic, environmental, and technological assessments, it can be readily adapted to evolving conditions. The treaty's provisions . . . incorporate innovative solutions to equity and technical problems. Indeed, the protocol's essence is that, far from being a static solution, it constitutes an ongoing process. This factor was clearly demonstrated in the events leading to the substantial strengthening and modification of the treaty at the Second Meeting of Parties in London in June 1990. As UNEP's [executive director, Mostafa] Tolba observed: "The mechanisms we design for the Protocol will—very likely—become the blueprint for the institutional apparatus designed to control greenhouse gases and adaptation to climate change."

NOTES AND QUESTIONS

1. The Role of Science. Richard Benedick does not attribute the success of the negotiations to the discovery of the ozone hole because its cause had not been established when the Protocol was signed. Others disagree, arguing that the ozone hole led to media and public interest that in turn influenced political perceptions. Benedick notes that close collaboration and communication between scientists and government officials played an important role in overcoming obstacles to agreement at several stages of the negotiations. For example, scientific assessment of the relative ozone-depleting potential of different types of CFCs and halons allowed the development of a weighting approach that permitted a broad array of CFCs and halons to be controlled as a "basket." This overcame the initial objections of the EC and Japan, who had argued that only a few chemicals should be controlled to avoid controls on others they deemed economically important. By assigning an "index number" to each chemical based on its ozone-depleting potential, the Protocol allows countries to choose the most economic mix of reductions with an incentive to concentrate on reducing substances thought to be most harmful. R. Benedick, Ozone Diplomacy 78-79 (1991). Scientists played an important role not only in the formulation of national policy but also as an informal transnational network outside government control.

2. Public Opinion: U.S. and European. Why did public opinion in the early 1970s prove to be such a potent catalyst for the aerosol ban in the United States while not being much of a factor in Europe? The British government played the leading role in opposing controls on ozone-depleting substances. Benedick notes that many Britons "tend to perceive Americans as either overreacting to environmental dangers or using ecology to mask commercial motives," citing U.S. opposition to the SST. Id. at 39. While environmental groups in Great Britain were "essentially uninterested in the ozone issue" until 1987, a group of visiting U.S. environmentalists got so much British press attention then that the British government asked the State Department to restrain them. Id.

3. *The Pursuit of Competitive Advantage.* Throughout the negotiations there was considerable jockeying among countries seeking to acquire an economic advantage over their international competition. Because the United States had taken unilateral action against CFCs in aerosols, U.S. manufacturers were more inclined to support international controls to reduce their perceived competitive disadvantage. As noted above, the EC had substantial excess capacity to produce CFCs, so it argued in favor of production, rather than consumption, controls, maintaining that the latter would be impracticable. Since most countries imported CFCs rather than producing them, the EC was greatly outnumbered, and a compromise freezing and then reducing both consumption and production was adopted.

4. *One Nation, One Vote?* While the framework established by the Vienna Convention had provided a one-nation, one-vote procedure for international decision-making, the United States was concerned that this could give small countries a disproportionate influence. Concerned that U.S. industry could be placed at a competitive disadvantage if it signed a treaty that became effective without the participation of other major CFC-producing countries, the United States proposed that the Montreal Protocol not enter into force until ratified by countries that account for 90 percent of CFC consumption. Id. at 89. The parties eventually agreed that the Protocol would enter into force when signed by at least 11 parties that constitute at least two-thirds of worldwide consumption (meaning the United States and at least four of the six other large consumers— Britain, France, Germany, Italy, Japan, and what was then the Soviet Union). The U.S. Senate ratified the Montreal Protocol by a vote of 83-0 in March 1988. The Protocol entered into force on January 1, 1989 after ratification by 29 nations accounting for 83 percent of global consumption. Id. at 117. As of 1992, 72 countries had signed the Protocol.

5. *Developing Countries and the Protocol.* Developing countries, who used a tiny but growing amount of CFCs, argued that it would be unfair to subject them to the same controls as industrialized countries who created the problem. Article 5 of the Protocol responds to these

concerns. It authorizes developing countries to increase CFC consumption to meet "basic domestic needs" up to a level of 0.3 kilograms per capita for ten years, followed by a 50 percent reduction phased in over ten years. Do these provisions weaken the Protocol because they allow increases in CFC use? Benedick notes that the 0.3 kilogram level would represent approximately 25-30 percent of existing per capita consumption levels in the United States and Europe and 50-60 percent of such consumption after the Protocol's reductions took effect. Id. at 93. Why would any developing country agree to such restrictions? How likely is it that developing countries will increase their consumption of CFCs to the maximum allowed under the Protocol?

6. Hats and Sunglasses.   Benedick reports fierce opposition to the U.S. negotiating position from OMB officials, who established an interagency working group to reexamine it. This opposition backfired after it was reported that Interior Secretary Donald Hodel had argued during a White House meeting that broad-brimmed hats and sunglasses could protect against ultraviolet radiation better than regulation of CFCs. Peterson, Administration Ozone Policy May Favor Sunglasses, Hats, Wash. Post, May 29, 1987, at A1. After this spawned much public ridicule, including a Herblock cartoon of fish wearing sunglasses, Hodel, while still arguing against regulation, claimed to have been misinterpreted. Benedick reports that President Reagan later surprised everyone by personally approving the tough U.S. position. He notes that a key development was a cost-benefit analysis from the President's Council of Economic Advisers showing that, "despite the scientific and economic uncertainties, the monetary benefits of preventing future deaths from skin cancer far outweighed costs of CFC controls as estimated by industry or by EPA." R. Benedick, Ozone Diplomacy 63 (1991).

7. The Role of U.S. Industry.   Why did U.S. industry play a supportive role in the negotiations? The same companies that supported controls had actively lobbied against regulatory action until mid-1986, and even had sought weakening amendments to the Clean Air Act. See S. Roan, The Ozone Crisis 1156 (1989). In 1986 the U.S. industry lobbying group on CFCs submitted a paper to EPA arguing that substitutes were not technically feasible. See Miller, Incentives for CFC Substitutes: Lessons for Other Greenhouse Gases, in Coping with Climate Change: Proceedings of the Second North American Conference on Preparing for Climate Change (1989). Nor is it apparent that the CFC manufacturers had achieved any technological breakthroughs beyond what was available in 1980. A. Makhijani, A. Makhijani, and A. Bickel, Saving Our Skins 13 (1988). What explains the seemingly sudden and dramatic change in industry position?

8. *Technology Forcing.* The response of industry to the Protocol is remarkable as an example of technology forcing. As late as the spring of 1986, CFC producers were aggressively insisting that substitutes were not feasible and that regulation would be ruinous for many industries. Miller, Cleaning the Air While Filling Corporate Coffers: Technology Forcing and Economic Growth, 1990 N.Y.U. Ann. Survey Am. L. 69 (1991). After the Protocol was signed, substitutes for CFCs were announced at an astonishing rate, and their projected costs declined steadily. By mid-1989, industry accepted the feasibility of a complete phaseout of CFCs, and EPA estimated that a total phaseout would cost less than it had projected for a 50 percent reduction only two years earlier. Some CFC substitutes may even offer superior performance, as the electronics industry found. After initially predicting that no substitute could be developed for CFCs used in cleaning circuit boards, the industry has developed substitutes that are better and less expensive than CFCs. Some companies have even produced circuit boards that do not need cleaning. Pollack, Moving Fast to Protect the Ozone Layer, N.Y. Times, May 15, 1991, at D1.

9. *The Amendment Process.* Benedick stresses that one of the most significant elements of the Protocol is that it is a flexible and dynamic instrument designed to adapt and to evolve. The Protocol provides that the parties must review and assess control measures at least every four years in light of available scientific and economic information. A two-thirds majority of voting parties can agree to revise the production or consumption targets for CFCs or halons without the need for repeating the ratification process. As discussed below, these provisions have become very important as new evidence demonstrates that ozone depletion has progressed far faster than originally thought.

C.   Accelerating the Phaseout

In March 1988 the Ozone Trends Panel, a team of more than 100 scientists from 10 countries, released the results of 16 months of research using newly developed methodology to analyze all previous measurements of the ozone layer. The Panel's alarming findings showed that significant ozone depletion already had occurred over heavily populated areas of the northern hemisphere, that a "large, sudden, and unexpected" decline in ozone levels had occurred over Antarctica, and that an ozone "hole" might soon be found over the Arctic and mid-latitudes of the northern hemisphere. The Panel was able to conclusively link CFCs and halons to ozone depletion for the first time. Kerr, Stratospheric Ozone Is Decreasing, 239 Science 1489 (1988).

These findings spurred further action to accelerate the phaseout of ozone-depleting chemicals. Reminded of its 1974 pledge, du Pont announced that it would stop production of CFCs and halons by the end of the century. The British government abandoned its long-standing resistance to controls and endorsed efforts to strengthen the Montreal Protocol. At a meeting in Helsinki in May 1989, the parties to the Protocol agreed that a total phaseout of CFCs and halons was necessary.

In June 1990 the parties met in London to consider measures to strengthen the Protocol. Noting that industrialized nations with less than one-quarter of the world's population consumed 88 percent of the world's CFCs, developing countries pressed for measures to compensate them for switching to CFC substitutes. The results of the London negotiations are described below.

Bryk, The Montreal Protocol and Recent Developments to Protect the Ozone Layer
15 Harv. Envtl. L. Rev. 275 (1991)

The Parties convened the London meeting with three major goals in mind: (1) to expedite the total phase-out of CFCs, (2) to establish a Funding Mechanism for assistance to developing countries, and (3) to add India and China as parties to the Protocol.

1. Phase-out

While many of the Parties, including members of the European Community, favored a total phase-out of CFCs by 1997, pressure from the United States, the Soviet Union and Japan resulted in a final agreement mandating a total elimination of CFC production and use by the year 2000. Similarly, proposals for a 50% cut from baseline 1986 levels by 1993 and an 85% cut by 1995 were watered down to a 20% cut by 1993, a 50% cut by 1995 and an 85% cut by 1997. As in the Montreal Protocol, a 10 to 15% leeway in these requirements extends to developing countries. The ten-year extension in implementation for these countries also applies. The Parties further agreed that in 1992 they will "review the situation with the objective of accelerating the reduction schedule."

The Parties agreed to specific reduction schedules for halons, carbon tetrachloride, methyl chloroform, and other fully halogenated CFCs. The production and consumption rates of halons will remain frozen at 1986 levels between 1992 and 1995, but they are to be reduced by 50% by 1995 and completely phased out by the year 2000. As with CFCs, developing countries have some leeway with halon requirements. However, with respect to halons only, the Parties may agree to permit higher production and consumption levels for any country, providing they are "necessary to satisfy essential uses for which no adequate alternatives are available." "Essential uses" are not defined.

Other fully halogenated CFCs are to be reduced 20% from 1989 rates by 1993, 85% by 1997, and completely phased out by the year 2000. The 1989 levels of carbon tetrachloride will be cut 85% by 1995 and phased out by the year 2000. Methyl chloroform production and consumption will be frozen at 1989 levels by 1993, cut 30% by 1995, cut 70% by the year 2000, and finally phased out in 2005. About fifteen countries also signed a resolution proposed by Finland mandating a stricter phase-out schedule, but this agreement exists outside the formal Protocol.

The Parties debated whether to make a declaration acknowledging and confirming that HCFCs are for interim use only. HCFCs have up to 95% less ozone-depleting power than CFCs, but they do deplete the ozone layer. Some Parties expressed fear that developing countries will invest too heavily in HCFC production, thus making their eventual phaseout in fifteen years more difficult.

The Parties also debated measures to ensure a stringent phaseout plan for HCFCs. Although they considered declaring that HCFCs would eventually be controlled, the entire issue was left for a later time. This is unfortunate, since at least a foreshadowing of future strict regulation of HCFCs is necessary now, in order to prevent later claims of ignorance as an excuse for delay.

2. The Funding Mechanism

The Parties established a multilateral trust fund of $240 million to assist developing countries in meeting the requirements of the Protocol. This money is designed to facilitate financial and technical cooperation, including the transfer of technology, and to cover incremental costs such as information distribution, country-specific studies, workshops, and training sessions. The Parties immediately set up an interim fund that will run for three years, after which the full Funding Mechanism should be established. Although a newly established Secretariat in Montreal will formally administer the fund, the World Bank will probably distribute money, $80 million of which is earmarked for equal distribution between India and China, with the remainder to be divided among other developing countries.

In addition to funding, actual technology is to be transferred; substitute products will not merely be subsidized. An Executive Committee will monitor the implementation of specific operational policies and administrative arrangements, including disbursement of funds. The United

States will hold a permanent seat on the Executive Committee, which will consist of seven representatives from developing countries and seven representatives from other countries. The Parties will appoint the members of the Executive Committee by joint decision. Decisions by the Committee are to be made by consensus whenever possible, or by a two-thirds majority of those present and voting, provided that the two-thirds majority constitutes a majority of both groups of seven.

3. India and China

India and China each currently produce over 20,000 tons of CFCs a year, and studies indicate that these figures will greatly increase over the next twenty years without an agreement.

In London, delegations from China and India both stated they would recommend to their governments that they join the Protocol. Prior to this agreement, the two nations had objected to joining the Protocol because they viewed CFC use and production as integral to their development process, and the industrialized nations had been unwilling to guarantee the technical and financial assistance needed to mitigate the impacts of compliance. . . . The environmental ministers from India and China agreed to recommend to their government that they join when the multilateral fund is approved and language is added which links developing countries' compliance obligations with financial compensation and technology transfer by industrialized countries.

NOTES AND QUESTIONS

1. The creation of a fund to compensate developing countries for the extra cost of CFC substitutes illustrates the importance of efforts to address the distributional impacts of regulations. Even measures that generate net benefits in the aggregate may create some perceived "losers." Many developing countries had balked at signing the Protocol until the fund was created. China has now signed the revised Protocol, and India is expected to follow suit. The United States initially opposed the fund, arguing that existing measures to aid developing countries were adequate and that even a modest ozone fund could create demands for much larger compensation in future agreements (such as a global warming convention). To accommodate U.S. concerns, the London agreement states that the financial mechanism "is without prejudice to any future arrangements that may be developed with respect to other environmental issues" (annex II, art. 10). See generally Bowser, History of the Montreal Protocol's Ozone Fund, 14 Intl. Envt. Rep. 636 (1991).

2. EPA's implementation of the Montreal Protocol is often cited as

one of the most significant examples of the use of market-based approaches to environmental regulation. Rather than attempting to determine the emissions reductions each of the five U.S. producers of CFCs was capable of achieving, EPA simply issued tradeable permits for CFC production based on each company's 1986 production level. By buying and selling the diminishing pool of CFC production rights, companies could ensure that reductions would be obtained in the most efficient manner. Seidel and Blank, Closing an Ozone Loophole, 1990 Envtl. Forum 18-20 (Nov.-Dec. 1990). As the annual supply of permits declined in accordance with Protocol requirements, CFC prices were expected to rise sharply, creating windfall profits of several billion dollars. After EPA questioned whether it had the authority to tax CFCs to capture some of the expected windfall, Congress imposed a CFC tax in the Omnibus Budget Reconciliation Act of 1989. The tax, which became effective in January 1990, more than doubled the pre-regulation price of CFCs. The tax rate increased by more than 20 percent in 1992 and will rise almost 60 percent more in 1993, according to a schedule provided in the Act. 26 U.S.C. §§4681-4682. See Orlando, Understanding the Excise Tax on Ozone-Depleting Chemicals, 42 Tax Executive 359 (1990). The tax is expected to raise almost $6 billion between 1990 and 1996. EPA officials believe that it has been responsible for faster-than-anticipated declines in CFC production. Id.

3. In 1990 Congress adopted a host of additional measures to speed the phaseout of ozone-depleting substances when it added subtitle VI to the Clean Air Act. These provisions both implement and go beyond the requirements of the Protocol and the London amendments. Congress provided for a complete phaseout by the year 2030 of the production of hydrochlorofluorocarbons (HCFCs), chemicals that are useful as CFC substitutes but that present some lesser risk of ozone depletion, and it banned their use in appliances as a refrigerant after 2020. §605. It also banned nonessential products containing CFCs (such as plastic party streamers and noise horns), §610, and required the establishment of a national program to maximize the recapture and recycling of ozone-depleting chemicals during the servicing and repair of appliances. §608. Effective July 1, 1992, the knowing release during service or repair operations of ozone-depleting substances used as refrigerants is prohibited. §608(c).

4. Since the London revisions were made, virtually every new piece of research has found that the ozone depletion problem is worse than previously reported. In 1991, NASA scientists reported that ozone depletion was occurring much faster than was anticipated and that a seasonal reduction of several percentage points had already been measured over mid-latitudes encompassing the United States. This rate of depletion could not be explained by atmospheric models, raising new concerns that even the amended international agreement might not be adequate

to prevent significant damage to the ozone layer. Kerr, Ozone Destruction Worsens, 252 Science 204 (1991). In 1992 NASA scientists found even more dramatic evidence that ozone depletion had progressed further than expected. The highest levels of ozone-destroying chlorine ever recorded were found in the stratosphere over eastern Canada and northern New England, and evidence of ozone depletion extended as far south as Cuba. Kerr, New Assaults Seen on Earth's Ozone Shield, 255 Science 797 (1992). As a result, measures to phase out ozone-depleting chemicals that were considered bold breakthroughs when adopted now appear to be inadequate to prevent serious damage to human health and the environment.

5. The discovery that ozone depletion is more severe than anticipated has spurred unilateral action to accelerate the phaseout of ozone-depleting chemicals. The European Community has banned production of halons and accelerated the timetable for CFC phaseout to 1997. In February 1992 EPA announced that it would accelerate the phaseout of most ozone-depleting substances to December 31, 1995, except for HCFCs, which would be banned in 2005. Environmentalists argued instead for an immediate ban on the production of halons and a ban on CFC production by the end of 1994. Schneider, Bush Orders End to Manufacture of Ozone-Harming Agents by 1996, N.Y. Times, Feb. 13, 1992, at B16. Companies that make refrigerators and air conditioners criticized the accelerated phaseout of HCFCs because HCFCs are leading candidates to replace CFCs in these products. Gutfeld and Naj, Industries Attack EPA Plan to Eliminate HCFCs, A Replacement for CFCs, by 2005, Wall St. J., Feb. 13, 1992, at B3. Section 606 of the 1990 Clean Air Act Amendments expressly authorizes EPA to adopt an accelerated phaseout schedule if it determines that it is necessary to protect human health and the environment. The unilateral actions by European governments and the United States are likely to result in further strengthening of the Protocol to phase out more chemicals on a shorter timetable.

6. Because CFCs and halons already present in the stratosphere will continue to destroy ozone for decades, scientists estimate that ozone destruction will continue into the next century and that the ozone hole could persist until 2050 or 2100. It is estimated that a 10 percent decrease in ozone levels will cause 300,000 new skin cancer cases and 1.5 million cases of cataracts each year. Hole in Ozone Layer May Persist for 100 Years Because of Long Chemical Lifetimes, NASA Says, 22 Env. Rep. 2073 (1991).

2. *Global Climate Change*

Many scientists believe that, as a result of the buildup of carbon dioxide and other gases in the atmosphere, the Earth is on the verge of un-

precedented global climate change. If predictions of a worldwide temperature increase of 3-8° Farenheit by the middle of the next century
prove accurate, many fear widespread disruption of the Earth's ecosystems, a rise in sea level, increased drought, and potentially vast environmental and economic damage.

A.   SCIENCE AND THE "GREENHOUSE EFFECT"

The "greenhouse effect" at the root of global warming is very much
a part of the evolution of climate and life on Earth. As Figure 9.1 indicates, carbon dioxide (CO_2) is known to have been present at a level
of about 280 ppm in the atmosphere in the mid-18th century prior to
the industrial revolution. Carbon dioxide, CFCs, and methane are the
most significant gases that have an effect crudely comparable to that of
the glass in a greenhouse—they allow visible light to pass through the

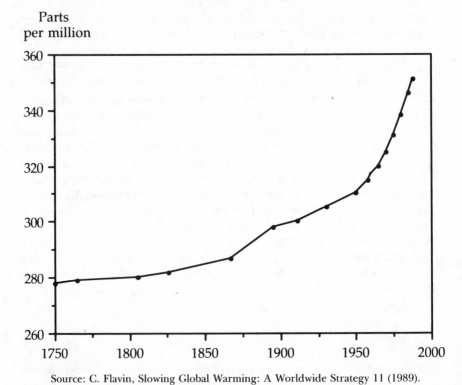

FIGURE 9.1
Atmospheric Concentration of Carbon Dioxide, 1750-1988

Source: C. Flavin, Slowing Global Warming: A Worldwide Strategy 11 (1989).

atmosphere. Heat radiated from the Earth is transmitted in a different form, as infrared rays, and much of it is trapped by these gases, resulting in a net warming effect.

Measurements of ice cores show much higher concentrations of carbon dioxide and much warmer temperatures than in previous epochs. Further physical proof of the greenhouse effect is provided by study of other planets: Mars, with virtually no atmosphere, is a frozen wasteland, while Venus, with an atmosphere largely comprised of carbon dioxide, is hot as an oven. Schneider, The Greenhouse Effect: Science and Policy, 243 Science 771 (1989).

While the greenhouse effect is a part of nature, the rapid increase in the atmospheric concentrations of greenhouse gases is directly caused by humankind's activities. The combustion of fossil fuels releases carbon dioxide; coal releases almost twice as much per unit of energy as natural gas, while oil is about halfway in between. Since trees store carbon dioxide as they grow, cutting and burning of trees, as is occurring on a vast scale in tropical rainforests, releases more carbon dioxide while reducing the amount of carbon dioxide being removed from the atmosphere by forests.

CFCs are another important greenhouse gas, although the damage they are doing to the ozone layer may largely offset their contribution to the greenhouse effect as ozone in the lower stratosphere is also a greenhouse gas. Although present in much lower concentrations than carbon dioxide (see Figure 9.2), CFCs are much more effective absorbers of infrared radiation per molecule. Methane, the other important greenhouse gas, is a very potent contributor to the greenhouse effect, but fortunately it has a much shorter atmospheric lifetime than carbon dioxide or CFCs (see Figure 9.2). While scientists are not certain about the causes of increased methane levels in the atmosphere, they suspect increased emissions from bovine flatulence (the livestock population surged after World War II), natural gas leaks, emissions from wet rice farming, and perhaps even the digestive process of termites. Andersen, Cows and Climate, 252 Science 1496 (1991). Air pollution also may be a contributor, as chemicals that remove methane increasingly are consumed instead by reactions with carbon monoxide.

The problem of controlling emissions of greenhouse gases is exacerbated by their distribution. Western industrialized countries accounted for over two-thirds of CFC use in the mid-1980s but only about 40 percent of greenhouse gas emissions, as indicated in Figure 9.3. The use of fossil fuels is increasing far more rapidly in developing countries than in industrialized nations. Developing countries are projected to account for more than 50 percent of carbon emissions from fossil fuels in a few decades.

The magnitude and pace of global warming are difficult to predict for many of the same reasons weather forecasts remain unreliable— localized climate is a chaotic system, subject to sudden and unanticipated

FIGURE 9.2

Major Greenhouse Gases and Their Characteristics

Gas	Atmospheric Concentration	Annual Increase	Life Span	Relative Greenhouse Efficiency	Current Greenhouse Contribution	Principal Sources of Gas
	(ppm)	(percent)	(years)	(CO$_2$=1)	(percent)	
Carbon Dioxide	351.3	.4	x[1]	1	57	
(Fossil Fuels)					(44)	Coal, Oil, Natural Gas,
(Biological)					(13)	Deforestation
Chlorofluoro-carbons	.000225	5	75-111	15,000	25	Foams, Aerosols, Refrigerants, Solvents
Methane	1.675	1	11	25	12	Wetlands, Rice, Fossil Fuels, Livestock
Nitrous Oxide	.31	.2	150	230	6	Fossil Fuels, Fertilizers, Deforestation

[1] Carbon dioxide is a stable molecule with a 2-4 year average residence time in the atmosphere.

Sources: Worldwatch Institute, based on various sources including EPA, Policy Options for Stabilizing Global Climate Change (1989, draft); Ramanathan et al., Trace Gas Trends and Their Potential Role in Climate Change, J. Geophysical Research (1985); Hansen et al., Greenhouse Effect of Chlorofluorocarbons and Other Trace Gases, J. Geophysical Research, in press; in C. Flavin, Slowing Global Warming: A Worldwide Strategy 13 (1989).

changes. Moreover, year-to-year variations in temperatures can mask long-term trends. Despite a growing consensus that some global warming will occur, there also is great uncertainty concerning the severity of its consequences. Some of the more likely effects include a gradual rise in sea level accompanied by flooding of coastlines and loss of wetlands, localized damage to agriculture and forests, and species loss. Warmer temperatures could exacerbate air pollution, increase the severity of tropical storms, and change the world in other, unexpected ways. Woodwell, The Effects of Global Warming, in J. Leggett, Global Warming: The Greenpeace Report 116-132 (1990); J. Smith and D. Tirpak, The Effects of Climate Change on the United States (1990).

    In an effort to reach international consensus on climate change, two U.N. agencies, the World Meteorological Organization and UNEP,

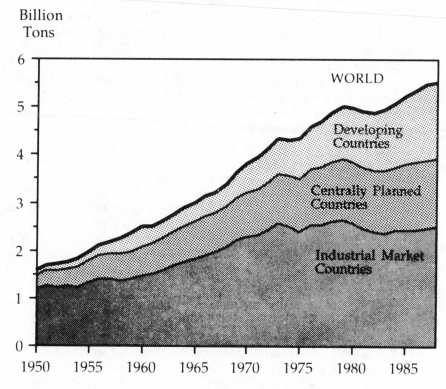

FIGURE 9.3
Carbon Emissions from Fossil Fuels, 1950-88

Source: C. Flavin, Slowing Global Warming: A Worldwide Strategy 25 (1989).

organized an Intergovernmental Panel on Climate Change (IPCC) in 1988. The IPCC prepared the following report on scientific knowledge about climate change under four alternative scenarios (A: Business-as-Usual, B: Low Emissions, C: Control Policies, and D: Accelerated Controls).

> **Intergovernmental Panel on Climate Change, Scientific Assessment**
> **xi, xii (1990)**

We are certain of the following:

—there is a natural greenhouse effect which already keeps the Earth warmer than it would otherwise be.

—emissions resulting from human activities are substantially increasing the atmospheric concentrations of the greenhouse gases: carbon dioxide, methane, chlorofluorocarbons (CFCs) and nitrous oxide. These increases will enhance the greenhouse effect, resulting on average in an additional warming of the Earth's surface. The main greenhouse gas, water vapor, will increase in response to global warming and further enhance it.

We calculate with confidence that:

—some gases are potentially more effective than others at changing climate, and their relative effectiveness can be estimated. Carbon dioxide has been responsible for over half the enhanced greenhouse effect in the past, and is likely to remain so in the future.

—atmospheric concentrations of the long-lived gases (carbon dioxide, nitrous oxide and the CFCs) adjust only slowly to changes in emissions. Continued emissions of these gases at present rates would commit us to increased concentrations for centuries ahead. The longer emissions continue to increase at present day rates, the greater reductions would have to be for concentrations to stabilize at a given level.

—the long-lived gases would require immediate reductions in emissions from human activities of over 60% to stabilize their concentrations at today's levels; methane would require a 15-20% reduction.

Based on current model results, we predict:

—under the IPCC Business-as-Usual (Scenario A) emissions of greenhouse gases, a rate of increase of global mean temperature during the next century of about 0.3°C per decade (with an uncertainty range of 0.2°C to 0.5°C per decade); this is greater than that seen over the past 10,000 years. This will result in a likely increase in global mean temperature of about 1°C above the present value by 2025 and 3°C before the end of the next century. The rise will not be steady because of the influence of other factors.

—under the other IPCC emission scenarios, which assume progressively increasing levels of controls, rates of increase in global mean temperature of about 0.2°C per decade (Scenario B), just above 0.1°C per decade (Scenario C) and about 0.1°C per decade (Scenario D).

—that land surfaces warm more rapidly than the ocean, and high northern latitudes warm more than the global mean in winter.

—regional climate changes different from the global mean, although our confidence in the prediction of the detail of regional changes is low. For example, temperature increases in Southern Europe and central North America are predicted to be higher than the global mean, accompanied on average by reduced summer precipitation and soil moisture. There are less consistent predictions for the tropics and the Southern Hemisphere.

—under the IPCC Business as Usual emissions scenario, an average rate of global mean sea level rise of about 6cm per decade over the next century (with an uncertainty range of 3 to 10cm per decade), mainly due to thermal expansion of the oceans and the melting of some land ice. The predicted rise is about 20cm in global mean sea level by 2030, and 65cm by the end of the next century. There will be significant regional variations.

There are many uncertainties in our predictions, particularly with regard to the timing, magnitude and regional patterns of climate change, due to our incomplete understanding of:

—sources and sinks of greenhouse gases, which affect predictions of future concentrations.

—clouds, which strongly influence the magnitude of climate change.

—oceans, which influence the timing and patterns of climate change.

—polar ice sheets, which affect predictions of sea level rise.

These processes are already partially understood, and we are confident that the uncertainties can be reduced by further research. However, the complexity of the system means that we cannot rule out surprises.

Our judgment is that:

—Global mean surface air temperature has increased by 0.3°C to 0.6°C over the last 100 years, with the five global-average warmest years being in the late 1980s. Over the same period global sea level has increased by 1020cm. These increases have not been smooth with time, nor uniform over the globe.

—The size of this warming is broadly consistent with predictions of climate models, but it is also of the same magnitude as natural climate variability. Thus the observed increase could be largely due to this natural variability; alternatively this variability and other human factors could have offset a still larger human induced greenhouse warming. The unequivocal detection of the enhanced greenhouse effect from observations is not likely for a decade or more.

—There is no firm evidence that climate has become more variable over the last few decades. However, with an increase in the mean temperature, episodes of high temperatures will most likely become more frequent in the future, and cold episodes less frequent.

—Ecosystems affect climate, and will be affected by a changing climate and by increasing carbon dioxide concentrations. Rapid changes in climate will change the composition of ecosystems; some species will benefit while others will be unable to migrate or adapt fast enough and may become extinct. Enhanced levels of carbon dioxide may increase productivity and efficiency of water use of vegetation. The effect of warming on biological processes, although poorly understood, may increase the atmospheric concentrations of natural greenhouse gases.

NOTES AND QUESTIONS

1. The potentially high cost of substantial reductions in fossil fuel emissions has led many to question whether we know enough to justify expensive control measures. See, e.g., F. Seitz, R. Jastrow, and W. Ni-

erenberg, eds., Scientific Perspectives on the Greenhouse Problem (1990); Rogers and Fiering, Climate Change: Do We Know Enough to Act?, 4 Forum for Applied Res. and Publ. Pol. 5 (1989). The IPCC report concludes that immediate emission reductions of more than 60 percent would be necessary just to stabilize concentrations of most greenhouse gases at today's levels. Yet the projected cost of even far more modest emissions reductions has horrified some economists. Michael Boskin, chairman of the President's Council of Economic Advisers, argued that a 20 percent emissions reduction by the year 2005 could cost the U.S. $100-200 billion per year and cause "substantially higher unemployment and lower economic growth." Davis, Bid to Slow Global Warming Could Cost U.S. $200 Billion a Year, Bush Aide Says, Wall St. J., Apr. 16, 1990, at B4.

2. Concern over the impact of global warming focuses not only on the size of temperature changes, but also on how rapidly they occur. The IPCC report predicts that if no action is taken to reduce emissions of greenhouse gases, global warming during the next century will be greater than has occurred over the last 10,000 years. While some experts argue that industrialized societies are no longer very vulnerable to climate change because little economically important activity takes place outdoors, others are concerned that natural systems are not as adaptable as humankind to rapid temperature changes. Over time technological innovation and increasing wealth may improve humankind's capacity to adapt to climate change, Ausubel, A Second Look at the Impacts of Climate Change, 79 Am. Scientist 210 (1991), but ecosystems may not be as adaptable.

3. In 1991 a report by a National Academy of Sciences panel endorsed the notion that public policy should emphasize adaptation to climate change rather than undertaking drastic measures to prevent it. National Academy of Sciences, Confronting Climate Change (1991). The report sparked two dissents from panel members who argued that it mistakenly sought to separate the ecological and economic effects of climate change. Dismissing concern about the severe damage to ecosystems that rapid climate change could cause, panel member William Nordhaus, a Yale University economist, countered that "Ninety percent of U.S. economic activity has no interaction" with natural systems. Because agriculture, "the part of the economy that is sensitive to climate change, accounts for just 3% of national output . . . there is no way to get a very large effect on the U.S. economy." Roberts, Academy Panel Split on Greenhouse Adaptation, 253 Science 1206 (1991). Economist Herman Daly responds that "the inelasticity of demand for food in general should convince anyone that the current 3% figure could soar to 90% in the event of a serious disruption of agriculture." Daly, Ecological Economics, 254 Science 358 (1991). While global warming is likely to have a dramatic effect on agriculture, many cultivars are replaced

every seven to ten years, making adaptation easier than one might imagine. Ausubel, Does Climate Still Matter?, 350 Nature 649 (1991). Droughts spawned by global warming would increase irrigation costs, but a carbon-rich atmosphere might contribute to higher crop yields.

4. Ultimately, the question of how one feels about the threat of climate change turns in large part on one's views concerning human-kind's relationship to nature. Some view the global warming problem through an economic perspective that considers nature "as an economic tool and a playground for humans" where "rapid, irrevocable changes in the global ecology are a liability only to the degree that they reduce productivity or upset the users of the playground." Passell, Warmer Globe, Greener Pastures?, N.Y. Times, Sept. 18, 1991, at D2. Others maintain that this perspective is singularly inappropriate for dealing with global warming because of the importance of intangible values implicated by climate change (such as biodiversity). What decisionmaking model would you suggest for evaluating proposed policy responses?

5. Studies indicate that global warming may have a devastating impact on efforts to preserve biodiversity. See, e.g., T. Lovejoy and R. Peter, eds., Global Warming and Biological Diversity (1992). Noting that ecosystems "could face significant environmental impacts" from global warming, the IPCC in 1992 reported a critical need for better information about the sensitivity of species and ecosystems to climate change. Stevens, Global Warming Threatens to Undo Decades of Conservation Efforts, N.Y. Times, Feb. 25, 1992, at C4. The World Wildlife Fund has identified several types of ecosystems placed at risk by global warming. Most immediately threatened are mangroves, coral reefs, and Arctic seas, while mountain ecosystems, coastal wetlands, Arctic tundra, and sub-arctic and temperate forests are highly vulnerable. Id.

6. As the IPCC confirms, the impacts of global warming will not be distributed evenly. The IPCC reports that the Maldives and certain Pacific islands may disappear under rising sea levels, while large areas of Bangladesh, Indonesia, Thailand, Egypt, and Louisiana could face severe flooding. An Alliance of Small Island States has been formed to lobby for strict controls on emissions of greenhouse gases. Stevens, In a Warming World, Who Comes Out Ahead?, N.Y. Times, Feb. 5, 1991, at C1, C8. Yet other parts of the world, like Northern Europe, may benefit from shifting rainfall patterns and more temperate climate conditions. What implications does the uneven (and uncertain) distribution of impacts have for efforts to obtain international agreement on measures to combat global warming?

7. The IPCC report notes that "the five global-average warmest years" in the 140 years that temperature records have been kept were in the 1980s (1988, 1987, 1983, 1989, and 1981). Convinced that a clear global warming trend had emerged, NASA scientist James Hansen predicted in 1989 that one of first three years of the decade of the 1990s

would be the warmest ever recorded. His prediction promptly came true when 1990 broke the temperature record set in 1988. Kerr, Global Temperature Hits Record Again, 251 Science 274 (1991). Climatologist Hugh Ellsaesser of Lawrence Livermore National Laboratory, who lost a $100 bet over Hansen's prediction, insists that Hansen simply "lucked out" because the temperature increase could be the product of natural temperature variability rather than a long-term trend. Other scientists believe that a clear long-term warming trend is emerging. This evidence has helped spur international efforts to negotiate a convention on climate change, as described below.

B. LEGAL AND POLICY RESPONSES TO GLOBAL WARMING

As noted above, substantial uncertainties surround assessments of global warming, including its timing, pace, magnitude, and distribution of impacts. Yet many scientists believe that global warming has the potential to cause an environmental catastrophe. Faced with a problem that involves both high risk and high uncertainty, how should society respond?

Stressing the uncertainties that surround global warming and the potentially high cost of control measures, the Bush Administration has refused to commit the United States to numerical targets for controlling emissions of greenhouse gases. Jessica Mathews argues that this policy is akin to driving a car over unknown terrain without headlights and refusing to slow down as it gets darker because nothing has been hit yet. She maintains that the United States should act as it did during the Cold War when it adopted defense policies designed to provide insurance against dangers of uncertain but potentially catastrophic magnitude. "There are too many unknowns for rigorous economic analysis," she notes, the risks are not reversible, and the uncertainties will not soon be removed. Mathews, Science, Uncertainty and Common Sense, Wash. Post, Nov. 3, 1991, at C7. There is broad agreement that countries should at least pursue a "no regrets" policy emphasizing measures (such as investments in energy efficiency) that reduce emissions of greenhouse gases while having positive net benefits in their own right.

The international community is now developing a coordinated global response to the global warming problem. In December 1988 the General Assembly of the United Nations adopted a resolution declaring that climate change is the "common concern of mankind" and calling for global action to combat the problem. In 1989 the European Community endorsed the notion that a worldwide agreement should be negotiated to establish an international response to global warming. Determining precisely what that response should be, however, has been more difficult than for the ozone depletion problem, in part because of the extent of worldwide dependence on fossil fuels.

At the end of 1990 the General Assembly adopted a resolution entitled Protection of Global Climate for Present and Future Generations of Mankind. Introduced by the island nation of Malta, the resolution established a process for negotiating an international framework convention on climate change. Pursuant to the resolution, the U.N. Secretary General established an ad hoc secretariat in Geneva to manage the negotiations with the assistance of UNEP and the World Meteorological Organization. The goal was to develop a framework convention on climate change that could be signed at the U.N. Conference on Environment and Development in Brazil in June 1992.

Citing uncertainties about the magnitude and timing of global warming, the United States has resisted European proposals to establish targets and timetables for stabilizing and reducing carbon dioxide emissions. U.S. officials argue that energy and environmental policies it has adopted for other reasons, such as reducing air pollution or preventing ozone depletion, should be considered sufficient to keep U.S. emissions of greenhouse gases at or below current levels through 2030. Gray and Rivkin, A "No Regrets" Environmental Policy, 83 Foreign Pol. 47 (1991); Morrissette and Platinga, The Global Warming Issue: Viewpoints of Different Countries, 103 Resources 2 (Spring 1991); K. Schmidt, How Industrialized Countries Are Responding to Climate Change, 3 Intl. Envtl. Aff. 292 (1991).

As concern over global warming grows, more countries have pledged unilateral action to stabilize or reduce emissions of greenhouse gases, leaving the United States increasingly isolated in its negotiating position. Germany has pledged a 25 percent reduction in carbon dioxide emissions by the year 2005, and New Zealand and Denmark have pledged 20 percent reductions by then. The British government, which had long supported the United States' "go slow" negotiating position, announced in 1991 that it would stabilize its carbon dioxide emissions at 1990 levels by the year 2005. Canada and France have made similar commitments. Japan, which initially supported the U.S. position, has pledged to stabilize per capita emissions by the year 2000.

At the fifth negotiating session for a global warming treaty in February 1992 the United States alone continued to oppose the establishment of firm targets for stabilizing carbon dioxide emissions, a position that threatens to block a meaningful agreement. Abramson, Global Warming Treaty Talks Bog Down, L.A. Times, Feb. 29, 1992 at A22. Virtually all other industrialized countries have announced unilateral policies to limit carbon dioxide emissions and are supporting a proposal to require stabilization of carbon dioxide emissions at 1990 levels by the year 2000. While the United States agreed to provide $75 million to help developing nations control emissions of greenhouse gases, it opposes specific targets or timetables for emission stabilization or reduction. Id. As a result, it may only be possible to sign a general framework agreement at the UN Conference on Environment and Development to be followed by further negotiations.

The Bush Administration's position emphasizes the potential economic risk associated with steep cuts in U.S. consumption of fossil fuels. Because the United States has a lower population density and larger domestic energy reserves than its major trading competitors, the United States has developed an economy that is arguably much more dependent on low energy prices. However, several studies suggest that cost-effective energy efficiency opportunities are immense and that it is at least technically possible to stabilize or even reduce carbon dioxide emissions for some time to come without incurring a substantial economic penalty. See, e.g., Office of Technology Assessment, Changing by Degrees (1991) (costs of achieving a 35 percent carbon dioxide reduction by 2015 range from negative to $115 billion per year); National Academy of Sciences, Policy Implications of Greenhouse Warming (1991) (substantial emission reductions possible with cost savings). EPA maintains that a tax on the carbon content of fossil fuels could stabilize emissions without reducing GNP if the revenues were used to reduce existing taxes on productive uses of capital. Stevens, New Studies Predict Profits in Heading Off Global Warming, N.Y. Times, Mar. 17, 1992, at C1.

Final agreement on global response to climate change will require resolution of a variety of complicated issues. Should firm target levels be established for controlling emissions of greenhouse gases and, if so, how should these targets be determined, and how can they be enforced? Should targets be set individually for different greenhouse gases, or should an overall target be established? While the United States maintains that it is more efficient to allow countries to choose the best means for reaching an overall target, other countries have argued for immediate limits on carbon dioxide emissions. At what levels should targets be set, and how should responsibility for achieving them be allocated among nations?

Differences in the magnitude and nature of greenhouse emissions in different countries make the task of developing a climate convention particularly challenging. Consider the following proposals for how such an agreement could be designed while taking these differences into account.

C. Flavin, Slowing Global Warming: A Worldwide Strategy
66 (1989)

As policymakers begin to consider the specifics of an international agreement on global warming, a host of complex issues arises. The first is whether to establish a broad carbon emissions limit for the world. Such a goal—cutting emissions by 20 percent by 2005—was proposed at the Toronto Conference. This was something of a compromise between the 50-80 percent cut needed to stabilize atmospheric carbon dioxide and the much more limited goals that policymakers seem willing to consider. So far, even countries such as Norway that are leading the way in addressing climate problems are mainly considering a freeze on carbon emissions.

While it is not feasible to achieve a cut as great as 50 percent in a period of 10-15 years, it is important that ambitious goals be established and that the industrial countries that dominate global carbon emissions embark immediately on a path of reducing them. And any plan that cuts carbon emissions is likely also to help in cutting back on two minor greenhouse gases, nitrous oxide and methane. Only by achieving a reduction of carbon emissions of at least 10 percent by 2000 can the world get on a course to achieve an eventual reduction of over 50 percent by mid-century.

In an effort to balance practicality and equity against the urgency of the problem, we have formulated a set of reduction targets based on today's per capita carbon emissions level. Countries such as the United States and the Soviet Union that currently produce carbon dioxide at a high rate would be required to reduce emissions by about 35 percent by the year 2000, while countries such as India or Kenya would be permitted to continue to increase emissions. Countries with carbon emissions between these levels, such as Italy and Japan, would have to reduce them less rapidly.

These targets can be met by pursuing [certain] technologies and policies. . . . The goals are designed to be ambitious and equitable, gradually narrowing the huge disparities that now exist between different nations' emissions levels. They are also practical, calling for a realizable 12-percent cut in global emissions by the year 2000. Under them, projected emissions of 6.4 billion tons are 38 percent below what they would reach if the world were to continue on its current path. While such a cut would not by itself stabilize the climate, it would put the world on a course toward stabilization of global carbon dioxide concentrations by mid-century. The growth in Third World emissions permitted under our program means that in order to eventually cut carbon emissions by 50 percent, progressively tighter standards will have to be developed in succeeding decades.

These goals put the onus on the industrial world to take a leadership role. Unless rapid reductions are achieved in wealthier countries, a stable climate could become unachievable for many decades. Indeed, if the industrial countries were simply to keep emissions level, Third World increases alone could lead to a 20-30 percent increase in global emissions by the year 2000 and a 50-70 percent increase by 2010. Unfortunately, there are as yet no industrial countries that are considering lowering carbon emissions by the needed 20-35 percent by the year 2000.

One of the most difficult issues posed by such goals is the constraints they place on the world's poorest nations. Since it is mainly deforestation that causes nations such as Brazil, Colombia, and Cote d'Ivoire to have such high per capita carbon emissions, the targets imply a major effort to slow forest clearing in these countries. This carbon reduction strategy will not reverse but will begin to slow growth in fossil fuel consumption in the Third World, something that is essential if the planet is to avoid vast increases in carbon emissions in the coming decades. China, for example, would be required to cut its projected growth rate of 3.5 percent per year to 1.5 percent. This change alone would reduce emissions estimated for the year 2000 by more than 200 million tons annually.

Some have suggested that the world community should directly adopt energy efficiency rather than carbon reduction goals, given the unique potential of efficiency. William U. Chandler of the Pacific Northwest Laboratory has suggested that nations commit to a goal of improving energy efficiency at a rate of at least 2 percent annually, with the goal by the year 2025 of making all countries as efficient as Denmark and Japan are today. This would allow the world to keep fossil fuel-related carbon emissions to about the current level, but would not permit reductions. While such goals are eminently sensible and achievable, they represent only part of what is required to stabilize the climate. In most countries improved energy efficiency is logically the centerpiece of a carbon reduction strategy, but investing in reforestation and the development of renewable energy sources is an essential complement to such programs. The potential of such programs should not be ignored in a global warming agreement.

One issue that must be addressed is how to pay for massive investments in energy efficiency and reforestation in developing countries that are now strapped with huge debts. Some mechanism will be needed to invest capital from industrial countries in Third World programs, stanching the hemorrhage of funds caused by the debt crisis. Many efficiency and forestry investments have broad economic and environmental value and can be justified on those grounds alone, but without sufficient capital they may nonetheless be neglected. One important mechanism might be the carbon tax mentioned earlier. If 10 percent of the revenues from such a tax were made available for Third World programs, this would create an annual fund of $28 billion. Such a "Global Atmosphere Fund" was in fact endorsed at [a meeting of experts convened by the Canadian government in Toronto in 1988].

The World Bank and institutions such as the U.S. Development Program can also play a role by increasing their lending for such projects and using climate protection as a consideration in reviewing loans. In recent years the bank, which lent $16 billion to Third World countries in 1988, has been increasingly receptive to lending for efficiency improvements, but few loans have been approved. Meanwhile, the World Bank is using global warming as justification for its extensive lending for natural gas development, a somewhat questionable greenhouse strategy.

Such institutions have their own agendas and are reluctant to take on an issue as far-reaching as global warming without a strong push from the international community. In a much-touted environmental speech in September 1989, Barber Conable, the president of the bank, emphasized the uncertainties of global warming and announced no significant new policy initiatives. It now seems clear that the world community will need to broaden the mandate for these lending institutions, forcibly enlisting them in the effort to sustain a livable climate.

> ## Nitze, A Proposed Structure for an International Convention on Climate Change
> ### 249 Science 607-608 (1990)

Whereas an international convention is in many respects a top-down undertaking, a more bottom-up process is preferable for developing policy responses. Only policies formulated at the national level will overcome widespread concern about economic costs and reflect the different circumstances of different countries. The convention should drive this process by requiring each party to prepare and distribute its own national plan for reducing greenhouse gas emissions and for adapting to future change while achieving its development objectives. The convention would contain general guidelines for preparing national plans, including the sectors and general issues to be covered. Each party would be free, however, to determine its own emissions reduction strategy consistent with any overall targets and timetables established by the convention.

The point is to require each party to make an initial determination of the national measures it is prepared to commit to and then to share that determination with other parties for analysis and discussion. From such analysis and discussion should emerge (i) an initial baseline emissions scenario based on implementation of the national plans, (ii) a more complete inventory of possible policy responses, and (iii) an initial indication of the additional financial and technical resources that might be required to implement the plans, particularly in developing countries.

As national plans are revised and updated, one would hope that various parties could be induced to make their plans more ambitious and effective in response to the information and feedback they receive from other parties and outside sources. Potential opportunities for asymmetrical reductions or emissions trades should become more apparent. The convention should require each party to prepare an initial plan within 1 year of its becoming subject to the convention and to update that plan every 2 years thereafter.

To obtain the participation of key developing countries such as China, India, and Brazil, the convention will have to contain strong provisions with respect to technology transfer and financial assistance. Despite the popularity of the sustainable development concept, developing country governments still perceive a direct conflict between their goals for economic development and measures to reduce greenhouse gas emissions in their countries. This perception is exaggerated. Developing countries collectively will be investing hundreds of billions of dollars for economic development over the next few decades. If this money is invested in systems that are energy and materials efficient, the environmental impact of a given level of economic development can be substantially reduced. For example, China's ratio of CO_2 emissions to gross national product (GNP) is roughly five times that of Japan. If China were to achieve even 60% of Japanese efficiency and carbon intensity levels in its new energy-producing and energy-consuming infrastructure, it could improve this ratio substantially in a relatively short time. The one major hurdle is obtaining the technical information, management assistance, and capital required to promote more efficient and less polluting supply and use of energy and other natural resources.

A climate convention could make an important contribution to overcoming this hurdle. First, the convention could establish a fund to meet all or part of the hard currency costs of preparing and updating the developing countries' national plans, referred to above. The fund would cover the costs of sending public and private sector experts from OECD countries and multilateral institutions to work with counterparts in developing countries in preparing the national plans and more detailed studies of energy, transport, agriculture, and other key sectors. The money required for such a fund might be in the order of a hundred million dollars per year, which could be contributed by the OECD countries proportionate to greenhouse gas emissions. Only developing countries that were parties to the convention could have access to the fund, which should provide a major incentive for developing countries to become parties.

The national plans and sectoral studies would have to identify capital requirements sector-by-sector and possible sources of capital, domestic and foreign. To help meet those requirements, the convention should contain provisions that encourage the private sector to furnish the capital required. The OECD countries would be obligated to arrange for sold loans from multilateral development banks, provide expanded political risk insurance, and even offer credit guarantees for projects meeting certain criteria. The developing countries would be obligated to provide a favorable investment climate for foreign investors making climate-related investments, including effective protection of intellectual property rights and patents, no prohibition on operating control, taxation of profits at a national rate or better, and foreign exchange priority for dividend and capital remittances within certain limits.

Finally, we come to the issues of targets and timetables for greenhouse gas emission reduction and their appropriate role. The purpose of short-term targets and timetables is not to set final goals. There is simply too much uncertainty about the science, regional impacts, and socioeconomic consequences of climate change for the United States and other key countries to commit to ambitious short-term emissions reduction goals within the next few years. Rather, the purpose of short-term targets and timetables is to catalyze a process—to induce governments and the private sector to take certain initial steps needed to set the stage for more far-reaching changes later on. Once this process has begun, we will be able to achieve much greater emissions reductions than we can imagine today, irrespective of what is written into international agreements.

The following is a set of targets and timetables for greenhouse gas emissions reductions that might be politically acceptable and yet sufficiently ambitious to begin to bring about results.

1. A short-term stabilization target placing an overall ceiling on the parties' emissions of all greenhouse gases (expressed in equivalent units) at their levels for the year the convention entered into force effective 10 years thereafter.

2. An OECD CO_2 stabilization subtarget that would require each OECD country to hold its emissions at their average level for the year the convention enters into effect and the previous 4 years effective 10 years after the convention enters into effect. The combination of a chlorofluorocarbon phase-out and stabilization of CO_2 emissions from industrialized countries would provide leeway for short-term emissions increases from developing countries.

3. An energy efficiency subtarget, whereby all parties would be obligated to improve the ratio of their carbon emissions to GNP by 2% per year over the same 10-year period. This rate of improvement, which was achieved by Japan and the United States during the 1973 to 1986 period, would allow individual parties to seek the combination of energy efficiency improvements and reductions in the carbon intensity of their overall fuel mix that best suits their particular circumstances. It would also allow parties with high GNP growth rates correspondingly high emissions.

4. A deforestation subtarget, whereby all parties agree to eliminate net loss of forests by the end of the 10-year period in question. Achieving

this goal would help preserve biodiversity and promote other environmental goals as well as reduce net carbon emissions.

To supplement and reinforce the targets and timetables proposed above, the convention should impose a general obligation on the parties to use the best available technology that is economically achievable to reduce emissions of greenhouse gases. This general obligation is particularly important for greenhouse gases such as methane and nitrous oxide, for which it is difficult to set targets because their sources and sinks are not yet well understood. An annex to the convention could describe specific technologies currently available for reducing emissions and their respective unit costs.

NOTES AND QUESTIONS

1. The Bush Administration has emphasized scientific uncertainty as a justification for refusing to commit to targets and timetables for reducing carbon dioxide emissions. Is this akin to refusing to slow down a car without headlights as darkness falls? How would you frame the policy options for purposes of a decision by the president? Suppose that experts convened by the National Academy of Sciences told you that with a substantial increase in research funding for atmospheric science, there was a good chance in five to ten years of substantially reducing the uncertainty surrounding the predicted magnitude and pace of global warming. What impact, if any, would this have on your decision?

2. What factors may make it more difficult to obtain international agreement on policy responses to global warming than for ozone depletion? One distinction is the number and shared interests of the countries most affected. (Compare the provisions of the Montreal Protocol with the approach suggested by Flavin.) Are there any differences that might make it *less* difficult? In particular, all substitutes for CFCs originally were thought to be more expensive, less acceptable environmentally (except for their risk to the ozone layer), inferior in providing their intended service, or all three. Is this true of measures to address global warming?

3. What mechanism should be established for enforcing an international agreement to control emissions of greenhouse gases? In March 1989, 17 nations, including France, Japan, and West Germany, called for the creation of a new international institution with the power to enforce a global warming convention. Flavin suggests making UNEP "a much more powerful agency" and allowing it to manage a global fund that could be used to ensure compliance by developing nations. Nitze argues for replacing IPCC with a permanent coordinating body, consisting of a bureau, an executive council, permanent committees, and a strong secretariat. What steps could be taken to induce compliance by

countries that fail to meet international targets? Levels of carbon dioxide emissions are closely related to levels of overall economic activity. Suppose that a country agrees to stabilize carbon dioxide emissions but unexpectedly strong economic growth results in far greater emissions than forecast. Should such a country be penalized and, if so, how?

4. Because much of the projected growth in greenhouse gas emissions is in developing countries, there is wide support for measures to provide financial and technical assistance to such countries to reduce their dependence on fossil fuels. In February 1992 the Intergovernmental Negotiation Committee agreed to use the Global Environmental Facility (GEF) as the vehicle for providing such assistance. The GEF was created in 1991 by the World Bank in cooperation with UNEP and UNDP. It administers a $1.5 billion Global Environmental Trust Fund to help finance international environmental protection projects and a separate Ozone Projects Trust Fund, which receives money from the Interim Multilateral Fund created to aid developing countries in complying with the Montreal Protocol. Arguing that the GEF is controlled by the large industrial nations, developing countries unsuccessfully opposed its selection as the vehicle for providing assistance for controls on greenhouse gas emissions.

5. Nitze argues that a "bottom-up" process is necessary for developing policy responses because each nation must decide for itself how best to cope with the economic trade-offs involved in controlling greenhouse gases. At what level of our federal system of government should such decisions be made? Several states and some localities have taken action to address global warming. Vermont, Oregon, Connecticut, California, Missouri, and New York are working to identify ways of substantially reducing their greenhouse gas emissions. New Jersey requires state agencies to buy the most energy-efficient equipment when justified by the savings achieved over its useful life. Los Angeles has a program of large-scale tree planting, and Irvine, California has banned the use of CFCs. D. Lashof and E. Washburn, The Statehouse Effect: State Policies to Cool the Greenhouse 15 (1990); ABA Section of Natural Resources, Energy, and Environmental Law, Natural Resources, Energy, and Environmental Law: 1991—The Year in Review 180-182 (1992). Do these state and local actions make sense, given the small contribution of even a large state to the total problem?

6. The Bush Administration's opposition to a cap on carbon dioxide emissions stems in part from suspicion that European nations less dependent on fossil fuels are seeking to gain an economic advantage over the United States. The administration has argued that any global warming convention should give the United States credit for CFC reductions it has mandated to prevent ozone depletion because CFCs also are a greenhouse gas. However, the IPCC concluded in 1992 that CFCs are not a potent greenhouse gas because their destruction of the ozone layer

contributes to global cooling, cancelling out much of their contribution to the greenhouse effect. Stevens, Washington, Odd Man Out, May Shift on Climate, N.Y. Times, Feb. 18, 1992, at C1, C11. Thus, good news about CFCs is bad news for the U.S. negotiating position.

7. Projections of growth in carbon dioxide emissions depend in large part on projections of future economic growth. EPA officials have argued that the United States could stabilize carbon dioxide emissions at relatively minor cost if more realistic growth projections are coupled with aggressive energy conservation measures that are cost-effective in their own right. In response to EPA's "green lights" program, companies accounting for 2 percent of office space in the United States have made voluntary commitments to improvements in energy efficiency. EPA officials maintain that this program could reduce emissions of carbon dioxide by 180 million tons, while Department of Energy officials estimate that it will only achieve one-sixth of that reduction.

8. In December 1991 representatives of the European Community reached tentative agreement on energy taxes designed to combat global warming. A tax based on the carbon content of fuels would be phased in at a level equivalent to $5 per barrel of oil by the year 2000. A separate tax would be levied on all energy consumption, a measure criticized for discouraging nuclear and hydropower projects, which do not contribute to emissions of greenhouse gases. Passell, Taxing Carbon: Taxing Politics, N.Y. Times, Feb. 26, 1992, at D2.

9. Should an international agreement to reduce greenhouse gas emissions incorporate a comprehensive emissions trading scheme? Supporters of such an idea include the U.S. Department of Justice, the President's Council of Economic Advisers, and Project 88. Department of Justice, A Comprehensive Approach to Addressing Potential Climate Change, Report of the Task Force on the Comprehensive Approach to Climate Change (1991); Project 88—Round II, Incentives for Action: Designing Market-Based Environmental Strategies (1991). Trading proposals would allow trades between countries (e.g., Japan might purchase the right to increase its emissions in return for additional reductions by Germany), between carbon dioxide sinks and sources (e.g., Brazil might choose to prevent deforestation in order to earn more CO_2 emission allowances), and between different types of greenhouse gases (e.g., a certain amount of carbon dioxide emissions reductions could offset an increase in methane emissions with an equivalent effect on global warming). A U.N. study released in 1992 endorsed a similar idea, proposing the creation of a kind of global EPA that would allocate tradeable emissions allowances. U.N. Conference on Trade and Development, Trading Entitlements to Control Carbon Emissions: A Practical Proposal to Combat Global Warming (1992). What advantages would such trading schemes have? What are some of the obstacles to such an approach? How could greenhouse gases like methane, whose sources are not well known, be

incorporated into such a scheme? On what basis should allowances be allocated among countries? Could an effective mechanism for monitoring and enforcement be established? Suppose Brazil agrees to protect 10,000 acres of forest but poor farmers move to other parts of the country to clear forest areas? How are various countries likely to react to such trading proposals? See J. Epstein and R. Gupta, Controlling the Greenhouse Effect: Five Global Regimes Compared (1990).

10. Some voluntary "trading" or "offsetting" already is occurring. For example, the Dutch Electricity Generating Board is establishing a $300 million fund to replant thousand of acres of forests in tropical countries as well as financing a $35 million project to reduce sulfur emissions from an aging power plant in Poland. M. Simons, Dutch Go Abroad to Help Clean Air, N.Y. Times, Dec. 3, 1990, at A5. The logic behind the latter investment is that while $35 million spent on further sulfur reductions would remove only 6,000 tons of sulfur in the Netherlands, where tight controls already exist, it would reduce sulfur emissions in Poland, where they are poorly controlled, by 45,000 tons. A private builder of coal-burning power plants in the United States, Applied Energy Services, has contracted with CARE to finance tree planting in Guatemala to absorb the additional carbon dioxide emissions one of its projects will generate.

11. The potential benefits of trading stem in part from the uneven distribution of sources of greenhouse gases. For example, "[f]ifteen percent of the methane fueling the greenhouse is livestock digestive gas," Andersen, Cows and Climate, 252 Science 1494 (1991). New Zealand is an unusually heavy offender in this regard because the country's 70 million sheep "are very efficient methane producers," with each producing up to five gallons of methane per day, for a total of nearly 2.5 billion gallons per week. David Lowe of the New Zealand Institute of Nuclear Sciences notes that humans are not nearly such significant contributors. He estimates that "you'd need a whole football team and a couple of kegs of beer" to equal one sheep. Brooks, The 70 Million Sheep Roving New Zealand Create Quite a Stink, Wall St. J., June 30, 1987, at A1.

PROBLEM EXERCISE: ESTABLISHING AN INTERNATIONAL PROGRAM TO REDUCE EMISSIONS OF GREENHOUSE GASES

Because the sources and effects of global warming are not distributed evenly among nations, reaching agreement on a global policy response is extraordinarily difficult. Consider how the characteristics of the following countries are likely to affect their position on global warming. How much support do you think each of the countries described below would give to a climate convention designed to control emissions of greenhouse gases?

United States: large fossil fuel resources, low energy efficiency relative to other major industrialized countries, energy policy based on promoting domestic production and maintaining low energy prices, large land area, high per capita income, carbon dioxide emissions forecast to increase by 15 percent and population by 6 percent by the year 2000.

Japan: small land area, densely populated, high per capita income, no fossil fuel reserves, very energy efficient, energy policy that emphasizes nuclear power, high energy taxes to discourage consumption.

China: very large population and low per capita income, large coal reserves but limited energy alternatives, very low state of technological development, highly subsidized energy prices, energy growth considered essential to development, rapid growth occurring in carbon dioxide emissions.

Saudi Arabia: small population living in desert area, high per capita income, vast oil reserves, economy entirely dependent on sales of oil.

Bangladesh: large population in low-lying coastal plain subject to floods (11 million people in an area that would be inundated by a three-foot rise in sea level), very poor.

Soviet Union: very large fossil fuel reserves including natural gas (much lower in carbon than coal or oil), very inefficient user of energy, large northern areas that may benefit from global warming by becoming more temperate.

Brazil: large population, large land area, vast natural resources, aggressively pro-development, heavily indebted, major contributor to buildup of carbon dioxide through deforestation of the Amazon (much of which is illegal), strong governmental support for development of alternatives to fossil fuels (including ethanol from sugar cane).

Based on the characteristics of each of the countries identified above, how is each likely to react to each of the following proposed approaches to an international climate convention?

1. A requirement that each country stabilize its carbon dioxide emissions (or emissions of all greenhouse gases adjusted for their global warming potential) at 1990 levels by the year 2000.

2. A requirement that each country reduce its total carbon dioxide emissions (or emissions of all greenhouse gases adjusted for their global warming potential) by an equal percentage.

3. A requirement that each country reduce its emissions of carbon dioxide (or emissions of all greenhouse gases adjusted for their global warming potential) either (a) by a fixed amount per capita or (b) to a fixed per capita level.

4. A requirement that each signatory achieve annual percentage

improvements in energy efficiency, to reduce energy use per unit of output.

5.   A structure comparable to the Montreal Protocol, with a percentage reduction in emissions required of industrialized countries by the year 2005 and more time given to developing countries to achieve less ambitious reductions.

6.   Emissions trading systems, in which countries are allocated tradeable emission allowances based on (a) existing emissions levels, (b) percentage of global GNP, (c) total population, or (d) land area.

7.   An international tax based on either (a) the carbon content of fuels, or (b) the energy produced by fossil fuels (a BTU charge) set high enough to discourage emissions, with some portion of the proceeds dedicated to support investments in renewable energy and energy efficiency in developing countries.

8.   A requirement that the costs of emissions reductions be shared based on either (a) the income levels of each country, with transfer payments being made by richer nations to poorer ones or (b) the amount of greenhouse gases they have emitted, in accordance with the "polluter pays" principle.

What arguments would you make in favor of, or in opposition to, each of these proposals?

An environmental scholar, Konrad van Moltke, has said that "[b]y any traditional standards there are no solutions to climate change." Do you agree?

C.   INTERNATIONAL TRADE AND THE ENVIRONMENT

The expansion of international trade and increasing global economic integration have raised environmental concerns in two major areas. First, the movement to reduce global trade barriers has raised concern that countries with strict environmental regulations will be placed at a competitive disadvantage in relation to countries with weak regulations. Second, a growing international trade in hazardous substances has raised concern that less developed countries are being subjected to environmental hazards that they are not adequately prepared to control. These issues raise important questions concerning global governance and the often contentious relationship between industrialized and developing nations.

1. The Environmental Impact of Trade Liberalization

As trade barriers have declined, international trade has grown rapidly, exceeding $4.3 trillion in 1991. Negotiations that could produce further, dramatic reductions in trade barriers are currently under way. The principal multilateral agreement governing trade relations, the General Agreement on Tariffs and Trade (GATT), 55 U.N.T.S. 194, will be revised substantially if the six-year-long Uruguay round of negotiations is successful. In 1988 the United States and Canada entered into a bilateral agreement that will eliminate most barriers to trade by 1998, Free Trade Agreement, United States-Canada, 27 I.L.M. 281 (1988). If negotiations between the United States and Mexico are successful, a North American Free Trade Agreement (NAFTA) eventually will phase out trade barriers throughout the continent.

These initiatives have sparked surprisingly vociferous environmental concern, particularly because of the prospect of a dramatic reduction in barriers to trade with Mexico. The Mexican government's *maquiladora* program, which provides duty-free import and export rights to foreign-owned businesses in border areas, has spawned both explosive growth and horrendous pollution along the United States-Mexico border. Nearly 2,000 manufacturing plants have sprung up in an area sorely lacking the infrastructure to provide basic health and environmental services. Rich, Bordering on Trouble, 1991 Envtl. Forum 26 (May-June 1991). With 3.3 million people crowded into an area with a capacity to treat only 16 percent of municipal and industrial waste, rates of typhoid and hepatitis have jumped dramatically. Solis and Nazario, U.S., Mexico Take on Border Pollution, Wall St. J., Feb. 25, 1992, at B1. Illegal disposal of hazardous waste is widespread, and groundwater contamination is becoming evident. McKeith, The Environment and Free Trade: Meeting Halfway at the Mexican Border," 10 Pac. Basin L.J. 183, 186 (1991).

Environmentalists argue that the *maquiladora* experience is but a preview of the environmental damage that would occur if relaxation of trade barriers is not accompanied by more stringent environmental protection measures. While the U.S. government has opposed efforts to link environmental concerns and trade negotiations, it promised to address border pollution problems in order to win congressional approval for "fast track" consideration of NAFTA. The Mexican government in turn has pledged to strengthen enforcement of its comprehensive environmental law, Ley General del Equilibrio Ecologico y Protección del Ambiente (General Law for Ecological Balance and Environmental Protection), which it adopted in 1988, and to increase environmental infrastructure investments. In 1992 the United States and Mexico announced agreement on a plan to clean up the border region. EPA, Environmental Plan for the Mexico-U.S. Border (1992). Under the plan, Mexico's environmental agency, the Secretaría de Desarrollo Urbano y

Ecologia (SEDUE), pledges to spend $460 million between 1992 to 1994 to provide wastewater treatment plants and to improve environmental monitoring and enforcement. EPA has pledged to seek $179 million for border-related projects. Environmental groups argue that these commitments are inadequate, that they are not legally binding, and that they will further subsidize polluters in the border area.

While the *maquiladora* experience illustrates some of the environmental problems that may accompany liberalization of trade barriers, concern over the environmental impact of free trade extends far beyond the problems of border areas. Many environmentalists are concerned that free trade will undermine U.S. environmental standards as domestic companies face increasing competition from firms in countries with weak environmental laws. They note that existing efforts to exclude goods on environmental grounds already are being challenged as protectionist barriers that violate existing international trade agreements. While not opposing all trade liberalization, environmentalists maintain that trade negotiations should be used to obtain commitments for stronger environmental standards.

Economists generally are strong supporters of free trade because they believe it increases efficiency by allowing countries to specialize in their areas of comparative advantage. They argue that protectionism can be damaging to the environment by subsidizing environmentally damaging production methods, such as greater chemical and water use by subsidized agriculture. Harvard Business School professor Michael Porter maintains that strict domestic environmental regulation actually enhances international competitiveness by encouraging technological innovation that improves the quality of products valued abroad. He notes that countries with the most stringent environmental regulations, such as Germany and Japan, are among the most competitive internationally and that the United States leads in trade in pesticides and environmental cleanup, precisely those areas where its regulations are the most stringent. Porter, America's Green Strategy, 264 Scientific American 168 (April 1991).

Not all economists are sanguine about the environmental impact of trade liberalization. Herman Daly, a senior economist with the Environment Department of the World Bank, argues that there is a clear conflict between free trade and national efforts to internalize environmental costs.

If one nation internalizes environmental and social costs to a high degree, . . . and then enters into free trade with a country that does not force its producers to internalize those costs, then the result will be that firms in the second country will have lower prices and will drive the competing firms in the first country out of business. [Daly, From Adjustment to Sustainable Development: The Obstacle of Free Trade (draft, 1992).]

Daly maintains that environmental externalities have become so important that this conflict should be resolved in favor of "tariffs to protect, not an inefficient industry, but an efficient national policy of internalizing external costs into prices." Id.

Economists Gene M. Grossman and Alan B. Krueger maintain that free trade ultimately will promote stricter environmental standards in developing countries. They note that developing countries can make rapid environmental progress as development enhances their capacity to invest in newer and cleaner technologies. Grossman and Krueger argue that public demand for environmental protection increases as national income rises. Based on World Health Organization data on levels of sulfur dioxide and smoke in 42 countries, Grossman and Krueger maintain that pollution levels generally increase until nations achieve a level of gross domestic product (GDP) between $4,000 and $5,000 per capita, but then decline steadily as a wealthier populace demands environmental protection. Grossman and Krueger, Environmental Impacts of a North American Free Trade Agreement 5 (Wilson School Discussion Paper in Economics 1991). Grossman argues that by contributing to economic growth in developing countries, free trade would "help them get to the point of mandating and enforcing environmental standards similar to those in the developed world." Grossman, In Poor Regions, Environmental Law Should Be Appropriate, N.Y. Times, Mar. 1, 1992, at F11. He also questions the notion that free trade will encourage relocation of industry to take advantage of lax regulation. Because environmental costs "average only 1 percent of total costs in all United States manufacturing and exceed 5 percent of costs in a mere handful of industries," Grossman maintains that they "are not large enough to have much influence on what gets produced where." Id.

Environmentalists are concerned that efforts to harmonize international trade laws could result in the invalidation of some strict domestic environmental standards as nontariff trade barriers. For example, as the largest exporter of agricultural products in the world, the United States has pushed to remove what it considers to be unjustified health or safety regulations that exclude U.S. products from foreign markets. This has sparked a lengthy feud with the EC over regulations banning the import of beef in which growth hormones have been used. While the EC maintains that the restrictions are designed to protect the health of consumers, the United States argues that they are protectionist trade barriers because the hormones pose no risk to health.

The General Agreement on Tariffs and Trade permits health and environmental regulations as long as they "are not applied in a manner which would constitute a means of arbitrary or unjustifiable discrimination between countries where the same conditions prevail, or a disguised restriction on international trade." GATT, art. XX. Thus, trade disputes often turn on whether a regulation discriminates against foreign products. While a GATT panel rejected a challenge to CERCLA's feed-stock tax because it applied equally to foreign and domestic chemical products, more difficult issues arise when ostensibly nondiscriminatory measures have a disproportionate impact on imported products, as with the EC's ban on hormone-treated beef and the U.S. ban on asbestos, nearly all of which is imported.

Conflicts over the trade implications of environmental standards can be avoided when the standards are themselves a product of international agreement. Several existing treaties, such as the Montreal Protocol, which regulates trade in CFCs, impose trade restrictions to protect the environment. The Convention on International Trade in Endangered Species of Wild Fauna and Flora (CITES) has been highly effective because it imposes strict controls on trade in endangered species. See generally Conference Report: Environmental Challenges to International Trade Policy (P. Petesch, ed. 1991).

NOTES AND QUESTIONS

1. The debate over the environmental impact of trade liberalization has been waged largely on theoretical grounds, with competing predictions of impact being made on the basis of scant data. How persuasive are the data obtained by Grossman and Krueger in suggesting that trade actually will stimulate stricter environmental standards in developing countries because air pollution levels generally are lower in countries with a GDP exceeding $5,000 per capita? Is it possible that this relationship is instead the product of more democratic political institutions in industrialized nations?

2. Daly's concerns about the impact of trade liberalization are not limited to its effects on national efforts to internalize environmental costs. He also argues that free trade threatens national aspirations to move toward a more just distribution of income, to foster community, to control the macroeconomy, and to keep the scale of the economy within ecological limits. Daly, above. To a large extent, Daly's objections are based on the notion that free trade reduces an individual nation's ability to control its own destiny. How should policymakers respond to this concern?

3. Can international trade agreements preempt domestic law? Recall Missouri v. Holland, 252 U.S. 416 (1920) (treaties have supremacy over state law). Could a president effectively repeal a domestic environmental law by agreeing to a treaty that preempts it? See Wirth, American Environmental Law and the International Legal System 32 Va. J. Intl. L.—(1992). David Wirth argues that because international law lacks many of domestic law's procedural protections for ensuring public disclosure, scrutiny, and participation in decision-making, the trend toward inter-

nationalization of environmental law may prove to be a mixed blessing for environmental interests.

4. Can an international agreement expand foreigners' standing to seek redress in the U.S. courts? In Corrosion Proof Fittings v. EPA, 947 F.2d 1201 (5th Cir. 1991), Canadian asbestos producers argued that they had standing to challenge EPA's asbestos ban because GATT gives them the right to challenge another country's environmental standards as de facto trade barriers. Noting that GATT establishes its own procedures for solving trade disputes, the court rejected this argument. The Fifth Circuit held that the Canadians did not fall within the zone of interests protected by U.S. law because TSCA does not require EPA to consider the extraterritorial effect of domestic regulation. The court noted that section 6(c)(1)(D) of TSCA expressly requires EPA to consider "the effect [of a rule] on the *national* economy," 15 U.S.C. §2605(c)(1)(D) (emphasis supplied), and that "[i]nternational concerns are conspicuously absent from the statute." 947 F.2d at 1209.

5. The Montreal Protocol's restrictions on international trade in CFCs initially were opposed by the EC as a possible violation of GATT. Under the Protocol parties are prohibited from importing CFCs or halons from nonparties and, beginning in January 1993, developing countries may not export them to nonparties. These restrictions were included in the Montreal Protocol after a GATT representative explained that they qualified for exceptions provided in Article XX(b)&(g) for standards "necessary to protect human, animal, or plant life or health" or "relating to the conservation or exhaustion of exhaustible natural resources." Benedick, Ozone Diplomacy 91 (1991).

6. Trade disputes have been spawned by U.S. environmental laws that use trade sanctions to promote environmental protection outside U.S. borders. The most prominent example is the Marine Mammal Protection Act of 1972 (MMPA). Designed to reduce the incidental kill of marine mammals in the course of commercial fishing, the MMPA requires the government to "ban the importation of commercial fish or products from fish which have been caught with commercial fishing technology which results in the incidental kill or incidental serious injury of ocean mammals in excess of United States standards." 16 U.S.C. §1371(a)(2). In order to import yellowfin tuna caught in a certain area of the Pacific Ocean, a country must demonstrate that the average incidental taking rate (in terms of dolphins killed each time the purse-seine nets are set) for its tuna fleet is no more than 1.25 times the average taking rate of U.S. vessels in the same period. While seemingly nondiscriminatory, these regulations have spawned international trade disputes because they represent a unilateral effort to promote extraterritorial environmental protection. In 1991 the United States imposed a ban on tuna imports from Mexico and four other countries after environmentalists won a judgment that such an embargo was required by the MMPA.

Earth Island Institute v. Mosbacher, 929 F.2d 1449 (9th Cir. 1991). Arguing that the embargo was inconsistent with GATT, the Mexican government then asked the GATT Council to convene a panel to hear its complaint. The panel rendered the following decision.

GATT Council, United States— Restrictions on Imports of Tuna
Report of the Panel 1991

[After describing the tuna embargo, the Panel noted that the MMPA also provides for an embargo of tuna products from any "intermediary nation" that fails within 90 days to prove that it has acted to ban tuna imports from the target country. Six months after the initial ban, the Pelly Amendment authorized the president to ban imports of all fish and wildlife products from the target country "for such duration as the President determines appropriate and to the extent that such prohibition is sanctioned by the General Agreement on Tariffs and Trade."]

The Panel proceeded to examine whether Article XX(b) or Article XX(g) could justify the MMPA provisions on imports of certain yellowfin tuna and yellowfin tuna products, and the import ban imposed under these provisions. The Panel noted that Article XX provides that:

Subject to the requirement that such measures are not applied in a manner which would constitute a means of arbitrary or unjustifiable discrimination between countries where the same conditions prevail, or a disguised restriction on international trade, nothing in this Agreement shall be construed to prevent the adoption or enforcement by any contracting party of measures . . .

(b) necessary to protect human, animal or plant life or health; . . .

(g) relating to the conservation of exhaustible natural resources if such measures are made effective in conjunction with restrictions on domestic production or consumption; . . .

The Panel noted that the United States considered the prohibition of imports of certain yellowfin tuna and certain yellowfin tuna products from Mexico, and the provisions of the MMPA on which this prohibition is based, to be justified by Article XX(b) because they served solely the purpose of protecting dolphin life and health and were "necessary" within the meaning of that provision because, in respect of the protection of dolphin life and health outside its jurisdiction, there was no alternative measure reasonably available to the United States to achieve this objective. Mexico considered that Article XX(b) was not applicable to a measure imposed to protect the life or health of animals outside the jurisdiction of the contracting party taking it and that the import prohibition imposed by the United States was not necessary because alternative means consistent with the General Agreement were available to it to protect dolphin lives or health, namely international co-operation between the countries concerned.

The Panel noted that the basic question raised by these arguments, namely whether Article XX(b) covers measures necessary to protect human, animal or plant life or health outside the jurisdiction of the contracting party taking the measure, is not clearly answered by the text of that provision. It refers to life and health protection generally without expressly limiting that protection to the jurisdiction of the contracting party concerned. The Panel therefore decided to analyze this issue in the light of the drafting history of Article XX(b), the purpose of this provision, and the consequences that the interpretations proposed by the parties would have for the operation of the General Agreement as a whole.

The Panel noted that the proposal for Article XX(b) dated from the Draft Charter of the International Trade Organization (ITO) proposed by the United States, which stated in Article 32, "Nothing in Chapter IV [on commercial policy] of this Charter shall be construed to prevent the adoption or enforcement by any Member of measures . . . (b) necessary to protect human, animal or plant life or health." In the New York Draft of the ITO Charter, the preamble had been revised to read as it does at present, and exception (b) read: "For the purpose of protecting human, animal or plant life or health, if corresponding domestic safeguards under similar conditions exist in the importing country." This added proviso reflected concerns regarding the abuse of sanitary regulations by importing countries. Later, Commission A of the Second Session of the Preparatory Committee in Geneva agreed to drop this proviso as unnecessary. Thus, the record indicates that the concerns of the drafters of Article XX(b) focused on the use of sanitary measures to safeguard life or health of humans, animals, or plants within the jurisdiction of the importing country.

The Panel further noted that Article XX(b) allows each contracting party to set its human, animal or plant life or health standards. The conditions set out in Article XX(b) which limit resort to this exception, namely that the measure taken must be "necessary" and not "constitute a means of arbitrary or unjustifiable discrimination or a disguised restriction on international trade," refer to the trade measure requiring justification under Article XX(b), not, however, to the life or health standard chosen by the contracting party. The Panel recalled the finding of a previous panel that this paragraph of Article XX was intended to allow contracting parties to impose trade restrictive measures inconsistent with the General Agreement to pursue overriding public policy goals to the extent that such inconsistencies were unavoidable. The Panel considered that if the broad interpretation of Article XX(b) suggested by the United States were accepted, each contracting party could unilaterally determine the life or health protection policies from which other contracting parties could not deviate without jeopardizing their rights under the General Agreement. The General Agreement would then no longer constitute a multilateral framework for trade among all contracting parties but would provide legal security only in respect of trade between a limited number of contracting parties with identical internal regulations.

The Panel considered that the United States' measures, even if Article XX(b) were interpreted to permit extrajurisdictional protection of life and health, would not meet the requirement of necessity set out in that provision. The United States had not demonstrated to the Panel—as required of the party invoking an Article XX exception—that it had exhausted all options reasonably available to it to pursue its dolphin protection objectives through measures consistent with the General Agreement, in particular through the negotiation of international cooperative arrangements, which would seem to be desirable in view of the fact that dolphins roam the waters of many states and the high seas. Moreover, even assuming that an import prohibition were the only resort reasonably available to the United States, the particular measure chosen could in the Panel's view not be considered to be necessary within the meaning of Article XX(b). The United States linked the maximum incidental dolphin taking rate which Mexico had to meet during a particular period in order to be able to export tuna to the United States to the taking rate actually recorded for United States fishermen during the same period. Consequently, the Mexican authorities could not know whether, at a given point of time, their policies conformed to the United States' dolphin protection standards. The Panel considered that a limitation on trade based on such unpredictable conditions could not be regarded as necessary to protect the health or life of dolphins.

On the basis of the above considerations, the Panel found that the United States' direct import prohibition imposed on certain yellowfin tuna and certain yellowfin tuna products of Mexico and the provisions of the MMPA under which it is imposed could not be justified under the exception in Article XX(b).

The Panel proceeded to examine whether the prohibition . . . could be justified under the exception in Article XX(g). The Panel noted the United States, in invoking Article XX(g) with respect to its direct import prohibition under the MMPA, had argued that the measures taken under the MMPA are measures primarily aimed at the conservation of dolphin, and that the import restrictions on certain tuna and tuna products under the MMPA are "primarily aimed at rendering effective restrictions on domestic production or consumption" of dolphin.

The Panel also noted that Mexico had argued that the United States measures were not justified under the exception in Article XX(g) because, inter alia, this provision could not be applied extrajurisdictionally.

The Panel noted that Article XX(g) required that the measures relating to the conservation of exhaustible natural resources be taken "in conjunction with restrictions on domestic production or consumption." A previous panel had found that a measure could only be considered to have been taken "in conjunction with" production restrictions "if it was primarily aimed at rendering effective these restrictions." A country can effectively control the production or consumption of an exhaustible natural resource only to the extent that the production or consumption is under its jurisdiction. This suggests that Article XX(g) was intended to permit contracting parties to take trade measures primarily aimed at rendering effective restrictions on production or consumption within their jurisdiction.

The Panel further noted that Article XX(g) allows each contracting party to adopt its own conservation policies. The conditions set out in Article XX(g) which limit resort to this exception, namely that the measures taken must be related to the conservation of exhaustible natural resources, and that they not "constitute a means of arbitrary or unjustifiable discrimination . . . or a disguised restriction on international trade" refer to the trade measure requiring justification under Article XX(g), not, however, to the conservation policies adopted by the contracting party. The Panel considered that if the extrajurisdictional interpretation of Article XX(g) suggested by the United States were accepted, each contracting party could unilaterally determine the conservation policies from which other contracting parties could not deviate without jeopardizing their rights under the General Agreement. The considerations that led the Panel to reject an extrajurisdictional application of Article XX(b) therefore apply also to Article XX(g).

The Panel did not consider that the United States measures, even if Article XX(g) could be applied extrajurisdictionally, would meet the conditions set out in that provision. A previous panel found that a measure could be considered as "relating to the conservation of exhaustible natural resources" within the meaning of Article XX(g) only if it was primarily aimed at such conservation. The Panel recalled that the United States linked the maximum incidental dolphin-taking rate which Mexico had to meet during a particular period in order to be able to export tuna to the United States to the taking rate actually recorded for United States fishermen during the same period. Consequently, the Mexican authorities could not know whether, at a given point in time, their conservation policies conformed to the United States conservation standards. The Panel considered that a limitation on trade based on such unpredictable conditions could not be regarded as being primarily aimed at the conservation of dolphins.

On the basis of the above considerations, the Panel found that the United States' direct import prohibition on certain yellowfin tuna products of Mexico directly imported from Mexico, and the provisions of the MMPA under which it is imposed, could not be justified under Article XX(g).

NOTES AND QUESTIONS

1. Does the panel's decision mean that the Article XX(b) exemption extends only to measures designed to protect resources within a nation's boundaries? If other countries choose to harm their own environment, does the United States have a legitimate interest in not trading with them? The draft UNCED Declaration endorses GATT's approach and states that "[u]nilateral actions to deal with environmental challenges outside the jurisdiction of the importing country should be avoided." Could restrictions designed solely to protect resources in another country ever be justified? What if the harm spills over into the global commons? Are there any circumstances in which import restrictions validly could be imposed under GATT solely to protect resources in the global commons?

2. The panel finds that the United States failed to meet the "necessity" requirement of Article XX(b) because it had not first exhausted all options to pursue dolphin protection consistent with GATT. What other options were open to the United States? Is the panel saying, in effect, that unilateral import restrictions will presumptively be invalid?

3. Why did the panel reject the U.S. claim that the tuna embargo was a valid conservation measure under Article XX(g)? Could the MMPA regulations be amended to satisfy these objections? In the first dispute involving the Canada-U.S. Free Trade Agreement, a trade panel found that regulations under Canada's Fisheries Act that required biological sampling of fish prior to export were invalid because their primary goal was not conservation. The panel indicated that regulations restricting trade would be upheld only if their *sole* purpose was conservation and only if there was no available alternative that was less restrictive. McKeith, The Environment and Free Trade, 10 Pac. Basin L.J. 183, 207 (1991).

4. Could this problem be resolved by implementing a "dolphin-safe" labeling scheme, as discussed in Chapter 2? Would such a scheme essentially let U.S. consumers decide whether they are willing to pay more to protect the global commons? In 1990 Congress enacted the Dolphin Consumer Protection Information Act, 16 U.S.C. §1385 (1990), which provides penalties for companies that use "dolphin safe" labels falsely. The GATT tuna panel went on to hold that this legislation was not inconsistent with U.S. obligations under GATT.

5. Hardly any U.S. tuna boats fish in the waters of the eastern

tropical Pacific Ocean. If the United States had little or no tuna industry of its own that was competing directly with the Mexican fleet, should it be more likely or less likely that the tuna embargo would be deemed a protectionist measure?

6. How is the methodology used to assess the validity of import restrictions under GATT similar to, or different from, the Supreme Court's formula for assessing the constitutionality of state restrictions on waste imports? Recall Philadelphia v. New Jersey, page 384 above, and its progeny. Note the importance of the principle of nondiscrimination for both. Is the Article XX(b) exception for health and safety measures equivalent to the "nuisance exception" to commerce clause doctrine? Is GATT's provision for measures to conserve natural resources in Article XX(g) the equivalent of the conservation cases discussed on page 393?

7. Despite this ruling in its favor, Mexico has sought to strengthen measures to protect the incidental taking of dolphins by its tuna fleet. A U.S. public relations firm hired by the Mexican government placed full-page ads in several U.S. newspapers featuring a picture of dolphins and the caption "A Longstanding Commitment Just Got Deeper." The ads announced that Mexico would require internationally certified observers on all tuna boats and would seek a law authorizing prison sentences for violators of its dolphin protection laws. The ads also announced that the government would seek to delay enforcing the GATT decision pending negotiations with the United States. In 1992, a U.S. district court directed that the tuna embargo be broadened, under the provisions of the Pelly Amendment, to prevent "tuna laundering" by 30 countries that purchase tuna from Mexico. Earth Island Institute v. Mosbacher, 785 F. Supp. 826 (N.D. Calif. 1992). While this would extend the embargo to more than half of the tuna imported into the United States, raising tuna prices from five to ten cents a can, Bradsher, U.S. Told to Ban Tuna Imports to Protect Dolphins, N.Y. Times, Jan. 15, 1992, at D16, a preliminary agreement has been reached to lift the embargo in return for a five-year moratorium on the use of purse-seine in the eastern tropical Pacific. Davis, U.S., Mexico, Venezuela Reach Accord to Protect Dolphins from Tuna Nets, Wall St. J., Mar. 20, 1992, at B10.

2. International Trade in Hazardous Substances

International trade in hazardous substances has exacerbated tensions between developing nations and the industrialized world. As industrialized countries adopt increasingly stringent environmental standards, countries without such standards have become inviting targets for the marketing and disposal of hazardous substances. Three types of activities—exports of hazardous waste, marketing of products banned in industrialized nations, and trade in other hazardous substances—raise environmental concerns explored below.

A. POLICY ISSUES

Exports of hazardous waste from industrialized nations have created international incidents when developing nations have discovered that they were the intended dumping grounds for toxic residue. When 8,000 drums of toxic waste, including 150 tons of PCBs, were dumped in a small Nigerian fishing village by an Italian firm, Nigeria recalled its ambassador to Italy and forced the firm to reclaim the waste. The waste, aboard the *Karin B.*, was then refused by five countries before being returned to Italy. Guinea jailed a Norwegian diplomat after a Norwegian ship dumped toxic waste there. After Panama refused a shipment of incinerator ash on board the *Khian Sea*, the shipper tried to dump it on a Haitian beach but was stopped after unloading 3,000 tons. The *Khian Sea* then roamed the oceans for 18 months, unable to find a willing recipient for its cargo. After visiting five continents and changing its name three times the boat reappeared, without its cargo, which probably was dumped in the Indian Ocean. French, A Most Deadly Trade, World-Watch 11 (July-Aug. 1990).

It is not difficult to understand why increasing quantities of hazardous waste are being exported by industrialized nations. Wendy Grieder of EPA's Office of International Activities notes that some developing countries charge as little as $40 per ton for disposal of wastes that can cost $250 to $300 per ton to dispose of in the United States. Chepesiuk, From Ash to Cash: The International Trade in Toxic Waste, E 31, 35 (July-Aug. 1991). While data on the volume of waste exports are sketchy, it is estimated that industrialized nations shipped three million tons of toxic waste to less developed countries between 1986 and 1988, Obstler, Toward a Working Solution to Global Pollution: Importing CERCLA to Regulate the Export of Hazardous Waste, 16 Yale J. Intl. L. 73, 76 (1991), and that the volume of exports is increasing.

The export of hazardous substances also is expanding. As regulation and increased consumer awareness reduce the domestic demand for such substances, producers of hazardous substances have intensified marketing efforts in developing countries. Products that are banned in the United States generally can be manufactured for export. For example, the pesticides heptachlor and chlordane, which have been banned by EPA, are currently being manufactured in the United States for export. Several other pesticides that have not been approved by EPA also are manufactured for export. Exports of such pesticides and other hazardous materials place workers at risk in developing countries, where regulatory standards are far less strict than in the United States. U.S.

consumers may continue to be exposed to pesticides banned as unreasonably dangerous under FIFRA when residues of such pesticides are present on imported fruits and vegetables, a phenomenon called the "circle of poison." See D. Weir and M. Shapiro, Circle of Poison: Pesticides and People in a Hungry World (1982).

Export markets are being aggressively pursued for products whose use is being phased out or discouraged to protect health in the United States. For example, while the United States is eliminating lead additives from gasoline to prevent lead poisoning, manufacturers of lead additives have expanded their sales to developing countries. In 1991 the Ethyl Corporation of Richmond, Virginia applied for permission to double production of lead additives at a plant in Sarnia, Canada to facilitate greater exports to South America. Although Canada also has banned lead additives in gasoline, fuel additives manufactured for export are exempt from the 1988 Canadian Environmental Protection Act's prohibition on the export of products banned domestically. Gorrie, Groups Oppose Canada's Export of Lead Additive, Toronto Star, Mar. 25, 1991, at D8. U.S. exports of cigarettes to developing countries have soared, easily offsetting substantial declines in domestic demand. In 1989 smoking in the United States dropped by 5 percent, while U.S. exports of tobacco rose 20 percent. Despite dramatic declines in smoking in the United States, tobacco use has soared by 75 percent worldwide during the past 20 years. The American Medical Association has charged that this dramatic increase is a result of U.S. trade policies that ignore the hazards of U.S. products sold abroad. Arguing that the United States has no business dictating how American companies should respond to foreign demand, the U.S. Cigarette Export Association has opposed efforts to require foreign-language health warning labels on cigarettes exported from the United States. A.M.A. Assails Nation's Export Policy on Tobacco, N.Y. Times, June 27, 1990, at A12. When Thailand sought to ban cigarette imports, the United States invoked GATT, and the ban was struck down because it did not apply to Thai cigarettes.

Critics of the international trade in hazardous substances argue that it is unfair or immoral for industrialized nations to export risks they are unwilling to bear to poor countries that are ill-prepared to handle them. Because "[m]ost developing countries have neither the technical capability nor the regulatory infrastructure to ensure safe handling and destruction of toxic waste," NRDC representatives argue that exports to such countries are "economically, environmentally, morally, and technically indefensible." Uva and Bloom, Exporting Pollution: The International Waste Trade, 31 Environment 4 (June 1989). Critics argue that the absence of effective controls on hazardous substance exports also promotes environmental damage, poisons relations between industrialized and developing countries, and puts U.S. consumers at risk through the "circle of poison."

Opponents of stricter regulation argue that it is paternalistic for the industrialized world to dictate environmental standards to less developed countries. They argue that it may be more efficient for developing countries to adopt less stringent environmental standards to promote development. In a controversial memorandum, Lawrence Summers, the World Bank's chief economist, wrote that "the economic logic behind dumping a load of toxic waste in the lowest wage country is impeccable" because lost earnings caused by a given amount of health damage would be lower there. Noting that "underpopulated countries in Africa are vastly *under*polluted," the memo argued that cancer risks should be of less concern there because life expectancy already is low. Weisskopf, World Bank Official's Irony Backfires, Wash. Post, Feb. 10, 1992, at A9. Brazil's environmental minister dubbed this reasoning "perfectly logical but totally insane." Cockburn, "Earth Summit" Is in Thrall to the Marketeers, L.A. Times, Mar. 1, 1992, at M5.

B. REGULATION OF INTERNATIONAL TRADE IN HAZARDOUS SUBSTANCES

One approach to the problems raised by international trade in hazardous substances is to emphasize the principle of informed consent in a manner similar to the informational approaches to regulation explored in Chapter 4. This is the approach most existing U.S. laws follow, as indicated in Figure 9.4. Section 3017 of RCRA requires persons seeking to export hazardous waste to notify EPA at least 60 days prior to shipment of the waste. The Secretary of State is then required to notify the government of the intended recipient and those of any countries through which the waste will pass in transit. Waste may not be exported until written consent has been obtained from the recipient's government, and copies of such consent must be attached to a manifest accompanying such shipments. Waste shipped pursuant to a bilateral agreement, such as the existing agreement between the United States and Canada (the largest recipient of U.S. hazardous waste exports), is exempt from the prior notification and consent requirements on the theory that the agreement already constitutes blanket consent to such shipments.

TSCA and FIFRA require that other countries be notified when regulatory action is taken against a chemical substance or when a pesticide's registration is canceled or suspended. Both statutes, however, permit products banned in the United States to be exported. Indeed, they actually insulate products manufactured solely for export from most domestic regulation. Under section 12(a) of TSCA, EPA can only regulate such products if it determines the risks they present *within the United States* are unreasonable, without considering their impact in countries importing them.

FIGURE 9.4
Provisions in U.S. Environmental Statutes Addressing International Trade in Hazardous Substances

Statutory Provision	Activities or Substances Covered	Requirements
RCRA §3017	Export of hazardous wastes	Prohibited unless notification is provided and the receiving country agrees to accept the waste or unless shipped in conformance with agreement between the United States and the receiving country
TSCA §12(a)	Chemical substances intended for export and so labeled unless found to present an unreasonable risk of injury to health or the environment within the United States	Exempt from all provisions of TSCA except for recordkeeping and reporting requirements imposed under §8
TSCA §12(b)	Chemical substances intended for export for which a data submission has been required under §4 or §5(b) or for which restrictions have been proposed or promulgated under §5 or §6	Notification of government of importing country of availability of data required to be submitted or of the existence of restrictions
FIFRA §17(a)	Unregistered pesticides produced solely for export to a foreign country	Exempt from most regulation when prepared and packed according to the specifications of a foreign purchaser when accompanied by a signed statement filed by the purchaser acknowledging that the pesticide is not registered in the United States
FIFRA §17(b)	Pesticides whose registration is canceled or suspended	Notification of governments of other countries and of appropriate international agencies of cancellation or suspension of registration

Continuing the trend of addressing international environmental problems through multilateral agreements, the Basel Convention on the Control of Transboundary Movement of Hazardous Wastes seeks to establish a framework for controlling hazardous waste exports. Signed in 1989, the Basel Convention builds on the informed consent model embodied in RCRA. Postponing the establishment of liability rules or uniform standards for waste management, the Convention adopts provisions to require tracking of waste shipments, to provide notification to importing countries, and to verify their acceptance of the waste. Its provisions and their relationship to RCRA are described in the following article.

Johnson, The Basel Convention: The Shape of Things to Come for United States Waste Exports?
21 Envtl. L. 299 (1991)

While the system for regulating waste exports established by the Basel Convention is similar to the United States system under RCRA, there are significant differences between the two systems. The Basel Convention expands the regulation of international solid waste exports in several ways: it is geared toward holding exporting countries accountable for the management of the waste that they export into receiving countries, increasing the ability of transit countries to limit use of their countries for the transportation of solid waste, encouraging waste minimization, and encouraging countries to share information and technology for safe waste management practices.

RCRA and the Basel Convention differ in the scope of waste exports covered. While RCRA's limitations apply only to exports of hazardous waste, the limitations of the Basel Convention apply to exports of hazardous waste, household waste, and residues from the incineration of household waste. The Basel Convention also establishes a broader definition of hazardous waste than does RCRA. Furthermore, while RCRA only regulates the export of waste defined to be hazardous in the United States, the Basel Convention regulates the export of waste defined to be hazardous in any of the countries that are parties to the Convention. Under RCRA, EPA does not have the authority to prohibit the export of wastes other than hazardous waste, as defined by RCRA, even though the receiving country may object to the shipment of those wastes to the country. Therefore, EPA can not impose any manifesting, export notification, record keeping or reporting requirements on persons who export wastes other than hazardous wastes as defined by RCRA. If the United States ratifies the Basel Convention, EPA's authority to impose limitations on the export of wastes other than hazardous wastes will have to be greatly increased.

RCRA's notification and consent requirements are less restrictive than the requirements of the Basel Convention. The Convention recognizes the interest of transit countries in having control over waste shipments through their countries and grants transit countries protection that is absent in RCRA. Under the Convention, an exporting country may not allow waste to be exported unless the receiving country and *any transit countries* have been notified of the shipment and have consented, in writing, to the shipment. EPA provides notification of waste shipments to transit countries and receiving countries under RCRA regulations, but only the consent of the receiving country is necessary before a waste shipment may proceed under RCRA.

Another safety net that the Convention includes to protect the interest of transit and receiving countries is a requirement that waste exporters must be covered by insurance, bonds, or guarantees as required by the receiving country, the exporting country, or any transit countries.

The Convention imposes additional limits on the export of wastes that are not imposed by RCRA. Most significantly, the Convention requires the exporting country to ensure that waste exported from the country is managed in an environmentally sound manner in the receiving country or elsewhere. Technical guidelines specifying what constitutes management "in an environmentally sound manner" are to be prepared by the Convention at the first meeting of the parties after the Convention enters into force. This requirement is important because it imposes a degree of responsibility on exporting countries for the management of their waste in receiving countries, and requires exporting countries to ensure that waste is not being exported from the country simply to avoid the high cost of managing the waste in an environmentally sound manner domestically. This may remove some of the incentive for exporting waste. Under RCRA, if a receiving country consents to accept a shipment of hazardous waste, EPA lacks the authority to prohibit the export of that waste, even if EPA knows that the waste will not be managed in an environmentally sound manner in the receiving country. If the United States ratifies the Basel Convention, EPA will need the authority to ban such shipments of waste.

The "environmentally sound management" requirement is one of several requirements imposed by the Basel Convention to hold exporting countries accountable for the hazards created by improper management of waste after it leaves the exporting country. The Convention imposes a duty on the exporting *country,* as well as the exporter, to ensure that waste will be returned to the exporting country if the waste shipment cannot be completed; RCRA imposes the duty to re-import solely on the exporter.

More importantly, the Convention requires countries that are parties to the Convention to adopt an international protocol setting out rules and procedures regarding liability and compensation for damage resulting from the transboundary movement and disposal of waste. These rules and procedures should provide a convenient and expeditious forum for countries that have suffered damage from the transboundary movement or disposal of waste.

The Convention also requires countries that are parties to the Convention to cooperate in the development and implementation of waste minimization techniques and to make information, standards, and technology regarding environmentally sound waste management and waste minimization practices available to other countries. To that end, the Convention proposes establishing regional waste management and waste minimization training and technology transfer centers. Finally, the Convention requires countries to place far broader restrictions on imports of solid waste than the United States currently places on such imports.

Whether ratifying and implementing the Basel Convention will reduce the volume of hazardous and non-hazardous solid waste exports from the United States and encourage environmentally sound management of waste will depend on questions that have not yet been resolved by the Convention. As noted earlier in this article, many persons choose to export waste from the United States to avoid the high cost of waste management in the United States, and to avoid the potential liability imposed by United States environmental laws. The Basel Convention took a step toward removing both of these incentives by requiring environmentally sound management of waste in the country to which waste is exported and by requiring the parties to the Convention to establish rules and procedures for international liability and compensation for damage resulting from the transboundary movement of waste.

However, the Convention postponed for future consideration determining what technical standards and procedures constitute "environmentally sound management of waste" and postponed actually establishing rules and procedures for international liability and compensation. If the parties to the Basel Convention establish a strong protocol on international liability that holds countries accountable for the hazards created by mismanagement of exported waste and if the parties to the Convention establish strict technical standards to define what constitutes "environmentally sound management" of waste, the Convention may effectively remove the incentives that make waste export an economically attractive alternative to domestic waste management.

The Convention also lays the groundwork for potentially more stringent restrictions on waste export in the future. Three years after the Convention enters into force, the parties are directed to consider a complete or partial ban on transboundary waste movement covered by the Convention, if necessary.

NOTES AND QUESTIONS

1. The Basel Convention postponed resolution of many difficult issues, including liability standards and determination of what constitutes "environmentally sound management." Implementation of the Convention will be complicated by the difficulty of defining hazardous waste. Because countries vary greatly in their decisions concerning what wastes are sufficiently hazardous to warrant controls, many countries will have to seek new authority to control waste covered by the Convention. The United States has signed the Convention and is seeking Senate ratification along with amendments to RCRA to provide EPA with additional authority to implement the terms of the Convention. For more information on the provisions of the Basel Convention, see generally Hackett, An Assessment of the Basel Convention on the Control of Transboundary Movements of Hazardous Wastes and Their Disposal, 5 Am. U.J. Intl. L. & Poly. 291 (1990).

2. EPA has been criticized for its failure to enforce aggressively RCRA's export requirements. Both the General Accounting Office and EPA's inspector general have found that many exporters fail to notify EPA or submit deficient or fraudulent manifests. For example, more than one-half of the manifests EPA received in 1987 for hazardous waste exports did not even show a port of exit. EPA had not established any monitoring program with U.S. Customs to detect illegal waste exports. The Agency subsequently beefed up its enforcement efforts, though problems remain.

3. The Basel Convention was signed on March 22, 1989 by 116 countries. While the Convention does not preclude any country from regulating or banning imports of hazardous wastes, many developing countries refused to sign it because they wanted more stringent controls to prevent illegal waste exports. The Basel Convention was developed under the auspices of UNEP and provides further evidence of the benefits of an institution devoted to promoting such agreements. Petsonk, The Role of the United Nations Environmental Programme (UNEP) in the Development of International Environmental Law, 5 Am. U.J. Intl. L. & Poly. 351, 373-381 (1990). On the other hand, some of the concerns about the Convention's inadequacies reflect the fact that UNEP has neither the resources nor the technical expertise to be an effective implementation agency.

4. The Bhopal tragedy highlighted the dangers of improper management of hazardous materials in developing countries. While Bhopal involved chemicals legal in the United States, the question whether the United States should continue to permit the export of products banned domestically has been receiving increasing attention. Amendments that would prohibit the export of such pesticides were included in farm bills that passed both houses of Congress in 1990 but were eliminated during

conference committee. U.S. chemical manufacturers have vigorously opposed such proposals by arguing that they would result in job losses in the United States without any corresponding gain in public health protection.

5. Proposals have been made to extend the principle of prior informed consent (PIC) beyond hazardous waste exports to cover exports of hazardous chemical products. The chemical industry opposes such proposals as unjustified interferences with the sovereignty of foreign states that will delay commercial transactions to the disadvantage of U.S. firms. See Walls, Chemical Exports and the Age of Consent: The High Cost of International Export Control Proposals, 20 Intl. L. & Pol. 753 (1988). Implementation of PIC is complicated because it can be extremely difficult to communicate scientific information about the hazards of chemicals in countries with widely varying social and cultural norms. See Kalmbach, International Labeling Requirements for the Export of Hazardous Chemicals: A Developing Nation's Perspective, 19 L. & Poly. in Intl. Bus. 811 (1987).

6. Enforcement of restrictions on trade in hazardous waste is much more difficult than enforcement of restriction on CFCs. The class and volume of substances affected by restrictions on trade in hazardous waste is much larger than the substances affected by CFC restrictions. It is far easier to control production of CFCs by a relatively small number of large firms than to regulate disposal of waste by thousands of small firms worldwide. CFCs are a valuable commodity unlikely to be "lost," while hazardous waste has negative value, creating significant incentives for corruption and losing paperwork. Petsonk, above, at 379-381. A strategy for improving incentives for proper management of waste exports might be to establish a market in waste import rights to be allocated among countries willing to be importers. Exporters would then have to buy rights, creating incentives for a functioning market in waste exports. Id.

7. One of the major limitations of the Basel Convention is the absence of any provision addressed to liability for improper disposal. Article 12 simply states that the parties shall develop rules and procedures for liability and damages. Indeed, once consent is given, it may be more difficult for a receiving country to seek compensation for costs if it subsequently finds that disposal is much more difficult or expensive than anticipated. (Can you think of a domestic comparison?) The Convention may also provide some shelter to multinational corporations insofar as responsibility is focused on governments. See Hackett, above, at 320-322.

8. Because of concerns about the adequacy of the Basel Convention, numerous proposals have been made to either strengthen the agreement or pursue entirely new approaches. See, e.g., Rabe, Exporting Hazardous Waste in North America, 1 Intl. Envtl. Aff. 108 (1990) (outright bans or tighter permit systems possible alternatives). Another possibility is to

allow claims by foreigners for damage from exports of hazardous waste from the United States. One commentator has argued that

> the statutory language of CERCLA implies that liability for releases of hazardous substances generated in the United States extends beyond our borders. The language suggests that CERCLA creates global, cradle to grave accountability of hazardous waste exports from the United States, and that foreign parties may pursue that accountability with an unrestricted, statutory right of action in United States federal district courts. [Obstler, Toward a Working Solution to Global Pollution, 16 Yale J. Intl. L. 73, 108 (1991).]

Would this strategy provide an effective solution to U.S. waste exports? What other consequences might it have?

9. In the case below, Wath, a British corporation, agreed to acquire waste material generated by a pesticide plant owned by the FMC Corporation in Baltimore, Maryland because it believed the material to be suitable for metals reclamation in England. After 20 containers of the material arrived in England, Wath discovered that it was highly contaminated with xylene and chlorinated phenols, despite FMC's assurances that it would be free from harmful impurities. British authorities then ordered Wath to take remedial action because of the hazardous character of the materials. Wath sued FMC in a British court, which held that the case should be brought in the United States, where all FMC's actions had occurred. Amlon, Wath's U.S. agent, then filed suit in federal court in New York asserting claims under the Alien Tort Statute and RCRA.

Amlon Metals, Inc. v. FMC Corp.
775 F. Supp. 668 (S.D.N.Y. 1991)

WILLIAM C. CONNER, District Judge.

This action stems from a commercial contract for the recycling of copper residue produced by defendant FMC Corporation ("FMC"). The matter is currently before the court on FMC's motion to dismiss plaintiffs' claims under the Resource Conservation and Recovery Act ("RCRA") and Alien Tort Statute, 28 U.S.C. §1350, on the grounds that this court lacks jurisdiction over the claims pursuant to Fed. R. Civ. P. 12(b)(1) and that the claims fail to state a claim upon which relief can be granted pursuant to Fed. R. Civ. P. 12(b)(6). . . .

When considering Alien Tort Statute claims on a 12(b)(1) motion, courts typically engage "in a more searching preliminary review of the merits than is required," for example under the more flexible "arising under formulation." Filartiga v. Pena-Irala, 630 F.2d 876 (2d Cir. 1980). This Court will do likewise.

An allegation of conduct constituting a treaty violation or a violation of the law of nations is a threshold jurisdictional requirement under the Alien Tort Statute, 28 U.S.C. §1350. See *Filartiga,* 630 F.2d at 880. If this requirement is not met, an action under section 1350 cannot be maintained. See id. at 887. Here, the complaint does not allege any treaty violation that is actionable under the Alien Tort Statute. Therefore, the complaint must allege facts that, if true, would constitute a violation of the law of nations.

Plaintiffs assert that the complaint does allege facts that constitute a violation of the law of nations. In particular, plaintiffs argue that FMC's conduct is violative of the Stockholm Principles, United Nations Conference on the Human Environment (adopted June 16, 1972), to which the U.S. is a signatory.[2] Plaintiffs also cite the Restatement (Third) of Foreign Relations Law §602(2) (1987), in support of their position.[3]

But these invocations of international law do not establish a violation of such law under the Alien Tort Statute. In *Filartiga,* one of the few cases to find the Statute applicable, the court stressed that "[i]t is only where the nations of the world have demonstrated that the wrong is of mutual and not merely several, concern, by means of express international accords, that a wrong generally recognized becomes an international law violation within the meaning of the statute." *Filartiga,* 630 F.2d at 888. Subsequent decisions have emphasized the narrow scope of *Filartiga's* holding. For example, in Zapata v. Quinn, 707 F.2d 691, 692 (2d Cir. 1983) (per curiam) the Second Circuit, citing *Filartiga,* held that the Alien Tort Statute "applies only to shockingly egregious violations of universally recognized principles of international law."

Plaintiffs' reliance on the Stockholm Principles is misplaced, since those Principles do not set forth any specific proscriptions, but rather refer only in a general sense to the responsibility of nations to insure

---

2. Principle 21, which plaintiffs aver is most explicit on the subject, states:

States have, in accordance with the Charter of the United Nations and the principles of international law, the sovereign right to exploit their own resources pursuant to their own environmental policies, and the responsibility to ensure that activities within their jurisdiction or control do not cause damage to the environment of other States or of areas beyond the limits of national jurisdiction.

3. The Restatement (Third) of Foreign Relations Law §602(2) (1987), in discussing the standards regarding "Remedies for Violation of Environmental Obligations," holds that:

[w]here pollution originating in a state has caused significant injury to persons outside that state, or has created a significant risk of such injury, the state of origin is obligated to accord to the person injured or exposed to such risk access to the same judicial or administrative remedies as are available in similar circumstances to persons within the state.

that activities within their jurisdiction do not cause damage to the environment beyond their borders. Nor does the Restatement of Foreign Relations law constitute a statement of universally recognized principles of international law. At most, as plaintiffs' own brief suggests, the Restatement iterates the existing *U.S.* view of the law of nations regarding global environmental protection.

Because the complaint contains no clear allegation of a violation of the law of nations, plaintiffs' second cause of action is dismissed. . . .

In their complaint, plaintiffs assert as their Second Claim for Relief a cause of action under RCRA's citizen suit provision, 42 U.S.C. §6972. Specifically, they seek injunctive relief and damages under Section 6972(a)(1)(B), which provides that any person may commence a civil action

> against any person . . . including any past or present generator, past or present transporter, or past or present owner or operator of a treatment, storage, or disposal facility, who has contributed or who is contributing to the past or present handling, storage, treatment, transportation, or disposal of any solid or hazardous waste which may present an imminent and substantial endangerment to health or to the environment.

Plaintiffs contend that they are entitled to relief under this provision because potentially toxic chemicals may evaporate from or leak out of containers in which they have stored the copper residue, posing an imminent and substantial danger to workers nearby and the community at large if the chemicals pollute the local water supply.

Defendant avers, however, that even accepting plaintiff's allegations as true, as this court must do on this motion, plaintiff's claim under section 6972(a)(1)(B) fails to state a claim upon which relief can be granted because RCRA does not extend to waste located within the territory of another sovereign nation. In support of its contention, defendant points to the well-established principle of American law "that legislation of Congress, unless a contrary intent appears, is meant to apply only within the territorial jurisdiction of the United States." EEOC v. Arabian American Oil Co.,—U.S.—,111 S. Ct. 1227, 1230 (1991) (quoting Foley Bros. v. Filardo, 336 U.S. 281, 285 (1949)). Defendant notes further that in applying this canon of construction, courts must determine whether "language in the [relevant act] gives any indication of a congressional purpose to extend its coverage beyond places over which the United States has sovereignty or some measure of legislative control." Id. (quoting *Foley Bros.*, 336 U.S. at 285). Thus, defendant maintains that courts must assume that Congress legislates against the backdrop of an underlying presumption against extraterritoriality and therefore must presume that the statute applies only within the United States unless it contains "the affirmative intention of Congress clearly expressed" that it applies abroad. Id. (quoting Benz v. Compania Naviera Hidalgo, S.A., 353 U.S. 138, 147 (1957)).

Plaintiffs attempt to work around this principle by pointing to a number of cases, most of which arise under the federal securities laws, that purport to grant jurisdiction based on the locus of conduct underlying the claim. . . .

While acknowledging that the endangerment alleged in the present action has occurred primarily in England, plaintiffs maintain that the conduct test should apply here because significant activities giving rise to the endangerment, including the generation of the waste, the making of the contract and the consignment of the waste to the carrier, took place in the U.S. In addition, plaintiffs aver that this case is distinguishable from *Arabian American Oil* and other cases cited by defendant because this case does not involve the application of "substantive" American law.[4]

Defendant responds by arguing that plaintiffs gain little by their reliance on *Leasco* and related cases.[5] Specifically, defendant maintains that nothing in the securities law cases relied on by plaintiffs suggests that the conduct test allows a court to apply a statute extraterritorially without determining that Congress in fact intended such extraterritorial application. The court agrees. . . .

Plaintiffs concede that nothing in RCRA suggests that Congress intended for its regulatory provisions to apply extraterritorially and that RCRA's "substantive" provisions "clearly do not apply abroad." Yet plaintiffs nonetheless contend that the citizen suit provision of RCRA should be applied extraterritorially. In particular, plaintiffs maintain that two aspects of RCRA, its export provision, 42 U.S.C. §6938, and the use of the term "any person" in its citizen suit provision, 42 U.S.C. §6972, support their view.

Yet plaintiffs adduce little evidence to bolster their position. Plaintiffs allege repeatedly that the citizen suit provision and the export provision were passed as part of a single bill, the Hazardous and Solid Waste Amendment of 1984. Even if they were passed at the same time, as

---

4. . . . In the instant case, plaintiffs aver that no such aspect of international comity is implicated since British authorities are telling plaintiffs how to manage the waste so that further injury does not occur and if FMC were forced to remove the waste such removal would have to be in compliance with the local regulatory regime for disposal. Thus plaintiffs maintain that British substantive law would control.

5. Defendant also maintains that the conduct test is inapplicable to the instant case. . . . Stated simply, defendant's point here is that the imminent and substantial endangerment provision is not triggered by conduct but by the existence of a condition of endangerment that exists entirely overseas and thus FMC's conduct cannot give rise to a cause of action under RCRA.

plaintiffs allege, the two provisions, as noted above, were certainly discussed separately, with a domestic emphasis attached to the remedial provision. Moreover, as defendant notes, the export provision and citizen suit provision were in fact just two of over 60 RCRA amendments passed simultaneously, addressing numerous topics as varied as land disposal practices, ground water monitoring and regulation of underground storage tanks.

As for plaintiffs' second argument, the use of the term "any person" in RCRA's citizen suit provision without more cannot be said to establish RCRA's extraterritorial applicability. This is especially so when, as defendant notes, other portions of the citizen suit provision itself reflect a domestic focus. Thus, for example, the citizen suit venue provision contained in section 6972(a)(1) provides that a citizen suit "shall be brought in the district court for the district in which the alleged endangerment may occur." RCRA contains nothing prescribing a venue for citizen suits concerning waste located in a foreign country. Similarly, section 6972(b)(2) provides that no citizen suit may be commenced until 90 days after the plaintiff has given notice of the endangerment to "the State in which the alleged endangerment may occur" and that a citizen suit cannot be commenced if the "State" has undertaken action to address the alleged endangerment. As with the venue provision, had Congress intended the citizen suit provision of RCRA to apply extraterritorially, it would have spoken to the question of what pre-suit notice would be required for waste located in the territory of another nation and would have addressed the effect on a citizen suit of a suit pending in that nation.

Also damaging to plaintiffs' position is defendant's citation of several other provisions of RCRA that tend to show that in adopting the statute, Congress was concerned with hazardous waste problems in the United States, not in foreign countries. For example, defendant notes that the first section of RCRA, setting forth the findings of Congress with respect to the issues that RCRA was passed to address, characterizes the problem of waste disposal as "a matter national in scope and concern." 42 U.S.C. §6901(a)(4). Among the congressional findings is that "alternatives to existing methods of land disposal must be developed since many of the cities in the United States will be running out of suitable solid disposal sites within five years unless immediate action is taken." 42 U.S.C. §6901(b)(8).

In addition, defendant notes that RCRA contains a number of provisions designed to limit the statute's encroachment on state sovereignty, but contains no parallel provisions protecting the sovereignty of other nations. For example, before commencing an action to redress "an imminent and substantial endangerment to health or environment," the administrator of the EPA must provide notice to "the affected State." 42 U.S.C. §6973(a); there is no analogous provision requiring notice to the appropriate authorities in a foreign country.

Having examined the relevant legislative history and the structure and language of RCRA, this court is unpersuaded by plaintiffs' claims.[11] Since there is little if any evidence to support plaintiffs' contention that Congress desired RCRA to apply extraterritorially, this court must decline to apply the statute in the instant case.

NOTES AND QUESTIONS

1. The Alien Tort Statute, 28 U.S.C. §1350, provides federal jurisdiction over actions by aliens for torts "committed in violation of the law of nations or a treaty of the United States." *Filartiga* involved a suit by Paraguayan citizens who had sought political asylum in the United States against a Paraguayan police official who had tortured and murdered their son. The Second Circuit held that deliberate torture perpetrated under color of official authority violated universally accepted norms of international human rights law. Under the *Amlon* court's interpretation of the Alien Tort Statute, can you imagine a successful claim ever being made under the Statute for conduct involving the export of hazardous materials? Under what circumstances?

2. The plaintiffs in *Amlon* did not contend that RCRA's regulatory provisions had extraterritorial application. Rather, they maintained that foreigners should be able to use RCRA's citizen suit provisions to seek redress for actions that occurred in the United States that allegedly caused imminent and substantial endangerment abroad. A related question that has arisen in other contexts is whether EPA may, should, or must consider the extraterritorial impact of its actions when regulating hazardous substances under domestic environmental law. As noted above, section 12(a) of TSCA prohibits EPA from considering the extraterritorial environmental risks of chemical products manufactured solely for export. In Corrosion Proof Fittings v. EPA, 947 F.2d 1201 (5th Cir. 1991), the Fifth Circuit suggested that EPA need not consider extrater-

---

11. It should be noted that both plaintiffs and defendant have articulated a number of policy arguments to support their respective positions. While plaintiff does argue convincingly that applying RCRA extraterritorially in the instant case would not foster international conflict but would likely promote international harmony and help alleviate foreign fears about United States waste exports, defendant has also argued persuasively against the application of RCRA on policy grounds. Stated simply, defendant posits a number of scenarios wherein extraterritorial application of RCRA could create awkward foreign relations difficulties. Thus, for example, under plaintiff's approach any time a foreign government consented to the import of a hazardous waste, foreign citizens who objected to their government's decision could sue in this country to have the waste removed.

ritorial impacts when regulating domestic chemical use under section 6(c) of TSCA. What rule should apply when regulating hazardous air pollutants under section 112 of the Clean Air Act? For example, should a risk assessment of arsenic emissions from a copper smelter in El Paso, Texas consider only cancer risks in the United States, or should it also consider risks to a large exposed population across the border in Mexico? See R. Luken, Setting Standards for Inorganic Arsenic Emissions from Primary Copper Smelters, in Conference on Valuing Health Risks, Costs and Benefits for Environmental Policymaking (1987).

3. Are U.S. courts capable of adequately assessing the merits of allegations of environmental damage occurring abroad? See In re Union Carbide Corp. Gas Plant Disaster, 634 F. Supp. 842 (S.D.N.Y. 1986), modified on appeal, 809 F.2d 195 (2d Cir. 1987).

4. One proposal for dealing with the problem of weak regulation in developing countries is to require multinational corporations to follow the "highest safety standard" applicable to them throughout their operations. This approach is sometimes cited as a means of avoiding accidents similar to the one that occurred at a Union Carbide chemical plant at Bhopal, India because the safety requirements at comparable U.S. plants were much more extensive. See American Society of International Law, Proceedings of the 79th Annual Meeting 303-322 (1985). The benefits and limitations of this approach are discussed in Gleckman, Proposed Requirements for Transnational Corporations to Disclose Information on Product and Process Hazards, 6 B.U. Intl. L.J. 89 (1988).

5. What are the potential sources of international "law" relevant to exports of hazardous substances from the United States? Can U.S. law be effective insofar as the requirements by definition apply outside U.S. boundaries? See Bent, Exporting Hazardous Industries: Should American Standards Apply?, 20 N.Y.U. J. Intl. L. & Pol. 777 (1988). Do voluntary codes of conduct potentially have any legal effect? How might a court consider such codes in any suit for negligence arising from inconsistent conduct? Are the provisions of a treaty like the Basel Convention likely to be more easily enforced than such codes?

6. One possible strategy for holding multinational companies accountable for damage caused by the export of hazardous substances is tort litigation by foreigners injured by exposure to such substances. In addition to the usual difficulties of proving causation in toxic tort cases, foreign plaintiffs face other formidable obstacles. American courts may refuse to hear cases brought by plaintiffs injured in foreign countries by invoking the doctrine of forum non conveniens, as illustrated by the litigation over the Bhopal tragedy, which was rejected by American courts. Because American tort law is perceived to be more generous to plaintiffs than the law in most foreign countries, the choice of forum can have a substantial impact on the prospects for recovery and the amount of

damages available. Consider the following case, in which banana workers in Costa Rica claimed that they had been injured by a pesticide that EPA had banned within the United States, but which continues to be produced in the United States for export abroad. The Costa Rican workers brought a tort action in Texas state court against the U.S. company that manufactured the pesticide. After the trial court dismissed the action, the plaintiffs appealed to the Texas Supreme Court. The court's 5-4 decision produced sharp disagreement among the justices, as indicated below.

Dow Chemical Co. v. Alfaro
786 S.W.2d 674 (Tex. 1990), cert. denied, 111 S. Ct. 671 (1991)

RAY, Justice:

Domingo Castro Alfaro, a Costa Rican resident and employee of the Standard Fruit Company, and eighty-one other Costa Rican employees and their wives brought suit against Dow Chemical company and Shell Oil Company. The employees claim that they suffered personal injuries as a result of exposure to dibromochloropropane (DBCP), a pesticide manufactured by Dow and Shell, which was allegedly furnished to Standard Fruit. The employees exposed to DBCP allegedly suffered several medical problems, including sterility.

Alfaro sued Dow and Shell in Harris County district court in April 1984. The amended petition alleged that the court had jurisdiction under article 4678 of the Revised Statutes. Following an unsuccessful attempt to remove the suit to federal court, Dow and Shell contested the jurisdiction of the trial court almost three years after the filing of the suit, and contended in the alternative that the case should be dismissed under the doctrine of forum non conveniens. Despite a finding of jurisdiction, the trial court dismissed the case on the ground of forum non conveniens.

Section 71.031 of the Civil Practice and Remedies Code provides:

(a) An action for damages for the death or personal injury of a citizen of this state, of the United States or of a foreign country may be enforced in the courts of this state, although the wrongful act, neglect, or default causing the death or injury takes place in a foreign state or country, if:

(1) a law of the foreign state or country or of this state gives a right to maintain an action for damages for the death or injury;

(2) the action is begun in this state within the time provided by the laws of this state for beginning the action; and

(3) in the case of a citizen of a foreign country, the country has equal treaty rights with the United States on behalf of its citizens.

(b) All matters pertaining to procedure in the prosecution or maintenance of the action in the courts of this state are governed by the law of this state.

(c) The court shall apply the rules of substantive law that are appropriate under the facts of the case.

Tex. Civ. Prac. & Rem. Code Ann. §71.031 (Vernon 1986). At issue is whether the language "may be enforced in the courts of this state" of Section 71.031(a) permits a trial court to relinquish jurisdiction under the doctrine of forum non conveniens. . . .

We conclude that the legislature has statutorily abolished the doctrine of forum non conveniens in suits brought under section 71.031. Accordingly, we affirm the judgment of the court of appeals, remanding the case to the trial court for further proceedings.

DOGGETT, Justice, concurring:

The dissenters argue that it is *inconvenient* and *unfair* for farmworkers allegedly suffering permanent physical and mental injuries, including irreversible sterility, to seek redress by suing a multinational corporation in a court three blocks away from its world headquarters and another corporation, which operates in Texas this country's largest chemical plant. Because the "doctrine" they advocate has nothing to do with fairness and convenience and everything to do with immunizing multinational corporations from accountability for their alleged torts causing injury abroad, I write separately.

I. THE FACTS

Respondents claim that while working on a banana plantation in Costa Rica for Standard Fruit Company, an American subsidiary of Dole Fresh Fruit Company, headquartered in Boca Raton, Florida, they were required to handle dibromochloropropane ["DBCP"], a pesticide allegedly manufactured and furnished to Standard Fruit by Shell Oil Company ["Shell"] and Dow Chemical Company ["Dow"]. The Environmental Protection Agency issued a notice of intent to cancel all food uses of DBCP on September 22, 1977. 42 Fed. Reg. 48026 (1977). It followed with an order suspending registrations of pesticides containing DBCP on November 3, 1977. 42 Fed. Reg. 57543 (1977). Before and after the E.P.A.'s ban of DBCP in the United States, Shell and Dow apparently shipped several hundred thousand gallons of the pesticide to Costa Rica for use by Standard Fruit. The Respondents, Domingo Castro Alfaro and other plantation workers, filed suit in a state district court in Houston, Texas, alleging that their handling of DBCP caused them serious personal injuries for which Shell and Dow were liable under the theories of products liability, strict liability and breach of warranty. . . .

Shell Oil Company is a multinational corporation with its world headquarters in Houston, Texas. Dow Chemical Company, though head-quartered in Midland, Michigan, conducts extensive operations from its Dow Chemical USA building located in Houston. Dow operates this country's largest chemical manufacturing plant within 60 miles of Houston in Freeport, Texas. The district court where this lawsuit was filed is three blocks away from Shell's world headquarters, One Shell Plaza in downtown Houston.

Shell has stipulated that all of its more than 100,000 documents relating to DBCP are located or will be produced in Houston. Shell's medical and scientific witnesses are in Houston. The majority of Dow's documents and witnesses are located in Michigan, which is far closer to Houston (both in terms of geography and communications linkages) than to Costa Rica. The respondents have agreed to be available in Houston for independent medical examinations, for depositions and for trial. Most of the respondents' treating doctors and co-workers have agreed to testify in Houston. Conversely, Shell and Dow have purport-edly refused to make their witnesses available in Costa Rica.

The banana plantation workers allegedly injured by DBCP were employed by an American company on American-owned land and grew Dole bananas for export solely to American tables. The chemical alleg-edly rendering the workers sterile was researched, formulated, tested, manufactured, labeled and shipped by an American company in the United States to another American company. The decision to manufacture DBCP for distribution and use in the third world was made by these two American companies in their corporate offices in the United States. Yet now Shell and Dow argue that the one part of this equation that should not be American is the legal consequences of their actions. . . .

Comity—deference shown to the interests of the foreign forum— is a consideration best achieved by rejecting forum non conveniens. Comity is not achieved when the United States allows its multinational corporations to adhere to a double standard when operating abroad and subsequently refuses to hold them accountable for those actions. As S. Jacob Scherr, Senior Project Attorney for the National Resources Defense Council, has noted:

> There is a sense of outrage on the part of many poor countries where citizens are the most vulnerable to exports of hazardous drugs, pesticides and food products. At the 1977 meeting of the UNEP Governing Council, Dr. J. C. Kiano, the Kenyan minister for water development, warned that developing nations will no longer tolerate being used as dumping grounds for products that had not been adequately tested "and that their peoples should not be used as guinea pigs for determining the safety of chemicals."

Comments, U.S. Exports Banned for Domestic Use, But Exported to Third World Countries, 6 Int'l Tr. L.J. 95, 98 (1980-81) [hereinafter "U.S. Exports Banned"].

Comity is best achieved by "avoiding the possibility of 'incurring the wrath and distrust of the Third World as it increasingly recognizes that it is being used as the industrial world's garbage can.' " Note, Hazardous Exports From A Human Rights Perspective, 14 Sw. U.L. Rev. 81, 101 (1983) [hereinafter "Hazardous Exports"] (quoting Hon. Michael D. Barnes (Representative in Congress representing Maryland)).

The factors announced in Gulf Oil [Corp. v. Gilbert, 330 U.S. 501 (1947)] fail to achieve fairness and convenience. The public interest factors are designed to favor dismissal and do little to promote the efficient administration of justice. It is clear that the application of forum non conveniens would produce muddled and unpredictable case law, and would be used by defendants to terminate litigation before a consideration of the merits ever occurs.

Public Policy & the Tort Liability of Multinational Corporations in United States Courts

The abolition of forum non conveniens will further important public policy considerations by providing a check on the conduct of multinational corporations (MNCs). See Economic Approach, 22 Geo. Wash. J. Int'l. L. & Econ. at 241. The misconduct of even a few multinational corporations can affect untold millions around the world. For example, after the United States imposed a domestic ban on the sale of cancer-producing TRIS-treated children's sleepwear, American companies exported approximately 2.4 million pieces to Africa, Asia and South America. A similar pattern occurred when a ban was proposed for baby pacifiers that had been linked to choking deaths in infants. Hazardous Exports, supra, 14 Sw. U.L. Rev. at 82. These examples of indifference by some corporations towards children abroad are not unusual.

The allegations against Shell and Dow, if proven true, would not be unique, since production of many chemicals banned for domestic use has thereafter continued for foreign marketing. Professor Thomas McGarity, a respected authority in the field of environmental law, explained:

> During the mid-1970s, the United States Environmental Protection Agency (EPA) began to restrict the use of some pesticides because of their environmental effects, and the Occupational Safety and Health Administration (OSHA) established workplace exposure standards for toxic and hazardous substances in the manufacture of pesticides. . . . [I]t is clear that many pesticides that have been severely restricted in the United States are used

without restriction in many Third World countries, with resulting harm to fieldworkers and the global environment.

McGarity, Bhopal and the Export of Hazardous Technologies, 20 Tex. Int'l L.J. 333, 334 (1985) (citations omitted). By 1976, "29 percent, or 161 million pounds, of all the pesticides exported by the United States were either unregistered or banned for domestic use." McWilliams, Tom Sawyer's Apology: A Reevaluation of United States Pesticide Export Policy, 8 Hastings Int'l & Compl. L. Rev. 61, 61 & n.4 (1984). It is estimated that these pesticides poison 750,000 people in developing countries each year, of which 22,500 die. Id. at 62. Some estimates place the death toll from the "improper marketing of pesticides at 400,000 lives a year." Id. at 62 n.7.

Some United States multinational corporations will undoubtedly continue to endanger human life and the environment with such activities until the economic consequences of these actions are such that it becomes unprofitable to operate in this manner. At present, the tort laws of many third world countries are not yet developed. An Economic Approach, supra, 22 Geo. Wash. J. Int'l L. & Econ. at 222-23. Industrialization "is occurring faster than the development of domestic infrastructures necessary to deal with the problems associated with industry." Exporting Hazardous Industries, supra, 20 Int'l L. & Pol. at 791. When a court dismisses a case against a United States multinational corporation, it often removes the most effective restraint on corporate misconduct. See An Economic Approach, supra, 22 Geo. Wash. J. Int'l L. & Econ. at 241.

The doctrine of forum non conveniens is obsolete in a world in which markets are global and in which ecologists have documented the delicate balance of all life on this planet. The parochial perspective embodied in the doctrine of forum non conveniens enables corporations to evade legal control merely because they are transnational. This perspective ignores the reality that actions of our corporations affecting those abroad will also affect Texans. Although DBCP is banned from use within the United States, it and other similarly banned chemicals have been consumed by Texans eating foods imported from Costa Rica and elsewhere. See D. Weir & M. Schapiro, Circle of Poison 28-30, 77, 82-83 (1981).[15] In the absence of meaningful tort liability in the United

---

[15]Less than one percent of the imported fruits and vegetables are inspected for pesticides. General Accounting Office, Pesticides: Better Sampling and Enforcement Needed on Imported Food, GAO/RCED-86-219 (Sept. 26, 1986), at 3. The GAO found that of the 7.3 billion pounds of bananas imported into the F.D.A.'s Dallas District (covering Texas) from countries other than Mexico in 1984, not a single sample was checked for illegal pesticide residues such as DBCP.

States for their actions, some multinational corporations will continue to operate without adequate regard for the human and environmental costs of their actions. This result cannot be allowed to repeat itself for decades to come.

GONZALEZ, Justice, dissenting.

Under the guise of statutory construction, the court today abolishes the doctrine of forum non conveniens in suits brought pursuant to section 71.032 of the Civil Practice and Remedies Code. This decision makes us one of the few states in the Union without such a procedural tool, and if the legislature fails to reinstate this doctrine, Texas will become an irresistible forum for all mass disaster lawsuits. See generally, Note, Foreign Plaintiffs and Forum Non Conveniens: Going Beyond *Reyno*, 64 Tex. L. Rev. 193 (1985). "Bhopal"-type litigation, with little or no connection to Texas, will *add* to our already crowded dockets, forcing our residents to wait in the corridors of our courthouses while foreign causes of action are tried. I would hold that section 71.031 of the Texas Civil Practice and Remedies Code *does not* confer upon foreign litigants an *absolute right* to bring suit in Texas. Because I believe that trial courts have the inherent power to apply forum non conveniens in appropriate cases, I would provide guidelines and set parameters for its use. I would thus modify the judgment of the court of appeals and remand the cause to the trial court for further proceedings.

This cause of action arose in Costa Rica where certain Costa Rican agricultural workers suffered injuries allegedly as a result of exposure to a pesticide manufactured by the defendants. The injured workers are seeking to enforce in Texas courts claims for personal injuries that occurred in Costa Rica. Several suits involving many of the same plaintiffs and essentially the same defendants have previously been filed in the United States and then dismissed on forum non conveniens grounds. . . .

In conclusion, I have no intent, much less "zeal," to implement social policy as Justice Doggett charges. That is not our role. It is clear that if anybody is trying to advance a particular social policy, it is Justice Doggett. I admire his altruism, and I too sympathize with the plight of the plaintiffs. However, the powers of this court are well-defined, and the sweeping implementations of social welfare policy Justice Doggett seeks to achieve by abolishing the doctrine of forum non conveniens are the exclusive domain of the legislature.

Id. at 53. Even when its meager inspection program discovers illegal pesticides, the F.D.A. rarely sanctions the shipper or producer. Id. at 4. The GAO found only eight instances over a six year period where any punitive action whatsoever was taken. Id. "United States consumers have suffered as pesticide-treated crops are imported to the United States, thus completing a circle of poison." McGarity, supra, 20 Tex. Int'l L.J. at 334.

NOTES AND QUESTIONS

1. The pesticide DBCP to which the plaintiffs had been exposed had been banned in the United States since 1977. What relevance, if any, should this have for plaintiffs' lawsuit?

2. Do you agree with Justice Doggett's claim that forum non conveniens is an obsolete doctrine in a world of global markets? A court's decision to invoke the doctrine to avoid hearing a case is often determinative of the outcome. In a portion of his concurring opinion not reproduced here, Justice Doggett cited a study that concluded that fewer than four percent of cases dismissed by American courts pursuant to the doctrine of forum non conveniens ever are litigated in foreign courts. Robertson, Forum Non Conveniens in America and England: "A Rather Fantastic Fiction," 103 Law Q. Rev. 398, 419 (1987). After the Bhopal litigation was rejected by courts in the United States, the Supreme Court of India approved a settlement in 1989 that would bar all actions against Union Carbide, the owner of the plant involved in the Bhopal tragedy, in return for a payment of $470 million to compensate the victims. Efforts are being made to overturn the settlement. More than 3,000 people were killed and more than 100,000 were injured by the gas leak.

3. Should foreign plaintiffs be permitted to forum shop in search of the most favorable court to hear their claims? In his dissent, Justice Gonzalez noted that the plaintiffs in *Alfaro* previously had filed three lawsuits that had been dismissed by courts in other states on forum non conveniens grounds—two in Florida federal courts and one in a federal court in California.

4. Foreigners can be sued in U.S. courts if it is reasonably foreseeable that actions they take outside the United States will cause harm here. See Ohio v. Wyandotte Chemicals Corp., 401 U.S. 493 (1971).

5. It is easy to understand why the Costa Rican plaintiffs preferred a U.S. forum for their claims. Under Costa Rican law they would have been limited to recoveries of no more than $1,500 each. Developments in the Law—International Environmental Law, 104 Harv. L. Rev. 1484, 1618 (1991). The *Alfaro* decision may have opened the door to similar lawsuits on behalf of foreigners allegedly injured by U.S. corporations. In October 1991 a toxic tort suit was filed against a U.S. company in Brownsville, Texas on behalf of a group of more than 60 Mexican children who are deformed or retarded. McClintock, In Matamoros, Residents' Rage at Polluting U.S.-Owned Companies Is Growing, Baltimore Sun, Jan. 19, 1992, at A8.

6. The California Supreme Court has declined to open California courts to foreign plaintiffs. In Stangvik v. Shiley, 819 P.2d 14 (1991), the court upheld the dismissal on forum non conveniens grounds of a products liability suit by Scandinavian families whose fathers had died after receiving allegedly defective heart valves manufactured by a Cal-

ifornia corporation. The court noted that a state statute authorized dismissals on forum non conveniens grounds and that California courts already were overcrowded with claims.

D. INTERNATIONAL DEVELOPMENT POLICY AND THE ENVIRONMENT

Environmentalists have been urging international development policy to shift to a model of "sustainable development" that respects the absorptive and regenerative capacities of ecosystems. Sustainable development is development that occurs on a scale that does not exceed the carrying capacity of the biosphere. While it is often difficult to define precisely what constitutes sustainable development, the concept has been valuable as a broad goal for shaping environmental policy debates. Efforts to move international development policy toward a sustainability model have focused on influencing the policies of federal agencies and international financial institutions.

1. Federal Agencies and the Extraterritorial Application of Environmental Law

As noted in the *Amlon Metals* case above, the traditional presumption is that federal statutes "apply only to conduct occurring within, or having effect within, the territory of the United States." Restatement (Second) of Foreign Relations Law of the United States §38. However, if Congress chooses to, it can give extraterritorial effect to U.S. legislation as long as it clearly indicates such an intent and does not violate principles of international comity. Thus, the extent to which U.S. environmental laws will have extraterritorial application depends on how clearly Congress has expressed its intent and courts' assessments of the reasonableness of such applications.

The question of whether or not U.S. environmental laws apply outside the United States has arisen most frequently in connection with the international activities of federal agencies subject to NEPA and the Endangered Species Act. Courts generally have examined the individual facts and circumstances of each case and each agency's activities without reaching any broad conclusions. In two early decisions courts assumed that NEPA was applicable to the extraterritorial activities of federal agencies without deciding the broader question. Sierra Club v. Adams, 578 F.2d 389, 392 (D.C. Cir. 1978) (assuming, without deciding, that NEPA applied to federal involvement in highway construction in Panama); National Organization for Reform of Marijuana Laws v. United States, 452 F. Supp. 1226, 1233 (D.D.C. 1978) (assuming NEPA applicable to U.S. herbicide spraying in Mexico for a marijuana eradication program, but denying injunction). In a case subsequently dismissed on appeal as moot, a district court observed that "NEPA *may* require federal agencies to prepare EISs for actions taken abroad, especially where the U.S. agency's action abroad has direct environmental impacts within [the United States], or where there has clearly been a total lack of environmental assessment by the federal agency or the foreign country involved." Greenpeace USA v. Stone, 748 F. Supp. 749, 761 (D. Haw. 1990), appeal dismissed as moot, 924 F.2d 175 (9th Cir. 1991) (emphasis in original). Environmental groups in that case sought to require preparation of an EIS for the transport of chemical weapons from Germany to Johnson Atoll. The court denied a motion for a preliminary injunction, relying heavily on the fact that an agreement already had been reached between President Bush and Chancellor Kohl that governed the timetable for removing the weapons.

Executive Order 12,114, 44 Fed. Reg. 1957 (1979), purports to preempt the application of NEPA to all federal agency actions outside of the United States by requiring preparation of a Global Commons Environmental Assessment (GCEA). The Executive Order requires that environmental assessments be performed for major federal actions that have a significant effect on either "the environment of the global commons outside the jurisdiction of any nation" or "the environment of a foreign nation not participating with the U.S. and not otherwise involved in the action." Citing foreign policy concerns, the court in Greenpeace USA v. Stone held that the Order could not preempt the extraterritorial application of NEPA, but on the merits it found no NEPA violation because the U.S. Army had prepared a lengthy report that adequately considered effects on the global commons.

In Environmental Defense Fund v. Massey, 772 F. Supp. 1296 (D.D.C. 1991), a federal district court dismissed a NEPA action challenging a decision by the National Science Foundation to build an incinerator in Antarctica for disposal of waste generated by its operations there. Finding no clear expression of congressional intent to apply NEPA beyond the territorial jurisdiction of the United States, the court held that NEPA did not apply outside of the United States. The court also held that a private right of action was not available to challenge alleged violations of Executive Order 12,114.

A case under review by the Supreme Court may decide the question whether agencies funding projects in foreign countries have a duty under the Endangered Species Act to consult with the Secretary of the Interior concerning the projects' impact on endangered species outside the U.S. Defenders of Wildlife v. Lujan, 911 F.2d 117 (8th Cir. 1990), cert. granted, 111 S. Ct. 2008 (1991). In the case under review, the Eighth Circuit had struck down the Interior Department's attempt to change its 1978 policy applying section 7 of the ESA extraterritorially. The court found that the ESA contained a "clear expression of congressional intent" to apply the consultation requirement to federal actions outside of the United States given the Act's concern for international species conservation. Foreign as well as domestic species can be listed as endangered under section 4 of the Act, and more than one-half of all species listed have a primary habitat outside the United States. The case involves challenges to State Department funding of a dam and irrigation project in Sri Lanka and the Aswan High Dam in Egypt. The Supreme Court also is considering whether plaintiffs have standing to pursue extraterritorial application of the ESA based on affidavits that two of their members had visited the countries and desire to return to see the endangered Nile crocodile and endangered Sri Lankan elephants and leopards.

NOTES AND QUESTIONS

1. Does NEPA require that an EIS be prepared for the North American Free Trade Agreement? Environmentalists have argued that an EIS is required. See McKeith, The Environment and Free Trade: Meeting Halfway at the Mexican Border, 10 Pac. Basin L. Rev. 183, 202 (1991). A lawsuit seeking to require preparation of an EIS was dismissed in Public Citizen v. Office of the United States Trade Representative, 782 F. Supp. 139 (D.D.C. 1992). The court held that the plaintiffs could not identify any specific action by the Trade Representative that caused sufficient harm to give them standing.

2. Could NEPA be used to force federal agencies to consider the implications of climate change for potentially affected projects in the United States (e.g., coastal developments)? Could NEPA force consideration of the impact of projects that will increase emissions of greenhouse gases (e.g., coal leasing on federal land) or global warming? What arguments are agencies likely to make in opposing such suggestions? See Prickett and Wirth, Environmental Impact Statements and Climate Change, 31 Environment 44 (Mar. 1989).

3. How can environmental organizations whose members reside in the United States satisfy standing requirements with respect to the extraterritorial actions of federal agencies?

2. International Financial Institutions and the Environment

International financial institutions play a major role in global development policies. These include the World Bank and other multilateral development banks (MDBs), institutions created by the industrialized countries to promote economic growth in the poorest of the developing countries. Private international financial institutions also play a role in efforts to prevent tropical deforestation and to preserve biological diversity through debt-for-nature swaps. Before examining efforts to enlist the MDBs in global environmental protection efforts, we consider debt-for-nature swaps and other efforts to prevent tropical deforestation.

A. DEBT-FOR-NATURE SWAPS AND THE PRESERVATION OF TROPICAL FORESTS

Tropical deforestation and the attendant loss of biodiversity has become one of the most widely recognized international environmental problems. A U.N. organization estimates that deforestation actually has accelerated during the last decade, with 40 percent more acreage being cleared in 1990 than in 1980. Booth, Tropical Forests Disappearing at Faster Rate, Wash. Post, Sept. 9, 1991, at A18. As tropical forests disappear, the Earth is losing an irreplaceable treasure trove of diverse habitats and species before we can even begin to grasp their value. The problem has become so urgent that a group of the world's leading tropical biologists has formed what has been called an "ecological SWAT team." Their mission is "to get to remote, uncharted sites in the tropics and then use satellite imagery, aerial reconnaissance, and field surveys to come up with an inventory of species in just a couple of weeks, instead of the usual months or years." Roberts, Ranking the Rain Forests, 251 Science 1559 (1991). While the use of such rapid assessment procedures worries scientists trained to use painstakingly methodical procedures for gathering data, no one questions the urgency of their mission.

Despite the lack of immediacy for most Americans, tropical deforestation has been a cover story in numerous magazines and a popular cause for fundraisers. However, it may also prove to be one of the most difficult issues to resolve. Third World officials argue with some justification that the industrialized countries decimated their own forests without complaint. Many economists argue that the United States still subsidizes timber harvests on public lands. R. Repetto, The Forests for the Trees? Government Policies and the Misuse of Forest Resources (1988). Solutions will require developing an attitude of cooperation and trust among the wealthiest and poorest countries, a process that is likely to take time and persistence.

Even sympathetic developing country governments have had difficulty enforcing limits on deforestation in the face of population and economic pressures. Brazil, for example, has lost the largest areas to deforestation in recent years despite a strong environment minister and the government's willingness to destroy small air strips used by miners to support remote forest developments. (Brazil's environment minister was fired in March 1992 after accusing other environmental officials of corruption.) Developing country officials have also responded angrily to public protests by international environmentalists. For example, Emil Salim, Indonesian Environment Minister, has said, "[W]ithout development, the rain forests will be destroyed; if you ban imports of tropical rain forest products, you keep us in poverty, and it is poverty that is a main cause for the destruction of the forests." See Wood, Tropical Deforestation: Balancing Regional Development Demands and Global Environmental Concerns, Global Environmental Change, Dec. 1990, at 23-41.

Several international organizations and agreements have some relevance to tropical deforestation. The United Nations Food and Agricultural Organization (FAO) and the International Tropical Timber Organization (ITTO) both have relevant missions but have historically been interested mainly in trade and commercial forestry rather than conservation. In response to this policy vacuum, FAO, the World Bank, the U.N. Environment Programme, and a U.S. research group, the World Resources Institute, sponsored the preparation of the Tropical Forest Action Plan in 1987. The Plan sought to develop a coherent research and funding plan as a starting point for international efforts to reverse deforestation. The plan was criticized by many nongovernmental organizations for insufficient attention to the importance of public participation issues. More focused national plans are now being prepared, and it appears that the process has been successful in contributing to a significant increase in international lending to forestry programs. R. Winterbottom, Taking Stock: The Tropical Forestry Action Plan After Five Years (1990).

Proposals have been made for an international forestry agreement, and the concept is supported by the United States. However, there are strong north-south differences about what a forestry convention should accomplish, and initial optimism about the prospects for an ambitious agreement has rapidly diminished.

A more modest but nevertheless important and innovative response to deforestation has been debt-for-nature swaps. The idea was first proposed by Thomas Lovejoy, then an official with the World Wildlife Fund-U.S., as a way to link the growing need for environmental protection and debt reduction in developing countries. Lovejoy, Aid Debtor Nations' Ecology, N.Y. Times, Oct. 4, 1984, at A31. Based partly on techniques developed for preserving ecologically significant lands in the

United States by such groups as the Nature Conservancy, Lovejoy proposed that conservation-minded nongovernmental organizations (NGOs) might purchase part of a developing country's debt at some greatly discounted price. The organization would then agree to forgive the debt in return for creation of a nature reserve or some other environmentally beneficial action. See generally Patterson, Debt for Nature Swaps and the Need for Alternatives, 32 Environment 5 (1990); Page, Debt for Nature Swaps: Experience Gained, Lessons Learned, 1 Intl. Envtl. Affairs 278 (1990); Deutscher Bundestag, Protecting the Tropical Forests: A High-Priority International Task (1990); Cody, Debt for Nature Swaps in Developing Countries (CRS Report for Congress, Sept. 1988).

The first debt-for-nature swap was concluded by a U.S. NGO, Conservation International (CI), with the government of Bolivia in 1987. CI had acquired $650,000 in Bolivian debt from an American bank for $100,000. CI then agreed to forgive the debt in return for promises from the Bolivian government to expand and protect the Beni Biosphere Reserve. Another 17 such swaps had taken place as of July 1991 involving 8 countries and nearly $100 million in foreign debt. Participating countries have in return made commitments worth over $60 million in funds for land acquisiton, training programs, and assistance to local conservation organizations. Hoskinson and Adams, The Next Generation of Debt-for-Nature Swaps (World Wildlife Fund, Sept. 1991).

The mechanics and details of the swap process have proved to be more varied and complex than the initial sponsors expected. For example, despite a favorable IRS ruling, tax consequences of swaps may be one reason few commercial banks have so far been willing to write down their debt. Rev. Rul. 87-124, 1987-2 I.R.C.B. 205. There are also concerns about the enforceability of developing countries' commitments. Some agreements have been viewed as undercutting the environmental ministries by relying totally on local NGOs. Loans are repaid in local currency and unless indexed to some effective inflationary measure may undergo a rapid decline in value. Developing countries also have been concerned that too many bond-based swaps could result in inflationary pressures; for this reason Costa Rica limited swaps to $15 million per year over a three-year period. Patterson, above.

Debt-for-nature swaps also must be viewed in the context of the enormity of both the debt and the conservation problems facing the developing world. Total debts of developing countries exceed $1 trillion; Costa Rica, the country most supportive of debt exchanges, has accomplished swaps approaching only 5 percent of its $1.5 billion debt. Swaps are most attractive when debt is heavily discounted; as swaps and other forms of debt restructuring take place, the remaining debt rises in value and swaps become less likely. Debt swaps therefore probably have a limited, albeit important, role.

Many other strategies are being pursued to protect tropical forests.

One of the most promising involves support for tourism and other activities consistent with sustainable use of the forest. In one recent agreement, a pharmaceutical company agreed to pay a Costa Rican conservation organization $1 million for the right to screen plants, microbes, and insects collected by native people and catalogued by a local scientific organization. Booth, U.S. Drug Firm Signs up to Farm Tropical Forests, Wash. Post, Sept. 21, 1991, at A3.

B. MULTILATERAL DEVELOPMENT BANKS

The multilateral development banks, which include the World Bank, the Asian Development Bank, the African Development Bank, and the Inter-American Development Bank, made more than $32 billion in loans in 1990. Their influence on the financing of international development projects greatly exceeds their direct lending, which serves as a catalyst for attracting funding from other sources. These projects often include construction of large dams, clearing of large forest areas, and other activities with major environmental impact. Until recently lending was done with minimal environmental review and even less public input.

The multilateral development banks are run by boards of governors composed of representatives from member countries with voting power based on each country's respective financial contribution to the bank. A board of executive directors has substantial delegated authority over significant policy decisions subject to approval of the board of governors. As the following articles explain, the MDBs are beginning to become aware of environmental concerns, in part because environmental organizations in the United States and Europe have been able to focus increasing public attention on the disparity between environmental requirements in developing countries and those established by U.S. law.

	Aufderheide and Rich, Environmental	
	Reform and the Multilateral Banks	
	World Poly. J. 303-305, 307 (Spring 1988)	

THE BANKS AND THE ENVIRONMENTALISTS

No other international or bilateral institutions have more influence on development financing and policy in the Third World than the multilateral development banks—the World Bank (or International Bank for Reconstruction and Development, as it is formally called), the Inter-American Development Bank, the Asian Development Bank, and the African Development Bank. In 1987, these four banks made loan commitments of more than $23 billion, mainly for projects and programs in the environmentally sensitive areas of agriculture, rural development, power and irrigation schemes, and road building. The impact of these banks is magnified by the fact that each dollar they lend typically raises two or three more from recipient country governments, aid agencies, and private banks. The multilateral development banks, especially the World Bank, also influence the development agenda worldwide by their funding of research, technology transfer, and other forms of institutional support. In addition, country-lending and sector-strategy reports drawn up by the development banks shape planning among commercial lenders, aid agencies, and borrowing nations. Finally, the macroeconomic conditions attached to World Bank loans require Third World countries to modify domestic policies and priorities, sometimes affecting entire sectors of their economies.

The multilateral development banks have long proclaimed a commitment to policies and procedures that are sensitive to environmental concerns. In practice, however, environmental protection has generally come to mean after-the-thought damage control. More often than not, environmental concerns have been ignored in project design and implementation. Or when they have been invoked, they frequently have been honored in the breach by government agencies eager to proceed with the most lucrative, politically useful parts of a project.

This trivializing of ecological damage, and the assumption that mitigating measures can "fix" problems, are predictable results of the narrow applications of neoclassical economic models used by development banks. As a result, there is a tendency to focus on those factors that can be expressed in dollar terms. For instance, to be approved, a development project must promise a favorable rate of return (typically 10 percent). In calculating the rate of return, economists rely on cost-benefit analyses that treat ecological destruction as an externality or a trade-off in exchange for other benefits. But this destruction has very real economic costs, even if they cannot be easily quantified. Another problem with this model is the narrow definition of social welfare it employs, one that assesses a country's economic progress in terms of increased gross national product or exports volume. This definition begs such vital questions as who controls and benefits from production for export, at what ecological and social cost, and to what degree export-led growth contributes to long-term development goals.

Moreover, the conventional neoclassical model has often led project planners to ignore crucial social and cultural elements that, in combination with ecological conditions, shape the dynamics of economic development. For example, the World Bank and Inter-American Development Bank have appraised road construction in the Brazilian Amazon mainly in terms of facilitating access to markets and lowering transportation costs. In doing so, the banks have given little consideration to the impact these penetration roads are likely to have on an inflationary economy such as Brazil's: the unleashing of enormous land speculation booms, which actually take land out of production, and the huge social costs associated with uncontrolled migration to lands lacking adequate facilities to support new populations.

The flaws of the development banks' economic approach have been apparent for years. Even neoclassical economic theorists acknowledge the limited usefulness of their models for making investment calculations when nonrenewable natural resources are involved. A more sophisticated use of neoclassical economics would improve the banks' ability to assess the potential negative effects of development projects. For instance, an effort might be made to quantify the long-term economic costs of some environmental impacts and include these costs in bank-loan preparation and appraisal work. Since [the Bank's] announcement of environmental reforms in May 1987, the World Bank staff has begun some research in this direction. It remains to be seen when and if the results of this research will be reflected in the Bank's operations. But even sincere efforts are likely to be frustrated by the fact that statistics and other economic indicators for developing countries are notoriously unreliable and often subject to political manipulation. And they are largely nonexistent for the critically important relationship between ecological destruction and declining economic productivity. . . .

At the core of the environmentalists' critique of bank policy is a very different conception of development. For the environmentalists, factors such as social cohesion, social equity, and the preservation of native cultures are vital to any program of sustainable development. Environmentalists also regard ecological concerns such as biological diversity as having a value that cannot be comprehended purely by economic analysis. They have been able to demonstrate convincingly that, over the long term, the neglect of these concerns can be disastrous.

NOTES AND QUESTIONS

1. Beginning in 1983, environmental groups launched a campaign to publicize the environmental damage caused by the lending policies of the multilateral development banks. Forging an unusual coalition with conservative critics of foreign aid, the environmentalists made the issue an important item on the agendas of congressional committees responsible for approving U.S. contributions to the MDBs. Responding to environmental critics, World Bank president Barber Conable announced in May 1987: "If the World Bank has been part of the problem in the past, it can and will be a strong force in finding solutions in the future." In order to put the environment "on the agenda" of the Bank, Conable announced that the Bank would increase its environmental staff sub-

stantially, finance more environmentally beneficial projects, and consult more closely with environmentalists.

2. Despite a tenfold increase in the World Bank's environmental staff by 1989, environmentalists argue that it will take time to change the prevailing culture at the Bank. For example, in March 1988 the Bank's Policy Planning and Research branch cosponsored a seminar on asbestos use in developing countries with the Asbestos Institute of North America, the lobbying arm of the Canadian asbestos industry. Unaware of the Asbestos Institute's industry connection, Bank officials viewed the seminar as an environmental initiative. It should have come as no surprise that the panelists the Institute selected gave ringing endorsements to increased asbestos use in the Third World while denouncing EPA for proposing to ban virtually all remaining uses of asbestos. The Bank's environmental staff created further controversy in April 1989 when a draft policy paper rejecting efforts to encourage developing countries to reduce emissions of greenhouse gases was leaked to the press.

3. World Bank policy is largely controlled by a 21-member board, on which each country's influence is roughly proportional to its financial contribution. As a consequence, no country or small group of countries has a veto; this effectively insulates the Bank from short-term political intervention, but it also impedes attempts at reform. The Bank is also traditionally very restrictive about disclosures of project and loan information, and it is not subject to the Freedom of Information Act or similar requirements of U.S. law. David Wirth argues that some form of neutral adjudicatory mechanism is needed for processing grievances against MDBs and for facilitating compliance with applicable standards. Wirth, Legitimacy, Accountability, and Partnership: A Model for Advocacy on Third World Environmental Issues, 100 Yale L.J. 2645, 2664 (1991). See also Rodgers, Looking a Gift Horse in the Mouth: The World Bank and Environmental Accountability, 3 Geo. Intl. Envtl. L. Rev. 457 (1990).

4. In December 1989 the International Development and Finance Act, 103 Stat. 2492 (1989), was enacted by Congress. The Act requires U.S. executive directors of MDBs to refrain from voting in favor of projects with a major effect on the environment unless an environmental assessment has been performed at least 120 days in advance of the vote. This legislation and other amendments to foreign aid laws require the U.S. representatives to the MDBs to promote the hiring of trained environmental staff, to develop and implement management plans to ensure environmental review of projects, to involve citizens' and indigenous peoples' organizations in project planning, and to increase the proportion of lending to environmental projects, including integrated pest management, solar energy, and small-scale mixed farming. 22 U.S.C. §§2621(a), (k). The Agency for International Development (AID) is further directed to analyze environmental impacts of proposed multilateral development loans and, where substantial adverse impacts are found,

to ensure a public investigation. 22 U.S.C. §262(m)(2)(A). Since 1989 the World Bank has required that an environmental assessment be prepared for virtually all major projects. World Bank Operational Directive 4.00 (1989). In 1991 the Bank broadened this directive to require consultation with nongovernmental organizations and the public in preparation of such assessments. World Bank Operational Directive 4.01 (1991). See Scott, Making a Bank Turn, 1992 Envtl. Forum 21 (Mar.-April 1992). Compare these provisions with those of the National Environmental Policy Act. Are they enforceable through litigation by environmental groups? Do they provide any assurance that the U.S. position will prevail? Critics of these provisions argue that they inject politics into World Bank decision-making in violation of article IV of the Bank's Articles of Agreement, which states that "[o]nly economic considerations shall be relevant" to such decisions.

5. Other efforts to reform MDB policy have tried to incorporate environmental considerations more effectively within the traditional accounting and financial systems used by MDBs. Economists concerned with promoting sustainable development have been promoting the concept of natural resources accounting. The objective is to assign values to resources and the services they provide (e.g., the water quality benefits of forests) so that analyses of development projects will more accurately reflect offsetting losses. See R. Repetto et al., Wasting Assets: Natural Resources in National Income Accounts (1989). What parallels might be cited in U.S. environmental regulations?

6. A Global Environmental Facility (GEF), sometimes referred to as the "Green Fund," was approved by the World Bank in November 1990. The GEF will help to promote multilateral funding for environmentally desirable projects. The Fund, which was established with contributions of more than $1.5 billion, is designed to enhance the attractiveness of investments with environmental benefits that fail to meet traditional lending criteria. Loans are available for four types of projects: biological diversity, forestry, global warming (including energy efficiency), and ozone depletion (where necessary to supplement the ozone fund). In 1992 the GEF made its first loan, to Poland to finance preservation of a forest. While environmentalists are in favor of such a fund, they have been sharply critical of the decision to house it in the World Bank. Bruce Rich of the EDF is quoted as saying that the fund is merely "a drop in the bucket" toward ameliorating the environmental damage the Bank has done through its ill-advised projects. World Bank Environment Fund, 251 Science 870 (1991).

7. Japan has announced the creation of its own $2 billion fund to help poor countries deal with environmental problems. The fund is viewed as an effort to defuse international resentment of Japan's trade surpluses and criticism of the environmental practices of Japanese companies in the Third World. Japan has pledged to provide $850 million

in loans from the fund to assist Mexico in efforts to control air pollution. Japan to Help Clean Mexican Air, N.Y. Times, June 19, 1990, at A3. Air pollution is now so bad in Mexico City that residents reportedly pay $1.60 per minute to breathe clean air at oxygen booths in the city's parks and malls. Best Things in Life Aren't Always Free in Mexico City, Wall St. J., May 8, 1991, at A1. In 1992 air pollution in Mexico City reached the highest levels ever recorded there, forcing an emergency shutdown of major segments of Mexican industry and the closing of schools.

8. Why should the World Bank have a poor environmental record? What are its institutional biases? One factor is a preference for large projects, which are theoretically more easily evaluated and administered than many small ones. This means, for example, a tendency to favor large central station power plants rather than highly decentralized investments in improving energy efficiency. The Bank is also dominated by economists and accountants who focus on traditional rate-of-return criteria that make it difficult to incorporate environmental concerns in project evaluations. The Bank is also usually responsive to the investment priorities of the recipient countries; they are themselves biased by traditional preferences for large, highly visible projects. Based on the U.S. experience, what strategies might be used to overcome some of these sources of bias?

9. Development planning in many developing countries is subject to oversight and not-so-subtle pressure from the MDBs, who exert considerable leverage on the ability of many countries to obtain critically needed financing. Leaders of developing countries often complain about the MDBs' tying loans to performance on larger social issues such as human rights or the environment, asserting that such arguments are "political." On the other hand, the MDBs have some right to impose loan conditions for the purpose of improving prospects for repayment. Where is the appropriate balance? One reason Congress has been willing to pass legislation supporting environmental reviews of the MDBs is a constituency generally hostile to foreign aid and therefore in favor of tighter conditions on loans. Professor Plater argues that Bank directors represent their governments and that no harm is done to the MDBs as institutions as long as governments do not attempt unilateral withdrawals or rescissions after a commitment has been made. Plater, Multilateral Development Banks, Environmental Diseconomies, and International Reform Pressures on the Lending Process: The Example of the Third World Dam-Building Projects, 9 Boston Col. Third World L.J. 169 (1989).

E. FUTURE DIRECTIONS FOR INTERNATIONAL ENVIRONMENTAL LAW

As this book goes to press, the nations of the world are assembling at the United Nations Conference on Environment and Development in Rio de Janeiro. Representatives from 160 nations, including scores of heads of state, are expected at the conference, which marks the twentieth anniversary of the Stockholm Declaration. Early expectations that this "Earth Summit" would culminate in the signing of conventions requiring profound responses to climate change and deforestation have been scaled back somewhat. But the agreements that will be a product of this summit, such as the declaration of global ecological principles reproduced above at page 1145, may establish a foundation for a new era of international environmental cooperation.

After two decades of remarkable developments, international environmental law has now developed a process for building consensus on global approaches to environmental problems. Some believe that the nations of the world may be on the verge of a new era of global cooperation in which national economic and foreign policies will be shaped by consideration of "their broader social and environmental effects." L. Caldwell, International Environmental Policy: Emergence and Dimensions 329 (2d ed. 1990). Others fear that economic nationalism may intensify, with environmental regulation used as a cover by nations jockeying for competitive advantage in the global economy.

Developing structures for effective implementation of cooperative responses to global environmental problems is one of the major challenges that lie ahead. With one-fourth of the world's people accounting for three-fourths of the world's consumption of natural resources, fundamental changes may be necessary in the relationship between the industrialized world and developing nations. Maurice Strong, secretary general of the Earth Summit, maintains that developing countries would need up to $125 billion per year in financial assistance ($70 billion more than all aid now currently received) to implement a global transition to a sustainable development path. Lewis, Balancing Industry with the Ecology, N.Y. Times, Mar. 12, 1992, at A3. While the industrialized world is unlikely to provide such a massive "earth increment" over and above existing assistance, proposals for global taxes on pollution or energy use are among the options now being debated.

While each generation believes that it lives at the most critical moment in history, observers of global environmental trends maintain that there is ample reason for ours to subscribe to this view. How the world responds to environmental concerns will affect not only the state of the environment, but also the future of global governance and the ability of the world community to live in peace and harmony.

NOTES AND QUESTIONS

1. Will concepts of national sovereignty have to change before a truly effective response can be made to global environmental problems? Consider the example of the Montreal Protocol. To what extent have its signatories given up some of their national sovereignty?

2. What is the relationship between environment and security? Would an effort to link these concerns be primarily a strategy to attract greater interest and support for environmental cooperation, or is it credible to view environmental problems as both a source of conflict and a basis for building cooperation? See generally J. Brown, ed., In the U.S. Interest (1990); S. Hoagland and S. Conbere, Environmental Stress and National Security (1991); J. Mathews, ed., Preserving the Global Environment (1991).

3. What is the relationship between environmental protection and economic development? The draft UNCED Declaration proclaims that "[p]eace, development and environmental protection are interdependent and indivisible." Draft UNCED Declaration, Principle 25. During the preparatory negotiations for the Rio Conference, developing countries pressed for greater recognition of their needs by the industrialized world. Representatives from developing countries argued not only that economic development was essential to environmental protection, but also that a transition to sustainable development would require a massive infusion of aid from the industrialized world. Responding to these concerns, the draft Declaration states that eradication of poverty is "an indispensable requirement for sustainable development, in order to decrease the disparities in standards of living and better meet the needs of the majority of the people of the world." Id., Principle 5.

4. What roles should law, lawyers, and legal institutions play in the evolution of international environmental cooperation? Does the legal discipline have any uniquely valuable skills to contribute to this process? Consider the following skeptical view:

> Ultimately, legal analysis will play at best a peripheral role in international environmental protection. The dirty work of pinpointing common interests lies within the expertise of diplomats, economists, financiers, and scientists, not lawyers. Law can do little but express the paramount objectives of these efforts—for example, the cessation of significant transboundary pollution and the payment of compensation for damages. The codification of abstract legal norms embodying the concerns of a few must give way to a focus on the matrix of shared interests attracting the ad-

herence of all. [Developments in the Law—International Environmental Law, 104 Harv. L. Rev. 1484, 1521 (1991).]

Is this view founded on too restrictive a conception of the role of lawyers in society? Or does it reflect a realistic and healthy aversion to what has been called "legal imperialism"?

=10=
‖ *Conclusion* ‖

The nation's success at fulfilling the promise of 1970—as measured by environmental trends data—has been mixed. After two decades of unprecedented environmental activism, some facets of the environment show remarkable improvement, while the quality of others has deteriorated sharply. . . . Taken as a whole, environmental trends data suggest that over the past two decades the United States has been fairly successful in protecting and improving environmental quality when the existence of a problem has been widely recognized and the sources of the problem well defined. In cases where general recognition of a problem emerged slowly over time, or where the sources of a problem were diverse and widely dispersed, progress has been slow and painful, at best.

—Council on Environmental Quality*

This book has provided a whirlwind tour of the complex maze that environmental law has become. Today, more than two decades after the momentous events of 1970—the signing of NEPA, the first Earth Day, and the creation of EPA—environmental protection has grown from a national concern to a global imperative. Environmental law continues to grow explosively, both nationally and internationally. At the end of this book, it is only natural to reflect on what environmental regulation has accomplished during nearly a quarter century of rapid growth and to assess its future prospects.

A. ENVIRONMENTAL PROGRESS

Clearly, much progress has been made, but it is equally clear that most of the laws have failed to live up to the lofty expectations that

---

*Environmental Quality: Twentieth Annual Report 7-8, 11 (1990).

accompanied their enactment. Looking back to the First Annual Report of the Council on Environmental Quality, one cannot help but be struck by how similar the problems outlined in the report are to today's environmental concerns. CEQ, Environmental Quality—1970, at 93 (1970). Although the ozone hole had not yet been discovered, the CEQ report devoted an entire chapter to concern that atmospheric pollution might cause global warming and climate change. New concerns, such as ozone depletion and radon, have been added to the environmental agenda. But with the possible exception of noise pollution, none of the environmental concerns outlined by CEQ in 1970 have vanished from the national agenda.

The CEQ was prescient in forecasting not only the significance of the policy changes launched in 1970, but also that environmental problems were bound to get worse before they got better. In the opening paragraphs of its first annual report CEQ noted that

> Historians may one day call 1970 the year of the environment. They may not be able to say that 1970 actually marked a significant change for the better in the quality of life; in the polluting and the fouling of the land, the water, and the air; or in health, working conditions, and recreational opportunity. Indeed, they are almost certain to see evidence of worsening environmental conditions in many parts of the country.
>
> Yet 1970 marks the beginning of a new emphasis on the environment—a turning point, a year when the quality of life has become more than a phrase; environment and pollution have become everyday words; and ecology has become almost a religion to some of the young. Environmental problems, standing for many years on the threshold of national prominence, are now at the center of nationwide concern. Action to improve the environment has been launched by government at all levels. And private groups, industry, and individuals have joined the attack. [CEQ, Environmental Quality—1970, at 5 (1970).]

What progress has been made in the past two decades? What have been the success stories and the failures, and what can be learned from them to help shape the development of better policy in the future? Consider first the views of Dr. Barry Commoner, an outspoken environmental scientist who has been a persistent critic of the current regulatory system.

	Commoner, Failure of the	
	Environmental Effort	
	18 Envtl. L. Rep. 10195	
	(1988)	

The enactment of the National Environmental Protection Act (NEPA), and the creation of the Environmental Protection Agency (EPA) to administer it in 1970, marked a turning point in the recent environmental history of the United States. Beginning in 1950, new forms of environmental pollution appeared and rapidly intensified: smog, acid rain, excess nitrate and phosphate in water supplies, pesticides and toxic chemicals in the food chain and our bodies, and dangerous accumulations of radioactive waste. Then, in 1970, pressed by a newly aroused public, Congress began a massive effort to undo the damage. Now, nearly 20 years later, the time has come to ask an important and perhaps embarrassing question: How far have we progressed toward the goal of restoring the quality of the environment?

The answer is in fact embarrassing. Apart from a few notable exceptions, environmental quality has improved only slightly, and in some cases has become worse. Since 1975, when most of the consistent environmental measurements began, overall improvement amounts to only about 15 percent. And at least in the case of air emissions (other than lead), since 1981—the advent of the current Administration—the annual rate of improvement has dropped from 1.52 percent per year to only 1.16 percent per year.

Although the massive national effort that began in 1970 has failed to restore the quality of the environment—or to even come close to that goal—the record shows that success is possible. In a few scattered instances, pollution levels have been significantly reduced, by 70 percent or more: lead in the air; DDT and PCBs in wildlife and people; mercury pollution in the Great Lakes; strontium 90 in the food chain; and in some local rivers, phosphate pollution. These few successes explain the far more common failures. Each of these pollutants has been effectively controlled not by high-tech devices, but by simply stopping its production or use. Air emissions of lead have declined by 86 percent because much less lead is now added to gasoline and therefore there is that much less in the environment. The environment levels of DDT and PCBs have dropped sharply because their production and use have been banned. Mercury is much less prevalent in the environment because it is no longer used in manufacturing chlorine. Strontium 90 has decayed to low levels because we and the Soviet Union have had the simple wisdom to stop the atmospheric nuclear bomb tests that produce it.

The lesson of both the few successes and the far more numerous failures is the same: environmental pollution is a nearly incurable disease, but it can be *prevented*. . . .

Most of our environmental problems are the inevitable result of the sweeping changes in the technology of production that transformed the U.S. economic system after World War II: the new large, high-powered, smog-generating cars; the shift from fuel-efficient railroads to gas-guzzling trucks and cars; the substitution of undegradable and hazardous petrochemical products for biodegradable and less toxic natural products; the substitution of fertilizers for manure and crop rotation and of toxic synthetic pesticides for ladybugs and birds.

By 1970 it was clear that these changes in the technology of production are the *root cause* of modern environmental pollution. Now this conclusion has been confirmed by the sharply divergent results of the effort to clean up the environment. Only in the few instances in which the technology of production has been changed—by eliminating lead from gasoline, mercury from chlorine production, DDT from agriculture, PCB from the electrical industry, and atmospheric nuclear explosions from the military enterprise—has the environment been substantially improved. When production technology remains unchanged, and an attempt is made to trap the pollutant in an appended control device—the automobile's catalyst or the power plant's scrubber—environmental improvement is at best only modest, and in some cases (such as nitrogen oxides) nil. When a pollutant is attacked at the point of origin, it can be eliminated; once it is produced, it is too late.

Unfortunately, the legislative base of the U.S. environmental program was created without reference to the origin of the crisis that it was supposed to solve. Our environmental laws do not discuss the origin of environmental pollutants—*why* we have been afflicted with the pollutants that the laws were designed to control. Not that theories weren't offered to the legislators. Some ecologists told them the country and the world are polluted because there are too many people, using more of the planet's resources than it can safely provide. A different point of view was heard from as well, but with a good deal of skepticism. I well remember the incredulity in Senator Muskie's voice during NEPA hearings when he asked me whether I was really testifying that the technology that generated post-World War II economic progress was also the cause of pollution. I was.

Because environmental legislation ignored the origin of the assault on environmental quality, it has dealt only with its subsequent effects. And, having defined the disease as a collection of symptoms, the legislation mandates only palliative measures. The notion of *preventing* pollution—the only measure that really works—appears but fitfully in the environmental laws and has never been given any administrative force.

This fundamental fault in our environmental laws has had a major impact on the operation of the agency that is chiefly responsible for administering and enforcing them—EPA.

The failed effort to deal with the automobile's most notorious environmental impact—photochemical smog—is an instructive example. That failure was recently commemorated on December 31, 1987, when dozens of urban areas were once again allowed to miss the deadline for meeting ambient air standards for carbon monoxide and ozone. Why has the effort to rid the environment of its automotive nemesis, which has generated a mass of environmental analyses, emission standards, administrative rulings, and litigation, nevertheless only ended in failure?

For more than 20 years we have understood the origin of photochemical smog: the high-compression engines introduced after World War II to drive the suddenly enlarged American cars necessarily run hot; they therefore convert oxygen and nitrogen in the cylinder air to nitrogen oxides. Once out the exhaust, nitrogen oxides are activated by sunlight and react with airborne fuel and other hydro-carbons—many of them otherwise relatively benign—to produce ozone and the other noxious components of photochemical smog.

EPA has tried to deal with the smog problem by aiming at everything except the crucial target: the engine's production of nitrogen oxides. The effort is largely designed to reduce emissions of the bewildering array of hydrocarbon sources. It has clearly failed; nitrogen oxide emissions have increased in the last decade, not only perpetuating smog but becoming a major source of acid rain as well.

Suppose, now, that guided by the few environmental successes, we seek to control automotive smog at its origin, the *production* of nitrogen oxides. The goal would be *zero* production of nitrogen oxides by cars and the complete elimination of this dominant source of smog. It is worth noting that this approach accords well with a corresponding approach to health: prevention of disease rather than curing or simply tolerating it. The preventive approach to disease is the source of some of the major advances in public health. The classical example is smallpox; widespread use of a preventive measure—vaccination—has now completely eradicated the disease. A zero incidence has actually been attained world-wide. Like smallpox, the great majority of the assaults on the environment are, in fact, preventable. After all, nearly all of them—the major exception is natural radiation—have been created, chiefly since 1950, by introducing inherently polluting forms of production technology. They are not the result of natural processes but of human action, and human action can once again change the technologies and undo their harm.

Is this approach to the automotive smog problem really practical? Can smogless engines that do not produce nitrogen oxides be built? They can. Indeed, they have been. Every pre-World War II car was driven by such an engine; that's why the country was then free of smog. In fact, nitrogen oxide production can be prevented without giving up the American car's precious over-powered engine (which is, nevertheless, a good idea). The so-called "stratified charge" engine can do just that. According to a 1974 National Science Foundation (NSF) study, prototypes were then already operating in Detroit, and tests showed that the engines would meet the 90 percent reduction in nitrogen oxide emissions required by the Clean Air Act Amendments. But, according to the NSF report, the engine would need to be considerably redesigned, requiring new fuel injector, fuel pump, ignition spark-plug system, cylinder head, piston, intake and exhaust manifolds. Unlike the addition of a catalytic converter to the exhaust system of the existing engine, this would mean extensive retooling in the manufacturing plants. According to the report, had the auto industry decided in 1975 to take this course, the stratified charge engine could now be driving most U.S. cars—and automotive nitrogen oxide emissions would have been sharply reduced instead of increasing.

In sum, the goal established by the 1970 Clean Air Act Amendments *could* have been met—but only if EPA had confronted the auto industry with a demand for fundamental changes in engine design. EPA was unwilling to take on this task. EPA's reluctance to tell the automobile industry what kind of engine it should build has helped to undermine the goal of the Clean Air Act.

There are other examples of how pollution can be attacked at its source—and thereby prevented. Had American farmers been required to reduce the present, often unproductively high, rate of nitrogen fertilization, nitrate water pollution would now be falling instead of increasing. If farms were required to shift from blindly repeated pesticide applications to integrated pest management, the rising level of pesticide pollution could be checked. If the railroads and mass transit were expanded; if the electric power system were decentralized and increasingly based on cogenerators and solar sources; if the pitifully small percentage of American homes that have been weatherized were increased—fuel consumption and the attendant air pollution could be sharply reduced. If brewers were forbidden to put plastic nooses on six-packs of beer; if supermarkets were not allowed to wrap polyvinyl chloride film around everything in sight and then stuff it into a plastic carrying bag; if McDonald's could rediscover the paper plate; if plastics were cut back to things where they are really needed, say, artificial hearts or video tape—then we could push back the petrochemical industry's toxic invasion of the biosphere.

Of course, all this is easier said than done. I am fully aware that what I am proposing is no small thing, easily accomplished by bureaucratic fiat. It means that sweeping changes in the major systems of production—agriculture, industry, power production, and transportation—would be undertaken for a *social* purpose: environmental improvement. As I have pointed out in explicit detail elsewhere, this represents social (as contrasted with private) governance of the means of production—an idea that is so foreign to what passes for our national ideology that even to mention it violates a deep-seated taboo.

It is not my purpose here to argue the merits of undertaking such a sweeping change in the country's deeply felt concept of political economy. Rather, I am interested in discussing the consequences, especially for EPA, of our failing to address the issue of environmental quality in these fundamental, if highly disturbing, terms. But first I wish to at least mention a major consequence that lies outside the realm of the environment but is related to it—the efficiency of the national economy. By now it is depressingly clear that the U.S. productive system, despite its past gains, is in a state of decline. Among the nations of the world, the United States has, for example, one of the lowest rates of annual improvement in a fundamental economic parameter—productivity. A good deal of this decline derives from the fact that the new, highly polluting post-World War II production technologies were based on large-scale, centralized, capital- and energy-intensive facilities. The country's overall economic efficiency is now heavily encumbered by the low capital productivity of these technologies (i.e., low output per unit of capital invested, as for example in a nuclear power plant as compared to a cogenerator), and their low energy productivity (i.e., low output per unit of energy used, as for example, in truck freight as compared to railroad freight). But the technological changes that reduce environmental impact can also improve economic productivity. Decentralized electric power systems, for example, by reducing fuel consumption, improve not only air pollution, but the economic efficiency of power production as well.

Now let us turn to the impact on EPA of the taboo against social intervention in the production system. Let me begin by reiterating the most immediate effect. The major consequence of this powerful taboo is the failure to reach the goals in environmental quality that motivated the environmental legislation of the 1970s.

The present, largely unsuccessful regulatory effort is based on a now well-established process. First, EPA must estimate the degree of harm represented by different levels of the numerous environmental pollutants. Next, some "acceptable" level of harm is chosen (for example, a cancer risk of one in a million) and emission and/or ambient concentration standards that can presumably achieve that risk level are established. Polluters are then expected to respond by introducing control measures (such as automobile exhaust catalysts or power plant stack scrubbers) that will bring emissions or ambient concentrations to the required levels. If the regulation survives the inevitable challenges from industry (and in recent years from the Administration itself), the polluters will invest in the appropriate control systems. Catalysts are appended to the cars, and scrubbers to the power plants and trash-burning incinerators. If all goes well—as it frequently does not—at least some areas of the country and some production facilities are then in compliance with the regulation.

The net result is that the "acceptable" pollution level is frozen in place. The industries, having heavily invested in equipment designed to just reach the required level, are unlikely to invest more in further improvements. The public, having been told that the accompanying hazard to health is "acceptable," is likely to be equally satisfied. Some optimistically inclined people will look upon exposure at the acceptable level as a kind of guarantee of health. Others, perhaps aware of the linear relation between pollution level and the risk to health, will con-

clude that we are doing as much as we can and will, in most cases, accept
the remaining risk fatalistically.

Clearly this process is the inverse of the preventive, public health
approach. It strikes not for the continuous improvement of environmental health, but for the social acceptance of some, hopefully low, risk
to health. In a way this is a return to the medieval approach to disease,
when illness—and death itself—was regarded as a debit on life that must
be incurred in payment for original sin. Now we have recast this philosophy into a more modern form: some level of pollution and some
risk to health is the unavoidable price that must be paid for the material
benefits of modern technology.

The preventive approach aims at progressively reducing the risk
to health; it does not mandate some socially convenient stopping point.
The medical professions, after all, did not decide that the smallpox
prevention program could quit when the risk reached one in a million.
In contrast, the present regulatory approach, by setting a standard of
"acceptable" exposure to the pollutant, erects an administrative barrier
that blocks further improvements in environmental quality. This is, I
believe, a major cost of our failure to confront the environmental crisis
at its source.

How do you decide when to stop, where to set the standard? The
current fashion is called risk/benefit. Since the pollutants' ultimate effect
can often be assessed by the number of lives lost (from cancer caused
by an environmental carcinogen, for instance), the risk/benefit analysis
requires that a value be placed on a human life. Some economists have
proposed that the value should be based on a person's lifelong earning
power. It then turns out that a woman's life is worth much less than a
man's, and that a black's life is worth much less than a white's. In effect,
the environmental harm is regarded as smaller if the people it kills are
poorer—a standard that could be used to justify situating heavily polluting operations in poor neighborhoods. And, in fact, this is an all too
common practice.

Thus, thinly veiled by a seemingly straightforward numerical com-
putation, there is a profound, unresolved moral question: Should poor
people be subjected to a more severe environmental burden than richer
people, simply because they lack the resources to evade it? Since in
practice the risk/benefit equation masquerades as science, it deprives
society of the duty to confront this moral question. It seems to me,
therefore, that one result of failing to adopt the preventive approach to
environmental quality is that the regulatory agencies have been driven
into positions that seriously diminish the force of social morality.

What happens when, by whatever means, standards are set but—
for the reasons described earlier—the required control measures fail to
achieve them? Something has to give way. Consider the scandalous situation in air pollution. In 1970 the Clean Air Act Amendments called

for a 90 percent reduction in urban carbon monoxide, hydrocarbon, and ozone levels, setting a 1977 deadline for achieving this goal. The penalty for failure is severe: loss of federal funding for development projects. In 1977, with compliance not even in sight, the deadline was moved to 1982; and when that was also missed, the deadline was once more delayed, to December 31, 1987. Now, with urban areas in which nearly 100 million people breathe substandard air still in noncompliance, they will be given up to 25 more years to comply.

So, step by embarrassing step, because we are unwilling to adopt the measures that can prevent air pollution, enforcement of the laboriously constructed standards evolves into a distant hope. It hardly requires a sociological survey to determine the response to this retrogressive policy: the polluters can justify their inaction and the public its apathy. It erodes the integrity of regulation and diminishes the public faith in the meaning of environmental legislation. This, too, is the price we pay for failing to attack environmental pollution at its origin.

Confronted with such environmental failures, regulatory agencies have become remarkably creative about finding new ways to retreat. The latest one is the Humpty Dumpty approach. You will remember that in *Through the Looking Glass* Alice gets into an argument with Humpty Dumpty, who claims that the word "glory" means "a nice knockdown argument." When Alice objects to this arbitrary redefinition, Humpty Dumpty says: "When I use a word it means just what I choose it to mean." Alice replies: "The question is whether you *can* make words mean so many different things." Humpty Dumpty's response is unanswerable: "The question is, which is to be master."

I am afraid to say that Humpty Dumpty's free-wheeling linguistic philosophy has begun to take hold in regulatory circles. Not long ago, for example, when tests of fly ash from trash-burning incinerators showed that it was sufficiently contaminated with toxic metals to qualify as a "hazardous substance," the New York State Department of Environmental Protection issued a remarkable pronouncement: Metal-contaminated fly ash is not a hazardous substance, it was declared, but a "special waste." Of course, this was not just a silly linguistic exercise. It meant that, unlike an ordinary hazardous substance, fly ash need not be consigned to an expensive Class I landfill—an additional cost that, according to a New York State official, might cripple the incinerator industry.

EPA and other regulatory agencies have put a great deal of effort into defining a "hazardous substance." Clearly the public must rely on the integrity of this definition in dealing with Superfund sites and a whole range of contaminated materials. The linguistic detoxification of fly ash may be a handy expedient for New York State—which may soon be emulated by EPA as well. But with Humpty Dumpty in charge, the public has good reason to doubt who is really the "master" that decides what environmental regulations mean. The loss of public confidence is another price that we pay for the failure to regulate the *cause* of environmental pollution instead of its symptoms. . . .

None of us are ready to prescribe what should be done to remedy the environmental failure. This will require the courage to challenge the taboo against even questioning the present dominance of private interests over the public interest. It will require good science and wise policies. But, I suggest that we know how to begin—by an open public discussion of what has gone wrong, and why. That is the necessary first step on the road toward realizing the nation's unswerving goal—restoring the quality of the environment.

NOTES AND QUESTIONS

1. Is Dr. Commoner too pessimistic in his assessment of the results of environmental regulation? Do you agree that changes in technology are the "root cause" of modern environmental problems? How does he propose to deal with this problem? If technology is the root cause of the problem, does the solution necessarily require that government intervene in the production process?

2. Dr. Commoner argues that the goals of the 1970 Clean Air Act could have been met "if EPA had confronted the auto industry with a demand for fundamental changes in engine design." Recall that President Nixon had sought to stimulate such changes by announcing a federal research and development effort to produce clean alternative vehicles. Why, do you think, was that not successful? How would you expect Dr. Commoner to react to the mobile source provisions of the 1990 Clean Air Act Amendments that seek to force the development not only of better emission controls but also cleaner fuels?

3. In large part, Dr. Commoner is arguing that greater effort should be placed on preventing pollution at its source. The concept of "pollution prevention" has now become so popular that it has almost achieved buzzword status. Is society in fact moving in the direction Dr. Commoner recommends? Is greater government regulation required to accomplish what Commoner wants? Note that he yearns for McDonald's to "rediscover the paper plate," which subsequently happened due to an unusual cooperative arrangement between the company and a national environmental group. Does this indicate that voluntary efforts may accomplish much of the changes that Commoner seeks?

4. Dr. Commoner is critical of approaches to regulation that seek to define an acceptable exposure to pollutants. How would Dr. Commoner determine how much protection to provide? How rapidly would he seek to require industry to develop environmentally benign technologies?

5. Dr. Commoner is critical of the use of risk assessment in envi-

ronmental regulation. Why? Is his critique founded primarily on a concern that risk assessments are unreliable, or does he have broader objections to their use?

6. Dr. Commoner cites Lewis Carroll's Through the Looking Glass to illustrate the difficulty of defining regulatory targets given the malleability of language. Is this problem the product of legislative unwillingness to make hard choices, the need to respond to unanticipated circumstances, or other factors?

7. Which perspective do you think is more closely reflected in Dr. Commoner's views—moral outrage or cool analysis? How do you think Dr. Commoner would react to informational approaches to regulation such as the Emergency Planning and Community Right to Know Act or Proposition 65's requirement that clear warning be given before individuals are knowingly exposed to carcinogens or reproductive toxins?

8. A somewhat more optimistic view of the results of the past decades of environmental regulation is presented in the Council on Environmental Quality's Twentieth Annual Report.

Council on Environmental Quality, Environmental Quality—Twentieth Annual Report
7 (1990)

FOR BETTER OR WORSE

In the two decades that followed the singular events of 1970, the nation's growing concern for the environment manifested itself in a dozen major—and several dozen minor—federal environmental laws. By 1989 the federal government had acquired regulatory responsibilities addressing air quality, water quality, drinking water, solid wastes, hazardous wastes, medical wastes, pesticides, toxic substances, endangered species, occupational safety and health, coastal zones, ocean pollution, and the upper atmosphere, among others.

One way to measure the nation's environmental progress since 1970 would be to look at 20-year data trends in those areas. Trends in pollutant emissions, biodiversity, and human health clearly are important measures of the relative success or failure of national efforts to protect the environment.

However, such trend data give only partial answers, and even those partial answers tell an inconsistent story. The nation's success at fulfilling the promise of 1970—as measured by environmental trends data—has been mixed. After two decades of unprecedented environmental activism, some facets of the environment show remarkable improvement, while the quality of others has deteriorated sharply.

For example, in response to the Clean Air Act of 1970, the Environmental Protection Agency (EPA) set national standards for the six most prevalent air pollutants: sulfur dioxide, nitrogen oxides, carbon monoxide, particulates, hydrocarbons, and lead. The federal and state governments then took a range of actions designed to reduce emissions of those pollutants so that the national health standards would be met nationwide.

For some of those common air pollutants, the 20-year record has been extraordinarily successful, especially in the case of lead. Between 1970 and 1987, total annual emissions of lead nationwide declined by 96 percent, from 203.8 million to 8.1 million tons, mainly due to the gradual phase-out of leaded gasoline. Today virtually all areas in the United States meet the national health standard for lead.

The United States also has made substantial progress in controlling sulfur dioxide (SO_2) and particulate matter (PM). Prior to 1970, emissions of SO_2 and PM had been increasing rapidly. But, between 1970 and 1987, total annual national emissions of SO_2 dropped by 28 percent, from 28.2 million to 20.4 million tons; particulate emissions declined by 61 percent, from 18.1 million to 7.0 million tons. As of 1987, most areas of the country met the national health standards for SO_2 and particulates.

The nation's record in controlling nitrogen oxides (NOx), ozone, and carbon monoxide (CO) is mixed. For example, total national emissions of NOx increased almost 8 percent between 1970 and 1987, rising from 18.1 million to 19.5 million tons, while the pre-1970 rate of growth dropped sharply. Despite the increase in total NOx emissions, almost all areas in the country meet the national health standard for NOx.

Total national hydrocarbon and CO emissions, which also had been growing rapidly, dropped by 28 percent and 38 percent, respectively, over the same period. Yet national health standards for both pollutants are still being exceeded in many U.S. cities. During 1989 EPA reported that approximately 110 U.S. urban areas failed to meet the national ozone standard, and about 50 areas did not meet the CO standard.

Despite continued air pollution problems in many places, primarily cities, the country's efforts to protect air quality have been substantial. Not only have total annual emissions of the most common air pollutants declined or remained fairly constant over the past two decades, but they have done so in spite of strong economic and population growth.

Since 1970 the population of the United States has grown by almost 22 percent. In 1970 the U.S. population totalled 205 million. Sometime during 1990, it will pass 250 million.

Over the same period, the U.S. economy has grown more than three times as fast as the population. In 1970 U.S. gross national product (GNP) was $2.42 trillion (measured in 1982 dollars). The Council of Economic Advisors estimates that U.S. GNP in 1989 was $4.17 trillion (measured in 1982 dollars), an increase of 72 percent. At least as far as the six most common air pollutants are concerned, the United States clearly has severed the linkage between economic growth and pollution growth, a linkage that seemed obvious and unbreakable to many people in 1970.

The nation's progress in controlling air pollution is especially noteworthy when evaluated in the context of skyrocketing growth in automobile use over the past 20 years. In 1970 the number of automobiles registered for use on U.S. roads was 89.2 million; by 1989 that number had jumped 56 percent to 139 million. Moreover, those automobiles were being driven many more miles. Between 1970 and 1987, the total vehicle miles traveled annually in this country rose from 920 billion to 1,313 billion, an increase of almost 48 percent.

There is no doubt that more needs to be done to control air pollution—especially CO and hydrocarbons—in this country. Millions of Americans still experience episodes of unhealthy air, and the Administration is committed to strengthening the Clean Air Act through the most cost-effective means to address this concern. But an evaluation of environmental progress must consider not only the current quality of the environment, but also what that quality would be had no action been taken. And undoubtedly, without the existing Clean Air Act, even intransigent problems like ozone and CO would have been very much worse.

If, on the other hand, the viability of wetlands and estuarine ecosystems is used to measure environmental progress, the nation's track record over the past two decades is less impressive. In 1970 the United States contained about 99 million acres of wetlands. No one knows exactly how many acres have been lost since then, but it is estimated that between the mid-1950s and mid-1970s losses exceeded 450,000 acres per year. Even though annual losses probably dropped after that time, wetlands destruction has continued at an unacceptable rate. In response to this problem, the President has announced that he is committed to the eventual goal of no net loss of wetlands. The President has directed a Domestic Policy Council task force to provide recommendations on wetlands policy following a series of public meetings this year.

Moreover, the quality of some coastal waters and estuaries apparently has declined over the last two decades. Between 1971 and 1985, shellfish harvest restrictions resulting from environmental contamination increased 14 percent to 7.5 million acres; by 1985 approximately 40 percent of the nation's shellfish beds were closed for some or all of the season. Closures were caused by environmental pollution ranging from inadequate or overwhelmed sewage treatment plants to urban water runoff to contamination from feedlots and other agricultural operations. Most recently, coastal beach closings and oil spills have focused public attention on coastal water quality.

Trends in waterfowl populations, which rely upon wetlands during breeding and migration, indicate the declining health of wetlands. Populations of mallard ducks have dropped by about 40 percent during the past 20 years. Mallards generally use a wide range of habitat for breeding, but filling, draining, and encroachment on wetlands has overtaxed even that species' ability to adapt. In short, both the quantity and quality of U.S. wetlands appear to have declined over the past two decades.

Population growth along U.S. coasts contributes to pressures on water quality and the decline of wetlands in many areas. In 1989, in fact, approximately 80 percent of the U.S. population lived in coastal counties (including those bordering the Great Lakes). Population growth usually leads to more polluted water runoff, the filling or draining of wetlands for development, and overtaxed wastewater treatment systems. Thus population growth—together with associated economic growth—contributes not only to direct wetlands losses, but also to a deterioration in water quality and the health of those wetlands that remain.

Wetlands losses result from other causes as well. Agricultural practices contributed to the vast majority of wetlands losses from the 1950s to the 1970s, and they continue to cause additional losses.

Other environmental trend data illustrates both the successes and shortcomings of national environmental protection efforts since 1970. For example, between 1972 and 1986 the number of Americans served by secondary wastewater treatment facilities, or better, increased from 85 million to 127 million. Consequently, the water quality in many stream and river segments in this country is much improved. On the other hand, concentrations of carbon dioxide (CO_2) in the atmosphere have increased at an average rate of about 1.4 percent a year since 1970, contributing to rising concerns about possible global climate change.

Taken as a whole, environmental trends data suggest that over the past two decades the United States has been fairly successful in protecting and improving environmental quality when the existence of a problem has been widely recognized and the sources of the problem well defined. In cases where general recognition of a problem emerged slowly over time, or where the sources of a problem were diverse and widely dispersed, progress has been slow and painful, at best.

NOTES AND QUESTIONS

1. Based on CEQ's assessment of environmental conditions and trends, what would you consider to be the most pressing problems to be addressed by environmental regulation?

2. The CEQ report concludes that environmental protection efforts have been least successful in dealing with problems that have emerged slowly and those that stem from widely dispersed sources. Do you agree? What examples, if any, can you think of that support this conclusion?

3. As noted above, economists approach environmental problems from a different perspective. Consider the views of a prominent environmental economist concerning the results of two decades of federal environmental regulation.

|| ***P. Portney, ed., Public Policies for Environmental Protection***
275-279 (1990) ||

[T]here are several ways by which one might measure progress in environmental policy. These include number of regulations issued, control measures put in place, enforcement actions taken, and, finally, actual physical improvements in environmental quality. . . . [W]here it is applicable, this last measure is by far the most important. After all, it does little good to issue regulations on time, ensure that affected sources comply promptly with them, and penalize those which do not if this flurry of activities does little to improve environmental conditions along one dimension or another.

When evaluated in this way—according to demonstrable environmental results—the record of federal environmental policy is a mixed one. Only in the case of air quality can widespread improvements be shown. There we have real reason to be encouraged. For most major metropolitan areas, ambient concentrations of almost all the common air pollutants have declined; this is particularly true for lead, sulfur dioxide, and particulate matter, three of the most worrisome pollutants from the standpoint of human health. Even in those areas where improvements have been slow or even nonexistent, one can fairly argue that things would be worse still were it not for nearly two decades of investments in pollution control required of automakers, industrial sources, municipalities, and others. While we have no widespread monitoring network to provide confirmatory evidence, it is likely that this prolonged period of controlling the common (or criteria) air pollutants has also resulted in substantial reductions in airborne concentrations of many less common hazardous air pollutants. . . .

As always, we must hedge our conclusions somewhat. First, ozone continues to be a stubborn air quality problem in many areas and will continue to be so for some time to come. It has proved far more difficult to control than the pollutants mentioned above. Second, we must remember that at least some of the improvements in air quality . . . are due to shifting patterns of industrial activity. To put it starkly, the slow and painful declines of the domestic steel, mining, and other heavy industries have contributed to the improvements in air quality in some areas. We would prefer that our environmental improvements not come at the expense of such losses.

10. Conclusion

It is hard to be as optimistic about the progress made in other environmental areas. . . . [I]mprovements in water quality have been much more sporadic and uneven. In some locations, particularly in urban areas where water quality had deteriorated badly throughout the 1950s and 1960s, dramatic turnarounds have taken place. Fishing and swimming are now possible in some places where they were unthinkable even ten years ago.

Yet such success stories are idiosyncratic rather than widespread. Moreover, water quality has deteriorated in many areas since 1972, when the federal government greatly stepped up its presence in water pollution control. In part this has been due to a reluctance on the part of Congress and the Environmental Protection Agency to take on the problems associated with non-point sources of water pollution, such as farms and the streets and parking lots in urban areas. Quite frankly, it is harder to whip up opposition to such sources than to industrial sources, and as a result their share of the overall water pollution picture has increased over time. Additional progress in water pollution control will depend in large part on summoning the political will and financial resources necessary to address these polluters.

It is premature to attempt any definitive evaluation of progress in cleaning up abandoned and active hazardous waste disposal sites. After all, the basic statutes—RCRA, enacted in 1976, and CERCLA (or Superfund), enacted in 1980—have not been in place as long as our air and water pollution control laws, and they were slower to be implemented once they were passed. Nevertheless, some tentative inferences are appropriate, and they suggest that all is not well.

To this point, at least, it would appear that the major impact of RCRA regulations (which deal in large part with currently operating hazardous waste disposal sites) has been to greatly reduce the number of such facilities. . . . [T]he number fell by nearly two-thirds following regulations stipulating that such facilities must have liability insurance to cover any clean-up costs that might be required following their eventual closure. While this makes it much more difficult to find permitted disposal sites, clearly such pruning is not all bad. To the extent the insurance requirement has weeded out sites which were operating in a careless fashion, it is encouraging to know that wastes will no longer be deposited there. On the other hand, we now must face the task of determining what remedial measures must be taken at those sites which did close, lest they find their way onto the National Priorities List (as some already have done).

It is much more difficult to ascertain the effects of RCRA regulations on those disposal sites that have continued to operate. To be sure, these facilities face new requirements concerning the technological safeguards that must be in place at each site, the groundwater monitoring they must do, and the reporting they must do in concert with those who generate, store, and/or transport hazardous wastes to the sites. In the long run, perhaps the most important feature of RCRA will be the phased prohibitions on land disposal of certain classes of hazardous wastes. Once the EPA determines which wastes can and cannot be safely disposed of even in secure landfills, other disposal options must be identified, or the generation of such wastes must be reduced. It will not be easy to find alternative means of disposal, since incineration—the most obvious alternative—is likely to be resisted by parties concerned about its risks or visual disamenities. . . .

Superfund may one day lend itself to easier evaluation. The program was put in place to clean up abandoned hazardous waste disposal sites, so we should be able to mark progress in part by looking at the number of cleanups that have taken place. A review of the record to date is not encouraging. Although the Superfund (CERCLA) Act was passed in 1980, the EPA has reported that through March 1989 work had been completed at only 41 sites, only 26 of which had been removed from the National Priorities List. Since the NPL now lists nearly 1,200 sites, and since the list of potential candidates for the NPL ranges from 30,000 to 400,000 . . . , the task ahead is sobering.

On the other hand, we must not fall into the trap of counting only finished cleanups. Emergency removals—the EPA's initial response upon ascertaining that a threat to health may exist at a site—have been much more frequent, numbering more than 1,300, counting actions at NPL and other sites. . . . [S]ome of these actions may remove the lion's share of the risks associated with a particular site; in fact, at some sites it might be wise to take no further action after an emergency removal has taken place, although the law makes it difficult to stop at that point.

The most difficult evaluative assignment concerns our laws governing pesticides and toxic substances and the regulations written pursuant to them. First of all, these laws are not directed at pollutants in the air or water or at the waste dumps that dot our landscape. Rather, they are intended to increase the information we possess about the pesticides and toxic substances society uses in a variety of ways. They are aimed at products rather than waste streams, in other words.

Nevertheless, . . . progress under both the Toxic Substances Control Act and the Federal Insecticide, Fungicide, and Rodenticide Act has been less than overwhelming. While new chemicals and pesticide introductions do include more testing data and other kinds of information than before, our record for testing products already in commerce at the time the laws were passed is not good. This is due to reasons both internal and external to the Environmental Protection Agency. As to the former, it has simply taken the EPA too long to gear up the TSCA program. On the other hand, certain features of TSCA—its requirement that any testing rules be promulgated as formal regulations, for instance—are not conducive to streamlined information-gathering. It will always be more difficult to keep score on TSCA and FIFRA than on the other environmental statutes.

Turning to environmental enforcement efforts, we encounter difficulties similar to those plaguing efforts to evaluate our pesticide and toxic substance laws. . . . [W]e have graduated in enforcement from worrying about forcing the installation of control equipment at regulated sources; we are now concerned with the more important but also more difficult problem of ensuring that that equipment is operated correctly and routinely. Unfortunately, for evidence on these important issues we often rely on information provided by the regulatees themselves (the environmental equivalent of the familiar problem of the fox guarding the chicken coop).

While scanty, the empirical evidence that does exist tells a mixed story. Some audits suggest that compliance with some standards is good; for example, a high percentage of industrial water polluters were found to be in compliance with the first-stage requirements issued under the Clean Water Act. On the other hand, municipal waste treatment plants—major water polluters in their own right—were found in one major study not only to be out of compliance often, but also to be significantly so for alarmingly long periods of time. Other enforcement areas of concern include (1) the performance of motor vehicles (the pollution control devices on which often deteriorate rapidly); (2) the persistence of violations at some sources which have repeatedly been cited for noncompliance, suggesting a lack of political will; and (3) poor compliance with groundwater monitoring and other requirements at hazardous waste disposal sites.

Although it cannot be measured like physical changes in air or water quality, or the number of hazardous waste sites, in one other respect federal environmental policy has had an important impact on life in the United States: I refer to the development of an environmental consciousness (or ethic) which colors virtually all decisions made by corporations, by federal, state, and local government operating units, and by many ordinary citizens. Environmental consciousness is not unrelated to quantitative measures of progress; indeed, without it less progress would have been made over the last twenty years than is reported above. Nevertheless, it is worth mentioning in its own right.

NOTES AND QUESTIONS

1. In what ways is Dr. Portney's assessment different from Dr. Commoner's? Can you tell which one is more pessimistic? What criteria does each use in attempting to measure the impact of environmental regulation?

2. In assessing the results of environmental regulation, how im-

portant should it be to consider the aggregate costs and benefits of regulation? Dr. Portney later notes that federal environmental legislation seems to be moving away from approaches that base standards on cost-benefit balancing, as indicated by recent amendments to CERCLA and the Clean Air Act. What factors account for this trend? Is society moving toward rejection of cost-benefit balancing as a means for determining how much environmental protection to provide, while embracing economic incentives approaches to reduce the cost of reaching independently determined environmental goals?

3. Having considered several perspectives, what do you think are the greatest success stories for environmental regulation? What have been its greatest failures? What factors account for the differences in results in different areas?

4. While environmental regulation seems poised to continue its rapid growth, there are divergent visions of its future, as explored below.

B. ENVIRONMENTAL PROSPECTS

Visions of the future world environment are many and varied, as articulated in the more than 20,000 pages of reports submitted to UNCED in 1992 by nations preparing to attend the Rio de Janeiro "Earth Summit." While developing nations articulated visions that often were substantially different from those of industrialized nations, discussions have focused in large part on two variables: technology and population growth. Developing nations are pressing the developed world for massive increases in financial assistance and technology transfers, while industrialized nations place more emphasis on controlling population growth. While environmentalists have had mixed feelings toward technology (some are perceived as rejecting modern technology, while others seek to channel it into environmentally benign avenues), technological innovations could play a key role in combatting future environmental problems. Former CEQ chairman Gus Speth, now executive director of the World Resources Institute, describes his vision of how new technology could be used to combat the planet's formidable environmental problems in the excerpt below.

Speth, The Greening of Technology
Wash. Post, Nov. 20, 1988, at D3

Despite the save-the-environment efforts of the past two decades, pollution is occurring today on a vast and unprecedented scale around the world. It reaches down to our groundwater, across national boundaries, and up to the stratosphere. For the first time in history, it has grown big enough to affect the global systems that control the climate and create the conditions for life.

The pollution-control laws of the early 1970s have bought us time; now far more is needed. The prescription, I believe, is straightforward but immensely challenging: societies can both reduce pollution and achieve expected economic growth only by bringing about a thoroughgoing transformation in the technologies of production and consumption. We must ditch 20th century technologies and rapidly adopt those of the 21st century. Our old environmental foe, modern technology, must become a friend.

To understand why this is so, consider the legacy of the pollution-prone technologies of this century. Four trends describe the situation:

The Trend from Modest Quantities of Pollutants to Huge Quantities.   The 20th century has witnessed explosive growth in human population and economic activity. World population has tripled. The world economy is 20 times larger today than in 1900.

With this growth have come huge changes in the quantities of pollutants released. This century's technologies have been raised on fossil fuels—first coal, then oil and natural gas; their use has jumped 10-fold in this period. One result is that over 200 million tons of sulfur and nitrogen oxide pollutants are added to the global atmosphere each year. Another is that Earth's atmosphere contains 25 percent more carbon dioxide—one of the greenhouse gases implicated in global warming and climate change.

The Trend from Natural Products to Synthetic Chemicals and Radioactive Substances.   Many of these substances are highly toxic in even minute quantities, and some persist and accumulate in biological systems or in the atmosphere.

Pesticides are released into the environment precisely because they are toxic. We use a billion pounds of pesticides each year in the United States, of which less than one percent reaches a pest. Ironically, other major products of the chemicals industry—chlorofluorocarbons—found wide use because they are not toxic, but unfortunately, as we have since discovered, they destroy the earth's protective ozone layer.

The Trend from First World to Third World.   A visit to any developing countries quickly shatters the myth that polluting technologies are predominately a problem of the highly industrialized countries. Cities in the Third World are consistently more polluted with sulfur dioxide and particulates than most cities in industrial countries.

A Combination of the First Three: The Trend from Local Effects to Global Effects.   When the volumes of pollution were much smaller and the pollutants similar to natural substances, impacts tended to be confined to limited geographic areas near sources. Today, the scale and intensity of pollution make its consequences truly global.

Nothing better illustrates this point than the atmosphere. Local air quality is improving in many cities, but it is worsening in others, and continues as a health threat almost everywhere. Meanwhile, acid rain, smog and other consequences of fossil fuel use are affecting plant and animal life over vast regions of the globe—killing forests and fish, damaging crops, changing the species composition of ecosystems.

Depletion of the stratosphere's ozone layer is a matter of such concern that an international treaty has been negotiated to reduce emissions of chlorofluorocarbons, but the latest measurements indicate the current treaty is already inadequate. And, probably most serious of all, the building of greenhouse gases in the atmosphere continues. This buildup is largely a consequence of the use of fossil fuels and chlorofluorocarbons, deforestation and various agricultural activities, and it now threatens societies with far-reaching climate change and rising sea levels. These closely linked assaults on the atmosphere probably constitute the most serious pollution threat in history.

The future could hold more of the same—a lot more. The scale and momentum of economic activity on the planet today are difficult to comprehend. It took all of human history to grow to the $600-billion world economy of 1900. Today the world economy grows by more than this amount every two years. By the middle of the next century, a scant lifetime away, our human world of five billion people will double to one of 10 billion, and our global economy of $13 trillion will be five times as large as today.

A LUDDITE RECANTS

Societies near and far have set two long-term goals for themselves—improving environmental quality, in part by reducing *current* pollution levels, and achieving large increases in economic activity. Reconciling these two goals will likely be one of the dominant challenges facing political leaders on all continents in the 1990s and beyond, and will require international cooperation on a scale seldom seen save in wartime.

What does this mean in practical terms? Imagine, just as a simple thought experiment, what would happen if greenhouse gases, industrial waste and other pollutants increased proportionately with the five-fold expansion in world economic activity projected for the middle of the next century. That would indeed happen if this growth merely replicates over and over today's prevailing technologies, broadly conceived. Seen this way, reconciling the economic and environmental goals societies have set for themselves will occur only if there is a transformation in technology—a shift, unprecedented in scope and pace to technologies high and low, soft and hard, that facilitate economic growth while sharply reducing the pressures on the natural environment.

In this limited sense at least, one might say that only technology can save us. That is a hard thing for a congenital Luddite like myself to say, but in a small victory of nurture over nature, I do now believe it. I do not diminish the importance of lifestyle changes—some go hand-in-hand with technological change—and I applaud the spread of more voluntary simplicity in our wasteful society. But economic growth has its imperatives; it will occur. The key question is: with what technologies? Only the population explosion rivals this question in fundamental importance to the planetary environment.

The good news is that many emerging technologies offer exciting opportunities and can help us move in the right direction. The bad news is that no "hidden hand" is operating to guide technology. We must think hard about the interventions that will be needed to bring about this greening of technology.

The two fundamental processes of technological transformation are discovery and application. The first is the realm of research and development. Science and engineering must have the financial support and the incentives to provide us with an accurate understanding of the Earth's systems and cycles and the effects of human actions. They must deliver to us a new agriculture, one redesigned to be sustainable both economically and ecologically, which stresses low inputs of commercial fertilizers, pesticides and energy. They must show us how industry and transportation can be transformed from an era of materials-intensive, high-throughput processes to an era that uses fuel and materials with great efficiency, generates little or no waste, recycles residuals, releases only benign products to the environment and is, hence, more "closed." And they must provide us with early and accurate assessments of possible, technological innovations and their consequences intended and unintended.

INSTITUTIONALIZING INNOVATION

Guiding and speeding the application of solution-oriented technologies will require institutional innovation. Imagine an Environmental Protection Agency organized not strictly by air pollution, water pollution, pesticides and so on, but by transportation, manufacturing, agriculture, energy and housing. These great sectors of economic services are technology-based and technology-driven. Today, EPA stands outside, imposing external "pollution control" standards. In the future, EPA must come inside and environmental factors must be integrated into the basic design of our transportation, energy and other systems. A new type of cooperation among the private sector, EPA, traditional Cabinet agencies, and environmental advocates must be forged. Together, they must work upstream to change the products, processes, policies and pressures that give rise to pollution.

Environmentalism began on the periphery of the economy, saving a bit of landscape here, bottling up some pollution there. The challenges ahead are such that it must spread as creed and code to permeate to the core of the economies of the world.

At the international level, institutional innovation will be needed to speed the process of agreement and concerted action. We will need upgraded international environmental agencies, new international treaties, environmental diplomats, and the integration of environmental concerns into our trade and other international economic relations.

Consider, for example, former Arizona governor Bruce Babbitt's recent suggestion that we begin restricting imports of products that are manufactured by processes that threaten the environment, much as we restrict the import of endangered species and harmful products. Should we import copper from countries where smelters are operated without pollution controls, or products made with chlorofluorocarbons or treated with pesticides banned here? In a similar vein, policies on technology transfer and development assistance must help developing countries leapfrog the wasteful and dangerous technologies characteristic of the industrial countries.

Technology-forcing regulations and economic incentives must both be harnessed. Most importantly, we must make the market mechanism work for us, guiding technological innovation that should not be micromanaged by government. Today, natural resource depletion and pollution are being subsidized on a grand scale around the globe. To get the prices right, we must begin by removing subsidies and making private companies and governments "internalize the externalities" so that prices reflect the true costs to society, including the costs of pollution.

For example, the costs to society of global warming could be very high. As a step toward honest pricing, a fee on carbon dioxide emissions from fossil fuel use, perhaps agreed to at the international level, could be imposed. A double benefit would occur if some revenues from the fee were used for programs to stem deforestation in the tropics.

The needed transition is technological, but the drive for it will come from another realm as well—from the hopes and fears of people, from their wonder at the natural world, from their dogged insistence that some things that seem very wrong are just that. People everywhere are offended by pollution. They sense intuitively that we have pressed beyond limits we should not have exceeded. With Thoreau, they know that heaven is under our feet as well as over our heads. Politicians around the globe are increasingly hearing the demand that things be set right. And that is very good news indeed.

NOTES AND QUESTIONS

1. Mr. Speth notes that there is no "hidden hand" operating to guide the development of technology in environmentally beneficial ways. What forces *are* operating to influence how technology develops? To what extent do existing environmental regulations help or hinder the development of environmentally superior technology? What types of collective action are best suited for stimulating such technological innovation?

2. The use of economic incentive approaches to regulation to stimulate the development of improved technology appears to be increasing. As noted above, even before the 1990 Amendments, Congress had amended the Clean Air Act to impose a pollution tax on manufacturers of chlorofluorocarbons (CFCs). The size of that tax increases automatically over time to encourage the rapid phaseout of substances that deplete the ozone layer. The Clean Air Act Amendments of 1990 incorporate an emissions trading scheme and a $25-per-ton tax on all pollutants to generate funds for administering a new permit program. Companies also are beginning to compete for consumers by touting their products as environmentally benign. To what extent will market forces such as these generate incentives for the development of environmentally superior technologies?

The draft UNCED Declaration, on which agreement was reached in April 1992, endorses efforts to enhance "the development, adaption, diffusion and transfer of technologies, including new and innovative technologies." Principle 9. Dodging any specific recommendations on the controversial issue of population control, the Declaration vaguely endorses adoption of "appropriate demographic policies." Principle 8.

4. While population control measures have not been a focus of environmental regulation in the industrialized world, population growth has played a prominent role in competing forecasts concerning the future health of the planet. Warning that population growth would soon overwhelm the Earth's carrying capacity, ecologist Paul Ehrlich attracted national attention in 1968 with his book, The Population Bomb, which forecast mass starvation and mineral shortages. Calling Erhlich a Malthusian, economist Julian Simon argued in The Ultimate Resource that "[n]atural resources are not finite" because human ingenuity continually finds more efficient ways to use them. In 1980 the two agreed to test their theories by betting $1,000 on whether the prices of five metals—

chrome, copper, nickel, tin, and tungsten—would be higher or lower in the year 1990. Erhlich argued that prices would rise with increased demand for a finite supply of the metals. Simon bet that prices would fall. In 1990 Simon won the bet when the prices of all five metals had declined in real terms due in part to the development of substitutes (such as plastics). The story of the bet is told in Tierney, A Bet on the Planet Earth, N.Y. Times Mag., Dec. 2, 1990, at 52. Tierney notes that Ehrlich, who lost the bet, has been highly popular with the public, while Simon, who won, has few followers.

Does the outcome of Ehrlich's bet with Simon prove that Ehrlich's ideas are wrong, or just that he is a poor gambler? Does Simon's argument imply that no action needs to be taken to avert environmental crises or just that we need not get too worried about the future because we can and will act to avert crises? The more people agree with Ehrlich, the more likely it is that society will impose stringent environmental protection measures. Is Simon's optimism more likely to prove correct the more people believe that Ehrlich is right and act to prevent environmental damage?

5. Paul Portney notes that one of the most significant impacts of environmental policy has been to stimulate "the development of an environmental consciousness (or ethic) which colors virtually all decisions made by corporations, by federal, state, and local government operating units, and by many ordinary citizens." P. Portney, Public Policies for Environmental Protection 279 (1990). This development may have an even more significant impact on the quality of the environment than will government regulation. Efforts to incorporate environmental concerns more explicitly in corporate decision-making intensified after the *Exxon Valdez* oil spill. The Coalition for Environmentally Responsible Economies (CERES), a group of environmentalists and institutional investors, drafted a set of principles of corporate environmental responsibility known as the Valdez Principles. See Carpency, The Valdez Principles: A Corporate Counselor's Perspective, 26 Wake Forest L. Rev. 11 (1991). Should companies adopt corporate environmental policies? What value might such codes of corporate conduct have? How can they be enforced?

6. The immense popularity of environmental concerns has caused some companies to court consumers with claims that their products provide environmental benefits. While it has been difficult to verify the claims that have been made by some companies, as noted in Chapter 3, it is also hard to determine whether this represents a genuine trend toward more environmentally responsible corporate behavior or just a short-run marketing fad. Jessica Mathews argues that corporations are changing their attitudes toward the environment, but that few have truly incorporated environmental concerns in their decision-making.

Mathews, Green, Inc.
Wash. Post, Mar. 15, 1991, at A23

When the government first required U.S. tuna fishermen to use dolphin-safe nets, the industry went on strike and burned the chief regulator in effigy in San Diego Harbor. Last year tuna canners voluntarily adopted even stricter practices. Now advertisements compare dolphin-purity. What the industry insisted was impossible a few years ago is the only way to do business today.

The shift symbolizes the recent birth of corporate environmentalism in the United States. It is a cultural change in mid-process, evolving rapidly though unevenly. Many companies have changed little: Business is business-as-usual, perhaps with a phony veneer of greenness. In others the changes in outlook and practice are profound. Environmentalists, put off by the former, too often fail to recognize the latter. Governments, which have to deal with both the ostriches and the eagles, have a tough job keeping pace, but there are a few innovative examples of appeals to enlightened self-interest in lieu of regulation.

Herewith a rough guide to the environmental evolution of American corporate culture.

Level 1—Exploit the Green Fad While It Lasts.   These are the folk who rush to slap on green labels whether the product deserves it or not. "Biodegradable" and "recyclable" are the most frequently abused. Internally, these companies appoint environmental officers who have neither access to executives above them nor clout with plant managers, but whose appointments are featured prominently in the annual report.

Level 2—Environmentalism Can Sometimes Be Good Business.   These companies may not have changed their basic attitudes, but under pressure to satisfy customers or critics have discovered that pollution reduction or improved environmental management can often buy valuable bragging rights at little or no cost. A lot of change in this category comes from businesses that know new laws and regulations are coming and see greater gain in getting out ahead of the new requirements than in paying lobbyists to fight them as they once would have done. The impetus still comes from external pressures, but the changes in practice are real.

Management style emphasizes scrupulous compliance with existing laws. Environmental audits are a favored tool. There is little inclination to go beyond the letter of the law. The motive is defensive, but it's a good defense.

Level 3—Environmentalism Is Here to Stay.   A still small number of companies see environmental concerns as a permanent feature of the business landscape. They figure that businesses that do the most to adapt to the new conditions will in the long run fare best. They believe that surprisingly often pollution prevention pays. Many set specific performance targets that go well beyond legal requirements. Environmental needs are integrated into R&D strategies, and process redesign replaces end-of-the-pipe controls.

Inside these firms, new policies are changing old attitudes. The chief environmental officer has direct access to top management. Employee performance reviews and bonuses include environmental criteria. Nearly always one individual—a highly committed CEO—is behind all of this change.

Level 4—The Environment Is a Strategic Business Opportunity. Beyond those whose business is directly environmental (pollution equipment vendors, for example) I don't know of any major American firm which believes that over the long run environmentalism will open as many doors as it closes and conducts strategic planning accordingly. Yet this belief is second nature to many Japanese and increasingly common in Europe. Japan, for example, has plunged headlong into the design of products and technologies that minimize greenhouse gas emissions despite scientific uncertainties about global warming.

There are at least two reasons for this difference between American companies and their principal competitors: low U.S. energy prices and the residue of 20 years of almost exclusively adversarial environmental policy making. Plenty of businessmen and environmentalists would still rather flog old enemies than see the other side as it exists today. Environmentalists who are pushing businesses to sign a code of conduct called the Valdez Principles must be aware that the name they have chosen asks businessmen to make an implicit admission of guilt by association.

The best place to find the same attitude on the other side is on the editorial page of The Wall Street Journal. My favorite recent example was a letter accusing environmental leaders of favoring "totalitarian regimes" because there was no "mass picketing of the Iraqi embassies" or "any expression of outrage" over Iraq's intentional oil spill. Such stuff would be merely ridiculous if a steady diet of it did not strengthen the worst myths. The Journal's editorial that day called for an end to western water subsidies. It included the requisite slap at the "environmental left" but conspicuously failed to acknowledge that environmentalists have been waging a lonely battle against water subsidies for a decade.

Fortunately, these are the extremes. The good news is that the constructive middle is expanding steadily. The Environmental Protection Agency's voluntary Green Lights program suggests what a less adversarial future might look like. Green Lights aims to make companies feel like heroes by making an investment that cuts their electricity use, lowers pollution and returns a quick, low-risk profit. (Yes, Virginia, there is a free lunch.) EPA expects to save more energy this way—perhaps as much as 10 percent of national electricity demand—than it could through regulation.

Businessmen and environmentalists will continue to disagree, but the changes now underway in the corporate world are of great potential import. Neither legislation nor litigation, essential as each is, can achieve what a heavy dose of cooperation and corporate initiative might produce.

NOTES AND QUESTIONS

1. The Valdez Principles seek an explicit acknowledgment that "corporations and shareholders have a direct responsibility for the environment." They ask companies to pledge to "minimize and strive to eliminate the release of any pollutant that may cause environmental damage" and to disclose to employees and the public environmental harm or hazards the company causes. If the regulatory system is working properly, why should corporations undertake any environmental obligations that extend beyond compliance with regulatory requirements?

2. While eschewing the Valdez Principles (in part due to concern that their name conveys the wrong impression), many corporations have adopted their own corporate environmental policies. See, e.g., Waste Management Inc., Environmental Policy (March 1990). Corporate officials have been particularly concerned about provisions in the Valdez Principles calling for independent audits of companies' environmental behavior and the appointment of a board member representing environmental concerns.

3. What forces or trends can you identify that are likely to affect the proportion of companies in each of the four categories that Jessica Mathews identifies? What actions by companies would convince you that they genuinely believe that the environment is a strategic business opportunity? What actions would make you believe that they are simply "exploiting the green fad while it lasts"?

C.   SOME CONCLUDING THOUGHTS

If these materials have left you with more questions than they have answered, then you may be developing a keen appreciation for some of the difficult policy choices posed by environmental regulation. The themes outlined in the early chapters of this book—moral outrage versus cool analysis, decision-making under uncertainty, winners and losers, implementation and institutional concerns, and differences in goals and means—are meant to convey some sense of why broad public support for environmental protection is not easily translated into effective policy.

Because environmental regulation raises many fundamental policy dilemmas for which there are no clear answers, it is hardly surprising that it has been such a persistent source of controversy. As we saw at the outset of this book, beneath the veneer of consensus on environmental values that permits politicians to declare the environment a "moral issue" lie deep divisions over policy. While a prominent senator now argues that the planet's health is so endangered that environmental protection should become "the central organizing principle for civilization," A. Gore, Earth in the Balance: Ecology and the Human Spirit 269 (1992), others depict environmentalists as power-hungry alarmists. Will, Earth Day's Hidden Agenda, Wash. Post, April 19, 1990, at A27.

These divisions are not simply the product of different interpretations of environmental "facts"; they also turn largely on differences of values concerning how much environmental risk society should tolerate, how that risk should be distributed, and how cautious society should be in the face of uncertainty. The difficulty of resolving such questions of value is reflected in the common law's long struggle between utilitarian and rights-based approaches to environmental problems. This tension persists today, even as public law has taken center stage in environmental protection efforts, in the fierce debate over competing approaches to regulatory policy.

While public law has overcome many of the common law's limitations, it faces difficulties of its own in designing and implementing regulatory policies that will affect human behavior in predictable ways. Nearly a quarter-century of experience with federal regulation has generated considerable knowledge that can be used to improve future regulatory policy. We have learned that regulation can affect human behavior in unintended and counterproductive ways, but that it also can stimulate technological innovation, expanding our capability to control environmental problems and reducing the costs of such controls. As the limitations of policies that emphasized command-and-control regulation become more evident, environmental law is becoming increasingly receptive to approaches that use economic incentives to affect behavior.

Improved scientific understanding of environmental problems has made us more acutely aware of the limits of our knowledge even as our desire to know more intensifies. We have come to realize that even small changes in human behavior can have an enormous impact on our environment, even if we cannot trace micro-level impacts with precision. This understanding is contributing to expanded notions of social responsibility embodied in laws that extend liability to parties more remotely connected to environmental damage or that seek to regulate increasingly smaller entities.

As legal responsibility for environmental protection expands, conflicts between environmental regulation and individual autonomy may arise more frequently. In such circumstances environmentalists may become the cool analysts while their opponents seek to muster moral outrage against perceived threats to their property. Recognition that concerns for fairness and respect for individual autonomy are at the root of much environmental regulation should provide some common ground for resolving these controversies as society decides how to control environmental risks and how to distribute the costs of regulation.

Many of the same policy dilemmas that have confronted national environmental policymaking are now appearing on a global scale as the international community seeks to develop a coordinated response to global environmental problems. How the world community addresses these issues will have a profound effect not only on what sort of physical environment our planet will have, but also on the public values and aspirations of the nations of the world and their citizens.

=== Appendix A ===
‖ *Glossary* ‖

The following glossary and the acronym list (Appendix B) may help you understand the terminology employed in environmental regulation. They are adapted from EPA, Glossary of Environmental Terms and Acronym List (1988). The definitions are intended to acquaint you with the basic concepts; they do not represent legal definitions of the terms.

Abatement. Reducing the degree of intensity of, or eliminating, pollution.

Acid deposition. A complex chemical and atmospheric phenomenon that occurs when emissions of sulfur and nitrogen compounds and other substances are transformed by chemical processes in the atmosphere, often far from the original sources, and then deposited on Earth in either a wet or dry form. The wet forms, popularly called "acid rain," can fall as rain, snow, or fog. The dry forms are acidic gases or particulates.

Acid rain. *See* Acid deposition.

Active ingredient. In any pesticide product, the component that kills, or otherwise controls, target pests. Pesticides are regulated primarily on the basis of their active ingredients.

Acute toxicity. The ability of a substance to cause poisonous effects resulting in severe biological harm or death soon after a single exposure or dose. Also, any severe poisonous effect resulting from a single short-term exposure to a toxic substance.

Administrative order. A legal document signed by EPA directing an individual, business, or other entity to take corrective action or refrain from an activity. It describes the violations and actions to be taken and can be enforced in court. Such orders may be issued, for example, as a result of an administrative complaint whereby the respondent is ordered to pay a penalty for violations of a statute.

Administrative order on consent. A legal agreement signed by EPA and an individual, business, or other entity through which the violator agrees to pay for correction of violations, take the required corrective or cleanup actions, or refrain from an activity. It describes the actions to be taken, may be subject to a comment period, applies to civil actions, and can be enforced in court.

Advanced waste water treatment. Any treatment of sewage that goes beyond the secondary or biological water treatment stage and includes the removal of nutrients such as phosphorus and nitrogen and a high percentage of suspended solids.

Advisory. A nonregulatory document that communicates risk information to persons who may have to make risk management decisions.

Airborne particulates. Total suspended particulate matter found in the atmosphere as solid particles or liquid droplets. The chemical composition of particulates varies widely depending on location and time of year. Airborne particulates include: windblown dust, emissions from industrial processes, smoke from the burning of wood and coal, and the exhaust of motor vehicles.

Air quality criteria. The levels of pollution and lengths of exposure above which adverse health and welfare effects may occur.

Air quality standards. The level of pollutants prescribed by regulations that may not be exceeded during a specified time in a defined area.

Ambient air quality standards. See Criteria pollutants; National ambient air quality standards.

Anthropogenic. Caused by or relating to the impact of human activity on the environment.

Anti-degradation clause. The part of federal air quality and water quality requirements prohibiting deterioration where pollution levels are above the legal limit.

Aquifer. An underground geological formation, or group of formations, containing usable amounts of groundwater that can supply wells and springs.

Area source. Any stationary source of hazardous air pollution that is not a major source. Such sources, which do not include motor vehicles, are to be regulated under sections 112(k) and 112(d) of the Clean Air Act.

Asbestos. A mineral fiber that can pollute air or water and cause cancer or asbestosis when inhaled. EPA has banned or severely restricted its use in manufacturing and construction.

Asbestosis. A disease associated with chronic exposure to and inhalation of asbestos fibers. The disease makes breathing progressively more difficult and can lead to death.

Ash. The mineral content of a product remaining after complete combustion.

Assimilation. The ability of a body of water to purify itself of pollutants.

Attainment area. An area considered to have air quality as good as or better than the national ambient air quality standards as defined in the Clean Air Act. An area may be an attainment area for one pollutant and a nonattainment area for others.

Background level. In air pollution control, the concentration of air pollutants in a definite area during a fixed period of time prior to the starting up of or the stoppage of a source of emission under control. In toxic substances monitoring, the average presence in the environment, originally referring to naturally occurring phenomena.

Banking. A system for recording qualified air emissions reductions for later use in bubble, offset, or netting transactions.

BEN. EPA's computer model for analyzing a violator's economic gain from not complying with the law.

Benthic organism (Benthos). A form of aquatic plant or animal life that is found on or near the bottom of a stream, lake, or ocean.

Benthic region. The bottom layer of a body of water.

Best available control technology (BACT). An emission limitation based on the maximum degree of emission reduction (considering energy, environmental, and economic impacts and other costs) achievable through application of production processes and available methods, systems, and techniques. In no event does BACT permit emissions in excess of those allowed under any applicable Clean Air Act provisions. Use of the BACT concept is allowable on a case-by-case basis for major new or modified emissions sources in attainment areas, and it applies to each regulated pollutant.

Bioaccumulative. Characterized by an increase in concentration of a substance in living organisms (that are very slowly metabolized or excreted) as they breathe contaminated air, drink contaminated water, or eat contaminated food.

Bioassay. The use of living organisms to measure the effect of a substance, factor, or condition by comparing before-and-after data. The term is often used to denote cancer bioassays.

Biochemical oxygen demand (BOD). A measure of the amount of oxygen consumed in the biological processes that break down organic matter in water. The greater the BOD, the greater the degree of pollution.

Biodegradable. Having the ability to break down or decompose rapidly under natural conditions and processes.

Biological treatment. A treatment technology that uses bacteria to consume waste. This treatment breaks down organic materials.

Biomass. All of the living material in a given area; often refers to vegetation. Also called "biota."

Biomonitoring. (1) The use of living organisms to test the suitability of effluent for discharge into receiving waters and to test the quality of such waters downstream from the discharge. (2) Analysis of blood, urine, tissues, and so on to measure chemical exposure in humans.

Biosphere. The portion of Earth and its atmosphere that can support life.

Biotic community. A naturally occurring assemblage of plants and animals that live in the same environment and are mutually sustaining and independent.

BOD5. The amount of dissolved oxygen consumed in five days by biological processes breaking down organic matter.

Bottle bill. Proposed or enacted legislation that requires a returnable deposit on beverage containers and provides for redemption in retail stores or other places. Such legislation is designed to discourage use of throw-away containers.

Bubble, The. A system under which existing emissions sources can propose alternate means to comply with a set of emissions limitations. Under the bubble concept, sources can control more than they are required to at one emission point where control costs are relatively low in return for a comparable relaxation of controls at a second emission point where costs are higher.

Bubble policy. *See* Emissions trading.

Buffer strips. Strips of grass or other erosion-resisting vegetation between or below cultivated strips or fields.

Cancellation. Refers to section 6(b) of the Federal Insecticide, Fungicide, and Rodenticide Act (FIFRA), which authorizes cancellation of a pesticide registration if unreasonable adverse effects to the environment and public health develop when a product is used according to widespread and commonly recognized practice or if its labeling or other material required to be submitted does not comply with FIFRA provisions.

Cap. A layer of clay or other highly impermeable material installed over the top of a closed landfill to prevent entry of rainwater and minimize production of leachate.

Carbon dioxide (CO_2). A colorless, odorless, nonpoisonous gas that results from fossil fuel combustion and is normally a part of the ambient air. Increasing levels of carbon dioxide in the atmosphere are contributing to the greenhouse effect.

Carbon monoxide (CO). A colorless, odorless, poisonous gas produced by incomplete fossil fuel combustion.

Carcinogen. Any substance that can cause or contribute to the production of cancer.

Carcinogenic. Cancer-producing.

Carrying capacity. (1) In recreation management, the amount of use a recreation area can sustain without deterioration of its quality. (2) In wildlife management, the maximum number of animals an area can support during a given period of the year.

Catalytic converter. An air pollution abatement device that removes pollutants from motor vehicle exhaust, either by oxidizing them into carbon dioxide and water or reducing them to nitrogen and oxygen.

Categorical exclusion. A class of actions that either individually or cumulatively would not have a significant effect on the human environment and therefore would not require preparation of an environmental assessment or environmental impact statement under the National Environmental Policy Act (NEPA).

Categorical pretreatment standard. A technology-based effluent limitation for an industrial facility that discharges into a municipal sewer system. Analogous in stringency to Best Availability Technology (BAT) for direct dischargers.

Characteristic. Any one of the four categories used in defining hazardous waste: ignitability, corrosivity, reactivity, and toxicity.

Chemical treatment. Any one of a variety of technologies that use chemicals or a variety of chemical processes to treat waste.

Chlorinated hydrocarbons. These include a class of persistent, broad-spectrum insecticides that linger in the environment and accumulate in the food chain. Among them are DDT, aldrin, dieldrin, heptachlor, chlordane, lindane, endrin, mirex, hexachloride, and toxaphene. Other examples include TCE, used as an industrial solvent.

Chlorinated solvent. An organic solvent containing chlorine atoms, for example, methylene chloride and 1,1,1-trichloromethane, which are used in aerosol spray containers and in traffic paint.

Chlorination. The application of chlorine to drinking water, sewage, or industrial waste to disinfect it or to oxidize undesirable compounds.

Chlorofluorocarbons (CFCs). A family of inert, nontoxic, and easily liquified chemicals used in refrigeration, air conditioning, packaging, and insulation or as solvents and aerosol propellants. Because CFCs are not destroyed in the lower atmosphere they drift into the upper atmosphere, where their chlorine components destroy ozone.

Chronic toxicity. The capacity of a substance to cause long-term poisonous human health effects.

Cleanup. Actions taken to deal with a release or threat of release of a hazardous substance that could affect humans or the environment. The term "cleanup" is sometimes used interchangeably with the terms remedial action, removal action, response action, or corrective action.

Clear cut. A forest management technique that involves harvesting all the trees in one area at one time. Under certain soil and slope conditions it can contribute sediment to water pollution.

Closed-loop recycling. Reclaiming or reusing wastewater for purposes other than drinking or cooking in an enclosed process.

Coastal zone. Lands and waters adjacent to the coast that exert an influence on the uses of the sea and its ecology, or, inversely, whose uses and ecology are affected by the sea.

Coefficient of haze. A measurement of visibility interference in the atmosphere.

Coliform index. A rating of the purity of water based on a count of fecal bacteria.

Combined sewers. A sewer system that carries both sewage and storm water runoff. Normally its entire flow goes to a waste treatment plant, but during a heavy storm, the storm water volume may be so great as to cause overflows. When this happens untreated mixtures of storm water and sewage may flow into receiving waters. Storm water runoff may also carry toxic chemicals from industrial areas or streets into the sewer system.

Comment period. Time provided for the public to review and comment on a proposed EPA action or rulemaking after it is published in the Federal Register.

Community water system. A public water system that serves at least 15 service connections used by year-round residents or regularly serves at least 25 year-round residents.

Compliance schedule. A negotiated agreement between a pollution source and a government agency that specifies dates and procedures by which a source will reduce emissions and thereby comply with a regulation.

Conditional registration. Under special circumstances, the Federal Insecticide, Fungicide, and Rodenticide Act permits registration of pesticide products that is "conditional" on the submission of additional data. These special circumstances include a finding by the EPA administrator that a new product or use of an existing pesticide will not significantly increase the risk of unreasonable adverse effects. A product containing a new (previously unregistered) active ingredient may be conditionally registered only if the administrator finds that such conditional registration is in the public interest, that a reasonable time for conducting the additional studies has not elapsed, and that the use of the pesticide for the period of conditional registration will not present an unreasonable risk.

Consent decree. A legal document, approved by a judge, that formalizes an agreement reached between EPA and potentially responsible parties (PRPs) through which PRPs will conduct all or part of a cleanup action at a Superfund site; cease or correct actions or processes that are polluting the environment; or otherwise comply with regulations where the PRP's failure to comply caused EPA to initiate regulatory enforcement actions. The consent decree describes the actions PRPs will take and may be subject to a public comment period.

Conservation. Avoiding waste of, and renewing when possible, human and natural resources; the protection, improvement, and use of natural resources according to principles that will assure their highest economic or social benefits.

Contaminant. Any physical, chemical, biological, or radiological substance or matter that has an adverse affect on air, water, or soil.

Contingency plan. A document setting out an organized, planned, and coordinated course of action to be followed in case of a fire, explosion, or other accident that releases toxic chemicals, hazardous wastes, or radioactive materials that threaten human health or the environment.

Conventional pollutants. Statutorily listed pollutants that are understood well by scientists. These may be in the form of organic waste, sediment, acid, bacteria and viruses, nutrients, oil and grease, or heat.

Corrosive. A chemical agent that reacts with the surface of a material, causing it to deteriorate or wear away.

Cost-effective alternative. An alternative control or corrective method identified after analysis as being the best available in terms of reliability, permanence, and economic considerations. Such analysis does not require EPA to choose the least expensive alternative. For example, when selecting a method for cleaning up a site on the Superfund National Priorities List, the Agency balances costs with the long-term effectiveness of the various methods proposed.

Cost recovery. A legal process by which potentially responsible parties who contributed to contamination at a Superfund site can be required to reimburse the Trust Fund for money spent during any cleanup actions by the federal government.

Criteria. Descriptive factors taken into account by EPA in setting standards for various pollutants. These factors are used to determine limits on allowable concentration levels and to limit the number of violations per year. When issued by EPA, the criteria provide guidance to the states on how to establish their standards.

Criteria pollutants. Six air pollutants known to be hazardous to human health: ozone, carbon monoxide, total suspended particulates, sulfur dioxide, lead, and nitrogen oxide. The term derives from the requirement that EPA describe the characteristics and potential health and welfare effects of these pollutants. It is on the basis of these criteria that standards are set or revised.

Curie. A quantitative measure of radioactivity equal to 3.7×10^{10} disintegrations per second.

Data call-in. A part of the process of developing key required test data, especially on the long-term, chronic effects of existing pesticides, in advance of scheduled Registration Standard reviews. Data call-in is an adjunct of the Registration Standards program intended to expedite reregistration and involves the "calling in" of data from manufacturers.

DDT. The first chlorinated hydrocarbon insecticide (chemical name: dichloro-diphenyl-trichloroethane). It has a half-life of 15 years and can collect in fatty tissues of certain animals. EPA banned registration and interstate sale of DDT for virtually all but emergency uses in the United States in 1972 because of its persistence in the environment and accumulation in the food chain.

Decomposition. The breakdown of matter by bacteria and fungi. It changes the chemical makeup and physical appearance of materials.

Degradation. The process by which a chemical is reduced to a less complex form.

Delegated state. A state (or other government entity) that has applied for and received authority to administer, within its territory, its state regulatory program as the federal program required under a particular federal statute. As used in connection with the NPDES program, the term does not connote any transfer of federal authority to a state.

Delisting. A decision to exclude a waste generated at a particular facility from listing as hazardous under RCRA subtitle C in response to a petition demonstrating that site-specific factors render the waste nonhazardous.

Dermal toxicity. The ability of a pesticide or toxic chemical to poison people or animals by contact with the skin.

Designated pollutant. An air pollutant that is neither a criteria nor a hazardous pollutant as described in the Clean Air Act but for which new sources performance standards exist. The Clean Air Act does require states to control these pollutants, which include acid mist, total reduced sulfur (TRS), and fluorides.

Designated uses. Those water uses identified in state water quality standards that must be achieved and maintained as required under the Clean Water Act. Uses can include cold water fisheries, public water supply, and agriculture.

Dilution ratio. The relationship between the volume of water in a stream and the volume of incoming water. It affects the ability of the stream to assimilate waste.

Dioxin. Any of a family of compounds known chemically as dibenzo-p-dioxins. Concern about them arises from their potential toxicity and contamination of commercial products. One of the more toxic manmade chemicals known.

Direct discharger. A municipal or industrial facility that introduces pollution through a defined conveyance or system; a point source.

Disposal. Final placement or destruction of toxic, radioactive, or other wastes; surplus or banned pesticides or other chemicals; polluted soils; and drums containing hazardous materials from removal actions or accidental releases. Disposal may be accomplished through use of approved secure landfills, surface impoundments, land farming, deep well injection, ocean dumping, or incineration.

Dissolved oxygen (DO). The oxygen freely available in water. Dissolved oxygen is vital to fish and other aquatic life and for the prevention of odors. Traditionally, the level of dissolved oxygen has been accepted as the single most important indicator of a water body's ability to support desirable aquatic life. Secondary and advanced waste treatment are generally designed to protect DO in waste-receiving waters.

Dissolved solids. Disintegrated organic and inorganic material contained in water. Excessive amounts make water unfit to drink or use in industrial processes.

Dredging. Removal of mud from the bottom of water bodies using a scooping machine. This disturbs the ecosystem and causes silting that can kill aquatic life. Dredging of contaminated muds can expose aquatic life to heavy metals and other toxics. Dredging activities may be subject to regulation under section 404 of the Clean Water Act.

Dump. A site used to dispose of solid wastes without environmental controls.

Ecological impact. The effect that a manmade or natural activity has on living organisms and their nonliving (abiotic) environment.

Ecology. The relationship of living things to one another and their environment, or the study of such relationships.

Ecosphere. The "bio-bubble" that contains life on Earth, in surface waters, and in the air.

Ecosystem. The interacting system of a biological community and its nonliving environmental surroundings.

Effluent. Wastewater—treated or untreated—that flows out of a treatment plant, sewer, or industrial outfall. Generally refers to wastes discharged into surface waters.

Effluent limitation. Restrictions established by a state or EPA on quantities, rates, and concentrations in wastewater discharges.

Electrostatic precipitator. An air pollution control device that removes particles from the gas stream (smoke) after combustion occurs. The ESP imparts an electrical charge to the particles, causing them to adhere to metal plates inside the precipitator. Rapping on the plates causes the particles to fall into a hopper for disposal.

Eminent domain. Government taking—or forced acquisition—of private land for public use, with compensation paid to the landowner.

Emission. Pollution discharged into the atmosphere from smokestacks, other vents, and surface areas of commercial or industrial facilities; from residential chimneys; and from motor vehicle, locomotive, or aircraft exhausts.

Emission inventory. A listing, by source, of the amount of air pollutants discharged into the atmosphere of a community. It is used to establish emission standards.

Emission standard. The maximum amount of air-polluting discharge legally allowed from a single source, mobile or stationary.

Emissions trading. An EPA policy that allows a plant complex with several facilities to decrease pollution from some facilities while increasing it from others, so long as total results are equal to or better than those required by previous limits. Facilities where this is done are treated as if they exist in a bubble in which total emissions are averaged out. Complexes that reduce emissions substantially may "bank" their "credits" or sell them to other industries.

Endangered species. Animals, birds, fish, plants, or other living organisms threatened with extinction by manmade or natural changes in their environment. Requirements for declaring a species endangered are contained in the Endangered Species Act.

Enforcement. EPA, state, or local legal actions to obtain compliance with environmental laws, rules, regulations, or agreements or obtain penalties or criminal sanctions for violations. Enforcement procedures may vary depending on the specific requirements of different environmental laws and related implementing regulatory requirements.

Enforcement decision document. A document that provides an explanation to the public of EPA's selection of the cleanup alternative at enforcement sites on the National Priorities List. Similar to a Record of Decision.

Environment. The sum of all external conditions affecting the life, development, and survival of an organism.

Environmental assessment. A written environmental analysis that is prepared pursuant to the National Environmental Policy Act to determine whether a federal action would significantly affect the environment and thus require preparation of a more detailed environmental impact statement.

Environmental audit. (1) An independent assessment of the current status of a party's compliance with applicable environmental requirements. (2) An independent evaluation of a party's environmental compliance policies, practices, and controls.

Environmental impact statement. A document required of federal agencies by the National Environmental Policy Act for major projects or legislative proposals significantly affecting the environment. A tool for decision-making, it describes in detail the positive and negative effects of the undertaking and must include an analysis of alternative actions.

EPA. The U.S. Environmental Protection Agency, established in 1970 by executive order.

Epidemiology. The study of diseases as they affect populations, including the distribution of disease or other health-related states and events in human populations, the factors (e.g., age, sex, occupation, economic status) that influence this distribution, and the application of this study to the control of health problems.

Erosion. The wearing away of land surface by wind or water. Erosion occurs naturally owing to weather or runoff but can be intensified by land-clearing practices related to farming, residential or industrial development, road building, or timber-cutting.

Estuary. Regions of interaction between rivers and nearshore ocean waters where tidal action and river flow create a mixing of fresh and salt water. These areas may include bays, mouths of rivers, salt marshes, and lagoons. These brackish water ecosystems shelter and feed marine life, birds, and wildlife.

Eutrophication. The slow aging process during which a lake, estuary, or bay evolves into a bog or marsh and eventually disappears. During the later stages of eutrophication, the water body is choked by abundant plant life as the result of increased amounts of nutritive compounds such as nitrogen and phosphorus. Human activities can accelerate the process.

Exceedance. Violation of environmental protection standards by exceeding allowable limits or concentration levels.

Exposure. The amount of radiation or pollutant present in an environment that represents a potential health threat to the living organisms in that environment.

Extremely hazardous substances. Any of hundreds of chemicals identified by EPA on the basis of toxicity and listed under the Emergency Planning and Community Right-to-Know Act. The list is subject to revision.

Fabric filter. A cloth device that catches dust particles from industrial emissions.

Feasibility study. (1) Analysis of the practicability of a proposal. The feasibility study usually recommends selection of a cost-effective alternative. It usually starts as soon as the remedial investigation is under way; together, they are commonly referred to as the "RI/FS." The term can apply to a variety of proposed corrective or regulatory actions. (2) In research, a small-scale investigation of a problem to ascertain whether or not a proposed research approach is likely to provide useful data.

Filling. Depositing dirt and mud or other materials into aquatic areas to create more dry land, usually for agricultural or commercial development purposes. Such activities often damage the ecology of the area.

Filtration. A treatment process, under the control of qualified operators, for removing solid (particulate) matter from water by passing the water through porous media such as sand or a manmade filter. The process is often used to remove particles that contain pathogenic organisms.

Finding of no significant impact. A document prepared by a federal agency that presents the reasons why a proposed action would not have a significant impact on the environment and thus would not require preparation of an Environmental Impact Statement. An FNSI is based on the results of an environmental assessment.

First draw. The water that immediately comes out when a tap is first opened. This water is likely to have the highest level of lead contamination from plumbing materials.

Flue gas. The air coming out of a chimney after combustion in the burner it is venting. It can include nitrogen oxides, carbon oxides, water vapor, sulfur oxides, particles, and many chemical pollutants.

Flue gas desulfurization. A technology that uses a sorbent, usually lime or limestone, to remove sulfur dioxide from the gases produced by burning fossil fuels. Flue gas desulfurization is currently the state-of-the-art technology in use in major SO_2 emitters, for example, power plants.

Fluorocarbons (FCs). Any of a number of organic compounds analogous to hydrocarbons in which one or more hydrogen atoms are replaced by fluorine. Once used in the United States as a propellant in aerosols, they are now primarily used in coolants and in some industrial processes. FCs containing chlorine are called chlorofluorocarbons (CFCs). They are believed to be depleting the ozone layer in the stratosphere, thereby allowing more harmful radiation to reach the Earth's surface.

Fly ash. Noncombustible residual particles from the combustion process carried by flue gas.

Food chain. A sequence of organisms, each of which uses the next lower member of the sequence as a food source.

Fresh water. Water that generally contains less than 1,000 milligrams per liter of dissolved solids.

Fuel economy standard. The Corporate Average Fuel Economy Standard (CAFE), which imposes financial penalties on motor vehicle manufacturers whose vehicles fail to average certain levels of fuel economy (in miles per gallon).

Fugitive emissions. Emissions not caught by a capture system.

Functional equivalent. A term used to describe EPA's decision-making process and its relationship to the environmental review conducted under the National Environmental Policy Act. A review is considered functionally equivalent when it addresses the substantive components of a NEPA review.

Fungicide. A pesticide used to control, prevent, or destroy fungi.

General permit. A permit applicable to a class or category of dischargers.

Generator. A facility or mobile source that emits pollutants or releases hazardous wastes.

Global climate change. Changes in worldwide climate and weather patterns of anthropogenic origin. These include changes in precipitation patterns, storm activity, and soil moisture induced by global warming, which increases the temperature of land masses more rapidly than oceans.

Global warming. An increase in worldwide temperature due to increased atmospheric concentrations of carbon dioxide and other gases that contribute to the greenhouse effect.

Greenhouse effect. The build-up of carbon dioxide or other trace gases that allows light from the sun's rays to heat the Earth but prevents a counterbalancing loss of heat.

Greenhouse gas. A gas whose presence in the upper atmosphere contributes to the greenhouse effect by allowing visible light to pass through the atmosphere while preventing heat radiating back from the Earth from escaping. Greenhouse gases from anthropogenic sources include carbon dioxide, nitrous oxide, methane, and CFCs. There also are even larger quantities of naturally occurring greenhouse gases, notably ozone and water vapor, whose concentrations may be affected by interactions with atmospheric pollutants.

Ground water. The supply of fresh water found beneath the Earth's surface, usually in aquifers, which is often used for supplying wells and springs. Because ground water is a major source of drinking water, there is growing concern over areas where leaching agricultural or industrial pollutants or substances from leaking underground storage tanks are contaminating ground water.

Habitat. The place where a population (e.g., human, animal, plant, microorganism) lives and its surroundings, both living and nonliving.

Hazard identification. A determination of whether or not a substance is capable of causing some form of adverse effect (e.g., determining if a substance is a carcinogen or reproductive toxin).

Hazardous air pollutants. Air pollutants that are not covered by ambient air quality standards but that present, or may present, a threat of adverse health or environmental effects. These include an initial list of 189 chemicals designated by Congress that is subject to revision by EPA.

Hazardous substance. Any material that poses a threat to human health or the environment. The term has a special meaning under CERCLA section 101(14), which broadly defines it to include any toxic water pollutant, hazardous waste, hazardous air pollutant, imminently hazardous chemical, or any substance designated by EPA to be reported if a designated quantity of the substance is spilled in the waters of the United States or if otherwise emitted to the environment.

Hazardous waste. A by-product of society that can pose a substantial or potential hazard to human health or the environment when improperly managed. Possesses at least one of four characteristics (ignitability, corrosivity, reactivity, or toxicity) or appears on special EPA lists.

Hazard ranking system (HRS). The principal screening tool used by EPA to evaluate risks to public health and the environment associated with abandoned or uncontrolled hazardous waste sites. The HRS calculates a score based on the potential for hazardous substances to cause harm to human health or the environment. This score is the primary factor in deciding if the site should be on the National Priorities List and, if so, what ranking it should have compared to other sites on the list.

Heavy metals. Metallic elements with high atomic weights, for example, mercury, chromium, cadmium, arsenic, and lead. They can damage living things at low concentrations and tend to accumulate in the food chain.

Herbicide. A chemical pesticide designed to control or destroy plants, weeds, or grasses.

High-level radioactive waste. Waste generated in the fuel of a nuclear reactor, found at nuclear reactors or nuclear fuel reprocessing plants. A serious threat to anyone who comes near the wastes without shielding.

Holding pond. A pond or reservoir, usually made of earth, built to store polluted runoff.

Hydrocarbons (HC). Chemical compounds that consist entirely of carbon and hydrogen.

Hydrogeology. The geology of ground water, with particular emphasis on the chemistry and movement of water.

Hydrology. The science dealing with the properties, distribution, and circulation of water.

Ignitable. Capable of burning or causing a fire.

Impoundment. A body of water or sludge confined by a dam, dike, floodgate, or other barrier.

Incineration. (1) Burning of certain types of solid, liquid, or gaseous materials. (2) A treatment technology involving destruction of waste by controlled burning at high temperatures, for example, burning sludge to remove the water and reduce the remaining residues to ash.

Incinerator. A furnace for burning wastes under controlled conditions.

Indicator. In biology, an organism, species, or community whose characteristics show the presence of specific environmental conditions.

Indirect discharge. Introduction of pollutants from a nondomestic source into a publicly owned waste treatment system. Indirect dischargers can be commercial or industrial facilities whose wastes go into the local sewers.

Indoor air. The air inside a habitable structure or conveyance.

Indoor air pollution. Chemical, physical, or biological contaminants in indoor air.

Inert ingredient. Pesticide components such as solvents, carriers, and surfactants that are not active against target pests. Not all inert ingredients are innocuous.

Injection well. A well into which fluids are injected for purposes such as waste disposal, improving the recovery of crude oil, or solution mining.

Injection zone. A geological formation, group of formations, or part of a formation receiving fluids through a well.

Inorganic chemicals. Chemical substances of mineral origin, not of basically carbon structure.

Insecticide. A pesticide compound specifically used to kill or control the growth of insects.

Inspection and maintenance. Activities to assure proper emissions-related operation of mobile sources of air pollutants, particularly automobile emissions controls. Also applies to wastewater treatment plants and other antipollution facilities and processes.

Integrated pest management. A mixture of pesticide-using and non-pesticide-using methods to control pests.

Interceptor sewers. Large sewer lines that, in a combined system, control the flow of the sewage to the treatment plant. In a storm, they allow some of the sewage to flow directly into a receiving stream, thus preventing an overload by a sudden surge of water into the sewers. They are also used in separate systems to collect the flows from main and trunk sewers and carry them to treatment points.

Interim (permit) status. The period during which treatment, storage, and disposal facilities coming under RCRA in 1980 were temporarily permitted to operate while awaiting denial or issuance of a permanent permit.

Interstitial monitoring. The continuous surveillance of the space between the walls of an underground storage tank.

Inversion. An atmospheric condition caused by a layer of warm air preventing the rise of cooling air trapped beneath it. This prevents the rise of pollutants that might otherwise be dispersed and can cause an air pollution episode.

In vitro. (1) "In glass"; a test-tube culture. (2) Any laboratory test using living cells taken from an organism.

In vivo. In the living body of a plant or animal. In vivo tests are those laboratory experiments carried out on whole animals or human volunteers.

Ionizing radiation. Radiation that can remove electrons from atoms, that is, alpha, beta, and gamma radiation.

Isotope. A variation of an element that has the same atomic number but a different weight because of its neutrons. Various isotopes of the same element may have different radioactive behaviors.

Land application. Discharge of wastewater onto the ground for treatment or reuse.

Land farming (of waste). A disposal process in which hazardous wastes are deposited on or in the soil in order to be naturally degraded by microbes.

Landfills. (1) Sanitary landfills are sites for the disposal of non-hazardous solid wastes that satisfy the criteria established by EPA under section 4004 of RCRA. Facilities that fail to meet these criteria are deemed "open dumps" under section 4004(14) of RCRA. (2) Land disposal sites for hazardous waste subject to regulation under RCRA subtitle C.

LD 50/Lethal dose. The dose of a toxicant that will kill 50 percent of test organisms within a designated period of time. The lower the LD 50, the more toxic the compound.

LD 0. The highest concentration of a toxic substance at which no test organisms die.

LD L0. The lowest concentration and dosage of a toxic substance that kills test organisms.

Leachate. A liquid that results from water's collecting contaminants as it trickles through wastes, agricultural pesticides, or fertilizers. Leaching may occur in farming areas, feedlots, and landfills, and may result in the entry of hazardous substances into surface water, ground water, or soil.

Leachate collection system. A system that gathers leachate and pumps it to the surface for treatment.

Leaching. The process by which soluble constituents are dissolved and carried down through the soil by a percolating fluid.

Lead (Pb). A heavy metal that is hazardous to health if breathed or swallowed. Its use in gasoline, paints, and plumbing compounds has been sharply restricted by federal regulations, but enormous quantities of it already released into the environment are causing significant problems.

Level of concern. The concentration in air of an extremely hazardous substance above which there may be serious immediate health effects to anyone exposed to it for short periods of time.

Limestone scrubbing. A process in which sulfur gases moving towards a smokestack are passed through a limestone-and-water solution to remove sulfur before it reaches the atmosphere.

Liner. (1) A relatively impermeable barrier designed to prevent leachate from leaking from a landfill. Liner materials include plastic and dense clay. (2) An insert or sleeve for sewer pipes to prevent leakage or infiltration.

Listed waste. Waste expressly listed as hazardous under subtitle C of RCRA because it is part of a waste stream that may pose a substantial threat to human health or the environment when managed improperly.

Local emergency planning committee. A committee appointed by the state emergency response commission, as required by section 301 of the Emergency Planning and Community Right-to-Know Act, to formulate a comprehensive emergency plan for its jurisdiction.

Lowest achievable emission rate. Under the Clean Air Act, this is the rate of emissions that reflects (a) the most stringent emission limitation contained in the implementation plan of any state for such source unless the owner or operator of the proposed source demonstrates such limitations are not achievable; or (b) the most stringent emissions limitation achieved in practice, whichever is more stringent. Application of this term does not permit a proposed new or modified source to emit pollutants in excess of existing new source standards.

Low-level radioactive waste. Radioactive wastes that are less hazardous than most of those generated by a nuclear reactor. These wastes usually are generated by hospitals, research laboratories, and certain industries.

Major modification. Any nonroutine physical or operational change in a stationary source that will result in a significant net increase in emissions. Threshold levels of significance vary depending on the pollutant emitted. Such a change may subject the source to PSD or new source review requirements under the Clean Air Act.

Major stationary source. Any stationary source that emits or has the potential to emit certain threshold levels of emissions to which PSD and new source requirements of the Clean Air Act are applicable.

Marsh. A type of wetland that does not accumulate appreciable peat deposits and is dominated by herbaceous vegetation. Marshes may be either fresh or saltwater and tidal or nontidal.

Material safety data sheet (MSDS). A compilation of information required under the OSHA Hazard Communication Standard on the identity of hazardous chemicals, health and physical hazards, exposure limits, and precautions. Section 311 of the Emergency Planning and Community Right-to-Know Act requires facilities to submit MSDSs under certain circumstances.

Maximum contaminant level. The maximum permissible level of a contaminant in water delivered to any user of a public water system under the Safe Drinking Water Act.

Maximum contaminant level goal. The maximum level of a contaminant in water at which no known or anticipated adverse effects on health occur and which includes an adequate margin of safety.

Media. Specific environments—air, water, soil—that are the subject of regulatory concern and activities.

Methane. A greenhouse gas that is colorless, nonpoisonous, and flammable and is created by anaerobic decomposition of organic compounds.

Mitigation. Measures taken to reduce adverse impacts on the environment.

Mobile source. A moving producer of air pollution. Refers mainly to vehicles used in transportation such as cars, trucks, motorcycles, and airplanes.

Modeling. An investigative technique using a mathematical or physical representation of a system or theory that accounts for all or some of its known properties. Models are often used to test the effect of changes of system components on the overall performance of the system.

Model plant. A theoretical description of a typical plant used for developing economic, environmental, and energy impact analyses as support for regulations or regulatory guidelines. It may incorporate features of existing and future plants to estimate the cost of incorporating pollution control technology as the first step in exploring the economic impact of a potential standard.

Monitoring. Periodic or continuous surveillance or testing to determine the level of compliance with statutory requirements or pollutant levels in various media or in humans, animals, and other living things.

Monitoring wells. Wells drilled at a hazardous waste management facility or Superfund site to collect ground water samples for the purpose of physical, chemical, or biological analysis to determine the amounts, types, and distribution of contaminants in the ground water beneath the site.

Mutagen. Any substance that can cause a change in genetic material.

Mutate. To bring about a change in the genetic constitution of a cell by altering its DNA structure. In turn, "mutagenesis" is any process by which cells are mutated.

National Ambient Air Quality Standards. Uniform, national air quality standards established by EPA that restrict ambient levels of certain pollutants to protect public health (primary standards) or public welfare (secondary standards).

National Contingency Plan. The federal plan that outlines procedures and standards for responding to releases of oil and hazardous substances including responses to sites designated for cleanup under the Superfund program.

National Emissions Standards for Hazardous Air Pollutants. National standards established by EPA that limit emissions of hazardous air pollutants.

National Pollutant Discharge Elimination System. The Clean Water Act's national permit program that regulates the discharge of pollutants into waters of the United States.

National Priorities List. EPA's list of the sites identified for possible long-term remedial action under CERCLA. Placement on the list is based primarily on the score a site receives from the Hazard Ranking System.

National Response Center. The federal operations center that receives notifications of all releases of oil and hazardous substances into the environment. The Center, open 24 hours a day, is operated by the U.S. Coast Guard, which evaluates all reports and notifies the appropriate agency.

National Response Team. Representatives of various federal agencies who, as a team, coordinate federal responses to nationally significant incidents of pollution and provide advice and technical assistance to the responding agency or agencies before and during a response action.

Navigable waters. Traditionally, waters sufficiently deep and wide for navigation but now including waters adjacent to or connected to waters navigable in fact.

Netting. Emission trading used to avoid PSD/NSR permit review requirements.

New source. Any stationary source built or modified after publication of final or proposed regulations that prescribe a standard of performance intended to apply to that type of emissions source.

New Source Performance Standards. Uniform national EPA air emissions and water effluent standards that limit the amount of pollution allowed from new sources or from existing sources that have been modified.

Nitrate. A compound containing nitrogen that can exist in the atmosphere or as a dissolved gas in water and that can have harmful effects on humans and animals. Nitrates in water can cause severe illness in infants and cows.

Nitric oxide (NO). A gas formed by combustion at a high temperature and under high pressure in an internal combustion engine. It changes into nitrogen dioxide in the ambient air and contributes to photochemical smog.

Nitrogen dioxide (NO_2). The result of nitric oxide combining with oxygen in the atmosphere. A major component of photochemical smog.

Nitrogen oxide (NOx). A product of combustion by mobile and stationary sources and a major contributor to the formation of ozone in the troposphere and acid deposition.

Nonattainment area. A geographic area that does not meet one or more of the National Ambient Air Quality Standards for the criteria pollutants designated in the Clean Air Act.

Noncommunity water system. A public water system that is not a community water system, for example, the water supply at a camp site or national park.

Nonconventional pollutant. Any pollutant that is not statutorily listed or that is poorly understood by the scientific community.

Nonpoint source. Pollution sources that are diffuse and do not have single point of origin or are not introduced into a receiving stream from a specific outlet. The pollutants are generally carried off the land by storm water runoff.

Nutrient. Any substance assimilated by living things that promotes growth. The term is generally applied to nitrogen and phosphorus in wastewater, but is also applied to other essential and trace elements.

Offsite facility. A hazardous waste treatment, storage, or disposal area that is located at a place away from the generating site.

Oil fingerprinting. A method that identifies sources of oil and allows spills to be traced to their source.

Oil spill. An accidental or intentional discharge of oil that reaches bodies of water. Can be controlled by chemical dispersion, combustion, mechanical containment, or adsorption.

Oncogenic. Causing tumors, whether benign or malignant.

Onsite facility. A hazardous waste treatment, storage, or disposal area that is located on the generating site.

Opacity. A measure of the amount of light obscured by particulate pollution in the air; clear window glass has a zero opacity, a brick wall has 100 percent opacity. Opacity is used as an indicator of changes in performance of particulate matter pollution control systems.

Open dump. A site where solid waste is disposed that does not satisfy criteria established by EPA under section 4004 of RCRA.

Operation and maintenance. (1) Activities conducted at a site after a Superfund site action is completed to ensure that the action is effective and operating properly. (2) Actions taken after construction to assure that facilities constructed to treat waste water will be properly operated, maintained, and managed to achieve efficiency levels and prescribed effluent limitations in an optimal manner.

Organic. (1) Derived from or relating to living organisms. (2) In chemistry, any compound containing carbon.

Organic chemicals and compounds. Animal- or plant-produced substances containing mainly carbon, hydrogen, and oxygen.

Organic matter. Carbonaceous waste contained in plant or animal matter and originating from domestic or industrial sources.

Organism. Any living thing.

Organophosphates. Pesticide chemicals that contain phosphorus; used to control insects. They are short-lived, but some can be toxic when first applied.

Organotins. Chemical compounds used in anti-foulant paints to protect the hulls of boats and ships, buoys, and dock pilings from marine organisms such as barnacles.

Outfall. The place where an effluent is discharged into receiving waters.

Overburden. The rock and soil cleared away before mining.

Oxidant. A substance containing oxygen that reacts chemically in air to produce a new substance. Oxidants contribute greatly to photochemical smog.

Ozone (O_3). A substance found in the stratosphere and the troposphere. In the stratosphere (the atmospheric layer beginning 7 to 10 miles above the Earth's surface) ozone is a form of oxygen found naturally that provides a protective layer shielding the Earth from ultraviolet radiation. In the troposphere (the layer extending up 7 to 10 miles from the Earth's surface), ozone is a chemical oxidant and a major component of photochemical smog. Ozone can seriously affect the human respiratory system and is one of the most widespread of all the criteria pollutants. Ozone in the troposphere is produced through complex chemical reactions of: nitrogen oxides, which are among the primary pollutants emitted by combustion sources; hydrocarbons, released into the atmosphere through the combustion, handling, and processing of petroleum products; and sunlight.

Ozone depletion. Destruction of the stratospheric ozone layer that shields the Earth from ultraviolet radiation. This destruction of ozone is caused by the breakdown of certain chlorine- and/or bromine-containing compounds (chlorofluorocarbons or halons), which break down when they reach the stratosphere and catalytically destroy ozone molecules.

Particulates. Fine liquid or solid particles such as dust, smoke, mist, fumes, or smog, found in air or emissions.

Pathogenic. Capable of causing disease.

Pathogens. Microorganisms that can cause disease in other organisms or in humans, animals, and plants. They may be bacteria, viruses, or parasites and are found in sewage, in runoff from animal farms or rural areas populated with domestic or wild animals, and in water used for swimming. Fish and shellfish contaminated by pathogens, or the contaminated water itself, can cause serious illness.

PCBs. A group of toxic, persistent chemicals (polychlorinated biphenyls) used in transformers and capacitators for insulating purposes and in gas pipeline systems as a lubricant. Further sale or use was banned by law in 1979.

Percolation. The movement of water downward and radially through the subsurface soil layers, usually continuing downward to the ground water.

Permit. An authorization, license, or equivalent control document issued by EPA or an approved state agency to implement the requirements of an environmental regulation.

Persistence. Refers to the length of time a compound, once introduced into the environment, stays there. A compound may persist for less than a second or indefinitely.

Pesticide. Substance or mixture of substances intended for preventing, destroying, repelling, or mitigating any pest. Also, any substance or mixture of substances intended for use as a plant regulator, defoliant, or desiccant.

Pesticide tolerance. The amount of pesticide residue allowed by law to remain in or on a harvested crop. EPA is supposed to set tolerances at levels well below the point at which the chemicals might be harmful to consumers.

pH. A measure of the acidity or alkalinity of a liquid or solid material.

Phosphates. Certain chemical compounds containing phosphorus.

Phosphorus. An essential chemical food element that can contribute to the eutrophication of lakes and other water bodies. Increased phosphorus levels result from discharge of phosphorus-containing materials into surface waters.

Photochemical oxidants. Air pollutants formed by the action of sunlight on oxides of nitrogen and hydrocarbons.

Photochemical smog. Air pollution caused by chemical reactions of various pollutants emitted from different sources.

Physical and chemical treatment. Processes generally used in large-scale wastewater treatment facilities. Physical processes may involve air-stripping or filtration. Chemical treatment includes coagulation, chlorination, and ozone addition. The term can also refer to treatment processes, treatment of toxic materials in surface waters and ground waters, oil spills, and some methods of dealing with hazardous materials on or in the ground.

Plume. (1) A visible or measurable discharge of a contaminant from a given point of origin. Can be visible or thermal in water or visible in the air as, for example, a plume of smoke. (2) The area of measurable and potentially harmful radiation leaking from a damaged reactor. (3) The distance from a toxic release considered dangerous for those exposed to the leaking fumes.

Point source. A stationary location or fixed facility from which pollutants are discharged or emitted. Also, any single identifiable source of pollution, for example, a pipe, ditch, ship, ore pit, or factory smokestack.

Pollutant. Generally, any substance introduced into the environment that adversely affects the usefulness of a resource.

Pollution. Generally, the presence of matter or energy whose nature, location, or quantity produces undesired environmental effects. Under the Clean Water Act, for example, the term is defined as the man-made or man-induced alteration of the physical, biological, and radiological integrity of water.

Polyvinyl chloride (PVC). A tough, environmentally indestructible plastic that releases hydrochloric acid when burned.

Postclosure period. The time period following the shutdown of a waste management or manufacturing facility. For monitoring purposes, this is often considered to be 30 years.

Potentially Responsible Party. Any individual or company—including an owner, operator, transporter, or generator—potentially liable under section 107 of CERCLA.

ppb, ppm. Parts per billion or parts per million, a way of expressing tiny concentrations of pollutants in air, water, soil, human tissue, and food or other products.

Precipitators. Air pollution control devices that collect particles from an emission.

Precursor. In photochemical terminology, a compound such as a volatile organic compound (VOC) that "precedes" an oxidant. Precursors react in sunlight to form ozone or other photochemical oxidants.

Preliminary assessment. The process of collecting and reviewing available information about a known or suspected waste site or release.

Pretreatment processes. Processes used to reduce, eliminate, or alter the nature of wastewater pollutants from nondomestic sources before they are discharged into publicly owned treatment works.

Prevention of Significant Deterioration. An EPA program in which state or federal permits are required that are intended to restrict emissions for new or modified sources in places where air quality is already better than required to meet primary and secondary ambient air quality standards.

Primary waste treatment. The first steps in wastewater treatment. Screens and sedimentation tanks are used to remove most materials that float or will settle. Primary treatment results in the removal of about 30 percent of carbonaceous biochemical oxygen demand from domestic sewage.

Publicly owned treatment works. A waste-treatment works owned by a state, unit of local government, or Indian tribe, usually designed to treat domestic wastewaters.

Public water system. A system that provides piped water for human consumption to at least 15 service connections or that regularly serves at least 25 individuals.

Radiation. Any form of energy propagated as rays, waves, or streams of energetic particles. The term is frequently used in relation to the emission of rays from the nucleus of an atom.

Radiation standards. Regulations that set maximum exposure limits for protection of the public from radioactive materials.

Radioactive substances. Substances that emit radiation.

Radionuclide. A radioactive element characterized according to its atomic mass and atomic number that can be manmade or naturally occurring. Radioisotopes can have a long life as soil or water pollutants and are believed to have potentially mutagenic effects on the human body.

Radon. A colorless, naturally occurring, radioactive, inert gaseous element formed by radioactive decay of radium atoms in soil or rocks.

Raw sewage. Untreated wastewater.

Reasonably available control technology (RACT). The lowest emissions limit that a particular source is capable of meeting by the application of control technology that is both reasonably available and technologically and economically feasible. RACT is usually applied to existing sources in nonattainment areas, and in most cases is less stringent than new source performance standards.

Receiving waters. A river, lake, ocean, stream, or other watercourse into which wastewater or treated effluent is discharged.

Recharge. The process by which water is added to a zone of saturation, usually by percolation from the soil surface, for example, the recharge of an aquifer.

Recharge area. A land area in which water reaches to the zone of saturation from surface infiltration, for example, an area where rainwater soaks through the earth to reach an aquifer.

Recommended Maximum Contaminant Level. The term formerly used for Maximum Contaminant Level Goal.

Record of Decision. A public document that explains which cleanup alternative(s) will be used at National Priorities List sites.

Recycle-reuse. The process of minimizing the generation of waste by recovering usable products that might otherwise become waste. Examples are the recycling of aluminum cans, wastepaper, and bottles.

Red border. An EPA document that is undergoing final review before being submitted for final management decision.

Registrant. Any manufacturer or formulator who obtains registration for a pesticide active ingredient or product.

Registration. Formal listing with EPA of a new pesticide before it can be sold or distributed in intrastate or interstate commerce. The product must be registered under the Federal Insecticide, Fungicide, and Rodenticide Act.

Remedial action. The actual construction or implementation phase of a Superfund site cleanup that follows remedial design.

Remedial design. A stage of the Superfund cleanup process that follows the remedial investigation feasibility study and includes development of engineering drawings and specifications for a site cleanup.

Remedial investigation. An in-depth study designed to gather the data necessary to determine the nature and extent of contamination at a Superfund site; establish criteria for cleaning up the site; identify preliminary alternatives for remedial actions; and support the technical and cost analyses of the alternatives. The remedial investigation is usually done with the feasibility study. Together they are usually referred to as the "RI/FS."

Remedial response. A long-term action that stops or substantially reduces a release or threat of a release of hazardous substances that is serious but not an immediate threat to public health.

Removal actions. Short-term immediate actions taken to address releases of hazardous substances that require expedited response.

Reportable quantity (RQ). The quantity of a hazardous substance that triggers reporting requirements under CERCLA. If a substance is released in amounts exceeding its RQ, the release must be reported to the National Response Center, the SERC, and community emergency coordinators for areas likely to be affected.

Reregistration. The reevaluation and relicensing of existing pesticides originally registered prior to the implementation of current scientific and regulatory standards. EPA reregisters pesticides through its Registration Standards Program.

Resource recovery. The process of obtaining matter or energy from materials formerly discarded.

Response action. A CERCLA-authorized action involving either a removal action or a remedial action response that may include but is not limited to: removing hazardous materials from a site to an EPA-approved hazardous waste facility for treatment, containment, or destruction; containing the waste safely on-site; destroying or treating the waste on-site; and identifying and removing the source of ground water contamination and halting further migration of contaminants.

Restricted use. When a pesticide is registered, some or all of its uses may be classified (under FIFRA regulations) for restricted use if the pesticide requires special handling because of its toxicity. Restricted-use pesticides may be applied only by trained, certified applicators or those under their direct supervision.

Riparian rights. Entitlement of a land owner to the water on or bordering his or her property, including the right to prevent diversion or misuse of upstream waters. Generally a matter of state law.

Risk assessment. The process of identifying and characterizing the nature and magnitude of the adverse effects of a substance or activity.

Risk communication. The exchange of information about health or environmental risks between risk assessors, risk managers, the general public, news media, interest groups, and so on.

Risk management. The process of evaluating alternative regulatory and nonregulatory responses to risk and selecting among them.

Rodenticide. A chemical or agent used to destroy rats or other rodent pests, or to prevent them from damaging food, crops, and so on.

Runoff. That part of precipitation, snow melt, or irrigation water that runs off the land into streams or other surface water. It can carry pollutants from the air and land into the receiving waters.

Salinity. The degree of salt in water.

Sanitary landfill. *See* Landfills.

Sanitary sewers. Underground pipes that carry off only domestic or industrial waste, not storm water.

Saturated zone. A subsurface area in which all pores and cracks are filled with water under pressure equal to or greater than that of the atmosphere.

Scrap. Materials discarded from manufacturing operations that may be suitable for reprocessing.

Scrubber. An air pollution device that uses a spray of water or reactant or a dry process to trap pollutants in emissions.

Secondary treatment. The second step in most publicly owned waste treatment systems, in which bacteria consume the organic parts of the waste. It is accomplished by bringing together waste, bacteria, and oxygen in trickling filters or in the activated sludge process. This treatment removes floating and settleable solids and about 90 percent of the oxygen-demanding substances and suspended solids. Disinfection is the final stage of secondary treatment.

Sedimentation. Letting solids settle out of wastewater by gravity during wastewater treatment.

Sedimentation tanks. Holding areas for wastewater where floating wastes are skimmed off and settled solids are removed for disposal.

Sediments. Soil, sand, and minerals washed from land into water, usually after rain. They pile up in reservoirs, rivers, and harbors, destroying fish-nesting areas and holes of water animals and clouding the water so that needed sunlight might not reach aquatic plants. Careless farming, mining, and building activities will expose sediment materials, allowing them to be washed off the land after rainfalls.

Septic tank. An underground storage tank for wastes from a home having no sewer line to a treatment plant. The waste goes directly from the home to the tank, where the organic waste is decomposed by bacteria and the sludge settles to the bottom. The effluent flows out of the tank into the ground through drains; the sludge is pumped out periodically.

Service connector. The pipe that carries tap water from the public water main to a building.

Settling tank. A holding area for wastewater where heavier particles sink to the bottom for removal and disposal.

Sewage. The waste and wastewater produced by residential and commercial establishments and discharged into sewers.

Sewage sludge. Sludge produced at a publicly owned treatment works, the disposal of which is regulated under the Clean Water Act.

Sewer. A channel or conduit that carries wastewater or stormwater runoff from the source to a treatment plant or receiving stream. Sanitary sewers carry household, industrial, and commercial waste. Storm sewers carry runoff from rain or snow. Combined sewers are used for both purposes.

Sewerage. The entire system of sewage collection, treatment, and disposal.

Significant deterioration. Pollution resulting from a new source in previously "clean" areas.

Silviculture. Management of forest land for timber. Sometimes contributes to water pollution, as in clear-cutting.

Site inspection. The collection of information from a Superfund site to determine the extent and severity of hazards posed by the site. It follows and is more extensive than a preliminary assessment. The purpose is to gather information necessary to score the site, using the Hazard Ranking System, and to determine if the site presents an immediate threat that requires prompt removal action.

Siting. The process of choosing a location for a facility.

Sludge. A semisolid residue from any of a number of air or water treatment processes. Sludge can be a hazardous waste.

Slurry. A watery mixture of insoluble matter that results from some pollution control techniques.

Smelter. A facility that melts or fuses ore, often with an accompanying chemical change, to separate the metal. Emissions are known to cause pollution. Smelting is the process involved.

Smog. Air pollution associated with oxidants.

Sole source aquifer. An aquifer that supplies 50 percent or more of the drinking water of an area.

Solid waste. Defined by RCRA to include "any garbage, refuse, sludge from a waste treatment plant, water supply treatment plant, or air pollution control facility and other discarded material, including solid, liquid, semisolid, or contained gaseous materials resulting from industrial, commercial, mining, and agricultural activities." EPA has had extreme difficulty in defining the boundaries of this definition, particularly when materials are reused in production processes.

Solvent. A substance (usually liquid) capable of dissolving or dispersing one or more other substances.

Sorption. The action of soaking up or attracting substances. A process used in many pollution control systems.

Special Review. Formerly known as Rebuttable Presumption Against Registration, this is the regulatory process through which existing pesticides suspected of posing unreasonable risks to human health, nontarget organisms, or the environment are referred for review by EPA. The review requires an intensive risk-benefit analysis with opportunity for public comment. If the risk of any use of a pesticide is found to outweigh social and economic benefits, regulatory action—ranging from label revisions and use-restriction to cancellation or suspended registration—can be initiated.

Species. A reproductively isolated aggregate of interbreeding populations of organisms.

Spoil. Dirt or rock that has been removed from its original location, destroying the composition of the soil in the process, as with strip-mining or dredging.

Stabilization. Conversion of the active organic matter in sludge into inert, harmless material.

Standards. Prescriptive norms that govern action and actual limits on the amount of pollutants or emissions produced. EPA, under most of its responsibilities, establishes minimum standards. States are allowed to be stricter.

State emergency response commission. The commission appointed by each state governor according to the requirements of the Emergency Planning and Community Right-to-Know Act. The SERCs designate emergency planning districts, appoint local emergency planning committees, and supervise and coordinate their activities.

State implementation plans. EPA-approved state plans for the establishment, regulation, and enforcement of air pollution standards.

Stationary sources. Fixed, nonmoving producers of pollution, mainly power plants and other facilities using industrial combustion processes.

Storage. Temporary holding of waste pending treatment or disposal. Storage places include containers, tanks, waste piles, and surface impoundments.

Storm sewer. A system of pipes (separate from sanitary sewers) that carry only water runoff from building and land surfaces.

Stratosphere. The portion of the atmosphere that is 10 to 25 miles above the Earth's surface.

Strip-mining. A process that uses machines to scrape soil or rock away from mineral deposits just under the Earth's surface.

Sulfur dioxide (SO_2). A heavy, pungent, colorless, gaseous air pollutant formed primarily by the combustion of fossil plants.

Sump. A pit or tank that catches liquid runoff for drainage or disposal.

Sump pump. A mechanism for removing water or wastewater from a sump or wet well.

Superfund. A fund set up under the Comprehensive Environmental Response, Compensation, and Liability Act (CERCLA) to help pay for cleanup of hazardous waste sites and for legal action to force those responsible for the sites to clean them up. Also sometimes used to refer to the program operated under the legislative authority of CERCLA that carries out EPA response activities.

Surface impoundment. Treatment, storage, or disposal of liquid hazardous wastes in ponds.

Surface water. All water naturally open to the atmosphere (rivers, lakes, reservoirs, streams, impoundments, seas, estuaries, and so on) and all springs, wells, or other collectors that are directly influenced by surface water.

Suspended solids. Small particles of solid pollutants that float on the surface of, or are suspended in, sewage or other liquids. They resist removal by conventional means.

Suspension. The act of suspending the use of a pesticide when EPA deems it necessary to do so in order to prevent an imminent hazard resulting from continued use of the pesticide. An emergency suspension takes effect immediately; under an ordinary suspension a registrant can request a hearing before the suspension goes into effect. Such a hearing process might take six months.

Swamp. A type of wetland that is dominated by woody vegetation and does not accumulate appreciable peat deposits. Swamps may be fresh or salt water and tidal or nontidal.

Synergism. The cooperative interaction of two or more chemicals or other phenomena producing a greater total effect than the sum of their individual effects.

Synthetic organic chemicals. Manmade organic chemicals. Some SOCs are volatile; others tend to stay dissolved in water rather than evaporate out of it.

Tailings. Residue of raw materials or waste separated out during the processing of crops or mineral ores.

Technology-based standards. Effluent limitations applicable to direct and indirect sources that are developed on a category-by-category basis using statutory factors, not including water-quality effects.

Teratogen. A substance that causes malformation or serious deviation from normal development of embryos and fetuses.

Tertiary treatment. Advanced cleaning of wastewater that goes beyond the secondary or biological stage. It removes nutrients such as phosphorus and nitrogen and most BOD and suspended solids.

Thermal pollution. Discharge of heated water from industrial processes that can affect the life processes of aquatic organisms.

Threshold limit value. This figure represents the air concentrations of chemical substances to which it is believed that workers may be exposed on a daily basis without adverse effect.

Threshold planning quantity. A quantity designated for each chemical on the list of extremely hazardous substances that triggers notification by facilities to the state emergency response commission that such facilities are subject to emergency planning under the Emergency Planning and Community Right-to-Know Act.

Tidal marsh. Low, flat marshlands traversed by channels and tidal hollows and subject to tidal inundation; normally, the only vegetation present is salt-tolerant bushes and grasses.

Tolerances. The permissible residue levels for pesticides in raw agricultural produce and processed foods. Whenever a pesticide is registered for use on a food or a feed crop, a tolerance (or exemption from the tolerance requirement) must be established. EPA establishes the tolerance levels, which are enforced by the Food and Drug Administration and the Department of Agriculture.

Topography. The physical features of a surface area, including relative elevations and the position of natural and manmade features.

Total suspended solids. A measure of the suspended solids in wastewater, effluent, or water bodies, determined by using tests for "total suspended non-filterable solids."

Toxic. Harmful to living organisms.

Toxic chemical release form. An information form required to be submitted by facilities that manufacture, process, or use (in quantities above a specific amount) chemicals listed under the Emergency Planning and Community Right-to-Know Act.

Toxicity. The degree of danger posed by a substance to animal or plant life.

Toxicology. The science and study of poison control.

Toxic pollutants. Materials contaminating the environment that cause death, disease, or birth defects in organisms that ingest or absorb them. The quantities and length of exposure necessary to cause these effects can vary widely.

Treatment, storage, and disposal facility. The site where a hazardous substance is treated, stored, or disposed. TSD facilities are regulated by EPA and states under RCRA.

Trichloroethylene (TCE). A stable, low-boiling, colorless liquid, toxic by inhalation. TCE is used as a solvent and as a metal degreasing agent and in other industrial applications.

Trihalomethane (THM). One of a family of organic compounds, named as derivatives of methane. THMs are generally the by-product of chlorination of drinking water that contains organic material.

Troposphere. The lower atmosphere; the portion of the atmosphere between 7 and 10 miles from the Earth's surface where clouds are formed.

Tundra. A type of ecosystem dominated by lichens, mosses, grasses, and woody plants. Tundra is found at high latitudes (arctic tundra) and high altitudes (alpine tundra). Arctic tundra is underlain by permafrost and is usually very wet.

Turbidity. (1) Haziness in air caused by the presence of particles and pollutants. (2) A similar cloudy condition in water due to suspended silt or organic matter.

Ultraviolet rays. Radiation from the sun, which can be useful or potentially harmful. Ultraviolet rays from one part of the spectrum enhance plant life and are useful in some medical and dental procedures; ultraviolet rays from other parts of the spectrum to which humans are exposed (for example, while getting a sun tan) can cause skin cancer or other tissue damage. The ozone layer in the stratosphere provides a protective shield that limits the amount of ultraviolet rays that reach the Earth's surface.

Underground Injection Control. The program under the Safe Drinking Water Act that regulates the use of underground injection wells to pump fluids into the ground.

Underground sources of drinking water. As defined in the UIC program, this term refers to aquifers that are currently being used as a source of drinking water and those that are capable of supplying a public water system. They have a total dissolved solids content of 10,000 milligrams per liter or less, and are not "exempted aquifers."

Underground storage tank. A tank located totally or partially underground that is designed to hold gasoline or other petroleum products or chemical solutions.

Unsaturated zone. The area above the water table where the soil pores are not fully saturated, although some water may be present.

Uranium. A radioactive heavy metal element used in nuclear reactors and the production of nuclear weapons. The term refers usually to U-238, the most abundant radium isotope, although a small percentage of naturally occurring uranium is U-235.

Urban runoff. Storm water from city streets and adjacent domestic or commercial properties that may carry pollutants of various kinds into the sewer systems or receiving waters.

Vaporization. The change of a substance from a liquid to a gas.

Variance. Government permission for a delay or exception in the application of a given law, ordinance, or regulation.

Vector. (1) An organism, often an insect or rodent, that carries disease. (2) An object that is used to transport genes into a host cell (vectors can be plasmids, viruses, or other bacteria). A gene is placed in the vector; the vector then "infects" the bacterium.

Vinyl chloride. A chemical compound, used in producing some plastics, that is believed to be carcinogenic.

Virus. The smallest form of microorganisms capable of causing disease.

Volatile. Capable of evaporating readily.

Volatile organic compound. Any organic compound that participates in atmospheric photochemical reactions except for those designated by the EPA administrator as having negligible photochemical reactivity.

Waste load allocation. The maximum load of pollutants each discharger of waste is allowed to release into a particular waterway. Discharge limits are usually required for each specific water quality criterion being, or expected to be, violated.

Waste treatment plant. A facility containing a series of tanks, screens, filters, and other processes by which pollutants are removed from water.

Waste treatment stream. The continuous movement of waste from generator to treater and disposer.

Wastewater. The spent or used water from individual homes, a community, a farm, or an industry that contains dissolved or suspended matter.

Water pollution. The presence in water of enough harmful or objectionable material to damage the water's quality.

Water quality criteria. Specific levels of water quality that, if reached, are expected to render a body of water suitable for its designated use. The criteria are based on specific levels of pollutants that would make the water harmful if used for drinking, swimming, farming, fish production, or industrial processes.

Water quality standards. State-adopted and EPA-approved ambient standards for water bodies. The standards cover the use of the water body and the water quality criteria that must be met to protect the designated use or uses.

Watershed. The land area that drains into a stream.

Water table. The level of ground water.

Well injection. The subsurface emplacement of fluids in a well.

Wetlands. An area that is regularly saturated by surface or ground water and subsequently is characterized by a prevalence of vegetation that is adapted for life in saturated soil conditions. Examples include swamps, bogs, fens, marshes, and estuaries.

Wildlife refuge. An area designated for the protection of wild animals within which hunting and fishing are either prohibited or strictly controlled.

Xenobiotic. Term for non-naturally occurring manmade substances found in the environment (i.e., synthetic material solvents, plastics).

═ APPENDIX B ═
‖ *List of Acronyms* ‖

AA Assistant Administrator or Associate Administrator
ACGIH American Council of Government Industrial Hygienists
ACL Alternate Concentration Limit
ADI Acceptable Daily Intake
ADR Alternative Dispute Resolution
AEA Atomic Energy Act
AEC Atomic Energy Commission
AHERA Asbestos Hazard Emergency Response Act
ALJ Administrative Law Judge
ANPR Advance Notice of Proposed Rulemaking
ANSI American National Standards Institute
ANWR Arctic National Wildlife Refuge
APA Administrative Procedure Act
ARAR Applicable or Relevant and Appropriate Standards, Limitations, Criteria, and Requirements
ATSDR Agency for Toxic Substances and Disease Registry (HHS)

BACT Best Available Control Technology
BADT Best Available Demonstrated Technology
BART Best Available Retrofit Technology
BAT Best Available Treatment
BATEA Best Available Technology Economically Achievable
BCT Best Control Technology or Best Conventional Pollutant Control Technology
BDAT Best Demonstrated Achievable Technology
BDT Best Demonstrated Technology
BLM Bureau of Land Management
BNA Bureau of National Affairs
BOD Biochemical Oxygen Demand
BPCT Best Practicable Control Technology
BPCTCA Best Practicable Control Technology Currently Available

BPJ Best Professional Judgment
BPT Best Practicable Technology, Best Practicable Control Technology, or Best Practicable Treatment
BTU British Thermal Unit

CAA Clean Air Act
CAFE Corporate Average Fuel Economy
CAG Carcinogenic Assessment Group
CAO Corrective Action Order
CAP Corrective Action Plan
CAS Chemical Abstract Service
CASAC Clean Air Scientific Advisory Committee
CBA Cost-Benefit Analysis
CBF Chesapeake Bay Foundation
CBO Congressional Budget Office
CDC Centers for Disease Control (HHS)
CEA Council of Economic Advisors
CEMS Continuous Emission Monitoring System
CEQ Council on Environmental Quality
CERCLA Comprehensive Environmental Response, Compensation, and Liability Act of 1980
CERCLIS Comprehensive Environmental Response, Compensation, and Liability Information System
CFCs Chlorofluorocarbons
CFR Code of Federal Regulations
CM Corrective Measure
CMA Chemical Manufacturers Association
COD Chemical Oxygen Demand
CPSA Consumer Product Safety Act
CPSC Consumer Product Safety Commission
CRS Congressional Research Service
CSO Combined Sewer Overflow
CWA Clean Water Act (also known as the FWPCA)
CZMA Coastal Zone Management Act

DDT Dichloro-diphenyl-trichloroethane
DMR Discharge Monitoring Report
DO Dissolved Oxygen
DOD Department of Defense
DOE Department of Energy
DOI Department of the Interior

DOJ Department of Justice
DOL Department of Labor
DOT Department of Transportation
DPA Deepwater Ports Act
DSAP Data Self Auditing Program

EA Environmental Assessment (NEPA)
EC European Community (Common Market)
ECRA Environment Cleanup Responsibility Act (New Jersey)
EDB Ethylene Dibromide
EDF Environmental Defense Fund
EEC European Economic Commission
EHA 2-Ethylhexanoic Acid
EHS Extremely Hazardous Substance
EI Emissions Inventory
EIS Environmental Impact Statement
ELI Environmental Law Institute
ELR Environmental Law Reporter
EO Executive Order
EP Extraction Procedure
EPA U.S. Environmental Protection Agency
EPCRTKA Emergency Planning and Community Right-to-Know
    Act
ERC Emissions Reduction Credit
ESA Endangered Species Act
ESC Endangered Species Committee
ETS Emergency Temporary Standard

FACA Federal Advisory Committee Act
FDA Food and Drug Administration
FDF Fundamentally Different Factors
FFDCA Federal Food, Drug, and Cosmetic Act
FHWA Federal Highway Administration
FIFRA Federal Insecticide, Fungicide, and Rodenticide Act
FIP Federal Implementation Plan
FLPMA Federal Land Policy and Management Act
FOIA Freedom of Information Act
FONSI Finding of No Significant Impact (NEPA)
FR Federal Register
FSA Food Security Act
FTC Federal Trade Commission

FWPCA Federal Water Pollution Control Act (also known as the Clean Water Act, or CWA)
FWS Fish and Wildlife Service (U.S.)
FY Fiscal Year

GAO General Accounting Office
GATT General Agreement on Tariffs and Trade
GCEA Global Commons Environment Assessment
GDP Gross Domestic Product

HCP Habitat Conservation Plan
HEPA High-Efficiency Particulate Air
HEW Health, Education, and Welfare (now HHS)
HHS Department of Health and Human Services (formerly HEW)
HLRW High-Level Radioactive Waste
HMTA Hazardous Materials Transportation Act
HRS Hazard Ranking System
HSWA Hazardous and Solid Waste Amendments
HUD Department of Housing and Urban Development
HWTC Hazardous Waste Treatment Council

IARC International Agency for Research on Cancer
ICS Individual Control Strategy
IG Inspector General
I/M Inspection/Maintenance
IPM Integrated Pest Management
ISC Interagency Scientific Committee
ITC Interagency Testing Committee
ITO International Trade Organization

LAER Lowest Achievable Emission Rate
LC Lethal Concentration
LEPC Local Emergency Planning Committee
LERC Local Emergency Response Committee
LLRWPA Low Level Radioactive Waste Policy Act
LOEL Lowest Observed Effect Level
LOIS Loss of Interim Status (SDWA)
LTU Land Treatment Unit
LUST Leaking Underground Storage Tank(s) (current usage omits the "L")

MACT Maximum Achievable Control Technology
MAER Maximum Allowable Emission Rate
MCL Maximum Contaminant Level
MCLG Maximum Contaminant Level Goal
MEPA Michigan Environmental Protection Act
MICROMORT A one-in-a-million chance of death from an environmental hazard
MIR Maximum Individual Risk
MMPA Marine Mammal Protection Act
MMT Million Metric Tons
MOU Memorandum of Understanding
MPRSA Marine Protection, Research, and Sanctuaries Act (Ocean Dumping Act)
MSDS Material Safety Data Sheet
MSHA Mine Safety and Health Administration (DOL)
MTBE Methyl Tertiary Butyl Ether
MTD Maximum Tolerated Dose

NAAQS National Ambient Air Quality Standards program (CAA)
NAFTA North American Free Trade Agreement
NAPAP National Acid Precipitation Assessment Program
NAS National Academy of Sciences
NBAR Non-Binding Allocation of Responsibility
NCP National Contingency Plan
NEPA National Environmental Policy Act
NESHAP National Emissions Standards for Hazardous Air Pollutants (CAA)
NFMA National Forests Management Act
NHANES National Health and Nutrition Examination Study
NHATS National Human Adipose Tissue Survey
NHTSA National Highway Traffic Safety Administration (DOT)
NIEHS National Institute of Environmental Health Sciences
NIH National Institutes of Health
NIMBY Not In My Backyard
NIOSH National Institute of Occupational Safety and Health
NIPDWR National Interim Primary Drinking Water Regulations
NMFS National Marine Fisheries Service
NOAA National Oceanic and Atmospheric Administration (DOC)
NOAEL No Observed Adverse Effect Level
NPDES National Pollutant Discharge Elimination System (CWA)
NPL National Priority List (CERCLA)

NPS National Park Service
NRC National Research Council, National Response Center, or Nuclear Regulatory Commission
NRDC Natural Resources Defense Council
NSF National Science Foundation
NSO Nonferrous Smelter Orders (CAA)
NSPS New Source Performance Standards (CAA)
NSR New Source Review
NSWMA National Solid Wastes Management Association
NTP National Toxicology Program
NWF National Wildlife Federation
NWPA Nuclear Waste Policy Act

OCS Outer Continental Shelf
OCSLA Outer Continental Shelf Lands Act
OECD Organization for Economic Cooperation and Development
OIRA Office of Information and Regulatory Affairs
OMB Office of Management and Budget
OPA 90 Oil Pollution Prevention, Response, Liability, and Compensation Act
OPP Office of Pesticide Programs
OSHA Occupational Safety and Health Administration (DOL)
OSH Act Occupational Safety and Health Act
OSM Office of Surface Mining (DOI)
OSTP Office of Science and Technology Policy (White House)
OTA Office of Technology Assessment (Congress)

PA Preliminary Assessment
PAH Polycyclic Aromatic Hydrocarbon
PCBs Polychlorinated Biphenyls
PEL Permissible Exposure Limit
PIC Prior Informed Consent
PM10 Particulate Matter (nominally 10mg and less)
PM15 Particulate Matter (nominally 15mg and less)
PMN Premanufacture Notification (TSCA)
POM Polycyclic Organic Matter
POTW Publicly Owned Treatment Works
ppb Parts per Billion
ppm Parts per Million
PPPA Poison Prevention Packaging Act

PRA Paperwork Reduction Act
PRP Potentially Responsible Party (CERCLA)
PSD Prevention of Significant Deterioration
PTE Potential to Emit
PVC Polyvinyl Chloride

QA/QC Quality Assistance/Quality Control
QOL Quality of Life (Nixon Administration)
QRA Quantitative Risk Assessment

RA Regulatory Analysis, Remedial Action, or Risk Assessment
RACM Reasonably Available Control Measures
RACT Reasonably Available Control Technology
RARG Regulatory Analysis Review Group
RB Red Border
RCRA Resource Conservation and Recovery Act
RD Remedial Design (CERCLA)
R&D Research and Development
RFA Regulatory Flexibility Act
RFP Reasonable Further Programs
RI Remedial Investigation
RIA Regulatory Impact Analysis
RI/FS Remedial Information/Feasibility Study
RMCL Recommended Maximum Contaminant Level (this phrase
    has been discontinued in favor of MCLG)
ROD Record of Decision (CERCLA)
RPAR Rebuttable Presumption Against Registration (FIFRA)
RQ Reportable Quantities

SAB Science Advisory Board (AO)
SAR Structure Activity Relationship
SARA Superfund Amendments and Reauthorization Act of 1986
SCS Soil Conservation Service
SDWA Safe Drinking Water Act
SERC State Emergency Planning Commission
SIC Standard Industrial Classification
SIP State Implementation Plan (CAA)
SMCRA Surface Mining Control and Reclamation Act
SNARL Suggested No Adverse Response Level
SNUR Significant New Use Rule (TSCA)
SQG Small Quantity Generator

STEL Short-Term Exposure Limit
SWDA Solid Waste Disposal Act
SWMU Solid Waste Management Unit

TCDD Dioxin (Tetrachlorodibenzo-p-dioxin)
TCE Trichloroethylene
TCLP Toxicity Characteristic Leachate Procedure
TDS Total Dissolved Solids
TKN Total Kjeldahl Nitrogen
TLV Threshold Limit Value
TMDL Total Maximum Daily Loading
TRI Toxic Release Inventory
TSCA Toxic Substances Control Act
TSD Treatment, Storage, and Disposal Facility (RCRA)
TVA Tennessee Valley Authority

UDMH Unsymmetrical Dimethylhydrazine
UIC Underground Injection Control
UMTRCA Uranium Mill Tailings Radiation Control Act
UN United Nations
UNEP United Nations Environment Programme
USC United States Code
USCA United States Code Annotated
UST Underground Storage Tank
UV Ultraviolet

VA Veterans Administration
VOC Volatile Organic Compound

WCED World Commission on Environment and Development
WHO World Health Organization
WIPP Waste Isolation Pilot Plan
WLA/TMDL Waste Load Allocation/Total Maximum Daily Load
WTA Willingness to Accept
WTP Willingness to Pay

Table of Cases

Index

References in italics are to principal excerpts.

Abbey, Edward, 27
Acid rain
  emissions trading, 823-826
  generally, *819-823*
  NAPAP study, 821
Accrual of cause of action, 639-640, 647
Ackerman, Bruce, 163-164, 176-177
Acquired Immune Deficiency Syndrome
      (AIDS), 494
Administrative compensation schemes,
      637-639
Administrative Conference of the United
      States, 507, 671, 683
Administrative law
  delegation and its dangers, 190
  exhaustion of administrative remedies
      requirement, 192
  impact of environmental cases on devel-
      opment of, 191
  informal rulemaking procedures, 674-
      676
  interest representation model, 188
  New Deal model of agency expertise,
      187
  notice and opportunity for comment,
      241, 260
  reviewability and ripeness, 733-735
Administrative Procedure Act, 185, 187,
      191, 496
  generally, 658
  judicial review provisions, 192, 669,
      715, 733
  §553 (informal rulemaking), 674
  §553(e) (petition), 671

Advance notice of proposed rulemaking,
      675
African Development Bank, 1230
Agencies, federal
  capture theory, 187
  discretion in implementing regulatory
      statutes, 153-154, 185-186
  external signals model of agency
      behavior, 188
  imbalance between responsibilities and
      resources, 112, 119
  lack of responsiveness to public, 187
  models of agency decision-making, 187-
      188
  as polluters, 7, 201-202
  as regulatory targets, 143-145
  responsibilities under environmental
      laws, 110-112
  wealth transfer model of agency
      behavior, 188-189
Agency-forcing mechanisms
  petitions, 671-674
    TSCA §21 petitions, 672-673
  statutory deadlines and citizen suits,
      666-671
  three models of
    coercive, 665-666
    ministerial, 665
    prescriptive, 665-666
Agency for International Development,
      1233
Agriculture
  effect of global warming on, 1170,
      1174-1175

1323